TRAINERS

FLAT STATISTICS 2019

Published in 2019 by Raceform Ltd
27 Kingfisher Court, Hambridge Road, Newbury, Berkshire RG14 5SJ

A catalogue record for this book is available from the British Library

ISBN 978-1-83950-006-0

Printed and bound in the UK by CPI Antony Rowe, Melksham

CONTENTS

WINNING TRAINERS

Flat statistics for the 2018 season for winning British-based trainers. Trainers with less than ten winners are shown with abbreviated statistics.

Winning horses preceded by an asterisk joined the stable during the course of the season.

An asterisk following the horse's name denotes a switch to another trainer during the season.

Course and Month tables are for the last five seasons starting on 1 January 2014 and ending on 31 Dec 2018.

LOUISE ALLAN

EXNING, SUFFOLK

	No. of Hrs	Races Run	1st	2nd	3rd	Unpl	Per cent	£1 Level Stake
2-y-o	*0*	*0*	*0*	*0*	*0*	*0*	*0.0*	*0.00*
3-y-o	*2*	*11*	*0*	*1*	*0*	*10*	*0.0*	*-11.00*
4-y-o+	*3*	*27*	*2*	*1*	*4*	*20*	*7.4*	*-18.00*
Totals	**5**	**38**	**2**	**2**	**4**	**30**	**5.3**	**-29.00**
2017	*2*	*5*	*0*	*1*	*0*	*4*	*0.0*	*-5.00*
2016	*0*							+

JOCKEYS

	W-R	Per cent	£1 Level Stake
Adam Kirby	1-1	100.0	+3.00
Callum Shepherd	1-2	50.0	+3.00

COURSE RECORD

	Total W-R	Non-Hndcps 2-y-o	Non-Hndcps 3-y-o+	Hndcps 2-y-o	Hndcps 3-y-o+	Per cent	£1 Level Stake
Chelmsford (A.W)	2-17	0-0	0-0	0-0	2-17	11.8	-8.00

WINNING HORSES

Horse	Races Run	1st	2nd	3rd	£
Hard Toffee (IRE)	11	2	0	3	6404
Total winning prize-money					**£6404**
Favourites	**0-1**		**0.0%**		**-1.00**

CONRAD ALLEN

NEWMARKET, SUFFOLK

	No. of Hrs	Races Run	1st	2nd	3rd	Unpl	Per cent	£1 Level Stake
2-y-o	*0*	*0*	*0*	*0*	*0*	*0*	*0.0*	*0.00*
3-y-o	*5*	*30*	*4*	*2*	*6*	*18*	*13.3*	*-1.00*
4-y-o+	*6*	*33*	*4*	*6*	*9*	*14*	*12.1*	*-15.50*
Totals	**11**	**63**	**8**	**8**	**15**	**32**	**12.7**	**-16.50**
2017	*10*	*83*	*6*	*6*	*9*	*62*	*7.2*	*-1.25*
2016	*15*	*73*	*7*	*5*	*5*	*56*	*9.6*	*-2.13*

JOCKEYS

	W-R	Per cent	£1 Level Stake
Sebastian Woods	2-9	22.2	-1.50
Martin Dwyer	2-11	18.2	+8.00
Charles Bishop	1-2	50.0	+3.00
Andrea Atzeni	1-4	25.0	+0.50
William Carver	1-8	12.5	-2.50
Robert Havlin	1-13	7.7	-8.00

COURSE RECORD

	Total W-R	Non-Hndcps 2-y-o	Non-Hndcps 3-y-o+	Hndcps 2-y-o	Hndcps 3-y-o+	Per cent	£1 Level Stake
Chelmsford (A.W)	3-14	0-0	0-2	0-0	3-12	21.4	+11.00
Kempton (A.W)	2-6	0-0	0-1	0-0	2-5	33.3	+1.00
Ffos Las	1-1	0-0	1-1	0-0	0-0	100.0	+4.00
Leicester	1-3	0-0	1-1	0-0	0-2	33.3	+2.00
Windsor	1-5	0-0	0-2	0-0	1-3	20.0	-0.50

WINNING HORSES

Horse	Races Run	1st	2nd	3rd	£
Busby (IRE)	11	2	0	5	9186
Ghalia Al Thumama	6	1	1	1	3752
Sonnet Rose (IRE)	19	3	4	8	10739
Sparkalex	9	1	1	0	5175
Voi	8	1	1	1	5531
Total winning prize-money					**£34383**
Favourites	**3-9**		**33.3%**		**2.50**

ERIC ALSTON

LONGTON, LANCS

	No. of Hrs	Races Run	1st	2nd	3rd	Unpl	Per cent	£1 Level Stake
2-y-o	*1*	*4*	*0*	*0*	*0*	*4*	*0.0*	*-4.00*
3-y-o	*6*	*25*	*1*	*2*	*4*	*18*	*4.0*	*-19.00*
4-y-o+	*11*	*99*	*13*	*11*	*13*	*62*	*13.1*	*-4.63*
Totals	**18**	**128**	**14**	**13**	**17**	**84**	**10.9**	**-27.63**
2017	*24*	*145*	*18*	*10*	*13*	*104*	*12.4*	*+14.50*
2016	*20*	*143*	*10*	*15*	*19*	*99*	*7.0*	*-70.25*

BY MONTH

2-y-o	W-R	Per cent	£1 Level Stake	**3-y-o**	W-R	Per cent	£1 Level Stake
January	0-0	0.0	0.00	January	0-0	0.0	0.00
February	0-0	0.0	0.00	February	0-0	0.0	0.00
March	0-0	0.0	0.00	March	0-0	0.0	0.00
April	0-0	0.0	0.00	April	0-1	0.0	-1.00
May	0-1	0.0	-1.00	May	0-3	0.0	-3.00
June	0-1	0.0	-1.00	June	0-5	0.0	-5.00
July	0-1	0.0	-1.00	July	0-4	0.0	-4.00
August	0-0	0.0	0.00	August	0-3	0.0	-3.00
September	0-1	0.0	-1.00	September	1-3	33.3	+3.00
October	0-0	0.0	0.00	October	0-3	0.0	-3.00
November	0-0	0.0	0.00	November	0-1	0.0	-1.00
December	0-0	0.0	0.00	December	0-2	0.0	-2.00

4-y-o+	W-R	Per cent	£1 Level Stake	**Totals**	W-R	Per cent	£1 Level Stake
January	0-3	0.0	-3.00	January	0-3	0.0	-3.00
February	0-2	0.0	-2.00	February	0-2	0.0	-2.00
March	0-2	0.0	-2.00	March	0-2	0.0	-2.00
April	3-9	33.3	+24.75	April	3-10	30.0	+23.75
May	4-15	26.7	+3.00	May	4-19	21.1	-1.00
June	1-19	5.3	-2.00	June	1-25	4.0	-8.00
July	1-7	14.3	-4.63	July	1-12	8.3	9.63
August	0-14	0.0	-14.00	August	0-17	0.0	-17.00
September	2-14	14.3	-0.50	September	3-18	16.7	+1.50
October	0-9	0.0	-9.00	October	0-12	0.0	-12.00
November	1-2	50.0	+1.75	November	1-3	33.3	+0.75
December	1-3	33.3	+3.00	December	1-5	20.0	+1.00

DISTANCE

2-y-o	W-R	Per cent	£1 Level Stake	3-y-o	W-R	Per cent	£1 Level Stake
5f-6f	0-3	0.0	-3.00	5f-6f	1-12	8.3	-6.00
7f-8f	0-1	0.0	-1.00	7f-8f	0-10	0.0	-10.00
9f-13f	0-0	0.0	0.00	9f-13f	0-3	0.0	-3.00
14f+	0-0	0.0	0.00	14f+	0-0	0.0	0.00

4-y-o+	W-R	Per cent	£1 Level Stake	Totals	W-R	Per cent	£1 Level Stake
5f-6f	10-71	14.1	-1.38	5f-6f	11-86	12.8	-10.38
7f-8f	3-18	16.7	+6.75	7f-8f	3-29	10.3	-4.25
9f-13f	0-10	0.0	-10.00	9f-13f	0-13	0.0	-13.00
14f+	0-0	0.0	0.00	14f+	0-0	0.0	0.00

TYPE OF RACE

Non-Handicaps	W-R	Per cent	£1 Level Stake	Handicaps	W-R	Per cent	£1 Level Stake
2-y-o	0-4	0.0	-4.00	2-y-o	0-0	0.0	0.00
3-y-o	0-6	0.0	-6.00	3-y-o	1-19	5.3	-13.00
4-y-o+	0-4	0.0	-4.00	4-y-o+	13-95	13.7	-0.63

RACE CLASS

	W-R	Per cent	£1 Level Stake
Class 1	0-2	0.0	-2.00
Class 2	1-5	20.0	+4.00
Class 3	1-6	16.7	0.00
Class 4	6-44	13.6	+13.88
Class 5	2-42	4.8	-35.75
Class 6	4-29	13.8	-7.75
Class 7	0-0	0.0	0.00

FIRST TIME OUT

	W-R	Per cent	£1 Level Stake
2-y-o	0-1	0.0	-1.00
3-y-o	0-6	0.0	-6.00
4-y-o+	3-11	27.3	+22.00
Totals	3-18	16.7	+15.00

JOCKEYS

	W-R	Per cent	£1 Level Stake
Rachel Richardson	4-32	12.5	-5.50
Jason Hart	4-48	8.3	-29.13
Robert Dodsworth	2-5	40.0	+21.25
Theodore Ladd	1-1	100.0	+3.50
Daniel Tudhope	1-1	100.0	+2.75
Shelley Birkett	1-3	33.3	+14.00
Martin Harley	1-5	20.0	-1.50

COURSE RECORD

	Total W-R	Non-Hndcps 2-y-o	Non-Hndcps 3-y-o+	Hndcps 2-y-o	Hndcps 3-y-o+	Per cent	£1 Level Stake
Catterick	3-11	0-0	0-0	0-0	3-11	27.3	+2.75
Thirsk	3-13	0-0	0-2	0-0	3-11	23.1	+5.00
Haydock	2-20	0-0	0-1	0-0	2-19	10.0	-14.13
Pontefract	1-2	0-0	0-1	0-0	1-1	50.0	+7.00
Nottingham	1-5	0-0	0-0	0-0	1-5	20.0	-1.00
Newcastle (A.W)	1-5	0-0	0-0	0-0	1-5	20.0	-1.25
Southwell (A.W)	1-7	0-0	0-0	0-0	1-7	14.3	-1.00
Ripon	1-8	0-1	0-1	0-0	1-6	12.5	+15.00
Chester	1-12	0-3	0-0	0-0	1-9	8.3	+5.00

WINNING HORSES

Horse	Races Run	1st	2nd	3rd	£
Acclaim The Nation (IRE)	10	2	2	1	18143
Boudica Bay (IRE)	6	1	1	2	3493
Bush Beauty (IRE)	10	1	1	0	6081
Casterbridge	10	1	1	3	3752
Jabbarockie	10	2	2	3	12938
Lydiate Lady	9	1	0	0	5693
Maid In India (IRE)	8	3	1	0	30837
Redrosezorro	11	3	2	1	10480
Total winning prize-money					**£91417**
Favourites	**7-18**		**38.9%**		**7.38**

MICHAEL APPLEBY

OAKHAM, RUTLAND

	No. of Hrs	Races Run	1st	2nd	3rd	Unpl	Per cent	£1 Level Stake
2-y-o	*18*	*63*	*10*	*4*	*6*	*43*	*15.9*	*+2.90*
3-y-o	*39*	*147*	*13*	*18*	*13*	*103*	*8.8*	*-72.88*
4-y-o+	*86*	*582*	*71*	*75*	*78*	*356*	*12.2*	*-90.54*
Totals	**143**	**792**	**94**	**97**	**97**	**502**	**11.9**	**-160.52**
2017	*145*	*853*	*91*	*82*	*100*	*576*	*10.7*	*-269.29*
2016	*138*	*787*	*70*	*63*	*70*	*584*	*8.9*	*-200.78*

BY MONTH

2-y-o	W-R	Per cent	£1 Level Stake	3-y-o	W-R	Per cent	£1 Level Stake
January	0-0	0.0	0.00	January	1-12	8.3	-8.25
February	0-0	0.0	0.00	February	0-4	0.0	-4.00
March	0-0	0.0	0.00	March	0-1	0.0	-1.00
April	0-1	0.0	-1.00	April	0-4	0.0	-4.00
May	0-1	0.0	-1.00	May	0-8	0.0	-8.00
June	1-3	33.3	+23.00	June	1-12	8.3	-3.00
July	1-8	12.5	-6.43	July	2-11	18.2	+4.00
August	0-5	0.0	-5.00	August	3-20	15.0	-10.63
September	1-7	14.3	+2.00	September	1-11	9.1	-4.50
October	3-21	14.3	-7.13	October	1-18	5.6	-13.50
November	1-11	9.1	-6.67	November	2-22	9.1	-13.75
December	3-6	50.0	+5.13	December	2-24	8.3	-6.25

4-y-o+	W-R	Per cent	£1 Level Stake	Totals	W-R	Per cent	£1 Level Stake
January	8-68	11.8	-36.79	January	9-80	11.3	-45.04
February	5-65	7.7	-38.25	February	5-69	7.2	-42.25
March	16-73	21.9	+64.42	March	16-74	21.6	+63.42
April	3-37	8.1	-24.50	April	3-42	7.1	-29.50
May	8-63	12.7	-15.25	May	8-72	11.1	-24.25
June	4-60	6.7	-21.50	June	6-75	8.0	-1.50
July	10-47	21.3	+11.08	July	13-66	19.7	+8.65
August	4-39	10.3	-12.00	August	7-64	10.9	-28.26
September	3-29	10.3	-14.25	September	5-47	10.6	-16.75
October	2-32	6.3	+10.50	October	6-71	8.5	-10.13
November	4-36	11.1	-3.38	November	7-69	10.1	-17.13
December	4-33	12.1	-10.00	December	9-63	14.3	-16.25

DISTANCE

2-y-o	W-R	Per cent	£1 Level Stake
5f-6f	7-41	17.1	+10.53
7f-8f	3-20	15.0	-5.63
9f-13f	0-2	0.0	-2.00
14f+	0-0	0.0	0.00

3-y-o	W-R	Per cent	£1 Level Stake
5f-6f	2-27	7.4	-20.25
7f-8f	6-76	7.9	-45.00
9f-13f	4-41	9.8	-19.63
14f+	1-3	33.3	+12.00

4-y-o+	W-R	Per cent	£1 Level Stake
5f-6f	27-175	15.4	+24.13
7f-8f	19-175	10.9	-5.58
9f-13f	23-190	12.1	-76.33
14f+	2-42	4.8	-32.75

Totals	W-R	Per cent	£1 Level Stake
5f-6f	36-243	14.8	+14.41
7f-8f	28-271	10.3	-56.21
9f-13f	27-233	11.6	-97.96
14f+	3-45	6.7	-20.75

TYPE OF RACE

Non-Handicaps	W-R	Per cent	£1 Level Stake
2-y-o	2-33	6.1	-5.43
3-y-o	2-58	3.4	-43.75
4-y-o+	8-70	11.4	-9.00

Handicaps	W-R	Per cent	£1 Level Stake
2-y-o	8-30	26.7	+8.33
3-y-o	11-89	12.4	-29.13
4-y-o+	63-512	12.3	-81.54

RACE CLASS

	W-R	Per cent	£1 Level Stake
Class 1	1-15	6.7	-10.67
Class 2	5-43	11.6	+11.50
Class 3	3-64	4.7	-35.50
Class 4	17-151	11.3	-41.13
Class 5	39-291	13.4	-49.66
Class 6	27-216	12.5	-30.30
Class 7	2-12	16.7	-4.75

FIRST TIME OUT

	W-R	Per cent	£1 Level Stake
2-y-o	5-18	27.8	+28.21
3-y-o	4-39	10.3	-17.88
4-y-o+	7-86	8.1	-45.25
Totals	16-143	11.2	-34.92

JOCKEYS

	W-R	Per cent	£1 Level Stake
Alistair Rawlinson	26-201	12.9	-30.13
Luke Morris	13-108	12.0	-39.25
Silvestre De Sousa	12-45	26.7	+8.83
Theodore Ladd	6-44	13.6	-15.25
Mark Crehan	5-15	33.3	+46.00
Oisin Murphy	4-10	40.0	+17.82
Robert Winston	4-28	14.3	-10.00
Kevin Lundie	4-70	5.7	-33.92
Nicola Currie	3-7	42.9	+38.00
Andrew Mullen	3-54	5.6	-44.43
Dougie Costello	2-5	40.0	+3.25
Gabriele Malune	2-15	13.3	+2.00
Finley Marsh	1-1	100.0	+3.00
Miss Becky Smith	1-1	100.0	+4.00
Joe Fanning	1-2	50.0	+2.33
Gerald Mosse	1-2	50.0	+4.50
Charles Bishop	1-3	33.3	+1.50
Liam Jones	1-4	25.0	+11.00
Miss Serena Brotherton	1-6	16.7	+9.00
David Egan	1-7	14.3	-2.50
Josephine Gordon	1-7	14.3	-5.27
Martin Dwyer	1-8	12.5	+18.00

COURSE RECORD

	Total W-R	Non-Hndcps 2-y-o	Non-Hndcps 3-y-o+	Hndcps 2-y-o	Hndcps 3-y-o+	Per cent	£1 Level Stake
Southwell (A.W)	20-152	0-2	3-26	3-6	14-118	13.2	-46.29
Wolvhptn (A.W)	15-131	0-1	3-33	1-5	11-92	11.5	-20.08
Chelmsford (A.W)	11-116	0-6	0-10	0-3	11-97	9.5	-42.67
Nottingham	8-56	1-5	0-5	0-3	7-43	14.3	-20.55
Pontefract	6-22	0-1	2-5	1-1	3-15	27.3	+6.33
Lingfield (A.W)	4-21	0-0	0-6	0-0	4-15	19.0	+14.50
Leicester	4-23	0-1	1-7	1-1	2-14	17.4	+9.75
Yarmouth	4-40	0-3	0-1	0-2	4-34	10.0	-12.25
Redcar	3-13	0-1	0-3	0-0	3-9	23.1	+9.50
Thirsk	2-18	0-1	0-1	0-0	2-16	11.1	-6.00
Doncaster	2-27	0-2	0-4	0-2	2-19	7.4	-17.00
Lingfield	1-1	0-0	0-0	0-0	1-1	100.0	+2.50
Salisbury	1-2	0-0	0-0	0-0	1-2	50.0	+1.00
Musselburgh	1-4	0-0	0-2	0-0	1-2	25.0	+13.00
Ripon	1-4	0-0	0-0	0-0	1-4	25.0	+3.50
Brighton	1-5	0-1	0-0	0-0	1-4	20.0	+0.50
Newmkt (Jly)	1-5	1-2	0-0	0-0	0-3	20.0	+21.00
Hamilton	1-6	0-0	0-1	0-0	1-5	16.7	-3.50
Windsor	1-6	0-0	1-3	0-0	0-3	16.7	+28.00
Newbury	1-8	0-1	0-1	0-0	1-6	12.5	-1.50
Bath	1-9	0-0	0-0	0-0	1-9	11.1	-5.00
Ascot	1-10	0-1	0-2	0-0	1-7	10.0	-5.50
Sandown	1-11	0-2	0-2	0-0	1-7	9.1	-8.25
Haydock	1-12	0-2	0-2	1-2	0-6	8.3	-6.50
Kempton (A.W)	1-16	0-0	0-1	0-0	1-15	6.3	-10.00
Catterick	1-20	0-0	0-5	1-3	0-12	5.0	-11.00

WINNING HORSES

Horse	Races Run	1st	2nd	3rd	£
Aquarius (IRE)	7	1	0	1	5175
Azam	11	2	1	3	11450
Barrington (IRE)	10	1	0	0	9338
Big Country (IRE)	8	3	2	1	90260
Brigadoon	13	1	2	2	3105
*Busy Street	7	1	3	2	3752
By Royal Approval (IRE)	1	1	0	0	3752
Case Key	11	1	2	1	3752
*Caspian Prince (IRE)	5	1	0	0	62250
Channel Packet	9	3	2	0	10092
Classic Pursuit	22	4	2	7	6728
Cockney Boy	11	1	2	1	3105
Constituent	5	1	0	0	3493
Courier	4	1	0	0	3752
Cryptonite (IRE)	8	1	1	3	4464
Debatable (IRE)	6	2	2	0	6849
Di's Gift	10	1	1	5	3105
*Dragon Beat (IRE)	1	1	0	0	3752
Dream Serenade	8	1	1	0	3105
Epitaph (IRE)	17	1	3	2	3752
*Eponina (IRE)	9	2	0	1	9574

Fantasy Keeper	2	1	0	0	6469
*Free Love	5	1	1	1	4787
Future Score (IRE)	1	1	0	0	4528
*Glory Of Paris (IRE)	2	1	1	0	5434
Greatest Journey	7	1	2	0	11828
Hakam (USA)	10	1	1	0	11972
It Must Be Faith	7	2	0	1	7995
Jackpot Royale	8	3	2	0	15687
Kafoo	7	1	0	1	3429
*Lads Order (IRE)	3	2	0	0	7407
*Lincoln Park	3	2	0	0	9962
Loch Ness Monster (IRE)	4	1	1	0	3881
Michele Strogoff	18	3	6	3	16399
Moi Aussie	6	1	0	0	3105
Moonraker	10	2	0	0	19666
Oyster Card	8	2	0	0	5369
Pearl Nation (USA)	3	1	0	0	3105
Raakid (IRE)	6	1	1	0	3105
Railport Dolly*	4	1	1	0	6728
Ramblow*	9	2	1	1	6857
Red Touch (USA)	5	1	0	0	3752
*Reveleon	6	1	0	2	3235
Saaheq	5	2	0	1	11256
Sean O'Casey (IRE)	8	1	1	0	3752
*Sesame (IRE)	4	1	0	1	3105
Shamrokh (IRE)	10	2	1	2	10868
Side Effect	7	1	1	1	3105
*Slipstream (IRE)	6	1	1	1	3105
Something Lucky (IRE)	20	6	6	3	25035
*Space Bandit	2	1	0	0	3752
Sputnik Planum (USA)	2	2	0	0	12162
Tan	14	4	1	4	15786
Tha'ir (IRE)*	7	3	1	1	10609
The Great Wall (USA)	5	1	1	0	6728
The Lock Master (IRE)	14	1	1	2	3105
What Usain	10	1	0	2	3752
Whenapoet	10	1	1	3	3493
Win Lose Draw (IRE)	4	1	1	0	3429
Zapper Cass (FR)	11	2	0	1	6987
Total winning prize-money					**£549334**
Favourites	**28-86**		**32.6%**		**-2.17**

CHARLIE APPLEBY

NEWMARKET, SUFFOLK

	No. of Hrs	Races Run	1st	2nd	3rd	Unpl	Per cent	£1 Level Stake
2-y-o	*43*	*93*	*22*	*16*	*15*	*40*	*23.7*	*-22.21*
3-y-o	*56*	*165*	*53*	*31*	*13*	*68*	*32.1*	*+17.97*
4-y-o+	*22*	*55*	*13*	*8*	*12*	*22*	*23.6*	*-13.08*
Totals	**121**	**313**	**88**	**55**	**40**	**130**	**28.1**	**-17.32**
2017	*140*	*378*	*106*	*62*	*48*	*160*	*28.0*	*+45.31*
2016	*119*	*331*	*70*	*61*	*44*	*155*	*21.1*	*-15.97*

BY MONTH

2-y-o	W-R	Per cent	£1 Level Stake	3-y-o	W-R	Per cent	£1 Level Stake
January	0-0	0.0	0.00	January	6-15	40.0	+1.64
February	0-0	0.0	0.00	February	2-8	25.0	-3.18
March	0-0	0.0	0.00	March	11-19	57.9	+9.12
April	1-1	100.0	+2.00	April	9-22	40.9	+12.16
May	1-10	10.0	-8.00	May	6-32	18.8	-18.35
June	2-14	14.3	-9.25	June	5-25	20.0	+6.00
July	6-13	46.2	+10.42	July	4-16	25.0	-2.47
August	1-10	10.0	-8.20	August	6-16	37.5	+14.05
September	2-15	13.3	-10.55	September	2-5	40.0	0.00
October	4-13	30.8	-1.83	October	2-5	40.0	+1.00
November	4-13	30.8	+5.00	November	0-1	0.0	-1.00
December	1-4	25.0	-1.80	December	0-1	0.0	-1.00

4-y-o+	W-R	Per cent	£1 Level Stake	Totals	W-R	Per cent	£1 Level Stake
January	1-3	33.3	-0.50	January	7-18	38.9	+1.14
February	0-0	0.0	0.00	February	2-8	25.0	-3.18
March	0-2	0.0	-2.00	March	11-21	52.4	+7.12
April	2-3	66.7	+1.16	April	12-26	46.2	+15.32
May	4-11	36.4	+1.51	May	11-53	20.8	-24.84
June	2-11	18.2	0.00	June	9-50	18.0	-3.25
July	2-11	18.2	-3.50	July	12-40	30.0	+4.45
August	1-5	20.0	-2.25	August	8-31	25.8	+3.60
September	0-3	0.0	-3.00	September	4-23	17.4	-13.55
October	0-2	0.0	-2.00	October	6-20	30.0	-2.83
November	1-3	33.3	-1.50	November	5-17	29.4	-2.50
December	0-1	0.0	-1.00	December	1-6	16.7	-2.00

DISTANCE

2-y-o	W-R	Per cent	£1 Level Stake	3-y-o	W-R	Per cent	£1 Level Stake
5f-6f	7-35	20.0	-14.48	5f-6f	3-14	21.4	-6.53
7f-8f	14-55	25.5	-12.23	7f-8f	20-67	29.9	-11.11
9f-13f	1-3	33.3	+4.50	9f-13f	26-71	36.6	+39.56
14f+	0-0	0.0	0.00	14f+	4-13	30.8	-3.95

4-y-o+	W-R	Per cent	£1 Level Stake	Totals	W-R	Per cent	£1 Level Stake
5f-6f	1-7	14.3	0.00	5f-6f	11-56	19.6	-21.01
7f-8f	1-6	16.7	-2.00	7f-8f	35-128	27.3	-25.34
9f-13f	10-30	33.3	-2.83	9f-13f	37-104	35.6	+41.23
14f+	1-12	8.3	-8.25	14f+	5-25	20.0	-12.20

TYPE OF RACE

Non-Handicaps	W-R	Per cent	£1 Level Stake	Handicaps	W-R	Per cent	£1 Level Stake
2-y-o	21-87	24.1	-17.88	2-y-o	1-6	16.7	-4.33
3-y-o	40-110	36.4	+22.80	3-y-o	13-55	23.6	-4.83
4-y-o+	6-22	27.3	-1.09	4-y-o+	7-33	21.2	-11.99

RACE CLASS

	W-R	Per cent	£1 Level Stake
Class 1	16-74	21.6	+2.16
Class 2	12-58	20.7	-4.27
Class 3	9-39	23.1	-7.59
Class 4	23-70	32.9	-6.53
Class 5	28-72	38.9	-1.09
Class 6	0-0	0.0	0.00
Class 7	0-0	0.0	0.00

FIRST TIME OUT

	W-R	Per cent	£1 Level Stake
2-y-o	13-43	30.2	+0.82
3-y-o	24-56	42.9	+20.82
4-y-o+	7-22	31.8	-1.18
Totals	44-121	36.4	+20.46

JOCKEYS

	W-R	Per cent	£1 Level Stake
William Buick	49-169	29.0	+4.52
James Doyle	16-51	31.4	+4.25
Tom Marquand	5-11	45.5	+2.45
Adam Kirby	4-18	22.2	-9.93
Brett Doyle	4-27	14.8	-18.95
Martin Harley	3-6	50.0	-0.66
George Wood	3-7	42.9	+4.50
Luke Morris	1-1	100.0	+5.00
Jack Mitchell	1-1	100.0	+6.50
Kieran O'Neill	1-2	50.0	+3.00
Connor Beasley	1-2	50.0	0.00

COURSE RECORD

	Total	Non-Hndcps		Hndcps		Per	£1 Level
	W-R	2-y-o	3-y-o+	2-y-o	3-y-o+	cent	Stake
Newmarket	12-51	1-14	7-20	0-0	4-17	23.5	-9.84
Kempton (A.W)	10-20	4-7	4-8	0-2	2-3	50.0	+1.80
Chelmsford (A.W)	8-20	2-5	4-8	0-1	2-6	40.0	-2.73
Lingfield (A.W)	8-20	0-2	7-15	0-0	1-3	40.0	+7.73
Newmkt (Jly)	8-34	4-17	1-7	0-1	3-9	23.5	+2.75
Newcastle (A.W)	6-13	1-3	5-10	0-0	0-0	46.2	+4.62
Ascot	6-32	1-4	4-14	0-0	1-14	18.8	-10.38
Wolvhptn (A.W)	5-16	1-4	2-7	0-0	2-5	31.3	-3.55
Newbury	4-10	0-3	3-4	1-1	0-2	40.0	+3.67
Nottingham	3-3	3-3	0-0	0-0	0-0	100.0	+7.50
Haydock	3-11	0-2	3-5	0-0	0-4	27.3	-2.85
Goodwood	3-13	1-2	2-6	0-1	0-4	23.1	-3.05
Sandown	3-14	1-5	0-5	0-0	2-4	21.4	-5.95
York	3-14	0-2	1-6	0-0	2-6	21.4	+8.50
Doncaster	2-13	0-0	2-7	0-0	0-6	15.4	-9.69
Salisbury	1-1	0-0	0-0	0-0	1-1	100.0	+0.80
Lingfield	1-2	1-1	0-1	0-0	0-0	50.0	+0.25
Epsom	1-6	0-1	1-4	0-0	0-1	16.7	+11.00
Yarmouth	1-7	1-6	0-1	0-0	0-0	14.3	-4.90

WINNING HORSES

Horse	Races Run	1st	2nd	3rd	£
African Jazz (IRE)	6	2	1	2	10221
Al Hilalee	1	1	0	0	7763
Art Du Val	1	1	0	0	4787
Art Song (USA)	1	1	0	0	3881
Aurum (IRE)	3	1	1	1	6469
Auxerre (IRE)	4	3	1	0	20658
Beyond Reason (IRE)	4	1	1	0	3881
Blue Point (IRE)	3	1	0	1	305525
Broderie	4	2	0	1	10480
Calliandra (IRE)	1	1	0	0	3752
Celestial Spheres (IRE)	3	1	1	0	7246
Ceratonia	2	1	0	0	6728
Court Poet	1	1	0	0	7375
Cross Counter	6	3	2	0	119942
D'bai (IRE)	6	1	2	1	35727
Dathanna (IRE)	3	2	0	0	25266
Divine Image (USA)	1	1	0	0	5175
Dubhe	1	1	0	0	12450
Emotionless (IRE)	1	1	0	0	20983
Espadrille	2	1	0	0	8345
Festival Of Ages (USA)	2	1	1	0	3881
Firebird Song (IRE)	2	1	0	1	3752
First Contact (IRE)	5	3	1	0	32792
Flag Festival	1	1	0	0	3752
Fountain Of Time (IRE)	4	2	1	0	7504
Ghostwatch (IRE)	8	4	2	1	128013
Good Fortune	5	1	1	2	3752
Hamada	4	4	0	0	103522
Jazirat (IRE)	3	1	1	1	5175
Key Victory (IRE)	2	1	0	0	28355
La Pelosa (IRE)	5	1	2	1	5822
Leading Spirit (IRE)	5	1	0	1	4140
Line of Duty (IRE)	3	1	2	0	15753
Lover's Knot	2	1	1	0	12938
Loxley (IRE)	3	1	1	0	5822
Masar (IRE)	3	2	0	1	884676
Moonlight Spirit (IRE)	1	1	0	0	6728
Nashirah	3	1	0	1	4916
Night Castle (IRE)	5	2	0	0	7504
Night Story	7	2	1	2	10480
Nordic Lights	4	2	0	0	10221
Oasis Charm	2	2	0	0	40829
Old Persian	6	4	1	0	259627
Poetic Charm	3	1	0	0	15563
Quorto (IRE)	2	2	0	0	50543
Rastrelli (FR)	2	1	0	0	9960
Roussel (IRE)	6	1	0	2	3752
Sayf Shamal (USA)	2	1	0	0	3881
Soliloquy	2	1	0	0	34026
Space Blues (IRE)	1	1	0	0	3881
Star Safari	2	1	0	0	6469
Strings Of Life	4	1	1	0	5175
Swiss Knight	4	1	1	0	6469
Symbolization (IRE)	4	1	1	0	16173
Tribal Quest (USA)	3	2	0	0	20054
White Desert (IRE)	5	1	2	1	5531
Wild Illusion	4	1	2	0	340260
Winds Of Fire (USA)	4	2	1	1	14102
Wuheida	1	1	0	0	59546
Ya Hala (IRE)	2	1	0	0	5563
Zakouski	1	1	0	0	3881

Total winning prize-money **£2821437**

Favourites **50-120** **41.7%** **-12.07**

MICHAEL ATTWATER

EPSOM, SURREY

	No. of Hrs	Races Run	1st	2nd	3rd	Unpl	Per cent	£1 Level Stake
2-y-o	*12*	*48*	*0*	*1*	*1*	*46*	*0.0*	*-48.00*
3-y-o	*15*	*86*	*0*	*6*	*6*	*74*	*0.0*	*-86.00*
4-y-o+	*13*	*125*	*5*	*12*	*27*	*81*	*4.0*	*-97.70*
Totals	**40**	**259**	**5**	**19**	**34**	**201**	**1.9**	**-231.70**
2017	*39*	*237*	*25*	*19*	*22*	*171*	*10.5*	*+12.91*
2016	*39*	*252*	*19*	*20*	*23*	*189*	*7.5*	*-47.00*

JOCKEYS

	W-R	Per cent	£1 Level Stake
Paddy Bradley	2-26	7.7	-10.50
Luke Morris	2-31	6.5	-25.20
Kieren Fox	1-68	1.5	-62.00

COURSE RECORD

	Total W-R	Non-Hndcps 2-y-o	Non-Hndcps 3-y-o+	Hndcps 2-y-o	Hndcps 3-y-o+	Per cent	£1 Level Stake
Wolvhptn (A.W)	2-13	0-2	1-4	0-0	1-7	15.4	-5.20
Lingfield (A.W)	2-74	0-8	1-10	0-3	1-53	2.7	-60.00
Brighton	1-18	0-1	0-0	0-0	1-17	5.6	-12.50

WINNING HORSES

Horse	Races Run	1st	2nd	3rd	£
Ask The Guru	15	1	0	4	3105
Just That Lord	11	2	0	4	9283
Monumental Man*	14	2	1	3	6210
Total winning prize-money					**£18598**
Favourites	**1-9**		**11.1%**		**-7.20**

JEAN-RENE AUVRAY

CALNE, WILTS

	No. of Hrs	Races Run	1st	2nd	3rd	Unpl	Per cent	£1 Level Stake
2-y-o	*0*	*0*	*0*	*0*	*0*	*0*	*0.0*	*0.00*
3-y-o	*1*	*4*	*0*	*0*	*1*	*3*	*0.0*	*-4.00*
4-y-o+	*3*	*21*	*1*	*1*	*0*	*17*	*4.8*	*-15.00*
Totals	**4**	**25**	**1**	**1**	**1**	**20**	**4.0**	**-19.00**
2017	*1*	*1*	*0*	*0*	*0*	*1*	*0.0*	*-1.00*
2016	*0*							*+*

JOCKEYS

	W-R	Per cent	£1 Level Stake
Mr James Harding	1-3	33.3	+3.00

COURSE RECORD

	Total W-R	Non-Hndcps 2-y-o	Non-Hndcps 3-y-o+	Hndcps 2-y-o	Hndcps 3-y-o+	Per cent	£1 Level Stake
Lingfield (A.W)	1-6	0-0	0-1	0-0	1-5	16.7	0.00

WINNING HORSES

Horse	Races Run	1st	2nd	3rd	£
Nafaayes (IRE)	11	1	1	0	2995
Total winning prize-money					**£2995**
Favourites	**0-0**		**0.0%**		**0.00**

ALAN BAILEY

NEWMARKET, SUFFOLK

	No. of Hrs	Races Run	1st	2nd	3rd	Unpl	Per cent	£1 Level Stake
2-y-o	*1*	*5*	*0*	*0*	*0*	*5*	*0.0*	*-5.00*
3-y-o	*4*	*28*	*1*	*3*	*2*	*22*	*3.6*	*-19.00*
4-y-o+	*11*	*72*	*9*	*9*	*9*	*45*	*12.5*	*-24.30*
Totals	**16**	**105**	**10**	**12**	**11**	**72**	**9.5**	**-48.30**
2017	*20*	*143*	*18*	*18*	*13*	*93*	*12.6*	*-6.00*
2016	*26*	*177*	*6*	*20*	*22*	*129*	*3.4*	*-101.00*

BY MONTH

2-y-o	W-R	Per cent	£1 Level Stake	**3-y-o**	W-R	Per cent	£1 Level Stake
January	0-0	0.0	0.00	January	0-0	0.0	0.00
February	0-0	0.0	0.00	February	0-0	0.0	0.00
March	0-0	0.0	0.00	March	0-1	0.0	-1.00
April	0-0	0.0	0.00	April	0-2	0.0	-2.00
May	0-0	0.0	0.00	May	0-1	0.0	-1.00
June	0-0	0.0	0.00	June	0-4	0.0	-4.00
July	0-0	0.0	0.00	July	0-1	0.0	-1.00
August	0-1	0.0	-1.00	August	0-4	0.0	-4.00
September	0-1	0.0	-1.00	September	0-3	0.0	-3.00
October	0-1	0.0	-1.00	October	1-5	20.0	+4.00
November	0-2	0.0	-2.00	November	0-5	0.0	-5.00
December	0-0	0.0	0.00	December	0-2	0.0	-2.00

4-y-o+	W-R	Per cent	£1 Level Stake	**Totals**	W-R	Per cent	£1 Level Stake
January	1-8	12.5	-5.80	January	1-8	12.5	-5.80
February	1-3	33.3	+1.00	February	1-3	33.3	+1.00
March	1-5	20.0	-0.50	March	1-6	16.7	-1.50
April	2-5	40.0	+4.50	April	2-7	28.6	+2.50
May	2-8	25.0	+7.00	May	2-9	22.2	+6.00
June	0-9	0.0	-9.00	June	0-13	0.0	-13.00
July	0-7	0.0	-7.00	July	0-8	0.0	-8.00
August	0-9	0.0	-9.00	August	0-14	0.0	-14.00
September	2-6	33.3	+6.50	September	2-10	20.0	+2.50
October	0-6	0.0	-6.00	October	1-12	8.3	-3.00
November	0-3	0.0	-3.00	November	0-10	0.0	-8.00
December	0-3	0.0	-3.00	December	0-5	0.0	-5.00

DISTANCE

2-y-o	W-R	Per cent	£1 Level Stake	**3-y-o**	W-R	Per cent	£1 Level Stake
5f-6f	0-2	0.0	-2.00	5f-6f	0-2	0.0	-2.00
7f-8f	0-3	0.0	-3.00	7f-8f	0-15	0.0	-15.00
9f-13f	0-0	0.0	0.00	9f-13f	1-11	9.1	-2.00
14f+	0-0	0.0	0.00	14f+	0-0	0.0	0.00

4-y-o+	W-R	Per cent	£1 Level Stake
5f-6f	2-30	6.7	-19.00
7f-8f	2-10	20.0	+4.50
9f-13f	5-26	19.2	-3.80
14f+	0-6	0.0	-6.00

Totals	W-R	Per cent	£1 Level Stake
5f-6f	2-34	5.9	-23.00
7f-8f	2-28	7.1	-13.50
9f-13f	6-37	16.2	-5.80
14f+	0-6	0.0	-6.00

TYPE OF RACE

Non-Handicaps

	W-R	Per cent	£1 Level Stake
2-y-o	0-3	0.0	-3.00
3-y-o	0-4	0.0	-4.00
4-y-o+	0-0	0.0	0.00

Handicaps

	W-R	Per cent	£1 Level Stake
2-y-o	0-2	0.0	-2.00
3-y-o	1-24	4.2	-15.00
4-y-o+	9-72	12.5	-24.30

RACE CLASS

	W-R	Per cent	£1 Level Stake
Class 1	0-0	0.0	0.00
Class 2	1-2	50.0	+3.50
Class 3	0-6	0.0	-6.00
Class 4	0-20	0.0	-20.00
Class 5	3-24	12.5	-2.00
Class 6	6-52	11.5	-22.80
Class 7	0-1	0.0	-1.00

FIRST TIME OUT

	W-R	Per cent	£1 Level Stake
2-y-o	0-1	0.0	-1.00
3-y-o	0-4	0.0	-4.00
4-y-o+	2-11	18.2	+0.20
Totals	2-16	12.5	-4.80

JOCKEYS

	W-R	Per cent	£1 Level Stake
Darragh Keenan	4-16	25.0	+8.50
Joey Haynes	2-10	20.0	+1.50
Josephine Gordon	1-7	14.3	-1.50
Harry Burns	1-11	9.1	-7.00
Jessica Cooley	1-15	6.7	-12.80
Joshua Bryan	1-21	4.8	-12.00

COURSE RECORD

	Total W-R	Non-Hndcps 2-y-o	Non-Hndcps 3-y-o+	Hndcps 2-y-o	Hndcps 3-y-o+	Per cent	£1 Level Stake
Newcastle (A.W)	2-4	0-0	0-0	0-0	2-4	50.0	+2.70
Chelmsford (A.W)	2-18	0-0	0-2	0-0	2-16	11.1	-5.00
Goodwood	1-1	0-0	0-0	0-0	1-1	100.0	+4.50
Sandown	1-3	0-1	0-0	0-0	1-2	33.3	+4.00
Kempton (A.W)	1-6	0-0	0-1	0-1	1-4	16.7	-1.50
Lingfield (A.W)	1-7	0-0	0-0	0-0	1-7	14.3	-2.00
Brighton	1-11	0-0	0-0	0-0	1-11	9.1	-5.00
Yarmouth	1-14	0-0	0-0	0-0	1-14	7.1	-5.00

WINNING HORSES

Horse	Races Run	1st	2nd	3rd	£
*Enigmatic (IRE)	8	2	1	2	22655
Esspeegee	8	3	1	0	9852
Gnaad (IRE)	6	1	0	2	4528
Grasmere (IRE)	9	1	1	0	3493
Lady Of York*	2	1	1	0	3105
Strictly Carter	12	1	0	3	3429
Widnes	12	1	1	1	3105
Total winning prize-money					**£50167**
Favourites	**1-7**		**14.3%**		**-4.80**

GEORGE BAKER

CHIDDINGFOLD, SURREY

	No. of Hrs	Races Run	1st	2nd	3rd	Unpl	Per cent	£1 Level Stake
2-y-o	*16*	*32*	*2*	*1*	*0*	*29*	*6.3*	*+105.00*
3-y-o	*16*	*86*	*3*	*9*	*13*	*60*	*3.5*	*-68.50*
4-y-o+	*11*	*52*	*2*	*8*	*7*	*35*	*3.8*	*-33.50*
Totals	**43**	**170**	**7**	**18**	**20**	**124**	**4.1**	**+3.00**
2017	*50*	*178*	*11*	*18*	*13*	*135*	*6.2*	*-110.02*
2016	*55*	*275*	*28*	*30*	*31*	*186*	*10.2*	*-62.88*

JOCKEYS

	W-R	Per cent	£1 Level Stake
Pat Cosgrave	2-29	6.9	+100.50
Trevor Whelan	2-54	3.7	-38.00
Jim Crowley	1-3	33.3	+12.00
Nicola Currie	1-7	14.3	0.00
Liam Keniry	1-26	3.8	-20.50

COURSE RECORD

	Total W-R	Non-Hndcps 2-y-o	Non-Hndcps 3-y-o+	Hndcps 2-y-o	Hndcps 3-y-o+	Per cent	£1 Level Stake
Lingfield	2-7	1-2	0-3	0-0	1-2	28.6	+9.00
Brighton	2-21	0-1	0-1	0-0	2-19	9.5	-12.00
Leicester	1-7	0-2	0-4	0-0	1-1	14.3	+8.00
Goodwood	1-8	1-4	0-0	0-0	0-4	12.5	+118.00
Kempton (A.W)	1-36	0-8	0-7	0-0	1-21	2.8	-29.00

WINNING HORSES

Horse	Races Run	1st	2nd	3rd	£
Confrerie (IRE)	11	1	2	1	3105
Feel Glorious	4	1	0	0	15753
Hit The Track Jack	3	1	0	0	3752
Infanta Isabella	3	1	1	0	5923
Mamillius	11	1	2	5	5531
Purple Jazz (IRE)	5	1	1	1	3105
The Lamplighter (FR)	11	1	2	1	6469
Total winning prize-money					**£43638**
Favourites	**1-9**		**11.1%**		**-5.50**

JOHN BALDING

SCROOBY, S YORKS

	No. of Hrs	Races Run	1st	2nd	3rd	Unpl	Per cent	£1 Level Stake
2-y-o	*1*	*1*	*0*	*0*	*0*	*1*	*0.0*	*-1.00*
3-y-o	*5*	*21*	*1*	*1*	*2*	*17*	*4.8*	*-17.50*
4-y-o+	*11*	*64*	*3*	*4*	*4*	*53*	*4.7*	*-15.50*
Totals	**17**	**86**	**4**	**5**	**6**	**71**	**4.7**	**-34.00**
2017	*13*	*83*	*11*	*7*	*7*	*57*	*13.3*	*+2.50*

2016	*16*	*89*	*8*	*12*	*8*	*61*	*9.0*	*-36.13*

JOCKEYS

	W-R	Per cent	£1 Level Stake
Lewis Edmunds	3-47	6.4	-21.00
Jason Watson	1-1	100.0	+25.00

COURSE RECORD

	Total W-R	Non-Hndcps 2-y-o	Non-Hndcps 3-y-o+	Hndcps 2-y-o	Hndcps 3-y-o+	Per cent	£1 Level Stake
Wolvhptn (A.W)	2-17	0-0	0-1	0-0	2-16	11.8	+24.00
Nottingham	1-9	0-0	0-1	0-0	1-8	11.1	-5.50
Southwell (A.W)	1-20	0-0	0-3	0-0	1-17	5.0	-12.50

WINNING HORSES

Horse	Races Run	1st	2nd	3rd	£
Showboating (IRE)	12	1	1	1	3752
Undercover Brother	10	1	1	1	3235
You're Cool	9	2	0	1	11062
Total winning prize-money					**£18049**
Favourites	**0-0**		**0.0%**		**0.00**

ANDREW BALDING

KINGSCLERE, HANTS

	No. of Hrs	Races Run	1st	2nd	3rd	Unpl	Per cent	£1 Level Stake
2-y-o	*66*	*180*	*24*	*24*	*25*	*106*	*13.3*	*+77.28*
3-y-o	*74*	*356*	*62*	*52*	*54*	*188*	*17.4*	*-68.75*
4-y-o+	*43*	*236*	*37*	*28*	*28*	*143*	*15.7*	*-63.88*
Totals	**183**	**772**	**123**	**104**	**107**	**437**	**15.9**	**-55.35**
2017	*160*	*677*	*93*	*100*	*71*	*411*	*13.7*	*-67.39*
2016	*160*	*731*	*107*	*103*	*96*	*425*	*14.6*	*-102.74*

BY MONTH

2-y-o	W-R	Per cent	£1 Level Stake	**3-y-o**	W-R	Per cent	£1 Level Stake
January	0-0	0.0	0.00	January	5-12	41.7	+3.96
February	0-0	0.0	0.00	February	5-12	41.7	-1.68
March	0-0	0.0	0.00	March	4-9	44.4	+0.96
April	0-0	0.0	0.00	April	5-44	11.4	-20.75
May	0-8	0.0	-8.00	May	4-49	8.2	-29.25
June	1-14	7.1	-11.00	June	12-57	21.1	+20.73
July	5-20	25.0	+0.42	July	5-42	11.9	-20.88
August	9-45	20.0	+35.20	August	13-49	26.5	+20.10
September	3-40	7.5	-28.08	September	6-35	17.1	-9.19
October	5-34	14.7	+73.75	October	1-23	4.3	-18.00
November	1-12	8.3	+22.00	November	1-12	8.3	-6.50
December	0-7	0.0	-7.00	December	1-12	8.3	-8.25

4-y-o+	W-R	Per cent	£1 Level Stake	**Totals**	W-R	Per cent	£1 Level Stake
January	2-19	10.5	-14.70	January	7-31	22.6	-10.74
February	1-12	8.3	-2.00	February	6-24	25.0	-3.68
March	0-10	0.0	-10.00	March	4-19	21.1	-9.04
April	1-12	8.3	-10.50	April	6-56	10.7	-31.25
May	0-37	0.0	-37.00	May	4-94	4.3	-74.25
June	7-35	20.0	+3.38	June	20-106	18.9	+13.11
July	5-30	16.7	-12.33	July	15-92	16.3	-32.79
August	8-32	25.0	+6.16	August	30-126	23.8	+61.46
September	11-28	39.3	+23.13	September	20-103	19.4	-14.14
October	1-14	7.1	-6.00	October	7-71	9.9	+49.75
November	1-6	16.7	-3.00	November	3-30	10.0	-9.50
December	0-1	0.0	-1.00	December	1-20	5.0	-9.25

DISTANCE

2-y-o	W-R	Per cent	£1 Level Stake	**3-y-o**	W-R	Per cent	£1 Level Stake
5f-6f	9-65	13.8	-8.38	5f-6f	13-49	26.5	+1.17
7f-8f	15-111	13.5	+89.66	7f-8f	25-147	17.0	-34.85
9f-13f	0-4	0.0	-4.00	9f-13f	21-142	14.8	-55.82
14f+	0-0	0.0	0.00	14f+	3-18	16.7	+20.75

4-y-o+	W-R	Per cent	£1 Level Stake	**Totals**	W-R	Per cent	£1 Level Stake
5f-6f	2-18	11.1	-10.50	5f-6f	24-132	18.2	-17.71
7f-8f	19-101	18.8	-6.17	7f-8f	59-359	16.4	+48.64
9f-13f	14-80	17.5	-17.50	9f-13f	35-226	15.5	-77.32
14f+	2-37	5.4	-29.70	14f+	5-55	9.1	-8.95

TYPE OF RACE

Non-Handicaps	W-R	Per cent	£1 Level Stake	**Handicaps**	W-R	Per cent	£1 Level Stake
2-y-o	23-159	14.5	+94.53	2-y-o	1-21	4.8	-17.25
3-y-o	22-148	14.9	-71.64	3-y-o	40-208	19.2	+2.89
4-y-o+	12-77	15.6	-31.03	4-y-o+	25-159	15.7	-32.85

RACE CLASS

	W-R	Per cent	£1 Level Stake
Class 1	10-98	10.2	-54.58
Class 2	18-140	12.9	-5.22
Class 3	13-87	14.9	-20.98
Class 4	37-191	19.4	+76.32
Class 5	32-192	16.7	-28.64
Class 6	12-60	20.0	-19.26
Class 7	1-4	25.0	-1.00

FIRST TIME OUT

	W-R	Per cent	£1 Level Stake
2-y-o	6-66	9.1	+121.00
3-y-o	8-74	10.8	-38.54
4-y-o+	2-43	4.7	-40.20
Totals	16-183	8.7	+42.26

JOCKEYS

	W-R	Per cent	£1 Level Stake
Oisin Murphy	35-198	17.7	-31.80
David Probert	24-163	14.7	+15.76
Jason Watson	22-98	22.4	-21.44
Rob Hornby	11-75	14.7	+8.26
Joshua Bryan	8-52	15.4	-9.00
William Cox	5-42	11.9	+1.45
James Doyle	3-8	37.5	+10.00
Graham Lee	3-10	30.0	+2.63
Martin Dwyer	3-34	8.8	-19.33
Franny Norton	2-6	33.3	+2.38
Jason Hart	1-1	100.0	+2.75
Joao Moreira	1-1	100.0	+4.50
Andrasch Starke	1-1	100.0	+9.00
Per-Anders Graberg	1-1	100.0	+4.50

Duran Fentiman	1-3	33.3	+31.00
William Buick	1-6	16.7	-1.00
Jim Crowley	1-15	6.7	-7.00

COURSE RECORD

	Total W-R	Non-Hndcps 2-y-o	3-y-o+	Hndcps 2-y-o	3-y-o+	Per cent	£1 Level Stake
Chester	12-43	2-4	2-10	0-1	8-28	27.9	+2.72
Chelmsford (A.W)	9-51	0-10	4-13	0-1	5-27	17.6	-24.13
Salisbury	8-32	3-13	1-8	0-1	4-10	25.0	+25.98
Wolvhptn (A.W)	8-33	1-7	3-13	0-1	4-12	24.2	+9.49
Lingfield (A.W)	7-43	0-3	5-17	0-0	2-23	16.3	-13.57
Kempton (A.W)	7-69	3-12	1-22	0-4	3-31	10.1	-18.12
Lingfield	6-16	0-3	2-7	0-0	4-6	37.5	+9.50
Doncaster	6-22	0-6	3-7	1-2	2-7	27.3	+31.75
Ascot	6-37	0-3	2-12	0-0	4-22	16.2	-3.00
Goodwood	5-39	0-8	2-13	0-3	3-15	12.8	-18.63
Haydock	4-19	0-0	2-10	0-0	2-9	21.1	-4.55
Sandown	4-27	1-5	0-7	0-1	3-14	14.8	+0.20
Newmkt (Jly)	4-33	1-9	0-5	0-1	3-18	12.1	-14.88
Brighton	3-12	0-2	1-1	0-1	2-8	25.0	-3.33
Nottingham	3-14	2-6	1-4	0-0	0-4	21.4	-1.02
Southwell (A.W)	3-16	0-0	0-4	0-0	3-12	18.8	-4.00
Windsor	3-22	1-7	2-8	0-0	0-7	13.6	-7.25
York	3-32	0-5	0-11	0-0	3-16	9.4	-4.00
Newbury	3-45	2-17	1-12	0-0	0-16	6.7	+25.00
Hamilton	2-4	1-2	0-1	0-0	1-1	50.0	+3.13
Thirsk	2-7	1-1	0-4	0-0	1-2	28.6	-1.68
Newcastle (A.W)	2-8	0-1	0-4	0-0	2-3	25.0	+4.50
Ffos Las	2-17	1-6	0-2	0-1	1-8	11.8	+1.67
Chepstow	2-18	0-3	0-6	0-0	2-9	11.1	-10.50
Newmarket	2-39	1-11	0-10	0-2	1-16	5.1	-1.25
Carlisle	1-1	0-0	0-0	0-0	1-1	100.0	+2.50
Pontefract	1-5	1-1	0-2	0-1	0-1	20.0	-2.25
Yarmouth	1-5	1-1	0-0	0-0	0-4	20.0	0.00
Ayr	1-7	1-2	0-2	0-0	0-3	14.3	+0.50
Bath	1-10	0-3	1-1	0-1	0-5	10.0	-2.00
Epsom	1-16	0-1	1-1	0-0	0-14	6.3	-13.13
Leicester	1-16	0-3	0-3	0-0	1-10	6.3	-11.00

WINNING HORSES

Horse	Races Run	1st	2nd	3rd	£
Absolutely So (IRE)	4	1	0	0	19407
Aiya (IRE)	5	2	0	2	7504
Bacacarat (IRE)	6	1	1	2	0
Beat The Bank	6	2	0	0	147446
Bell Rock	1	1	0	0	5175
Belle Meade (IRE)	7	1	0	1	6469
Berkshire Blue (IRE)	5	2	0	0	25236
Berkshire Boy (IRE)	7	1	0	1	5531
Berkshire Royal	9	3	3	1	24910
Bye Bye Hong Kong (USA)	4	1	1	1	3752
Carouse (IRE)*	2	2	0	0	6857
Chai Chai (IRE)	7	1	0	1	6081
Cleonte (IRE)	6	1	1	1	22131
Count Octave	5	1	1	2	4949
Crossing The Line	6	4	2	0	72093
Dancing Star	7	1	2	1	34026
Danzan (IRE)	6	2	2	2	12162
Dashing Willoughby	3	1	1	0	6728
Dawn Dancer	10	1	3	3	3752
Diocletian (IRE)	4	1	0	1	31125
Dixieland Diva (USA)	6	1	0	1	3105
Donjuan Triumphant (IRE)	8	1	1	1	22684
Dream Catching (IRE)	10	2	2	2	6857
Duration (IRE)	9	1	0	1	3493
Duretto	4	1	0	2	20983
Dutch Treat	7	1	2	0	6728
Face Like Thunder*	8	1	0	1	4399
Firelight (FR)	6	2	0	0	9057
Flashcard (IRE)	2	2	0	0	10544
Flintrock (GER)	3	1	0	1	5531
Forseti	5	1	0	0	5111
Fox Tal	3	1	0	1	5434
Foxtrot Lady	9	4	3	0	95214
Genetics (FR)	9	3	1	1	33254
Good Birthday (IRE)	3	1	1	0	5434
Grace And Danger (IRE)	1	1	0	0	3881
Hairdryer	2	1	0	0	3752
Happy Power (IRE)	4	2	0	1	12550
Here Comes When (IRE)	4	1	0	0	35727
Highland Pass	9	2	1	2	12550
Horseplay	4	1	2	0	52740
Indomitable (IRE)	4	1	2	0	5852
Intimate Art (IRE)	2	1	0	0	5531
Intransigent	9	1	1	1	7470
Isomer (USA)	10	2	2	1	22642
Ka Ying Star	4	3	0	1	52661
Kabrit (IRE)	8	1	1	2	3752
Lady Perignon	4	1	0	1	3752
Landa Beach (IRE)	1	1	0	0	5434
Lariat	3	1	0	2	6474
Lissitzky (IRE)	4	1	1	0	3752
Look Around	4	2	0	0	20894
Lord Vetinari	7	2	1	0	11256
Lorelina	7	3	0	0	43431
Luna Eclipse (IRE)	5	3	0	1	19407
Macaque	9	1	3	1	6728
Maggie Jonks	5	1	0	0	3817
Maid Up	8	4	1	2	65950
Make Music	9	2	0	2	20086
Master Of Wine (GER)	3	1	1	0	6469
Morando (FR)	5	1	1	1	0
Natural History	4	1	1	1	5531
Never Do Nothing (IRE)	3	2	0	1	9380
Night Of Glory	6	1	0	0	3881
Pak Choi	5	1	1	0	3752
Papa Stour (USA)	9	1	2	1	3752
Pass The Gin	7	1	0	1	5852
Perfect Illusion	8	2	0	0	6857
Pivoine (IRE)	7	2	0	0	56025
Poet's Vanity	6	1	1	0	13695
Rebel Streak	9	3	1	1	47517
Rectory Road	1	1	0	0	3881
Rux Ruxx (IRE)	8	1	2	2	3752

Seasearch	7	2	2	0	5418
Shailene (IRE)	6	2	1	1	11191
Silver Swift	4	1	0	0	3493
Soldier To Follow	6	1	0	0	5175
Straight Right (FR)	4	2	0	0	44185
Strict Tempo	6	1	1	2	3881
Twin Star (IRE)*	5	1	1	1	7470
Whitefountainfairy (IRE)	4	1	0	0	3752
Zwayyan	8	1	2	1	22642
Total winning prize-money					**£1390802**
Favourites	**50-133**		**37.6%**		**-14.80**

RON BARR

SEAMER, N YORKS

	No. of Hrs	Races Run	1st	2nd	3rd	Unpl	Per cent	£1 Level Stake
2-y-o	*0*	*0*	*0*	*0*	*0*	*0*	*0.0*	*0.00*
3-y-o	*3*	*10*	*0*	*0*	*0*	*10*	*0.0*	*-10.00*
4-y-o+	*8*	*61*	*3*	*5*	*3*	*50*	*4.9*	*-39.50*
Totals	**11**	**71**	**3**	**5**	**3**	**60**	**4.2**	**-49.50**
2017	*6*	*51*	*2*	*4*	*5*	*40*	*3.9*	*-12.67*
2016	*9*	*68*	*6*	*1*	*7*	*54*	*8.8*	*-30.50*

JOCKEYS

	W-R	Per cent	£1 Level Stake
Jamie Gormley	2-14	14.3	-2.50
Jane Elliott	1-3	33.3	+7.00

COURSE RECORD

	Total W-R	Non-Hndcps 2-y-o	Non-Hndcps 3-y-o+	Hndcps 2-y-o	Hndcps 3-y-o+	Per cent	£1 Level Stake
Wetherby	1-3	0-0	0-0	0-0	1-3	33.3	+2.50
Redcar	1-11	0-0	0-1	0-0	1-10	9.1	-5.00
Catterick	1-16	0-0	0-4	0-0	1-12	6.3	-6.00

WINNING HORSES

Horse	Races Run	1st	2nd	3rd	£
Leodis (IRE)	1	1	0	0	3493
Mitchum	11	2	0	0	6987
Total winning prize-money					**£10480**
Favourites	**0-1**		**0.0%**		**-1.00**

BRIAN BARR

LONGBURTON, DORSET

	No. of Hrs	Races Run	1st	2nd	3rd	Unpl	Per cent	£1 Level Stake
2-y-o	*2*	*11*	*0*	*2*	*2*	*7*	*0.0*	*-11.00*
3-y-o	*4*	*10*	*0*	*0*	*0*	*10*	*0.0*	*-10.00*
4-y-o+	*12*	*62*	*4*	*8*	*4*	*46*	*6.5*	*-23.50*
Totals	**18**	**83**	**4**	**10**	**6**	**63**	**4.8**	**-44.50**
2017	*26*	*115*	*3*	*8*	*8*	*95*	*2.6*	*-69.00*
2016	*12*	*48*	*2*	*8*	*2*	*36*	*4.2*	*-34.00*

JOCKEYS

	W-R	Per cent	£1 Level Stake
Trevor Whelan	3-26	11.5	+8.00
Finley Marsh	1-3	33.3	+1.50

COURSE RECORD

	Total W-R	Non-Hndcps 2-y-o	Non-Hndcps 3-y-o+	Hndcps 2-y-o	Hndcps 3-y-o+	Per cent	£1 Level Stake
Bath	2-9	0-1	0-0	0-0	2-8	22.2	+1.50
Leicester	1-4	0-0	1-2	0-1	0-1	25.0	+13.00
Lingfield (A.W)	1-18	0-0	0-5	0-1	1-12	5.6	-7.00

WINNING HORSES

Horse	Races Run	1st	2nd	3rd	£
Majorette	7	1	2	0	3105
Mulsanne Chase	3	1	1	0	4011
Toolatetodelegate	17	2	4	0	6210
Total winning prize-money					**£13326**
Favourites	**1-5**		**20.0%**		**-2.25**

DAVID BARRON

MAUNBY, N YORKS

	No. of Hrs	Races Run	1st	2nd	3rd	Unpl	Per cent	£1 Level Stake
2-y-o	*11*	*27*	*1*	*1*	*3*	*22*	*3.7*	*-23.00*
3-y-o	*14*	*63*	*5*	*5*	*7*	*46*	*7.9*	*-34.79*
4-y-o+	*35*	*225*	*21*	*10*	*21*	*171*	*9.3*	*-48.00*
Totals	**60**	**315**	**27**	**16**	**31**	**239**	**8.6**	**-105.79**
2017	*78*	*430*	*50*	*58*	*53*	*267*	*11.6*	*-91.98*
2016	*67*	*354*	*37*	*42*	*32*	*243*	*10.5*	*-54.02*

BY MONTH

2-y-o	W-R	Per cent	£1 Level Stake	3-y-o	W-R	Per cent	£1 Level Stake
January	0-0	0.0	0.00	January	1-4	25.0	+5.00
February	0-0	0.0	0.00	February	0-6	0.0	-6.00
March	0-0	0.0	0.00	March	3-8	37.5	+5.21
April	0-1	0.0	-1.00	April	0-6	0.0	-6.00
May	1-2	50.0	+2.00	May	0-9	0.0	-9.00
June	0-5	0.0	-5.00	June	0-7	0.0	-7.00
July	0-5	0.0	-5.00	July	1-4	25.0	+2.00
August	0-6	0.0	-6.00	August	0-4	0.0	-4.00
September	0-3	0.0	-3.00	September	0-6	0.0	-6.00
October	0-1	0.0	-1.00	October	0-4	0.0	-4.00
November	0-2	0.0	-2.00	November	0-2	0.0	-2.00
December	0-2	0.0	-2.00	December	0-3	0.0	-3.00

4-y-o+	W-R	Per cent	£1 Level Stake	Totals	W-R	Per cent	£1 Level Stake
January	2-14	14.3	-5.00	January	3-18	16.7	0.00
February	1-10	10.0	-5.00	February	1-16	6.3	-11.00
March	1-12	8.3	-6.50	March	4-20	20.0	-1.29
April	1-19	5.3	-14.50	April	1-26	3.8	-21.50
May	2-31	6.5	-10.00	May	3-42	7.1	-17.00

June	3-25	12.0	+10.50	June	3-37	8.1	-1.50
July	4-27	14.8	+2.00	July	5-36	13.9	-1.00
August	3-30	10.0	+5.00	August	3-40	7.5	-5.00
September	1-26	3.8	-18.50	September	1-35	2.9	-27.50
October	0-11	0.0	-11.00	October	0-16	0.0	-16.00
November	1-11	9.1	-1.00	November	1-15	6.7	-3.00
December	2-9	22.2	+6.00	December	2-14	14.3	+3.00

DISTANCE

2-y-o	W-R	Per cent	£1 Level Stake	3-y-o	W-R	Per cent	£1 Level Stake
5f-6f	1-24	4.2	-20.00	5f-6f	2-33	6.1	-22.67
7f-8f	0-3	0.0	-3.00	7f-8f	3-27	11.1	-9.13
9f-13f	0-0	0.0	0.00	9f-13f	0-3	0.0	-3.00
14f+	0-0	0.0	0.00	14f+	0-0	0.0	0.00

4-y-o+	W-R	Per cent	£1 Level Stake	Totals	W-R	Per cent	£1 Level Stake
5f-6f	13-112	11.6	-18.50	5f-6f	16-169	9.5	-61.17
7f-8f	6-90	6.7	-33.50	7f-8f	9-120	7.5	-45.63
9f-13f	2-20	10.0	+7.00	9f-13f	2-23	8.7	+4.00
14f+	0-3	0.0	-3.00	14f+	0-3	0.0	-3.00

TYPE OF RACE

Non-Handicaps	W-R	Per cent	£1 Level Stake	Handicaps	W-R	Per cent	£1 Level Stake
2-y-o	1-22	4.5	-18.00	2-y-o	0-5	0.0	-5.00
3-y-o	4-24	16.7	-4.79	3-y-o	1-39	2.6	-30.00
4-y-o+	3-17	17.6	+13.00	4-y-o+	18-208	8.7	-61.00

RACE CLASS

	W-R	Per cent	£1 Level Stake
Class 1	3-11	27.3	+19.00
Class 2	3-38	7.9	-4.50
Class 3	4-46	8.7	-1.00
Class 4	5-68	7.4	-40.13
Class 5	8-92	8.7	-51.67
Class 6	4-60	6.7	-27.50
Class 7	0-0	0.0	0.00

FIRST TIME OUT

	W-R	Per cent	£1 Level Stake
2-y-o	0-11	0.0	-11.00
3-y-o	2-14	14.3	+4.00
4-y-o+	3-35	8.6	-15.00
Totals	5-60	8.3	-22.00

JOCKEYS

	W-R	Per cent	£1 Level Stake
Ben Curtis	19-140	13.6	+11.21
Jason Hart	2-14	14.3	-3.50
Jane Elliott	2-19	10.5	-3.50
Robert Winston	1-3	33.3	+1.00
Nicola Currie	1-4	25.0	+3.00
Joe Fanning	1-9	11.1	+2.00
Dougie Costello	1-15	6.7	-5.00

COURSE RECORD

	Total W-R	Non-Hndcps 2-y-o	Non-Hndcps 3-y-o+	Hndcps 2-y-o	Hndcps 3-y-o+	Per cent	£1 Level Stake
Southwell (A.W)	6-23	0-1	2-3	0-0	4-19	26.1	+11.88
Wolvhptn (A.W)	4-29	0-1	1-6	0-1	3-21	13.8	-2.67
Pontefract	2-8	0-0	1-1	0-0	1-7	25.0	+21.00
Ripon	2-18	1-7	0-1	0-0	1-10	11.1	-3.00
Newcastle (A.W)	2-40	0-2	1-7	0-1	1-30	5.0	-21.50
Newmkt (Jly)	1-4	0-0	0-0	0-0	1-4	25.0	+1.50
Catterick	1-7	0-0	0-0	0-0	1-7	14.3	+2.00
Leicester	1-7	0-0	1-3	0-0	0-4	14.3	-1.00
Ascot	1-8	0-0	1-1	0-0	0-7	12.5	-3.00
York	1-8	0-0	0-1	0-0	1-7	12.5	+9.00
Chelmsford (A.W)	1-11	0-0	0-1	0-0	1-10	9.1	-4.00
Hamilton	1-12	0-0	0-3	0-0	1-9	8.3	-2.00
Ayr	1-15	0-0	0-0	0-1	1-14	6.7	-12.00
Redcar	1-15	0-2	0-2	0-1	1-10	6.7	-7.50
Doncaster	1-16	0-1	0-2	0-0	1-13	6.3	-11.50
Thirsk	1-30	0-4	0-4	0-0	1-22	3.3	-19.00

WINNING HORSES

Horse	Races Run	1st	2nd	3rd	£
Above The Rest (IRE)	9	2	0	2	64597
Black Salt	9	2	0	2	9833
Bolder Bob (IRE)	5	2	0	0	26145
Carpet Time (IRE)	7	1	1	1	3752
Clon Coulis (IRE)	6	2	0	0	62036
Dirchill (IRE)*	9	2	0	1	8604
Fake News	4	1	0	0	6728
Gifted Zebedee (IRE)	2	1	0	0	3881
Glorious Politics	5	1	0	1	5531
Granny Roz	4	1	0	2	3752
Gunmetal (IRE)	5	3	0	0	72564
Handsome Dude	9	1	0	1	5531
Kodi Beach	7	1	0	1	3752
Kripke (IRE)	5	1	1	2	8345
Liquid (IRE)*	9	1	0	0	3752
Magical Molly Joe	7	1	0	0	3105
Mr Coco Bean (USA)	7	1	0	2	3105
Queen In Waiting (IRE)	6	1	0	1	16173
Robben Rainbow	12	1	0	1	3493
Tember	12	1	1	0	4140
Total winning prize-money					**£318819**
Favourites	**2-23**		**8.7%**		**-19.17**

REBECCA BASTIMAN

COWTHORPE, N YORKS

	No. of Hrs	Races Run	1st	2nd	3rd	Unpl	Per cent	£1 Level Stake
2-y-o	*1*	*5*	*0*	*0*	*1*	*4*	*0.0*	*-5.00*
3-y-o	*6*	*33*	*1*	*1*	*2*	*29*	*3.0*	*-30.00*
4-y-o+	*25*	*276*	*26*	*31*	*34*	*185*	*9.4*	*-66.50*
Totals	**32**	**314**	**27**	**32**	**37**	**218**	**8.6**	**-101.50**
2017	*26*	*223*	*22*	*27*	*25*	*149*	*9.9*	*-86.75*
2016	*25*	*215*	*15*	*19*	*20*	*160*	*7.0*	*-66.50*

BY MONTH

2-y-o	W-R	Per cent	£1 Level Stake	3-y-o	W-R	Per cent	£1 Level Stake
January	0-0	0.0	0.00	January	0-0	0.0	0.00
February	0-0	0.0	0.00	February	0-0	0.0	0.00

	W-R	Per cent	£1 Level Stake		W-R	Per cent	£1 Level Stake
March	0-0	0.0	0.00	March	0-2	0.0	-2.00
April	0-1	0.0	-1.00	April	0-3	0.0	-3.00
May	0-1	0.0	-1.00	May	0-5	0.0	-5.00
June	0-1	0.0	-1.00	June	0-5	0.0	-5.00
July	0-0	0.0	0.00	July	1-6	16.7	-3.00
August	0-1	0.0	-1.00	August	0-7	0.0	-7.00
September	0-1	0.0	-1.00	September	0-3	0.0	-3.00
October	0-0	0.0	0.00	October	0-2	0.0	-2.00
November	0-0	0.0	0.00	November	0-0	0.0	0.00
December	0-0	0.0	0.00	December	0-0	0.0	0.00

4-y-o+	W-R	Per cent	£1 Level Stake	Totals	W-R	Per cent	£1 Level Stake
January	0-14	0.0	-14.00	January	0-14	0.0	-14.00
February	4-25	16.0	+28.00	February	4-25	16.0	+28.00
March	3-28	10.7	-11.25	March	3-30	10.0	-13.25
April	2-24	8.3	+13.00	April	2-28	7.1	+9.00
May	5-37	13.5	-17.75	May	5-43	11.6	-23.75
June	1-27	3.7	-23.75	June	1-33	3.0	-29.75
July	3-32	9.4	-9.50	July	4-38	10.5	-12.50
August	2-22	9.1	-13.50	August	2-30	6.7	-21.50
September	3-30	10.0	+4.00	September	3-34	8.8	0.00
October	3-24	12.5	-8.75	October	3-26	11.5	-10.75
November	0-10	0.0	-10.00	November	0-10	0.0	-10.00
December	0-3	0.0	-3.00	December	0-3	0.0	-3.00

DISTANCE

2-y-o	W-R	Per cent	£1 Level Stake	3-y-o	W-R	Per cent	£1 Level Stake
5f-6f	0-5	0.0	-5.00	5f-6f	1-21	4.8	-18.00
7f-8f	0-0	0.0	0.00	7f-8f	0-9	0.0	-9.00
9f-13f	0-0	0.0	0.00	9f-13f	0-3	0.0	-3.00
14f+	0-0	0.0	0.00	14f+	0-0	0.0	0.00

4-y-o+	W-R	Per cent	£1 Level Stake	Totals	W-R	Per cent	£1 Level Stake
5f-6f	11-94	11.7	-18.63	5f-6f	12-120	10.0	-41.63
7f-8f	14-151	9.3	-22.38	7f-8f	14-160	8.8	-31.38
9f-13f	1-31	3.2	-25.50	9f-13f	1-34	2.9	-28.50
14f+	0-0	0.0	0.00	14f+	0-0	0.0	0.00

TYPE OF RACE

Non-Handicaps	W-R	Per cent	£1 Level Stake	Handicaps	W-R	Per cent	£1 Level Stake
2-y-o	0-3	0.0	-3.00	2-y-o	0-2	0.0	-2.00
3-y-o	0-4	0.0	-4.00	3-y-o	1-29	3.4	-26.00
4-y-o+	1-5	20.0	-2.12	4-y-o+	25-271	9.2	-64.38

RACE CLASS

	W-R	Per cent	£1 Level Stake
Class 1	0-0	0.0	0.00
Class 2	2-17	11.8	+12.75
Class 3	1-15	6.7	+6.00
Class 4	3-47	6.4	-33.00
Class 5	12-106	11.3	-48.25
Class 6	6-119	5.0	-51.50
Class 7	3-10	30.0	+12.50

FIRST TIME OUT

	W-R	Per cent	£1 Level Stake
2-y-o	0-1	0.0	-1.00
3-y-o	0-6	0.0	-6.00
4-y-o+	1-25	4.0	-4.00
Totals	1-32	3.1	-11.00

JOCKEYS

	W-R	Per cent	£1 Level Stake
Daniel Tudhope	10-57	17.5	-12.63
Jamie Gormley	4-18	22.2	-3.38
Jason Hart	3-53	5.7	-8.00
David Allan	2-6	33.3	+4.75
Theodore Ladd	2-13	15.4	+12.00
Miss Becky Smith	1-1	100.0	+2.25
Gary Mahon	1-3	33.3	+1.00
Royston Ffrench	1-6	16.7	+20.00
Callum Rodriguez	1-6	16.7	-1.00
Lewis Edmunds	1-14	7.1	-8.50
Connor Beasley	1-14	7.1	+15.00

COURSE RECORD

	Total W-R	Non-Hndcps 2-y-o	Non-Hndcps 3-y-o+	Hndcps 2-y-o	Hndcps 3-y-o+	Per cent	£1 Level Stake
Wolvhptn (A.W)	6-45	0-0	0-1	0-0	6-44	13.3	+18.75
Hamilton	5-26	0-0	0-0	0-0	5-26	19.2	-4.63
Musselburgh	5-29	0-1	0-1	0-1	5-26	17.2	-7.75
Thirsk	3-15	0-0	0-1	0-1	3-13	20.0	+26.50
Ayr	3-35	0-0	0-0	0-0	3-35	8.6	-19.75
Pontefract	2-9	0-0	0-0	0-0	2-9	22.2	-1.50
Beverley	2-29	0-1	1-3	0-0	1-25	6.9	-13.13
Ripon	1-16	0-1	0-0	0-0	1-15	6.3	+10.00

WINNING HORSES

Horse	Races Run	1st	2nd	3rd	£
*Amazing Grazing (IRE)	7	1	1	1	4787
Be Bold	14	1	2	2	3398
Berlios (IRE)*	13	1	5	1	3182
Clergyman	15	2	2	1	5369
Edgar Allan Poe (IRE)	13	1	2	2	5434
Elerfaan (IRE)	3	1	1	0	4140
Gone With The Wind (GER)	17	2	0	1	4528
Harbour Patrol (IRE)	15	2	1	0	6503
Hayadh	14	2	1	1	20184
Hitman	12	1	2	1	4075
Jacob's Pillow	9	2	0	1	8432
Logi (IRE)	13	3	3	2	15105
Natajack	9	1	0	2	4140
Roaring Forties (IRE)	14	1	1	0	3170
Royal Brave (IRE)	14	3	1	3	28242
Zeshov (IRE)	17	2	2	5	7633
Zumurud (IRE)	7	1	0	1	3881
Total winning prize-money					**£132203**
Favourites	**12-30**		**40.0%**		**15.63**

BRIAN BAUGH

AUDLEY, STAFFS

	No. of Hrs	Races Run	1st	2nd	3rd	Unpl	Per cent	£1 Level Stake
2-y-o	*2*	*2*	*0*	*0*	*0*	*2*	*0.0*	*-2.00*

3-y-o	*0*	*0*	*0*	*0*	*0*	*0*	*0.0*	*0.00*
4-y-o+	*3*	*24*	*2*	*5*	*3*	*14*	*8.3*	*-14.50*
Totals	**5**	**26**	**2**	**5**	**3**	**16**	**7.7**	**-16.50**
2017	*3*	*23*	*1*	*1*	*3*	*18*	*4.3*	*-15.50*
2016	*7*	*36*	*3*	*3*	*5*	*25*	*8.3*	*-6.00*

JOCKEYS

	W-R	Per cent	£1 Level Stake
Luke Morris	2-6	33.3	+3.50

COURSE RECORD

	Total W-R	Non-Hndcps 2-y-o	Non-Hndcps 3-y-o+	Hndcps 2-y-o	Hndcps 3-y-o+	Per cent	£1 Level Stake
Chepstow	2-3	0-0	0-0	0-0	2-3	66.7	+6.50

WINNING HORSES

Horse	Races Run	1st	2nd	3rd	£
David's Beauty (IRE)	11	2	5	1	6210
Total winning prize-money					**£6210**
Favourites	**0-1**		**0.0%**		**-1.00**

RALPH BECKETT

KIMPTON, HANTS

	No. of Hrs	Races Run	1st	2nd	3rd	Unpl	Per cent	£1 Level Stake
2-y-o	*55*	*161*	*27*	*26*	*18*	*90*	*16.8*	*-35.31*
3-y-o	*52*	*258*	*46*	*47*	*34*	*131*	*17.8*	*-23.82*
4-y-o+	*23*	*103*	*15*	*16*	*10*	*62*	*14.6*	*-19.38*
Totals	**130**	**522**	**88**	**89**	**62**	**283**	**16.9**	**-78.51**
2017	*136*	*464*	*66*	*59*	*69*	*269*	*14.2*	*-103.21*
2016	*133*	*506*	*101*	*70*	*55*	*279*	*20.0*	*+7.55*

BY MONTH

2-y-o	W-R	Per cent	£1 Level Stake	3-y-o	W-R	Per cent	£1 Level Stake
January	0-0	0.0	0.00	January	1-10	10.0	-2.00
February	0-0	0.0	0.00	February	1-2	50.0	+0.50
March	0-0	0.0	0.00	March	0-7	0.0	-7.00
April	1-3	33.3	+3.00	April	6-29	20.7	+33.00
May	0-7	0.0	-7.00	May	7-41	17.1	-0.08
June	1-7	14.3	-5.67	June	5-44	11.4	-26.32
July	2-18	11.1	0.00	July	7-35	20.0	-12.32
August	3-30	10.0	-18.00	August	7-35	20.0	-13.84
September	9-37	24.3	+18.63	September	5-27	18.5	-1.00
October	7-29	24.1	5.42	October	5-20	25.0	+8.50
November	3-22	13.6	-15.09	November	2-7	28.6	-2.27
December	1-8	12.5	-5.75	December	0-1	0.0	-1.00

4-y-o+	W-R	Per cent	£1 Level Stake	Totals	W-R	Per cent	£1 Level Stake
January	1-10	10.0	-7.50	January	2-20	10.0	-9.50
February	0-1	0.0	-1.00	February	1-3	33.3	-0.50
March	0-4	0.0	-4.00	March	0-11	0.0	-11.00
April	2-8	25.0	-2.75	April	9-40	22.5	+33.25
May	3-15	20.0	+5.75	May	10-63	15.9	-1.33
June	2-18	11.1	-7.00	June	8-69	11.6	-38.99
July	2-11	18.2	-3.50	July	11-64	17.2	-15.82
August	2-11	18.2	+4.63	August	12-76	15.8	-27.21
September	1-11	9.1	+4.00	September	15-75	20.0	+21.63
October	0-7	0.0	-7.00	October	12-56	21.4	-3.92
November	2-6	33.3	0.00	November	7-35	20.0	-2.27
December	0-1	0.0	-1.00	December	1-10	10.0	-2.00

DISTANCE

2-y-o	W-R	Per cent	£1 Level Stake	3-y-o	W-R	Per cent	£1 Level Stake
5f-6f	7-56	12.5	-19.92	5f-6f	6-38	15.8	-0.40
7f-8f	17-98	17.3	-19.52	7f-8f	15-84	17.9	-1.33
9f-13f	3-7	42.9	+4.13	9f-13f	23-120	19.2	-13.00
14f+	0-0	0.0	0.00	14f+	2-16	12.5	-9.09

4-y-o+	W-R	Per cent	£1 Level Stake	Totals	W-R	Per cent	£1 Level Stake
5f-6f	0-4	0.0	-4.00	5f-6f	13-98	13.3	-24.32
7f-8f	5-31	16.1	-7.13	7f-8f	37-213	17.4	-27.98
9f-13f	8-49	16.3	-4.63	9f-13f	34-176	19.3	-13.50
14f+	2-19	10.5	-3.63	14f+	4-35	11.4	-12.72

TYPE OF RACE

Non-Handicaps	W-R	Per cent	£1 Level Stake	Handicaps	W-R	Per cent	£1 Level Stake
2-y-o	24-135	17.8	-21.31	2-y-o	3-26	11.5	-14.00
3-y-o	12-96	12.5	-22.99	3-y-o	34-162	21.0	-0.83
4-y-o+	6-30	20.0	+5.00	4-y-o+	9-73	12.3	-24.38

RACE CLASS

	W-R	Per cent	£1 Level Stake
Class 1	9-51	17.6	+3.03
Class 2	7-52	13.5	-3.00
Class 3	13-58	22.4	+5.38
Class 4	22-127	17.3	-24.93
Class 5	31-199	15.6	-61.99
Class 6	6-35	17.1	+3.00
Class 7	0-0	0.0	0.00

FIRST TIME OUT

	W-R	Per cent	£1 Level Stake
2-y-o	11-55	20.0	+5.66
3-y-o	6-52	11.5	+6.50
4-y-o+	4-23	17.4	-9.75
Totals	21-130	16.2	+2.41

JOCKEYS

	W-R	Per cent	£1 Level Stake
Harry Bentley	44-207	21.3	-0.27
Richard Kingscote	12-73	16.4	-20.38
Oisin Murphy	8-57	14.0	-25.52
Louis Steward	6-52	11.5	+9.00
Silvestre De Sousa	4-8	50.0	+9.07
Daniel Tudhope	4-9	44.4	+15.30
Ryan Moore	2-8	25.0	+4.00
Kevin Stott	2-11	18.2	-3.25
William Buick	1-1	100.0	+0.67
Graham Lee	1-3	33.3	+6.00
P J McDonald	1-6	16.7	-3.38
David Probert	1-6	16.7	-2.25
Josephine Gordon	1-7	14.3	-2.50
Stevie Donohoe	1-12	8.3	-3.00

COURSE RECORD

	Total W-R	Non-Hndcps 2-y-o	Non-Hndcps 3-y-o+	Hndcps 2-y-o	Hndcps 3-y-o+	Per cent	£1 Level Stake
Kempton (A.W)	13-65	4-23	0-7	0-5	9-30	20.0	-2.48
Newmarket	8-29	2-9	2-7	2-3	2-10	27.6	+12.41
Goodwood	5-20	2-4	1-5	0-0	2-11	25.0	+24.00
Salisbury	5-30	2-11	1-6	0-0	2-13	16.7	-7.75
Lingfield (A.W)	5-38	1-8	3-16	0-2	1-12	13.2	-4.13
Newcastle (A.W)	4-10	0-2	0-1	0-1	4-6	40.0	+5.50
Chepstow	4-12	0-2	0-4	0-0	4-6	33.3	-3.51
Chelmsford (A.W)	4-23	1-2	0-4	0-2	3-15	17.4	-7.72
Windsor	4-23	0-3	2-6	0-0	2-14	17.4	-4.75
Wolvhptn (A.W)	4-26	1-7	0-3	0-1	3-15	15.4	-9.88
Pontefract	3-5	1-1	1-1	0-1	1-2	60.0	+4.48
Ayr	3-7	2-3	1-3	0-0	0-1	42.9	+19.63
York	3-15	1-2	0-3	0-0	2-10	20.0	+4.75
Leicester	3-18	1-4	1-2	0-2	1-10	16.7	-6.33
Ffos Las	2-9	1-4	1-2	0-2	0-1	22.2	-2.25
Epsom	2-10	0-0	0-2	0-0	2-8	20.0	-3.25
Nottingham	2-14	0-4	2-7	0-2	0-1	14.3	-9.25
Doncaster	2-17	1-6	0-4	0-0	1-7	11.8	-10.88
Newmkt (Jly)	2-18	1-8	0-2	0-0	1-8	11.1	+3.00
Newbury	2-28	2-10	0-7	0-0	0-11	7.1	-17.00
Ripon	1-2	1-1	0-0	0-0	0-1	50.0	+2.00
Thirsk	1-4	0-0	1-3	0-0	0-1	25.0	-1.20
Yarmouth	1-4	0-0	0-1	0-0	1-3	25.0	+9.00
Bath	1-7	0-3	0-1	0-1	1-2	14.3	-4.90
Chester	1-10	0-0	0-5	1-1	0-4	10.0	-6.25
Lingfield	1-10	0-3	1-4	0-2	0-1	10.0	-7.25
Ascot	1-17	0-2	1-5	0-0	0-10	5.9	-9.50
Sandown	1-17	0-6	0-6	0-0	1-5	5.9	-11.00

WINNING HORSES

Horse	Races Run	1st	2nd	3rd	£
Akvavera	7	2	1	0	15807
Albizzia	6	1	1	1	3752
Antonia De Vega (IRE)	3	2	0	0	36118
Blazing Saddles	5	1	0	1	9704
Blizzard	7	1	1	0	3105
Brasca	2	1	1	0	7375
Breath Caught	6	2	2	1	17100
Briyouni (FR)	10	1	0	0	3105
Ceilidhs Dream	4	1	0	0	6469
Chaleur	4	2	1	1	36559
Considered Opinion	8	2	3	0	9283
Construct	7	1	3	0	3881
Cross My Mind (IRE)	12	3	1	2	13423
Dancing Vega (IRE)	1	1	0	0	3752
Dave Dexter	8	3	1	1	46652
Dazzling Rock (IRE)	7	1	1	0	5434
Desirous	4	1	2	0	3881
Di Fede (IRE)	7	2	1	1	32136
Diocles Of Rome (IRE)	8	2	3	0	10221
*Dolphin Vista (IRE)	2	1	1	0	36862
Edge Of The World (IRE)*	5	2	1	1	7569
Fearless Warrior (FR)	4	1	1	2	5822
Feliciana De Vega	1	1	0	0	5175
Font Vert (FR)	8	1	0	1	3105
Fragrant Belle	1	1	0	0	3752
Fresh Terms	9	3	2	2	13811
Frown	9	2	2	1	13779
Gilded Hour (IRE)	3	1	0	2	3752
Glance	4	1	1	0	4528
Gripper	7	1	1	1	5434
Guildhall	3	1	0	1	6728
Here And Now	5	1	0	1	43575
Isabel De Urbina (IRE)	6	2	0	0	56365
*Junius Brutus (FR)	4	1	1	0	9452
Manuela De Vega (IRE)	2	2	0	0	38247
Mesquite	9	2	2	1	13456
Mighty Mac (IRE)	5	1	0	0	3105
Mitchum Swagger	4	1	0	1	20983
Mount Moriah	3	1	0	0	22684
Nine Below Zero	9	1	2	3	5387
Nivaldo (IRE)	2	2	0	0	8668
Pacify	8	1	1	1	12450
Parisian (IRE)	2	1	0	0	3105
Plait	1	1	0	0	3817
Podemos (GER)	7	2	1	1	12938
*Poyle Charlotte	10	2	2	2	7504
Prevent	9	1	2	0	6469
Princess Salamah (IRE)	2	1	0	1	3752
Queen Power (IRE)	1	1	0	0	7763
Richenza (FR)	6	1	2	1	10350
Rock Eagle	5	3	1	0	82204
Sam Cooke (IRE)	3	1	2	0	9704
Sand Share	2	1	0	1	5822
Scintilating	3	1	0	0	5111
Skymax (GER)	4	1	1	1	24900
Star Story	1	1	0	0	3752
Stormwave (IRE)	1	1	0	0	5111
Taurean Star (IRE)	3	1	0	0	31125
Thimbleweed	5	2	1	1	8992
Time Change	2	1	0	1	12450
Victory Chime (IRE)	6	3	0	0	20701
Zilara (IRE)	6	1	2	1	3752

Total winning prize-money **£881768**

Favourites **41-113** **36.3%** **-7.84**

MICHAEL BELL

NEWMARKET, SUFFOLK

	No. of Hrs	Races Run	1st	2nd	3rd	Unpl	Per cent	£1 Level Stake
2-y-o	*46*	*129*	*16*	*11*	*15*	*87*	*12.4*	*+0.20*
3-y-o	*36*	*184*	*30*	*26*	*24*	*104*	*16.3*	*-41.81*
4-y-o+	*12*	*66*	*10*	*7*	*12*	*37*	*15.2*	*-34.03*
Totals	**94**	**379**	**56**	**44**	**51**	**228**	**14.8**	**-75.64**
2017	*76*	*346*	*53*	*61*	*40*	*192*	*15.3*	*-73.34*
2016	*74*	*323*	*37*	*51*	*55*	*179*	*11.5*	*-134.77*

BY MONTH

2-y-o	W-R	Per cent	£1 Level Stake
January	0-0	0.0	0.00
February	0-0	0.0	0.00
March	0-0	0.0	0.00
April	0-1	0.0	-1.00
May	3-13	23.1	-5.40
June	3-19	15.8	+1.88
July	3-16	18.8	+14.75
August	2-21	9.5	-11.00
September	2-17	11.8	-12.46
October	1-30	3.3	-28.56
November	2-7	28.6	+47.00
December	0-5	0.0	-5.00

3-y-o	W-R	Per cent	£1 Level Stake
January	2-9	22.2	-3.25
February	1-6	16.7	-4.09
March	2-9	22.2	+7.75
April	3-19	15.8	+10.00
May	3-20	15.0	+1.25
June	2-31	6.5	-24.88
July	6-24	25.0	-5.75
August	7-34	20.6	-5.59
September	3-18	16.7	-8.75
October	1-12	8.3	-6.50
November	0-2	0.0	-2.00
December	0-0	0.0	0.00

4-y-o+	W-R	Per cent	£1 Level Stake
January	1-6	16.7	-2.75
February	1-1	100.0	+0.91
March	1-4	25.0	-1.38
April	0-5	0.0	-5.00
May	0-6	0.0	-6.00
June	0-8	0.0	-8.00
July	4-7	57.1	+7.75
August	2-13	15.4	-9.07
September	1-9	11.1	-3.50
October	0-4	0.0	-4.00
November	0-2	0.0	-2.00
December	0-1	0.0	-1.00

Totals	W-R	Per cent	£1 Level Stake
January	3-15	20.0	-6.00
February	2-7	28.6	-3.18
March	3-13	23.1	+6.37
April	3-25	12.0	+4.00
May	6-39	15.4	-10.15
June	5-58	8.6	-31.00
July	13-47	27.7	+16.75
August	11-68	16.2	-25.66
September	6-44	13.6	-24.71
October	2-46	4.3	-39.06
November	2-11	18.2	-4.00
December	0-6	0.0	-1.00

DISTANCE

2-y-o	W-R	Per cent	£1 Level Stake
5f-6f	10-67	14.9	-5.36
7f-8f	5-59	8.5	+7.13
9f-13f	1-3	33.3	-1.56
14f+	0-0	0.0	0.00

3-y-o	W-R	Per cent	£1 Level Stake
5f-6f	3-26	11.5	-6.75
7f-8f	10-73	13.7	-17.97
9f-13f	15-78	19.2	-16.09
14f+	2-7	28.6	-1.00

4-y-o+	W-R	Per cent	£1 Level Stake
5f-6f	2-11	18.2	-6.67
7f-8f	1-19	5.3	-17.09
9f-13f	7-26	26.9	-0.27
14f+	0-10	0.0	-10.00

Totals	W-R	Per cent	£1 Level Stake
5f-6f	15-104	14.4	-18.78
7f-8f	16-151	10.6	-27.93
9f-13f	23-107	21.5	-17.92
14f+	2-17	11.8	-11.00

TYPE OF RACE

Non-Handicaps	W-R	Per cent	£1 Level Stake
2-y-o	14-109	12.8	+9.45
3-y-o	4-40	10.0	-18.88
4-y-o+	3-9	33.3	-2.36

Handicaps	W-R	Per cent	£1 Level Stake
2-y-o	2-20	10.0	-9.25
3-y-o	26-144	18.1	-22.93
4-y-o+	7-57	12.3	-31.67

RACE CLASS

	W-R	Per cent	£1 Level Stake
Class 1	4-24	16.7	+14.73
Class 2	1-40	2.5	-37.25
Class 3	3-30	10.0	-19.75
Class 4	18-115	15.7	-46.17
Class 5	23-125	18.4	+25.15
Class 6	7-43	16.3	-10.34
Class 7	0-2	0.0	-2.00

FIRST TIME OUT

	W-R	Per cent	£1 Level Stake
2-y-o	5-46	10.9	+31.50
3-y-o	5-36	13.9	-9.25
4-y-o+	1-12	8.3	-9.38
Totals	11-94	11.7	+12.87

JOCKEYS

	W-R	Per cent	£1 Level Stake
Hayley Turner	11-91	12.1	+4.38
Cameron Noble	9-50	18.0	-9.22
Jamie Spencer	5-36	13.9	-4.15
Silvestre De Sousa	4-19	21.1	+8.44
Daniel Tudhope	4-21	19.0	+4.29
Andrea Atzeni	3-7	42.9	+2.38
Oisin Murphy	3-12	25.0	-2.00
James Doyle	3-15	20.0	-5.15
David Allan	2-3	66.7	+2.41
Joe Fanning	2-4	50.0	+14.00
P J McDonald	2-5	40.0	+0.50
Adam Kirby	2-8	25.0	-2.59
Sara Del Fabbro	2-9	22.2	-4.67
Clifford Lee	1-1	100.0	+2.50
Duran Fentiman	1-1	100.0	+1.75
Jim Crowley	1-2	50.0	+3.50
Stevie Donohoe	1-2	50.0	+1.00

COURSE RECORD

	Total W-R	Non-Hndcps 2-y-o	Non-Hndcps 3-y-o+	Hndcps 2-y-o	Hndcps 3-y-o+	Per cent	£1 Level Stake
Yarmouth	7-24	2-9	0-1	0-1	5-13	29.2	+19.68
Wolvhptn (A.W)	5-18	2-5	1-4	0-0	2-9	27.8	+56.75
Kempton (A.W)	5-22	0-4	2-3	0-2	3-13	22.7	-9.81
Chelmsford (A.W)	5-33	2-8	0-4	0-2	3-19	15.2	-17.06
Catterick	4-9	0-2	1-1	0-1	3-5	44.4	+1.66
Windsor	4-19	1-6	1-4	0-0	2-9	21.1	-3.40
Newmkt (Jly)	4-29	2-12	0-3	0-2	2-12	13.8	+5.13
Sandown	3-12	0-1	0-3	0-0	3-8	25.0	-1.50
Lingfield	2-7	0-3	0-1	0-0	2-3	28.6	+1.00
Beverley	2-10	0-1	0-1	0-0	2-8	20.0	+4.00
Doncaster	2-16	0-3	0-3	1-2	1-8	12.5	-9.00
Leicester	2-16	0-6	0-0	1-1	1-9	12.5	-5.00
Bath	1-4	0-1	0-1	0-0	1-2	25.0	-2.00
Musselburgh	1-4	0-0	0-0	0-0	1-4	25.0	-0.50
Ripon	1-4	1-3	0-0	0-0	0-1	25.0	-1.00
Brighton	1-6	1-1	0-1	0-0	0-4	16.7	-3.50
Haydock	1-9	1-2	0-0	0-1	0-6	11.1	-7.71
Nottingham	1-9	1-4	0-2	0-2	0-1	11.1	-6.00
York	1-9	0-2	1-1	0-1	0-5	11.1	+4.00
Chepstow	1-10	0-3	1-2	0-0	0-5	10.0	-7.63
Ascot	1-17	1-7	0-3	0-1	0-6	5.9	-11.00
Newmarket	1-17	0-7	0-0	0-2	1-8	5.9	-11.50
Lingfield (A.W)	1-17	0-0	0-5	0-0	1-12	5.9	-13.25

WINNING HORSES

Horse	Races Run	1st	2nd	3rd	£
Allmankind	4	1	1	1	6081
Arabian Jazz (IRE)	8	2	2	1	9208
Artair (IRE)	8	1	0	2	4787
Artarmon (IRE)	10	4	2	1	38296
Balladeer	3	1	0	0	6081
Choice Encounter*	6	1	2	1	6469
Christopher Wood (IRE)	8	1	2	1	5531
Demurrer (USA)	3	1	0	1	3105
Eightsome Reel	1	1	0	0	3752
Fabricate	5	2	1	0	59546
Flying Sparkle (IRE)	4	1	1	1	3752
Freebe Rocks (IRE)*	11	2	3	2	6857
Geetanjali (IRE)	15	4	4	3	14232
Girls Talk (IRE)	4	1	0	0	3105
Highlight Reel (IRE)	12	1	0	3	6469
Hot Off The Press (IRE)	6	1	1	0	3105
Immortal Romance (IRE)	3	1	0	0	3752
India	8	3	2	0	27401
James Watt (IRE)	6	2	0	1	10221
Lady Aria	4	1	2	1	4787
Letmestopyouthere (IRE)	8	2	1	2	10480
Main Desire (IRE)	5	1	0	0	28355
Maori Bob (IRE)	10	3	0	5	10803
Master Brewer (FR)	3	1	0	0	5175
Neverbeen To Paris (IRE)	9	2	0	2	7785
Nuremberg (IRE)	1	1	0	0	6728
Nurse Nightingale	3	1	1	0	3752
Poetry	4	1	1	0	3881
Porcelain Girl (IRE)	7	2	0	2	10480
Pretty Pollyanna	5	2	0	1	49185
Queen Of Connaught	7	2	0	1	13456
Revived	7	1	0	1	3752
*Royal Reserve	7	1	1	0	6728
Sacred Act	3	1	0	1	3881
Sheriff*	3	1	0	1	3752
Stage Play (IRE)	5	1	2	0	3881
Youthful	1	1	0	0	3752
Total winning prize-money					**£402363**
Favourites	**26-57**		**45.6%**		**13.58**

ALAN BERRY

COCKERHAM, LANCS

	No. of Hrs	Races Run	1st	2nd	3rd	Unpl	Per cent	£1 Level Stake
2-y-o	*4*	*19*	*0*	*1*	*1*	*17*	*0.0*	*-19.00*
3-y-o	*3*	*20*	*0*	*0*	*1*	*19*	*0.0*	*-20.00*
4-y-o+	*15*	*85*	*1*	*2*	*3*	*79*	*1.2*	*-72.00*
Totals	**22**	**124**	**1**	**3**	**5**	**115**	**0.8**	**-111.00**
2017	*6*	*14*	*2*	*2*	*1*	*9*	*14.3*	*+4.00*
2016	*6*	*8*	*0*	*0*	*0*	*8*	*0.0*	*-8.00*

JOCKEYS

	W-R	Per cent	£1 Level Stake
Harrison Shaw	1-5	20.0	+8.00

COURSE RECORD

	Total W-R	Non-Hndcps 2-y-o	Non-Hndcps 3-y-o+	Hndcps 2-y-o	Hndcps 3-y-o+	Per cent	£1 Level Stake
Ayr	1-4	0-0	0-0	0-0	1-4	25.0	+9.00

WINNING HORSES

Horse	Races Run	1st	2nd	3rd	£
Economic Crisis (IRE)	18	1	2	2	6728
Total winning prize-money					**£6728**
Favourites	**0-0**		**0.0%**		**0.00**

JOHN BERRY

NEWMARKET, SUFFOLK

	No. of Hrs	Races Run	1st	2nd	3rd	Unpl	Per cent	£1 Level Stake
2-y-o	*0*	*0*	*0*	*0*	*0*	*0*	*0.0*	*0.00*
3-y-o	*4*	*10*	*0*	*1*	*0*	*9*	*0.0*	*-10.00*
4-y-o+	*6*	*40*	*3*	*4*	*8*	*25*	*7.5*	*-24.80*
Totals	**10**	**50**	**3**	**5**	**8**	**34**	**6.0**	**-34.80**
2017	*12*	*55*	*11*	*5*	*6*	*33*	*20.0*	*+15.33*
2016	*13*	*46*	*7*	*5*	*5*	*29*	*15.2*	*-5.50*

JOCKEYS

	W-R	Per cent	£1 Level Stake
Rob Hornby	1-2	50.0	+7.00
Mr Ross Birkett	1-2	50.0	+2.00
J F Egan	1-14	7.1	-11.80

COURSE RECORD

	Total W-R	Non-Hndcps 2-y-o	Non-Hndcps 3-y-o+	Hndcps 2-y-o	Hndcps 3-y-o+	Per cent	£1 Level Stake
Brighton	3-11	0-0	0-0	0-0	3-11	27.3	+4.20

WINNING HORSES

Horse	Races Run	1st	2nd	3rd	£
Roy Rocket (FR)	13	3	1	3	9205
Total winning prize-money					**£9205**
Favourites	**1-5**		**20.0%**		**-2.80**

SUZI BEST

LEWES, EAST SUSSEX

	No. of Hrs	Races Run	1st	2nd	3rd	Unpl	Per cent	£1 Level Stake
2-y-o	*3*	*14*	*0*	*0*	*1*	*13*	*0.0*	*-14.00*
3-y-o	*1*	*3*	*0*	*0*	*0*	*3*	*0.0*	*-3.00*
4-y-o+	*15*	*82*	*4*	*4*	*2*	*71*	*4.9*	*-50.88*

Totals	**19**	**99**	**4**	**4**	**3**	**87**	**4.0**	**-67.88**
2017	*2*	*3*	*1*	*0*	*0*	*2*	*33.3*	*+12.00*
2016	*0*							*+*

JOCKEYS

	W-R	Per cent	£1 Level Stake
Jim Crowley	1-1	100.0	+2.50
Gary Mahon	1-2	50.0	+6.00
Charles Bishop	1-6	16.7	-3.38
Harry Burns	1-12	8.3	+5.00

COURSE RECORD

	Total W-R	Non-Hndcps 2-y-o	3-y-o+	Hndcps 2-y-o	3-y-o+	Per cent	£1 Level Stake
Kempton (A.W)	2-17	0-1	0-0	0-2	2-14	11.8	+8.00
Lingfield (A.W)	1-20	0-1	0-0	0-0	1-19	5.0	-17.38
Chelmsford (A.W)	1-25	0-2	0-2	0-1	1-20	4.0	-21.50

WINNING HORSES

Horse	Races Run	1st	2nd	3rd	£
Ertidaad (IRE)*	7	2	1	0	4852
New Street (IRE)	10	1	1	1	3493
Outrath (IRE)	6	1	1	0	2588
Total winning prize-money					**£10933**
Favourites	**2-4**		**50.0%**		**1.88**

JOHN BEST

OAD STREET, KENT

	No. of Hrs	Races Run	1st	2nd	3rd	Unpl	Per cent	£1 Level Stake
2-y-o	*5*	*10*	*0*	*0*	*2*	*8*	*0.0*	*-10.00*
3-y-o	*6*	*24*	*0*	*1*	*1*	*22*	*0.0*	*-24.00*
4-y-o+	*13*	*90*	*3*	*4*	*8*	*75*	*3.3*	*-75.00*
Totals	**24**	**124**	**3**	**5**	**11**	**105**	**2.4**	**-109.00**
2017	*32*	*207*	*24*	*21*	*22*	*139*	*11.6*	*-2.15*
2016	*35*	*184*	*17*	*27*	*20*	*118*	*9.2*	*-41.38*

JOCKEYS

	W-R	Per cent	£1 Level Stake
Hayley Turner	1-1	100.0	+3.00
Jamie Spencer	1-2	50.0	+3.00
Joey Haynes	1-22	4.5	-16.00

COURSE RECORD

	Total W-R	Non-Hndcps 2-y-o	3-y-o+	Hndcps 2-y-o	3-y-o+	Per cent	£1 Level Stake
Nottingham	1-1	0-0	0-0	0-0	1-1	100.0	+3.00
Windsor	1-7	0-0	0-0	0-0	1-7	14.3	-2.00
Chelmsford (A.W)	1-18	0-0	0-1	0-0	1-17	5.6	-12.00

WINNING HORSES

Horse	Races Run	1st	2nd	3rd	£
Chance To Dream (IRE)	5	1	1	0	5531
Ourmullion*	12	2	0	3	12162
Total winning prize-money					**£17693**
Favourites	**0-1**		**0.0%**		**-1.00**

JAMES BETHELL

MIDDLEHAM MOOR, N YORKS

	No. of Hrs	Races Run	1st	2nd	3rd	Unpl	Per cent	£1 Level Stake
2-y-o	*8*	*27*	*3*	*5*	*5*	*14*	*11.1*	*+19.00*
3-y-o	*10*	*49*	*5*	*2*	*13*	*29*	*10.2*	*-15.00*
4-y-o+	*17*	*95*	*9*	*9*	*9*	*68*	*9.5*	*-13.75*
Totals	**35**	**171**	**17**	**16**	**27**	**111**	**9.9**	**-9.75**
2017	*29*	*169*	*20*	*23*	*24*	*102*	*11.8*	*-47.09*
2016	*28*	*146*	*15*	*15*	*19*	*97*	*10.3*	*-33.59*

BY MONTH

2-y-o	W-R	Per cent	£1 Level Stake	**3-y-o**	W-R	Per cent	£1 Level Stake
January	0-0	0.0	0.00	January	0-2	0.0	-2.00
February	0-0	0.0	0.00	February	0-0	0.0	0.00
March	0-0	0.0	0.00	March	0-1	0.0	-1.00
April	0-0	0.0	0.00	April	0-4	0.0	-4.00
May	0-1	0.0	-1.00	May	1-12	8.3	+1.00
June	1-1	100.0	+33.00	June	1-6	16.7	-1.50
July	0-5	0.0	-5.00	July	0-6	0.0	-6.00
August	0-7	0.0	-7.00	August	1-6	16.7	0.00
September	0-5	0.0	-5.00	September	2-5	40.0	+5.50
October	0-3	0.0	-3.00	October	0-5	0.0	-5.00
November	2-4	50.0	+8.00	November	0-1	0.0	-1.00
December	0-1	0.0	-1.00	December	0-1	0.0	-1.00

4-y-o+	W-R	Per cent	£1 Level Stake	**Totals**	W-R	Per cent	£1 Level Stake
January	0-6	0.0	-6.00	January	0-8	0.0	-8.00
February	0-3	0.0	-3.00	February	0-3	0.0	-3.00
March	1-5	20.0	+6.00	March	1-6	16.7	+5.00
April	1-5	20.0	+1.00	April	1-9	11.1	-3.00
May	3-14	21.4	+9.75	May	4-27	14.8	+9.75
June	0-15	0.0	-15.00	June	2-22	9.1	+16.50
July	1-9	11.1	+6.00	July	1-20	5.0	-5.00
August	1-12	8.3	-7.00	August	2-25	8.0	-14.00
September	1-11	9.1	+2.00	September	3-21	14.3	+2.50
October	0-7	0.0	-7.00	October	0-15	0.0	-15.00
November	1-7	14.3	+0.50	November	3-12	25.0	-0.50
December	0-1	0.0	-1.00	December	0-3	0.0	-2.00

DISTANCE

2-y-o	W-R	Per cent	£1 Level Stake	**3-y-o**	W-R	Per cent	£1 Level Stake
5f-6f	3-17	17.6	+29.00	5f-6f	3-24	12.5	0.00
7f-8f	0-10	0.0	-10.00	7f-8f	1-13	7.7	-8.50
9f-13f	0-0	0.0	0.00	9f-13f	1-11	9.1	-5.50
14f+	0-0	0.0	0.00	14f+	0-1	0.0	-1.00

4-y-o+	W-R	Per cent	£1 Level Stake	**Totals**	W-R	Per cent	£1 Level Stake
5f-6f	0-8	0.0	-8.00	5f-6f	6-49	12.2	+21.00

7f-8f	3-39	7.7	-5.50	7f-8f	4-62	6.5	-24.00
9f-13f	2-17	11.8	-8.25	9f-13f	3-28	10.7	-13.75
14f+	4-31	12.9	+8.00	14f+	4-32	12.5	+7.00

TYPE OF RACE

Non-Handicaps	W-R	Per cent	£1 Level Stake	Handicaps	W-R	Per cent	£1 Level Stake
2-y-o	2-22	9.1	+18.00	2-y-o	1-5	20.0	+1.00
3-y-o	0-15	0.0	-15.00	3-y-o	5-34	14.7	0.00
4-y-o+	0-7	0.0	-7.00	4-y-o+	9-88	10.2	-6.75

RACE CLASS / FIRST TIME OUT

RACE CLASS	W-R	Per cent	£1 Level Stake	FIRST TIME OUT	W-R	Per cent	£1 Level Stake
Class 1	0-1	0.0	-1.00	2-y-o	1-8	12.5	+26.00
Class 2	0-15	0.0	-15.00	3-y-o	0-10	0.0	-10.00
Class 3	2-18	11.1	+20.50	4-y-o+	2-17	11.8	+2.00
Class 4	4-55	7.3	-18.25				
Class 5	8-65	12.3	-1.50	Totals	3-35	8.6	+18.00
Class 6	3-16	18.8	+6.50				
Class 7	0-1	0.0	-1.00				

JOCKEYS

	W-R	Per cent	£1 Level Stake
P J McDonald	6-35	17.1	+11.75
Daniel Tudhope	4-19	21.1	+3.50
Kevin Stott	3-29	10.3	+26.00
Josephine Gordon	2-10	20.0	+9.00
George Wood	1-4	25.0	+9.00
David Allan	1-6	16.7	-1.00

COURSE RECORD

	Total W-R	Non-Hndcps 2-y-o	Non-Hndcps 3-y-o+	Hndcps 2-y-o	Hndcps 3-y-o+	Per cent	£1 Level Stake
Newcastle (A.W)	4-43	0-5	0-6	0-1	4-31	9.3	+1.50
Catterick	3-9	0-1	0-1	0-0	3-7	33.3	+17.50
Doncaster	3-16	1-1	0-4	0-1	2-10	18.8	+0.50
Pontefract	2-6	0-1	0-1	0-0	2-4	33.3	+1.75
Leicester	1-2	0-1	0-0	0-0	1-1	50.0	+3.00
Wolvhptn (A.W)	1-8	0-1	0-0	1-1	0-6	12.5	-2.00
Ripon	1-8	0-3	0-0	0-0	1-5	12.5	0.00
Thirsk	1-9	0-1	0-1	0-0	1-7	11.1	+4.00
York	1-10	1-2	0-0	0-1	0-7	10.0	+24.00

WINNING HORSES

Horse	Races Run	1st	2nd	3rd	£
Airton	9	1	1	1	6728
Cale Lane	8	2	0	2	7504
Cray (IRE)	9	1	2	1	3881
Edgewood	3	1	1	0	4663
Firby (IRE)	6	1	0	2	3493
Harrogate (IRE)	9	1	0	4	4757
Hesslewood (IRE)	5	1	1	0	9704
Mudawwan (IRE)	8	1	1	0	3752
New Society (IRE)	8	2	1	2	11580
On Fire	5	1	1	0	4528
Portledge (IRE)	8	2	0	2	9283
Rich Approach (IRE)	5	1	0	1	3105
Thankyou Very Much	4	1	2	0	3105
Ulshaw Bridge (IRE)	8	1	2	2	7763
Total winning prize-money					**£83846**
Favourites	**3-12**		**25.0%**		**-0.88**

HARRIET BETHELL

ARNOLD, E YORKS

	No. of Hrs	Races Run	1st	2nd	3rd	Unpl	Per cent	£1 Level Stake
2-y-o	*0*	*0*	*0*	*0*	*0*	*0*	*0.0*	*0.00*
3-y-o	*0*	*0*	*0*	*0*	*0*	*0*	*0.0*	*0.00*
4-y-o+	*6*	*28*	*4*	*2*	*1*	*21*	*14.3*	*+33.00*
Totals	**6**	**28**	**4**	**2**	**1**	**21**	**14.3**	**+33.00**
2017	*2*	*5*	*0*	*0*	*1*	*4*	*0.0*	*-5.00*
2016	*5*	*14*	*0*	*0*	*2*	*12*	*0.0*	*-14.00*

JOCKEYS

	W-R	Per cent	£1 Level Stake
Alistair Rawlinson	2-7	28.6	+2.00
Cam Hardie	1-1	100.0	+40.00
Josephine Gordon	1-10	10.0	+1.00

COURSE RECORD

	Total W-R	Non-Hndcps 2-y-o	Non-Hndcps 3-y-o+	Hndcps 2-y-o	Hndcps 3-y-o+	Per cent	£1 Level Stake
Lingfield	1-1	0-0	1-1	0-0	0-0	100.0	+1.50
Redcar	1-1	0-0	0-0	0-0	1-1	100.0	+40.00
Chelmsford (A.W)	1-5	0-0	0-0	0-0	1-5	20.0	+6.00
Wolvhptn (A.W)	1-10	0-0	1-2	0-0	0-8	10.0	-3.50

WINNING HORSES

Horse	Races Run	1st	2nd	3rd	£
Lopes Dancer (IRE)	6	1	1	0	4399
Steel Helmet (IRE)	12	1	1	0	3429
Viewpoint (IRE)	2	2	0	0	6210
Total winning prize-money					**£14038**
Favourites	**2-2**		**100.0%**		**4.25**

GEORGE BEWLEY

COLBY, CUMBRIA

	No. of Hrs	Races Run	1st	2nd	3rd	Unpl	Per cent	£1 Level Stake
2-y-o	*0*	*0*	*0*	*0*	*0*	*0*	*0.0*	*0.00*
3-y-o	*0*	*0*	*0*	*0*	*0*	*0*	*0.0*	*0.00*
4-y-o+	*2*	*5*	*1*	*1*	*1*	*2*	*20.0*	*+10.00*
Totals	**2**	**5**	**1**	**1**	**1**	**2**	**20.0**	**+10.00**
2017	*2*	*4*	*0*	*0*	*0*	*4*	*0.0*	*-4.00*
2016	*0*							

JOCKEYS

	W-R	Per cent	£1 Level Stake
James Sullivan	1-2	50.0	+13.00

COURSE RECORD

	Total W-R	Non-Hndcps 2-y-o	Non-Hndcps 3-y-o+	Hndcps 2-y-o	Hndcps 3-y-o+	Per cent	£1 Level Stake
Hamilton	1-1	0-0	0-0	0-0	1-1	100.0	+14.00

WINNING HORSES

Horse	Races Run	1st	2nd	3rd	£
Mitcd (IRE)	3	1	1	0	3493
Total winning prize-money					**£3493**
Favourites	**0-4**		**0.0%**		**-4.00**

MICHAEL BLAKE

TROWBRIDGE, WILTS

	No. of Hrs	Races Run	1st	2nd	3rd	Unpl	Per cent	£1 Level Stake
2-y-o	*0*	*0*	*0*	*0*	*0*	*0*	*0.0*	*0.00*
3-y-o	*3*	*9*	*1*	*0*	*0*	*8*	*11.1*	*+25.00*
4-y-o+	*6*	*33*	*3*	*2*	*3*	*25*	*9.1*	*+14.00*
Totals	**9**	**42**	**4**	**2**	**3**	**33**	**9.5**	**+39.00**
2017	*8*	*30*	*5*	*4*	*1*	*20*	*16.7*	*+9.13*
2016	*10*	*54*	*6*	*6*	*4*	*38*	*11.1*	*+7.00*

JOCKEYS

	W-R	Per cent	£1 Level Stake
Mitch Godwin	2-11	18.2	+31.00
Megan Nicholls	1-1	100.0	+33.00
William Cox	1-19	5.3	-14.00

COURSE RECORD

	Total W-R	Non-Hndcps 2-y-o	Non-Hndcps 3-y-o+	Hndcps 2-y-o	Hndcps 3-y-o+	Per cent	£1 Level Stake
Lingfield (A.W)	1-1	0-0	0-0	0-0	1-1	100.0	+33.00
Leicester	1-2	0-0	0-0	0-0	1-2	50.0	+3.00
Brighton	1-5	0-0	0-0	0-0	1-5	20.0	+16.00
Wolvhptn (A.W)	1-9	0-0	0-0	0-0	1-9	11.1	+12.00

WINNING HORSES

Horse	Races Run	1st	2nd	3rd	£
Bounty Pursuit	11	1	2	3	4399
Captain George (IRE)	4	1	0	0	3105
Kaaber (USA)	4	1	0	0	3105
*Mouchee (IRE)	3	1	0	0	3752
Total winning prize-money					**£14361**
Favourites	**0-0**		**0.0%**		**0.00**

MICHAEL BLANSHARD

UPPER LAMBOURN, BERKS

	No. of Hrs	Races Run	1st	2nd	3rd	Unpl	Per cent	£1 Level Stake
2-y-o	*6*	*20*	*0*	*0*	*0*	*20*	*0.0*	*-20.00*
3-y-o	*4*	*12*	*0*	*0*	*4*	*8*	*0.0*	*-12.00*
4-y-o+	*7*	*55*	*4*	*4*	*5*	*42*	*7.3*	*-22.17*
Totals	**17**	**87**	**4**	**4**	**9**	**70**	**4.6**	**-54.17**
2017	*19*	*103*	*2*	*4*	*7*	*89*	*1.9*	*-65.00*
2016	*20*	*108*	*6*	*10*	*12*	*80*	*5.6*	*-72.00*

JOCKEYS

	W-R	Per cent	£1 Level Stake
Rob Hornby	2-29	6.9	-11.67
Charles Bishop	1-8	12.5	-0.50
Josephine Gordon	1-9	11.1	-1.00

COURSE RECORD

	Total W-R	Non-Hndcps 2-y-o	Non-Hndcps 3-y-o+	Hndcps 2-y-o	Hndcps 3-y-o+	Per cent	£1 Level Stake
Lingfield	1-4	0-1	0-0	0-0	1-3	25.0	+0.33
Salisbury	1-4	0-2	0-0	0-0	1-2	25.0	+9.00
Lingfield (A.W)	1-25	0-3	0-2	0-2	1-18	4.0	-17.50
Kempton (A.W)	1-26	0-7	0-3	0-2	1-14	3.8	-18.00

WINNING HORSES

Horse	Races Run	1st	2nd	3rd	£
Accomplice	10	1	1	2	3752
Famous Dynasty (IRE)	16	2	3	2	6210
Garcon De Soleil	7	1	0	1	3493
Total winning prize-money					**£13455**
Favourites	**0-1**		**0.0%**		**-1.00**

GILLIAN BOANAS

LINGDALE, REDCAR & CLEVELAND

	No. of Hrs	Races Run	1st	2nd	3rd	Unpl	Per cent	£1 Level Stake
2-y-o	*0*	*0*	*0*	*0*	*0*	*0*	*0.0*	*0.00*
3-y-o	*1*	*4*	*0*	*1*	*0*	*3*	*0.0*	*-4.00*
4-y-o+	*3*	*21*	*1*	*4*	*6*	*10*	*4.8*	*-13.00*
Totals	**4**	**25**	**1**	**5**	**6**	**13**	**4.0**	**-17.00**
2017	*3*	*13*	*2*	*0*	*2*	*9*	*15.4*	*+3.00*
2016	*0*							

JOCKEYS

	W-R	Per cent	£1 Level Stake
Oliver Stammers	1-12	8.3	-4.00

COURSE RECORD

	Total W-R	Non-Hndcps 2-y-o	Non-Hndcps 3-y-o+	Hndcps 2-y-o	Hndcps 3-y-o+	Per cent	£1 Level Stake
Newcastle (A.W)	1-10	0-0	0-1	0-0	1-9	10.0	-2.00

WINNING HORSES

Horse	Races Run	1st	2nd	3rd	£
St Andrews (IRE)	10	1	2	3	3105
Total winning prize-money					**£3105**
Favourites	**0-7**		**0.0%**		**-7.00**

MARTIN BOSLEY

CHALFONT ST GILES, BUCKS

	No. of Hrs	Races Run	1st	2nd	3rd	Unpl	Per cent	£1 Level Stake
2-y-o	*1*	*3*	*0*	*0*	*0*	*3*	*0.0*	*-3.00*
3-y-o	*1*	*1*	*0*	*0*	*0*	*1*	*0.0*	*-1.00*
4-y-o+	*9*	*42*	*5*	*1*	*2*	*34*	*11.9*	*+46.00*
Totals	**11**	**46**	**5**	**1**	**2**	**38**	**10.9**	**+42.00**
2017	*9*	*37*	*4*	*3*	*1*	*29*	*10.8*	*-9.00*
2016	*7*	*28*	*1*	*3*	*3*	*21*	*3.6*	*-18.50*

JOCKEYS

	W-R	Per cent	£1 Level Stake
George Wood	2-7	28.6	+61.00
Robert Havlin	2-17	11.8	-2.50
Franny Norton	1-2	50.0	+3.50

COURSE RECORD

	Total W-R	Non-Hndcps 2-y-o	Non-Hndcps 3-y-o+	Hndcps 2-y-o	Hndcps 3-y-o+	Per cent	£1 Level Stake
Kempton (A.W)	2-11	0-0	0-0	0-0	2-11	18.2	+9.50
Bath	1-1	0-0	0-0	0-0	1-1	100.0	+4.50
Chelmsford (A.W)	1-6	0-1	0-0	0-0	1-5	16.7	+45.00
Lingfield (A.W)	1-11	0-1	0-4	0-0	1-6	9.1	0.00

WINNING HORSES

Horse	Races Run	1st	2nd	3rd	£
Catheadans Fury	9	2	1	0	6598
Exceeding Power	8	3	0	0	18469
Total winning prize-money					**£25067**
Favourites	**1-1**		**100.0%**		**2.50**

MARCO BOTTI

NEWMARKET, SUFFOLK

	No. of Hrs	Races Run	1st	2nd	3rd	Unpl	Per cent	£1 Level Stake
2-y-o	*41*	*126*	*13*	*16*	*13*	*84*	*10.3*	*-19.72*
3-y-o	*40*	*163*	*12*	*22*	*24*	*105*	*7.4*	*-78.28*
4-y-o+	*17*	*84*	*9*	*15*	*7*	*53*	*10.7*	*13.00*
Totals	**98**	**373**	**34**	**53**	**44**	**242**	**9.1**	**-111.90**
2017	*98*	*325*	*40*	*43*	*47*	*194*	*12.3*	*-23.98*
2016	*106*	*397*	*52*	*54*	*51*	*239*	*13.1*	*-122.69*

BY MONTH

2-y-o	W-R	Per cent	£1 Level Stake	**3-y-o**	W-R	Per cent	£1 Level Stake
January	0-0	0.0	0.00	January	2-18	11.1	+0.25
February	0-0	0.0	0.00	February	1-8	12.5	-5.38
March	0-0	0.0	0.00	March	1-14	7.1	-12.78
April	0-0	0.0	0.00	April	2-24	8.3	+3.00
May	0-5	0.0	-5.00	May	0-18	0.0	-18.00
June	1-12	8.3	-4.00	June	1-13	7.7	-9.25
July	0-10	0.0	-10.00	July	2-10	20.0	+4.38
August	5-21	23.8	+42.42	August	0-7	0.0	-7.00
September	3-21	14.3	-6.90	September	0-15	0.0	-15.00
October	1-29	3.4	-24.00	October	1-10	10.0	+1.00
November	3-18	16.7	-2.25	November	1-14	7.1	-10.50
December	0-10	0.0	-10.00	December	1-12	8.3	-9.00

4-y-o+	W-R	Per cent	£1 Level Stake	**Totals**	W-R	Per cent	£1 Level Stake
January	1-10	10.0	-7.00	January	3-28	10.7	-6.75
February	0-5	0.0	-5.00	February	1-13	7.7	-10.38
March	2-8	25.0	+12.00	March	3-22	13.6	-0.78
April	1-6	16.7	+2.00	April	3-30	10.0	+5.00
May	0-10	0.0	-10.00	May	0-33	0.0	-33.00
June	2-8	25.0	-0.40	June	4-33	12.1	-13.65
July	2-8	25.0	+18.00	July	4-28	14.3	+12.38
August	1-8	12.5	-2.50	August	6-36	16.7	+32.92
September	0-8	0.0	-8.00	September	3-44	6.8	-29.90
October	0-8	0.0	-8.00	October	2-47	4.3	-31.00
November	0-4	0.0	-4.00	November	4-36	11.1	-14.50
December	0-1	0.0	-1.00	December	1-23	4.3	-10.00

DISTANCE

2-y-o	W-R	Per cent	£1 Level Stake	**3-y-o**	W-R	Per cent	£1 Level Stake
5f-6f	5-40	12.5	-4.45	5f-6f	0-19	0.0	-19.00
7f-8f	8-83	9.6	-12.27	7f-8f	5-90	5.6	-59.53
9f-13f	0-3	0.0	-3.00	9f-13f	6-51	11.8	-0.50
14f+	0-0	0.0	0.00	14f+	1-3	33.3	+0.75

4-y-o+	W-R	Per cent	£1 Level Stake	**Totals**	W-R	Per cent	£1 Level Stake
5f-6f	3-14	21.4	+16.50	5f-6f	8-73	11.0	-6.95
7f-8f	2-31	6.5	-23.40	7f-8f	15-204	7.4	-95.20
9f-13f	4-34	11.8	-2.00	9f-13f	10-88	11.4	-5.50
14f+	0-5	0.0	-5.00	14f+	1-8	12.5	-4.25

TYPE OF RACE

Non-Handicaps	W-R	Per cent	£1 Level Stake	**Handicaps**	W-R	Per cent	£1 Level Stake
2-y-o	9-105	8.6	-20.53	2-y-o	4-21	19.0	+0.80
3-y-o	5-60	8.3	-35.53	3-y-o	7-103	6.8	-42.75
4-y-o+	3-16	18.8	+15.50	4-y-o+	6-68	8.8	-29.40

RACE CLASS / FIRST TIME OUT

RACE CLASS	W-R	Per cent	£1 Level Stake	FIRST TIME OUT	W-R	Per cent	£1 Level Stake
Class 1	3-16	18.8	+15.50	2-y-o	2-41	4.9	+10.00

Class 2	5-44	11.4	-10.90	3-y-o	3-40	7.5	-19.13
Class 3	1-21	4.8	+13.00	4-y-o+	2-17	11.8	-11.90
Class 4	7-74	9.5	-35.80				
Class 5	13-184	7.1	-81.88	Totals	7-98	7.1	-21.03
Class 6	5-34	14.7	-11.82				
Class 7	0-0	0.0	0.00				

JOCKEYS

	W-R	Per cent	£1 Level Stake
Marc Monaghan	13-101	12.9	+8.65
Andrea Atzeni	5-21	23.8	+0.95
Gabriele Malune	5-65	7.7	-25.50
Gerald Mosse	3-27	11.1	+11.50
Luke Morris	3-28	10.7	-11.00
Antonio Fresu	2-42	4.8	-29.00
Dane O'Neill	1-1	100.0	+8.00
William Buick	1-2	50.0	+3.50
Daniel Muscutt	1-23	4.3	-16.00

COURSE RECORD

	Total W-R	Non-Hndcps 2-y-o	Non-Hndcps 3-y-o+	Hndcps 2-y-o	Hndcps 3-y-o+	Per cent	£1 Level Stake
Chelmsford (A.W)	10-68	4-17	2-15	0-3	4-33	14.7	+21.45
Kempton (A.W)	9-104	1-28	1-15	2-7	5-54	8.7	-30.75
Wolvhptn (A.W)	6-65	0-21	2-18	2-4	2-22	9.2	-44.60
York	2-8	0-0	2-2	0-0	0-6	25.0	+18.00
Lingfield (A.W)	2-28	0-4	0-5	0-1	2-18	7.1	-19.50
Ascot	1-5	0-0	1-2	0-0	0-3	20.0	+0.50
Windsor	1-7	1-4	0-1	0-0	0-2	14.3	+10.00
Newmkt (Jly)	1-8	1-6	0-1	0-0	0-1	12.5	0.00
Newcastle (A.W)	1-11	1-4	0-3	0-0	0-4	9.1	-6.00
Nottingham	1-16	1-8	0-3	0-1	0-4	6.3	-8.00

WINNING HORSES

Horse	Races Run	1st	2nd	3rd	£
Acclafrith (IRE)	4	1	1	1	3105
Aljazzi	3	1	0	1	106757
American Endeavour (USA)	7	1	1	0	3752
Artieshow (USA)	5	1	0	0	3881
Be Like Me (IRE)	6	1	2	2	3752
Blame Me Forever (USA)	6	1	0	0	4399
Burcan (FR)	1	1	0	0	11828
Capla Rock (IRE)	6	1	0	1	3881
Crowned Eagle	7	1	2	0	31125
Domitilla	2	1	0	0	5531
Dylan Mouth (IRE)	4	1	1	0	36862
Fares Kodiac (IRE)	4	2	0	1	9574
Fox Coach (IRE)	4	2	2	0	30016
Galactic Spirit	2	1	0	0	3752
Houlton	7	1	0	3	3493
Jellmood	8	1	2	0	8086
Kyllachy Gala*	9	1	1	2	15563
Lady Al Thumama	3	1	0	0	3752
Mulhima (IRE)	3	1	0	2	3752
Muthhila (IRE)	8	1	2	0	3105
My Maharani (IRE)	6	1	0	0	4528
Rambaldi (IRE)	4	1	0	0	3105
Raven's Lady	6	2	2	0	52424
Roma Bangkok	1	1	0	0	9704
Seprani*	9	1	2	2	5531
So Hi Class (IRE)	9	1	2	0	3105
Sonja Henie (IRE)	2	1	0	0	3881
Volevo Lui	5	3	0	0	19051
Yusra	5	1	1	1	5434
Total winning prize-money					**£402729**
Favourites	**9-22**		**40.9%**		**3.60**

ROY BOWRING

EDWINSTOWE, NOTTS

	No. of Hrs	Races Run	1st	2nd	3rd	Unpl	Per cent	£1 Level Stake
2-y-o	*0*	*0*	*0*	*0*	*0*	*0*	*0.0*	*0.00*
3-y-o	*2*	*4*	*0*	*0*	*0*	*4*	*0.0*	*-4.00*
4-y-o+	*11*	*56*	*7*	*7*	*2*	*40*	*12.5*	*-0.70*
Totals	**13**	**60**	**7**	**7**	**2**	**44**	**11.7**	**-4.70**
2017	*11*	*79*	*8*	*7*	*8*	*56*	*10.1*	*-22.75*
2016	*16*	*104*	*9*	*6*	*15*	*74*	*8.7*	*-46.00*

JOCKEYS

	W-R	Per cent	£1 Level Stake
Robert Winston	4-18	22.2	-0.20
Kieran O'Neill	2-4	50.0	+18.50
Liam Keniry	1-5	20.0	+10.00

COURSE RECORD

	Total W-R	Non-Hndcps 2-y-o	Non-Hndcps 3-y-o+	Hndcps 2-y-o	Hndcps 3-y-o+	Per cent	£1 Level Stake
Southwell (A.W)	3-24	0-0	0-2	0-0	3-22	12.5	-14.20
Pontefract	1-2	0-0	0-0	0-0	1-2	50.0	+15.00
Catterick	1-4	0-0	0-0	0-0	1-4	25.0	+11.00
Wolvhptn (A.W)	1-5	0-0	0-0	0-0	1-5	20.0	0.00
Newcastle (A.W)	1-5	0-0	0-0	0-0	1-5	20.0	+3.50

WINNING HORSES

Horse	Races Run	1st	2nd	3rd	£
Ace Master	8	1	1	0	1941
Foolaad	13	5	1	0	65161
Little Choosey	4	1	0	0	3105
Total winning prize-money					**£70207**
Favourites	**2-5**		**40.0%**		**-0.70**

JIM BOYLE

EPSOM, SURREY

	No. of Hrs	Races Run	1st	2nd	3rd	Unpl	Per cent	£1 Level Stake
2-y-o	*5*	*21*	*1*	*2*	*3*	*15*	*4.8*	*-8.00*
3-y-o	*10*	*59*	*9*	*6*	*4*	*40*	*15.3*	*+1.50*
4-y-o+	*12*	*87*	*5*	*8*	*15*	*59*	*5.7*	*-59.00*

Totals	**27**	**167**	**15**	**16**	**22**	**114**	**9.0**	**-65.50**
2017	*25*	*192*	*14*	*15*	*17*	*145*	*7.3*	*-70.15*
2016	*27*	*170*	*20*	*13*	*22*	*115*	*11.8*	*-20.00*

BY MONTH

2-y-o	W-R	Per cent	£1 Level Stake	3-y-o	W-R	Per cent	£1 Level Stake
January	0-0	0.0	0.00	January	1-2	50.0	+4.00
February	0-0	0.0	0.00	February	1-1	100.0	+6.00
March	0-0	0.0	0.00	March	0-2	0.0	-2.00
April	0-0	0.0	0.00	April	0-4	0.0	-4.00
May	0-1	0.0	-1.00	May	2-8	25.0	+1.50
June	0-3	0.0	-3.00	June	0-7	0.0	-7.00
July	1-4	25.0	+9.00	July	2-7	28.6	+2.50
August	0-2	0.0	-2.00	August	2-9	22.2	+13.00
September	0-1	0.0	-1.00	September	1-4	25.0	+2.50
October	0-3	0.0	-3.00	October	0-5	0.0	-5.00
November	0-7	0.0	-7.00	November	0-4	0.0	-4.00
December	0-0	0.0	0.00	December	0-6	0.0	-6.00

4-y-o+	W-R	Per cent	£1 Level Stake	Totals	W-R	Per cent	£1 Level Stake
January	0-13	0.0	-13.00	January	1-15	6.7	-9.00
February	0-8	0.0	-8.00	February	1-9	11.1	-2.00
March	0-5	0.0	-5.00	March	0-7	0.0	-7.00
April	0-8	0.0	-8.00	April	0-12	0.0	-12.00
May	3-15	20.0	+3.00	May	5-24	20.8	+3.50
June	0-6	0.0	-6.00	June	0-16	0.0	-16.00
July	2-9	22.2	+1.00	July	5-20	25.0	+12.50
August	0-4	0.0	-4.00	August	2-15	13.3	+7.00
September	0-7	0.0	-7.00	September	1-12	8.3	-5.50
October	0-6	0.0	-6.00	October	0-14	0.0	-14.00
November	0-3	0.0	-3.00	November	0-14	0.0	-7.00
December	0-3	0.0	-3.00	December	0-9	0.0	-9.00

DISTANCE

2-y-o	W-R	Per cent	£1 Level Stake	3-y-o	W-R	Per cent	£1 Level Stake
5f-6f	0-10	0.0	-10.00	5f-6f	3-22	13.6	-2.00
7f-8f	1-11	9.1	+2.00	7f-8f	5-18	27.8	+16.00
9f-13f	0-0	0.0	0.00	9f-13f	1-19	5.3	-12.50
14f+	0-0	0.0	0.00	14f+	0-0	0.0	0.00

4-y-o+	W-R	Per cent	£1 Level Stake	Totals	W-R	Per cent	£1 Level Stake
5f-6f	0-19	0.0	-19.00	5f-6f	3-51	5.9	-31.00
7f-8f	4-55	7.3	-35.00	7f-8f	10-84	11.9	-17.00
9f-13f	1-13	7.7	-5.00	9f-13f	2-32	6.3	-17.50
14f+	0-0	0.0	0.00	14f+	0-0	0.0	0.00

TYPE OF RACE

Non-Handicaps	W-R	Per cent	£1 Level Stake	Handicaps	W-R	Per cent	£1 Level Stake
2-y-o	1-17	5.9	-4.00	2-y-o	0-4	0.0	-4.00
3-y-o	1-2	50.0	+2.50	3-y-o	8-57	14.0	-1.00
4-y-o+	0-4	0.0	-4.00	4-y-o+	5-83	6.0	-55.00

RACE CLASS

	W-R	Per cent	£1 Level Stake
Class 1	0-0	0.0	0.00
Class 2	0-3	0.0	-3.00
Class 3	1-14	7.1	-8.00
Class 4	5-20	25.0	+19.50
Class 5	4-43	9.3	-24.50
Class 6	5-80	6.3	-42.50
Class 7	0-7	0.0	-7.00

FIRST TIME OUT

	W-R	Per cent	£1 Level Stake
2-y-o	0-5	0.0	-5.00
3-y-o	2-10	20.0	+0.50
4-y-o+	1-12	8.3	-8.00
Totals	3-27	11.1	-12.50

JOCKEYS

	W-R	Per cent	£1 Level Stake
Pat Cosgrave	6-29	20.7	+19.50
Charlie Bennett	5-67	7.5	-34.50
William Buick	1-1	100.0	+4.00
Josephine Gordon	1-6	16.7	+1.00
Paddy Bradley	1-15	6.7	-9.00
Isobel Francis	1-18	5.6	-15.50

COURSE RECORD

	Total W-R	Non-Hndcps 2-y-o	Non-Hndcps 3-y-o+	Hndcps 2-y-o	Hndcps 3-y-o+	Per cent	£1 Level Stake
Lingfield	5-14	1-3	0-1	0-0	4-10	35.7	+25.00
Epsom	3-11	0-0	0-0	0-0	3-11	27.3	+4.00
Lingfield (A.W)	3-35	0-3	1-2	0-1	2-29	8.6	-20.00
Newbury	2-4	0-0	0-0	0-0	2-4	50.0	+17.50
Chelmsford (A.W)	1-17	0-1	0-0	0-0	1-16	5.9	-13.00
Kempton (A.W)	1-29	0-5	0-2	0-2	1-20	3.4	-22.00

WINNING HORSES

Horse	Races Run	1st	2nd	3rd	£
Black Bess	6	1	0	2	7246
Broughtons Knight	2	1	0	0	5434
Duke Of North (IRE)	9	2	1	1	9704
*Exec Chef (IRE)	4	3	0	1	14814
Hateya (IRE)	9	3	1	1	15105
Isle Of Wolves	5	1	0	1	3105
Man Of Harlech	12	1	0	2	5531
Quick Recovery	13	3	1	1	9315
Total winning prize-money					**£70254**
Favourites	**2-12**		**16.7%**		**-5.50**

MILTON BRADLEY

SEDBURY, GLOUCS

	No. of Hrs	Races Run	1st	2nd	3rd	Unpl	Per cent	£1 Level Stake
2-y-o	*3*	*19*	*0*	*0*	*1*	*18*	*0.0*	*-19.00*
3-y-o	*2*	*19*	*0*	*0*	*0*	*19*	*0.0*	*-19.00*
4-y-o+	*16*	*160*	*4*	*9*	*8*	*138*	*2.5*	*-86.00*
Totals	**21**	**198**	**4**	**9**	**9**	**175**	**2.0**	**-124.00**
2017	*20*	*210*	*9*	*16*	*19*	*165*	*4.3*	*-103.00*
2016	*18*	*200*	*13*	*10*	*22*	*155*	*6.5*	*-93.07*

JOCKEYS

	W-R	Per cent	£1 Level Stake
Liam Keniry	2-14	14.3	+13.00
Kerrie Raybould	2-30	6.7	+17.00

COURSE RECORD

	Total W-R	Non-Hndcps 2-y-o	Non-Hndcps 3-y-o+	Hndcps 2-y-o	Hndcps 3-y-o+	Per cent	£1 Level Stake
Goodwood	1-1	0-0	0-0	0-0	1-1	100.0	+5.00
Windsor	1-7	0-1	0-0	0-0	1-6	14.3	+14.00
Lingfield (A.W)	1-23	0-0	0-0	0-0	1-23	4.3	-17.00
Wolvhptn (A.W)	1-56	0-0	0-2	0-1	1-53	1.8	-15.00

WINNING HORSES

Horse	Races Run	1st	2nd	3rd	£
Englishman	9	2	1	0	12259
Indian Affair	21	1	2	0	3752
Rising Sunshine (IRE)	19	1	0	4	3105
Total winning prize-money					**£19116**
Favourites	**0-2**		**0.0%**		**-2.00**

JOHN BRIDGER

LIPHOOK, HANTS

	No. of Hrs	Races Run	1st	2nd	3rd	Unpl	Per cent	£1 Level Stake
2-y-o	*5*	*21*	*2*	*1*	*2*	*16*	*9.5*	*+9.00*
3-y-o	*5*	*27*	*1*	*1*	*0*	*25*	*3.7*	*-21.50*
4-y-o+	*16*	*166*	*14*	*15*	*13*	*123*	*8.4*	*-45.25*
Totals	**26**	**214**	**17**	**17**	**15**	**164**	**7.9**	**-57.75**
2017	*26*	*239*	*18*	*20*	*27*	*174*	*7.5*	*-95.63*
2016	*27*	*236*	*17*	*18*	*25*	*175*	*7.2*	*-101.00*

BY MONTH

2-y-o	W-R	Per cent	£1 Level Stake	**3-y-o**	W-R	Per cent	£1 Level Stake
January	0-0	0.0	0.00	January	0-0	0.0	0.00
February	0-0	0.0	0.00	February	0-0	0.0	0.00
March	0-0	0.0	0.00	March	0-0	0.0	0.00
April	0-1	0.0	-1.00	April	0-4	0.0	-4.00
May	0-1	0.0	-1.00	May	0-4	0.0	-4.00
June	0-3	0.0	-3.00	June	0-2	0.0	-2.00
July	0-3	0.0	-3.00	July	0-2	0.0	-2.00
August	1-4	25.0	+17.00	August	1-4	25.0	+1.50
September	0-4	0.0	-4.00	September	0-2	0.0	-2.00
October	1-2	50.0	+7.00	October	0-7	0.0	-7.00
November	0-2	0.0	-2.00	November	0-1	0.0	-1.00
December	0-1	0.0	-1.00	December	0-1	0.0	-1.00

4-y-o+	W-R	Per cent	£1 Level Stake	**Totals**	W-R	Per cent	£1 Level Stake
January	1-14	7.1	-9.00	January	1-14	7.1	-9.00
February	1-12	8.3	-3.00	February	1-12	8.3	-3.00
March	0-7	0.0	-7.00	March	0-7	0.0	-7.00
April	2-16	12.5	-1.50	April	2-21	9.5	-6.50
May	4-15	26.7	+12.00	May	4-20	20.0	+7.00
June	2-15	13.3	+14.75	June	2-20	10.0	+9.75
July	1-18	5.6	-13.50	July	1-23	4.3	-18.50
August	1-17	5.9	-7.00	August	3-25	12.0	+11.50
September	0-12	0.0	-12.00	September	0-18	0.0	-18.00
October	1-17	5.9	-8.00	October	2-26	7.7	-8.00
November	0-13	0.0	-13.00	November	0-16	0.0	-14.00
December	1-10	10.0	+2.00	December	1-12	8.3	+1.00

DISTANCE

2-y-o	W-R	Per cent	£1 Level Stake	**3-y-o**	W-R	Per cent	£1 Level Stake
5f-6f	2-17	11.8	+13.00	5f-6f	1-20	5.0	-14.50
7f-8f	0-4	0.0	-4.00	7f-8f	0-4	0.0	-4.00
9f-13f	0-0	0.0	0.00	9f-13f	0-3	0.0	-3.00
14f+	0-0	0.0	0.00	14f+	0-0	0.0	0.00

4-y-o+	W-R	Per cent	£1 Level Stake	**Totals**	W-R	Per cent	£1 Level Stake
5f-6f	7-85	8.2	-37.75	5f-6f	10-122	8.2	-39.25
7f-8f	5-54	9.3	+5.50	7f-8f	5-62	8.1	-2.50
9f-13f	2-26	7.7	-12.00	9f-13f	2-29	6.9	-15.00
14f+	0-1	0.0	-1.00	14f+	0-1	0.0	-1.00

TYPE OF RACE

Non-Handicaps	W-R	Per cent	£1 Level Stake	**Handicaps**	W-R	Per cent	£1 Level Stake
2-y-o	1-17	5.9	-8.00	2-y-o	1-4	25.0	+17.00
3-y-o	0-10	0.0	-10.00	3-y-o	1-17	5.9	-11.50
4-y-o+	0-8	0.0	-8.00	4-y-o+	14-158	8.9	-37.25

RACE CLASS

	W-R	Per cent	£1 Level Stake
Class 1	0-1	0.0	-1.00
Class 2	0-6	0.0	-6.00
Class 3	1-7	14.3	+1.00
Class 4	1-10	10.0	0.00
Class 5	5-73	6.8	-41.75
Class 6	10-112	8.9	-5.00
Class 7	0-5	0.0	-5.00

FIRST TIME OUT

	W-R	Per cent	£1 Level Stake
2-y-o	1-5	20.0	+16.00
3-y-o	0-5	0.0	-5.00
4-y-o+	0-16	0.0	-16.00
Totals	1-26	3.8	-5.00

JOCKEYS

	W-R	Per cent	£1 Level Stake
Kieran O'Neill	11-92	12.0	+17.25
Liam Jones	2-14	14.3	+7.00
Mitch Godwin	2-18	11.1	-4.00
Sophie Ralston	1-3	33.3	+1.00
Hollie Doyle	1-8	12.5	0.00

COURSE RECORD

	Total W-R	Non-Hndcps 2-y-o	Non-Hndcps 3-y-o+	Hndcps 2-y-o	Hndcps 3-y-o+	Per cent	£1 Level Stake
Lingfield	4-21	0-2	0-3	1-1	3-15	19.0	+34.25
Windsor	4-28	1-5	0-4	0-0	3-19	14.3	+4.00
Lingfield (A.W)	4-59	0-0	0-9	0-0	4-50	6.8	-25.00
Brighton	3-22	0-2	0-0	0-0	3-20	13.6	-0.50

Goodwood	2-19	0-1	0-0	0-0	2-18	10.5	-5.50

WINNING HORSES

Horse	Races Run	1st	2nd	3rd	£
*Aegean Mist	4	2	0	0	6857
Betsalottie	15	2	2	0	6210
Bookmaker	16	1	1	1	3105
Delicate Kiss	14	1	2	2	3105
Firenze Rosa (IRE)	15	1	1	0	5175
Flowing Clarets	12	1	2	1	3105
Flying Sakhee	9	2	1	0	6210
Live Dangerously	9	2	0	0	6210
Pettochside	12	1	1	1	9704
Porto Ferro (IRE)	21	3	4	2	13035
Shifting Star (IRE)	12	1	0	0	3752
Total winning prize-money					**£66468**
Favourites	**0-6**		**0.0%**		**-6.00**

DAVID BRIDGWATER

ICOMB, GLOUCS

	No. of Hrs	Races Run	1st	2nd	3rd	Unpl	Per cent	£1 Level Stake
2-y-o	*1*	*3*	*0*	*0*	*0*	*3*	*0.0*	*-3.00*
3-y-o	*1*	*3*	*0*	*0*	*0*	*3*	*0.0*	*-3.00*
4-y-o+	*10*	*45*	*1*	*4*	*8*	*32*	*2.2*	*-37.00*
Totals	**12**	**51**	**1**	**4**	**8**	**38**	**2.0**	**-43.00**
2017	*9*	*51*	*2*	*2*	*8*	*39*	*3.9*	*-37.00*
2016	*9*	*37*	*5*	*7*	*5*	*20*	*13.5*	*-2.50*

JOCKEYS

	W-R	Per cent	£1 Level Stake
Poppy Bridgwater	1-38	2.6	-30.00

COURSE RECORD

	Total W-R	Non-Hndcps 2-y-o	Non-Hndcps 3-y-o+	Hndcps 2-y-o	Hndcps 3-y-o+	Per cent	£1 Level Stake
Chelmsford (A.W)	1-10	0-0	0-2	0-0	1-8	10.0	-2.00

WINNING HORSES

Horse	Races Run	1st	2nd	3rd	£
Zephyros (GER)	6	1	2	0	3493
Total winning prize-money					**£3493**
Favourites	**1-9**		**11.1%**		**-6.00**

MARK BRISBOURNE

GREAT NESS, SHROPSHIRE

	No. of Hrs	Races Run	1st	2nd	3rd	Unpl	Per cent	£1 Level Stake
2-y-o	*0*	*0*	*0*	*0*	*0*	*0*	*0.0*	*0.00*
3-y-o	*1*	*2*	*0*	*0*	*0*	*2*	*0.0*	*-2.00*
4-y-o+	*7*	*54*	*3*	*3*	*4*	*44*	*5.6*	*+40.00*
Totals	**8**	**56**	**3**	**3**	**4**	**46**	**5.4**	**+38.00**
2017	*12*	*88*	*3*	*5*	*9*	*71*	*3.4*	*-67.50*
2016	*15*	*94*	*1*	*3*	*8*	*82*	*1.1*	*-77.00*

JOCKEYS

	W-R	Per cent	£1 Level Stake
Eoin Walsh	2-14	14.3	+54.00
Liam Jones	1-15	6.7	+11.00

COURSE RECORD

	Total W-R	Non-Hndcps 2-y-o	Non-Hndcps 3-y-o+	Hndcps 2-y-o	Hndcps 3-y-o+	Per cent	£1 Level Stake
Kempton (A.W)	1-3	0-0	0-0	0-0	1-3	33.3	+31.00
Chester	1-4	0-0	0-1	0-0	1-3	25.0	+22.00
Wolvhptn (A.W)	1-43	0-0	0-2	0-0	1-41	2.3	-9.00

WINNING HORSES

Horse	Races Run	1st	2nd	3rd	£
Ice Canyon	15	1	2	2	7698
Storm Lightning	12	2	0	1	5693
Total winning prize-money					**£13391**
Favourites	**0-0**		**0.0%**		**0.00**

ROBYN BRISLAND

NEWMARKET, SUFFOLK

	No. of Hrs	Races Run	1st	2nd	3rd	Unpl	Per cent	£1 Level Stake
2-y-o	*4*	*7*	*0*	*0*	*0*	*7*	*0.0*	*-7.00*
3-y-o	*11*	*39*	*2*	*1*	*2*	*34*	*5.1*	*0.00*
4-y-o+	*12*	*54*	*5*	*7*	*6*	*34*	*9.3*	*-24.17*
Totals	**27**	**100**	**7**	**8**	**8**	**75**	**7.0**	**-31.17**
2017	*22*	*92*	*9*	*17*	*11*	*54*	*9.8*	*-42.88*
2016	*19*	*87*	*12*	*12*	*10*	*53*	*13.8*	*+43.13*

JOCKEYS

	W-R	Per cent	£1 Level Stake
Sean Levey	1-2	50.0	+24.00
Kieran Shoemark	1-2	50.0	+11.00
David Egan	1-3	33.3	+1.33
Jason Watson	1-4	25.0	+1.50
Andrew Mullen	1-4	25.0	+6.00
Martin Harley	1-6	16.7	-3.00
Gabriele Malune	1-10	10.0	-3.00

COURSE RECORD

	Total W-R	Non-Hndcps 2-y-o	Non-Hndcps 3-y-o+	Hndcps 2-y-o	Hndcps 3-y-o+	Per cent	£1 Level Stake
Chelmsford (A.W)	2-26	0-0	0-6	0-0	2-20	7.7	-18.67
Wetherby	1-1	0-0	0-0	0-0	1-1	100.0	+9.00
Yarmouth	1-6	0-1	0-1	0-0	1-4	16.7	+1.00
Nottingham	1-8	0-0	0-1	0-0	1-7	12.5	+18.00
Southwell (A.W)	1-8	0-1	0-0	0-0	1-7	12.5	-2.50
Wolvhptn (A.W)	1-11	0-0	1-2	0-0	0-9	9.1	+2.00

WINNING HORSES

Horse	Races Run	1st	2nd	3rd	£
Apache Blaze	7	1	0	1	3493
Harbour Storm	2	1	0	0	3752
Katie Gale	12	1	2	4	3752
Navajo Star (IRE)	15	3	4	0	14232
Navajo Storm (IRE)	2	1	0	0	3105
Total winning prize-money					**£28334**
Favourites	**0-5**		**0.0%**		**-5.00**

ANTONY BRITTAIN

WARTHILL, N YORKS

	No. of Hrs	Races Run	1st	2nd	3rd	Unpl	Per cent	£1 Level Stake
2-y-o	*4*	*21*	*2*	*1*	*1*	*17*	*9.5*	*-4.50*
3-y-o	*10*	*61*	*3*	*8*	*6*	*44*	*4.9*	*-32.38*
4-y-o+	*19*	*181*	*16*	*19*	*19*	*126*	*8.8*	*-52.25*
Totals	**33**	**263**	**21**	**28**	**26**	**187**	**8.0**	**-89.13**
2017	*33*	*207*	*12*	*16*	*18*	*161*	*5.8*	*-97.75*
2016	*22*	*105*	*5*	*11*	*9*	*80*	*4.8*	*-33.00*

BY MONTH

2-y-o	W-R	Per cent	£1 Level Stake	**3-y-o**	W-R	Per cent	£1 Level Stake
January	0-0	0.0	0.00	January	0-4	0.0	-4.00
February	0-0	0.0	0.00	February	0-1	0.0	-1.00
March	0-0	0.0	0.00	March	1-3	33.3	+12.00
April	0-1	0.0	-1.00	April	0-7	0.0	-7.00
May	0-2	0.0	-2.00	May	0-8	0.0	-8.00
June	0-5	0.0	-5.00	June	1-7	14.3	-4.38
July	0-0	0.0	0.00	July	1-9	11.1	+2.00
August	0-1	0.0	-1.00	August	0-5	0.0	-5.00
September	0-3	0.0	-3.00	September	0-7	0.0	-7.00
October	1-5	20.0	-1.50	October	0-3	0.0	-3.00
November	1-3	33.3	+10.00	November	0-4	0.0	-4.00
December	0-1	0.0	-1.00	December	0-3	0.0	-3.00

4-y-o+	W-R	Per cent	£1 Level Stake	**Totals**	W-R	Per cent	£1 Level Stake
January	4-19	21.1	+5.25	January	4-23	17.4	+1.25
February	2-21	9.5	+14.00	February	2-22	9.1	+13.00
March	0-11	0.0	-11.00	March	1-14	7.1	+1.00
April	1-10	10.0	+7.00	April	1-18	5.6	-1.00
May	1-23	4.3	-17.00	May	1-33	3.0	-27.00
June	1-16	6.3	-10.50	June	2-28	7.1	-19.88
July	0-12	0.0	-12.00	July	1-21	4.8	-10.00
August	2-12	16.7	+4.50	August	2-18	11.1	-1.50
September	1-19	5.3	-15.50	September	1-29	3.4	-25.50
October	2-12	16.7	+0.25	October	3-20	15.0	-4.25
November	1-17	5.9	-13.25	November	2-24	8.3	-17.25
December	1-9	11.1	-4.00	December	1-13	7.7	-7.00

DISTANCE

2-y-o	W-R	Per cent	£1 Level Stake	**3-y-o**	W-R	Per cent	£1 Level Stake
5f-6f	2-14	14.3	+2.50	5f-6f	3-37	8.1	-8.38
7f-8f	0-7	0.0	-7.00	7f-8f	0-21	0.0	-21.00
9f-13f	0-0	0.0	0.00	9f-13f	0-3	0.0	-3.00
14f+	0-0	0.0	0.00	14f+	0-0	0.0	0.00

4-y-o+	W-R	Per cent	£1 Level Stake	**Totals**	W-R	Per cent	£1 Level Stake
5f-6f	7-61	11.5	-26.50	5f-6f	12-112	10.7	-32.38
7f-8f	8-82	9.8	+0.25	7f-8f	8-110	7.3	-27.75
9f-13f	1-36	2.8	-24.00	9f-13f	1-39	2.6	-27.00
14f+	0-2	0.0	-2.00	14f+	0-2	0.0	-2.00

TYPE OF RACE

Non-Handicaps	W-R	Per cent	£1 Level Stake	**Handicaps**	W-R	Per cent	£1 Level Stake
2-y-o	0-11	0.0	-11.00	2-y-o	2-10	20.0	+6.50
3-y-o	0-9	0.0	-9.00	3-y-o	3-52	5.8	-23.38
4-y-o+	0-2	0.0	-2.00	4-y-o+	16-179	8.9	-50.25

RACE CLASS

	W-R	Per cent	£1 Level Stake
Class 1	0-0	0.0	0.00
Class 2	0-0	0.0	0.00
Class 3	0-1	0.0	-1.00
Class 4	1-23	4.3	+3.00
Class 5	3-94	3.2	-74.75
Class 6	17-137	12.4	-8.38
Class 7	0-8	0.0	-8.00

FIRST TIME OUT

	W-R	Per cent	£1 Level Stake
2-y-o	0-4	0.0	-4.00
3-y-o	1-10	10.0	+1.00
4-y-o+	1-19	5.3	-11.00
Totals	2-33	6.1	-14.00

JOCKEYS

	W-R	Per cent	£1 Level Stake
Cam Hardie	17-227	7.5	-84.13
Kieran Schofield	2-4	50.0	+8.00
Eoin Walsh	1-3	33.3	+8.00
William Cox	1-13	7.7	-5.00

COURSE RECORD

	Total W-R	Non-Hndcps 2-y-o	Non-Hndcps 3-y-o+	Hndcps 2-y-o	Hndcps 3-y-o+	Per cent	£1 Level Stake
Newcastle (A.W)	7-64	0-4	0-1	2-5	5-54	10.9	-5.50
Wolvhptn (A.W)	7-96	0-2	0-3	0-1	7-90	7.3	-24.50
Southwell (A.W)	3-14	0-0	0-0	0-0	3-14	21.4	+2.25
Wetherby	1-1	0-0	0-0	0-0	1-1	100.0	+4.50
Leicester	1-4	0-0	0-0	0-0	1-4	25.0	+7.00
Redcar	1-12	0-1	0-0	0-0	1-11	8.3	-3.50
Thirsk	1-12	0-0	0-1	0-0	1-11	8.3	-9.38

WINNING HORSES

Horse	Races Run	1st	2nd	3rd	£
Another Angel (IRE)	12	3	3	1	9315
Beathybeatbybeat	18	2	6	3	6210
Canford Bay (IRE)	11	2	3	0	7245
International Law	7	1	0	0	6081
Klopp	5	1	0	0	3105
Lucky Lodge	22	5	2	2	16561

Horse	Races Run	1st	2nd	3rd	£
Mutabaahy (IRE)	16	2	5	3	6503
*One One Seven (IRE)	7	1	0	1	3105
*Qaaraat	6	1	1	1	4787
Sooqaan	16	3	1	0	9315
Total winning prize-money					**£72227**
Favourites	**7-12**		**58.3%**		**12.88**

JULIA BROOKE

MIDDLEHAM, N YORKS

	No. of Hrs	Races Run	1st	2nd	3rd	Unpl	Per cent	£1 Level Stake
2-y-o	*0*	*0*	*0*	*0*	*0*	*0*	*0.0*	*0.00*
3-y-o	*0*	*0*	*0*	*0*	*0*	*0*	*0.0*	*0.00*
4-y-o+	*6*	*22*	*1*	*0*	*2*	*19*	*4.5*	*-13.00*
Totals	**6**	**22**	**1**	**0**	**2**	**19**	**4.5**	**-13.00**
2017	*4*	*11*	*0*	*0*	*0*	*11*	*0.0*	*-11.00*
2016	*5*	*6*	*0*	*0*	*0*	*6*	*0.0*	*-6.00*

JOCKEYS

	W-R	Per cent	£1 Level Stake
Nathan Evans	1-4	25.0	+5.00

COURSE RECORD

	Total W-R	Non-Hndcps 2-y-o	Non-Hndcps 3-y-o+	Hndcps 2-y-o	Hndcps 3-y-o+	Per cent	£1 Level Stake
Southwell (A.W)	1-4	0-0	0-0	0-0	1-4	25.0	+5.00

WINNING HORSES

Horse	Races Run	1st	2nd	3rd	£
*Piazon	6	1	0	1	3105
Total winning prize-money					**£3105**
Favourites	**0-1**		**0.0%**		**-1.00**

ROY BROTHERTON

ELMLEY CASTLE, WORCS

	No. of Hrs	Races Run	1st	2nd	3rd	Unpl	Per cent	£1 Level Stake
2-y-o	*0*	*0*	*0*	*0*	*0*	*0*	*0.0*	*0.00*
3-y-o	*2*	*6*	*0*	*0*	*0*	*6*	*0.0*	*-6.00*
4-y-o+	*4*	*32*	*2*	*1*	*5*	*24*	*6.3*	*-4.00*
Totals	**6**	**38**	**2**	**1**	**5**	**30**	**5.3**	**-10.00**
2017	*9*	*44*	*2*	*1*	*6*	*35*	*4.5*	*-19.00*
2016	*11*	*49*	*4*	*3*	*1*	*41*	*8.2*	*+0.88*

JOCKEYS

	W-R	Per cent	£1 Level Stake
Eoin Walsh	2-21	9.5	+7.00

COURSE RECORD

	Total W-R	Non-Hndcps 2-y-o	Non-Hndcps 3-y-o+	Hndcps 2-y-o	Hndcps 3-y-o+	Per cent	£1 Level Stake
Bath	2-8	0-0	0-0	0-0	2-8	25.0	+20.00

WINNING HORSES

Horse	Races Run	1st	2nd	3rd	£
Filament Of Gold (USA)	11	2	0	3	6210
Total winning prize-money					**£6210**
Favourites	**0-0**		**0.0%**		**0.00**

ALAN BROWN

YEDINGHAM, N YORKS

	No. of Hrs	Races Run	1st	2nd	3rd	Unpl	Per cent	£1 Level Stake
2-y-o	*2*	*8*	*0*	*0*	*0*	*8*	*0.0*	*-8.00*
3-y-o	*1*	*3*	*0*	*0*	*0*	*3*	*0.0*	*-3.00*
4-y-o+	*7*	*56*	*5*	*4*	*7*	*39*	*8.9*	*+8.50*
Totals	**10**	**67**	**5**	**4**	**7**	**50**	**7.5**	**-2.50**
2017	*9*	*76*	*4*	*7*	*8*	*57*	*5.3*	*-45.25*
2016	*8*	*73*	*7*	*6*	*6*	*54*	*9.6*	*+0.50*

JOCKEYS

	W-R	Per cent	£1 Level Stake
Andrew Mullen	2-21	9.5	+3.00
Mr Tom Midgley	1-3	33.3	+10.00
Kieran Schofield	1-3	33.3	+16.00
Hollie Doyle	1-4	25.0	+4.50

COURSE RECORD

	Total W-R	Non-Hndcps 2-y-o	Non-Hndcps 3-y-o+	Hndcps 2-y-o	Hndcps 3-y-o+	Per cent	£1 Level Stake
Carlisle	1-2	0-0	0-0	0-0	1-2	50.0	+11.00
Hamilton	1-3	0-0	0-0	0-0	1-3	33.3	+10.00
Wetherby	1-4	0-0	0-0	0-0	1-4	25.0	+15.00
Southwell (A.W)	1-5	0-0	0-0	0-0	1-5	20.0	+3.50
Redcar	1-10	0-1	0-5	0-1	1-3	10.0	+1.00

WINNING HORSES

Horse	Races Run	1st	2nd	3rd	£
Imperial Legend (IRE)	16	2	3	3	6987
Meandmyshadow	8	2	0	1	6598
*Warrior's Spirit (IRE)	6	1	0	1	3120
Total winning prize-money					**£16705**
Favourites	**0-0**		**0.0%**		**0.00**

DAVID BROWN

AVERHAM PARK, NOTTS

	No. of Hrs	Races Run	1st	2nd	3rd	Unpl	Per cent	£1 Level Stake
2-y-o	*6*	*22*	*0*	*2*	*0*	*20*	*0.0*	*-22.00*

3-y-o	*16*	*70*	*7*	*7*	*10*	*46*	*10.0*	*+5.35*
4-y-o+	*8*	*35*	*1*	*4*	*6*	*24*	*2.9*	*-31.00*
Totals	**30**	**127**	**8**	**13**	**16**	**90**	**6.3**	**-47.65**
2017	*49*	*237*	*15*	*26*	*27*	*169*	*6.3*	*-80.75*
2016	*46*	*230*	*25*	*22*	*18*	*164*	*10.9*	*+18.33*

JOCKEYS

	W-R	Per cent	£1 Level Stake
Andrew Mullen	2-11	18.2	-2.00
Jason Watson	2-20	10.0	-11.50
Jimmy Quinn	1-2	50.0	+49.00
Harrison Shaw	1-3	33.3	0.90
Richard Kingscote	1-4	25.0	+2.00
Sean Levey	1-5	20.0	-2.25

COURSE RECORD

	Total W-R	Non-Hndcps 2-y-o	Non-Hndcps 3-y-o+	Hndcps 2-y-o	Hndcps 3-y-o+	Per cent	£1 Level Stake
Wolvhptn (A.W)	3-14	0-1	0-0	0-0	3-13	21.4	-1.25
Southwell (A.W)	2-19	0-1	1-2	0-0	1-16	10.5	-10.00
Ripon	1-2	0-1	0-0	0-0	1-1	50.0	+2.50
Newcastle (A.W)	1-8	0-0	0-0	0-1	1-7	12.5	-5.90
Chelmsford (A.W)	1-12	0-0	0-0	0-1	1-11	8.3	+39.00

WINNING HORSES

Horse	Races Run	1st	2nd	3rd	£
Fortunate Vision*	4	1	0	0	3752
Hard Graft	5	1	0	2	3752
Hic Bibi*	7	1	0	0	5434
Medici Oro	7	1	0	2	3105
One More Chance (IRE)*	5	1	0	1	3752
Sky Gypsy	7	1	0	2	3105
Snaffled (IRE)	8	2	2	1	6857
Total winning prize-money					**£29757**
Favourites	**4-13**		**30.8%**		**0.35**

DAI BURCHELL

BRIERY HILL, BLAENAU GWENT

	No. of Hrs	Races Run	1st	2nd	3rd	Unpl	Per cent	£1 Level Stake
2-y-o	*0*	*0*	*0*	*0*	*0*	*0*	*0.0*	*0.00*
3-y-o	*1*	*1*	*0*	*0*	*0*	*1*	*0.0*	*-1.00*
4-y-o+	*3*	*13*	*1*	*0*	*1*	*11*	*7.7*	*0.00*
Totals	**4**	**14**	**1**	**0**	**1**	**12**	**7.1**	**-1.00**
2017	*10*	*25*	*0*	*0*	*4*	*21*	*0.0*	*-25.00*
2016	*4*	*11*	*2*	*1*	*0*	*8*	*18.2*	*+12.00*

JOCKEYS

	W-R	Per cent	£1 Level Stake
Hollie Doyle	1-7	14.3	+6.00

COURSE RECORD

	Total W-R	Non-Hndcps 2-y-o	Non-Hndcps 3-y-o+	Hndcps 2-y-o	Hndcps 3-y-o+	Per cent	£1 Level Stake
Wolvhptn (A.W)	1-5	0-0	0-0	0-0	1-5	20.0	+8.00

WINNING HORSES

Horse	Races Run	1st	2nd	3rd	£
Cooperess	7	1	0	0	2264
Total winning prize-money					**£2264**
Favourites	**1-2**		**50.0%**		**1.75**

PAUL BURGOYNE

SHEPTON MONTAGUE, SOMERSET

	No. of Hrs	Races Run	1st	2nd	3rd	Unpl	Per cent	£1 Level Stake
2-y-o	*0*	*0*	*0*	*0*	*0*	*0*	*0.0*	*0.00*
3-y-o	*0*	*0*	*0*	*0*	*0*	*0*	*0.0*	*0.00*
4-y-o+	*1*	*3*	*1*	*0*	*1*	*1*	*33.3*	*+0.75*
Totals	**1**	**3**	**1**	**0**	**1**	**1**	**33.3**	**+0.75**
2017	*6*	*42*	*1*	*0*	*3*	*38*	*2.4*	*-34.00*
2016	*8*	*49*	*2*	*7*	*3*	*37*	*4.1*	*-23.00*

JOCKEYS

	W-R	Per cent	£1 Level Stake
Oisin Murphy	1-1	100.0	+2.75

COURSE RECORD

	Total W-R	Non-Hndcps 2-y-o	Non-Hndcps 3-y-o+	Hndcps 2-y-o	Hndcps 3-y-o+	Per cent	£1 Level Stake
Kempton (A.W)	1-2	0-0	0-0	0-0	1-2	50.0	+1.75

WINNING HORSES

Horse	Races Run	1st	2nd	3rd	£
Runaiocht (IRE)*	3	1	0	1	2588
Total winning prize-money					**£2588**
Favourites	**0-0**		**0.0%**		**0.00**

K R BURKE

MIDDLEHAM MOOR, N YORKS

	No. of Hrs	Races Run	1st	2nd	3rd	Unpl	Per cent	£1 Level Stake
2-y-o	*58*	*236*	*26*	*28*	*31*	*150*	*11.0*	*-29.76*
3-y-o	*50*	*267*	*24*	*45*	*36*	*162*	*9.0*	*-106.88*
4-y-o+	*24*	*131*	*20*	*15*	*13*	*81*	*15.3*	*+70.83*
Totals	**132**	**634**	**70**	**88**	**80**	**393**	**11.0**	**-65.81**
2017	*129*	*617*	*74*	*63*	*83*	*397*	*12.0*	*+0.68*
2016	*126*	*587*	*68*	*54*	*60*	*405*	*11.6*	*-16.74*

BY MONTH

2-y-o	W-R	Per cent	£1 Level Stake
January	0-0	0.0	0.00
February	0-0	0.0	0.00
March	0-1	0.0	-1.00
April	0-3	0.0	-3.00
May	1-12	8.3	-5.00
June	6-25	24.0	+16.50
July	2-34	5.9	-22.50
August	6-34	17.6	+12.16
September	4-59	6.8	-38.00
October	5-44	11.4	-14.92
November	1-16	6.3	+25.00
December	1-8	12.5	+1.00

3-y-o	W-R	Per cent	£1 Level Stake
January	2-15	13.3	+14.00
February	2-9	22.2	+15.25
March	2-15	13.3	-3.88
April	3-30	10.0	-16.88
May	0-47	0.0	-47.00
June	3-40	7.5	-12.50
July	6-21	28.6	+6.88
August	2-19	10.5	-6.50
September	1-28	3.6	-25.25
October	1-20	5.0	-16.25
November	2-13	15.4	-4.75
December	0-10	0.0	-10.00

4-y-o+	W-R	Per cent	£1 Level Stake
January	4-23	17.4	+3.00
February	1-10	10.0	-6.50
March	2-17	11.8	+21.33
April	2-13	15.4	+16.00
May	2-15	13.3	-8.25
June	1-8	12.5	-4.75
July	1-7	14.3	+3.00
August	1-7	14.3	+16.00
September	2-15	13.3	+7.00
October	2-9	22.2	+7.00
November	1-3	33.3	+12.00
December	1-4	25.0	+5.00

Totals	W-R	Per cent	£1 Level Stake
January	6-38	15.8	+17.00
February	3-19	15.8	+8.75
March	4-33	12.1	+16.45
April	5-46	10.9	-3.88
May	3-74	4.1	-60.25
June	10-73	13.7	-0.75
July	9-62	14.5	-12.62
August	9-60	15.0	+21.66
September	7-102	6.9	-56.25
October	8-73	11.0	-24.17
November	4-32	12.5	+7.25
December	2-22	9.1	-5.00

DISTANCE

2-y-o	W-R	Per cent	£1 Level Stake
5f-6f	13-132	9.8	-45.67
7f-8f	13-98	13.3	+21.91
9f-13f	0-6	0.0	-6.00
14f+	0-0	0.0	0.00

3-y-o	W-R	Per cent	£1 Level Stake
5f-6f	10-68	14.7	-1.88
7f-8f	10-121	8.3	-40.63
9f-13f	4-77	5.2	-63.38
14f+	0-1	0.0	-1.00

4-y-o+	W-R	Per cent	£1 Level Stake
5f-6f	3-16	18.8	+0.50
7f-8f	10-78	12.8	+23.33
9f-13f	7-37	18.9	+47.00
14f+	0-0	0.0	0.00

Totals	W-R	Per cent	£1 Level Stake
5f-6f	26-216	12.0	-47.05
7f-8f	33-297	11.1	+4.61
9f-13f	11-120	9.2	-22.38
14f+	0-1	0.0	-1.00

TYPE OF RACE

Non-Handicaps

	W-R	Per cent	£1 Level Stake
2-y-o	24-185	13.0	+13.49
3-y-o	9-99	9.1	-45.63
4-y-o+	2-12	16.7	-4.00

Handicaps

	W-R	Per cent	£1 Level Stake
2-y-o	2-51	3.9	-43.25
3-y-o	15-168	8.9	-61.25
4-y-o+	18-119	15.1	+74.83

RACE CLASS

	W-R	Per cent	£1 Level Stake
Class 1	1-44	2.3	-40.25
Class 2	8-53	15.1	+22.00
Class 3	4-57	7.0	-21.67
Class 4	16-160	10.0	+18.00
Class 5	34-253	13.4	-7.29
Class 6	7-66	10.6	-35.59
Class 7	0-1	0.0	-1.00

FIRST TIME OUT

	W-R	Per cent	£1 Level Stake
2-y-o	5-58	8.6	-19.00
3-y-o	3-50	6.0	-35.88
4-y-o+	3-24	12.5	+22.50
Totals	11-132	8.3	-32.38

JOCKEYS

	W-R	Per cent	£1 Level Stake
Ben Curtis	25-127	19.7	+56.83
Clifford Lee	23-222	10.4	-15.26
Richard Kingscote	4-15	26.7	+22.75
Jonathan Fisher	3-19	15.8	+22.00
Daniel Tudhope	2-8	25.0	+7.75
Andrew Elliott	2-8	25.0	+10.00
Russell Harris	2-11	18.2	+0.50
Michael Stainton	2-14	14.3	-6.25
Shane Kelly	1-2	50.0	+19.00
Nicola Currie	1-3	33.3	+1.00
Tom Marquand	1-4	25.0	-1.25
Jason Watson	1-5	20.0	+1.00
David Egan	1-13	7.7	-9.00
Rhona Pindar	1-27	3.7	-24.38
P J McDonald	1-58	1.7	-52.50

COURSE RECORD

	Total W-R	Non-Hndcps 2-y-o	Non-Hndcps 3-y-o+	Hndcps 2-y-o	Hndcps 3-y-o+	Per cent	£1 Level Stake
Southwell (A.W)	12-49	1-2	4-12	0-5	7-30	24.5	+63.38
Wolvhptn (A.W)	9-62	4-16	2-9	0-7	3-30	14.5	+21.87
Carlisle	6-23	3-11	0-0	0-3	3-9	26.1	+21.25
Haydock	4-36	1-13	1-5	0-1	2-17	11.1	-13.00
Newcastle (A.W)	4-64	2-15	1-19	0-4	1-26	6.3	-5.75
Nottingham	3-23	3-8	0-1	0-3	0-11	13.0	-6.25
Doncaster	3-35	2-8	0-12	0-3	1-12	8.6	-17.50
Windsor	2-8	0-3	1-1	0-0	1-4	25.0	+7.63
Pontefract	2-10	2-3	0-4	0-1	0-2	20.0	-5.42
Catterick	2-11	0-2	1-4	0-1	1-4	18.2	+13.00
Yarmouth	2-12	1-2	0-0	0-2	1-8	16.7	+17.00
Musselburgh	2-13	0-4	0-0	0-1	2-8	15.4	-4.75
Newmarket	2-15	0-6	1-5	0-1	1-3	13.3	-3.25
Chelmsford (A.W)	2-16	1-5	0-1	1-3	0-7	12.5	-7.25
Leicester	2-20	0-3	0-5	0-3	2-9	10.0	-7.75
York	2-22	2-14	0-2	0-2	0-4	9.1	-1.00
Ayr	2-23	0-6	0-2	1-1	1-14	8.7	-11.00
Ripon	2-29	1-11	0-5	0-1	1-12	6.9	+1.00
Brighton	1-2	0-0	0-0	0-0	1-2	50.0	+0.75
Chepstow	1-2	0-1	0-0	0-0	1-1	50.0	+6.00
Newmkt (Jly)	1-6	0-2	0-0	0-0	1-4	16.7	-2.00
Newbury	1-8	0-3	0-1	0-1	1-3	12.5	-4.00
Ascot	1-10	0-4	0-2	0-0	1-4	10.0	0.00
Lingfield (A.W)	1-14	0-1	0-2	0-0	1-11	7.1	-10.50
Thirsk	1-18	1-10	0-3	0-2	0-3	5.6	-15.25

WINNING HORSES

Horse	Races Run	1st	2nd	3rd	£
Absolutio (FR)	3	1	0	0	3752
Angel Palanas	12	4	1	3	17337
Assimile (IRE)	11	2	2	1	6857
Borderforce (FR)	6	1	0	0	15563
Broken Force (USA)	8	1	2	1	5175
Chains Of Love (IRE)	4	1	0	1	9704
Chasing The Rain	3	1	0	0	3752
Comedy (IRE)	4	2	0	0	7633
Commanding Officer	3	1	1	0	43575
Constant	5	1	1	0	4787
Copper Baked (FR)	6	1	1	0	5531
Darwina*	8	1	1	0	3752
Divinity	6	2	0	1	8733
Dizzy G (IRE)	6	3	0	0	17111
Double Reflection	10	2	5	1	14524
Enzo's Lad (IRE)	8	1	2	1	3752
Four Kingdoms (IRE)*	3	1	0	1	3105
Havana Mariposa	9	1	3	0	5693
Helen Sherbet	9	1	0	3	5531
Humble Gratitude	7	1	1	0	7116
Jay Kay	7	1	0	0	4140
Jenoow (IRE)	8	1	0	2	3105
Kadar (USA)	1	1	0	0	6469
Kelly's Dino (FR)	10	4	2	2	35656
Koduro (IRE)	3	1	0	0	4205
Laurens (FR)	4	1	1	0	151345
Life Of Riley	8	1	2	0	3881
Line House	7	1	1	0	3881
Little Kim	6	1	0	0	4205
London Protocol (FR)	7	1	0	0	9704
Lonely Boy	6	1	1	3	3105
Lord Oberon	7	3	3	0	20083
Lumi (IRE)	7	1	1	2	3752
Made Of Honour (IRE)	5	2	0	0	14149
Mardle	3	1	0	0	6728
Midsummer Knight	8	2	3	2	19925
Mistress Of Love (USA)	4	1	0	1	2911
Mjjack (IRE)	6	2	0	1	25229
Myboyhenry (IRE)	4	1	0	2	16173
Play Mate	4	1	0	1	3817
Praxidice	3	1	0	0	4205
Riviere Argentee (FR)*	4	2	0	0	8604
Self Assessment (IRE)	4	1	1	0	3105
Shallow Hal	6	2	2	0	19444
Shine So Bright*	2	1	0	0	3881
So Hi Storm (IRE)	11	2	0	3	9898
Star Of Zaam (IRE)	5	1	2	0	3752
Sunday Prospect (FR)	5	1	0	2	3752
Swissterious	7	1	2	0	4787
True Mason	5	1	1	1	3881
Total winning prize-money					**£600755**
Favourites	**20-57**		**35.1%**		**2.56**

OWEN BURROWS

LAMBOURN, BERKS

	No. of Hrs	Races Run	1st	2nd	3rd	Unpl	Per cent	£1 Level Stake
2-y-o	*18*	*34*	*4*	*6*	*8*	*16*	*11.8*	*-14.25*
3-y-o	*37*	*122*	*27*	*15*	*20*	*60*	*22.1*	*+0.03*
4-y-o+	*9*	*26*	*7*	*2*	*1*	*16*	*26.9*	*+23.48*
Totals	**64**	**182**	**38**	**23**	**29**	**92**	**20.9**	**+9.26**
2017	*53*	*151*	*27*	*26*	*23*	*74*	*17.9*	*-28.12*
2016	*41*	*110*	*16*	*21*	*16*	*57*	*14.5*	*-47.37*

BY MONTH

2-y-o	W-R	Per cent	£1 Level Stake
January	0-0	0.0	0.00
February	0-0	0.0	0.00
March	0-0	0.0	0.00
April	0-0	0.0	0.00
May	0-0	0.0	0.00
June	0-3	0.0	-3.00
July	0-2	0.0	-2.00
August	0-3	0.0	-3.00
September	0-3	0.0	-3.00
October	1-10	10.0	-3.50
November	3-10	30.0	+3.25
December	0-3	0.0	-3.00

3-y-o	W-R	Per cent	£1 Level Stake
January	0-0	0.0	0.00
February	0-0	0.0	0.00
March	0-0	0.0	0.00
April	1-7	14.3	+19.00
May	4-24	16.7	-8.50
June	7-26	26.9	-1.17
July	3-18	16.7	-10.25
August	0-8	0.0	-8.00
September	8-19	42.1	+6.45
October	3-15	20.0	+4.00
November	1-5	20.0	-1.50
December	0-0	0.0	0.00

4-y-o+	W-R	Per cent	£1 Level Stake
January	0-0	0.0	0.00
February	0-0	0.0	0.00
March	1-1	100.0	+1.50
April	0-3	0.0	-3.00
May	0-3	0.0	-3.00
June	2-7	28.6	-2.02
July	0-2	0.0	-2.00
August	1-1	100.0	+7.00
September	2-5	40.0	+22.50
October	1-4	25.0	+2.50
November	0-0	0.0	0.00
December	0-0	0.0	0.00

Totals	W-R	Per cent	£1 Level Stake
January	0-0	0.0	0.00
February	0-0	0.0	0.00
March	1-1	100.0	+1.50
April	1-10	10.0	+16.00
May	4-27	14.8	-11.50
June	9-36	25.0	-6.19
July	3-22	13.6	-14.25
August	1-12	8.3	-4.00
September	10-27	37.0	+25.95
October	5-29	17.2	+3.00
November	4-15	26.7	-1.50
December	0-3	0.0	0.00

DISTANCE

2-y-o	W-R	Per cent	£1 Level Stake
5f-6f	1-13	7.7	-9.00
7f-8f	3-19	15.8	-3.25
9f-13f	0-2	0.0	-2.00
14f+	0-0	0.0	0.00

3-y-o	W-R	Per cent	£1 Level Stake
5f-6f	4-20	20.0	-9.77
7f-8f	16-73	21.9	+15.71
9f-13f	7-29	24.1	-5.91
14f+	0-0	0.0	0.00

4-y-o+	W-R	Per cent	£1 Level Stake
5f-6f	1-5	20.0	+3.00
7f-8f	3-10	30.0	+16.38
9f-13f	2-8	25.0	+5.00
14f+	1-3	33.3	-0.90

Totals	W-R	Per cent	£1 Level Stake
5f-6f	6-38	15.8	-15.77
7f-8f	22-102	21.6	+28.84
9f-13f	9-39	23.1	-2.91
14f+	1-3	33.3	-0.90

TYPE OF RACE

Non-Handicaps	W-R	Per cent	£1 Level Stake	Handicaps	W-R	Per cent	£1 Level Stake
2-y-o	3-32	9.4	-18.75	2-y-o	1-2	50.0	+4.50
3-y-o	16-75	21.3	-0.82	3-y-o	11-47	23.4	+0.85
4-y-o+	3-7	42.9	+4.88	4-y-o+	4-19	21.1	+18.60

RACE CLASS

	W-R	Per cent	£1 Level Stake
Class 1	2-18	11.1	-9.83
Class 2	3-10	30.0	+1.75
Class 3	4-22	18.2	+32.88
Class 4	7-54	13.0	-28.43
Class 5	21-76	27.6	+11.40
Class 6	1-2	50.0	+1.50
Class 7	0-0	0.0	0.00

FIRST TIME OUT

	W-R	Per cent	£1 Level Stake
2-y-o	1-18	5.6	-11.50
3-y-o	8-37	21.6	+16.88
4-y-o+	2-9	22.2	+14.50
Totals	11-64	17.2	+19.88

JOCKEYS

	W-R	Per cent	£1 Level Stake
Jim Crowley	17-77	22.1	-12.81
Dane O'Neill	8-43	18.6	+8.13
Jason Watson	4-6	66.7	+15.86
David Probert	3-22	13.6	+4.07
Graham Lee	1-1	100.0	+3.00
Daniel Tudhope	1-1	100.0	+5.50
Frankie Dettori	1-1	100.0	+1.38
Silvestre De Sousa	1-1	100.0	+1.63
Gerald Mosse	1-2	50.0	+6.00
Kieran Shoemark	1-5	20.0	-0.50

COURSE RECORD

	Total W-R	Non-Hndcps 2-y-o	Non-Hndcps 3-y-o+	Hndcps 2-y-o	Hndcps 3-y-o+	Per cent	£1 Level Stake
Chelmsford (A.W)	5-27	1-5	2-10	0-0	2-12	18.5	+11.62
Lingfield (A.W)	4-11	1-5	3-5	0-0	0-1	36.4	+7.13
Newmarket	4-14	0-1	2-5	0-0	2-8	28.6	+23.00
Kempton (A.W)	4-20	1-7	2-6	0-0	1-7	20.0	-0.25
Nottingham	3-7	0-2	2-4	0-0	1-1	42.9	+7.00
Ascot	3-12	0-0	1-7	0-0	2-5	25.0	-0.63
Lingfield	2-4	0-1	2-3	0-0	0-0	50.0	+2.38
Leicester	2-6	0-0	0-2	0-0	2-4	33.3	+0.60
Sandown	2-8	0-0	2-5	0-0	0-3	25.0	-2.33
Ayr	1-1	0-0	0-0	0-0	1-1	100.0	+5.50
Bath	1-2	0-0	1-1	0-0	0-1	50.0	-0.43
Brighton	1-2	0-0	0-0	0-1	1-1	50.0	+3.50
Doncaster	1-5	0-0	1-3	0-0	0-2	20.0	-3.27
Salisbury	1-5	0-1	0-3	0-0	1-1	20.0	-2.90
York	1-6	0-0	0-1	0-0	1-5	16.7	-3.25
Goodwood	1-7	0-0	1-6	0-0	0-1	14.3	-4.90
Newmkt (Jly)	1-7	0-0	0-5	0-0	1-2	14.3	-2.00
Wolvhptn (A.W)	1-10	0-4	0-2	1-1	0-3	10.0	-3.50

WINNING HORSES

Horse	Races Run	1st	2nd	3rd	£
Alfarqad (USA)	1	1	0	0	3881
Althaaqib (USA)	6	1	0	0	3752
Anasheed	3	1	1	0	9704
Bawaasil	5	1	1	1	3752
Dawaam (USA)	1	1	0	0	3752
Elwazir	3	2	0	0	14232
Etisalat	5	1	0	1	3752
Fakhoor (IRE)	5	1	0	2	6469
Ganayem (IRE)	4	2	0	0	9057
Habub (USA)	1	1	0	0	6469
Kasbaan	3	1	0	0	3752
Katleen (USA)	4	1	0	1	4140
Khamry	5	2	0	0	7633
Laraaib (IRE)	4	1	1	0	34026
Mafaaheem (IRE)	3	1	1	0	15563
Manthoor (IRE)	4	1	1	0	3105
Mizaah (IRE)	1	1	0	0	9704
Multamis (IRE)	4	1	1	0	3752
Naqaawa (IRE)	5	2	0	1	9574
Okool (FR)	2	1	0	0	5757
Raheeb (IRE)	2	1	0	1	4204
Sawwaah	5	2	1	1	19407
Tabdeed	3	2	0	0	22556
Tashaaboh (IRE)	4	1	2	0	3752
Thammin	4	1	0	0	8345
Wadilsafa	4	3	0	0	42128
Warsaan	3	1	1	0	4528
Watheerah (USA)	2	1	1	0	7116
Wohileh	5	1	3	0	3752
Zaajer	5	1	0	2	3752
Total winning prize-money					**£281366**
Favourites	**16-40**		**40.0%**		**0.13**

JOHN BUTLER

NEWMARKET, SUFFOLK

	No. of Hrs	Races Run	1st	2nd	3rd	Unpl	Per cent	£1 Level Stake
2-y-o	*3*	*9*	*0*	*0*	*1*	*8*	*0.0*	*-9.00*
3-y-o	*14*	*64*	*5*	*2*	*5*	*52*	*7.8*	*-3.00*
4-y-o+	*51*	*287*	*27*	*26*	*23*	*210*	*9.4*	*-81.13*
Totals	**68**	**360**	**32**	**28**	**29**	**270**	**8.9**	**-93.13**
2017	*58*	*286*	*33*	*22*	*24*	*207*	*11.5*	*-44.75*
2016	*39*	*145*	*18*	*14*	*19*	*93*	*12.4*	*+61.22*

BY MONTH

2-y-o	W-R	Per cent	£1 Level Stake	3-y-o	W-R	Per cent	£1 Level Stake
January	0-0	0.0	0.00	January	0-2	0.0	-2.00
February	0-0	0.0	0.00	February	1-3	33.3	+3.00
March	0-0	0.0	0.00	March	0-1	0.0	-1.00
April	0-0	0.0	0.00	April	0-5	0.0	-5.00

	W-R	Per cent	£1 Level Stake
May	0-0	0.0	0.00
June	0-2	0.0	-2.00
July	0-0	0.0	0.00
August	0-0	0.0	0.00
September	0-1	0.0	-1.00
October	0-3	0.0	-3.00
November	0-3	0.0	-3.00
December	0-0	0.0	0.00

	W-R	Per cent	£1 Level Stake
May	0-2	0.0	-2.00
June	1-5	20.0	+7.00
July	0-9	0.0	-9.00
August	0-9	0.0	-9.00
September	1-10	10.0	+5.00
October	1-8	12.5	+13.00
November	1-10	10.0	-3.00
December	0-0	0.0	0.00

4-y-o+	W-R	Per cent	£1 Level Stake
January	1-24	4.2	-22.47
February	1-20	5.0	-14.50
March	3-21	14.3	-7.63
April	3-25	12.0	+7.33
May	4-28	14.3	-10.75
June	4-32	12.5	-13.88
July	1-16	6.3	-3.00
August	3-33	9.1	-2.00
September	2-29	6.9	-10.50
October	2-26	7.7	+3.75
November	3-25	12.0	+0.50
December	0-8	0.0	-8.00

Totals	W-R	Per cent	£1 Level Stake
January	1-26	3.8	-24.47
February	2-23	8.7	-11.50
March	3-22	13.6	-8.63
April	3-30	10.0	+2.33
May	4-30	13.3	-12.75
June	5-39	12.8	-8.88
July	1-25	4.0	-12.00
August	3-42	7.1	-11.00
September	3-40	7.5	-6.50
October	3-37	8.1	+13.75
November	4-38	10.5	-2.50
December	0-8	0.0	-8.00

DISTANCE

2-y-o	W-R	Per cent	£1 Level Stake
5f-6f	0-2	0.0	-2.00
7f-8f	0-7	0.0	-7.00
9f-13f	0-0	0.0	0.00
14f+	0-0	0.0	0.00

3-y-o	W-R	Per cent	£1 Level Stake
5f-6f	2-23	8.7	-4.00
7f-8f	1-29	3.4	-14.00
9f-13f	2-12	16.7	+15.00
14f+	0-0	0.0	0.00

4-y-o+	W-R	Per cent	£1 Level Stake
5f-6f	7-61	11.5	-40.72
7f-8f	8-130	6.2	-61.42
9f-13f	9-76	11.8	-1.50
14f+	3-20	15.0	+22.50

Totals	W-R	Per cent	£1 Level Stake
5f-6f	9-86	10.5	-46.72
7f-8f	9-166	5.4	-82.42
9f-13f	11-88	12.5	+13.50
14f+	3-20	15.0	+22.50

TYPE OF RACE

Non-Handicaps

	W-R	Per cent	£1 Level Stake
2-y-o	0-8	0.0	-8.00
3-y-o	0-16	0.0	-16.00
4-y-o+	1-13	7.7	-1.00

Handicaps

	W-R	Per cent	£1 Level Stake
2-y-o	0-1	0.0	-1.00
3-y-o	5-48	10.4	+13.00
4-y-o+	26-274	9.5	-80.13

RACE CLASS

	W-R	Per cent	£1 Level Stake
Class 1	0-0	0.0	0.00
Class 2	0-5	0.0	-5.00
Class 3	3-20	15.0	+34.00
Class 4	2-48	4.2	-39.00
Class 5	4-87	4.6	-51.63
Class 6	22-186	11.8	-19.04
Class 7	1-14	7.1	-12.47

FIRST TIME OUT

	W-R	Per cent	£1 Level Stake
2-y-o	0-3	0.0	-3.00
3-y-o	0-14	0.0	-14.00
4-y-o+	5-51	9.8	-11.22
Totals	5-68	7.4	-28.22

JOCKEYS

	W-R	Per cent	£1 Level Stake
Adam Kirby	7-38	18.4	+10.83
Liam Keniry	5-43	11.6	-22.13
Tim Clark	4-75	5.3	-31.00
David Egan	2-5	40.0	+10.75
Paddy Mathers	2-8	25.0	+28.00
Daniel Muscutt	2-8	25.0	+10.50
Robert Winston	2-19	10.5	-13.97
J F Egan	2-21	9.5	+13.00
P J McDonald	1-2	50.0	+1.00
Harry Bentley	1-2	50.0	+21.00
Joey Haynes	1-4	25.0	-1.75
Charles Bishop	1-5	20.0	-1.25
Nicola Currie	1-6	16.7	-3.63
Danny Brock	1-15	6.7	-8.50

COURSE RECORD

	Total W-R	Non-Hndcps 2-y-o	Non-Hndcps 3-y-o+	Hndcps 2-y-o	Hndcps 3-y-o+	Per cent	£1 Level Stake
Wolvhptn (A.W)	8-80	0-1	1-4	0-0	7-75	10.0	+2.50
Lingfield (A.W)	7-46	0-0	0-3	0-0	7-43	15.2	-9.79
Kempton (A.W)	5-64	0-2	0-2	0-1	5-59	7.8	-28.75
Newcastle (A.W)	2-12	0-0	0-1	0-0	2-11	16.7	+14.00
Yarmouth	2-15	0-0	0-2	0-0	2-13	13.3	-0.75
Bath	1-2	0-0	0-0	0-0	1-2	50.0	+1.75
Ripon	1-3	0-0	0-0	0-0	1-3	33.3	+18.00
Doncaster	1-4	0-0	0-0	0-0	1-4	25.0	+22.00
Leicester	1-7	0-1	0-1	0-0	1-5	14.3	-4.63
Brighton	1-12	0-0	0-3	0-0	1-9	8.3	-2.00
Southwell (A.W)	1-12	0-0	0-1	0-0	1-11	8.3	-10.47
Nottingham	1-13	0-3	0-1	0-0	1-9	7.7	-9.50
Chelmsford (A.W)	1-43	0-0	0-4	0-0	1-39	2.3	-38.50

WINNING HORSES

Horse	Races Run	1st	2nd	3rd	£
*Amherst Rock	6	1	0	0	3105
At Your Service	1	1	0	0	3105
Cat Royale (IRE)	17	1	2	2	3105
Connemera Queen	11	2	0	1	6210
Declamation (IRE)*	6	1	0	1	2588
Deleyll	5	2	0	0	6210
Denmead*	6	1	1	1	6469
Fashaak (IRE)	7	1	0	0	4464
Father Ailbe (IRE)	4	1	1	2	3105
Forbidding (USA)	10	1	0	0	3493
Foxy Locks*	10	1	0	0	3105
Genuine Approval (IRE)	7	1	1	0	3105
Haveoneyerself (IRE)	13	1	0	1	3752
Island Flame (IRE)*	6	1	1	1	3105
King Crimson	14	2	3	0	7245
Mime Dance	13	1	1	0	3105
*Pushkin Museum (IRE)	5	1	0	0	3105
Red Invader (IRE)*	5	1	1	0	3105

Ruby Gates (IRE)*	10	2	1	0	6857
Soar Above*	7	2	0	0	6210
The Grand Visir	1	1	0	0	7246
Time To Sea (IRE)	3	1	1	0	3235
Tom's Rock (IRE)	8	1	1	2	5531
Unforgiving Minute*	9	1	2	2	7246
Waneen (IRE)*	6	1	2	0	3105
Weloof (FR)	8	1	2	0	3429
Windsor Beach (IRE)	5	1	0	0	9338
Total winning prize-money					**£123678**
Favourites	**12-32**		**37.5%**		**6.37**

PADDY BUTLER

EAST CHILTINGTON, E SUSSEX

	No. of Hrs	Races Run	1st	2nd	3rd	Unpl	Per cent	£1 Level Stake
2-y-o	*1*	*2*	*0*	*0*	*0*	*2*	*0.0*	*-2.00*
3-y-o	*0*	*0*	*0*	*0*	*0*	*0*	*0.0*	*0.00*
4-y-o+	*12*	*51*	*4*	*0*	*1*	*46*	*7.8*	*-9.50*
Totals	**13**	**53**	**4**	**0**	**1**	**48**	**7.5**	**-11.50**
2017	*12*	*57*	*2*	*3*	*2*	*50*	*3.5*	*-37.00*
2016	*15*	*64*	*0*	*2*	*1*	*61*	*0.0*	*-64.00*

JOCKEYS

	W-R	Per cent	£1 Level Stake
Jason Watson	4-13	30.8	+28.50

COURSE RECORD

	Total W-R	Non-Hndcps 2-y-o	Non-Hndcps 3-y-o+	Hndcps 2-y-o	Hndcps 3-y-o+	Per cent	£1 Level Stake
Lingfield (A.W)	2-22	0-1	0-0	0-1	2-20	9.1	+2.50
Brighton	1-6	0-0	0-0	0-0	1-6	16.7	0.00
Kempton (A.W)	1-14	0-0	0-0	0-0	1-14	7.1	-3.00

WINNING HORSES

Horse	Races Run	1st	2nd	3rd	£
Mercers	15	4	0	1	12420
Total winning prize-money					**£12420**
Favourites	**0-0**		**0.0%**		**0.00**

JULIE CAMACHO

NORTON, N YORKS

	No. of Hrs	Races Run	1st	2nd	3rd	Unpl	Per cent	£1 Level Stake
2-y-o	*5*	*11*	*2*	*2*	*3*	*4*	*18.2*	*-1.70*
3-y-o	*11*	*41*	*6*	*5*	*2*	*28*	*14.6*	*+6.00*
4-y-o+	*20*	*117*	*20*	*15*	*12*	*69*	*17.1*	*+2.87*
Totals	**36**	**169**	**28**	**22**	**17**	**101**	**16.6**	**+7.17**
2017	*27*	*142*	*17*	*17*	*9*	*99*	*12.0*	*-48.92*
2016	*17*	*121*	*9*	*12*	*22*	*78*	*7.4*	*-58.92*

BY MONTH

2-y-o	W-R	Per cent	£1 Level Stake	3-y-o	W-R	Per cent	£1 Level Stake
January	0-0	0.0	0.00	January	0-0	0.0	0.00
February	0-0	0.0	0.00	February	0-0	0.0	0.00
March	0-0	0.0	0.00	March	0-0	0.0	0.00
April	0-0	0.0	0.00	April	1-2	50.0	+8.00
May	0-1	0.0	-1.00	May	1-6	16.7	-2.25
June	0-2	0.0	-2.00	June	0-4	0.0	-4.00
July	1-1	100.0	+0.80	July	0-8	0.0	-8.00
August	0-0	0.0	0.00	August	3-8	37.5	+8.25
September	0-1	0.0	-1.00	September	0-4	0.0	-4.00
October	1-3	33.3	+4.50	October	0-6	0.0	-6.00
November	0-2	0.0	-2.00	November	1-1	100.0	+16.00
December	0-1	0.0	-1.00	December	0-2	0.0	-2.00

4-y-o+	W-R	Per cent	£1 Level Stake	Totals	W-R	Per cent	£1 Level Stake
January	2-7	28.6	+7.00	January	2-7	28.6	+7.00
February	1-7	14.3	+2.00	February	1-7	14.3	+2.00
March	2-10	20.0	0.00	March	2-10	20.0	0.00
April	0-6	0.0	-6.00	April	1-8	12.5	+2.00
May	2-11	18.2	-2.50	May	3-18	16.7	-5.75
June	3-19	15.8	-7.72	June	3-25	12.0	-13.72
July	3-14	21.4	+7.00	July	4-23	17.4	-0.20
August	1-16	6.3	-6.00	August	4-24	16.7	+2.25
September	0-8	0.0	-8.00	September	0-13	0.0	-13.00
October	2-8	25.0	+5.33	October	3-17	17.6	+3.83
November	3-5	60.0	+11.75	November	4-8	50.0	+27.75
December	1-6	16.7	0.00	December	1-9	11.1	-2.00

DISTANCE

2-y-o	W-R	Per cent	£1 Level Stake	3-y-o	W-R	Per cent	£1 Level Stake
5f-6f	2-9	22.2	+0.30	5f-6f	4-20	20.0	+18.75
7f-8f	0-2	0.0	-2.00	7f-8f	0-10	0.0	-10.00
9f-13f	0-0	0.0	0.00	9f-13f	2-11	18.2	-2.75
14f+	0-0	0.0	0.00	14f+	0-0	0.0	0.00

4-y-o+	W-R	Per cent	£1 Level Stake	Totals	W-R	Per cent	£1 Level Stake
5f-6f	12-64	18.8	+16.24	5f-6f	18-93	19.4	+35.29
7f-8f	8-46	17.4	-6.38	7f-8f	8-58	13.8	-18.38
9f-13f	0-7	0.0	-7.00	9f-13f	2-18	11.1	-9.75
14f+	0-0	0.0	0.00	14f+	0-0	0.0	0.00

TYPE OF RACE

Non-Handicaps	W-R	Per cent	£1 Level Stake	Handicaps	W-R	Per cent	£1 Level Stake
2-y-o	2-9	22.2	+0.30	2-y-o	0-2	0.0	-2.00
3-y-o	2-14	14.3	-0.25	3-y-o	4-27	14.8	+6.25
4-y-o+	2-6	33.3	+0.91	4-y-o+	18-111	16.2	+1.96

RACE CLASS / FIRST TIME OUT

RACE CLASS	W-R	Per cent	£1 Level Stake	FIRST TIME OUT	W-R	Per cent	£1 Level Stake
Class 1	1-5	20.0	0.00	2-y-o	0-5	0.0	-5.00

Class 2	1-5	20.0	+2.50	3-y-o	2-11	18.2	+16.00
Class 3	3-18	16.7	+10.91	4-y-o+	4-20	20.0	+7.00
Class 4	7-39	17.9	-8.13				
Class 5	9-65	13.8	-13.62	Totals	6-36	16.7	+18.00
Class 6	7-36	19.4	+16.50				
Class 7	0-1	0.0	-1.00				

JOCKEYS

	W-R	Per cent	£1 Level Stake
Paul Mulrennan	9-40	22.5	-1.07
Callum Rodriguez	6-34	17.6	+7.58
Conor McGovern	4-15	26.7	+12.25
Jason Hart	2-4	50.0	+5.50
Graham Lee	2-23	8.7	-4.09
David Allan	1-1	100.0	+9.00
Marc Monaghan	1-1	100.0	+7.00
Kieran O'Neill	1-1	100.0	+6.50
Luke Morris	1-4	25.0	+5.00
Paul Hanagan	1-5	20.0	+0.50

COURSE RECORD

	Total W-R	Non-Hndcps 2-y-o	3-y-o+	Hndcps 2-y-o	3-y-o+	Per cent	£1 Level Stake
Newcastle (A.W)	8-47	0-2	0-4	0-2	8-39	17.0	+13.25
Catterick	4-10	0-0	0-0	0-0	4-10	40.0	+5.21
Redcar	4-19	0-2	1-3	0-0	3-14	21.1	+3.00
Chelmsford (A.W)	2-7	0-0	0-0	0-0	2-7	28.6	+6.00
Doncaster	2-8	0-0	0-1	0-0	2-7	25.0	+3.00
Thirsk	2-17	0-1	1-1	0-0	1-15	11.8	+6.00
Ripon	1-1	1-1	0-0	0-0	0-0	100.0	+0.80
Sandown	1-1	0-0	1-1	0-0	0-0	100.0	+4.00
Hamilton	1-2	0-0	0-1	0-0	1-1	50.0	+5.00
Newmarket	1-2	1-1	0-1	0-0	0-0	50.0	+5.50
Beverley	1-5	0-0	1-1	0-0	0-4	20.0	-3.09
Wolvhptn (A.W)	1-13	0-0	0-1	0-0	1-12	7.7	-4.50

WINNING HORSES

Horse	Races Run	1st	2nd	3rd	£
*Bill Cody (IRE)	8	2	2	0	10221
Brockholes	9	2	3	2	13456
Burtonwood	11	3	0	0	10255
Chosen World	8	2	0	1	6857
Dalton	7	2	1	0	17725
Dandy Bird (IRE)	2	1	0	0	3105
Deansgate (IRE)	9	2	1	2	11426
Dreamofdiscovery (IRE)	1	1	0	0	3105
I Know How (IRE)	4	1	0	1	3235
Judicial (IRE)	6	2	1	0	48412
Lorton	5	2	1	1	85046
Makanah	7	2	1	0	8216
Mythical Spirit (IRE)	6	3	3	0	14329
Royal Prospect (IRE)	1	1	0	0	7439
Spirit Of Wedza (IRE)	12	2	1	3	10544
Total winning prize-money					**£253371**
Favourites	**7-13**		**53.8%**		**7.33**

JENNIE CANDLISH

BASFORD GREEN, STAFFS

	No. of Hrs	Races Run	1st	2nd	3rd	Unpl	Per cent	£1 Level Stake
2-y-o	*2*	*6*	*0*	*0*	*0*	*6*	*0.0*	*-6.00*
3-y-o	*0*	*0*	*0*	*0*	*0*	*0*	*0.0*	*0.00*
4-y-o+	*10*	*69*	*12*	*7*	*10*	*40*	*17.4*	*+1.67*
Totals	**12**	**75**	**12**	**7**	**10**	**46**	**16.0**	**-4.33**
2017	*14*	*74*	*13*	*7*	*6*	*48*	*17.6*	*-0.92*
2016	*10*	*53*	*9*	*8*	*3*	*33*	*17.0*	*+0.75*

BY MONTH

2-y-o	W-R	Per cent	£1 Level Stake	3-y-o	W-R	Per cent	£1 Level Stake
January	0-0	0.0	0.00	January	0-0	0.0	0.00
February	0-0	0.0	0.00	February	0-0	0.0	0.00
March	0-0	0.0	0.00	March	0-0	0.0	0.00
April	0-0	0.0	0.00	April	0-0	0.0	0.00
May	0-2	0.0	-2.00	May	0-0	0.0	0.00
June	0-2	0.0	-2.00	June	0-0	0.0	0.00
July	0-0	0.0	0.00	July	0-0	0.0	0.00
August	0-1	0.0	-1.00	August	0-0	0.0	0.00
September	0-1	0.0	-1.00	September	0-0	0.0	0.00
October	0-0	0.0	0.00	October	0-0	0.0	0.00
November	0-0	0.0	0.00	November	0-0	0.0	0.00
December	0-0	0.0	0.00	December	0-0	0.0	0.00

4-y-o+	W-R	Per cent	£1 Level Stake	Totals	W-R	Per cent	£1 Level Stake
January	2-3	66.7	+9.25	January	2-3	66.7	+9.25
February	3-6	50.0	+3.92	February	3-6	50.0	+3.92
March	3-5	60.0	+8.00	March	3-5	60.0	+8.00
April	2-5	40.0	+15.50	April	2-5	40.0	+15.50
May	1-9	11.1	-1.00	May	1-11	9.1	-3.00
June	0-3	0.0	-3.00	June	0-5	0.0	-5.00
July	0-6	0.0	-6.00	July	0-6	0.0	-6.00
August	0-6	0.0	-6.00	August	0-7	0.0	-7.00
September	1-10	10.0	-3.00	September	1-11	9.1	-4.00
October	0-6	0.0	-6.00	October	0-6	0.0	-6.00
November	0-5	0.0	-5.00	November	0-5	0.0	-5.00
December	0-5	0.0	-5.00	December	0-5	0.0	-5.00

DISTANCE

2-y-o	W-R	Per cent	£1 Level Stake	3-y-o	W-R	Per cent	£1 Level Stake
5f-6f	0-5	0.0	-5.00	5f-6f	0-0	0.0	0.00
7f-8f	0-1	0.0	-1.00	7f-8f	0-0	0.0	0.00
9f-13f	0-0	0.0	0.00	9f-13f	0-0	0.0	0.00
14f+	0-0	0.0	0.00	14f+	0-0	0.0	0.00

4-y-o+	W-R	Per cent	£1 Level Stake	Totals	W-R	Per cent	£1 Level Stake
5f-6f	0-9	0.0	-9.00	5f-6f	0-14	0.0	-14.00
7f-8f	2-10	20.0	+5.00	7f-8f	2-11	18.2	+4.00
9f-13f	10-48	20.8	+7.67	9f-13f	10-48	20.8	+7.67
14f+	0-2	0.0	-2.00	14f+	0-2	0.0	-2.00

TYPE OF RACE

Non-Handicaps

	W-R	Per cent	£1 Level Stake
2-y-o	0-5	0.0	-5.00
3-y-o	0-0	0.0	0.00
4-y-o+	0-0	0.0	0.00

Handicaps

	W-R	Per cent	£1 Level Stake
2-y-o	0-1	0.0	-1.00
3-y-o	0-0	0.0	0.00
4-y-o+	12-69	17.4	+1.67

RACE CLASS

	W-R	Per cent	£1 Level Stake
Class 1	0-0	0.0	0.00
Class 2	0-2	0.0	-2.00
Class 3	0-7	0.0	-7.00
Class 4	0-18	0.0	-18.00
Class 5	4-28	14.3	+2.63
Class 6	8-20	40.0	+20.04
Class 7	0-0	0.0	0.00

FIRST TIME OUT

	W-R	Per cent	£1 Level Stake
2-y-o	0-2	0.0	-2.00
3-y-o	0-0	0.0	0.00
4-y-o+	3-10	30.0	+10.25
Totals	3-12	25.0	+8.25

JOCKEYS

	W-R	Per cent	£1 Level Stake
Joe Fanning	6-23	26.1	+6.92
Rossa Ryan	3-10	30.0	+12.00
Edward Greatrex	2-8	25.0	+3.75
Callum Shepherd	1-5	20.0	+2.00

COURSE RECORD

	Total W-R	Non-Hndcps 2-y-o	Non-Hndcps 3-y-o+	Hndcps 2-y-o	Hndcps 3-y-o+	Per cent	£1 Level Stake
Wolvhptn (A.W)	5-18	0-0	0-0	0-0	5-18	27.8	+17.00
Southwell (A.W)	4-10	0-0	0-0	0-0	4-10	40.0	+6.17
Bath	1-2	0-0	0-0	0-0	1-2	50.0	+6.00
Lingfield (A.W)	1-2	0-0	0-0	0-0	1-2	50.0	+2.50
Ffos Las	1-2	0-0	0-0	0-0	1-2	50.0	+5.00

WINNING HORSES

Horse	Races Run	1st	2nd	3rd	£
Aqua Libre	8	2	1	1	6275
Star Ascending (IRE)	15	6	0	1	20313
Sunshineandbubbles	19	4	4	2	13714
Total winning prize-money					**£40302**
Favourites	**11-35**		**31.4%**		**-8.18**

BY MONTH

2-y-o	W-R	Per cent	£1 Level Stake
January	0-0	0.0	0.00
February	0-0	0.0	0.00
March	0-0	0.0	0.00
April	0-0	0.0	0.00
May	0-0	0.0	0.00
June	1-6	16.7	+4.00
July	0-5	0.0	-5.00
August	0-1	0.0	-1.00
September	0-8	0.0	-8.00
October	0-9	0.0	-9.00
November	0-4	0.0	-4.00
December	0-5	0.0	-5.00

3-y-o	W-R	Per cent	£1 Level Stake
January	1-4	25.0	+1.50
February	0-0	0.0	0.00
March	0-0	0.0	0.00
April	1-5	20.0	-2.80
May	1-11	9.1	-4.50
June	2-20	10.0	-9.00
July	1-11	9.1	-6.50
August	3-5	60.0	+17.25
September	1-16	6.3	-7.00
October	1-17	5.9	-2.00
November	0-2	0.0	-2.00
December	1-1	100.0	+6.00

4-y-o+	W-R	Per cent	£1 Level Stake
January	1-5	20.0	-2.75
February	0-0	0.0	0.00
March	0-0	0.0	0.00
April	1-2	50.0	+1.50
May	1-15	6.7	-12.63
June	2-14	14.3	-0.50
July	1-8	12.5	-1.00
August	2-7	28.6	+0.75
September	3-12	25.0	-3.46
October	1-11	9.1	-8.25
November	0-2	0.0	-2.00
December	1-2	50.0	+0.25

Totals	W-R	Per cent	£1 Level Stake
January	2-9	22.2	-1.25
February	0-0	0.0	0.00
March	0-0	0.0	0.00
April	2-7	28.6	-1.30
May	2-26	7.7	-17.13
June	5-40	12.5	-5.50
July	2-24	8.3	-12.50
August	5-13	38.5	+17.00
September	4-36	11.1	-18.46
October	2-37	5.4	-19.25
November	0-8	0.0	-4.00
December	2-8	25.0	+6.25

DISTANCE

2-y-o	W-R	Per cent	£1 Level Stake
5f-6f	1-21	4.8	-11.00
7f-8f	0-17	0.0	-17.00
9f-13f	0-0	0.0	0.00
14f+	0-0	0.0	0.00

3-y-o	W-R	Per cent	£1 Level Stake
5f-6f	2-27	7.4	-15.50
7f-8f	7-41	17.1	+7.45
9f-13f	3-20	15.0	+3.00
14f+	0-4	0.0	-4.00

4-y-o+	W-R	Per cent	£1 Level Stake
5f-6f	6-21	28.6	+6.32
7f-8f	4-33	12.1	-20.75
9f-13f	3-24	12.5	-13.65
14f+	0-0	0.0	0.00

Totals	W-R	Per cent	£1 Level Stake
5f-6f	9-69	13.0	-20.18
7f-8f	11-91	12.1	-30.30
9f-13f	6-44	13.6	-10.65
14f+	0-4	0.0	-4.00

HENRY CANDY

KINGSTON WARREN, OXON

	No. of Hrs	Races Run	1st	2nd	3rd	Unpl	Per cent	£1 Level Stake
2-y-o	*12*	*38*	*1*	*2*	*5*	*30*	*2.6*	*-28.00*
3-y-o	*31*	*92*	*12*	*9*	*7*	*64*	*13.0*	*-9.05*
4-y-o+	*21*	*78*	*13*	*10*	*8*	*47*	*16.7*	*-28.08*
Totals	**64**	**208**	**26**	**21**	**20**	**141**	**12.5**	**-65.13**
2017	*55*	*201*	*32*	*33*	*21*	*115*	*15.9*	*-42.96*
2016	*55*	*225*	*22*	*21*	*29*	*152*	*9.8*	*-64.88*

TYPE OF RACE

Non-Handicaps

	W-R	Per cent	£1 Level Stake
2-y-o	1-33	3.0	-23.00
3-y-o	5-41	12.2	-15.30
4-y-o+	5-25	20.0	-10.81

Handicaps

	W-R	Per cent	£1 Level Stake
2-y-o	0-5	0.0	-5.00
3-y-o	7-51	13.7	+6.25
4-y-o+	8-53	15.1	-17.27

RACE CLASS

	W-R	Per cent	£1 Level Stake
Class 1	4-29	13.8	-17.06
Class 2	0-14	0.0	-14.00

FIRST TIME OUT

	W-R	Per cent	£1 Level Stake
2-y-o	1-12	8.3	-2.00
3-y-o	3-31	9.7	-16.80

Class 3	2-22	9.1	-12.63	4-y-o+	2-21	9.5	-15.25
Class 4	9-52	17.3	-20.70				
Class 5	9-77	11.7	-8.75	Totals	6-64	9.4	-34.05
Class 6	2-14	14.3	+8.00				
Class 7	0-0	0.0	0.00				

JOCKEYS

	W-R	Per cent	£1 Level Stake
Fran Berry	11-93	11.8	-14.00
Harry Bentley	8-32	25.0	-4.98
Andrea Atzeni	2-3	66.7	+4.75
Martin Harley	2-8	25.0	+1.50
Georgia Cox	1-2	50.0	+0.50
Ryan Moore	1-5	20.0	-2.90
Nicola Currie	1-23	4.3	-8.00

COURSE RECORD

	Total W-R	Non-Hndcps 2-y-o	Non-Hndcps 3-y-o+	Hndcps 2-y-o	Hndcps 3-y-o+	Per cent	£1 Level Stake
Kempton (A.W)	5-37	0-8	1-9	0-1	4-19	13.5	-4.50
Salisbury	3-7	0-1	1-4	0-0	2-2	42.9	+5.85
Newmkt (Jly)	3-13	0-0	1-4	0-0	2-9	23.1	+3.00
Lingfield (A.W)	2-6	0-0	2-3	0-1	0-2	33.3	+5.25
Goodwood	2-11	0-1	1-4	0-0	1-6	18.2	+1.00
Sandown	2-11	1-3	0-2	0-0	1-6	18.2	+6.00
York	1-3	0-0	1-2	0-0	0-1	33.3	-1.56
Lingfield	1-4	0-0	0-3	0-0	1-1	25.0	-1.63
Wolvhptn (A.W)	1-5	0-0	0-1	0-0	1-4	20.0	+2.00
Brighton	1-5	0-0	0-1	0-0	1-4	20.0	+10.00
Nottingham	1-6	0-2	0-1	0-0	1-3	16.7	-1.50
Chelmsford (A.W)	1-6	0-1	1-2	0-0	0-3	16.7	-3.50
Doncaster	1-7	0-0	1-3	0-1	0-3	14.3	-4.80
Newmarket	1-16	0-4	1-5	0-1	0-6	6.3	-13.25
Windsor	1-18	0-3	0-4	0-0	1-11	5.6	-14.50

WINNING HORSES

Horse	Races Run	1st	2nd	3rd	£
Be My Angel	3	1	1	0	3752
Chain Of Daisies	5	1	0	0	31191
Choosey (IRE)	6	1	0	0	3881
Cuban Spirit	5	1	0	0	3105
Eula Varner	2	1	0	1	3817
Hidden Affair	2	2	0	0	12938
Katie Lee (IRE)	5	1	1	0	3752
King Of Nepal	7	2	2	0	12938
Kurious	3	1	0	0	4528
Let Rip (IRE)	2	1	1	0	3752
Limato (IRE)	7	3	0	0	119091
Mt Augustus	6	1	1	0	9962
Ornamental	1	1	0	0	5531
Ortiz	5	1	1	1	6469
Past Master	6	2	2	0	10933
Rebecca Rocks	3	2	0	0	12777
Sarstedt	5	1	0	0	3105
Skill Set (IRE)	2	1	1	0	8345
Sovereign Duke (GER)	3	1	0	0	3881
Vibrant Chords	4	1	0	0	10583
Total winning prize-money					**£274331**
Favourites	**11-26**		**42.3%**		**0.87**

DON CANTILLON

NEWMARKET, SUFFOLK

	No. of Hrs	Races Run	1st	2nd	3rd	Unpl	Per cent	£1 Level Stake
2-y-o	*0*	*0*	*0*	*0*	*0*	*0*	*0.0*	*0.00*
3-y-o	*1*	*13*	*1*	*1*	*5*	*6*	*7.7*	*-5.50*
4-y-o+	*3*	*12*	*3*	*4*	*2*	*3*	*25.0*	*-0.38*
Totals	**4**	**25**	**4**	**5**	**7**	**9**	**16.0**	**-5.88**
2017	*6*	*36*	*5*	*5*	*6*	*20*	*13.9*	*-15.50*
2016	*5*	*25*	*5*	*6*	*0*	*14*	*20.0*	*+16.50*

JOCKEYS

	W-R	Per cent	£1 Level Stake
Adam Kirby	2-4	50.0	+2.63
Rossa Ryan	2-10	20.0	+2.50

COURSE RECORD

	Total W-R	Non-Hndcps 2-y-o	Non-Hndcps 3-y-o+	Hndcps 2-y-o	Hndcps 3-y-o+	Per cent	£1 Level Stake
Kempton (A.W)	2-7	0-0	0-1	0-0	2-6	28.6	+3.13
Wolvhptn (A.W)	1-7	0-0	0-1	0-0	1-6	14.3	-2.00
Chelmsford (A.W)	1-7	0-0	0-1	0-0	1-6	14.3	-3.00

WINNING HORSES

Horse	Races Run	1st	2nd	3rd	£
Navarra Princess (IRE)	13	1	1	5	3105
Western Way (IRE)	8	3	2	1	12065
Total winning prize-money					**£15170**
Favourites	**2-8**		**25.0%**		**-1.38**

RUTH CARR

HUBY, N YORKS

	No. of Hrs	Races Run	1st	2nd	3rd	Unpl	Per cent	£1 Level Stake
2-y-o	*1*	*7*	*1*	*0*	*1*	*5*	*14.3*	*+8.00*
3-y-o	*16*	*100*	*1*	*7*	*9*	*83*	*1.0*	*-91.00*
4-y-o+	*42*	*477*	*38*	*50*	*43*	*345*	*8.0*	*-162.92*
Totals	**59**	**584**	**40**	**57**	**53**	**433**	**6.8**	**-245.92**
2017	*52*	*480*	*49*	*48*	*51*	*331*	*10.2*	*-33.75*
2016	*43*	*412*	*42*	*51*	*34*	*284*	*10.2*	*-86.60*

BY MONTH

2-y-o	W-R	Per cent	£1 Level Stake	3-y-o	W-R	Per cent	£1 Level Stake
January	0-0	0.0	0.00	January	0-0	0.0	0.00
February	0-0	0.0	0.00	February	0-0	0.0	0.00
March	0-0	0.0	0.00	March	1-5	20.0	+4.00
April	0-0	0.0	0.00	April	0-8	0.0	-8.00

	W-R	Per cent	£1 Level Stake
May	0-3	0.0	-3.00
June	0-0	0.0	0.00
July	0-0	0.0	0.00
August	1-1	100.0	+14.00
September	0-1	0.0	-1.00
October	0-2	0.0	-2.00
November	0-0	0.0	0.00
December	0-0	0.0	0.00

	W-R	Per cent	£1 Level Stake
May	0-15	0.0	-15.00
June	0-8	0.0	-8.00
July	0-11	0.0	-11.00
August	0-13	0.0	-13.00
September	0-8	0.0	-8.00
October	0-14	0.0	-14.00
November	0-11	0.0	-11.00
December	0-7	0.0	-7.00

4-y-o+	W-R	Per cent	£1 Level Stake
January	0-1	0.0	-1.00
February	0-4	0.0	-4.00
March	5-25	20.0	+17.50
April	3-55	5.5	-13.50
May	7-78	9.0	-23.75
June	3-66	4.5	-41.50
July	7-71	9.9	-31.00
August	4-62	6.5	-27.50
September	3-49	6.1	-12.50
October	4-35	11.4	-7.17
November	1-21	4.8	-14.50
December	1-10	10.0	-4.00

Totals	W-R	Per cent	£1 Level Stake
January	0-1	0.0	-1.00
February	0-4	0.0	-4.00
March	6-30	20.0	+21.50
April	3-63	4.8	-21.50
May	7-96	7.3	-41.75
June	3-74	4.1	-49.50
July	7-82	8.5	-42.00
August	5-76	6.6	-26.50
September	3-58	5.2	-21.50
October	4-51	7.8	-23.17
November	1-32	3.1	-25.50
December	1-17	5.9	-11.00

DISTANCE

2-y-o	W-R	Per cent	£1 Level Stake
5f-6f	1-6	16.7	+9.00
7f-8f	0-1	0.0	-1.00
9f-13f	0-0	0.0	0.00
14f+	0-0	0.0	0.00

3-y-o	W-R	Per cent	£1 Level Stake
5f-6f	1-47	2.1	-38.00
7f-8f	0-44	0.0	-44.00
9f-13f	0-8	0.0	-8.00
14f+	0-1	0.0	-1.00

4-y-o+	W-R	Per cent	£1 Level Stake
5f-6f	25-289	8.7	-92.92
7f-8f	9-142	6.3	-62.50
9f-13f	4-45	8.9	-6.50
14f+	0-1	0.0	-1.00

Totals	W-R	Per cent	£1 Level Stake
5f-6f	27-342	7.9	-121.92
7f-8f	9-187	4.8	-107.50
9f-13f	4-53	7.5	-14.50
14f+	0-2	0.0	-2.00

TYPE OF RACE

Non-Handicaps

	W-R	Per cent	£1 Level Stake
2-y-o	0-3	0.0	-3.00
3-y-o	1-22	4.5	-13.00
4-y-o+	2-17	11.8	-7.50

Handicaps

	W-R	Per cent	£1 Level Stake
2-y-o	1-4	25.0	+11.00
3-y-o	0-78	0.0	-78.00
4-y-o+	36-460	7.8	-155.42

RACE CLASS

	W-R	Per cent	£1 Level Stake
Class 1	1-4	25.0	+2.00
Class 2	0-31	0.0	-31.00
Class 3	6-43	14.0	+15.75
Class 4	4-112	3.6	-86.00
Class 5	7-184	3.8	-108.75
Class 6	22-204	10.8	-31.92
Class 7	0-6	0.0	-6.00

FIRST TIME OUT

	W-R	Per cent	£1 Level Stake
2-y-o	0-1	0.0	-1.00
3-y-o	1-16	6.3	-7.00
4-y-o+	5-42	11.9	+7.00
Totals	6-59	10.2	-1.00

JOCKEYS

	W-R	Per cent	£1 Level Stake
James Sullivan	18-334	5.4	-171.00
Jack Garritty	8-80	10.0	-9.75
Barry McHugh	3-23	13.0	+1.50
Jane Elliott	2-27	7.4	-15.50
Ella McCain	1-1	100.0	+14.00
Jack Mitchell	1-1	100.0	+3.50
Mr Patrick Millman	1-1	100.0	+6.00
Sebastian Woods	1-2	50.0	+1.25
P J McDonald	1-3	33.3	+8.00
Franny Norton	1-3	33.3	+12.00
Callum Rodriguez	1-4	25.0	+0.33
Jamie Gormley	1-8	12.5	-1.50
Miss Emily Bullock	1-16	6.3	-13.75

COURSE RECORD

	Total W-R	Non-Hndcps 2-y-o	Non-Hndcps 3-y-o+	Hndcps 2-y-o	Hndcps 3-y-o+	Per cent	£1 Level Stake
Newcastle (A.W)	8-79	0-0	1-9	0-0	7-70	10.1	-2.67
Ripon	4-31	0-1	0-1	0-0	4-29	12.9	+8.75
Ayr	4-34	0-0	0-0	0-0	4-34	11.8	-12.25
Pontefract	3-23	0-0	0-0	0-0	3-23	13.0	-3.75
Catterick	3-46	0-0	1-2	0-0	2-44	6.5	-26.50
Wolvhptn (A.W)	3-51	0-0	0-7	0-0	3-44	5.9	-27.50
Carlisle	2-12	0-0	0-0	0-0	2-12	16.7	+1.50
Nottingham	2-19	0-0	0-2	1-2	1-15	10.5	+11.00
Hamilton	2-25	0-1	0-0	0-1	2-23	8.0	+1.50
Redcar	2-33	0-0	0-7	0-0	2-26	6.1	-19.50
Wetherby	1-6	0-0	0-0	0-0	1-6	16.7	+0.50
Yarmouth	1-6	0-0	0-0	0-0	1-6	16.7	-1.50
York	1-8	0-0	1-1	0-0	0-7	12.5	-2.00
Doncaster	1-19	0-1	0-2	0-0	1-16	5.3	-14.00
Musselburgh	1-20	0-0	0-0	0-0	1-20	5.0	-7.00
Southwell (A.W)	1-24	0-0	0-1	0-0	1-23	4.2	-19.50
Thirsk	1-57	0-0	0-1	0-0	1-56	1.8	-42.00

WINNING HORSES

Horse	Races Run	1st	2nd	3rd	£
Abushamah (IRE)	17	1	1	1	4464
Adventureman	10	2	2	0	6210
Be Perfect (USA)	18	2	2	5	9024
Bobby Joe Leg	10	1	1	0	3752
Brian Ryan*	2	1	0	0	3493
Chaplin Bay (IRE)	14	1	1	3	6728
Cosmic Chatter	8	1	0	1	3120
Cupid's Arrow (IRE)	14	1	1	0	3493
Danish Duke (IRE)	13	1	0	1	3105
Explain	14	1	1	1	7439
Foxtrot Knight	16	1	5	1	3881
Foxy Rebel	9	1	0	1	3235
Fuel Injection	9	1	0	1	3105
Katheefa (USA)	17	1	4	1	4140
Kibaar	15	2	1	2	6275
Kingstreet Lady	18	3	5	2	10092

Lexington Place	17	1	2	3	3369
Liberatum	9	1	2	1	5531
Mark's Choice (IRE)	7	1	0	1	3881
Mutamaded (IRE)	8	2	0	0	18675
Mutarakez (IRE)	13	1	0	2	7763
Ower Fly	14	1	3	0	9338
Pipers Note	13	2	2	0	20909
Racquet	12	2	0	0	6772
Sovereign Debt (IRE)	5	1	0	0	28355
Sureyoutoldme (IRE)	5	1	1	0	4399
Tadaany (IRE)	17	2	0	1	6598
Vallarta (IRE)	15	3	0	1	12420
Zebulon (IRE)	14	1	1	0	3105
Total winning prize-money					**£212671**
Favourites	**7-31**		**22.6%**		**-1.17**

TONY CARROLL

CROPTHORNE, WORCS

	No. of Hrs	Races Run	1st	2nd	3rd	Unpl	Per cent	£1 Level Stake
2-y-o	*10*	*37*	*0*	*0*	*1*	*36*	*0.0*	*-37.00*
3-y-o	*10*	*42*	*3*	*4*	*1*	*34*	*7.1*	*+3.00*
4-y-o+	*67*	*454*	*58*	*57*	*63*	*275*	*12.8*	*-70.71*
Totals	**87**	**533**	**61**	**61**	**65**	**345**	**11.4**	**-104.71**
2017	*104*	*581*	*31*	*50*	*68*	*431*	*5.3*	*-344.88*
2016	*102*	*613*	*54*	*55*	*69*	*434*	*8.8*	*-164.47*

BY MONTH

2-y-o	W-R	Per cent	£1 Level Stake	**3-y-o**	W-R	Per cent	£1 Level Stake
January	0-0	0.0	0.00	January	0-0	0.0	0.00
February	0-0	0.0	0.00	February	0-0	0.0	0.00
March	0-0	0.0	0.00	March	0-1	0.0	-1.00
April	0-0	0.0	0.00	April	0-0	0.0	0.00
May	0-1	0.0	-1.00	May	0-4	0.0	-4.00
June	0-4	0.0	-4.00	June	0-4	0.0	-4.00
July	0-3	0.0	-3.00	July	0-2	0.0	-2.00
August	0-5	0.0	-5.00	August	0-6	0.0	-6.00
September	0-6	0.0	-6.00	September	2-6	33.3	+30.00
October	0-6	0.0	-6.00	October	1-10	10.0	-1.00
November	0-6	0.0	-6.00	November	0-6	0.0	-6.00
December	0-6	0.0	-6.00	December	0-3	0.0	-3.00

4-y-o+	W-R	Per cent	£1 Level Stake	**Totals**	W-R	Per cent	£1 Level Stake
January	3-38	7.9	-8.00	January	3-38	7.9	-8.00
February	5-47	10.6	+9.33	February	5-47	10.6	+9.33
March	2-31	6.5	-14.50	March	2-32	6.3	-15.50
April	7-22	31.8	+26.33	April	7-22	31.8	+26.33
May	3-34	8.8	-21.67	May	3-39	7.7	-26.67
June	7-43	16.3	-6.92	June	7-51	13.7	-14.92
July	4-30	13.3	-9.75	July	4-35	11.4	-14.75
August	6-55	10.9	-22.13	August	6-66	9.1	-33.13
September	11-60	18.3	-6.42	September	13-72	18.1	+17.58
October	4-47	8.5	-3.50	October	5-63	7.9	-10.50
November	1-24	4.2	-21.00	November	1-36	2.8	-27.00
December	5-23	21.7	+7.50	December	5-32	15.6	+4.50

DISTANCE

2-y-o	W-R	Per cent	£1 Level Stake	**3-y-o**	W-R	Per cent	£1 Level Stake
5f-6f	0-24	0.0	-24.00	5f-6f	1-12	8.3	+3.00
7f-8f	0-13	0.0	-13.00	7f-8f	1-19	5.3	-10.00
9f-13f	0-0	0.0	0.00	9f-13f	1-10	10.0	+11.00
14f+	0-0	0.0	0.00	14f+	0-1	0.0	-1.00

4-y-o+	W-R	Per cent	£1 Level Stake	**Totals**	W-R	Per cent	£1 Level Stake
5f-6f	27-184	14.7	-67.88	5f-6f	28-220	12.7	-88.88
7f-8f	18-135	13.3	+15.67	7f-8f	19-167	11.4	-7.33
9f-13f	13-120	10.8	-3.50	9f-13f	14-130	10.8	+7.50
14f+	0-15	0.0	-15.00	14f+	0-16	0.0	-16.00

TYPE OF RACE

Non-Handicaps	W-R	Per cent	£1 Level Stake	**Handicaps**	W-R	Per cent	£1 Level Stake
2-y-o	0-24	0.0	-24.00	2-y-o	0-13	0.0	-13.00
3-y-o	0-6	0.0	-6.00	3-y-o	3-36	8.3	+9.00
4-y-o+	0-18	0.0	-18.00	4-y-o+	58-436	13.3	-52.71

RACE CLASS

	W-R	Per cent	£1 Level Stake
Class 1	0-1	0.0	-1.00
Class 2	2-21	9.5	-6.00
Class 3	0-21	0.0	-21.00
Class 4	7-82	8.5	-38.17
Class 5	22-133	16.5	+20.71
Class 6	27-242	11.2	-45.75
Class 7	3-33	9.1	-13.50

FIRST TIME OUT

	W-R	Per cent	£1 Level Stake
2-y-o	0-10	0.0	-10.00
3-y-o	0-10	0.0	-10.00
4-y-o+	7-67	10.4	+31.50
Totals	7-87	8.0	+11.50

JOCKEYS

	W-R	Per cent	£1 Level Stake
Poppy Bridgwater	20-96	20.8	-18.42
George Downing	9-84	10.7	-20.33
Sophie Ralston	6-27	22.2	-2.42
Aled Beech	5-16	31.3	+52.00
Tom Marquand	4-48	8.3	-6.00
Luke Morris	3-28	10.7	-2.50
David Probert	3-36	8.3	-5.50
Rossa Ryan	1-3	33.3	+7.00
Silvestre De Sousa	1-3	33.3	+2.00
Elisha Whittington	1-3	33.3	+9.00
Dane O'Neill	1-4	25.0	+5.50
Jason Watson	1-4	25.0	-1.38
Franny Norton	1-4	25.0	+5.00
Nicola Currie	1-5	20.0	+10.00
Adam Kirby	1-6	16.7	+1.00
Miss Sarah Bowen	1-6	16.7	+7.00
Toby Eley	1-8	12.5	+1.00
Robert Winston	1-14	7.1	-9.67

COURSE RECORD

	Total W-R	Non-Hndcps 2-y-o	Non-Hndcps 3-y-o+	Hndcps 2-y-o	Hndcps 3-y-o+	Per cent	£1 Level Stake
Brighton	12-62	0-1	0-0	0-0	12-61	19.4	-16.96
Wolvhptn (A.W)	11-86	0-2	0-7	0-4	11-73	12.8	-1.67
Kempton (A.W)	7-75	0-4	0-4	0-4	7-63	9.3	-16.75
Bath	6-24	0-0	0-0	0-2	6-22	25.0	+11.58
Lingfield (A.W)	5-56	0-2	0-7	0-0	5-47	8.9	-6.50
Southwell (A.W)	4-16	0-0	0-1	0-0	4-15	25.0	+40.00
Goodwood	3-22	0-2	0-0	0-0	3-20	13.6	-13.92
Windsor	2-30	0-6	0-2	0-0	2-22	6.7	-11.50
Chelmsford (A.W)	2-35	0-0	0-0	0-0	2-35	5.7	-24.50
Salisbury	1-4	0-2	0-0	0-0	1-2	25.0	+0.50
Newmkt (Jly)	1-5	0-0	0-0	0-0	1-5	20.0	0.00
Yarmouth	1-8	0-0	0-1	0-0	1-7	12.5	-4.50
Epsom	1-9	0-0	0-0	0-0	1-9	11.1	+6.00
Leicester	1-9	0-0	0-0	0-0	1-9	11.1	-2.00
Haydock	1-10	0-1	0-0	0-0	1-9	10.0	-5.50
Newbury	1-10	0-0	0-0	0-0	1-10	10.0	+3.00
Lingfield	1-11	0-1	0-1	0-0	1-9	9.1	-6.00
Chepstow	1-17	0-1	0-1	0-0	1-15	5.9	-12.00

WINNING HORSES

Horse	Races Run	1st	2nd	3rd	£
Altaira	11	1	0	2	3105
Baltic Prince (IRE)	16	4	3	3	17984
*Chetan	1	1	0	0	3105
De Vegas Kid (IRE)	12	5	1	3	16819
Essaka (IRE)	11	2	1	3	6857
Foresee (GER)	6	1	0	2	4528
Henry Croft	6	1	1	0	3429
Ilhabela Fact	5	2	0	1	9574
Imbucato	9	2	1	2	6210
Jeremy's Jet (IRE)	13	1	2	4	2911
Long Call	4	1	0	1	3493
*Madrinho (IRE)	17	3	3	3	11644
Mister Music	11	4	1	0	25776
Nelson River	3	1	1	0	3105
Oeil De Tigre (FR)	10	3	2	1	17078
Papa Delta	7	3	0	2	7633
Poetic Force (IRE)	12	1	5	0	3752
Pour La Victoire (IRE)	18	5	6	3	24730
Prominna	7	1	1	1	3105
Red Alert	10	2	1	2	16202
River Dart (IRE)	6	1	0	0	3105
Rowlestonerendezvu	4	1	1	0	3105
*Scrafton	7	2	0	1	6857
*Silverturnstogold	5	1	1	0	3105
Sir Jamie	9	2	2	1	6210
Sugar Plum Fairy	7	1	0	0	3105
Time Medicean	8	1	2	1	3105
Toni's A Star	12	3	2	0	11062
*Upavon	4	1	0	1	5887
Wiley Post	8	2	1	3	7504
Windsorlot (IRE)	14	2	3	1	6724
Total winning prize-money					**£250809**
Favourites	**22-46**		**47.8%**		**25.62**

DECLAN CARROLL

MALTON, N YORKS

	No. of Hrs	Races Run	1st	2nd	3rd	Unpl	Per cent	£1 Level Stake
2-y-o	*11*	*57*	*9*	*6*	*3*	*39*	*15.8*	*+22.08*
3-y-o	*9*	*69*	*8*	*5*	*4*	*52*	*11.6*	*-1.38*
4-y-o+	*16*	*147*	*17*	*13*	*15*	*101*	*11.6*	*-23.67*
Totals	**36**	**273**	**34**	**24**	**22**	**192**	**12.5**	**-2.97**
2017	*28*	*240*	*33*	*24*	*21*	*161*	*13.8*	*-13.54*
2016	*24*	*219*	*25*	*14*	*23*	*157*	*11.4*	*+100.88*

BY MONTH

2-y-o	W-R	Per cent	£1 Level Stake	3-y-o	W-R	Per cent	£1 Level Stake
January	0-0	0.0	0.00	January	0-1	0.0	-1.00
February	0-0	0.0	0.00	February	0-1	0.0	-1.00
March	0-1	0.0	-1.00	March	0-1	0.0	-1.00
April	0-2	0.0	-2.00	April	1-5	20.0	+4.00
May	0-4	0.0	-4.00	May	1-8	12.5	-0.50
June	0-8	0.0	-8.00	June	0-7	0.0	-7.00
July	1-6	16.7	+28.00	July	0-6	0.0	-6.00
August	3-13	23.1	+1.58	August	1-12	8.3	-8.00
September	1-7	14.3	+0.50	September	1-6	16.7	+6.00
October	1-6	16.7	+2.00	October	2-7	28.6	+14.38
November	2-8	25.0	+2.00	November	1-10	10.0	-6.25
December	1-2	50.0	+3.00	December	1-5	20.0	+5.00

4-y-o+	W-R	Per cent	£1 Level Stake	Totals	W-R	Per cent	£1 Level Stake
January	1-9	11.1	+6.00	January	1-10	10.0	+5.00
February	1-4	25.0	+1.00	February	1-5	20.0	0.00
March	2-7	28.6	+3.75	March	2-9	22.2	+1.75
April	1-10	10.0	+3.00	April	2-17	11.8	+5.00
May	2-19	10.5	-7.50	May	3-31	9.7	-12.00
June	2-16	12.5	-3.00	June	2-31	6.5	-18.00
July	2-18	11.1	-3.75	July	3-30	10.0	+18.25
August	2-16	12.5	+5.00	August	6-41	14.6	-1.42
September	2-20	10.0	-13.80	September	4-33	12.1	-7.30
October	1-9	11.1	+2.00	October	4-22	18.2	+18.38
November	1-10	10.0	-7.38	November	4-28	14.3	-13.63
December	0-9	0.0	-9.00	December	2-16	12.5	-4.00

DISTANCE

2-y-o	W-R	Per cent	£1 Level Stake	3-y-o	W-R	Per cent	£1 Level Stake
5f-6f	6-46	13.0	+15.58	5f-6f	6-38	15.8	+16.63
7f-8f	3-11	27.3	+6.50	7f-8f	2-19	10.5	-6.00
9f-13f	0-0	0.0	0.00	9f-13f	0-12	0.0	-12.00
14f+	0-0	0.0	0.00	14f+	0-0	0.0	0.00

4-y-o+	W-R	Per cent	£1 Level Stake	Totals	W-R	Per cent	£1 Level Stake
5f-6f	4-30	13.3	-4.50	5f-6f	16-114	14.0	+27.71
7f-8f	6-59	10.2	-17.42	7f-8f	11-89	12.4	-16.92
9f-13f	7-46	15.2	+10.25	9f-13f	7-58	12.1	-1.75
14f+	0-12	0.0	-12.00	14f+	0-12	0.0	-12.00

TYPE OF RACE

Non-Handicaps

	W-R	Per cent	£1 Level Stake
2-y-o	2-34	5.9	+1.83
3-y-o	0-13	0.0	-13.00
4-y-o+	4-12	33.3	+6.46

Handicaps

	W-R	Per cent	£1 Level Stake
2-y-o	7-23	30.4	+20.25
3-y-o	8-56	14.3	+11.63
4-y-o+	13-135	9.6	-30.13

RACE CLASS

	W-R	Per cent	£1 Level Stake
Class 1	0-8	0.0	-8.00
Class 2	2-16	12.5	0.00
Class 3	2-12	16.7	-1.50
Class 4	4-63	6.3	-28.17
Class 5	13-95	13.7	+23.95
Class 6	13-77	16.9	+12.75
Class 7	0-2	0.0	-2.00

FIRST TIME OUT

	W-R	Per cent	£1 Level Stake
2-y-o	0-11	0.0	-11.00
3-y-o	1-9	11.1	0.00
4-y-o+	2-16	12.5	+6.00
Totals	3-36	8.3	-5.00

JOCKEYS

	W-R	Per cent	£1 Level Stake
Ger O'Neill	13-76	17.1	+20.00
Paddy Mathers	4-13	30.8	+16.13
Jason Hart	3-14	21.4	+5.20
Stevie Donohoe	3-14	21.4	+34.75
Callum Shepherd	3-14	21.4	+10.63
Kevin Stott	3-28	10.7	-3.50
Daniel Tudhope	2-15	13.3	-6.17
Tony Hamilton	1-6	16.7	-1.00
David Nolan	1-17	5.9	-12.00
Tom Eaves	1-19	5.3	-10.00

COURSE RECORD

	Total W-R	Non-Hndcps 2-y-o	Non-Hndcps 3-y-o+	Hndcps 2-y-o	Hndcps 3-y-o+	Per cent	£1 Level Stake
Southwell (A.W)	6-36	0-0	0-1	0-0	6-35	16.7	-1.88
Redcar	5-19	0-2	1-2	2-3	2-12	26.3	+12.75
Catterick	3-12	0-2	1-1	0-1	2-8	25.0	+1.57
Wetherby	2-5	0-0	1-2	0-0	1-3	40.0	+9.00
Ayr	2-13	0-1	0-0	1-1	1-11	15.4	+9.75
Pontefract	2-13	1-5	0-0	0-0	1-8	15.4	-0.17
Wolvhptn (A.W)	2-14	0-3	0-2	2-3	0-6	14.3	-4.00
Thirsk	2-17	1-1	0-3	1-2	0-11	11.8	+26.00
Doncaster	2-23	0-3	1-3	0-0	1-17	8.7	-3.00
Carlisle	1-5	0-2	0-0	0-1	1-2	20.0	+7.00
Ripon	1-5	0-1	0-0	0-1	1-3	20.0	+7.00
Chelmsford (A.W)	1-6	0-0	0-0	0-1	1-5	16.7	+4.00
Haydock	1-9	0-1	0-0	0-1	1-7	11.1	+2.00
Beverley	1-16	0-4	0-1	0-0	1-11	6.3	-12.00
York	1-16	0-4	0-3	0-0	1-9	6.3	-7.00
Nottingham	1-22	0-2	0-2	0-3	1-15	4.5	-17.00
Newcastle (A.W)	1-23	0-1	0-2	1-5	0-15	4.3	-18.00

WINNING HORSES

Horse	Races Run	1st	2nd	3rd	£
Bee Machine (IRE)	15	3	0	1	6987
Bold Spirit	15	2	0	0	7504
God Willing	10	1	2	1	3235
Honey Gg	10	2	4	0	6275
House Deposit	7	2	0	0	6891
Jackamundo (FR)	4	1	0	0	4787
Jem Scuttle (USA)	7	2	2	0	6857
Justanotherbottle (IRE)	8	2	1	0	19407
Machree (IRE)	11	3	0	0	19472
Monsieur Jimmy*	9	1	1	1	3881
Motahassen (IRE)	8	1	1	0	4205
Musharrif	15	2	4	2	11115
Music Seeker (IRE)	13	1	0	1	4787
Raypeteafterme	7	1	1	0	4528
Saigon City	3	1	0	1	12938
Save The Bees	13	1	1	0	4852
Shawaamekh	5	1	1	2	5111
Shearian	15	2	1	0	6210
Titus	7	2	0	2	48362
Tobeeornottobee	11	2	0	2	6275
World Order (IRE)	8	1	2	0	5822
Total winning prize-money					**£199501**
Favourites	**6-33**		**18.2%**		**-13.67**

ANTHONY CARSON

NEWMARKET, SUFFOLK

	No. of Hrs	Races Run	1st	2nd	3rd	Unpl	Per cent	£1 Level Stake
2-y-o	*4*	*9*	*0*	*0*	*1*	*8*	*0.0*	*-9.00*
3-y-o	*1*	*6*	*1*	*0*	*1*	*4*	*16.7*	*+28.00*
4-y-o+	*10*	*81*	*6*	*6*	*9*	*60*	*7.4*	*-18.25*
Totals	**15**	**96**	**7**	**6**	**11**	**72**	**7.3**	**+0.75**
2017	*12*	*83*	*12*	*9*	*13*	*49*	*14.5*	*+4.08*
2016	*14*	*82*	*11*	*10*	*6*	*55*	*13.4*	*+50.75*

JOCKEYS

	W-R	Per cent	£1 Level Stake
David Probert	2-8	25.0	-0.25
William Carson	2-46	4.3	-17.00
Gerald Mosse	1-1	100.0	+20.00
Cieren Fallon	1-1	100.0	+4.00
Kieran O'Neill	1-4	25.0	+30.00

COURSE RECORD

	Total W-R	Non-Hndcps 2-y-o	Non-Hndcps 3-y-o+	Hndcps 2-y-o	Hndcps 3-y-o+	Per cent	£1 Level Stake
Chelmsford (A.W)	3-21	0-1	0-0	0-1	3-19	14.3	+13.00
Goodwood	1-2	0-1	0-0	0-0	1-1	50.0	+2.50
Lingfield	1-4	0-0	0-1	0-0	1-3	25.0	-0.75
Yarmouth	1-11	0-2	0-0	0-0	1-9	9.1	+10.00
Wolvhptn (A.W)	1-12	0-0	0-0	0-0	1-12	8.3	+22.00

WINNING HORSES

Horse	Races Run	1st	2nd	3rd	£
Curious Fox	16	2	2	3	9833
Gulland Rock	15	1	0	1	3105
Hawatif (IRE)	5	1	0	1	4399
Mossy's Lodge*	12	1	1	2	2264
Pammi*	6	1	0	1	3105
Tundra	8	1	0	0	3493
Total winning prize-money					**£26199**
Favourites	**1-2**		**50.0%**		**1.25**

LEE CARTER

EPSOM, SURREY

	No. of Hrs	Races Run	1st	2nd	3rd	Unpl	Per cent	£1 Level Stake
2-y-o	*1*	*3*	*0*	*0*	*0*	*3*	*0.0*	*-3.00*
3-y-o	*3*	*10*	*0*	*0*	*1*	*9*	*0.0*	*-10.00*
4-y-o+	*13*	*88*	*5*	*5*	*4*	*73*	*5.7*	*-50.00*
Totals	**17**	**101**	**5**	**5**	**5**	**85**	**5.0**	**-63.00**
2017	*28*	*161*	*7*	*15*	*17*	*121*	*4.3*	*-109.50*
2016	*35*	*198*	*16*	*15*	*17*	*150*	*8.1*	*-68.38*

JOCKEYS

	W-R	Per cent	£1 Level Stake
Paddy Bradley	3-21	14.3	+0.50
Rossa Ryan	1-9	11.1	-5.50
Charlie Bennett	1-18	5.6	-5.00

COURSE RECORD

	Total W-R	Non-Hndcps 2-y-o	Non-Hndcps 3-y-o+	Hndcps 2-y-o	Hndcps 3-y-o+	Per cent	£1 Level Stake
Chelmsford (A.W)	2-11	0-0	0-0	0-0	2-11	18.2	-3.00
Wolvhptn (A.W)	1-9	0-0	0-0	0-0	1-9	11.1	+1.00
Kempton (A.W)	1-29	0-2	0-4	0-0	1-23	3.4	-22.00
Lingfield (A.W)	1-37	0-1	0-1	0-0	1-35	2.7	-24.00

WINNING HORSES

Horse	Races Run	1st	2nd	3rd	£
*Art Of Swing (IRE)	8	1	1	0	3105
First Experience	7	1	0	0	3105
*Ross Raith Rover	10	2	0	0	6598
Spiritual Star (IRE)	9	1	0	0	3105
Total winning prize-money					**£15913**
Favourites	**0-1**		**0.0%**		**-1.00**

PATRICK CHAMINGS

BAUGHURST, HANTS

	No. of Hrs	Races Run	1st	2nd	3rd	Unpl	Per cent	£1 Level Stake
2-y-o	*4*	*9*	*0*	*0*	*0*	*9*	*0.0*	*-9.00*
3-y-o	*8*	*42*	*0*	*3*	*4*	*35*	*0.0*	*-42.00*
4-y-o+	*16*	*70*	*9*	*10*	*4*	*47*	*12.9*	*-17.75*
Totals	**28**	**121**	**9**	**13**	**8**	**91**	**7.4**	**-68.75**
2017	*25*	*124*	*10*	*12*	*15*	*87*	*8.1*	*-68.93*
2016	*25*	*150*	*15*	*15*	*16*	*104*	*10.0*	*-55.50*

JOCKEYS

	W-R	Per cent	£1 Level Stake
Joey Haynes	6-43	14.0	-9.75
Tyler Saunders	1-4	25.0	+1.00
Hector Crouch	1-10	10.0	-4.00
David Probert	1-16	6.3	-8.00

COURSE RECORD

	Total W-R	Non-Hndcps 2-y-o	Non-Hndcps 3-y-o+	Hndcps 2-y-o	Hndcps 3-y-o+	Per cent	£1 Level Stake
Newbury	2-4	0-0	0-0	0-0	2-4	50.0	+10.00
Ascot	2-5	0-0	0-0	0-0	2-5	40.0	+2.88
Lingfield	2-5	0-1	1-2	0-0	1-2	40.0	+9.00
Sandown	1-2	0-0	0-0	0-0	1-2	50.0	+0.88
Southwell (A.W)	1-2	0-0	0-0	0-0	1-2	50.0	+9.00
Windsor	1-12	0-1	0-4	0-0	1-7	8.3	-9.50

WINNING HORSES

Horse	Races Run	1st	2nd	3rd	£
Mister Freeze (IRE)	6	1	0	1	3105
Scottish Glen	5	1	0	0	3105
What A Welcome	7	6	0	0	32313
Wild Dancer	4	1	1	1	3752
Total winning prize-money					**£42275**
Favourites	**3-9**		**33.3%**		**-0.75**

MICK CHANNON

WEST ILSLEY, BERKS

	No. of Hrs	Races Run	1st	2nd	3rd	Unpl	Per cent	£1 Level Stake
2-y-o	*45*	*220*	*31*	*26*	*27*	*136*	*14.1*	*-39.51*
3-y-o	*43*	*311*	*42*	*26*	*44*	*199*	*13.5*	*-38.34*
4-y-o+	*19*	*148*	*19*	*17*	*31*	*81*	*12.8*	*-39.29*
Totals	**107**	**679**	**92**	**69**	**102**	**416**	**13.5**	**-117.14**
2017	*108*	*588*	*59*	*49*	*74*	*406*	*10.0*	*-132.60*
2016	*94*	*625*	*71*	*79*	*65*	*409*	*11.4*	*-139.14*

BY MONTH

2-y-o	W-R	Per cent	£1 Level Stake	3-y-o	W-R	Per cent	£1 Level Stake
January	0-0	0.0	0.00	January	2-7	28.6	+2.50
February	0-0	0.0	0.00	February	0-7	0.0	-7.00
March	2-2	100.0	+5.25	March	2-16	12.5	-7.25
April	4-15	26.7	-1.50	April	9-30	30.0	+21.63
May	8-28	28.6	+21.82	May	1-48	2.1	-42.50
June	4-27	14.8	-7.29	June	5-37	13.5	-12.34
July	3-30	10.0	-6.88	July	4-28	14.3	+5.25
August	3-33	9.1	-8.17	August	6-48	12.5	-4.50
September	3-47	6.4	-30.00	September	4-42	9.5	-11.00

	W-R	Per cent	£1 Level Stake
October	4-30	13.3	-4.75
November	0-5	0.0	-5.00
December	0-3	0.0	-3.00

	W-R	Per cent	£1 Level Stake
October	6-31	19.4	+22.75
November	1-12	8.3	-6.50
December	2-5	40.0	+0.63

4-y-o+	W-R	Per cent	£1 Level Stake
January	2-10	20.0	+5.00
February	1-13	7.7	-10.50
March	1-13	7.7	-6.00
April	1-14	7.1	-12.00
May	2-28	7.1	-15.50
June	3-15	20.0	-2.17
July	4-17	23.5	+3.63
August	3-17	17.6	+3.75
September	1-9	11.1	-4.50
October	1-7	14.3	+4.00
November	0-5	0.0	-5.00
December	0-0	0.0	0.00

Totals	W-R	Per cent	£1 Level Stake
January	4-17	23.5	+7.50
February	1-20	5.0	-17.50
March	5-31	16.1	-8.00
April	14-59	23.7	+8.13
May	11-104	10.6	-36.18
June	12-79	15.2	-21.80
July	11-75	14.7	+2.00
August	12-98	12.2	-8.92
September	8-98	8.2	-45.50
October	11-68	16.2	+22.00
November	1-22	4.5	-11.50
December	2-8	25.0	+0.63

DISTANCE

2-y-o	W-R	Per cent	£1 Level Stake
5f-6f	27-150	18.0	+7.65
7f-8f	4-66	6.1	-43.17
9f-13f	0-4	0.0	-4.00
14f+	0-0	0.0	0.00

3-y-o	W-R	Per cent	£1 Level Stake
5f-6f	16-97	16.5	-4.88
7f-8f	8-84	9.5	-20.59
9f-13f	16-114	14.0	-4.88
14f+	2-16	12.5	-8.00

4-y-o+	W-R	Per cent	£1 Level Stake
5f-6f	1-10	10.0	-8.00
7f-8f	6-56	10.7	-17.00
9f-13f	10-58	17.2	+0.88
14f+	2-24	8.3	-15.17

Totals	W-R	Per cent	£1 Level Stake
5f-6f	44-257	17.1	-5.23
7f-8f	18-206	8.7	-80.76
9f-13f	26-176	14.8	-8.00
14f+	4-40	10.0	-23.17

TYPE OF RACE

Non-Handicaps

	W-R	Per cent	£1 Level Stake
2-y-o	26-167	15.6	-23.51
3-y-o	13-85	15.3	-27.97
4-y-o+	1-32	3.1	-23.00

Handicaps

	W-R	Per cent	£1 Level Stake
2-y-o	5-53	9.4	-16.00
3-y-o	29-226	12.8	-10.38
4-y-o+	18-116	15.5	-16.29

RACE CLASS

	W-R	Per cent	£1 Level Stake
Class 1	1-54	1.9	-43.00
Class 2	8-69	11.6	+11.25
Class 3	12-76	15.8	+18.25
Class 4	19-113	16.8	-18.25
Class 5	31-228	13.6	-63.72
Class 6	21-136	15.4	-18.68
Class 7	0-3	0.0	-3.00

FIRST TIME OUT

	W-R	Per cent	£1 Level Stake
2-y-o	11-45	24.4	+26.82
3-y-o	5-43	11.6	-16.75
4-y-o+	2-19	10.5	-4.00
Totals	18-107	16.8	+6.07

JOCKEYS

	W-R	Per cent	£1 Level Stake
Charles Bishop	23-133	17.3	-0.63
Franny Norton	13-55	23.6	+34.96
Silvestre De Sousa	11-47	23.4	+4.48
David Egan	8-39	20.5	+15.29
Scott McCullagh	8-77	10.4	-33.63
Andrea Atzeni	5-35	14.3	+1.50
Callum Shepherd	5-46	10.9	-18.25
Ben Curtis	3-13	23.1	-4.13
Graham Lee	3-17	17.6	+12.25
Nicola Currie	3-19	15.8	+3.50
J F Egan	2-51	3.9	-35.50
Darragh Keenan	1-1	100.0	+4.00
Miss Nell McCann	1-1	100.0	+10.00
James Doyle	1-2	50.0	+3.00
Gerald Mosse	1-2	50.0	+9.00
Kieran O'Neill	1-2	50.0	+3.00
Nathan Evans	1-5	20.0	-1.50
Hollie Doyle	1-9	11.1	-4.00
George Downing	1-34	2.9	-29.50

COURSE RECORD

	Total W-R	Non-Hndcps 2-y-o	Non-Hndcps 3-y-o+	Hndcps 2-y-o	Hndcps 3-y-o+	Per cent	£1 Level Stake
Leicester	2-15	1-6	0-1	0-2	1-6	13.3	-9.13
Ripon	2-15	2-5	0-3	0-1	0-6	13.3	-8.75
Chepstow	2-17	1-4	0-4	0-0	1-9	11.8	+3.50
Haydock	2-18	1-5	0-1	1-4	0-8	11.1	-5.38
Newmarket	2-18	0-6	0-4	0-1	2-7	11.1	+8.00
Catterick	1-7	0-1	0-1	1-2	0-3	14.3	-2.00
Yarmouth	1-13	0-2	0-0	0-3	1-8	7.7	-7.50
York	1-14	1-6	0-0	0-1	0-7	7.1	+3.00
Ffos Las	1-15	0-1	0-1	1-3	0-10	6.7	-10.00
Newmkt (Jly)	1-18	0-2	0-2	0-2	1-12	5.6	-7.00
Doncaster	1-19	1-6	0-3	0-1	0-9	5.3	-14.00
Sandown	1-19	0-8	0-2	0-1	1-8	5.3	-15.25
Ascot	1-20	0-9	0-1	0-0	1-10	5.0	-9.00
Brighton	1-28	0-6	0-3	0-2	1-17	3.6	-20.00
Bath	10-18	4-6	3-4	0-0	3-8	55.6	+31.25
Windsor	7-29	1-10	0-5	0-0	6-14	24.1	+7.33
Salisbury	7-31	1-9	1-5	1-2	4-15	22.6	+17.38
Goodwood	7-44	3-12	1-10	0-3	3-19	15.9	+3.58
Nottingham	5-19	2-4	1-2	0-2	2-11	26.3	+18.66
Wolvhptn (A.W)	5-32	1-4	1-9	0-0	3-19	15.6	-1.25
Lingfield (A.W)	5-35	1-3	0-9	0-1	4-22	14.3	-14.13
Redcar	4-19	3-6	0-3	0-2	1-8	21.1	-1.18
Lingfield	4-23	2-5	1-8	0-1	1-9	17.4	-8.29
Pontefract	3-10	0-1	1-2	0-0	2-7	30.0	+14.75
Beverley	3-16	1-7	1-4	0-0	1-5	18.8	+1.00
Chelmsford (A.W)	3-16	0-0	1-4	0-1	2-11	18.8	+1.00
Newbury	3-37	0-17	2-10	0-2	1-8	8.1	-17.25
Kempton (A.W)	3-46	0-5	0-6	1-8	2-27	6.5	-27.00
Carlisle	2-6	0-1	1-1	0-1	1-3	33.3	-0.50
Epsom	2-9	0-2	0-0	0-2	2-5	22.2	+4.00

WINNING HORSES

Horse	Races Run	1st	2nd	3rd	£
Adorable (IRE)	3	1	0	1	5531
Azor Ahai	4	1	1	0	4205
Barbill (IRE)	9	1	2	1	5531
Beer With The Boys	9	1	0	3	3881
Big Boots (IRE)	10	1	3	0	4663

Billy Ray	7	2	1	1	16431
Can Can Sixty Two*	8	2	0	1	13197
Caravela (IRE)	7	2	1	2	22655
Certain Lad	4	2	0	1	10933
Chairmanoftheboard (IRE)	2	1	0	0	4787
Charming Guest (IRE)	12	3	0	2	12938
Chikoko Trail*	7	1	0	1	4528
Chynna	9	1	2	3	9704
Converter (IRE)	3	1	1	0	3881
Cotubanama	10	2	0	1	11321
Dan's Dream	5	2	0	0	39039
Dancing Jo	7	1	1	1	3105
Diamond Dougal (IRE)	7	1	2	0	5531
Dusty	10	1	1	3	3105
Eden Rose	9	1	2	1	3105
Ettie Hart (IRE)	6	1	0	2	3429
Fannie By Gaslight	9	2	1	2	19246
Fitzwilly	18	2	2	6	7504
Gospel	3	1	1	0	3881
Hats Off To Larry	8	3	0	1	15466
Helvetian	17	2	2	3	19407
Iconic Belle*	20	4	3	3	16949
Izzer (IRE)	8	2	1	1	12450
Jazeel (IRE)	11	2	0	3	37594
Jungle Inthebungle (IRE)	7	2	1	0	25540
Jungle Juice (IRE)	7	1	1	2	3752
Kinks	10	2	1	1	8992
Knockabout Queen*	5	1	0	1	3752
Koeman	9	2	1	1	16950
Macho Mover (IRE)	13	2	1	2	6210
Maksab (IRE)	8	1	0	1	31125
Marietta Robusti (IRE)*	8	3	1	1	13585
Mobsta (IRE)	6	1	0	2	7439
Modern Millie	1	1	0	0	6469
Patchouli	4	1	0	0	3752
Pattie	13	2	2	2	23335
Red Flower (IRE)	2	1	0	0	3493
Sayesse*	15	1	2	1	4464
So Near So Farhh	9	2	2	1	7116
Social Butterfly (IRE)	12	4	1	1	12310
Solesmes*	9	2	1	1	12557
Summer Icon	15	1	3	4	12938
Swinging Jean	1	1	0	0	3752
Tarrzan (IRE)*	1	1	0	0	3409
The Night King*	2	1	0	0	3429
The Night Porter	6	3	0	1	22890
Tricksy Spirit	13	1	1	1	5387
Two Blondes (IRE)	12	2	1	4	11256
Valentino Sunrise	15	2	1	2	7892
Westbrook Bertie	6	1	0	0	5757
Why We Dream (IRE)	8	2	1	2	10027
Zain City (IRE)	5	1	1	2	3881
Total winning prize-money					**£605456**
Favourites	**25-76**		**32.9%**		**-0.27**

JANE CHAPPLE-HYAM

DALHAM, SUFFOLK

	No. of Hrs	Races Run	1st	2nd	3rd	Unpl	Per cent	£1 Level Stake
2-y-o	*10*	*27*	*0*	*1*	*2*	*24*	*0.0*	*-27.00*
3-y-o	*12*	*59*	*5*	*5*	*10*	*39*	*8.5*	*+13.75*
4-y-o+	*12*	*50*	*4*	*6*	*5*	*35*	*8.0*	*-26.00*
Totals	**34**	**136**	**9**	**12**	**17**	**98**	**6.6**	**-39.25**
2017	*32*	*107*	*11*	*16*	*11*	*68*	*10.3*	*+59.75*
2016	*28*	*139*	*12*	*15*	*16*	*96*	*8.6*	*-35.50*

JOCKEYS

	W-R	Per cent	£1 Level Stake
Ray Dawson	3-22	13.6	+2.50
J F Egan	2-27	7.4	+18.00
Graham Lee	1-1	100.0	+3.50
Frankie Dettori	1-1	100.0	+3.00
Paul Mulrennan	1-2	50.0	+1.75
Brett Doyle	1-9	11.1	+6.00

COURSE RECORD

	Total W-R	Non-Hndcps 2-y-o	Non-Hndcps 3-y-o+	Hndcps 2-y-o	Hndcps 3-y-o+	Per cent	£1 Level Stake
Newmkt (Jly)	3-14	0-5	2-3	0-0	1-6	21.4	+40.00
Beverley	1-1	0-0	0-0	0-0	1-1	100.0	+14.00
Goodwood	1-1	0-0	0-0	0-0	1-1	100.0	+3.00
Doncaster	1-2	0-0	0-0	0-0	1-2	50.0	+1.75
Haydock	1-6	0-2	0-1	0-0	1-3	16.7	-1.50
Lingfield (A.W)	1-12	0-0	0-5	0-0	1-7	8.3	-6.00
Yarmouth	1-13	0-4	0-0	0-0	1-9	7.7	-3.50

WINNING HORSES

Horse	Races Run	1st	2nd	3rd	£
Amourice (IRE)	9	2	1	3	30431
Gold Chest (USA)	2	2	0	0	32236
*Mythological (IRE)	5	1	0	1	3170
*Suzi's Connoisseur	2	1	0	0	5531
Uber Cool (IRE)	7	3	0	0	26446
Total winning prize-money					**£97814**
Favourites	**1-4**		**25.0%**		**0.00**

PETER CHAPPLE-HYAM

NEWMARKET, SUFFOLK

	No. of Hrs	Races Run	1st	2nd	3rd	Unpl	Per cent	£1 Level Stake
2-y-o	*9*	*27*	*1*	*1*	*3*	*22*	*3.7*	*-22.50*
3-y-o	*10*	*28*	*5*	*3*	*1*	*19*	*17.9*	*+3.21*
4-y-o+	*6*	*25*	*5*	*7*	*4*	*9*	*20.0*	*+9.33*
Totals	**25**	**80**	**11**	**11**	**8**	**50**	**13.8**	**-9.96**
2017	*22*	*72*	*7*	*4*	*7*	*52*	*9.7*	*-33.97*
2016	*31*	*90*	*10*	*7*	*11*	*62*	*11.1*	*-36.43*

BY MONTH

2-y-o	W-R	Per cent	£1 Level Stake	3-y-o	W-R	Per cent	£1 Level Stake
January	0-0	0.0	0.00	January	0-1	0.0	-1.00
February	0-0	0.0	0.00	February	0-0	0.0	0.00
March	0-0	0.0	0.00	March	0-0	0.0	0.00
April	0-0	0.0	0.00	April	1-5	20.0	-3.09
May	0-2	0.0	-2.00	May	2-8	25.0	+14.00
June	0-1	0.0	-1.00	June	0-1	0.0	-1.00
July	0-2	0.0	-2.00	July	0-0	0.0	0.00
August	0-5	0.0	-5.00	August	0-4	0.0	-4.00
September	1-6	16.7	-1.50	September	1-4	25.0	-1.20
October	0-9	0.0	-9.00	October	1-5	20.0	-0.50
November	0-2	0.0	-2.00	November	0-0	0.0	0.00
December	0-0	0.0	0.00	December	0-0	0.0	0.00

4-y-o+	W-R	Per cent	£1 Level Stake	Totals	W-R	Per cent	£1 Level Stake
January	0-1	0.0	-1.00	January	0-2	0.0	-2.00
February	0-0	0.0	0.00	February	0-0	0.0	0.00
March	0-2	0.0	-2.00	March	0-2	0.0	-2.00
April	0-1	0.0	-1.00	April	1-6	16.7	-4.09
May	2-3	66.7	+19.83	May	4-13	30.8	+31.83
June	0-4	0.0	-4.00	June	0-6	0.0	-6.00
July	1-3	33.3	0.00	July	1-5	20.0	-2.00
August	1-4	25.0	+2.00	August	1-13	7.7	-7.00
September	1-2	50.0	+0.50	September	3-12	25.0	-2.20
October	0-4	0.0	-4.00	October	1-18	5.6	-13.50
November	0-1	0.0	-1.00	November	0-3	0.0	-1.00
December	0-0	0.0	0.00	December	0-0	0.0	0.00

DISTANCE

2-y-o	W-R	Per cent	£1 Level Stake	3-y-o	W-R	Per cent	£1 Level Stake
5f-6f	0-12	0.0	-12.00	5f-6f	0-2	0.0	-2.00
7f-8f	1-13	7.7	-8.50	7f-8f	1-12	8.3	-1.00
9f-13f	0-2	0.0	-2.00	9f-13f	4-14	28.6	+6.21
14f+	0-0	0.0	0.00	14f+	0-0	0.0	0.00

4-y-o+	W-R	Per cent	£1 Level Stake	Totals	W-R	Per cent	£1 Level Stake
5f-6f	2-9	22.2	+14.50	5f-6f	2-23	8.7	+0.50
7f-8f	1-3	33.3	0.00	7f-8f	3-28	10.7	-9.50
9f-13f	2-13	15.4	-5.17	9f-13f	6-29	20.7	-0.96
14f+	0-0	0.0	0.00	14f+	0-0	0.0	0.00

TYPE OF RACE

Non-Handicaps	W-R	Per cent	£1 Level Stake	Handicaps	W-R	Per cent	£1 Level Stake
2-y-o	1-20	5.0	-15.50	2-y-o	0-7	0.0	-7.00
3-y-o	3-12	25.0	+3.71	3-y-o	2-16	12.5	-0.50
4-y-o+	2-9	22.2	+15.00	4-y-o+	3-16	18.8	-5.67

RACE CLASS

	W-R	Per cent	£1 Level Stake
Class 1	1-10	10.0	+11.00
Class 2	0-5	0.0	-5.00
Class 3	0-5	0.0	-5.00
Class 4	6-29	20.7	-5.70
Class 5	3-25	12.0	-1.17
Class 6	1-6	16.7	-4.09
Class 7	0-0	0.0	0.00

FIRST TIME OUT

	W-R	Per cent	£1 Level Stake
2-y-o	0-9	0.0	-9.00
3-y-o	3-10	30.0	+5.71
4-y-o+	1-6	16.7	-3.00
Totals	4-25	16.0	-6.29

JOCKEYS

	W-R	Per cent	£1 Level Stake
Jack Mitchell	3-29	10.3	+4.91
Tom Queally	1-1	100.0	+3.50
David Allan	1-1	100.0	+10.00
Paul Hanagan	1-1	100.0	+1.80
Sebastian Woods	1-1	100.0	+0.83
Mr Finian Maguire	1-1	100.0	+5.00
James Doyle	1-2	50.0	+1.00
Silvestre De Sousa	1-2	50.0	+0.50
Andrea Atzeni	1-3	33.3	+1.50

COURSE RECORD

	Total W-R	Non-Hndcps 2-y-o	Non-Hndcps 3-y-o+	Hndcps 2-y-o	Hndcps 3-y-o+	Per cent	£1 Level Stake
Haydock	2-7	0-1	1-2	0-0	1-4	28.6	+25.00
Chester	1-1	0-0	1-1	0-0	0-0	100.0	+1.80
Epsom	1-1	0-0	0-0	0-0	1-1	100.0	+5.00
Leicester	1-2	0-0	0-0	0-0	1-2	50.0	-0.17
Lingfield (A.W)	1-3	0-0	1-1	0-1	0-1	33.3	-1.09
Kempton (A.W)	1-4	0-0	0-0	0-0	1-4	25.0	-1.50
Chelmsford (A.W)	1-4	0-1	1-1	0-0	0-2	25.0	-1.00
Pontefract	1-5	0-1	0-1	0-1	1-2	20.0	-0.50
Nottingham	1-6	0-0	1-3	0-1	0-2	16.7	+5.00
Newmarket	1-10	1-5	0-3	0-1	0-1	10.0	-5.50

WINNING HORSES

Horse	Races Run	1st	2nd	3rd	£
Amuletum	5	1	2	1	4334
Blooriedotcom (IRE)	6	1	2	0	4852
Classical Times	4	1	2	1	26654
Deja (FR)	2	2	0	0	11674
Fivetwoeight	5	1	1	1	6469
*La Figlia (IRE)	3	1	0	0	8345
Lubinka (IRE)	2	1	0	0	3105
M C Muldoon (IRE)	5	1	0	0	4528
Medalla De Oro	7	1	2	1	7487
Sh Boom	2	1	0	0	5175
Total winning prize-money					**£82623**
Favourites	**4-7**		**57.1%**		**2.04**

ROGER CHARLTON

BECKHAMPTON, WILTS

	No. of Hrs	Races Run	1st	2nd	3rd	Unpl	Per cent	£1 Level Stake
2-y-o	*41*	*84*	*12*	*5*	*7*	*60*	*14.3*	*-5.10*
3-y-o	*43*	*156*	*30*	*17*	*18*	*90*	*19.2*	*-25.72*

4-y-o+	*18*	*67*	*6*	*7*	*11*	*43*	*9.0*	*-45.72*
Totals	**102**	**307**	**48**	**29**	**36**	**193**	**15.6**	**-76.54**
2017	*90*	*321*	*65*	*37*	*27*	*190*	*20.2*	*+2.75*
2016	*70*	*250*	*48*	*38*	*27*	*136*	*19.2*	*-49.31*

BY MONTH

2-y-o	W-R	Per cent	£1 Level Stake
January	0-0	0.0	0.00
February	0-0	0.0	0.00
March	0-0	0.0	0.00
April	0-0	0.0	0.00
May	0-0	0.0	0.00
June	0-4	0.0	-4.00
July	1-5	20.0	-1.00
August	0-8	0.0	-8.00
September	3-15	20.0	+33.00
October	3-23	13.0	-14.00
November	4-19	21.1	-8.10
December	1-10	10.0	-3.00

3-y-o	W-R	Per cent	£1 Level Stake
January	1-3	33.3	-1.27
February	0-2	0.0	-2.00
March	2-7	28.6	-3.67
April	1-5	20.0	-2.13
May	1-16	6.3	-11.50
June	8-23	34.8	+5.09
July	6-24	25.0	+18.50
August	3-23	13.0	-9.75
September	2-21	9.5	-13.75
October	2-21	9.5	-4.75
November	4-8	50.0	+2.50
December	0-3	0.0	-3.00

4-y-o+	W-R	Per cent	£1 Level Stake
January	0-3	0.0	-3.00
February	0-0	0.0	0.00
March	0-0	0.0	0.00
April	0-4	0.0	-4.00
May	0-12	0.0	-12.00
June	2-9	22.2	-1.47
July	1-11	9.1	-8.63
August	1-12	8.3	-9.13
September	1-7	14.3	-1.50
October	1-7	14.3	-4.00
November	0-1	0.0	-1.00
December	0-1	0.0	-1.00

Totals	W-R	Per cent	£1 Level Stake
January	1-6	16.7	-4.27
February	0-2	0.0	-2.00
March	2-7	28.6	-3.67
April	1-9	11.1	-6.13
May	1-28	3.6	-23.50
June	10-36	27.8	-0.38
July	8-40	20.0	+8.87
August	4-43	9.3	-26.88
September	6-43	14.0	+17.75
October	6-51	11.8	-22.75
November	8-28	28.6	+1.50
December	1-14	7.1	-4.00

DISTANCE

2-y-o	W-R	Per cent	£1 Level Stake
5f-6f	3-16	18.8	-4.84
7f-8f	9-64	14.1	+3.74
9f-13f	0-4	0.0	-4.00
14f+	0-0	0.0	0.00

3-y-o	W-R	Per cent	£1 Level Stake
5f-6f	5-20	25.0	-9.71
7f-8f	9-45	20.0	-17.06
9f-13f	13-86	15.1	-3.46
14f+	3-5	60.0	+4.50

4-y-o+	W-R	Per cent	£1 Level Stake
5f-6f	1-15	6.7	-12.00
7f-8f	0-8	0.0	-8.00
9f-13f	4-38	10.5	-25.72
14f+	1-6	16.7	0.00

Totals	W-R	Per cent	£1 Level Stake
5f-6f	9-51	17.6	-26.55
7f-8f	18-117	15.4	-21.32
9f-13f	17-128	13.3	-33.18
14f+	4-11	36.4	+4.50

TYPE OF RACE

Non-Handicaps

	W-R	Per cent	£1 Level Stake
2-y-o	12-81	14.8	-2.10
3-y-o	18-85	21.2	-1.03
4-y-o+	3-24	12.5	-17.56

Handicaps

	W-R	Per cent	£1 Level Stake
2-y-o	0-3	0.0	-3.00
3-y-o	12-71	16.9	-24.69
4-y-o+	3-43	7.0	-31.75

RACE CLASS

	W-R	Per cent	£1 Level Stake
Class 1	4-32	12.5	-17.47
Class 2	3-27	11.1	-13.50
Class 3	6-31	19.4	-7.07
Class 4	8-76	10.5	-52.38
Class 5	23-119	19.3	+16.38
Class 6	4-22	18.2	-2.50
Class 7	0-0	0.0	0.00

FIRST TIME OUT

	W-R	Per cent	£1 Level Stake
2-y-o	4-41	9.8	-28.26
3-y-o	6-43	14.0	+0.52
4-y-o+	1-18	5.6	-12.00
Totals	11-102	10.8	-39.74

JOCKEYS

	W-R	Per cent	£1 Level Stake
Kieran Shoemark	14-111	12.6	-55.69
Adam McNamara	10-55	18.2	+16.77
Silvestre De Sousa	5-15	33.3	-6.00
Andrea Atzeni	4-15	26.7	-6.80
Trevor Whelan	2-9	22.2	+30.50
James Doyle	2-10	20.0	-4.75
George Wood	1-2	50.0	+1.00
Robert Winston	1-2	50.0	+4.00
Hollie Doyle	1-3	33.3	+5.00
Jack Mitchell	1-3	33.3	+1.00
Tom Marquand	1-4	25.0	-1.38
Jamie Spencer	1-4	25.0	-0.75
Oisin Murphy	1-5	20.0	-1.00
Edward Greatrex	1-5	20.0	-3.60
Ryan Moore	1-7	14.3	-3.75
Harry Burns	1-8	12.5	-3.50
David Probert	1-10	10.0	-8.60

COURSE RECORD

	Total W-R	Non-Hndcps 2-y-o	Non-Hndcps 3-y-o+	Hndcps 2-y-o	Hndcps 3-y-o+	Per cent	£1 Level Stake
Kempton (A.W)	7-54	3-18	0-12	0-1	4-23	13.0	-20.13
Wolvhptn (A.W)	6-41	1-12	3-12	0-0	2-17	14.6	-18.11
Lingfield (A.W)	4-17	1-4	1-6	0-0	2-7	23.5	-7.97
Yarmouth	3-5	0-0	2-2	0-0	1-3	60.0	+1.40
Newcastle (A.W)	3-6	1-2	1-3	0-0	1-1	50.0	+3.28
Windsor	3-20	0-2	2-11	0-0	1-7	15.0	-11.63
Newbury	3-22	2-10	1-10	0-0	0-2	13.6	+20.00
Wetherby	2-2	0-0	0-0	0-0	2-2	100.0	+5.38
Ripon	2-3	0-0	2-3	0-0	0-0	66.7	+0.90
Ascot	2-9	0-0	2-6	0-0	0-3	22.2	-2.75
Nottingham	2-9	1-4	1-2	0-0	0-3	22.2	-5.21
Ffos Las	2-13	2-4	0-2	0-1	0-6	15.4	+31.00
Salisbury	2-15	0-6	1-5	0-0	1-4	13.3	-2.82
Brighton	1-1	1-1	0-0	0-0	0-0	100.0	+2.75
Pontefract	1-2	0-0	1-2	0-0	0-0	50.0	-0.83
Bath	1-3	0-0	1-1	0-0	0-2	33.3	-1.60
Chester	1-3	0-0	1-1	0-0	0-2	33.3	+2.50
Goodwood	1-9	0-0	1-5	0-0	0-4	11.1	-4.50
Newmkt (Jly)	1-13	0-1	1-4	0-0	0-8	7.7	-11.47
Chelmsford (A.W)	1-15	0-8	0-1	0-1	1-5	6.7	-11.75

WINNING HORSES

Horse	Races Run	1st	2nd	3rd	£
Al Kherb*	4	2	0	0	7633
Aspetar (FR)	4	2	0	2	29272
Blakeney Point	6	1	0	0	22117
Blue Mist	4	1	2	0	9704
Breathless Times	9	4	0	1	34416
Buffer Zone	4	1	0	1	3752
Catan (GER)	4	2	0	1	8280
Chippie Hill (IRE)	2	1	0	0	3105
Extra Elusive	4	2	1	0	13219
Fashion's Star (IRE)	1	1	0	0	10271
Great Bear	1	1	0	0	3752
Great Beyond	6	1	0	0	6728
Guild	4	1	0	0	3752
Headman	2	1	1	0	5531
Herculean	3	1	1	1	4528
Kassar (IRE)	7	1	1	1	11972
L'Explora (USA)	3	1	1	0	3752
Lady Adelaide (IRE)	2	1	1	0	3881
Low Profile*	3	1	0	0	5434
Lumen	6	1	0	0	3105
Magellan*	5	2	1	0	12938
Momkin (IRE)	3	1	1	1	6728
Mubariz	3	1	0	0	6469
Polish	6	1	1	1	9704
Projection	7	1	1	3	39697
Red Impression	2	2	0	0	7633
Regina Pacis (IRE)	6	2	0	2	9283
Savaanah (IRE)	6	3	2	0	21606
Second Step (IRE)	3	1	1	1	22684
Thorn	3	1	0	0	3752
Timespan	5	1	1	1	3752
Total Commitment (IRE)	3	1	0	0	3881
True Destiny	7	2	0	1	6210
Universal Command	4	1	0	1	3752
Withhold	1	1	0	0	92385
Total winning prize-money					**£444678**
Favourites	**28-58**		**48.3%**		**5.71**

TOM CLOVER

NEWMARKET, SUFFOLK

	No. of Hrs	Races Run	1st	2nd	3rd	Unpl	Per cent	£1 Level Stake
2-y-o	*17*	*70*	*2*	*7*	*13*	*48*	*2.9*	*-51.25*
3-y-o	*9*	*39*	*1*	*7*	*9*	*22*	*2.6*	*-33.00*
4-y-o+	*5*	*25*	*4*	*5*	*1*	*15*	*16.0*	*-7.75*
Totals	**31**	**134**	**7**	**19**	**23**	**85**	**5.2**	**-92.00**
2017	*16*	*81*	*7*	*12*	*13*	*49*	*8.6*	*-38.75*
2016	*1*	*1*	*0*	*1*	*0*	*0*	*0.0*	*-1.00*

JOCKEYS

	W-R	Per cent	£1 Level Stake
Adam Kirby	1-2	50.0	+1.25
Aaron Jones	1-4	25.0	+2.00
Andrea Atzeni	1-4	25.0	+0.50
Martin Harley	1-8	12.5	-2.00
Josephine Gordon	1-12	8.3	+3.00
Pat Cosgrave	1-16	6.3	-12.50
Jack Mitchell	1-32	3.1	-28.25

COURSE RECORD

	Total W-R	Non-Hndcps 2-y-o	Non-Hndcps 3-y-o+	Hndcps 2-y-o	Hndcps 3-y-o+	Per cent	£1 Level Stake
Brighton	1-4	0-0	0-0	0-0	1-4	25.0	-0.50
Newmkt (Jly)	1-7	0-4	0-0	0-1	1-2	14.3	-2.50
Windsor	1-10	1-4	0-2	0-0	0-4	10.0	+5.00
Yarmouth	1-13	0-4	0-1	0-0	1-8	7.7	-7.00
Lingfield (A.W)	1-13	0-4	0-1	0-1	1-7	7.7	-7.00
Wolvhptn (A.W)	1-15	0-5	0-2	0-4	1-4	6.7	-11.75
Chelmsford (A.W)	1-17	0-7	0-2	1-5	0-3	5.9	-13.25

WINNING HORSES

Horse	Races Run	1st	2nd	3rd	£
Balgair	7	2	3	0	10221
Castle Talbot (IRE)	6	1	0	1	3105
Gypsy Spirit	10	1	1	5	3752
Maestro Mac (IRE)	3	1	0	0	3752
Obrigada	1	1	0	0	3105
Storm Shelter (IRE)	7	1	1	0	3493
Total winning prize-money					**£27428**
Favourites	**3-7**		**42.9%**		**3.50**

DENIS COAKLEY

WEST ILSLEY, BERKS

	No. of Hrs	Races Run	1st	2nd	3rd	Unpl	Per cent	£1 Level Stake
2-y-o	*5*	*13*	*1*	*0*	*2*	*10*	*7.7*	*-5.00*
3-y-o	*8*	*39*	*1*	*4*	*3*	*31*	*2.6*	*-31.00*
4-y-o+	*11*	*63*	*4*	*9*	*14*	*36*	*6.3*	*-35.25*
Totals	**24**	**115**	**6**	**13**	**19**	**77**	**5.2**	**-71.25**
2017	*19*	*85*	*8*	*8*	*15*	*54*	*9.4*	*-1.50*
2016	*16*	*76*	*3*	*7*	*7*	*59*	*3.9*	*-49.50*

JOCKEYS

	W-R	Per cent	£1 Level Stake
Fran Berry	2-14	14.3	-0.50
Harry Burns	1-4	25.0	-0.25
Finley Marsh	1-6	16.7	-0.50
David Egan	1-8	12.5	+5.00
Charles Bishop	1-12	8.3	-4.00

COURSE RECORD

	Total W-R	Non-Hndcps 2-y-o	3-y-o+	Hndcps 2-y-o	3-y-o+	Per cent	£1 Level Stake
Newbury	2-9	1-1	0-1	0-0	1-7	22.2	+12.00
Leicester	1-3	0-0	0-1	0-0	1-2	33.3	+5.00
Sandown	1-4	0-0	0-1	0-0	1-3	25.0	+1.50
Bath	1-11	0-0	0-1	0-0	1-10	9.1	-5.50
Windsor	1-11	0-1	0-3	0-0	1-7	9.1	-7.25

WINNING HORSES

Horse	Races Run	1st	2nd	3rd	£
Keeper's Choice (IRE)	8	2	1	1	13197
Sheila's Showcase	4	1	0	1	0
Sweet Charity	6	1	2	0	4399
Tiar Na Nog (IRE)	7	1	2	1	3105
Yogiyogiyogi (IRE)	13	1	1	2	3105
Total winning prize-money					**£23806**
Favourites	**0-2**		**0.0%**		**-2.00**

PAUL COLE

WHATCOMBE, OXON

	No. of Hrs	Races Run	1st	2nd	3rd	Unpl	Per cent	£1 Level Stake
2-y-o	*18*	*55*	*7*	*6*	*11*	*31*	*12.7*	*+39.00*
3-y-o	*13*	*64*	*3*	*3*	*11*	*47*	*4.7*	*-36.50*
4-y-o+	*11*	*79*	*8*	*10*	*6*	*55*	*10.1*	*-7.84*
Totals	**42**	**198**	**18**	**19**	**28**	**133**	**9.1**	**-5.34**
2017	*44*	*184*	*25*	*27*	*19*	*112*	*13.6*	*+7.75*
2016	*46*	*219*	*29*	*38*	*29*	*123*	*13.2*	*-33.75*

BY MONTH

2-y-o	W-R	Per cent	£1 Level Stake	3-y-o	W-R	Per cent	£1 Level Stake
January	0-0	0.0	0.00	January	0-3	0.0	-3.00
February	0-0	0.0	0.00	February	0-1	0.0	-1.00
March	0-0	0.0	0.00	March	0-2	0.0	-2.00
April	0-0	0.0	0.00	April	0-3	0.0	-3.00
May	0-4	0.0	-4.00	May	0-6	0.0	-6.00
June	2-6	33.3	+38.25	June	0-11	0.0	-11.00
July	1-8	12.5	-4.50	July	1-10	10.0	-6.50
August	1-11	9.1	-7.25	August	0-7	0.0	-7.00
September	0-6	0.0	-6.00	September	1-9	11.1	+8.00
October	1-9	11.1	-6.50	October	0-5	0.0	-5.00
November	1-6	16.7	+28.00	November	1-5	20.0	+2.00
December	1-5	20.0	+1.00	December	0-2	0.0	-2.00

4-y-o+	W-R	Per cent	£1 Level Stake	Totals	W-R	Per cent	£1 Level Stake
January	0-1	0.0	-1.00	January	0-4	0.0	-4.00
February	0-0	0.0	0.00	February	0-1	0.0	-1.00
March	0-1	0.0	-1.00	March	0-3	0.0	-3.00
April	1-10	10.0	+3.00	April	1-13	7.7	0.00
May	0-10	0.0	-10.00	May	0-20	0.0	-20.00
June	2-14	14.3	-2.09	June	4-31	12.9	+25.16
July	1-11	9.1	-7.25	July	3-29	10.3	-18.25
August	2-10	20.0	+1.75	August	3-28	10.7	-12.50
September	2-12	16.7	+18.75	September	3-27	11.1	+20.75
October	0-7	0.0	-7.00	October	1-21	4.8	-18.50
November	0-3	0.0	-3.00	November	2-14	14.3	-1.00
December	0-0	0.0	0.00	December	1-7	14.3	-2.00

DISTANCE

2-y-o	W-R	Per cent	£1 Level Stake	3-y-o	W-R	Per cent	£1 Level Stake
5f-6f	5-31	16.1	+25.25	5f-6f	0-22	0.0	-22.00
7f-8f	1-23	4.3	-19.25	7f-8f	1-28	3.6	-24.50
9f-13f	1-1	100.0	+33.00	9f-13f	2-14	14.3	+10.00
14f+	0-0	0.0	0.00	14f+	0-0	0.0	0.00

4-y-o+	W-R	Per cent	£1 Level Stake	Totals	W-R	Per cent	£1 Level Stake
5f-6f	4-26	15.4	+17.50	5f-6f	9-79	11.4	+20.75
7f-8f	2-30	6.7	-14.25	7f-8f	4-81	4.9	-58.00
9f-13f	2-22	9.1	-10.09	9f-13f	5-37	13.5	+32.91
14f+	0-1	0.0	-1.00	14f+	0-1	0.0	-1.00

TYPE OF RACE

Non-Handicaps	W-R	Per cent	£1 Level Stake	Handicaps	W-R	Per cent	£1 Level Stake
2-y-o	7-46	15.2	+48.00	2-y-o	0-9	0.0	-9.00
3-y-o	0-10	0.0	-10.00	3-y-o	3-54	5.6	-26.50
4-y-o+	1-6	16.7	-3.25	4-y-o+	7-73	9.6	-4.59

RACE CLASS

	W-R	Per cent	£1 Level Stake
Class 1	0-4	0.0	-4.00
Class 2	3-23	13.0	+18.75
Class 3	1-27	3.7	-23.25
Class 4	5-55	9.1	-19.00
Class 5	8-69	11.6	+40.41
Class 6	1-20	5.0	-17.25
Class 7	0-0	0.0	0.00

FIRST TIME OUT

	W-R	Per cent	£1 Level Stake
2-y-o	2-18	11.1	+29.00
3-y-o	0-13	0.0	-13.00
4-y-o+	1-11	9.1	+2.00
Totals	3-42	7.1	+18.00

JOCKEYS

	W-R	Per cent	£1 Level Stake
David Probert	4-13	30.8	+38.50
Raul Da Silva	4-69	5.8	-11.50
Rossa Ryan	2-10	20.0	+16.00
Robert Havlin	2-10	20.0	-4.00
Tom Eaves	1-1	100.0	+2.25
Gary Mahon	1-1	100.0	+1.75
Cameron Noble	1-3	33.3	+25.00
Darragh Keenan	1-5	20.0	-2.25
Silvestre De Sousa	1-5	20.0	-3.09
P J McDonald	1-7	14.3	+6.00

COURSE RECORD

	Total W-R	Non-Hndcps 2-y-o	3-y-o+	Hndcps 2-y-o	3-y-o+	Per cent	£1 Level Stake
Lingfield (A.W)	2-10	1-2	0-0	0-0	1-8	20.0	-1.25
Goodwood	2-11	1-3	0-0	0-0	1-8	18.2	+1.75

Leicester	2-12	1-2	0-3	0-0	1-7	16.7	+32.50
Wolvhptn (A.W)	2-17	1-4	0-3	0-4	1-6	11.8	+24.00
Kempton (A.W)	2-34	1-8	0-4	0-2	1-20	5.9	-18.50
Catterick	1-1	1-1	0-0	0-0	0-0	100.0	+2.25
Ayr	1-2	0-0	0-0	0-0	1-2	50.0	+26.00
Chepstow	1-2	0-0	1-1	0-0	0-1	50.0	+0.75
Epsom	1-2	0-1	0-0	0-0	1-1	50.0	+1.75
Chelmsford (A.W)	1-4	0-0	0-1	0-0	1-3	25.0	+13.00
Lingfield	1-7	0-0	0-2	0-0	1-5	14.3	-5.09
Salisbury	1-7	1-2	0-0	0-0	0-5	14.3	-3.50
Windsor	1-19	0-7	0-0	0-0	1-12	5.3	-9.00

WINNING HORSES

Horse	Races Run	1st	2nd	3rd	£
Arctic Sea	13	1	0	3	3752
Assassinate (IRE)	9	1	2	0	3105
Baron Bolt	7	3	2	0	27618
Cool Reflection (IRE)	5	1	2	0	3881
Duke Of Hazzard (FR)	6	1	2	1	18903
Li Kui	12	1	2	4	4787
Mercenary Rose (IRE)	1	1	0	0	4787
Over The Guns (IRE)	3	1	0	1	4528
Pink Phantom	6	2	0	0	9186
Plunger	7	1	0	3	6553
Port Douglas (IRE)	5	1	0	0	3752
Rotherwick (IRE)	9	1	1	2	5531
Shir Khan	2	1	0	0	4140
Spirit Of Belle*	5	1	1	0	6469
Walkman (IRE)*	2	1	0	0	5111
Total winning prize-money					**£112103**
Favourites	**3-12**		**25.0%**		**-4.84**

PAUL COLLINS

SALTBURN, CLEVELAND

	No. of Hrs	Races Run	1st	2nd	3rd	Unpl	Per cent	£1 Level Stake
2-y-o	*1*	*3*	*0*	*0*	*0*	*3*	*0.0*	*-3.00*
3-y-o	*1*	*1*	*0*	*0*	*0*	*1*	*0.0*	*-1.00*
4-y-o+	*2*	*12*	*2*	*2*	*0*	*8*	*16.7*	*+1.50*
Totals	**4**	**16**	**2**	**2**	**0**	**12**	**12.5**	**-2.50**
2017	*5*	*21*	*1*	*3*	*3*	*14*	*4.8*	*-19.27*
2016	*0*							

JOCKEYS

	W-R	Per cent	£1 Level Stake
Paddy Vaughan	1-2	50.0	+8.00
Conor McGovern	1-7	14.3	-3.50

COURSE RECORD

	Total W-R	Non-Hndcps 2-y-o	3-y-o+	Hndcps 2-y-o	3-y-o+	Per cent	£1 Level Stake
Leicester	1-1	0-0	0-0	0-0	1-1	100.0	+9.00
Carlisle	1-4	0-0	0-0	0-0	1-4	25.0	-0.50

WINNING HORSES

Horse	Races Run	1st	2nd	3rd	£
Roys Dream	11	2	2	0	6987
Total winning prize-money					**£6987**
Favourites	**1-1**		**100.0%**		**2.50**

JACQUELINE COWARD

DALBY, NORTH YORKS

	No. of Hrs	Races Run	1st	2nd	3rd	Unpl	Per cent	£1 Level Stake
2-y-o	*0*	*0*	*0*	*0*	*0*	*0*	*0.0*	*0.00*
3-y-o	*1*	*4*	*0*	*0*	*0*	*4*	*0.0*	*-4.00*
4-y-o+	*6*	*40*	*5*	*3*	*4*	*28*	*12.5*	*-19.38*
Totals	**7**	**44**	**5**	**3**	**4**	**32**	**11.4**	**-23.38**
2017	*3*	*15*	*2*	*1*	*2*	*10*	*13.3*	*-3.25*
2016	*3*	*15*	*1*	*0*	*2*	*12*	*6.7*	*-11.50*

JOCKEYS

	W-R	Per cent	£1 Level Stake
Miss Joanna Mason	3-9	33.3	+5.13
Nathan Evans	2-17	11.8	-10.50

COURSE RECORD

	Total W-R	Non-Hndcps 2-y-o	3-y-o+	Hndcps 2-y-o	3-y-o+	Per cent	£1 Level Stake
Ayr	2-7	0-0	0-0	0-0	2-7	28.6	-1.13
Epsom	1-1	0-0	0-0	0-0	1-1	100.0	+3.50
Goodwood	1-1	0-0	0-0	0-0	1-1	100.0	+6.00
Wolvhptn (A.W)	1-5	0-0	0-0	0-0	1-5	20.0	-1.75

WINNING HORSES

Horse	Races Run	1st	2nd	3rd	£
Coviglia (IRE)	11	3	3	0	9704
Tapis Libre	7	2	0	1	12967
Total winning prize-money					**£22671**
Favourites	**3-4**		**75.0%**		**5.13**

ROBERT COWELL

SIX MILE BOTTOM, CAMBS

	No. of Hrs	Races Run	1st	2nd	3rd	Unpl	Per cent	£1 Level Stake
2-y-o	*29*	*99*	*5*	*10*	*13*	*71*	*5.1*	*-80.67*
3-y-o	*24*	*109*	*14*	*15*	*16*	*64*	*12.8*	*-10.39*
4-y-o+	*25*	*140*	*15*	*17*	*18*	*90*	*10.7*	*-48.13*
Totals	**78**	**348**	**34**	**42**	**47**	**225**	**9.8**	**-139.19**
2017	*70*	*294*	*43*	*33*	*37*	*181*	*14.6*	*-27.26*
2016	*79*	*340*	*34*	*29*	*46*	*231*	*10.0*	*-114.41*

BY MONTH

2-y-o	W-R	Per cent	£1 Level Stake
January	0-0	0.0	0.00
February	0-0	0.0	0.00
March	0-1	0.0	-1.00
April	0-5	0.0	-5.00
May	1-12	8.3	-8.75
June	0-9	0.0	-9.00
July	0-13	0.0	-13.00
August	0-11	0.0	-11.00
September	2-9	22.2	-5.42
October	1-19	5.3	-12.50
November	1-12	8.3	-7.00
December	0-8	0.0	-8.00

3-y-o	W-R	Per cent	£1 Level Stake
January	0-5	0.0	-5.00
February	4-5	80.0	+5.53
March	2-8	25.0	-2.75
April	0-3	0.0	-3.00
May	3-15	20.0	+3.50
June	0-15	0.0	-15.00
July	2-17	11.8	+11.00
August	1-16	6.3	+1.00
September	0-9	0.0	-9.00
October	2-10	20.0	+9.33
November	0-3	0.0	-3.00
December	0-3	0.0	-3.00

4-y-o+	W-R	Per cent	£1 Level Stake
January	0-4	0.0	-4.00
February	0-1	0.0	-1.00
March	1-6	16.7	-3.00
April	1-14	7.1	-10.50
May	4-22	18.2	-0.50
June	2-29	6.9	-14.00
July	1-17	5.9	-4.00
August	0-11	0.0	-11.00
September	4-14	28.6	+3.88
October	2-15	13.3	+3.00
November	0-5	0.0	-5.00
December	0-2	0.0	-2.00

Totals	W-R	Per cent	£1 Level Stake
January	0-9	0.0	-9.00
February	4-6	66.7	+4.53
March	3-15	20.0	-6.75
April	1-22	4.5	-18.50
May	8-49	16.3	-5.75
June	2-53	3.8	-38.00
July	3-47	6.4	-6.00
August	1-38	2.6	-21.00
September	6-32	18.8	-10.54
October	5-44	11.4	-0.17
November	1-20	5.0	-8.00
December	0-13	0.0	-5.00

DISTANCE

2-y-o	W-R	Per cent	£1 Level Stake
5f-6f	4-93	4.3	-81.17
7f-8f	1-6	16.7	+0.50
9f-13f	0-0	0.0	0.00
14f+	0-0	0.0	0.00

3-y-o	W-R	Per cent	£1 Level Stake
5f-6f	12-96	12.5	-16.39
7f-8f	2-13	15.4	+6.00
9f-13f	0-0	0.0	0.00
14f+	0-0	0.0	0.00

4-y-o+	W-R	Per cent	£1 Level Stake
5f-6f	15-139	10.8	-47.13
7f-8f	0-1	0.0	-1.00
9f-13f	0-0	0.0	0.00
14f+	0-0	0.0	0.00

Totals	W-R	Per cent	£1 Level Stake
5f-6f	31-328	9.5	-144.69
7f-8f	3-20	15.0	+5.50
9f-13f	0-0	0.0	0.00
14f+	0-0	0.0	0.00

TYPE OF RACE

Non-Handicaps

	W-R	Per cent	£1 Level Stake
2-y-o	5-84	6.0	-65.67
3-y-o	9-42	21.4	+5.73
4-y-o+	1-15	6.7	-12.00

Handicaps

	W-R	Per cent	£1 Level Stake
2-y-o	0-15	0.0	-15.00
3-y-o	5-67	7.5	-16.13
4-y-o+	14-125	11.2	-36.13

RACE CLASS

	W-R	Per cent	£1 Level Stake
Class 1	1-14	7.1	-11.00
Class 2	7-66	10.6	-26.13
Class 3	4-48	8.3	-17.72
Class 4	6-68	8.8	-41.38
Class 5	15-115	13.0	-9.47
Class 6	1-37	2.7	-33.50
Class 7	0-0	0.0	0.00

FIRST TIME OUT

	W-R	Per cent	£1 Level Stake
2-y-o	0-29	0.0	-29.00
3-y-o	3-24	12.5	-8.13
4-y-o+	3-25	12.0	-3.75
Totals	6-78	7.7	-40.88

JOCKEYS

	W-R	Per cent	£1 Level Stake
Joe Fanning	6-8	75.0	+22.87
Eoin Walsh	5-61	8.2	-45.48
Ryan Moore	2-8	25.0	-2.63
Jim Crowley	2-14	14.3	-7.33
Gerald Mosse	2-15	13.3	-3.50
Tom Eaves	1-1	100.0	+16.00
Pat Dobbs	1-1	100.0	+8.00
William Buick	1-2	50.0	+7.00
Paul Hanagan	1-3	33.3	+10.00
Robert Havlin	1-3	33.3	+3.00
J F Egan	1-4	25.0	+13.00
Andrea Atzeni	1-5	20.0	+6.00
Daniel Tudhope	1-5	20.0	-1.00
Edward Greatrex	1-5	20.0	+0.50
Jamie Spencer	1-6	16.7	-1.00
Silvestre De Sousa	1-7	14.3	-3.50
P J McDonald	1-8	12.5	-1.50
Franny Norton	1-8	12.5	-4.75
Oisin Murphy	1-15	6.7	-2.00
Tom Marquand	1-16	6.3	-12.25
Jonathan Fisher	1-20	5.0	-10.50
Luke Morris	1-44	2.3	-41.13

COURSE RECORD

	Total W-R	Non-Hndcps 2-y-o	Non-Hndcps 3-y-o+	Hndcps 2-y-o	Hndcps 3-y-o+	Per cent	£1 Level Stake
Lingfield (A.W)	6-23	0-5	4-7	0-2	2-9	26.1	-5.97
Chelmsford (A.W)	5-46	1-7	0-3	0-4	4-32	10.9	-7.00
Newcastle (A.W)	4-25	1-4	2-4	0-1	1-16	16.0	-10.42
Musselburgh	3-5	1-2	1-2	0-0	1-1	60.0	+4.91
Leicester	2-8	1-4	0-0	0-0	1-4	25.0	-1.33
Doncaster	2-15	1-4	1-6	0-0	0-5	13.3	-5.50
Windsor	2-18	0-7	1-4	0-0	1-7	11.1	-3.50
Yarmouth	2-23	0-7	0-3	0-0	2-13	8.7	-3.63
Newmkt (Jly)	1-6	0-1	0-1	0-0	1-4	16.7	+3.00
Brighton	1-7	0-2	0-0	0-0	1-5	14.3	-3.75
Goodwood	1-7	0-2	0-0	0-1	1-4	14.3	-2.00
Sandown	1-8	0-2	0-0	0-0	1-6	12.5	+0.50
Bath	1-9	0-1	0-2	0-0	1-6	11.1	+0.50
Southwell (A.W)	1-9	0-0	1-2	0-2	0-5	11.1	+8.00
Ascot	1-18	0-3	0-0	0-0	1-15	5.6	-5.00
Nottingham	1-18	0-6	0-2	0-1	1-9	5.6	-5.00

WINNING HORSES

Horse	Races Run	1st	2nd	3rd	£
Blame Roberta (USA)	6	2	0	1	11644
Blue De Vega (GER)	17	1	1	3	28013

Cowboy Soldier (IRE)	6	2	2	1	22642
Dazzle Gold (USA)	3	1	1	0	3235
Dollar Value (USA)	9	1	1	0	5434
Dubai Silk	2	1	0	1	3752
Encore D'Or	12	3	2	1	37176
*Global Applause	2	2	0	0	35134
Grandfather Tom	15	3	2	2	12388
Green Fortune*	6	1	1	1	7439
Leo Minor (USA)	12	1	3	2	6469
Madam Devious	7	1	1	3	3752
Misty Spirit	7	1	0	0	4140
*Mr Pocket (IRE)	2	1	0	0	5531
Nomorecalls (IRE)	4	2	1	0	7504
Ocelot	10	2	1	1	7633
Peace Dreamer (IRE)	3	1	0	0	3752
Pocket Dynamo (USA)	4	1	2	0	7116
Raucous	7	1	2	1	15563
Reeves	6	1	2	1	3752
Rocket Action	2	1	0	1	4787
Storm Over (IRE)	5	1	0	0	25876
Victors Lady (IRE)	4	1	1	0	4787
Zamjar	9	2	1	0	11062
Total winning prize-money					**£278581**
Favourites	**8-24**		**33.3%**		**-3.77**

CLIVE COX

LAMBOURN, BERKS

	No. of Hrs	Races Run	1st	2nd	3rd	Unpl	Per cent	£1 Level Stake
2-y-o	*45*	*123*	*15*	*24*	*16*	*68*	*12.2*	*-68.75*
3-y-o	*54*	*244*	*43*	*30*	*19*	*152*	*17.6*	*+46.78*
4-y-o+	*25*	*119*	*10*	*17*	*9*	*82*	*8.4*	*-60.18*
Totals	**124**	**486**	**68**	**71**	**44**	**302**	**14.0**	**-82.15**
2017	*103*	*380*	*60*	*54*	*52*	*213*	*15.8*	*-10.15*
2016	*100*	*435*	*65*	*54*	*52*	*264*	*14.9*	*-51.45*

BY MONTH

2-y-o	W-R	Per cent	£1 Level Stake	**3-y-o**	W-R	Per cent	£1 Level Stake
January	0-0	0.0	0.00	January	0-0	0.0	0.00
February	0-0	0.0	0.00	February	0-4	0.0	-4.00
March	0-0	0.0	0.00	March	0-3	0.0	-3.00
April	0-0	0.0	0.00	April	2-15	13.3	-8.25
May	3-12	25.0	+7.50	May	8-40	20.0	+7.50
June	0-16	0.0	-16.00	June	6-44	13.6	-3.25
July	1-10	10.0	-8.82	July	7-26	26.9	+21.60
August	2-19	10.5	-14.75	August	6-40	15.0	-7.00
September	5-18	27.8	-3.96	September	5-28	17.9	+24.00
October	2-21	9.5	-13.80	October	3-21	14.3	+11.75
November	2-15	13.3	-6.92	November	3-11	27.3	+11.55
December	0-12	0.0	-12.00	December	3-12	25.0	-4.13

4-y-o+	W-R	Per cent	£1 Level Stake	**Totals**	W-R	Per cent	£1 Level Stake
January	0-5	0.0	-5.00	January	0-5	0.0	-5.00
February	2-6	33.3	+0.38	February	2-10	20.0	-3.62
March	1-5	20.0	+4.00	March	1-8	12.5	+1.00
April	0-5	0.0	-5.00	April	2-20	10.0	-13.25
May	2-14	14.3	-5.56	May	13-66	19.7	+9.44
June	0-16	0.0	-16.00	June	6-76	7.9	-35.25
July	0-10	0.0	-10.00	July	8-46	17.4	+2.78
August	2-19	10.5	-1.00	August	10-78	12.8	-22.75
September	1-14	7.1	-8.00	September	11-60	18.3	+12.04
October	2-15	13.3	-4.00	October	7-57	12.3	-6.05
November	0-7	0.0	-7.00	November	5-33	15.2	+4.55
December	0-3	0.0	-3.00	December	3-27	11.1	-7.13

DISTANCE

2-y-o	W-R	Per cent	£1 Level Stake	**3-y-o**	W-R	Per cent	£1 Level Stake
5f-6f	13-84	15.5	-37.58	5f-6f	13-89	14.6	+11.50
7f-8f	2-39	5.1	-31.17	7f-8f	22-102	21.6	+21.03
9f-13f	0-0	0.0	0.00	9f-13f	8-53	15.1	+14.25
14f+	0-0	0.0	0.00	14f+	0-0	0.0	0.00

4-y-o+	W-R	Per cent	£1 Level Stake	**Totals**	W-R	Per cent	£1 Level Stake
5f-6f	5-52	9.6	-20.56	5f-6f	31-225	13.8	-46.64
7f-8f	3-41	7.3	-21.00	7f-8f	27-182	14.8	-31.14
9f-13f	2-24	8.3	-16.63	9f-13f	10-77	13.0	-2.38
14f+	0-2	0.0	-2.00	14f+	0-2	0.0	-2.00

TYPE OF RACE

Non-Handicaps	W-R	Per cent	£1 Level Stake	**Handicaps**	W-R	Per cent	£1 Level Stake
2-y-o	11-112	9.8	-73.08	2-y-o	4-11	36.4	+4.33
3-y-o	6-83	7.2	-53.77	3-y-o	37-161	23.0	+100.55
4-y-o+	2-29	6.9	-18.55	4-y-o+	8-90	8.9	-41.63

RACE CLASS

	W-R	Per cent	£1 Level Stake
Class 1	2-45	4.4	-37.56
Class 2	8-54	14.8	+14.50
Class 3	7-51	13.7	-20.54
Class 4	26-142	18.3	-19.96
Class 5	22-168	13.1	-14.72
Class 6	3-26	11.5	-3.88
Class 7	0-0	0.0	0.00

FIRST TIME OUT

	W-R	Per cent	£1 Level Stake
2-y-o	3-45	6.7	-25.50
3-y-o	8-54	14.8	-21.75
4-y-o+	4-25	16.0	-5.18
Totals	15-124	12.1	-52.43

JOCKEYS

	W-R	Per cent	£1 Level Stake
Adam Kirby	40-228	17.5	-36.31
Hector Crouch	12-94	12.8	+5.13
Amelia Glass	5-26	19.2	+25.00
William Buick	2-7	28.6	-1.25
David Probert	2-18	11.1	+7.00
Hollie Doyle	1-3	33.3	+4.00
Jason Watson	1-3	33.3	+4.00
Daniel Tudhope	1-3	33.3	-1.71
Ryan Moore	1-5	20.0	-1.25
James Doyle	1-5	20.0	-2.00

Dane O'Neill	1-6	16.7	-2.75
Oisin Murphy	1-7	14.3	-1.00

COURSE RECORD

	Total W-R	Non-Hndcps 2-y-o	Non-Hndcps 3-y-o+	Hndcps 2-y-o	Hndcps 3-y-o+	Per cent	£1 Level Stake
Kempton (A.W)	12-73	0-18	2-16	1-4	9-35	16.4	+0.88
Windsor	8-48	1-8	2-13	0-0	5-27	16.7	+7.23
Lingfield (A.W)	6-22	0-2	0-2	1-1	5-17	27.3	+11.38
Ascot	6-31	3-8	0-6	0-0	3-17	19.4	+8.50
Haydock	5-17	2-6	0-5	0-1	3-5	29.4	+9.49
Sandown	5-20	1-4	0-2	1-1	3-13	25.0	-0.69
Goodwood	4-26	1-7	0-4	0-0	3-15	15.4	-5.00
Wolvhptn (A.W)	3-41	0-8	1-14	0-1	2-18	7.3	-14.63
Lingfield	2-8	0-0	1-4	0-0	1-4	25.0	+5.00
Newmkt (Jly)	2-8	0-1	0-0	0-0	2-7	25.0	+3.25
Chelmsford (A.W)	2-10	0-2	0-4	1-1	1-3	20.0	-2.25
York	2-10	0-0	1-2	0-1	1-7	20.0	-4.81
Newmarket	2-21	1-5	0-7	0-0	1-9	9.5	-12.00
Leicester	2-22	1-7	0-3	0-0	1-12	9.1	-5.50
Ayr	1-2	0-0	0-0	0-0	1-2	50.0	+10.00
Brighton	1-2	0-0	0-0	0-0	1-2	50.0	+2.50
Epsom	1-6	0-0	0-2	0-0	1-4	16.7	+7.00
Bath	1-12	0-3	0-3	0-0	1-6	8.3	-6.00
Nottingham	1-17	0-3	1-4	0-1	0-9	5.9	-12.00
Salisbury	1-24	1-9	0-4	0-0	0-11	4.2	-22.00
Newbury	1-36	0-15	0-8	0-0	1-13	2.8	-32.50

WINNING HORSES

Horse	Races Run	1st	2nd	3rd	£
Autumn Leaves*	5	1	0	0	4528
Awesome	6	1	1	1	5531
Bobby Wheeler (IRE)	3	1	0	0	6469
Chagatai (IRE)	9	2	0	0	12938
Cloak And Dagger (IRE)	5	1	1	1	6728
Come On Come On (IRE)	6	1	1	2	3881
Connect	4	1	0	1	31125
Crack On Crack On	5	3	1	0	83343
Dark Power (IRE)	6	1	1	0	9057
Dark Shadow (IRE)	6	1	1	0	4528
Del Parco	6	1	0	1	5531
Emerald Approach (IRE)	3	1	1	0	6081
Existential (IRE)	5	1	0	1	3881
Get Back Get Back (IRE)	5	2	1	1	7504
Getchagetchagetcha	3	1	0	0	9057
Golden Force	4	1	2	0	4787
Grey Galleon (USA)	9	1	1	0	5175
Harry Angel (IRE)	4	1	1	0	70888
He's Amazing (IRE)	7	1	1	0	12938
Heartwarming	5	1	2	0	4528
House Of Kings (IRE)	3	1	1	1	6728
Hulcote	4	1	0	2	7116
Icart Point	3	3	0	0	14749
Isle Of Man	4	1	0	1	3105
Kick On Kick On	5	1	0	2	7246
King's Slipper	8	2	3	0	10221
Koditime (IRE)	6	1	1	0	12450
Konchek	7	1	1	1	9704
Lethal Lunch	7	2	1	1	12647
Little Miss Lilly	9	1	1	0	3105
Little Palaver	11	1	0	1	3752
Maid Of Spirit (IRE)	2	1	0	0	3752
Moon Song	7	2	1	0	9283
Now Children (IRE)	5	2	1	0	24434
Perfect Clarity	5	1	0	0	22684
Perfect Refuge	9	1	1	2	3752
Prince Ahwahnee	5	1	1	0	5531
Private Rocket (IRE)	4	1	1	1	9338
Reticent Angel (IRE)	7	2	2	1	8863
Salute The Soldier (GER)	4	2	1	0	13132
Shades Of Blue (IRE)	2	1	0	1	6728
Silca Mistress	10	4	2	0	22351
Simply Breathless	8	3	1	2	30922
Snazzy Jazzy (IRE)	5	1	0	0	37350
Sounds Approving (IRE)	6	1	1	0	3752
Swift And Sure (IRE)	4	1	2	0	4787
Tamerlane (IRE)	5	2	0	0	6857
Tis Marvellous	6	1	0	0	22131
Welcoming (FR)	3	1	1	1	6469
Wise Counsel	4	1	0	1	6469
Total winning prize-money					**£637906**
Favourites	**23-76**		**30.3%**		**-15.11**

TONY COYLE

NORTON, N YORKS

	No. of Hrs	Races Run	1st	2nd	3rd	Unpl	Per cent	£1 Level Stake
2-y-o	*17*	*71*	*2*	*7*	*6*	*56*	*2.8*	*-61.00*
3-y-o	*3*	*9*	*0*	*0*	*1*	*8*	*0.0*	*-9.00*
4-y-o+	*13*	*57*	*5*	*6*	*7*	*39*	*8.8*	*-5.00*
Totals	**33**	**137**	**7**	**13**	**14**	**103**	**5.1**	**-75.00**
2017	*35*	*171*	*12*	*8*	*9*	*142*	*7.0*	*+3.50*
2016	*29*	*184*	*8*	*13*	*22*	*141*	*4.3*	*-50.42*

JOCKEYS

	W-R	Per cent	£1 Level Stake
Dougie Costello	3-25	12.0	+3.00
Ben Curtis	1-2	50.0	+11.00
Joe Fanning	1-4	25.0	+7.00
Kevin Stott	1-5	20.0	0.00
Barry McHugh	1-46	2.2	-41.00

COURSE RECORD

	Total W-R	Non-Hndcps 2-y-o	Non-Hndcps 3-y-o+	Hndcps 2-y-o	Hndcps 3-y-o+	Per cent	£1 Level Stake
Catterick	2-12	0-2	0-1	0-1	2-8	16.7	+11.50
Hamilton	1-5	0-2	0-0	0-0	1-3	20.0	+6.00
Newcastle (A.W)	1-7	0-2	1-1	0-1	0-3	14.3	+6.00
York	1-9	1-8	0-0	0-0	0-1	11.1	-4.00
Thirsk	1-14	0-8	0-3	1-1	0-2	7.1	-9.00
Beverley	1-16	0-8	0-1	0-0	1-7	6.3	-11.50

WINNING HORSES

Horse	Races Run	1st	2nd	3rd	£
Broken Spear	10	2	3	2	19407
Caspian Prince (IRE)*	2	1	0	1	18903
Flower Power	13	3	1	2	10092
Little Pippin	2	1	0	0	3493
Total winning prize-money					**£51895**
Favourites	**1-3**		**33.3%**		**1.50**

RAY CRAGGS

SEDGEFIELD, CO DURHAM

	No. of Hrs	Races Run	1st	2nd	3rd	Unpl	Per cent	£1 Level Stake
2-y-o	*1*	*1*	*0*	*0*	*0*	*1*	*0.0*	*-1.00*
3-y-o	*1*	*2*	*2*	*0*	*0*	*0*	*100.0*	*+105.50*
4-y-o+	*2*	*15*	*2*	*3*	*3*	*7*	*13.3*	*+10.50*
Totals	**4**	**18**	**4**	**3**	**3**	**8**	**22.2**	**+115.00**
2017	*2*	*2*	*0*	*0*	*0*	*2*	*0.0*	*-2.00*
2016	*2*	*12*	*1*	*0*	*1*	*10*	*8.3*	*+3.00*

JOCKEYS

	W-R	Per cent	£1 Level Stake
James Sullivan	2-4	50.0	+103.50
Oliver Stammers	1-2	50.0	+2.50
Connor Beasley	1-3	33.3	+18.00

COURSE RECORD

	Total W-R	Non-Hndcps 2-y-o	Non-Hndcps 3-y-o+	Hndcps 2-y-o	Hndcps 3-y-o+	Per cent	£1 Level Stake
Southwell (A.W)	3-4	0-0	2-2	0-0	1-2	75.0	+124.50
Newcastle (A.W)	1-11	0-1	0-0	0-0	1-10	9.1	-6.50

WINNING HORSES

Horse	Races Run	1st	2nd	3rd	£
Amouri Gleam	2	2	0	0	7504
Coral Queen	7	1	2	2	3493
Glasgon	8	1	1	1	3493
Total winning prize-money					**£14490**
Favourites	**1-3**		**33.3%**		**1.50**

PETER CRATE

NEWDIGATE, SURREY

	No. of Hrs	Races Run	1st	2nd	3rd	Unpl	Per cent	£1 Level Stake
2-y-o	*0*	*0*	*0*	*0*	*0*	*0*	*0.0*	*0.00*
3-y-o	*1*	*4*	*0*	*0*	*0*	*4*	*0.0*	*-4.00*
4-y-o+	*1*	*12*	*1*	*3*	*2*	*6*	*8.3*	*+3.00*
Totals	**2**	**16**	**1**	**3**	**2**	**10**	**6.3**	**-1.00**
2017	*5*	*46*	*2*	*9*	*6*	*29*	*4.3*	*-38.25*
2016	*7*	*57*	*5*	*4*	*2*	*46*	*8.8*	*-12.00*

JOCKEYS

	W-R	Per cent	£1 Level Stake
Tom Queally	1-5	20.0	+10.00

COURSE RECORD

	Total W-R	Non-Hndcps 2-y-o	Non-Hndcps 3-y-o+	Hndcps 2-y-o	Hndcps 3-y-o+	Per cent	£1 Level Stake
Lingfield (A.W)	1-10	0-0	0-2	0-0	1-8	10.0	+5.00

WINNING HORSES

Horse	Races Run	1st	2nd	3rd	£
Sandfrankskipsgo	12	1	3	2	3105
Total winning prize-money					**£3105**
Favourites	**0-0**		**0.0%**		**0.00**

SIMON CRISFORD

NEWMARKET, SUFFOLK

	No. of Hrs	Races Run	1st	2nd	3rd	Unpl	Per cent	£1 Level Stake
2-y-o	*35*	*90*	*17*	*19*	*13*	*41*	*18.9*	*-23.33*
3-y-o	*48*	*185*	*43*	*33*	*26*	*83*	*23.2*	*+20.74*
4-y-o+	*17*	*62*	*10*	*17*	*8*	*27*	*16.1*	*-25.65*
Totals	**100**	**337**	**70**	**69**	**47**	**151**	**20.8**	**-28.24**
2017	*77*	*253*	*43*	*37*	*36*	*137*	*17.0*	*+32.28*
2016	*67*	*203*	*32*	*31*	*24*	*116*	*15.8*	*-38.27*

BY MONTH

2-y-o	W-R	Per cent	£1 Level Stake	**3-y-o**	W-R	Per cent	£1 Level Stake
January	0-0	0.0	0.00	January	1-7	14.3	+4.00
February	0-0	0.0	0.00	February	0-3	0.0	-3.00
March	0-0	0.0	0.00	March	3-5	60.0	+10.11
April	0-0	0.0	0.00	April	0-17	0.0	-17.00
May	2-3	66.7	+12.50	May	2-23	8.7	-16.75
June	0-8	0.0	-8.00	June	8-33	24.2	-1.43
July	0-6	0.0	-6.00	July	4-20	20.0	-0.67
August	2-13	15.4	-3.13	August	6-18	33.3	+10.65
September	3-23	13.0	-13.88	September	5-18	27.8	+3.73
October	6-19	31.6	+3.13	October	7-16	43.8	+17.75
November	3-13	23.1	-6.45	November	5-15	33.3	+14.25
December	1-5	20.0	-1.50	December	2-10	20.0	-0.90

4-y-o+	W-R	Per cent	£1 Level Stake	**Totals**	W-R	Per cent	£1 Level Stake
January	3-8	37.5	+8.50	January	4-15	26.7	+12.50
February	0-4	0.0	-4.00	February	0-7	0.0	-7.00
March	0-5	0.0	-5.00	March	3-10	30.0	+5.11
April	2-6	33.3	-0.88	April	2-23	8.7	-17.88
May	1-9	11.1	-5.50	May	5-35	14.3	-9.75
June	2-8	25.0	-2.15	June	10-49	20.4	-11.58
July	1-7	14.3	-4.25	July	5-33	15.2	-10.92
August	0-5	0.0	-5.00	August	8-36	22.2	+2.52
September	0-6	0.0	-6.00	September	8-47	17.0	-16.15
October	1-3	33.3	-0.38	October	14-38	36.8	+20.50

November	0-1	0.0	-1.00	November	8-29	27.6	+13.25
December	0-0	0.0	0.00	December	3-15	20.0	-0.90

DISTANCE

2-y-o	W-R	Per cent	£1 Level Stake	3-y-o	W-R	Per cent	£1 Level Stake
5f-6f	7-33	21.2	+0.50	5f-6f	5-18	27.8	+11.83
7f-8f	10-53	18.9	-19.82	7f-8f	26-105	24.8	+1.54
9f-13f	0-4	0.0	-4.00	9f-13f	11-55	20.0	+11.37
14f+	0-0	0.0	0.00	14f+	1-7	14.3	-4.00

4-y-o+	W-R	Per cent	£1 Level Stake	Totals	W-R	Per cent	£1 Level Stake
5f-6f	1-13	7.7	-5.00	5f-6f	13-64	20.3	+7.33
7f-8f	3-20	15.0	-10.25	7f-8f	39-178	21.9	-28.53
9f-13f	4-22	18.2	-8.25	9f-13f	15-81	18.5	-0.88
14f+	2-7	28.6	-2.15	14f+	3-14	21.4	-6.15

TYPE OF RACE

Non-Handicaps	W-R	Per cent	£1 Level Stake	Handicaps	W-R	Per cent	£1 Level Stake
2-y-o	14-82	17.1	-25.77	2-y-o	3-8	37.5	+2.45
3-y-o	24-104	23.1	+5.99	3-y-o	19-81	23.5	+14.75
4-y-o+	5-14	35.7	+0.48	4-y-o+	5-48	10.4	-26.13

RACE CLASS

	W-R	Per cent	£1 Level Stake
Class 1	3-16	18.8	-1.75
Class 2	3-27	11.1	-10.63
Class 3	5-45	11.1	-29.57
Class 4	25-89	28.1	+2.36
Class 5	32-153	20.9	+7.35
Class 6	2-7	28.6	+6.00
Class 7	0-0	0.0	0.00

FIRST TIME OUT

	W-R	Per cent	£1 Level Stake
2-y-o	6-35	17.1	-7.38
3-y-o	7-48	14.6	-3.47
4-y-o+	5-17	29.4	+5.50
Totals	18-100	18.0	-5.35

JOCKEYS

	W-R	Per cent	£1 Level Stake
Silvestre De Sousa	12-39	30.8	+14.62
Jack Mitchell	12-55	21.8	+7.33
Robert Havlin	7-35	20.0	+3.11
James Doyle	6-19	31.6	+2.50
Andrea Atzeni	6-30	20.0	-14.21
Jim Crowley	5-14	35.7	+0.81
Oisin Murphy	4-18	22.2	+0.82
William Buick	3-13	23.1	-1.75
Joe Fanning	2-2	100.0	+9.00
Kieran Shoemark	2-8	25.0	-1.50
Graham Lee	2-9	22.2	+8.50
Pat Cosgrave	2-13	15.4	-5.00
P J McDonald	1-1	100.0	+0.18
Miss Serena Brotherton	1-1	100.0	+5.00
Cameron Noble	1-2	50.0	+7.00
David Egan	1-3	33.3	-0.90
Ryan Moore	1-4	25.0	-1.25
Paul Hanagan	1-7	14.3	-2.00
Franny Norton	1-11	9.1	-7.50

COURSE RECORD

	Total W-R	Non-Hndcps 2-y-o	Non-Hndcps 3-y-o+	Hndcps 2-y-o	Hndcps 3-y-o+	Per cent	£1 Level Stake
Chelmsford (A.W)	10-47	2-14	4-16	0-1	4-16	21.3	-8.04
Kempton (A.W)	8-37	0-6	3-9	1-1	4-21	21.6	-1.52
Wolvhptn (A.W)	8-38	2-9	2-16	1-1	3-12	21.1	+2.25
Newcastle (A.W)	6-17	2-5	4-7	0-0	0-5	35.3	+6.23
Nottingham	4-12	3-5	0-4	0-0	1-3	33.3	+11.21
Lingfield (A.W)	4-23	1-3	0-8	0-0	3-12	17.4	-7.75
Catterick	3-6	0-1	2-3	1-2	0-0	50.0	+6.18
Ripon	3-6	1-1	1-1	0-0	1-4	50.0	+4.47
Southwell (A.W)	3-11	0-0	3-6	0-0	0-5	27.3	+8.61
Windsor	3-17	0-2	2-7	0-1	1-7	17.6	+16.50
Leicester	2-4	0-1	2-3	0-0	0-0	50.0	-0.61
Doncaster	2-6	0-1	0-1	0-0	2-4	33.3	-0.50
Yarmouth	2-6	0-2	0-1	0-0	2-3	33.3	+0.13
Ascot	2-9	0-0	1-4	0-0	1-5	22.2	+5.50
Newmarket	2-10	1-6	0-1	0-0	1-3	20.0	-5.65
Thirsk	1-1	0-0	1-1	0-0	0-0	100.0	+0.29
Ffos Las	1-1	0-0	1-1	0-0	0-0	100.0	+5.00
Epsom	1-4	0-2	1-1	0-0	0-1	25.0	-0.25
Salisbury	1-6	1-3	0-1	0-2	0-0	16.7	-4.88
Newmkt (Jly)	1-6	1-5	0-0	0-0	0-1	16.7	-3.13
Newbury	1-7	0-0	1-3	0-0	0-4	14.3	-4.13
Sandown	1-10	0-2	0-2	0-0	1-6	10.0	-7.25
Goodwood	1-13	0-5	1-6	0-0	0-2	7.7	-10.90

WINNING HORSES

Horse	Races Run	1st	2nd	3rd	£
Aldana	4	2	1	0	9186
Alnadir (USA)	3	1	0	1	6469
Archetype (FR)	3	1	0	0	9704
Awalii (FR)	4	1	0	0	3881
Bobby K (IRE)	7	3	2	1	19020
Cape Liberty (IRE)	5	1	1	0	3752
Century Dream (IRE)	5	2	0	1	72022
Cool Exhibit	1	1	0	0	3881
Craving (IRE)	5	1	1	2	3752
Eden Gardens (IRE)	4	1	0	0	3881
Enthaar*	4	1	0	2	3752
Eyecatcher (IRE)	6	1	2	1	4399
Ghost Queen	7	1	1	1	4787
Given Choice (IRE)	7	2	1	0	8539
Global Conqueror	6	2	1	0	14814
Honey Man (IRE)	7	2	2	1	14771
How Far (IRE)	7	3	0	1	15752
Imperial Charm	3	1	0	2	5175
Jadeyra	4	1	0	0	3752
Jash (IRE)	3	2	1	0	9962
Mannaal (IRE)	2	1	0	0	3881
Maybe Today	6	1	4	1	3752
Mordin (IRE)	8	2	5	0	9412
Mutafani	4	2	0	1	12938
Nobleman's Nest	4	1	0	0	7876
Ostilio	6	3	3	0	98025
Outbox	3	3	0	0	41337

Persian Sun	4	1	0	0	4528
Pride's Gold (USA)	9	2	2	3	3752
Reconcile (IRE)	2	1	1	0	3752
Red Mist	3	2	0	0	13939
Ring Dancer	4	1	1	1	3752
Romaana	4	1	2	0	5111
Saroog	6	2	3	0	11644
Shamsaya (IRE)	2	1	0	1	6469
Smart Champion	2	1	0	0	5111
Spinning Melody (USA)	1	1	0	0	7310
Sporting Chance	5	2	1	0	21800
Starry Eyes (USA)	2	1	0	1	6081
Sun Hat (IRE)	4	3	0	0	13035
Time To Blossom	4	1	1	1	6239
Trolius (IRE)	3	3	0	0	6752
Turn 'n Twirl (USA)	1	1	0	0	3752
Wazin	6	1	0	1	3752
We Know (IRE)	6	1	2	0	5531
Well Suited (IRE)	3	1	1	0	5175
Total winning prize-money					**£535957**
Favourites	**36-86**		**41.9%**		**3.51**

ANDREW CROOK

MIDDLEHAM MOOR, N YORKS

	No. of Hrs	Races Run	1st	2nd	3rd	Unpl	Per cent	£1 Level Stake
2-y-o	*3*	*16*	*0*	*0*	*2*	*14*	*0.0*	*-16.00*
3-y-o	*2*	*9*	*0*	*0*	*1*	*8*	*0.0*	*-9.00*
4-y-o+	*11*	*41*	*3*	*1*	*3*	*34*	*7.3*	*-19.50*
Totals	**16**	**66**	**3**	**1**	**6**	**56**	**4.5**	**-44.50**
2017	*8*	*31*	*1*	*2*	*2*	*26*	*3.2*	*-25.00*
2016	*9*	*36*	*1*	*3*	*4*	*28*	*2.8*	*-30.50*

JOCKEYS

	W-R	Per cent	£1 Level Stake
Kevin Stott	2-7	28.6	+10.50
David Allan	1-2	50.0	+2.00

COURSE RECORD

	Total W-R	Non-Hndcps 2-y-o	Non-Hndcps 3-y-o+	Hndcps 2-y-o	Hndcps 3-y-o+	Per cent	£1 Level Stake
Ayr	1-2	0-0	0-0	0-1	1-1	50.0	+2.00
Thirsk	1-4	0-1	0-2	0-0	1-1	25.0	+5.50
Redcar	1-10	0-0	0-1	0-3	1-6	10.0	-2.00

WINNING HORSES

Horse	Races Run	1st	2nd	3rd	£
Racemaker	10	3	1	2	17596
Total winning prize-money					**£17596**
Favourites	**1-2**		**50.0%**		**2.00**

LUCA CUMANI

NEWMARKET, SUFFOLK

	No. of Hrs	Races Run	1st	2nd	3rd	Unpl	Per cent	£1 Level Stake
2-y-o	*14*	*37*	*6*	*4*	*6*	*21*	*16.2*	*-0.11*
3-y-o	*18*	*87*	*14*	*8*	*17*	*48*	*16.1*	*-22.91*
4-y-o+	*10*	*46*	*5*	*7*	*3*	*31*	*10.9*	*-24.25*
Totals	**42**	**170**	**25**	**19**	**26**	**100**	**14.7**	**-47.27**
2017	*56*	*234*	*39*	*37*	*29*	*127*	*16.7*	*-62.21*
2016	*72*	*255*	*38*	*36*	*38*	*142*	*14.9*	*-81.63*

BY MONTH

2-y-o	W-R	Per cent	£1 Level Stake	**3-y-o**	W-R	Per cent	£1 Level Stake
January	0-0	0.0	0.00	January	0-0	0.0	0.00
February	0-0	0.0	0.00	February	0-0	0.0	0.00
March	0-0	0.0	0.00	March	0-0	0.0	0.00
April	0-0	0.0	0.00	April	0-6	0.0	-6.00
May	0-0	0.0	0.00	May	1-12	8.3	-4.00
June	0-0	0.0	0.00	June	3-21	14.3	-10.13
July	0-2	0.0	-2.00	July	4-15	26.7	-4.08
August	1-6	16.7	-4.27	August	4-16	25.0	-4.50
September	3-14	21.4	+3.67	September	1-9	11.1	-7.20
October	2-12	16.7	+5.50	October	1-7	14.3	+14.00
November	0-3	0.0	-3.00	November	0-1	0.0	-1.00
December	0-0	0.0	0.00	December	0-0	0.0	0.00

4-y-o+	W-R	Per cent	£1 Level Stake	**Totals**	W-R	Per cent	£1 Level Stake
January	0-0	0.0	0.00	January	0-0	0.0	0.00
February	0-0	0.0	0.00	February	0-0	0.0	0.00
March	0-0	0.0	0.00	March	0-0	0.0	0.00
April	0-2	0.0	-2.00	April	0-8	0.0	-8.00
May	1-6	16.7	-4.00	May	2-18	11.1	-8.00
June	1-7	14.3	-3.75	June	4-28	14.3	-13.88
July	1-7	14.3	-2.50	July	5-24	20.8	-8.58
August	1-9	11.1	-3.00	August	6-31	19.4	-11.77
September	1-6	16.7	0.00	September	5-29	17.2	-3.53
October	0-6	0.0	-6.00	October	3-25	12.0	+13.50
November	0-3	0.0	-3.00	November	0-7	0.0	-4.00
December	0-0	0.0	0.00	December	0-0	0.0	0.00

DISTANCE

2-y-o	W-R	Per cent	£1 Level Stake	**3-y-o**	W-R	Per cent	£1 Level Stake
5f-6f	0-2	0.0	-2.00	5f-6f	0-1	0.0	-1.00
7f-8f	6-34	17.6	+2.89	7f-8f	1-22	4.5	-18.75
9f-13f	0-1	0.0	-1.00	9f-13f	13-62	21.0	-1.16
14f+	0-0	0.0	0.00	14f+	0-2	0.0	-2.00

4-y-o+	W-R	Per cent	£1 Level Stake	**Totals**	W-R	Per cent	£1 Level Stake
5f-6f	1-12	8.3	-7.50	5f-6f	1-15	6.7	-10.50
7f-8f	1-10	10.0	-4.00	7f-8f	8-66	12.1	-19.86
9f-13f	2-21	9.5	-15.75	9f-13f	15-84	17.9	-17.91
14f+	1-3	33.3	+3.00	14f+	1-5	20.0	+1.00

TYPE OF RACE

Non-Handicaps	W-R	Per cent	£1 Level Stake	Handicaps	W-R	Per cent	£1 Level Stake
2-y-o	5-33	15.2	-1.11	2-y-o	1-4	25.0	+1.00
3-y-o	4-41	9.8	-25.46	3-y-o	10-46	21.7	+2.55
4-y-o+	2-23	8.7	-13.75	4-y-o+	3-23	13.0	-10.50

RACE CLASS / FIRST TIME OUT

RACE CLASS	W-R	Per cent	£1 Level Stake	FIRST TIME OUT	W-R	Per cent	£1 Level Stake
Class 1	2-18	11.1	-8.75	2-y-o	0-14	0.0	-14.00
Class 2	0-15	0.0	-15.00	3-y-o	1-18	5.6	-10.00
Class 3	6-23	26.1	+14.92	4-y-o+	0-10	0.0	-10.00
Class 4	9-53	17.0	-20.03				
Class 5	8-55	14.5	-12.40	Totals	1-42	2.4	-34.00
Class 6	0-6	0.0	-6.00				
Class 7	0-0	0.0	0.00				

JOCKEYS

	W-R	Per cent	£1 Level Stake
Jamie Spencer	11-63	17.5	+15.54
Andrea Atzeni	4-11	36.4	+3.25
Robert Winston	2-3	66.7	+4.80
Ryan Moore	2-5	40.0	0.00
Adam Kirby	1-2	50.0	+0.75
James Doyle	1-2	50.0	-0.33
Gerald Mosse	1-2	50.0	+0.75
Daniel Tudhope	1-4	25.0	+1.00
Pat Cosgrave	1-5	20.0	-3.27
Luke Morris	1-26	3.8	-22.75

COURSE RECORD

	Total W-R	Non-Hndcps 2-y-o	Non-Hndcps 3-y-o+	Hndcps 2-y-o	Hndcps 3-y-o+	Per cent	£1 Level Stake
Doncaster	5-13	1-2	1-5	0-1	3-5	38.5	+32.50
Leicester	4-10	2-2	0-1	0-0	2-7	40.0	+3.42
Newmkt (Jly)	4-15	0-3	1-5	0-0	3-7	26.7	-1.08
Brighton	3-7	1-2	0-1	0-0	2-4	42.9	-0.02
Chelmsford (A.W)	2-14	0-4	1-5	0-0	1-5	14.3	-5.00
Redcar	1-3	0-0	0-1	1-1	0-1	33.3	+2.00
Lingfield	1-4	0-0	1-3	0-0	0-1	25.0	+4.00
Bath	1-5	0-0	0-2	0-0	1-3	20.0	-3.20
Goodwood	1-5	0-0	1-3	0-0	0-2	20.0	-2.13
Haydock	1-7	0-1	1-4	0-0	0-2	14.3	-3.75
Windsor	1-7	0-1	0-3	0-0	1-3	14.3	-5.00
Yarmouth	1-9	1-6	0-1	0-0	0-2	11.1	+2.00

WINNING HORSES

Horse	Races Run	1st	2nd	3rd	£
Alwaysandforever (IRE)	8	1	3	1	7439
Ashington	6	2	3	0	17227
Coolongolook	7	2	0	2	12970
Drill	8	2	2	2	18113
Ernest Aldrich	3	1	0	0	3752
Fairlight (IRE)	5	2	0	1	15784
Faro Angel (IRE)	3	2	0	0	13197
Felix	3	1	1	1	4787
Floria Tosca (IRE)	9	2	0	3	9962
Four White Socks	5	1	1	1	5175
God Given	6	2	1	0	92437
Gorgeous Noora (IRE)	6	1	1	1	12938
Prejudice	5	1	0	1	4399
Recollect	5	1	0	1	6728
Saving Grace	6	2	1	1	10480
Stormy Road (IRE)	3	1	1	0	3752
Warsaw Road (IRE)	7	1	1	1	16173
Total winning prize-money					**£255313**
Favourites	**12-26**		**46.2%**		**2.49**

KEN CUNNINGHAM-BROWN

DANEBURY, HANTS

	No. of Hrs	Races Run	1st	2nd	3rd	Unpl	Per cent	£1 Level Stake
2-y-o	*2*	*2*	*0*	*0*	*0*	*2*	*0.0*	*-2.00*
3-y-o	*1*	*2*	*0*	*0*	*0*	*2*	*0.0*	*-2.00*
4-y-o+	*9*	*88*	*4*	*16*	*8*	*60*	*4.5*	*-43.00*
Totals	**12**	**92**	**4**	**16**	**8**	**64**	**4.3**	**-47.00**
2017	*12*	*66*	*3*	*5*	*7*	*51*	*4.5*	*-38.00*
2016	*8*	*50*	*5*	*5*	*2*	*38*	*10.0*	*-1.00*

JOCKEYS

	W-R	Per cent	£1 Level Stake
Jason Watson	2-7	28.6	+15.50
Joshua Bryan	1-7	14.3	-1.50
Hector Crouch	1-18	5.6	-1.00

COURSE RECORD

	Total W-R	Non-Hndcps 2-y-o	Non-Hndcps 3-y-o+	Hndcps 2-y-o	Hndcps 3-y-o+	Per cent	£1 Level Stake
Bath	2-13	0-0	0-0	0-0	2-13	15.4	0.00
Sandown	1-1	0-0	0-0	0-0	1-1	100.0	+14.00
Lingfield (A.W)	1-16	0-0	0-2	0-0	1-14	6.3	+1.00

WINNING HORSES

Horse	Races Run	1st	2nd	3rd	£
Red Tycoon (IRE)	11	1	0	0	3752
Vincenzo Coccotti (USA)	13	1	4	0	3105
Waseem Faris (IRE)	11	2	2	0	10221
Total winning prize-money					**£17078**
Favourites	**0-1**		**0.0%**		**-1.00**

PAUL D'ARCY

NEWMARKET, SUFFOLK

	No. of Hrs	Races Run	1st	2nd	3rd	Unpl	Per cent	£1 Level Stake
2-y-o	*2*	*12*	*0*	*0*	*3*	*9*	*0.0*	*-12.00*

3-y-o	*7*	*25*	*3*	*1*	*1*	*20*	*12.0*	*+12.00*
4-y-o+	*7*	*23*	*3*	*1*	*5*	*14*	*13.0*	*-9.38*
Totals	**16**	**60**	**6**	**2**	**9**	**43**	**10.0**	**-9.38**
2017	*15*	*102*	*4*	*10*	*10*	*78*	*3.9*	*-70.00*
2016	*15*	*71*	*7*	*7*	*4*	*53*	*9.9*	*-35.75*

JOCKEYS

	W-R	Per cent	£1 Level Stake
William Carson	2-13	15.4	+19.00
Sean Levey	1-2	50.0	+1.25
Tim Clark	1-5	20.0	0.00
Luke Morris	1-5	20.0	-2.63
Adam Kirby	1-6	16.7	+2.00

COURSE RECORD

	Total W-R	Non-Hndcps 2-y-o	3-y-o+	Hndcps 2-y-o	3-y-o+	Per cent	£1 Level Stake
Windsor	1-1	0-0	0-0	0-0	1-1	100.0	+2.25
Newmkt (Jly)	1-1	0-0	0-0	0-0	1-1	100.0	+10.00
Ascot	1-4	0-0	0-1	0-0	1-3	25.0	+4.00
Lingfield (A.W)	1-4	0-1	0-0	0-0	1-3	25.0	+17.00
Wolvhptn (A.W)	1-9	0-1	1-1	0-1	0-6	11.1	-6.63
Kempton (A.W)	1-10	0-1	0-1	0-1	1-7	10.0	-5.00

WINNING HORSES

Horse	Races Run	1st	2nd	3rd	£
Nampara	7	2	0	0	7633
Shadow Warrior	7	1	0	3	5531
*Soar Above	1	1	0	0	3105
Spring Loaded (IRE)	5	1	0	1	62250
*Unforgiving Minute	1	1	0	0	3105
Total winning prize-money					**£81624**
Favourites	**2-3**		**66.7%**		**2.63**

LUKE DACE

PULBOROUGH, W SUSSEX

	No. of Hrs	Races Run	1st	2nd	3rd	Unpl	Per cent	£1 Level Stake
2-y-o	*3*	*13*	*0*	*0*	*1*	*12*	*0.0*	*-13.00*
3-y-o	*2*	*9*	*0*	*0*	*0*	*9*	*0.0*	*-9.00*
4-y-o+	*2*	*24*	*4*	*3*	*0*	*17*	*16.7*	*-5.13*
Totals	**7**	**46**	**4**	**3**	**1**	**38**	**8.7**	**-27.13**
2017	*4*	*20*	*1*	*3*	*2*	*14*	*5.0*	*-3.00*
2016	*7*	*37*	*4*	*4*	*0*	*29*	*10.8*	*+2.00*

JOCKEYS

	W-R	Per cent	£1 Level Stake
Poppy Bridgwater	1-1	100.0	+5.00
Nicola Currie	1-3	33.3	-0.13
Silvestre De Sousa	1-4	25.0	0.00
Nicky Mackay	1-5	20.0	+1.00

COURSE RECORD

	Total W-R	Non-Hndcps 2-y-o	3-y-o+	Hndcps 2-y-o	3-y-o+	Per cent	£1 Level Stake
Chester	1-1	0-0	0-0	0-0	1-1	100.0	+5.00
Newmkt (Jly)	1-1	0-0	0-0	0-0	1-1	100.0	+5.00
Lingfield	1-2	0-0	0-0	0-0	1-2	50.0	+2.00
Salisbury	1-3	0-0	0-0	0-1	1-2	33.3	-0.13

WINNING HORSES

Horse	Races Run	1st	2nd	3rd	£
Ravenous	14	2	3	0	14399
The Secrets Out	10	2	0	0	8280
Total winning prize-money					**£22679**
Favourites	**1-1**		**100.0%**		**1.88**

KEITH DALGLEISH

CARLUKE, S LANARKS

	No. of Hrs	Races Run	1st	2nd	3rd	Unpl	Per cent	£1 Level Stake
2-y-o	*29*	*132*	*21*	*21*	*14*	*76*	*15.9*	*+51.15*
3-y-o	*37*	*206*	*22*	*12*	*29*	*142*	*10.7*	*+24.76*
4-y-o+	*59*	*397*	*30*	*37*	*49*	*281*	*7.6*	*-172.50*
Totals	**125**	**735**	**73**	**70**	**92**	**499**	**9.9**	**-96.59**
2017	*129*	*815*	*86*	*97*	*88*	*540*	*10.6*	*-259.17*
2016	*108*	*664*	*82*	*86*	*60*	*434*	*12.3*	*-96.56*

BY MONTH

2-y-o	W-R	Per cent	£1 Level Stake	**3-y-o**	W-R	Per cent	£1 Level Stake
January	0-0	0.0	0.00	January	3-6	50.0	+18.50
February	0-0	0.0	0.00	February	1-2	50.0	-0.47
March	0-1	0.0	-1.00	March	0-3	0.0	-3.00
April	0-2	0.0	-2.00	April	0-12	0.0	-12.00
May	0-7	0.0	-7.00	May	1-17	5.9	-5.00
June	2-15	13.3	0.00	June	2-35	5.7	-23.00
July	3-12	25.0	-0.58	July	4-31	12.9	-13.65
August	4-28	14.3	-11.65	August	2-28	7.1	-8.13
September	3-27	11.1	-5.67	September	3-23	13.0	+22.50
October	6-25	24.0	+28.42	October	3-29	10.3	+31.00
November	1-9	11.1	+25.00	November	1-12	8.3	-7.00
December	2-6	33.3	+25.63	December	2-8	25.0	+25.00

4-y-o+	W-R	Per cent	£1 Level Stake	**Totals**	W-R	Per cent	£1 Level Stake
January	1-20	5.0	-15.00	January	4-26	15.4	+3.50
February	0-16	0.0	-16.00	February	1-18	5.6	-16.47
March	1-26	3.8	-23.00	March	1-30	3.3	-27.00
April	3-15	20.0	+37.00	April	3-29	10.3	+23.00
May	3-63	4.8	-48.00	May	4-87	4.6	-60.00
June	2-73	2.7	-64.25	June	6-123	4.9	-87.25
July	7-58	12.1	-30.08	July	14-101	13.9	-44.31
August	6-42	14.3	+16.00	August	12-98	12.2	-3.78
September	3-39	7.7	-15.00	September	9-89	10.1	+1.83
October	3-30	10.0	-4.67	October	12-84	14.3	+54.75

	W-R	Per cent	£1 Level Stake		W-R	Per cent	£1 Level Stake
November	0-7	0.0	-7.00	November	2-28	7.1	-14.00
December	1-8	12.5	-2.50	December	5-22	22.7	+22.50

DISTANCE

2-y-o	W-R	Per cent	£1 Level Stake	3-y-o	W-R	Per cent	£1 Level Stake
5f-6f	11-99	11.1	-12.61	5f-6f	5-48	10.4	-18.47
7f-8f	9-30	30.0	+60.76	7f-8f	8-94	8.5	-27.25
9f-13f	1-3	33.3	+3.00	9f-13f	9-60	15.0	+74.47
14f+	0-0	0.0	0.00	14f+	0-4	0.0	-4.00

4-y-o+	W-R	Per cent	£1 Level Stake	Totals	W-R	Per cent	£1 Level Stake
5f-6f	3-44	6.8	-19.17	5f-6f	19-191	9.9	-50.25
7f-8f	13-155	8.4	-77.17	7f-8f	30-279	10.8	-43.66
9f-13f	13-162	8.0	-53.17	9f-13f	23-225	10.2	+24.30
14f+	1-36	2.8	-23.00	14f+	1-40	2.5	-27.00

TYPE OF RACE

Non-Handicaps	W-R	Per cent	£1 Level Stake	Handicaps	W-R	Per cent	£1 Level Stake
2-y-o	16-95	16.8	+41.42	2-y-o	5-37	13.5	+9.73
3-y-o	3-36	8.3	-7.00	3-y-o	19-170	11.2	+31.76
4-y-o+	1-16	6.3	-9.00	4-y-o+	29-381	7.6	-163.50

RACE CLASS

	W-R	Per cent	£1 Level Stake
Class 1	2-19	10.5	-3.00
Class 2	2-66	3.0	-48.00
Class 3	4-55	7.3	-5.00
Class 4	17-157	10.8	-17.46
Class 5	30-263	11.4	+12.81
Class 6	18-175	10.3	-35.94
Class 7	0-0	0.0	0.00

FIRST TIME OUT

	W-R	Per cent	£1 Level Stake
2-y-o	2-29	6.9	+14.00
3-y-o	3-37	8.1	-11.00
4-y-o+	2-59	3.4	-50.00
Totals	7-125	5.6	-47.00

JOCKEYS

	W-R	Per cent	£1 Level Stake
Callum Rodriguez	17-51	33.3	+104.78
Connor Beasley	15-128	11.7	+13.93
Joe Fanning	9-91	9.9	-14.08
Rowan Scott	7-92	7.6	-40.33
Phillip Makin	4-92	4.3	-65.92
Graham Lee	3-48	6.3	+31.00
P J McDonald	2-5	40.0	+1.38
Andrew Breslin	2-5	40.0	+12.00
James Sullivan	2-12	16.7	+5.00
Jason Hart	2-16	12.5	+3.00
Paul Mulrennan	2-16	12.5	-7.47
Dougie Costello	2-19	10.5	-8.00
Adam Kirby	1-3	33.3	-0.38
Gavin Ashton	1-3	33.3	+2.00
Paul Hanagan	1-3	33.3	+1.00
Silvestre De Sousa	1-5	20.0	0.00
Tony Hamilton	1-10	10.0	-2.00
Andrew Mullen	1-17	5.9	-13.50

COURSE RECORD

	Total W-R	Non-Hndcps 2-y-o	Non-Hndcps 3-y-o+	Hndcps 2-y-o	Hndcps 3-y-o+	Per cent	£1 Level Stake
Ayr	13-135	4-16	2-8	0-7	7-104	9.6	-16.94
Hamilton	11-111	2-19	0-4	0-5	9-83	9.9	-34.13
Musselburgh	10-95	2-9	0-2	2-8	6-76	10.5	-48.52
Newcastle (A.W)	7-72	1-11	1-5	0-2	5-54	9.7	-15.70
Thirsk	6-21	1-2	0-4	0-1	5-14	28.6	+45.46
Catterick	5-23	1-3	1-2	0-3	3-15	21.7	+51.33
Redcar	4-17	3-8	0-2	0-1	1-6	23.5	+44.00
Southwell (A.W)	4-31	0-2	0-2	0-1	4-26	12.9	+3.03
Wolvhptn (A.W)	4-46	1-3	0-1	0-1	3-41	8.7	-26.75
Carlisle	2-40	1-5	0-3	0-0	1-32	5.0	-28.00
Kempton (A.W)	1-4	0-1	0-0	1-2	0-1	25.0	+25.00
Newmarket	1-6	0-1	0-1	1-1	0-3	16.7	-1.00
Chelmsford (A.W)	1-7	0-0	0-0	0-0	1-7	14.3	0.00
Beverley	1-9	0-2	0-0	0-0	1-7	11.1	-4.00
Lingfield (A.W)	1-12	0-1	0-0	1-2	0-9	8.3	-9.38
Doncaster	1-13	0-0	0-0	0-0	1-13	7.7	-1.00
Ripon	1-18	0-3	0-3	0-0	1-12	5.6	-5.00

WINNING HORSES

Horse	Races Run	1st	2nd	3rd	£
Acker Bilk (IRE)*	5	2	2	0	3752
Alabanza	7	2	1	2	7633
Beechwood Ella (IRE)	2	1	0	0	5757
Beechwood Izzy (IRE)	5	1	1	0	4528
Boston George (IRE)	2	1	0	0	3105
Caballero (IRE)	8	2	2	1	22427
Chapman Billy	3	1	0	0	6728
Che Bella (IRE)	6	1	1	0	5693
Chookie Dunedin	12	1	0	3	6728
Crazy Tornado (IRE)	13	2	0	0	6987
Dark Defender	10	1	0	2	6728
Dark Lochnagar (USA)	2	1	0	0	4528
Diamonique	7	2	1	1	11451
El Hombre	9	1	0	3	7246
Epona	7	1	2	2	3817
Euro Nightmare (IRE)	9	1	1	1	28355
Falcon's Fire (IRE)	18	1	4	2	3105
Forever A Lady (IRE)	12	1	1	2	4722
Fuente	5	1	1	1	4140
Glengarry	2	1	0	0	5531
Good Boy Alfie	7	2	0	2	11774
Handsome Bob (IRE)	14	3	0	0	11290
Howzer Black (IRE)	8	1	1	1	5434
I Could Do Better (IRE)	1	1	0	0	4528
Iconic Code	8	1	0	0	4140
Iron Sky	8	3	1	0	17208
Jack Blane	18	1	1	4	3493
Jacob Black	12	4	4	1	9574
Lang Toun Lady (IRE)	8	1	1	1	3105
Lexington Palm (IRE)	4	1	0	0	4787
Lomu (IRE)	6	1	2	0	8022
Maulesden May (IRE)	7	1	1	1	4399
Mirsaale	5	1	0	1	18675

Horse	Races Run	1st	2nd	3rd	£
Mixboy (FR)	5	1	1	0	6728
Morticia	6	1	1	0	4787
Picture Painter (IRE)*	4	1	1	1	3105
Qasr	7	1	0	1	3170
Ray Purchase	5	2	1	2	6210
Rita's Man (IRE)*	8	1	1	1	4033
Riverside Walk	4	1	0	1	4464
Rock N Rolla (IRE)	7	2	0	1	8022
Saint Equiano	6	1	1	1	6728
Starplex*	5	1	0	0	9704
Summer Daydream (IRE)	3	2	0	0	103447
Theatre Of War (IRE)	6	1	3	1	3105
Tough Remedy (IRE)	7	3	0	1	14814
Universal Gleam	5	1	1	1	4140
Valkenburg	6	1	0	1	3493
War Department (IRE)	15	2	2	0	7504
What's The Story	8	1	0	1	9704
Woodside Wonder	13	3	3	1	14102
Zoravan (USA)	20	1	2	3	4140
Total winning prize-money					**£480790**
Favourites	**29-100**		**29.0%**		**-32.48**

VICTOR DARTNALL

BRAYFORD, DEVON

	No. of Hrs	Races Run	1st	2nd	3rd	Unpl	Per cent	£1 Level Stake
2-y-o	*0*	*0*	*0*	*0*	*0*	*0*	*0.0*	*0.00*
3-y-o	*1*	*2*	*0*	*0*	*0*	*2*	*0.0*	*-2.00*
4-y-o+	*1*	*8*	*1*	*2*	*1*	*4*	*12.5*	*-3.50*
Totals	**2**	**10**	**1**	**2**	**1**	**6**	**10.0**	**-5.50**
2017	*3*	*12*	*1*	*1*	*0*	*10*	*8.3*	*+22.00*
2016	*3*	*15*	*2*	*4*	*1*	*8*	*13.3*	*+1.25*

JOCKEYS

	W-R	Per cent	£1 Level Stake
William Cox	1-7	14.3	-2.50

COURSE RECORD

	Total W-R	Non-Hndcps 2-y-o	Non-Hndcps 3-y-o+	Hndcps 2-y-o	Hndcps 3-y-o+	Per cent	£1 Level Stake
Kempton (A.W)	1-5	0-0	0-0	0-0	1-5	20.0	-0.50

WINNING HORSES

Horse	Races Run	1st	2nd	3rd	£
Howardian Hills (IRE)	8	1	2	1	3105
Total winning prize-money					**£3105**
Favourites	**2-9**		**22.2%**		**-3.50**

TOM DASCOMBE

MALPAS, CHESHIRE

	No. of Hrs	Races Run	1st	2nd	3rd	Unpl	Per cent	£1 Level Stake
2-y-o	*39*	*199*	*37*	*29*	*41*	*92*	*18.6*	*+80.79*
3-y-o	*33*	*202*	*24*	*24*	*22*	*132*	*11.9*	*+43.99*
4-y-o+	*15*	*93*	*16*	*13*	*3*	*61*	*17.2*	*+7.47*
Totals	**87**	**494**	**77**	**66**	**66**	**285**	**15.6**	**+132.25**
2017	*109*	*506*	*59*	*59*	*51*	*337*	*11.7*	*-158.52*
2016	*105*	*569*	*75*	*62*	*58*	*373*	*13.2*	*+14.80*

BY MONTH

2-y-o	W-R	Per cent	£1 Level Stake	3-y-o	W-R	Per cent	£1 Level Stake
January	0-0	0.0	0.00	January	0-2	0.0	-2.00
February	0-0	0.0	0.00	February	0-2	0.0	-2.00
March	0-0	0.0	0.00	March	1-1	100.0	+1.38
April	2-9	22.2	-0.92	April	3-16	18.8	+0.67
May	2-18	11.1	-10.50	May	4-32	12.5	+6.50
June	3-23	13.0	-6.25	June	4-35	11.4	-19.56
July	6-32	18.8	+0.91	July	4-32	12.5	-7.75
August	8-37	21.6	-1.27	August	4-27	14.8	+90.75
September	7-48	14.6	+76.88	September	2-25	8.0	-12.00
October	9-25	36.0	+28.94	October	2-23	8.7	-5.00
November	0-6	0.0	-6.00	November	0-5	0.0	-5.00
December	0-1	0.0	-1.00	December	0-2	0.0	-2.00

4-y-o+	W-R	Per cent	£1 Level Stake	Totals	W-R	Per cent	£1 Level Stake
January	3-8	37.5	+23.67	January	3-10	30.0	+21.67
February	3-8	37.5	+3.73	February	3-10	30.0	+1.73
March	1-9	11.1	-5.00	March	2-10	20.0	-3.62
April	3-7	42.9	+13.00	April	8-32	25.0	+12.75
May	1-16	6.3	-14.00	May	7-66	10.6	-18.00
June	1-13	7.7	-7.00	June	8-71	11.3	-32.81
July	0-5	0.0	-5.00	July	10-69	14.5	-11.84
August	1-11	9.1	0.00	August	13-75	17.3	+89.48
September	0-6	0.0	-6.00	September	9-79	11.4	+58.88
October	0-2	0.0	-2.00	October	11-50	22.0	+21.94
November	0-1	0.0	-1.00	November	0-12	0.0	-6.00
December	3-7	42.9	+7.07	December	3-10	30.0	+5.07

DISTANCE

2-y-o	W-R	Per cent	£1 Level Stake	3-y-o	W-R	Per cent	£1 Level Stake
5f-6f	22-127	17.3	-26.42	5f-6f	2-37	5.4	-24.56
7f-8f	15-72	20.8	+107.21	7f-8f	7-84	8.3	-42.25
9f-13f	0-0	0.0	0.00	9f-13f	15-73	20.5	+118.79
14f+	0-0	0.0	0.00	14f+	0-8	0.0	-8.00

4-y-o+	W-R	Per cent	£1 Level Stake	Totals	W-R	Per cent	£1 Level Stake
5f-6f	9-27	33.3	+32.07	5f-6f	33-191	17.3	-18.91
7f-8f	5-40	12.5	-15.61	7f-8f	27-196	13.8	+49.35
9f-13f	2-26	7.7	-9.00	9f-13f	17-99	17.2	+109.79
14f+	0-0	0.0	0.00	14f+	0-8	0.0	-8.00

TYPE OF RACE

Non-Handicaps	W-R	Per cent	£1 Level Stake	Handicaps	W-R	Per cent	£1 Level Stake
2-y-o	25-140	17.9	+72.63	2-y-o	12-59	20.3	+8.17
3-y-o	10-53	18.9	+105.99	3-y-o	14-149	9.4	-62.00
4-y-o+	8-20	40.0	+8.47	4-y-o+	8-73	11.0	-1.00

RACE CLASS

	W-R	Per cent	£1 Level Stake
Class 1	5-30	16.7	+1.63
Class 2	11-67	16.4	-14.70
Class 3	11-60	18.3	+11.87
Class 4	26-169	15.4	-46.51
Class 5	20-142	14.1	+188.02
Class 6	4-26	15.4	-8.06
Class 7	0-0	0.0	0.00

FIRST TIME OUT

	W-R	Per cent	£1 Level Stake
2-y-o	5-39	12.8	-13.42
3-y-o	4-33	12.1	+1.38
4-y-o+	5-15	33.3	+23.67
Totals	14-87	16.1	+11.63

JOCKEYS

	W-R	Per cent	£1 Level Stake
Richard Kingscote	42-275	15.3	-71.28
Martin Harley	7-31	22.6	+32.50
Paddy Pilley	6-42	14.3	+84.33
Alistair Rawlinson	5-35	14.3	+0.50
P J McDonald	4-11	36.4	+19.50
Liam Jones	4-25	16.0	-0.75
David Probert	2-6	33.3	+101.50
Franny Norton	2-7	28.6	+7.00
Elisha Whittington	2-13	15.4	-4.00
Robert Winston	1-2	50.0	-0.56
Hector Crouch	1-3	33.3	+5.00
Ben Curtis	1-5	20.0	-2.50

COURSE RECORD

	Total W-R	Non-Hndcps 2-y-o	Non-Hndcps 3-y-o+	Hndcps 2-y-o	Hndcps 3-y-o+	Per cent	£1 Level Stake
Wolvhptn (A.W)	18-96	3-19	7-16	0-6	8-55	18.8	+112.80
Haydock	16-96	7-25	3-15	2-9	4-47	16.7	+88.70
Chester	7-66	4-23	1-5	0-7	2-31	10.6	-32.50
Lingfield (A.W)	6-16	0-0	3-10	0-0	3-6	37.5	+23.61
Newbury	4-10	2-3	0-0	0-1	2-6	40.0	+13.25
York	4-20	1-7	1-1	2-4	0-8	20.0	+5.20
Redcar	3-9	2-4	0-0	0-1	1-4	33.3	+3.91
Nottingham	3-10	0-4	0-0	3-4	0-2	30.0	+7.83
Beverley	2-5	0-3	0-0	1-1	1-1	40.0	+4.00
Bath	2-6	1-4	0-0	0-0	1-2	33.3	-0.25
Ripon	2-9	1-4	0-1	1-2	0-2	22.2	-2.83
Sandown	2-13	1-5	0-1	1-2	0-5	15.4	-3.00
Ayr	1-3	0-1	0-0	1-1	0-1	33.3	+3.50
Chepstow	1-3	1-2	0-0	0-0	0-1	33.3	-1.60
Newcastle (A.W)	1-5	0-1	1-3	0-0	0-1	20.0	+12.00
Ascot	1-7	1-4	0-1	0-0	0-2	14.3	+0.50
Thirsk	1-8	0-1	1-3	0-1	0-3	12.5	-5.00
Goodwood	1-10	0-2	0-1	1-2	0-5	10.0	-2.00
Newmarket	1-11	1-5	0-2	0-2	0-2	9.1	-7.25
Doncaster	1-21	0-6	1-5	0-1	0-9	4.8	-18.63

WINNING HORSES

Horse	Races Run	1st	2nd	3rd	£
Arcanada (IRE)	9	3	0	1	35627
Arthur Kitt	4	2	1	0	57508
Barnaby Brook (CAN)*	6	1	4	0	3105
Barristan The Bold	8	2	1	2	12321
Big Time Maybe (IRE)*	6	1	2	1	3105
Blyton	12	3	4	2	25876
Calder Prince (IRE)	7	1	0	0	7246
Celestial Force (IRE)	5	2	0	0	10609
Charlie D (USA)	9	2	1	3	9283
Dance On The Day (IRE)	5	2	1	0	9704
*Doctor Sardonicus	5	2	0	0	19131
Dragons Tail (IRE)	12	1	1	1	11828
Drogon (IRE)	6	1	2	1	6469
Epaulement (IRE)	8	2	4	0	12809
Finniston Farm	9	1	2	0	8715
Finoah (IRE)	11	1	2	5	4528
Fire Diamond	9	1	1	0	3752
Five Angels (IRE)	6	1	0	0	3881
Five Helmets (IRE)	10	1	1	2	4033
Great Scot	4	3	0	0	26782
Iconic Choice	9	5	0	1	46412
Jackstar (IRE)	1	1	0	0	5175
Jensue (IRE)	9	1	2	0	4464
Jonah Jones (IRE)	4	2	0	1	16173
Kachy	8	4	1	1	61625
Light My Fire (IRE)	4	2	1	1	7633
Lola's Theme	6	2	1	0	26575
Metatron (IRE)	2	1	0	1	4140
New Day Dawn (IRE)	5	1	1	0	4852
No I'm Easy (IRE)	9	1	1	0	7116
Poppy Love	7	1	0	1	3105
Proschema (IRE)	8	2	1	1	13456
Quantatmental (IRE)	9	3	0	1	11774
Rajinsky (IRE)	5	1	1	2	4528
Red Force One	8	3	0	2	17143
Reflektor (IRE)	5	2	0	0	19074
Sha La La La Lee	6	1	2	0	3752
She Can Boogie (IRE)	9	3	1	2	21830
Silver Character (IRE)	9	1	1	0	3752
Sir Victor (IRE)	7	2	1	1	9833
Slowmo (IRE)	6	1	0	2	5434
Teodoro (IRE)	5	2	0	0	43167
Wild Edric	5	2	1	0	12627
Total winning prize-money					**£629952**
Favourites	**21-73**		**28.8%**		**-24.17**

TRISTAN DAVIDSON

IRTHINGTON, CUMBRIA

	No. of Hrs	Races Run	1st	2nd	3rd	Unpl	Per cent	£1 Level Stake
2-y-o	*0*	*0*	*0*	*0*	*0*	*0*	*0.0*	*0.00*
3-y-o	*1*	*1*	*0*	*0*	*0*	*1*	*0.0*	*-1.00*
4-y-o+	*3*	*14*	*6*	*4*	*2*	*2*	*42.9*	*+19.50*
Totals	**4**	**15**	**6**	**4**	**2**	**3**	**40.0**	**+18.50**
2017	*0*							
2016	*0*							

JOCKEYS

	W-R	Per cent	£1 Level Stake
Jason Hart	3-4	75.0	+18.50
Rachel Richardson	3-6	50.0	+5.00

COURSE RECORD

	Total W-R	Non-Hndcps 2-y-o	Non-Hndcps 3-y-o+	Hndcps 2-y-o	Hndcps 3-y-o+	Per cent	£1 Level Stake
Carlisle	2-3	0-0	0-0	0-0	2-3	66.7	+6.00
Beverley	1-1	0-0	0-0	0-0	1-1	100.0	+1.00
Hamilton	1-1	0-0	0-0	0-0	1-1	100.0	+2.00
Newcastle (A.W)	1-1	0-0	0-0	0-0	1-1	100.0	+5.50
Ayr	1-2	0-0	0-0	0-0	1-2	50.0	+11.00

WINNING HORSES

Horse	Races Run	1st	2nd	3rd	£
*Island Song (IRE)	6	5	1	0	18049
*Rubenesque (IRE)	5	1	1	2	4205
Total winning prize-money					**£22254**
Favourites	**8-16**		**50.0%**		**3.67**

JOHN DAVIES

PIERCEBRIDGE, DURHAM

	No. of Hrs	Races Run	1st	2nd	3rd	Unpl	Per cent	£1 Level Stake
2-y-o	*2*	*8*	*0*	*0*	*2*	*6*	*0.0*	*-8.00*
3-y-o	*2*	*8*	*0*	*0*	*2*	*6*	*0.0*	*-8.00*
4-y-o+	*7*	*38*	*4*	*2*	*7*	*25*	*10.5*	*-20.00*
Totals	**11**	**54**	**4**	**2**	**11**	**37**	**7.4**	**-36.00**
2017	*15*	*67*	*8*	*6*	*6*	*47*	*11.9*	*-32.04*
2016	*16*	*71*	*8*	*2*	*10*	*50*	*11.3*	*+7.50*

JOCKEYS

	W-R	Per cent	£1 Level Stake
Kevin Stott	2-2	100.0	+5.50
Phillip Makin	1-8	12.5	-3.50
Sam James	1-33	3.0	-27.00

COURSE RECORD

	Total W-R	Non-Hndcps 2-y-o	Non-Hndcps 3-y-o+	Hndcps 2-y-o	Hndcps 3-y-o+	Per cent	£1 Level Stake
Newcastle (A.W)	2-17	0-2	0-3	0-1	2-11	11.8	-9.50
Wetherby	1-4	0-0	0-0	0-0	1-4	25.0	+2.00
Thirsk	1-8	0-0	0-0	0-0	1-8	12.5	-3.50

WINNING HORSES

Horse	Races Run	1st	2nd	3rd	£
Alfred Richardson	10	3	0	3	14717
Mango Chutney	8	1	1	3	3752
Total winning prize-money					**£18469**
Favourites	**1-2**		**50.0%**		**1.00**

DOMINIC FFRENCH DAVIS

LAMBOURN, BERKS

	No. of Hrs	Races Run	1st	2nd	3rd	Unpl	Per cent	£1 Level Stake
2-y-o	*0*	*0*	*0*	*0*	*0*	*0*	*0.0*	*0.00*
3-y-o	*7*	*31*	*1*	*5*	*2*	*23*	*3.2*	*-16.00*
4-y-o+	*9*	*60*	*9*	*7*	*5*	*38*	*15.0*	*+4.00*
Totals	**16**	**91**	**10**	**12**	**7**	**61**	**11.0**	**-12.00**
2017	*10*	*65*	*2*	*5*	*11*	*47*	*3.1*	*-20.00*
2016	*10*	*69*	*9*	*7*	*6*	*47*	*13.0*	*+6.63*

BY MONTH

2-y-o	W-R	Per cent	£1 Level Stake
January	0-0	0.0	0.00
February	0-0	0.0	0.00
March	0-0	0.0	0.00
April	0-0	0.0	0.00
May	0-0	0.0	0.00
June	0-0	0.0	0.00
July	0-0	0.0	0.00
August	0-0	0.0	0.00
September	0-0	0.0	0.00
October	0-0	0.0	0.00
November	0-0	0.0	0.00
December	0-0	0.0	0.00

3-y-o	W-R	Per cent	£1 Level Stake
January	0-0	0.0	0.00
February	0-0	0.0	0.00
March	0-0	0.0	0.00
April	0-0	0.0	0.00
May	0-2	0.0	-2.00
June	0-3	0.0	-3.00
July	0-4	0.0	-4.00
August	0-4	0.0	-4.00
September	0-6	0.0	-6.00
October	0-7	0.0	-7.00
November	0-1	0.0	-1.00
December	1-4	25.0	+11.00

4-y-o+	W-R	Per cent	£1 Level Stake
January	1-6	16.7	+7.00
February	0-4	0.0	-4.00
March	0-2	0.0	-2.00
April	0-2	0.0	-2.00
May	1-5	20.0	-0.50
June	0-7	0.0	-7.00
July	3-8	37.5	+11.50
August	2-9	22.2	+4.00
September	1-6	16.7	-0.50
October	0-7	0.0	-7.00
November	1-3	33.3	+5.50
December	0-1	0.0	-1.00

Totals	W-R	Per cent	£1 Level Stake
January	1-6	16.7	+7.00
February	0-4	0.0	-4.00
March	0-2	0.0	-2.00
April	0-2	0.0	-2.00
May	1-7	14.3	-2.50
June	0-10	0.0	-10.00
July	3-12	25.0	+7.50
August	2-13	15.4	0.00
September	1-12	8.3	-6.50
October	0-14	0.0	-14.00
November	1-4	25.0	+4.50
December	1-5	20.0	+10.00

DISTANCE

2-y-o	W-R	Per cent	£1 Level Stake
5f-6f	0-0	0.0	0.00
7f-8f	0-0	0.0	0.00
9f-13f	0-0	0.0	0.00
14f+	0-0	0.0	0.00

3-y-o	W-R	Per cent	£1 Level Stake
5f-6f	1-5	20.0	+10.00
7f-8f	0-8	0.0	-8.00
9f-13f	0-17	0.0	-17.00
14f+	0-1	0.0	-1.00

4-y-o+	W-R	Per cent	£1 Level Stake
5f-6f	3-17	17.6	+11.00
7f-8f	4-13	30.8	+12.50
9f-13f	2-28	7.1	-17.50
14f+	0-2	0.0	-2.00

Totals	W-R	Per cent	£1 Level Stake
5f-6f	4-22	18.2	+21.00
7f-8f	4-21	19.0	+4.50
9f-13f	2-45	4.4	-34.50
14f+	0-3	0.0	-3.00

TYPE OF RACE

Non-Handicaps	W-R	Per cent	£1 Level Stake	Handicaps	W-R	Per cent	£1 Level Stake
2-y-o	0-0	0.0	0.00	2-y-o	0-0	0.0	0.00
3-y-o	0-12	0.0	-12.00	3-y-o	1-19	5.3	-4.00
4-y-o+	0-0	0.0	0.00	4-y-o+	9-60	15.0	+4.00

RACE CLASS

	W-R	Per cent	£1 Level Stake
Class 1	0-0	0.0	0.00
Class 2	0-7	0.0	-7.00
Class 3	1-6	16.7	-0.50
Class 4	3-18	16.7	+6.50
Class 5	3-37	8.1	-13.50
Class 6	2-21	9.5	-10.50
Class 7	1-2	50.0	+13.00

FIRST TIME OUT

	W-R	Per cent	£1 Level Stake
2-y-o	0-0	0.0	0.00
3-y-o	0-7	0.0	-7.00
4-y-o+	1-9	11.1	+2.00
Totals	1-16	6.3	-5.00

JOCKEYS

	W-R	Per cent	£1 Level Stake
Liam Keniry	3-13	23.1	+9.00
J F Egan	2-14	14.3	-3.00
Rob Hornby	2-20	10.0	-8.50
Luke Morris	1-1	100.0	+7.50
Fergus Sweeney	1-1	100.0	+14.00
Poppy Bridgwater	1-4	25.0	+7.00

COURSE RECORD

	Total W-R	Non-Hndcps 2-y-o	Non-Hndcps 3-y-o+	Hndcps 2-y-o	Hndcps 3-y-o+	Per cent	£1 Level Stake
Chelmsford (A.W)	3-11	0-0	0-1	0-0	3-10	27.3	+17.00
Lingfield (A.W)	2-10	0-0	0-2	0-0	2-8	20.0	+11.50
Lingfield	1-3	0-0	0-1	0-0	1-2	33.3	+1.50
Newbury	1-5	0-0	0-0	0-0	1-5	20.0	-3.00
Sandown	1-6	0-0	0-0	0-0	1-6	16.7	-0.50
Kempton (A.W)	1-11	0-0	0-2	0-0	1-9	9.1	0.00
Wolvhptn (A.W)	1-13	0-0	0-1	0-0	1-12	7.7	-6.50

WINNING HORSES

Horse	Races Run	1st	2nd	3rd	£
Anonymous John (IRE)	17	3	2	2	13035
Distant Applause (IRE)	4	1	0	1	2911
Majboor (IRE)	6	4	1	0	27904
Midnight Mood	9	2	3	1	6598
Total winning prize-money					**£50448**
Favourites	**1-4**		**25.0%**		**-2.00**

GEOFFREY DEACON

COMPTON, BERKS

	No. of Hrs	Races Run	1st	2nd	3rd	Unpl	Per cent	£1 Level Stake
2-y-o	*0*	*0*	*0*	*0*	*0*	*0*	*0.0*	*0.00*
3-y-o	*2*	*11*	*0*	*0*	*2*	*9*	*0.0*	*-11.00*
4-y-o+	*7*	*38*	*1*	*2*	*3*	*32*	*2.6*	*-12.00*
Totals	**9**	**49**	**1**	**2**	**5**	**41**	**2.0**	**-23.00**
2017	*17*	*89*	*5*	*8*	*14*	*62*	*5.6*	*-47.00*
2016	*17*	*83*	*3*	*5*	*8*	*67*	*3.6*	*-56.50*

JOCKEYS

	W-R	Per cent	£1 Level Stake
Trevor Whelan	1-11	9.1	+15.00

COURSE RECORD

	Total W-R	Non-Hndcps 2-y-o	Non-Hndcps 3-y-o+	Hndcps 2-y-o	Hndcps 3-y-o+	Per cent	£1 Level Stake
Salisbury	1-2	0-0	0-1	0-0	1-1	50.0	+24.00

WINNING HORSES

Horse	Races Run	1st	2nd	3rd	£
Picket Line	9	1	1	0	3493
Total winning prize-money					**£3493**
Favourites	**0-0**		**0.0%**		**0.00**

DAVID DENNIS

HANLEY SWAN, WORCESTERSHIRE

	No. of Hrs	Races Run	1st	2nd	3rd	Unpl	Per cent	£1 Level Stake
2-y-o	*0*	*0*	*0*	*0*	*0*	*0*	*0.0*	*0.00*
3-y-o	*5*	*25*	*1*	*3*	*2*	*19*	*4.0*	*-18.00*
4-y-o+	*4*	*14*	*1*	*1*	*2*	*10*	*7.1*	*-7.00*
Totals	**9**	**39**	**2**	**4**	**4**	**29**	**5.1**	**-25.00**
2017	*11*	*46*	*4*	*4*	*1*	*36*	*8.7*	*-6.25*
2016	*20*	*98*	*1*	*10*	*9*	*78*	*1.0*	*-92.00*

JOCKEYS

	W-R	Per cent	£1 Level Stake
David Egan	1-3	33.3	+4.00
William Cox	1-9	11.1	-2.00

COURSE RECORD

	Total W-R	Non-Hndcps 2-y-o	Non-Hndcps 3-y-o+	Hndcps 2-y-o	Hndcps 3-y-o+	Per cent	£1 Level Stake
Brighton	1-1	0-0	0-0	0-0	1-1	100.0	+6.00
Leicester	1-3	0-0	0-0	0-0	1-3	33.3	+4.00

WINNING HORSES

Horse	Races Run	1st	2nd	3rd	£
Danecase	11	1	1	1	3752
Swissal (IRE)	10	1	1	1	3752
Total winning prize-money					**£7504**
Favourites	**1-13**		**7.7%**		**-10.75**

SCOTT DIXON

BABWORTH, NOTTS

	No. of Hrs	Races Run	1st	2nd	3rd	Unpl	Per cent	£1 Level Stake
2-y-o	*2*	*19*	*2*	*2*	*3*	*12*	*10.5*	*-11.09*
3-y-o	*13*	*81*	*8*	*8*	*11*	*54*	*9.9*	*-7.50*
4-y-o+	*24*	*227*	*14*	*26*	*18*	*168*	*6.2*	*-87.00*
Totals	**39**	**327**	**24**	**36**	**32**	**234**	**7.3**	**-105.59**
2017	*49*	*391*	*31*	*30*	*44*	*285*	*7.9*	*+3.70*
2016	*51*	*352*	*18*	*29*	*26*	*278*	*5.1*	*-138.64*

BY MONTH

2-y-o	W-R	Per cent	£1 Level Stake
January	0-0	0.0	0.00
February	0-0	0.0	0.00
March	0-1	0.0	-1.00
April	0-1	0.0	-1.00
May	0-1	0.0	-1.00
June	0-3	0.0	-3.00
July	1-2	50.0	-0.09
August	0-3	0.0	-3.00
September	0-3	0.0	-3.00
October	0-2	0.0	-2.00
November	0-0	0.0	0.00
December	1-3	33.3	+3.00

3-y-o	W-R	Per cent	£1 Level Stake
January	0-10	0.0	-10.00
February	0-5	0.0	-5.00
March	2-5	40.0	+8.50
April	1-4	25.0	+8.00
May	1-7	14.3	+10.00
June	1-7	14.3	+2.00
July	1-7	14.3	+0.50
August	0-7	0.0	-7.00
September	0-4	0.0	-4.00
October	0-7	0.0	-7.00
November	1-7	14.3	-2.50
December	1-11	9.1	-1.00

4-y-o+	W-R	Per cent	£1 Level Stake
January	3-18	16.7	+22.00
February	2-13	15.4	+7.00
March	1-25	4.0	-17.00
April	0-20	0.0	-20.00
May	2-19	10.5	+1.00
June	1-17	5.9	-12.50
July	2-25	8.0	+4.25
August	2-27	7.4	-13.25
September	0-16	0.0	-16.00
October	1-17	5.9	-12.50
November	0-17	0.0	-17.00
December	0-13	0.0	-13.00

Totals	W-R	Per cent	£1 Level Stake
January	3-28	10.7	+12.00
February	2-18	11.1	+2.00
March	3-31	9.7	-9.50
April	1-25	4.0	-13.00
May	3-27	11.1	+10.00
June	2-27	7.4	-13.50
July	4-34	11.8	+4.66
August	2-37	5.4	-23.25
September	0-23	0.0	-23.00
October	1-26	3.8	-21.50
November	1-24	4.2	-19.50
December	2-27	7.4	-14.00

DISTANCE

2-y-o	W-R	Per cent	£1 Level Stake
5f-6f	2-19	10.5	-11.09
7f-8f	0-0	0.0	0.00
9f-13f	0-0	0.0	0.00
14f+	0-0	0.0	0.00

3-y-o	W-R	Per cent	£1 Level Stake
5f-6f	4-36	11.1	-1.50
7f-8f	2-25	8.0	-0.50
9f-13f	2-18	11.1	-3.50
14f+	0-2	0.0	-2.00

4-y-o+	W-R	Per cent	£1 Level Stake
5f-6f	9-129	7.0	-44.75
7f-8f	4-71	5.6	-25.25
9f-13f	1-25	4.0	-15.00
14f+	0-2	0.0	-2.00

Totals	W-R	Per cent	£1 Level Stake
5f-6f	15-184	8.2	-57.34
7f-8f	6-96	6.3	-25.75
9f-13f	3-43	7.0	-18.50
14f+	0-4	0.0	-4.00

TYPE OF RACE

Non-Handicaps

	W-R	Per cent	£1 Level Stake
2-y-o	2-14	14.3	-6.09
3-y-o	1-18	5.6	-13.50
4-y-o+	0-5	0.0	-5.00

Handicaps

	W-R	Per cent	£1 Level Stake
2-y-o	0-5	0.0	-5.00
3-y-o	7-63	11.1	+6.00
4-y-o+	14-222	6.3	-82.00

RACE CLASS

	W-R	Per cent	£1 Level Stake
Class 1	0-5	0.0	-5.00
Class 2	0-11	0.0	-11.00
Class 3	0-15	0.0	-15.00
Class 4	3-47	6.4	-8.50
Class 5	6-95	6.3	-48.59
Class 6	15-151	9.9	-14.50
Class 7	0-3	0.0	-3.00

FIRST TIME OUT

	W-R	Per cent	£1 Level Stake
2-y-o	0-2	0.0	-2.00
3-y-o	1-13	7.7	+4.00
4-y-o+	2-24	8.3	+11.00
Totals	3-39	7.7	+13.00

JOCKEYS

	W-R	Per cent	£1 Level Stake
Kieran O'Neill	8-99	8.1	-3.59
Theodore Ladd	8-111	7.2	-54.00
Luke Morris	2-18	11.1	-2.00
Tom Eaves	1-2	50.0	+7.00
Nicola Currie	1-3	33.3	+3.00
Richard Kingscote	1-3	33.3	+14.00
James Sullivan	1-4	25.0	+5.00
Mr Gareth Newmarch	1-4	25.0	+0.50
Paddy Mathers	1-6	16.7	+1.50

COURSE RECORD

	Total W-R	Non-Hndcps 2-y-o	Non-Hndcps 3-y-o+	Hndcps 2-y-o	Hndcps 3-y-o+	Per cent	£1 Level Stake
Southwell (A.W)	11-134	1-2	1-13	0-2	9-117	8.2	-37.25
Thirsk	4-12	0-0	0-0	0-0	4-12	33.3	+22.25
Nottingham	3-24	0-0	0-1	0-0	3-23	12.5	+3.50
Wolvhptn (A.W)	2-24	0-1	0-3	0-1	2-19	8.3	-10.50
Catterick	2-25	1-2	0-0	0-0	1-23	8.0	-18.59
Redcar	1-6	0-0	0-1	0-2	1-3	16.7	+11.00
Chester	1-7	0-0	0-1	0-0	1-6	14.3	+19.00

WINNING HORSES

Horse	Races Run	1st	2nd	3rd	£
Albert Boy (IRE)	11	1	3	2	3398
Best Iamayuz	10	2	2	2	6857
Break The Silence	15	1	3	1	3493
Champagne Mondays	10	1	0	2	3493
Coiste Bodhar (IRE)	21	1	3	2	3105
Crosse Fire	24	1	5	2	5693
Deia Glory	9	1	2	1	4787
Krystallite	10	2	2	0	6210
Love Rat	10	1	2	1	3493
Optimickstickhill	12	1	1	0	3398
Pearl Noir	15	2	1	2	6767

Penny Dreadful	9	1	1	0	3398
Samovar	15	3	4	2	13908
Sans Souci Bay	13	1	1	0	5852
Sir Geoffrey (IRE)	14	1	0	0	3105
Socialites Red	13	1	0	2	3881
*Sociologist (FR)	4	1	0	0	3752
Thundercloud	8	2	0	2	6728
Total winning prize-money					**£91318**
Favourites	**4-16**		**25.0%**		**-1.34**

MICHAEL DODS

DENTON, CO DURHAM

	No. of Hrs	Races Run	1st	2nd	3rd	Unpl	Per cent	£1 Level Stake
2-y-o	*33*	*104*	*14*	*9*	*13*	*68*	*13.5*	*+25.53*
3-y-o	*28*	*143*	*17*	*16*	*11*	*98*	*11.9*	*-39.92*
4-y-o+	*27*	*198*	*21*	*26*	*28*	*122*	*10.6*	*-51.25*
Totals	**88**	**445**	**52**	**51**	**52**	**288**	**11.7**	**-65.64**
2017	*74*	*432*	*62*	*51*	*52*	*267*	*14.4*	*-40.44*
2016	*84*	*487*	*50*	*57*	*58*	*321*	*10.3*	*-148.88*

BY MONTH

2-y-o	W-R	Per cent	£1 Level Stake	3-y-o	W-R	Per cent	£1 Level Stake
January	0-0	0.0	0.00	January	0-4	0.0	-4.00
February	0-0	0.0	0.00	February	0-3	0.0	-3.00
March	0-0	0.0	0.00	March	0-2	0.0	-2.00
April	0-0	0.0	0.00	April	2-13	15.4	+2.50
May	0-3	0.0	-3.00	May	1-19	5.3	-6.00
June	0-9	0.0	-9.00	June	4-24	16.7	-5.25
July	2-15	13.3	+4.75	July	5-25	20.0	+7.33
August	6-27	22.2	+5.65	August	3-26	11.5	-10.00
September	3-21	14.3	+15.75	September	1-14	7.1	-10.50
October	1-19	5.3	-2.00	October	0-11	0.0	-11.00
November	1-7	14.3	+14.00	November	1-2	50.0	+2.00
December	1-3	33.3	-0.63	December	0-0	0.0	0.00

4-y-o+	W-R	Per cent	£1 Level Stake	Totals	W-R	Per cent	£1 Level Stake
January	1-2	50.0	+7.00	January	1-6	16.7	+3.00
February	0-1	0.0	-1.00	February	0-4	0.0	-4.00
March	0-4	0.0	-4.00	March	0-6	0.0	-6.00
April	1-21	4.8	-4.00	April	3-34	8.8	-1.50
May	1-25	4.0	-19.50	May	2-47	4.3	-28.50
June	4-29	13.8	+6.50	June	8-62	12.9	-7.75
July	4-23	17.4	-4.50	July	11-63	17.5	+7.58
August	4-33	12.1	-8.25	August	13-86	15.1	-12.60
September	4-27	14.8	-6.50	September	8-62	12.9	-1.25
October	1-23	4.3	-11.00	October	2-53	3.8	-24.00
November	0-7	0.0	-7.00	November	2-16	12.5	-5.00
December	1-3	33.3	+1.00	December	2-6	33.3	+1.00

DISTANCE

2-y-o	W-R	Per cent	£1 Level Stake	3-y-o	W-R	Per cent	£1 Level Stake
5f-6f	10-70	14.3	+5.78	5f-6f	10-61	16.4	+12.00
7f-8f	4-34	11.8	+19.75	7f-8f	7-60	11.7	-29.92
9f-13f	0-0	0.0	0.00	9f-13f	0-22	0.0	-22.00
14f+	0-0	0.0	0.00	14f+	0-0	0.0	0.00

4-y-o+	W-R	Per cent	£1 Level Stake	Totals	W-R	Per cent	£1 Level Stake
5f-6f	6-99	6.1	-62.00	5f-6f	26-230	11.3	-44.22
7f-8f	7-57	12.3	-0.75	7f-8f	18-151	11.9	-10.92
9f-13f	7-38	18.4	+12.25	9f-13f	7-60	11.7	-9.75
14f+	1-4	25.0	-0.75	14f+	1-4	25.0	-0.75

TYPE OF RACE

Non-Handicaps	W-R	Per cent	£1 Level Stake	Handicaps	W-R	Per cent	£1 Level Stake
2-y-o	12-91	13.2	+26.78	2-y-o	2-13	15.4	-1.25
3-y-o	4-34	11.8	-8.50	3-y-o	13-109	11.9	-31.42
4-y-o+	3-13	23.1	+11.50	4-y-o+	18-185	9.7	-62.75

RACE CLASS

	W-R	Per cent	£1 Level Stake
Class 1	3-8	37.5	+16.50
Class 2	3-51	5.9	-39.25
Class 3	11-45	24.4	+31.83
Class 4	9-104	8.7	-13.25
Class 5	16-168	9.5	-46.60
Class 6	10-69	14.5	-14.88
Class 7	0-0	0.0	0.00

FIRST TIME OUT

	W-R	Per cent	£1 Level Stake
2-y-o	5-33	15.2	+52.33
3-y-o	4-28	14.3	+6.00
4-y-o+	2-27	7.4	-1.00
Totals	11-88	12.5	+57.33

JOCKEYS

	W-R	Per cent	£1 Level Stake
Callum Rodriguez	25-187	13.4	-21.21
Paul Mulrennan	8-66	12.1	-16.25
Connor Beasley	6-46	13.0	+20.00
Paula Muir	5-53	9.4	-31.25
Andrew Mullen	4-57	7.0	-15.00
Franny Norton	1-1	100.0	+2.50
Ben Curtis	1-2	50.0	+6.00
Miss Sophie Dods	1-2	50.0	+19.00
Tom Eaves	1-6	16.7	-4.43

COURSE RECORD

	Total W-R	Non-Hndcps 2-y-o	Non-Hndcps 3-y-o+	Hndcps 2-y-o	Hndcps 3-y-o+	Per cent	£1 Level Stake
Ayr	9-58	2-8	2-5	0-2	5-43	15.5	-2.75
Newcastle (A.W)	7-50	3-14	2-10	0-1	2-25	14.0	-3.29
Haydock	6-20	0-1	0-1	0-0	6-18	30.0	+29.75
York	4-35	0-1	0-1	0-2	4-31	11.4	-3.17
Thirsk	4-50	0-14	0-3	1-1	3-32	8.0	-26.75
Ripon	3-21	2-4	1-3	0-1	0-13	14.3	+9.50
Carlisle	3-31	0-11	0-1	1-1	2-18	9.7	-11.00
Leicester	2-5	1-1	0-3	0-0	1-1	40.0	+5.50
Beverley	2-12	1-1	0-2	0-0	1-9	16.7	-2.75
Catterick	2-17	1-8	0-0	0-2	1-7	11.8	-10.93
Redcar	2-41	2-17	0-5	0-2	0-17	4.9	+2.00
Yarmouth	1-2	0-0	0-0	0-0	1-2	50.0	+1.75
Newmarket	1-3	0-1	1-1	0-0	0-1	33.3	+2.50
Wolvhptn (A.W)	1-4	0-1	0-0	0-0	1-3	25.0	+0.50

Ascot	1-4	0-0	1-2	0-0	0-2	25.0	+8.00
Southwell (A.W)	1-8	0-0	0-0	0-0	1-8	12.5	-4.00
Hamilton	1-19	0-2	0-3	0-0	1-14	5.3	-12.50
Pontefract	1-19	0-1	0-2	0-1	1-15	5.3	-13.00
Doncaster	1-21	0-4	0-1	0-0	1-16	4.8	-10.00

WINNING HORSES

Horse	Races Run	1st	2nd	3rd	£
Arcavallo (IRE)	7	1	0	0	6469
Archi's Affaire	3	1	0	1	22410
Bandola (IRE)	8	2	0	1	6275
Bartle Hall	4	1	0	0	3881
Billy No Mates (IRE)	5	2	0	0	8216
Boundary Lane	5	1	1	1	4140
Byron's Choice	4	3	0	0	25769
Camacho Chief (IRE)	8	2	1	1	15057
Dakota Gold	12	1	1	2	31125
Davy's Dilemma	5	1	1	2	9704
Dutch Pursuit (IRE)	2	1	0	0	3105
Flint Hill	6	1	1	0	4205
Gale Force Maya	3	1	0	0	4787
Get Knotted (IRE)	10	1	3	1	15563
Heath Charnock	1	1	0	0	3817
Intense Romance (IRE)	8	3	2	0	73282
Kings Gift (IRE)	7	1	0	1	9057
Kings Gold (IRE)	6	1	2	0	3398
Kolossus	6	1	0	1	4787
Limoncino (IRE)	1	1	0	0	3493
Mabs Cross	5	1	2	1	34026
Mecca's Spirit (IRE)	8	1	0	0	3493
Miningggold	12	1	1	3	3105
Mister Belvedere	6	2	3	0	24930
Mooltazem (IRE)	12	2	3	0	16819
Mustaqbal (IRE)	10	2	0	3	4852
Myrmidons (IRE)	1	1	0	0	5175
Proud Archi (IRE)	11	2	1	0	19412
Que Amoro (IRE)	6	2	1	1	10395
Queens Gift (IRE)	6	2	2	1	7633
Reinforced	6	1	0	1	3493
Ride The Monkey (IRE)	2	1	0	0	6469
Rumshak (IRE)	6	1	0	0	5434
Snowdon	5	1	2	0	3105
Super Major (IRE)	8	1	1	1	3398
Thirlmere	2	1	0	0	3752
Wahoo	5	2	0	0	14879
Zahraa	6	1	0	0	3752
Total winning prize-money					**£432662**
Favourites	**15-42**		**35.7%**		**11.03**

CONOR DORE

HUBBERT'S BRIDGE, LINCS

	No. of Hrs	Races Run	1st	2nd	3rd	Unpl	Per cent	£1 Level Stake
2-y-o	*5*	*14*	*1*	*0*	*0*	*13*	*7.1*	*-5.00*
3-y-o	*0*	*0*	*0*	*0*	*0*	*0*	*0.0*	*0.00*
4-y-o+	*9*	*29*	*0*	*2*	*2*	*25*	*0.0*	*-29.00*
Totals	**14**	**43**	**1**	**2**	**2**	**38**	**2.3**	**-34.00**
2017	*20*	*129*	*6*	*5*	*10*	*108*	*4.7*	*-58.88*
2016	*26*	*246*	*22*	*22*	*23*	*179*	*8.9*	*-117.45*

JOCKEYS

	W-R	Per cent	£1 Level Stake
Liam Keniry	1-7	14.3	+2.00

COURSE RECORD

	Total W-R	Non-Hndcps 2-y-o	Non-Hndcps 3-y-o+	Hndcps 2-y-o	Hndcps 3-y-o+	Per cent	£1 Level Stake
Leicester	1-1	1-1	0-0	0-0	0-0	100.0	+8.00

WINNING HORSES

Horse	Races Run	1st	2nd	3rd	£
*Knockabout Queen	3	1	0	0	3752
Total winning prize-money					**£3752**
Favourites	**0-0**		**0.0%**		**0.00**

SIMON DOW

ASHTEAD, SURREY

	No. of Hrs	Races Run	1st	2nd	3rd	Unpl	Per cent	£1 Level Stake
2-y-o	*4*	*12*	*1*	*0*	*0*	*11*	*8.3*	*-8.50*
3-y-o	*11*	*72*	*7*	*9*	*9*	*47*	*9.7*	*-29.67*
4-y-o+	*14*	*83*	*10*	*11*	*10*	*51*	*12.0*	*-28.82*
Totals	**29**	**167**	**18**	**20**	**19**	**109**	**10.8**	**-66.99**
2017	*28*	*149*	*19*	*11*	*14*	*105*	*12.8*	*+1.20*
2016	*29*	*144*	*14*	*14*	*11*	*105*	*9.7*	*-8.29*

BY MONTH

2-y-o	W-R	Per cent	£1 Level Stake	**3-y-o**	W-R	Per cent	£1 Level Stake
January	0-0	0.0	0.00	January	2-7	28.6	+1.50
February	0-0	0.0	0.00	February	2-4	50.0	+6.50
March	0-0	0.0	0.00	March	0-5	0.0	-5.00
April	0-0	0.0	0.00	April	1-4	25.0	+11.00
May	0-1	0.0	-1.00	May	0-7	0.0	-7.00
June	0-1	0.0	-1.00	June	0-6	0.0	-6.00
July	0-1	0.0	-1.00	July	1-8	12.5	-3.67
August	1-2	50.0	+1.50	August	1-11	9.1	-7.00
September	0-0	0.0	0.00	September	0-9	0.0	-9.00
October	0-3	0.0	-3.00	October	0-6	0.0	-6.00
November	0-2	0.0	-2.00	November	0-2	0.0	-2.00
December	0-2	0.0	-2.00	December	0-3	0.0	-3.00

4-y-o+	W-R	Per cent	£1 Level Stake	**Totals**	W-R	Per cent	£1 Level Stake
January	2-11	18.2	-2.25	January	4-18	22.2	-0.75
February	2-10	20.0	-2.75	February	4-14	28.6	+3.75
March	3-9	33.3	+9.35	March	3-14	21.4	+4.35
April	1-5	20.0	-0.67	April	2-9	22.2	+10.33
May	1-7	14.3	+4.00	May	1-15	6.7	-4.00
June	0-10	0.0	-10.00	June	0-17	0.0	-17.00

July	0-5	0.0	-5.00	July	1-14	7.1	-9.67
August	0-10	0.0	-10.00	August	2-23	8.7	-15.50
September	0-6	0.0	-6.00	September	0-15	0.0	-15.00
October	0-5	0.0	-5.00	October	0-14	0.0	-14.00
November	0-1	0.0	-1.00	November	0-5	0.0	-3.00
December	1-4	25.0	+0.50	December	1-9	11.1	-2.50

DISTANCE

2-y-o	W-R	Per cent	£1 Level Stake	3-y-o	W-R	Per cent	£1 Level Stake
5f-6f	0-4	0.0	-4.00	5f-6f	0-11	0.0	-11.00
7f-8f	1-8	12.5	-4.50	7f-8f	6-43	14.0	-5.00
9f-13f	0-0	0.0	0.00	9f-13f	1-18	5.6	-13.67
14f+	0-0	0.0	0.00	14f+	0-0	0.0	0.00
4-y-o+	W-R	Per cent	£1 Level Stake	**Totals**	W-R	Per cent	£1 Level Stake
5f-6f	5-28	17.9	-2.90	5f-6f	5-43	11.6	-17.90
7f-8f	1-30	3.3	-25.50	7f-8f	8-81	9.9	-35.00
9f-13f	2-22	9.1	-14.75	9f-13f	3-40	7.5	-28.42
14f+	2-3	66.7	+14.33	14f+	2-3	66.7	+14.33

TYPE OF RACE

Non-Handicaps	W-R	Per cent	£1 Level Stake	Handicaps	W-R	Per cent	£1 Level Stake
2-y-o	0-10	0.0	-10.00	2-y-o	1-2	50.0	+1.50
3-y-o	1-18	5.6	-15.00	3-y-o	6-54	11.1	-14.67
4-y-o+	1-2	50.0	+1.25	4-y-o+	9-81	11.1	-30.07

RACE CLASS / FIRST TIME OUT

	W-R	Per cent	£1 Level Stake		W-R	Per cent	£1 Level Stake
Class 1	0-1	0.0	-1.00	2-y-o	0-4	0.0	-4.00
Class 2	0-26	0.0	-26.00	3-y-o	2-11	18.2	-3.00
Class 3	1-15	6.7	-10.00	4-y-o+	2-14	14.3	+2.25
Class 4	6-39	15.4	-3.65				
Class 5	7-51	13.7	-15.33	Totals	4-29	13.8	-4.75
Class 6	4-34	11.8	-10.00				
Class 7	0-1	0.0	-1.00				

JOCKEYS

	W-R	Per cent	£1 Level Stake
Tom Marquand	7-49	14.3	-9.42
Oisin Murphy	3-12	25.0	-1.50
Luke Morris	2-7	28.6	+0.60
Adam Kirby	2-11	18.2	-2.17
Silvestre De Sousa	1-4	25.0	+11.00
Charles Bishop	1-8	12.5	-4.50
Harry Bentley	1-12	8.3	-8.00
Nicky Mackay	1-17	5.9	-6.00

COURSE RECORD

	Total W-R	Non-Hndcps 2-y-o	Non-Hndcps 3-y-o+	Hndcps 2-y-o	Hndcps 3-y-o+	Per cent	£1 Level Stake
Kempton (A.W)	8-57	0-6	1-7	0-0	7-44	14.0	-15.65
Lingfield (A.W)	4-40	0-2	1-9	0-0	3-29	10.0	-24.67
Epsom	2-16	0-0	0-0	0-0	2-16	12.5	+3.00
Brighton	1-3	0-0	0-0	0-0	1-3	33.3	+8.00
Wolvhptn (A.W)	1-5	0-0	0-0	0-0	1-5	20.0	+0.50
Windsor	1-5	0-0	0-1	0-0	1-4	20.0	-0.67
Chelmsford (A.W)	1-7	0-1	0-0	1-1	0-5	14.3	-3.50

WINNING HORSES

Horse	Races Run	1st	2nd	3rd	£
Bobby Biscuit (USA)	8	1	0	1	3881
Chica De La Noche	11	1	2	2	3105
Corazon Espinado (IRE)	13	4	3	2	22868
Dutiful Son (IRE)*	1	1	0	0	3105
El Borracho (IRE)	13	1	4	3	3752
Le Torrent	3	2	0	0	6857
Native Fighter (IRE)	10	2	3	2	10221
Ojala (IRE)	2	1	0	1	9338
Recuerdame (USA)	5	1	0	0	4787
Roundabout Magic (IRE)	17	2	3	3	6857
Sparkalot	5	2	0	1	12938
Total winning prize-money					**£87709**
Favourites	**6-17**		**35.3%**		**2.93**

DAVID W DRINKWATER

HANLEY CASTLE, WORCS

	No. of Hrs	Races Run	1st	2nd	3rd	Unpl	Per cent	£1 Level Stake
2-y-o	*0*	*0*	*0*	*0*	*0*	*0*	*0.0*	*0.00*
3-y-o	*0*	*0*	*0*	*0*	*0*	*0*	*0.0*	*0.00*
4-y-o+	*4*	*27*	*2*	*4*	*3*	*18*	*7.4*	*-14.00*
Totals	**4**	**27**	**2**	**4**	**3**	**18**	**7.4**	**-14.00**
2017	*3*	*20*	*3*	*0*	*1*	*16*	*15.0*	*-0.50*
2016	*3*	*20*	*1*	*1*	*0*	*18*	*5.0*	*-3.00*

JOCKEYS

	W-R	Per cent	£1 Level Stake
Martin Harley	1-1	100.0	+5.00
Ellie MacKenzie	1-2	50.0	+5.00

COURSE RECORD

	Total W-R	Non-Hndcps 2-y-o	Non-Hndcps 3-y-o+	Hndcps 2-y-o	Hndcps 3-y-o+	Per cent	£1 Level Stake
Lingfield	2-5	0-0	0-0	0-0	2-5	40.0	+8.00

WINNING HORSES

Horse	Races Run	1st	2nd	3rd	£
Ashpan Sam	7	1	0	1	5531
Dear Bruin (IRE)	12	1	1	1	3105
Total winning prize-money					**£8636**
Favourites	**0-2**		**0.0%**		**-2.00**

ANN DUFFIELD

CONSTABLE BURTON, N YORKS

	No. of Hrs	Races Run	1st	2nd	3rd	Unpl	Per cent	£1 Level Stake
2-y-o	*7*	*24*	*0*	*1*	*3*	*20*	*0.0*	*-24.00*
3-y-o	*13*	*72*	*4*	*9*	*7*	*52*	*5.6*	*-51.50*
4-y-o+	*12*	*81*	*11*	*8*	*10*	*52*	*13.6*	*+28.50*
Totals	**32**	**177**	**15**	**18**	**20**	**124**	**8.5**	**-47.00**
2017	*51*	*244*	*13*	*12*	*18*	*201*	*5.3*	*-72.75*
2016	*75*	*302*	*23*	*27*	*44*	*208*	*7.6*	*-167.33*

BY MONTH

2-y-o	W-R	Per cent	£1 Level Stake	**3-y-o**	W-R	Per cent	£1 Level Stake
January	0-0	0.0	0.00	January	1-3	33.3	+2.50
February	0-0	0.0	0.00	February	0-1	0.0	-1.00
March	0-0	0.0	0.00	March	0-3	0.0	-3.00
April	0-0	0.0	0.00	April	0-4	0.0	-4.00
May	0-1	0.0	-1.00	May	2-7	28.6	+3.50
June	0-1	0.0	-1.00	June	1-13	7.7	-8.50
July	0-2	0.0	-2.00	July	0-7	0.0	-7.00
August	0-7	0.0	-7.00	August	0-13	0.0	-13.00
September	0-5	0.0	-5.00	September	0-7	0.0	-7.00
October	0-4	0.0	-4.00	October	0-6	0.0	-6.00
November	0-4	0.0	-4.00	November	0-6	0.0	-6.00
December	0-0	0.0	0.00	December	0-2	0.0	-2.00

4-y-o+	W-R	Per cent	£1 Level Stake	**Totals**	W-R	Per cent	£1 Level Stake
January	1-6	16.7	+1.00	January	2-9	22.2	+3.50
February	1-2	50.0	+6.00	February	1-3	33.3	+5.00
March	1-5	20.0	-1.00	March	1-8	12.5	-4.00
April	0-3	0.0	-3.00	April	0-7	0.0	-7.00
May	0-10	0.0	-10.00	May	2-18	11.1	-7.50
June	3-11	27.3	+51.00	June	4-25	16.0	+41.50
July	3-13	23.1	+6.00	July	3-22	13.6	-3.00
August	1-12	8.3	-7.50	August	1-32	3.1	-27.50
September	0-7	0.0	-7.00	September	0-19	0.0	-19.00
October	0-6	0.0	-6.00	October	0-16	0.0	-16.00
November	1-4	25.0	+1.00	November	1-14	7.1	-5.00
December	0-2	0.0	-2.00	December	0-4	0.0	-4.00

DISTANCE

2-y-o	W-R	Per cent	£1 Level Stake	**3-y-o**	W-R	Per cent	£1 Level Stake
5f-6f	0-17	0.0	-17.00	5f-6f	2-33	6.1	21.00
7f-8f	0-7	0.0	-7.00	7f-8f	1-25	4.0	-20.50
9f-13f	0-0	0.0	0.00	9f-13f	1-13	7.7	-6.00
14f+	0-0	0.0	0.00	14f+	0-1	0.0	-1.00

4-y-o+	W-R	Per cent	£1 Level Stake	**Totals**	W-R	Per cent	£1 Level Stake
5f-6f	11-44	25.0	+65.50	5f-6f	13-94	13.8	+24.50
7f-8f	0-29	0.0	-29.00	7f-8f	1-61	1.6	-56.50
9f-13f	0-8	0.0	-8.00	9f-13f	1-21	4.8	-14.00
14f+	0-0	0.0	0.00	14f+	0-1	0.0	-1.00

TYPE OF RACE

Non-Handicaps	W-R	Per cent	£1 Level Stake	**Handicaps**	W-R	Per cent	£1 Level Stake
2-y-o	0-18	0.0	-18.00	2-y-o	0-6	0.0	-6.00
3-y-o	1-13	7.7	-9.50	3-y-o	3-59	5.1	-42.00
4-y-o+	1-4	25.0	+6.00	4-y-o+	10-77	13.0	+22.50

RACE CLASS

	W-R	Per cent	£1 Level Stake
Class 1	0-0	0.0	0.00
Class 2	0-1	0.0	-1.00
Class 3	0-2	0.0	-2.00
Class 4	1-20	5.0	-13.00
Class 5	3-61	4.9	-45.50
Class 6	11-89	12.4	+18.50
Class 7	0-4	0.0	-4.00

FIRST TIME OUT

	W-R	Per cent	£1 Level Stake
2-y-o	0-7	0.0	-7.00
3-y-o	0-13	0.0	13.00
4-y-o+	2-12	16.7	+3.00
Totals	2-32	6.3	-17.00

JOCKEYS

	W-R	Per cent	£1 Level Stake
Joe Fanning	6-51	11.8	-21.50
Franny Norton	2-18	11.1	-6.00
David Egan	1-1	100.0	+3.50
Paul Mulrennan	1-2	50.0	+3.00
Andrew Breslin	1-4	25.0	+3.00
Dougie Costello	1-6	16.7	+4.00
Connor Beasley	1-8	12.5	+43.00
Graham Lee	1-16	6.3	-10.00
Jack Garritty	1-16	6.3	-11.00

COURSE RECORD

	Total W-R	Non-Hndcps 2-y-o	Non-Hndcps 3-y-o+	Hndcps 2-y-o	Hndcps 3-y-o+	Per cent	£1 Level Stake
Newcastle (A.W)	4-42	0-4	0-2	0-3	4-33	9.5	-16.50
Beverley	3-14	0-3	0-0	0-0	3-11	21.4	-0.50
Catterick	3-17	0-2	2-2	0-1	1-12	17.6	+47.50
Carlisle	2-6	0-1	0-0	0-0	2-5	33.3	+5.00
Musselburgh	1-3	0-0	0-0	0-0	1-3	33.3	+1.50
Wolvhptn (A.W)	1-10	0-0	0-1	0-0	1-9	10.0	-6.00
Hamilton	1-12	0-0	0-1	0-0	1-11	8.3	-5.00

WINNING HORSES

Horse	Races Run	1st	2nd	3rd	£
Arnold	9	2	0	2	7245
Bibbidibobbidiboo (IRE)	10	2	4	1	6987
Highly Focussed (IRE)	11	4	1	0	12420
Lady Lintera (IRE)	2	1	0	1	3105
Nifty Niece (IRE)	10	2	0	0	6987
Rosina	10	1	1	2	6081
Troop	4	1	1	0	3493
Uncle Charlie (IRE)	6	2	0	1	8410
Total winning prize-money					**£54728**
Favourites	**0-12**		**0.0%**		**-12.00**

ED DUNLOP

NEWMARKET, SUFFOLK

	No. of Hrs	Races Run	1st	2nd	3rd	Unpl	Per cent	£1 Level Stake
2-y-o	*29*	*91*	*3*	*8*	*11*	*68*	*3.3*	*-60.25*
3-y-o	*42*	*219*	*13*	*26*	*22*	*158*	*5.9*	*-146.95*
4-y-o+	*17*	*98*	*13*	*16*	*9*	*60*	*13.3*	*-31.88*
Totals	**88**	**408**	**29**	**50**	**42**	**286**	**7.1**	**-239.08**
2017	*105*	*478*	*52*	*58*	*54*	*314*	*10.9*	*-215.95*
2016	*86*	*385*	*51*	*49*	*39*	*246*	*13.2*	*-109.26*

BY MONTH

2-y-o	W-R	Per cent	£1 Level Stake	**3-y-o**	W-R	Per cent	£1 Level Stake
January	0-0	0.0	0.00	January	0-4	0.0	-4.00
February	0-0	0.0	0.00	February	1-3	33.3	+3.00
March	0-0	0.0	0.00	March	0-5	0.0	-5.00
April	0-0	0.0	0.00	April	0-19	0.0	-19.00
May	0-1	0.0	-1.00	May	2-36	5.6	-25.75
June	0-14	0.0	-14.00	June	1-35	2.9	-29.00
July	0-13	0.0	-13.00	July	2-28	7.1	-14.00
August	3-18	16.7	+12.75	August	4-35	11.4	-15.70
September	0-16	0.0	-16.00	September	2-23	8.7	-13.50
October	0-17	0.0	-17.00	October	1-17	5.9	-10.00
November	0-10	0.0	-10.00	November	0-9	0.0	-9.00
December	0-2	0.0	-2.00	December	0-5	0.0	-5.00

4-y-o+	W-R	Per cent	£1 Level Stake	**Totals**	W-R	Per cent	£1 Level Stake
January	2-6	33.3	+1.75	January	2-10	20.0	-2.25
February	2-6	33.3	+1.33	February	3-9	33.3	+4.33
March	1-13	7.7	-9.75	March	1-18	5.6	-14.75
April	0-4	0.0	-4.00	April	0-23	0.0	-23.00
May	2-16	12.5	+2.00	May	4-53	7.5	-24.75
June	3-16	18.8	+2.75	June	4-65	6.2	-40.25
July	2-12	16.7	-3.83	July	4-53	7.5	-30.83
August	1-10	10.0	-7.13	August	8-63	12.7	-10.08
September	0-6	0.0	-6.00	September	2-45	4.4	-35.50
October	0-9	0.0	-9.00	October	1-43	2.3	-36.00
November	0-0	0.0	0.00	November	0-19	0.0	-9.00
December	0-0	0.0	0.00	December	0-7	0.0	-5.00

DISTANCE

2-y-o	W-R	Per cent	£1 Level Stake	**3-y-o**	W-R	Per cent	£1 Level Stake
5f-6f	1-37	2.7	-27.00	5f-6f	0-20	0.0	-20.00
7f-8f	2-52	3.8	-31.25	7f-8f	5-92	5.4	-60.00
9f-13f	0-2	0.0	-2.00	9f-13f	5-87	5.7	-55.00
14f+	0-0	0.0	0.00	14f+	3-20	15.0	-11.95

4-y-o+	W-R	Per cent	£1 Level Stake	**Totals**	W-R	Per cent	£1 Level Stake
5f-6f	0-2	0.0	-2.00	5f-6f	1-59	1.7	-49.00
7f-8f	3-28	10.7	-14.63	7f-8f	10-172	5.8	-105.88
9f-13f	5-48	10.4	-22.17	9f-13f	10-137	7.3	-79.17
14f+	5-20	25.0	+6.92	14f+	8-40	20.0	-5.03

TYPE OF RACE

Non-Handicaps	W-R	Per cent	£1 Level Stake	**Handicaps**	W-R	Per cent	£1 Level Stake
2-y-o	1-73	1.4	-63.00	2-y-o	2-18	11.1	+2.75
3-y-o	0-39	0.0	-39.00	3-y-o	13-180	7.2	-107.95
4-y-o+	1-7	14.3	-5.67	4-y-o+	12-91	13.2	-26.21

RACE CLASS / FIRST TIME OUT

RACE CLASS	W-R	Per cent	£1 Level Stake	FIRST TIME OUT	W-R	Per cent	£1 Level Stake
Class 1	0-10	0.0	-10.00	2-y-o	0-29	0.0	-29.00
Class 2	2-37	5.4	-26.67	3-y-o	0-42	0.0	-42.00
Class 3	2-26	7.7	-8.00	4-y-o+	3-17	17.6	-7.92
Class 4	5-111	4.5	-81.33				
Class 5	14-163	8.6	-82.75	Totals	3-88	3.4	-78.92
Class 6	6-61	9.8	-30.33				
Class 7	0-0	0.0	0.00				

JOCKEYS

	W-R	Per cent	£1 Level Stake
Robert Havlin	6-33	18.2	-2.00
Ben Curtis	4-19	21.1	-0.20
James Doyle	3-29	10.3	-19.08
Miss Sophie Smith	2-7	28.6	+6.50
Luke Morris	2-12	16.7	+8.75
Edward Greatrex	2-18	11.1	-0.50
Jim Crowley	2-23	8.7	-9.00
Frankie Dettori	1-3	33.3	+6.00
Ryan Moore	1-5	20.0	-2.13
Oisin Murphy	1-7	14.3	-5.67
Martin Harley	1-9	11.1	-3.00
Charles Bishop	1-10	10.0	-6.25
Fran Berry	1-15	6.7	-6.00
David Probert	1-15	6.7	-9.50
Gerald Mosse	1-46	2.2	-40.00

COURSE RECORD

	Total W-R	Non-Hndcps 2-y-o	Non-Hndcps 3-y-o+	Hndcps 2-y-o	Hndcps 3-y-o+	Per cent	£1 Level Stake
Chelmsford (A.W)	7-47	1-6	0-7	0-2	6-32	14.9	-10.71
Beverley	3-12	0-1	0-1	0-0	3-10	25.0	+0.80
Wolvhptn (A.W)	3-33	0-4	0-3	0-0	3-26	9.1	-22.00
Chepstow	2-7	0-0	0-0	0-0	2-7	28.6	+6.50
Doncaster	2-13	0-2	0-2	0-0	2-9	15.4	+2.50
Nottingham	2-16	0-4	0-0	1-1	1-11	12.5	+3.25
Lingfield (A.W)	2-30	0-6	1-3	0-0	1-21	6.7	-24.67
Ffos Las	1-2	0-0	0-0	0-0	1-2	50.0	+3.50
York	1-5	0-0	0-1	0-0	1-4	20.0	+7.00
Leicester	1-8	0-1	0-1	0-2	1-4	12.5	-2.00
Redcar	1-9	0-0	0-2	0-1	1-6	11.1	-2.00
Salisbury	1-10	0-4	0-1	1-1	0-4	10.0	-6.25
Newcastle (A.W)	1-20	0-1	0-1	0-1	1-17	5.0	-14.00
Newmkt (Jly)	1-22	0-11	0-1	0-1	1-9	4.5	-13.00
Kempton (A.W)	1-40	0-6	0-1	0-7	1-26	2.5	-34.00

WINNING HORSES

Horse	Races Run	1st	2nd	3rd	£
Amazing Red (IRE)	7	2	0	1	40463
Amplification (USA)	8	1	0	2	3752
Arnarson	9	2	1	1	9574
Conflagration	5	1	0	1	3105
Dagueneau (IRE)	8	2	4	0	10355
Dubai Frame	6	1	1	1	3105
Global Angel	4	1	0	0	3429
Global Art	10	1	0	4	4787
Grandscape	10	1	1	0	3369
Hallalulu	5	2	0	0	7698
King Kevin	12	2	3	1	7633
Manjaam (IRE)	9	1	1	0	9704
Melodies	3	1	1	0	5531
Mudallel (IRE)	9	1	2	1	8345
Perla Blanca (USA)	4	1	1	0	3619
Qaswarah (IRE)*	4	1	0	1	3752
Red Verdon (USA)	7	1	4	0	11972
Roxy Art (IRE)	6	1	2	0	7375
Sageness (IRE)	7	1	0	0	5293
Sanam	8	3	0	0	11385
Teenage Gal (IRE)	8	1	1	1	3752
Vision Clear (GER)	8	1	2	1	4348
Total winning prize-money					**£172346**
Favourites	**9-35**		**25.7%**		**-10.07**

HARRY DUNLOP

LAMBOURN, BERKS

	No. of Hrs	Races Run	1st	2nd	3rd	Unpl	Per cent	£1 Level Stake
2-y-o	*13*	*45*	*1*	*2*	*1*	*41*	*2.2*	*-28.00*
3-y-o	*19*	*91*	*7*	*11*	*10*	*63*	*7.7*	*-22.75*
4-y-o+	*9*	*46*	*3*	*3*	*5*	*35*	*6.5*	*-28.00*
Totals	**41**	**182**	**11**	**16**	**16**	**139**	**6.0**	**-78.75**
2017	*43*	*173*	*9*	*15*	*15*	*134*	*5.2*	*-93.68*
2016	*50*	*200*	*19*	*24*	*30*	*127*	*9.5*	*-12.63*

BY MONTH

2-y-o	W-R	Per cent	£1 Level Stake
January	0-0	0.0	0.00
February	0-0	0.0	0.00
March	0-0	0.0	0.00
April	0-0	0.0	0.00
May	0-2	0.0	-2.00
June	0-2	0.0	-2.00
July	1-4	25.0	+13.00
August	0-6	0.0	-6.00
September	0-10	0.0	-10.00
October	0-12	0.0	-12.00
November	0-8	0.0	-8.00
December	0-1	0.0	-1.00

3-y-o	W-R	Per cent	£1 Level Stake
January	0-2	0.0	-2.00
February	0-3	0.0	-3.00
March	0-3	0.0	-3.00
April	0-8	0.0	-8.00
May	1-15	6.7	-7.00
June	2-17	11.8	0.00
July	1-8	12.5	+18.00
August	0-9	0.0	-9.00
September	1-10	10.0	-6.75
October	2-11	18.2	+3.00
November	0-4	0.0	-4.00
December	0-1	0.0	-1.00

4-y-o+	W-R	Per cent	£1 Level Stake
January	1-6	16.7	-2.00
February	0-2	0.0	-2.00
March	0-3	0.0	-3.00
April	0-4	0.0	-4.00
May	0-7	0.0	-7.00
June	0-5	0.0	-5.00
July	1-6	16.7	+1.00
August	1-5	20.0	+2.00
September	0-4	0.0	-4.00
October	0-3	0.0	-3.00
November	0-1	0.0	-1.00
December	0-0	0.0	0.00

Totals	W-R	Per cent	£1 Level Stake
January	1-8	12.5	-4.00
February	0-5	0.0	-5.00
March	0-6	0.0	-6.00
April	0-12	0.0	-12.00
May	1-24	4.2	-16.00
June	2-24	8.3	-7.00
July	3-18	16.7	+32.00
August	1-20	5.0	-13.00
September	1-24	4.2	-20.75
October	2-26	7.7	-12.00
November	0-13	0.0	-5.00
December	0-2	0.0	-1.00

DISTANCE

2-y-o	W-R	Per cent	£1 Level Stake
5f-6f	1-15	6.7	+2.00
7f-8f	0-26	0.0	-26.00
9f-13f	0-4	0.0	-4.00
14f+	0-0	0.0	0.00

3-y-o	W-R	Per cent	£1 Level Stake
5f-6f	0-11	0.0	-11.00
7f-8f	1-31	3.2	-24.00
9f-13f	4-41	9.8	-12.75
14f+	2-8	25.0	+25.00

4-y-o+	W-R	Per cent	£1 Level Stake
5f-6f	1-17	5.9	-10.00
7f-8f	0-14	0.0	-14.00
9f-13f	2-13	15.4	-2.00
14f+	0-2	0.0	-2.00

Totals	W-R	Per cent	£1 Level Stake
5f-6f	2-43	4.7	-19.00
7f-8f	1-71	1.4	-64.00
9f-13f	6-58	10.3	-18.75
14f+	2-10	20.0	+23.00

TYPE OF RACE

Non-Handicaps

	W-R	Per cent	£1 Level Stake
2-y-o	1-40	2.5	-23.00
3-y-o	2-39	5.1	-25.00
4-y-o+	0-7	0.0	-7.00

Handicaps

	W-R	Per cent	£1 Level Stake
2-y-o	0-5	0.0	-5.00
3-y-o	5-52	9.6	+2.25
4-y-o+	3-39	7.7	-21.00

RACE CLASS

	W-R	Per cent	£1 Level Stake
Class 1	1-12	8.3	-4.00
Class 2	0-6	0.0	-6.00
Class 3	1-8	12.5	+18.00
Class 4	2-24	8.3	0.00
Class 5	4-87	4.6	-63.00
Class 6	3-45	6.7	-23.75
Class 7	0-0	0.0	0.00

FIRST TIME OUT

	W-R	Per cent	£1 Level Stake
2-y-o	0-13	0.0	-13.00
3-y-o	1-19	5.3	-11.00
4-y-o+	1-9	11.1	-5.00
Totals	2-41	4.9	-29.00

JOCKEYS

	W-R	Per cent	£1 Level Stake
Jim Crowley	3-7	42.9	+29.25
Kieran O'Neill	2-6	33.3	+5.00
Nicola Currie	2-13	15.4	+1.00
Richard Kingscote	1-5	20.0	+3.00
Charles Bishop	1-9	11.1	+2.00
Pat Cosgrave	1-12	8.3	-6.00
Hector Crouch	1-29	3.4	-12.00

COURSE RECORD

	Total W-R	Non-Hndcps 2-y-o	Non-Hndcps 3-y-o+	Hndcps 2-y-o	Hndcps 3-y-o+	Per cent	£1 Level Stake
Lingfield (A.W)	2-22	0-1	0-9	0-0	2-12	9.1	-11.75
Kempton (A.W)	2-38	0-15	0-4	0-0	2-19	5.3	-27.00
Doncaster	1-3	0-0	1-2	0-1	0-0	33.3	+3.00
Newmkt (Jly)	1-3	1-1	0-0	0-0	0-2	33.3	+14.00
Chepstow	1-7	0-1	0-1	0-0	1-5	14.3	0.00
Lingfield	1-7	0-1	1-3	0-1	0-2	14.3	+1.00
Newbury	1-8	0-0	0-3	0-0	1-5	12.5	-1.00
Sandown	1-8	0-2	0-1	0-0	1-5	12.5	+18.00
Salisbury	1-14	0-5	0-4	0-0	1-5	7.1	-3.00

WINNING HORSES

Horse	Races Run	1st	2nd	3rd	£
Flight Of Fantasy	6	2	1	0	10480
Golden Image	5	1	2	0	3493
Goldino Bello (FR)	4	1	0	0	5175
Jackfinbar (FR)	3	1	0	0	18675
Just An Idea (IRE)	9	1	0	1	3752
Knight To Behold (IRE)	2	1	0	0	34026
Looking For Carl	7	1	1	1	3105
Pact Of Steel	12	1	2	2	3105
Pirate King	5	1	0	1	3752
Space Talk	6	1	4	0	3752
Total winning prize-money					**£89315**
Favourites	**1-8**		**12.5%**		**-4.00**

ALEXANDRA DUNN

WEST BUCKLAND, SOMERSET

	No. of Hrs	Races Run	1st	2nd	3rd	Unpl	Per cent	£1 Level Stake
2-y-o	*0*	*0*	*0*	*0*	*0*	*0*	*0.0*	*0.00*
3-y-o	*5*	*25*	*0*	*0*	*2*	*23*	*0.0*	*-25.00*
4-y-o+	*25*	*172*	*15*	*7*	*16*	*133*	*8.7*	*-11.50*
Totals	**30**	**197**	**15**	**7**	**18**	**156**	**7.6**	**-36.50**
2017	*9*	*17*	*1*	*0*	*1*	*15*	*5.9*	*-11.00*
2016	*8*	*23*	*3*	*2*	*5*	*13*	*13.0*	*-5.75*

BY MONTH

2-y-o	W-R	Per cent	£1 Level Stake	3-y-o	W-R	Per cent	£1 Level Stake
January	0-0	0.0	0.00	January	0-0	0.0	0.00
February	0-0	0.0	0.00	February	0-0	0.0	0.00
March	0-0	0.0	0.00	March	0-0	0.0	0.00
April	0-0	0.0	0.00	April	0-0	0.0	0.00
May	0-0	0.0	0.00	May	0-0	0.0	0.00
June	0-0	0.0	0.00	June	0-0	0.0	0.00
July	0-0	0.0	0.00	July	0-4	0.0	-4.00
August	0-0	0.0	0.00	August	0-9	0.0	-9.00
September	0-0	0.0	0.00	September	0-7	0.0	-7.00
October	0-0	0.0	0.00	October	0-1	0.0	-1.00
November	0-0	0.0	0.00	November	0-1	0.0	-1.00
December	0-0	0.0	0.00	December	0-3	0.0	-3.00

4-y-o+	W-R	Per cent	£1 Level Stake	Totals	W-R	Per cent	£1 Level Stake
January	2-8	25.0	+23.00	January	2-8	25.0	+23.00
February	2-23	8.7	+14.00	February	2-23	8.7	+14.00
March	0-8	0.0	-8.00	March	0-8	0.0	-8.00
April	0-23	0.0	-23.00	April	0-23	0.0	-23.00
May	1-12	8.3	-3.50	May	1-12	8.3	-3.50
June	1-10	10.0	+2.00	June	1-10	10.0	+2.00
July	3-16	18.8	+7.50	July	3-20	15.0	+3.50
August	2-15	13.3	+1.00	August	2-24	8.3	-8.00
September	2-14	14.3	0.00	September	2-21	9.5	-7.00
October	0-16	0.0	-16.00	October	0-17	0.0	-17.00
November	1-14	7.1	-8.50	November	1-15	6.7	-9.50
December	1-13	7.7	0.00	December	1-16	6.3	-3.00

DISTANCE

2-y-o	W-R	Per cent	£1 Level Stake	3-y-o	W-R	Per cent	£1 Level Stake
5f-6f	0-0	0.0	0.00	5f-6f	0-1	0.0	-1.00
7f-8f	0-0	0.0	0.00	7f-8f	0-9	0.0	-9.00
9f-13f	0-0	0.0	0.00	9f-13f	0-13	0.0	-13.00
14f+	0-0	0.0	0.00	14f+	0-2	0.0	-2.00

4-y-o+	W-R	Per cent	£1 Level Stake	Totals	W-R	Per cent	£1 Level Stake
5f-6f	0-10	0.0	-10.00	5f-6f	0-11	0.0	-11.00
7f-8f	3-18	16.7	+5.50	7f-8f	3-27	11.1	-3.50
9f-13f	8-99	8.1	-8.00	9f-13f	8-112	7.1	-21.00
14f+	4-45	8.9	+1.00	14f+	4-47	8.5	-1.00

TYPE OF RACE

Non-Handicaps	W-R	Per cent	£1 Level Stake	Handicaps	W-R	Per cent	£1 Level Stake
2-y-o	0-0	0.0	0.00	2-y-o	0-0	0.0	0.00
3-y-o	0-4	0.0	-4.00	3-y-o	0-21	0.0	-21.00
4-y-o+	0-7	0.0	-7.00	4-y-o+	15-165	9.1	-4.50

RACE CLASS

	W-R	Per cent	£1 Level Stake
Class 1	0-0	0.0	0.00
Class 2	0-6	0.0	-6.00
Class 3	0-10	0.0	-10.00
Class 4	4-31	12.9	+6.50
Class 5	6-49	12.2	+35.50
Class 6	5-99	5.1	-60.50
Class 7	0-2	0.0	-2.00

FIRST TIME OUT

	W-R	Per cent	£1 Level Stake
2-y-o	0-0	0.0	0.00
3-y-o	0-5	0.0	-5.00
4-y-o+	1-25	4.0	-4.00
Totals	1-30	3.3	-9.00

JOCKEYS

	W-R	Per cent	£1 Level Stake
Rossa Ryan	8-49	16.3	+21.50
Liam Keniry	4-30	13.3	+38.00
Stephen Cummins	1-4	25.0	0.00
George Wood	1-6	16.7	+7.00
Miss Hannah Welch	1-9	11.1	-4.00

COURSE RECORD

	Total W-R	Non-Hndcps 2-y-o	Non-Hndcps 3-y-o+	Hndcps 2-y-o	Hndcps 3-y-o+	Per cent	£1 Level Stake
Wolvhptn (A.W)	5-38	0-0	0-1	0-0	5-37	13.2	-1.50
Chelmsford (A.W)	3-22	0-0	0-0	0-0	3-22	13.6	+4.00
Kempton (A.W)	3-39	0-0	0-2	0-0	3-37	7.7	+3.00
Chepstow	1-4	0-0	0-0	0-0	1-4	25.0	+8.00
Southwell (A.W)	1-8	0-0	0-0	0-0	1-8	12.5	+5.00
Brighton	1-9	0-0	0-1	0-0	1-8	11.1	-4.00
Lingfield (A.W)	1-22	0-0	0-2	0-0	1-20	4.5	+4.00

WINNING HORSES

Horse	Races Run	1st	2nd	3rd	£
Argus (IRE)	11	2	0	1	10221
Azari	11	1	0	0	3752
*Cry Wolf	10	3	1	2	18663
*De Little Engine (IRE)	11	3	1	1	9704
Diamond Reflection (IRE)	15	1	1	2	3105
Enmeshing	12	1	1	4	3752
French Mix (USA)	17	3	1	3	7504
Gang Warfare	8	1	0	1	5531
Total winning prize-money					**£62232**
Favourites	**0-5**		**0.0%**		**-5.00**

CHRISTINE DUNNETT

HINGHAM, NORFOLK

	No. of Hrs	Races Run	1st	2nd	3rd	Unpl	Per cent	£1 Level Stake
2-y-o	*1*	*1*	*0*	*0*	*0*	*1*	*0.0*	*-1.00*
3-y-o	*8*	*45*	*5*	*6*	*6*	*28*	*11.1*	*+28.00*
4-y-o+	*7*	*57*	*2*	*1*	*6*	*48*	*3.5*	*+3.00*
Totals	**16**	**103**	**7**	**7**	**12**	**77**	**6.8**	**+30.00**
2017	*17*	*85*	*0*	*3*	*4*	*78*	*0.0*	*-85.00*
2016	*16*	*69*	*2*	*1*	*4*	*62*	*2.9*	*-45.00*

JOCKEYS

	W-R	Per cent	£1 Level Stake
Kieran O'Neill	2-14	14.3	+31.00
Jimmy Quinn	2-21	9.5	+18.00
Joey Haynes	1-2	50.0	+19.00
Gabriele Malune	1-3	33.3	+10.00
Kevin Lundie	1-4	25.0	+11.00

COURSE RECORD

	Total W-R	Non-Hndcps 2-y-o	Non-Hndcps 3-y-o+	Hndcps 2-y-o	Hndcps 3-y-o+	Per cent	£1 Level Stake
Yarmouth	4-36	0-1	0-1	0-0	4-34	11.1	+37.00
Chelmsford (A.W)	2-29	0-0	0-2	0-0	2-27	6.9	-3.00
Nottingham	1-4	0-0	0-0	0-0	1-4	25.0	+30.00

WINNING HORSES

Horse	Races Run	1st	2nd	3rd	£
Agent Of Fortune	9	3	2	0	9315
Drop Kick Murphi (IRE)	15	1	0	4	3235
Hidden Dream (IRE)	10	1	1	1	3493
*Kraka (IRE)	8	1	1	4	3105
Percy Toplis	13	1	0	0	3105
Total winning prize-money					**£22253**
Favourites	**0-0**		**0.0%**		**0.00**

SEAMUS DURACK

UPPER LAMBOURN, BERKSHIRE

	No. of Hrs	Races Run	1st	2nd	3rd	Unpl	Per cent	£1 Level Stake
2-y-o	*3*	*14*	*0*	*1*	*0*	*13*	*0.0*	*-11.00*
3-y-o	*8*	*37*	*2*	*3*	*1*	*31*	*5.4*	*-22.90*
4-y-o+	*13*	*58*	*4*	*4*	*9*	*41*	*6.9*	*+12.63*
Totals	**24**	**109**	**6**	**8**	**10**	**85**	**5.5**	**-24.27**
2017	*21*	*93*	*7*	*10*	*7*	*68*	*7.5*	*-61.67*
2016	*18*	*78*	*9*	*7*	*7*	*55*	*11.5*	*-25.03*

JOCKEYS

	W-R	Per cent	£1 Level Stake
James Doyle	1-1	100.0	+1.10
Luke Morris	1-3	33.3	+9.00
Finley Marsh	1-3	33.3	-0.38
Oisin Murphy	1-5	20.0	-1.00
David Probert	1-9	11.1	+4.00
Shane Kelly	1-28	3.6	+23.00

COURSE RECORD

	Total W-R	Non-Hndcps 2-y-o	Non-Hndcps 3-y-o+	Hndcps 2-y-o	Hndcps 3-y-o+	Per cent	£1 Level Stake
Kempton (A.W)	3-28	0-0	0-6	0-2	3-20	10.7	+40.00
Newcastle (A.W)	1-4	0-0	0-1	0-0	1-3	25.0	-1.90
Bath	1-5	0-0	0-0	0-0	1-5	20.0	-2.38
Wolvhptn (A.W)	1-12	0-0	0-2	0-0	1-10	8.3	0.00

WINNING HORSES

Horse	Races Run	1st	2nd	3rd	£
Alfredo (IRE)	5	1	1	0	6469
Apex Predator (IRE)	9	1	0	0	3105
Cayirli (FR)	5	1	0	0	15563
High Wells	7	1	2	0	3752
Para Mio (IRE)	5	1	1	0	3493
Pipes Of Peace (IRE)	5	1	1	2	46688
Total winning prize-money					**£79070**
Favourites	**2-7**		**28.6%**		**-2.27**

CHRIS DWYER

NEWMARKET, SUFFOLK

	No. of Hrs	Races Run	1st	2nd	3rd	Unpl	Per cent	£1 Level Stake
2-y-o	*3*	*11*	*2*	*2*	*0*	*7*	*18.2*	*+2.63*
3-y-o	*5*	*37*	*7*	*2*	*4*	*24*	*18.9*	*-1.20*

4-y-o+	*12*	*126*	*17*	*17*	*15*	*77*	*13.5*	*-10.04*
Totals	**20**	**174**	**26**	**21**	**19**	**108**	**14.9**	**-8.61**
2017	*22*	*189*	*24*	*29*	*30*	*106*	*12.7*	*-40.80*
2016	*28*	*203*	*32*	*22*	*19*	*128*	*15.8*	*+66.51*

BY MONTH

2-y-o	W-R	Per cent	£1 Level Stake
January	0-0	0.0	0.00
February	0-0	0.0	0.00
March	0-0	0.0	0.00
April	0-1	0.0	-1.00
May	1-3	33.3	-0.38
June	1-1	100.0	+10.00
July	0-1	0.0	-1.00
August	0-1	0.0	-1.00
September	0-1	0.0	-1.00
October	0-2	0.0	-2.00
November	0-1	0.0	-1.00
December	0-0	0.0	0.00

3-y-o	W-R	Per cent	£1 Level Stake
January	0-0	0.0	0.00
February	2-2	100.0	+2.55
March	2-4	50.0	+5.00
April	0-2	0.0	-2.00
May	0-5	0.0	-5.00
June	1-3	33.3	+0.75
July	1-6	16.7	-0.50
August	0-5	0.0	-5.00
September	1-2	50.0	+11.00
October	0-5	0.0	-5.00
November	0-3	0.0	-3.00
December	0-0	0.0	0.00

4-y-o+	W-R	Per cent	£1 Level Stake
January	0-0	0.0	0.00
February	0-8	0.0	-8.00
March	1-16	6.3	-12.25
April	0-14	0.0	-14.00
May	3-14	21.4	+3.75
June	2-12	16.7	-3.25
July	0-11	0.0	-11.00
August	2-15	13.3	+13.00
September	6-14	42.9	+15.38
October	1-15	6.7	-4.00
November	2-7	28.6	+10.33
December	0-0	0.0	0.00

Totals	W-R	Per cent	£1 Level Stake
January	0-0	0.0	0.00
February	2-10	20.0	-5.45
March	3-20	15.0	-7.25
April	0-17	0.0	-17.00
May	4-22	18.2	-1.63
June	4-16	25.0	+7.50
July	1-18	5.6	-12.50
August	2-21	9.5	+7.00
September	7-17	41.2	+25.38
October	1-22	4.5	-11.00
November	2-11	18.2	+7.33
December	0-0	0.0	0.00

DISTANCE

2-y-o	W-R	Per cent	£1 Level Stake
5f-6f	2-9	22.2	+4.63
7f-8f	0-2	0.0	-2.00
9f-13f	0-0	0.0	0.00
14f+	0-0	0.0	0.00

3-y-o	W-R	Per cent	£1 Level Stake
5f-6f	7-28	25.0	+7.80
7f-8f	0-9	0.0	-9.00
9f-13f	0-0	0.0	0.00
14f+	0-0	0.0	0.00

4-y-o+	W-R	Per cent	£1 Level Stake
5f-6f	11-77	14.3	-12.79
7f-8f	3-38	7.9	-6.25
9f-13f	3-11	27.3	+9.00
14f+	0-0	0.0	0.00

Totals	W-R	Per cent	£1 Level Stake
5f-6f	20-114	17.5	-0.36
7f-8f	3-49	6.1	-17.25
9f-13f	3-11	27.3	+9.00
14f+	0-0	0.0	0.00

TYPE OF RACE

Non-Handicaps

	W-R	Per cent	£1 Level Stake
2-y-o	2-8	25.0	+5.63
3-y-o	0-13	0.0	-13.00
4-y-o+	0-3	0.0	-3.00

Handicaps

	W-R	Per cent	£1 Level Stake
2-y-o	0-3	0.0	-3.00
3-y-o	7-24	29.2	+11.80
4-y-o+	17-123	13.8	-7.04

RACE CLASS

	W-R	Per cent	£1 Level Stake
Class 1	0-6	0.0	-6.00
Class 2	1-12	8.3	-6.50
Class 3	2-20	10.0	-5.25
Class 4	10-49	20.4	+34.75
Class 5	6-43	14.0	-12.45
Class 6	7-44	15.9	-13.17
Class 7	0-0	0.0	0.00

FIRST TIME OUT

	W-R	Per cent	£1 Level Stake
2-y-o	0-3	0.0	-3.00
3-y-o	1-5	20.0	-2.25
4-y-o+	0-12	0.0	-12.00
Totals	1-20	5.0	-17.25

JOCKEYS

	W-R	Per cent	£1 Level Stake
Lewis Edmunds	11-60	18.3	+8.42
Silvestre De Sousa	6-45	13.3	-17.13
Josephine Gordon	3-13	23.1	+20.00
Nicola Currie	2-11	18.2	+3.75
David Egan	1-2	50.0	+3.00
Seamus Cronin	1-4	25.0	+3.00
Darragh Keenan	1-6	16.7	-1.67
Irineu Goncalves	1-11	9.1	-6.00

COURSE RECORD

	Total W-R	Non-Hndcps 2-y-o	Non-Hndcps 3-y-o+	Hndcps 2-y-o	Hndcps 3-y-o+	Per cent	£1 Level Stake
Yarmouth	7-38	1-5	0-1	0-0	6-32	18.4	+34.00
Brighton	4-8	0-0	0-0	0-0	4-8	50.0	+8.38
Lingfield (A.W)	3-13	0-0	0-5	0-0	3-8	23.1	+0.80
Wolvhptn (A.W)	3-19	0-0	0-1	0-0	3-18	15.8	-7.00
Chelmsford (A.W)	3-33	1-1	0-1	0-2	2-29	9.1	-23.13
Kempton (A.W)	2-19	0-1	0-1	0-0	2-17	10.5	-10.92
Chester	1-1	0-0	0-0	0-0	1-1	100.0	+4.50
Ascot	1-2	0-0	0-0	0-0	1-2	50.0	+9.00
Lingfield	1-3	0-0	0-0	0-0	1-3	33.3	+0.75
Southwell (A.W)	1-6	0-0	0-1	0-0	1-5	16.7	+7.00

WINNING HORSES

Horse	Races Run	1st	2nd	3rd	£
Arcanista (IRE)	13	3	3	0	12388
Arzaak (IRE)	15	3	1	0	17790
Bint Dandy (IRE)	13	2	0	0	11062
Dark Side Dream	13	1	2	3	3752
Erissimus Maximus (FR)*	9	1	1	3	12938
*Faithful Promise	8	1	0	2	4140
Phoenix Star (IRE)	2	1	0	0	4787
Right About Now (IRE)	13	3	1	3	10997
Rock On Baileys	16	6	1	2	45959
Rose Berry	13	1	3	5	5531
The Lacemaker	16	3	3	1	9315
The Last Party	5	1	2	0	4787

Total winning prize-money **£143446**

Favourites **9-17** **52.9%** **12.63**

TIM EASTERBY

GREAT HABTON, N YORKS

	No. of Hrs	Races Run	1st	2nd	3rd	Unpl	Per cent	£1 Level Stake
2-y-o	*49*	*207*	*12*	*19*	*15*	*161*	*5.8*	*-109.35*
3-y-o	*51*	*339*	*42*	*44*	*33*	*220*	*12.4*	*-18.20*
4-y-o+	*57*	*539*	*64*	*64*	*64*	*346*	*11.9*	*-45.82*
Totals	**157**	**1085**	**118**	**127**	**112**	**727**	**10.9**	**-173.37**
2017	*146*	*930*	*86*	*91*	*88*	*664*	*9.2*	*-238.55*
2016	*117*	*807*	*76*	*82*	*82*	*564*	*9.4*	*-213.08*

BY MONTH

2-y-o	W-R	Per cent	£1 Level Stake
January	0-0	0.0	0.00
February	0-0	0.0	0.00
March	0-0	0.0	0.00
April	1-5	20.0	+21.00
May	2-12	16.7	-4.75
June	1-28	3.6	-23.00
July	0-27	0.0	-27.00
August	3-44	6.8	-33.00
September	1-46	2.2	-42.60
October	3-37	8.1	-9.00
November	1-8	12.5	+9.00
December	0-0	0.0	0.00

3-y-o	W-R	Per cent	£1 Level Stake
January	0-0	0.0	0.00
February	0-0	0.0	0.00
March	0-2	0.0	-2.00
April	1-31	3.2	-26.50
May	7-51	13.7	-11.17
June	5-42	11.9	-7.90
July	10-74	13.5	+30.67
August	10-64	15.6	-1.30
September	5-42	11.9	+7.50
October	4-27	14.8	-1.50
November	0-6	0.0	-6.00
December	0-0	0.0	0.00

4-y-o+	W-R	Per cent	£1 Level Stake
January	2-6	33.3	+11.00
February	0-2	0.0	-2.00
March	0-0	0.0	0.00
April	0-37	0.0	-37.00
May	8-70	11.4	-21.50
June	21-86	24.4	+78.25
July	12-78	15.4	+14.16
August	7-81	8.6	-37.42
September	6-82	7.3	-36.40
October	6-73	8.2	+2.00
November	2-22	9.1	-14.92
December	0-2	0.0	-2.00

Totals	W-R	Per cent	£1 Level Stake
January	2-6	33.3	+11.00
February	0-2	0.0	-2.00
March	0-2	0.0	-2.00
April	2-73	2.7	-42.50
May	17-133	12.8	-37.42
June	27-156	17.3	+47.35
July	22-179	12.3	+17.83
August	20-189	10.6	-71.72
September	12-170	7.1	-71.50
October	13-137	9.5	-8.50
November	3-36	8.3	-20.92
December	0-2	0.0	-2.00

DISTANCE

2-y-o	W-R	Per cent	£1 Level Stake
5f-6f	8-140	5.7	-72.35
7f-8f	4-65	6.2	-35.00
9f-13f	0-2	0.0	-2.00
14f+	0-0	0.0	0.00

3-y-o	W-R	Per cent	£1 Level Stake
5f-6f	19-144	13.2	-40.81
7f-8f	8-112	7.1	-15.50
9f-13f	12-73	16.4	+37.52
14f+	3-10	30.0	+0.60

4-y-o+	W-R	Per cent	£1 Level Stake
5f-6f	20-187	10.7	-21.67
7f-8f	22-155	14.2	+15.41
9f-13f	20-162	12.3	-12.65
14f+	2-35	5.7	-26.92

Totals	W-R	Per cent	£1 Level Stake
5f-6f	47-471	10.0	-134.83
7f-8f	34-332	10.2	-35.09
9f-13f	32-237	13.5	+22.87
14f+	5-45	11.1	-26.32

TYPE OF RACE

Non-Handicaps	W-R	Per cent	£1 Level Stake
2-y-o	10-157	6.4	-78.35
3-y-o	5-47	10.6	-15.67
4-y-o+	1-10	10.0	-3.50

Handicaps	W-R	Per cent	£1 Level Stake
2-y-o	2-50	4.0	-31.00
3-y-o	37-292	12.7	-2.53
4-y-o+	63-529	11.9	-42.32

RACE CLASS

	W-R	Per cent	£1 Level Stake
Class 1	3-16	18.8	+5.50
Class 2	9-138	6.5	-57.92
Class 3	11-155	7.1	-38.50
Class 4	32-255	12.5	-49.38
Class 5	34-326	10.4	-104.09
Class 6	29-195	14.9	+72.02
Class 7	0-0	0.0	0.00

FIRST TIME OUT

	W-R	Per cent	£1 Level Stake
2-y-o	1-49	2.0	-23.00
3-y-o	0-51	0.0	-51.00
4-y-o+	5-57	8.8	-21.00
Totals	6-157	3.8	-95.00

JOCKEYS

	W-R	Per cent	£1 Level Stake
David Allan	49-396	12.4	-71.76
Rachel Richardson	18-242	7.4	-64.92
James Sullivan	8-54	14.8	+11.35
Miss Emily Easterby	7-30	23.3	+0.42
Jason Hart	6-38	15.8	-11.50
Duran Fentiman	6-114	5.3	-34.00
Robert Dodsworth	4-40	10.0	+15.50
Jamie Gormley	3-14	21.4	+4.00
Nathan Evans	3-15	20.0	+17.00
Rob Hornby	2-8	25.0	+20.00
Tony Hamilton	2-13	15.4	-0.50
Jack Garritty	2-16	12.5	-3.13
Yuga Kawada	1-1	100.0	+2.25
Daniel Tudhope	1-4	25.0	-2.67
P J McDonald	1-5	20.0	-1.75
Miss Jessica Gillam	1-5	20.0	+8.00
Ben Robinson	1-6	16.7	0.00
Andrew Mullen	1-10	10.0	-1.50
Paul Hanagan	1-11	9.1	-6.67
Cam Hardie	1-24	4.2	-14.50

COURSE RECORD

	Total W-R	Non-Hndcps 2-y-o	Non-Hndcps 3-y-o+	Hndcps 2-y-o	Hndcps 3-y-o+	Per cent	£1 Level Stake
Hamilton	12-36	3-5	0-0	0-0	9-31	33.3	+9.40
Beverley	12-76	1-17	0-7	0-1	11-51	15.8	-25.33
Redcar	12-103	0-21	1-5	0-4	11-73	11.7	+2.72
Ripon	10-95	1-15	1-7	0-1	8-72	10.5	-33.07
York	8-90	1-14	0-3	0-3	7-70	8.9	-2.50
Catterick	7-74	0-8	1-3	1-5	5-58	9.5	-14.77
Chester	6-42	0-3	0-2	0-1	6-36	14.3	+16.50
Thirsk	6-90	1-15	0-9	0-5	5-61	6.7	-36.40
Haydock	5-51	0-4	0-2	0-4	5-41	9.8	-11.00
Ayr	5-53	0-3	0-0	0-3	5-47	9.4	+4.41
Musselburgh	4-36	1-3	0-1	0-2	3-30	11.1	-7.25

Pontefract	4-50	0-7	1-3	0-1	3-39	8.0	-37.67
Newcastle (A.W)	4-58	0-11	0-3	0-6	4-38	6.9	-26.50
Leicester	3-15	0-2	0-0	1-1	2-12	20.0	+12.00
Nottingham	3-21	0-0	0-0	0-5	3-16	14.3	-5.67
Wolvhptn (A.W)	3-32	0-1	0-2	0-0	3-29	9.4	+19.50
Doncaster	3-37	0-6	0-2	0-1	3-28	8.1	+2.00
Carlisle	3-62	0-15	0-1	0-4	3-42	4.8	-46.50
Newmkt (Jly)	2-5	0-0	1-1	0-1	1-3	40.0	+6.25
Wetherby	2-14	0-2	1-3	0-0	1-9	14.3	+9.00
Southwell (A.W)	2-15	1-1	0-1	0-0	1-13	13.3	+10.50
Salisbury	1-1	0-0	0-0	0-0	1-1	100.0	+5.50
Sandown	1-2	1-1	0-1	0-0	0-0	50.0	+2.50

WINNING HORSES

Horse	Races Run	1st	2nd	3rd	£
Aasheq (IRE)	12	3	2	3	33509
Airplane (IRE)	9	2	1	0	6598
Amadeus Grey (IRE)	6	1	3	0	4140
Angels	9	2	1	0	7763
Autumn Flight (IRE)	4	1	1	1	5434
Balestra	4	2	2	0	5111
Big Ace	11	1	3	0	5434
Bollin Joan	10	3	1	2	10717
Bollin Ted	9	2	1	3	7152
Bossipop	16	1	2	2	11828
Breathable	9	1	3	0	2995
Brother McGonagall	11	3	0	1	13316
Computable	13	1	1	1	6081
Confessional	14	3	2	3	22512
Contrebasse	7	1	1	0	3752
Copper Knight (IRE)	13	3	0	0	59748
Dance King	13	1	0	0	15563
Dellaguista (IRE)	3	1	1	0	6081
Duke Of Yorkshire	9	2	1	0	8672
Eeh Bah Gum (IRE)	9	5	1	0	62076
Excellent Times	6	1	2	2	6469
Excessable	12	1	1	0	8007
Fashion Theory	10	1	3	0	16173
Flying Pursuit	10	1	1	1	31125
Ghayyar (IRE)	13	2	0	1	9624
Give It Some Teddy	12	3	0	2	41727
Gremoboy	3	1	0	0	3752
Gullane One (IRE)	5	2	1	0	7892
Hyanna*	2	1	0	0	4528
Just Hiss	7	1	0	4	18675
King Of The Celts (IRE)	7	1	0	0	2995
Lever Du Soleil (FR)	5	1	0	4	3493
Look Out Louis	4	1	0	0	5434
Make Me	9	1	3	3	4528
Midnight Malibu (IRE)	16	3	2	2	22769
Mikmak	12	2	4	2	25100
Mischief Managed (IRE)	11	3	3	4	10609
Mukhayyam	16	2	2	1	18419
Multellie	15	3	3	2	19545
Munthany (USA)	13	1	0	2	3493
My Reward	7	1	0	1	15398
Nuns Walk	15	3	5	2	20714
Off Piste	5	1	0	1	4528
Packington Lane	10	1	1	2	4348
Parole (IRE)	4	1	0	1	8345
Parys Mountain (IRE)	15	3	1	3	22124
Poet's Dawn	12	1	3	0	5041
Power Sail	8	2	1	2	4787
Regal Mirage (IRE)	8	2	1	2	9828
Relight My Fire	10	1	1	1	3369
Revenge	14	1	5	1	3170
Scoundrel	12	1	1	2	3105
*Shortbackandsides (IRE)	8	1	2	1	5693
Sir Derrick (IRE)	13	2	1	1	6891
Staxton	9	1	1	1	28013
Stormin Tom (IRE)	14	2	5	1	12167
Suitcase 'N' Taxi	13	2	1	0	9898
Supaulette (IRE)	14	2	1	2	6598
Super Kid	15	1	1	1	5531
Symposing (IRE)	10	1	0	1	4787
The Knot Is Tied (IRE)*	12	4	2	0	17854
Timetodock	5	1	0	0	3493
Travel Lightly	6	1	1	0	3493
Twilight (IRE)	13	4	1	2	13585
*Uncle Norman (FR)	4	1	0	0	3752
Vintage Brut	9	3	1	0	28355
Vive La Difference (IRE)	11	2	2	1	12162
Wells Farhh Go (IRE)	4	1	0	0	85065
Total winning prize-money					**£914933**
Favourites	**29-120**		**24.2%**		**-38.81**

MICHAEL EASTERBY

SHERIFF HUTTON, N YORKS

	No. of Hrs	Races Run	1st	2nd	3rd	Unpl	Per cent	£1 Level Stake
2-y-o	*25*	*77*	*7*	*3*	*6*	*61*	*9.1*	*+86.25*
3-y-o	*23*	*140*	*13*	*13*	*10*	*104*	*9.3*	*-46.72*
4-y-o+	*41*	*282*	*32*	*29*	*22*	*199*	*11.3*	*-66.07*
Totals	**89**	**499**	**52**	**45**	**38**	**364**	**10.4**	**-26.54**
2017	*78*	*498*	*46*	*48*	*46*	*357*	*9.2*	*-194.22*
2016	*68*	*476*	*61*	*52*	*55*	*308*	*12.8*	*-6.29*

BY MONTH

2-y-o	W-R	Per cent	£1 Level Stake	**3-y-o**	W-R	Per cent	£1 Level Stake
January	0-0	0.0	0.00	January	2-6	33.3	+3.25
February	0-0	0.0	0.00	February	1-3	33.3	+8.00
March	0-0	0.0	0.00	March	0-4	0.0	-4.00
April	0-2	0.0	-2.00	April	0-11	0.0	-11.00
May	0-5	0.0	-5.00	May	0-19	0.0	-19.00
June	1-5	20.0	+5.00	June	3-16	18.8	-0.25
July	0-5	0.0	-5.00	July	3-18	16.7	-2.59
August	0-10	0.0	-10.00	August	2-12	16.7	+5.88
September	1-13	7.7	+38.00	September	0-19	0.0	-19.00
October	3-18	16.7	+77.00	October	1-19	5.3	-12.00
November	1-13	7.7	-9.75	November	0-6	0.0	-6.00
December	1-6	16.7	-2.00	December	1-7	14.3	+10.00

4-y-o+	W-R	Per cent	£1 Level Stake
January	3-14	21.4	+9.88
February	0-8	0.0	-8.00
March	1-20	5.0	-15.00
April	5-27	18.5	+11.63
May	5-39	12.8	+2.38
June	2-32	6.3	-16.00
July	4-25	16.0	+4.50
August	6-33	18.2	-3.75
September	4-40	10.0	-17.20
October	1-28	3.6	-23.50
November	1-10	10.0	-5.00
December	0-6	0.0	-6.00

Totals	W-R	Per cent	£1 Level Stake
January	5-20	25.0	+13.13
February	1-11	9.1	0.00
March	1-24	4.2	-19.00
April	5-40	12.5	-1.37
May	5-63	7.9	-21.62
June	6-53	11.3	-11.25
July	7-48	14.6	-3.09
August	8-55	14.5	-7.87
September	5-72	6.9	+1.80
October	5-65	7.7	+41.50
November	2-29	6.9	-11.00
December	2-19	10.5	+4.00

DISTANCE

2-y-o	W-R	Per cent	£1 Level Stake
5f-6f	2-35	5.7	+50.00
7f-8f	5-40	12.5	+38.25
9f-13f	0-2	0.0	-2.00
14f+	0-0	0.0	0.00

3-y-o	W-R	Per cent	£1 Level Stake
5f-6f	6-56	10.7	-0.13
7f-8f	6-73	8.2	-38.34
9f-13f	1-11	9.1	-8.25
14f+	0-0	0.0	0.00

4-y-o+	W-R	Per cent	£1 Level Stake
5f-6f	12-79	15.2	+19.88
7f-8f	10-131	7.6	-50.38
9f-13f	6-61	9.8	-37.75
14f+	4-11	36.4	+2.18

Totals	W-R	Per cent	£1 Level Stake
5f-6f	20-170	11.8	+69.75
7f-8f	21-244	8.6	-50.47
9f-13f	7-74	9.5	-48.00
14f+	4-11	36.4	+2.18

TYPE OF RACE

Non-Handicaps	W-R	Per cent	£1 Level Stake
2-y-o	4-60	6.7	+91.00
3-y-o	0-25	0.0	-25.00
4-y-o+	1-12	8.3	-7.00

Handicaps	W-R	Per cent	£1 Level Stake
2-y-o	3-17	17.6	-4.75
3-y-o	13-115	11.3	-21.72
4-y-o+	31-270	11.5	-59.07

RACE CLASS

	W-R	Per cent	£1 Level Stake
Class 1	1-2	50.0	+3.00
Class 2	3-45	6.7	-29.38
Class 3	5-57	8.8	-16.20
Class 4	11-106	10.4	-35.63
Class 5	15-170	8.8	+68.75
Class 6	17-118	14.4	-16.09
Class 7	0-1	0.0	-1.00

FIRST TIME OUT

	W-R	Per cent	£1 Level Stake
2-y-o	1-25	4.0	+56.00
3-y-o	2-23	8.7	-11.00
4-y-o+	5-41	12.2	+5.50
Totals	8-89	9.0	+50.50

JOCKEYS

	W-R	Per cent	£1 Level Stake
Nathan Evans	22-233	9.4	+33.66
Harrison Shaw	12-105	11.4	+1.88
James Sullivan	4-15	26.7	+2.00
Miss Serena Brotherton	3-5	60.0	+5.50
Miss Joanna Mason	3-14	21.4	-1.75
Mr Alexander Fielding	2-8	25.0	+18.00
Ger O'Neill	1-1	100.0	+0.80
David Allan	1-2	50.0	+3.00
Hayley Turner	1-3	33.3	-0.13
Scott McCullagh	1-4	25.0	+3.00
Paul Mulrennan	1-8	12.5	-1.50
Cam Hardie	1-29	3.4	-19.00

COURSE RECORD

	Total W-R	Non-Hndcps 2-y-o	Non-Hndcps 3-y-o+	Hndcps 2-y-o	Hndcps 3-y-o+	Per cent	£1 Level Stake
Newcastle (A.W)	8-66	1-13	0-6	2-3	5-44	12.1	+65.13
York	5-28	0-4	0-0	0-0	5-24	17.9	+22.50
Wolvhptn (A.W)	5-37	0-3	0-4	0-3	5-27	13.5	-1.25
Carlisle	4-21	0-0	0-4	0-0	4-17	19.0	+13.00
Haydock	3-11	1-2	0-0	0-0	2-9	27.3	+11.63
Chelmsford (A.W)	3-20	0-1	0-1	0-1	3-17	15.0	-3.75
Southwell (A.W)	3-37	0-2	0-3	1-2	2-30	8.1	-11.00
Beverley	3-38	1-9	0-4	0-0	2-25	7.9	+24.75
Hamilton	2-7	0-0	0-0	0-0	2-7	28.6	-1.09
Ripon	2-14	0-1	0-0	0-0	2-13	14.3	-4.00
Redcar	2-21	1-7	0-2	0-0	1-12	9.5	-8.13
Windsor	1-1	0-0	0-0	0-0	1-1	100.0	+2.50
Chepstow	1-2	0-0	0-0	0-0	1-2	50.0	+0.88
Epsom	1-2	0-0	0-0	0-0	1-2	50.0	+4.00
Lingfield (A.W)	1-6	0-0	0-0	0-0	1-6	16.7	-3.00
Chester	1-10	0-1	0-1	0-1	1-7	10.0	-4.50
Musselburgh	1-11	0-0	0-0	0-2	1-9	9.1	-7.00
Nottingham	1-12	0-0	0-0	0-0	1-12	8.3	+3.00
Pontefract	1-21	0-3	0-4	0-1	1-13	4.8	-14.00
Ayr	1-23	0-2	0-0	0-0	1-21	4.3	-21.20
Doncaster	1-25	0-4	1-3	0-0	0-18	4.0	-20.00
Catterick	1-26	0-2	0-3	0-0	1-21	3.8	-19.00
Thirsk	1-30	0-5	0-2	0-2	1-21	3.3	-26.00

WINNING HORSES

Horse	Races Run	1st	2nd	3rd	£
Airglow (IRE)	13	3	1	1	20442
Apalis (FR)	2	2	0	0	7245
Aphaea	3	1	0	1	2995
Arrowtown	5	3	1	0	29628
Astraea	8	1	0	1	3493
Bad Dog	9	1	1	0	3752
Bop It	10	1	1	1	3105
Bosham	14	3	2	1	20442
Carlton Frankie	7	2	0	0	20173
Decima (IRE)	7	1	0	1	3057
Desert Dream	12	1	2	1	4205
Elysian Flame	3	1	0	0	6469
Gulf Of Poets	8	2	0	1	26700
Harvest Day	11	3	2	0	14038
Itlaaq	9	3	0	2	10232
Jack Berry House	1	1	0	0	3817
Kannapolis (IRE)	7	1	2	3	3105
Ladies First	6	2	2	0	14167
Lady Lavinia	9	1	1	1	3493
Magic City (IRE)	11	1	0	0	9359
Major Snugfit	4	1	0	0	4140
Maldonado (FR)	4	1	0	0	2995

Horse	Races Run	1st	2nd	3rd	£
Melgate Magic	8	1	0	0	3105
Melgate Majeure	6	2	0	1	6210
Miss Sheridan (IRE)	14	2	1	1	10933
Perfect Pasture	5	1	1	0	20983
Qaffaal (USA)	9	1	1	0	12938
Quick Look	12	2	1	0	22412
Rapid Applause	8	2	0	1	10760
Rolladice	5	1	0	0	3881
Up Ten Down Two (IRE)	6	1	0	0	2995
Weld Al Emarat	7	1	2	1	3752
Where's Jeff	6	2	1	1	3493
Total winning prize-money					**£318514**
Favourites	**15-48**		**31.3%**		**-2.92**

ROBERT EDDERY

NEWMARKET, SUFFOLK

	No. of Hrs	Races Run	1st	2nd	3rd	Unpl	Per cent	£1 Level Stake
2-y-o	*7*	*30*	*0*	*4*	*2*	*24*	*0.0*	*-30.00*
3-y-o	*7*	*29*	*2*	*1*	*1*	*25*	*6.9*	*-9.50*
4-y-o+	*10*	*61*	*6*	*4*	*3*	*48*	*9.8*	*-13.67*
Totals	**24**	**120**	**8**	**9**	**6**	**97**	**6.7**	**-53.17**
2017	*19*	*106*	*9*	*7*	*9*	*81*	*8.5*	*-39.59*
2016	*23*	*101*	*6*	*12*	*12*	*71*	*5.9*	*-63.00*

JOCKEYS

	W-R	Per cent	£1 Level Stake
Darragh Keenan	4-55	7.3	-7.67
Andrew Breslin	2-3	66.7	+6.00
Martin Harley	2-18	11.1	-7.50

COURSE RECORD

	Total W-R	Non-Hndcps 2-y-o	Non-Hndcps 3-y-o+	Hndcps 2-y-o	Hndcps 3-y-o+	Per cent	£1 Level Stake
Southwell (A.W)	3-12	0-1	0-1	0-1	3-9	25.0	+18.33
Newbury	1-2	0-1	0-0	0-0	1-1	50.0	+4.00
Salisbury	1-2	0-1	0-0	0-0	1-1	50.0	+6.00
Leicester	1-4	0-0	1-1	0-2	0-1	25.0	+13.00
Newmarket	1-7	0-4	0-1	0-0	1-2	14.3	-4.00
Lingfield (A.W)	1-8	0-0	0-1	0-1	1-6	12.5	-5.50

WINNING HORSES

Horse	Races Run	1st	2nd	3rd	£
Colwood	2	1	0	0	3752
*Country'N'Western (FR)	3	1	1	0	3752
Equimou	16	1	0	0	5757
Fiery Breath	6	1	0	0	3105
Graceful Lady	13	2	1	1	12809
Teaser	4	1	1	0	3105
Tynecastle Park	5	1	1	1	3493
Total winning prize-money					**£35773**
Favourites	**2-4**		**50.0%**		**1.50**

LUCINDA EGERTON

MALTON, N YORKS

	No. of Hrs	Races Run	1st	2nd	3rd	Unpl	Per cent	£1 Level Stake
2-y-o	*0*	*0*	*0*	*0*	*0*	*0*	*0.0*	*0.00*
3-y-o	*0*	*0*	*0*	*0*	*0*	*0*	*0.0*	*0.00*
4-y-o+	*7*	*34*	*2*	*1*	*6*	*25*	*5.9*	*+4.00*
Totals	**7**	**34**	**2**	**1**	**6**	**25**	**5.9**	**+4.00**
2017	*7*	*17*	*0*	*0*	*1*	*16*	*0.0*	*-17.00*
2016	*5*	*9*	*0*	*0*	*0*	*9*	*0.0*	*-9.00*

JOCKEYS

	W-R	Per cent	£1 Level Stake
Paula Muir	2-10	20.0	+28.00

COURSE RECORD

	Total W-R	Non-Hndcps 2-y-o	Non-Hndcps 3-y-o+	Hndcps 2-y-o	Hndcps 3-y-o+	Per cent	£1 Level Stake
Nottingham	1-4	0-0	0-0	0-0	1-4	25.0	0.00
Newcastle (A.W)	1-12	0-0	0-5	0-0	1-7	8.3	+22.00

WINNING HORSES

Horse	Races Run	1st	2nd	3rd	£
Orobas (IRE)	12	2	1	4	6404
Total winning prize-money					**£6404**
Favourites	**1-3**		**33.3%**		**1.00**

BRIAN ELLISON

NORTON, N YORKS

	No. of Hrs	Races Run	1st	2nd	3rd	Unpl	Per cent	£1 Level Stake
2-y-o	*17*	*69*	*4*	*8*	*5*	*52*	*5.8*	*-20.50*
3-y-o	*7*	*45*	*4*	*3*	*4*	*34*	*8.9*	*-25.75*
4-y-o+	*40*	*211*	*27*	*23*	*26*	*134*	*12.8*	*-29.30*
Totals	**64**	**325**	**35**	**34**	**35**	**220**	**10.8**	**-75.55**
2017	*82*	*399*	*28*	*39*	*42*	*289*	*7.0*	*-98.17*
2016	*105*	*471*	*60*	*50*	*55*	*305*	*12.7*	*-81.20*

BY MONTH

2-y-o	W-R	Per cent	£1 Level Stake	**3-y-o**	W-R	Per cent	£1 Level Stake
January	0-0	0.0	0.00	January	0-2	0.0	-2.00
February	0-0	0.0	0.00	February	0-0	0.0	0.00
March	0-0	0.0	0.00	March	0-0	0.0	0.00
April	0-4	0.0	-4.00	April	0-4	0.0	-4.00
May	1-8	12.5	+18.00	May	1-7	14.3	-2.50
June	2-16	12.5	-1.50	June	1-10	10.0	-2.00
July	1-10	10.0	-2.00	July	1-7	14.3	-3.75
August	0-13	0.0	13.00	August	1-4	25.0	-0.50
September	0-9	0.0	-9.00	September	0-4	0.0	-4.00
October	0-4	0.0	-4.00	October	0-3	0.0	-3.00
November	0-3	0.0	-3.00	November	0-3	0.0	-3.00

	W-R	Per cent	£1 Level Stake
December	0-2	0.0	-2.00

	W-R	Per cent	£1 Level Stake
December	0-1	0.0	-1.00

4-y-o+	W-R	Per cent	£1 Level Stake
January	2-5	40.0	+9.50
February	0-2	0.0	-2.00
March	2-12	16.7	+16.00
April	0-19	0.0	-19.00
May	4-24	16.7	-2.63
June	2-37	5.4	-15.00
July	3-28	10.7	-3.00
August	9-33	27.3	+13.21
September	3-22	13.6	-9.72
October	1-13	7.7	-5.00
November	1-9	11.1	-4.67
December	0-7	0.0	-7.00

Totals	W-R	Per cent	£1 Level Stake
January	2-7	28.6	+7.50
February	0-2	0.0	-2.00
March	2-12	16.7	+16.00
April	0-27	0.0	-27.00
May	6-39	15.4	+12.87
June	5-63	7.9	-18.50
July	5-45	11.1	-8.75
August	10-50	20.0	-0.29
September	3-35	8.6	-22.72
October	1-20	5.0	-12.00
November	1-15	6.7	-7.67
December	0-10	0.0	-8.00

DISTANCE

2-y-o	W-R	Per cent	£1 Level Stake
5f-6f	4-55	7.3	-6.50
7f-8f	0-14	0.0	-14.00
9f-13f	0-0	0.0	0.00
14f+	0-0	0.0	0.00

3-y-o	W-R	Per cent	£1 Level Stake
5f-6f	1-26	3.8	-21.50
7f-8f	1-12	8.3	-4.00
9f-13f	1-4	25.0	-0.75
14f+	1-3	33.3	+0.50

4-y-o+	W-R	Per cent	£1 Level Stake
5f-6f	6-51	11.8	-3.79
7f-8f	11-71	15.5	-1.76
9f-13f	3-57	5.3	-41.50
14f+	7-32	21.9	+17.75

Totals	W-R	Per cent	£1 Level Stake
5f-6f	11-132	8.3	-31.79
7f-8f	12-97	12.4	-19.76
9f-13f	4-61	6.6	-42.25
14f+	8-35	22.9	+18.25

TYPE OF RACE

Non-Handicaps

	W-R	Per cent	£1 Level Stake
2-y-o	4-55	7.3	-6.50
3-y-o	1-9	11.1	-4.50
4-y-o+	1-17	5.9	-14.37

Handicaps

	W-R	Per cent	£1 Level Stake
2-y-o	0-14	0.0	-14.00
3-y-o	3-36	8.3	-21.25
4-y-o+	26-194	13.4	-14.93

RACE CLASS

	W-R	Per cent	£1 Level Stake
Class 1	0-4	0.0	-4.00
Class 2	3-20	15.0	+15.00
Class 3	2-14	14.3	+0.33
Class 4	3-74	4.1	-55.50
Class 5	19-121	15.7	+18.41
Class 6	8-89	9.0	-46.79
Class 7	0-3	0.0	-3.00

FIRST TIME OUT

	W-R	Per cent	£1 Level Stake
2-y-o	1-17	5.9	+9.00
3-y-o	0-7	0.0	-7.00
4-y-o+	5-40	12.5	+21.50
Totals	6-64	9.4	+23.50

JOCKEYS

	W-R	Per cent	£1 Level Stake
Ben Robinson	16-165	9.7	-47.00
Ben Curtis	4-9	44.4	+14.38
Callum Rodriguez	3-11	27.3	-0.42
Kieran Schofield	3-36	8.3	-21.13
Daniel Tudhope	1-1	100.0	+2.00
Miss Becky Smith	1-1	100.0	+5.50
Callum Shepherd	1-2	50.0	+0.63
Yuga Kawada	1-3	33.3	+5.00
Phil Dennis	1-4	25.0	+4.00
Josephine Gordon	1-4	25.0	+15.00
Miss Abbie McCain	1-4	25.0	+0.50
Stevie Donohoe	1-8	12.5	+2.00
David Allan	1-9	11.1	+12.00

COURSE RECORD

	Total	Non-Hndcps		Hndcps		Per	£1 Level
	W-R	2-y-o	3-y-o+	2-y-o	3-y-o+	cent	Stake
Newcastle (A.W)	11-80	1-11	0-7	0-4	10-58	13.8	-0.59
Carlisle	4-14	1-3	0-0	0-0	3-11	28.6	+10.00
Beverley	3-31	1-15	1-6	0-0	1-10	9.7	+7.50
Ayr	2-5	0-0	0-0	0-0	2-5	40.0	+22.00
Thirsk	2-9	0-3	0-0	0-0	2-6	22.2	-2.13
Chester	2-11	0-1	0-0	0-0	2-10	18.2	+5.00
Nottingham	2-18	0-2	0-0	0-0	2-16	11.1	-7.50
Southwell (A.W)	2-22	0-1	1-2	0-2	1-17	9.1	-14.88
Newmkt (Jly)	1-1	0-0	0-0	0-0	1-1	100.0	+2.00
Newmarket	1-4	0-1	0-0	0-0	1-3	25.0	+0.33
Chelmsford (A.W)	1-4	0-0	0-0	0-1	1-3	25.0	+4.00
Doncaster	1-10	0-0	0-1	0-0	1-9	10.0	-2.00
Musselburgh	1-12	0-1	0-0	0-1	1-10	8.3	-7.67
Pontefract	1-12	0-1	0-2	0-0	1-9	8.3	-7.50
Catterick	1-18	1-3	0-3	0-2	0-10	5.6	-10.00

WINNING HORSES

Horse	Races Run	1st	2nd	3rd	£
Archive (FR)	9	1	1	2	4205
Bal De Rio (FR)	4	2	0	1	7892
Baraweez (IRE)	9	2	0	0	49178
Burn Some Dust (IRE)	5	2	0	0	6840
Eastern Racer (IRE)	8	3	1	1	13520
*First Flight (IRE)	7	1	0	1	18675
Kalissi	7	1	1	1	3493
Little Jo	6	4	1	1	23547
Little Legs	4	1	1	1	7561
Moltoir (IRE)	9	1	0	1	4663
*Monsieur Jimmy	5	1	2	0	3120
Moonlit Sands (IRE)	9	1	1	2	3170
Pea Shooter	11	2	1	2	6857
Pearl Of Qatar	5	1	0	0	4033
Pickett's Charge	12	3	1	2	10067
Royal Flag	8	1	3	1	4140
Serenity Now (IRE)	8	2	1	0	6724
Snookered (IRE)	9	1	1	2	4205
Sugarloaf Mountain (IRE)	6	2	0	0	10868
Tallinski (IRE)	8	1	1	0	3881
The Mackem Bullet (IRE)	6	1	2	2	5175
Traveltalk (IRE)	10	1	2	1	3493
Total winning prize-money					**£208307**
Favourites	**24-65**		**36.9%**		**-5.86**

DAVID ELSWORTH

NEWMARKET, SUFFOLK

	No. of Hrs	Races Run	1st	2nd	3rd	Unpl	Per cent	£1 Level Stake
2-y-o	*9*	*21*	*2*	*1*	*1*	*17*	*9.5*	*-13.00*
3-y-o	*12*	*65*	*9*	*8*	*10*	*38*	*13.8*	*-24.79*
4-y-o+	*12*	*75*	*17*	*14*	*3*	*41*	*22.7*	*+38.04*
Totals	**33**	**161**	**28**	**23**	**14**	**96**	**17.4**	**+0.25**
2017	*39*	*184*	*24*	*20*	*24*	*115*	*13.0*	*-22.99*
2016	*38*	*189*	*27*	*18*	*26*	*117*	*14.3*	*-18.79*

BY MONTH

2-y-o	W-R	Per cent	£1 Level Stake
January	0-0	0.0	0.00
February	0-0	0.0	0.00
March	0-0	0.0	0.00
April	0-0	0.0	0.00
May	0-0	0.0	0.00
June	0-0	0.0	0.00
July	0-0	0.0	0.00
August	0-4	0.0	-4.00
September	1-3	33.3	+2.00
October	0-4	0.0	-4.00
November	0-4	0.0	-4.00
December	1-6	16.7	-3.00

3-y-o	W-R	Per cent	£1 Level Stake
January	3-8	37.5	+1.88
February	0-2	0.0	-2.00
March	0-3	0.0	-3.00
April	1-8	12.5	-3.00
May	1-8	12.5	-3.67
June	1-10	10.0	-2.00
July	0-7	0.0	-7.00
August	1-5	20.0	-2.50
September	1-8	12.5	-3.50
October	0-5	0.0	-5.00
November	1-1	100.0	+5.00
December	0-0	0.0	0.00

4-y-o+	W-R	Per cent	£1 Level Stake
January	1-3	33.3	+1.00
February	1-4	25.0	+13.00
March	1-3	33.3	-1.75
April	0-6	0.0	-6.00
May	1-15	6.7	+6.00
June	5-11	45.5	+6.29
July	2-9	22.2	+4.00
August	2-9	22.2	+5.50
September	3-9	33.3	+9.00
October	0-5	0.0	-5.00
November	1-1	100.0	+6.00
December	0-0	0.0	0.00

Totals	W-R	Per cent	£1 Level Stake
January	4-11	36.4	+2.88
February	1-6	16.7	+11.00
March	1-6	16.7	-4.75
April	1-14	7.1	-9.00
May	2-23	8.7	+2.33
June	6-21	28.6	+4.29
July	2-16	12.5	-3.00
August	3-18	16.7	-1.00
September	5-20	25.0	+7.50
October	0-14	0.0	-14.00
November	2-6	33.3	+11.00
December	1-6	16.7	0.00

DISTANCE

2-y-o	W-R	Per cent	£1 Level Stake
5f-6f	1-5	20.0	-2.00
7f-8f	1-16	6.3	-11.00
9f-13f	0-0	0.0	0.00
14f+	0-0	0.0	0.00

3-y-o	W-R	Per cent	£1 Level Stake
5f-6f	3-17	17.6	-4.13
7f-8f	6-32	18.8	-4.67
9f-13f	0-16	0.0	-16.00
14f+	0-0	0.0	0.00

4-y-o+	W-R	Per cent	£1 Level Stake
5f-6f	2-9	22.2	-5.92
7f-8f	7-26	26.9	+28.21
9f-13f	8-33	24.2	+22.75
14f+	0-7	0.0	-7.00

Totals	W-R	Per cent	£1 Level Stake
5f-6f	6-31	19.4	-12.05
7f-8f	14-74	18.9	+12.54
9f-13f	8-49	16.3	+6.75
14f+	0-7	0.0	-7.00

TYPE OF RACE

Non-Handicaps	W-R	Per cent	£1 Level Stake
2-y-o	2-17	11.8	-9.00
3-y-o	4-21	19.0	-8.63
4-y-o+	7-35	20.0	+7.41

Handicaps	W-R	Per cent	£1 Level Stake
2-y-o	0-4	0.0	-4.00
3-y-o	5-44	11.4	-16.17
4-y-o+	10-40	25.0	+30.63

RACE CLASS

	W-R	Per cent	£1 Level Stake
Class 1	5-30	16.7	+9.33
Class 2	7-27	25.9	+21.08
Class 3	2-18	11.1	-6.00
Class 4	3-27	11.1	-13.63
Class 5	11-47	23.4	+1.46
Class 6	0-12	0.0	-12.00
Class 7	0-0	0.0	0.00

FIRST TIME OUT

	W-R	Per cent	£1 Level Stake
2-y-o	0-9	0.0	-9.00
3-y-o	4-12	33.3	+2.38
4-y-o+	2-12	16.7	+9.00
Totals	6-33	18.2	+2.38

JOCKEYS

	W-R	Per cent	£1 Level Stake
Gerald Mosse	7-24	29.2	+9.33
Silvestre De Sousa	5-26	19.2	-5.54
Sean Levey	4-20	20.0	+7.63
Hollie Doyle	3-7	42.9	+4.50
Mr George Eddery	2-3	66.7	+12.00
Ryan Moore	2-8	25.0	+7.00
Jason Watson	2-8	25.0	+4.50
Paul Mulrennan	1-1	100.0	+0.83
David Probert	1-7	14.3	-4.00
Hayley Turner	1-14	7.1	+7.00

COURSE RECORD

	Total W-R	Non-Hndcps 2-y-o	Non-Hndcps 3-y-o+	Hndcps 2-y-o	Hndcps 3-y-o+	Per cent	£1 Level Stake
Kempton (A.W)	7-38	2-8	3-8	0-3	2-19	18.4	-12.88
Lingfield (A.W)	5-23	0-2	4-14	0-0	1-7	21.7	+10.38
Ascot	3-12	0-0	0-6	0-0	3-6	25.0	+21.50
Goodwood	2-5	0-0	1-2	0-0	1-3	40.0	+5.50
Haydock	2-5	0-0	0-2	0-0	2-3	40.0	+5.00
Sandown	2-6	0-0	0-0	0-0	2-6	33.3	+7.00
Newmkt (Jly)	2-15	0-4	1-3	0-0	1-8	13.3	-3.67
Catterick	1-1	0-0	0-0	0-0	1-1	100.0	+8.50
Hamilton	1-1	0-0	1-1	0-0	0-0	100.0	+0.83
Lingfield	1-1	0-0	0-0	0-0	1-1	100.0	+3.33
Epsom	1-6	0-0	0-0	0-0	1-6	16.7	-2.25
Newbury	1-7	0-0	1-3	0-0	0-4	14.3	-2.00

WINNING HORSES

Horse	Races Run	1st	2nd	3rd	£
Ay Ay (IRE)	6	1	1	0	11972
Brancaster (IRE)	7	2	0	0	8907
Cosmopolitan Queen	9	2	0	1	8280
Country'N'Western (FR)*	5	1	0	0	4617
Dance Teacher (IRE)*	4	1	0	0	6469

Dandhu	4	1	1	0	11828
Dash Of Spice	5	2	2	0	87150
Enzemble (IRE)*	3	1	1	1	3881
Galloway Hills	10	1	2	1	3752
Lady Dancealot (IRE)	10	2	2	3	14814
Master The World (IRE)	10	2	1	0	79394
Merlin Magic	3	1	0	0	15563
Morning Has Broken (IRE)	7	2	1	2	7633
No Nonsense	2	1	0	0	3881
Ripp Orf (IRE)	16	4	7	1	82182
Sir Dancealot (IRE)	10	4	1	1	312834
Total winning prize-money					**£663157**
Favourites	**9-26**		**34.6%**		**0.46**

JAMES EUSTACE

NEWMARKET, SUFFOLK

	No. of Hrs	Races Run	1st	2nd	3rd	Unpl	Per cent	£1 Level Stake
2-y-o	*1*	*1*	*0*	*0*	*0*	*1*	*0.0*	*-1.00*
3-y-o	*4*	*21*	*2*	*1*	*5*	*13*	*9.5*	*-9.50*
4-y-o+	*10*	*50*	*7*	*1*	*4*	*38*	*14.0*	*+17.75*
Totals	**15**	**72**	**9**	**2**	**9**	**52**	**12.5**	**+7.25**
2017	*24*	*92*	*7*	*10*	*14*	*61*	*7.6*	*-24.09*
2016	*25*	*108*	*14*	*11*	*12*	*71*	*13.0*	*-33.77*

JOCKEYS

	W-R	Per cent	£1 Level Stake
Ryan Tate	6-57	10.5	+4.75
Luke Morris	2-5	40.0	+5.00
Aled Beech	1-4	25.0	+3.50

COURSE RECORD

	Total W-R	Non-Hndcps 2-y-o	Non-Hndcps 3-y-o+	Hndcps 2-y-o	Hndcps 3-y-o+	Per cent	£1 Level Stake
Kempton (A.W)	7-22	0-0	0-2	0-0	7-20	31.8	+23.75
Newmarket	1-2	0-0	0-0	0-0	1-2	50.0	+5.50
Windsor	1-2	0-0	0-0	0-0	1-2	50.0	+24.00

WINNING HORSES

Horse	Races Run	1st	2nd	3rd	£
Coverham (IRE)	11	4	1	1	15137
Directory	10	2	1	4	6857
Envoy	6	3	0	0	15807
Total winning prize-money					**£37801**
Favourites	**0-0**		**0.0%**		**0.00**

DAVID EVANS

PANDY, MONMOUTHS

	No. of Hrs	Races Run	1st	2nd	3rd	Unpl	Per cent	£1 Level Stake
2-y-o	*32*	*147*	*6*	*14*	*12*	*114*	*4.1*	*-91.54*
3-y-o	*30*	*202*	*18*	*37*	*21*	*124*	*8.9*	*-59.97*
4-y-o+	*31*	*266*	*18*	*39*	*27*	*182*	*6.8*	*-127.47*
Totals	**93**	**615**	**42**	**90**	**60**	**420**	**6.8**	**-278.98**
2017	*112*	*883*	*81*	*114*	*104*	*582*	*9.2*	*-324.12*
2016	*108*	*720*	*70*	*94*	*97*	*456*	*9.7*	*-241.98*

BY MONTH

2-y-o	W-R	Per cent	£1 Level Stake	**3-y-o**	W-R	Per cent	£1 Level Stake
January	0-0	0.0	0.00	January	3-22	13.6	-2.00
February	0-0	0.0	0.00	February	4-16	25.0	+41.00
March	0-1	0.0	-1.00	March	1-14	7.1	-7.00
April	2-18	11.1	-12.17	April	2-18	11.1	-9.50
May	0-17	0.0	-17.00	May	0-22	0.0	-22.00
June	1-18	5.6	+16.00	June	2-22	9.1	-9.00
July	2-22	9.1	-15.38	July	2-11	18.2	-0.80
August	1-23	4.3	-14.00	August	1-18	5.6	-16.17
September	0-14	0.0	-14.00	September	1-16	6.3	-4.00
October	0-16	0.0	-16.00	October	0-12	0.0	-12.00
November	0-13	0.0	-13.00	November	1-19	5.3	-7.00
December	0-5	0.0	-5.00	December	1-12	8.3	-5.50

4-y-o+	W-R	Per cent	£1 Level Stake	**Totals**	W-R	Per cent	£1 Level Stake
January	0-23	0.0	-23.00	January	3-45	6.7	-25.00
February	3-26	11.5	+5.50	February	7-42	16.7	+46.50
March	1-25	4.0	-13.00	March	2-40	5.0	-21.00
April	3-20	15.0	-5.00	April	7-56	12.5	-26.67
May	2-27	7.4	-14.00	May	2-66	3.0	-53.00
June	2-19	10.5	-8.50	June	5-59	8.5	-1.50
July	2-25	8.0	-20.17	July	6-58	10.3	-42.35
August	2-29	6.9	-18.80	August	4-70	5.7	-48.97
September	2-25	8.0	+11.00	September	3-55	5.5	-7.00
October	0-17	0.0	-17.00	October	0-45	0.0	-45.00
November	0-14	0.0	-14.00	November	1-46	2.2	-21.00
December	1-16	6.3	-10.50	December	2-33	6.1	-16.00

DISTANCE

2-y-o	W-R	Per cent	£1 Level Stake	**3-y-o**	W-R	Per cent	£1 Level Stake
5f-6f	3-98	3.1	-88.42	5f-6f	7-85	8.2	-40.57
7f-8f	3-48	6.3	-2.13	7f-8f	7-88	8.0	-7.00
9f-13f	0-1	0.0	-1.00	9f-13f	4-29	13.8	-12.40
14f+	0-0	0.0	0.00	14f+	0-0	0.0	0.00

4-y-o+	W-R	Per cent	£1 Level Stake	**Totals**	W-R	Per cent	£1 Level Stake
5f-6f	8-100	8.0	-38.50	5f-6f	18-283	6.4	-167.49
7f-8f	7-103	6.8	-59.97	7f-8f	17-239	7.1	-69.10
9f-13f	3-55	5.5	-21.00	9f-13f	7-85	8.2	-34.40
14f+	0-8	0.0	-8.00	14f+	0-8	0.0	-8.00

TYPE OF RACE

Non-Handicaps	W-R	Per cent	£1 Level Stake	**Handicaps**	W-R	Per cent	£1 Level Stake
2-y-o	4-101	4.0	-58.29	2-y-o	2-46	4.3	-33.25
3-y-o	4-39	10.3	-23.57	3-y-o	14-163	8.6	-36.40
4-y-o+	3-21	14.3	+2.83	4-y-o+	15-245	6.1	-130.30

RACE CLASS

	W-R	Per cent	£1 Level Stake
Class 1	1-9	11.1	0.00
Class 2	2-44	4.5	-29.00
Class 3	1-52	1.9	-50.17
Class 4	6-100	6.0	-44.83
Class 5	15-192	7.8	-87.55
Class 6	17-214	7.9	-63.43
Class 7	0-4	0.0	-4.00

FIRST TIME OUT

	W-R	Per cent	£1 Level Stake
2-y-o	1-32	3.1	+2.00
3-y-o	4-30	13.3	+16.00
4-y-o+	1-31	3.2	-25.50
Totals	6-93	6.5	-7.50

JOCKEYS

	W-R	Per cent	£1 Level Stake
Fran Berry	9-100	9.0	-29.67
Rossa Ryan	8-47	17.0	+7.70
Gabriele Malune	4-44	9.1	-13.00
Silvestre De Sousa	3-24	12.5	-10.50
Adam Kirby	3-28	10.7	-18.07
J F Egan	3-38	7.9	-25.50
Kieran O'Neill	2-16	12.5	+8.00
Rhona Pindar	1-1	100.0	+11.00
Hollie Doyle	1-5	20.0	+14.00
Hayley Turner	1-5	20.0	+29.00
Paddy Bradley	1-5	20.0	+7.00
Sean Levey	1-7	14.3	+19.00
Brett Doyle	1-7	14.3	-4.13
Eoin Walsh	1-11	9.1	-9.17
Nicola Currie	1-13	7.7	-9.25
P J McDonald	1-14	7.1	-11.90
Katherine Begley	1-30	3.3	-23.50

COURSE RECORD

	Total W-R	Non-Hndcps 2-y-o	Non-Hndcps 3-y-o+	Hndcps 2-y-o	Hndcps 3-y-o+	Per cent	£1 Level Stake
Chepstow	6-35	0-5	1-1	0-0	5-29	17.1	-9.97
Wolvhptn (A.W)	6-115	0-11	1-13	0-10	5-81	5.2	-48.50
Lingfield (A.W)	5-50	0-3	2-12	0-1	3-34	10.0	-13.50
Southwell (A.W)	4-44	0-1	0-6	0-2	4-35	9.1	+12.50
Chelmsford (A.W)	3-40	1-3	0-2	0-2	2-33	7.5	-29.00
Kempton (A.W)	3-44	1-6	1-3	0-10	1-25	6.8	-17.67
Brighton	2-9	0-0	0-1	0-1	2-7	22.2	+4.50
Lingfield	2-14	0-2	1-4	1-3	0-5	14.3	-8.42
Newbury	2-19	1-8	0-1	0-2	1-8	10.5	+22.00
Ffos Las	2-40	0-6	0-0	1-8	1-26	5.0	-14.00
Hamilton	1-3	0-0	1-1	0-0	0-2	33.3	-0.90
Thirsk	1-4	1-2	0-0	0-1	0-1	25.0	-1.13
Sandown	1-5	0-0	0-0	0-0	1-5	20.0	0.00
Newmkt (Jly)	1-9	0-0	0-1	0-0	1-8	11.1	-1.00
Bath	1-14	0-3	0-1	0-1	1-9	7.1	-8.50
Leicester	1-19	0-6	0-5	0-1	1-7	5.3	-16.50
Windsor	1-44	0-15	0-3	0-0	1-26	2.3	-41.90

WINNING HORSES

Horse	Races Run	1st	2nd	3rd	£
*Anif (IRE)	1	1	0	0	3105
Bahamian Dollar	10	1	1	4	6969
Bond Angel	10	2	1	2	6210
Brexit Time (IRE)	3	1	2	0	4140
Brockey Rise (IRE)	20	2	3	1	3105
Cherubic	8	2	0	2	6857
Daily Trader	10	1	1	0	3105
Dougan	13	1	2	0	5531
Essenaitch (IRE)	14	1	2	2	3752
Felisa	6	1	1	0	3105
Go Annie Go*	10	1	3	2	3398
Gracious John (IRE)	18	2	2	3	41082
Harry Beau	19	3	3	2	10609
Herm (IRE)	10	1	2	0	3105
Istanbul Pasha (IRE)*	6	1	0	0	3105
Joegogo (IRE)	20	1	2	2	5531
*Kodiline (IRE)	8	1	0	0	3752
Lady Prancealot (IRE)	5	1	1	1	4528
Last Page	5	1	1	0	3752
Lihou	9	1	2	0	5822
Los Camachos (IRE)	13	1	4	3	3105
Miniature Daffodil (IRE)	8	2	1	2	6857
Mouchee (IRE)*	7	1	3	1	3752
North Korea (IRE)*	9	1	2	0	3752
One Kiss	7	1	1	0	3170
Renny's Lady (IRE)	7	2	1	1	8992
Room To Improve (IRE)	1	1	0	0	4787
Satchville Flyer	20	1	4	2	3752
Sea Fox (IRE)	17	3	1	4	27300
Sonnetist	12	1	1	1	3752
The Establishment	10	1	2	1	5531
*The Groove	9	1	4	1	3105
Total winning prize-money					**£208418**
Favourites	**10-35**		**28.6%**		**-11.68**

NIKKI EVANS

PANDY, MONMOUTHS

	No. of Hrs	Races Run	1st	2nd	3rd	Unpl	Per cent	£1 Level Stake
2-y-o	*1*	*2*	*0*	*0*	*0*	*2*	*0.0*	*-2.00*
3-y-o	*2*	*5*	*0*	*0*	*0*	*5*	*0.0*	*-5.00*
4-y-o+	*17*	*75*	*1*	*5*	*3*	*66*	*1.3*	*-70.50*
Totals	**20**	**82**	**1**	**5**	**3**	**73**	**1.2**	**-77.50**
2017	*22*	*77*	*1*	*5*	*5*	*66*	*1.3*	*-26.00*
2016	*21*	*78*	*3*	*3*	*6*	*66*	*3.8*	*-35.00*

JOCKEYS

	W-R	Per cent	£1 Level Stake
Stephen Cummins	1-4	25.0	+0.50

COURSE RECORD

	Total W-R	Non-Hndcps 2-y-o	Non-Hndcps 3-y-o+	Hndcps 2-y-o	Hndcps 3-y-o+	Per cent	£1 Level Stake
Lingfield	1-2	0-0	0-0	0-0	1-2	50.0	+2.50

WINNING HORSES

Horse	Races Run	1st	2nd	3rd	£
Maroc	7	1	3	0	3105
Total winning prize-money					**£3105**
Favourites	**0-1**		**0.0%**		**-1.00**

JAMES EWART

LANGHOLM, DUMFRIES & G'WAY

	No. of Hrs	Races Run	1st	2nd	3rd	Unpl	Per cent	£1 Level Stake
2-y-o	*0*	*0*	*0*	*0*	*0*	*0*	*0.0*	*0.00*
3-y-o	*3*	*20*	*1*	*3*	*1*	*15*	*5.0*	*-16.50*
4-y-o+	*7*	*21*	*3*	*1*	*3*	*14*	*14.3*	*-13.13*
Totals	**10**	**41**	**4**	**4**	**4**	**29**	**9.8**	**-29.63**
2017	*7*	*28*	*1*	*1*	*3*	*23*	*3.6*	*-21.00*
2016	*1*	*3*	*0*	*1*	*0*	*2*	*0.0*	*-3.00*

JOCKEYS

	W-R	Per cent	£1 Level Stake
Liam Keniry	3-9	33.3	-1.13
Ben Robinson	1-1	100.0	+2.50

COURSE RECORD

	Total W-R	Non-Hndcps 2-y-o	Non-Hndcps 3-y-o+	Hndcps 2-y-o	Hndcps 3-y-o+	Per cent	£1 Level Stake
Southwell (A.W)	3-8	0-0	0-4	0-0	3-4	37.5	-0.13
Newcastle (A.W)	1-10	0-0	0-2	0-0	1-8	10.0	-6.50

WINNING HORSES

Horse	Races Run	1st	2nd	3rd	£
Da Capo Dandy (IRE)	4	3	1	0	6210
I Am Dandy (IRE)	11	1	3	1	3235
Total winning prize-money					**£9445**
Favourites	**9-16**		**56.3%**		**8.95**

LES EYRE

CATWICK, N YORKS

	No. of Hrs	Races Run	1st	2nd	3rd	Unpl	Per cent	£1 Level Stake
2-y-o	*4*	*10*	*0*	*0*	*0*	*10*	*0.0*	*-10.00*
3-y-o	*5*	*29*	*1*	*1*	*2*	*25*	*3.4*	*-24.00*
4-y-o+	*17*	*126*	*17*	*10*	*10*	*89*	*13.5*	*-14.20*
Totals	**26**	**165**	**18**	**11**	**12**	**124**	**10.9**	**-48.20**
2017	*17*	*150*	*18*	*16*	*15*	*101*	*12.0*	*-5.04*
2016	*17*	*127*	*10*	*15*	*11*	*91*	*7.9*	*-46.75*

BY MONTH

2-y-o	W-R	Per cent	£1 Level Stake	**3-y-o**	W-R	Per cent	£1 Level Stake
January	0-0	0.0	0.00	January	1-1	100.0	+4.00
February	0-0	0.0	0.00	February	0-1	0.0	-1.00
March	0-0	0.0	0.00	March	0-2	0.0	-2.00
April	0-1	0.0	-1.00	April	0-2	0.0	-2.00
May	0-1	0.0	-1.00	May	0-2	0.0	-2.00
June	0-0	0.0	0.00	June	0-1	0.0	-1.00
July	0-0	0.0	0.00	July	0-4	0.0	-4.00
August	0-1	0.0	-1.00	August	0-2	0.0	-2.00
September	0-1	0.0	-1.00	September	0-4	0.0	-4.00
October	0-3	0.0	-3.00	October	0-3	0.0	-3.00
November	0-3	0.0	-3.00	November	0-4	0.0	-4.00
December	0-0	0.0	0.00	December	0-3	0.0	-3.00

4-y-o+	W-R	Per cent	£1 Level Stake	**Totals**	W-R	Per cent	£1 Level Stake
January	0-3	0.0	-3.00	January	1-4	25.0	+1.00
February	0-6	0.0	-6.00	February	0-7	0.0	-7.00
March	1-5	20.0	-1.50	March	1-7	14.3	-3.50
April	0-9	0.0	-9.00	April	0-12	0.0	-12.00
May	6-23	26.1	+23.75	May	6-26	23.1	+20.75
June	4-17	23.5	+15.50	June	4-18	22.2	+14.50
July	2-17	11.8	-2.00	July	2-21	9.5	-6.00
August	0-12	0.0	-12.00	August	0-15	0.0	-15.00
September	4-15	26.7	-0.95	September	4-20	20.0	-5.95
October	0-10	0.0	-10.00	October	0-16	0.0	-16.00
November	0-8	0.0	-8.00	November	0-15	0.0	-12.00
December	0-1	0.0	-1.00	December	0-4	0.0	-4.00

DISTANCE

2-y-o	W-R	Per cent	£1 Level Stake	**3-y-o**	W-R	Per cent	£1 Level Stake
5f-6f	0-6	0.0	-6.00	5f-6f	0-10	0.0	-10.00
7f-8f	0-4	0.0	-4.00	7f-8f	1-7	14.3	-2.00
9f-13f	0-0	0.0	0.00	9f-13f	0-12	0.0	-12.00
14f+	0-0	0.0	0.00	14f+	0-0	0.0	0.00

4-y-o+	W-R	Per cent	£1 Level Stake	**Totals**	W-R	Per cent	£1 Level Stake
5f-6f	6-32	18.8	+4.50	5f-6f	6-48	12.5	-11.50
7f-8f	9-72	12.5	-12.20	7f-8f	10-83	12.0	-18.20
9f-13f	2-22	9.1	-6.50	9f-13f	2-34	5.9	-18.50
14f+	0-0	0.0	0.00	14f+	0-0	0.0	0.00

TYPE OF RACE

Non-Handicaps	W-R	Per cent	£1 Level Stake	**Handicaps**	W-R	Per cent	£1 Level Stake
2-y-o	0-9	0.0	-9.00	2-y-o	0-1	0.0	-1.00
3-y-o	0-3	0.0	-3.00	3-y-o	1-26	3.8	-21.00
4-y-o+	1-3	33.3	+0.50	4-y-o+	16-123	13.0	-14.70

RACE CLASS

	W-R	Per cent	£1 Level Stake
Class 1	0-1	0.0	-1.00
Class 2	1-8	12.5	-2.50
Class 3	4-18	22.2	+10.00
Class 4	5-48	10.4	-11.50
Class 5	7-57	12.3	-15.20
Class 6	1-33	3.0	-28.00
Class 7	0-0	0.0	0.00

FIRST TIME OUT

	W-R	Per cent	£1 Level Stake
2-y-o	0-4	0.0	-4.00
3-y-o	1-5	20.0	0.00
4-y-o+	2-17	11.8	+7.50
Totals	3-26	11.5	+3.50

JOCKEYS

	W-R	Per cent	£1 Level Stake
Silvestre De Sousa	5-13	38.5	+14.00
Joe Fanning	4-23	17.4	+0.25
Jane Elliott	3-23	13.0	+6.25
Daniel Tudhope	2-6	33.3	+9.00
Mr James Harding	1-3	33.3	+0.50
James Sullivan	1-5	20.0	+1.00
Robert Winston	1-11	9.1	0.00
David Allan	1-15	6.7	-13.20

COURSE RECORD

	Total W-R	Non-Hndcps 2-y-o	Non-Hndcps 3-y-o+	Hndcps 2-y-o	Hndcps 3-y-o+	Per cent	£1 Level Stake
Beverley	6-28	0-1	0-1	0-0	6-26	21.4	+14.55
Pontefract	3-20	0-1	0-0	0-0	3-19	15.0	-1.25
Ripon	2-7	0-0	0-0	0-0	2-7	28.6	+4.00
Chester	1-2	0-0	0-0	0-0	1-2	50.0	+1.50
Southwell (A.W)	1-3	0-0	0-0	0-0	1-3	33.3	+2.00
Nottingham	1-5	0-0	0-0	0-0	1-5	20.0	+6.00
Redcar	1-5	0-0	0-0	0-0	1-5	20.0	+1.00
York	1-6	0-0	0-0	0-0	1-6	16.7	-0.50
Doncaster	1-7	0-2	0-1	0-0	1-4	14.3	+3.00
Newcastle (A.W)	1-21	0-3	1-3	0-1	0-14	4.8	-17.50

WINNING HORSES

Horse	Races Run	1st	2nd	3rd	£
Cote D'Azur	11	1	0	1	9704
Dawaaleeb (USA)	9	3	1	2	20397
Detachment	11	3	2	0	10502
El Principe	3	1	0	0	6553
Golden Guest	10	1	1	0	3752
Highly Sprung (IRE)	7	2	0	1	7763
Hilborough	11	1	0	2	3105
Intense Style (IRE)	10	1	1	2	5865
Make On Madam (IRE)	12	1	0	2	4033
Sandra's Secret (IRE)	8	3	2	1	40463
Van Gerwen	11	1	2	0	4033
Total winning prize-money					**£116170**
Favourites	**6-15**		**40.0%**		**5.80**

RICHARD FAHEY

MUSLEY BANK, N YORKS

	No. of Hrs	Races Run	1st	2nd	3rd	Unpl	Per cent	£1 Level Stake
2-y-o	*108*	*493*	*54*	*65*	*62*	*312*	*11.0*	*-160.93*
3-y-o	*82*	*571*	*79*	*79*	*67*	*345*	*13.8*	*+4.24*
4-y-o+	*66*	*535*	*57*	*55*	*62*	*360*	*10.7*	*-92.36*
Totals	**256**	**1599**	**190**	**199**	**191**	**1017**	**11.9**	**-249.05**
2017	*298*	*1749*	*200*	*220*	*218*	*1109*	*11.4*	*-505.32*
2016	*294*	*1739*	*198*	*194*	*223*	*1121*	*11.4*	*-396.09*

BY MONTH

2-y-o	W-R	Per cent	£1 Level Stake
January	0-0	0.0	0.00
February	0-0	0.0	0.00
March	0-2	0.0	-2.00
April	2-14	14.3	-0.50
May	9-44	20.5	+8.88
June	8-60	13.3	-9.34
July	12-82	14.6	-17.58
August	12-101	11.9	-24.51
September	2-82	2.4	-56.00
October	6-60	10.0	-32.38
November	1-31	3.2	-26.50
December	2-17	11.8	-1.00

3-y-o	W-R	Per cent	£1 Level Stake
January	1-17	5.9	-12.50
February	2-16	12.5	+3.00
March	3-24	12.5	+1.00
April	7-40	17.5	-1.50
May	11-75	14.7	-18.37
June	14-85	16.5	+49.50
July	15-83	18.1	-2.80
August	10-80	12.5	-27.09
September	6-66	9.1	-5.50
October	5-51	9.8	+20.00
November	2-22	9.1	-6.00
December	3-12	25.0	+4.50

4-y-o+	W-R	Per cent	£1 Level Stake
January	1-23	4.3	-19.25
February	1-22	4.5	-13.00
March	5-30	16.7	+8.00
April	8-44	18.2	+15.75
May	8-79	10.1	-30.21
June	12-88	13.6	+0.13
July	9-68	13.2	-5.75
August	6-59	10.2	+5.23
September	3-62	4.8	-29.25
October	3-44	6.8	-19.00
November	1-14	7.1	-3.00
December	0-2	0.0	-2.00

Totals	W-R	Per cent	£1 Level Stake
January	2-40	5.0	-31.75
February	3-38	7.9	-10.00
March	8-56	14.3	+7.00
April	17-98	17.3	+13.75
May	28-198	14.1	-39.70
June	34-233	14.6	+40.29
July	36-233	15.5	-26.13
August	28-240	11.7	-46.37
September	11-210	5.2	-90.75
October	14-155	9.0	-31.38
November	4-67	6.0	-9.00
December	5-31	16.1	+2.50

DISTANCE

2-y-o	W-R	Per cent	£1 Level Stake
5f-6f	42-338	12.4	-84.05
7f-8f	12-148	8.1	-69.88
9f-13f	0-7	0.0	-7.00
14f+	0-0	0.0	0.00

3-y-o	W-R	Per cent	£1 Level Stake
5f-6f	32-193	16.6	+9.01
7f-8f	31-255	12.2	-8.27
9f-13f	16-120	13.3	+6.50
14f+	0-3	0.0	-3.00

4-y-o+	W-R	Per cent	£1 Level Stake
5f-6f	15-155	9.7	-15.25
7f-8f	26-223	11.7	-15.02
9f-13f	12-125	9.6	-42.25
14f+	4-32	12.5	-19.83

Totals	W-R	Per cent	£1 Level Stake
5f-6f	89-686	13.0	-90.29
7f-8f	69-626	11.0	-93.17
9f-13f	28-252	11.1	-42.75
14f+	4-35	11.4	-22.83

TYPE OF RACE

Non-Handicaps

	W-R	Per cent	£1 Level Stake
2-y-o	43-351	12.3	-86.80
3-y-o	14-98	14.3	+2.29
4-y-o+	13-64	20.3	+10.35

Handicaps

	W-R	Per cent	£1 Level Stake
2-y-o	11-142	7.7	-74.13
3-y-o	65-473	13.7	+1.95
4-y-o+	44-471	9.3	-102.71

RACE CLASS

	W-R	Per cent	£1 Level Stake
Class 1	8-94	8.5	-25.42

FIRST TIME OUT

	W-R	Per cent	£1 Level Stake
2-y-o	11-108	10.2	-12.25

Class 2	16-266	6.0	-103.50
Class 3	29-213	13.6	-3.50
Class 4	51-386	13.2	-59.62
Class 5	65-487	13.3	-50.08
Class 6	21-152	13.8	-4.93
Class 7	0-1	0.0	-1.00

3-y-o	15-82	18.3	+12.63
4-y-o+	6-66	9.1	-21.50
Totals	32-256	12.5	-21.12

JOCKEYS

	W-R	Per cent	£1 Level Stake
Paul Hanagan	70-555	12.6	-55.61
Tony Hamilton	30-313	9.6	-57.25
David Nolan	12-54	22.2	+14.42
Connor Murtagh	12-97	12.4	-28.25
Jack Garritty	9-76	11.8	12.04
Paddy Mathers	9-125	7.2	-83.27
Barry McHugh	8-37	21.6	+36.25
Sebastian Woods	6-70	8.6	-17.50
P J McDonald	4-21	19.0	+4.50
Oisin Murphy	3-3	100.0	+12.00
Silvestre De Sousa	3-11	27.3	+4.75
Daniel Tudhope	3-13	23.1	-6.87
Connor Beasley	3-13	23.1	+12.50
Oakley Brown	3-35	8.6	-11.13
Graham Lee	2-5	40.0	+3.50
Russell Harris	2-13	15.4	+4.00
Megan Nicholls	2-13	15.4	-1.00
Richard Kingscote	1-1	100.0	+1.00
Kieran O'Neill	1-2	50.0	+10.00
Miss Serena Brotherton	1-2	50.0	+9.00
Gerald Mosse	1-3	33.3	+0.75
Adam McNamara	1-4	25.0	+7.00
Rhiain Ingram	1-5	20.0	+4.50
Joe Fanning	1-6	16.7	-1.00
Andrew Mullen	1-7	14.3	+1.00
James Sullivan	1-8	12.5	+7.00

COURSE RECORD

	Total	Non-Hndcps		Hndcps		Per	£1 Level
	W-R	2-y-o	3-y-o+	2-y-o	3-y-o+	cent	Stake
Newcastle (A.W)	16-117	2-17	1-17	1-13	12-70	13.7	-7.38
York	16-136	2-33	1-8	2-9	11-86	11.8	+24.00
Pontefract	12-68	5-16	0-5	2-5	5-42	17.6	+25.88
Chester	12-112	2-14	3-9	0-9	7-80	10.7	-41.22
Hamilton	11-60	3-16	1-6	0-6	7-32	18.3	+0.55
Ripon	11-64	3-21	0-0	0-3	8-40	17.2	+14.75
Wolvhptn (A.W)	11-101	5-21	3-13	0-15	3-52	10.9	-27.43
Musselburgh	10-49	2-7	0-4	2-5	6-33	20.4	+21.13
Thirsk	10-60	2-18	4-7	0-3	4-32	16.7	+16.55
Doncaster	10-77	2-13	1-8	0-2	7-54	13.0	+8.25
Ayr	10-83	3-14	0-2	1-8	6-59	12.0	-29.25
Beverley	7-80	2-31	1-7	0-1	4-41	8.8	-52.95
Southwell (A.W)	6-42	1-4	2-6	0-5	3-27	14.3	-13.75
Nottingham	6-43	1-11	0-5	1-9	4-18	14.0	+10.08
Carlisle	6-53	2-19	1-3	1-3	2-28	11.3	-14.13
Redcar	6-55	3-25	1-8	0-3	2-19	10.9	-21.13
Haydock	6-58	1-14	1-5	0-5	4-34	10.3	-14.67
Leicester	4-38	1-8	1-3	0-7	2-20	10.5	-22.09
Catterick	4-49	0-11	0-5	0-9	4-24	8.2	-24.75
Chelmsford (A.W)	3-51	0-2	0-7	0-10	3-32	5.9	-23.00
Wetherby	2-10	0-2	0-1	0-0	2-7	20.0	+15.00
Epsom	2-16	1-1	1-3	0-2	0-10	12.5	-0.50
Newmarket	2-31	0-5	1-4	0-2	1-20	6.5	-15.00
Lingfield (A.W)	2-32	0-4	1-10	0-4	1-14	6.3	-13.00
Lingfield	1-1	0-0	1-1	0-0	0-0	100.0	+2.25
Newbury	1-11	0-6	1-2	0-0	0-3	9.1	-7.25
Newmkt (Jly)	1-12	0-2	0-1	0-2	1-7	8.3	-4.00
Ascot	1-27	0-8	1-4	0-0	0-15	3.7	+2.00
Goodwood	1-27	0-5	0-2	1-1	0-19	3.7	-22.00

WINNING HORSES

Horse	Races Run	1st	2nd	3rd	£
Absolute Dream (IRE)	8	1	2	1	4528
Aljady (FR)	4	2	1	0	14167
Amadeus (IRE)	6	1	0	1	3105
Amazing Michele (FR)	13	2	1	4	15580
Amber Spark (IRE)	7	1	1	1	6081
Andok (IRE)	11	2	1	0	8539
Aurag (IRE)	7	1	0	1	5434
Axe Axelrod (USA)	4	1	2	0	3752
Ballymore Castle (IRE)*	4	1	0	0	3493
Baronial Pride	6	1	1	3	5434
Billy Bond	9	2	2	0	6663
Borodin (IRE)	7	2	2	1	18858
Brian The Snail (IRE)	9	1	0	0	7763
Call Him Al (IRE)	10	1	0	1	3105
Cameo Star (IRE)	11	1	1	1	0
Charming Kid	5	1	0	1	12450
Claire Underwood (IRE)	4	2	2	0	9283
Clubbable	9	2	1	0	38326
Cognac Blue	9	1	1	2	3493
Constantino (IRE)	10	1	1	2	7246
Coolagh Forest (IRE)	2	1	0	0	3752
Cosmic Law (IRE)	9	2	0	1	43819
Crotchet	10	2	3	2	20083
Crownthorpe	10	1	1	1	9338
Dance Diva	7	1	1	1	22684
Delph Crescent (IRE)	10	3	1	0	29872
Doctor Cross (IRE)	6	1	0	1	3752
Dose	14	2	2	3	8173
Dubai Acclaim (IRE)	9	2	3	0	7569
Eljayeff (IRE)	4	2	1	0	9380
Equitant	9	2	1	2	15461
Essenza (IRE)	12	1	4	1	3752
Exhort	10	2	3	0	22290
Firewater	8	1	0	0	3170
Flawless Jewel (FR)	4	1	1	0	6469
Fool For You (IRE)	9	2	4	1	19666
Forest Ranger (IRE)	5	2	1	0	104914
Gabrial (IRE)	15	1	2	3	9338
*Gabrial The Devil (IRE)	8	2	3	1	14102
Gabrial The One (IRE)	6	1	1	2	3881
Gabrial The Saint (IRE)	7	2	0	0	24278
Gabrial The Tiger (IRE)	13	2	0	1	7504

Gabrial The Wire	8	1	2	0	5852
Gabrial's Kaka (IRE)	6	1	1	0	5865
Gabrial's Star*	1	1	0	0	3752
Gabrials Centurion (IRE)	8	1	1	3	4399
Gallipoli (IRE)	11	1	2	3	6728
Gangland	5	1	1	1	4663
George Bowen (IRE)	10	2	2	0	39840
Get The Rhythm	4	1	0	0	5175
Gin In The Inn (IRE)	10	2	1	1	19517
Golconda Prince (IRE)	11	1	0	3	3752
Golden Circle (IRE)	4	1	2	0	3881
Good Tyne Girl (IRE)*	7	2	0	1	7116
Grise Lightning (FR)	8	1	0	0	4787
Heaven's Guest (IRE)	7	1	0	1	5531
Illusions	8	1	0	2	6469
Indomeneo	10	1	2	1	6728
International Man	9	1	1	1	8645
Inviolable Spirit (IRE)	11	1	1	3	4011
*Joe's Spirit (IRE)	3	1	0	0	7439
Kimberella	15	2	2	4	30320
King Of Tonga (IRE)	4	1	1	2	6728
Knowing Glance (IRE)	6	1	0	0	4852
Kodyanna (IRE)	8	2	0	2	31491
La Sioux (IRE)	13	2	0	0	8345
Lady In Question (IRE)	8	1	2	3	5531
Lucky Lucky Man (IRE)	11	2	2	1	27020
Luis Vaz De Torres (IRE)	7	2	0	1	14749
Mabo	4	1	0	0	3105
Maybride	3	1	0	0	16173
Metallic Black	4	1	0	0	4852
Militia	7	2	1	1	11256
More Than This	3	3	0	0	22222
Mr Buttons (IRE)	4	1	2	1	4205
Mr Diamond (IRE)	8	2	1	1	20377
Mr Lupton (IRE)	11	3	2	0	93506
Mrs Hoo (IRE)	6	1	1	1	5822
Nicki's Angel (IRE)	3	1	0	0	3235
Ninetythreetwenty (IRE)	3	2	0	0	19150
Northwest Frontier (IRE)	9	3	1	1	17337
Odds On Oli	18	2	3	4	7181
Pacino	6	1	0	0	3752
Paddy Power (IRE)	11	1	0	0	9962
Paramount Love	7	1	0	1	6469
Penwortham (IRE)	7	1	0	1	6081
Picture No Sound (IRE)	3	1	0	0	12450
Posh Perfect	9	1	1	0	4528
Powerallied (IRE)	9	1	3	1	11828
Primeiro Boy (IRE)	9	1	2	0	3493
Private Matter	10	1	0	2	6728
Quayside	4	1	1	0	4852
Queen Penn	10	1	1	3	14006
Red Balloons	7	2	1	1	151421
Red Hot (FR)	7	1	0	0	3235
Rene Mathis (GER)	11	2	0	0	9833
Requinto Dawn (IRE)	12	1	4	0	6728
Right Action	14	2	1	2	15234
Roderick	4	2	1	0	7375
Rotherhithe	2	1	0	0	4011
Royal Connoisseur (IRE)	9	1	2	0	3105
Royal Cosmic	6	1	1	0	3493
Sabre	5	1	2	1	3752
Sands Of Mali (FR)	5	2	1	0	409730
Scofflaw*	10	2	0	0	17984
Scotch Myst	9	1	2	1	3105
Sempre Presto (IRE)	8	2	1	2	7763
Sioux Frontier (IRE)	7	1	0	1	4140
Society Queen (IRE)	4	2	1	0	13779
Society Red	9	2	1	1	19003
Sootability (IRE)	4	1	0	1	5822
Space Traveller	5	2	0	0	9186
Spanish Mane (IRE)*	7	2	0	1	6598
Spray The Sea (IRE)	8	2	0	0	4140
Starlight Romance (IRE)	7	1	2	0	9704
Stewardess (IRE)	10	2	2	0	8604
Suegioo (FR)	11	1	1	0	6469
Swiss Belle	6	1	0	1	3105
The Feathered Nest (IRE)	4	1	0	1	7698
The Navigator	4	1	0	0	3881
The Right Choice (IRE)	9	2	0	2	7633
Third Time Lucky (IRE)	12	1	1	3	9704
Vange	3	1	1	0	11828
Ventura Dragon (IRE)	5	1	0	0	7763
Ventura Gold (IRE)	14	3	0	2	10997
Ventura Ocean (IRE)	6	1	2	0	6469
Wasntexpectingthat	6	1	1	2	3170
Windsor Cross (IRE)	8	2	0	0	11027
Wirral Girl (IRE)	11	1	2	2	3752
Withernsea (IRE)	10	1	1	0	3781
Zap	9	1	1	0	31125
Zip Along (IRE)	4	3	0	0	25848
Total winning prize-money					**£2048298**
Favourites	**50-143**		**35.0%**		**-10.25**

CHRIS FAIRHURST

MIDDLEHAM, N YORKS

	No. of Hrs	Races Run	1st	2nd	3rd	Unpl	Per cent	£1 Level Stake
2-y-o	*1*	*1*	*0*	*0*	*0*	*1*	*0.0*	*-1.00*
3-y-o	*4*	*26*	*4*	*2*	*4*	*16*	*15.4*	*+18.00*
4-y-o+	*6*	*31*	*3*	*1*	*0*	*27*	*9.7*	*-10.50*
Totals	**11**	**58**	**7**	**3**	**4**	**44**	**12.1**	**+6.50**
2017	*11*	*62*	*8*	*5*	*8*	*41*	*12.9*	*+18.60*
2016	*11*	*61*	*3*	*3*	*8*	*47*	*4.9*	*+7.00*

JOCKEYS

	W-R	Per cent	£1 Level Stake
Jason Hart	2-4	50.0	+10.00
Michael Stainton	2-13	15.4	+3.00
Paula Muir	2-14	14.3	-4.50
James Sullivan	1-1	100.0	+16.00

COURSE RECORD

	Total W-R	Non-Hndcps 2-y-o	3-y-o+	Hndcps 2-y-o	3-y-o+	Per cent	£1 Level Stake
Ripon	2-5	0-0	0-1	0-0	2-4	40.0	+19.00
Thirsk	2-12	0-0	0-0	0-0	2-12	16.7	+8.50
Chester	1-1	0-0	0-0	0-0	1-1	100.0	+4.00
Doncaster	1-7	0-0	0-1	0-0	1-6	14.3	+4.00
Redcar	1-7	0-0	0-2	0-0	1-5	14.3	-3.00

WINNING HORSES

Horse	Races Run	1st	2nd	3rd	£
Benadalid	7	2	2	2	21643
Florenza	7	1	0	0	9057
Mountain Breath	4	2	0	0	10739
The Armed Man	10	2	1	0	14426
Total winning prize-money					**£55865**
Favourites	**0-1**		**0.0%**		**-1.00**

JAMES FANSHAWE

NEWMARKET, SUFFOLK

	No. of Hrs	Races Run	1st	2nd	3rd	Unpl	Per cent	£1 Level Stake
2-y-o	*10*	*23*	*3*	*2*	*3*	*15*	*13.0*	*+7.91*
3-y-o	*35*	*152*	*19*	*26*	*24*	*83*	*12.5*	*-63.31*
4-y-o+	*27*	*133*	*16*	*27*	*16*	*74*	*12.0*	*-52.63*
Totals	**72**	**308**	**38**	**55**	**43**	**172**	**12.3**	**-108.03**
2017	*66*	*273*	*34*	*49*	*42*	*146*	*12.5*	*-103.61*
2016	*63*	*243*	*43*	*35*	*32*	*133*	*17.7*	*-36.02*

BY MONTH

2-y-o	W-R	Per cent	£1 Level Stake
January	0-0	0.0	0.00
February	0-0	0.0	0.00
March	0-0	0.0	0.00
April	0-0	0.0	0.00
May	0-0	0.0	0.00
June	0-1	0.0	-1.00
July	0-0	0.0	0.00
August	1-4	25.0	+17.00
September	1-5	20.0	+3.00
October	0-7	0.0	-7.00
November	0-5	0.0	-5.00
December	1-1	100.0	+0.91

3-y-o	W-R	Per cent	£1 Level Stake
January	1-3	33.3	+2.50
February	0-0	0.0	0.00
March	0-1	0.0	-1.00
April	3-9	33.3	+13.00
May	0-22	0.0	-22.00
June	3-17	17.6	-7.50
July	2-17	11.8	-10.59
August	1-20	5.0	-17.13
September	3-19	15.8	-1.00
October	3-21	14.3	-4.55
November	1-13	7.7	-11.27
December	2-10	20.0	-3.77

4-y-o+	W-R	Per cent	£1 Level Stake
January	1-5	20.0	-1.50
February	2-5	40.0	+1.00
March	0-5	0.0	-5.00
April	0-10	0.0	-10.00
May	1-23	4.3	-20.25
June	4-24	16.7	-8.38
July	0-11	0.0	-11.00
August	2-16	12.5	-10.75
September	5-18	27.8	+22.25
October	1-9	11.1	-2.00
November	0-4	0.0	-4.00
December	0-3	0.0	-3.00

Totals	W-R	Per cent	£1 Level Stake
January	2-8	25.0	+1.00
February	2-5	40.0	+1.00
March	0-6	0.0	-6.00
April	3-19	15.8	+3.00
May	1-45	2.2	-42.25
June	7-42	16.7	-16.88
July	2-28	7.1	-21.59
August	4-40	10.0	-10.88
September	9-42	21.4	+24.25
October	4-37	10.8	-13.55
November	1-22	4.5	-15.27
December	3-14	21.4	-6.77

DISTANCE

2-y-o	W-R	Per cent	£1 Level Stake
5f-6f	2-8	25.0	+21.00
7f-8f	1-15	6.7	-13.09
9f-13f	0-0	0.0	0.00
14f+	0-0	0.0	0.00

3-y-o	W-R	Per cent	£1 Level Stake
5f-6f	3-16	18.8	+2.75
7f-8f	7-62	11.3	-26.25
9f-13f	9-71	12.7	-36.81
14f+	0-3	0.0	-3.00

4-y-o+	W-R	Per cent	£1 Level Stake
5f-6f	8-26	30.8	+11.25
7f-8f	2-32	6.3	-18.00
9f-13f	2-47	4.3	-33.00
14f+	4-28	14.3	-12.88

Totals	W-R	Per cent	£1 Level Stake
5f-6f	13-50	26.0	+35.00
7f-8f	10-109	9.2	-57.34
9f-13f	11-118	9.3	-69.81
14f+	4-31	12.9	-15.88

TYPE OF RACE

Non-Handicaps	W-R	Per cent	£1 Level Stake
2-y-o	2-21	9.5	+1.91
3-y-o	7-83	8.4	-50.74
4-y-o+	4-28	14.3	-7.25

Handicaps	W-R	Per cent	£1 Level Stake
2-y-o	1-2	50.0	+6.00
3-y-o	12-69	17.4	-12.57
4-y-o+	12-105	11.4	-45.38

RACE CLASS

	W-R	Per cent	£1 Level Stake
Class 1	2-18	11.1	-7.25
Class 2	5-35	14.3	-9.13
Class 3	6-41	14.6	-12.88
Class 4	11-69	15.9	-1.47
Class 5	12-128	9.4	-71.22
Class 6	2-17	11.8	-6.09
Class 7	0-0	0.0	0.00

FIRST TIME OUT

	W-R	Per cent	£1 Level Stake
2-y-o	1-10	10.0	+11.00
3-y-o	3-35	8.6	-13.00
4-y-o+	3-27	11.1	-17.75
Totals	7-72	9.7	-19.75

JOCKEYS

	W-R	Per cent	£1 Level Stake
George Wood	16-114	14.0	-20.16
Daniel Muscutt	9-103	8.7	-50.97
Oisin Murphy	4-15	26.7	+9.88
Tom Queally	3-20	15.0	-9.00
Ryan Moore	1-1	100.0	+1.50
Richard Kingscote	1-1	100.0	+1.88
Charles Bishop	1-2	50.0	+0.38
Adam Kirby	1-6	16.7	-4.27
David Probert	1-7	14.3	-3.75
P J McDonald	1-8	12.5	-2.50

COURSE RECORD

	Total W-R	Non-Hndcps 2-y-o	3-y-o+	Hndcps 2-y-o	3-y-o+	Per cent	£1 Level Stake
Kempton (A.W)	12-73	1-5	3-18	0-0	8-50	16.4	-22.91
Lingfield (A.W)	5-33	0-5	2-12	1-2	2-14	15.2	-12.77
Chester	3-3	0-0	0-0	0-0	3-3	100.0	+14.13

Haydock	3-7	0-0	2-3	0-0	1-4	42.9	+16.50
Doncaster	3-18	0-0	2-8	0-0	1-10	16.7	+7.91
Chelmsford (A.W)	3-20	0-0	0-10	0-0	3-10	15.0	-9.25
Yarmouth	2-18	1-2	0-3	0-0	1-13	11.1	+10.00
Newbury	1-6	0-0	0-1	0-0	1-5	16.7	-1.50
Sandown	1-6	0-0	0-2	0-0	1-4	16.7	-3.50
Goodwood	1-7	0-0	0-4	0-0	1-3	14.3	-3.75
Windsor	1-8	0-0	1-5	0-0	0-3	12.5	-5.25
Lingfield	1-10	0-0	0-5	0-0	1-5	10.0	-5.50
Newmkt (Jly)	1-10	0-0	0-0	0-0	1-10	10.0	-6.00
Nottingham	1-17	0-3	1-8	0-0	0-6	5.9	-14.13

WINNING HORSES

Horse	Races Run	1st	2nd	3rd	£
Blue Reflection	7	1	0	1	3105
Bombyx	5	1	1	2	5531
Carnival Rose	2	1	0	0	3235
Charles Fox	5	1	0	0	3752
Excelled (IRE)	3	1	0	1	6081
Fondest	5	2	0	0	11321
Indian Tygress	6	3	2	0	13973
Insurgence	7	2	1	1	12000
Keyhaven	4	1	0	0	4787
Lady Bergamot (FR)	7	2	1	1	44551
Lord George (IRE)	8	1	1	1	15563
Magical Dreamer (IRE)	6	3	1	0	35328
Mainsail Atlantic (USA)	9	1	3	2	3752
Master Archer (IRE)	9	2	5	0	12162
Mazzini	11	3	1	2	46202
Merchant Of Venice	2	1	0	0	3881
Preening	5	1	1	2	7116
Ptarmigan Ridge	8	1	4	0	6081
Regicide (IRE)	6	1	1	0	5531
Sleeping Lion (USA)	5	2	0	1	11968
Spanish Archer (FR)	4	1	2	0	3881
The Pinto Kid (FR)	7	2	1	0	8086
The Tin Man	4	2	0	0	205404
Voluminous	7	1	1	1	3752
Zest (IRE)	5	1	0	1	14318
Total winning prize-money					**£491361**
Favourites	**17-56**		**30.4%**		**-9.98**

JOHNNY FARRELLY

ENMORE, SOMERSET

	No. of Hrs	Races Run	1st	2nd	3rd	Unpl	Per cent	£1 Level Stake
2-y-o	*0*	*0*	*0*	*0*	*0*	*0*	*0.0*	*0.00*
3-y-o	*1*	*3*	*0*	*0*	*0*	*3*	*0.0*	*-3.00*
4-y-o+	*17*	*67*	*5*	*2*	*3*	*57*	*7.5*	*+35.25*
Totals	**18**	**70**	**5**	**2**	**3**	**60**	**7.1**	**+32.25**
2017	*12*	*30*	*2*	*4*	*1*	*23*	*6.7*	*-16.50*
2016	*7*	*27*	*5*	*2*	*3*	*17*	*18.5*	*+20.67*

JOCKEYS

	W-R	Per cent	£1 Level Stake
Stevie Donohoe	3-24	12.5	+64.25
David Probert	1-2	50.0	+8.00
Darragh Keenan	1-6	16.7	-2.00

COURSE RECORD

	Total W-R	Non-Hndcps 2-y-o	Non-Hndcps 3-y-o+	Hndcps 2-y-o	Hndcps 3-y-o+	Per cent	£1 Level Stake
Wolvhptn (A.W)	4-23	0-0	0-1	0-0	4-22	17.4	+75.25
Chelmsford (A.W)	1-9	0-0	0-0	0-0	1-9	11.1	-5.00

WINNING HORSES

Horse	Races Run	1st	2nd	3rd	£
False Id	6	1	0	0	3105
Hell Of A Lady	6	1	0	0	3105
Lake Shore Drive (IRE)	1	1	0	0	3752
Stringybark Creek	5	2	0	1	6534
Total winning prize-money					**£16496**
Favourites	**12-25**		**48.0%**		**10.03**

JULIA FEILDEN

EXNING, SUFFOLK

	No. of Hrs	Races Run	1st	2nd	3rd	Unpl	Per cent	£1 Level Stake
2-y-o	*3*	*10*	*0*	*1*	*0*	*9*	*0.0*	*-10.00*
3-y-o	*9*	*61*	*9*	*5*	*9*	*37*	*14.8*	*+8.00*
4-y-o+	*17*	*132*	*8*	*14*	*18*	*92*	*6.1*	*-62.00*
Totals	**29**	**203**	**17**	**20**	**27**	**138**	**8.4**	**-64.00**
2017	*29*	*206*	*11*	*19*	*19*	*156*	*5.3*	*-111.42*
2016	*34*	*202*	*21*	*23*	*20*	*138*	*10.4*	*-52.73*

BY MONTH

2-y-o	W-R	Per cent	£1 Level Stake	3-y-o	W-R	Per cent	£1 Level Stake
January	0-0	0.0	0.00	January	0-2	0.0	-2.00
February	0-0	0.0	0.00	February	0-2	0.0	-2.00
March	0-0	0.0	0.00	March	0-2	0.0	-2.00
April	0-0	0.0	0.00	April	1-6	16.7	+3.00
May	0-0	0.0	0.00	May	1-4	25.0	+2.50
June	0-2	0.0	-2.00	June	1-7	14.3	-0.50
July	0-3	0.0	-3.00	July	1-6	16.7	-2.50
August	0-1	0.0	-1.00	August	3-11	27.3	+11.50
September	0-1	0.0	-1.00	September	0-6	0.0	-6.00
October	0-3	0.0	-3.00	October	0-8	0.0	-8.00
November	0-0	0.0	0.00	November	1-3	33.3	+1.00
December	0-0	0.0	0.00	December	1-4	25.0	+13.00

4-y-o+	W-R	Per cent	£1 Level Stake	Totals	W-R	Per cent	£1 Level Stake
January	1-16	6.3	-7.00	January	1-18	5.6	-9.00
February	1-10	10.0	-5.50	February	1-12	8.3	-7.50
March	2-11	18.2	+17.00	March	2-13	15.4	+15.00
April	1-9	11.1	-1.00	April	2-15	13.3	+2.00

	W-R	Per cent	£1 Level Stake		W-R	Per cent	£1 Level Stake
May	2-14	14.3	-2.00	May	3-18	16.7	+0.50
June	0-13	0.0	-13.00	June	1-22	4.5	-15.50
July	0-10	0.0	-10.00	July	1-19	5.3	-15.50
August	0-12	0.0	-12.00	August	3-24	12.5	-1.50
September	0-6	0.0	-6.00	September	0-13	0.0	-13.00
October	0-11	0.0	-11.00	October	0-22	0.0	-22.00
November	0-8	0.0	-8.00	November	1-11	9.1	-7.00
December	1-12	8.3	-3.50	December	2-16	12.5	+9.50

DISTANCE

2-y-o	W-R	Per cent	£1 Level Stake	3-y-o	W-R	Per cent	£1 Level Stake
5f-6f	0-4	0.0	-4.00	5f-6f	4-15	26.7	+7.00
7f-8f	0-6	0.0	-6.00	7f-8f	4-28	14.3	+12.00
9f-13f	0-0	0.0	0.00	9f-13f	1-17	5.9	-10.00
14f+	0-0	0.0	0.00	14f+	0-1	0.0	-1.00

4-y-o+	W-R	Per cent	£1 Level Stake	Totals	W-R	Per cent	£1 Level Stake
5f-6f	0-9	0.0	-9.00	5f-6f	4-28	14.3	-6.00
7f-8f	6-84	7.1	-36.00	7f-8f	10-118	8.5	-30.00
9f-13f	2-34	5.9	-12.00	9f-13f	3-51	5.9	-22.00
14f+	0-5	0.0	-5.00	14f+	0-6	0.0	-6.00

TYPE OF RACE

Non-Handicaps	W-R	Per cent	£1 Level Stake	Handicaps	W-R	Per cent	£1 Level Stake
2-y-o	0-7	0.0	-7.00	2-y-o	0-3	0.0	-3.00
3-y-o	0-13	0.0	-13.00	3-y-o	9-48	18.8	+21.00
4-y-o+	0-5	0.0	-5.00	4-y-o+	8-127	6.3	-57.00

RACE CLASS

	W-R	Per cent	£1 Level Stake
Class 1	0-0	0.0	0.00
Class 2	0-1	0.0	-1.00
Class 3	0-6	0.0	-6.00
Class 4	1-18	5.6	-13.50
Class 5	4-58	6.9	-20.50
Class 6	11-118	9.3	-25.00
Class 7	1-2	50.0	+2.00

FIRST TIME OUT

	W-R	Per cent	£1 Level Stake
2-y-o	0-3	0.0	-3.00
3-y-o	1-9	11.1	0.00
4-y-o+	0-17	0.0	-17.00
Totals	1-29	3.4	-20.00

JOCKEYS

	W-R	Per cent	£1 Level Stake
Shelley Birkett	11-117	9.4	-23.50
Jamie Spencer	1-1	100.0	+4.50
Hector Crouch	1-1	100.0	+7.50
Joshua Bryan	1-2	50.0	+5.00
Jimmy Quinn	1-5	20.0	+1.50
Josephine Gordon	1-5	20.0	+5.00
Mr Ross Birkett	1-10	10.0	-2.00

COURSE RECORD

	Total W-R	Non-Hndcps 2-y-o	Non-Hndcps 3-y-o+	Hndcps 2-y-o	Hndcps 3-y-o+	Per cent	£1 Level Stake
Southwell (A.W)	6-33	0-0	0-2	0-0	6-31	18.2	+27.50
Yarmouth	4-48	0-3	0-3	0-2	4-40	8.3	-24.00
Newcastle (A.W)	2-11	0-0	0-0	0-0	2-11	18.2	-0.50
Kempton (A.W)	2-21	0-1	0-3	0-1	2-16	9.5	-7.50
Brighton	1-15	0-1	0-0	0-0	1-14	6.7	-8.50
Lingfield (A.W)	1-15	0-0	0-1	0-0	1-14	6.7	+2.00
Chelmsford (A.W)	1-23	0-0	0-3	0-0	1-20	4.3	-16.00

WINNING HORSES

Horse	Races Run	1st	2nd	3rd	£
Boxatricks (IRE)	8	1	1	0	2911
Candesta (USA)	8	1	1	0	3105
Casey Banter	6	1	1	1	3105
Gas Monkey	4	1	2	0	3105
Go On Gal (IRE)	13	1	1	1	3105
Limerick Lord (IRE)	17	3	0	6	9205
Lulu Star (IRE)	11	1	1	3	3493
Majestic Moon (IRE)	13	1	3	0	3752
Oceanus (IRE)	13	1	0	3	3752
Oud Metha Bridge (IRE)	13	1	4	4	6469
Terri Rules (IRE)	13	4	0	1	13456
*Wilson (IRE)	6	1	0	0	3752
Total winning prize-money					**£59210**
Favourites	**1-7**		**14.3%**		**-3.50**

ROGER FELL

NAWTON, N YORKS

	No. of Hrs	Races Run	1st	2nd	3rd	Unpl	Per cent	£1 Level Stake
2-y-o	*11*	*46*	*2*	*3*	*3*	*38*	*4.3*	*-22.13*
3-y-o	*16*	*98*	*11*	*12*	*10*	*65*	*11.2*	*+12.33*
4-y-o+	*34*	*329*	*43*	*33*	*32*	*221*	*13.1*	*-24.77*
Totals	**61**	**473**	**56**	**48**	**45**	**324**	**11.8**	**-34.57**
2017	*51*	*360*	*34*	*39*	*30*	*257*	*9.4*	*-76.22*
2016	*24*	*80*	*8*	*10*	*5*	*57*	*10.0*	*-1.38*

BY MONTH

2-y-o	W-R	Per cent	£1 Level Stake	3-y-o	W-R	Per cent	£1 Level Stake
January	0-0	0.0	0.00	January	3-7	42.9	+44.50
February	0-0	0.0	0.00	February	0-3	0.0	-3.00
March	0-2	0.0	-2.00	March	1-6	16.7	+17.00
April	0-1	0.0	-1.00	April	0-6	0.0	-6.00
May	0-1	0.0	-1.00	May	0-12	0.0	-12.00
June	0-0	0.0	0.00	June	1-8	12.5	-5.00
July	0-4	0.0	-4.00	July	2-6	33.3	+1.08
August	0-8	0.0	-8.00	August	2-17	11.8	7.25
September	0-12	0.0	-12.00	September	0-11	0.0	-11.00
October	0-8	0.0	-8.00	October	1-12	8.3	-6.00
November	1-7	14.3	+14.00	November	1-7	14.3	+3.00
December	1-3	33.3	-0.13	December	0-3	0.0	-3.00

4-y-o+	W-R	Per cent	£1 Level Stake	Totals	W-R	Per cent	£1 Level Stake
January	3-16	18.8	+11.00	January	6-23	26.1	+55.50
February	0-11	0.0	-11.00	February	0-14	0.0	-14.00
March	1-15	6.7	-3.00	March	2-23	8.7	+12.00

April	4-29	13.8	+21.25	April	4-36	11.1	+14.25
May	6-38	15.8	-5.65	May	6-51	11.8	-18.65
June	9-52	17.3	+2.00	June	10-60	16.7	-3.00
July	6-34	17.6	+10.50	July	8-44	18.2	+7.58
August	5-44	11.4	-29.75	August	7-69	10.1	-45.00
September	4-31	12.9	+0.50	September	4-54	7.4	-22.50
October	3-31	9.7	-14.13	October	4-51	7.8	-28.13
November	2-20	10.0	+1.50	November	4-34	11.8	+4.50
December	0-8	0.0	-8.00	December	1-14	7.1	-11.00

DISTANCE

2-y-o	W-R	Per cent	£1 Level Stake	3-y-o	W-R	Per cent	£1 Level Stake
5f-6f	2-34	5.9	-10.13	5f-6f	2-35	5.7	-25.25
7f-8f	0-12	0.0	-12.00	7f-8f	6-28	21.4	+56.83
9f-13f	0-0	0.0	0.00	9f-13f	3-34	8.8	-18.25
14f+	0-0	0.0	0.00	14f+	0-1	0.0	-1.00

4-y-o+	W-R	Per cent	£1 Level Stake	Totals	W-R	Per cent	£1 Level Stake
5f-6f	18-100	18.0	+32.75	5f-6f	22-169	13.0	-2.63
7f-8f	19-180	10.6	-36.90	7f-8f	25-220	11.4	+7.93
9f-13f	6-48	12.5	-19.63	9f-13f	9-82	11.0	-37.88
14f+	0-1	0.0	-1.00	14f+	0-2	0.0	-2.00

TYPE OF RACE

Non-Handicaps	W-R	Per cent	£1 Level Stake	Handicaps	W-R	Per cent	£1 Level Stake
2-y-o	0-26	0.0	-26.00	2-y-o	2-20	10.0	+3.88
3-y-o	1-9	11.1	+1.00	3-y-o	10-89	11.2	+11.33
4-y-o+	3-16	18.8	-4.00	4-y-o+	40-313	12.8	-20.77

RACE CLASS

	W-R	Per cent	£1 Level Stake
Class 1	0-3	0.0	-3.00
Class 2	5-39	12.8	+17.50
Class 3	3-55	5.5	-41.50
Class 4	17-128	13.3	-23.53
Class 5	18-140	12.9	+17.00
Class 6	13-105	12.4	+1.96
Class 7	0-3	0.0	-3.00

FIRST TIME OUT

	W-R	Per cent	£1 Level Stake
2-y-o	0-11	0.0	-11.00
3-y-o	1-16	6.3	+10.00
4-y-o+	1-34	2.9	-17.00
Totals	2-61	3.3	-18.00

JOCKEYS

	W-R	Per cent	£1 Level Stake
Ben Sanderson	15-93	16.1	+19.58
Tony Hamilton	15-185	8.1	-82.00
Ben Curtis	10-40	25.0	+31.63
Cameron Noble	4-13	30.8	+23.00
Paula Muir	2-11	18.2	+1.50
Cam Hardie	2-30	6.7	+14.00
David Egan	1-2	50.0	+0.10
Paul Hanagan	1-2	50.0	+6.00
Shane Kelly	1-3	33.3	+18.00
Silvestre De Sousa	1-3	33.3	+0.50
Connor Murtagh	1-4	25.0	+0.50
David Allan	1-6	16.7	-2.25
Tristan Price	1-6	16.7	+7.00
Jamie Gormley	1-16	6.3	-13.13

COURSE RECORD

	Total W-R	Non-Hndcps 2-y-o	Non-Hndcps 3-y-o+	Hndcps 2-y-o	Hndcps 3-y-o+	Per cent	£1 Level Stake
Southwell (A.W)	8-43	0-1	1-1	1-1	6-40	18.6	+46.72
Newcastle (A.W)	6-79	0-6	1-4	0-6	5-63	7.6	-18.75
Haydock	5-19	0-0	0-2	0-0	5-17	26.3	+5.50
Carlisle	5-24	0-1	0-0	0-1	5-22	20.8	+1.50
Hamilton	4-12	0-0	0-0	0-0	4-12	33.3	+4.33
Redcar	3-16	0-2	1-4	0-0	2-10	18.8	+2.25
Doncaster	3-20	0-1	0-1	1-1	2-17	15.0	+15.50
Ayr	3-21	0-1	0-0	0-1	3-19	14.3	-10.88
Catterick	3-24	0-4	1-2	0-0	2-18	12.5	-11.00
Ripon	3-30	0-1	0-0	0-0	3-29	10.0	-12.75
Newmarket	2-3	0-0	0-1	0-0	2-2	66.7	+18.50
Nottingham	2-9	0-0	0-0	0-1	2-8	22.2	+0.50
Beverley	2-29	0-3	0-4	0-0	2-22	6.9	-9.50
Newmkt (Jly)	1-2	0-0	0-0	0-0	1-2	50.0	+6.00
Ascot	1-4	0-0	0-0	0-0	1-4	25.0	+17.00
Leicester	1-5	0-0	0-1	0-0	1-4	20.0	+0.50
Wolvhptn (A.W)	1-13	0-0	0-0	0-0	1-13	7.7	+13.00
Pontefract	1-17	0-1	0-2	0-1	1-13	5.9	-11.00
York	1-24	0-0	0-0	0-2	1-22	4.2	-19.00
Thirsk	1-32	0-2	0-1	0-1	1-28	3.1	-26.00

WINNING HORSES

Horse	Races Run	1st	2nd	3rd	£
*Ad Libitum	16	2	4	1	9898
Burnt Sugar (IRE)	7	2	0	0	168075
Club Wexford (IRE)	13	3	0	2	19925
*Daawy (IRE)	6	3	0	1	18049
Dapper Man (IRE)	18	5	3	1	21412
Elixsoft (IRE)	7	2	2	1	6857
Florencio*	12	2	2	3	12291
Geography Teacher (IRE)	10	1	1	0	3105
Guardia Svizzera (IRE)	14	3	1	1	11127
Harome (IRE)	10	2	2	1	16819
Hawaam (IRE)	7	1	0	0	5822
Imagine If (IRE)	7	1	0	1	3752
Kody Ridge (IRE)*	8	2	0	1	7245
Memories Galore (IRE)	5	1	0	0	11321
Mulligatawny (IRE)	14	1	1	2	9338
Muntadab (IRE)	13	3	3	1	44215
Muqarred (USA)	6	1	1	0	3105
My Boy Lewis (IRE)	7	1	1	1	4787
Plansina	15	4	1	2	7892
Presidential (IRE)	17	5	2	3	13197
Remmy D (IRE)	2	1	0	0	3493
Sienna Says	22	1	3	4	3493
Tadaawol	18	3	0	1	18372
Zihaam	15	2	3	2	7267
Zodiakos (IRE)	13	1	2	1	3105
Zylan (IRE)	14	3	2	0	15095
Total winning prize-money					**£449057**
Favourites	**17-40**		**42.5%**		**11.60**

CHARLIE FELLOWES

NEWMARKET, SUFFOLK

	No. of Hrs	Races Run	1st	2nd	3rd	Unpl	Per cent	£1 Level Stake
2-y-o	*16*	*49*	*3*	*2*	*9*	*35*	*6.1*	*-31.00*
3-y-o	*17*	*84*	*12*	*7*	*9*	*56*	*14.3*	*-11.65*
4-y-o+	*15*	*81*	*10*	*9*	*12*	*50*	*12.3*	*-24.42*
Totals	**48**	**214**	**25**	**18**	**30**	**141**	**11.7**	**-67.07**
2017	*46*	*194*	*29*	*22*	*20*	*123*	*14.9*	*-17.56*
2016	*36*	*137*	*25*	*16*	*15*	*81*	*18.2*	*+33.61*

BY MONTH

2-y-o	W-R	Per cent	£1 Level Stake
January	0-0	0.0	0.00
February	0-0	0.0	0.00
March	1-1	100.0	+5.00
April	0-0	0.0	0.00
May	0-3	0.0	-3.00
June	0-5	0.0	-5.00
July	0-7	0.0	-7.00
August	0-8	0.0	-8.00
September	1-9	11.1	-3.50
October	1-13	7.7	-6.50
November	0-1	0.0	-1.00
December	0-2	0.0	-2.00

3-y-o	W-R	Per cent	£1 Level Stake
January	0-2	0.0	-2.00
February	1-2	50.0	+2.50
March	0-3	0.0	-3.00
April	0-10	0.0	-10.00
May	1-10	10.0	-2.00
June	2-13	15.4	-6.00
July	0-5	0.0	-5.00
August	3-13	23.1	+12.25
September	2-7	28.6	+9.00
October	2-14	14.3	-4.50
November	0-1	0.0	-1.00
December	1-4	25.0	-1.90

4-y-o+	W-R	Per cent	£1 Level Stake
January	1-7	14.3	-4.63
February	1-10	10.0	-2.00
March	0-7	0.0	-7.00
April	0-9	0.0	-9.00
May	4-14	28.6	+0.70
June	2-15	13.3	+3.00
July	0-4	0.0	-4.00
August	2-7	28.6	+6.50
September	0-6	0.0	-6.00
October	0-2	0.0	-2.00
November	0-0	0.0	0.00
December	0-0	0.0	0.00

Totals	W-R	Per cent	£1 Level Stake
January	1-9	11.1	-6.63
February	2-12	16.7	+0.50
March	1-11	9.1	-5.00
April	0-19	0.0	-19.00
May	5-27	18.5	-4.30
June	4-33	12.1	-8.00
July	0-16	0.0	-16.00
August	5-28	17.9	+10.75
September	3-22	13.6	-0.50
October	3-29	10.3	-13.00
November	0-2	0.0	-1.00
December	1-6	16.7	-1.90

DISTANCE

2-y-o	W-R	Per cent	£1 Level Stake
5f-6f	1-33	3.0	-27.00
7f-8f	2-15	13.3	-3.00
9f-13f	0-1	0.0	-1.00
14f+	0-0	0.0	0.00

3-y-o	W-R	Per cent	£1 Level Stake
5f-6f	1-10	10.0	+3.00
7f-8f	7-43	16.3	-8.00
9f-13f	3-24	12.5	-4.65
14f+	1-7	14.3	-2.00

4-y-o+	W-R	Per cent	£1 Level Stake
5f-6f	0-2	0.0	-2.00
7f-8f	7-55	12.7	-14.67
9f-13f	3-20	15.0	-3.75
14f+	0-4	0.0	-4.00

Totals	W-R	Per cent	£1 Level Stake
5f-6f	2-45	4.4	-26.00
7f-8f	16-113	14.2	-25.67
9f-13f	6-45	13.3	-9.40
14f+	1-11	9.1	-6.00

TYPE OF RACE

Non-Handicaps

	W-R	Per cent	£1 Level Stake
2-y-o	2-37	5.4	-25.50
3-y-o	1-35	2.9	-32.90
4-y-o+	3-23	13.0	+0.51

Handicaps

	W-R	Per cent	£1 Level Stake
2-y-o	1-12	8.3	-5.50
3-y-o	11-49	22.4	+21.25
4-y-o+	7-58	12.1	-24.93

RACE CLASS

	W-R	Per cent	£1 Level Stake
Class 1	3-23	13.0	+0.50
Class 2	4-35	11.4	-6.75
Class 3	4-11	36.4	+11.75
Class 4	7-45	15.6	-18.55
Class 5	6-78	7.7	-34.40
Class 6	1-22	4.5	-19.63
Class 7	0-0	0.0	0.00

FIRST TIME OUT

	W-R	Per cent	£1 Level Stake
2-y-o	2-16	12.5	-4.50
3-y-o	1-17	5.9	-14.90
4-y-o+	1-15	6.7	-12.63
Totals	4-48	8.3	-32.03

JOCKEYS

	W-R	Per cent	£1 Level Stake
Stevie Donohoe	14-144	9.7	-54.33
Richard Kingscote	2-4	50.0	+4.75
Aled Beech	2-22	9.1	-6.00
David Egan	1-1	100.0	+4.00
Daniel Tudhope	1-1	100.0	+1.25
Fran Berry	1-2	50.0	+6.00
David Probert	1-2	50.0	+4.00
Ben Curtis	1-3	33.3	+2.50
James Doyle	1-3	33.3	-1.00
Jim Crowley	1-4	25.0	-0.25

COURSE RECORD

	Total W-R	Non-Hndcps 2-y-o	Non-Hndcps 3-y-o+	Hndcps 2-y-o	Hndcps 3-y-o+	Per cent	£1 Level Stake
Nottingham	3-13	0-3	1-2	0-0	2-8	23.1	+1.75
Thirsk	2-5	0-0	0-2	0-0	2-3	40.0	-0.55
Doncaster	2-6	0-1	0-0	0-0	2-5	33.3	+2.75
Newmkt (Jly)	2-6	0-2	1-2	0-1	1-1	33.3	+1.50
Wolvhptn (A.W)	2-16	0-2	1-6	0-2	1-6	12.5	-5.90
Chelmsford (A.W)	2-19	0-3	1-6	0-1	1-9	10.5	0.00
Lingfield (A.W)	2-21	0-2	0-8	0-0	2-11	9.5	-13.50
Kempton (A.W)	2-32	0-2	0-7	0-3	2-20	6.3	-16.00
Carlisle	1-3	0-1	0-0	0-1	1-1	33.3	+10.00
Goodwood	1-4	0-0	0-1	0-0	1-3	25.0	+11.00
Leicester	1-4	0-1	0-0	0-1	1-2	25.0	+0.50
Southwell (A.W)	1-5	0-0	0-1	0-0	1-4	20.0	-2.63
Sandown	1-6	0-2	0-0	0-0	1-4	16.7	0.00
Newbury	1-7	1-3	0-2	0-0	0-2	14.3	-1.50
Newcastle (A.W)	1-7	1-2	0-3	0-0	0-2	14.3	-1.00
Windsor	1-10	0-3	0-4	1-1	0-2	10.0	-3.50

WINNING HORSES

Horse	Races Run	1st	2nd	3rd	£
Buckland Beau	12	1	1	3	5434

Carnwennan (IRE)	6	1	1	2	15563
Carolinae	11	2	3	1	54983
Chiefofchiefs	5	1	0	0	9338
Crimson Rosette (IRE)	6	2	1	2	35622
Divine Gift (IRE)	5	1	0	2	4787
Escalator	7	4	0	0	56095
Feathery	8	1	1	2	5693
Haverland (IRE)	10	1	1	1	4205
Jeremiah	5	1	1	1	7310
King Ottokar (FR)	2	1	0	0	5531
Mia Tesoro (IRE)	7	1	1	0	22684
Paco's Prince	4	1	0	0	3752
Ramsbury	1	1	0	0	3752
Repercussion	6	1	0	0	14232
Snazzy (IRE)	6	1	0	2	12938
Spun Gold	9	1	1	1	3105
Treasure Me	8	2	0	2	9283
Vice Marshal (IRE)	5	1	0	0	3752
Total winning prize-money					**£278059**
Favourites	**7-17**		**41.2%**		**-0.33**

MARJORIE FIFE

STILLINGTON, N YORKS

	No. of Hrs	Races Run	1st	2nd	3rd	Unpl	Per cent	£1 Level Stake
2-y-o	*1*	*2*	*0*	*0*	*0*	*2*	*0.0*	*-2.00*
3-y-o	*3*	*19*	*0*	*1*	*2*	*16*	*0.0*	*-19.00*
4-y-o+	*23*	*164*	*17*	*17*	*13*	*117*	*10.4*	*-42.75*
Totals	**27**	**185**	**17**	**18**	**15**	**135**	**9.2**	**-63.75**
2017	*33*	*210*	*16*	*20*	*19*	*155*	*7.6*	*-88.00*
2016	*29*	*191*	*19*	*19*	*19*	*134*	*9.9*	*-35.58*

BY MONTH

2-y-o	W-R	Per cent	£1 Level Stake	3-y-o	W-R	Per cent	£1 Level Stake
January	0-0	0.0	0.00	January	0-0	0.0	0.00
February	0-0	0.0	0.00	February	0-0	0.0	0.00
March	0-0	0.0	0.00	March	0-0	0.0	0.00
April	0-0	0.0	0.00	April	0-2	0.0	-2.00
May	0-0	0.0	0.00	May	0-0	0.0	0.00
June	0-0	0.0	0.00	June	0-5	0.0	-5.00
July	0-0	0.0	0.00	July	0-1	0.0	-1.00
August	0-0	0.0	0.00	August	0-4	0.0	-4.00
September	0-1	0.0	-1.00	September	0-5	0.0	-5.00
October	0-1	0.0	-1.00	October	0-1	0.0	-1.00
November	0-0	0.0	0.00	November	0-0	0.0	0.00
December	0-0	0.0	0.00	December	0-1	0.0	-1.00

4-y-o+	W-R	Per cent	£1 Level Stake	Totals	W-R	Per cent	£1 Level Stake
January	1-11	9.1	+4.00	January	1-11	9.1	+4.00
February	1-5	20.0	-1.50	February	1-5	20.0	-1.50
March	1-5	20.0	0.00	March	1-5	20.0	0.00
April	2-14	14.3	+11.50	April	2-16	12.5	+9.50
May	1-20	5.0	-14.50	May	1-20	5.0	-14.50
June	2-28	7.1	-16.50	June	2-33	6.1	-21.50
July	1-15	6.7	-8.00	July	1-16	6.3	-9.00
August	4-21	19.0	+9.00	August	4-25	16.0	+5.00
September	1-17	5.9	-12.50	September	1-23	4.3	-18.50
October	2-13	15.4	-3.75	October	2-15	13.3	-5.75
November	1-12	8.3	-7.50	November	1-12	8.3	-7.50
December	0-3	0.0	-3.00	December	0-4	0.0	-4.00

DISTANCE

2-y-o	W-R	Per cent	£1 Level Stake	3-y-o	W-R	Per cent	£1 Level Stake
5f-6f	0-0	0.0	0.00	5f-6f	0-7	0.0	-7.00
7f-8f	0-1	0.0	-1.00	7f-8f	0-8	0.0	-8.00
9f-13f	0-1	0.0	-1.00	9f-13f	0-4	0.0	-4.00
14f+	0-0	0.0	0.00	14f+	0-0	0.0	0.00

4-y-o+	W-R	Per cent	£1 Level Stake	Totals	W-R	Per cent	£1 Level Stake
5f-6f	5-57	8.8	-12.00	5f-6f	5-64	7.8	-19.00
7f-8f	4-38	10.5	-8.75	7f-8f	4-47	8.5	-17.75
9f-13f	7-56	12.5	-24.00	9f-13f	7-61	11.5	-29.00
14f+	1-13	7.7	+2.00	14f+	1-13	7.7	+2.00

TYPE OF RACE

Non-Handicaps	W-R	Per cent	£1 Level Stake	Handicaps	W-R	Per cent	£1 Level Stake
2-y-o	0-2	0.0	-2.00	2-y-o	0-0	0.0	0.00
3-y-o	0-4	0.0	-4.00	3-y-o	0-15	0.0	-15.00
4-y-o+	1-9	11.1	-5.25	4-y-o+	16-155	10.3	-37.50

RACE CLASS

	W-R	Per cent	£1 Level Stake
Class 1	0-0	0.0	0.00
Class 2	0-10	0.0	-10.00
Class 3	0-14	0.0	-14.00
Class 4	2-37	5.4	-10.00
Class 5	9-69	13.0	-15.75
Class 6	6-54	11.1	-13.00
Class 7	0-1	0.0	-1.00

FIRST TIME OUT

	W-R	Per cent	£1 Level Stake
2-y-o	0-1	0.0	-1.00
3-y-o	0-3	0.0	-3.00
4-y-o+	3-23	13.0	+17.50
Totals	3-27	11.1	+13.50

JOCKEYS

	W-R	Per cent	£1 Level Stake
Miss Becky Smith	6-16	37.5	+25.00
Harrison Shaw	2-17	11.8	-4.50
Barry McHugh	2-24	8.3	+12.00
Luke Morris	1-1	100.0	+3.50
Daniel Tudhope	1-3	33.3	+2.50
P J McDonald	1-4	25.0	+2.00
Hollie Doyle	1-5	20.0	-1.50
Sebastian Woods	1-5	20.0	0.00
Ben Curtis	1-6	16.7	-2.25
Faye McManoman	1-24	4.2	-20.50

COURSE RECORD

	Total W-R	Non-Hndcps 2-y-o	Non-Hndcps 3-y-o+	Hndcps 2-y-o	Hndcps 3-y-o+	Per cent	£1 Level Stake
Ayr	3-18	0-0	0-0	0-0	3-18	16.7	+1.00
Chelmsford (A.W)	2-4	0-0	0-0	0-0	2-4	50.0	+4.00
Beverley	2-9	0-0	0-0	0-0	2-9	22.2	+10.50

Southwell (A.W)	2-19	0-0	0-1	0-0	2-18	10.5	+1.00
Salisbury	1-1	0-0	0-0	0-0	1-1	100.0	+5.00
Newbury	1-2	0-0	0-0	0-0	1-2	50.0	+5.00
Newmkt (Jly)	1-2	0-0	0-0	0-0	1-2	50.0	+4.00
Pontefract	1-3	0-0	0-0	0-0	1-3	33.3	+1.50
Goodwood	1-4	0-0	0-0	0-0	1-4	25.0	-1.00
Musselburgh	1-6	0-0	1-1	0-0	0-5	16.7	-2.25
Ripon	1-6	0-0	0-0	0-0	1-6	16.7	+15.00
Carlisle	1-8	0-0	0-1	0-0	1-7	12.5	-4.50

WINNING HORSES

Horse	Races Run	1st	2nd	3rd	£
Adam's Ale	3	1	0	0	5693
B Fifty Two (IRE)	13	1	1	1	3881
Inexes	12	1	1	1	4140
Luv U Whatever	27	4	4	4	15799
*My Amigo	12	1	2	1	12699
Palindrome (USA)	12	2	2	1	6229
Perfect Words (IRE)	14	1	0	0	3105
*Red Charmer (IRE)	9	4	1	0	15419
Samtu (IRE)*	6	1	0	1	3752
*Squire	1	1	0	0	3493
Total winning prize-money					**£74210**
Favourites	**5-19**		**26.3%**		**-0.75**

JOHN FLINT

KENFIG HILL, BRIDGEND

	No. of Hrs	Races Run	1st	2nd	3rd	Unpl	Per cent	£1 Level Stake
2-y-o	*0*	*0*	*0*	*0*	*0*	*0*	*0.0*	*0.00*
3-y-o	*6*	*33*	*1*	*3*	*3*	*26*	*3.0*	*-25.00*
4-y-o+	*15*	*95*	*8*	*10*	*5*	*72*	*8.4*	*-25.00*
Totals	**21**	**128**	**9**	**13**	**8**	**98**	**7.0**	**-50.00**
2017	*23*	*100*	*8*	*4*	*9*	*79*	*8.0*	*-46.33*
2016	*11*	*64*	*10*	*4*	*8*	*42*	*15.6*	*+27.50*

JOCKEYS

	W-R	Per cent	£1 Level Stake
William Cox	6-55	10.9	+3.00
Rossa Ryan	1-4	25.0	+2.50
Charlie Bennett	1-4	25.0	+4.00
Nicola Currie	1-5	20.0	+0.50

COURSE RECORD

	Total W-R	Non-Hndcps 2-y-o	Non-Hndcps 3-y-o+	Hndcps 2-y-o	Hndcps 3-y-o+	Per cent	£1 Level Stake
Windsor	3-14	0-0	1-3	0-0	2-11	21.4	+16.00
Lingfield (A.W)	2-7	0-0	1-1	0-0	1-6	28.6	+9.00
Chepstow	2-25	0-0	0-2	0-0	2-23	8.0	-12.50
Kempton (A.W)	1-12	0-0	0-0	0-0	1-12	8.3	+1.00
Wolvhptn (A.W)	1-23	0-0	1-7	0-0	0-16	4.3	-16.50

WINNING HORSES

Horse	Races Run	1st	2nd	3rd	£
Air Of York (IRE)	18	3	3	0	9315
*Carp Kid (IRE)	8	1	2	1	3752
Crindle Carr (IRE)	12	1	0	1	3105
Field Of Vision (IRE)	13	1	4	1	3752
Love And Be Loved	4	1	0	0	3105
*Outer Space	12	2	0	2	3105
Total winning prize-money					**£26134**
Favourites	**1-8**		**12.5%**		**-5.00**

DAVID FLOOD

CHISELDON, WILTSHIRE

	No. of Hrs	Races Run	1st	2nd	3rd	Unpl	Per cent	£1 Level Stake
2-y-o	*1*	*3*	*0*	*0*	*0*	*3*	*0.0*	*-3.00*
3-y-o	*1*	*8*	*1*	*0*	*0*	*7*	*12.5*	*+9.00*
4-y-o+	*3*	*19*	*0*	*4*	*2*	*13*	*0.0*	*-19.00*
Totals	**5**	**30**	**1**	**4**	**2**	**23**	**3.3**	**-13.00**
2017	*4*	*28*	*1*	*3*	*2*	*21*	*3.6*	*-15.00*
2016	*5*	*18*	*1*	*1*	*0*	*16*	*5.6*	*-1.00*

JOCKEYS

	W-R	Per cent	£1 Level Stake
David Probert	1-8	12.5	+9.00

COURSE RECORD

	Total W-R	Non-Hndcps 2-y-o	Non-Hndcps 3-y-o+	Hndcps 2-y-o	Hndcps 3-y-o+	Per cent	£1 Level Stake
Kempton (A.W)	1-9	0-2	0-0	0-0	1-7	11.1	+8.00

WINNING HORSES

Horse	Races Run	1st	2nd	3rd	£
Kendergarten Kop (IRE)	8	1	0	0	3105
Total winning prize-money					**£3105**
Favourites	**0-3**		**0.0%**		**-3.00**

JOANNE FOSTER

MENSTON, W YORKS

	No. of Hrs	Races Run	1st	2nd	3rd	Unpl	Per cent	£1 Level Stake
2-y-o	*0*	*0*	*0*	*0*	*0*	*0*	*0.0*	*0.00*
3-y-o	*0*	*0*	*0*	*0*	*0*	*0*	*0.0*	*0.00*
4-y-o+	*2*	*5*	*1*	*1*	*0*	*3*	*20.0*	*+18.00*
Totals	**2**	**5**	**1**	**1**	**0**	**3**	**20.0**	**+18.00**
2017	*2*	*2*	*0*	*0*	*0*	*2*	*0.0*	*-2.00*
2016	*1*	*2*	*0*	*0*	*0*	*2*	*0.0*	*-2.00*

JOCKEYS

	W-R	Per cent	£1 Level Stake
Phillip Makin	1-3	33.3	+20.00

COURSE RECORD

	Total W-R	Non-Hndcps 2-y-o	Non-Hndcps 3-y-o+	Hndcps 2-y-o	Hndcps 3-y-o+	Per cent	£1 Level Stake
Southwell (A.W)	1-3	0-0	0-0	0-0	1-3	33.3	+20.00

WINNING HORSES

Horse	Races Run	1st	2nd	3rd	£
Brotherly Company (IRE)	4	1	1	0	3752
Total winning prize-money					**£3752**
Favourites	**1-1**		**100.0%**		**1.10**

JIMMY FOX

COLLINGBOURNE DUCIS, WILTS

	No. of Hrs	Races Run	1st	2nd	3rd	Unpl	Per cent	£1 Level Stake
2-y-o	*1*	*4*	*0*	*0*	*0*	*4*	*0.0*	*-4.00*
3-y-o	*3*	*17*	*1*	*2*	*2*	*12*	*5.9*	*+34.00*
4-y-o+	*9*	*40*	*1*	*2*	*4*	*33*	*2.5*	*+27.00*
Totals	**13**	**61**	**2**	**4**	**6**	**49**	**3.3**	**+57.00**
2017	*16*	*74*	*7*	*2*	*9*	*56*	*9.5*	*-41.25*
2016	*17*	*84*	*5*	*11*	*13*	*55*	*6.0*	*-51.50*

JOCKEYS

	W-R	Per cent	£1 Level Stake
John Fahy	1-1	100.0	+66.00
Kieran O'Neill	1-25	4.0	+26.00

COURSE RECORD

	Total W-R	Non-Hndcps 2-y-o	Non-Hndcps 3-y-o+	Hndcps 2-y-o	Hndcps 3-y-o+	Per cent	£1 Level Stake
Lingfield (A.W)	2-12	0-0	1-3	0-0	1-9	16.7	+106.00

WINNING HORSES

Horse	Races Run	1st	2nd	3rd	£
Millie May	5	1	0	0	3105
Sweet And Dandy (IRE)	8	1	2	1	3752
Total winning prize-money					**£6857**
Favourites	**0-0**		**0.0%**		**0.00**

SUZZANNE FRANCE

NORTON, N YORKS

	No. of Hrs	Races Run	1st	2nd	3rd	Unpl	Per cent	£1 Level Stake
2-y-o	*0*	*0*	*0*	*0*	*0*	*0*	*0.0*	*0.00*
3-y-o	*1*	*7*	*0*	*0*	*0*	*7*	*0.0*	*-7.00*
4-y-o+	*6*	*37*	*1*	*2*	*2*	*32*	*2.7*	*-11.00*
Totals	**7**	**44**	**1**	**2**	**2**	**39**	**2.3**	**-18.00**
2017	*6*	*39*	*1*	*5*	*2*	*31*	*2.6*	*-5.00*
2016	*4*	*31*	*1*	*1*	*3*	*26*	*3.2*	*-16.00*

JOCKEYS

	W-R	Per cent	£1 Level Stake
Tom Eaves	1-5	20.0	+21.00

COURSE RECORD

	Total W-R	Non-Hndcps 2-y-o	Non-Hndcps 3-y-o+	Hndcps 2-y-o	Hndcps 3-y-o+	Per cent	£1 Level Stake
Thirsk	1-1	0-0	0-0	0-0	1-1	100.0	+25.00

WINNING HORSES

Horse	Races Run	1st	2nd	3rd	£
Ad Vitam (IRE)	10	1	1	1	3398
Total winning prize-money					**£3398**
Favourites	**0-0**		**0.0%**		**0.00**

KEVIN FROST

NEWCASTLE-UNDER-LYME, STAFFS

	No. of Hrs	Races Run	1st	2nd	3rd	Unpl	Per cent	£1 Level Stake
2-y-o	*1*	*2*	*0*	*0*	*0*	*2*	*0.0*	*-2.00*
3-y-o	*12*	*42*	*4*	*0*	*5*	*33*	*9.5*	*-15.50*
4-y-o+	*15*	*86*	*9*	*11*	*10*	*56*	*10.5*	*-31.25*
Totals	**28**	**130**	**13**	**11**	**15**	**91**	**10.0**	**-48.75**
2017	*22*	*119*	*7*	*5*	*6*	*101*	*5.9*	*-66.63*
2016	*21*	*81*	*5*	*3*	*5*	*68*	*6.2*	*-21.75*

BY MONTH

2-y-o	W-R	Per cent	£1 Level Stake	**3-y-o**	W-R	Per cent	£1 Level Stake
January	0-0	0.0	0.00	January	0-0	0.0	0.00
February	0-0	0.0	0.00	February	0-2	0.0	-2.00
March	0-0	0.0	0.00	March	0-0	0.0	0.00
April	0-0	0.0	0.00	April	0-1	0.0	-1.00
May	0-0	0.0	0.00	May	0-8	0.0	-8.00
June	0-0	0.0	0.00	June	0-6	0.0	-6.00
July	0-0	0.0	0.00	July	1-4	25.0	-1.00
August	0-0	0.0	0.00	August	3-4	75.0	+19.50
September	0-0	0.0	0.00	September	0-3	0.0	-3.00
October	0-0	0.0	0.00	October	0-5	0.0	-5.00
November	0-1	0.0	-1.00	November	0-3	0.0	-3.00
December	0-1	0.0	-1.00	December	0-6	0.0	-6.00

4-y-o+	W-R	Per cent	£1 Level Stake	**Totals**	W-R	Per cent	£1 Level Stake
January	0-8	0.0	-8.00	January	0-8	0.0	-8.00
February	1-6	16.7	+1.00	February	1-8	12.5	-1.00
March	0-4	0.0	-4.00	March	0-4	0.0	-4.00
April	1-4	25.0	-0.25	April	1-5	20.0	-1.25
May	0-5	0.0	-5.00	May	0-13	0.0	-13.00
June	1-11	9.1	-4.00	June	1-17	5.9	-10.00
July	1-5	20.0	-1.75	July	2-9	22.2	-2.75

August	0-4	0.0	-4.00	August	3-8	37.5	+15.50
September	2-10	20.0	+10.50	September	2-13	15.4	+7.50
October	2-6	33.3	+3.25	October	2-11	18.2	-1.75
November	0-10	0.0	-10.00	November	0-14	0.0	-13.00
December	1-13	7.7	-9.00	December	1-20	5.0	-15.00

DISTANCE

2-y-o	W-R	Per cent	£1 Level Stake	3-y-o	W-R	Per cent	£1 Level Stake
5f-6f	0-0	0.0	0.00	5f-6f	1-10	10.0	+5.00
7f-8f	0-2	0.0	-2.00	7f-8f	0-15	0.0	-15.00
9f-13f	0-0	0.0	0.00	9f-13f	3-17	17.6	-5.50
14f+	0-0	0.0	0.00	14f+	0-0	0.0	0.00

4-y-o+	W-R	Per cent	£1 Level Stake	Totals	W-R	Per cent	£1 Level Stake
5f-6f	0-5	0.0	-5.00	5f-6f	1-15	6.7	0.00
7f-8f	6-43	14.0	-15.75	7f-8f	6-60	10.0	-32.75
9f-13f	3-32	9.4	-4.50	9f-13f	6-49	12.2	-10.00
14f+	0-6	0.0	-6.00	14f+	0-6	0.0	-6.00

TYPE OF RACE

Non-Handicaps	W-R	Per cent	£1 Level Stake	Handicaps	W-R	Per cent	£1 Level Stake
2-y-o	0-2	0.0	-2.00	2-y-o	0-0	0.0	0.00
3-y-o	0-15	0.0	-15.00	3-y-o	4-27	14.8	-0.50
4-y-o+	1-4	25.0	-0.75	4-y-o+	8-82	9.8	-30.50

RACE CLASS / FIRST TIME OUT

RACE CLASS	W-R	Per cent	£1 Level Stake	FIRST TIME OUT	W-R	Per cent	£1 Level Stake
Class 1	0-0	0.0	0.00	2-y-o	0-1	0.0	-1.00
Class 2	0-4	0.0	-4.00	3-y-o	0-12	0.0	-12.00
Class 3	2-5	40.0	+15.50	4-y-o+	1-15	6.7	+2.00
Class 4	2-8	25.0	+0.50				
Class 5	2-35	5.7	-27.75	Totals	1-28	3.6	-11.00
Class 6	7-78	9.0	-33.00				
Class 7	0-0	0.0	0.00				

JOCKEYS

	W-R	Per cent	£1 Level Stake
Clifford Lee	3-24	12.5	+3.75
Rossa Ryan	2-3	66.7	+3.25
Joshua Bryan	2-12	16.7	-5.50
Jack Mitchell	2-12	16.7	-1.00
Jason Watson	1-3	33.3	+0.25
J F Egan	1-6	16.7	-1.50
Liam Jones	1-10	10.0	+5.00
Dougie Costello	1-15	6.7	-8.00

COURSE RECORD

	Total W-R	Non-Hndcps 2-y-o	Non-Hndcps 3-y-o+	Hndcps 2-y-o	Hndcps 3-y-o+	Per cent	£1 Level Stake
Wolvhptn (A.W)	8-65	0-2	1-9	0-0	7-54	12.3	-27.00
York	1-1	0-0	0-0	0-0	1-1	100.0	+16.00
Pontefract	1-4	0-0	0-2	0-0	1-2	25.0	-0.50
Lingfield (A.W)	1-6	0-0	0-0	0-0	1-6	16.7	-2.00
Nottingham	1-9	0-0	0-3	0-0	1-6	11.1	+6.00
Chelmsford (A.W)	1-9	0-0	0-0	0-0	1-9	11.1	-5.25

WINNING HORSES

Horse	Races Run	1st	2nd	3rd	£
Arrowzone	12	1	2	1	3105
*Calvinist	6	1	3	0	3105
Documenting	9	2	1	0	9283
*Francis Xavier (IRE)	2	2	0	0	24741
Poppy Jag (IRE)	10	1	0	1	3235
Shamlan (IRE)	9	1	0	2	3170
Showdance Kid	10	2	2	1	6534
The Throstles	11	3	0	0	12388
Total winning prize-money					**£65561**
Favourites	**9-14**		**64.3%**		**13.75**

HARRY FRY

SEABOROUGH, DORSET

	No. of Hrs	Races Run	1st	2nd	3rd	Unpl	Per cent	£1 Level Stake
2-y-o	*0*	*0*	*0*	*0*	*0*	*0*	*0.0*	*0.00*
3-y-o	*0*	*0*	*0*	*0*	*0*	*0*	*0.0*	*0.00*
4-y-o+	*11*	*34*	*4*	*7*	*1*	*22*	*11.8*	*-20.85*
Totals	**11**	**34**	**4**	**7**	**1**	**22**	**11.8**	**-20.85**
2017	*3*	*7*	*3*	*0*	*0*	*4*	*42.9*	*+0.75*
2016	*0*							

JOCKEYS

	W-R	Per cent	£1 Level Stake
Fran Berry	3-15	20.0	-7.35
Jamie Spencer	1-5	20.0	+0.50

COURSE RECORD

	Total W-R	Non-Hndcps 2-y-o	Non-Hndcps 3-y-o+	Hndcps 2-y-o	Hndcps 3-y-o+	Per cent	£1 Level Stake
Goodwood	1-1	0-0	0-0	0-0	1-1	100.0	+4.50
Newcastle (A.W)	1-1	0-0	0-0	0-0	1-1	100.0	+2.50
Lingfield (A.W)	1-4	0-0	1-2	0-0	0-2	25.0	-1.25
Kempton (A.W)	1-7	0-0	1-3	0-0	0-4	14.3	-5.60

WINNING HORSES

Horse	Races Run	1st	2nd	3rd	£
American Gigolo	7	3	1	0	23196
Shraaoh (IRE)	3	1	1	0	9452
Total winning prize-money					**£32648**
Favourites	**25-61**		**41.0%**		**1.29**

IVAN FURTADO

WISETON, NOTTINGHAMSHIRE

	No. of Hrs	Races Run	1st	2nd	3rd	Unpl	Per cent	£1 Level Stake
2-y-o	*15*	*56*	*6*	*4*	*6*	*40*	*10.7*	*+50.63*
3-y-o	*19*	*65*	*12*	*3*	*5*	*45*	*18.5*	*+46.58*

4-y-o+	*37*	*158*	*15*	*14*	*12*	*117*	*9.5*	*-42.63*
Totals	**71**	**279**	**33**	**21**	**23**	**202**	**11.8**	**+54.58**
2017	*37*	*190*	*23*	*14*	*16*	*137*	*12.1*	*-15.50*
2016	*43*	*204*	*17*	*19*	*17*	*151*	*8.3*	*-94.38*

BY MONTH

2-y-o	W-R	Per cent	£1 Level Stake
January	0-0	0.0	0.00
February	0-0	0.0	0.00
March	0-0	0.0	0.00
April	0-0	0.0	0.00
May	0-1	0.0	-1.00
June	1-6	16.7	+15.00
July	0-5	0.0	-5.00
August	1-9	11.1	+42.00
September	1-17	5.9	+4.00
October	2-11	18.2	0.00
November	0-2	0.0	-2.00
December	1-5	20.0	-2.38

3-y-o	W-R	Per cent	£1 Level Stake
January	1-9	11.1	+2.00
February	1-3	33.3	+4.00
March	0-3	0.0	-3.00
April	1-9	11.1	-5.25
May	1-4	25.0	+11.00
June	2-8	25.0	+14.50
July	1-3	33.3	+1.50
August	1-7	14.3	-5.17
September	2-4	50.0	+16.00
October	0-4	0.0	-4.00
November	0-3	0.0	-3.00
December	2-8	25.0	+18.00

4-y-o+	W-R	Per cent	£1 Level Stake
January	3-13	23.1	+4.38
February	2-11	18.2	+0.25
March	2-19	10.5	-3.00
April	1-17	5.9	-13.25
May	0-15	0.0	-15.00
June	2-13	15.4	-3.75
July	2-12	16.7	-4.25
August	0-13	0.0	-13.00
September	0-11	0.0	-11.00
October	2-14	14.3	+25.00
November	1-6	16.7	+5.00
December	0-14	0.0	-14.00

Totals	W-R	Per cent	£1 Level Stake
January	4-22	18.2	+6.38
February	3-14	21.4	+4.25
March	2-22	9.1	-6.00
April	2-26	7.7	-18.50
May	1-20	5.0	-5.00
June	5-27	18.5	+25.75
July	3-20	15.0	-7.75
August	2-29	6.9	+23.83
September	3-32	9.4	+9.00
October	4-29	13.8	+21.00
November	1-11	9.1	+2.00
December	3-27	11.1	+4.00

DISTANCE

2-y-o	W-R	Per cent	£1 Level Stake
5f-6f	4-35	11.4	+46.63
7f-8f	2-21	9.5	+4.00
9f-13f	0-0	0.0	0.00
14f+	0-0	0.0	0.00

3-y-o	W-R	Per cent	£1 Level Stake
5f-6f	9-29	31.0	+62.83
7f-8f	3-27	11.1	-7.25
9f-13f	0-8	0.0	-8.00
14f+	0-1	0.0	-1.00

4-y-o+	W-R	Per cent	£1 Level Stake
5f-6f	2-23	8.7	-4.00
7f-8f	8-82	9.8	-27.88
9f-13f	5-50	10.0	-7.75
14f+	0-3	0.0	-3.00

Totals	W-R	Per cent	£1 Level Stake
5f-6f	15-87	17.2	+105.46
7f-8f	13-130	10.0	-31.13
9f-13f	5-58	8.6	-15.75
14f+	0-4	0.0	-4.00

TYPE OF RACE

Non-Handicaps

	W-R	Per cent	£1 Level Stake
2-y-o	3-50	6.0	+24.63
3-y-o	3-17	17.6	+20.00
4-y-o+	0-16	0.0	-16.00

Handicaps

	W-R	Per cent	£1 Level Stake
2-y-o	3-6	50.0	+26.00
3-y-o	9-48	18.8	+26.58
4-y-o+	15-142	10.6	-26.63

RACE CLASS

	W-R	Per cent	£1 Level Stake
Class 1	0-0	0.0	0.00
Class 2	0-4	0.0	-4.00
Class 3	0-8	0.0	-8.00
Class 4	10-69	14.5	+65.58
Class 5	13-114	11.4	+1.25
Class 6	9-77	11.7	-2.25
Class 7	1-7	14.3	+2.00

FIRST TIME OUT

	W-R	Per cent	£1 Level Stake
2-y-o	0-15	0.0	-15.00
3-y-o	1-19	5.3	-2.00
4-y-o+	3-37	8.1	-18.75
Totals	4-71	5.6	-35.75

JOCKEYS

	W-R	Per cent	£1 Level Stake
Gabriele Malune	9-74	12.2	+22.25
P J McDonald	4-23	17.4	+3.38
Jane Elliott	3-17	17.6	+8.00
Trevor Whelan	2-7	28.6	+65.00
Silvestre De Sousa	2-7	28.6	-1.42
Shane Gray	2-9	22.2	+19.00
David Nolan	2-17	11.8	-10.50
Adam Kirby	1-1	100.0	+3.00
Jim Crowley	1-1	100.0	+5.00
Andrea Atzeni	1-1	100.0	+2.75
Jason Hart	1-4	25.0	+9.00
Nicky Mackay	1-4	25.0	+7.00
Franny Norton	1-4	25.0	+17.00
Kieran O'Neill	1-4	25.0	-1.38
Luke Morris	1-8	12.5	0.00
Tony Hamilton	1-9	11.1	-4.50

COURSE RECORD

	Total W-R	Non-Hndcps 2-y-o	Non-Hndcps 3-y-o+	Hndcps 2-y-o	Hndcps 3-y-o+	Per cent	£1 Level Stake
Southwell (A.W)	7-37	0-0	0-6	0-0	7-31	18.9	+29.75
Wolvhptn (A.W)	5-51	1-8	0-4	0-1	4-38	9.8	-26.25
Newcastle (A.W)	4-27	0-6	1-5	0-0	3-16	14.8	+9.50
Redcar	3-8	1-4	0-2	0-0	2-2	37.5	+33.50
Doncaster	3-13	0-1	1-3	0-1	2-8	23.1	+11.75
Yarmouth	2-8	0-0	0-0	0-0	2-8	25.0	+6.83
Leicester	2-9	1-2	0-2	0-0	1-5	22.2	+45.75
Kempton (A.W)	2-17	0-1	1-2	1-1	0-13	11.8	-5.00
Goodwood	1-1	0-0	0-0	1-1	0-0	100.0	+3.00
Epsom	1-2	0-0	0-0	0-0	1-2	50.0	+1.25
Chester	1-3	0-1	0-0	1-2	0-0	33.3	+18.00
Catterick	1-5	0-0	0-0	0-0	1-5	20.0	+21.00
Lingfield (A.W)	1-11	0-0	0-0	0-0	1-11	9.1	-7.50

WINNING HORSES

Horse	Races Run	1st	2nd	3rd	£
African Trader (USA)*	5	1	0	0	3509
Alba Del Sole (IRE)	9	1	1	0	3881
Belisa (IRE)	5	2	0	0	11515
Check 'Em Tuesday (IRE)	5	1	0	0	2313
Eternal Sun	5	2	0	0	7504
Feel The Wrath (IRE)	2	1	0	0	3105

*Fly True	5	1	0	0	3105
Frank's Legacy*	8	1	0	1	3105
Freed From Desire	10	1	2	2	4464
Haadhir	7	1	2	3	3752
Illustrissime (USA)	9	1	2	1	7097
Laith Alareen	5	4	0	0	16270
Murdanova (IRE)	4	2	0	0	9283
Oneroa (IRE)	4	1	1	1	5531
Raven Banner (IRE)	7	2	3	0	8280
Sheila's Treat (IRE)	5	1	0	0	3752
Shelneverwalkalone	3	1	2	0	3105
Sparklealot (IRE)	6	3	0	0	19278
Swissie	4	1	0	1	3105
Sword Exceed (GER)	6	1	0	0	5531
Tagle (IRE)	4	1	0	0	3105
Terrier Spirit (IRE)*	1	1	0	0	3752
Vee Man Ten	4	1	0	1	3752
Zaeem	5	1	1	0	5531
Total winning prize-money					**£143625**
Favourites	**7-32**		**21.9%**		**-10.17**

JOHN GALLAGHER

CHASTLETON, OXON

	No. of Hrs	Races Run	1st	2nd	3rd	Unpl	Per cent	£1 Level Stake
2-y-o	*6*	*24*	*0*	*1*	*2*	*21*	*0.0*	*-24.00*
3-y-o	*8*	*45*	*3*	*0*	*1*	*41*	*6.7*	*-9.00*
4-y-o+	*13*	*90*	*10*	*5*	*11*	*64*	*11.1*	*-4.25*
Totals	**27**	**159**	**13**	**6**	**14**	**126**	**8.2**	**-37.25**
2017	*22*	*151*	*12*	*19*	*18*	*102*	*7.9*	*-50.17*
2016	*23*	*136*	*12*	*10*	*12*	*102*	*8.8*	*-39.63*

BY MONTH

2-y-o	W-R	Per cent	£1 Level Stake	3-y-o	W-R	Per cent	£1 Level Stake
January	0-0	0.0	0.00	January	0-1	0.0	-1.00
February	0-0	0.0	0.00	February	0-2	0.0	-2.00
March	0-0	0.0	0.00	March	0-1	0.0	-1.00
April	0-2	0.0	-2.00	April	0-5	0.0	-5.00
May	0-4	0.0	-4.00	May	1-5	20.0	+3.00
June	0-3	0.0	-3.00	June	0-6	0.0	-6.00
July	0-4	0.0	-4.00	July	0-4	0.0	-4.00
August	0-4	0.0	-4.00	August	1-5	20.0	+8.00
September	0-6	0.0	-6.00	September	1-7	14.3	+8.00
October	0-1	0.0	-1.00	October	0-3	0.0	-3.00
November	0-0	0.0	0.00	November	0-3	0.0	-3.00
December	0-0	0.0	0.00	December	0-3	0.0	-3.00

4-y-o+	W-R	Per cent	£1 Level Stake	Totals	W-R	Per cent	£1 Level Stake
January	2-6	33.3	-0.25	January	2-7	28.6	-1.25
February	0-3	0.0	-3.00	February	0-5	0.0	-5.00
March	0-4	0.0	-4.00	March	0-5	0.0	-5.00
April	2-9	22.2	+20.00	April	2-16	12.5	+13.00
May	0-11	0.0	-11.00	May	1-20	5.0	-12.00
June	2-5	40.0	+10.00	June	2-14	14.3	+1.00
July	1-7	14.3	-0.50	July	1-15	6.7	-8.50
August	2-12	16.7	-3.50	August	3-21	14.3	+0.50
September	0-12	0.0	-12.00	September	1-25	4.0	-10.00
October	0-12	0.0	-12.00	October	0-16	0.0	-16.00
November	1-6	16.7	+15.00	November	1-9	11.1	+12.00
December	0-3	0.0	-3.00	December	0-6	0.0	-6.00

DISTANCE

2-y-o	W-R	Per cent	£1 Level Stake	3-y-o	W-R	Per cent	£1 Level Stake
5f-6f	0-22	0.0	-22.00	5f-6f	3-22	13.6	+14.00
7f-8f	0-2	0.0	-2.00	7f-8f	0-12	0.0	-12.00
9f-13f	0-0	0.0	0.00	9f-13f	0-10	0.0	-10.00
14f+	0-0	0.0	0.00	14f+	0-1	0.0	-1.00

4-y-o+	W-R	Per cent	£1 Level Stake	Totals	W-R	Per cent	£1 Level Stake
5f-6f	4-43	9.3	-19.00	5f-6f	7-87	8.0	-27.00
7f-8f	3-26	11.5	+9.00	7f-8f	3-40	7.5	-5.00
9f-13f	3-18	16.7	+8.75	9f-13f	3-28	10.7	-1.25
14f+	0-3	0.0	-3.00	14f+	0-4	0.0	-4.00

TYPE OF RACE

Non-Handicaps	W-R	Per cent	£1 Level Stake	Handicaps	W-R	Per cent	£1 Level Stake
2-y-o	0-19	0.0	-19.00	2-y-o	0-5	0.0	-5.00
3-y-o	0-11	0.0	-11.00	3-y-o	3-34	8.8	+2.00
4-y-o+	0-9	0.0	-9.00	4-y-o+	10-81	12.3	+4.75

RACE CLASS

	W-R	Per cent	£1 Level Stake
Class 1	0-3	0.0	-3.00
Class 2	1-14	7.1	-1.00
Class 3	2-12	16.7	+2.50
Class 4	0-22	0.0	-22.00
Class 5	1-55	1.8	-47.00
Class 6	9-51	17.6	+35.25
Class 7	0-2	0.0	-2.00

FIRST TIME OUT

	W-R	Per cent	£1 Level Stake
2-y-o	0-6	0.0	-6.00
3-y-o	0-8	0.0	-8.00
4-y-o+	1-13	7.7	-10.00
Totals	1-27	3.7	-24.00

JOCKEYS

	W-R	Per cent	£1 Level Stake
Joey Haynes	3-27	11.1	+8.00
Ben Curtis	2-16	12.5	-10.25
Joao Moreira	1-1	100.0	+12.00
Rhiain Ingram	1-3	33.3	+12.00
Silvestre De Sousa	1-4	25.0	+4.00
P J McDonald	1-5	20.0	+16.00
Gabriele Malune	1-10	10.0	-3.50
Finley Marsh	1-11	9.1	-7.50
Hector Crouch	1-17	5.9	-12.00
Charlie Bennett	1-18	5.6	-9.00

COURSE RECORD

	Total W-R	Non-Hndcps 2-y-o	Non-Hndcps 3-y-o+	Hndcps 2-y-o	Hndcps 3-y-o+	Per cent	£1 Level Stake
Brighton	6-28	0-3	0-1	0-1	6-23	21.4	+18.50
Kempton (A.W)	3-15	0-0	0-1	0-0	3-14	20.0	+11.75
Ascot	1-5	0-0	0-0	0-0	1-5	20.0	+8.00

Epsom	1-6	0-0	0-0	0-0	1-6	16.7	+2.00
Chelmsford (A.W)	1-8	0-0	0-0	0-0	1-8	12.5	+13.00
Windsor	1-14	0-3	0-1	0-0	1-10	7.1	-7.50

WINNING HORSES

Horse	Races Run	1st	2nd	3rd	£
Andalusite	16	2	1	1	6922
Bahamian Sunrise	13	1	1	3	15563
Cruel Clever Cat	10	1	0	1	3105
Green Power	9	1	0	0	22131
Harrison Stickle	5	1	0	1	3105
Iley Boy	11	3	1	0	3105
Junoesque	12	2	0	2	6210
Quench Dolly	9	1	0	1	7246
Rivas Rob Roy	10	1	0	0	3752
Total winning prize-money					**£71139**
Favourites	**2-9**		**22.2%**		**-3.25**

MRS ILKA GANSERA-LEVEQUE

NEWMARKET, SUFFOLK

	No. of Hrs	Races Run	1st	2nd	3rd	Unpl	Per cent	£1 Level Stake
2-y-o	*2*	*3*	*0*	*0*	*0*	*3*	*0.0*	*-3.00*
3-y-o	*5*	*20*	*2*	*1*	*2*	*15*	*10.0*	*-11.75*
4-y-o+	*2*	*4*	*0*	*0*	*0*	*4*	*0.0*	*-4.00*
Totals	**9**	**27**	**2**	**1**	**2**	**22**	**7.4**	**-18.75**
2017	*10*	*46*	*4*	*6*	*3*	*33*	*8.7*	*-1.00*
2016	*8*	*30*	*3*	*2*	*0*	*25*	*10.0*	*+5.50*

JOCKEYS

	W-R	Per cent	£1 Level Stake
Antonio Fresu	2-13	15.4	-4.75

COURSE RECORD

	Total W-R	Non-Hndcps 2-y-o	Non-Hndcps 3-y-o+	Hndcps 2-y-o	Hndcps 3-y-o+	Per cent	£1 Level Stake
Wolvhptn (A.W)	2-5	0-0	0-0	0-0	2-5	40.0	+3.25

WINNING HORSES

Horse	Races Run	1st	2nd	3rd	£
Decoration Of War (IRE)	4	2	1	0	6857
Total winning prize-money					**£6857**
Favourites	**1-4**		**25.0%**		**-1.75**

SUE GARDNER

LONGDOWN, DEVON

	No. of Hrs	Races Run	1st	2nd	3rd	Unpl	Per cent	£1 Level Stake
2-y-o	*0*	*0*	*0*	*0*	*0*	*0*	*0.0*	*0.00*
3-y-o	*0*	*0*	*0*	*0*	*0*	*0*	*0.0*	*0.00*
4-y-o+	*5*	*15*	*2*	*1*	*1*	*11*	*13.3*	*+1.00*
Totals	**5**	**15**	**2**	**1**	**1**	**11**	**13.3**	**+1.00**
2017	*0*							
2016	*1*	*1*	*0*	*0*	*0*	*1*	*0.0*	*-1.00*

JOCKEYS

	W-R	Per cent	£1 Level Stake
Jamie Spencer	1-1	100.0	+2.00
Megan Nicholls	1-8	12.5	+5.00

COURSE RECORD

	Total W-R	Non-Hndcps 2-y-o	Non-Hndcps 3-y-o+	Hndcps 2-y-o	Hndcps 3-y-o+	Per cent	£1 Level Stake
Chepstow	2-4	0-0	1-1	0-0	1-3	50.0	+12.00

WINNING HORSES

Horse	Races Run	1st	2nd	3rd	£
Coeur Blimey (IRE)	4	1	0	0	3752
Zillion (IRE)	3	1	0	0	4140
Total winning prize-money					**£7892**
Favourites	**1-3**		**33.3%**		**-0.38**

PAUL GEORGE

CREDITON, DEVON

	No. of Hrs	Races Run	1st	2nd	3rd	Unpl	Per cent	£1 Level Stake
2-y-o	*8*	*23*	*1*	*0*	*2*	*20*	*4.3*	*+11.00*
3-y-o	*5*	*12*	*1*	*1*	*1*	*9*	*8.3*	*-4.50*
4-y-o+	*9*	*22*	*4*	*1*	*3*	*14*	*18.2*	*+20.00*
Totals	**22**	**57**	**6**	**2**	**6**	**43**	**10.5**	**+26.50**
2017	*0*							
2016	*0*							

JOCKEYS

	W-R	Per cent	£1 Level Stake
Rhiain Ingram	4-33	12.1	+30.00
Luke Morris	2-6	33.3	+14.50

COURSE RECORD

	Total W-R	Non-Hndcps 2-y-o	Non-Hndcps 3-y-o+	Hndcps 2-y-o	Hndcps 3-y-o+	Per cent	£1 Level Stake
Lingfield	2-2	1-1	0-0	0-0	1-1	100.0	+41.00
Bath	1-1	0-0	0-0	0-0	1-1	100.0	+10.00
Chepstow	1-1	0-0	0-0	0-0	1-1	100.0	+6.50
Windsor	1-3	0-0	0-0	0-0	1-3	33.3	+10.00
Ffos Las	1-7	0-1	0-1	0-2	1-3	14.3	+2.00

WINNING HORSES

Horse	Races Run	1st	2nd	3rd	£
Knightshayes	4	1	0	2	3105
*Princess Way (IRE)	4	3	0	0	6340
*Secret Return (IRE)	5	1	1	1	5531
*Zapateado	5	1	1	1	3105
Total winning prize-money					**£18081**
Favourites	**0-1**		**0.0%**		**-1.00**

KAREN GEORGE

HIGHER EASTINGTON, DEVON

	No. of Hrs	Races Run	1st	2nd	3rd	Unpl	Per cent	£1 Level Stake
2-y-o	*3*	*6*	*0*	*0*	*1*	*5*	*0.0*	*-6.00*
3-y-o	*4*	*17*	*1*	*2*	*2*	*12*	*5.9*	*-4.00*
4-y-o+	*5*	*15*	*2*	*2*	*2*	*9*	*13.3*	*-5.50*
Totals	**12**	**38**	**3**	**4**	**5**	**26**	**7.9**	**-15.50**
2017	*11*	*37*	*0*	*3*	*3*	*31*	*0.0*	*-37.00*
2016	*3*	*10*	*0*	*0*	*0*	*10*	*0.0*	*-10.00*

JOCKEYS

	W-R	Per cent	£1 Level Stake
Rhiain Ingram	3-33	9.1	-10.50

COURSE RECORD

	Total W-R	Non-Hndcps 2-y-o	Non-Hndcps 3-y-o+	Hndcps 2-y-o	Hndcps 3-y-o+	Per cent	£1 Level Stake
Leicester	1-2	0-0	0-1	0-0	1-1	50.0	+2.50
Chepstow	1-4	0-0	0-1	0-0	1-3	25.0	+9.00
Lingfield (A.W)	1-8	0-0	0-1	0-0	1-7	12.5	-3.00

WINNING HORSES

Horse	Races Run	1st	2nd	3rd	£
Counterfeit*	2	1	0	0	3105
Secret Return (IRE)*	6	2	1	2	6728
Total winning prize-money					**£9833**
Favourites	**0-0**		**0.0%**		**0.00**

ED DE GILES

LEDBURY, H'FORDS

	No. of Hrs	Races Run	1st	2nd	3rd	Unpl	Per cent	£1 Level Stake
2-y-o	*3*	*6*	*0*	*0*	*0*	*6*	*0.0*	*-6.00*
3-y-o	*9*	*46*	*3*	*5*	*2*	*36*	*6.5*	*-31.75*
4-y-o+	*21*	*154*	*15*	*17*	*10*	*112*	*9.7*	*-12.00*
Totals	**33**	**206**	**18**	**22**	**12**	**154**	**8.7**	**-49.75**
2017	*33*	*214*	*23*	*23*	*17*	*151*	*10.7*	*-27.13*
2016	*32*	*200*	*29*	*22*	*17*	*132*	*14.5*	*+12.40*

BY MONTH

2-y-o	W-R	Per cent	£1 Level Stake	3-y-o	W-R	Per cent	£1 Level Stake
January	0-0	0.0	0.00	January	0-0	0.0	0.00
February	0-0	0.0	0.00	February	0-0	0.0	0.00
March	0-0	0.0	0.00	March	0-1	0.0	-1.00
April	0-0	0.0	0.00	April	0-3	0.0	-3.00
May	0-0	0.0	0.00	May	1-4	25.0	+2.50
June	0-0	0.0	0.00	June	1-6	16.7	-2.75
July	0-0	0.0	0.00	July	0-4	0.0	-4.00
August	0-0	0.0	0.00	August	0-6	0.0	-6.00
September	0-0	0.0	0.00	September	0-4	0.0	-4.00
October	0-3	0.0	-3.00	October	1-10	10.0	-5.50
November	0-1	0.0	-1.00	November	0-3	0.0	-3.00
December	0-2	0.0	-2.00	December	0-5	0.0	-5.00

4-y-o+	W-R	Per cent	£1 Level Stake	Totals	W-R	Per cent	£1 Level Stake
January	0-3	0.0	-3.00	January	0-3	0.0	-3.00
February	0-1	0.0	-1.00	February	0-1	0.0	-1.00
March	0-10	0.0	-10.00	March	0-11	0.0	-11.00
April	0-7	0.0	-7.00	April	0-10	0.0	-10.00
May	2-20	10.0	-4.50	May	3-24	12.5	-2.00
June	6-26	23.1	+57.00	June	7-32	21.9	+54.25
July	2-17	11.8	-5.50	July	2-21	9.5	-9.50
August	1-12	8.3	+5.00	August	1-18	5.6	-1.00
September	2-19	10.5	-10.50	September	2-23	8.7	-14.50
October	2-21	9.5	-14.50	October	3-34	8.8	-23.00
November	0-14	0.0	-14.00	November	0-18	0.0	-17.00
December	0-4	0.0	-4.00	December	0-11	0.0	-9.00

DISTANCE

2-y-o	W-R	Per cent	£1 Level Stake	3-y-o	W-R	Per cent	£1 Level Stake
5f-6f	0-0	0.0	0.00	5f-6f	0-1	0.0	-1.00
7f-8f	0-6	0.0	-6.00	7f-8f	1-19	5.3	-12.50
9f-13f	0-0	0.0	0.00	9f-13f	1-23	4.3	-18.50
14f+	0-0	0.0	0.00	14f+	1-3	33.3	+0.25

4-y-o+	W-R	Per cent	£1 Level Stake	Totals	W-R	Per cent	£1 Level Stake
5f-6f	5-29	17.2	+2.00	5f-6f	5-30	16.7	+1.00
7f-8f	6-60	10.0	+19.50	7f-8f	7-85	8.2	+1.00
9f-13f	4-54	7.4	-22.50	9f-13f	5-77	6.5	-41.00
14f+	0-11	0.0	-11.00	14f+	1-14	7.1	-10.75

TYPE OF RACE

Non-Handicaps	W-R	Per cent	£1 Level Stake	Handicaps	W-R	Per cent	£1 Level Stake
2-y-o	0-5	0.0	-5.00	2-y-o	0-1	0.0	-1.00
3-y-o	0-14	0.0	-14.00	3-y-o	3-32	9.4	-17.75
4-y-o+	0-5	0.0	-5.00	4-y-o+	15-149	10.1	-7.00

RACE CLASS

	W-R	Per cent	£1 Level Stake
Class 1	0-0	0.0	0.00
Class 2	0-5	0.0	-5.00
Class 3	0-7	0.0	-7.00
Class 4	4-48	8.3	27.25
Class 5	9-85	10.6	-11.50
Class 6	4-59	6.8	-1.50
Class 7	1-2	50.0	+2.50

FIRST TIME OUT

	W-R	Per cent	£1 Level Stake
2-y-o	0-3	0.0	-3.00
3-y-o	0-9	0.0	-9.00
4-y-o+	3-21	14.3	+4.00
Totals	3-33	9.1	-8.00

JOCKEYS

	W-R	Per cent	£1 Level Stake
Callum Shepherd	9-74	12.2	-18.00
Pat Cosgrave	2-11	18.2	+1.25
Kieran O'Neill	2-12	16.7	+9.50

	W-R	Per cent	£1 Level Stake
Gabriele Malune	1-2	50.0	+39.00
Seamus Cronin	1-4	25.0	-0.50
Dougie Costello	1-4	25.0	+2.00
Rob Hornby	1-10	10.0	-5.00
William Cox	1-22	4.5	-11.00

COURSE RECORD

	Total W-R	Non-Hndcps 2-y-o	Non-Hndcps 3-y-o+	Hndcps 2-y-o	Hndcps 3-y-o+	Per cent	£1 Level Stake
Chepstow	7-22	0-0	0-2	0-0	7-20	31.8	+38.00
Kempton (A.W)	3-50	0-3	0-7	0-1	3-39	6.0	-33.00
Haydock	2-4	0-0	0-0	0-0	2-4	50.0	+5.75
Chelmsford (A.W)	2-6	0-0	0-0	0-0	2-6	33.3	+3.00
Bath	2-14	0-0	0-0	0-0	2-14	14.3	+38.00
Epsom	1-2	0-0	0-0	0-0	1-2	50.0	+1.50
Sandown	1-9	0-0	0-0	0-0	1-9	11.1	-4.00

WINNING HORSES

Horse	Races Run	1st	2nd	3rd	£
Bombastic (IRE)	9	1	0	1	7116
Bombero (IRE)	10	1	2	1	3752
Coachella (IRE)	11	2	3	0	6534
Croquembouche (IRE)	8	1	0	0	3752
Delirium (IRE)	8	1	1	1	3752
Liberisque	11	1	3	0	2911
Pike Corner Cross (IRE)	15	1	1	1	3105
Quantum Dot (IRE)	8	3	0	1	10609
Sexy Beast	8	1	2	1	9704
So Hoity Toity	6	1	0	0	3752
Swanton Blue (IRE)	11	2	1	1	9186
Treacherous	8	2	1	2	10221
Zlatan (IRE)	15	1	6	0	6469
Total winning prize-money					**£80863**
Favourites	**2-13**		**15.4%**		**-7.50**

JAMES GIVEN

WILLOUGHTON, LINCS

	No. of Hrs	Races Run	1st	2nd	3rd	Unpl	Per cent	£1 Level Stake
2-y-o	*15*	*62*	*0*	*3*	*6*	*53*	*0.0*	*-62.00*
3-y-o	*11*	*51*	*5*	*3*	*12*	*31*	*9.8*	*-34.18*
4-y-o+	*5*	*36*	*3*	*4*	*3*	*26*	*8.3*	*+17.00*
Totals	**31**	**149**	**8**	**10**	**21**	**110**	**5.4**	**-79.18**
2017	*34*	*206*	*18*	*25*	*24*	*139*	*8.7*	*-111.67*
2016	*47*	*262*	*24*	*30*	*36*	*171*	*9.2*	*-57.25*

JOCKEYS

	W-R	Per cent	£1 Level Stake
Paul Mulrennan	3-13	23.1	+32.75
Richard Kingscote	2-14	14.3	-5.25
Barry McHugh	2-33	6.1	-28.68
P J McDonald	1-5	20.0	+6.00

COURSE RECORD

	Total W-R	Non-Hndcps 2-y-o	Non-Hndcps 3-y-o+	Hndcps 2-y-o	Hndcps 3-y-o+	Per cent	£1 Level Stake
Southwell (A.W)	3-17	0-2	2-3	0-1	1-11	17.6	+21.32
Chelmsford (A.W)	3-22	0-4	0-2	0-2	3-14	13.6	-2.25
Pontefract	1-3	0-0	0-1	0-0	1-2	33.3	+5.00
Kempton (A.W)	1-5	0-0	0-0	0-0	1-5	20.0	-1.25

WINNING HORSES

Horse	Races Run	1st	2nd	3rd	£
Becker*	7	2	0	4	11062
Blyton Lass	7	1	1	1	3429
Cool Spirit	3	1	1	0	3752
Gift In Time (IRE)*	4	1	0	2	3752
Poppy May (IRE)	11	2	2	0	6016
Tawny Port	10	1	0	3	7763
Total winning prize-money					**£35774**
Favourites	**1-7**		**14.3%**		**-5.56**

JIM GOLDIE

UPLAWMOOR, E RENFREWS

	No. of Hrs	Races Run	1st	2nd	3rd	Unpl	Per cent	£1 Level Stake
2-y-o	*0*	*0*	*0*	*0*	*0*	*0*	*0.0*	*0.00*
3-y-o	*10*	*76*	*11*	*8*	*8*	*49*	*14.5*	*-8.77*
4-y-o+	*30*	*323*	*31*	*35*	*35*	*220*	*9.6*	*+27.60*
Totals	**40**	**399**	**42**	**43**	**43**	**269**	**10.5**	**+18.83**
2017	*43*	*370*	*35*	*36*	*38*	*260*	*9.5*	*-85.29*
2016	*46*	*337*	*20*	*24*	*33*	*260*	*5.9*	*-130.75*

BY MONTH

2-y-o	W-R	Per cent	£1 Level Stake
January	0-0	0.0	0.00
February	0-0	0.0	0.00
March	0-0	0.0	0.00
April	0-0	0.0	0.00
May	0-0	0.0	0.00
June	0-0	0.0	0.00
July	0-0	0.0	0.00
August	0-0	0.0	0.00
September	0-0	0.0	0.00
October	0-0	0.0	0.00
November	0-0	0.0	0.00
December	0-0	0.0	0.00

3-y-o	W-R	Per cent	£1 Level Stake
January	1-2	50.0	-0.27
February	1-2	50.0	+1.00
March	0-5	0.0	-5.00
April	0-3	0.0	-3.00
May	0-5	0.0	-5.00
June	3-7	42.9	+14.50
July	0-8	0.0	-8.00
August	1-11	9.1	-4.00
September	3-12	25.0	+12.50
October	0-10	0.0	-10.00
November	2-9	22.2	+0.50
December	0-2	0.0	-2.00

4-y-o+	W-R	Per cent	£1 Level Stake
January	4-15	26.7	+3.48
February	2-8	25.0	+4.00
March	0-23	0.0	-23.00
April	0-9	0.0	-9.00
May	4-38	10.5	+9.00
June	6-53	11.3	-13.25
July	5-54	9.3	+17.88

Totals	W-R	Per cent	£1 Level Stake
January	5-17	29.4	+3.21
February	3-10	30.0	+5.00
March	0-28	0.0	-28.00
April	0-12	0.0	-12.00
May	4-43	9.3	+4.00
June	9-60	15.0	+1.25
July	5-62	8.1	+9.88

August	4-40	10.0	+6.00	August	5-51	9.8	+2.00
September	3-29	10.3	-7.00	September	6-41	14.6	+5.50
October	1-27	3.7	+54.00	October	1-37	2.7	+44.00
November	1-16	6.3	-12.50	November	3-25	12.0	-12.00
December	1-11	9.1	-2.00	December	1-13	7.7	-4.00

DISTANCE

2-y-o	W-R	Per cent	£1 Level Stake	3-y-o	W-R	Per cent	£1 Level Stake
5f-6f	0-0	0.0	0.00	5f-6f	6-46	13.0	-9.27
7f-8f	0-0	0.0	0.00	7f-8f	2-12	16.7	-1.50
9f-13f	0-0	0.0	0.00	9f-13f	3-18	16.7	+2.00
14f+	0-0	0.0	0.00	14f+	0-0	0.0	0.00

4-y-o+	W-R	Per cent	£1 Level Stake	Totals	W-R	Per cent	£1 Level Stake
5f-6f	16-141	11.3	+2.88	5f-6f	22-187	11.8	-6.39
7f-8f	4-82	4.9	-42.00	7f-8f	6-94	6.4	-43.50
9f-13f	8-68	11.8	+0.73	9f-13f	11-86	12.8	+2.73
14f+	3-32	9.4	+66.00	14f+	3-32	9.4	+66.00

TYPE OF RACE

Non-Handicaps	W-R	Per cent	£1 Level Stake	Handicaps	W-R	Per cent	£1 Level Stake
2-y-o	0-0	0.0	0.00	2-y-o	0-0	0.0	0.00
3-y-o	0-16	0.0	-16.00	3-y-o	11-60	18.3	+7.23
4-y-o+	0-5	0.0	-5.00	4-y-o+	31-318	9.7	+32.60

RACE CLASS

	W-R	Per cent	£1 Level Stake
Class 1	0-2	0.0	-2.00
Class 2	4-42	9.5	+7.50
Class 3	1-33	3.0	-16.00
Class 4	13-91	14.3	+69.00
Class 5	14-101	13.9	+6.33
Class 6	10-127	7.9	-43.00
Class 7	0-3	0.0	-3.00

FIRST TIME OUT

	W-R	Per cent	£1 Level Stake
2-y-o	0-0	0.0	0.00
3-y-o	1-10	10.0	-8.27
4-y-o+	3-30	10.0	-14.27
Totals	4-40	10.0	-22.54

JOCKEYS

	W-R	Per cent	£1 Level Stake
Phil Dennis	11-107	10.3	+30.48
Jamie Gormley	9-63	14.3	-6.38
Barry McHugh	6-41	14.6	+6.00
Alistair Rawlinson	4-24	16.7	+22.50
George Downing	2-21	9.5	+24.00
P J McDonald	2-24	8.3	-5.27
Joe Fanning	1-1	100.0	+6.50
Silvestre De Sousa	1-2	50.0	+9.00
Paul Mulrennan	1-3	33.3	+1.50
Clifford Lee	1-4	25.0	+5.00
Robert Winston	1-5	20.0	+8.00
Harrison Shaw	1-6	16.7	+3.00
Corey Madden	1-8	12.5	+1.00
Daniel Tudhope	1-21	4.8	-17.50

COURSE RECORD

	Total W-R	Non-Hndcps 2-y-o	Non-Hndcps 3-y-o+	Hndcps 2-y-o	Hndcps 3-y-o+		
Newcastle (A.W)	16-110	0-0	0-6	0-0	16-104	14.5	[illegible]
Ayr	10-126	0-0	0-2	0-0	10-124	7.9	[illegible]
Hamilton	5-30	0-0	0-7	0-0	5-23	16.7	+7[illegible]
Musselburgh	5-43	0-0	0-1	0-0	5-42	11.6	-4.13
Goodwood	2-3	0-0	0-0	0-0	2-3	66.7	+21.00
Wolvhptn (A.W)	2-21	0-0	0-1	0-0	2-20	9.5	-9.00
York	1-8	0-0	0-1	0-0	1-7	12.5	+13.00
Redcar	1-12	0-0	0-0	0-0	1-12	8.3	-3.00

WINNING HORSES

Horse	Races Run	1st	2nd	3rd	£
Braes Of Lochalsh	11	1	2	1	4140
Brendan (IRE)	13	1	2	1	3493
Eternalist	13	3	1	2	10997
Euchen Glen	6	2	1	2	150376
Fintry Flyer	10	1	1	0	3105
Jeffrey Harris	10	1	1	1	3105
Jessie Allan (IRE)	20	3	2	1	10938
Lord Of The Glen	16	2	3	1	9671
Lotara	11	1	2	1	3493
*Loud And Clear	7	2	1	1	11062
Oriental Lilly	19	5	1	2	23774
*Pammi	10	2	3	1	6598
Party Fears Too (IRE)	8	2	0	2	10868
Primo's Comet	13	3	1	2	13423
*Restive (IRE)	8	1	0	0	4075
*Sarvi	5	1	0	0	8345
Sir Chauvelin	9	1	1	1	62250
Star Cracker (IRE)	23	1	3	4	3105
Testa Rossa (IRE)	18	2	1	3	10918
Theglasgowwarrior	18	4	2	5	24582
Tommy G	21	3	2	3	60143
Total winning prize-money					**£438461**
Favourites	**11-27**		**40.7%**		**11.33**

STEVE GOLLINGS

SCAMBLESBY, LINCS

	No. of Hrs	Races Run	1st	2nd	3rd	Unpl	Per cent	£1 Level Stake
2-y-o	*0*	*0*	*0*	*0*	*0*	*0*	*0.0*	*0.00*
3-y-o	*1*	*2*	*0*	*0*	*0*	*2*	*0.0*	*-2.00*
4-y-o+	*8*	*39*	*5*	*5*	*4*	*25*	*12.8*	*-4.00*
Totals	**9**	**41**	**5**	**5**	**4**	**27**	**12.2**	**-6.00**
2017	*6*	*28*	*4*	*7*	*5*	*12*	*14.3*	*-11.25*
2016	*10*	*29*	*5*	*4*	*3*	*17*	*17.2*	*+0.13*

JOCKEYS

	W-R	Per cent	£1 Level Stake
Joe Fanning	1-1	100.0	+10.00
Mr Simon Walker	1-1	100.0	+3.00

	25.0	+2.00
	20.0	+1.00
	1.1	-1.00

	Total W-R	Non-Hndcps 2-y-o	3-y-o+	Hndcps 2-y-o	3-y-o+	Per cent	£1 Level Stake
					2-13	15.4	+1.00
					1-1	100.0	+10.00
			0-0	0-0	1-3	33.3	+1.00
Southwell (A.W)	1-8	0-0	0-1	0-0	1-7	12.5	-2.00

WINNING HORSES

Horse	Races Run	1st	2nd	3rd	£
Handiwork	4	1	0	0	5531
Molten Lava (IRE)	11	2	2	2	3105
Nevada	6	1	1	1	3120
With Hindsight (IRE)	6	1	1	1	3429
Total winning prize-money					**£15185**
Favourites	**1-3**		**33.3%**		**1.00**

CHRIS GORDON

MORESTEAD, HAMPSHIRE

	No. of Hrs	Races Run	1st	2nd	3rd	Unpl	Per cent	£1 Level Stake
2-y-o	*0*	*0*	*0*	*0*	*0*	*0*	*0.0*	*0.00*
3-y-o	*2*	*5*	*0*	*0*	*2*	*3*	*0.0*	*-5.00*
4-y-o+	*7*	*28*	*1*	*5*	*2*	*20*	*3.6*	*-19.00*
Totals	**9**	**33**	**1**	**5**	**4**	**23**	**3.0**	**-24.00**
2017	*13*	*45*	*3*	*4*	*3*	*35*	*6.7*	*-1.00*
2016	*8*	*32*	*2*	*1*	*1*	*28*	*6.3*	*-7.00*

JOCKEYS

	W-R	Per cent	£1 Level Stake
Charles Bishop	1-18	5.6	-9.00

COURSE RECORD

	Total W-R	Non-Hndcps 2-y-o	3-y-o+	Hndcps 2-y-o	3-y-o+	Per cent	£1 Level Stake
Kempton (A.W)	1-8	0-0	0-0	0-0	1-8	12.5	+1.00

WINNING HORSES

Horse	Races Run	1st	2nd	3rd	£
Tarseekh*	6	1	1	1	2588
Total winning prize-money					**£2588**
Favourites	**15-40**		**37.5%**		**-1.51**

JOHN GOSDEN

NEWMARKET, SUFFOLK

	No. of Hrs	Races Run	1st	2nd	3rd	Unpl	Per cent	£1 Level Stake
2-y-o	*89*	*228*	*52*	*49*	*24*	*102*	*22.8*	*-28.48*
3-y-o	*105*	*394*	*104*	*72*	*56*	*162*	*26.4*	*-27.86*
4-y-o+	*25*	*83*	*21*	*10*	*10*	*42*	*25.3*	*-2.37*
Totals	**219**	**705**	**177**	**131**	**90**	**306**	**25.1**	**-58.71**
2017	*225*	*690*	*138*	*91*	*102*	*358*	*20.0*	*-81.86*
2016	*211*	*613*	*142*	*106*	*78*	*287*	*23.2*	*+7.64*

BY MONTH

2-y-o	W-R	Per cent	£1 Level Stake	3-y-o	W-R	Per cent	£1 Level Stake
January	0-0	0.0	0.00	January	6-24	25.0	-3.78
February	0-0	0.0	0.00	February	4-11	36.4	+7.03
March	0-0	0.0	0.00	March	3-17	17.6	-10.57
April	0-0	0.0	0.00	April	17-50	34.0	+18.40
May	1-4	25.0	-1.00	May	20-72	27.8	+1.80
June	4-10	40.0	+1.23	June	11-57	19.3	-24.73
July	7-22	31.8	-2.02	July	9-39	23.1	-16.68
August	5-22	22.7	-6.59	August	11-39	28.2	-6.80
September	9-45	20.0	-1.52	September	9-34	26.5	+7.10
October	9-55	16.4	-22.39	October	7-28	25.0	+2.85
November	9-42	21.4	-1.73	November	3-16	18.8	-5.27
December	8-28	28.6	+5.55	December	4-7	57.1	+2.80

4-y-o+	W-R	Per cent	£1 Level Stake	Totals	W-R	Per cent	£1 Level Stake
January	0-1	0.0	-1.00	January	6-25	24.0	-4.78
February	1-2	50.0	+4.00	February	5-13	38.5	+11.03
March	0-5	0.0	-5.00	March	3-22	13.6	-15.57
April	3-5	60.0	+7.20	April	20-55	36.4	+25.60
May	7-20	35.0	-1.13	May	28-96	29.2	-0.33
June	3-18	16.7	-4.96	June	18-85	21.2	-28.46
July	1-7	14.3	-5.20	July	17-68	25.0	-23.90
August	2-6	33.3	+7.36	August	18-67	26.9	-6.03
September	1-7	14.3	-5.47	September	19-86	22.1	+0.11
October	2-9	22.2	-5.17	October	18-92	19.6	-24.71
November	1-3	33.3	+7.00	November	13-61	21.3	+1.73
December	0-0	0.0	0.00	December	12-35	34.3	+2.80

DISTANCE

2-y-o	W-R	Per cent	£1 Level Stake	3-y-o	W-R	Per cent	£1 Level Stake
5f-6f	13-36	36.1	+9.39	5f-6f	3-18	16.7	-9.15
7f-8f	37-176	21.0	-31.86	7f-8f	43-165	26.1	-39.54
9f-13f	2-16	12.5	-6.00	9f-13f	56-194	28.9	+33.38
14f+	0-0	0.0	0.00	14f+	2-17	11.8	-12.55

4-y-o+	W-R	Per cent	£1 Level Stake	Totals	W-R	Per cent	£1 Level Stake
5f-6f	1-5	20.0	-3.09	5f-6f	17-59	28.8	-2.85
7f-8f	2-20	10.0	-11.00	7f-8f	82-361	22.7	-82.40
9f-13f	13-48	27.1	+12.14	9f-13f	71-258	27.5	+39.52
14f+	5-10	50.0	-0.42	14f+	7-27	25.9	-12.97

TYPE OF RACE

Non-Handicaps	W-R	Per cent	£1 Level Stake	Handicaps	W-R	Per cent	£1 Level Stake
2-y-o	48-209	23.0	-27.06	2-y-o	4-19	21.1	-1.42
3-y-o	77-265	29.1	+5.62	3-y-o	27-129	20.9	-33.49

4-y-o+	14-46	30.4	-7.15	4-y-o+	7-37	18.9	+4.78

RACE CLASS

	W-R	Per cent	£1 Level Stake
Class 1	34-130	26.2	-13.96
Class 2	12-80	15.0	-17.74
Class 3	20-78	25.6	-18.95
Class 4	37-173	21.4	-40.58
Class 5	66-234	28.2	+17.94
Class 6	8-10	80.0	+15.58
Class 7	0-0	0.0	0.00

FIRST TIME OUT

	W-R	Per cent	£1 Level Stake
2-y-o	17-89	19.1	-15.72
3-y-o	28-105	26.7	-2.07
4-y-o+	11-25	44.0	+9.14
Totals	56-219	25.6	-8.65

JOCKEYS

	W-R	Per cent	£1 Level Stake
Robert Havlin	89-309	28.8	-3.19
Frankie Dettori	40-134	29.9	-9.49
Nicky Mackay	12-83	14.5	-14.87
Kieran O'Neill	9-48	18.8	+14.00
Oisin Murphy	8-20	40.0	+6.17
Jim Crowley	8-36	22.2	-9.30
James Doyle	5-24	20.8	-8.99
William Buick	2-12	16.7	-3.75
Adam Kirby	1-1	100.0	+2.00
Martin Harley	1-1	100.0	+2.00
Andrea Atzeni	1-7	14.3	-5.20
Dane O'Neill	1-14	7.1	-12.09

COURSE RECORD

	Total W-R	Non-Hndcps 2-y-o	Non-Hndcps 3-y-o+	Hndcps 2-y-o	Hndcps 3-y-o+	Per cent	£1 Level Stake
Kempton (A.W)	20-70	5-26	11-28	1-5	3-11	28.6	+8.93
Newcastle (A.W)	15-40	5-11	7-23	1-1	2-5	37.5	-3.55
Wolvhptn (A.W)	15-52	3-17	8-22	2-5	2-8	28.8	-3.69
Lingfield (A.W)	14-46	2-11	10-27	0-0	2-8	30.4	+17.05
Ascot	13-59	4-9	7-32	0-0	2-18	22.0	-13.26
Newmarket	13-75	4-25	7-32	0-3	2-15	17.3	+3.03
Chelmsford (A.W)	12-54	3-12	7-24	0-2	2-16	22.2	-18.77
Newmkt (Jly)	10-53	4-21	1-14	0-0	5-18	18.9	-17.07
York	9-23	0-3	7-13	0-0	2-7	39.1	+11.95
Yarmouth	9-25	4-14	4-6	0-0	1-5	36.0	+2.98
Sandown	9-32	5-11	4-11	0-0	0-10	28.1	-4.73
Newbury	8-27	3-10	2-10	0-0	3-7	29.6	+9.33
Windsor	6-17	1-3	3-7	0-1	2-6	35.3	-3.31
Haydock	5-15	3-7	0-5	0-0	2-3	33.3	+1.01
Epsom	3-8	0-1	2-5	0-0	1-2	37.5	+3.04
Wetherby	2-3	0-0	2-3	0-0	0-0	66.7	+2.00
Brighton	2-4	0-1	1-2	0-0	1-1	50.0	+0.10
Salisbury	2-10	0-2	2-6	0-0	0-2	20.0	+4.80
Goodwood	2-18	0-4	1-9	0-0	1-5	11.1	-14.47
Doncaster	2-23	1-9	0-5	0-1	1-8	8.7	-11.64
Chepstow	1-1	0-0	1-1	0-0	0-0	100.0	+0.91
Redcar	1-2	1-2	0-0	0-0	0-0	50.0	+2.50
Lingfield	1-3	0-0	1-3	0-0	0-0	33.3	+0.75
Southwell (A.W)	1-6	0-1	1-3	0-0	0-2	16.7	-2.00
Leicester	1-10	0-3	1-4	0-0	0-3	10.0	-7.25
Nottingham	1-21	0-5	1-9	0-1	0-6	4.8	-19.33

WINNING HORSES

Horse	Races Run	1st	2nd	3rd	£
Aim Of Artemis (IRE)	3	1	0	0	3881
Alfaatik	1	1	0	0	3752
Almashriq (USA)	1	1	0	0	3752
Almoghared (IRE)	5	1	1	0	3752
Angel's Hideaway (IRE)	8	2	2	1	33207
Argentello (IRE)	9	4	1	3	34290
Award Winning (IRE)	3	1	0	0	4787
Azano	3	1	1	0	4916
Battle For Glory (USA)	1	1	0	0	5175
Boar Slam (USA)	5	2	0	0	32388
Beatboxer (USA)	3	2	0	0	12291
Ben Vrackie	7	1	2	2	3752
Bowditch (IRE)	1	1	0	0	3752
Briscola	2	1	1	0	3752
Buffalo River (USA)	4	1	2	1	3881
Calyx	2	2	0	0	90240
Casey Jones (IRE)	6	3	0	1	15914
Cassini (IRE)	2	1	0	0	3752
Corelli (USA)	3	2	0	1	22154
Coronet	4	1	2	1	70888
Court House (IRE)	6	2	3	0	11386
Cracksman	3	2	1	0	975412
Crossed Baton	4	2	1	0	33530
Culpability (USA)	2	1	1	0	5175
Daafr (IRE)	6	1	1	1	6728
Daarik (IRE)	2	1	0	0	3817
Derrymore (IRE)	2	1	0	0	3752
Dive For Gold	5	1	1	0	4787
Dolcissimo (IRE)	8	1	5	0	5434
Dreamfield	4	1	1	0	7763
Dubai Warrior	1	1	0	0	4787
Duneflower (IRE)	2	1	1	0	3817
Emaraaty	4	1	1	0	3752
Emblazoned (IRE)	5	2	1	2	7504
Enable	1	1	0	0	39697
Enbihaar (IRE)	3	1	0	1	6469
Entitle	2	1	0	0	3752
Fennaan (IRE)	8	2	0	0	12572
Fightwithme (IRE)	4	1	1	2	8821
First Eleven	6	2	1	2	68978
Frederickbarbarosa (IRE)	5	1	2	0	4787
Gaudi (IRE)	2	1	1	0	3752
George Villiers (IRE)	4	1	2	0	6728
Ghazawaat (FR)	3	1	1	0	9767
Glencadam Glory	4	1	0	0	3752
Gumriyah	4	1	1	0	6728
Hameem	5	2	3	0	13456
Hasanoanda*	6	3	0	0	16302
Highgarden	6	1	1	1	34026
Hinde Street (USA)	3	1	0	1	3752
Holy Heart (IRE)	2	1	0	1	3881
Honest Albert	1	1	0	0	3235
Humanitarian (USA)	2	1	1	0	3752

Il Primo Sole	3	1	0	0	3881
Jamih	3	1	1	0	5175
Jawwaal	8	2	0	1	6987
Keltie	4	1	0	1	3881
Kessaar (IRE)	6	3	1	0	81346
Kick On	3	1	1	0	6469
Kimblewick (IRE)	1	1	0	0	3881
King Of Comedy (IRE)	2	1	1	0	6469
Kings Shield (USA)	4	1	0	1	15563
Kosciuszko (IRE)	2	1	0	0	4528
Lady Baker (USA)	5	1	1	0	9704
Lady Lawyer (USA)	1	1	0	0	3881
Lah Ti Dar	5	3	1	1	73583
Legends Of War (USA)	6	2	1	0	14491
Lord North (IRE)	1	1	0	0	7116
Main Street	3	1	1	0	8086
Margie's Choice (GER)*	6	1	1	1	3752
Marhaba Milliar (IRE)	3	2	1	0	13973
Mehdaayih	3	1	1	0	4787
Mister Ambassador (USA)	4	1	0	0	3752
Monarchs Glen	2	1	0	0	56710
Mr Marrakech	2	2	0	0	9057
Muchly	2	1	0	1	5434
Muntahaa (IRE)	4	1	0	1	311250
New King	2	1	0	0	3752
Nordic Passage (IRE)	2	1	1	0	3235
Ode To Autumn	7	2	2	0	9139
Oscar's Ridge (IRE)	3	1	1	1	5434
Panmolle	4	1	2	0	3752
Pennywhistle (IRE)	4	1	0	2	3881
Perfection	8	3	1	1	32096
Petit Palais	2	1	0	0	3105
Pouvoir Magique (FR)	3	1	0	0	24900
Precious Ramotswe	5	2	0	1	60806
Raa Atoll	5	2	1	0	13585
Reeth (IRE)	6	1	0	1	3881
Roaring Lion (USA)	7	4	0	2	1800188
Rococo	5	1	0	3	7763
Royal Line	3	2	0	1	59138
Sacred Path	4	1	2	0	4140
Scottish Jig (USA)	6	3	0	3	28215
Sevenna Star (IRE)	5	2	0	0	43449
Shambolic (IRE)	3	2	0	0	11903
She's Got You	2	1	0	0	3752
Sophie Gray (IRE)	2	1	0	0	3752
Spanish Aria	6	1	1	1	7116
Sparkle Roll (FR)	2	1	0	0	4787
Star Of Bengal	3	1	0	1	3752
Stradivarius (IRE)	5	5	0	0	1088832
Stream Of Stars	3	1	1	0	9704
Stream Song	5	1	0	1	5531
Stylehunter	6	2	2	0	13456
Sucellus	1	1	0	0	3752
Surya	8	3	1	0	29479
Taqdeer (IRE)	2	1	0	0	31125
Tivoli (IRE)	4	1	1	0	5822
Tobruk (IRE)	5	1	1	1	3752
Too Darn Hot	4	4	0	0	358966
Turgenev	4	2	1	0	10221
Utmost (USA)	3	1	0	0	25520
Waldstern	3	1	1	0	5175
War Eagle (IRE)	5	1	1	0	3752
Weekender	5	1	2	1	16173
Whitlock	7	2	2	0	8280
Wissahickon (USA)	6	5	0	0	171632
Without Parole	5	3	0	0	331961

Total winning prize-money **£6624537**

Favourites **101-228** **44.3%** **-9.03**

WARREN GREATREX

UPPER LAMBOURN, BERKS

	No. of Hrs	Races Run	1st	2nd	3rd	Unpl	Per cent	£1 Level Stake
2-y-o	*0*	*0*	*0*	*0*	*0*	*0*	*0.0*	*0.00*
3-y-o	*2*	*6*	*1*	*0*	*0*	*5*	*16.7*	*+2.00*
4-y-o+	*6*	*17*	*9*	*2*	*1*	*5*	*52.9*	*+9.16*
Totals	**8**	**23**	**10**	**2**	**1**	**10**	**43.5**	**+11.16**
2017	*6*	*9*	*0*	*3*	*1*	*5*	*0.0*	*-9.00*
2016	*5*	*8*	*2*	*1*	*1*	*4*	*25.0*	*+11.00*

BY MONTH

2-y-o	W-R	Per cent	£1 Level Stake	3-y-o	W-R	Per cent	£1 Level Stake
January	0-0	0.0	0.00	January	0-0	0.0	0.00
February	0-0	0.0	0.00	February	0-0	0.0	0.00
March	0-0	0.0	0.00	March	0-1	0.0	-1.00
April	0-0	0.0	0.00	April	0-0	0.0	0.00
May	0-0	0.0	0.00	May	0-1	0.0	-1.00
June	0-0	0.0	0.00	June	1-2	50.0	+6.00
July	0-0	0.0	0.00	July	0-1	0.0	-1.00
August	0-0	0.0	0.00	August	0-0	0.0	0.00
September	0-0	0.0	0.00	September	0-0	0.0	0.00
October	0-0	0.0	0.00	October	0-0	0.0	0.00
November	0-0	0.0	0.00	November	0-0	0.0	0.00
December	0-0	0.0	0.00	December	0-1	0.0	-1.00

4-y-o+	W-R	Per cent	£1 Level Stake	Totals	W-R	Per cent	£1 Level Stake
January	0-1	0.0	-1.00	January	0-1	0.0	-1.00
February	3-3	100.0	+8.50	February	3-3	100.0	+8.50
March	0-0	0.0	0.00	March	0-1	0.0	-1.00
April	0-1	0.0	-1.00	April	0-1	0.0	-1.00
May	2-2	100.0	+3.42	May	2-3	66.7	+2.42
June	1-2	50.0	+0.50	June	2-4	50.0	+6.50
July	1-3	33.3	-1.39	July	1-4	25.0	-2.39
August	2-4	50.0	+1.13	August	2-4	50.0	+1.13
September	0-1	0.0	-1.00	September	0-1	0.0	-1.00
October	0-0	0.0	0.00	October	0-0	0.0	0.00
November	0-0	0.0	0.00	November	0-0	0.0	0.00
December	0-0	0.0	0.00	December	0-1	0.0	-1.00

DISTANCE

2-y-o	W-R	Per cent	£1 Level Stake	3-y-o	W-R	Per cent	£1 Level Stake
5f-6f	0-0	0.0	0.00	5f-6f	0-0	0.0	0.00

	W-R	Per cent	£1 Level Stake		W-R	Per cent	£1 Level Stake
7f-8f	0-0	0.0	0.00	7f-8f	1-3	33.3	+5.00
9f-13f	0-0	0.0	0.00	9f-13f	0-2	0.0	-2.00
14f+	0-0	0.0	0.00	14f+	0-1	0.0	-1.00

4-y-o+	W-R	Per cent	£1 Level Stake	Totals	W-R	Per cent	£1 Level Stake
5f-6f	0-0	0.0	0.00	5f-6f	0-0	0.0	0.00
7f-8f	0-0	0.0	0.00	7f-8f	1-3	33.3	+5.00
9f-13f	1-5	20.0	-3.50	9f-13f	1-7	14.3	-5.50
14f+	8-12	66.7	+12.66	14f+	8-13	61.5	+11.66

TYPE OF RACE

Non-Handicaps	W-R	Per cent	£1 Level Stake	Handicaps	W-R	Per cent	£1 Level Stake
2-y-o	0-0	0.0	0.00	2-y-o	0-0	0.0	0.00
3-y-o	1-2	50.0	+6.00	3-y-o	0-4	0.0	-4.00
4-y-o+	0-1	0.0	-1.00	4-y-o+	9-16	56.3	+10.16

RACE CLASS

	W-R	Per cent	£1 Level Stake
Class 1	0-0	0.0	0.00
Class 2	0-1	0.0	-1.00
Class 3	0-0	0.0	0.00
Class 4	1-4	25.0	0.00
Class 5	3-9	33.3	+3.00
Class 6	6-9	66.7	+9.16
Class 7	0-0	0.0	0.00

FIRST TIME OUT

	W-R	Per cent	£1 Level Stake
2-y-o	0-0	0.0	0.00
3-y-o	1-2	50.0	+6.00
4-y-o+	1-6	16.7	-2.25
Totals	2-8	25.0	+3.75

JOCKEYS

	W-R	Per cent	£1 Level Stake
Edward Greatrex	5-11	45.5	+2.28
Shane Kelly	1-1	100.0	+3.00
Andrea Atzeni	1-1	100.0	+1.63
Richard Kingscote	1-1	100.0	+2.75
Charles Bishop	1-2	50.0	+0.50
Thomas Greatrex	1-4	25.0	+4.00

COURSE RECORD

	Total W-R	Non-Hndcps 2-y-o	Non-Hndcps 3-y-o+	Hndcps 2-y-o	Hndcps 3-y-o+	Per cent	£1 Level Stake
Nottingham	2-2	0-0	0-0	0-0	2-2	100.0	+3.13
Wolvhptn (A.W)	2-4	0-0	0-1	0-0	2-3	50.0	+3.50
Haydock	1-1	0-0	1-1	0-0	0-0	100.0	+7.00
Lingfield	1-1	0-0	0-0	0-0	1-1	100.0	+0.61
Yarmouth	1-1	0-0	0-0	0-0	1-1	100.0	+0.67
Southwell (A.W)	1-1	0-0	0-0	0-0	1-1	100.0	+3.00
Chepstow	1-2	0-0	0-0	0-0	1-2	50.0	+1.75
Chelmsford (A.W)	1-4	0-0	0-0	0-0	1-4	25.0	-1.50

WINNING HORSES

Horse	Races Run	1st	2nd	3rd	£
*Bailarico (IRE)	5	5	0	0	16431
Bodes Well (IRE)	3	1	0	0	5175
Final Choice*	4	1	1	0	3493
Great Return	5	3	1	1	12388
Total winning prize-money					**£37487**
Favourites		**25-63**		**39.7%**	**-3.87**

OLIVER GREENALL

OLDCASTLE HEATH, CHESHIRE

	No. of Hrs	Races Run	1st	2nd	3rd	Unpl	Per cent	£1 Level Stake
2-y-o	*3*	*10*	*0*	*0*	*1*	*9*	*0.0*	*-10.00*
3-y-o	*0*	*0*	*0*	*0*	*0*	*0*	*0.0*	*0.00*
4-y-o+	*10*	*32*	*2*	*1*	*3*	*25*	*6.3*	*-13.27*
Totals	**13**	**42**	**2**	**1**	**4**	**34**	**4.8**	**-23.27**
2017	*14*	*85*	*6*	*8*	*7*	*64*	*7.1*	*-46.75*
2016	*6*	*24*	*3*	*1*	*1*	*19*	*12.5*	*-10.00*

JOCKEYS

	W-R	Per cent	£1 Level Stake
Ross Turner	1-2	50.0	-0.27
Paddy Pilley	1-2	50.0	+15.00

COURSE RECORD

	Total W-R	Non-Hndcps 2-y-o	Non-Hndcps 3-y-o+	Hndcps 2-y-o	Hndcps 3-y-o+	Per cent	£1 Level Stake
Nottingham	1-2	0-0	0-0	0-1	1-1	50.0	+15.00
Haydock	1-3	0-1	0-0	0-0	1-2	33.3	-1.27

WINNING HORSES

Horse	Races Run	1st	2nd	3rd	£
Fort Jefferson	4	2	0	0	8733
Total winning prize-money					**£8733**
Favourites	**6-19**		**31.6%**		**-4.77**

DAVID C GRIFFITHS

BAWTRY, S YORKS

	No. of Hrs	Races Run	1st	2nd	3rd	Unpl	Per cent	£1 Level Stake
2-y-o	*3*	*9*	*0*	*0*	*1*	*8*	*0.0*	*-9.00*
3-y-o	*10*	*67*	*6*	*2*	*4*	*55*	*9.0*	*-45.17*
4-y-o+	*18*	*190*	*14*	*17*	*13*	*145*	*7.4*	*-75.67*
Totals	**31**	**266**	**20**	**19**	**18**	**208**	**7.5**	**-129.84**
2017	*28*	*198*	*22*	*14*	*15*	*145*	*11.1*	*-17.67*
2016	*25*	*114*	*7*	*6*	*10*	*91*	*6.1*	*-69.50*

BY MONTH

2-y-o	W-R	Per cent	£1 Level Stake	3-y-o	W-R	Per cent	£1 Level Stake
January	0-0	0.0	0.00	January	1-6	16.7	-3.00
February	0-0	0.0	0.00	February	1-7	14.3	-5.00
March	0-0	0.0	0.00	March	2-3	66.7	+3.33
April	0-0	0.0	0.00	April	0-4	0.0	-4.00
May	0-0	0.0	0.00	May	0-8	0.0	-8.00
June	0-2	0.0	-2.00	June	0-7	0.0	-7.00
July	0-2	0.0	-2.00	July	0-8	0.0	-8.00
August	0-2	0.0	-2.00	August	1-3	33.3	+2.50
September	0-1	0.0	-1.00	September	1-6	16.7	-1.00

	W-R	Per cent	£1 Level Stake		W-R	Per cent	£1 Level Stake
October	0-0	0.0	0.00	October	0-5	0.0	-5.00
November	0-0	0.0	0.00	November	0-5	0.0	-5.00
December	0-2	0.0	-2.00	December	0-5	0.0	-5.00

4-y-o+	W-R	Per cent	£1 Level Stake	Totals	W-R	Per cent	£1 Level Stake
January	2-10	20.0	+8.50	January	3-16	18.8	+5.50
February	3-18	16.7	-6.25	February	4-25	16.0	-11.25
March	1-11	9.1	-7.25	March	3-14	21.4	-3.92
April	2-16	12.5	+1.00	April	2-20	10.0	-3.00
May	1-19	5.3	-14.67	May	1-27	3.7	-22.67
June	0-17	0.0	-17.00	June	0-26	0.0	-26.00
July	2-21	9.5	-8.00	July	2-31	6.5	-18.00
August	1-19	5.3	+2.00	August	2-24	8.3	+2.50
September	1-19	5.3	-15.00	September	2-26	7.7	-17.00
October	1-16	6.3	+5.00	October	1-21	4.8	0.00
November	0-13	0.0	-13.00	November	0-18	0.0	-18.00
December	0-11	0.0	-11.00	December	0-18	0.0	-16.00

DISTANCE

2-y-o	W-R	Per cent	£1 Level Stake	3-y-o	W-R	Per cent	£1 Level Stake
5f-6f	0-9	0.0	-9.00	5f-6f	6-48	12.5	-26.17
7f-8f	0-0	0.0	0.00	7f-8f	0-11	0.0	-11.00
9f-13f	0-0	0.0	0.00	9f-13f	0-5	0.0	-5.00
14f+	0-0	0.0	0.00	14f+	0-3	0.0	-3.00

4-y-o+	W-R	Per cent	£1 Level Stake	Totals	W-R	Per cent	£1 Level Stake
5f-6f	13-133	9.8	-39.67	5f-6f	19-190	10.0	-74.84
7f-8f	1-53	1.9	-32.00	7f-8f	1-64	1.6	-43.00
9f-13f	0-4	0.0	-4.00	9f-13f	0-9	0.0	-9.00
14f+	0-0	0.0	0.00	14f+	0-3	0.0	-3.00

TYPE OF RACE

Non-Handicaps	W-R	Per cent	£1 Level Stake	Handicaps	W-R	Per cent	£1 Level Stake
2-y-o	0-8	0.0	-8.00	2-y-o	0-1	0.0	-1.00
3-y-o	0-18	0.0	-18.00	3-y-o	6-49	12.2	-27.17
4-y-o+	2-21	9.5	-12.67	4-y-o+	12-169	7.1	-63.00

RACE CLASS

	W-R	Per cent	£1 Level Stake
Class 1	1-13	7.7	-9.00
Class 2	0-19	0.0	-19.00
Class 3	1-23	4.3	-10.00
Class 4	3-50	6.0	-34.25
Class 5	5-98	5.1	-68.00
Class 6	9-61	14.8	+7.92
Class 7	1-2	50.0	+2.50

FIRST TIME OUT

	W-R	Per cent	£1 Level Stake
2-y-o	0-3	0.0	-3.00
3-y-o	1-10	10.0	-7.00
4-y-o+	0-18	0.0	-18.00
Totals	1-31	3.2	-28.00

JOCKEYS

	W-R	Per cent	£1 Level Stake
David Allan	4-41	9.8	-20.25
Andrea Atzeni	2-6	33.3	+11.00
Oisin Murphy	2-8	25.0	-1.67
Dougie Costello	2-10	20.0	-1.50
Tom Marquand	2-23	8.7	+7.00
Josephine Gordon	1-3	33.3	+1.00
George Wood	1-4	25.0	+0.33
Jim Crowley	1-4	25.0	+1.00
Martin Dwyer	1-8	12.5	+1.50
Fran Berry	1-9	11.1	-6.25
P J McDonald	1-9	11.1	-7.00
Andrew Mullen	1-12	8.3	-7.00
Phil Dennis	1-23	4.3	-2.00

COURSE RECORD

	Total W-R	Non-Hndcps 2-y-o	Non-Hndcps 3-y-o+	Hndcps 2-y-o	Hndcps 3-y-o+	Per cent	£1 Level Stake
Southwell (A.W)	7-63	0-2	0-8	0-1	7-52	11.1	-31.75
Chelmsford (A.W)	3-10	0-0	1-1	0-0	2-9	30.0	+12.83
Lingfield (A.W)	3-20	0-0	0-1	0-0	3-19	15.0	-11.42
Beverley	2-14	0-0	1-3	0-0	1-11	14.3	-2.00
Bath	1-6	0-0	0-0	0-0	1-6	16.7	-1.00
Brighton	1-6	0-0	0-0	0-0	1-6	16.7	+15.00
Redcar	1-7	0-0	0-1	0-0	1-6	14.3	-2.00
Catterick	1-14	0-1	0-2	0-0	1-11	7.1	+7.00
Wolvhptn (A.W)	1-20	0-1	0-5	0-0	1-14	5.0	-10.50

WINNING HORSES

Horse	Races Run	1st	2nd	3rd	£
Aguerooo (IRE)*	5	1	0	1	3493
Angel Force (IRE)	13	1	1	0	4399
Archimedes (IRE)	26	4	1	2	12420
*Bondi Beach Boy	7	1	3	0	4033
Brother Tiger	7	1	3	0	5531
Fieldsman (USA)	25	1	4	4	3105
Magic Pulse (IRE)	10	3	0	1	12162
Pearl Acclaim (IRE)	21	2	1	2	9024
Take Cover	7	1	2	1	34026
Tavener	19	3	0	0	18987
Warrior's Valley	9	2	1	3	5418
Total winning prize-money					**£112598**
Favourites	**6-14**		**42.9%**		**3.33**

RAE GUEST

NEWMARKET, SUFFOLK

	No. of Hrs	Races Run	1st	2nd	3rd	Unpl	Per cent	£1 Level Stake
2-y-o	*5*	*23*	*1*	*0*	*0*	*22*	*4.3*	*-6.00*
3-y-o	*12*	*76*	*14*	*9*	*7*	*46*	*18.4*	*-7.58*
4-y-o+	*9*	*64*	*5*	*5*	*2*	*52*	*7.8*	*-32.84*
Totals	**26**	**163**	**20**	**14**	**9**	**120**	**12.3**	**-46.42**
2017	*31*	*141*	*18*	*18*	*13*	*92*	*12.8*	*-56.42*
2016	*27*	*127*	*13*	*11*	*17*	*85*	*10.2*	*-24.39*

BY MONTH

2-y-o	W-R	Per cent	£1 Level Stake	3-y-o	W-R	Per cent	£1 Level Stake
January	0-0	0.0	0.00	January	0-6	0.0	-6.00
February	0-0	0.0	0.00	February	0-3	0.0	-3.00
March	0-0	0.0	0.00	March	0-0	0.0	0.00

	W-R	Per cent	£1 Level Stake		W-R	Per cent	£1 Level Stake
April	0-0	0.0	0.00	April	1-4	25.0	+5.00
May	0-0	0.0	0.00	May	2-9	22.2	+3.50
June	0-1	0.0	-1.00	June	1-6	16.7	-2.50
July	0-1	0.0	-1.00	July	1-2	50.0	+2.50
August	0-2	0.0	-2.00	August	0-10	0.0	-10.00
September	0-3	0.0	-3.00	September	3-12	25.0	+5.00
October	1-6	16.7	+11.00	October	3-14	21.4	-3.70
November	0-8	0.0	-8.00	November	2-7	28.6	+0.63
December	0-2	0.0	-2.00	December	1-3	33.3	+1.00

4-y-o+	W-R	Per cent	£1 Level Stake	Totals	W-R	Per cent	£1 Level Stake
January	0-5	0.0	-5.00	January	0-11	0.0	-11.00
February	1-4	25.0	+9.00	February	1-7	14.3	+6.00
March	1-3	33.3	+7.00	March	1-3	33.3	+7.00
April	0-2	0.0	-2.00	April	1-6	16.7	+3.00
May	1-7	14.3	-3.25	May	3-16	18.8	+0.25
June	0-6	0.0	-6.00	June	1-13	7.7	-9.50
July	2-9	22.2	-4.59	July	3-12	25.0	-3.09
August	0-4	0.0	-4.00	August	0-16	0.0	-16.00
September	0-11	0.0	-11.00	September	3-26	11.5	-9.00
October	0-4	0.0	-4.00	October	4-24	16.7	+3.30
November	0-7	0.0	-7.00	November	2-22	9.1	-6.37
December	0-2	0.0	-2.00	December	1-7	14.3	-1.00

DISTANCE

2-y-o	W-R	Per cent	£1 Level Stake	3-y-o	W-R	Per cent	£1 Level Stake
5f-6f	1-14	7.1	+3.00	5f-6f	5-22	22.7	+3.00
7f-8f	0-9	0.0	-9.00	7f-8f	2-24	8.3	-12.00
9f-13f	0-0	0.0	0.00	9f-13f	6-29	20.7	+0.63
14f+	0-0	0.0	0.00	14f+	1-1	100.0	+0.80

4-y-o+	W-R	Per cent	£1 Level Stake	Totals	W-R	Per cent	£1 Level Stake
5f-6f	4-38	10.5	-10.59	5f-6f	10-74	13.5	-4.59
7f-8f	1-21	4.8	-17.25	7f-8f	3-54	5.6	-38.25
9f-13f	0-5	0.0	-5.00	9f-13f	6-34	17.6	-4.37
14f+	0-0	0.0	0.00	14f+	1-1	100.0	+0.80

TYPE OF RACE

Non-Handicaps	W-R	Per cent	£1 Level Stake	Handicaps	W-R	Per cent	£1 Level Stake
2-y-o	1-17	5.9	0.00	2-y-o	0-6	0.0	-6.00
3-y-o	1-19	5.3	-10.00	3-y-o	13-57	22.8	+2.42
4-y-o+	0-7	0.0	-7.00	4-y-o+	5-57	8.8	-25.84

RACE CLASS

	W-R	Per cent	£1 Level Stake
Class 1	0-7	0.0	-7.00
Class 2	0-10	0.0	-10.00
Class 3	1-9	11.1	-5.25
Class 4	3-24	12.5	-10.59
Class 5	6-54	11.1	0.00
Class 6	10-57	17.5	-11.58
Class 7	0-2	0.0	-2.00

FIRST TIME OUT

	W-R	Per cent	£1 Level Stake
2-y-o	1-5	20.0	+12.00
3-y-o	1-12	8.3	-6.00
4-y-o+	1-9	11.1	5.25
Totals	3-26	11.5	+0.75

JOCKEYS

	W-R	Per cent	£1 Level Stake
Martin Harley	6-27	22.2	+11.38
David Probert	4-26	15.4	-3.00
Silvestre De Sousa	3-9	33.3	-0.09
Oisin Murphy	2-3	66.7	+1.30
Dane O'Neill	1-3	33.3	+4.00
Fran Berry	1-5	20.0	+1.00
Shane Kelly	1-6	16.7	+11.00
William Carson	1-12	8.3	-5.50
Sebastian Woods	1-12	8.3	-6.50

COURSE RECORD

	Total W-R	Non-Hndcps 2-y-o	Non-Hndcps 3-y-o+	Hndcps 2-y-o	Hndcps 3-y-o+	Per cent	£1 Level Stake
Kempton (A.W)	6-21	1-3	0-3	0-1	5-14	28.6	+18.13
Brighton	3-6	0-1	0-1	0-0	3-4	50.0	+8.50
Wolvhptn (A.W)	3-22	0-2	0-3	0-1	3-16	13.6	+1.50
Bath	2-6	0-1	0-0	0-0	2-5	33.3	-1.59
Chelmsford (A.W)	2-36	0-2	0-5	0-4	2-25	5.6	-24.20
Chepstow	1-1	0-0	0-0	0-0	1-1	100.0	+6.00
Ripon	1-3	0-0	1-1	0-0	0-2	33.3	+6.00
Yarmouth	1-9	0-1	0-0	0-0	1-8	11.1	-5.25
Lingfield (A.W)	1-11	0-1	0-3	0-0	1-7	9.1	-7.50

WINNING HORSES

Horse	Races Run	1st	2nd	3rd	£
Alaskan Bay (IRE)	8	2	1	0	3105
Dame Nellie	10	4	1	1	12809
Dance Legend	6	1	1	0	5822
Dupioni (IRE)	3	1	0	0	3881
Kachumba	13	4	0	2	3752
Midnightly	9	2	0	0	8151
Roman Spinner	9	1	3	2	3752
Salt Whistle Bay (IRE)	6	1	1	0	7246
Show Stealer	10	2	0	0	11062
*Thistimelastyear	4	1	0	0	3105
Wallflower (IRE)	9	1	2	1	3105
Total winning prize-money					**£65790**
Favourites	**7-11**		**63.6%**		**9.83**

RICHARD GUEST

INGMANTHORPE, W YORKS

	No. of Hrs	Races Run	1st	2nd	3rd	Unpl	Per cent	£1 Level Stake
2-y-o	*2*	*8*	*0*	*0*	*0*	*8*	*0.0*	*-8.00*
3-y-o	*8*	*48*	*5*	*4*	*4*	*35*	*10.4*	*-5.00*
4-y-o+	*18*	*178*	*16*	*15*	*16*	*130*	*9.0*	*-55.92*
Totals	**28**	**234**	**21**	**19**	**20**	**173**	**9.0**	**-68.92**
2017	*42*	*375*	*33*	*26*	*44*	*272*	*8.8*	*-130.68*
2016	*33*	*351*	*34*	*32*	*20*	*264*	*9.7*	*-67.40*

BY MONTH

2-y-o	W-R	Per cent	£1 Level Stake	3-y-o	W-R	Per cent	£1 Level Stake
January	0-0	0.0	0.00	January	0-3	0.0	-3.00
February	0-0	0.0	0.00	February	0-0	0.0	0.00
March	0-0	0.0	0.00	March	0-0	0.0	0.00
April	0-0	0.0	0.00	April	0-8	0.0	-8.00
May	0-0	0.0	0.00	May	0-3	0.0	-3.00
June	0-0	0.0	0.00	June	0-7	0.0	-7.00
July	0-0	0.0	0.00	July	0-3	0.0	-3.00
August	0-1	0.0	-1.00	August	2-8	25.0	+23.50
September	0-0	0.0	0.00	September	1-7	14.3	-3.75
October	0-3	0.0	-3.00	October	0-2	0.0	-2.00
November	0-3	0.0	-3.00	November	2-4	50.0	+4.25
December	0-1	0.0	-1.00	December	0-3	0.0	-3.00

4-y-o+	W-R	Per cent	£1 Level Stake	Totals	W-R	Per cent	£1 Level Stake
January	4-18	22.2	+6.70	January	4-21	19.0	+3.70
February	1-12	8.3	-6.00	February	1-12	8.3	-6.00
March	1-26	3.8	-21.50	March	1-26	3.8	-21.50
April	0-13	0.0	-13.00	April	0-21	0.0	-21.00
May	0-10	0.0	-10.00	May	0-13	0.0	-13.00
June	0-12	0.0	-12.00	June	0-19	0.0	-19.00
July	0-11	0.0	-11.00	July	0-14	0.0	-14.00
August	2-17	11.8	0.00	August	4-26	15.4	+22.50
September	2-20	10.0	+19.50	September	3-27	11.1	+15.75
October	2-15	13.3	-7.50	October	2-20	10.0	-12.50
November	3-13	23.1	+4.88	November	5-20	25.0	+9.13
December	1-11	9.1	-6.00	December	1-15	6.7	-9.00

DISTANCE

2-y-o	W-R	Per cent	£1 Level Stake	3-y-o	W-R	Per cent	£1 Level Stake
5f-6f	0-2	0.0	-2.00	5f-6f	1-13	7.7	+13.00
7f-8f	0-5	0.0	-5.00	7f-8f	2-26	7.7	-16.75
9f-13f	0-1	0.0	-1.00	9f-13f	2-9	22.2	-1.25
14f+	0-0	0.0	0.00	14f+	0-0	0.0	0.00

4-y-o+	W-R	Per cent	£1 Level Stake	Totals	W-R	Per cent	£1 Level Stake
5f-6f	7-53	13.2	-6.30	5f-6f	8-68	11.8	+4.70
7f-8f	6-87	6.9	-28.13	7f-8f	8-118	6.8	-49.88
9f-13f	3-38	7.9	-21.50	9f-13f	5-48	10.4	-23.75
14f+	0-0	0.0	0.00	14f+	0-0	0.0	0.00

TYPE OF RACE

Non-Handicaps	W-R	Per cent	£1 Level Stake	Handicaps	W-R	Per cent	£1 Level Stake
2-y-o	0-6	0.0	-6.00	2-y-o	0-2	0.0	-2.00
3-y-o	0-5	0.0	-5.00	3-y-o	5-43	11.6	0.00
4-y-o+	0-11	0.0	-11.00	4-y-o+	16-167	9.6	-44.92

RACE CLASS

	W-R	Per cent	£1 Level Stake
Class 1	0-0	0.0	0.00
Class 2	2-10	20.0	+3.20
Class 3	1-3	33.3	+2.00
Class 4	1-10	10.0	-2.00
Class 5	2-41	4.9	-29.50
Class 6	14-159	8.8	-37.63
Class 7	1-11	9.1	-5.00

FIRST TIME OUT

	W-R	Per cent	£1 Level Stake
2-y-o	0-2	0.0	-2.00
3-y-o	0-8	0.0	-8.00
4-y-o+	2-18	11.1	-4.80
Totals	2-28	7.1	-14.80

JOCKEYS

	W-R	Per cent	£1 Level Stake
Philip Prince	5-43	11.6	+11.25
Gerald Mosse	3-6	50.0	+19.00
Ben Sanderson	2-6	33.3	+5.50
Joe Fanning	2-13	15.4	-7.63
Franny Norton	2-14	14.3	-3.50
Ger O'Neill	1-1	100.0	+2.25
Robert Winston	1-2	50.0	+0.20
Andrew Elliott	1-3	33.3	+23.00
Jack Osborn	1-5	20.0	+6.00
Cam Hardie	1-6	16.7	-0.50
Connor Murtagh	1-12	8.3	-6.00
Connor Beasley	1-22	4.5	-17.50

COURSE RECORD

	Total W-R	Non-Hndcps 2-y-o	Non-Hndcps 3-y-o+	Hndcps 2-y-o	Hndcps 3-y-o+	Per cent	£1 Level Stake
Newcastle (A.W)	5-43	0-1	0-3	0-0	5-39	11.6	-18.63
Wolvhptn (A.W)	4-33	0-0	0-7	0-1	4-25	12.1	-13.75
Chelmsford (A.W)	4-45	0-0	0-0	0-1	4-44	8.9	-27.80
Kempton (A.W)	3-20	0-1	0-0	0-0	3-19	15.0	-1.00
Thirsk	1-2	0-0	0-0	0-0	1-2	50.0	+24.00
Windsor	1-2	0-0	0-0	0-0	1-2	50.0	+9.00
Musselburgh	1-6	0-0	0-0	0-0	1-6	16.7	+28.00
Beverley	1-11	0-0	0-1	0-0	1-10	9.1	-7.75
Southwell (A.W)	1-15	0-0	0-3	0-0	1-12	6.7	-4.00

WINNING HORSES

Horse	Races Run	1st	2nd	3rd	£
Amazing Grazing (IRE)*	5	1	0	3	3752
Another Situation (USA)*	7	1	1	0	3398
Breathoffreshair	11	1	1	1	3105
*Exchequer (IRE)	10	3	2	0	19559
Harry George (IRE)	6	3	0	0	9315
Mr Potter	26	1	3	6	4140
Outlaw Torn (IRE)	27	3	2	0	9509
Tellovoi (IRE)	21	2	2	4	3105
Udontdodou	9	2	1	0	46688
Whatwouldyouknow (IRE)	11	4	2	0	12809
Total winning prize-money					**£115380**
Favourites	**5-20**		**25.0%**		**-3.18**

WILLIAM HAGGAS

NEWMARKET, SUFFOLK

	No. of Hrs	Races Run	1st	2nd	3rd	Unpl	Per cent	£1 Level Stake
2-y-o	*63*	*178*	*36*	*28*	*23*	*90*	*20.2*	*-25.41*
3-y-o	*82*	*326*	*79*	*59*	*29*	*159*	*24.2*	*-58.47*
4-y-o+	*30*	*153*	*30*	*18*	*26*	*78*	*19.6*	*-23.34*
Totals	**175**	**657**	**145**	**105**	**78**	**327**	**22.1**	**-107.22**
2017	*160*	*590*	*158*	*78*	*76*	*276*	*26.8*	*+15.10*
2016	*156*	*596*	*137*	*107*	*89*	*263*	*23.0*	*-78.79*

BY MONTH

2-y-o	W-R	Per cent	£1 Level Stake
January	0-0	0.0	0.00
February	0-0	0.0	0.00
March	0-0	0.0	0.00
April	1-3	33.3	+0.25
May	2-9	22.2	-5.23
June	2-11	18.2	-5.15
July	2-16	12.5	-9.13
August	3-24	12.5	-13.84
September	9-45	20.0	+22.95
October	10-44	22.7	-11.42
November	5-20	25.0	-6.34
December	2-6	33.3	+2.50

3-y-o	W-R	Per cent	£1 Level Stake
January	2-13	15.4	-8.00
February	1-6	16.7	-2.50
March	2-6	33.3	-2.33
April	6-23	26.1	-8.68
May	14-46	30.4	+8.88
June	6-56	10.7	-40.00
July	18-51	35.3	+11.62
August	11-47	23.4	-10.96
September	10-36	27.8	+5.25
October	6-29	20.7	-9.75
November	3-10	30.0	+1.00
December	0-3	0.0	-3.00

4-y-o+	W-R	Per cent	£1 Level Stake
January	1-3	33.3	-1.60
February	0-1	0.0	-1.00
March	5-8	62.5	+9.76
April	1-3	33.3	-0.50
May	6-29	20.7	+0.38
June	5-25	20.0	-4.25
July	3-20	15.0	-4.00
August	4-25	16.0	-5.00
September	2-19	10.5	-10.50
October	0-12	0.0	-12.00
November	1-6	16.7	-3.13
December	2-2	100.0	+8.50

Totals	W-R	Per cent	£1 Level Stake
January	3-16	18.8	-9.60
February	1-7	14.3	-3.50
March	7-14	50.0	+7.43
April	8-29	27.6	-8.93
May	22-84	26.2	+4.03
June	13-92	14.1	-49.40
July	23-87	26.4	-1.51
August	18-96	18.8	-29.80
September	21-100	21.0	+17.70
October	16-85	18.8	-33.17
November	9-36	25.0	-2.13
December	4-11	36.4	+5.50

DISTANCE

2-y-o	W-R	Per cent	£1 Level Stake
5f-6f	18-85	21.2	-19.97
7f-8f	17-92	18.5	-6.02
9f-13f	1-1	100.0	+0.57
14f+	0-0	0.0	0.00

3-y-o	W-R	Per cent	£1 Level Stake
5f-6f	5-32	15.6	-20.70
7f-8f	41-194	21.1	-51.18
9f-13f	32-96	33.3	+14.41
14f+	1-4	25.0	-1.00

4-y-o+	W-R	Per cent	£1 Level Stake
5f-6f	4-26	15.4	-9.88
7f-8f	17-65	26.2	+13.60
9f-13f	7-46	15.2	-17.60
14f+	2-16	12.5	-9.47

Totals	W-R	Per cent	£1 Level Stake
5f-6f	27-143	18.9	-50.55
7f-8f	75-351	21.4	-43.60
9f-13f	40-143	28.0	-2.62
14f+	3-20	15.0	-10.47

TYPE OF RACE

Non-Handicaps	W-R	Per cent	£1 Level Stake
2-y-o	32-149	21.5	-15.21
3-y-o	52-192	27.1	-25.81
4-y-o+	10-63	15.9	-31.59

Handicaps	W-R	Per cent	£1 Level Stake
2-y-o	4-29	13.8	-10.20
3-y-o	27-134	20.1	-32.67
4-y-o+	20-90	22.2	+8.25

RACE CLASS

	W-R	Per cent	£1 Level Stake
Class 1	18-94	19.1	-26.13
Class 2	21-108	19.4	-9.82
Class 3	17-63	27.0	+5.45
Class 4	38-180	21.1	-25.96
Class 5	48-190	25.3	-41.26
Class 6	3-22	13.6	-7.50
Class 7	0-0	0.0	0.00

FIRST TIME OUT

	W-R	Per cent	£1 Level Stake
2-y-o	6-63	9.5	-11.54
3-y-o	14-82	17.1	-31.16
4-y-o+	9-30	30.0	+2.54
Totals	29-175	16.6	-40.16

JOCKEYS

	W-R	Per cent	£1 Level Stake
James Doyle	52-182	28.6	+7.94
Jim Crowley	13-49	26.5	-0.54
Daniel Tudhope	10-52	19.2	-20.70
Tom Marquand	9-42	21.4	-7.02
Oisin Murphy	7-19	36.8	+8.27
Ryan Moore	6-20	30.0	-2.49
Liam Jones	6-34	17.6	-17.76
Tom Queally	4-6	66.7	+6.25
Ben Curtis	4-11	36.4	+3.17
Joe Fanning	4-13	30.8	+2.00
Martin Harley	4-18	22.2	+35.00
Paul Hanagan	3-11	27.3	-5.76
Dane O'Neill	3-24	12.5	-13.50
Georgia Cox	3-42	7.1	-25.13
Charles Bishop	2-8	25.0	-2.13
Harry Bentley	2-10	20.0	-3.42
Fran Berry	2-11	18.2	-4.00
Andrea Atzeni	2-11	18.2	-5.93
Richard Kingscote	2-12	16.7	-6.90
David Allan	1-2	50.0	+2.50
Franny Norton	1-2	50.0	+2.50
Josephine Gordon	1-2	50.0	+0.75
Adam Kirby	1-4	25.0	+2.50
P J McDonald	1-6	16.7	-4.09
Silvestre De Sousa	1-6	16.7	-2.25
William Buick	1-13	7.7	-9.50

COURSE RECORD

	Total W-R	Non-Hndcps 2-y-o	Non-Hndcps 3-y-o+	Hndcps 2-y-o	Hndcps 3-y-o+	Per cent	£1 Level Stake
Newbury	16-49	3-19	8-18	1-1	4-11	32.7	+20.12
Wolvhptn (A.W)	15-37	5-8	8-19	0-1	2-9	40.5	+9.97
Chelmsford (A.W)	12-61	1-8	5-24	0-3	6-26	19.7	-25.06
Kempton (A.W)	9-48	2-13	0-11	2-5	5-19	18.8	-14.89

Newcastle (A.W)	7-18	0-1	4-10	1-2	2-5	38.9	+1.43
Goodwood	7-37	1-6	2-16	0-2	4-13	18.9	+0.57
Haydock	6-28	0-3	3-14	0-1	3-10	21.4	-7.63
Lingfield (A.W)	6-28	1-7	4-17	0-0	1-4	21.4	-5.90
Yarmouth	6-33	4-16	1-3	0-1	1-13	18.2	-12.13
Nottingham	5-15	2-5	3-8	0-1	0-1	33.3	+0.21
Ripon	4-9	0-3	3-5	0-0	1-1	44.4	+0.16
Lingfield	4-12	1-2	2-8	0-0	1-2	33.3	-0.84
Redcar	4-13	1-5	1-3	0-1	2-4	30.8	+0.85
Sandown	4-15	1-3	2-6	0-0	1-6	26.7	+1.75
Windsor	4-17	1-6	2-6	0-1	1-4	23.5	-8.42
Ascot	4-27	0-2	1-9	0-0	3-16	14.8	-10.75
Newmarket	4-39	2-13	1-13	0-2	1-11	10.3	+9.67
Chester	3-10	1-1	2-4	0-1	0-4	30.0	+1.21
Thirsk	3-15	1-4	2-7	0-0	0-4	20.0	-7.83
Newmkt (Jly)	3-24	0-4	1-9	0-1	2-10	12.5	-10.00
York	3-33	0-3	2-10	0-1	1-19	9.1	-20.75
Catterick	2-3	1-1	1-1	0-0	0-1	66.7	+0.36
Chepstow	2-6	0-0	2-3	0-0	0-3	33.3	+1.25
Salisbury	2-6	1-2	0-1	0-1	1-2	33.3	+0.96
Leicester	2-14	1-4	0-6	0-1	1-3	14.3	-7.90
Ayr	1-2	1-1	0-1	0-0	0-0	50.0	+3.50
Hamilton	1-3	0-0	0-2	0-0	1-1	33.3	+0.50
Southwell (A.W)	1-3	0-0	1-2	0-0	0-1	33.3	+1.50
Epsom	1-4	1-1	0-3	0-0	0-0	25.0	-1.63
Wetherby	1-4	0-0	0-1	0-0	1-3	25.0	+3.00
Musselburgh	1-5	0-0	0-1	0-0	1-4	20.0	-2.50
Pontefract	1-9	0-0	1-5	0-1	0-3	11.1	-4.00
Doncaster	1-18	0-6	0-3	0-2	1-7	5.6	-12.00

WINNING HORSES

Horse	Races Run	1st	2nd	3rd	£
Across Dubai	5	1	0	1	15563
Addeybb (IRE)	5	2	0	1	118960
Al Muffrih (IRE)	2	1	0	0	6728
Alexana	3	2	1	0	13456
Alexanderthegreat (FR)*	7	2	1	0	6857
Alfarris (FR)	5	2	2	0	59626
Aplomb (IRE)	2	1	0	0	4787
Astronaut	5	1	0	1	4528
Awe	3	1	1	0	5175
Awesometank	4	2	1	0	42091
Beauty Filly	7	1	3	1	12450
Beshaayir	7	3	0	0	39374
*Big Kitten (USA)	2	1	0	0	6081
Boerhan	3	1	0	0	0
Canford Heights (IRE)	5	2	0	0	22427
Carrie's Vision	7	1	1	0	3752
Cavatina	10	1	1	1	7375
Completion (IRE)	9	2	3	2	12097
Cosmic Love	5	1	1	1	3752
Cristal Spirit	5	1	1	1	3105
Croque Monsieur	7	1	1	1	5434
Dal Harraild	4	1	1	0	12938
Dal Horrisgle	2	1	0	0	3752
Dalaalaat (IRE)	2	1	0	0	6469
Deputise	8	4	1	1	24247
Diagnostic	3	1	0	2	93375
Dramatic Queen (USA)	5	2	0	1	38247
Dynamic	5	1	1	0	9338
Extra Large	6	1	0	0	3752
Eyelool (IRE)	5	2	2	0	10997
Fanaar (IRE)	6	1	2	0	5434
Feline Groovy (USA)	5	1	1	0	5531
Field Gun (USA)	5	1	3	0	4787
First Thought	8	1	0	1	3105
Flarepath	2	1	0	0	3752
Frankellina	1	1	0	0	4787
Give And Take	3	1	1	0	56710
Hakeem	6	2	1	2	13456
Headway	3	1	0	0	25520
Heart Of Grace (JPN)	4	2	0	0	8927
Hidden Message (USA)	2	1	0	0	4787
Humbolt Current	6	3	0	0	15332
Ice Gala	5	1	1	2	6728
Improve (IRE)	4	1	1	0	4852
Island Of Life (USA)	10	3	2	3	27562
Jahaafel (FR)	4	1	0	0	3752
Jahbath	3	2	1	0	7763
Juthoor (IRE)	5	1	0	1	5822
King Of Hearts (IRE)	4	3	1	0	90377
Klassique	5	3	1	0	41346
Life On Earth (USA)	7	2	1	0	10305
Listen To The Wind (IRE)	2	1	1	0	3752
Luxor	4	2	0	1	10221
Magical Sight	3	1	1	0	6469
Magnetic Charm	4	1	0	1	3752
Mankib	6	3	0	0	43624
Martineo*	4	1	0	2	3752
Mashaheer	3	1	1	0	3881
Mosalim (IRE)	4	1	1	0	5175
Move Swiftly	6	2	3	1	19505
Muneyra	4	1	2	0	3752
Muthmir (IRE)	7	1	1	2	20983
Nicklaus	8	3	0	1	19650
Nomoathaj (IRE)	3	1	0	0	3881
Original Choice (IRE)	9	2	0	3	37704
*Pablo Escobarr (IRE)	2	1	1	0	11972
Politicise (IRE)	3	1	1	0	5531
Prabeni*	6	1	1	2	3881
Pretty Baby (IRE)	4	3	1	0	72580
Queen Of Bermuda (IRE)	7	3	1	0	48118
Rainbow Heart (IRE)	2	1	0	1	3881
Regina Nostra	4	1	0	2	3752
Restive Spirit	7	2	1	0	9452
Reverend Jacobs*	5	2	0	0	18500
Rhigolter Rose (IRE)	6	1	1	1	3752
Saint Diana (JPN)	5	1	4	0	9704
Sea Of Class (IRE)	4	3	1	0	266537
Second Thought (IRE)	2	1	1	0	28355
Seniority	6	3	0	0	138658
Senza Limiti (IRE)	1	1	0	0	5111
Sharamm (IRE)	3	1	2	0	3881
Skardu	1	1	0	0	6469
Snow Wind (IRE)	5	2	0	0	9733
Squats (IRE)	13	1	0	0	12450
Sweet Nature (IRE)	5	1	1	0	3752
Swiss Air	4	1	1	0	3752

Talaaqy (IRE)	4	1	0	1	5111
Tanseeq	2	1	0	0	3752
The Grand Visir*	3	1	0	0	16173
The Night Watch	2	1	0	0	4787
Three Weeks (USA)*	5	1	0	0	5531
True Hero	3	1	1	0	5563
Ummalnar	2	2	0	0	12226
Urban Fox	3	1	1	0	28013
Victory Bond	5	2	1	0	136472
Young Rascal (FR)	5	4	0	0	100440
Total winning prize-money					**£2121358**
Favourites	**73-192**		**38.0%**		**-6.26**

ALEX HALES

EDGCOTE, NORTHAMPTONSHIRE

	No. of Hrs	Races Run	1st	2nd	3rd	Unpl	Per cent	£1 Level Stake
2-y-o	*1*	*4*	*0*	*0*	*0*	*4*	*0.0*	*-4.00*
3-y-o	*0*	*0*	*0*	*0*	*0*	*0*	*0.0*	*0.00*
4-y-o+	*10*	*41*	*3*	*3*	*6*	*29*	*7.3*	*-17.09*
Totals	**11**	**45**	**3**	**3**	**6**	**33**	**6.7**	**-21.09**
2017	*8*	*47*	*7*	*8*	*6*	*26*	*14.9*	*+85.00*
2016	*6*	*13*	*0*	*2*	*2*	*9*	*0.0*	*-13.00*

JOCKEYS

	W-R	Per cent	£1 Level Stake
Martin Harley	3-7	42.9	+16.91

COURSE RECORD

	Total W-R	Non-Hndcps 2-y-o	Non-Hndcps 3-y-o+	Hndcps 2-y-o	Hndcps 3-y-o+	Per cent	£1 Level Stake
Doncaster	1-1	0-0	0-0	0-0	1-1	100.0	+18.00
Leicester	1-3	0-1	0-0	0-0	1-2	33.3	-1.09
Goodwood	1-4	0-0	0-0	0-0	1-4	25.0	-1.00

WINNING HORSES

Horse	Races Run	1st	2nd	3rd	£
Methag (FR)	7	1	1	1	3752
Panko (IRE)	5	2	0	1	9962
Total winning prize-money					**£13714**
Favourites	**3-10**		**30.0%**		**-3.93**

MIKE HAMMOND

KYRE, WORCS

	No. of Hrs	Races Run	1st	2nd	3rd	Unpl	Per cent	£1 Level Stake
2-y-o	*0*	*0*	*0*	*0*	*0*	*0*	*0.0*	*0.00*
3-y-o	*0*	*0*	*0*	*0*	*0*	*0*	*0.0*	*0.00*
4-y-o+	*9*	*13*	*1*	*1*	*2*	*9*	*7.7*	*+8.00*
Totals	**9**	**13**	**1**	**1**	**2**	**9**	**7.7**	**+8.00**
2017	*1*	*1*	*0*	*0*	*0*	*1*	*0.0*	*-1.00*
2016	*1*	*3*	*0*	*0*	*0*	*3*	*0.0*	*-3.00*

JOCKEYS

	W-R	Per cent	£1 Level Stake
Rob Hornby	1-6	16.7	+15.00

COURSE RECORD

	Total W-R	Non-Hndcps 2-y-o	Non-Hndcps 3-y-o+	Hndcps 2-y-o	Hndcps 3-y-o+	Per cent	£1 Level Stake
Wolvhptn (A.W)	1-10	0-0	0-1	0-0	1-9	10.0	+11.00

WINNING HORSES

Horse	Races Run	1st	2nd	3rd	£
Sevilla	2	1	1	0	3105
Total winning prize-money					**£3105**
Favourites	**0-0**		**0.0%**		**0.00**

MICKY HAMMOND

MIDDLEHAM, N YORKS

	No. of Hrs	Races Run	1st	2nd	3rd	Unpl	Per cent	£1 Level Stake
2-y-o	*5*	*17*	*0*	*1*	*0*	*16*	*0.0*	*-17.00*
3-y-o	*5*	*26*	*1*	*2*	*0*	*23*	*3.8*	*-17.00*
4-y-o+	*22*	*78*	*8*	*11*	*5*	*54*	*10.3*	*+19.75*
Totals	**32**	**121**	**9**	**14**	**5**	**93**	**7.4**	**-14.25**
2017	*37*	*151*	*9*	*12*	*11*	*119*	*6.0*	*-14.00*
2016	*47*	*249*	*11*	*20*	*25*	*193*	*4.4*	*-71.25*

JOCKEYS

	W-R	Per cent	£1 Level Stake
Franny Norton	3-9	33.3	+1.25
P J McDonald	2-19	10.5	-5.50
Dougie Costello	1-4	25.0	+63.00
Miss Becky Smith	1-8	12.5	-4.75
Rob J Fitzpatrick	1-8	12.5	-4.25
Andrew Mullen	1-10	10.0	-1.00

COURSE RECORD

	Total W-R	Non-Hndcps 2-y-o	Non-Hndcps 3-y-o+	Hndcps 2-y-o	Hndcps 3-y-o+	Per cent	£1 Level Stake
Pontefract	5-31	0-4	0-0	0-0	5-27	16.1	-8.25
Redcar	2-13	0-2	0-3	0-2	2-6	15.4	-0.50
Carlisle	1-6	0-0	0-0	0-0	1-6	16.7	-1.50
York	1-6	0-0	0-0	0-1	1-5	16.7	+61.00

WINNING HORSES

Horse	Races Run	1st	2nd	3rd	£
Almunther (IRE)	7	1	1	0	3881
Becky The Thatcher	6	2	3	0	10674
Indian Vision (IRE)	4	2	1	0	6987
Jo's Girl (IRE)	5	1	0	0	3881
Le Maitre Chat (USA)	3	1	0	0	9962
Quoteline Direct	10	2	2	1	7625
Total winning prize-money					**£43010**
Favourites	**9-33**		**27.3%**		**-10.87**

RICHARD HANNON

EAST EVERLEIGH, WILTS

	No. of Hrs	Races Run	1st	2nd	3rd	Unpl	Per cent	£1 Level Stake
2-y-o	*150*	*647*	*81*	*98*	*69*	*399*	*12.5*	*-206.96*
3-y-o	*102*	*538*	*63*	*66*	*67*	*340*	*11.7*	*-121.32*
4-y-o+	*37*	*216*	*28*	*26*	*24*	*138*	*13.0*	*-16.98*
Totals	**289**	**1401**	**172**	**190**	**160**	**877**	**12.3**	**-345.26**
2017	*268*	*1354*	*194*	*176*	*164*	*818*	*14.3*	*-78.24*
2016	*297*	*1357*	*172*	*183*	*165*	*834*	*12.7*	*-211.92*

BY MONTH

2-y-o	W-R	Per cent	£1 Level Stake	**3-y-o**	W-R	Per cent	£1 Level Stake
January	0-0	0.0	0.00	January	1-18	5.6	-14.50
February	0-0	0.0	0.00	February	2-11	18.2	-6.00
March	0-0	0.0	0.00	March	2-12	16.7	-6.50
April	2-8	25.0	-2.13	April	8-53	15.1	+38.50
May	7-42	16.7	-8.80	May	13-107	12.1	+14.31
June	9-72	12.5	-12.84	June	8-96	8.3	-57.38
July	14-88	15.9	-13.69	July	13-66	19.7	+8.92
August	19-126	15.1	-35.69	August	14-89	15.7	-18.53
September	14-129	10.9	-59.28	September	2-38	5.3	-32.15
October	9-112	8.0	-63.77	October	0-28	0.0	-28.00
November	5-37	13.5	-5.75	November	0-11	0.0	-11.00
December	2-33	6.1	-5.00	December	0-9	0.0	-9.00

4-y-o+	W-R	Per cent	£1 Level Stake	**Totals**	W-R	Per cent	£1 Level Stake
January	0-10	0.0	-10.00	January	1-28	3.6	-24.50
February	1-5	20.0	-1.25	February	3-16	18.8	-7.25
March	4-11	36.4	+8.33	March	6-23	26.1	+1.83
April	4-23	17.4	+11.50	April	14-84	16.7	+47.87
May	5-38	13.2	-13.17	May	25-187	13.4	-7.66
June	2-34	5.9	-4.00	June	19-202	9.4	-74.22
July	2-22	9.1	-12.50	July	29-176	16.5	-17.27
August	3-27	11.1	+1.00	August	36-242	14.9	-53.22
September	4-22	18.2	+9.60	September	20-189	10.6	-81.83
October	3-16	18.8	+1.50	October	12-156	7.7	-90.27
November	0-5	0.0	-5.00	November	5-53	9.4	-16.00
December	0-3	0.0	-3.00	December	2-45	4.4	-12.00

DISTANCE

2-y-o	W-R	Per cent	£1 Level Stake	**3-y-o**	W-R	Per cent	£1 Level Stake
5f-6f	49-337	14.5	-75.80	5f-6f	16-114	14.0	-38.57
7f-8f	31-303	10.2	-126.41	7f-8f	38-306	12.4	-23.28
9f-13f	1-7	14.3	-4.75	9f-13f	9-114	7.9	-55.48
14f+	0-0	0.0	0.00	14f+	0-4	0.0	-4.00

4-y-o+	W-R	Per cent	£1 Level Stake	**Totals**	W-R	Per cent	£1 Level Stake
5f-6f	4-29	13.8	-8.67	5f-6f	69-480	14.4	-123.04
7f-8f	15-121	12.4	+1.06	7f-8f	84-730	11.5	-148.63
9f-13f	9-66	13.6	-9.38	9f-13f	19-187	10.2	-69.61
14f+	0-0	0.0	0.00	14f+	0-4	0.0	-4.00

TYPE OF RACE

Non-Handicaps	W-R	Per cent	£1 Level Stake	**Handicaps**	W-R	Per cent	£1 Level Stake
2-y-o	64-493	13.0	-154.97	2-y-o	17-154	11.0	-51.99
3-y-o	22-160	13.8	+24.09	3-y-o	41-378	10.8	-145.42
4-y-o+	9-59	15.3	-3.56	4-y-o+	19-157	12.1	-13.42

RACE CLASS

	W-R	Per cent	£1 Level Stake
Class 1	14-126	11.1	+44.83
Class 2	17-173	9.8	-65.84
Class 3	19-149	12.8	-46.10
Class 4	50-387	12.9	-89.29
Class 5	57-468	12.2	-162.35
Class 6	15-98	15.3	-26.52
Class 7	0-0	0.0	0.00

FIRST TIME OUT

	W-R	Per cent	£1 Level Stake
2-y-o	17-150	11.3	-25.38
3-y-o	10-102	9.8	-23.67
4-y-o+	4-37	10.8	-1.50
Totals	31-289	10.7	-50.55

JOCKEYS

	W-R	Per cent	£1 Level Stake
Tom Marquand	50-399	12.5	-108.38
Rossa Ryan	17-159	10.7	-79.57
Sean Levey	17-181	9.4	+6.49
Silvestre De Sousa	12-31	38.7	+17.93
Jim Crowley	8-46	17.4	-7.61
Thore Hammer Hansen	7-40	17.5	+6.85
Pat Dobbs	6-44	13.6	+1.88
Ryan Moore	6-70	8.6	-43.93
Hollie Doyle	6-86	7.0	-31.00
Oisin Murphy	5-19	26.3	+2.75
Harry Bentley	5-19	26.3	+22.25
Andrea Atzeni	4-17	23.5	-6.09
Seamus Cronin	4-36	11.1	-26.01
Clifford Lee	3-4	75.0	+15.00
Hayley Turner	3-8	37.5	+10.00
James Doyle	3-18	16.7	-7.25
P J McDonald	2-4	50.0	+7.75
Tom Queally	2-9	22.2	+18.00
Phillip Makin	2-9	22.2	+14.75
Frankie Dettori	2-9	22.2	-2.75
Gary Mahon	2-40	5.0	-32.67
Dane O'Neill	2-46	4.3	-36.00
Trevor Whelan	1-1	100.0	+8.00
Edward Greatrex	1-1	100.0	+3.50
Mr Simon Walker	1-2	50.0	+0.10
Fran Berry	1-6	16.7	-2.25

COURSE RECORD

	Total W-R	Non-Hndcps 2-y-o	Non-Hndcps 3-y-o+	Hndcps 2-y-o	Hndcps 3-y-o+	Per cent	£1 Level Stake
Kempton (A.W)	16-162	6-41	3-27	0-20	7-74	9.9	-61.99
Windsor	15-81	9-32	0-15	1-4	5-30	18.5	-12.14
Wolvhptn (A.W)	13-76	5-31	3-8	2-13	3-24	17.1	+4.99
Lingfield (A.W)	13-78	3-17	2-15	1-7	7-39	16.7	-21.59
Brighton	12-36	5-15	0-2	1-1	6-18	33.3	+30.29

Newbury	11-110	5-51	2-20	1-8	3-31	10.0	-30.55
Newmkt (Jly)	10-77	1-25	1-7	1-8	7-37	13.0	-24.62
Sandown	9-56	4-19	0-7	1-2	4-28	16.1	+6.13
Salisbury	9-79	4-33	2-10	0-8	3-28	11.4	-38.92
Lingfield	6-32	2-8	3-11	0-1	1-12	18.8	-12.38
Leicester	6-47	5-20	0-4	1-7	0-16	12.8	-12.27
Doncaster	6-66	1-28	1-14	2-8	2-16	9.1	-22.13
Newmarket	6-69	0-27	3-17	1-6	2-19	8.7	+66.75
Chelmsford (A.W)	5-67	1-22	1-6	1-12	2-27	7.5	-42.06
Chester	4-13	2-5	1-4	0-2	1-2	30.8	+8.75
Nottingham	4-41	1-11	1-4	0-11	2-15	9.8	-22.38
Goodwood	4-71	2-25	1-11	0-9	1-26	5.6	-37.00
York	3-30	2-12	0-3	1-4	0-11	10.0	-11.50
Haydock	3-38	0-12	1-4	0-2	2-20	7.9	-26.92
Redcar	2-6	0-3	2-2	0-1	0-0	33.3	+4.00
Ripon	2-10	0-3	1-2	1-1	0-4	20.0	-5.89
Chepstow	2-17	1-5	1-2	0-0	0-10	11.8	-9.00
Ffos Las	2-18	1-9	0-1	0-6	1-2	11.1	-9.50
Bath	2-24	1-9	0-1	1-4	0-10	8.3	-12.25
Hamilton	1-1	0-0	1-1	0-0	0-0	100.0	+1.75
Musselburgh	1-2	0-1	1-1	0-0	0-0	50.0	+19.00
Thirsk	1-3	1-2	0-0	0-0	0-1	33.3	-1.09
Wetherby	1-4	0-0	0-0	0-0	1-4	25.0	-0.50
Beverley	1-5	1-3	0-0	0-0	0-2	20.0	+2.00
Yarmouth	1-10	0-2	0-1	1-4	0-3	10.0	-5.50
Ascot	1-52	1-16	0-14	0-1	0-21	1.9	-48.75

WINNING HORSES

Horse	Races Run	1st	2nd	3rd	£
Aim Power (IRE)	6	1	0	1	3752
Ajrar	7	1	2	0	3752
Al Barg (IRE)	4	1	0	2	5531
Anna Nerium	6	2	1	0	62381
Aspire Tower (IRE)	6	1	2	2	5175
Ateem (FR)	8	1	2	0	5531
Balata Bay	7	1	1	0	4787
Balletomane	2	1	1	0	3752
Bathsheba Bay (IRE)	7	1	0	2	7246
Bezos (IRE)*	4	1	0	1	3105
Big Baby Bull (IRE)	6	2	1	0	9977
Billesdon Brook	5	1	0	0	310487
Blanchefleur (IRE)	7	1	1	1	4528
Boitron (FR)	3	3	0	0	23000
Bombshell Bay	11	2	1	4	6210
Brexitmeansbrexit	13	1	4	2	3752
Brian Epstein (IRE)	3	1	0	0	5822
Bullingdon	7	1	1	1	7310
Buridan (FR)	5	2	1	0	15849
Canton Queen (IRE)	4	1	0	0	6469
Chonburi	9	1	0	0	3752
Come On Leicester (IRE)	8	2	1	3	12550
Contrast (IRE)*	6	1	0	1	7246
Critical Data (IRE)	10	2	1	4	8216
Department Of War (IRE)	3	1	0	1	4528
Dirty Rascal (IRE)	8	2	5	0	11012
Doctor Jazz (IRE)	6	1	1	0	3105
Dotted Swiss (IRE)*	10	2	1	2	10221
Dragon Moon (USA)	7	2	0	1	7504
Drakefell (IRE)	5	1	0	1	3752
Elsaabiqaat	6	1	2	0	4528
Elysium Dream	10	1	2	0	6080
Embour (IRE)	6	3	0	0	24712
Enchanted Linda	4	2	0	0	7892
Equal Sum	2	1	1	0	4787
Euginio (IRE)	9	2	2	1	45854
Fast And Hot (IRE)	4	1	0	0	3817
Floating Artist	3	1	1	0	6728
Flying Dragon (FR)	3	1	0	1	4528
Flying North	10	3	0	0	20798
Fox Champion (IRE)	2	1	1	0	3881
Fox Power (IRE)	6	1	1	3	3752
Ginger Fox	5	1	2	1	3752
Ginger Nut (IRE)	8	3	2	1	170640
Good Luck Fox (IRE)	5	2	0	0	8280
He'Zanarab (IRE)	4	2	0	1	13456
Himself	6	2	0	1	10997
Hua Hin (IRE)	4	1	0	0	4205
In The Cove (IRE)	9	1	0	1	3105
Its The Only Way (IRE)	9	3	1	0	10739
Jaayiz (IRE)	7	1	0	1	4140
K Club (IRE)	10	2	1	2	9574
Kuwait Currency (USA)	5	2	0	0	22183
Leoube (IRE)	8	1	2	0	3752
Leroy Leroy	5	1	3	0	11828
Letsbe Avenue (IRE)	5	2	0	0	9509
London Rock (IRE)	11	1	1	0	3493
Maaward (IRE)	3	2	0	0	10350
Magical Wish (IRE)	5	1	3	0	3752
Masaru	2	1	0	0	3752
Maypole	10	3	4	0	15105
Medahim (IRE)	8	1	0	0	15753
Mordred (IRE)	7	1	2	1	5852
Motafaawit (IRE)	3	1	1	1	6081
Motakhayyel	1	1	0	0	3752
Mouille Point	4	1	0	0	3752
Moyassar	6	1	4	1	7375
Mushtaq (IRE)	9	2	1	2	12000
Naughty Rascal (IRE)	4	2	1	0	12809
Nayel (IRE)	5	2	0	0	16528
Neverland Rock	5	1	0	1	5175
No More Thrills	6	2	1	0	8927
Oh This Is Us (IRE)	9	2	3	1	50129
Peak Princess (IRE)	8	1	0	1	6469
Penarth Pier (IRE)	5	1	0	0	3752
Pepita (IRE)	9	2	1	1	29412
Pesto	3	1	0	0	6469
Popsicle (IRE)	11	1	2	0	3105
Princely*	3	1	0	1	4787
Production	4	1	0	1	12450
Promising (IRE)	7	1	2	0	3752
Qaysar (FR)	4	2	0	0	18919
Raymond Tusk (IRE)	6	2	2	0	29916
Red Starlight	8	3	1	3	34561
Repton (IRE)	9	1	1	0	6469
Riviera Nights	4	2	0	2	8798

Horse	Races Run	1st	2nd	3rd	£
Rogue	8	2	2	0	19282
Rollicking (IRE)	9	1	1	4	3752
Rum Runner	9	2	0	0	19664
See The Sea (IRE)	4	1	0	0	4399
Sergio Leone (IRE)	9	1	2	0	3619
Shoyd	6	1	0	0	3105
Sotomayor	14	1	3	1	4787
St Ouen (IRE)	9	1	0	0	3752
Star Of Southwold (FR)*	5	1	0	0	6469
Star Terms	5	2	2	0	17725
Straight Ash (IRE)*	7	1	1	0	3105
Sweet Pearl	4	1	1	0	3881
Tabarrak (IRE)	7	3	0	1	59104
The Paddocks (IRE)	6	1	1	0	6469
Tigre Du Terre (FR)	4	2	1	1	50721
Tomily (IRE)	14	2	0	3	27534
Topical	4	1	0	2	5175
Typhoon Ten (IRE)	3	1	0	0	5822
Urban Icon	2	2	0	0	8863
Ventura Magic*	5	1	0	0	3105
Vitamin (IRE)	5	1	0	0	9704
Wahash (IRE)	7	1	1	0	7246
Walkinthesand (IRE)	2	1	1	0	8715
War Glory (IRE)	11	1	2	3	43575
Watan	4	2	1	0	22222
Water Diviner (IRE)	10	2	4	1	8216
Wedding Date	8	2	2	1	15709
Well Done Fox	9	3	3	0	61821
Wicked Sea (IRE)	12	1	1	1	3493
Yafta	6	2	3	0	65151
Zalshah	15	1	1	2	5757
Total winning prize-money					**£1859205**
Favourites	**68-171**		**39.8%**		**6.07**

GEOFFREY HARKER

THIRKLEBY, N YORKS

	No. of Hrs	Races Run	1st	2nd	3rd	Unpl	Per cent	£1 Level Stake
2-y-o	*0*	*0*	*0*	*0*	*0*	*0*	*0.0*	*0.00*
3-y-o	*2*	*7*	*0*	*0*	*1*	*6*	*0.0*	*-7.00*
4-y-o+	*10*	*63*	*7*	*8*	*5*	*43*	*11.1*	*+19.00*
Totals	**12**	**70**	**7**	**8**	**6**	**49**	**10.0**	**+12.00**
2017	*10*	*69*	*2*	*9*	*5*	*53*	*2.9*	*-29.50*
2016	*8*	*54*	*6*	*7*	*2*	*39*	*11.1*	*-0.50*

JOCKEYS

	W-R	Per cent	£1 Level Stake
Sam James	4-29	13.8	+14.50
Ben Sanderson	1-2	50.0	+5.50
Kevin Stott	1-6	16.7	+15.00
David Allan	1-11	9.1	-1.00

COURSE RECORD

	Total W-R	Non-Hndcps 2-y-o	Non-Hndcps 3-y-o+	Hndcps 2-y-o	Hndcps 3-y-o+	Per cent	£1 Level Stake
Redcar	2-11	0-0	2-4	0-0	0-7	18.2	+20.00
Catterick	2-13	0-0	0-2	0-0	2-11	15.4	+2.50
Newmkt (Jly)	1-3	0-0	0-0	0-0	1-3	33.3	+4.00
Carlisle	1-4	0-0	0-0	0-0	1-4	25.0	+3.50
Nottingham	1-6	0-0	0-0	0-0	1-6	16.7	+15.00

WINNING HORSES

Horse	Races Run	1st	2nd	3rd	£
Extrasolar	16	3	1	0	12809
Mambila (FR)	1	1	0	0	4528
Scottish Summit (IRE)	8	2	3	0	6469
Shamaheart (IRE)	9	1	1	1	4399
Total winning prize-money					**£28205**
Favourites	**0-5**		**0.0%**		**-5.00**

GRACE HARRIS

SHIRENEWTON, MONMOUTHSHIRE

	No. of Hrs	Races Run	1st	2nd	3rd	Unpl	Per cent	£1 Level Stake
2-y-o	*2*	*3*	*0*	*0*	*0*	*3*	*0.0*	*-3.00*
3-y-o	*4*	*22*	*1*	*3*	*3*	*13*	*4.5*	*-17.00*
4-y-o+	*8*	*56*	*4*	*2*	*3*	*47*	*7.1*	*+30.50*
Totals	**14**	**81**	**5**	**5**	**6**	**63**	**6.2**	**+10.50**
2017	*10*	*85*	*6*	*3*	*5*	*71*	*7.1*	*-13.00*
2016	*14*	*75*	*1*	*4*	*1*	*69*	*1.3*	*-71.00*

JOCKEYS

	W-R	Per cent	£1 Level Stake
Cameron Noble	2-18	11.1	+54.00
Oisin Murphy	1-1	100.0	+3.00
Theodore Ladd	1-2	50.0	+1.50
Hollie Doyle	1-5	20.0	+7.00

COURSE RECORD

	Total W-R	Non-Hndcps 2-y-o	Non-Hndcps 3-y-o+	Hndcps 2-y-o	Hndcps 3-y-o+	Per cent	£1 Level Stake
Chepstow	3-21	0-0	0-1	0-0	3-20	14.3	+63.00
Salisbury	1-8	0-2	0-1	0-0	1-5	12.5	-4.50
Bath	1-10	0-1	0-0	0-0	1-9	10.0	-6.00

WINNING HORSES

Horse	Races Run	1st	2nd	3rd	£
*Bungee Jump (IRE)	11	1	3	2	5531
Living Leader	11	1	2	0	3752
Mooroverthebridge	9	2	0	0	6598
Tally's Son	8	1	0	0	3752
Total winning prize-money					**£19633**
Favourites	**1-2**		**50.0%**		**2.00**

SHAUN HARRIS

CARBURTON, NOTTS

	No. of Hrs	Races Run	1st	2nd	3rd	Unpl	Per cent	£1 Level Stake
2-y-o	*1*	*3*	*0*	*0*	*0*	*3*	*0.0*	*-3.00*
3-y-o	*1*	*3*	*0*	*0*	*0*	*3*	*0.0*	*-3.00*
4-y-o+	*9*	*67*	*3*	*5*	*5*	*53*	*4.5*	*-42.00*
Totals	**11**	**73**	**3**	**5**	**5**	**59**	**4.1**	**-48.00**
2017	*29*	*201*	*14*	*10*	*18*	*159*	*7.0*	*-62.00*
2016	*32*	*219*	*11*	*18*	*17*	*173*	*5.0*	*-146.77*

JOCKEYS

	W-R	Per cent	£1 Level Stake
Charlie Bennett	3-32	9.4	-7.00

COURSE RECORD

	Total W-R	Non-Hndcps 2-y-o	Non-Hndcps 3-y-o+	Hndcps 2-y-o	Hndcps 3-y-o+	Per cent	£1 Level Stake
Chelmsford (A.W)	1-9	0-0	0-0	0-0	1-9	11.1	+8.00
Lingfield (A.W)	1-10	0-0	0-0	0-0	1-10	10.0	-6.50
Wolvhptn (A.W)	1-13	0-0	0-0	0-0	1-13	7.7	-8.50

WINNING HORSES

Horse	Races Run	1st	2nd	3rd	£
Roy's Legacy	18	2	2	1	6210
Song Of Love (IRE)	8	1	1	1	3429
Total winning prize-money					**£9639**
Favourites	**0-3**		**0.0%**		**-3.00**

RONALD HARRIS

EARLSWOOD, MONMOUTHS

	No. of Hrs	Races Run	1st	2nd	3rd	Unpl	Per cent	£1 Level Stake
2-y-o	*9*	*45*	*2*	*5*	*2*	*36*	*4.4*	*-21.00*
3-y-o	*6*	*32*	*7*	*4*	*2*	*19*	*21.9*	*+26.20*
4-y-o+	*14*	*141*	*17*	*12*	*13*	*99*	*12.1*	*-1.25*
Totals	**29**	**218**	**26**	**21**	**17**	**154**	**11.9**	**+3.95**
2017	*31*	*223*	*22*	*20*	*13*	*168*	*9.9*	*+20.00*
2016	*36*	*272*	*22*	*21*	*28*	*200*	*8.1*	*-57.25*

BY MONTH

2-y-o	W-R	Per cent	£1 Level Stake
January	0-0	0.0	0.00
February	0-0	0.0	0.00
March	0-1	0.0	-1.00
April	0-4	0.0	-4.00
May	0-7	0.0	-7.00
June	1-9	11.1	-2.00
July	0-5	0.0	-5.00
August	0-5	0.0	-5.00
September	1-6	16.7	+11.00
October	0-3	0.0	-3.00
November	0-1	0.0	-1.00
December	0-4	0.0	-4.00

3-y-o	W-R	Per cent	£1 Level Stake
January	0-3	0.0	-3.00
February	0-0	0.0	0.00
March	0-1	0.0	-1.00
April	0-3	0.0	-3.00
May	0-2	0.0	-2.00
June	4-6	66.7	+26.60
July	1-4	25.0	-1.90
August	0-6	0.0	-6.00
September	0-1	0.0	-1.00
October	1-4	25.0	+13.00
November	0-1	0.0	-1.00
December	1-1	100.0	+5.50

4-y-o+	W-R	Per cent	£1 Level Stake
January	0-6	0.0	-6.00
February	1-8	12.5	+9.00
March	2-5	40.0	+4.50
April	1-12	8.3	-6.50
May	2-20	10.0	-3.50
June	1-13	7.7	-8.00
July	1-10	10.0	+7.00
August	3-14	21.4	+5.50
September	1-14	7.1	-9.50
October	4-20	20.0	+21.50
November	0-13	0.0	-13.00
December	1-6	16.7	-2.25

Totals	W-R	Per cent	£1 Level Stake
January	0-9	0.0	-9.00
February	1-8	12.5	+9.00
March	2-7	28.6	+2.50
April	1-19	5.3	-13.50
May	2-29	6.9	-12.50
June	6-28	21.4	+16.60
July	2-19	10.5	+0.10
August	3-25	12.0	-5.50
September	2-21	9.5	+0.50
October	5-27	18.5	+31.50
November	0-15	0.0	-14.00
December	2-11	18.2	+3.25

DISTANCE

2-y-o	W-R	Per cent	£1 Level Stake
5f-6f	2-43	4.7	-19.00
7f-8f	0-2	0.0	-2.00
9f-13f	0-0	0.0	0.00
14f+	0-0	0.0	0.00

3-y-o	W-R	Per cent	£1 Level Stake
5f-6f	5-22	22.7	+27.60
7f-8f	2-10	20.0	-1.40
9f-13f	0-0	0.0	0.00
14f+	0-0	0.0	0.00

4-y-o+	W-R	Per cent	£1 Level Stake
5f-6f	14-110	12.7	-3.00
7f-8f	3-31	9.7	+1.75
9f-13f	0-0	0.0	0.00
14f+	0-0	0.0	0.00

Totals	W-R	Per cent	£1 Level Stake
5f-6f	21-175	12.0	+5.60
7f-8f	5-43	11.6	-1.65
9f-13f	0-0	0.0	0.00
14f+	0-0	0.0	0.00

TYPE OF RACE

Non-Handicaps

	W-R	Per cent	£1 Level Stake
2-y-o	1-33	3.0	-26.00
3-y-o	0-8	0.0	-8.00
4-y-o+	1-8	12.5	-3.00

Handicaps

	W-R	Per cent	£1 Level Stake
2-y-o	1-12	8.3	+5.00
3-y-o	7-24	29.2	+34.20
4-y-o+	16-133	12.0	+1.75

RACE CLASS

	W-R	Per cent	£1 Level Stake
Class 1	0-9	0.0	-9.00
Class 2	2-11	18.2	+11.00
Class 3	0-6	0.0	-6.00
Class 4	3-38	7.9	-12.00
Class 5	7-71	9.9	-29.55
Class 6	14-82	17.1	+50.50
Class 7	0-1	0.0	-1.00

FIRST TIME OUT

	W-R	Per cent	£1 Level Stake
2-y-o	0-9	0.0	-9.00
3-y-o	1-6	16.7	+0.50
4-y-o+	2-14	14.3	-4.50
Totals	3-29	10.3	-13.00

JOCKEYS

	W-R	Per cent	£1 Level Stake
David Probert	12-87	13.8	+0.35
P J McDonald	2-4	50.0	+16.75
Liam Jones	2-9	22.2	+18.00

Jason Watson	2-10	20.0	+9.50
Franny Norton	2-15	13.3	-5.50
Robbie Downey	1-2	50.0	+9.00
Adam Kirby	1-5	20.0	-1.25
Liam Keniry	1-5	20.0	+12.00
Tim Clark	1-6	16.7	+11.00
Oisin Murphy	1-7	14.3	-4.90
Nicky Mackay	1-8	12.5	-1.00

COURSE RECORD

	Total W-R	Non-Hndcps 2-y-o	Non-Hndcps 3-y-o+	Hndcps 2-y-o	Hndcps 3-y-o+	Per cent	£1 Level Stake
Bath	5-43	0-7	1-5	0-1	4-30	11.6	-14.00
Wolvhptn (A.W)	5-45	0-6	0-0	0-1	5-38	11.1	-3.25
Kempton (A.W)	4-27	0-3	0-2	0-4	4 18	14.8	+12.75
Chepstow	3-18	0-5	0-0	0-0	3-13	16.7	-0.15
Brighton	2-7	0-1	0-0	0-0	2-6	28.6	+12.50
Lingfield	2-9	1-1	0-2	0-1	1-5	22.2	+0.10
Goodwood	1-4	0-0	0-0	0-0	1-4	25.0	+13.00
Salisbury	1-5	0-0	0-0	0-0	1-5	20.0	+12.00
Ffos Las	1-6	0-0	0-0	1-3	0-3	16.7	+11.00
Chelmsford (A.W)	1-9	0-1	0-1	0-2	1-5	11.1	-3.50
Windsor	1-9	0-3	0-0	0-0	1-6	11.1	0.00

WINNING HORSES

Horse	Races Run	1st	2nd	3rd	£
Broadhaven Honey (IRE)	11	3	2	1	9962
Country Rose (IRE)	6	1	2	0	3752
Equally Fast	6	1	0	1	3752
Eye Of The Water (IRE)	9	1	1	1	3170
Fantasy Justifier (IRE)	17	2	4	0	6598
Glamorous Dream (IRE)	10	2	1	1	7245
Glamorous Rocket (IRE)	12	4	3	1	16431
*Kyllachy Dragon (IRE)	1	1	0	0	3752
Powerful Dream (IRE)	16	2	1	6	7181
Secret Potion	14	1	1	3	3105
The Daley Express (IRE)	9	2	1	0	10853
Under The Covers	8	2	0	0	31353
Union Rose	12	1	0	1	3170
Viola Park	18	3	3	1	9315
Total winning prize-money					**£119639**
Favourites	**3-10**		**30.0%**		**-2.05**

BEN HASLAM

MIDDLEHAM MOOR, N YORKS

	No. of Hrs	Races Run	1st	2nd	3rd	Unpl	Per cent	£1 Level Stake
2-y-o	*7*	*30*	*0*	*1*	*2*	*27*	*0.0*	*-30.00*
3-y-o	*11*	*75*	*6*	*6*	*9*	*54*	*8.0*	*-16.25*
4-y-o+	*10*	*46*	*6*	*9*	*5*	*26*	*13.0*	*+9.00*
Totals	**28**	**151**	**12**	**16**	**16**	**107**	**7.9**	**-37.25**
2017	*25*	*109*	*11*	*11*	*18*	*69*	*10.1*	*+3.83*
2016	*26*	*101*	*2*	*6*	*14*	*79*	*2.0*	*-64.50*

BY MONTH

2-y-o	W-R	Per cent	£1 Level Stake	3-y-o	W-R	Per cent	£1 Level Stake
January	0-0	0.0	0.00	January	0-3	0.0	-3.00
February	0-0	0.0	0.00	February	0-6	0.0	-6.00
March	0-0	0.0	0.00	March	3-7	42.9	+3.25
April	0-1	0.0	-1.00	April	0-6	0.0	-6.00
May	0-5	0.0	-5.00	May	0-8	0.0	-8.00
June	0-3	0.0	-3.00	June	0-10	0.0	-10.00
July	0-5	0.0	-5.00	July	0-3	0.0	-3.00
August	0-3	0.0	-3.00	August	0-10	0.0	-10.00
September	0-5	0.0	-5.00	September	1-9	11.1	+20.00
October	0-5	0.0	-5.00	October	0-4	0.0	-4.00
November	0-3	0.0	-3.00	November	2-6	33.3	+13.50
December	0-0	0.0	0.00	December	0-3	0.0	-3.00

4-y-o+	W-R	Per cent	£1 Level Stake	Totals	W-R	Per cent	£1 Level Stake
January	0-1	0.0	-1.00	January	0-4	0.0	-4.00
February	0-2	0.0	-2.00	February	0-8	0.0	-8.00
March	2-4	50.0	+10.00	March	5-11	45.5	+13.25
April	0-5	0.0	-5.00	April	0-12	0.0	-12.00
May	1-8	12.5	0.00	May	1-21	4.8	-13.00
June	0-4	0.0	-4.00	June	0-17	0.0	-17.00
July	1-4	25.0	+0.50	July	1-12	8.3	-7.50
August	1-6	16.7	+15.00	August	1-19	5.3	+2.00
September	0-4	0.0	-4.00	September	1-18	5.6	+11.00
October	0-2	0.0	-2.00	October	0-11	0.0	-11.00
November	1-4	25.0	+3.50	November	3-13	23.1	+17.00
December	0-2	0.0	-2.00	December	0-5	0.0	-5.00

DISTANCE

2-y-o	W-R	Per cent	£1 Level Stake	3-y-o	W-R	Per cent	£1 Level Stake
5f-6f	0-20	0.0	-20.00	5f-6f	4-42	9.5	-0.50
7f-8f	0-10	0.0	-10.00	7f-8f	1-27	3.7	-24.75
9f-13f	0-0	0.0	0.00	9f-13f	1-6	16.7	+9.00
14f+	0-0	0.0	0.00	14f+	0-0	0.0	0.00

4-y-o+	W-R	Per cent	£1 Level Stake	Totals	W-R	Per cent	£1 Level Stake
5f-6f	2-18	11.1	+7.50	5f-6f	6-80	7.5	-13.00
7f-8f	3-22	13.6	-0.50	7f-8f	4-59	6.8	-35.25
9f-13f	1-5	20.0	+3.00	9f-13f	2-11	18.2	+12.00
14f+	0-1	0.0	-1.00	14f+	0-1	0.0	-1.00

TYPE OF RACE

Non-Handicaps	W-R	Per cent	£1 Level Stake	Handicaps	W-R	Per cent	£1 Level Stake
2-y-o	0-22	0.0	-22.00	2-y-o	0-8	0.0	-8.00
3-y-o	1-13	7.7	-10.50	3-y-o	5-62	8.1	-5.75
4-y-o+	2-11	18.2	+17.50	4-y-o+	4-35	11.4	-8.50

RACE CLASS / FIRST TIME OUT

RACE CLASS	W-R	Per cent	£1 Level Stake	FIRST TIME OUT	W-R	Per cent	£1 Level Stake
Class 1	1-3	33.3	+18.00	2-y-o	0-7	0.0	-7.00

	W-R	Per cent	£1 Level Stake
Class 2	1-1	100.0	+6.50
Class 3	1-4	25.0	+11.00
Class 4	1-10	10.0	-1.00
Class 5	4-63	6.3	-48.75
Class 6	4-68	5.9	-21.00
Class 7	0-2	0.0	-2.00

	W-R	Per cent	£1 Level Stake
3-y-o	0-11	0.0	-11.00
4-y-o+	2-10	20.0	+4.00
Totals	2-28	7.1	-14.00

JOCKEYS

	W-R	Per cent	£1 Level Stake
Paul Mulrennan	4-29	13.8	-8.25
Andrew Mullen	3-11	27.3	+37.50
Graham Lee	3-43	7.0	-5.50
Mr Dylan McDonagh	1-3	33.3	+1.50
Luke Morris	1-4	25.0	-1.50

COURSE RECORD

	Total W-R	Non-Hndcps 2-y-o	Non-Hndcps 3-y-o+	Hndcps 2-y-o	Hndcps 3-y-o+	Per cent	£1 Level Stake
Newcastle (A.W)	6-59	0-6	0-6	0-6	6-41	10.2	-3.75
Hamilton	2-12	0-2	0-1	0-0	2-9	16.7	+0.50
Lingfield (A.W)	1-2	0-0	1-2	0-0	0-0	50.0	+0.50
Pontefract	1-4	0-1	1-1	0-0	0-2	25.0	+17.00
Redcar	1-7	0-1	0-1	0-0	1-5	14.3	+8.00
Wolvhptn (A.W)	1-12	0-1	1-4	0-0	0-7	8.3	-4.50

WINNING HORSES

Horse	Races Run	1st	2nd	3rd	£
Castle Hill Cassie (IRE)	8	3	2	1	33612
Cherry Oak (IRE)	11	1	2	2	3105
Displaying Amber	8	1	0	2	3105
Epeius (IRE)	9	1	1	1	3993
*Hasanoanda	2	1	0	0	9704
Lord Caprio (IRE)	4	1	1	0	3752
Porrima (IRE)	7	1	1	0	3752
Prancing Oscar (IRE)	7	1	0	1	3493
Rey Loopy (IRE)	7	1	2	0	3752
The Bull (IRE)	7	1	0	0	3105
Total winning prize-money					**£71373**
Favourites	**3-12**		**25.0%**		**-4.45**

PETER HEDGER

HOOK, HAMPSHIRE

	No. of Hrs	Races Run	1st	2nd	3rd	Unpl	Per cent	£1 Level Stake
2-y-o	*1*	*5*	*0*	*0*	*0*	*5*	*0.0*	*-5.00*
3-y-o	*0*	*0*	*0*	*0*	*0*	*0*	*0.0*	*0.00*
4-y-o+	*11*	*62*	*11*	*6*	*7*	*38*	*17.7*	*+50.00*
Totals	**12**	**67**	**11**	**6**	**7**	**43**	**16.4**	**+45.00**
2017	*15*	*85*	*8*	*8*	*14*	*55*	*9.4*	*-19.75*
2016	*16*	*100*	*9*	*17*	*13*	*61*	*9.0*	*-40.63*

BY MONTH

2-y-o	W-R	Per cent	£1 Level Stake
January	0-0	0.0	0.00
February	0-0	0.0	0.00
March	0-0	0.0	0.00
April	0-0	0.0	0.00
May	0-0	0.0	0.00
June	0-2	0.0	-2.00
July	0-1	0.0	-1.00
August	0-1	0.0	-1.00
September	0-0	0.0	0.00
October	0-1	0.0	-1.00
November	0-0	0.0	0.00
December	0-0	0.0	0.00

3-y-o	W-R	Per cent	£1 Level Stake
January	0-0	0.0	0.00
February	0-0	0.0	0.00
March	0-0	0.0	0.00
April	0-0	0.0	0.00
May	0-0	0.0	0.00
June	0-0	0.0	0.00
July	0-0	0.0	0.00
August	0-0	0.0	0.00
September	0-0	0.0	0.00
October	0-0	0.0	0.00
November	0-0	0.0	0.00
December	0-0	0.0	0.00

4-y-o+	W-R	Per cent	£1 Level Stake
January	2-6	33.3	+7.00
February	0-5	0.0	-5.00
March	0-4	0.0	-4.00
April	1-5	20.0	+21.00
May	2-7	28.6	+2.50
June	2-5	40.0	+5.50
July	0-2	0.0	-2.00
August	0-7	0.0	-7.00
September	0-7	0.0	-7.00
October	3-9	33.3	+37.50
November	0-1	0.0	-1.00
December	1-4	25.0	+2.50

Totals	W-R	Per cent	£1 Level Stake
January	2-6	33.3	+7.00
February	0-5	0.0	5.00
March	0-4	0.0	-4.00
April	1-5	20.0	+21.00
May	2-7	28.6	+2.50
June	2-7	28.6	+3.50
July	0-3	0.0	-3.00
August	0-8	0.0	-8.00
September	0-7	0.0	-7.00
October	3-10	30.0	+36.50
November	0-1	0.0	-1.00
December	1-4	25.0	+2.50

DISTANCE

2-y-o	W-R	Per cent	£1 Level Stake
5f-6f	0-5	0.0	-5.00
7f-8f	0-0	0.0	0.00
9f-13f	0-0	0.0	0.00
14f+	0-0	0.0	0.00

3-y-o	W-R	Per cent	£1 Level Stake
5f-6f	0-0	0.0	0.00
7f-8f	0-0	0.0	0.00
9f-13f	0-0	0.0	0.00
14f+	0-0	0.0	0.00

4-y-o+	W-R	Per cent	£1 Level Stake
5f-6f	4-12	33.3	+9.00
7f-8f	4-20	20.0	+24.50
9f-13f	2-18	11.1	+2.50
14f+	1-12	8.3	+14.00

Totals	W-R	Per cent	£1 Level Stake
5f-6f	4-17	23.5	+4.00
7f-8f	4-20	20.0	+24.50
9f-13f	2-18	11.1	+2.50
14f+	1-12	8.3	+14.00

TYPE OF RACE

Non-Handicaps

	W-R	Per cent	£1 Level Stake
2-y-o	0-4	0.0	-4.00
3-y-o	0-0	0.0	0.00
4-y-o+	0-6	0.0	-6.00

Handicaps

	W-R	Per cent	£1 Level Stake
2-y-o	0-1	0.0	-1.00
3-y-o	0-0	0.0	0.00
4-y-o+	11-56	19.6	+56.00

RACE CLASS

	W-R	Per cent	£1 Level Stake
Class 1	0-0	0.0	0.00
Class 2	2-9	22.2	+23.00
Class 3	3-20	15.0	-6.00
Class 4	0-14	0.0	-14.00
Class 5	2-12	16.7	+8.50
Class 6	4-12	33.3	+33.50
Class 7	0-0	0.0	0.00

FIRST TIME OUT

	W-R	Per cent	£1 Level Stake
2-y-o	0-1	0.0	-1.00
3-y-o	0-0	0.0	0.00
4-y-o+	3-11	27.3	+28.00
Totals	3-12	25.0	+27.00

JOCKEYS

	W-R	Per cent	£1 Level Stake
Charles Bishop	3-18	16.7	+21.00
Tom Marquand	3-20	15.0	-5.50
Franny Norton	1-1	100.0	+5.00
Andrea Atzeni	1-1	100.0	+5.00
Hayley Turner	1-1	100.0	+16.00
Mr Simon Walker	1-2	50.0	+1.50
Joe Fanning	1-3	33.3	+23.00

COURSE RECORD

	Total W-R	Non-Hndcps 2-y-o	Non-Hndcps 3-y-o+	Hndcps 2-y-o	Hndcps 3-y-o+	Per cent	£1 Level Stake
Windsor	3-8	0-2	0-1	0-0	3-5	37.5	+6.00
Bath	2-3	0-1	0-0	0-0	2-2	66.7	+40.00
Lingfield (A.W)	2-13	0-0	0-1	0-0	2-12	15.4	-0.50
Doncaster	1-2	0-0	0-0	0-0	1-2	50.0	+1.50
Epsom	1-3	0-0	0-0	0-0	1-3	33.3	+3.00
Newbury	1-4	0-0	0-0	0-0	1-4	25.0	+22.00
Kempton (A.W)	1-19	0-0	0-3	0-0	1-16	5.3	-12.00

WINNING HORSES

Horse	Races Run	1st	2nd	3rd	£
Bridge Builder	4	2	1	0	6210
Medburn Cutler	3	1	0	0	25876
Medburn Dream	2	2	0	0	38564
Mr Mac	8	2	0	1	6275
Silent Echo	8	2	2	0	14879
Tralee Hills	7	2	0	0	7435
Total winning prize-money					**£99239**
Favourites	**2-4**		**50.0%**		**3.00**

NICKY HENDERSON

UPPER LAMBOURN, BERKS

	No. of Hrs	Races Run	1st	2nd	3rd	Unpl	Per cent	£1 Level Stake
2-y-o	*0*	*0*	*0*	*0*	*0*	*0*	*0.0*	*0.00*
3-y-o	*1*	*2*	*1*	*0*	*0*	*1*	*50.0*	*+5.00*
4-y-o+	*3*	*6*	*1*	*1*	*1*	*3*	*16.7*	*+1.00*
Totals	**4**	**8**	**2**	**1**	**1**	**4**	**25.0**	**+6.00**
2017	*5*	*5*	*1*	*0*	*0*	*4*	*20.0*	*-2.00*
2016	*6*	*13*	*1*	*0*	*2*	*10*	*7.7*	*-1.00*

JOCKEYS

	W-R	Per cent	£1 Level Stake
Adam Kirby	1-2	50.0	+5.00
Luke Morris	1-4	25.0	+3.00

COURSE RECORD

	Total W-R	Non-Hndcps 2-y-o	Non-Hndcps 3-y-o+	Hndcps 2-y-o	Hndcps 3-y-o+	Per cent	£1 Level Stake
Chelmsford (A.W)	1-1	0-0	1-1	0-0	0-0	100.0	+6.00
Lingfield (A.W)	1-1	0-0	1-1	0-0	0-0	100.0	+6.00

WINNING HORSES

Horse	Races Run	1st	2nd	3rd	£
Twist (IRE)	2	1	0	0	3752
Verdana Blue (IRE)	2	1	1	0	9704
Total winning prize-money					**£13456**
Favourites	**98-211**		**46.4%**		**-10.95**

MICHAEL HERRINGTON

COLD KIRBY, N YORKS

	No. of Hrs	Races Run	1st	2nd	3rd	Unpl	Per cent	£1 Level Stake
2-y-o	*0*	*0*	*0*	*0*	*0*	*0*	*0.0*	*0.00*
3-y-o	*3*	*13*	*0*	*1*	*2*	*10*	*0.0*	*-13.00*
4-y-o+	*14*	*106*	*11*	*19*	*14*	*62*	*10.4*	*-28.75*
Totals	**17**	**119**	**11**	**20**	**16**	**72**	**9.2**	**-41.75**
2017	*15*	*122*	*10*	*17*	*13*	*82*	*8.2*	*-54.75*
2016	*14*	*111*	*12*	*6*	*15*	*78*	*10.8*	*-21.00*

BY MONTH

2-y-o	W-R	Per cent	£1 Level Stake	3-y-o	W-R	Per cent	£1 Level Stake
January	0-0	0.0	0.00	January	0-0	0.0	0.00
February	0-0	0.0	0.00	February	0-0	0.0	0.00
March	0-0	0.0	0.00	March	0-0	0.0	0.00
April	0-0	0.0	0.00	April	0-1	0.0	-1.00
May	0-0	0.0	0.00	May	0-2	0.0	-2.00
June	0-0	0.0	0.00	June	0-2	0.0	-2.00
July	0-0	0.0	0.00	July	0-2	0.0	-2.00
August	0-0	0.0	0.00	August	0-2	0.0	-2.00
September	0-0	0.0	0.00	September	0-3	0.0	-3.00
October	0-0	0.0	0.00	October	0-0	0.0	0.00
November	0-0	0.0	0.00	November	0-0	0.0	0.00
December	0-0	0.0	0.00	December	0-1	0.0	-1.00

4-y-o+	W-R	Per cent	£1 Level Stake	Totals	W-R	Per cent	£1 Level Stake
January	1-10	10.0	-5.00	January	1-10	10.0	-5.00
February	1-10	10.0	+11.00	February	1-10	10.0	+11.00
March	3-12	25.0	+5.75	March	3-12	25.0	+5.75
April	4-11	36.4	+13.75	April	4-12	33.3	+12.75
May	0-17	0.0	-17.00	May	0-19	0.0	-19.00
June	0-9	0.0	-9.00	June	0-11	0.0	-11.00
July	0-6	0.0	-6.00	July	0-8	0.0	-8.00
August	0-8	0.0	-8.00	August	0-10	0.0	-10.00
September	0-2	0.0	-2.00	September	0-5	0.0	-5.00
October	1-7	14.3	-3.25	October	1-7	14.3	-3.25
November	1-11	9.1	-6.00	November	1-11	9.1	-6.00
December	0-3	0.0	-3.00	December	0-4	0.0	-4.00

DISTANCE

2-y-o	W-R	Per cent	£1 Level Stake	3-y-o	W-R	Per cent	£1 Level Stake
5f-6f	0-0	0.0	0.00	5f-6f	0-0	0.0	0.00
7f-8f	0-0	0.0	0.00	7f-8f	0-7	0.0	-7.00
9f-13f	0-0	0.0	0.00	9f-13f	0-6	0.0	-6.00

	W-R	Per cent	£1 Level Stake		W-R	Per cent	£1 Level Stake
14f+	0-0	0.0	0.00	14f+	0-0	0.0	0.00
4-y-o+	W-R	Per cent	£1 Level Stake	**Totals**	W-R	Per cent	£1 Level Stake
5f-6f	9-73	12.3	-6.00	5f-6f	9-73	12.3	-6.00
7f-8f	2-30	6.7	-19.75	7f-8f	2-37	5.4	-26.75
9f-13f	0-3	0.0	-3.00	9f-13f	0-9	0.0	-9.00
14f+	0-0	0.0	0.00	14f+	0-0	0.0	0.00

TYPE OF RACE

Non-Handicaps	W-R	Per cent	£1 Level Stake	Handicaps	W-R	Per cent	£1 Level Stake
2-y-o	0-0	0.0	0.00	2-y-o	0-0	0.0	0.00
3-y-o	0-7	0.0	-7.00	3-y-o	0-6	0.0	-6.00
4-y-o+	1-11	9.1	-5.50	4-y-o+	10-95	10.5	-23.25

RACE CLASS

	W-R	Per cent	£1 Level Stake
Class 1	0-1	0.0	-1.00
Class 2	0-0	0.0	0.00
Class 3	0-3	0.0	-3.00
Class 4	0-22	0.0	-22.00
Class 5	3-59	5.1	-37.00
Class 6	8-34	23.5	+21.25
Class 7	0-0	0.0	0.00

FIRST TIME OUT

	W-R	Per cent	£1 Level Stake
2-y-o	0-0	0.0	0.00
3-y-o	0-3	0.0	-3.00
4-y-o+	1-14	7.1	-5.00
Totals	1-17	5.9	-8.00

JOCKEYS

	W-R	Per cent	£1 Level Stake
Jason Hart	2-4	50.0	+5.75
Tom Eaves	2-12	16.7	-1.75
Andrew Mullen	2-20	10.0	-7.00
James Sullivan	1-1	100.0	+20.00
Kieran Shoemark	1-1	100.0	+4.50
Mr Kaine Wood	1-2	50.0	+7.00
Harrison Shaw	1-3	33.3	+2.00
George Wood	1-7	14.3	-3.25

COURSE RECORD

	Total W-R	Non-Hndcps 2-y-o	Non-Hndcps 3-y-o+	Hndcps 2-y-o	Hndcps 3-y-o+	Per cent	£1 Level Stake
Wolvhptn (A.W)	6-30	0-0	0-6	0-0	6-24	20.0	+20.00
Southwell (A.W)	2-18	0-0	0-2	0-0	2-16	11.1	-5.00
Kempton (A.W)	1-2	0-0	0-0	0-0	1-2	50.0	+1.75
Lingfield (A.W)	1-3	0-0	1-3	0-0	0-0	33.3	+2.50
Newcastle (A.W)	1-30	0-0	0-3	0-0	1-27	3.3	-25.00

WINNING HORSES

Horse	Races Run	1st	2nd	3rd	£
Dazeekha	4	2	0	0	6210
Duke Cosimo	15	2	2	2	6857
Kommander Kirkup	17	2	5	0	6857
Mishaal (IRE)	9	1	1	2	3105
Newstead Abbey*	10	1	3	0	3105
Street Poet (IRE)	9	2	4	0	6210
*The Amber Fort (USA)	10	1	3	1	3619

Total winning prize-money			**£35963**
Favourites	**3-16**	**18.8%**	**-4.75**

PETER HIATT

HOOK NORTON, OXON

	No. of Hrs	Races Run	1st	2nd	3rd	Unpl	Per cent	£1 Level Stake
2-y-o	*1*	*2*	*0*	*0*	*0*	*2*	*0.0*	*-2.00*
3-y-o	*2*	*13*	*0*	*0*	*2*	*11*	*0.0*	*-13.00*
4-y-o+	*7*	*58*	*6*	*5*	*8*	*39*	*10.3*	*+8.00*
Totals	**10**	**73**	**6**	**5**	**10**	**52**	**8.2**	**-7.00**
2017	*15*	*96*	*7*	*4*	*7*	*78*	*7.3*	*-23.00*
2016	*18*	*119*	*10*	*6*	*20*	*81*	*8.4*	*+33.13*

JOCKEYS

	W-R	Per cent	£1 Level Stake
Finley Marsh	2-4	50.0	+24.75
Adam Kirby	1-1	100.0	+14.00
James Doyle	1-1	100.0	+1.75
Poppy Bridgwater	1-2	50.0	+13.00
William Carson	1-16	6.3	-11.50

COURSE RECORD

	Total W-R	Non-Hndcps 2-y-o	Non-Hndcps 3-y-o+	Hndcps 2-y-o	Hndcps 3-y-o+	Per cent	£1 Level Stake
Wolvhptn (A.W)	3-15	0-0	0-2	0-0	3-13	20.0	+28.75
Newbury	1-1	0-0	0-0	0-0	1-1	100.0	+14.00
Nottingham	1-2	0-0	0-1	0-0	1-1	50.0	+0.75
Chelmsford (A.W)	1-8	0-0	0-0	0-0	1-8	12.5	-3.50

WINNING HORSES

Horse	Races Run	1st	2nd	3rd	£
Baashiq (IRE)	10	1	0	2	3105
Monarch Maid	21	1	4	6	3429
Raashdy (IRE)	8	1	0	0	3105
Red Tea	7	2	1	0	34848
Wildomar	3	1	0	0	3105

Total winning prize-money			**£47592**
Favourites	**1-4**	**25.0%**	**-1.25**

PHILIP HIDE

FINDON, W SUSSEX

	No. of Hrs	Races Run	1st	2nd	3rd	Unpl	Per cent	£1 Level Stake
2-y-o	*0*	*0*	*0*	*0*	*0*	*0*	*0.0*	*0.00*
3-y-o	*4*	*17*	*0*	*1*	*1*	*15*	*0.0*	*-17.00*
4-y-o+	*11*	*55*	*5*	*9*	*9*	*32*	*9.1*	*-11.59*
Totals	**15**	**72**	**5**	**10**	**10**	**47**	**6.9**	**-28.59**
2017	*19*	*118*	*17*	*13*	*15*	*73*	*14.4*	*-3.79*
2016	*18*	*78*	*7*	*11*	*5*	*54*	*9.0*	*+3.57*

JOCKEYS

	W-R	Per cent	£1 Level Stake
Jason Watson	3-14	21.4	-1.59
Harry Bentley	1-4	25.0	+6.00
Charlie Bennett	1-7	14.3	+14.00

COURSE RECORD

	Total W-R	Non-Hndcps 2-y-o	Non-Hndcps 3-y-o+	Hndcps 2-y-o	Hndcps 3-y-o+	Per cent	£1 Level Stake
Brighton	3-23	0-0	0-2	0-0	3-21	13.0	-10.59
Ascot	1-1	0-0	0-0	0-0	1-1	100.0	+20.00
Kempton (A.W)	1-10	0-0	0-2	0-0	1-8	10.0	0.00

WINNING HORSES

Horse	Races Run	1st	2nd	3rd	£
Archimento*	6	2	0	2	6857
Black Caesar (IRE)	12	1	3	2	3752
Buzz Lightyere*	8	1	2	0	6728
Dragons Voice*	3	1	0	0	6469
Total winning prize-money					**£23806**
Favourites	**1-10**		**10.0%**		**-8.09**

CHARLES HILLS

LAMBOURN, BERKS

	No. of Hrs	Races Run	1st	2nd	3rd	Unpl	Per cent	£1 Level Stake
2-y-o	*55*	*172*	*16*	*26*	*23*	*107*	*9.3*	*-62.88*
3-y-o	*63*	*275*	*35*	*22*	*29*	*188*	*12.7*	*-9.09*
4-y-o+	*18*	*94*	*11*	*11*	*7*	*65*	*11.7*	*-0.61*
Totals	**136**	**541**	**62**	**59**	**59**	**360**	**11.5**	**-72.58**
2017	*143*	*590*	*70*	*68*	*67*	*384*	*11.9*	*-161.41*
2016	*133*	*543*	*76*	*75*	*72*	*319*	*14.0*	*-192.65*

BY MONTH

2-y-o	W-R	Per cent	£1 Level Stake
January	0-0	0.0	0.00
February	0-0	0.0	0.00
March	0-1	0.0	-1.00
April	0-2	0.0	-2.00
May	2-13	15.4	-9.08
June	1-20	5.0	-17.00
July	1-17	5.9	-14.80
August	5-39	12.8	+19.88
September	3-34	8.8	-22.88
October	2-28	7.1	-11.50
November	2-10	20.0	+3.50
December	0-8	0.0	-8.00

3-y-o	W-R	Per cent	£1 Level Stake
January	0-5	0.0	-5.00
February	1-9	11.1	+17.00
March	0-6	0.0	-6.00
April	3-23	13.0	-9.78
May	5-43	11.6	+7.00
June	1-41	2.4	-20.00
July	5-33	15.2	-9.48
August	5-34	14.7	-1.13
September	10-40	25.0	+6.28
October	5-27	18.5	+26.00
November	0-8	0.0	-8.00
December	0-6	0.0	-6.00

4-y-o+	W-R	Per cent	£1 Level Stake
January	0-1	0.0	-1.00
February	0-2	0.0	-2.00
March	0-1	0.0	-1.00
April	2-10	20.0	+14.75
May	6-19	31.6	+13.41
June	0-14	0.0	-14.00
July	0-14	0.0	-14.00
August	2-9	22.2	+1.23
September	1-13	7.7	+13.00
October	0-8	0.0	-8.00
November	0-3	0.0	-3.00
December	0-0	0.0	0.00

Totals	W-R	Per cent	£1 Level Stake
January	0-6	0.0	-6.00
February	1-11	9.1	+15.00
March	0-8	0.0	-8.00
April	5-35	14.3	+2.97
May	13-75	17.3	+11.33
June	2-75	2.7	-51.00
July	6-64	9.4	-38.28
August	12-82	14.6	+19.98
September	14-87	16.1	-3.60
October	7-63	11.1	+6.50
November	2-21	9.5	-11.00
December	0-14	0.0	-6.00

DISTANCE

2-y-o	W-R	Per cent	£1 Level Stake
5f-6f	7-99	7.1	-78.58
7f-8f	9-73	12.3	+15.70
9f-13f	0-0	0.0	0.00
14f+	0-0	0.0	0.00

3-y-o	W-R	Per cent	£1 Level Stake
5f-6f	7-52	13.5	+3.50
7f-8f	13-111	11.7	-13.59
9f-13f	14-108	13.0	+1.00
14f+	1-4	25.0	0.00

4-y-o+	W-R	Per cent	£1 Level Stake
5f-6f	5-25	20.0	+12.14
7f-8f	2-37	5.4	-27.00
9f-13f	4-29	13.8	+17.25
14f+	0-3	0.0	-3.00

Totals	W-R	Per cent	£1 Level Stake
5f-6f	19-176	10.8	-62.94
7f-8f	24-221	10.9	-24.89
9f-13f	18-137	13.1	+18.25
14f+	1-7	14.3	-3.00

TYPE OF RACE

Non-Handicaps

	W-R	Per cent	£1 Level Stake
2-y-o	12-145	8.3	-65.38
3-y-o	15-120	12.5	+10.63
4-y-o+	4-22	18.2	+7.14

Handicaps

	W-R	Per cent	£1 Level Stake
2-y-o	4-27	14.8	+2.50
3-y-o	20-155	12.9	-19.72
4-y-o+	7-72	9.7	-7.75

RACE CLASS

	W-R	Per cent	£1 Level Stake
Class 1	3-46	6.5	-36.86
Class 2	8-58	13.8	+5.38
Class 3	7-59	11.9	-12.50
Class 4	11-138	8.0	-71.33
Class 5	29-192	15.1	+61.23
Class 6	4-48	8.3	-18.50
Class 7	0-0	0.0	0.00

FIRST TIME OUT

	W-R	Per cent	£1 Level Stake
2-y-o	3-55	5.5	-3.50
3-y-o	7-63	11.1	+16.22
4-y-o+	2-18	11.1	-11.59
Totals	12-136	8.8	+1.13

JOCKEYS

	W-R	Per cent	£1 Level Stake
Callum Shepherd	15-124	12.1	-2.42
Jim Crowley	10-65	15.4	-6.37
Dane O'Neill	5-20	25.0	+4.07
Paul Hanagan	4-19	21.1	+8.25
Oisin Murphy	4-20	20.0	+14.72
William Buick	4-22	18.2	+14.75
Jason Watson	3-16	18.8	-4.00
William Cox	2-9	22.2	+7.50
David Probert	2-10	20.0	+2.25
Luke Morris	2-15	13.3	+1.50
Jamie Spencer	2-17	11.8	+1.50

Robert Winston	2-30	6.7	+9.00
Gerald Mosse	2-40	5.0	-12.33
Tom Marquand	1-2	50.0	+2.50
Charlie Bennett	1-4	25.0	+4.50
Ryan Moore	1-7	14.3	-5.50
James Doyle	1-12	8.3	-7.50
P J McDonald	1-12	8.3	-8.00

COURSE RECORD

	Total W-R	Non-Hndcps 2-y-o	3-y-o+	Hndcps 2-y-o	3-y-o+	Per cent	£1 Level Stake
Kempton (A.W)	7-57	1-14	3-10	0-8	3-25	12.3	-10.38
Wolvhptn (A.W)	5-33	2-6	1-13	1-2	1-12	15.2	-6.08
Bath	4-17	0-4	1-2	0-1	3-10	23.5	-6.10
Leicester	4-17	0-2	2-4	0-1	2-10	23.5	+16.00
Newmkt (Jly)	4-21	2-6	0-4	1-1	1-10	19.0	+17.88
Windsor	4-37	0-12	0-8	0-1	4-16	10.8	-0.50
Salisbury	3-15	0-7	2-5	0-0	1-3	20.0	+23.88
Newcastle (A.W)	3-19	0-4	1-6	1-1	1-8	15.8	+16.25
Doncaster	3-24	1-11	1-5	0-1	1-7	12.5	+8.38
Chelmsford (A.W)	3-27	0-5	1-5	0-0	2-17	11.1	+3.50
Goodwood	3-28	1-7	2-10	0-1	0-10	10.7	-21.15
Catterick	2-2	0-0	0-0	1-1	1-1	100.0	+17.50
Ffos Las	2-11	1-5	1-2	0-2	0-2	18.2	+11.91
Chester	2-12	0-1	0-3	0-0	2-8	16.7	-2.75
Haydock	2-12	0-1	2-5	0-0	0-6	16.7	+2.91
York	2-18	1-7	0-4	0-0	1-7	11.1	-7.00
Chepstow	1-4	0-1	0-1	0-0	1-2	25.0	-1.25
Ayr	1-5	1-2	0-0	0-0	0-3	20.0	-2.00
Lingfield	1-5	1-1	0-3	0-1	0-0	20.0	-3.33
Beverley	1-6	0-1	0-1	0-0	1-4	16.7	+4.00
Epsom	1-6	0-1	0-0	0-0	1-5	16.7	+2.50
Ripon	1-7	0-1	0-3	0-0	1-3	14.3	+3.00
Nottingham	1-15	0-6	1-3	0-0	0-6	6.7	-5.00
Newmarket	1-27	0-7	1-11	0-1	0-8	3.7	-22.00
Newbury	1-37	1-17	0-10	0-1	0-9	2.7	-33.75

WINNING HORSES

Horse	Races Run	1st	2nd	3rd	£
A Momentofmadness	9	3	1	1	74078
Afaak	7	1	1	1	31125
Always A Drama (IRE)	2	1	0	0	3881
Arthenia (IRE)	7	1	0	0	5434
Artistic Rifles (IRE)	6	1	0	0	9338
Autumn War (IRE)	4	2	0	1	9057
Bartholomeu Dias	8	2	1	2	10998
Battaash (IRE)	4	2	1	0	233645
Breath Of Air	3	1	0	1	6469
Burning Lake (IRE)	6	1	0	0	3105
Chuck Willis (IRE)	4	1	1	1	5046
Clematis (USA)	1	1	0	0	3881
Dark Jedi (IRE)	3	1	2	0	4140
Delicious	6	1	0	1	3105
Equilateral	5	2	0	0	13204
Eraad (IRE)	6	1	0	1	5175
Gemini	7	2	0	1	7181
Glory Fighter	4	1	1	0	6301
Groveman*	9	2	2	2	7569
Here's Alice (IRE)	6	1	0	0	3752
Jallota	1	1	0	0	9338
Jetstream (IRE)*	5	1	0	1	4140
Khaadem (IRE)	3	2	0	1	16380
Livvys Dream (IRE)	8	3	1	0	11644
Makambe (IRE)*	9	2	2	2	10480
Mapped (USA)	8	1	1	1	5822
Metatrons Cube (IRE)*	8	1	1	2	5531
Mirbat	5	1	0	0	5434
Motagally	3	1	0	0	3752
Mutawaffer (IRE)	4	1	1	0	6728
Never Surrender (IRE)	10	1	2	1	5175
Phoenix Of Spain (IRE)	5	2	2	0	60462
Plutonian (IRE)	6	1	2	0	7439
Pogo (IRE)	8	1	2	2	9704
Porth Swtan (IRE)	6	3	0	0	53767
Puds	9	2	1	1	11515
Red Bravo (IRE)	3	1	0	0	5175
Rhosneigr (IRE)	6	1	0	1	4399
Shanghai Silver (IRE)	7	2	1	0	10706
Smooth Sailing	3	1	0	0	4787
Solar Gold (IRE)	7	1	2	2	3752
Spoof	6	1	0	1	21165
Tamreer	2	1	0	0	4787
Time For A Toot (IRE)	4	1	1	0	4787
Wufud	4	1	1	0	3752
Total winning prize-money					**£737105**
Favourites	**18-49**		**36.7%**		**-7.72**

MARK HOAD

LEWES, E SUSSEX

	No. of Hrs	Races Run	1st	2nd	3rd	Unpl	Per cent	£1 Level Stake
2-y-o	*0*	*0*	*0*	*0*	*0*	*0*	*0.0*	*0.00*
3-y-o	*0*	*0*	*0*	*0*	*0*	*0*	*0.0*	*0.00*
4-y-o+	*6*	*27*	*2*	*3*	*4*	*17*	*7.4*	*-5.00*
Totals	**6**	**27**	**2**	**3**	**4**	**17**	**7.4**	**-5.00**
2017	*12*	*46*	*1*	*3*	*3*	*37*	*2.2*	*-39.00*
2016	*12*	*44*	*0*	*0*	*5*	*39*	*0.0*	*-44.00*

JOCKEYS

	W-R	Per cent	£1 Level Stake
Jack Mitchell	1-3	33.3	+4.00
Kieran O'Neill	1-6	16.7	+9.00

COURSE RECORD

	Total W-R	Non-Hndcps 2-y-o	3-y-o+	Hndcps 2-y-o	3-y-o+	Per cent	£1 Level Stake
Chelmsford (A.W)	1-4	0-0	0-0	0-0	1-4	25.0	+3.00
Lingfield (A.W)	1-13	0-0	0-2	0-0	1-11	7.7	+2.00

WINNING HORSES

Horse	Races Run	1st	2nd	3rd	£
Hurricane Alert	19	2	3	4	6534
Total winning prize-money					**£6534**
Favourites	**0-0**		**0.0%**		**0.00**

PHILIP HOBBS

WITHYCOMBE, SOMERSET

	No. of Hrs	Races Run	1st	2nd	3rd	Unpl	Per cent	£1 Level Stake
2-y-o	*0*	*0*	*0*	*0*	*0*	*0*	*0.0*	*0.00*
3-y-o	*0*	*0*	*0*	*0*	*0*	*0*	*0.0*	*0.00*
4-y-o+	*2*	*6*	*1*	*0*	*0*	*5*	*16.7*	*-4.27*
Totals	**2**	**6**	**1**	**0**	**0**	**5**	**16.7**	**-4.27**
2017	*3*	*8*	*2*	*2*	*2*	*2*	*25.0*	*-1.25*
2016	*3*	*5*	*0*	*0*	*3*	*2*	*0.0*	*-5.00*

JOCKEYS

	W-R	Per cent	£1 Level Stake
Martin Harley	1-1	100.0	+0.73

COURSE RECORD

	Total W-R	Non-Hndcps 2-y-o	Non-Hndcps 3-y-o+	Hndcps 2-y-o	Hndcps 3-y-o+	Per cent	£1 Level Stake
Catterick	1-1	0-0	1-1	0-0	0-0	100.0	+0.73

WINNING HORSES

Horse	Races Run	1st	2nd	3rd	£
St Malo (USA)*	1	1	0	0	3493
Total winning prize-money					**£3493**
Favourites	**49-123**		**39.8%**		**-3.45**

RON HODGES

CHARLTON MACKRELL, SOMERSET

	No. of Hrs	Races Run	1st	2nd	3rd	Unpl	Per cent	£1 Level Stake
2-y-o	*0*	*0*	*0*	*0*	*0*	*0*	*0.0*	*0.00*
3-y-o	*0*	*0*	*0*	*0*	*0*	*0*	*0.0*	*0.00*
4-y-o+	*5*	*45*	*4*	*5*	*7*	*29*	*8.9*	*-13.00*
Totals	**5**	**45**	**4**	**5**	**7**	**29**	**8.9**	**-13.00**
2017	*7*	*55*	*8*	*4*	*3*	*40*	*14.5*	*+20.00*
2016	*10*	*65*	*5*	*5*	*5*	*50*	*7.7*	*-23.50*

JOCKEYS

	W-R	Per cent	£1 Level Stake
Kieran O'Neill	2-12	16.7	+7.00
Finley Marsh	1-1	100.0	+8.00
David Probert	1-13	7.7	-9.00

COURSE RECORD

	Total W-R	Non-Hndcps 2-y-o	Non-Hndcps 3-y-o+	Hndcps 2-y-o	Hndcps 3-y-o+	Per cent	£1 Level Stake
Salisbury	1-3	0-0	0-0	0-0	1-3	33.3	+12.00
Chepstow	1-5	0-0	0-0	0-0	1-5	20.0	+4.00
Lingfield (A.W)	1-9	0-0	0-0	0-0	1-9	11.1	-5.00
Bath	1-14	0-0	0-0	0-0	1-14	7.1	-10.00

WINNING HORSES

Horse	Races Run	1st	2nd	3rd	£
Evening Starlight	4	1	0	0	3105
Here's Two	7	1	0	1	3817
Met By Moonlight	11	1	1	3	5387
Mister Musicmaster	13	1	2	2	3752
Total winning prize-money					**£16061**
Favourites	**0-2**		**0.0%**		**-2.00**

SARAH HOLLINSHEAD

UPPER LONGDON, STAFFS

	No. of Hrs	Races Run	1st	2nd	3rd	Unpl	Per cent	£1 Level Stake
2-y-o	*2*	*10*	*0*	*0*	*0*	*10*	*0.0*	*-10.00*
3-y-o	*2*	*26*	*1*	*4*	*4*	*17*	*3.8*	*-13.00*
4-y-o+	*9*	*60*	*2*	*2*	*6*	*50*	*3.3*	*-43.00*
Totals	**13**	**96**	**3**	**6**	**10**	**77**	**3.1**	**-66.00**
2017	*19*	*82*	*7*	*3*	*5*	*67*	*8.5*	*-39.30*
2016	*18*	*93*	*3*	*5*	*5*	*80*	*3.2*	*-27.00*

JOCKEYS

	W-R	Per cent	£1 Level Stake
Gabriele Malune	2-21	9.5	+5.00
Richard Kingscote	1-5	20.0	-1.00

COURSE RECORD

	Total W-R	Non-Hndcps 2-y-o	Non-Hndcps 3-y-o+	Hndcps 2-y-o	Hndcps 3-y-o+	Per cent	£1 Level Stake
Wolvhptn (A.W)	2-56	0-1	0-3	0-1	2-51	3.6	-39.00
Thirsk	1-2	0-0	0-0	0-0	1-2	50.0	+11.00

WINNING HORSES

Horse	Races Run	1st	2nd	3rd	£
Final Attack (IRE)	16	2	1	5	6210
Jenny Ren	11	1	1	0	3398
Total winning prize-money					**£9608**
Favourites	**0-1**		**0.0%**		**-1.00**

STEPH HOLLINSHEAD

UPPER LONGDON, STAFFS

	No. of Hrs	Races Run	1st	2nd	3rd	Unpl	Per cent	£1 Level Stake
2-y-o	*4*	*23*	*0*	*1*	*0*	*22*	*0.0*	*-23.00*

3-y-o	*8*	*58*	*2*	*6*	*3*	*47*	*3.4*	*-39.00*
4-y-o+	*11*	*57*	*0*	*3*	*2*	*52*	*0.0*	*-57.00*
Totals	**23**	**138**	**2**	**10**	**5**	**121**	**1.4**	**-119.00**
2017	*20*	*102*	*7*	*6*	*16*	*73*	*6.9*	*-54.00*
2016	*17*	*111*	*9*	*9*	*9*	*84*	*8.1*	*-26.75*

JOCKEYS

	W-R	Per cent	£1 Level Stake
Kieran O'Neill	1-12	8.3	-4.00
Toby Eley	1-47	2.1	-36.00

COURSE RECORD

	Total W-R	Non-Hndcps 2-y-o	3-y-o+	Hndcps 2-y-o	3-y-o+	Per cent	£1 Level Stake
Chelmsford (A.W)	1-11	0-0	0-0	0-0	1-11	9.1	-3.00
Nottingham	1-12	0-3	0-1	0-0	1-8	8.3	-1.00

WINNING HORSES

Horse	Races Run	1st	2nd	3rd	£
Enchanting Enya (IRE)	13	1	1	1	3493
The Golden Cue	11	1	1	1	3235
Total winning prize-money					**£6728**
Favourites	**0-4**		**0.0%**		**-4.00**

JOHN HOLT

PECKLETON, LEICS

	No. of Hrs	Races Run	1st	2nd	3rd	Unpl	Per cent	£1 Level Stake
2-y-o	*1*	*2*	*0*	*0*	*0*	*2*	*0.0*	*-2.00*
3-y-o	*2*	*13*	*0*	*1*	*2*	*10*	*0.0*	*-13.00*
4-y-o+	*3*	*20*	*1*	*1*	*2*	*16*	*5.0*	*-10.00*
Totals	**6**	**35**	**1**	**2**	**4**	**28**	**2.9**	**-25.00**
2017	*9*	*61*	*1*	*2*	*4*	*54*	*1.6*	*-57.25*
2016	*8*	*53*	*3*	*3*	*5*	*42*	*5.7*	*-12.00*

JOCKEYS

	W-R	Per cent	£1 Level Stake
Megan Ellingworth	1-6	16.7	+4.00

COURSE RECORD

	Total W-R	Non-Hndcps 2-y-o	3-y-o+	Hndcps 2-y-o	3-y-o+	Per cent	£1 Level Stake
Kempton (A.W)	1-2	0-0	0-0	0-0	1-2	50.0	+8.00

WINNING HORSES

Horse	Races Run	1st	2nd	3rd	£
Barnsdale*	6	1	0	1	2588
Total winning prize-money					**£2588**
Favourites	**0-1**		**0.0%**		**-1.00**

EVE JOHNSON HOUGHTON

BLEWBURY, OXON

	No. of Hrs	Races Run	1st	2nd	3rd	Unpl	Per cent	£1 Level Stake
2-y-o	*24*	*83*	*9*	*12*	*13*	*49*	*10.8*	*-42.26*
3-y-o	*29*	*164*	*15*	*19*	*20*	*110*	*9.1*	*-77.65*
4-y-o+	*23*	*126*	*13*	*11*	*16*	*85*	*10.3*	*-33.00*
Totals	**76**	**373**	**37**	**42**	**49**	**244**	**9.9**	**-152.91**
2017	*74*	*375*	*52*	*47*	*45*	*230*	*13.9*	*+33.39*
2016	*55*	*329*	*41*	*32*	*42*	*214*	*12.5*	*+10.44*

BY MONTH

2-y-o	W-R	Per cent	£1 Level Stake	3-y-o	W-R	Per cent	£1 Level Stake
January	0-0	0.0	0.00	January	0-4	0.0	-4.00
February	0-0	0.0	0.00	February	1-3	33.3	+10.00
March	0-0	0.0	0.00	March	0-1	0.0	-1.00
April	0-2	0.0	-2.00	April	3-14	21.4	+0.88
May	2-11	18.2	-7.38	May	4-30	13.3	-13.50
June	2-10	20.0	-5.09	June	1-28	3.6	-24.25
July	1-16	6.3	-3.00	July	3-23	13.0	-2.77
August	4-16	25.0	+3.21	August	2-22	9.1	-11.50
September	0-11	0.0	-11.00	September	1-14	7.1	-6.50
October	0-9	0.0	-9.00	October	0-15	0.0	-15.00
November	0-4	0.0	-4.00	November	0-5	0.0	-5.00
December	0-4	0.0	-4.00	December	0-5	0.0	-5.00

4-y-o+	W-R	Per cent	£1 Level Stake	Totals	W-R	Per cent	£1 Level Stake
January	2-8	25.0	+1.75	January	2-12	16.7	-2.25
February	1-6	16.7	-2.25	February	2-9	22.2	+7.75
March	0-4	0.0	-4.00	March	0-5	0.0	-5.00
April	2-12	16.7	-0.50	April	5-28	17.9	-1.62
May	2-18	11.1	-4.50	May	8-59	13.6	-25.38
June	2-21	9.5	+22.00	June	5-59	8.5	-7.34
July	2-6	33.3	-0.88	July	6-45	13.3	-6.65
August	0-14	0.0	-14.00	August	6-52	11.5	-22.29
September	1-13	7.7	-9.00	September	2-38	5.3	-26.50
October	1-10	10.0	-7.63	October	1-34	2.9	-31.63
November	0-5	0.0	-5.00	November	0-14	0.0	-10.00
December	0-9	0.0	-9.00	December	0-18	0.0	-14.00

DISTANCE

2-y-o	W-R	Per cent	£1 Level Stake	3-y-o	W-R	Per cent	£1 Level Stake
5f-6f	8-54	14.8	-15.63	5f-6f	0-21	0.0	-21.00
7f-8f	1-29	3.4	-26.63	7f-8f	8-82	9.8	-31.13
9f-13f	0-0	0.0	0.00	9f-13f	7-60	11.7	-24.52
14f+	0-0	0.0	0.00	14f+	0-1	0.0	-1.00

4-y-o+	W-R	Per cent	£1 Level Stake	Totals	W-R	Per cent	£1 Level Stake
5f-6f	4-32	12.5	-10.25	5f-6f	12-107	11.2	-46.88
7f-8f	5-47	10.6	+4.88	7f-8f	14-158	8.9	-52.88
9f-13f	4-41	9.8	-21.63	9f-13f	11-101	10.9	-46.15
14f+	0-6	0.0	-6.00	14f+	0-7	0.0	-7.00

TYPE OF RACE

Non-Handicaps	W-R	Per cent	£1 Level Stake	Handicaps	W-R	Per cent	£1 Level Stake
2-y-o	8-70	11.4	-42.26	2-y-o	1-13	7.7	0.00
3-y-o	5-34	14.7	-2.38	3-y-o	10-130	7.7	-75.27
4-y-o+	1-23	4.3	+11.00	4-y-o+	12-103	11.7	-44.00

RACE CLASS

	W-R	Per cent	£1 Level Stake
Class 1	2-19	10.5	+18.75
Class 2	5-42	11.9	-11.75
Class 3	4-32	12.5	-11.09
Class 4	8-85	9.4	-49.25
Class 5	12-133	9.0	-59.44
Class 6	6-62	9.7	-40.13
Class 7	0-0	0.0	0.00

FIRST TIME OUT

	W-R	Per cent	£1 Level Stake
2-y-o	0-24	0.0	-24.00
3-y-o	5-29	17.2	+2.88
4-y-o+	4-23	17.4	-1.75
Totals	9-76	11.8	-22.87

JOCKEYS

	W-R	Per cent	£1 Level Stake
Charles Bishop	23-194	11.9	-76.66
Edward Greatrex	10-71	14.1	-1.13
Martin Dwyer	2-16	12.5	+1.50
William Carson	1-4	25.0	+9.00
Georgia Dobie	1-19	5.3	-16.63

COURSE RECORD

	Total W-R	Non-Hndcps 2-y-o	Non-Hndcps 3-y-o+	Hndcps 2-y-o	Hndcps 3-y-o+	Per cent	£1 Level Stake
Windsor	5-28	1-7	1-1	0-0	3-20	17.9	+0.58
Lingfield (A.W)	5-39	0-9	1-11	0-0	4-19	12.8	-14.63
Brighton	4-28	1-2	0-1	0-1	3-24	14.3	-16.38
Kempton (A.W)	4-52	1-6	0-7	0-2	3-37	7.7	-26.13
Chelmsford (A.W)	3-13	2-4	0-1	1-2	0-6	23.1	+4.38
Wolvhptn (A.W)	3-19	0-2	2-4	0-1	1-12	15.8	+0.13
Epsom	2-11	0-1	0-0	0-0	2-10	18.2	-5.77
Ascot	2-13	0-4	1-2	0-0	1-7	15.4	+26.50
Yarmouth	1-5	0-0	0-0	0-0	1-5	20.0	-1.25
Newmkt (Jly)	1-5	0-1	0-0	0-0	1-4	20.0	+1.00
Chepstow	1-10	0-0	0-0	0-0	1-10	10.0	-6.00
Nottingham	1-11	0-2	0-3	0-0	1-6	9.1	-6.00
Leicester	1-13	1-2	0-2	0-2	0-7	7.7	0.00
Goodwood	1-17	0-5	1-4	0-2	0-6	5.9	-13.25
Salisbury	1-17	1-5	0-1	0-1	0-10	5.9	-15.09
Sandown	1-19	1-2	0-1	0-0	0-16	5.3	-16.00
Newbury	1-24	0-7	0-9	0-0	1-8	4.2	-16.00

WINNING HORSES

Horse	Races Run	1st	2nd	3rd	£
Accidental Agent	4	1	0	1	367197
Buckingham (IRE)	7	3	0	1	37132
Caiya	4	1	0	0	3752
Camomile Lawn (IRE)	6	1	1	3	3752
Count Calabash (IRE)	4	2	1	0	25510
Dorella (GER)	6	1	1	1	3752
Ferik (IRE)	1	1	0	0	3105
Goring (GER)	10	2	1	1	23944
Hedging (IRE)	12	1	0	1	5531
*Hyanna	7	2	3	1	17466
Ice Age (IRE)	9	2	0	2	32345
Key Player	3	1	1	0	3752
Kirkland Forever	8	2	1	2	6210
Last Enchantment (IRE)*	9	1	2	3	4528
Liva (IRE)*	7	1	0	0	7116
Lively Lydia	5	2	0	1	9574
Magnolia Springs (IRE)	4	1	0	0	25520
New Rich	10	1	1	1	3105
Oberyn Martell	5	2	1	0	12291
Optimum Time (IRE)	11	3	0	0	13035
Pont Vert	4	1	0	0	5175
Roser Moter (IRE)*	7	1	0	0	3105
Statuario	8	1	0	2	5531
Tin Hat (IRE)	12	1	2	5	4140
Vixen (IRE)	3	2	0	0	6857
Total winning prize-money					**£633425**
Favourites	**16-38**		**42.1%**		**4.84**

PAUL HOWLING

COWLINGE, SUFFOLK

	No. of Hrs	Races Run	1st	2nd	3rd	Unpl	Per cent	£1 Level Stake
2-y-o	*2*	*6*	*0*	*0*	*0*	*6*	*0.0*	*-6.00*
3-y-o	*4*	*13*	*1*	*1*	*1*	*10*	*7.7*	*+28.00*
4-y-o+	*10*	*35*	*1*	*6*	*2*	*26*	*2.9*	*-20.00*
Totals	**16**	**54**	**2**	**7**	**3**	**42**	**3.7**	**+2.00**
2017	*0*							
2016	*0*							

JOCKEYS

	W-R	Per cent	£1 Level Stake
Mr Matthew Johnson	1-1	100.0	+40.00
Joey Haynes	1-47	2.1	-32.00

COURSE RECORD

	Total W-R	Non-Hndcps 2-y-o	Non-Hndcps 3-y-o+	Hndcps 2-y-o	Hndcps 3-y-o+	Per cent	£1 Level Stake
Lingfield (A.W)	1-10	0-1	0-0	0-0	1-9	10.0	+5.00
Chelmsford (A.W)	1-16	0-3	0-1	0-0	1-12	6.3	+25.00

WINNING HORSES

Horse	Races Run	1st	2nd	3rd	£
*Declamation (IRE)	1	1	0	0	3105
*Holy Tiber (IRE)	8	1	1	1	3369
Total winning prize-money					**£6474**
Favourites	**0-3**		**0.0%**		**-3.00**

JO HUGHES

LAMBOURN, BERKS

	No. of Hrs	Races Run	1st	2nd	3rd	Unpl	Per cent	£1 Level Stake
2-y-o	*12*	*35*	*1*	*1*	*0*	*33*	*2.9*	*-20.00*
3-y-o	*11*	*53*	*2*	*3*	*5*	*43*	*3.8*	*-46.70*
4-y-o+	*9*	*56*	*5*	*5*	*12*	*34*	*8.9*	*-24.29*
Totals	**32**	**144**	**8**	**9**	**17**	**110**	**5.6**	**-90.99**
2017	*29*	*135*	*14*	*15*	*12*	*93*	*10.4*	*-33.75*
2016	*26*	*91*	*5*	*7*	*10*	*68*	*5.5*	*-10.00*

JOCKEYS

	W-R	Per cent	£1 Level Stake
Harry Burns	3-25	12.0	-1.13
J F Egan	2-11	18.2	+5.80
Robert Winston	1-1	100.0	+3.50
Richard Kingscote	1-2	50.0	+2.33
Dougie Costello	1-23	4.3	-19.50

COURSE RECORD

	Total W-R	Non-Hndcps 2-y-o	Non-Hndcps 3-y-o+	Hndcps 2-y-o	Hndcps 3-y-o+	Per cent	£1 Level Stake
Wolvhptn (A.W)	3-38	0-3	0-7	0-4	3-24	7.9	-18.17
Lingfield (A.W)	2-17	0-5	0-1	0-0	2-11	11.8	-3.50
Southwell (A.W)	1-5	0-0	1-1	0-0	0-4	20.0	-3.20
Kempton (A.W)	1-12	0-0	0-0	1-3	0-9	8.3	+3.00
Bath	1-15	0-5	0-1	0-0	1-9	6.7	-12.13

WINNING HORSES

Horse	Races Run	1st	2nd	3rd	£
Caledonia Laird	12	1	1	1	3105
Cape Greco (USA)	5	1	1	1	3105
Compass Hill (USA)	6	1	0	4	3105
Flying Tiger Hero (IRE)	1	1	0	0	3881
Grandee Daisy	5	1	0	0	3105
Rock Icon	11	3	2	3	10609
Total winning prize-money					**£26910**
Favourites	**3-8**		**37.5%**		**1.63**

BY MONTH

2-y-o	W-R	Per cent	£1 Level Stake	3-y-o	W-R	Per cent	£1 Level Stake
January	0-0	0.0	0.00	January	1-6	16.7	0.00
February	0-0	0.0	0.00	February	0-3	0.0	-3.00
March	0-1	0.0	-1.00	March	2-10	20.0	-3.64
April	0-2	0.0	-2.00	April	2-16	12.5	-7.50
May	0-23	0.0	-23.00	May	5-28	17.9	+2.50
June	5-23	21.7	-8.00	June	2-18	11.1	+0.50
July	2-23	8.7	-18.52	July	4-19	21.1	+16.99
August	5-23	21.7	-8.50	August	2-15	13.3	-3.00
September	4-33	12.1	-11.63	September	1-13	7.7	-10.75
October	4-35	11.4	-12.77	October	3-12	25.0	+5.63
November	3-16	18.8	-0.25	November	1-10	10.0	-6.50
December	1-11	9.1	-8.38	December	2-5	40.0	+9.50

4-y-o+	W-R	Per cent	£1 Level Stake	Totals	W-R	Per cent	£1 Level Stake
January	0-4	0.0	-4.00	January	1-10	10.0	-4.00
February	0-2	0.0	-2.00	February	0-5	0.0	-5.00
March	2-10	20.0	+5.00	March	4-21	19.0	+0.36
April	1-14	7.1	-9.50	April	3-32	9.4	-19.00
May	1-16	6.3	-12.00	May	6-67	9.0	-32.50
June	1-12	8.3	-9.75	June	8-53	15.1	-17.25
July	3-17	17.6	-7.20	July	9-59	15.3	-8.73
August	1-12	8.3	-7.50	August	8-50	16.0	-19.00
September	0-8	0.0	-8.00	September	5-54	9.3	-30.38
October	2-7	28.6	+7.50	October	9-54	16.7	+0.36
November	2-7	28.6	+7.75	November	6-33	18.2	+1.25
December	0-2	0.0	-2.00	December	3-18	16.7	+7.50

DISTANCE

2-y-o	W-R	Per cent	£1 Level Stake	3-y-o	W-R	Per cent	£1 Level Stake
5f-6f	18-128	14.1	-66.55	5f-6f	11-70	15.7	-17.52
7f-8f	6-62	9.7	-27.50	7f-8f	4-44	9.1	+0.50
9f-13f	0-0	0.0	0.00	9f-13f	10-38	26.3	+20.75
14f+	0-0	0.0	0.00	14f+	0-3	0.0	-3.00

4-y-o+	W-R	Per cent	£1 Level Stake	Totals	W-R	Per cent	£1 Level Stake
5f-6f	2-17	11.8	-4.20	5f-6f	31-215	14.4	-88.27
7f-8f	1-38	2.6	-27.00	7f-8f	11-144	7.6	-54.00
9f-13f	8-39	20.5	-2.00	9f-13f	18-77	23.4	+18.75
14f+	2-17	11.8	-8.50	14f+	2-20	10.0	-11.50

TYPE OF RACE

Non-Handicaps	W-R	Per cent	£1 Level Stake	Handicaps	W-R	Per cent	£1 Level Stake
2-y-o	18-138	13.0	-71.67	2-y-o	6-52	11.5	-22.38
3-y-o	8-38	21.1	+7.74	3-y-o	17-117	14.5	-7.01
4-y-o+	0-8	0.0	-8.00	4-y-o+	13-103	12.6	-33.70

RACE CLASS / FIRST TIME OUT

RACE CLASS	W-R	Per cent	£1 Level Stake	FIRST TIME OUT	W-R	Per cent	£1 Level Stake
Class 1	0-13	0.0	-13.00	2-y-o	2-42	4.8	-26.00

RICHARD HUGHES

UPPER LAMBOURN, BERKS

	No. of Hrs	Races Run	1st	2nd	3rd	Unpl	Per cent	£1 Level Stake
2-y-o	*42*	*190*	*24*	*27*	*36*	*103*	*12.6*	*-94.05*
3-y-o	*27*	*155*	*25*	*24*	*21*	*84*	*16.1*	*+0.73*
4-y-o+	*19*	*111*	*13*	*17*	*14*	*67*	*11.7*	*-41.70*
Totals	**88**	**456**	**62**	**68**	**71**	**254**	**13.6**	**-135.02**
2017	*93*	*519*	*63*	*91*	*59*	*306*	*12.1*	*-167.27*
2016	*70*	*356*	*36*	*38*	*48*	*234*	*10.1*	*-153.04*

Class 2	2-35	5.7	-26.00	3-y-o	7-27	25.9	+16.36
Class 3	5-51	9.8	-12.50	4-y-o+	0-19	0.0	-19.00
Class 4	15-111	13.5	-24.65				
Class 5	31-171	18.1	-25.49	Totals	9-88	10.2	-28.64
Class 6	9-75	12.0	-33.38				
Class 7	0-0	0.0	0.00				

JOCKEYS

	W-R	Per cent	£1 Level Stake
Shane Kelly	38-286	13.3	-116.29
Finley Marsh	7-42	16.7	-7.00
Nicola Currie	6-41	14.6	+5.25
Pat Dobbs	2-8	25.0	-1.20
Jamie Spencer	2-10	20.0	+3.50
George Rooke	2-13	15.4	-6.00
Stevie Donohoe	1-2	50.0	+6.00
Adam Kirby	1-3	33.3	+5.00
Andrea Atzeni	1-3	33.3	-1.27
David Egan	1-6	16.7	-2.00
Stephen Cummins	1-14	7.1	+7.00

COURSE RECORD

	Total W-R	Non-Hndcps 2-y-o	3-y-o+	Hndcps 2-y-o	3-y-o+	Per cent	£1 Level Stake
Chelmsford (A.W)	14-48	5-15	2-8	3-7	4-18	29.2	+12.47
Brighton	9-17	4-6	1-1	0-0	4-10	52.9	+18.57
Wolvhptn (A.W)	8-50	1-12	3-6	0-8	4-24	16.0	-8.00
Kempton (A.W)	6-62	1-17	0-4	3-11	2-30	9.7	-17.50
Chepstow	4-8	2-3	0-0	0-0	2-5	50.0	+1.80
Lingfield (A.W)	4-38	1-5	0-5	0-4	3-24	10.5	-19.00
Ffos Las	3-12	0-2	1-2	0-4	2-4	25.0	+13.18
Southwell (A.W)	3-14	0-2	1-2	0-1	2-9	21.4	+4.75
Chester	2-4	1-1	0-0	0-0	1-3	50.0	+7.50
Salisbury	2-16	1-6	0-1	0-1	1-8	12.5	-7.00
Newbury	2-18	0-8	0-0	0-1	2-9	11.1	-0.50
Bath	2-19	1-7	0-1	0-2	1-9	10.5	-7.00
Yarmouth	1-3	1-2	0-0	0-0	0-1	33.3	-1.27
Newmarket	1-14	0-7	0-0	0-2	1-5	7.1	-5.00
Windsor	1-28	0-14	0-4	0-0	1-10	3.6	-23.00

WINNING HORSES

Horse	Races Run	1st	2nd	3rd	£
Amitie Waltz (FR)	4	2	0	0	7569
Appenzeller (USA)	7	2	1	0	8863
Beepeecee*	4	1	0	1	3105
Believe It (IRE)	4	1	0	0	6469
*Bid Adieu (IRE)	10	2	2	3	9283
Big Brave Bob	7	1	0	3	3105
*Creek Harbour (IRE)	1	1	0	0	3752
Ellen Gates	7	1	4	0	3105
Fayrouz Rose (IRE)	3	1	0	0	3105
Fintas	3	2	0	0	13326
George Of Hearts (FR)	6	1	1	1	5175
Gold Filigree (IRE)	9	3	1	1	37704
Hellovaqueen	5	1	0	0	4140
Hollydaze (IRE)	5	1	2	0	5531
Jack Taylor (IRE)	16	2	3	3	7504
Jashma (IRE)	15	2	4	1	11063
Kath's Legacy	8	1	1	1	3752
Kath's Lustre	14	2	1	2	9186
Lady Madison (IRE)	2	1	0	0	6081
More Than Likely	8	3	2	1	14879
*Motajaasid (IRE)	6	2	0	1	7504
Odyssa (IRE)	9	1	1	0	4528
Pink Iceburg (IRE)	6	1	1	2	3752
Prince Of Rome (IRE)	6	2	1	1	11256
Rock Bottom	4	1	1	2	3752
Rosamour (IRE)	7	1	3	1	4031
Rustang (FR)	8	4	0	1	21445
Secratario (FR)*	4	2	0	1	6534
Shaybani (IRE)	5	2	1	0	9186
Soghan (IRE)	4	1	2	0	6469
Stanley	7	1	2	2	8022
Sunsprite (IRE)	5	3	0	1	28030
Top Breeze (IRE)	2	1	1	0	3881
Torolight	5	1	0	1	3105
Twenty Times (IRE)	7	2	0	1	11062
Um Shama (IRE)*	7	1	1	1	3105
Uncle Jerry	11	2	3	2	11256
Winter Light	6	2	2	1	9833
Wolf Hunter (IRE)	8	1	0	3	3105
Total winning prize-money					**£326553**
Favourites	**19-56**		**33.9%**		**-6.14**

ROGER INGRAM

EPSOM, SURREY

	No. of Hrs	Races Run	1st	2nd	3rd	Unpl	Per cent	£1 Level Stake
2-y-o	*1*	*2*	*0*	*0*	*0*	*2*	*0.0*	*-2.00*
3-y-o	*4*	*24*	*0*	*1*	*2*	*21*	*0.0*	*-24.00*
4-y-o+	*8*	*38*	*1*	*1*	*0*	*36*	*2.6*	*-29.00*
Totals	**13**	**64**	**1**	**2**	**2**	**59**	**1.6**	**-55.00**
2017	*19*	*85*	*3*	*6*	*6*	*70*	*3.5*	*-22.00*
2016	*17*	*94*	*3*	*4*	*8*	*79*	*3.2*	*-38.00*

JOCKEYS

	W-R	Per cent	£1 Level Stake
Rhiain Ingram	1-48	2.1	-39.00

COURSE RECORD

	Total W-R	Non-Hndcps 2-y-o	3-y-o+	Hndcps 2-y-o	3-y-o+	Per cent	£1 Level Stake
Chelmsford (A.W)	1-12	0-0	0-1	0-0	1-11	8.3	-3.00

WINNING HORSES

Horse	Races Run	1st	2nd	3rd	£
Dukes Meadow	11	1	0	0	3493
Total winning prize-money					**£3493**
Favourites	**0-0**		**0.0%**		**0.00**

DEAN IVORY

RADLETT, HERTS

	No. of Hrs	Races Run	1st	2nd	3rd	Unpl	Per cent	£1 Level Stake
2-y-o	*13*	*55*	*0*	*2*	*1*	*52*	*0.0*	*-55.00*
3-y-o	*18*	*83*	*9*	*14*	*11*	*49*	*10.8*	*-24.65*
4-y-o+	*32*	*221*	*30*	*21*	*24*	*146*	*13.6*	*+25.38*
Totals	**63**	**359**	**39**	**37**	**36**	**247**	**10.9**	**-54.27**
2017	*54*	*387*	*38*	*39*	*34*	*276*	*9.8*	*-23.88*
2016	*50*	*318*	*34*	*34*	*26*	*224*	*10.7*	*-117.13*

BY MONTH

2-y-o	W-R	Per cent	£1 Level Stake
January	0-0	0.0	0.00
February	0-0	0.0	0.00
March	0-0	0.0	0.00
April	0-7	0.0	-7.00
May	0-3	0.0	-3.00
June	0-4	0.0	-4.00
July	0-8	0.0	-8.00
August	0-7	0.0	-7.00
September	0-9	0.0	-9.00
October	0-10	0.0	-10.00
November	0-5	0.0	-5.00
December	0-2	0.0	-2.00

3-y-o	W-R	Per cent	£1 Level Stake
January	0-5	0.0	-5.00
February	3-6	50.0	+14.25
March	1-5	20.0	+10.00
April	1-11	9.1	-7.00
May	2-14	14.3	-5.00
June	0-4	0.0	-4.00
July	0-3	0.0	-3.00
August	1-7	14.3	-4.90
September	0-7	0.0	-7.00
October	0-9	0.0	-9.00
November	1-6	16.7	+2.00
December	0-6	0.0	-6.00

4-y-o+	W-R	Per cent	£1 Level Stake
January	4-22	18.2	+3.50
February	2-13	15.4	+1.00
March	3-16	18.8	-3.75
April	2-11	18.2	+2.88
May	1-15	6.7	-11.00
June	4-23	17.4	+28.75
July	2-23	8.7	-15.75
August	2-14	14.3	-5.00
September	0-18	0.0	-18.00
October	2-22	9.1	+15.00
November	6-25	24.0	+26.75
December	2-19	10.5	+1.00

Totals	W-R	Per cent	£1 Level Stake
January	4-27	14.8	-1.50
February	5-19	26.3	+15.25
March	4-21	19.0	+6.25
April	3-29	10.3	-11.12
May	3-32	9.4	-19.00
June	4-31	12.9	+20.75
July	2-34	5.9	-26.75
August	3-28	10.7	-16.90
September	0-34	0.0	-34.00
October	2-41	4.9	-4.00
November	7-36	19.4	+28.75
December	2-27	7.4	-5.00

DISTANCE

2-y-o	W-R	Per cent	£1 Level Stake
5f-6f	0-40	0.0	-40.00
7f-8f	0-15	0.0	-15.00
9f-13f	0-0	0.0	0.00
14f+	0-0	0.0	0.00

3-y-o	W-R	Per cent	£1 Level Stake
5f-6f	5-36	13.9	-9.75
7f-8f	4-36	11.1	-3.90
9f-13f	0-11	0.0	-11.00
14f+	0-0	0.0	0.00

4-y-o+	W-R	Per cent	£1 Level Stake
5f-6f	12-63	19.0	-12.38
7f-8f	15-116	12.9	+28.25
9f-13f	3-40	7.5	+11.50
14f+	0-2	0.0	-2.00

Totals	W-R	Per cent	£1 Level Stake
5f-6f	17-139	12.2	-62.13
7f-8f	19-167	11.4	+9.35
9f-13f	3-51	5.9	+0.50
14f+	0-2	0.0	-2.00

TYPE OF RACE

Non-Handicaps

	W-R	Per cent	£1 Level Stake
2-y-o	0-43	0.0	-43.00
3-y-o	4-32	12.5	-3.65
4-y-o+	5-36	13.9	-18.62

Handicaps

	W-R	Per cent	£1 Level Stake
2-y-o	0-12	0.0	-12.00
3-y-o	5-51	9.8	-21.00
4-y-o+	25-185	13.5	+44.00

RACE CLASS

	W-R	Per cent	£1 Level Stake
Class 1	1-24	4.2	-20.00
Class 2	7-36	19.4	-10.02
Class 3	6-18	33.3	+22.50
Class 4	6-75	8.0	+11.25
Class 5	9-115	7.8	-54.75
Class 6	10-89	11.2	-1.25
Class 7	0-2	0.0	-2.00

FIRST TIME OUT

	W-R	Per cent	£1 Level Stake
2-y-o	0-13	0.0	-13.00
3-y-o	3-18	16.7	+15.00
4-y-o+	3-32	9.4	-17.50
Totals	6-63	9.5	-15.50

JOCKEYS

	W-R	Per cent	£1 Level Stake
Robert Winston	21-111	18.9	+20.22
Jack Duern	10-118	8.5	-50.25
Rob Hornby	3-32	9.4	+32.50
Dane O'Neill	1-3	33.3	+8.00
Adam Kirby	1-6	16.7	-1.00
Franny Norton	1-7	14.3	+8.00
Robert Havlin	1-8	12.5	-1.50
Martin Dwyer	1-29	3.4	-25.25

COURSE RECORD

	Total W-R	Non-Hndcps 2-y-o	Non-Hndcps 3-y-o+	Hndcps 2-y-o	Hndcps 3-y-o+	Per cent	£1 Level Stake
Chelmsford (A.W)	11-70	0-4	3-9	0-4	8-53	15.7	-25.02
Lingfield (A.W)	9-45	0-5	1-7	0-2	8-31	20.0	+22.75
Kempton (A.W)	9-68	0-7	3-15	0-1	6-45	13.2	+26.50
Wolvhptn (A.W)	4-49	0-6	1-9	0-2	3-32	8.2	-28.25
Brighton	2-9	0-0	0-0	0-0	2-9	22.2	+28.00
Windsor	2-30	0-7	1-6	0-0	1-17	6.7	-21.25
Goodwood	1-7	0-1	0-0	0-0	1-6	14.3	-2.00
Newmarket	1-7	0-1	0-3	0-0	1-3	14.3	+19.00

WINNING HORSES

Horse	Races Run	1st	2nd	3rd	£
Angel Of The South (IRE)	12	1	3	1	6409
Blaze Of Hearts (IRE)	11	2	0	2	7504
Daddy's Daughter (CAN)	1	1	0	0	5175
Dor's Law	11	1	2	4	3105
Eirene	8	1	1	2	21788
Eljaddaaf (IRE)	14	3	2	2	26287
Flaming Spear (IRE)	6	2	0	0	87770
Lancelot Du Lac (ITY)	8	2	0	0	35160
Lucymai	15	4	2	2	62328
Mimram	10	1	3	2	3105

Nezar (IRE)	11	1	1	2	3752
One Cool Daddy (USA)	2	1	1	0	3881
Soaring Spirits (IRE)	15	3	1	1	9315
Spring Romance (IRE)	7	4	2	0	14361
Tangramm	10	1	2	0	5531
Tropics (USA)	13	3	0	1	51752
Varsovian	10	3	1	1	9962
Villette (IRE)	8	3	0	0	18631
Wotadoll	14	2	5	2	6598
Total winning prize-money					**£382474**
Favourites	**9-24**		**37.5%**		**9.50**

TINA JACKSON

LIVERTON, CLEVELAND

	No. of Hrs	Races Run	1st	2nd	3rd	Unpl	Per cent	£1 Level Stake
2-y-o	*1*	*2*	*0*	*0*	*0*	*2*	*0.0*	*-2.00*
3-y-o	*1*	*4*	*0*	*0*	*0*	*4*	*0.0*	*-4.00*
4-y-o+	*8*	*52*	*3*	*1*	*5*	*43*	*5.8*	*-20.50*
Totals	**10**	**58**	**3**	**1**	**5**	**49**	**5.2**	**-26.50**
2017	*7*	*59*	*7*	*10*	*3*	*38*	*11.9*	*+35.50*
2016	*7*	*36*	*0*	*4*	*4*	*28*	*0.0*	*-36.00*

JOCKEYS

	W-R	Per cent	£1 Level Stake
Nathan Evans	2-14	14.3	+10.00
Sophie Ralston	1-9	11.1	-1.50

COURSE RECORD

	Total W-R	Non-Hndcps 2-y-o	Non-Hndcps 3-y-o+	Hndcps 2-y-o	Hndcps 3-y-o+	Per cent	£1 Level Stake
Wetherby	1-1	0-0	0-0	0-0	1-1	100.0	+14.00
Doncaster	1-4	0-0	0-0	0-0	1-4	25.0	+3.50
Ripon	1-8	0-0	0-1	0-0	1-7	12.5	+1.00

WINNING HORSES

Horse	Races Run	1st	2nd	3rd	£
Point Of Woods	11	1	0	1	3752
Thomas Cranmer (USA)	12	2	1	0	16712
Total winning prize-money					**£20464**
Favourites	**0-4**		**0.0%**		**-4.00**

IAIN JARDINE

CARRUTHERSTOWN, D'FRIES & G'WAY

	No. of Hrs	Races Run	1st	2nd	3rd	Unpl	Per cent	£1 Level Stake
2-y-o	*15*	*71*	*3*	*2*	*6*	*60*	*4.2*	*-25.70*
3-y-o	*20*	*141*	*7*	*22*	*23*	*89*	*5.0*	*-89.67*
4-y-o+	*37*	*247*	*22*	*29*	*31*	*165*	*8.9*	*-96.88*
Totals	**72**	**459**	**32**	**53**	**60**	**314**	**7.0**	**-212.25**
2017	*70*	*430*	*52*	*49*	*46*	*283*	*12.1*	*-90.69*
2016	*46*	*261*	*36*	*31*	*22*	*171*	*13.8*	*+42.50*

BY MONTH

2-y-o	W-R	Per cent	£1 Level Stake	3-y-o	W-R	Per cent	£1 Level Stake
January	0-0	0.0	0.00	January	0-2	0.0	-2.00
February	0-0	0.0	0.00	February	0-2	0.0	-2.00
March	0-0	0.0	0.00	March	0-2	0.0	-2.00
April	0-0	0.0	0.00	April	0-7	0.0	-7.00
May	0-5	0.0	-5.00	May	0-10	0.0	-10.00
June	2-13	15.4	+30.50	June	2-16	12.5	+4.50
July	1-8	12.5	-6.20	July	2-20	10.0	-8.50
August	0-12	0.0	-12.00	August	1-22	4.5	-14.00
September	0-13	0.0	-13.00	September	2-28	7.1	-16.67
October	0-16	0.0	-16.00	October	0-22	0.0	-22.00
November	0-2	0.0	-2.00	November	0-6	0.0	-6.00
December	0-2	0.0	-2.00	December	0-4	0.0	-4.00

4-y-o+	W-R	Per cent	£1 Level Stake	Totals	W-R	Per cent	£1 Level Stake
January	1-19	5.3	-13.00	January	1-21	4.8	-15.00
February	1-11	9.1	-3.50	February	1-13	7.7	-5.50
March	1-10	10.0	-1.50	March	1-12	8.3	-3.50
April	1-8	12.5	-5.25	April	1-15	6.7	-12.25
May	1-32	3.1	-28.50	May	1-47	2.1	-43.50
June	4-38	10.5	-13.38	June	8-67	11.9	+21.62
July	4-28	14.3	-4.75	July	7-56	12.5	-19.45
August	4-37	10.8	-6.50	August	5-71	7.0	-32.50
September	3-30	10.0	-2.00	September	5-71	7.0	-31.67
October	1-21	4.8	-14.50	October	1-59	1.7	-52.50
November	1-7	14.3	+2.00	November	1-15	6.7	-4.00
December	0-6	0.0	-6.00	December	0-12	0.0	-10.00

DISTANCE

2-y-o	W-R	Per cent	£1 Level Stake	3-y-o	W-R	Per cent	£1 Level Stake
5f-6f	3-48	6.3	-2.70	5f-6f	4-69	5.8	-47.00
7f-8f	0-23	0.0	-23.00	7f-8f	1-45	2.2	-37.00
9f-13f	0-0	0.0	0.00	9f-13f	2-27	7.4	-5.67
14f+	0-0	0.0	0.00	14f+	0-0	0.0	0.00

4-y-o+	W-R	Per cent	£1 Level Stake	Totals	W-R	Per cent	£1 Level Stake
5f-6f	3-26	11.5	-9.00	5f-6f	10-143	7.0	-58.70
7f-8f	8-66	12.1	-1.50	7f-8f	9-134	6.7	-61.50
9f-13f	6-109	5.5	-67.50	9f-13f	8-136	5.9	-73.17
14f+	5-46	10.9	-18.88	14f+	5-46	10.9	-18.88

TYPE OF RACE

Non-Handicaps	W-R	Per cent	£1 Level Stake	Handicaps	W-R	Per cent	£1 Level Stake
2-y-o	3-56	5.4	-10.70	2-y-o	0-15	0.0	-15.00
3-y-o	0-23	0.0	-23.00	3-y-o	7-118	5.9	-66.67
4-y-o+	0-12	0.0	-12.00	4-y-o+	22-235	9.4	-84.88

RACE CLASS / FIRST TIME OUT

RACE CLASS	W-R	Per cent	£1 Level Stake	FIRST TIME OUT	W-R	Per cent	£1 Level Stake
Class 1	0-3	0.0	-3.00	2-y-o	0-15	0.0	-15.00

Class 2	2-26	7.7	-14.50
Class 3	4-40	10.0	-4.88
Class 4	14-90	15.6	+19.38
Class 5	5-163	3.1	-123.00
Class 6	7-136	5.1	-85.25
Class 7	0-1	0.0	-1.00

3-y-o	1-20	5.0	-3.00
4-y-o+	0-37	0.0	-37.00
Totals	1-72	1.4	-55.00

JOCKEYS

	W-R	Per cent	£1 Level Stake
Jamie Gormley	14-172	8.1	-80.12
Joe Fanning	8-32	25.0	+12.88
Phillip Makin	2-14	14.3	-4.50
Andrew Mullen	2-29	6.9	+20.00
Jason Watson	1-2	50.0	+5.00
Adam Kirby	1-3	33.3	+3.50
Kieran O'Neill	1-3	33.3	+14.00
Miss Serena Brotherton	1-4	25.0	+2.50
Tom Eaves	1-15	6.7	-5.00
Callum Rodriguez	1-23	4.3	-18.50

COURSE RECORD

	Total W-R	Non-Hndcps 2-y-o	Non-Hndcps 3-y-o+	Hndcps 2-y-o	Hndcps 3-y-o+	Per cent	£1 Level Stake
Ayr	6-70	0-7	0-5	0-2	6-56	8.6	-26.00
Haydock	4-17	0-1	0-0	0-0	4-16	23.5	+8.50
Hamilton	4-59	2-9	0-3	0-2	2-45	6.8	-44.20
Musselburgh	3-51	0-8	0-2	0-1	3-40	5.9	-33.63
Newcastle (A.W)	3-69	0-4	0-7	0-3	3-55	4.3	-48.75
Chester	2-12	0-0	0-0	0-0	2-12	16.7	-4.17
Doncaster	2-14	1-1	0-1	0-0	1-12	14.3	+44.00
Wolvhptn (A.W)	2-22	0-0	0-3	0-0	2-19	9.1	-6.50
Carlisle	2-22	0-2	0-1	0-0	2-19	9.1	-4.00
Chelmsford (A.W)	1-5	0-0	0-0	0-1	1-4	20.0	+2.00
Southwell (A.W)	1-15	0-0	0-4	0-0	1-11	6.7	-9.00
Thirsk	1-16	0-4	0-1	0-1	1-10	6.3	-9.50
Catterick	1-20	0-3	0-1	0-0	1-16	5.0	-14.00

WINNING HORSES

Horse	Races Run	1st	2nd	3rd	£
Akkadian Empire	9	1	2	0	3105
Alemaratalyoum (IRE)	10	4	1	0	45963
Archipeligo	18	1	1	0	3105
Bedrock	6	1	1	0	12450
Falmouth Light (FR)	7	1	1	2	7763
Golden Jeffrey (SWI)	5	1	1	0	5693
Hediddodinthe (IRE)*	6	1	1	0	3105
I Believe In You	7	2	1	1	10868
Jabbaar	14	2	5	6	11612
Marnie James	8	3	1	2	44240
Mcoring	13	2	1	4	10286
Must See The Doc	4	1	0	0	4787
Newmarket Warrior (IRE)	14	2	2	1	10318
Smugglers Creek (IRE)	17	2	1	2	7245
Something Brewing (FR)	10	1	0	1	3493
Stone The Crows	6	1	0	1	7439
Super Florence (IRE)	14	1	4	3	5111
Thorntoun Care*	10	1	0	4	3369
Tor	9	1	1	1	8022
Yes You (IRE)	11	3	1	1	15590
Total winning prize-money					**£223572**

Favourites	**16-56**	**28.6%**	**-17.11**

WILLIAM JARVIS

NEWMARKET, SUFFOLK

	No. of Hrs	Races Run	1st	2nd	3rd	Unpl	Per cent	£1 Level Stake
2-y-o	*7*	*26*	*3*	*1*	*3*	*19*	*11.5*	*-6.00*
3-y-o	*8*	*39*	*11*	*5*	*7*	*16*	*28.2*	*+62.95*
4-y-o+	*7*	*34*	*1*	*3*	*8*	*22*	*2.9*	*-31.13*
Totals	**22**	**99**	**15**	**9**	**18**	**57**	**15.2**	**+25.82**
2017	*21*	*92*	*7*	*9*	*11*	*65*	*7.6*	*-32.10*
2016	*21*	*93*	*11*	*9*	*15*	*58*	*11.8*	*+13.25*

BY MONTH

2-y-o	W-R	Per cent	£1 Level Stake
January	0-0	0.0	0.00
February	0-0	0.0	0.00
March	0-0	0.0	0.00
April	0-1	0.0	-1.00
May	0-1	0.0	-1.00
June	0-3	0.0	-3.00
July	1-3	33.3	+4.00
August	0-5	0.0	-5.00
September	0-4	0.0	-4.00
October	1-5	20.0	-2.00
November	1-3	33.3	+7.00
December	0-1	0.0	-1.00

3-y-o	W-R	Per cent	£1 Level Stake
January	0-1	0.0	-1.00
February	0-1	0.0	-1.00
March	0-1	0.0	-1.00
April	1-3	33.3	+12.00
May	2-6	33.3	+35.00
June	2-8	25.0	+11.75
July	2-3	66.7	+4.50
August	2-6	33.3	+0.20
September	1-3	33.3	+2.00
October	0-0	0.0	0.00
November	1-5	20.0	+2.50
December	0-2	0.0	-2.00

4-y-o+	W-R	Per cent	£1 Level Stake
January	1-5	20.0	-2.13
February	0-3	0.0	-3.00
March	0-1	0.0	-1.00
April	0-3	0.0	-3.00
May	0-5	0.0	-5.00
June	0-5	0.0	-5.00
July	0-2	0.0	-2.00
August	0-2	0.0	-2.00
September	0-2	0.0	-2.00
October	0-2	0.0	-2.00
November	0-2	0.0	-2.00
December	0-2	0.0	-2.00

Totals	W-R	Per cent	£1 Level Stake
January	1-6	16.7	-3.13
February	0-4	0.0	-4.00
March	0-2	0.0	-2.00
April	1-7	14.3	+8.00
May	2-12	16.7	+29.00
June	2-16	12.5	+3.75
July	3-8	37.5	+6.50
August	2-13	15.4	-6.80
September	1-9	11.1	-4.00
October	1-7	14.3	-4.00
November	2-10	20.0	+0.50
December	0-5	0.0	-4.00

DISTANCE

2-y-o	W-R	Per cent	£1 Level Stake
5f-6f	2-18	11.1	-8.00
7f-8f	1-8	12.5	+2.00
9f-13f	0-0	0.0	0.00
14f+	0-0	0.0	0.00

3-y-o	W-R	Per cent	£1 Level Stake
5f-6f	1-5	20.0	+10.00
7f-8f	4-21	19.0	+18.70
9f-13f	6-13	46.2	+34.25
14f+	0-0	0.0	0.00

4-y-o+	W-R	Per cent	£1 Level Stake
5f-6f	0-2	0.0	-2.00

Totals	W-R	Per cent	£1 Level Stake
5f-6f	3-25	12.0	0.00

7f-8f	0-11	0.0	-11.00	7f-8f	5-40	12.5	+9.70
9f-13f	1-19	5.3	-16.13	9f-13f	7-32	21.9	+18.12
14f+	0-2	0.0	-2.00	14f+	0-2	0.0	-2.00

TYPE OF RACE

Non-Handicaps	W-R	Per cent	£1 Level Stake	Handicaps	W-R	Per cent	£1 Level Stake
2-y-o	0-18	0.0	-18.00	2-y-o	3-8	37.5	+12.00
3-y-o	2-18	11.1	+12.00	3-y-o	9-21	42.9	+50.95
4-y-o+	0-3	0.0	-3.00	4-y-o+	1-31	3.2	-28.13

RACE CLASS

	W-R	Per cent	£1 Level Stake
Class 1	1-6	16.7	+9.00
Class 2	1-9	11.1	-6.25
Class 3	2-7	28.6	+12.00
Class 4	5-32	15.6	-7.43
Class 5	5-30	16.7	+16.50
Class 6	1-15	6.7	+2.00
Class 7	0-0	0.0	0.00

FIRST TIME OUT

	W-R	Per cent	£1 Level Stake
2-y-o	0-7	0.0	-7.00
3-y-o	1-8	12.5	+7.00
4-y-o+	1-7	14.3	-4.13
Totals	2-22	9.1	-4.13

JOCKEYS

	W-R	Per cent	£1 Level Stake
Silvestre De Sousa	3-9	33.3	+3.00
Kieran Shoemark	3-10	30.0	+33.75
Josephine Gordon	3-31	9.7	-9.80
Eoin Walsh	2-4	50.0	+16.50
Robert Havlin	1-1	100.0	+1.88
Andrew Breslin	1-3	33.3	+4.00
Luke Morris	1-4	25.0	+6.00
David Probert	1-9	11.1	-1.50

COURSE RECORD

	Total W-R	Non-Hndcps 2-y-o	Non-Hndcps 3-y-o+	Hndcps 2-y-o	Hndcps 3-y-o+	Per cent	£1 Level Stake
Sandown	3-5	0-1	0-0	0-0	3-4	60.0	+8.00
Bath	2-2	0-0	1-1	1-1	0-0	100.0	+16.00
Catterick	1-1	0-0	0-0	1-1	0-0	100.0	+6.00
Chester	1-1	0-0	1-1	0-0	0-0	100.0	+14.00
Nottingham	1-2	0-1	0-0	1-1	0-0	50.0	+8.00
Epsom	1-3	0-0	0-0	0-0	1-3	33.3	-0.80
Windsor	1-4	0-1	0-1	0-0	1-2	25.0	-0.50
Newmarket	1-6	0-0	0-1	0-1	1-4	16.7	+20.00
Chelmsford (A.W)	1-8	0-1	0-1	0-0	1-6	12.5	-5.13
Newmkt (Jly)	1-10	0-3	0-0	0-1	1-6	10.0	-7.25
Kempton (A.W)	1-14	0-3	0-2	0-1	1-8	7.1	-6.50
Yarmouth	1-14	0-3	0-0	0-1	1-10	7.1	+3.00

WINNING HORSES

Horse	Races Run	1st	2nd	3rd	£
Arigato	9	3	2	2	15526
Chief Ironside	7	2	0	3	28000
Knight Errant (IRE)	8	4	0	1	22664
Lady Katy	6	1	0	1	6728
Michaels Choice	5	1	0	1	3752
Mrs Gallagher	4	1	0	0	22684
Queen Constantine (GER)	6	1	1	1	3881
*Rampant Lion (IRE)	3	1	1	1	6469
Wimpole Hall	9	1	0	4	5693
Total winning prize-money					**£115397**
Favourites	**5-13**		**38.5%**		**1.32**

J R JENKINS

ROYSTON, HERTS

	No. of Hrs	Races Run	1st	2nd	3rd	Unpl	Per cent	£1 Level Stake
2-y-o	*2*	*5*	*0*	*0*	*0*	*5*	*0.0*	*-5.00*
3-y-o	*7*	*34*	*5*	*1*	*3*	*25*	*14.7*	*+9.25*
4-y-o+	*27*	*129*	*6*	*10*	*13*	*100*	*4.7*	*-93.25*
Totals	**36**	**168**	**11**	**11**	**16**	**130**	**6.5**	**-89.00**
2017	*36*	*217*	*6*	*11*	*18*	*182*	*2.8*	*-178.25*
2016	*37*	*262*	*17*	*20*	*28*	*196*	*6.5*	*-72.50*

BY MONTH

2-y-o	W-R	Per cent	£1 Level Stake	3-y-o	W-R	Per cent	£1 Level Stake
January	0-0	0.0	0.00	January	1-2	50.0	+19.00
February	0-0	0.0	0.00	February	0-3	0.0	-3.00
March	0-0	0.0	0.00	March	0-1	0.0	-1.00
April	0-0	0.0	0.00	April	1-2	50.0	+1.25
May	0-0	0.0	0.00	May	0-3	0.0	-3.00
June	0-0	0.0	0.00	June	0-3	0.0	-3.00
July	0-0	0.0	0.00	July	0-4	0.0	-4.00
August	0-0	0.0	0.00	August	2-4	50.0	+7.00
September	0-0	0.0	0.00	September	0-4	0.0	-4.00
October	0-2	0.0	-2.00	October	0-3	0.0	-3.00
November	0-1	0.0	-1.00	November	1-3	33.3	+5.00
December	0-2	0.0	-2.00	December	0-2	0.0	-2.00

4-y-o+	W-R	Per cent	£1 Level Stake	Totals	W-R	Per cent	£1 Level Stake
January	1-13	7.7	-7.50	January	2-15	13.3	+11.50
February	0-11	0.0	-11.00	February	0-14	0.0	-14.00
March	2-14	14.3	-4.25	March	2-15	13.3	-5.25
April	0-14	0.0	-14.00	April	1-16	6.3	-12.75
May	0-16	0.0	-16.00	May	0-19	0.0	-19.00
June	0-10	0.0	-10.00	June	0-13	0.0	-13.00
July	0-15	0.0	-15.00	July	0-19	0.0	-19.00
August	0-7	0.0	-7.00	August	2-11	18.2	0.00
September	0-3	0.0	-3.00	September	0-7	0.0	-7.00
October	2-9	22.2	+6.50	October	2-14	14.3	+1.50
November	1-10	10.0	-5.00	November	2-14	14.3	0.00
December	0-7	0.0	-7.00	December	0-11	0.0	-9.00

DISTANCE

2-y-o	W-R	Per cent	£1 Level Stake	3-y-o	W-R	Per cent	£1 Level Stake
5f-6f	0-1	0.0	-1.00	5f-6f	4-23	17.4	+12.25
7f-8f	0-4	0.0	-4.00	7f-8f	1-7	14.3	+1.00
9f-13f	0-0	0.0	0.00	9f-13f	0-4	0.0	-4.00

14f+	0-0	0.0	0.00	14f+	0-0	0.0	0.00
4-y-o+	W-R	Per cent	£1 Level Stake	**Totals**	W-R	Per cent	£1 Level Stake
5f-6f	0-32	0.0	-32.00	5f-6f	4-56	7.1	-20.75
7f-8f	1-45	2.2	-40.00	7f-8f	2-56	3.6	-43.00
9f-13f	4-48	8.3	-22.75	9f-13f	4-52	7.7	-26.75
14f+	1-4	25.0	+1.50	14f+	1-4	25.0	+1.50

TYPE OF RACE

Non-Handicaps	W-R	Per cent	£1 Level Stake	Handicaps	W-R	Per cent	£1 Level Stake
2-y-o	0-5	0.0	-5.00	2-y-o	0-0	0.0	0.00
3-y-o	0-9	0.0	-9.00	3-y-o	5-25	20.0	+18.25
4-y-o+	0-12	0.0	-12.00	4-y-o+	6-117	5.1	-81.25

RACE CLASS

	W-R	Per cent	£1 Level Stake
Class 1	0-0	0.0	0.00
Class 2	0-0	0.0	0.00
Class 3	0-0	0.0	0.00
Class 4	0-0	0.0	0.00
Class 5	0-39	0.0	-39.00
Class 6	10-118	8.5	-42.75
Class 7	1-11	9.1	-7.25

FIRST TIME OUT

	W-R	Per cent	£1 Level Stake
2-y-o	0-2	0.0	-2.00
3-y-o	1-7	14.3	+14.00
4-y-o+	1-27	3.7	-21.50
Totals	2-36	5.6	-9.50

JOCKEYS

	W-R	Per cent	£1 Level Stake
David Probert	6-15	40.0	+24.50
Franny Norton	3-18	16.7	+10.00
Martin Harley	1-7	14.3	-1.50
Kieren Fox	1-13	7.7	-7.00

COURSE RECORD

	Total W-R	Non-Hndcps 2-y-o	Non-Hndcps 3-y-o+	Hndcps 2-y-o	Hndcps 3-y-o+	Per cent	£1 Level Stake
Kempton (A.W)	6-39	0-3	0-3	0-0	6-33	15.4	+9.75
Chelmsford (A.W)	4-27	0-0	0-1	0-0	4-26	14.8	-2.25
Lingfield (A.W)	1-30	0-1	0-3	0-0	1-26	3.3	-24.50

WINNING HORSES

Horse	Races Run	1st	2nd	3rd	£
Carvelas (IRE)	16	2	1	3	6922
Chloellie	11	5	1	0	15914
Karam Albaari (IRE)	12	1	1	1	3105
Tilsworth Lukey	13	1	3	3	2588
Wally's Wisdom*	3	1	0	0	3105
Zahirah	11	1	1	2	3105
Total winning prize-money					**£34739**
Favourites	**3-7**		**42.9%**		**5.50**

LINDA JEWELL

SUTTON VALENCE, KENT

	No. of Hrs	Races Run	1st	2nd	3rd	Unpl	Per cent	£1 Level Stake
2-y-o	*1*	*2*	*0*	*0*	*1*	*1*	*0.0*	*-2.00*
3-y-o	*2*	*9*	*0*	*0*	*0*	*9*	*0.0*	*-9.00*
4-y-o+	*1*	*8*	*3*	*0*	*1*	*4*	*37.5*	*+9.50*
Totals	**4**	**19**	**3**	**0**	**2**	**14**	**15.8**	**-1.50**
2017	*4*	*16*	*1*	*1*	*1*	*13*	*6.3*	*+1.00*
2016	*6*	*25*	*1*	*1*	*4*	*19*	*4.0*	*-14.00*

JOCKEYS

	W-R	Per cent	£1 Level Stake
Robert Winston	3-6	50.0	+11.50

COURSE RECORD

	Total W-R	Non-Hndcps 2-y-o	Non-Hndcps 3-y-o+	Hndcps 2-y-o	Hndcps 3-y-o+	Per cent	£1 Level Stake
Newbury	1-1	0-0	0-0	0-0	1-1	100.0	+4.50
Chelmsford (A.W)	1-2	0-0	0-0	0-0	1-2	50.0	+2.00
Kempton (A.W)	1-3	0-1	0-0	0-0	1-2	33.3	+5.00

WINNING HORSES

Horse	Races Run	1st	2nd	3rd	£
Breden (IRE)	8	3	0	1	26480
Total winning prize-money					**£26480**
Favourites	**0-1**		**0.0%**		**-1.00**

BRETT JOHNSON

EPSOM, SURREY

	No. of Hrs	Races Run	1st	2nd	3rd	Unpl	Per cent	£1 Level Stake
2-y-o	*1*	*3*	*0*	*0*	*0*	*3*	*0.0*	*-3.00*
3-y-o	*1*	*2*	*0*	*0*	*0*	*2*	*0.0*	*-2.00*
4-y-o+	*12*	*74*	*11*	*14*	*6*	*43*	*14.9*	*+16.75*
Totals	**14**	**79**	**11**	**14**	**6**	**48**	**13.9**	**+11.75**
2017	*13*	*68*	*6*	*4*	*10*	*48*	*8.8*	*+1.13*
2016	*12*	*43*	*2*	*1*	*0*	*40*	*4.7*	*-27.00*

BY MONTH

2-y-o	W-R	Per cent	£1 Level Stake	**3-y-o**	W-R	Per cent	£1 Level Stake
January	0-0	0.0	0.00	January	0-0	0.0	0.00
February	0-0	0.0	0.00	February	0-0	0.0	0.00
March	0-0	0.0	0.00	March	0-0	0.0	0.00
April	0-0	0.0	0.00	April	0-0	0.0	0.00
May	0-0	0.0	0.00	May	0-0	0.0	0.00
June	0-0	0.0	0.00	June	0-0	0.0	0.00
July	0-0	0.0	0.00	July	0-0	0.0	0.00
August	0-0	0.0	0.00	August	0-0	0.0	0.00
September	0-1	0.0	-1.00	September	0-0	0.0	0.00
October	0-1	0.0	-1.00	October	0-0	0.0	0.00

	W-R	Per cent	£1 Level Stake
November	0-1	0.0	-1.00
December	0-0	0.0	0.00

	W-R	Per cent	£1 Level Stake
November	0-0	0.0	0.00
December	0-2	0.0	-2.00

4-y-o+	W-R	Per cent	£1 Level Stake
January	2-7	28.6	+23.00
February	1-8	12.5	-2.50
March	2-7	28.6	+11.50
April	2-8	25.0	+2.50
May	2-5	40.0	+8.00
June	0-9	0.0	-9.00
July	0-5	0.0	-5.00
August	0-2	0.0	-2.00
September	1-3	33.3	+7.00
October	0-8	0.0	-8.00
November	0-6	0.0	-6.00
December	1-6	16.7	-2.75

Totals	W-R	Per cent	£1 Level Stake
January	2-7	28.6	+23.00
February	1-8	12.5	-2.50
March	2-7	28.6	+11.50
April	2-8	25.0	+2.50
May	2-5	40.0	+8.00
June	0-9	0.0	-9.00
July	0-5	0.0	-5.00
August	0-2	0.0	-2.00
September	1-4	25.0	+6.00
October	0-9	0.0	-9.00
November	0-7	0.0	-6.00
December	1-8	12.5	-4.75

DISTANCE

2-y-o	W-R	Per cent	£1 Level Stake
5f-6f	0-0	0.0	0.00
7f-8f	0-3	0.0	-3.00
9f-13f	0-0	0.0	0.00
14f+	0-0	0.0	0.00

3-y-o	W-R	Per cent	£1 Level Stake
5f-6f	0-0	0.0	0.00
7f-8f	0-1	0.0	-1.00
9f-13f	0-1	0.0	-1.00
14f+	0-0	0.0	0.00

4-y-o+	W-R	Per cent	£1 Level Stake
5f-6f	2-14	14.3	+4.50
7f-8f	3-30	10.0	-5.50
9f-13f	6-22	27.3	+25.75
14f+	0-8	0.0	-8.00

Totals	W-R	Per cent	£1 Level Stake
5f-6f	2-14	14.3	+4.50
7f-8f	3-34	8.8	-9.50
9f-13f	6-23	26.1	+24.75
14f+	0-8	0.0	-8.00

TYPE OF RACE

Non-Handicaps

	W-R	Per cent	£1 Level Stake
2-y-o	0-3	0.0	-3.00
3-y-o	0-2	0.0	-2.00
4-y-o+	1-8	12.5	-5.50

Handicaps

	W-R	Per cent	£1 Level Stake
2-y-o	0-0	0.0	0.00
3-y-o	0-0	0.0	0.00
4-y-o+	10-66	15.2	+22.25

RACE CLASS

	W-R	Per cent	£1 Level Stake
Class 1	0-0	0.0	0.00
Class 2	0-2	0.0	-2.00
Class 3	0-0	0.0	0.00
Class 4	2-17	11.8	-2.50
Class 5	4-23	17.4	+19.50
Class 6	5-37	13.5	-3.25
Class 7	0-0	0.0	0.00

FIRST TIME OUT

	W-R	Per cent	£1 Level Stake
2-y-o	0-1	0.0	-1.00
3-y-o	0-1	0.0	-1.00
4-y-o+	3-12	25.0	+23.00
Totals	3-14	21.4	+21.00

JOCKEYS

	W-R	Per cent	£1 Level Stake
Callum Shepherd	8-36	22.2	+41.00
Rossa Ryan	2-12	16.7	-1.50
Ray Dawson	1-1	100.0	+2.25

COURSE RECORD

	Total W-R	Non-Hndcps 2-y-o	Non-Hndcps 3-y-o+	Hndcps 2-y-o	Hndcps 3-y-o+	Per cent	£1 Level Stake
Lingfield (A.W)	5-16	0-0	1-3	0-0	4-13	31.3	+24.25
Kempton (A.W)	2-32	0-2	0-5	0-0	2-25	6.3	-10.00
Wolvhptn (A.W)	1-3	0-0	0-1	0-0	1-2	33.3	+7.00
Windsor	1-5	0-0	0-0	0-0	1-5	20.0	+3.00
Lingfield	1-7	0-0	0-0	0-0	1-7	14.3	-2.00
Chelmsford (A.W)	1-8	0-0	0-1	0-0	1-7	12.5	-2.50

WINNING HORSES

Horse	Races Run	1st	2nd	3rd	£
Cayuga	7	3	1	0	10609
Compton Abbey*	4	1	0	0	3105
Dangerous Ends	5	1	1	0	3752
Jackblack	4	1	0	0	3105
Lacan (IRE)	11	2	1	1	12162
Rakematiz	8	2	3	1	6275
Very Honest (IRE)	10	1	2	1	3752
Total winning prize-money					**£42760**
Favourites	**2-8**		**25.0%**		**-2.25**

MARK JOHNSTON

MIDDLEHAM MOOR, N YORKS

	No. of Hrs	Races Run	1st	2nd	3rd	Unpl	Per cent	£1 Level Stake
2-y-o	*103*	*461*	*84*	*56*	*61*	*258*	*18.2*	*-134.04*
3-y-o	*95*	*676*	*102*	*97*	*109*	*368*	*15.1*	*-139.23*
4-y-o+	*29*	*303*	*40*	*38*	*33*	*191*	*13.2*	*-65.90*
Totals	**227**	**1440**	**226**	**191**	**203**	**817**	**15.7**	**-339.17**
2017	*217*	*1379*	*215*	*187*	*164*	*807*	*15.6*	*-223.79*
2016	*237*	*1413*	*195*	*206*	*175*	*836*	*13.8*	*-317.31*

BY MONTH

2-y-o	W-R	Per cent	£1 Level Stake
January	0-0	0.0	0.00
February	0-0	0.0	0.00
March	0-3	0.0	-3.00
April	3-13	23.1	-3.00
May	13-41	31.7	+5.95
June	18-63	28.6	-5.53
July	16-61	26.2	-1.51
August	12-68	17.6	-17.65
September	12-86	14.0	-34.11
October	5-79	6.3	-55.44
November	2-34	5.9	-17.25
December	3-13	23.1	-2.50

3-y-o	W-R	Per cent	£1 Level Stake
January	3-20	15.0	-10.90
February	1-18	5.6	-14.75
March	9-47	19.1	-3.63
April	4-40	10.0	-16.15
May	17-104	16.3	-13.47
June	19-116	16.4	-24.77
July	22-116	19.0	-14.05
August	8-79	10.1	-41.50
September	7-63	11.1	-15.13
October	7-44	15.9	+24.80
November	2-17	11.8	-5.00
December	3-12	25.0	-4.68

4-y-o+	W-R	Per cent	£1 Level Stake
January	3-9	33.3	+5.25
February	6-14	42.9	+19.63
March	2-30	6.7	-20.50
April	3-20	15.0	0.00
May	8-55	14.5	-11.25
June	7-53	13.2	-23.27

Totals	W-R	Per cent	£1 Level Stake
January	6-29	20.7	-5.65
February	7-32	21.9	+4.88
March	11-80	13.8	-27.13
April	10-73	13.7	-19.15
May	38-200	19.0	-18.77
June	44-232	19.0	-53.57

July	4-30	13.3	-1.25
August	4-38	10.5	+5.00
September	1-25	4.0	-21.25
October	0-16	0.0	-16.00
November	2-7	28.6	+3.75
December	0-6	0.0	-6.00

July	42-207	20.3	-16.81
August	24-185	13.0	-54.15
September	20-174	11.5	-70.49
October	12-139	8.6	-46.64
November	6-58	10.3	-1.25
December	6-31	19.4	-10.68

DISTANCE

2-y-o	W-R	Per cent	£1 Level Stake
5f-6f	36-184	19.6	-45.61
7f-8f	45-250	18.0	-73.91
9f-13f	3-27	11.1	-14.52
14f+	0-0	0.0	0.00

3-y-o	W-R	Per cent	£1 Level Stake
5f-6f	6-65	9.2	-38.17
7f-8f	38-260	14.6	-82.39
9f-13f	52-310	16.8	-11.74
14f+	6-41	14.6	-6.93

4-y-o+	W-R	Per cent	£1 Level Stake
5f-6f	0-8	0.0	-8.00
7f-8f	14-90	15.6	-6.27
9f-13f	14-124	11.3	-21.50
14f+	12-81	14.8	-30.13

Totals	W-R	Per cent	£1 Level Stake
5f-6f	42-257	16.3	-91.78
7f-8f	97-600	16.2	-162.57
9f-13f	69-461	15.0	-47.76
14f+	18-122	14.8	-37.06

TYPE OF RACE

Non-Handicaps	W-R	Per cent	£1 Level Stake
2-y-o	72-352	20.5	-78.76
3-y-o	24-158	15.2	-51.07
4-y-o+	3-29	10.3	-18.88

Handicaps	W-R	Per cent	£1 Level Stake
2-y-o	12-109	11.0	-55.28
3-y-o	78-518	15.1	-88.16
4-y-o+	37-274	13.5	-47.02

RACE CLASS

	W-R	Per cent	£1 Level Stake
Class 1	12-106	11.3	-54.94
Class 2	35-289	12.1	-73.07
Class 3	32-169	18.9	-24.15
Class 4	65-375	17.3	-87.64
Class 5	66-394	16.8	-89.80
Class 6	16-107	15.0	-9.56
Class 7	0-0	0.0	0.00

FIRST TIME OUT

	W-R	Per cent	£1 Level Stake
2-y-o	18-103	17.5	-18.70
3-y-o	11-95	11.6	-48.83
4-y-o+	3-29	10.3	-14.50
Totals	32-227	14.1	-82.03

JOCKEYS

	W-R	Per cent	£1 Level Stake
Joe Fanning	55-360	15.3	-107.95
Franny Norton	49-318	15.4	-93.16
P J McDonald	34-210	16.2	-49.98
Silvestre De Sousa	28-135	20.7	-10.11
James Doyle	8-32	25.0	-2.74
Oliver Stammers	6-48	12.5	+0.25
Adam Kirby	5-21	23.8	0.45
William Buick	5-37	13.5	-19.00
Andrew Breslin	5-39	12.8	-3.00
Ryan Moore	4-19	21.1	-6.38
Richard Kingscote	4-24	16.7	-7.75
Jason Hart	3-27	11.1	+11.50
Jack Mitchell	2-5	40.0	+3.00
Frankie Dettori	2-7	28.6	+16.10
Jane Elliott	2-8	25.0	+12.00
Dane O'Neill	2-10	20.0	+3.00
Harry Bentley	2-13	15.4	-5.50
J F Egan	2-17	11.8	-8.17
Daniel Tudhope	1-4	25.0	-2.43
C Y Ho	1-5	20.0	+2.00
Sharna Armstrong	1-5	20.0	+1.50
Oisin Murphy	1-8	12.5	-5.90
Andrea Atzeni	1-8	12.5	+2.00
David Probert	1-8	12.5	-2.50
Andrew Mullen	1-9	11.1	-5.50
Jim Crowley	1-10	10.0	-7.00

COURSE RECORD

	Total W-R	Non-Hndcps 2-y-o	Non-Hndcps 3-y-o+	Hndcps 2-y-o	Hndcps 3-y-o+	Per cent	£1 Level Stake
Chelmsford (A.W)	22-111	5-22	4-12	1-6	12-71	19.8	+5.81
Lingfield (A.W)	15-67	3-5	4-22	2-4	6-36	22.4	+10.15
Goodwood	12-71	4-16	1-9	0-5	7-41	16.9	-24.67
Haydock	11-59	4-18	0-3	0-0	7-38	18.6	+2.03
Bath	10-23	4-9	0-2	0-0	6-12	43.5	+4.96
York	10-51	5-14	1-6	0-4	4-27	19.6	+26.35
Wolvhptn (A.W)	10-100	1-21	2-9	2-13	5-57	10.0	-35.72
Musselburgh	9-37	3-10	0-1	0-0	6-26	24.3	+25.43
Doncaster	8-39	5-15	0-3	1-5	2-16	20.5	-1.75
Beverley	8-46	6-15	1-4	0-1	1-26	17.4	-24.44
Newmkt (Jly)	7-43	1-10	0-3	1-3	5-27	16.3	-11.67
Hamilton	7-44	1-10	1-6	0-2	5-26	15.9	-10.08
Chester	7-45	3-9	0-6	0-2	4-28	15.6	-13.38
Windsor	6-20	4-6	0-1	0-1	2-12	30.0	+2.83
Epsom	6-24	3-5	1-5	0-1	2-13	25.0	-2.59
Pontefract	6-37	1-10	3-13	1-2	1-12	16.2	-17.94
Nottingham	6-41	2-13	0-6	1-6	3-16	14.6	-20.43
Newmarket	6-51	2-17	3-10	0-7	1-17	11.8	-15.88
Southwell (A.W)	5-23	0-1	0-4	0-2	5-16	21.7	+5.25
Leicester	5-26	2-7	0-1	0-3	3-15	19.2	-5.31
Kempton (A.W)	5-54	2-16	1-6	1-9	1-23	9.3	-40.17
Newcastle (A.W)	5-83	0-17	1-16	1-12	3-38	6.0	-63.71
Carlisle	4-21	0-8	1-2	0-0	3-11	19.0	-5.50
Newbury	4-22	2-5	0-5	0-0	2-12	18.2	-1.90
Yarmouth	4-22	2-4	0-1	1-3	1-14	18.2	-6.55
Redcar	4-24	0-6	1-1	0-1	3-16	16.7	-1.70
Ripon	4-35	0-4	0-6	0-0	4-25	11.4	+1.00
Ascot	4-52	3-11	0-8	0-1	1-32	7.7	-24.50
Catterick	3-30	2-6	0-1	0-7	1-16	10.0	-18.50
Ayr	3-34	0-9	1-4	0-1	2-20	8.8	-24.17
Salisbury	2-11	0-4	1-3	0-1	1-3	18.2	-4.50
Chepstow	2-12	0-3	0-0	0-0	2-9	16.7	-0.50
Thirsk	2-17	1-5	0-3	0-4	1-5	11.8	-7.75
Brighton	2-24	0-9	0-0	0-1	2-14	8.3	-14.67
Wetherby	1-5	0-1	0-0	0-0	1-4	20.0	+7.00
Sandown	1-26	1-10	0-2	0-1	0-13	3.8	-22.00

WINNING HORSES

Horse	Races Run	1st	2nd	3rd	£
Abareeq	5	1	1	0	7763
Accordance	4	1	2	0	15753
Aclimatise	9	2	1	1	23288

Addicted To You (IRE)	2	1	0	0	8345
Alhawdaj (USA)	1	1	0	0	3881
Angelina D'Or (GER)*	7	1	2	3	3105
Aquarium	22	5	2	4	43265
Arctic Sound	6	4	1	0	50608
Aussie View (IRE)	7	1	2	1	3752
Austin Powers (IRE)	6	1	1	3	3752
Austrian School (IRE)	11	2	5	2	19137
Axel Jacklin	11	1	1	1	3170
Baghdad (FR)	3	2	0	1	68056
Baileys Excelerate (FR)	3	1	0	0	10583
Bayshore Freeway (IRE)	9	3	2	3	23936
Big Kitten (USA)*	1	1	0	0	3752
Blown By Wind	7	3	1	0	23965
Book Of Dreams (IRE)	7	3	0	0	40540
Branscombe	13	2	4	1	8539
Burgonet	6	3	2	0	25000
Cape Islay (FR)	5	2	1	1	10350
Cardsharp	10	1	0	1	31191
Chapelli	7	2	0	1	14491
Charles Kingsley	2	1	0	0	5434
Claramara (IRE)	7	1	1	2	3105
Communique (IRE)	14	5	2	1	178919
Cupboard Love	7	2	0	1	14232
Dalileo (IRE)	7	2	0	1	8636
Danzay (IRE)	15	1	3	4	5175
Dark Vision (IRE)	4	3	0	0	128040
Deep Intrigue	4	2	1	1	10760
Delft Dancer	8	1	3	1	4528
Desert Friend (IRE)	3	2	0	0	10350
Diva D (IRE)	6	1	0	1	3105
Diviner (IRE)	9	2	1	1	7892
Dr Richard Kimble (IRE)	15	3	2	3	17602
Eesha's Smile (IRE)	5	2	0	0	8668
Elegiac	12	3	5	2	81291
Fire Fighting (IRE)	12	2	0	2	19411
Firlinfeu	10	1	1	1	4075
Gateway	5	1	1	1	3235
Hibernicus (IRE)	4	2	0	0	10674
I Am A Dreamer	11	2	1	1	22154
I'll Have Another (IRE)	6	2	2	2	8280
If We Can Can	6	1	0	0	3493
Illusional	8	1	1	1	3752
Indian Sounds (IRE)	7	2	0	2	11418
Juneau (IRE)	18	4	4	1	16237
Just Wait (IRE)	3	1	1	0	4140
Kalagia (IRE)	15	2	6	3	12970
Kilbarchan (GER)	7	3	1	0	16690
Lake Volta (IRE)	16	1	2	4	28355
Liberatrix (IRE)	5	1	1	0	7375
Living Legend (IRE)	2	1	0	0	3752
Love Dreams (IRE)	12	2	2	0	31735
Lucky Deal	11	3	1	3	44386
Main Edition (IRE)	6	4	0	1	90650
Making Miracles	9	2	2	2	67943
Mambo Dancer	17	3	3	2	15105
Marie's Diamond (IRE)	6	2	1	1	10639
Masham Star (IRE)	24	2	2	2	22154
Massam	7	2	2	1	20350
Matterhorn (IRE)	5	3	1	1	18987
Mildenberger	2	1	1	0	22684
Mister Chiang	5	1	2	0	7763
Natalie's Joy	3	2	0	0	14461
Nayef Road (IRE)	6	2	1	1	16819
New Winds	5	2	0	1	10027
No Lippy (IRE)	8	3	1	0	31142
Nyaleti (IRE)	5	1	0	0	28355
Octave (IRE)	6	2	1	0	10221
On A May Day (IRE)	12	2	0	3	6857
One Second	2	1	0	0	3752
Persian Moon (IRE)	7	3	1	1	26941
Poet's Prince	11	3	3	1	25617
Poet's Society	30	6	3	3	90712
Poetic Steps (FR)	16	1	3	0	3105
Port Of Leith (IRE)	8	1	1	2	3752
Prairie Spy (IRE)	6	2	0	1	9191
Quintada	3	1	0	1	3752
Rainbow Rebel (IRE)	16	5	2	2	105549
Rampant Lion (IRE)*	8	1	1	1	5434
Rastacap	13	1	2	1	3752
Ravenhoe (IRE)	28	4	3	4	12420
Rebel Assault (IRE)	17	1	1	4	9338
River Glades	9	1	1	2	4787
Royal Big Night (USA)	7	1	2	1	4528
Rufus King	13	1	2	2	22642
Sea Youmzain (IRE)	9	3	0	2	23293
Seductive Moment (GER)	5	2	0	0	7504
Showroom (FR)	1	1	0	0	4464
Sky Cross (IRE)	2	1	0	0	4787
Sky Defender	5	1	1	1	4787
Snax	4	1	0	0	5693
Sofia's Rock (FR)*	11	1	1	1	10997
Soldier In Action (FR)	12	1	0	0	15753
Spirit Kingdom (USA)	9	1	0	2	5822
Star Of The East (IRE)	17	4	3	2	58798
The British Lion (IRE)	10	1	0	1	5387
The Last Debutante	10	1	3	0	3752
The Trader (IRE)	5	2	0	0	10121
Themaxwecan (IRE)	1	1	0	0	3752
Threading (IRE)	8	1	1	1	28355
Ticklish (FR)	3	1	1	1	3752
Tight Lines	10	1	3	2	8022
Vale Of Kent (IRE)	18	6	2	2	56322
Ventura Knight (IRE)	13	3	0	2	35494
Victoria Drummond (IRE)	7	2	0	3	12162
Victory Command (IRE)	9	4	1	2	28830
Viscount Loftus (IRE)	11	1	1	1	5693
Vivid Diamond (IRE)	3	1	1	0	5563
Watersmeet	11	4	0	1	54924
West End Charmer (IRE)	3	2	0	0	7892
Winged Spur (IRE)	16	4	2	2	18954
X Rated (IRE)	15	1	1	5	4852
Total winning prize-money					**£2351245**
Favourites	**87-217**		**40.1%**		**1.21**

SHAUN KEIGHTLEY

WALTHAM-ON-THE-WOLDS, LEICS

	No. of Hrs	Races Run	1st	2nd	3rd	Unpl	Per cent	£1 Level Stake
2-y-o	*4*	*11*	*1*	*0*	*0*	*10*	*9.1*	*-8.38*
3-y-o	*5*	*25*	*0*	*1*	*2*	*22*	*0.0*	*-25.00*
4-y-o+	*5*	*23*	*1*	*3*	*1*	*18*	*4.3*	*-19.75*
Totals	**14**	**59**	**2**	**4**	**3**	**50**	**3.4**	**-53.13**
2017	*0*							
2016	*0*							

JOCKEYS

	W-R	Per cent	£1 Level Stake
Silvestre De Sousa	1-1	100.0	+2.25
Liam Jones	1-14	7.1	-11.38

COURSE RECORD

	Total W-R	Non-Hndcps 2-y-o	Non-Hndcps 3-y-o+	Hndcps 2-y-o	Hndcps 3-y-o+	Per cent	£1 Level Stake
Epsom	1-2	0-0	0-0	0-0	1-2	50.0	+1.25
Chelmsford (A.W)	1-7	1-1	0-0	0-0	0-6	14.3	-4.38

WINNING HORSES

Horse	Races Run	1st	2nd	3rd	£
*Dance Teacher (IRE)	5	1	1	0	7116
San Carlos	2	1	0	0	4204
Total winning prize-money					**£11320**
Favourites	**1-1**		**100.0%**		**1.63**

GAY KELLEWAY

EXNING, SUFFOLK

	No. of Hrs	Races Run	1st	2nd	3rd	Unpl	Per cent	£1 Level Stake
2-y-o	*10*	*36*	*2*	*4*	*6*	*24*	*5.6*	*-16.25*
3-y-o	*13*	*111*	*12*	*27*	*12*	*60*	*10.8*	*-2.75*
4-y-o+	*15*	*123*	*13*	*13*	*13*	*84*	*10.6*	*+20.13*
Totals	**38**	**270**	**27**	**44**	**31**	**168**	**10.0**	**+1.13**
2017	*38*	*236*	*15*	*23*	*34*	*164*	*6.4*	*-88.58*
2016	*37*	*220*	*21*	*26*	*31*	*142*	*9.5*	*-45.50*

BY MONTH

2-y-o	W-R	Per cent	£1 Level Stake
January	0-0	0.0	0.00
February	0-0	0.0	0.00
March	0-0	0.0	0.00
April	0-1	0.0	-1.00
May	0-4	0.0	-4.00
June	0-4	0.0	-4.00
July	0-5	0.0	-5.00
August	0-0	0.0	0.00
September	0-5	0.0	-5.00
October	0-6	0.0	-6.00
November	1-8	12.5	+9.00
December	1-3	33.3	-0.25

3-y-o	W-R	Per cent	£1 Level Stake
January	1-2	50.0	+1.50
February	0-3	0.0	-3.00
March	0-6	0.0	-6.00
April	0-13	0.0	-13.00
May	5-18	27.8	+39.25
June	0-15	0.0	-15.00
July	2-20	10.0	+2.50
August	1-10	10.0	+1.00
September	0-10	0.0	-10.00
October	2-7	28.6	-0.50
November	1-4	25.0	+3.50
December	0-3	0.0	-3.00

4-y-o+	W-R	Per cent	£1 Level Stake
January	3-18	16.7	+23.50
February	0-8	0.0	-8.00
March	0-3	0.0	-3.00
April	1-9	11.1	-5.75
May	2-12	16.7	+2.88
June	2-10	20.0	+31.50
July	0-14	0.0	-14.00
August	2-13	15.4	+2.00
September	0-10	0.0	-10.00
October	1-11	9.1	+6.00
November	0-8	0.0	-8.00
December	2-7	28.6	+3.00

Totals	W-R	Per cent	£1 Level Stake
January	4-20	20.0	+25.00
February	0-11	0.0	-11.00
March	0-9	0.0	-9.00
April	1-23	4.3	-19.75
May	7-34	20.6	+38.13
June	2-29	6.9	+12.50
July	2-39	5.1	-16.50
August	3-23	13.0	+3.00
September	0-25	0.0	-25.00
October	3-24	12.5	-0.50
November	2-20	10.0	-4.50
December	3-13	23.1	0.00

DISTANCE

2-y-o	W-R	Per cent	£1 Level Stake
5f-6f	1-22	4.5	-19.25
7f-8f	1-14	7.1	+3.00
9f-13f	0-0	0.0	0.00
14f+	0-0	0.0	0.00

3-y-o	W-R	Per cent	£1 Level Stake
5f-6f	6-46	13.0	+23.50
7f-8f	5-51	9.8	-29.25
9f-13f	1-14	7.1	+3.00
14f+	0-0	0.0	0.00

4-y-o+	W-R	Per cent	£1 Level Stake
5f-6f	1-17	5.9	-6.00
7f-8f	9-66	13.6	+1.63
9f-13f	1-24	4.2	+2.00
14f+	2-16	12.5	+22.50

Totals	W-R	Per cent	£1 Level Stake
5f-6f	8-85	9.4	-1.75
7f-8f	15-131	11.5	-24.62
9f-13f	2-38	5.3	+5.00
14f+	2-16	12.5	+22.50

TYPE OF RACE

Non-Handicaps

	W-R	Per cent	£1 Level Stake
2-y-o	2-28	7.1	-8.25
3-y-o	3-27	11.1	-18.25
4-y-o+	0-8	0.0	-8.00

Handicaps

	W-R	Per cent	£1 Level Stake
2-y-o	0-8	0.0	-8.00
3-y-o	9-84	10.7	+15.50
4-y-o+	13-115	11.3	+28.13

RACE CLASS

	W-R	Per cent	£1 Level Stake
Class 1	0-3	0.0	-3.00
Class 2	1-18	5.6	+16.00
Class 3	3-11	27.3	+29.88
Class 4	2-46	4.3	-37.00
Class 5	11-104	10.6	-18.25
Class 6	10-87	11.5	+15.50
Class 7	0-1	0.0	1.00

FIRST TIME OUT

	W-R	Per cent	£1 Level Stake
2-y-o	1-10	10.0	+7.00
3-y-o	1-13	7.7	-9.50
4-y-o+	2-15	13.3	+0.50
Totals	4-38	10.5	-2.00

JOCKEYS

	W-R	Per cent	£1 Level Stake
Silvestre De Sousa	4-16	25.0	+4.38
Josephine Gordon	4-28	14.3	-6.50
Aaron Jones	4-39	10.3	+20.50
Toby Eley	3-7	42.9	+5.75
Rossa Ryan	3-10	30.0	+9.00

Gerald Mosse	2-20	10.0	+4.50
Dane O'Neill	1-3	33.3	+2.50
Daniel Muscutt	1-4	25.0	+30.00
Tom Eaves	1-5	20.0	+21.00
Gina Mangan	1-7	14.3	+4.00
Jason Hart	1-9	11.1	+8.00
Shane Kelly	1-9	11.1	+1.00
William Cox	1-12	8.3	-2.00

COURSE RECORD

	Total W-R	Non-Hndcps 2-y-o	3-y-o+	Hndcps 2-y-o	3-y-o+	Per cent	£1 Level Stake
Wolvhptn (A.W)	6-30	0-2	0-5	0-1	6-22	20.0	+32.75
Yarmouth	4-17	0-1	0-1	0-0	4-15	23.5	+20.50
Southwell (A.W)	3-10	1-1	0-2	0-0	2-7	30.0	+24.75
Leicester	3-17	0-2	2-5	0-2	1-8	17.6	+0.50
Chelmsford (A.W)	3-35	0-1	0-3	0-0	3-31	8.6	-16.63
Kempton (A.W)	2-28	1-1	0-1	0-1	1-25	7.1	-3.50
York	1-1	0-0	0-0	0-0	1-1	100.0	+11.00
Redcar	1-4	0-1	1-3	0-0	0-0	25.0	-1.75
Bath	1-7	0-0	0-0	0-1	1-6	14.3	+3.00
Newcastle (A.W)	1-8	0-2	0-2	0-0	1-4	12.5	+26.00
Brighton	1-17	0-2	0-0	0-1	1-14	5.9	-7.00
Lingfield (A.W)	1-20	0-1	0-1	0-1	1-17	5.0	-12.50

WINNING HORSES

Horse	Races Run	1st	2nd	3rd	£
Angel Of The North (IRE)*	10	1	0	0	3105
Billy Booth (IRE)	7	2	0	1	6210
Capla Demon	9	1	3	2	5434
Cosmelli (ITY)	8	2	0	0	54249
Crystal Deauville (FR)	10	2	3	1	7504
Global Academy (IRE)	8	1	1	0	5531
Global Spectrum	1	1	0	0	3881
*Global Wonder (IRE)	9	1	4	1	3105
Johni Boxit*	10	1	3	1	3105
Lady Alavesa	13	2	5	3	3752
Reedanjas (IRE)	4	1	0	1	4399
*Robero	11	2	1	2	8539
Robsdelight (IRE)	9	1	3	0	3493
Scale Force	3	1	0	1	4399
Stosur (IRE)	15	1	1	4	3752
Topmeup	17	2	3	1	6210
Ubla (IRE)	17	2	2	0	3170
Vettori Rules	7	1	0	0	0
Yeah Baby Yeah (IRE)	9	2	3	0	25388
Total winning prize-money					**£155226**
Favourites	**5-20**		**25.0%**		**-4.88**

STEF KENIRY

MIDDLEHAM, N YORKS

	No. of Hrs	Races Run	1st	2nd	3rd	Unpl	Per cent	£1 Level Stake
2-y-o	*4*	*17*	*0*	*0*	*0*	*17*	*0.0*	*-17.00*
3-y-o	*2*	*5*	*0*	*0*	*0*	*5*	*0.0*	*-5.00*
4-y-o+	*9*	*27*	*4*	*3*	*0*	*20*	*14.8*	*+11.50*
Totals	**15**	**49**	**4**	**3**	**0**	**42**	**8.2**	**-10.50**
2017	*0*							
2016	*0*							

JOCKEYS

	W-R	Per cent	£1 Level Stake
Liam Keniry	2-21	9.5	-1.50
Joe Fanning	1-1	100.0	+8.00
Jonathan Fisher	1-1	100.0	+9.00

COURSE RECORD

	Total W-R	Non-Hndcps 2-y-o	3-y-o+	Hndcps 2-y-o	3-y-o+	Per cent	£1 Level Stake
Redcar	3-9	0-2	0-1	0-0	3-6	33.3	+14.50
Wolvhptn (A.W)	1-2	0-0	0-0	0-0	1-2	50.0	+13.00

WINNING HORSES

Horse	Races Run	1st	2nd	3rd	£
*Betancourt (IRE)	6	2	1	0	6598
Gilmer (IRE)	7	1	0	0	3493
Icario (FR)	4	1	2	0	4399
Total winning prize-money					**£14490**
Favourites	**1-8**		**12.5%**		**-5.90**

NEIL KING

BARBURY CASTLE, WILTS

	No. of Hrs	Races Run	1st	2nd	3rd	Unpl	Per cent	£1 Level Stake
2-y-o	*0*	*0*	*0*	*0*	*0*	*0*	*0.0*	*0.00*
3-y-o	*0*	*0*	*0*	*0*	*0*	*0*	*0.0*	*0.00*
4-y-o+	*5*	*9*	*2*	*1*	*1*	*5*	*22.2*	*+7.75*
Totals	**5**	**9**	**2**	**1**	**1**	**5**	**22.2**	**+7.75**
2017	*4*	*13*	*3*	*3*	*1*	*6*	*23.1*	*-4.25*
2016	*8*	*29*	*5*	*4*	*1*	*19*	*17.2*	*+26.00*

JOCKEYS

	W-R	Per cent	£1 Level Stake
Silvestre De Sousa	1-1	100.0	+2.75
Trevor Whelan	1-2	50.0	+11.00

COURSE RECORD

	Total W-R	Non-Hndcps 2-y-o	3-y-o+	Hndcps 2-y-o	3-y-o+	Per cent	£1 Level Stake
Goodwood	1-1	0-0	0-0	0-0	1-1	100.0	+2.75
Lingfield	1-1	0-0	0-0	0-0	1-1	100.0	+12.00

WINNING HORSES

Horse	Races Run	1st	2nd	3rd	£
Cubswin (IRE)	2	1	1	0	5531
Lil Rockerfeller (USA)	1	1	0	0	31125
Total winning prize-money					**£36656**
Favourites	**18-38**		**47.4%**		**8.50**

ALAN KING

BARBURY CASTLE, WILTS

	No. of Hrs	Races Run	1st	2nd	3rd	Unpl	Per cent	£1 Level Stake
2-y-o	*15*	*46*	*3*	*5*	*5*	*33*	*6.5*	*-31.38*
3-y-o	*21*	*99*	*14*	*13*	*17*	*55*	*14.1*	*-28.00*
4-y-o+	*31*	*116*	*21*	*13*	*17*	*65*	*18.1*	*-13.38*
Totals	**67**	**261**	**38**	**31**	**39**	**153**	**14.6**	**-72.76**
2017	*51*	*177*	*19*	*21*	*26*	*111*	*10.7*	*-59.71*
2016	*51*	*195*	*21*	*26*	*28*	*120*	*10.8*	*-74.76*

BY MONTH

2-y-o	W-R	Per cent	£1 Level Stake	3-y-o	W-R	Per cent	£1 Level Stake
January	0-0	0.0	0.00	January	0-0	0.0	0.00
February	0-0	0.0	0.00	February	0-3	0.0	-3.00
March	0-0	0.0	0.00	March	0-4	0.0	-4.00
April	0-0	0.0	0.00	April	1-6	16.7	-1.00
May	0-0	0.0	0.00	May	1-11	9.1	-6.50
June	2-8	25.0	+2.63	June	3-19	15.8	-6.63
July	0-9	0.0	-9.00	July	3-15	20.0	+5.50
August	0-6	0.0	-6.00	August	2-18	11.1	-6.75
September	0-8	0.0	-8.00	September	0-11	0.0	-11.00
October	1-13	7.7	-9.00	October	2-8	25.0	+3.88
November	0-2	0.0	-2.00	November	1-2	50.0	0.00
December	0-0	0.0	0.00	December	1-2	50.0	+1.50

4-y-o+	W-R	Per cent	£1 Level Stake	Totals	W-R	Per cent	£1 Level Stake
January	0-3	0.0	-3.00	January	0-3	0.0	-3.00
February	6-11	54.5	+11.88	February	6-14	42.9	+8.88
March	1-7	14.3	-3.25	March	1-11	9.1	-7.25
April	0-15	0.0	-15.00	April	1-21	4.8	-16.00
May	2-17	11.8	-9.32	May	3-28	10.7	-15.82
June	3-18	16.7	-9.46	June	8-45	17.8	-13.46
July	2-8	25.0	-0.10	July	5-32	15.6	-3.60
August	2-10	20.0	+3.38	August	4-34	11.8	-9.37
September	1-5	20.0	+8.00	September	1-24	4.2	-11.00
October	0-7	0.0	-7.00	October	3-28	10.7	-12.12
November	0-4	0.0	-4.00	November	1-8	12.5	-4.00
December	4-11	36.4	+14.50	December	5-13	38.5	+16.00

DISTANCE

2-y-o	W-R	Per cent	£1 Level Stake	3-y-o	W-R	Per cent	£1 Level Stake
5f-6f	2-8	25.0	+2.63	5f-6f	0-0	0.0	0.00
7f-8f	0-35	0.0	-35.00	7f-8f	1-15	6.7	-12.50
9f-13f	1-3	33.3	+1.00	9f-13f	12-76	15.8	-13.50
14f+	0-0	0.0	0.00	14f+	1-8	12.5	-2.00

4-y-o+	W-R	Per cent	£1 Level Stake	Totals	W-R	Per cent	£1 Level Stake
5f-6f	0-0	0.0	0.00	5f-6f	2-8	25.0	+2.63
7f-8f	0-2	0.0	-2.00	7f-8f	1-52	1.9	-49.50
9f-13f	17-74	23.0	+9.22	9f-13f	30-153	19.6	-3.28
14f+	4-40	10.0	-20.60	14f+	5-48	10.4	-22.60

TYPE OF RACE

Non-Handicaps	W-R	Per cent	£1 Level Stake	Handicaps	W-R	Per cent	£1 Level Stake
2-y-o	3-45	6.7	-30.38	2-y-o	0-1	0.0	-1.00
3-y-o	2-28	7.1	-17.13	3-y-o	12-71	16.9	-10.88
4-y-o+	3-16	18.8	-8.16	4-y-o+	18-100	18.0	-5.22

RACE CLASS

	W-R	Per cent	£1 Level Stake
Class 1	0-11	0.0	-11.00
Class 2	3-36	8.3	-14.75
Class 3	6-32	18.8	-10.75
Class 4	12-65	18.5	-4.85
Class 5	14-98	14.3	-23.90
Class 6	3-19	15.8	-7.50
Class 7	0-0	0.0	0.00

FIRST TIME OUT

	W-R	Per cent	£1 Level Stake
2-y-o	0-15	0.0	-15.00
3-y-o	1-21	4.8	-16.50
4-y-o+	4-31	12.9	-10.13
Totals	5-67	7.5	-41.63

JOCKEYS

	W-R	Per cent	£1 Level Stake
Martin Harley	22-146	15.1	-33.18
Tom Marquand	5-28	17.9	-3.00
David Probert	3-8	37.5	+19.50
Joe Fanning	1-1	100.0	+1.38
James Doyle	1-1	100.0	+0.18
Joshua Bryan	1-1	100.0	+1.88
Ryan Moore	1-3	33.3	0.00
Andrea Atzeni	1-4	25.0	-0.75
David Egan	1-7	14.3	-4.38
Hollie Doyle	1-7	14.3	-4.38
William Carson	1-16	6.3	-11.00

COURSE RECORD

	Total W-R	Non-Hndcps 2-y-o	Non-Hndcps 3-y-o+	Hndcps 2-y-o	Hndcps 3-y-o+	Per cent	£1 Level Stake
Kempton (A.W)	8-30	0-4	1-3	0-0	7-23	26.7	+20.63
Wolvhptn (A.W)	5-30	0-2	1-11	0-0	4-17	16.7	-10.25
Sandown	3-12	0-5	0-0	0-0	3-7	25.0	-1.97
Windsor	3-12	1-3	0-2	0-0	2-7	25.0	+7.00
Lingfield (A.W)	3-23	0-4	0-7	0-0	3-12	13.0	+1.25
Leicester	2-11	0-2	0-2	0-0	2-7	18.2	-4.00
Newbury	2-20	0-3	0-2	0-0	2-15	10.0	-10.63
Catterick	1-1	0-0	1-1	0-0	0-0	100.0	+0.67
Newcastle (A.W)	1-4	0-0	0-0	0-0	1-4	25.0	-0.75
Newmkt (Jly)	1-4	0-1	0-0	0-0	1-3	25.0	-1.00
Ffos Las	1-4	0-0	1-1	0-0	0-3	25.0	+4.00
Chepstow	1-5	0-0	0-1	0-0	1-4	20.0	-1.00
York	1-5	1-2	0-0	0-0	0-3	20.0	-2.38
Southwell (A.W)	1-5	0-1	0-0	0-0	1-4	20.0	-2.38
Doncaster	1-7	0-1	0-0	0-0	1-6	14.3	+6.00
Newmarket	1-9	1-4	0-0	0-0	0-5	11.1	-5.00
Goodwood	1-13	0-4	0-1	0-0	1-8	7.7	-10.63
Nottingham	1-14	0-4	0-2	0-0	1-8	7.1	-11.50
Chelmsford (A.W)	1-15	0-1	1-5	0-0	0-9	6.7	-13.82

WINNING HORSES

Horse	Races Run	1st	2nd	3rd	£
Beringer	8	2	3	1	13445
Caspar The Cub (IRE)	12	4	3	3	29025
Coeur De Lion	8	1	2	1	9704
Cosmeapolitan	7	2	1	1	22809
Dunkerron	7	2	1	0	14491
Elgin	4	2	0	1	10286
Elysees (IRE)	10	2	0	2	7633
Giveaway Glance	5	1	0	1	5531
Giving Glances	7	2	2	0	10463
Gravina	7	1	0	4	4528
Inn The Bull (GER)	7	3	0	0	13973
Just In Time	6	3	1	0	38426
Lady Persephone (FR)	6	1	1	0	3752
Lexington Law (IRE)	5	2	0	0	12000
Manor Park	5	1	0	1	3752
Nylon Speed (IRE)	1	1	0	0	3752
Our Power (IRE)	4	1	1	0	3817
Outofthequestion	7	2	1	3	7504
Redicean	3	2	0	0	17503
Seaborough (IRE)	5	1	1	0	3235
Sula Island	6	1	1	2	3105
The Olympian (IRE)	3	1	2	0	6469
Total winning prize-money					**£245203**
Favourites	**58-141**		**41.1%**		**-18.64**

PHILIP KIRBY

EAST APPLETON, N YORKS

	No. of Hrs	Races Run	1st	2nd	3rd	Unpl	Per cent	£1 Level Stake
2-y-o	*3*	*6*	*0*	*0*	*0*	*6*	*0.0*	*-6.00*
3-y-o	*9*	*72*	*3*	*7*	*5*	*57*	*4.2*	*-57.50*
4-y-o+	*25*	*153*	*16*	*12*	*12*	*112*	*10.5*	*+32.95*
Totals	**37**	**231**	**19**	**19**	**17**	**175**	**8.2**	**-30.55**
2017	*33*	*147*	*10*	*10*	*16*	*110*	*6.8*	*-49.50*
2016	*30*	*168*	*8*	*10*	*13*	*136*	*4.8*	*-108.50*

BY MONTH

2-y-o	W-R	Per cent	£1 Level Stake	3-y-o	W-R	Per cent	£1 Level Stake
January	0-0	0.0	0.00	January	2-2	100.0	+7.00
February	0-0	0.0	0.00	February	0-2	0.0	-2.00
March	0-0	0.0	0.00	March	0-2	0.0	-2.00
April	0-0	0.0	0.00	April	1-11	9.1	-5.50
May	0-0	0.0	0.00	May	0-3	0.0	-3.00
June	0-0	0.0	0.00	June	0-3	0.0	-3.00
July	0-1	0.0	-1.00	July	0-8	0.0	-8.00
August	0-0	0.0	0.00	August	0-7	0.0	-7.00
September	0-1	0.0	-1.00	September	0-9	0.0	-9.00
October	0-1	0.0	-1.00	October	0-14	0.0	-14.00
November	0-3	0.0	-3.00	November	0-4	0.0	-4.00
December	0-0	0.0	0.00	December	0-7	0.0	-7.00

4-y-o+	W-R	Per cent	£1 Level Stake	Totals	W-R	Per cent	£1 Level Stake
January	1-10	10.0	-6.75	January	3-12	25.0	+0.25
February	0-7	0.0	-7.00	February	0-9	0.0	-9.00
March	4-14	28.6	+80.20	March	4-16	25.0	+78.20
April	3-23	13.0	-5.50	April	4-34	11.8	-11.00
May	0-13	0.0	-13.00	May	0-16	0.0	-16.00
June	0-19	0.0	-19.00	June	0-22	0.0	-22.00
July	2-10	20.0	+11.00	July	2-19	10.5	+2.00
August	2-11	18.2	+8.00	August	2-18	11.1	+1.00
September	1-15	6.7	-9.00	September	1-25	4.0	-19.00
October	1-12	8.3	-1.00	October	1-27	3.7	-16.00
November	1-14	7.1	-10.00	November	1-21	4.8	-14.00
December	1-5	20.0	+5.00	December	1-12	8.3	-2.00

DISTANCE

2-y-o	W-R	Per cent	£1 Level Stake	3-y-o	W-R	Per cent	£1 Level Stake
5f-6f	0-0	0.0	0.00	5f-6f	0-9	0.0	-9.00
7f-8f	0-5	0.0	-5.00	7f-8f	1-12	8.3	-8.00
9f-13f	0-1	0.0	-1.00	9f-13f	2-43	4.7	-32.50
14f+	0-0	0.0	0.00	14f+	0-8	0.0	-8.00

4-y-o+	W-R	Per cent	£1 Level Stake	Totals	W-R	Per cent	£1 Level Stake
5f-6f	1-13	7.7	-10.50	5f-6f	1-22	4.5	-19.50
7f-8f	2-42	4.8	+46.00	7f-8f	3-59	5.1	+33.00
9f-13f	7-67	10.4	-10.50	9f-13f	9-111	8.1	-44.00
14f+	6-31	19.4	+7.95	14f+	6-39	15.4	-0.05

TYPE OF RACE

Non-Handicaps	W-R	Per cent	£1 Level Stake	Handicaps	W-R	Per cent	£1 Level Stake
2-y-o	0-6	0.0	-6.00	2-y-o	0-0	0.0	0.00
3-y-o	0-6	0.0	-6.00	3-y-o	3-66	4.5	-51.50
4-y-o+	1-6	16.7	+4.00	4-y-o+	15-147	10.2	+28.95

RACE CLASS

	W-R	Per cent	£1 Level Stake
Class 1	0-0	0.0	0.00
Class 2	1-9	11.1	+1.00
Class 3	1-11	9.1	-5.50
Class 4	4-45	8.9	-19.50
Class 5	8-75	10.7	+58.20
Class 6	5-90	5.6	-63.75
Class 7	0-1	0.0	-1.00

FIRST TIME OUT

	W-R	Per cent	£1 Level Stake
2-y-o	0-3	0.0	-3.00
3-y-o	1-9	11.1	-4.00
4-y-o+	2-25	8.0	-16.25
Totals	3-37	8.1	-23.25

JOCKEYS

	W-R	Per cent	£1 Level Stake
P J McDonald	4-19	21.1	-3.30
Paula Muir	2-6	33.3	+18.00
Bruce Lynn	1-1	100.0	+2.25
Robert Winston	1-1	100.0	+9.00
Adam Kirby	1-3	33.3	+1.00
Jack Mitchell	1-5	20.0	+4.00
Rossa Ryan	1-6	16.7	-1.00

Jimmy Quinn	1-6	16.7	-0.50
Connor Murtagh	1-6	16.7	+5.00
Callum Rodriguez	1-7	14.3	+1.00
Shane Gray	1-8	12.5	+73.00
William Cox	1-9	11.1	-5.00
Paddy Aspell	1-13	7.7	-6.00
Kevin Stott	1-20	5.0	-14.00
Andrew Mullen	1-29	3.4	-22.00

COURSE RECORD

	Total W-R	Non-Hndcps 2-y-o	3-y-o+	Hndcps 2-y-o	3-y-o+	Per cent	£1 Level Stake
Southwell (A.W)	5-27	0-0	0-3	0-0	5-24	18.5	-9.55
Pontefract	2-8	0-0	0-0	0-0	2-8	25.0	+6.00
Wolvhptn (A.W)	2-18	0-0	0-1	0-0	2-17	11.1	-9.00
Redcar	2-18	0-3	0-3	0-0	2-12	11.1	0.00
Catterick	2-24	0-0	0-0	0-0	2-24	8.3	-1.00
Newcastle (A.W)	2-42	0-2	1-3	0-0	1-37	4.8	+49.00
Leicester	1-2	0-0	0-0	0-0	1-2	50.0	+3.50
Doncaster	1-8	0-0	0-0	0-0	1-8	12.5	-2.50
Chester	1-10	0-0	0-0	0-0	1-10	10.0	-1.00
Thirsk	1-13	0-0	0-2	0-0	1-11	7.7	-5.00

WINNING HORSES

Horse	Races Run	1st	2nd	3rd	£
Archippos	9	1	0	1	5531
Captain Bob (IRE)	11	1	0	1	3752
Good Time Ahead (IRE)	9	1	1	1	6081
Ice Galley (IRE)	6	1	1	0	3493
Man Of Verve (IRE)	11	2	0	1	6857
Mr Carbonator	15	2	3	1	8636
Pumaflor (IRE)	10	1	0	1	6469
Rayna's World (IRE)	6	1	1	1	7561
Richard Strauss (IRE)	13	1	2	3	4787
Shine Baby Shine	1	1	0	0	2995
Stargazer (IRE)	8	1	3	0	16173
The Resdev Way	17	4	2	0	16173
Wemyss Point	3	1	0	1	5175
Zig Zag (IRE)	7	1	1	0	3398
Total winning prize-money					**£97081**
Favourites	**12-31**		**38.7%**		**4.49**

SYLVESTER KIRK

UPPER LAMBOURN, BERKS

	No. of Hrs	Races Run	1st	2nd	3rd	Unpl	Per cent	£1 Level Stake
2-y-o	*15*	*63*	*5*	*3*	*7*	*48*	*7.9*	*-21.00*
3-y-o	*22*	*180*	*17*	*19*	*18*	*126*	*9.4*	*-64.50*
4-y-o+	*9*	*44*	*2*	*4*	*5*	*33*	*4.5*	*-33.50*
Totals	**46**	**287**	**24**	**26**	**30**	**207**	**8.4**	**-119.00**
2017	*54*	*321*	*29*	*39*	*36*	*217*	*9.0*	*-80.29*
2016	*53*	*368*	*40*	*45*	*37*	*245*	*10.9*	*-82.42*

BY MONTH

2-y-o	W-R	Per cent	£1 Level Stake	3-y-o	W-R	Per cent	£1 Level Stake
January	0-0	0.0	0.00	January	0-1	0.0	-1.00
February	0-0	0.0	0.00	February	0-1	0.0	-1.00
March	0-0	0.0	0.00	March	0-0	0.0	0.00
April	0-1	0.0	-1.00	April	1-13	7.7	-7.00
May	0-4	0.0	-4.00	May	3-21	14.3	+2.50
June	0-6	0.0	-6.00	June	1-24	4.2	-15.50
July	0-10	0.0	-10.00	July	1-19	5.3	-15.50
August	1-8	12.5	+7.00	August	4-28	14.3	+1.00
September	4-13	30.8	+14.00	September	5-27	18.5	-8.00
October	0-9	0.0	-9.00	October	0-23	0.0	-23.00
November	0-9	0.0	-9.00	November	2-15	13.3	+11.00
December	0-3	0.0	-3.00	December	0-8	0.0	-8.00

4-y-o+	W-R	Per cent	£1 Level Stake	Totals	W-R	Per cent	£1 Level Stake
January	0-1	0.0	-1.00	January	0-2	0.0	-2.00
February	0-3	0.0	-3.00	February	0-4	0.0	-4.00
March	0-2	0.0	-2.00	March	0-2	0.0	-2.00
April	0-2	0.0	-2.00	April	1-16	6.3	-10.00
May	1-9	11.1	-2.00	May	4-34	11.8	-3.50
June	0-8	0.0	-8.00	June	1-38	2.6	-29.50
July	0-7	0.0	-7.00	July	1-36	2.8	-32.50
August	1-2	50.0	+1.50	August	6-38	15.8	+9.50
September	0-4	0.0	-4.00	September	9-44	20.5	+2.00
October	0-2	0.0	-2.00	October	0-34	0.0	-34.00
November	0-1	0.0	-1.00	November	2-25	8.0	+10.00
December	0-3	0.0	-3.00	December	0-14	0.0	-11.00

DISTANCE

2-y-o	W-R	Per cent	£1 Level Stake	3-y-o	W-R	Per cent	£1 Level Stake
5f-6f	3-32	9.4	-13.00	5f-6f	2-30	6.7	-21.50
7f-8f	2-29	6.9	-6.00	7f-8f	6-63	9.5	-19.25
9f-13f	0-2	0.0	-2.00	9f-13f	7-73	9.6	-25.75
14f+	0-0	0.0	0.00	14f+	2-14	14.3	+2.00

4-y-o+	W-R	Per cent	£1 Level Stake	Totals	W-R	Per cent	£1 Level Stake
5f-6f	0-5	0.0	-5.00	5f-6f	5-67	7.5	-39.50
7f-8f	0-19	0.0	-19.00	7f-8f	8-111	7.2	-44.25
9f-13f	1-15	6.7	-8.00	9f-13f	8-90	8.9	-35.75
14f+	1-5	20.0	-1.50	14f+	3-19	15.8	+0.50

TYPE OF RACE

Non-Handicaps	W-R	Per cent	£1 Level Stake	Handicaps	W-R	Per cent	£1 Level Stake
2-y-o	3-41	7.3	-18.00	2-y-o	2-22	9.1	-3.00
3-y-o	1-16	6.3	-12.25	3-y-o	16-164	9.8	-52.25
4-y-o+	0-8	0.0	-8.00	4-y-o+	2-36	5.6	-25.50

RACE CLASS / FIRST TIME OUT

RACE CLASS	W-R	Per cent	£1 Level Stake	FIRST TIME OUT	W-R	Per cent	£1 Level Stake
Class 1	0-3	0.0	-3.00	2-y-o	1-15	6.7	-10.50

Class 2	1-14	7.1	-3.00
Class 3	1-17	5.9	-14.00
Class 4	7-53	13.2	-3.50
Class 5	7-86	8.1	-41.25
Class 6	7-113	6.2	-70.25
Class 7	1-1	100.0	+16.00

3-y-o	1-22	4.5	-16.00
4-y-o+	1-9	11.1	-2.00
Totals	3-46	6.5	-28.50

JOCKEYS

	W-R	Per cent	£1 Level Stake
David Egan	4-38	10.5	-8.75
Luke Morris	4-39	10.3	+7.00
Jason Watson	3-14	21.4	+2.00
Tom Marquand	2-18	11.1	-6.00
Cam Hardie	1-1	100.0	+14.00
Yuga Kawada	1-1	100.0	+10.00
Mr Simon Walker	1-1	100.0	+2.00
Jim Crowley	1-4	25.0	-0.50
Nicola Currie	1-4	25.0	+1.50
Andrea Atzeni	1-4	25.0	0.00
Edward Greatrex	1-4	25.0	-1.00
Callum Shepherd	1-5	20.0	-1.00
Martin Dwyer	1-10	10.0	-4.00
Liam Keniry	1-14	7.1	-11.25
Gary Mahon	1-21	4.8	-14.00

COURSE RECORD

	Total	Non-Hndcps		Hndcps		Per	£1 Level
	W-R	2-y-o	3-y-o+	2-y-o	3-y-o+	cent	Stake
Chelmsford (A.W)	5-37	1-5	0-4	1-3	3-25	13.5	-9.25
Wolvhptn (A.W)	5-52	0-5	0-1	0-4	5-42	9.6	-20.00
Goodwood	2-12	0-3	0-0	0-0	2-9	16.7	+3.50
Brighton	2-19	1-4	0-0	0-1	1-14	10.5	-1.50
Kempton (A.W)	2-45	0-9	0-3	0-4	2-29	4.4	-19.00
Newcastle (A.W)	1-2	0-0	0-0	0-1	1-1	50.0	+2.00
Epsom	1-4	0-0	0-1	1-1	0-2	25.0	+4.00
Bath	1-5	0-0	0-1	0-0	1-4	20.0	+0.50
Newmarket	1-7	0-0	0-1	0-0	1-6	14.3	-4.00
Chepstow	1-8	1-2	0-0	0-0	0-6	12.5	+7.00
Leicester	1-9	0-0	1-2	0-3	0-4	11.1	-5.25
Salisbury	1-11	0-3	0-1	0-0	1-7	9.1	-7.00
Lingfield (A.W)	1-15	0-2	0-1	0-0	1-12	6.7	-9.00

WINNING HORSES

Horse	Races Run	1st	2nd	3rd	£
Ainne	9	1	0	1	2588
Bubble And Squeak	8	2	1	2	19206
George (IRE)	11	3	1	0	21801
Gift Of Hera	5	1	1	1	3105
Gravity Wave (IRE)	10	2	1	1	7504
Hackle Setter (USA)	5	2	0	1	11903
Irene May (IRE)	2	2	0	0	12809
Lamb Chop	9	1	1	1	4787
Lyford (IRE)*	10	1	3	2	3429
Masters Apprentice (IRE)	10	1	1	0	3493
Nayslayer (IRE)	10	1	1	3	22642
Sassie (IRE)	9	2	1	1	8086
Sauchiehall Street (IRE)	9	3	1	0	9704
Three Little Birds	12	2	2	4	7504
Total winning prize-money					**£138561**
Favourites	**5-16**		**31.3%**		**0.00**

STUART KITTOW

BLACKBOROUGH, DEVON

	No. of Hrs	Races Run	1st	2nd	3rd	Unpl	Per cent	£1 Level Stake
2-y-o	*1*	*4*	*0*	*1*	*0*	*3*	*0.0*	*-4.00*
3-y-o	*9*	*46*	*5*	*2*	*4*	*35*	*10.9*	*-14.63*
4-y-o+	*11*	*54*	*4*	*4*	*11*	*35*	*7.4*	*-25.63*
Totals	**21**	**104**	**9**	**7**	**15**	**73**	**8.7**	**-44.26**
2017	*25*	*102*	*9*	*11*	*9*	*73*	*8.8*	*-30.19*
2016	*24*	*109*	*12*	*9*	*10*	*78*	*11.0*	*-33.25*

JOCKEYS

	W-R	Per cent	£1 Level Stake
Fran Berry	2-3	66.7	+6.50
David Egan	2-7	28.6	+8.88
Andrea Atzeni	1-3	33.3	+4.50
Silvestre De Sousa	1-4	25.0	+1.00
Adam Kirby	1-5	20.0	-2.13
Jim Crowley	1-5	20.0	+1.00
Liam Keniry	1-11	9.1	+2.00

COURSE RECORD

	Total	Non-Hndcps		Hndcps		Per	£1 Level
	W-R	2-y-o	3-y-o+	2-y-o	3-y-o+	cent	Stake
Haydock	2-4	0-0	0-0	0-0	2-4	50.0	+4.88
Salisbury	2-10	0-1	0-3	0-0	2-6	20.0	+8.50
Windsor	2-14	0-1	0-5	0-0	2-8	14.3	-1.50
Chelmsford (A.W)	1-3	0-0	0-0	0-0	1-3	33.3	-0.13
Ffos Las	1-9	0-0	0-2	0-1	1-6	11.1	-5.00
Wolvhptn (A.W)	1-10	0-0	1-4	0-0	0-6	10.0	+3.00

WINNING HORSES

Horse	Races Run	1st	2nd	3rd	£
Bakht A Rawan (IRE)	7	1	1	0	3752
Beyond Equal	7	4	1	0	22221
Dora's Field (IRE)	5	1	0	0	3493
Nordic Combined (IRE)*	5	1	0	1	3752
Trotter	10	1	1	3	3752
Youkan (IRE)	5	1	0	1	6469
Total winning prize-money					**£43439**
Favourites	**4-7**		**57.1%**		**7.75**

WILLIAM KNIGHT

PATCHING, W SUSSEX

	No. of Hrs	Races Run	1st	2nd	3rd	Unpl	Per cent	£1 Level Stake
2-y-o	*7*	*27*	*2*	*3*	*2*	*20*	*7.4*	*+6.50*

3-y-o	*17*	*100*	*8*	*5*	*10*	*77*	*8.0*	*-3.15*
4-y-o+	*17*	*124*	*14*	*8*	*14*	*87*	*11.3*	*-28.45*
Totals	**41**	**251**	**24**	**16**	**26**	**184**	**9.6**	**-25.10**
2017	*37*	*185*	*19*	*14*	*19*	*133*	*10.3*	*-62.90*
2016	*49*	*248*	*29*	*21*	*32*	*166*	*11.7*	*-39.90*

BY MONTH

2-y-o	W-R	Per cent	£1 Level Stake
January	0-0	0.0	0.00
February	0-0	0.0	0.00
March	0-0	0.0	0.00
April	0-0	0.0	0.00
May	0-0	0.0	0.00
June	0-0	0.0	0.00
July	0-5	0.0	-5.00
August	1-7	14.3	+0.50
September	1-8	12.5	+18.00
October	0-4	0.0	-4.00
November	0-2	0.0	-2.00
December	0-1	0.0	-1.00

3-y-o	W-R	Per cent	£1 Level Stake
January	0-4	0.0	-4.00
February	0-2	0.0	-2.00
March	0-0	0.0	0.00
April	0-13	0.0	-13.00
May	1-14	7.1	+12.00
June	2-13	15.4	-7.15
July	0-9	0.0	-9.00
August	2-10	20.0	+32.00
September	2-13	15.4	-5.00
October	1-10	10.0	+5.00
November	0-7	0.0	-7.00
December	0-5	0.0	-5.00

4-y-o+	W-R	Per cent	£1 Level Stake
January	2-5	40.0	+3.25
February	2-7	28.6	+3.25
March	2-12	16.7	-4.40
April	1-15	6.7	-9.50
May	1-18	5.6	-8.00
June	2-12	16.7	+13.20
July	0-9	0.0	-9.00
August	1-12	8.3	-8.00
September	2-13	15.4	+2.75
October	1-13	7.7	-4.00
November	0-7	0.0	-7.00
December	0-1	0.0	-1.00

Totals	W-R	Per cent	£1 Level Stake
January	2-9	22.2	-0.75
February	2-9	22.2	+1.25
March	2-12	16.7	-4.40
April	1-28	3.6	-22.50
May	2-32	6.3	+4.00
June	4-25	16.0	+6.05
July	0-23	0.0	-23.00
August	4-29	13.8	+24.50
September	5-34	14.7	+15.75
October	2-27	7.4	-3.00
November	0-16	0.0	-14.00
December	0-7	0.0	-6.00

DISTANCE

2-y-o	W-R	Per cent	£1 Level Stake
5f-6f	2-10	20.0	+23.50
7f-8f	0-17	0.0	-17.00
9f-13f	0-0	0.0	0.00
14f+	0-0	0.0	0.00

3-y-o	W-R	Per cent	£1 Level Stake
5f-6f	1-17	5.9	+9.00
7f-8f	2-33	6.1	-9.00
9f-13f	3-42	7.1	-15.15
14f+	2-8	25.0	+12.00

4-y-o+	W-R	Per cent	£1 Level Stake
5f-6f	1-13	7.7	+10.00
7f-8f	3-37	8.1	-23.80
9f-13f	5-43	11.6	-9.75
14f+	5-31	16.1	-4.90

Totals	W-R	Per cent	£1 Level Stake
5f-6f	4-40	10.0	+42.50
7f-8f	5-87	5.7	-49.80
9f-13f	8-85	9.4	-24.90
14f+	7-39	17.9	+7.10

TYPE OF RACE

Non-Handicaps	W-R	Per cent	£1 Level Stake
2-y-o	2-22	9.1	+11.50
3-y-o	1-31	3.2	-10.00
4-y-o+	0-5	0.0	-5.00

Handicaps	W-R	Per cent	£1 Level Stake
2-y-o	0-5	0.0	-5.00
3-y-o	7-69	10.1	+6.85
4-y-o+	14-119	11.8	-23.45

RACE CLASS

	W-R	Per cent	£1 Level Stake
Class 1	0-2	0.0	-2.00
Class 2	3-33	9.1	+21.00
Class 3	1-32	3.1	-19.00
Class 4	7-42	16.7	+40.60
Class 5	10-88	11.4	-22.05
Class 6	3-53	5.7	-42.65
Class 7	0-1	0.0	-1.00

FIRST TIME OUT

	W-R	Per cent	£1 Level Stake
2-y-o	0-7	0.0	-7.00
3-y-o	0-17	0.0	-17.00
4-y-o+	2-17	11.8	-8.75
Totals	2-41	4.9	-32.75

JOCKEYS

	W-R	Per cent	£1 Level Stake
Jason Watson	6-27	22.2	+6.15
Martin Harley	5-35	14.3	-13.75
Adam Kirby	2-10	20.0	+1.50
Silvestre De Sousa	2-19	10.5	-6.00
Luke Morris	2-29	6.9	+4.50
Jimmy Quinn	1-4	25.0	+17.00
Oisin Murphy	1-5	20.0	+8.00
Nicola Currie	1-5	20.0	+16.00
Tom Queally	1-7	14.3	+16.00
Jim Crowley	1-7	14.3	-1.50
Charles Bishop	1-9	11.1	-5.00
Callum Shepherd	1-19	5.3	+7.00

COURSE RECORD

	Total W-R	Non-Hndcps 2-y-o	Non-Hndcps 3-y-o+	Hndcps 2-y-o	Hndcps 3-y-o+	Per cent	£1 Level Stake
Kempton (A.W)	8-76	0-4	1-8	0-1	7-63	10.5	-3.30
Lingfield (A.W)	5-34	0-3	0-6	0-0	5-25	14.7	+8.10
Chelmsford (A.W)	3-22	0-0	0-0	0-0	3-22	13.6	-1.50
Brighton	2-8	0-0	0-1	0-0	2-7	25.0	-3.15
Chepstow	1-1	1-1	0-0	0-0	0-0	100.0	+6.50
Newcastle (A.W)	1-3	0-0	0-0	0-0	1-3	33.3	+20.00
Wolvhptn (A.W)	1-6	0-1	0-1	0-0	1-4	16.7	-1.50
Newbury	1-12	1-5	0-1	0-1	0-5	8.3	+14.00
Windsor	1-16	0-1	0-7	0-0	1-8	6.3	-12.25
Goodwood	1-22	0-2	0-4	0-0	1-16	4.5	-1.00

WINNING HORSES

Horse	Races Run	1st	2nd	3rd	£
Arab Moon	10	1	0	2	9338
*Archimento	5	2	1	1	10221
Author's Dream	6	3	0	0	14057
Dancing Warrior	3	1	0	0	3752
Gavlar	11	1	1	2	6469
Goodwood Showman	7	1	1	1	3752
Kingston Kurrajong	15	2	1	3	7504
Progressive Dawn	3	1	0	0	6469
Queen Of Dreams (IRE)	6	1	0	1	3752
Secret Art (IRE)	8	2	1	1	29951
Seinesational	14	4	0	2	18113
Sir Busker (IRE)	5	1	2	0	6469

	Races Run	1st	2nd	3rd	£
Solar Flair	11	1	1	0	18675
Soto Sizzler	7	1	1	1	46688
Unit Of Assessment (IRE)	5	2	0	1	6857
Total winning prize-money					**£192067**
Favourites	**6-17**		**35.3%**		**0.40**

DANIEL KUBLER

LAMBOURN, BERKS

	No. of Hrs	Races Run	1st	2nd	3rd	Unpl	Per cent	£1 Level Stake
2-y-o	*5*	*25*	*3*	*2*	*1*	*19*	*12.0*	*+4.63*
3-y-o	*9*	*32*	*3*	*1*	*3*	*25*	*9.4*	*-16.90*
4-y-o+	*6*	*34*	*2*	*5*	*3*	*24*	*5.9*	*-24.00*
Totals	**20**	**91**	**8**	**8**	**7**	**68**	**8.8**	**-36.27**
2017	*26*	*131*	*10*	*12*	*7*	*102*	*7.6*	*-73.69*
2016	*28*	*116*	*10*	*3*	*14*	*88*	*8.6*	*-51.65*

JOCKEYS

	W-R	Per cent	£1 Level Stake
Robert Winston	2-17	11.8	+9.50
David Egan	1-1	100.0	+6.50
Paul Hanagan	1-1	100.0	+5.00
Kieran O'Neill	1-1	100.0	+5.00
Richard Kingscote	1-1	100.0	+1.63
William Carson	1-4	25.0	-1.90
George Downing	1-29	3.4	-25.00

COURSE RECORD

	Total W-R	Non-Hndcps 2-y-o	Non-Hndcps 3-y-o+	Hndcps 2-y-o	Hndcps 3-y-o+	Per cent	£1 Level Stake
Newcastle (A.W)	3-7	0-0	0-1	1-1	2-5	42.9	+5.63
Brighton	2-6	0-0	0-0	0-0	2-6	33.3	+3.60
Redcar	1-1	0-0	0-0	1-1	0-0	100.0	+5.00
Wolvhptn (A.W)	1-12	0-0	1-5	0-2	0-5	8.3	-6.50
Kempton (A.W)	1-17	0-1	0-5	1-1	0-10	5.9	+4.00

WINNING HORSES

Horse	Races Run	1st	2nd	3rd	£
Chitra	9	3	2	0	9704
Chizz De Biz (IRE)	5	1	0	0	3105
Involved	3	1	1	0	3105
Nyala	9	1	0	2	3105
Outrage	12	2	3	1	9452
Total winning prize-money					**£28471**
Favourites	**2-2**		**100.0%**		**2.73**

DAVID LANIGAN

NEWMARKET, SUFFOLK

	No. of Hrs	Races Run	1st	2nd	3rd	Unpl	Per cent	£1 Level Stake
2-y-o	*12*	*31*	*2*	*1*	*1*	*27*	*6.5*	*+12.50*
3-y-o	*13*	*47*	*11*	*6*	*5*	*25*	*23.4*	*+14.03*
4-y-o+	*3*	*11*	*3*	*2*	*1*	*5*	*27.3*	*+2.00*
Totals	**28**	**89**	**16**	**9**	**7**	**57**	**18.0**	**+28.53**
2017	*29*	*111*	*9*	*12*	*11*	*79*	*8.1*	*-64.27*
2016	*32*	*113*	*15*	*12*	*15*	*71*	*13.3*	*-54.18*

BY MONTH

2-y-o	W-R	Per cent	£1 Level Stake	3-y-o	W-R	Per cent	£1 Level Stake
January	0-0	0.0	0.00	January	1-5	20.0	+16.00
February	0-0	0.0	0.00	February	0-1	0.0	-1.00
March	0-0	0.0	0.00	March	0-0	0.0	0.00
April	0-0	0.0	0.00	April	0-2	0.0	-2.00
May	0-0	0.0	0.00	May	1-11	9.1	-9.50
June	0-3	0.0	-3.00	June	2-9	22.2	-0.77
July	0-6	0.0	-6.00	July	4-6	66.7	+8.30
August	0-2	0.0	-2.00	August	1-7	14.3	-3.50
September	1-3	33.3	+38.00	September	1-4	25.0	+0.50
October	0-9	0.0	-9.00	October	0-1	0.0	-1.00
November	1-8	12.5	-5.50	November	1-1	100.0	+7.00
December	0-0	0.0	0.00	December	0-0	0.0	0.00

4-y-o+	W-R	Per cent	£1 Level Stake	Totals	W-R	Per cent	£1 Level Stake
January	0-0	0.0	0.00	January	1-5	20.0	+16.00
February	0-0	0.0	0.00	February	0-1	0.0	-1.00
March	0-0	0.0	0.00	March	0-0	0.0	0.00
April	0-1	0.0	-1.00	April	0-3	0.0	-3.00
May	1-1	100.0	+5.00	May	2-12	16.7	-4.50
June	2-2	100.0	+5.00	June	4-14	28.6	+1.23
July	0-1	0.0	-1.00	July	4-13	30.8	+1.30
August	0-2	0.0	-2.00	August	1-11	9.1	-7.50
September	0-2	0.0	-2.00	September	2-9	22.2	+36.50
October	0-2	0.0	-2.00	October	0-12	0.0	-12.00
November	0-0	0.0	0.00	November	2-9	22.2	+7.00
December	0-0	0.0	0.00	December	0-0	0.0	0.00

DISTANCE

2-y-o	W-R	Per cent	£1 Level Stake	3-y-o	W-R	Per cent	£1 Level Stake
5f-6f	0-11	0.0	-11.00	5f-6f	0-0	0.0	0.00
7f-8f	2-19	10.5	+24.50	7f-8f	0-14	0.0	-14.00
9f-13f	0-1	0.0	-1.00	9f-13f	11-33	33.3	+28.03
14f+	0-0	0.0	0.00	14f+	0-0	0.0	0.00

4-y-o+	W-R	Per cent	£1 Level Stake	Totals	W-R	Per cent	£1 Level Stake
5f-6f	0-0	0.0	0.00	5f-6f	0-11	0.0	-11.00
7f-8f	0-1	0.0	-1.00	7f-8f	2-34	5.9	+9.50
9f-13f	3-10	30.0	+3.00	9f-13f	14-44	31.8	+30.03
14f+	0-0	0.0	0.00	14f+	0-0	0.0	0.00

TYPE OF RACE

Non-Handicaps	W-R	Per cent	£1 Level Stake	Handicaps	W-R	Per cent	£1 Level Stake
2-y-o	2-27	7.4	+16.50	2-y-o	0-4	0.0	-4.00
3-y-o	3-18	16.7	+9.50	3-y-o	8-29	27.6	+4.53
4-y-o+	0-1	0.0	-1.00	4-y-o+	3-10	30.0	+3.00

RACE CLASS

	W-R	Per cent	£1 Level Stake
Class 1	1-2	50.0	+3.00
Class 2	0-0	0.0	0.00
Class 3	1-3	33.3	+5.00
Class 4	5-16	31.3	+39.73
Class 5	6-51	11.8	-12.70
Class 6	3-17	17.6	-6.50
Class 7	0-0	0.0	0.00

FIRST TIME OUT

	W-R	Per cent	£1 Level Stake
2-y-o	0-12	0.0	-12.00
3-y-o	1-13	7.7	+8.00
4-y-o+	1-3	33.3	+3.00
Totals	2-28	7.1	-1.00

JOCKEYS

	W-R	Per cent	£1 Level Stake
Daniel Muscutt	4-8	50.0	+4.50
Stevie Donohoe	4-44	9.1	-10.20
James Doyle	2-2	100.0	+3.50
Fran Berry	2-6	33.3	+4.00
Pat Cosgrave	2-11	18.2	+31.73
Franny Norton	1-2	50.0	+3.00
Shane Kelly	1-3	33.3	+5.00

COURSE RECORD

	Total W-R	Non-Hndcps 2-y-o	Non-Hndcps 3-y-o+	Hndcps 2-y-o	Hndcps 3-y-o+	Per cent	£1 Level Stake
Newcastle (A.W)	3-3	1-1	0-0	0-0	2-2	100.0	+6.50
Wolvhptn (A.W)	3-13	0-4	0-1	0-1	3-7	23.1	-1.00
Lingfield (A.W)	2-5	0-0	1-1	0-0	1-4	40.0	+24.00
Redcar	1-1	0-0	1-1	0-0	0-0	100.0	+0.50
Hamilton	1-3	0-0	0-0	0-0	1-3	33.3	-1.20
Yarmouth	1-3	1-1	0-0	0-0	0-2	33.3	+38.00
Leicester	1-4	0-0	0-0	0-0	1-4	25.0	+2.00
Windsor	1-5	0-2	0-0	0-0	1-3	20.0	-3.27
Newmkt (Jly)	1-6	0-3	1-1	0-0	0-2	16.7	-1.00
Chelmsford (A.W)	1-13	0-3	0-6	0-1	1-3	7.7	-9.50
Kempton (A.W)	1-16	0-7	0-3	0-1	1-5	6.3	-9.50

WINNING HORSES

Horse	Races Run	1st	2nd	3rd	£
Atticus Boy (IRE)	8	3	2	2	11644
Lacustre	3	1	1	0	9767
Lexington Empire	7	3	0	2	10415
Light Of Joy (USA)	4	3	1	0	19278
Millions Memories	2	1	0	0	4787
Roundabout Kitten (USA)	4	1	0	0	3752
Sunset Flash (IRE)	2	1	0	0	3105
Worth Waiting	4	3	1	0	32679

Total winning prize-money **£95427**

Favourites **5-12** **41.7%** **-1.47**

SOPHIE LEECH

ELTON, GLOUCS

	No. of Hrs	Races Run	1st	2nd	3rd	Unpl	Per cent	£1 Level Stake
2-y-o	*1*	*1*	*0*	*0*	*0*	*1*	*0.0*	*-1.00*
3-y-o	*1*	*3*	*0*	*0*	*0*	*3*	*0.0*	*-3.00*
4-y-o+	*9*	*40*	*4*	*5*	*9*	*22*	*10.0*	*-18.00*
Totals	**11**	**44**	**4**	**5**	**9**	**26**	**9.1**	**-22.00**
2017	*9*	*35*	*2*	*1*	*6*	*26*	*5.7*	*+10.00*
2016	*12*	*46*	*8*	*3*	*7*	*28*	*17.4*	*+20.00*

JOCKEYS

	W-R	Per cent	£1 Level Stake
David Probert	4-12	33.3	+10.00

COURSE RECORD

	Total W-R	Non-Hndcps 2-y-o	Non-Hndcps 3-y-o+	Hndcps 2-y-o	Hndcps 3-y-o+	Per cent	£1 Level Stake
Wolvhptn (A.W)	2-13	0-0	0-0	0-1	2-12	15.4	2.50
Leicester	1-4	0-0	0-1	0-0	1-3	25.0	+1.00
Chepstow	1-9	0-0	0-0	0-0	1-9	11.1	-2.50

WINNING HORSES

Horse	Races Run	1st	2nd	3rd	£
Perfect Symphony (IRE)	8	1	2	2	3493
Wahaab (IRE)	11	1	0	2	3752
*Yasir (USA)	7	2	1	2	6210

Total winning prize-money **£13455**

Favourites **0-6** **0.0%** **-6.00**

NICK LITTMODEN

NEWMARKET, SUFFOLK

	No. of Hrs	Races Run	1st	2nd	3rd	Unpl	Per cent	£1 Level Stake
2-y-o	*3*	*10*	*0*	*0*	*0*	*10*	*0.0*	*-10.00*
3-y-o	*0*	*0*	*0*	*0*	*0*	*0*	*0.0*	*0.00*
4-y-o+	*6*	*29*	*5*	*2*	*2*	*19*	*17.2*	*-2.09*
Totals	**9**	**39**	**5**	**2**	**2**	**29**	**12.8**	**-12.09**
2017	*1*	*2*	*0*	*0*	*0*	*2*	*0.0*	*-2.00*
2016	*0*							

JOCKEYS

	W-R	Per cent	£1 Level Stake
Tom Marquand	3-6	50.0	+16.50
Adam Kirby	2-3	66.7	+1.41

COURSE RECORD

	Total W-R	Non-Hndcps 2-y-o	Non-Hndcps 3-y-o+	Hndcps 2-y-o	Hndcps 3-y-o+	Per cent	£1 Level Stake
Lingfield (A.W)	5-15	0-0	1-2	0-0	4-13	33.3	+11.91

WINNING HORSES

Horse	Races Run	1st	2nd	3rd	£
Fearsome	12	4	0	1	18566
Toriano	10	1	1	0	3752

Total winning prize-money **£22318**

Favourites **2-3** **66.7%** **1.41**

BERNARD LLEWELLYN

FOCHRIW, CAERPHILLY

	No. of Hrs	Races Run	1st	2nd	3rd	Unpl	Per cent	£1 Level Stake
2-y-o	*0*	*0*	*0*	*0*	*0*	*0*	*0.0*	*0.00*
3-y-o	*1*	*2*	*0*	*0*	*0*	*2*	*0.0*	*-2.00*
4-y-o+	*14*	*71*	*2*	*9*	*9*	*51*	*2.8*	*-52.00*
Totals	**15**	**73**	**2**	**9**	**9**	**53**	**2.7**	**-54.00**
2017	*13*	*69*	*7*	*6*	*6*	*50*	*10.1*	*-13.50*
2016	*19*	*85*	*11*	*9*	*6*	*59*	*12.9*	*+18.67*

JOCKEYS

	W-R	Per cent	£1 Level Stake
Martin Harley	1-4	25.0	+11.00
Stevie Donohoe	1-8	12.5	-4.00

COURSE RECORD

	Total W-R	Non-Hndcps 2-y-o	Non-Hndcps 3-y-o+	Hndcps 2-y-o	Hndcps 3-y-o+	Per cent	£1 Level Stake
Chelmsford (A.W)	1-6	0-0	0-0	0-0	1-6	16.7	-2.00
Ffos Las	1-8	0-0	0-0	0-0	1-8	12.5	+7.00

WINNING HORSES

Horse	Races Run	1st	2nd	3rd	£
Ascot Day (FR)	5	1	1	0	3170
Edge (IRE)	12	1	2	2	3429
Total winning prize-money					**£6599**
Favourites	**2-6**		**33.3%**		**0.63**

NATALIE LLOYD-BEAVIS

EAST GARSTON, BERKS

	No. of Hrs	Races Run	1st	2nd	3rd	Unpl	Per cent	£1 Level Stake
2-y-o	*1*	*3*	*0*	*0*	*0*	*3*	*0.0*	*-3.00*
3-y-o	*1*	*2*	*1*	*0*	*0*	*1*	*50.0*	*+8.00*
4-y-o+	*5*	*11*	*0*	*0*	*0*	*11*	*0.0*	*-11.00*
Totals	**7**	**16**	**1**	**0**	**0**	**15**	**6.3**	**-6.00**
2017	*10*	*21*	*0*	*1*	*1*	*19*	*0.0*	*-21.00*
2016	*11*	*55*	*3*	*1*	*4*	*47*	*5.5*	*-34.50*

JOCKEYS

	W-R	Per cent	£1 Level Stake
Raul Da Silva	1-2	50.0	+8.00

COURSE RECORD

	Total W-R	Non-Hndcps 2-y-o	Non-Hndcps 3-y-o+	Hndcps 2-y-o	Hndcps 3-y-o+	Per cent	£1 Level Stake
Southwell (A.W)	1-1	0-0	0-0	0-0	1-1	100.0	+9.00

WINNING HORSES

Horse	Races Run	1st	2nd	3rd	£
Precious Silk (IRE)	2	1	0	0	3105
Total winning prize-money					**£3105**
Favourites	**0-1**		**0.0%**		**-1.00**

JOHN E LONG

ROYSTON, HERTS

	No. of Hrs	Races Run	1st	2nd	3rd	Unpl	Per cent	£1 Level Stake
2-y-o	*0*	*0*	*0*	*0*	*0*	*0*	*0.0*	*0.00*
3-y-o	*2*	*3*	*1*	*0*	*0*	*2*	*33.3*	*+48.00*
4-y-o+	*7*	*19*	*3*	*0*	*1*	*15*	*15.8*	*+35.00*
Totals	**9**	**22**	**4**	**0**	**1**	**17**	**18.2**	**+83.00**
2017	*5*	*38*	*1*	*1*	*2*	*34*	*2.6*	*-23.00*
2016	*7*	*43*	*3*	*5*	*2*	*33*	*7.0*	*-3.50*

JOCKEYS

	W-R	Per cent	£1 Level Stake
Rob J Fitzpatrick	2-5	40.0	+28.00
Rob Hornby	1-2	50.0	+49.00
Hollie Doyle	1-4	25.0	+17.00

COURSE RECORD

	Total W-R	Non-Hndcps 2-y-o	Non-Hndcps 3-y-o+	Hndcps 2-y-o	Hndcps 3-y-o+	Per cent	£1 Level Stake
Sandown	1-1	0-0	0-0	0-0	1-1	100.0	+6.00
Brighton	1-3	0-0	0-0	0-0	1-3	33.3	+23.00
Chelmsford (A.W)	1-3	0-0	0-0	0-0	1-3	33.3	+18.00
Kempton (A.W)	1-6	0-0	0-0	0-0	1-6	16.7	+45.00

WINNING HORSES

Horse	Races Run	1st	2nd	3rd	£
*Choral Music	2	1	0	0	3752
Lyrica's Lion (IRE)*	3	2	0	0	7633
*Magicinthemaking (USA)	2	1	0	1	4140
Total winning prize-money					**£15525**
Favourites	**0-1**		**0.0%**		**-1.00**

DAVID LOUGHNANE

MARKET DRAYTON, SHROPSHIRE

	No. of Hrs	Races Run	1st	2nd	3rd	Unpl	Per cent	£1 Level Stake
2-y-o	*10*	*37*	*2*	*3*	*7*	*25*	*5.4*	*-28.50*
3-y-o	*15*	*87*	*7*	*4*	*8*	*68*	*8.0*	*+17.00*
4-y-o+	*23*	*170*	*19*	*15*	*23*	*113*	*11.2*	*-13.50*
Totals	**48**	**294**	**28**	**22**	**38**	**206**	**9.5**	**-25.00**
2017	*32*	*193*	*16*	*18*	*20*	*138*	*8.3*	*+12.38*
2016	*33*	*233*	*26*	*25*	*29*	*153*	*11.2*	*+3.96*

BY MONTH

2-y-o	W-R	Per cent	£1 Level Stake	3-y-o	W-R	Per cent	£1 Level Stake
January	0-0	0.0	0.00	January	0-2	0.0	-2.00
February	0-0	0.0	0.00	February	0-2	0.0	-2.00
March	0-1	0.0	-1.00	March	0-2	0.0	-2.00
April	0-1	0.0	-1.00	April	1-11	9.1	+10.00
May	0-4	0.0	-4.00	May	1-16	6.3	+10.00
June	1-6	16.7	-3.50	June	0-12	0.0	-12.00
July	0-2	0.0	-2.00	July	1-7	14.3	+1.00
August	1-4	25.0	+2.00	August	0-9	0.0	-9.00
September	0-10	0.0	-10.00	September	1-10	10.0	+1.00
October	0-3	0.0	-3.00	October	1-5	20.0	+5.00
November	0-1	0.0	-1.00	November	1-5	20.0	+12.00
December	0-5	0.0	-5.00	December	1-6	16.7	+5.00

4-y-o+	W-R	Per cent	£1 Level Stake	Totals	W-R	Per cent	£1 Level Stake
January	1-14	7.1	-3.00	January	1-16	6.3	-5.00
February	1-7	14.3	-3.00	February	1-9	11.1	-5.00
March	1-3	33.3	+0.25	March	1-6	16.7	-2.75
April	1-10	10.0	-4.00	April	2-22	9.1	+5.00
May	2-20	10.0	-3.00	May	3-40	7.5	+3.00
June	2-20	10.0	+7.00	June	3-38	7.9	-8.50
July	1-13	7.7	-7.00	July	2-22	9.1	-8.00
August	2-25	8.0	-12.50	August	3-38	7.9	-19.50
September	2-18	11.1	-4.75	September	3-38	7.9	-13.75
October	0-20	0.0	-20.00	October	1-28	3.6	-18.00
November	2-9	22.2	+14.00	November	3-15	20.0	+26.00
December	4-11	36.4	+22.50	December	5-22	22.7	+27.50

DISTANCE

2-y-o	W-R	Per cent	£1 Level Stake	3-y-o	W-R	Per cent	£1 Level Stake
5f-6f	2-24	8.3	-15.50	5f-6f	2-14	14.3	+20.00
7f-8f	0-13	0.0	-13.00	7f-8f	3-43	7.0	+6.00
9f-13f	0-0	0.0	0.00	9f-13f	2-30	6.7	-9.00
14f+	0-0	0.0	0.00	14f+	0-0	0.0	0.00

4-y-o+	W-R	Per cent	£1 Level Stake	Totals	W-R	Per cent	£1 Level Stake
5f-6f	2-39	5.1	-18.50	5f-6f	6-77	7.8	-14.00
7f-8f	12-85	14.1	-3.50	7f-8f	15-141	10.6	-10.50
9f-13f	5-44	11.4	+10.50	9f-13f	7-74	9.5	+1.50
14f+	0-2	0.0	-2.00	14f+	0-2	0.0	-2.00

TYPE OF RACE

Non-Handicaps	W-R	Per cent	£1 Level Stake	Handicaps	W-R	Per cent	£1 Level Stake
2-y-o	2-35	5.7	-26.50	2-y-o	0-2	0.0	-2.00
3-y-o	1-19	5.3	-8.00	3-y-o	6-68	8.8	+25.00
4-y-o+	0-10	0.0	-10.00	4-y-o+	19-160	11.9	-3.50

RACE CLASS

	W-R	Per cent	£1 Level Stake
Class 1	0-3	0.0	-3.00
Class 2	1-7	14.3	+4.00
Class 3	0-14	0.0	-14.00
Class 4	4-73	5.5	-35.50
Class 5	10-122	8.2	-14.75
Class 6	11-70	15.7	+33.25
Class 7	2-5	40.0	+5.00

FIRST TIME OUT

	W-R	Per cent	£1 Level Stake
2-y-o	0-10	0.0	-10.00
3-y-o	1-15	6.7	-4.00
4-y-o+	1-23	4.3	-12.00
Totals	2-48	4.2	-26.00

JOCKEYS

	W-R	Per cent	£1 Level Stake
Stevie Donohoe	5-18	27.8	+14.25
Ben Curtis	4-38	10.5	+4.50
David Egan	2-12	16.7	+1.50
P J McDonald	2-12	16.7	+16.00
Sam James	2-16	12.5	-1.00
Laura Coughlan	2-26	7.7	-12.75
Mark Crehan	1-1	100.0	+6.00
David Probert	1-1	100.0	+6.50
Ger O'Neill	1-2	50.0	+15.00
Joe Fanning	1-3	33.3	+8.00
Tom Eaves	1-5	20.0	+16.00
John Fahy	1-7	14.3	-1.00
Cameron Noble	1-7	14.3	+10.00
Trevor Whelan	1-8	12.5	+3.00
Thomas Greatrex	1-8	12.5	-4.00
Edward Greatrex	1-9	11.1	+1.00
Luke Morris	1-12	8.3	+1.00

COURSE RECORD

	Total W-R	Non-Hndcps 2-y-o	Non-Hndcps 3-y-o+	Hndcps 2-y-o	Hndcps 3-y-o+	Per cent	£1 Level Stake
Wolvhptn (A.W)	10-86	1-11	0-14	0-0	9-61	11.6	+1.50
Beverley	3-10	0-0	0-0	0-0	3-10	30.0	+25.75
Newcastle (A.W)	2-7	0-0	0-0	0-1	2-6	28.6	+3.00
Catterick	2-11	0-1	0-0	0-0	2-10	18.2	+6.50
Kempton (A.W)	2-17	0-2	0-2	0-0	2-13	11.8	+15.00
Nottingham	2-19	0-2	0-2	0-0	2-15	10.5	+7.00
Brighton	1-1	0-0	0-0	0-0	1-1	100.0	+12.00
Salisbury	1-1	0-0	0-0	0-0	1-1	100.0	+2.50
Carlisle	1-6	1-2	0-0	0-0	0-4	16.7	-3.50
Lingfield (A.W)	1-8	0-1	0-0	0-1	1-6	12.5	-4.75
Leicester	1-10	0-1	0-0	0-0	1-9	10.0	0.00
Chester	1-18	0-5	1-4	0-0	0-9	5.6	-7.00
Haydock	1-34	0-7	0-1	0-0	1-26	2.9	-17.00

WINNING HORSES

Horse	Races Run	1st	2nd	3rd	£
Baby Steps	5	1	0	2	4205
Baliuta Acha	12	2	1	0	10760
Berlusca (IRE)	18	2	3	4	8604
*Careyanne	11	2	2	2	6210
Critical Thinking (IRE)	18	5	4	3	18598
*False Id	11	3	1	0	8992
Fizzy Feet (IRE)	5	1	1	1	3752
Harbour Pilot	9	1	0	2	3752
*Kaser (IRE)	3	1	0	2	3752
*Raven's Raft (IRE)	6	1	0	2	3105
Rockesbury	16	2	1	1	8957

Seamster	14	1	1	4	3235
Signore Piccolo	10	1	0	1	5757
Star Quality	8	1	0	0	15563
*Stringybark Creek	12	4	0	2	14512
Total winning prize-money					**£119754**
Favourites	**4-14**		**28.6%**		**3.00**

DANIEL MARK LOUGHNANE

ROCK, WORCS

	No. of Hrs	Races Run	1st	2nd	3rd	Unpl	Per cent	£1 Level Stake
2-y-o	*8*	*33*	*1*	*3*	*3*	*26*	*3.0*	*-24.00*
3-y-o	*18*	*83*	*5*	*4*	*12*	*62*	*6.0*	*-46.50*
4-y-o+	*32*	*220*	*18*	*34*	*35*	*132*	*8.2*	*-109.75*
Totals	**58**	**336**	**24**	**41**	**50**	**220**	**7.1**	**-180.25**
2017	*61*	*328*	*21*	*35*	*41*	*230*	*6.4*	*-121.50*
2016	*65*	*365*	*36*	*38*	*37*	*254*	*9.9*	*-86.94*

BY MONTH

2-y-o	W-R	Per cent	£1 Level Stake	3-y-o	W-R	Per cent	£1 Level Stake
January	0-0	0.0	0.00	January	0-6	0.0	-6.00
February	0-0	0.0	0.00	February	0-4	0.0	-4.00
March	0-0	0.0	0.00	March	0-0	0.0	0.00
April	0-1	0.0	-1.00	April	1-2	50.0	+6.00
May	0-4	0.0	-4.00	May	0-9	0.0	-9.00
June	0-5	0.0	-5.00	June	0-8	0.0	-8.00
July	0-1	0.0	-1.00	July	2-11	18.2	-1.00
August	1-2	50.0	+7.00	August	0-10	0.0	-10.00
September	0-3	0.0	-3.00	September	1-15	6.7	-8.50
October	0-4	0.0	-4.00	October	0-5	0.0	-5.00
November	0-5	0.0	-5.00	November	0-6	0.0	-6.00
December	0-8	0.0	-8.00	December	1-7	14.3	+5.00

4-y-o+	W-R	Per cent	£1 Level Stake	Totals	W-R	Per cent	£1 Level Stake
January	3-32	9.4	-19.50	January	3-38	7.9	-25.50
February	4-20	20.0	-4.13	February	4-24	16.7	-8.13
March	2-18	11.1	-9.63	March	2-18	11.1	-9.63
April	3-16	18.8	-4.00	April	4-19	21.1	+1.00
May	0-20	0.0	-20.00	May	0-33	0.0	-33.00
June	1-18	5.6	-12.00	June	1-31	3.2	-25.00
July	0-18	0.0	-18.00	July	2-30	6.7	-20.00
August	2-18	11.1	+1.50	August	3-30	10.0	-1.50
September	1-21	4.8	-8.00	September	2-39	5.1	-19.50
October	1-14	7.1	-1.00	October	1-23	4.3	-10.00
November	0-14	0.0	-14.00	November	0-25	0.0	-20.00
December	1-11	9.1	-1.00	December	2-26	7.7	+4.00

DISTANCE

2-y-o	W-R	Per cent	£1 Level Stake	3-y-o	W-R	Per cent	£1 Level Stake
5f-6f	0-20	0.0	-20.00	5f-6f	0-12	0.0	-12.00
7f-8f	1-13	7.7	-4.00	7f-8f	2-42	4.8	-27.50
9f-13f	0-0	0.0	0.00	9f-13f	3-29	10.3	-7.00
14f+	0-0	0.0	0.00	14f+	0-0	0.0	0.00

4-y-o+	W-R	Per cent	£1 Level Stake	Totals	W-R	Per cent	£1 Level Stake
5f-6f	5-52	9.6	-19.50	5f-6f	5-84	6.0	-51.50
7f-8f	9-107	8.4	-53.75	7f-8f	12-162	7.4	-85.25
9f-13f	3-54	5.6	-35.00	9f-13f	6-83	7.2	-42.00
14f+	1-7	14.3	-1.50	14f+	1-7	14.3	-1.50

TYPE OF RACE

Non-Handicaps	W-R	Per cent	£1 Level Stake	Handicaps	W-R	Per cent	£1 Level Stake
2-y-o	0-20	0.0	-20.00	2-y-o	1-13	7.7	-4.00
3-y-o	0-17	0.0	-17.00	3-y-o	5-66	7.6	-29.50
4-y-o+	2-11	18.2	-5.50	4-y-o+	16-209	7.7	-114.25

RACE CLASS

	W-R	Per cent	£1 Level Stake
Class 1	0-0	0.0	0.00
Class 2	0-2	0.0	-2.00
Class 3	1-7	14.3	+6.00
Class 4	3-57	5.3	-33.63
Class 5	8-100	8.0	-58.63
Class 6	12-165	7.3	-87.00
Class 7	0-5	0.0	-5.00

FIRST TIME OUT

	W-R	Per cent	£1 Level Stake
2-y-o	0-8	0.0	-8.00
3-y-o	1-18	5.6	-10.00
4-y-o+	4-32	12.5	-13.75
Totals	5-58	8.6	-31.75

JOCKEYS

	W-R	Per cent	£1 Level Stake
Edward Greatrex	4-23	17.4	-11.25
Kieran O'Neill	3-17	17.6	+2.50
Andrew Mullen	3-27	11.1	-14.50
Eoin Walsh	3-47	6.4	-28.50
Oisin Murphy	2-8	25.0	+5.00
Luke Morris	2-15	13.3	-4.50
Liam Jones	2-51	3.9	-23.00
Jessica Cooley	1-5	20.0	+8.00
Silvestre De Sousa	1-5	20.0	+1.50
P J McDonald	1-7	14.3	-0.50
Megan Nicholls	1-7	14.3	+5.00
Ryan Holmes	1-13	7.7	-9.00

COURSE RECORD

	Total W-R	Non-Hndcps 2-y-o	3-y-o+	Hndcps 2-y-o	3-y-o+	Per cent	£1 Level Stake
Wolvhptn (A.W)	11-107	0-7	1-8	0-3	10-89	10.3	-39.00
Kempton (A.W)	5-45	0-1	1-4	1-5	3-35	11.1	-7.00
Lingfield (A.W)	2-32	0-1	0-4	0-1	2-26	6.3	-24.25
Doncaster	1-4	0-2	0-0	0-0	1-2	25.0	+9.00
Haydock	1-6	0-0	0-0	0-0	1-6	16.7	+2.00
Bath	1-7	0-0	0-0	0-1	1-6	14.3	-1.00
Newcastle (A.W)	1-16	0-0	0-4	0-1	1-11	6.3	-11.00
Chelmsford (A.W)	1-18	0-0	0-0	0-1	1-17	5.6	-12.50
Brighton	1-21	0-0	0-0	0-0	1-21	4.8	-16.50

WINNING HORSES

Horse	Races Run	1st	2nd	3rd	£
Big Amigo (IRE)*	11	1	2	1	3105

Big Lachie	16	3	5	1	20442
Chocolate Box (IRE)	6	1	0	1	5693
Dark Alliance (IRE)	15	4	2	2	9283
Deeley's Double (FR)	2	1	0	0	3752
Destinys Rock	9	1	0	6	3105
Dream Magic (IRE)	10	1	1	1	3752
*Ember's Glow	6	1	1	1	3105
*Harbour Approach	7	1	1	2	3752
Little Miss Kodi (IRE)	15	1	1	3	3105
Lord Murphy (IRE)	22	1	4	6	3105
Moxy Mares	5	1	1	1	4852
Onefootinfront	6	2	1	1	6210
Pensax Boy	4	1	0	0	5531
Precision Prince (IRE)	7	1	1	0	3105
*Seaforth (IRE)	5	1	1	0	3105
Tigerwolf (IRE)	15	2	6	3	6857
Total winning prize-money					**£91859**
Favourites	**8-29**		**27.6%**		**-2.75**

SHAUN LYCETT

LEAFIELD, OXON

	No. of Hrs	Races Run	1st	2nd	3rd	Unpl	Per cent	£1 Level Stake
2-y-o	*0*	*0*	*0*	*0*	*0*	*0*	*0.0*	*0.00*
3-y-o	*1*	*1*	*0*	*0*	*0*	*1*	*0.0*	*-1.00*
4-y-o+	*5*	*23*	*3*	*3*	*2*	*14*	*13.0*	*-6.63*
Totals	**6**	**24**	**3**	**3**	**2**	**15**	**12.5**	**-7.63**
2017	*9*	*31*	*1*	*3*	*3*	*24*	*3.2*	*-23.00*
2016	*10*	*52*	*3*	*3*	*6*	*40*	*5.8*	*-31.75*

JOCKEYS

	W-R	Per cent	£1 Level Stake
Kieran Shoemark	2-11	18.2	+2.50
Silvestre De Sousa	1-1	100.0	+1.88

COURSE RECORD

	Total W-R	Non-Hndcps 2-y-o	Non-Hndcps 3-y-o+	Hndcps 2-y-o	Hndcps 3-y-o+	Per cent	£1 Level Stake
Wolvhptn (A.W)	2-11	0-0	0-0	0-0	2-11	18.2	+0.38
Chelmsford (A.W)	1-4	0-0	0-0	0-0	1-4	25.0	+1.00

WINNING HORSES

Horse	Races Run	1st	2nd	3rd	£
The King's Steed	14	3	2	2	9639
Total winning prize-money					**£9639**
Favourites	**1-6**		**16.7%**		**-3.13**

JOHN MACKIE

CHURCH BROUGHTON, DERBYS

	No. of Hrs	Races Run	1st	2nd	3rd	Unpl	Per cent	£1 Level Stake
2-y-o	*1*	*3*	*0*	*0*	*0*	*3*	*0.0*	*-3.00*
3-y-o	*5*	*20*	*1*	*5*	*5*	*9*	*5.0*	*-15.50*
4-y-o+	*14*	*88*	*7*	*6*	*8*	*67*	*8.0*	*-47.67*
Totals	**20**	**111**	**8**	**11**	**13**	**79**	**7.2**	**-66.17**
2017	*18*	*111*	*19*	*12*	*14*	*66*	*17.1*	*+46.50*
2016	*21*	*126*	*13*	*17*	*15*	*81*	*10.3*	*-23.92*

JOCKEYS

	W-R	Per cent	£1 Level Stake
Silvestre De Sousa	2-3	66.7	+2.33
Jimmy Quinn	2-18	11.1	+2.00
David Allan	1-4	25.0	+3.00
Ben Curtis	1-5	20.0	-2.00
Andrew Mullen	1-10	10.0	-5.50
Joe Fanning	1-11	9.1	-6.00

COURSE RECORD

	Total W-R	Non-Hndcps 2-y-o	Non-Hndcps 3-y-o+	Hndcps 2-y-o	Hndcps 3-y-o+	Per cent	£1 Level Stake
Southwell (A.W)	4-14	0-0	0-0	0-0	4-14	28.6	-0.67
Musselburgh	1-2	0-0	0-0	0-0	1-2	50.0	+2.50
Newbury	1-2	0-0	0-0	0-0	1-2	50.0	+7.00
Nottingham	1-15	0-1	0-1	0-0	1-13	6.7	-8.00
Wolvhptn (A.W)	1-22	0-1	0-2	0-0	1-19	4.5	-11.00

WINNING HORSES

Horse	Races Run	1st	2nd	3rd	£
Art Echo	10	1	1	0	3752
Custard The Dragon	9	1	1	1	9960
Lunar Jet	7	1	1	2	7763
Monks Stand (USA)	12	3	0	0	10933
Polyphony (IRE)	6	1	2	0	3105
Tristram	6	1	0	0	3881
Total winning prize-money					**£39394**
Favourites	**3-8**		**37.5%**		**0.33**

MICHAEL MADGWICK

DENMEAD, HANTS

	No. of Hrs	Races Run	1st	2nd	3rd	Unpl	Per cent	£1 Level Stake
2-y-o	*2*	*7*	*0*	*0*	*0*	*7*	*0.0*	*-7.00*
3-y-o	*8*	*19*	*1*	*1*	*1*	*16*	*5.3*	*+15.00*
4-y-o+	*8*	*42*	*1*	*9*	*2*	*30*	*2.4*	*-31.00*
Totals	**18**	**68**	**2**	**10**	**3**	**53**	**2.9**	**-23.00**
2017	*14*	*80*	*4*	*4*	*6*	*66*	*5.0*	*-41.75*
2016	*13*	*95*	*5*	*6*	*14*	*70*	*5.3*	*-54.00*

JOCKEYS

	W-R	Per cent	£1 Level Stake
Fran Berry	1-2	50.0	+32.00
Scott McCullagh	1-7	14.3	+4.00

COURSE RECORD

	Total W-R	Non-Hndcps 2-y-o	Non-Hndcps 3-y-o+	Hndcps 2-y-o	Hndcps 3-y-o+	Per cent	£1 Level Stake
Kempton (A.W)	2-25	0-1	0-2	0-0	2-22	8.0	+20.00

WINNING HORSES

Horse	Races Run	1st	2nd	3rd	£
*Dono Di Dio	5	1	1	0	3752
*Family Fortunes	7	1	4	0	3752
Total winning prize-money					**£7504**
Favourites	**0-2**		**0.0%**		**-2.00**

HEATHER MAIN

KINGSTON LISLE, OXON

	No. of Hrs	Races Run	1st	2nd	3rd	Unpl	Per cent	£1 Level Stake
2-y-o	*9*	*21*	*2*	*0*	*0*	*19*	*9.5*	*+12.33*
3-y-o	*9*	*45*	*4*	*3*	*6*	*32*	*8.9*	*-16.50*
4-y-o+	*11*	*94*	*15*	*9*	*7*	*62*	*16.0*	*+4.08*
Totals	**29**	**160**	**21**	**12**	**13**	**113**	**13.1**	**-0.09**
2017	*17*	*88*	*13*	*8*	*14*	*53*	*14.8*	*+50.75*
2016	*10*	*53*	*4*	*4*	*6*	*39*	*7.5*	*+5.50*

BY MONTH

2-y-o	W-R	Per cent	£1 Level Stake	3-y-o	W-R	Per cent	£1 Level Stake
January	0-0	0.0	0.00	January	0-1	0.0	-1.00
February	0-0	0.0	0.00	February	1-2	50.0	+9.00
March	0-0	0.0	0.00	March	0-2	0.0	-2.00
April	0-1	0.0	-1.00	April	0-3	0.0	-3.00
May	0-1	0.0	-1.00	May	0-7	0.0	-7.00
June	0-1	0.0	-1.00	June	1-8	12.5	0.00
July	0-2	0.0	-2.00	July	1-9	11.1	-2.50
August	0-4	0.0	-4.00	August	0-4	0.0	-4.00
September	0-3	0.0	-3.00	September	0-1	0.0	-1.00
October	0-3	0.0	-3.00	October	0-3	0.0	-3.00
November	2-2	100.0	+31.33	November	0-4	0.0	-4.00
December	0-4	0.0	-4.00	December	1-1	100.0	+2.00

4-y-o+	W-R	Per cent	£1 Level Stake	Totals	W-R	Per cent	£1 Level Stake
January	1-1	100.0	+3.00	January	1-2	50.0	+2.00
February	1-1	100.0	+2.25	February	2-3	66.7	+11.25
March	2-6	33.3	+13.00	March	2-8	25.0	+11.00
April	1-4	25.0	+9.00	April	1-8	12.5	+5.00
May	1-13	7.7	-9.00	May	1-21	4.8	-17.00
June	2-10	20.0	-6.26	June	3-19	15.8	-7.26
July	1-9	11.1	-6.25	July	2-20	10.0	-10.75
August	1-10	10.0	-3.00	August	1-18	5.6	-11.00
September	2-14	14.3	+5.00	September	2-18	11.1	+1.00
October	1-13	7.7	-8.67	October	1-19	5.3	-14.67
November	1-8	12.5	-1.00	November	3-14	21.4	-5.00
December	1-5	20.0	+6.00	December	2-10	20.0	+8.00

DISTANCE

2-y-o	W-R	Per cent	£1 Level Stake	3-y-o	W-R	Per cent	£1 Level Stake
5f-6f	0-9	0.0	-9.00	5f-6f	0-1	0.0	-1.00
7f-8f	2-9	22.2	+24.33	7f-8f	4-27	14.8	+1.50
9f-13f	0-3	0.0	-3.00	9f-13f	0-15	0.0	-15.00
14f+	0-0	0.0	0.00	14f+	0-2	0.0	-2.00

4-y-o+	W-R	Per cent	£1 Level Stake	Totals	W-R	Per cent	£1 Level Stake
5f-6f	1-5	20.0	-1.00	5f-6f	1-15	6.7	-11.00
7f-8f	5-38	13.2	+3.66	7f-8f	11-74	14.9	+29.49
9f-13f	8-41	19.5	+4.42	9f-13f	8-59	13.6	-13.58
14f+	1-10	10.0	-3.00	14f+	1-12	8.3	-5.00

TYPE OF RACE

Non-Handicaps	W-R	Per cent	£1 Level Stake	Handicaps	W-R	Per cent	£1 Level Stake
2-y-o	2-17	11.8	+16.33	2-y-o	0-4	0.0	-4.00
3-y-o	0-15	0.0	-15.00	3-y-o	4-30	13.3	-1.50
4-y-o+	1-3	33.3	-1.16	4-y-o+	14-91	15.4	+5.24

RACE CLASS

	W-R	Per cent	£1 Level Stake
Class 1	0-0	0.0	0.00
Class 2	1-14	7.1	-6.00
Class 3	4-19	21.1	+9.25
Class 4	4-51	7.8	-10.92
Class 5	9-48	18.8	+16.41
Class 6	3-28	10.7	-8.83
Class 7	0-0	0.0	0.00

FIRST TIME OUT

	W-R	Per cent	£1 Level Stake
2-y-o	0-9	0.0	-9.00
3-y-o	0-9	0.0	-9.00
4-y-o+	3-11	27.3	+8.00
Totals	3-29	10.3	-10.00

JOCKEYS

	W-R	Per cent	£1 Level Stake
David Egan	5-30	16.7	-9.50
Luke Morris	5-30	16.7	+5.16
P J McDonald	3-9	33.3	+9.00
William Buick	1-1	100.0	+6.00
Phillip Makin	1-1	100.0	+7.00
Ellie MacKenzie	1-2	50.0	+27.00
Robert Havlin	1-4	25.0	+2.50
Charles Bishop	1-5	20.0	+2.00
Georgia Cox	1-7	14.3	+6.00
Ben Curtis	1-8	12.5	-5.25
Fran Berry	1-9	11.1	+4.00

COURSE RECORD

	Total W-R	Non-Hndcps 2-y-o	Non-Hndcps 3-y-o+	Hndcps 2-y-o	Hndcps 3-y-o+	Per cent	£1 Level Stake
Newcastle (A.W)	5-17	2-2	0-2	0-0	3-13	29.4	+35.33
Wolvhptn (A.W)	5-22	0-1	1-5	0-0	4-16	22.7	+12.17
Lingfield (A.W)	3-11	0-1	0-2	0-0	3-8	27.3	+9.25
Southwell (A.W)	1-1	0-0	0-0	0-0	1-1	100.0	+10.00
Nottingham	1-2	0-0	0-0	0-0	1-2	50.0	+5.00
Haydock	1-3	0-0	0-0	0-0	1-3	33.3	+1.00
Newmarket	1-7	0-0	0-0	0-0	1-7	14.3	0.00
Leicester	1-8	0-3	0-1	0-0	1-4	12.5	-5.25
Chepstow	1-10	0-0	0-0	0-0	1-10	10.0	-8.09
Kempton (A.W)	1-17	0-1	0-2	0-3	1-11	5.9	-4.00
Newbury	1-18	0-7	0-1	0-0	1-10	5.6	-11.50

WINNING HORSES

Horse	Races Run	1st	2nd	3rd	£
C Note (IRE)	13	2	0	0	16303
Dashing Poet	10	3	2	0	12356
Fair Selene	8	1	0	0	3105
First Flight (IRE)*	4	1	0	0	3105
Island Brave (IRE)	9	4	1	0	89551
Island Cloud	10	2	2	2	11385
Island Glen (USA)	2	1	0	0	3105
Island Sound	6	1	0	0	5434
Keswick	11	2	0	1	9283
Marshal Dan (IRE)	11	2	1	3	7504
Merweb (IRE)	5	1	2	1	3752
Mostawaa	2	1	0	0	4787
Total winning prize-money					**£169670**
Favourites	**6-14**		**42.9%**		**3.49**

CHARLIE MANN

UPPER LAMBOURN, BERKS

	No. of Hrs	Races Run	1st	2nd	3rd	Unpl	Per cent	£1 Level Stake
2-y-o	*0*	*0*	*0*	*0*	*0*	*0*	*0.0*	*0.00*
3-y-o	*0*	*0*	*0*	*0*	*0*	*0*	*0.0*	*0.00*
4-y-o+	*4*	*15*	*6*	*2*	*1*	*6*	*40.0*	*+18.16*
Totals	**4**	**15**	**6**	**2**	**1**	**6**	**40.0**	**+18.16**
2017	*1*	*1*	*0*	*0*	*0*	*1*	*0.0*	*-1.00*
2016	*2*	*6*	*2*	*1*	*0*	*3*	*33.3*	*+26.50*

JOCKEYS

	W-R	Per cent	£1 Level Stake
Shane Kelly	2-4	50.0	+2.50
Jim Crowley	1-1	100.0	+0.91
Silvestre De Sousa	1-1	100.0	+2.75
Fran Berry	1-3	33.3	+10.00
Franny Norton	1-3	33.3	+5.00

COURSE RECORD

	Total W-R	Non-Hndcps 2-y-o	Non-Hndcps 3-y-o+	Hndcps 2-y-o	Hndcps 3-y-o+	Per cent	£1 Level Stake
Wolvhptn (A.W)	3-4	0-0	0-0	0-0	3-4	75.0	+6.25
Kempton (A.W)	1-1	0-0	0-0	0-0	1-1	100.0	+0.91
Lingfield (A.W)	1-3	0-0	0-0	0-0	1-3	33.3	+10.00
Chelmsford (A.W)	1-5	0-0	0-0	0-0	1-5	20.0	+3.00

WINNING HORSES

Horse	Races Run	1st	2nd	3rd	£
Bear Valley (IRE)*	4	1	1	0	10997
Leoro (IRE)	5	2	1	0	6210
Oregon Gift	5	3	0	1	9315
Total winning prize-money					**£26522**
Favourites	**5-16**		**31.3%**		**-4.49**

GEORGE MARGARSON

NEWMARKET, SUFFOLK

	No. of Hrs	Races Run	1st	2nd	3rd	Unpl	Per cent	£1 Level Stake
2-y-o	*5*	*20*	*1*	*6*	*1*	*12*	*5.0*	*-16.50*
3-y-o	*9*	*53*	*8*	*3*	*6*	*36*	*15.1*	*+35.63*
4-y-o+	*4*	*39*	*3*	*3*	*6*	*26*	*7.7*	*-17.00*
Totals	**18**	**112**	**12**	**12**	**13**	**74**	**10.7**	**+2.13**
2017	*20*	*111*	*11*	*12*	*7*	*81*	*9.9*	*-22.50*
2016	*25*	*129*	*9*	*14*	*9*	*96*	*7.0*	*-73.06*

BY MONTH

2-y-o	W-R	Per cent	£1 Level Stake	3-y-o	W-R	Per cent	£1 Level Stake
January	0-0	0.0	0.00	January	1-4	25.0	-1.63
February	0-0	0.0	0.00	February	0-1	0.0	-1.00
March	0-0	0.0	0.00	March	0-0	0.0	0.00
April	0-0	0.0	0.00	April	1-5	20.0	-0.50
May	0-2	0.0	-2.00	May	0-7	0.0	-7.00
June	0-3	0.0	-3.00	June	1-9	11.1	+25.00
July	0-2	0.0	-2.00	July	0-6	0.0	-6.00
August	0-3	0.0	-3.00	August	1-8	12.5	-4.25
September	0-5	0.0	-5.00	September	2-6	33.3	+11.00
October	1-4	25.0	-0.50	October	2-6	33.3	+21.00
November	0-1	0.0	-1.00	November	0-0	0.0	0.00
December	0-0	0.0	0.00	December	0-1	0.0	-1.00

4-y-o+	W-R	Per cent	£1 Level Stake	Totals	W-R	Per cent	£1 Level Stake
January	0-3	0.0	-3.00	January	1-7	14.3	-4.63
February	0-6	0.0	-6.00	February	0-7	0.0	-7.00
March	0-3	0.0	-3.00	March	0-3	0.0	-3.00
April	0-5	0.0	-5.00	April	1-10	10.0	-5.50
May	1-8	12.5	-4.25	May	1-17	5.9	-13.25
June	1-4	25.0	-0.75	June	2-16	12.5	+21.25
July	0-3	0.0	-3.00	July	0-11	0.0	-11.00
August	0-0	0.0	0.00	August	1-11	9.1	-7.25
September	0-2	0.0	-2.00	September	2-13	15.4	+4.00
October	0-1	0.0	-1.00	October	3-11	27.3	+19.50
November	1-1	100.0	+14.00	November	1-2	50.0	+14.00
December	0-3	0.0	-3.00	December	0-4	0.0	-4.00

DISTANCE

2-y-o	W-R	Per cent	£1 Level Stake	3-y-o	W-R	Per cent	£1 Level Stake
5f-6f	1-12	8.3	-8.50	5f-6f	2-15	13.3	-3.00
7f-8f	0-8	0.0	-8.00	7f-8f	3-22	13.6	+35.38
9f-13f	0-0	0.0	0.00	9f-13f	3-16	18.8	+3.25
14f+	0-0	0.0	0.00	14f+	0-0	0.0	0.00

4-y-o+	W-R	Per cent	£1 Level Stake	Totals	W-R	Per cent	£1 Level Stake
5f-6f	0-3	0.0	-3.00	5f-6f	3-30	10.0	-14.50
7f-8f	3-35	8.6	-13.00	7f-8f	6-65	9.2	+14.38
9f-13f	0-1	0.0	-1.00	9f-13f	3-17	17.6	+2.25
14f+	0-0	0.0	0.00	14f+	0-0	0.0	0.00

TYPE OF RACE

Non-Handicaps	W-R	Per cent	£1 Level Stake	Handicaps	W-R	Per cent	£1 Level Stake
2-y-o	0-16	0.0	-16.00	2-y-o	1-4	25.0	-0.50
3-y-o	1-15	6.7	-10.50	3-y-o	7-38	18.4	+46.13
4-y-o+	0-0	0.0	0.00	4-y-o+	3-39	7.7	-17.00

RACE CLASS

	W-R	Per cent	£1 Level Stake
Class 1	0-4	0.0	-4.00
Class 2	2-9	22.2	+5.75
Class 3	0-8	0.0	-8.00
Class 4	1-24	4.2	+10.00
Class 5	2-33	6.1	-26.13
Class 6	6-33	18.2	+19.50
Class 7	1-1	100.0	+5.00

FIRST TIME OUT

	W-R	Per cent	£1 Level Stake
2-y-o	0-5	0.0	-5.00
3-y-o	1-9	11.1	+25.00
4-y-o+	0-4	0.0	-4.00
Totals	1-18	5.6	+16.00

JOCKEYS

	W-R	Per cent	£1 Level Stake
Jane Elliott	7-55	12.7	+27.50
Oisin Murphy	2-5	40.0	+1.88
David Egan	1-1	100.0	+2.75
Miss Rosie Margarson	1-4	25.0	+11.00
Tom Queally	1-14	7.1	-8.00

COURSE RECORD

	Total W-R	Non-Hndcps 2-y-o	Non-Hndcps 3-y-o+	Hndcps 2-y-o	Hndcps 3-y-o+	Per cent	£1 Level Stake
Wolvhptn (A.W)	3-11	0-1	0-0	0-0	3-10	27.3	-1.63
Yarmouth	3-28	0-5	0-6	0-0	3-17	10.7	+20.75
Kempton (A.W)	2-18	0-2	0-2	0-1	2-13	11.1	+9.00
Lingfield (A.W)	2-21	0-0	1-3	0-0	1-18	9.5	-10.50
Southwell (A.W)	1-1	0-0	0-0	0-0	1-1	100.0	+14.00
Chelmsford (A.W)	1-8	0-1	0-0	1-2	0-5	12.5	-4.50

WINNING HORSES

Horse	Races Run	1st	2nd	3rd	£
Caribbean Spring (IRE)	11	3	1	2	9205
City Guest (IRE)	5	1	0	0	3105
Midnight Guest (IRE)*	11	2	0	1	5046
Protected Guest	8	3	0	1	35473
Technological	9	2	2	0	7504
Windy Guest	8	1	2	0	3493
Total winning prize-money					**£63826**
Favourites	**3-10**		**30.0%**		**-0.88**

CHRISTOPHER MASON

CAEWENT, MONMOUTHSHIRE

	No. of Hrs	Races Run	1st	2nd	3rd	Unpl	Per cent	£1 Level Stake
2-y-o	*3*	*13*	*0*	*0*	*1*	*12*	*0.0*	*-13.00*
3-y-o	*2*	*11*	*0*	*0*	*2*	*9*	*0.0*	*-11.00*
4-y-o+	*2*	*25*	*1*	*2*	*4*	*18*	*4.0*	*-21.25*
Totals	**7**	**49**	**1**	**2**	**7**	**39**	**2.0**	**-45.25**
2017	*2*	*15*	*4*	*0*	*2*	*9*	*26.7*	*+13.50*
2016	*4*	*24*	*1*	*3*	*1*	*19*	*4.2*	*-15.00*

JOCKEYS

	W-R	Per cent	£1 Level Stake
Nicola Currie	1-9	11.1	-5.25

COURSE RECORD

	Total W-R	Non-Hndcps 2-y-o	Non-Hndcps 3-y-o+	Hndcps 2-y-o	Hndcps 3-y-o+	Per cent	£1 Level Stake
Chepstow	1-15	0-3	0-1	0-0	1-11	6.7	-11.25

WINNING HORSES

Horse	Races Run	1st	2nd	3rd	£
Jaganory (IRE)	16	1	2	2	3105
Total winning prize-money					**£3105**
Favourites	**1-3**		**33.3%**		**0.75**

PHILIP MCBRIDE

NEWMARKET, SUFFOLK

	No. of Hrs	Races Run	1st	2nd	3rd	Unpl	Per cent	£1 Level Stake
2-y-o	*7*	*26*	*1*	*3*	*2*	*20*	*3.8*	*-17.00*
3-y-o	*8*	*53*	*6*	*4*	*7*	*36*	*11.3*	*-20.05*
4-y-o+	*7*	*27*	*2*	*1*	*5*	*19*	*7.4*	*-16.50*
Totals	**22**	**106**	**9**	**8**	**14**	**75**	**8.5**	**-53.55**
2017	*29*	*134*	*12*	*11*	*15*	*95*	*9.0*	*-72.05*
2016	*31*	*127*	*15*	*11*	*15*	*86*	*11.8*	*-59.26*

JOCKEYS

	W-R	Per cent	£1 Level Stake
Rossa Ryan	3-8	37.5	+5.70
Jason Hart	3-8	37.5	+11.25
Stevie Donohoe	1-12	8.3	-6.50
Danny Brock	1-14	7.1	-9.00
David Probert	1-14	7.1	-5.00

COURSE RECORD

	Total W-R	Non-Hndcps 2-y-o	Non-Hndcps 3-y-o+	Hndcps 2-y-o	Hndcps 3-y-o+	Per cent	£1 Level Stake
Chelmsford (A.W)	4-20	0-2	1-2	0-3	3-13	20.0	-3.55
Wolvhptn (A.W)	3-20	1-5	1-5	0-1	1-9	15.0	+4.50
Newcastle (A.W)	1-2	0-0	0-1	0-0	1-1	50.0	+4.00
Lingfield (A.W)	1-4	0-0	0-1	0-0	1-3	25.0	+1.50

WINNING HORSES

Horse	Races Run	1st	2nd	3rd	£
Broughtons Story	10	1	0	3	3105
Image	8	4	0	2	22577
Minnelli	3	1	0	0	3752

Onefootinparadise	9	1	1	0	3105
Priscilla's Dream	5	1	1	0	3752
Suzi's Connoisseur	2	1	0	0	3493
Total winning prize-money					**£39784**
Favourites	**2-4**		**50.0%**		**1.95**

DONALD MCCAIN

CHOLMONDELEY, CHESHIRE

	No. of Hrs	Races Run	1st	2nd	3rd	Unpl	Per cent	£1 Level Stake
2-y-o	*4*	*8*	*1*	*0*	*1*	*6*	*12.5*	*+93.00*
3-y-o	*4*	*8*	*0*	*1*	*1*	*6*	*0.0*	*-8.00*
4-y-o+	*11*	*33*	*2*	*1*	*0*	*30*	*6.1*	*-16.00*
Totals	**19**	**49**	**3**	**2**	**2**	**42**	**6.1**	**+69.00**
2017	*17*	*63*	*7*	*5*	*4*	*47*	*11.1*	*+4.00*
2016	*12*	*31*	*2*	*2*	*5*	*22*	*6.5*	*+7.00*

JOCKEYS

	W-R	Per cent	£1 Level Stake
Ella McCain	2-12	16.7	+5.00
Andrew Mullen	1-11	9.1	+90.00

COURSE RECORD

	Total W-R	Non-Hndcps 2-y-o	Non-Hndcps 3-y-o+	Hndcps 2-y-o	Hndcps 3-y-o+	Per cent	£1 Level Stake
Wolvhptn (A.W)	2-10	0-1	1-2	0-0	1-7	20.0	+7.00
Pontefract	1-4	1-1	0-0	0-0	0-3	25.0	+97.00

WINNING HORSES

Horse	Races Run	1st	2nd	3rd	£
*Barnaby Brook (CAN)	7	2	0	0	9722
Our Rodney (IRE)	3	1	0	0	5175
Total winning prize-money					**£14897**
Favourites	**33-83**		**39.8%**		**5.59**

PHIL MCENTEE

NEWMARKET, SUFFOLK

	No. of Hrs	Races Run	1st	2nd	3rd	Unpl	Per cent	£1 Level Stake
2-y-o	*4*	*15*	*1*	*1*	*0*	*13*	*6.7*	*-5.00*
3-y-o	*6*	*38*	*2*	*5*	*8*	*23*	*5.3*	*-27.00*
4-y-o+	*20*	*213*	*26*	*17*	*19*	*150*	*12.2*	*+15.63*
Totals	**30**	**266**	**29**	**23**	**27**	**186**	**10.9**	**-16.37**
2017	*31*	*210*	*13*	*25*	*19*	*153*	*6.2*	*-122.04*
2016	*37*	*220*	*24*	*21*	*25*	*150*	*10.9*	*-20.67*

BY MONTH

2-y-o	W-R	Per cent	£1 Level Stake	3-y-o	W-R	Per cent	£1 Level Stake
January	0-0	0.0	0.00	January	0-3	0.0	-3.00
February	0-0	0.0	0.00	February	0-1	0.0	-1.00
March	0-0	0.0	0.00	March	0-4	0.0	-4.00
April	0-0	0.0	0.00	April	0-1	0.0	-1.00
May	0-0	0.0	0.00	May	0-2	0.0	-2.00
June	0-0	0.0	0.00	June	1-3	33.3	+4.00
July	0-0	0.0	0.00	July	0-5	0.0	-5.00
August	0-1	0.0	-1.00	August	0-3	0.0	-3.00
September	0-2	0.0	-2.00	September	0-0	0.0	0.00
October	0-1	0.0	-1.00	October	0-4	0.0	-4.00
November	1-6	16.7	+4.00	November	0-4	0.0	-4.00
December	0-5	0.0	-5.00	December	1-8	12.5	-4.00

4-y-o+	W-R	Per cent	£1 Level Stake	Totals	W-R	Per cent	£1 Level Stake
January	6-27	22.2	-4.38	January	6-30	20.0	-7.38
February	2-22	9.1	-3.00	February	2-23	8.7	-4.00
March	5-31	16.1	+4.00	March	5-35	14.3	0.00
April	2-13	15.4	+11.00	April	2-14	14.3	+10.00
May	1-11	9.1	-4.00	May	1-13	7.7	-6.00
June	4-19	21.1	+32.50	June	5-22	22.7	+36.50
July	1-17	5.9	-10.00	July	1-22	4.5	-15.00
August	0-9	0.0	-9.00	August	0-13	0.0	-13.00
September	2-14	14.3	-3.50	September	2-16	12.5	-5.50
October	2-16	12.5	+19.00	October	2-21	9.5	+14.00
November	1-16	6.3	+1.00	November	2-26	7.7	-3.00
December	0-18	0.0	-18.00	December	1-31	3.2	-22.00

DISTANCE

2-y-o	W-R	Per cent	£1 Level Stake	3-y-o	W-R	Per cent	£1 Level Stake
5f-6f	1-4	25.0	+6.00	5f-6f	2-21	9.5	-10.00
7f-8f	0-8	0.0	-8.00	7f-8f	0-3	0.0	-3.00
9f-13f	0-3	0.0	-3.00	9f-13f	0-11	0.0	-11.00
14f+	0-0	0.0	0.00	14f+	0-3	0.0	-3.00

4-y-o+	W-R	Per cent	£1 Level Stake	Totals	W-R	Per cent	£1 Level Stake
5f-6f	11-73	15.1	+39.63	5f-6f	14-98	14.3	+35.63
7f-8f	15-126	11.9	-10.00	7f-8f	15-137	10.9	-21.00
9f-13f	0-12	0.0	-12.00	9f-13f	0-26	0.0	-26.00
14f+	0-2	0.0	-2.00	14f+	0-5	0.0	-5.00

TYPE OF RACE

Non-Handicaps	W-R	Per cent	£1 Level Stake	Handicaps	W-R	Per cent	£1 Level Stake
2-y-o	0-5	0.0	-5.00	2-y-o	1-10	10.0	0.00
3-y-o	1-10	10.0	-6.00	3-y-o	1-28	3.6	-21.00
4-y-o+	1-6	16.7	-3.12	4-y-o+	25-207	12.1	+18.75

RACE CLASS

	W-R	Per cent	£1 Level Stake
Class 1	0-1	0.0	-1.00
Class 2	1-7	14.3	+19.00
Class 3	1-17	5.9	-9.00
Class 4	5-48	10.4	+36.00
Class 5	6-54	11.1	-22.13
Class 6	15-129	11.6	-31.75
Class 7	1-10	10.0	-7.50

FIRST TIME OUT

	W-R	Per cent	£1 Level Stake
2-y-o	1-4	25.0	+6.00
3-y-o	0-6	0.0	-6.00
4-y-o+	3-20	15.0	+2.50
Totals	4-30	13.3	+2.50

JOCKEYS

	W-R	Per cent	£1 Level Stake
Nicola Currie	14-107	13.1	+29.63
Rossa Ryan	5-30	16.7	-4.50
Callum Shepherd	3-15	20.0	+11.00
Danny Brock	2-30	6.7	-12.00
Oisin Murphy	1-1	100.0	+4.00
Cameron Noble	1-2	50.0	+0.50
Silvestre De Sousa	1-2	50.0	+5.00
Adam Kirby	1-3	33.3	0.00
Darragh Keenan	1-9	11.1	+17.00

COURSE RECORD

	Total W-R	Non-Hndcps 2-y-o	Non-Hndcps 3-y-o+	Hndcps 2-y-o	Hndcps 3-y-o+	Per cent	£1 Level Stake
Wolvhptn (A.W)	5-34	0-2	0-3	0-1	5-28	14.7	-5.50
Chelmsford (A.W)	5-78	0-3	0-3	1-4	4-68	6.4	-35.75
Yarmouth	4-22	0-0	0-0	0-0	4-22	18.2	+1.50
Kempton (A.W)	4-29	0-0	0-0	0-1	4-28	13.8	+2.50
Lingfield (A.W)	4-46	0-0	1-5	0-1	3-40	8.7	-20.63
Southwell (A.W)	3-14	0-0	1-2	0-2	2-10	21.4	+11.00
Brighton	2-15	0-0	0-0	0-0	2-15	13.3	-1.50
Windsor	1-3	0-0	0-0	0-0	1-3	33.3	+31.00
Newmarket	1-4	0-0	0-1	0-0	1-3	25.0	+22.00

WINNING HORSES

Horse	Races Run	1st	2nd	3rd	£
Bernie's Boy	20	5	2	3	19892
Emily Goldfinch	15	4	2	1	41411
Gentlemen	9	1	1	0	6728
*Global Melody	3	1	0	0	3752
*Inshaa	2	1	1	0	3105
London (FR)	16	1	2	0	7561
Malaysian Boleh	29	2	2	6	6534
Mother Of Dragons (IRE)	19	1	4	4	3105
Pearl Spectre (USA)	18	1	1	1	5693
Spare Parts (IRE)	19	7	2	1	28916
Swiss Cross	18	1	1	2	3105
Tasaaboq	14	1	1	0	3105
*Valley Belle (IRE)	5	1	1	0	3493
*Wild Acclaim (IRE)	13	2	1	2	6210
Total winning prize-money					**£142610**
Favourites	**4-15**		**26.7%**		**-2.50**

LUKE MCJANNET

NEWMARKET, SUFFOLK

	No. of Hrs	Races Run	1st	2nd	3rd	Unpl	Per cent	£1 Level Stake
2-y-o	*3*	*5*	*0*	*0*	*0*	*5*	*0.0*	*-5.00*
3-y-o	*4*	*22*	*0*	*0*	*1*	*21*	*0.0*	*-22.00*
4-y-o+	*6*	*25*	*2*	*0*	*2*	*21*	*8.0*	*+6.00*
Totals	**13**	**52**	**2**	**0**	**3**	**47**	**3.8**	**-21.00**
2017	*14*	*50*	*0*	*5*	*5*	*39*	*0.0*	*-50.00*
2016	*0*							

JOCKEYS

	W-R	Per cent	£1 Level Stake
Noel Garbutt	2-25	8.0	+6.00

COURSE RECORD

	Total W-R	Non-Hndcps 2-y-o	Non-Hndcps 3-y-o+	Hndcps 2-y-o	Hndcps 3-y-o+	Per cent	£1 Level Stake
Southwell (A.W)	1-4	0-0	0-0	0-0	1-4	25.0	+6.00
Chelmsford (A.W)	1-8	0-1	0-1	0-0	1-6	12.5	+13.00

WINNING HORSES

Horse	Races Run	1st	2nd	3rd	£
*Arabian Oasis	7	1	0	1	3752
Diana Lady (CHI)	5	1	0	0	3429
Total winning prize-money					**£7181**
Favourites	**0-0**		**0.0%**		**0.00**

KAREN MCLINTOCK

INGOE, NORTHUMBERLAND

	No. of Hrs	Races Run	1st	2nd	3rd	Unpl	Per cent	£1 Level Stake
2-y-o	*0*	*0*	*0*	*0*	*0*	*0*	*0.0*	*0.00*
3-y-o	*5*	*20*	*4*	*1*	*2*	*13*	*20.0*	*+12.50*
4-y-o+	*13*	*84*	*16*	*14*	*6*	*48*	*19.0*	*+11.28*
Totals	**18**	**104**	**20**	**15**	**8**	**61**	**19.2**	**+23.78**
2017	*15*	*76*	*8*	*3*	*8*	*57*	*10.5*	*+10.50*
2016	*9*	*68*	*11*	*9*	*9*	*39*	*16.2*	*+8.50*

BY MONTH

2-y-o	W-R	Per cent	£1 Level Stake	3-y-o	W-R	Per cent	£1 Level Stake
January	0-0	0.0	0.00	January	0-1	0.0	-1.00
February	0-0	0.0	0.00	February	0-0	0.0	0.00
March	0-0	0.0	0.00	March	0-0	0.0	0.00
April	0-0	0.0	0.00	April	0-0	0.0	0.00
May	0-0	0.0	0.00	May	1-3	33.3	+10.00
June	0-0	0.0	0.00	June	0-4	0.0	-4.00
July	0-0	0.0	0.00	July	0-0	0.0	0.00
August	0-0	0.0	0.00	August	0-3	0.0	-3.00
September	0-0	0.0	0.00	September	2-4	50.0	+11.00
October	0-0	0.0	0.00	October	1-4	25.0	+0.50
November	0-0	0.0	0.00	November	0-1	0.0	-1.00
December	0-0	0.0	0.00	December	0-0	0.0	0.00

4-y-o+	W-R	Per cent	£1 Level Stake	Totals	W-R	Per cent	£1 Level Stake
January	2-9	22.2	-2.75	January	2-10	20.0	-3.75
February	1-7	14.3	-5.09	February	1-7	14.3	-5.09
March	2-8	25.0	+1.00	March	2-8	25.0	+1.00
April	0-2	0.0	-2.00	April	0-2	0.0	-2.00
May	3-12	25.0	+9.50	May	4-15	26.7	+19.50
June	3-14	21.4	-2.13	June	3-18	16.7	-6.13
July	0-1	0.0	-1.00	July	0-1	0.0	-1.00
August	3-10	30.0	+11.75	August	3-13	23.1	+8.75

September	1-10	10.0	+1.00	September	3-14	21.4	+12.00
October	0-3	0.0	-3.00	October	1-7	14.3	-2.50
November	0-5	0.0	-5.00	November	0-6	0.0	-6.00
December	1-3	33.3	+9.00	December	1-3	33.3	+9.00

DISTANCE

2-y-o	W-R	Per cent	£1 Level Stake	3-y-o	W-R	Per cent	£1 Level Stake
5f-6f	0-0	0.0	0.00	5f-6f	2-11	18.2	+8.50
7f-8f	0-0	0.0	0.00	7f-8f	1-6	16.7	+2.50
9f-13f	0-0	0.0	0.00	9f-13f	1-3	33.3	+1.50
14f+	0-0	0.0	0.00	14f+	0-0	0.0	0.00
4-y-o+	W-R	Per cent	£1 Level Stake	**Totals**	W-R	Per cent	£1 Level Stake
5f-6f	2-10	20.0	+11.00	5f-6f	4-21	19.0	+19.50
7f-8f	5-27	18.5	+1.38	7f-8f	6-33	18.2	+3.88
9f-13f	7-40	17.5	-8.00	9f-13f	8-43	18.6	-6.50
14f+	2-7	28.6	+6.91	14f+	2-7	28.6	+6.91

TYPE OF RACE

Non-Handicaps	W-R	Per cent	£1 Level Stake	Handicaps	W-R	Per cent	£1 Level Stake
2-y-o	0-0	0.0	0.00	2-y-o	0-0	0.0	0.00
3-y-o	0-0	0.0	0.00	3-y-o	4-20	20.0	+12.50
4-y-o+	0-5	0.0	-5.00	4-y-o+	16-79	20.3	+16.28

RACE CLASS

	W-R	Per cent	£1 Level Stake
Class 1	0-0	0.0	0.00
Class 2	3-11	27.3	+1.41
Class 3	2-14	14.3	-5.13
Class 4	4-24	16.7	+8.50
Class 5	7-31	22.6	+14.25
Class 6	4-23	17.4	+5.75
Class 7	0-1	0.0	-1.00

FIRST TIME OUT

	W-R	Per cent	£1 Level Stake
2-y-o	0-0	0.0	0.00
3-y-o	1-5	20.0	+8.00
4-y-o+	2-13	15.4	+2.50
Totals	3-18	16.7	+10.50

JOCKEYS

	W-R	Per cent	£1 Level Stake
Jamie Gormley	9-26	34.6	+27.75
Connor Beasley	3-13	23.1	+21.00
Silvestre De Sousa	2-6	33.3	+3.38
Ben Curtis	1-1	100.0	+5.50
Paul Mulrennan	1-2	50.0	+1.50
Jason Hart	1-3	33.3	+9.00
Joe Fanning	1-5	20.0	-3.09
Sebastian Woods	1-5	20.0	-1.00
P J McDonald	1-9	11.1	-6.25

COURSE RECORD

	Total W-R	Non-Hndcps 2-y-o	Non-Hndcps 3-y-o+	Hndcps 2-y-o	Hndcps 3-y-o+	Per cent	£1 Level Stake
Newcastle (A.W)	7-36	0-0	0-2	0-0	7-34	19.4	+6.00
Hamilton	3-13	0-0	0-0	0-0	3-13	23.1	+14.00
Musselburgh	2-2	0-0	0-0	0-0	2-2	100.0	+13.00
Ripon	2-5	0-0	0-0	0-0	2-5	40.0	+4.38
Beverley	1-2	0-0	0-0	0-0	1-2	50.0	+1.75
York	1-2	0-0	0-0	0-0	1-2	50.0	+4.50
Carlisle	1-3	0-0	0-0	0-0	1-3	33.3	+8.00
Southwell (A.W)	1-3	0-0	0-0	0-0	1-3	33.3	-0.25
Wolvhptn (A.W)	1-8	0-0	0-0	0-0	1-8	12.5	-6.09
Pontefract	1-8	0-0	0-0	0-0	1-8	12.5	+0.50

WINNING HORSES

Horse	Races Run	1st	2nd	3rd	£
Avenue Of Stars	10	2	1	0	7698
Big Les (IRE)	6	2	0	1	16431
Dubawi Fifty	5	2	1	1	27580
Grey Mist	1	1	0	0	3493
Gurkha Friend	6	2	2	0	24900
Rockwood	12	1	0	2	4399
*Rose Tinted Spirit	5	2	0	0	11256
Senatus (FR)	3	1	1	0	3105
Trinity Star (IRE)	5	1	2	0	3881
Weather Front (USA)	9	4	2	1	12628
Zabeel Star (IRE)	14	2	2	2	12259
Total winning prize-money					**£127630**
Favourites	**10-19**		**52.6%**		**10.88**

GRAEME MCPHERSON

UPPER ODDINGTON, GLOUCS

	No. of Hrs	Races Run	1st	2nd	3rd	Unpl	Per cent	£1 Level Stake
2-y-o	*0*	*0*	*0*	*0*	*0*	*0*	*0.0*	*0.00*
3-y-o	*0*	*0*	*0*	*0*	*0*	*0*	*0.0*	*0.00*
4-y-o+	*3*	*6*	*1*	*0*	*1*	*4*	*16.7*	*-2.75*
Totals	**3**	**6**	**1**	**0**	**1**	**4**	**16.7**	**-2.75**
2017	*6*	*14*	*2*	*3*	*1*	*8*	*14.3*	*+9.00*
2016	*6*	*20*	*2*	*2*	*0*	*16*	*10.0*	*-3.00*

JOCKEYS

	W-R	Per cent	£1 Level Stake
Liam Keniry	1-5	20.0	-1.75

COURSE RECORD

	Total W-R	Non-Hndcps 2-y-o	Non-Hndcps 3-y-o+	Hndcps 2-y-o	Hndcps 3-y-o+	Per cent	£1 Level Stake
Nottingham	1-2	0-0	0-0	0-0	1-2	50.0	+1.25

WINNING HORSES

Horse	Races Run	1st	2nd	3rd	£
Stynes (IRE)	1	1	0	0	3235
Total winning prize-money					**£3235**
Favourites	**1-10**		**10.0%**		**-6.75**

MARTYN MEADE

MANTON, WILTS

	No. of Hrs	Races Run	1st	2nd	3rd	Unpl	Per cent	£1 Level Stake
2-y-o	*19*	*39*	*8*	*4*	*6*	*21*	*20.5*	*+19.10*
3-y-o	*15*	*65*	*9*	*4*	*13*	*39*	*13.8*	*-6.25*
4-y-o+	*6*	*17*	*1*	*1*	*1*	*14*	*5.9*	*-12.50*
Totals	**40**	**121**	**18**	**9**	**20**	**74**	**14.9**	**+0.35**
2017	*27*	*81*	*13*	*9*	*9*	*50*	*16.0*	*+35.37*
2016	*32*	*133*	*21*	*19*	*18*	*75*	*15.8*	*-45.78*

BY MONTH

2-y-o	W-R	Per cent	£1 Level Stake	3-y-o	W-R	Per cent	£1 Level Stake
January	0-0	0.0	0.00	January	0-4	0.0	-4.00
February	0-0	0.0	0.00	February	3-7	42.9	+6.00
March	0-0	0.0	0.00	March	0-2	0.0	-2.00
April	0-0	0.0	0.00	April	1-6	16.7	-0.50
May	1-2	50.0	+3.00	May	0-6	0.0	-6.00
June	1-2	50.0	+15.00	June	1-13	7.7	-8.50
July	1-4	25.0	-1.90	July	0-5	0.0	-5.00
August	0-2	0.0	-2.00	August	3-9	33.3	+19.75
September	1-8	12.5	-0.50	September	0-7	0.0	-7.00
October	0-8	0.0	-8.00	October	0-5	0.0	-5.00
November	0-8	0.0	-8.00	November	1-1	100.0	+6.00
December	4-5	80.0	+21.50	December	0-0	0.0	0.00

4-y-o+	W-R	Per cent	£1 Level Stake	Totals	W-R	Per cent	£1 Level Stake
January	0-0	0.0	0.00	January	0-4	0.0	-4.00
February	0-1	0.0	-1.00	February	3-8	37.5	+5.00
March	0-3	0.0	-3.00	March	0-5	0.0	-5.00
April	0-2	0.0	-2.00	April	1-8	12.5	-2.50
May	0-4	0.0	-4.00	May	1-12	8.3	-7.00
June	1-4	25.0	+0.50	June	3-19	15.8	+7.00
July	0-1	0.0	-1.00	July	1-10	10.0	-7.90
August	0-2	0.0	-2.00	August	3-13	23.1	+15.75
September	0-0	0.0	0.00	September	1-15	6.7	-7.50
October	0-0	0.0	0.00	October	0-13	0.0	-13.00
November	0-0	0.0	0.00	November	1-9	11.1	+6.00
December	0-0	0.0	0.00	December	4-5	80.0	0.00

DISTANCE

2-y-o	W-R	Per cent	£1 Level Stake	3-y-o	W-R	Per cent	£1 Level Stake
5f-6f	5-12	41.7	+22.60	5f-6f	2-5	40.0	+20.00
7f-8f	3-25	12.0	-1.50	7f-8f	2-26	7.7	-18.00
9f-13f	0-2	0.0	-2.00	9f-13f	5-34	14.7	-8.25
14f+	0-0	0.0	0.00	14f+	0-0	0.0	0.00

4-y-o+	W-R	Per cent	£1 Level Stake	Totals	W-R	Per cent	£1 Level Stake
5f-6f	0-5	0.0	-5.00	5f-6f	7-22	31.8	+37.60
7f-8f	1-6	16.7	-1.50	7f-8f	6-57	10.5	-21.00
9f-13f	0-5	0.0	-5.00	9f-13f	5-41	12.2	-15.25
14f+	0-1	0.0	-1.00	14f+	0-1	0.0	-1.00

TYPE OF RACE

Non-Handicaps	W-R	Per cent	£1 Level Stake	Handicaps	W-R	Per cent	£1 Level Stake
2-y-o	7-37	18.9	+13.60	2-y-o	1-2	50.0	+5.50
3-y-o	4-34	11.8	0.00	3-y-o	5-31	16.1	-6.25
4-y-o+	1-11	9.1	-6.50	4-y-o+	0-6	0.0	-6.00

RACE CLASS

	W-R	Per cent	£1 Level Stake
Class 1	2-21	9.5	-14.40
Class 2	0-6	0.0	-6.00
Class 3	1-13	7.7	-8.50
Class 4	5-37	13.5	+1.50
Class 5	8-39	20.5	+26.25
Class 6	2-5	40.0	+1.50
Class 7	0-0	0.0	0.00

FIRST TIME OUT

	W-R	Per cent	£1 Level Stake
2-y-o	4-19	21.1	+9.50
3-y-o	3-15	20.0	-1.50
4-y-o+	0-6	0.0	-6.00
Totals	7-40	17.5	+2.00

JOCKEYS

	W-R	Per cent	£1 Level Stake
Rob Hornby	4-14	28.6	+16.00
Callum Shepherd	4-23	17.4	+23.25
Oisin Murphy	4-31	12.9	-10.50
Frankie Dettori	2-5	40.0	+1.60
Dane O'Neill	1-2	50.0	+3.50
Richard Kingscote	1-2	50.0	+3.00
Charles Bishop	1-3	33.3	+1.00
Fran Berry	1-8	12.5	-4.50

COURSE RECORD

	Total W-R	Non-Hndcps 2-y-o	Non-Hndcps 3-y-o+	Hndcps 2-y-o	Hndcps 3-y-o+	Per cent	£1 Level Stake
Wolvhptn (A.W)	5-9	2-4	3-4	0-0	0-1	55.6	+24.00
Salisbury	3-5	0-0	1-2	1-1	1-2	60.0	+28.00
Newbury	2-15	2-7	0-4	0-0	0-4	13.3	+7.00
Epsom	1-2	0-0	1-1	0-0	0-1	50.0	+2.50
Newmkt (Jly)	1-3	1-1	0-1	0-0	0-1	33.3	-0.90
Doncaster	1-5	0-0	0-0	0-0	1-5	20.0	+0.50
Lingfield (A.W)	1-5	1-1	0-4	0-0	0-0	20.0	-2.00
Chelmsford (A.W)	1-6	0-1	0-2	0-0	1-3	16.7	+1.00
Windsor	1-7	0-1	0-4	0-0	1-2	14.3	-3.00
Sandown	1-8	0-2	0-2	0-0	1-4	12.5	-4.25
Kempton (A.W)	1-12	1-5	0-2	0-1	0-4	8.3	-8.50

WINNING HORSES

Horse	Races Run	1st	2nd	3rd	£
Advertise	4	2	2	0	45368
Airwaves	2	2	0	0	6987
Confiding	3	1	0	2	4787
Crackling (IRE)	1	1	0	0	3105
Engrossed (IRE)	2	1	0	0	3752
Fabianski (IRE)*	3	1	0	1	3752
Headland	4	1	0	0	3817
Infrastructure	7	1	2	1	15563

Loyal Promise (IRE)	4	1	1	1	3752
Michael Corleone	8	1	0	1	3752
Monoxide	5	1	1	0	5531
Rise Hall	5	1	0	1	4787
Ship Of The Fen	5	1	0	2	5531
Solar Echo (IRE)	7	1	0	2	4528
*Vj Day (USA)	3	1	0	0	5531
Wilamina (IRE)	4	1	1	1	51039
Total winning prize-money					**£171582**
Favourites	**3-15**		**20.0%**		**-5.90**

BRIAN MEEHAN

MANTON, WILTS

	No. of Hrs	Races Run	1st	2nd	3rd	Unpl	Per cent	£1 Level Stake
2-y-o	*30*	*114*	*8*	*15*	*12*	*79*	*7.0*	*-46.75*
3-y-o	*25*	*105*	*9*	*6*	*12*	*78*	*8.6*	*-17.97*
4-y-o+	*9*	*38*	*4*	*4*	*3*	*27*	*10.5*	*+25.25*
Totals	**64**	**257**	**21**	**25**	**27**	**184**	**8.2**	**-39.47**
2017	*57*	*247*	*28*	*27*	*29*	*163*	*11.3*	*-77.86*
2016	*64*	*248*	*26*	*20*	*32*	*170*	*10.5*	*-32.37*

BY MONTH

2-y-o	W-R	Per cent	£1 Level Stake	**3-y-o**	W-R	Per cent	£1 Level Stake
January	0-0	0.0	0.00	January	0-3	0.0	-3.00
February	0-0	0.0	0.00	February	0-0	0.0	0.00
March	0-0	0.0	0.00	March	0-0	0.0	0.00
April	0-3	0.0	-3.00	April	2-10	20.0	+49.00
May	1-13	7.7	-3.00	May	1-18	5.6	-14.75
June	0-15	0.0	-15.00	June	1-16	6.3	-12.25
July	3-17	17.6	-8.25	July	1-19	5.3	-15.88
August	2-19	10.5	+10.00	August	3-17	17.6	-8.59
September	0-22	0.0	-22.00	September	1-10	10.0	-0.50
October	2-20	10.0	-0.50	October	0-12	0.0	-12.00
November	0-2	0.0	-2.00	November	0-0	0.0	0.00
December	0-3	0.0	-3.00	December	0-0	0.0	0.00

4-y-o+	W-R	Per cent	£1 Level Stake	**Totals**	W-R	Per cent	£1 Level Stake
January	0-2	0.0	-2.00	January	0-5	0.0	-5.00
February	0-0	0.0	0.00	February	0-0	0.0	0.00
March	1-2	50.0	+7.00	March	1-2	50.0	+7.00
April	0-1	0.0	-1.00	April	2-14	14.3	+45.00
May	0-9	0.0	-9.00	May	2-40	5.0	-26.75
June	2-7	28.6	+30.25	June	3-38	7.9	+3.00
July	0-4	0.0	4.00	July	4-40	10.0	-28.13
August	0-4	0.0	-4.00	August	5-40	12.5	-2.59
September	0-4	0.0	-4.00	September	1-36	2.8	-26.50
October	0-3	0.0	-3.00	October	2-35	5.7	-15.50
November	0-1	0.0	-1.00	November	0-3	0.0	-1.00
December	1-1	100.0	+16.00	December	1-4	25.0	+16.00

DISTANCE

2-y-o	W-R	Per cent	£1 Level Stake	**3-y-o**	W-R	Per cent	£1 Level Stake
5f-6f	4-62	6.5	-44.25	5f-6f	1-4	25.0	+4.00
7f-8f	4-50	8.0	-0.50	7f-8f	4-57	7.0	+4.13
9f-13f	0-2	0.0	-2.00	9f-13f	4-42	9.5	-24.09
14f+	0-0	0.0	0.00	14f+	0-2	0.0	-2.00

4-y-o+	W-R	Per cent	£1 Level Stake	**Totals**	W-R	Per cent	£1 Level Stake
5f-6f	1-3	33.3	+31.00	5f-6f	6-69	8.7	-9.25
7f-8f	2-22	9.1	-9.75	7f-8f	10-129	7.8	-6.12
9f-13f	1-11	9.1	+6.00	9f-13f	5-55	9.1	-20.09
14f+	0-2	0.0	-2.00	14f+	0-4	0.0	-4.00

TYPE OF RACE

Non-Handicaps	W-R	Per cent	£1 Level Stake	**Handicaps**	W-R	Per cent	£1 Level Stake
2-y-o	8-92	8.7	-24.75	2-y-o	0-22	0.0	-22.00
3-y-o	5-46	10.9	+20.66	3-y-o	4-59	6.8	-38.63
4-y-o+	1-12	8.3	+5.00	4-y-o+	3-26	11.5	+20.25

RACE CLASS

	W-R	Per cent	£1 Level Stake
Class 1	1-24	4.2	-7.00
Class 2	2-30	6.7	+13.00
Class 3	2-31	6.5	-17.00
Class 4	7-87	8.0	+19.00
Class 5	5-72	6.9	-51.63
Class 6	4-13	30.8	+4.16
Class 7	0-0	0.0	0.00

FIRST TIME OUT

	W-R	Per cent	£1 Level Stake
2-y-o	4-30	13.3	+26.00
3-y-o	2-25	8.0	+34.00
4-y-o+	1-9	11.1	+25.00
Totals	7-64	10.9	+85.00

JOCKEYS

	W-R	Per cent	£1 Level Stake
Jim Crowley	4-28	14.3	+77.50
Nicky Mackay	3-9	33.3	+4.53
Joe Fanning	2-6	33.3	+0.38
Dane O'Neill	2-10	20.0	+0.50
William Buick	2-13	15.4	-7.75
Oisin Murphy	2-28	7.1	-21.00
Edward Greatrex	1-2	50.0	+0.88
Adam McNamara	1-7	14.3	+2.00
Nicola Currie	1-12	8.3	-2.50
Harry Bentley	1-12	8.3	-2.00
James Doyle	1-13	7.7	+8.00
Tom Marquand	1-14	7.1	+3.00

COURSE RECORD

	Total W-R	Non-Hndcps 2-y-o	Non-Hndcps 3-y-o+	Hndcps 2-y-o	Hndcps 3-y-o+	Per cent	£1 Level Stake
Newbury	3-45	2-21	1-15	0-2	0-7	6.7	+20.63
Ffos Las	2-5	1-2	0-1	0-0	1-2	40.0	+7.00
Brighton	2-8	1-6	0-0	0-0	1-2	25.0	+4.00
Lingfield (A.W)	2-10	1-2	0-3	0-1	1-4	20.0	+1.63
Lingfield	1-3	0-0	1-2	0-0	0-1	33.3	-1.47
Redcar	1-3	0-1	0-0	0-1	1-1	33.3	+0.13
Yarmouth	1-4	0-1	0-0	0-1	1-2	25.0	-0.75
Epsom	1-5	1-4	0-1	0-0	0-0	20.0	-1.50
Leicester	1-7	0-2	1-2	0-0	0-3	14.3	-4.13
Salisbury	1-8	1-5	0-1	0-0	0-2	12.5	+9.00

Kempton (A.W)	1-8	0-3	1-2	0-2	0-1	12.5	+9.00
Wolvhptn (A.W)	1-10	0-2	1-2	0-0	0-6	10.0	-6.75
Bath	1-10	1-5	0-0	0-0	0-5	10.0	0.00
Windsor	1-11	0-4	0-1	0-1	1-5	9.1	-7.25
Chelmsford (A.W)	1-12	0-2	1-6	0-0	0-4	8.3	-4.00
Ascot	1-15	0-5	0-5	0-0	1-5	6.7	+19.00

WINNING HORSES

Horse	Races Run	1st	2nd	3rd	£
Adjutant	7	2	0	0	8636
Almurr (IRE)	8	1	2	0	5434
Athmad (IRE)	3	1	0	0	4787
Bacchus	3	1	0	0	108938
Boa Nova (IRE)	4	1	1	0	6469
Breanski*	3	1	1	0	5531
Carlini (IRE)	8	1	0	1	3752
Contingency Fee*	5	1	0	0	3105
Greenback Boogie (IRE)	11	1	3	3	4528
Kaloor	1	1	0	0	5111
Malangen (IRE)*	2	1	0	0	3493
Napanook	7	1	4	1	3752
Nkosikazi	8	1	0	2	4690
No Way Jose (IRE)	6	1	0	1	3752
Palavecino (FR)	2	1	0	0	4787
Spark Plug (IRE)	7	1	1	1	25520
Spirit Of Appin	5	2	1	0	12557
Tadbir (IRE)	5	1	1	0	8086
Take The Helm	3	1	1	0	31125
Total winning prize-money					**£254053**
Favourites	**6-23**		**26.1%**		**-6.47**

DAVID MENUISIER

PULBOROUGH, W SUSSEX

	No. of Hrs	Races Run	1st	2nd	3rd	Unpl	Per cent	£1 Level Stake
2-y-o	*3*	*7*	*0*	*0*	*0*	*7*	*0.0*	*-7.00*
3-y-o	*18*	*81*	*7*	*5*	*10*	*59*	*8.6*	*-37.25*
4-y-o+	*8*	*37*	*5*	*1*	*5*	*26*	*13.5*	*-10.25*
Totals	**29**	**125**	**12**	**6**	**15**	**92**	**9.6**	**-54.50**
2017	*25*	*91*	*8*	*11*	*10*	*61*	*8.8*	*-29.77*
2016	*22*	*99*	*15*	*17*	*9*	*58*	*15.2*	*+21.00*

BY MONTH

2-y-o	W-R	Per cent	£1 Level Stake	3-y-o	W-R	Per cent	£1 Level Stake
January	0-0	0.0	0.00	January	0-0	0.0	0.00
February	0-0	0.0	0.00	February	0-0	0.0	0.00
March	0-0	0.0	0.00	March	0-1	0.0	-1.00
April	0-0	0.0	0.00	April	0-15	0.0	-15.00
May	0-0	0.0	0.00	May	0-12	0.0	-12.00
June	0-0	0.0	0.00	June	2-12	16.7	+10.00
July	0-0	0.0	0.00	July	2-12	16.7	-7.00
August	0-0	0.0	0.00	August	2-10	20.0	+1.75
September	0-4	0.0	-4.00	September	1-10	10.0	-5.00
October	0-3	0.0	-3.00	October	0-7	0.0	-7.00
November	0-0	0.0	0.00	November	0-1	0.0	-1.00
December	0-0	0.0	0.00	December	0-1	0.0	-1.00

4-y-o+	W-R	Per cent	£1 Level Stake	Totals	W-R	Per cent	£1 Level Stake
January	0-0	0.0	0.00	January	0-0	0.0	0.00
February	0-0	0.0	0.00	February	0-0	0.0	0.00
March	0-1	0.0	-1.00	March	0-2	0.0	-2.00
April	0-3	0.0	-3.00	April	0-18	0.0	-18.00
May	2-6	33.3	+1.25	May	2-18	11.1	-10.75
June	0-5	0.0	-5.00	June	2-17	11.8	+5.00
July	1-7	14.3	-1.00	July	3-19	15.8	-8.00
August	0-4	0.0	-4.00	August	2-14	14.3	-2.25
September	2-5	40.0	+8.50	September	3-19	15.8	-0.50
October	0-4	0.0	-4.00	October	0-14	0.0	-14.00
November	0-1	0.0	-1.00	November	0-2	0.0	-2.00
December	0-1	0.0	-1.00	December	0-2	0.0	-2.00

DISTANCE

2-y-o	W-R	Per cent	£1 Level Stake	3-y-o	W-R	Per cent	£1 Level Stake
5f-6f	0-0	0.0	0.00	5f-6f	0-2	0.0	-2.00
7f-8f	0-5	0.0	-5.00	7f-8f	3-27	11.1	+1.50
9f-13f	0-2	0.0	-2.00	9f-13f	4-46	8.7	-30.75
14f+	0-0	0.0	0.00	14f+	0-6	0.0	-6.00

4-y-o+	W-R	Per cent	£1 Level Stake	Totals	W-R	Per cent	£1 Level Stake
5f-6f	0-0	0.0	0.00	5f-6f	0-2	0.0	-2.00
7f-8f	1-11	9.1	-2.00	7f-8f	4-43	9.3	-5.50
9f-13f	3-18	16.7	-3.50	9f-13f	7-66	10.6	-36.25
14f+	1-8	12.5	-4.75	14f+	1-14	7.1	-10.75

TYPE OF RACE

Non-Handicaps	W-R	Per cent	£1 Level Stake	Handicaps	W-R	Per cent	£1 Level Stake
2-y-o	0-7	0.0	-7.00	2-y-o	0-0	0.0	0.00
3-y-o	0-38	0.0	-38.00	3-y-o	7-43	16.3	+0.75
4-y-o+	1-2	50.0	+4.00	4-y-o+	4-35	11.4	-14.25

RACE CLASS

	W-R	Per cent	£1 Level Stake
Class 1	1-4	25.0	+2.00
Class 2	3-13	23.1	-2.75
Class 3	2-14	14.3	-3.50
Class 4	4-32	12.5	+2.25
Class 5	1-43	2.3	-38.00
Class 6	1-19	5.3	-14.50
Class 7	0-0	0.0	0.00

FIRST TIME OUT

	W-R	Per cent	£1 Level Stake
2-y-o	0-3	0.0	-3.00
3-y-o	0-18	0.0	-18.00
4-y-o+	2-8	25.0	+4.25
Totals	2-29	6.9	-16.75

JOCKEYS

	W-R	Per cent	£1 Level Stake
Fran Berry	8-49	16.3	+6.00
Andrea Atzeni	1-3	33.3	+1.00
David Nolan	1-4	25.0	+1.00

Jim Crowley	1-5	20.0	-1.75
Jason Watson	1-5	20.0	-1.75

COURSE RECORD

	Total W-R	Non-Hndcps 2-y-o	Non-Hndcps 3-y-o+	Hndcps 2-y-o	Hndcps 3-y-o+	Per cent	£1 Level Stake
Newmkt (Jly)	4-8	0-0	0-0	0-0	4-8	50.0	+5.25
Sandown	3-12	0-1	0-2	0-0	3-9	25.0	+22.50
York	2-6	0-0	1-2	0-0	1-4	33.3	+4.00
Haydock	1-4	0-0	0-0	0-0	1-4	25.0	+1.00
Leicester	1-4	0-2	0-0	0-0	1-2	25.0	+0.50
Nottingham	1-8	0-0	0-3	0-0	1-5	12.5	-4.75

WINNING HORSES

Horse	Races Run	1st	2nd	3rd	£
Danceteria (FR)	6	4	0	0	40108
*Dragons Voice	3	1	0	0	6469
History Writer (IRE)	8	1	1	1	9338
Nuits St Georges (IRE)	7	1	1	1	4852
Psychotic	7	1	0	0	3105
Slunovrat (FR)	3	1	0	0	7763
Thundering Blue (USA)	6	2	1	1	86727
Vintager	4	1	1	1	28013
Total winning prize-money					**£186375**
Favourites	**3-9**		**33.3%**		**1.25**

REBECCA MENZIES

MORDON, DURHAM

	No. of Hrs	Races Run	1st	2nd	3rd	Unpl	Per cent	£1 Level Stake
2-y-o	*1*	*2*	*0*	*0*	*0*	*2*	*0.0*	*-2.00*
3-y-o	*5*	*15*	*1*	*0*	*0*	*14*	*6.7*	*-7.50*
4-y-o+	*17*	*113*	*13*	*14*	*11*	*75*	*11.5*	*-2.00*
Totals	**23**	**130**	**14**	**14**	**11**	**91**	**10.8**	**-11.50**
2017	*23*	*117*	*15*	*10*	*15*	*77*	*12.8*	*+42.13*
2016	*15*	*82*	*6*	*12*	*13*	*51*	*7.3*	*-32.13*

BY MONTH

2-y-o	W-R	Per cent	£1 Level Stake	3-y-o	W-R	Per cent	£1 Level Stake
January	0-0	0.0	0.00	January	0-1	0.0	-1.00
February	0-0	0.0	0.00	February	0-0	0.0	0.00
March	0-0	0.0	0.00	March	0-2	0.0	-2.00
April	0-0	0.0	0.00	April	0-2	0.0	-2.00
May	0-0	0.0	0.00	May	0-1	0.0	-1.00
June	0-0	0.0	0.00	June	0-2	0.0	-2.00
July	0-0	0.0	0.00	July	0-0	0.0	0.00
August	0-0	0.0	0.00	August	0-0	0.0	0.00
September	0-0	0.0	0.00	September	0-3	0.0	-3.00
October	0-0	0.0	0.00	October	0-3	0.0	-3.00
November	0-1	0.0	-1.00	November	1-1	100.0	+6.50
December	0-1	0.0	-1.00	December	0-0	0.0	0.00

4-y-o+	W-R	Per cent	£1 Level Stake	Totals	W-R	Per cent	£1 Level Stake
January	1-13	7.7	-6.50	January	1-14	7.1	-7.50
February	0-7	0.0	-7.00	February	0-7	0.0	-7.00
March	0-5	0.0	-5.00	March	0-7	0.0	-7.00
April	0-7	0.0	-7.00	April	0-9	0.0	-9.00
May	1-12	8.3	+5.00	May	1-13	7.7	+4.00
June	1-11	9.1	+1.00	June	1-13	7.7	-1.00
July	2-13	15.4	-3.00	July	2-13	15.4	-3.00
August	2-10	20.0	0.00	August	2-10	20.0	0.00
September	2-6	33.3	+23.00	September	2-9	22.2	+20.00
October	1-12	8.3	-1.00	October	1-15	6.7	-4.00
November	2-9	22.2	+1.50	November	3-11	27.3	+8.00
December	1-8	12.5	-3.00	December	1-9	11.1	-3.00

DISTANCE

2-y-o	W-R	Per cent	£1 Level Stake	3-y-o	W-R	Per cent	£1 Level Stake
5f-6f	0-1	0.0	-1.00	5f-6f	0-6	0.0	-6.00
7f-8f	0-1	0.0	-1.00	7f-8f	1-9	11.1	-1.50
9f-13f	0-0	0.0	0.00	9f-13f	0-0	0.0	0.00
14f+	0-0	0.0	0.00	14f+	0-0	0.0	0.00

4-y-o+	W-R	Per cent	£1 Level Stake	Totals	W-R	Per cent	£1 Level Stake
5f-6f	3-28	10.7	+20.50	5f-6f	3-35	8.6	+13.50
7f-8f	5-33	15.2	-8.00	7f-8f	6-43	14.0	-10.50
9f-13f	4-40	10.0	-14.50	9f-13f	4-40	10.0	-14.50
14f+	1-12	8.3	0.00	14f+	1-12	8.3	0.00

TYPE OF RACE

Non-Handicaps	W-R	Per cent	£1 Level Stake	Handicaps	W-R	Per cent	£1 Level Stake
2-y-o	0-0	0.0	0.00	2-y-o	0-2	0.0	-2.00
3-y-o	1-7	14.3	+0.50	3-y-o	0-8	0.0	-8.00
4-y-o+	0-12	0.0	-12.00	4-y-o+	13-101	12.9	+10.00

RACE CLASS

	W-R	Per cent	£1 Level Stake
Class 1	0-4	0.0	-4.00
Class 2	2-6	33.3	+26.50
Class 3	0-7	0.0	-7.00
Class 4	1-12	8.3	-6.50
Class 5	1-31	3.2	-23.50
Class 6	9-67	13.4	+1.00
Class 7	1-3	33.3	+2.00

FIRST TIME OUT

	W-R	Per cent	£1 Level Stake
2-y-o	0-1	0.0	-1.00
3-y-o	1-5	20.0	+2.50
4-y-o+	1-17	5.9	-10.50
Totals	2-23	8.7	-9.00

JOCKEYS

	W-R	Per cent	£1 Level Stake
P J McDonald	4-25	16.0	+8.50
Cam Hardie	3-20	15.0	+14.50
Alistair Rawlinson	2-4	50.0	+9.00
Paul Hanagan	2-7	28.6	+9.50
Gerald Mosse	1-1	100.0	+10.00
Paula Muir	1-8	12.5	-3.00
Andrew Mullen	1-10	10.0	-5.00

COURSE RECORD

	Total W-R	Non-Hndcps 2-y-o	Non-Hndcps 3-y-o+	Hndcps 2-y-o	Hndcps 3-y-o+	Per cent	£1 Level Stake
Newcastle (A.W)	5-37	0-0	1-7	0-0	4-30	13.5	-1.50
Musselburgh	3-10	0-0	0-0	0-0	3-10	30.0	+4.50
Wolvhptn (A.W)	3-20	0-0	0-2	0-1	3-17	15.0	-6.50
Wetherby	1-1	0-0	0-0	0-0	1-1	100.0	+11.00
Doncaster	1-5	0-0	0-1	0-0	1-4	20.0	+21.00
Thirsk	1-11	0-0	0-2	0-0	1-9	9.1	+6.00

WINNING HORSES

Horse	Races Run	1st	2nd	3rd	£
Celtic Artisan (IRE)	14	2	4	0	6275
Landing Night (IRE)	14	1	2	1	5693
*Mossy's Lodge	11	2	2	2	6016
Pantomime (IRE)	10	1	0	1	3493
Searanger (USA)	9	1	2	2	3398
*Thaayer	1	1	0	0	3752
Trautmann (IRE)	15	4	2	3	6210
Von Blucher (IRE)	11	2	1	0	28691
Total winning prize-money					**£63528**
Favourites	**5-14**		**35.7%**		**1.71**

PAUL MIDGLEY

WESTOW, N YORKS

	No. of Hrs	Races Run	1st	2nd	3rd	Unpl	Per cent	£1 Level Stake
2-y-o	*5*	*18*	*0*	*0*	*0*	*18*	*0.0*	*-18.00*
3-y-o	*8*	*45*	*0*	*3*	*4*	*38*	*0.0*	*-45.00*
4-y-o+	*39*	*345*	*39*	*32*	*43*	*230*	*11.3*	*-34.02*
Totals	**52**	**408**	**39**	**35**	**47**	**286**	**9.6**	**-97.02**
2017	*46*	*363*	*34*	*27*	*32*	*270*	*9.4*	*-29.75*
2016	*39*	*310*	*26*	*32*	*38*	*213*	*8.4*	*-125.75*

BY MONTH

2-y-o	W-R	Per cent	£1 Level Stake	3-y-o	W-R	Per cent	£1 Level Stake
January	0-0	0.0	0.00	January	0-0	0.0	0.00
February	0-0	0.0	0.00	February	0-1	0.0	-1.00
March	0-1	0.0	-1.00	March	0-4	0.0	-4.00
April	0-1	0.0	-1.00	April	0-7	0.0	-7.00
May	0-2	0.0	-2.00	May	0-11	0.0	-11.00
June	0-1	0.0	-1.00	June	0-3	0.0	-3.00
July	0-3	0.0	-3.00	July	0-6	0.0	-6.00
August	0-2	0.0	-2.00	August	0-6	0.0	-6.00
September	0-3	0.0	-3.00	September	0-4	0.0	-4.00
October	0-5	0.0	-5.00	October	0-3	0.0	-3.00
November	0-0	0.0	0.00	November	0-0	0.0	0.00
December	0-0	0.0	0.00	December	0-0	0.0	0.00

4-y-o+	W-R	Per cent	£1 Level Stake	Totals	W-R	Per cent	£1 Level Stake
January	0-4	0.0	-4.00	January	0-4	0.0	-4.00
February	1-5	20.0	+21.00	February	1-6	16.7	+20.00
March	0-27	0.0	-27.00	March	0-32	0.0	-32.00
April	2-32	6.3	+8.00	April	2-40	5.0	0.00
May	7-46	15.2	-11.88	May	7-59	11.9	-24.88
June	5-48	10.4	-7.38	June	5-52	9.6	-11.38
July	5-43	11.6	-16.88	July	5-52	9.6	-25.88
August	11-48	22.9	+13.60	August	11-56	19.6	+5.60
September	3-54	5.6	-21.00	September	3-61	4.9	-28.00
October	4-33	12.1	+11.50	October	4-41	9.8	+3.50
November	1-3	33.3	+2.00	November	1-3	33.3	+2.00
December	0-2	0.0	-2.00	December	0-2	0.0	-2.00

DISTANCE

2-y-o	W-R	Per cent	£1 Level Stake	3-y-o	W-R	Per cent	£1 Level Stake
5f-6f	0-18	0.0	-18.00	5f-6f	0-43	0.0	-43.00
7f-8f	0-0	0.0	0.00	7f-8f	0-2	0.0	-2.00
9f-13f	0-0	0.0	0.00	9f-13f	0-0	0.0	0.00
14f+	0-0	0.0	0.00	14f+	0-0	0.0	0.00

4-y-o+	W-R	Per cent	£1 Level Stake	Totals	W-R	Per cent	£1 Level Stake
5f-6f	35-325	10.8	-59.03	5f-6f	35-386	9.1	-120.03
7f-8f	3-11	27.3	+13.00	7f-8f	3-13	23.1	+11.00
9f-13f	1-7	14.3	+14.00	9f-13f	1-7	14.3	+14.00
14f+	0-2	0.0	-2.00	14f+	0-2	0.0	-2.00

TYPE OF RACE

Non-Handicaps	W-R	Per cent	£1 Level Stake	Handicaps	W-R	Per cent	£1 Level Stake
2-y-o	0-16	0.0	-16.00	2-y-o	0-2	0.0	-2.00
3-y-o	0-5	0.0	-5.00	3-y-o	0-40	0.0	-40.00
4-y-o+	7-24	29.2	+32.11	4-y-o+	32-321	10.0	-66.13

RACE CLASS

	W-R	Per cent	£1 Level Stake
Class 1	0-6	0.0	-6.00
Class 2	3-51	5.9	-3.00
Class 3	10-59	16.9	-2.65
Class 4	11-120	9.2	-19.38
Class 5	9-119	7.6	-57.25
Class 6	6-53	11.3	-8.75
Class 7	0-0	0.0	0.00

FIRST TIME OUT

	W-R	Per cent	£1 Level Stake
2-y-o	0-5	0.0	-5.00
3-y-o	0-8	0.0	-8.00
4-y-o+	1-39	2.6	-13.00
Totals	1-52	1.9	-26.00

JOCKEYS

	W-R	Per cent	£1 Level Stake
Luke Morris	6-47	12.8	+6.35
Kevin Stott	5-20	25.0	+26.13
Dougie Costello	5-34	14.7	+22.25
Paul Mulrennan	4-34	11.8	-13.00
Joe Fanning	4-36	11.1	-17.88
Graham Lee	4-63	6.3	-37.50
Phillip Makin	3-16	18.8	+6.88
Ben Robinson	2-5	40.0	+23.00
Pat Cosgrave	1-1	100.0	+4.50
Connor Beasley	1-4	25.0	-0.25
Callum Rodriguez	1-5	20.0	0.00

Daniel Tudhope	1-7	14.3	-2.00
James Sullivan	1-10	10.0	+3.00
Mr Tom Midgley	1-12	8.3	-4.50

COURSE RECORD

	Total	Non-Hndcps		Hndcps		Per	£1 Level
	W-R	2-y-o	3-y-o+	2-y-o	3-y-o+	cent	Stake
Thirsk	6-26	0-1	1-1	0-0	5-24	23.1	+27.75
Beverley	5-37	0-3	1-6	0-0	4-28	13.5	-13.00
Ayr	3-14	0-0	0-0	0-0	3-14	21.4	-2.63
Pontefract	3-26	0-2	0-0	0-0	3-24	11.5	+5.50
Newcastle (A.W)	3-34	0-1	0-3	0-1	3-29	8.8	-13.50
Newmarket	2-4	0-0	0-0	0-0	2-4	50.0	+6.00
Hamilton	2-18	0-0	1-2	0-0	1-16	11.1	-1.75
Musselburgh	2-24	0-0	1-5	0-1	1-18	8.3	-8.00
Doncaster	2-27	0-0	0-1	0-0	2-26	7.4	-7.00
Chester	1-3	0-0	0-0	0-0	1-3	33.3	-0.38
Lingfield (A.W)	1-3	0-0	1-2	0-0	0-1	33.3	+18.00
Windsor	1-5	0-0	0-0	0-0	1-5	20.0	0.00
Newmkt (Jly)	1-6	0-0	1-1	0-0	0-5	16.7	+3.00
Carlisle	1-8	0-1	0-0	0-0	1-7	12.5	-4.88
Epsom	1-8	0-0	0-0	0-0	1-8	12.5	+5.00
Nottingham	1-9	0-0	1-1	0-0	0-8	11.1	-6.90
Haydock	1-15	0-0	0-1	0-0	1-14	6.7	-11.25
Catterick	1-16	0-4	0-1	0-0	1-11	6.3	-11.00
Wolvhptn (A.W)	1-17	0-0	0-2	0-0	1-15	5.9	+9.00
Redcar	1-17	0-1	0-1	0-0	1-15	5.9	0.00

WINNING HORSES

Horse	Races Run	1st	2nd	3rd	£
Araqeel	7	1	0	0	3493
Buccaneers Vault (IRE)	13	2	0	2	10156
Captain Colby (USA)	8	2	1	1	17555
Desert Ace (IRE)	16	3	0	1	17983
Down Time (USA)	7	1	0	0	3105
Hee Haw (IRE)	14	1	0	4	4852
Line Of Reason (IRE)	14	1	2	3	9704
Manshood (IRE)	12	1	2	1	3752
Merry Banter	12	3	1	2	16334
Move In Time	9	1	2	2	7763
Mr Orange (IRE)	12	3	0	0	25000
One Boy (IRE)	12	1	2	0	2588
Urvar (IRE)	11	3	1	1	48225
Rantan (IRE)	9	1	0	2	3398
Start Time (IRE)	8	2	0	1	9623
Tanasoq (IRE)	13	4	2	0	84084
Tarboosh	10	4	2	0	58881
Twentysvnthlancers	14	2	2	1	5693
Tylery Wonder (IRE)	15	1	2	2	3752
War Whisper (IRE)	9	2	2	0	10997
Total winning prize-money					**£346938**
Favourites	**7-19**		**36.8%**		**3.97**

ROD MILLMAN

KENTISBEARE, DEVON

	No. of Hrs	Races Run	1st	2nd	3rd	Unpl	Per cent	£1 Level Stake
2-y-o	*13*	*60*	*6*	*2*	*6*	*46*	*10.0*	*-7.13*
3-y-o	*13*	*99*	*8*	*10*	*16*	*64*	*8.1*	*-50.38*
4-y-o+	*17*	*120*	*13*	*12*	*13*	*82*	*10.8*	*-52.50*
Totals	**43**	**279**	**27**	**24**	**35**	**192**	**9.7**	**-110.01**
2017	*41*	*261*	*31*	*24*	*29*	*176*	*11.9*	*+55.88*
2016	*37*	*231*	*21*	*23*	*25*	*162*	*9.1*	*-71.88*

BY MONTH

2-y-o	W-R	Per cent	£1 Level Stake	**3-y-o**	W-R	Per cent	£1 Level Stake
January	0-0	0.0	0.00	January	0-0	0.0	0.00
February	0-0	0.0	0.00	February	0-0	0.0	0.00
March	0-0	0.0	0.00	March	0-0	0.0	0.00
April	1-6	16.7	-3.13	April	2-10	20.0	+2.50
May	0-9	0.0	-9.00	May	2-15	13.3	-2.00
June	1-8	12.5	+13.00	June	3-14	21.4	+2.63
July	2-7	28.6	+13.50	July	0-16	0.0	-16.00
August	1-6	16.7	-2.50	August	1-13	7.7	-6.50
September	1-10	10.0	-5.00	September	0-15	0.0	-15.00
October	0-12	0.0	-12.00	October	0-10	0.0	-10.00
November	0-1	0.0	-1.00	November	0-3	0.0	-3.00
December	0-1	0.0	-1.00	December	0-3	0.0	-3.00

4-y-o+	W-R	Per cent	£1 Level Stake	**Totals**	W-R	Per cent	£1 Level Stake
January	0-2	0.0	-2.00	January	0-2	0.0	-2.00
February	0-4	0.0	-4.00	February	0-4	0.0	-4.00
March	1-5	20.0	+0.50	March	1-5	20.0	+0.50
April	1-14	7.1	-5.00	April	4-30	13.3	-5.63
May	0-13	0.0	-13.00	May	2-37	5.4	-24.00
June	2-17	11.8	-7.50	June	6-39	15.4	+8.13
July	3-12	25.0	0.00	July	5-35	14.3	-2.50
August	2-15	13.3	-8.50	August	4-34	11.8	-17.50
September	3-16	18.8	+3.50	September	4-41	9.8	-16.50
October	0-15	0.0	-15.00	October	0-37	0.0	-37.00
November	1-4	25.0	+1.50	November	1-8	12.5	-1.50
December	0-3	0.0	-3.00	December	0-7	0.0	-6.00

DISTANCE

2-y-o	W-R	Per cent	£1 Level Stake	**3-y-o**	W-R	Per cent	£1 Level Stake
5f-6f	3-35	8.6	-8.13	5f-6f	6-35	17.1	+1.13
7f-8f	3-23	13.0	+1.00	7f-8f	1-34	2.9	-25.00
9f-13f	0-2	0.0	-2.00	9f-13f	0-27	0.0	-27.00
14f+	0-0	0.0	0.00	14f+	1-3	33.3	+0.50

4-y-o+	W-R	Per cent	£1 Level Stake	**Totals**	W-R	Per cent	£1 Level Stake
5f-6f	5-34	14.7	-11.50	5f-6f	14-104	13.5	-16.50
7f-8f	4-45	8.9	-23.50	7f-8f	8-102	7.8	-47.50
9f-13f	4-35	11.4	-11.50	9f-13f	4-64	6.3	-40.50
14f+	0-6	0.0	-6.00	14f+	1-9	11.1	-5.50

TYPE OF RACE

Non-Handicaps

	W-R	Per cent	£1 Level Stake
2-y-o	2-38	5.3	-14.13
3-y-o	0-10	0.0	-10.00
4-y-o+	0-4	0.0	-4.00

Handicaps

	W-R	Per cent	£1 Level Stake
2-y-o	4-22	18.2	+7.00
3-y-o	8-89	9.0	-40.38
4-y-o+	13-116	11.2	-48.50

RACE CLASS

	W-R	Per cent	£1 Level Stake
Class 1	0-5	0.0	-5.00
Class 2	1-24	4.2	-15.00
Class 3	0-27	0.0	-27.00
Class 4	9-82	11.0	-16.13
Class 5	13-81	16.0	-8.38
Class 6	4-58	6.9	-36.50
Class 7	0-2	0.0	-2.00

FIRST TIME OUT

	W-R	Per cent	£1 Level Stake
2-y-o	0-13	0.0	-13.00
3-y-o	1-13	7.7	-4.00
4-y-o+	1-17	5.9	-8.00
Totals	2-43	4.7	-25.00

JOCKEYS

	W-R	Per cent	£1 Level Stake
Oisin Murphy	5-36	13.9	+5.50
Kieran O'Neill	3-9	33.3	+15.00
Finley Marsh	3-11	27.3	+4.50
William Carson	3-28	10.7	-16.13
Theodore Ladd	2-7	28.6	+20.50
Jason Watson	2-22	9.1	-12.50
Rob Hornby	1-1	100.0	+4.00
Franny Norton	1-2	50.0	+1.00
Ellie MacKenzie	1-2	50.0	+2.00
David Egan	1-4	25.0	+0.50
Jim Crowley	1-4	25.0	+1.00
Charles Bishop	1-4	25.0	-1.38
Gerald Mosse	1-5	20.0	+1.00
Mr Patrick Millman	1-13	7.7	-9.50
J F Egan	1-23	4.3	-17.50

COURSE RECORD

	Total W-R	Non-Hndcps 2-y-o	Non-Hndcps 3-y-o+	Hndcps 2-y-o	Hndcps 3-y-o+	Per cent	£1 Level Stake
Salisbury	5-33	1-10	0-1	1-1	3-21	15.2	-11.63
Ffos Las	4-22	0-7	0-1	0-1	4-13	18.2	-2.00
Bath	4-27	1-6	0-0	0-1	3-20	14.8	+14.00
Chelmsford (A.W)	3-8	0-0	0-0	0-0	3-8	37.5	+9.50
Leicester	2-10	0-1	0-2	1-1	1-6	20.0	+9.50
Windsor	2-36	0-8	0-1	1-1	1-26	5.6	-26.50
Kempton (A.W)	2-37	0-0	0-4	0-3	2-30	5.4	-25.38
Newmkt (Jly)	1-4	0-0	0-0	1-1	0-3	25.0	+1.50
Newmarket	1-7	0-0	0-0	0-2	1-5	14.3	-1.50
Sandown	1-9	0-0	0-1	0-1	1-7	11.1	-5.00
Goodwood	1-14	0-0	0-1	0-2	1-11	7.1	-9.50
Newbury	1-22	0-4	0-2	0-1	1-15	4.5	-13.00

WINNING HORSES

Horse	Races Run	1st	2nd	3rd	£
Airshow	8	2	2	0	10221
Biotic	10	3	0	1	13071
Crystal Casque	9	1	1	4	4787
Duke Of Bronte	4	1	0	1	16173
Glory Of Paris (IRE)*	13	1	2	2	4399
Greeley (IRE)	9	3	0	0	16787
Hawridge Flyer	10	1	3	3	6469
Master Carpenter (IRE)	9	1	0	0	8022
Master Grey (IRE)	9	1	2	1	3493
Mawde (IRE)	4	1	0	0	4787
Ragstone View (IRE)	9	1	1	1	3752
Sir Plato (IRE)	12	2	2	0	11062
Sir Roderic (IRE)	14	1	0	3	3752
Spot Lite	12	3	0	3	9623
Steeve	11	1	2	4	5111
Sufficient	7	1	0	2	3817
Sweet Pursuit	10	3	2	0	11774
Total winning prize-money					**£137100**
Favourites	**7-20**		**35.0%**		**4.63**

ISMAIL MOHAMMED

NEWMARKET, SUFFOLK

	No. of Hrs	Races Run	1st	2nd	3rd	Unpl	Per cent	£1 Level Stake
2-y-o	*7*	*24*	*1*	*3*	*3*	*17*	*4.2*	*-20.50*
3-y-o	*7*	*46*	*6*	*6*	*10*	*24*	*13.0*	*-23.70*
4-y-o+	*6*	*35*	*7*	*3*	*3*	*22*	*20.0*	*-4.95*
Totals	**20**	**105**	**14**	**12**	**16**	**63**	**13.3**	**-49.15**
2017	*31*	*120*	*15*	*25*	*8*	*72*	*12.5*	*-29.73*
2016	*34*	*123*	*23*	*17*	*14*	*69*	*18.7*	*+60.60*

BY MONTH

2-y-o	W-R	Per cent	£1 Level Stake
January	0-0	0.0	0.00
February	0-0	0.0	0.00
March	0-0	0.0	0.00
April	0-0	0.0	0.00
May	0-1	0.0	-1.00
June	0-4	0.0	-4.00
July	0-2	0.0	-2.00
August	0-3	0.0	-3.00
September	0-6	0.0	-6.00
October	1-6	16.7	-2.50
November	0-2	0.0	-2.00
December	0-0	0.0	0.00

3-y-o	W-R	Per cent	£1 Level Stake
January	0-0	0.0	0.00
February	0-0	0.0	0.00
March	0-1	0.0	-1.00
April	0-4	0.0	-4.00
May	1-8	12.5	-0.50
June	1-8	12.5	-3.00
July	1-4	25.0	-1.90
August	3-7	42.9	+0.70
September	0-6	0.0	-6.00
October	0-6	0.0	-6.00
November	0-2	0.0	-2.00
December	0-0	0.0	0.00

4-y-o+	W-R	Per cent	£1 Level Stake
January	1-1	100.0	+1.20
February	1-2	50.0	+4.50
March	0-1	0.0	-1.00

Totals	W-R	Per cent	£1 Level Stake
January	1-1	100.0	+1.20
February	1-2	50.0	+4.50
March	0-2	0.0	-2.00

	W-R	Per cent	£1 Level Stake
April	0-3	0.0	-3.00
May	0-4	0.0	-4.00
June	1-4	25.0	+1.00
July	0-5	0.0	-5.00
August	2-5	40.0	+0.25
September	2-4	50.0	+7.10
October	0-4	0.0	-4.00
November	0-2	0.0	-2.00
December	0-0	0.0	0.00

	W-R	Per cent	£1 Level Stake
April	0-7	0.0	-7.00
May	1-13	7.7	-5.50
June	2-16	12.5	-6.00
July	1-11	9.1	-8.90
August	5-15	33.3	-2.05
September	2-16	12.5	-4.90
October	1-16	6.3	-12.50
November	0-6	0.0	-4.00
December	0-0	0.0	0.00

DISTANCE

2-y-o	W-R	Per cent	£1 Level Stake
5f-6f	0-5	0.0	-5.00
7f-8f	1-19	5.3	-15.50
9f-13f	0-0	0.0	0.00
14f+	0-0	0.0	0.00

3-y-o	W-R	Per cent	£1 Level Stake
5f-6f	0-1	0.0	-1.00
7f-8f	4-25	16.0	-12.70
9f-13f	1-16	6.3	-8.50
14f+	1-4	25.0	-1.50

4-y-o+	W-R	Per cent	£1 Level Stake
5f-6f	2-8	25.0	+3.50
7f-8f	5-24	20.8	-5.45
9f-13f	0-2	0.0	-2.00
14f+	0-1	0.0	-1.00

Totals	W-R	Per cent	£1 Level Stake
5f-6f	2-14	14.3	-2.50
7f-8f	10-68	14.7	-33.65
9f-13f	1-18	5.6	-10.50
14f+	1-5	20.0	-2.50

TYPE OF RACE

Non-Handicaps

	W-R	Per cent	£1 Level Stake
2-y-o	0-21	0.0	-21.00
3-y-o	1-20	5.0	-15.00
4-y-o+	1-2	50.0	+0.20

Handicaps

	W-R	Per cent	£1 Level Stake
2-y-o	1-3	33.3	+0.50
3-y-o	5-26	19.2	-8.70
4-y-o+	6-33	18.2	-5.15

RACE CLASS

	W-R	Per cent	£1 Level Stake
Class 1	0-3	0.0	-3.00
Class 2	1-8	12.5	-3.00
Class 3	1-7	14.3	-4.80
Class 4	5-26	19.2	-3.20
Class 5	5-51	9.8	-32.90
Class 6	2-10	20.0	-2.25
Class 7	0-0	0.0	0.00

FIRST TIME OUT

	W-R	Per cent	£1 Level Stake
2-y-o	0-7	0.0	-7.00
3-y-o	0-7	0.0	-7.00
4-y-o+	2-6	33.3	+2.70
Totals	2-20	10.0	-11.30

JOCKEYS

	W-R	Per cent	£1 Level Stake
Oisin Murphy	3-13	23.1	-2.90
Silvestre De Sousa	2-5	40.0	-0.30
Ben Curtis	2-7	28.6	-2.70
Aaron Jones	1-1	100.0	+8.00
Jim Crowley	1-1	100.0	+1.50
Daniel Muscutt	1-2	50.0	+3.00
David Probert	1-3	33.3	-0.25
George Wood	1-4	25.0	+3.50
Gerald Mosse	1-4	25.0	-0.50
Edward Greatrex	1-5	20.0	+1.50

COURSE RECORD

	Total W-R	Non-Hndcps 2-y-o	Non-Hndcps 3-y-o+	Hndcps 2-y-o	Hndcps 3-y-o+	Per cent	£1 Level Stake
Newcastle (A.W)	4-9	0-1	1-2	0-0	3-6	44.4	+6.80
Yarmouth	2-6	0-2	1-1	0-0	1-3	33.3	+1.50
Wolvhptn (A.W)	2-10	0-0	0-2	0-0	2-8	20.0	-5.15
Bath	1-1	0-0	0-0	0-0	1-1	100.0	+8.00
Newmarket	1-3	0-0	0-1	1-1	0-1	33.3	+0.50
Redcar	1-5	0-0	0-1	0-1	1-3	20.0	+2.50
Newbury	1-6	0-1	0-2	0-0	1-3	16.7	-3.00
Haydock	1-7	0-2	0-1	0-0	1-4	14.3	-4.50
Chelmsford (A.W)	1-10	0-1	0-1	0-0	1-8	10.0	-7.80

WINNING HORSES

Horse	Races Run	1st	2nd	3rd	£
Al Fajir Mukbile (IRE)	6	1	2	0	4528
Amazour (IRE)	7	2	0	0	23002
Comporta	9	1	0	4	3105
Counter Spirit (IRE)	7	2	2	1	6857
Glenglade	7	2	2	1	13876
Good Effort (IRE)	7	1	1	2	5531
Ifubelieveindreams (IRE)	6	1	0	1	5923
Nibras Again	10	2	1	1	10383
Nibras Galaxy (IRE)	10	2	2	3	8474
Total winning prize-money					**£81679**
Favourites	**7-16**		**43.8%**		**0.85**

LAURA MONGAN

EPSOM, SURREY

	No. of Hrs	Races Run	1st	2nd	3rd	Unpl	Per cent	£1 Level Stake
2-y-o	*2*	*3*	*0*	*0*	*1*	*2*	*0.0*	*-3.00*
3-y-o	*4*	*23*	*0*	*2*	*4*	*17*	*0.0*	*-23.00*
4-y-o+	*11*	*91*	*7*	*10*	*11*	*62*	*7.7*	*-28.50*
Totals	**17**	**117**	**7**	**12**	**16**	**81**	**6.0**	**-54.50**
2017	*23*	*106*	*5*	*9*	*7*	*84*	*4.7*	*-52.42*
2016	*23*	*120*	*13*	*9*	*12*	*86*	*10.8*	*+13.75*

JOCKEYS

	W-R	Per cent	£1 Level Stake
Liam Jones	3-14	21.4	+6.00
Luke Morris	2-12	16.7	+4.00
Edward Greatrex	1-4	25.0	+17.00
Sophie Ralston	1-11	9.1	-5.50

COURSE RECORD

	Total W-R	Non-Hndcps 2-y-o	Non-Hndcps 3-y-o+	Hndcps 2-y-o	Hndcps 3-y-o+	Per cent	£1 Level Stake
Brighton	3-16	0-0	0-0	0-0	3-16	18.8	+6.50
Lingfield (A.W)	3-38	0-1	0-9	0-0	3-28	7.9	-19.00
Salisbury	1-4	0-0	0-0	0-0	1-4	25.0	+17.00

WINNING HORSES

Horse	Races Run	1st	2nd	3rd	£
Ablaze	7	1	0	0	3493
*Impart	15	3	3	0	9315
Narjes	16	2	3	2	6210
With Approval (IRE)	10	1	1	2	3105
Total winning prize-money					**£22123**
Favourites	**1-4**		**25.0%**		**-1.13**

J S MOORE

UPPER LAMBOURN, BERKS

	No. of Hrs	Races Run	1st	2nd	3rd	Unpl	Per cent	£1 Level Stake
2-y-o	*19*	*66*	*2*	*3*	*8*	*53*	*3.0*	*-10.50*
3-y-o	*16*	*66*	*0*	*2*	*4*	*60*	*0.0*	*-66.00*
4-y-o+	*4*	*24*	*0*	*4*	*5*	*15*	*0.0*	*-24.00*
Totals	**39**	**156**	**2**	**9**	**17**	**128**	**1.3**	**-100.50**
2017	*42*	*157*	*6*	*12*	*23*	*116*	*3.8*	*-87.50*
2016	*52*	*221*	*8*	*13*	*31*	*169*	*3.6*	*-83.38*

JOCKEYS

	W-R	Per cent	£1 Level Stake
John Fahy	2-31	6.5	+24.50

COURSE RECORD

	Total W-R	Non-Hndcps 2-y-o	Non-Hndcps 3-y-o+	Hndcps 2-y-o	Hndcps 3-y-o+	Per cent	£1 Level Stake
Ripon	1-1	1-1	0-0	0-0	0-0	100.0	+3.50
Chepstow	1-11	1-4	0-1	0-0	0-6	9.1	+40.00

WINNING HORSES

Horse	Races Run	1st	2nd	3rd	£
Hope Again	1	1	0	0	3105
The Big Bad (IRE)*	3	1	1	0	3105
Total winning prize-money					**£6210**
Favourites	**0-1**		**0.0%**		**-1.00**

GARY MOORE

LOWER BEEDING, W SUSSEX

	No. of Hrs	Races Run	1st	2nd	3rd	Unpl	Per cent	£1 Level Stake
2-y-o	*16*	*46*	*1*	*1*	*4*	*40*	*2.2*	*-40.50*
3-y-o	*18*	*64*	*4*	*6*	*6*	*48*	*6.3*	*-42.00*
4-y-o+	*50*	*216*	*19*	*34*	*19*	*143*	*8.8*	*-39.55*
Totals	**84**	**326**	**24**	**41**	**29**	**231**	**7.4**	**-122.05**
2017	*72*	*349*	*41*	*47*	*40*	*221*	*11.7*	*+65.00*
2016	*70*	*359*	*38*	*28*	*43*	*250*	*10.6*	*-149.54*

BY MONTH

2-y-o	W-R	Per cent	£1 Level Stake	**3-y-o**	W-R	Per cent	£1 Level Stake
January	0-0	0.0	0.00	January	0-4	0.0	-4.00
February	0-0	0.0	0.00	February	0-1	0.0	-1.00
March	0-0	0.0	0.00	March	1-1	100.0	+3.00
April	0-0	0.0	0.00	April	0-2	0.0	-2.00
May	0-2	0.0	-2.00	May	1-5	20.0	+0.50
June	0-5	0.0	-5.00	June	0-11	0.0	-11.00
July	0-2	0.0	-2.00	July	0-4	0.0	-4.00
August	0-6	0.0	-6.00	August	2-13	15.4	-0.50
September	0-7	0.0	-7.00	September	0-6	0.0	-6.00
October	1-17	5.9	-11.50	October	0-5	0.0	-5.00
November	0-5	0.0	-5.00	November	0-4	0.0	-4.00
December	0-2	0.0	-2.00	December	0-8	0.0	-8.00

4-y-o+	W-R	Per cent	£1 Level Stake	**Totals**	W-R	Per cent	£1 Level Stake
January	2-15	13.3	-9.30	January	2-19	10.5	-13.30
February	1-16	6.3	-12.25	February	1-17	5.9	-13.25
March	1-10	10.0	-6.00	March	2-11	18.2	-3.00
April	1-9	11.1	-6.00	April	1-11	9.1	-8.00
May	4-28	14.3	+33.50	May	5-35	14.3	+32.00
June	1-23	4.3	-18.00	June	1-39	2.6	-34.00
July	2-20	10.0	+21.00	July	2-26	7.7	+15.00
August	1-29	3.4	-25.00	August	3-48	6.3	-31.50
September	2-14	14.3	+9.00	September	2-27	7.4	-4.00
October	1-21	4.8	-11.00	October	2-43	4.7	-27.50
November	0-15	0.0	-15.00	November	0-24	0.0	-19.00
December	3-16	18.8	-0.50	December	3-26	11.5	-8.50

DISTANCE

2-y-o	W-R	Per cent	£1 Level Stake	**3-y-o**	W-R	Per cent	£1 Level Stake
5f-6f	1-21	4.8	-15.50	5f-6f	1-9	11.1	-5.00
7f-8f	0-21	0.0	-21.00	7f-8f	0-33	0.0	-33.00
9f-13f	0-4	0.0	-4.00	9f-13f	3-22	13.6	-4.00
14f+	0-0	0.0	0.00	14f+	0-0	0.0	0.00

4-y-o+	W-R	Per cent	£1 Level Stake	**Totals**	W-R	Per cent	£1 Level Stake
5f-6f	2-14	14.3	-5.00	5f-6f	4-44	9.1	-25.50
7f-8f	4-54	7.4	-23.00	7f-8f	4-108	3.7	-77.00
9f-13f	8-99	8.1	-14.00	9f-13f	11-125	8.8	-22.00
14f+	5-49	10.2	+2.45	14f+	5-49	10.2	+2.45

TYPE OF RACE

Non-Handicaps	W-R	Per cent	£1 Level Stake	**Handicaps**	W-R	Per cent	£1 Level Stake
2-y-o	1-41	2.4	-35.50	2-y-o	0-5	0.0	-5.00
3-y-o	0-14	0.0	-14.00	3-y-o	4-50	8.0	-28.00
4-y-o+	2-16	12.5	-12.80	4-y-o+	17-200	8.5	-26.75

RACE CLASS

	W-R	Per cent	£1 Level Stake
Class 1	0-2	0.0	-2.00
Class 2	0-21	0.0	-21.00
Class 3	3-21	14.3	+64.00
Class 4	6-67	9.0	-19.50
Class 5	5-104	4.8	-80.25

FIRST TIME OUT

	W-R	Per cent	£1 Level Stake
2-y-o	0-16	0.0	-16.00
3-y-o	2-18	11.1	-5.50
4-y-o+	2-50	4.0	-7.80
Totals	4-84	4.8	-29.30

Class 6	10-104	9.6	-56.30
Class 7	0-7	0.0	-7.00

JOCKEYS

	W-R	Per cent	£1 Level Stake
Hector Crouch	13-137	9.5	-21.05
Adam Kirby	3-23	13.0	-6.50
Jim Crowley	2-6	33.3	+2.00
Liam Keniry	2-6	33.3	+4.00
Jason Watson	2-20	10.0	-4.50
Kieran O'Neill	1-5	20.0	-1.00
David Probert	1-7	14.3	+27.00

COURSE RECORD

	Total W-R	Non-Hndcps 2-y-o	Non-Hndcps 3-y-o+	Hndcps 2-y-o	Hndcps 3-y-o+	Per cent	£1 Level Stake
Lingfield (A.W)	6-51	0-3	1-6	0-0	5-42	11.8	-28.80
Brighton	4-48	0-5	0-1	0-1	4-41	8.3	-19.00
Chelmsford (A.W)	3-30	0-3	1-1	0-2	2-24	10.0	-19.50
Kempton (A.W)	3-62	0-4	0-6	0-0	3-52	4.8	-16.25
Lingfield	2-16	0-1	0-2	0-0	2-13	12.5	-5.50
Goodwood	2-27	0-6	0-3	0-0	2-18	7.4	-11.50
Newmarket	1-5	0-0	0-0	0-0	1-5	20.0	+36.00
Salisbury	1-6	1-4	0-1	0-0	0-1	16.7	-0.50
Sandown	1-12	0-3	0-0	0-0	1-9	8.3	-5.00
Epsom	1-15	0-2	0-1	0-0	1-12	6.7	+2.00

WINNING HORSES

Horse	Races Run	1st	2nd	3rd	£
Age Of Wisdom (IRE)	8	3	1	0	16195
Ban Shoof	9	1	4	2	3105
Canberra Cliffs (IRE)	6	1	1	0	12450
Clara Peeters	4	1	1	0	5111
Deebaj (IRE)	3	1	1	0	3105
Good Luck Charm	10	1	0	1	3752
Guns Of Leros (USA)	4	1	0	0	9704
Hint Of Grey (IRE)	4	1	0	1	3105
Hollywood Road (IRE)	6	1	0	2	5531
Kafeel (USA)	5	1	1	0	3105
*King Athelstan (IRE)	5	1	2	1	3105
Le Précieux (FR)	2	1	0	0	3169
Lord Clenaghcastle (IRE)	7	2	0	0	11644
Pride Of Angels	7	2	3	0	9283
*Rocksette	4	1	0	1	3105
Rydan (IRE)	12	2	1	3	11903
Sing Out Loud (IRE)*	7	1	1	0	6728
*Spring Praise (IRE)	2	1	0	0	3493
Swift Fox	7	1	0	1	3105
Total winning prize-money					**£120698**
Favourites	**25-75**		**33.3%**		**-6.78**

PATRICK MORRIS

PRESCOT, MERSEYSIDE

	No. of Hrs	Races Run	1st	2nd	3rd	Unpl	Per cent	£1 Level Stake
2-y-o	*0*	*0*	*0*	*0*	*0*	*0*	*0.0*	*0.00*
3-y-o	*1*	*2*	*0*	*0*	*0*	*2*	*0.0*	*-2.00*
4-y-o+	*12*	*78*	*6*	*6*	*8*	*58*	*7.7*	*-36.59*
Totals	**13**	**80**	**6**	**6**	**8**	**60**	**7.5**	**-38.59**
2017	*16*	*87*	*8*	*11*	*13*	*55*	*9.2*	*-16.00*
2016	*8*	*45*	*1*	*7*	*5*	*32*	*2.2*	*-33.00*

JOCKEYS

	W-R	Per cent	£1 Level Stake
Stevie Donohoe	1-1	100.0	+6.00
Rossa Ryan	1-4	25.0	-2.09
Shane Kelly	1-7	14.3	0.00
Fran Berry	1-8	12.5	+4.00
Connor Murtagh	1-10	10.0	-3.00
Callum Rodriguez	1-13	7.7	-6.50

COURSE RECORD

	Total W-R	Non-Hndcps 2-y-o	Non-Hndcps 3-y-o+	Hndcps 2-y-o	Hndcps 3-y-o+	Per cent	£1 Level Stake
Wolvhptn (A.W)	5-56	0-0	2-7	0-0	3-49	8.9	-21.59
Newcastle (A.W)	1-13	0-0	0-0	0-0	1-13	7.7	-6.00

WINNING HORSES

Horse	Races Run	1st	2nd	3rd	£
Bell Heather (IRE)	9	1	1	3	3105
Energia Flavio (BRZ)	14	2	1	2	6210
Pushkin Museum (IRE)*	9	2	0	0	6210
Top Offer	19	1	3	1	3105
Total winning prize-money					**£18630**
Favourites	**1-3**		**33.3%**		**-1.09**

HUGHIE MORRISON

EAST ILSLEY, BERKS

	No. of Hrs	Races Run	1st	2nd	3rd	Unpl	Per cent	£1 Level Stake
2-y-o	*17*	*62*	*6*	*7*	*3*	*46*	*9.7*	*-35.72*
3-y-o	*30*	*202*	*24*	*22*	*29*	*127*	*11.9*	*-35.13*
4-y-o+	*25*	*130*	*14*	*12*	*14*	*90*	*10.8*	*-41.63*
Totals	**72**	**394**	**44**	**41**	**46**	**263**	**11.2**	**-112.48**
2017	*71*	*331*	*43*	*39*	*35*	*214*	*13.0*	*-70.66*
2016	*72*	*351*	*44*	*46*	*31*	*230*	*12.5*	*-67.88*

BY MONTH

2-y-o	W-R	Per cent	£1 Level Stake	**3-y-o**	W-R	Per cent	£1 Level Stake
January	0-0	0.0	0.00	January	0-2	0.0	-2.00
February	0-0	0.0	0.00	February	0-3	0.0	-3.00
March	0-0	0.0	0.00	March	2-3	66.7	+10.50

April	0-0	0.0	0.00	April	2-21	9.5	-10.00
May	0-2	0.0	-2.00	May	3-26	11.5	+17.00
June	0-5	0.0	-5.00	June	3-27	11.1	-11.75
July	0-5	0.0	-5.00	July	1-31	3.2	-21.00
August	4-13	30.8	+5.03	August	6-32	18.8	-2.72
September	1-11	9.1	-6.00	September	3-29	10.3	-9.17
October	0-14	0.0	-14.00	October	4-22	18.2	+3.00
November	1-9	11.1	-5.75	November	0-4	0.0	-4.00
December	0-3	0.0	-3.00	December	0-2	0.0	-2.00

4-y-o+	W-R	Per cent	£1 Level Stake	Totals	W-R	Per cent	£1 Level Stake
January	0-4	0.0	-4.00	January	0-6	0.0	-6.00
February	1-6	16.7	0.00	February	1-9	11.1	-3.00
March	1-4	25.0	-0.75	March	3-7	42.9	+9.75
April	0-7	0.0	-7.00	April	2-28	7.1	-17.00
May	1-17	5.9	-4.00	May	4-45	8.9	+11.00
June	1-16	6.3	-13.63	June	4-48	8.3	-30.38
July	3-11	27.3	+2.25	July	4-47	8.5	-23.75
August	3-16	18.8	+8.25	August	13-61	21.3	+10.56
September	3-21	14.3	-1.75	September	7-61	11.5	-16.92
October	0-16	0.0	-16.00	October	4-52	7.7	-27.00
November	1-9	11.1	-2.00	November	2-22	9.1	-6.00
December	0-3	0.0	-3.00	December	0-8	0.0	-5.00

DISTANCE

2-y-o	W-R	Per cent	£1 Level Stake	3-y-o	W-R	Per cent	£1 Level Stake
5f-6f	1-19	5.3	-16.00	5f-6f	4-17	23.5	+12.00
7f-8f	5-41	12.2	-17.72	7f-8f	8-73	11.0	-15.50
9f-13f	0-2	0.0	-2.00	9f-13f	11-104	10.6	-29.63
14f+	0-0	0.0	0.00	14f+	1-8	12.5	-2.00

4-y-o+	W-R	Per cent	£1 Level Stake	Totals	W-R	Per cent	£1 Level Stake
5f-6f	0-7	0.0	-7.00	5f-6f	5-43	11.6	-11.00
7f-8f	3-35	8.6	-6.50	7f-8f	16-149	10.7	-39.72
9f-13f	6-57	10.5	-19.38	9f-13f	17-163	10.4	-51.01
14f+	5-31	16.1	-8.75	14f+	6-39	15.4	-10.75

TYPE OF RACE

Non-Handicaps	W-R	Per cent	£1 Level Stake	Handicaps	W-R	Per cent	£1 Level Stake
2-y-o	4-48	8.3	-38.72	2-y-o	2-14	14.3	+3.00
3-y-o	3-61	4.9	-43.67	3-y-o	21-141	14.9	+8.53
4-y-o+	3-18	16.7	+9.63	4-y-o+	11-112	9.8	-32.00

RACE CLASS

	W-R	Per cent	£1 Level Stake
Class 1	3-10	30.0	-1.63
Class 2	2-51	3.9	-32.00
Class 3	8-33	24.2	+13.75
Class 4	10-89	11.2	-40.01
Class 5	13-123	10.6	-40.09
Class 6	8-85	9.4	-9.50
Class 7	0-3	0.0	-3.00

FIRST TIME OUT

	W-R	Per cent	£1 Level Stake
2-y-o	0-17	0.0	-17.00
3-y-o	1-30	3.3	-23.00
4-y-o+	1-25	4.0	-22.63
Totals	2-72	2.8	-62.63

JOCKEYS

	W-R	Per cent	£1 Level Stake
Charlie Bennett	9-129	7.0	-46.00
Oisin Murphy	6-27	22.2	+13.50
Liam Keniry	4-17	23.5	+18.25
Richard Kingscote	3-12	25.0	-4.79
Robert Havlin	3-22	13.6	-15.06
Ryan Moore	2-2	100.0	+3.13
Adam Kirby	2-11	18.2	-0.50
Jason Watson	2-12	16.7	-0.50
P J McDonald	2-18	11.1	-3.00
Theodore Ladd	2-18	11.1	-8.75
Dane O'Neill	1-2	50.0	+7.00
Miss Serena Brotherton	1-2	50.0	+1.75
Gerald Mosse	1-3	33.3	+3.50
David Probert	1-3	33.3	+2.50
James Doyle	1-4	25.0	-0.75
Fran Berry	1-8	12.5	+1.00
Robert Winston	1-8	12.5	+3.00
Kieran O'Neill	1-12	8.3	-6.50
Jim Crowley	1-13	7.7	-9.25

COURSE RECORD

	Total W-R	Non-Hndcps 2-y-o	Non-Hndcps 3-y-o+	Hndcps 2-y-o	Hndcps 3-y-o+	Per cent	£1 Level Stake
Kempton (A.W)	7-48	1-5	1-12	1-2	4-29	14.6	-11.01
Southwell (A.W)	4-15	1-1	0-3	0-0	3-11	26.7	+1.25
Epsom	3-12	1-2	0-0	1-1	1-9	25.0	+7.00
Sandown	3-13	0-1	1-3	0-0	2-9	23.1	-2.25
Nottingham	3-18	0-2	0-1	0-0	3-15	16.7	+7.50
Newbury	3-33	0-9	0-9	0-1	3-14	9.1	-13.00
Salisbury	2-7	0-2	0-0	0-0	2-5	28.6	+15.00
Doncaster	2-14	0-0	0-2	0-2	2-10	14.3	-3.50
Newmarket	2-16	0-2	1-4	0-1	1-9	12.5	-4.25
Goodwood	2-23	0-3	1-6	0-1	1-13	8.7	-6.50
Wolvhptn (A.W)	2-32	0-4	1-8	0-2	1-18	6.3	-12.50
Pontefract	1-3	0-0	0-1	0-0	1-2	33.3	+2.50
Wetherby	1-3	0-0	0-1	0-0	1-2	33.3	+5.00
York	1-5	0-0	1-1	0-0	0-4	20.0	-2.63
Chepstow	1-7	0-0	0-1	0-0	1-6	14.3	-4.63
Newmkt (Jly)	1-7	1-1	0-2	0-0	0-4	14.3	-5.47
Brighton	1-9	0-0	0-0	0-0	1-9	11.1	+8.00
Ffos Las	1-11	0-3	0-1	0-2	1-5	9.1	-8.00
Leicester	1-14	0-3	0-3	0-0	1-8	7.1	-5.00
Windsor	1-18	0-3	0-5	0-1	1-9	5.6	-10.00
Chelmsford (A.W)	1-20	0-3	0-3	0-0	1-14	5.0	-13.00
Lingfield (A.W)	1-24	0-3	0-8	0-0	1-13	4.2	-15.00

WINNING HORSES

Horse	Races Run	1st	2nd	3rd	£
Affair	10	1	3	1	3493
Belated Breath	10	4	1	2	26366
Bella Ragazza	6	3	1	0	45752
Bossiney Bay (IRE)	8	1	0	1	5693
Buzz (FR)	7	3	1	0	65363

Horse	Races Run	1st	2nd	3rd	£
Candidate (IRE)	9	1	1	1	3752
Compton Mill	9	1	1	1	6239
Corgi	6	1	3	1	9338
Cousin Khee	12	2	1	3	13779
Deadly Accurate*	10	1	1	1	7116
Dorian Gray (IRE)	8	3	1	1	10156
Finale	4	1	0	0	3493
Geranium	7	1	0	1	3105
Indian Viceroy	8	2	2	0	10027
Jedhi	10	2	1	3	19315
Korcho	5	1	0	0	3105
Majestic Mac	6	1	0	0	4528
Marmelo	1	1	0	0	28355
Mums Hope	3	1	1	0	5175
Nearly Caught (IRE)	4	2	0	0	45637
Pastoral Player	9	1	0	2	12699
Pippin	5	2	1	1	7245
Pursuing Steed	9	1	0	0	3752
Quicksand (IRE)	3	1	0	1	6469
Racehorse	11	1	0	1	3493
Requited (IRE)	8	1	1	0	4787
Sod's Law	7	2	0	2	13090
Starcaster	7	1	0	2	5531
Temple Church (IRE)	6	1	0	2	7439
Total winning prize-money					**£384292**
Favourites	**16-46**		**34.8%**		**-4.73**

MOHAMED MOUBARAK

EXNING, SUFFOLK

	No. of Hrs	Races Run	1st	2nd	3rd	Unpl	Per cent	£1 Level Stake
2-y-o	*8*	*21*	*2*	*0*	*2*	*17*	*9.5*	*+151.00*
3-y-o	*4*	*15*	*2*	*1*	*0*	*12*	*13.3*	*+2.25*
4-y-o+	*3*	*12*	*0*	*2*	*0*	*10*	*0.0*	*-12.00*
Totals	**15**	**48**	**4**	**3**	**2**	**39**	**8.3**	**+141.25**
2017	*15*	*61*	*2*	*6*	*3*	*50*	*3.3*	*-27.00*
2016	*2*	*2*	*0*	*1*	*1*	*0*	*0.0*	*-2.00*

JOCKEYS

	W-R	Per cent	£1 Level Stake
Robert Havlin	1-4	25.0	+17.00
George Wood	1-5	20.0	+10.00
Luke Morris	1-6	16.7	-3.75
Darragh Keenan	1-7	14.3	+144.00

COURSE RECORD

	Total W-R	Non-Hndcps 2-y-o	Non-Hndcps 3-y-o+	Hndcps 2-y-o	Hndcps 3-y-o+	Per cent	£1 Level Stake
Windsor	1-3	0-1	1-1	0-0	0-1	33.3	+12.00
Thirsk	1-5	0-1	1-4	0-0	0-0	20.0	-2.75
Yarmouth	1-5	1-1	0-1	0-1	0-2	20.0	+16.00
Chelmsford (A.W)	1-9	1-4	0-1	0-1	0-3	11.1	+142.00

WINNING HORSES

Horse	Races Run	1st	2nd	3rd	£
Sharp Style (FR)	3	2	1	0	8280
Taylormade	3	1	0	0	3105
The Meter	2	1	0	0	6728
Total winning prize-money					**£18113**
Favourites	**1-1**		**100.0%**		**1.25**

WILLIAM MUIR

LAMBOURN, BERKS

	No. of Hrs	Races Run	1st	2nd	3rd	Unpl	Per cent	£1 Level Stake
2-y-o	*11*	*41*	*5*	*4*	*2*	*29*	*12.2*	*-17.63*
3-y-o	*11*	*64*	*10*	*5*	*7*	*42*	*15.6*	*+16.45*
4-y-o+	*11*	*78*	*8*	*4*	*9*	*57*	*10.3*	*-19.25*
Totals	**33**	**183**	**23**	**13**	**18**	**128**	**12.6**	**-20.43**
2017	*45*	*262*	*25*	*30*	*24*	*183*	*9.5*	*-36.27*
2016	*50*	*258*	*27*	*26*	*38*	*166*	*10.5*	*-32.42*

BY MONTH

2-y-o	W-R	Per cent	£1 Level Stake	**3-y-o**	W-R	Per cent	£1 Level Stake
January	0-0	0.0	0.00	January	0-1	0.0	-1.00
February	0-0	0.0	0.00	February	0-6	0.0	-6.00
March	0-0	0.0	0.00	March	0-3	0.0	-3.00
April	0-0	0.0	0.00	April	0-2	0.0	-2.00
May	0-3	0.0	-3.00	May	1-7	14.3	-2.00
June	0-3	0.0	-3.00	June	1-6	16.7	+35.00
July	0-3	0.0	-3.00	July	3-13	23.1	-2.00
August	0-7	0.0	-7.00	August	3-12	25.0	+2.70
September	2-8	25.0	-1.13	September	2-9	22.2	-0.25
October	1-8	12.5	-4.25	October	0-2	0.0	-2.00
November	2-4	50.0	+8.75	November	0-3	0.0	-3.00
December	0-5	0.0	-5.00	December	0-0	0.0	0.00

4-y-o+	W-R	Per cent	£1 Level Stake	**Totals**	W-R	Per cent	£1 Level Stake
January	0-2	0.0	-2.00	January	0-3	0.0	-3.00
February	0-2	0.0	-2.00	February	0-8	0.0	-8.00
March	0-1	0.0	-1.00	March	0-4	0.0	-4.00
April	0-2	0.0	-2.00	April	0-4	0.0	-4.00
May	0-11	0.0	-11.00	May	1-21	4.8	-16.00
June	0-12	0.0	-12.00	June	1-21	4.8	+20.00
July	2-7	28.6	+6.25	July	5-23	21.7	+1.25
August	2-10	20.0	+2.50	August	5-29	17.2	-1.80
September	1-8	12.5	-3.00	September	5-25	20.0	-4.38
October	2-11	18.2	+12.00	October	3-21	14.3	+5.75
November	1-7	14.3	-2.00	November	3-14	21.4	-5.00
December	0-5	0.0	-5.00	December	0-10	0.0	-5.00

DISTANCE

2-y-o	W-R	Per cent	£1 Level Stake	**3-y-o**	W-R	Per cent	£1 Level Stake
5f-6f	2-17	11.8	-5.13	5f-6f	3-12	25.0	+1.20
7f-8f	2-19	10.5	-11.25	7f-8f	5-28	17.9	+33.75

	W-R	Per cent	£1 Level Stake		W-R	Per cent	£1 Level Stake
9f-13f	1-5	20.0	-1.25	9f-13f	0-19	0.0	-19.00
14f+	0-0	0.0	0.00	14f+	2-5	40.0	+0.50

4-y-o+	W-R	Per cent	£1 Level Stake	Totals	W-R	Per cent	£1 Level Stake
5f-6f	4-35	11.4	-1.75	5f-6f	9-64	14.1	-5.68
7f-8f	1-18	5.6	-13.00	7f-8f	8-65	12.3	+9.50
9f-13f	3-22	13.6	-1.50	9f-13f	4-46	8.7	-21.75
14f+	0-3	0.0	-3.00	14f+	2-8	25.0	-2.50

TYPE OF RACE

Non-Handicaps	W-R	Per cent	£1 Level Stake	Handicaps	W-R	Per cent	£1 Level Stake
2-y-o	3-30	10.0	-14.38	2-y-o	2-11	18.2	-3.25
3-y-o	0-18	0.0	-18.00	3-y-o	10-46	21.7	+34.45
4-y-o+	0-1	0.0	-1.00	4-y-o+	8-77	10.4	-18.25

RACE CLASS

	W-R	Per cent	£1 Level Stake
Class 1	0-0	0.0	0.00
Class 2	0-1	0.0	-1.00
Class 3	0-4	0.0	-4.00
Class 4	5-38	13.2	-13.63
Class 5	4-75	5.3	-45.50
Class 6	14-65	21.5	+44.70
Class 7	0-0	0.0	0.00

FIRST TIME OUT

	W-R	Per cent	£1 Level Stake
2-y-o	1-11	9.1	-2.00
3-y-o	1-11	9.1	-6.00
4-y-o+	0-11	0.0	-11.00
Totals	2-33	6.1	-19.00

JOCKEYS

	W-R	Per cent	£1 Level Stake
Martin Dwyer	8-78	10.3	+3.75
Nicola Currie	5-22	22.7	+13.50
Jason Watson	2-5	40.0	+1.20
J F Egan	1-1	100.0	+9.00
Daniel Tudhope	1-1	100.0	+2.75
James Doyle	1-2	50.0	+0.88
George Wood	1-3	33.3	+2.00
Silvestre De Sousa	1-3	33.3	-0.25
Finley Marsh	1-4	25.0	0.00
Fran Berry	1-8	12.5	0.00
Franny Norton	1-9	11.1	-6.25

COURSE RECORD

	Total W-R	Non-Hndcps 2-y-o	Non-Hndcps 3-y-o+	Hndcps 2-y-o	Hndcps 3-y-o+	Per cent	£1 Level Stake
Lingfield (A.W)	5-22	1-2	0-2	0-0	4-18	22.7	+39.00
Ffos Las	2-10	0-2	0-1	1-2	1-5	20.0	0.00
Chelmsford (A.W)	2-15	1-3	0-0	0-1	1-11	13.3	-7.13
Kempton (A.W)	2-20	0-4	0-3	1-2	1-11	10.0	-12.25
Wolvhptn (A.W)	2-28	0-6	0-6	0-1	2-15	7.1	-4.50
Beverley	1-1	0-0	0-0	0-0	1-1	100.0	+1.75
Epsom	1-1	0-0	0-0	0-0	1-1	100.0	+2.75
Pontefract	1-1	1-1	0-0	0-0	0-0	100.0	+2.75
Newmkt (Jly)	1-3	0-2	0-0	0-0	1-1	33.3	+5.00
Sandown	1-4	0-1	0-0	0-0	1-3	25.0	+0.50
Brighton	1-5	0-0	0-0	0-0	1-5	20.0	-2.80
Nottingham	1-6	0-0	0-0	0-0	1-6	16.7	+1.00
Lingfield	1-8	0-0	0-2	0-0	1-6	12.5	-2.50
Bath	1-11	0-1	0-1	0-0	1-9	9.1	-6.00
Windsor	1-14	0-2	0-2	0-2	1-8	7.1	-4.00

WINNING HORSES

Horse	Races Run	1st	2nd	3rd	£
Cent Flying	10	3	1	2	10027
Cuttin' Edge (IRE)	6	1	0	0	3105
Data Protection	9	3	0	2	7763
General Zoff	7	2	2	1	6210
Hold Still (IRE)	5	1	0	0	5822
Hollander	9	1	0	2	3105
Jack's Point	5	1	1	1	7375
Javelin	12	1	2	0	3105
Just Hubert (IRE)	4	1	0	0	5175
Lorna Cole (IRE)	2	1	1	0	3752
Max Guevara (IRE)	11	1	1	1	3105
Miss M (IRE)	10	1	1	2	3752
Peace And Plenty	7	2	0	0	11450
Prezzie*	4	1	0	0	3105
Secret Agent	11	2	2	0	6340
Spin Top	11	1	0	3	3105
Total winning prize-money					**£86296**
Favourites	**5-15**		**33.3%**		**2.70**

NEIL MULHOLLAND

LIMPLEY STOKE, WILTS

	No. of Hrs	Races Run	1st	2nd	3rd	Unpl	Per cent	£1 Level Stake
2-y-o	*2*	*5*	*0*	*0*	*0*	*5*	*0.0*	*-5.00*
3-y-o	*6*	*23*	*0*	*0*	*0*	*23*	*0.0*	*-23.00*
4-y-o+	*35*	*109*	*19*	*12*	*15*	*63*	*17.4*	*+24.63*
Totals	**43**	**137**	**19**	**12**	**15**	**91**	**13.9**	**-3.37**
2017	*44*	*140*	*16*	*9*	*12*	*103*	*11.4*	*-53.97*
2016	*29*	*97*	*12*	*16*	*13*	*56*	*12.4*	*-47.83*

BY MONTH

2-y-o	W-R	Per cent	£1 Level Stake	3-y-o	W-R	Per cent	£1 Level Stake
January	0-0	0.0	0.00	January	0-3	0.0	-3.00
February	0-0	0.0	0.00	February	0-3	0.0	-3.00
March	0-0	0.0	0.00	March	0-0	0.0	0.00
April	0-0	0.0	0.00	April	0-5	0.0	-5.00
May	0-0	0.0	0.00	May	0-4	0.0	-4.00
June	0-2	0.0	-2.00	June	0-0	0.0	0.00
July	0-1	0.0	-1.00	July	0-0	0.0	0.00
August	0-1	0.0	-1.00	August	0-1	0.0	-1.00
September	0-0	0.0	0.00	September	0-2	0.0	-2.00
October	0-0	0.0	0.00	October	0-3	0.0	-3.00
November	0-1	0.0	-1.00	November	0-1	0.0	-1.00
December	0-0	0.0	0.00	December	0-1	0.0	-1.00

4-y-o+	W-R	Per cent	£1 Level Stake	Totals	W-R	Per cent	£1 Level Stake
January	3-13	23.1	+11.00	January	3-16	18.8	+8.00
February	3-13	23.1	0.00	February	3-16	18.8	-3.00

	W-R	Per cent	£1 Level Stake		W-R	Per cent	£1 Level Stake
March	1-10	10.0	+1.00	March	1-10	10.0	+1.00
April	3-12	25.0	+2.88	April	3-17	17.6	-2.12
May	3-14	21.4	+7.00	May	3-18	16.7	+3.00
June	1-11	9.1	+10.00	June	1-13	7.7	+8.00
July	3-8	37.5	+13.00	July	3-9	33.3	+12.00
August	2-9	22.2	-1.25	August	2-11	18.2	-3.25
September	0-7	0.0	-7.00	September	0-9	0.0	-9.00
October	0-9	0.0	-9.00	October	0-12	0.0	-12.00
November	0-2	0.0	-2.00	November	0-4	0.0	-3.00
December	0-1	0.0	-1.00	December	0-2	0.0	-2.00

DISTANCE

2-y-o	W-R	Per cent	£1 Level Stake	3-y-o	W-R	Per cent	£1 Level Stake
5f-6f	0-4	0.0	-4.00	5f-6f	0-5	0.0	-5.00
7f-8f	0-1	0.0	-1.00	7f-8f	0-14	0.0	-14.00
9f-13f	0-0	0.0	0.00	9f-13f	0-4	0.0	-4.00
14f+	0-0	0.0	0.00	14f+	0-0	0.0	0.00

4-y-o+	W-R	Per cent	£1 Level Stake	Totals	W-R	Per cent	£1 Level Stake
5f-6f	0-4	0.0	-4.00	5f-6f	0-13	0.0	-13.00
7f-8f	5-20	25.0	+24.25	7f-8f	5-35	14.3	+9.25
9f-13f	9-68	13.2	-16.38	9f-13f	9-72	12.5	-20.38
14f+	5-17	29.4	+20.75	14f+	5-17	29.4	+20.75

TYPE OF RACE

Non-Handicaps	W-R	Per cent	£1 Level Stake	Handicaps	W-R	Per cent	£1 Level Stake
2-y-o	0-5	0.0	-5.00	2-y-o	0-0	0.0	0.00
3-y-o	0-8	0.0	-8.00	3-y-o	0-15	0.0	-15.00
4-y-o+	0-4	0.0	-4.00	4-y-o+	19-105	18.1	+28.63

RACE CLASS

	W-R	Per cent	£1 Level Stake
Class 1	0-0	0.0	0.00
Class 2	0-1	0.0	-1.00
Class 3	0-1	0.0	-1.00
Class 4	3-19	15.8	+11.50
Class 5	8-47	17.0	+12.38
Class 6	8-67	11.9	-23.25
Class 7	0-2	0.0	-2.00

FIRST TIME OUT

	W-R	Per cent	£1 Level Stake
2-y-o	0-2	0.0	-2.00
3-y-o	0-6	0.0	-6.00
4-y-o+	7-35	20.0	+23.25
Totals	7-43	16.3	+15.25

JOCKEYS

	W-R	Per cent	£1 Level Stake
Adam Kirby	8-23	34.8	+21.13
Timmy Murphy	3-4	75.0	+26.50
Jamie Spencer	2-8	25.0	-2.00
Shane Kelly	2-9	22.2	+16.00
Rob Hornby	1-3	33.3	+8.00
Gabriele Malune	1-5	20.0	+3.00
Silvestre De Sousa	1-7	14.3	-2.50
Dougie Costello	1-10	10.0	-5.50

COURSE RECORD

	Total W-R	Non-Hndcps 2-y-o	3-y-o+	Hndcps 2-y-o	3-y-o+	Per cent	£1 Level Stake
Wolvhptn (A.W)	6-42	0-3	0-2	0-0	6-37	14.3	-5.38
Kempton (A.W)	5-34	0-0	0-6	0-0	5-28	14.7	-0.75
Lingfield (A.W)	3-8	0-0	0-0	0-0	3-8	37.5	+2.75
Windsor	2-8	0-0	0-1	0-0	2-7	25.0	+5.00
Sandown	1-2	0-0	0-0	0-0	1-2	50.0	+19.00
Chepstow	1-7	0-0	0-0	0-0	1-7	14.3	+4.00
Chelmsford (A.W)	1-7	0-0	0-1	0-0	1-6	14.3	+1.00

WINNING HORSES

Horse	Races Run	1st	2nd	3rd	£
American Patrol (IRE)	9	2	1	0	6210
Cape Banjo (USA)	7	1	0	1	3752
Dream Machine (IRE)	5	1	1	0	5531
Happy Escape*	4	3	0	1	11256
Just Fred (IRE)	4	1	0	0	3429
Masquerade Bling (IRE)	11	1	1	1	3493
Master Burbidge	2	1	0	1	3105
Penny Poet (IRE)	6	1	3	2	3105
Seven Clans (IRE)	4	2	0	0	7504
The Detainee	3	1	0	1	3105
The Way You Dance (IRE)	4	2	1	1	6857
Vis A Vis	3	2	0	0	12938
Willyegolassiego	3	1	0	0	3752
Total winning prize-money					**£74037**
Favourites	**19-72**		**26.4%**		**-25.45**

LAWRENCE MULLANEY

GREAT HABTON, N YORKS

	No. of Hrs	Races Run	1st	2nd	3rd	Unpl	Per cent	£1 Level Stake
2-y-o	*4*	*11*	*0*	*0*	*1*	*10*	*0.0*	*-11.00*
3-y-o	*4*	*30*	*3*	*1*	*4*	*22*	*10.0*	*-15.63*
4-y-o+	*28*	*169*	*15*	*16*	*15*	*123*	*8.9*	*-41.00*
Totals	**36**	**210**	**18**	**17**	**20**	**155**	**8.6**	**-67.63**
2017	*11*	*81*	*10*	*5*	*13*	*53*	*12.3*	*-21.42*
2016	*11*	*83*	*7*	*8*	*8*	*59*	*8.4*	*-0.13*

BY MONTH

2-y-o	W-R	Per cent	£1 Level Stake	3-y-o	W-R	Per cent	£1 Level Stake
January	0-0	0.0	0.00	January	0-1	0.0	-1.00
February	0-0	0.0	0.00	February	0-0	0.0	0.00
March	0-0	0.0	0.00	March	0-1	0.0	-1.00
April	0-0	0.0	0.00	April	0-2	0.0	-2.00
May	0-0	0.0	0.00	May	0-5	0.0	-5.00
June	0-1	0.0	-1.00	June	0-4	0.0	-4.00
July	0-0	0.0	0.00	July	1-3	33.3	-0.13
August	0-2	0.0	-2.00	August	1-3	33.3	+0.50
September	0-1	0.0	-1.00	September	1-3	33.3	+5.00
October	0-3	0.0	-3.00	October	0-1	0.0	-1.00
November	0-1	0.0	-1.00	November	0-4	0.0	-4.00
December	0-3	0.0	-3.00	December	0-3	0.0	-3.00

4-y-o+	W-R	Per cent	£1 Level Stake
January	0-0	0.0	0.00
February	0-0	0.0	0.00
March	1-5	20.0	+1.50
April	0-8	0.0	-8.00
May	2-12	16.7	+6.00
June	4-31	12.9	-7.00
July	2-33	6.1	-25.75
August	3-33	9.1	+3.25
September	1-23	4.3	-2.00
October	2-19	10.5	-4.00
November	0-5	0.0	-5.00
December	0-0	0.0	0.00

Totals	W-R	Per cent	£1 Level Stake
January	0-1	0.0	-1.00
February	0-0	0.0	0.00
March	1-6	16.7	+0.50
April	0-10	0.0	-10.00
May	2-17	11.8	+1.00
June	4-36	11.1	-12.00
July	3-36	8.3	-25.88
August	4-38	10.5	+1.75
September	2-27	7.4	+2.00
October	2-23	8.7	-8.00
November	0-10	0.0	-9.00
December	0-6	0.0	-3.00

DISTANCE

2-y-o	W-R	Per cent	£1 Level Stake
5f-6f	0-7	0.0	-7.00
7f-8f	0-4	0.0	-4.00
9f-13f	0-0	0.0	0.00
14f+	0-0	0.0	0.00

3-y-o	W-R	Per cent	£1 Level Stake
5f-6f	3-21	14.3	-6.63
7f-8f	0-7	0.0	-7.00
9f-13f	0-2	0.0	-2.00
14f+	0-0	0.0	0.00

4-y-o+	W-R	Per cent	£1 Level Stake
5f-6f	1-10	10.0	-5.50
7f-8f	5-63	7.9	-19.75
9f-13f	8-76	10.5	+1.50
14f+	1-20	5.0	-17.25

Totals	W-R	Per cent	£1 Level Stake
5f-6f	4-38	10.5	-19.13
7f-8f	5-74	6.8	-30.75
9f-13f	8-78	10.3	-0.50
14f+	1-20	5.0	-17.25

TYPE OF RACE

Non-Handicaps

	W-R	Per cent	£1 Level Stake
2-y-o	0-8	0.0	-8.00
3-y-o	0-9	0.0	-9.00
4-y-o+	0-6	0.0	-6.00

Handicaps

	W-R	Per cent	£1 Level Stake
2-y-o	0-3	0.0	-3.00
3-y-o	3-21	14.3	-6.63
4-y-o+	15-163	9.2	-35.00

RACE CLASS

	W-R	Per cent	£1 Level Stake
Class 1	0-1	0.0	-1.00
Class 2	0-3	0.0	-3.00
Class 3	2-11	18.2	+14.50
Class 4	3-28	10.7	-4.50
Class 5	8-60	13.3	+12.75
Class 6	5-106	4.7	-85.38
Class 7	0-1	0.0	-1.00

FIRST TIME OUT

	W-R	Per cent	£1 Level Stake
2-y-o	0-4	0.0	-4.00
3-y-o	0-4	0.0	-4.00
4-y-o+	4-28	14.3	-9.00
Totals	4-36	11.1	-17.00

JOCKEYS

	W-R	Per cent	£1 Level Stake
Paula Muir	7-32	21.9	+58.00
Faye McManoman	6-22	27.3	+8.63
Daniel Tudhope	2-21	9.5	-13.25
Jason Watson	1-2	50.0	+5.00
Mr Dylan McDonagh	1-3	33.3	+0.50
Graham Lee	1-17	5.9	-13.50

COURSE RECORD

	Total W-R	Non-Hndcps 2-y-o	Non-Hndcps 3-y-o+	Hndcps 2-y-o	Hndcps 3-y-o+	Per cent	£1 Level Stake
Doncaster	2-9	0-0	0-0	0-0	2-9	22.2	+8.50
Carlisle	2-11	0-0	0-0	0-0	2-11	18.2	+22.50
York	2-14	0-1	0-0	0-0	2-13	14.3	+1.50
Thirsk	2-18	0-2	0-2	0-0	2-14	11.1	-5.00
Beverley	2-20	0-0	0-3	0-0	2-17	10.0	-13.63
Hamilton	2-26	0-0	0-0	0-0	2-26	7.7	-15.50
Chester	1-1	0-0	0-0	0-0	1-1	100.0	+20.00
Haydock	1-3	0-1	0-0	0-0	1-2	33.3	+0.75
Ripon	1-8	0-0	0-1	0-0	1-7	12.5	-5.25
Catterick	1-13	0-1	0-0	0-0	1-12	7.7	-9.50
Redcar	1-14	0-1	0-2	0-0	1-11	7.1	-7.00
Newcastle (A.W)	1-27	0-0	0-5	0-2	1-20	3.7	-19.00

WINNING HORSES

Horse	Races Run	1st	2nd	3rd	£
*Auxiliary	6	1	2	0	3493
Beverley Bullet	13	2	1	0	10868
Bogardus (IRE)	6	1	0	1	4205
Buyer Beware (IRE)	5	1	0	0	3369
Dark Intention (IRE)	10	2	0	1	20286
Duck Egg Blue (IRE)	8	1	1	0	5434
Framley Garth (IRE)	12	3	1	2	17466
Lagenda	7	1	0	0	4852
Life Knowledge (IRE)	7	1	2	0	3493
Our Little Pony	10	3	1	1	15733
Princess Nearco (IRE)	6	1	1	0	4075
*Urban Spirit (IRE)	6	1	2	1	3105
Total winning prize-money					**£96379**
Favourites	**6-23**		**26.1%**		**-2.13**

MICHAEL MULLINEAUX

ALPRAHAM, CHESHIRE

	No. of Hrs	Races Run	1st	2nd	3rd	Unpl	Per cent	£1 Level Stake
2-y-o	*0*	*0*	*0*	*0*	*0*	*0*	*0.0*	*0.00*
3-y-o	*3*	*17*	*0*	*0*	*1*	*16*	*0.0*	*-17.00*
4-y-o+	*14*	*121*	*5*	*8*	*5*	*103*	*4.1*	*-31.50*
Totals	**17**	**138**	**5**	**8**	**6**	**119**	**3.6**	**-48.50**
2017	*22*	*132*	*9*	*10*	*6*	*107*	*6.8*	*-23.75*
2016	*18*	*108*	*6*	*8*	*6*	*88*	*5.6*	*+36.00*

JOCKEYS

	W-R	Per cent	£1 Level Stake
James Sullivan	2-2	100.0	+18.50
Callum Rodriguez	1-3	33.3	+14.00
Miss Michelle Mullineaux	1-10	10.0	+16.00
Laura Coughlan	1-16	6.3	+10.00

COURSE RECORD

	Total W-R	Non-Hndcps 2-y-o	Non-Hndcps 3-y-o+	Hndcps 2-y-o	Hndcps 3-y-o+	Per cent	£1 Level Stake
Newcastle (A.W)	2-11	0-0	0-0	0-0	2-11	18.2	+23.00
Leicester	1-7	0-0	0-1	0-0	1-6	14.3	+19.00
Chepstow	1-14	0-0	0-0	0-0	1-14	7.1	+12.00
Wolvhptn (A.W)	1-23	0-0	0-2	0-0	1-21	4.3	-19.50

WINNING HORSES

Horse	Races Run	1st	2nd	3rd	£
Jacksonfire	12	1	0	0	3752
Peachey Carnehan	15	2	3	1	6210
Secretinthepark	11	1	1	1	3752
Teepee Time	15	1	1	0	3619
Total winning prize-money					**£17333**
Favourites	**1-2**		**50.0%**		**1.50**

SEAMUS MULLINS

WILSFORD-CUM-LAKE, WILTS

	No. of Hrs	Races Run	1st	2nd	3rd	Unpl	Per cent	£1 Level Stake
2-y-o	*3*	*5*	*1*	*0*	*0*	*4*	*20.0*	*+29.00*
3-y-o	*5*	*13*	*1*	*0*	*1*	*11*	*7.7*	*-5.50*
4-y-o+	*4*	*14*	*0*	*1*	*2*	*11*	*0.0*	*-14.00*
Totals	**12**	**32**	**2**	**1**	**3**	**26**	**6.3**	**+9.50**
2017	*9*	*23*	*1*	*1*	*0*	*21*	*4.3*	*-12.00*
2016	*13*	*18*	*0*	*0*	*2*	*16*	*0.0*	*-18.00*

JOCKEYS

	W-R	Per cent	£1 Level Stake
Rob Hornby	1-7	14.3	+27.00
Hollie Doyle	1-9	11.1	-1.50

COURSE RECORD

	Total W-R	Non-Hndcps 2-y-o	Non-Hndcps 3-y-o+	Hndcps 2-y-o	Hndcps 3-y-o+	Per cent	£1 Level Stake
Brighton	1-3	0-0	1-1	0-0	0-2	33.3	+4.50
Goodwood	1-6	1-2	0-3	0-0	0-1	16.7	+28.00

WINNING HORSES

Horse	Races Run	1st	2nd	3rd	£
Happy Ending (IRE)	6	1	0	1	3105
The Pink'N	3	1	0	0	7375
Total winning prize-money					**£10480**
Favourites	**10-24**		**41.7%**		**8.57**

AMY MURPHY

NEWMARKET, SUFFOLK

	No. of Hrs	Races Run	1st	2nd	3rd	Unpl	Per cent	£1 Level Stake
2-y-o	*16*	*66*	*5*	*10*	*6*	*44*	*7.6*	*-37.25*
3-y-o	*14*	*64*	*5*	*4*	*3*	*52*	*7.8*	*-22.72*
4-y-o+	*15*	*60*	*7*	*5*	*6*	*42*	*11.7*	*-25.25*
Totals	**45**	**190**	**17**	**19**	**15**	**138**	**8.9**	**-85.22**
2017	*18*	*88*	*6*	*6*	*3*	*73*	*6.8*	*-38.05*
2016	*3*	*8*	*2*	*1*	*0*	*5*	*25.0*	*+15.50*

BY MONTH

2-y-o	W-R	Per cent	£1 Level Stake	3-y-o	W-R	Per cent	£1 Level Stake
January	0-0	0.0	0.00	January	0-3	0.0	-3.00
February	0-0	0.0	0.00	February	1-2	50.0	+3.50
March	0-0	0.0	0.00	March	0-1	0.0	-1.00
April	0-2	0.0	-2.00	April	0-1	0.0	-1.00
May	2-14	14.3	-4.25	May	1-7	14.3	+10.00
June	2-11	18.2	-0.50	June	0-9	0.0	-9.00
July	0-10	0.0	-10.00	July	0-5	0.0	-5.00
August	0-9	0.0	-9.00	August	3-11	27.3	+7.78
September	1-7	14.3	+1.50	September	0-10	0.0	-10.00
October	0-7	0.0	-7.00	October	0-8	0.0	-8.00
November	0-2	0.0	-2.00	November	0-4	0.0	-4.00
December	0-4	0.0	-4.00	December	0-3	0.0	-3.00

4-y-o+	W-R	Per cent	£1 Level Stake	Totals	W-R	Per cent	£1 Level Stake
January	3-9	33.3	+8.50	January	3-12	25.0	+5.50
February	1-7	14.3	-1.50	February	2-9	22.2	+2.00
March	0-2	0.0	-2.00	March	0-3	0.0	-3.00
April	0-0	0.0	0.00	April	0-3	0.0	-3.00
May	0-6	0.0	-6.00	May	3-27	11.1	-0.25
June	0-7	0.0	-7.00	June	2-27	7.4	-16.50
July	1-7	14.3	-3.75	July	1-22	4.5	-18.75
August	1-5	20.0	-1.50	August	4-25	16.0	-2.72
September	1-3	33.3	+2.00	September	2-20	10.0	-6.50
October	0-2	0.0	-2.00	October	0-17	0.0	-17.00
November	0-3	0.0	-3.00	November	0-9	0.0	-7.00
December	0-9	0.0	-9.00	December	0-16	0.0	-12.00

DISTANCE

2-y-o	W-R	Per cent	£1 Level Stake	3-y-o	W-R	Per cent	£1 Level Stake
5f-6f	5-50	10.0	-21.25	5f-6f	4-20	20.0	+15.78
7f-8f	0-16	0.0	-16.00	7f-8f	0-19	0.0	-19.00
9f-13f	0-0	0.0	0.00	9f-13f	1-22	4.5	-16.50
14f+	0-0	0.0	0.00	14f+	0-3	0.0	-3.00

4-y-o+	W-R	Per cent	£1 Level Stake	Totals	W-R	Per cent	£1 Level Stake
5f-6f	1-19	5.3	-15.50	5f-6f	10-89	11.2	-20.97
7f-8f	0-6	0.0	-6.00	7f-8f	0-41	0.0	-41.00
9f-13f	6-23	26.1	+8.25	9f-13f	7-45	15.6	-8.25
14f+	0-12	0.0	-12.00	14f+	0-15	0.0	-15.00

TYPE OF RACE

Non-Handicaps	W-R	Per cent	£1 Level Stake	Handicaps	W-R	Per cent	£1 Level Stake
2-y-o	5-53	9.4	-24.25	2-y-o	0-13	0.0	-13.00
3-y-o	2-12	16.7	-5.06	3-y-o	3-52	5.8	-17.67

4-y-o+	0-1	0.0	-1.00

4-y-o+	7-59	11.9	-24.25

RACE CLASS

	W-R	Per cent	£1 Level Stake
Class 1	0-2	0.0	-2.00
Class 2	0-3	0.0	-3.00
Class 3	0-6	0.0	-6.00
Class 4	2-21	9.5	-10.00
Class 5	7-88	8.0	-57.31
Class 6	8-67	11.9	-3.92
Class 7	0-3	0.0	-3.00

FIRST TIME OUT

	W-R	Per cent	£1 Level Stake
2-y-o	0-16	0.0	-16.00
3-y-o	1-14	7.1	-8.50
4-y-o+	2-15	13.3	-5.75
Totals	3-45	6.7	-30.25

JOCKEYS

	W-R	Per cent	£1 Level Stake
Tom Marquand	3-4	75.0	+8.44
Martin Harley	3-12	25.0	+6.00
Gerald Mosse	1-2	50.0	+1.75
Silvestre De Sousa	1-5	20.0	-1.50
Lewis Edmunds	1-6	16.7	-2.75
Oisin Murphy	1-7	14.3	-2.00
Darragh Keenan	1-7	14.3	-1.00
Dougie Costello	1-8	12.5	-3.00
Nicola Currie	1-10	10.0	-5.67
Rhiain Ingram	1-10	10.0	+3.00
Jack Mitchell	1-14	7.1	-9.00
Gabriele Malune	1-15	6.7	-6.50
Lemos de Souza	1-30	3.3	-13.00

COURSE RECORD

	Total W-R	Non-Hndcps 2-y-o	Non-Hndcps 3-y-o+	Hndcps 2-y-o	Hndcps 3-y-o+	Per cent	£1 Level Stake
Kempton (A.W)	3-14	0-2	0-1	0-3	3-8	21.4	+4.00
Brighton	3-15	1-7	0-0	0-1	2-7	20.0	-2.17
Goodwood	2-6	1-3	0-0	0-1	1-2	33.3	+2.75
Beverley	2-7	2-3	0-0	0-0	0-4	28.6	+7.50
Chelmsford (A.W)	2-29	0-4	0-3	0-2	2-20	6.9	-7.00
Redcar	1-3	0-0	0-1	0-0	1-2	33.3	+10.00
Newmkt (Jly)	1-5	1-3	0-0	0-0	0-2	20.0	+0.50
Lingfield	1-11	0-3	1-2	0-0	0-6	9.1	-9.56
Yarmouth	1-13	0-1	0-0	0-1	1-11	7.7	-9.75
Lingfield (A.W)	1-22	0-1	1-3	0-0	0-18	4.5	-16.50

WINNING HORSES

Horse	Races Run	1st	2nd	3rd	£
Aaliya	5	1	0	2	3752
Blessed To Empress (IRE)	10	2	1	1	6534
Entertaining Ben	14	1	2	2	3752
Esprit De Baileys (FR)	5	2	2	0	8280
Happy Odyssey (IRE)	5	1	4	0	5175
Islay Mist	11	1	0	1	3105
Kapono	3	1	0	1	4528
Lazarus (IRE)	9	1	0	1	3105
Marble Statue	1	1	0	0	4270
One One Seven (IRE)*	3	1	0	0	3170
Sandkissed (IRE)	9	1	2	0	3493
Thaqaffa (IRE)	6	3	1	1	10221
Thegreatestshowman	7	1	1	1	3752
Total winning prize-money					**£63137**
Favourites	**4-19**		**21.1%**		**-11.41**

OLLY MURPHY

WILMCOTE, WARKS

	No. of Hrs	Races Run	1st	2nd	3rd	Unpl	Per cent	£1 Level Stake
2-y-o	*2*	*6*	*0*	*0*	*0*	*6*	*0.0*	*-6.00*
3-y-o	*1*	*1*	*0*	*0*	*0*	*1*	*0.0*	*-1.00*
4-y-o+	*19*	*50*	*8*	*4*	*9*	*29*	*16.0*	*-24.09*
Totals	**22**	**57**	**8**	**4**	**9**	**36**	**14.0**	**-31.09**
2017	*10*	*23*	*3*	*2*	*2*	*16*	*13.0*	*-13.27*
2016	*0*							

JOCKEYS

	W-R	Per cent	£1 Level Stake
Luke Morris	4-22	18.2	-10.63
Ms L O'Neill	1-1	100.0	+1.25
Hayley Turner	1-1	100.0	+7.00
Megan Nicholls	1-1	100.0	+1.75
Jamie Spencer	1-6	16.7	-4.47

COURSE RECORD

	Total W-R	Non-Hndcps 2-y-o	Non-Hndcps 3-y-o+	Hndcps 2-y-o	Hndcps 3-y-o+	Per cent	£1 Level Stake
Wolvhptn (A.W)	3-14	0-1	0-0	0-0	3-13	21.4	-7.59
Bath	1-2	0-0	0-0	0-0	1-2	50.0	+6.00
Chelmsford (A.W)	1-4	0-0	0-0	0-0	1-4	25.0	-1.63
Southwell (A.W)	1-4	0-0	0-0	0-0	1-4	25.0	0.00
Brighton	1-5	0-0	0-0	0-0	1-5	20.0	-2.63
Lingfield (A.W)	1-9	0-0	1-1	0-0	0-8	11.1	-6.25

WINNING HORSES

Horse	Races Run	1st	2nd	3rd	£
Avocet (USA)*	6	2	0	3	5693
Carraigin Aonair (IRE)	3	1	0	1	3105
Compatriot (IRE)	4	2	1	0	6165
*Dutch Uncle	2	1	0	0	3105
Napping	4	1	0	0	3752
*World Of Good	2	1	0	0	3105
Total winning prize-money					**£24925**
Favourites	**38-107**		**35.5%**		**-24.97**

MIKE MURPHY

WESTONING, BEDS

	No. of Hrs	Races Run	1st	2nd	3rd	Unpl	Per cent	£1 Level Stake
2-y-o	*4*	*12*	*0*	*1*	*1*	*10*	*0.0*	*-12.00*
3-y-o	*4*	*29*	*7*	*6*	*1*	*15*	*24.1*	*+23.50*
4-y-o+	*13*	*77*	*11*	*5*	*6*	*55*	*14.3*	*-11.40*

Totals	21	118	18	12	8	80	15.3	+0.10
2017	*25*	*123*	*11*	*16*	*7*	*88*	*8.9*	*-34.43*
2016	*21*	*121*	*9*	*8*	*4*	*100*	*7.4*	*-41.00*

BY MONTH

2-y-o	W-R	Per cent	£1 Level Stake
January	0-0	0.0	0.00
February	0-0	0.0	0.00
March	0-0	0.0	0.00
April	0-0	0.0	0.00
May	0-0	0.0	0.00
June	0-1	0.0	-1.00
July	0-1	0.0	-1.00
August	0-1	0.0	-1.00
September	0-2	0.0	-2.00
October	0-4	0.0	-4.00
November	0-1	0.0	-1.00
December	0-2	0.0	-2.00

3-y-o	W-R	Per cent	£1 Level Stake
January	0-0	0.0	0.00
February	0-0	0.0	0.00
March	0-3	0.0	-3.00
April	0-1	0.0	-1.00
May	0-2	0.0	-2.00
June	2-3	66.7	+9.75
July	1-5	20.0	+1.50
August	1-4	25.0	+13.00
September	1-2	50.0	+7.50
October	1-4	25.0	-0.50
November	0-3	0.0	-3.00
December	1-2	50.0	+1.25

4-y-o+	W-R	Per cent	£1 Level Stake
January	3-6	50.0	+20.88
February	0-3	0.0	-3.00
March	1-9	11.1	-4.00
April	1-5	20.0	+1.50
May	0-7	0.0	-7.00
June	1-10	10.0	-6.50
July	1-8	12.5	-2.50
August	0-5	0.0	-5.00
September	1-7	14.3	-3.50
October	2-11	18.2	+2.00
November	1-6	16.7	-4.27
December	0-0	0.0	0.00

Totals	W-R	Per cent	£1 Level Stake
January	3-6	50.0	+20.88
February	0-3	0.0	-3.00
March	1-12	8.3	-7.00
April	1-6	16.7	+0.50
May	0-9	0.0	-9.00
June	3-14	21.4	+2.25
July	2-14	14.3	-2.00
August	1-10	10.0	+7.00
September	2-11	18.2	+2.00
October	3-19	15.8	-2.50
November	1-10	10.0	-7.27
December	1-4	25.0	+1.25

DISTANCE

2-y-o	W-R	Per cent	£1 Level Stake
5f-6f	0-3	0.0	-3.00
7f-8f	0-9	0.0	-9.00
9f-13f	0-0	0.0	0.00
14f+	0-0	0.0	0.00

3-y-o	W-R	Per cent	£1 Level Stake
5f-6f	3-13	23.1	+6.25
7f-8f	2-9	22.2	+3.75
9f-13f	2-7	28.6	+13.50
14f+	0-0	0.0	0.00

4-y-o+	W-R	Per cent	£1 Level Stake
5f-6f	5-36	13.9	-4.27
7f-8f	5-24	20.8	+2.88
9f-13f	1-16	6.3	-9.00
14f+	0-1	0.0	-1.00

Totals	W-R	Per cent	£1 Level Stake
5f-6f	8-52	15.4	-1.02
7f-8f	7-42	16.7	-2.37
9f-13f	3-23	13.0	+4.50
14f+	0-1	0.0	-1.00

TYPE OF RACE

Non-Handicaps

	W-R	Per cent	£1 Level Stake
2-y-o	0-9	0.0	-9.00
3-y-o	0-9	0.0	-9.00
4-y-o+	1-6	16.7	-2.50

Handicaps

	W-R	Per cent	£1 Level Stake
2-y-o	0-3	0.0	-3.00
3-y-o	7-20	35.0	+32.50
4-y-o+	10-71	14.1	-8.90

RACE CLASS

	W-R	Per cent	£1 Level Stake
Class 1	0-0	0.0	0.00
Class 2	1-6	16.7	-2.75
Class 3	1-9	11.1	0.00
Class 4	4-27	14.8	-4.25
Class 5	7-43	16.3	+2.60
Class 6	5-31	16.1	+6.50
Class 7	0-2	0.0	-2.00

FIRST TIME OUT

	W-R	Per cent	£1 Level Stake
2-y-o	0-4	0.0	-4.00
3-y-o	0-4	0.0	-4.00
4-y-o+	3-13	23.1	+17.50
Totals	3-21	14.3	+9.50

JOCKEYS

	W-R	Per cent	£1 Level Stake
Nicola Currie	5-29	17.2	+2.38
Gabriele Malune	4-12	33.3	+12.75
Shane Kelly	2-12	16.7	+8.00
Ger O'Neill	1-1	100.0	+2.50
Mr Charlie Todd	1-1	100.0	+5.00
Luke Catton	1-2	50.0	-0.27
Theodore Ladd	1-2	50.0	+1.25
Hayley Turner	1-4	25.0	+13.00
Rossa Ryan	1-5	20.0	+2.00
Andrea Atzeni	1-8	12.5	-4.50

COURSE RECORD

	Total W-R	Non-Hndcps 2-y-o	Non-Hndcps 3-y-o+	Hndcps 2-y-o	Hndcps 3-y-o+	Per cent	£1 Level Stake
Chelmsford (A.W)	4-30	0-5	0-5	0-0	4-20	13.3	-3.63
Yarmouth	3-8	0-0	0-0	0-0	3-8	37.5	+11.00
Nottingham	2-3	0-0	0-1	0-0	2-2	66.7	+7.25
Leicester	2-6	0-0	0-0	0-1	2-5	33.3	+9.50
Beverley	1-1	0-0	1-1	0-0	0-0	100.0	+2.50
Newcastle (A.W)	1-1	0-0	0-0	0-0	1-1	100.0	+0.73
Newmkt (Jly)	1-1	0-0	0-0	0-0	1-1	100.0	+16.00
Salisbury	1-3	0-0	0-0	0-0	1-3	33.3	+0.50
Windsor	1-10	0-0	0-1	0-0	1-9	10.0	-1.00
Wolvhptn (A.W)	1-11	0-1	0-2	0-1	1-7	9.1	-7.75
Kempton (A.W)	1-12	0-2	0-1	0-0	1-9	8.3	-3.00

WINNING HORSES

Horse	Races Run	1st	2nd	3rd	£
Desert Fox	11	2	1	1	7827
Just Maybe	2	1	0	0	3235
Kodiac Express (IRE)	13	3	4	1	16690
Lily Ash (IRE)	11	3	1	2	9315
Overtrumped	3	1	0	0	4528
Rio Ronaldo (IRE)	9	1	1	0	5757
Titan Goddess	12	2	0	0	16849
Yaa Mous	9	3	2	0	27029
Young John (IRE)	9	2	1	0	7371
Total winning prize-money					**£98601**
Favourites	**4-13**		**30.8%**		**-1.02**

ANABEL K MURPHY

WILMCOTE, WARWICKS

	No. of Hrs	Races Run	1st	2nd	3rd	Unpl	Per cent	£1 Level Stake
2-y-o	*0*	*0*	*0*	*0*	*0*	*0*	*0.0*	*0.00*
3-y-o	*0*	*0*	*0*	*0*	*0*	*0*	*0.0*	*0.00*
4-y-o+	*3*	*5*	*1*	*0*	*0*	*4*	*20.0*	*+3.00*
Totals	**3**	**5**	**1**	**0**	**0**	**4**	**20.0**	**+3.00**
2017	*12*	*56*	*2*	*6*	*6*	*42*	*3.6*	*-47.50*
2016	*11*	*72*	*5*	*14*	*2*	*50*	*6.9*	*-34.50*

JOCKEYS

	W-R	Per cent	£1 Level Stake
Luke Morris	1-1	100.0	+7.00

COURSE RECORD

	Total W-R	Non-Hndcps 2-y-o	3-y-o+	Hndcps 2-y-o	3-y-o+	Per cent	£1 Level Stake
Lingfield (A.W)	1-2	0-0	0-0	0-0	1-2	50.0	+6.00

WINNING HORSES

Horse	Races Run	1st	2nd	3rd	£
Krazy Paving*	2	1	0	0	3105
Total winning prize-money					**£3105**
Favourites	**0-0**		**0.0%**		**0.00**

BARRY MURTAGH

LOW BRAITHWAITE, CUMBRIA

	No. of Hrs	Races Run	1st	2nd	3rd	Unpl	Per cent	£1 Level Stake
2-y-o	*1*	*5*	*0*	*0*	*0*	*5*	*0.0*	*-5.00*
3-y-o	*0*	*0*	*0*	*0*	*0*	*0*	*0.0*	*0.00*
4-y-o+	*4*	*12*	*1*	*0*	*0*	*11*	*8.3*	*-8.00*
Totals	**5**	**17**	**1**	**0**	**0**	**16**	**5.9**	**-13.00**
2017	*4*	*17*	*3*	*0*	*0*	*14*	*17.6*	*+24.50*
2016	*4*	*14*	*0*	*0*	*0*	*14*	*0.0*	*-14.00*

JOCKEYS

	W-R	Per cent	£1 Level Stake
Callum Rodriguez	1-1	100.0	+3.00

COURSE RECORD

	Total W-R	Non-Hndcps 2-y-o	3-y-o+	Hndcps 2-y-o	3-y-o+	Per cent	£1 Level Stake
Newcastle (A.W)	1-9	0-1	0-0	0-1	1-7	11.1	-5.00

WINNING HORSES

Horse	Races Run	1st	2nd	3rd	£
Symbolic Star (IRE)	8	1	0	0	3493
Total winning prize-money					**£3493**
Favourites	**0-0**		**0.0%**		**0.00**

TONY NEWCOMBE

YARNSCOMBE, DEVON

	No. of Hrs	Races Run	1st	2nd	3rd	Unpl	Per cent	£1 Level Stake
2-y-o	*0*	*0*	*0*	*0*	*0*	*0*	*0.0*	*0.00*
3-y-o	*1*	*3*	*0*	*0*	*0*	*3*	*0.0*	*-3.00*
4-y-o+	*17*	*70*	*4*	*5*	*5*	*56*	*5.7*	*+2.00*
Totals	**18**	**73**	**4**	**5**	**5**	**59**	**5.5**	**-1.00**
2017	*18*	*63*	*2*	*1*	*4*	*56*	*3.2*	*-51.00*
2016	*10*	*61*	*6*	*3*	*3*	*48*	*9.8*	*-10.00*

JOCKEYS

	W-R	Per cent	£1 Level Stake
Eoin Walsh	3-40	7.5	+24.00
Franny Norton	1-2	50.0	+6.00

COURSE RECORD

	Total W-R	Non-Hndcps 2-y-o	3-y-o+	Hndcps 2-y-o	3-y-o+	Per cent	£1 Level Stake
Lingfield (A.W)	2-8	0-0	0-0	0-0	2-8	25.0	+22.00
Bath	1-15	0-0	0-0	0-0	1-15	6.7	-7.00
Chelmsford (A.W)	1-15	0-0	0-1	0-0	1-14	6.7	+19.00

WINNING HORSES

Horse	Races Run	1st	2nd	3rd	£
Dubai Waves	4	1	0	1	3105
Kay Sera	6	1	0	0	3105
Kodiac Pearl (IRE)	8	1	3	1	3105
War Of Succession	7	1	1	1	3752
Total winning prize-money					**£13067**
Favourites	**0-0**		**0.0%**		**0.00**

PAUL NICHOLLS

DITCHEAT, SOMERSET

	No. of Hrs	Races Run	1st	2nd	3rd	Unpl	Per cent	£1 Level Stake
2-y-o	*4*	*14*	*1*	*1*	*2*	*10*	*7.1*	*-7.50*
3-y-o	*0*	*0*	*0*	*0*	*0*	*0*	*0.0*	*0.00*
4-y-o+	*7*	*25*	*6*	*3*	*3*	*13*	*24.0*	*-7.00*
Totals	**11**	**39**	**7**	**4**	**5**	**23**	**17.9**	**-14.50**
2017	*5*	*17*	*4*	*6*	*4*	*3*	*23.5*	*+11.80*
2016	*1*	*2*	*0*	*0*	*1*	*1*	*0.0*	*-2.00*

JOCKEYS

	W-R	Per cent	£1 Level Stake
Megan Nicholls	7-37	18.9	-12.50

COURSE RECORD

	Total W-R	Non-Hndcps 2-y-o	3-y-o+	Hndcps 2-y-o	3-y-o+	Per cent	£1 Level Stake
Lingfield (A.W)	2-3	0-0	0-0	0-0	2-3	66.7	+1.25
Chepstow	2-4	1-2	0-1	0-0	1-1	50.0	+6.00

Haydock	1-2	0-0	0-0	0-0	1-2	50.0	+1.75
Salisbury	1-3	0-2	0-0	0-0	1-1	33.3	+0.50
Bath	1-5	0-1	0-0	0-0	1-4	20.0	-2.00

WINNING HORSES

Horse	Races Run	1st	2nd	3rd	£
Cliffs Of Dover	7	3	0	1	13585
Divin Bere (FR)	2	1	0	0	4787
Moabit (GER)	1	1	0	0	15563
Volpone Jelois (FR)*	7	1	2	1	3752
Whataguy	3	1	0	1	3752
Total winning prize-money					**£41439**
Favourites	**60-152**		**39.5%**		**-20.37**

ADRIAN NICHOLLS

SESSAY, N YORKS

	No. of Hrs	Races Run	1st	2nd	3rd	Unpl	Per cent	£1 Level Stake
2-y-o	*6*	*23*	*2*	*2*	*4*	*15*	*8.7*	*-3.00*
3-y-o	*1*	*2*	*0*	*0*	*0*	*2*	*0.0*	*-2.00*
4-y-o+	*7*	*44*	*5*	*4*	*7*	*28*	*11.4*	*+23.50*
Totals	**14**	**69**	**7**	**6**	**11**	**45**	**10.1**	**+18.50**
2017	*4*	*15*	*0*	*0*	*0*	*15*	*0.0*	*-15.00*
2016	*0*							

JOCKEYS

	W-R	Per cent	£1 Level Stake
Andrew Mullen	5-32	15.6	+45.00
Ben Sanderson	1-6	16.7	-0.50
Barry McHugh	1-15	6.7	-10.00

COURSE RECORD

	Total W-R	Non-Hndcps 2-y-o	Non-Hndcps 3-y-o+	Hndcps 2-y-o	Hndcps 3-y-o+	Per cent	£1 Level Stake
Wolvhptn (A.W)	2-14	0-0	0-1	0-1	2-12	14.3	+14.50
Doncaster	1-2	1-1	0-1	0-0	0-0	50.0	+10.00
Catterick	1-4	0-1	0-0	0-0	1-3	25.0	+9.00
Carlisle	1-5	1-3	0-0	0-0	0-2	20.0	+3.00
Southwell (A.W)	1-5	0-1	0-1	0-0	1-3	20.0	0.00
Newcastle (A.W)	1-10	0-2	0-1	0-1	1-6	10.0	+11.00

WINNING HORSES

Horse	Races Run	1st	2nd	3rd	£
Hafeet Alain (IRE)	4	1	0	2	3752
*Sfumato	5	1	0	1	5111
Sir Lancelott	20	1	4	4	3105
Vivernus (USA)	8	3	0	1	13585
Xtara (IRE)	7	1	1	2	4205
Total winning prize-money					**£29758**
Favourites	**0-4**		**0.0%**		**-4.00**

PETER NIVEN

BARTON-LE-STREET, N YORKS

	No. of Hrs	Races Run	1st	2nd	3rd	Unpl	Per cent	£1 Level Stake
2-y-o	*1*	*1*	*0*	*0*	*0*	*1*	*0.0*	*-1.00*
3-y-o	*1*	*6*	*0*	*0*	*0*	*6*	*0.0*	*-6.00*
4-y-o+	*7*	*45*	*1*	*0*	*2*	*42*	*2.2*	*-39.00*
Totals	**9**	**52**	**1**	**0**	**2**	**49**	**1.9**	**-46.00**
2017	*13*	*70*	*5*	*5*	*3*	*57*	*7.1*	*-14.50*
2016	*12*	*65*	*10*	*8*	*6*	*41*	*15.4*	*-3.38*

JOCKEYS

	W-R	Per cent	£1 Level Stake
Sebastian Woods	1-3	33.3	+3.00

COURSE RECORD

	Total W-R	Non-Hndcps 2-y-o	Non-Hndcps 3-y-o+	Hndcps 2-y-o	Hndcps 3-y-o+	Per cent	£1 Level Stake
Ripon	1-3	0-0	1-2	0-0	0-1	33.3	+3.00

WINNING HORSES

Horse	Races Run	1st	2nd	3rd	£
Metronomic (IRE)	13	1	0	1	3881
Total winning prize-money					**£3881**
Favourites	**1-1**		**100.0%**		**2.25**

LUCY NORMILE

DUNCRIEVIE, PERTH & KINROSS

	No. of Hrs	Races Run	1st	2nd	3rd	Unpl	Per cent	£1 Level Stake
2-y-o	*1*	*3*	*0*	*0*	*0*	*3*	*0.0*	*-3.00*
3-y-o	*0*	*0*	*0*	*0*	*0*	*0*	*0.0*	*0.00*
4-y-o+	*6*	*26*	*2*	*7*	*3*	*14*	*7.7*	*-17.00*
Totals	**7**	**29**	**2**	**7**	**3**	**17**	**6.9**	**-20.00**
2017	*7*	*38*	*2*	*4*	*9*	*23*	*5.3*	*-26.00*
2016	*6*	*23*	*2*	*1*	*3*	*17*	*8.7*	*-5.50*

JOCKEYS

	W-R	Per cent	£1 Level Stake
Jamie Gormley	2-7	28.6	+2.00

COURSE RECORD

	Total W-R	Non-Hndcps 2-y-o	Non-Hndcps 3-y-o+	Hndcps 2-y-o	Hndcps 3-y-o+	Per cent	£1 Level Stake
Hamilton	1-6	0-0	0-0	0-0	1-6	16.7	-1.00
Ayr	1-18	0-1	0-0	0-0	1-17	5.6	-14.00

WINNING HORSES

Horse	Races Run	1st	2nd	3rd	£
Granite City Doc	6	1	3	1	3493
Royal Regent	6	1	0	0	4787

Total winning prize-money			**£8280**
Favourites	**0-4**	**0.0%**	**-4.00**

JEREMY NOSEDA

NEWMARKET, SUFFOLK

	No. of Hrs	Races Run	1st	2nd	3rd	Unpl	Per cent	£1 Level Stake
2-y-o	*10*	*35*	*5*	*5*	*6*	*19*	*14.3*	*-20.66*
3-y-o	*15*	*45*	*9*	*4*	*6*	*26*	*20.0*	*-17.19*
4-y-o+	*5*	*17*	*5*	*2*	*3*	*7*	*29.4*	*+4.25*
Totals	**30**	**97**	**19**	**11**	**15**	**52**	**19.6**	**-33.60**
2017	*39*	*122*	*28*	*19*	*13*	*62*	*23.0*	*-25.67*
2016	*34*	*109*	*19*	*20*	*11*	*59*	*17.4*	*-47.85*

BY MONTH

2-y-o	W-R	Per cent	£1 Level Stake	**3-y-o**	W-R	Per cent	£1 Level Stake
January	0-0	0.0	0.00	January	1-3	33.3	-0.75
February	0-0	0.0	0.00	February	2-2	100.0	+0.33
March	0-0	0.0	0.00	March	2-3	66.7	+2.13
April	0-0	0.0	0.00	April	0-6	0.0	-6.00
May	0-0	0.0	0.00	May	0-2	0.0	-2.00
June	0-0	0.0	0.00	June	0-7	0.0	-7.00
July	0-4	0.0	-4.00	July	2-4	50.0	+10.00
August	3-8	37.5	+3.22	August	2-9	22.2	-4.90
September	2-10	20.0	-6.88	September	0-7	0.0	-7.00
October	0-5	0.0	-5.00	October	0-1	0.0	-1.00
November	0-6	0.0	-6.00	November	0-1	0.0	-1.00
December	0-2	0.0	-2.00	December	0-0	0.0	0.00

4-y-o+	W-R	Per cent	£1 Level Stake	**Totals**	W-R	Per cent	£1 Level Stake
January	1-2	50.0	-0.50	January	2-5	40.0	-1.25
February	1-1	100.0	+1.50	February	3-3	100.0	+1.83
March	0-4	0.0	-4.00	March	2-7	28.6	-1.87
April	0-1	0.0	-1.00	April	0-7	0.0	-7.00
May	0-1	0.0	-1.00	May	0-3	0.0	-3.00
June	1-1	100.0	+10.00	June	1-8	12.5	+3.00
July	1-3	33.3	-0.75	July	3-11	27.3	+5.25
August	0-1	0.0	-1.00	August	5-18	27.8	-2.68
September	1-2	50.0	+2.00	September	3-19	15.8	-11.88
October	0-1	0.0	-1.00	October	0-7	0.0	-7.00
November	0-0	0.0	0.00	November	0-7	0.0	-1.00
December	0-0	0.0	0.00	December	0-2	0.0	0.00

DISTANCE

2-y-o	W-R	Per cent	£1 Level Stake	**3-y-o**	W-R	Per cent	£1 Level Stake
5f-6f	3-17	17.6	-12.49	5f-6f	2-10	20.0	-5.90
7f-8f	2-18	11.1	-8.17	7f-8f	7-27	25.9	-3.29
9f-13f	0-0	0.0	0.00	9f-13f	0-7	0.0	-7.00
14f+	0-0	0.0	0.00	14f+	0-1	0.0	-1.00

4-y-o+	W-R	Per cent	£1 Level Stake	**Totals**	W-R	Per cent	£1 Level Stake
5f-6f	2-3	66.7	+10.25	5f-6f	7-30	23.3	-8.14
7f-8f	2-5	40.0	+0.50	7f-8f	11-50	22.0	-10.96
9f-13f	1-9	11.1	-6.50	9f-13f	1-16	6.3	-13.50
14f+	0-0	0.0	0.00	14f+	0-1	0.0	-1.00

TYPE OF RACE

Non-Handicaps	W-R	Per cent	£1 Level Stake	**Handicaps**	W-R	Per cent	£1 Level Stake
2-y-o	5-30	16.7	-15.66	2-y-o	0-5	0.0	-5.00
3-y-o	7-27	25.9	-12.19	3-y-o	2-18	11.1	-5.00
4-y-o+	1-5	20.0	-3.00	4-y-o+	4-12	33.3	+7.75

RACE CLASS

	W-R	Per cent	£1 Level Stake
Class 1	1-9	11.1	-6.38
Class 2	3-13	23.1	-4.25
Class 3	2-13	15.4	+0.50
Class 4	4-22	18.2	-5.17
Class 5	9-38	23.7	-16.31
Class 6	0-2	0.0	-2.00
Class 7	0-0	0.0	0.00

FIRST TIME OUT

	W-R	Per cent	£1 Level Stake
2-y-o	0-10	0.0	-10.00
3-y-o	3-15	20.0	-9.40
4-y-o+	2-5	40.0	+7.50
Totals	5-30	16.7	-11.90

JOCKEYS

	W-R	Per cent	£1 Level Stake
Ryan Moore	7-13	53.8	+2.92
Jamie Spencer	4-11	36.4	+3.38
James Doyle	2-9	22.2	-5.71
Daniel Tudhope	1-1	100.0	+2.00
Kieran Shoemark	1-2	50.0	-0.50
Adam Kirby	1-4	25.0	+7.00
Luke Morris	1-4	25.0	-2.78
Robert Havlin	1-7	14.3	-4.90
Shane Kelly	1-10	10.0	+1.00

COURSE RECORD

	Total W-R	Non-Hndcps 2-y-o	Non-Hndcps 3-y-o+	Hndcps 2-y-o	Hndcps 3-y-o+	Per cent	£1 Level Stake
Kempton (A.W)	5-20	3-6	2-7	0-1	0-6	25.0	-4.13
Newcastle (A.W)	3-4	1-2	2-2	0-0	0-0	75.0	+1.10
Chelmsford (A.W)	3-9	0-3	0-1	0-0	3-5	33.3	+8.25
Doncaster	2-7	0-2	2-4	0-1	0-0	28.6	-1.90
Lingfield (A.W)	2-11	0-2	1-5	0-0	1-4	18.2	-7.42
Nottingham	1-1	0-0	0-0	0-0	1-1	100.0	+1.00
Newmkt (Jly)	1-4	1-3	0-0	0-0	0-1	25.0	-2.00
Ascot	1-5	0-2	0-0	0-0	1-3	20.0	+6.00
Wolvhptn (A.W)	1-7	0-1	1-3	0-2	0-1	14.3	-5.50

WINNING HORSES

Horse	Races Run	1st	2nd	3rd	£
Abe Lincoln (USA)	5	2	0	2	10998
Alexa Rose (USA)	4	1	1	2	5822
Betty F	5	1	0	2	3752
Cenotaph (USA)	4	3	1	0	97035
Garrus (IRE)	5	2	0	1	9315
Gronkowski (USA)	3	3	0	0	91587
Kamikaze Lord (USA)	3	1	1	0	3881
Missy Mischief (USA)	3	1	1	0	3752
Perfect Hustler (USA)	6	1	2	1	8345

Querelle (USA)	4	1	0	0	3881
Walk In The Sun (USA)*	2	2	0	0	7633
Zain Hana	7	1	1	1	6469
Total winning prize-money					**£252470**
Favourites	**15-26**		**57.7%**		**4.40**

JEDD O'KEEFFE

MIDDLEHAM MOOR, N YORKS

	No. of Hrs	Races Run	1st	2nd	3rd	Unpl	Per cent	£1 Level Stake
2-y-o	*10*	*37*	*2*	*3*	*5*	*27*	*5.4*	*-25.25*
3-y-o	*16*	*75*	*5*	*7*	*11*	*52*	*6.7*	*-51.50*
4-y-o+	*13*	*76*	*11*	*10*	*7*	*48*	*14.5*	*-25.41*
Totals	**39**	**188**	**18**	**20**	**23**	**127**	**9.6**	**-102.16**
2017	*34*	*175*	*20*	*23*	*22*	*110*	*11.4*	*-11.03*
2016	*26*	*131*	*15*	*15*	*14*	*87*	*11.5*	*-50.80*

BY MONTH

2-y-o	W-R	Per cent	£1 Level Stake	**3-y-o**	W-R	Per cent	£1 Level Stake
January	0-0	0.0	0.00	January	0-1	0.0	-1.00
February	0-0	0.0	0.00	February	0-1	0.0	-1.00
March	0-0	0.0	0.00	March	0-2	0.0	-2.00
April	0-0	0.0	0.00	April	1-7	14.3	-3.00
May	0-2	0.0	-2.00	May	0-12	0.0	-12.00
June	0-7	0.0	-7.00	June	1-6	16.7	-2.75
July	0-6	0.0	-6.00	July	1-6	16.7	-3.75
August	2-12	16.7	-0.25	August	1-7	14.3	-2.00
September	0-7	0.0	-7.00	September	1-11	9.1	-2.00
October	0-3	0.0	-3.00	October	0-14	0.0	-14.00
November	0-0	0.0	0.00	November	0-8	0.0	-8.00
December	0-0	0.0	0.00	December	0-0	0.0	0.00

4-y-o+	W-R	Per cent	£1 Level Stake	**Totals**	W-R	Per cent	£1 Level Stake
January	2-2	100.0	+4.13	January	2-3	66.7	+3.13
February	0-1	0.0	-1.00	February	0-2	0.0	-2.00
March	0-2	0.0	-2.00	March	0-4	0.0	-4.00
April	0-5	0.0	-5.00	April	1-12	8.3	-8.00
May	5-10	50.0	+9.10	May	5-24	20.8	-4.90
June	2-13	15.4	-1.64	June	3-26	11.5	-11.39
July	1-8	12.5	+1.50	July	2-20	10.0	-8.25
August	1-11	9.1	-6.50	August	4-30	13.3	-8.75
September	0-10	0.0	-10.00	September	1-28	3.6	-19.00
October	0-7	0.0	-7.00	October	0-24	0.0	-24.00
November	0-6	0.0	-6.00	November	0-14	0.0	-14.00
December	0-1	0.0	-1.00	December	0-1	0.0	-1.00

DISTANCE

2-y-o	W-R	Per cent	£1 Level Stake	**3-y-o**	W-R	Per cent	£1 Level Stake
5f-6f	1-23	4.3	-20.25	5f-6f	0-6	0.0	-6.00
7f-8f	1-14	7.1	-5.00	7f-8f	2-42	4.8	-35.75
9f-13f	0-0	0.0	0.00	9f-13f	3-27	11.1	-9.75
14f+	0-0	0.0	0.00	14f+	0-0	0.0	0.00

4-y-o+	W-R	Per cent	£1 Level Stake	**Totals**	W-R	Per cent	£1 Level Stake
5f-6f	3-15	20.0	-7.54	5f-6f	4-44	9.1	-33.79
7f-8f	5-40	12.5	-7.00	7f-8f	8-96	8.3	-47.75
9f-13f	3-18	16.7	-7.88	9f-13f	6-45	13.3	-17.63
14f+	0-3	0.0	-3.00	14f+	0-3	0.0	-3.00

TYPE OF RACE

Non-Handicaps	W-R	Per cent	£1 Level Stake	**Handicaps**	W-R	Per cent	£1 Level Stake
2-y-o	2-26	7.7	-14.25	2-y-o	0-11	0.0	-11.00
3-y-o	2-17	11.8	-10.75	3-y-o	3-58	5.2	-40.75
4-y-o+	1-2	50.0	+1.50	4-y-o+	10-74	13.5	-26.91

RACE CLASS

	W-R	Per cent	£1 Level Stake
Class 1	0-1	0.0	-1.00
Class 2	2-22	9.1	-7.50
Class 3	2-19	10.5	-0.50
Class 4	1-46	2.2	-43.25
Class 5	7-67	10.4	-34.38
Class 6	6-33	18.2	-15.54
Class 7	0-0	0.0	0.00

FIRST TIME OUT

	W-R	Per cent	£1 Level Stake
2-y-o	0-10	0.0	-10.00
3-y-o	1-16	6.3	-12.00
4-y-o+	3-13	23.1	+4.50
Totals	4-39	10.3	-17.50

JOCKEYS

	W-R	Per cent	£1 Level Stake
Jack Garritty	10-92	10.9	-44.88
Andrew Mullen	2-6	33.3	+0.10
Jamie Gormley	1-3	33.3	-1.64
Daniel Tudhope	1-3	33.3	+0.25
Clifford Lee	1-4	25.0	+1.00
Antonio Fresu	1-4	25.0	+0.50
P J McDonald	1-12	8.3	-3.00
Graham Lee	1-23	4.3	-13.50

COURSE RECORD

	Total W-R	Non-Hndcps 2-y-o	Non-Hndcps 3-y-o+	Hndcps 2-y-o	Hndcps 3-y-o+	Per cent	£1 Level Stake
Newcastle (A.W)	4-44	0-3	1-5	0-2	3-34	9.1	-19.38
Hamilton	3-8	0-1	0-0	0-0	3-7	37.5	+2.36
Ayr	2-9	0-1	0-0	0-0	2-8	22.2	-0.50
Beverley	2-15	1-6	0-1	0-0	1-8	13.3	-3.90
Epsom	1-1	0-0	0-0	0-0	1-1	100.0	+9.00
Wetherby	1-3	0-0	1-1	0-0	0-2	33.3	+1.00
Carlisle	1-6	0-1	0-0	0-1	1-4	16.7	-2.75
Thirsk	1-9	0-2	0-3	0-0	1-4	11.1	-4.50
Catterick	1-10	0-1	1-2	0-2	0-5	10.0	-7.75
Ripon	1-10	1-5	0-0	0-0	0-5	10.0	-7.25
Doncaster	1-15	0-1	0-1	0-1	1-12	6.7	-10.50

WINNING HORSES

Horse	Races Run	1st	2nd	3rd	£
Air Raid	6	1	0	0	4787
*Breanski	6	2	0	0	28623

Desert Ruler	7	2	1	0	7892
Dream Poet	6	1	1	1	4464
Evie Speed (IRE)	6	1	1	0	5175
French Resistance (IRE)	8	1	1	1	3493
Only Spoofing (IRE)	11	3	0	2	6663
Rare Groove (IRE)	6	2	1	0	14491
Rebel State (IRE)	13	1	5	1	3105
Remember The Days (IRE)	8	1	1	0	3817
Saisons D'Or (IRE)	8	1	2	2	3493
Shared Equity	7	1	1	2	31125
Whitkirk	8	1	0	0	3752
Total winning prize-money					**£120880**
Favourites	**10-30**		**33.3%**		**-0.59**

DAVID O'MEARA

UPPER HELMSLEY, N YORKS

	No. of Hrs	Races Run	1st	2nd	3rd	Unpl	Per cent	£1 Level Stake
2-y-o	*32*	*141*	*17*	*18*	*11*	*94*	*12.1*	*-28.72*
3-y-o	*38*	*251*	*32*	*35*	*22*	*161*	*12.7*	*-21.17*
4-y-o+	*78*	*683*	*64*	*97*	*75*	*446*	*9.4*	*-249.90*
Totals	**148**	**1075**	**113**	**150**	**108**	**701**	**10.5**	**-299.79**
2017	*174*	*1078*	*109*	*125*	*131*	*710*	*10.1*	*-247.14*
2016	*164*	*975*	*103*	*124*	*115*	*633*	*10.6*	*-336.62*

BY MONTH

2-y-o	W-R	Per cent	£1 Level Stake	3-y-o	W-R	Per cent	£1 Level Stake
January	0-0	0.0	0.00	January	0-1	0.0	-1.00
February	0-0	0.0	0.00	February	0-2	0.0	-2.00
March	1-2	50.0	+2.00	March	0-7	0.0	-7.00
April	0-5	0.0	-5.00	April	3-17	17.6	+1.25
May	1-10	10.0	-2.00	May	3-36	8.3	-22.00
June	1-12	8.3	+5.00	June	4-39	10.3	-16.13
July	4-18	22.2	+10.88	July	6-38	15.8	-11.42
August	4-26	15.4	-10.75	August	5-37	13.5	+1.38
September	2-18	11.1	-13.38	September	6-35	17.1	+5.25
October	2-20	10.0	0.00	October	4-25	16.0	+29.50
November	2-18	11.1	-3.47	November	0-8	0.0	-8.00
December	0-12	0.0	-12.00	December	1-6	16.7	+9.00

4-y-o+	W-R	Per cent	£1 Level Stake	Totals	W-R	Per cent	£1 Level Stake
January	0-33	0.0	-33.00	January	0-34	0.0	-34.00
February	0-21	0.0	-21.00	February	0-23	0.0	-23.00
March	0-22	0.0	-22.00	March	1-31	3.2	-27.00
April	6-35	17.1	+10.03	April	9-57	15.8	+6.28
May	10-86	11.6	-30.42	May	14-132	10.6	-54.42
June	11-107	10.3	-46.67	June	16-158	10.1	-57.80
July	19-91	20.9	+14.67	July	29-147	19.7	+14.13
August	8-79	10.1	-34.96	August	17-142	12.0	-44.33
September	6-73	8.2	+5.00	September	14-126	11.1	-3.13
October	1-58	1.7	-47.00	October	7-103	6.8	-17.50
November	3-45	6.7	-11.56	November	5-71	7.0	-19.56
December	0-33	0.0	-33.00	December	1-51	2.0	-24.00

DISTANCE

2-y-o	W-R	Per cent	£1 Level Stake	3-y-o	W-R	Per cent	£1 Level Stake
5f-6f	14-97	14.4	-18.47	5f-6f	16-127	12.6	-2.42
7f-8f	3-44	6.8	-10.25	7f-8f	15-103	14.6	-4.75
9f-13f	0-0	0.0	0.00	9f-13f	1-21	4.8	-14.00
14f+	0-0	0.0	0.00	14f+	0-0	0.0	0.00

4-y-o+	W-R	Per cent	£1 Level Stake	Totals	W-R	Per cent	£1 Level Stake
5f-6f	22-190	11.6	-62.59	5f-6f	52-414	12.6	-83.48
7f-8f	30-321	9.3	-94.39	7f-8f	48-468	10.3	-109.39
9f-13f	9-158	5.7	-86.71	9f-13f	10-179	5.6	-100.71
14f+	3-14	21.4	-6.21	14f+	3-14	21.4	-6.21

TYPE OF RACE

Non-Handicaps	W-R	Per cent	£1 Level Stake	Handicaps	W-R	Per cent	£1 Level Stake
2-y-o	14-104	13.5	-18.47	2-y-o	3-37	8.1	-10.25
3-y-o	8-55	14.5	-14.63	3-y-o	24-196	12.2	-6.54
4-y-o+	12-98	12.2	-47.11	4-y-o+	52-585	8.9	-202.79

RACE CLASS

	W-R	Per cent	£1 Level Stake
Class 1	2-48	4.2	-32.00
Class 2	5-164	3.0	-122.50
Class 3	15-157	9.6	-41.92
Class 4	29-273	10.6	-66.67
Class 5	43-285	15.1	-5.14
Class 6	19-146	13.0	-29.56
Class 7	0-2	0.0	-2.00

FIRST TIME OUT

	W-R	Per cent	£1 Level Stake
2-y-o	4-32	12.5	+18.00
3-y-o	4-38	10.5	-18.25
4-y-o+	5-78	6.4	-32.00
Totals	13-148	8.8	-32.25

JOCKEYS

	W-R	Per cent	£1 Level Stake
Daniel Tudhope	39-295	13.2	-80.15
David Nolan	28-183	15.3	-16.13
Conor McGovern	13-129	10.1	-51.25
Martin Harley	8-68	11.8	-11.38
Shane Gray	6-62	9.7	+12.50
Phillip Makin	3-31	9.7	-2.50
Adam Kirby	3-37	8.1	+4.00
Harry Bentley	2-22	9.1	-16.75
Sam James	2-50	4.0	-26.50
Scott McCullagh	1-2	50.0	+24.00
Ben Curtis	1-4	25.0	-1.00
William Carver	1-4	25.0	+1.00
Silvestre De Sousa	1-4	25.0	-1.50
Liam Keniry	1-6	16.7	+7.00
Jim Crowley	1-7	14.3	-4.63
Joe Fanning	1-12	8.3	+5.00
David Probert	1-19	5.3	-14.50
Paddy Vaughan	1-25	4.0	-12.00

COURSE RECORD

	Total W-R	Non-Hndcps 2-y-o	Non-Hndcps 3-y-o+	Hndcps 2-y-o	Hndcps 3-y-o+	Per cent	£1 Level Stake
Ripon	15-66	3-9	2-6	0-1	10-50	22.7	+46.50
Wolvhptn (A.W)	9-98	1-9	1-15	1-8	6-66	9.2	-45.88
Hamilton	8-35	0-2	2-4	0-1	6-28	22.9	-0.75
Beverley	8-47	1-10	3-5	0-1	4-31	17.0	+3.88
Ayr	7-42	0-2	1-2	0-1	6-37	16.7	+11.83
Haydock	7-48	0-0	2-8	0-1	5-39	14.6	+6.58
Thirsk	7-59	2-7	0-11	0-1	5-40	11.9	+7.63
Catterick	6-39	3-13	0-3	0-1	3-22	15.4	-15.00
Musselburgh	5-25	1-6	0-0	1-2	3-17	20.0	-3.25
Chelmsford (A.W)	5-47	1-2	1-4	0-2	3-39	10.6	+4.44
Pontefract	4-37	0-5	1-4	0-1	3-27	10.8	-24.75
Redcar	4-45	0-5	3-8	0-1	1-31	8.9	-19.83
Doncaster	4-49	0-4	0-7	0-0	4-38	8.2	-17.50
Newcastle (A.W)	4-84	0-12	1-16	1-7	2-49	4.8	-24.75
Nottingham	3-12	1-1	0-1	0-0	2-10	25.0	+4.00
Leicester	3-24	0-2	1-5	0-1	2-16	12.5	-10.50
Wetherby	2-10	0-0	0-0	0-0	2-10	20.0	-0.75
Epsom	2-16	0-0	0-1	0-0	2-15	12.5	+1.50
Kempton (A.W)	2-24	0-0	0-1	0-1	2-22	8.3	+2.00
Lingfield	1-2	0-0	0-1	0-0	1-1	50.0	-0.33
Newmkt (Jly)	1-7	0-1	0-2	0-1	1-3	14.3	-4.38
Newmarket	1-10	1-1	0-3	0-0	0-6	10.0	+3.00
Chester	1-11	0-0	0-0	0-0	1-11	9.1	-4.00
Carlisle	1-22	0-2	0-0	0-1	1-19	4.5	-15.00
Southwell (A.W)	1-23	0-1	1-8	0-2	0-12	4.3	-21.47
Lingfield (A.W)	1-44	0-1	0-13	0-1	1-29	2.3	-37.00
York	1-69	0-4	1-4	0-1	0-60	1.4	-66.00

WINNING HORSES

Horse	Races Run	1st	2nd	3rd	£
Acrux*	12	4	1	2	15461
Addis Ababa (IRE)	5	1	2	1	3752
Agincourt (IRE)	6	2	1	0	8604
Aleef (IRE)	15	1	2	2	4140
Alsvinder	16	4	2	0	23375
Areen Heart (FR)	16	2	6	2	10572
Battle Commence (IRE)	6	1	0	0	4787
Beryl The Petal (IRE)	10	1	2	3	3881
Billy Dylan (IRE)	13	2	1	2	11774
Black Isle Boy (IRE)	8	1	1	0	5693
Blue Gardenia (IRE)	5	1	2	1	17013
Cascella (IRE)	8	1	1	0	3493
Clenymistra (IRE)	12	1	2	2	3105
Cold Stare (IRE)	9	1	1	0	8715
Consequences (IRE)	11	1	1	0	5531
Conversant (IRE)	6	1	0	0	3752
Dalshand (FR)	10	2	1	1	8151
Dancing Rave	7	1	3	0	4140
Dosc (IRE)	3	1	2	0	4787
Escobar (IRE)	9	1	2	2	10997
Fastman (IRE)	4	2	1	0	7763
Fayez (IRE)	17	1	1	2	8927
Fighting Spirit (IRE)	12	1	0	0	3105
Fire Leopard	7	1	0	0	4722
Hajjam	12	3	2	2	25488
*Havana Star (IRE)	4	1	0	0	3105
Highland Acclaim (IRE)	21	2	3	3	20054
Highland Bobby	7	1	0	0	3493
Ingleby Hollow	11	2	4	1	8280
Ingleby Molly (IRE)	11	1	1	2	3105
Intisaab	8	1	1	1	14006
Jacbequick*	13	2	3	1	7633
Kharbetation (IRE)	10	1	2	0	3752
Kuwait Station (IRE)	6	2	0	1	8668
Lamloom (IRE)	11	2	3	1	12938
Laubali	11	3	1	0	11256
Leodis Dream (IRE)	3	2	1	0	8539
Liamba	11	1	4	1	4787
Lord Glitters (FR)	6	1	3	1	56710
Lovin (USA)	2	1	0	0	7375
Lucifugous (IRE)	8	1	0	1	3105
Macho Lady (IRE)	8	1	0	0	3105
Major Crispies*	10	1	2	0	3105
Makawee (IRE)	4	1	0	1	3493
Mayson Mac	6	2	1	0	8086
Me Before You (IRE)	12	1	2	1	3429
*Montague (IRE)	11	2	6	0	8863
Mujassam	25	5	3	5	23806
Muscika	13	2	2	1	16431
Mutadaffeq (IRE)	11	1	1	2	5693
Mythical Madness	24	1	4	1	10350
*Nature Boy (IRE)	3	1	0	1	4033
Primero (FR)	5	1	0	0	11972
Prince Elzaam (IRE)	6	2	2	0	9315
Safrani (IRE)	7	1	0	1	3170
Salateen	17	2	4	1	23124
Saryshagann (FR)	14	2	0	1	11256
Smart Illusion (IRE)	7	1	1	1	3105
Stonific (IRE)	14	2	2	0	13844
Summerghand (IRE)	13	5	1	3	40981
Three Saints Bay (IRE)	10	3	1	2	16987
Tidal Surge (IRE)*	5	1	0	1	3105
Trading Point (FR)	4	2	0	0	13182
Valentino Dancer	6	1	0	1	4787
*Vigee Le Brun (IRE)	12	1	2	2	3105
Waarif (IRE)	15	4	4	1	66941
Watchable	15	2	3	1	20213
Weellan	13	3	2	2	17188
Total winning prize-money					**£741203**
Favourites	**42-133**		**31.6%**		**-16.91**

JONJO O'NEILL

CHELTENHAM, GLOUCS

	No. of Hrs	Races Run	1st	2nd	3rd	Unpl	Per cent	£1 Level Stake
2-y-o	*2*	*5*	*0*	*0*	*1*	*4*	*0.0*	*-5.00*
3-y-o	*0*	*0*	*0*	*0*	*0*	*0*	*0.0*	*0.00*
4-y-o+	*14*	*44*	*5*	*7*	*5*	*27*	*11.4*	*-10.75*
Totals	**16**	**49**	**5**	**7**	**6**	**31**	**10.2**	**-15.75**

2017	*20*	*72*	*4*	*9*	*11*	*48*	*5.6*	*-54.50*
2016	*14*	*51*	*3*	*4*	*6*	*38*	*5.9*	*-11.00*

JOCKEYS

	W-R	Per cent	£1 Level Stake
Fran Berry	4-23	17.4	+4.25
Martin Harley	1-6	16.7	0.00

COURSE RECORD

	Total W-R	Non-Hndcps 2-y-o	Non-Hndcps 3-y-o+	Hndcps 2-y-o	Hndcps 3-y-o+	Per cent	£1 Level Stake
Salisbury	1-1	0-0	0-0	0-0	1-1	100.0	+4.00
Lingfield (A.W)	1-2	0-0	0-0	0-0	1-2	50.0	+7.00
Chepstow	1-4	0-0	0-1	0-0	1-3	25.0	+2.00
Bath	1-5	0-0	0-0	0-0	1-5	20.0	-1.75
Wolvhptn (A.W)	1-13	0-0	0-4	0-1	1-8	7.7	-3.00

WINNING HORSES

Horse	Races Run	1st	2nd	3rd	£
Desert Cross	4	2	0	1	8377
Spiritual Man (IRE)	12	2	3	1	6210
Storm Melody*	5	1	0	0	3105
Total winning prize-money					**£17692**
Favourites	**12-48**		**25.0%**		**-15.30**

JOHN O'SHEA

ELTON, GLOUCS

	No. of Hrs	Races Run	1st	2nd	3rd	Unpl	Per cent	£1 Level Stake
2-y-o	*2*	*2*	*0*	*0*	*0*	*2*	*0.0*	*-2.00*
3-y-o	*0*	*0*	*0*	*0*	*0*	*0*	*0.0*	*0.00*
4-y-o+	*15*	*148*	*14*	*12*	*15*	*106*	*9.5*	*+8.95*
Totals	**17**	**150**	**14**	**12**	**15**	**108**	**9.3**	**+6.95**
2017	*24*	*159*	*15*	*10*	*13*	*121*	*9.4*	*-60.00*
2016	*25*	*183*	*13*	*9*	*21*	*139*	*7.1*	*-99.30*

BY MONTH

2-y-o	W-R	Per cent	£1 Level Stake	3-y-o	W-R	Per cent	£1 Level Stake
January	0-0	0.0	0.00	January	0-0	0.0	0.00
February	0-0	0.0	0.00	February	0-0	0.0	0.00
March	0-0	0.0	0.00	March	0-0	0.0	0.00
April	0-0	0.0	0.00	April	0-0	0.0	0.00
May	0-0	0.0	0.00	May	0-0	0.0	0.00
June	0-0	0.0	0.00	June	0-0	0.0	0.00
July	0-0	0.0	0.00	July	0-0	0.0	0.00
August	0-0	0.0	0.00	August	0-0	0.0	0.00
September	0-0	0.0	0.00	September	0-0	0.0	0.00
October	0-0	0.0	0.00	October	0-0	0.0	0.00
November	0-0	0.0	0.00	November	0-0	0.0	0.00
December	0-2	0.0	-2.00	December	0-0	0.0	0.00

4-y-o+	W-R	Per cent	£1 Level Stake	Totals	W-R	Per cent	£1 Level Stake
January	3-12	25.0	+27.50	January	3-12	25.0	+27.50
February	1-15	6.7	-6.00	February	1-15	6.7	-6.00
March	0-9	0.0	-9.00	March	0-9	0.0	-9.00
April	1-17	5.9	-6.00	April	1-17	5.9	-6.00
May	2-21	9.5	+18.00	May	2-21	9.5	+18.00
June	2-15	13.3	-7.25	June	2-15	13.3	-7.25
July	3-17	17.6	+3.70	July	3-17	17.6	+3.70
August	2-17	11.8	+13.00	August	2-17	11.8	+13.00
September	0-3	0.0	-3.00	September	0-3	0.0	-3.00
October	0-10	0.0	-10.00	October	0-10	0.0	-10.00
November	0-4	0.0	-4.00	November	0-4	0.0	-4.00
December	0-8	0.0	-8.00	December	0-10	0.0	-8.00

DISTANCE

2-y-o	W-R	Per cent	£1 Level Stake	3-y-o	W-R	Per cent	£1 Level Stake
5f-6f	0-2	0.0	-2.00	5f-6f	0-0	0.0	0.00
7f-8f	0-0	0.0	0.00	7f-8f	0-0	0.0	0.00
9f-13f	0-0	0.0	0.00	9f-13f	0-0	0.0	0.00
14f+	0-0	0.0	0.00	14f+	0-0	0.0	0.00

4-y-o+	W-R	Per cent	£1 Level Stake	Totals	W-R	Per cent	£1 Level Stake
5f-6f	6-69	8.7	+10.75	5f-6f	6-71	8.5	+8.75
7f-8f	2-37	5.4	-17.00	7f-8f	2-37	5.4	-17.00
9f-13f	6-40	15.0	+17.20	9f-13f	6-40	15.0	+17.20
14f+	0-2	0.0	-2.00	14f+	0-2	0.0	-2.00

TYPE OF RACE

Non-Handicaps	W-R	Per cent	£1 Level Stake	Handicaps	W-R	Per cent	£1 Level Stake
2-y-o	0-2	0.0	-2.00	2-y-o	0-0	0.0	0.00
3-y-o	0-0	0.0	0.00	3-y-o	0-0	0.0	0.00
4-y-o+	0-4	0.0	-4.00	4-y-o+	14-144	9.7	+12.95

RACE CLASS

	W-R	Per cent	£1 Level Stake
Class 1	0-0	0.0	0.00
Class 2	0-2	0.0	-2.00
Class 3	0-0	0.0	0.00
Class 4	2-16	12.5	+22.00
Class 5	2-61	3.3	-46.25
Class 6	9-67	13.4	+32.20
Class 7	1-4	25.0	+1.00

FIRST TIME OUT

	W-R	Per cent	£1 Level Stake
2-y-o	0-2	0.0	-2.00
3-y-o	0-0	0.0	0.00
4-y-o+	2-15	13.3	+19.50
Totals	2-17	11.8	+17.50

JOCKEYS

	W-R	Per cent	£1 Level Stake
Rossa Ryan	6-30	20.0	+9.95
Robert Havlin	2-10	20.0	+27.00
Luke Morris	2-17	11.8	-8.00
Miss Brodie Hampson	1-4	25.0	+22.00
Fran Berry	1-7	14.3	+2.00
Kate Leahy	1-14	7.1	+9.00
Ben Robinson	1-20	5.0	-7.00

COURSE RECORD

	Total W-R	Non-Hndcps 2-y-o	Non-Hndcps 3-y-o+	Hndcps 2-y-o	Hndcps 3-y-o+	Per cent	£1 Level Stake
Chepstow	5-30	0-0	0-2	0-0	5-28	16.7	+17.45

Kempton (A.W)	3-29	0-0	0-0	0-0	3-29	10.3	-6.50
Wolvhptn (A.W)	2-37	0-2	0-0	0-0	2-35	5.4	+2.00
Ffos Las	1-2	0-0	0-0	0-0	1-2	50.0	+5.00
Lingfield	1-4	0-0	0-0	0-0	1-4	25.0	+22.00
Lingfield (A.W)	1-12	0-0	0-2	0-0	1-10	8.3	-1.00
Bath	1-18	0-0	0-0	0-0	1-18	5.6	-14.00

WINNING HORSES

Horse	Races Run	1st	2nd	3rd	£
Ambitious Boy	6	1	0	0	2995
Clement (IRE)	11	1	0	0	3752
Dalness Express	11	1	1	4	2588
Frozen Lake (USA)	10	1	2	1	3105
General Brook (IRE)	12	5	3	0	15526
Kinglami	20	2	1	3	9283
Major Valentine	14	1	1	1	5531
Swendab (IRE)	16	1	2	2	3493
Warofindependence (USA)	14	1	0	3	3105
Total winning prize-money					**£49378**
Favourites	**3-8**		**37.5%**		**3.20**

JAMIE OSBORNE

UPPER LAMBOURN, BERKS

	No. of Hrs	Races Run	1st	2nd	3rd	Unpl	Per cent	£1 Level Stake
2-y-o	*20*	*81*	*4*	*4*	*6*	*67*	*4.9*	*-53.75*
3-y-o	*37*	*156*	*22*	*20*	*23*	*91*	*14.1*	*-5.05*
4-y-o+	*33*	*169*	*21*	*24*	*11*	*112*	*12.4*	*-38.27*
Totals	**90**	**406**	**47**	**48**	**40**	**270**	**11.6**	**-97.07**
2017	*88*	*395*	*46*	*52*	*43*	*254*	*11.6*	*-33.05*
2016	*73*	*376*	*48*	*60*	*44*	*224*	*12.8*	*-57.82*

BY MONTH

2-y-o	W-R	Per cent	£1 Level Stake
January	0-0	0.0	0.00
February	0-0	0.0	0.00
March	0-0	0.0	0.00
April	0-0	0.0	0.00
May	0-2	0.0	-2.00
June	1-8	12.5	-2.00
July	0-7	0.0	-7.00
August	0-13	0.0	-13.00
September	1-19	5.3	-16.00
October	1-11	9.1	+7.75
November	0-14	0.0	-14.00
December	1-7	14.3	+8.00

3-y-o	W-R	Per cent	£1 Level Stake
January	2-26	7.7	-20.77
February	1-12	8.3	+3.00
March	3-14	21.4	-5.00
April	0-6	0.0	-6.00
May	3-10	30.0	+26.50
June	1-17	5.9	-13.50
July	1-6	16.7	+3.00
August	4-12	33.3	+8.63
September	0-15	0.0	-15.00
October	3-14	21.4	+8.50
November	3-10	30.0	+7.60
December	1-14	7.1	-2.00

4-y-o+	W-R	Per cent	£1 Level Stake
January	3-32	9.4	-17.11
February	4-18	22.2	+3.75
March	4-26	15.4	-9.25
April	0-3	0.0	-3.00
May	1-13	7.7	+13.00
June	0-11	0.0	-11.00
July	3-12	25.0	+7.75
August	0-8	0.0	-8.00
September	3-15	20.0	+0.83
October	3-15	20.0	+0.75
November	0-11	0.0	-11.00
December	0-5	0.0	-5.00

Totals	W-R	Per cent	£1 Level Stake
January	5-58	8.6	-37.88
February	5-30	16.7	+6.75
March	7-40	17.5	-14.25
April	0-9	0.0	-9.00
May	4-25	16.0	+37.50
June	2-36	5.6	-26.50
July	4-25	16.0	+3.75
August	4-33	12.1	-12.37
September	4-49	8.2	-30.17
October	7-40	17.5	+1.50
November	3-35	8.6	-3.40
December	2-26	7.7	-7.00

DISTANCE

2-y-o	W-R	Per cent	£1 Level Stake
5f-6f	1-46	2.2	-40.00
7f-8f	2-33	6.1	-15.00
9f-13f	1-2	50.0	+1.25
14f+	0-0	0.0	0.00

3-y-o	W-R	Per cent	£1 Level Stake
5f-6f	6-35	17.1	-13.15
7f-8f	9-67	13.4	-7.40
9f-13f	7-54	13.0	+15.50
14f+	0-0	0.0	0.00

4-y-o+	W-R	Per cent	£1 Level Stake
5f-6f	9-59	15.3	-8.04
7f-8f	6-64	9.4	-30.00
9f-13f	2-32	6.3	-24.36
14f+	4-14	28.6	+24.13

Totals	W-R	Per cent	£1 Level Stake
5f-6f	16-140	11.4	-61.19
7f-8f	17-164	10.4	-52.40
9f-13f	10-88	11.4	-7.61
14f+	4-14	28.6	+24.13

TYPE OF RACE

Non-Handicaps	W-R	Per cent	£1 Level Stake
2-y-o	3-59	5.1	-46.75
3-y-o	8-64	12.5	-27.77
4-y-o+	6-35	17.1	-6.23

Handicaps	W-R	Per cent	£1 Level Stake
2-y-o	1-22	4.5	-7.00
3-y-o	14-92	15.2	+22.72
4-y-o+	15-134	11.2	-32.04

RACE CLASS

	W-R	Per cent	£1 Level Stake
Class 1	0-5	0.0	-5.00
Class 2	3-34	8.8	-6.00
Class 3	5-32	15.6	+19.75
Class 4	6-63	9.5	-13.25
Class 5	17-150	11.3	-71.00
Class 6	16-119	13.4	-18.57
Class 7	0-3	0.0	-3.00

FIRST TIME OUT

	W-R	Per cent	£1 Level Stake
2-y-o	0-20	0.0	-20.00
3-y-o	4-37	10.8	-22.50
4-y-o+	2-33	6.1	-21.50
Totals	6-90	6.7	-64.00

JOCKEYS

	W-R	Per cent	£1 Level Stake
Dougie Costello	15-186	8.1	-89.17
Nicola Currie	11-85	12.9	-7.63
Rossa Ryan	4-21	19.0	-2.25
Jason Hart	2-2	100.0	+11.50
Adam Kirby	2-11	18.2	-5.00
Jamie Spencer	2-17	11.8	-11.38
James Doyle	1-1	100.0	+4.00
James Sullivan	1-1	100.0	+2.50
Mr Alex Ferguson	1-1	100.0	+2.25
Miss Gina Andrews	1-1	100.0	+12.00
Miss Alexandra Bell	1-1	100.0	+8.00
Martin Dwyer	1-2	50.0	+0.10
Oisin Murphy	1-3	33.3	+1.50

Tom Marquand	1-3	33.3	+2.00
William Buick	1-3	33.3	+1.50
Jack Dinsmore	1-6	16.7	+20.00
Joe Fanning	1-8	12.5	+7.00

COURSE RECORD

	Total W-R	Non-Hndcps 2-y-o	3-y-o+	Hndcps 2-y-o	3-y-o+	Per cent	£1 Level Stake
Chelmsford (A.W)	11-77	0-11	4-10	1-7	6-49	14.3	+6.97
Lingfield (A.W)	7-61	0-7	3-25	0-1	4-28	11.5	-22.11
Ascot	5-19	0-2	0-0	0-0	5-17	26.3	+33.75
Kempton (A.W)	5-62	0-8	2-11	0-5	3-38	8.1	-36.75
Wolvhptn (A.W)	5-67	1-8	2-22	0-1	2-36	7.5	-42.19
Windsor	3-17	0-6	0-4	0-0	3-7	17.6	+2.00
Ffos Las	2-9	0-0	0-3	0-3	2-3	22.2	+2.75
Southwell (A.W)	2-10	0-0	1-3	0-0	1-7	20.0	-3.13
Redcar	1-1	0-0	1-1	0-0	0-0	100.0	+3.50
Wetherby	1-2	0-0	0-1	0-0	1-1	50.0	+21.00
Leicester	1-3	0-0	1-2	0-1	0-0	33.3	+0.50
Goodwood	1-4	1-2	0-1	0-0	0-1	25.0	+2.00
Salisbury	1-7	1-4	0-1	0-0	0-2	14.3	-4.00
Lingfield	1-11	0-2	0-5	0-2	1-2	9.1	-8.38
Bath	1-14	0-1	0-3	0-1	1-9	7.1	-11.00

WINNING HORSES

Horse	Races Run	1st	2nd	3rd	£
*Acrux	5	1	1	0	3752
Alifax	3	1	0	1	3752
Arabic Culture (USA)	8	1	0	0	3105
Born To Finish (IRE)	12	2	5	1	7504
Breakfast (IRE)*	7	1	0	1	3235
Cliffs Of Capri	10	3	2	0	19973
Darkest Light	6	1	0	0	3429
Every Chance (IRE)*	2	1	1	0	3105
*Faraasah (IRE)	2	1	0	0	3105
Haraz (IRE)*	6	1	1	0	3429
Jersey Wonder (IRE)	3	2	1	0	8539
Kion (IRE)	7	2	2	1	9186
Long John Silver (IRE)	4	1	0	0	6728
Lush Life (IRE)	4	2	0	0	11515
Mans Not Trot (IRE)	8	1	3	1	3105
Montague (IRE)*	3	1	0	0	3105
*Monumental Man	8	1	4	0	3105
Mr Reckless (IRE)	7	2	1	2	13974
Preacher Man (IRE)	3	1	1	0	5434
Raising Sand	7	1	0	0	112050
Reckless Endeavour (IRE)*	10	1	1	2	11972
Red Warrior (IRE)	1	1	0	0	5531
*Rippling Waters (FR)	5	1	0	0	3881
Rusper Dreams (IRE)	5	1	0	0	3493
Sam Missile (IRE)	10	1	2	1	7763
Sicario (IRE)	10	2	1	1	7245
Society Shock (IRE)	9	1	0	1	6553
Strategic Heights (IRE)*	8	1	1	2	3105
Turn Of Luck (IRE)	8	1	1	1	3105
Vegas Boy (IRE)	10	2	2	2	10480
Volatile	10	3	1	1	17642
Volturnus*	4	2	0	0	6987
Voyager Blue	4	2	0	0	22900
Your Band	7	1	3	0	3105
Total winning prize-money					**£344892**
Favourites	**16-48**		**33.3%**		**-2.65**

EMMA OWEN

NETHER WINCHENDON, BUCKS

	No. of Hrs	Races Run	1st	2nd	3rd	Unpl	Per cent	£1 Level Stake
2-y-o	*1*	*1*	*0*	*0*	*0*	*1*	*0.0*	*-1.00*
3-y-o	*2*	*5*	*0*	*0*	*0*	*5*	*0.0*	*-5.00*
4-y-o+	*11*	*52*	*4*	*6*	*3*	*39*	*7.7*	*-16.00*
Totals	**14**	**58**	**4**	**6**	**3**	**45**	**6.9**	**-22.00**
2017	*13*	*74*	*4*	*7*	*8*	*55*	*5.4*	*-14.00*
2016	*16*	*78*	*2*	*8*	*9*	*59*	*2.6*	*-64.50*

JOCKEYS

	W-R	Per cent	£1 Level Stake
Adam Kirby	2-8	25.0	+2.00
P J McDonald	1-3	33.3	+2.00
Eoin Walsh	1-7	14.3	+14.00

COURSE RECORD

	Total W-R	Non-Hndcps 2-y-o	3-y-o+	Hndcps 2-y-o	3-y-o+	Per cent	£1 Level Stake
Kempton (A.W)	3-22	0-1	0-5	0-0	3-16	13.6	-7.00
Chelmsford (A.W)	1-10	0-0	0-0	0-0	1-10	10.0	+11.00

WINNING HORSES

Horse	Races Run	1st	2nd	3rd	£
Divine Messenger	5	1	3	0	3105
*Ertidaad (IRE)	6	1	0	1	2588
Higher Court (USA)	2	1	1	0	3752
Sea The Waves	4	1	0	1	3105
Total winning prize-money					**£12550**
Favourites	**1-2**		**50.0%**		**2.50**

HUGO PALMER

NEWMARKET, SUFFOLK

	No. of Hrs	Races Run	1st	2nd	3rd	Unpl	Per cent	£1 Level Stake
2-y-o	*34*	*114*	*18*	*18*	*10*	*68*	*15.8*	*-43.81*
3-y-o	*67*	*329*	*59*	*35*	*35*	*198*	*17.9*	*+54.63*
4-y-o+	*15*	*65*	*10*	*8*	*8*	*39*	*15.4*	*+7.75*
Totals	**116**	**508**	**87**	**61**	**53**	**305**	**17.1**	**+18.57**
2017	*134*	*493*	*77*	*69*	*51*	*295*	*15.6*	*-126.71*
2016	*102*	*344*	*71*	*54*	*49*	*169*	*20.6*	*+13.28*

BY MONTH

2-y-o	W-R	Per cent	£1 Level Stake	3-y-o	W-R	Per cent	£1 Level Stake
January	0-0	0.0	0.00	January	0-15	0.0	-15.00

February	0-0	0.0	0.00	February	1-9	11.1	-7.27
March	0-0	0.0	0.00	March	1-11	9.1	-8.00
April	0-1	0.0	-1.00	April	4-23	17.4	-7.95
May	0-5	0.0	-5.00	May	10-45	22.2	+14.35
June	2-16	12.5	-13.31	June	6-42	14.3	+85.22
July	3-20	15.0	-9.75	July	5-51	9.8	-33.51
August	2-16	12.5	-11.85	August	7-39	17.9	-7.72
September	2-20	10.0	-10.00	September	12-47	25.5	+5.87
October	4-18	22.2	-2.75	October	8-31	25.8	+25.00
November	0-6	0.0	-6.00	November	5-12	41.7	+7.63
December	5-12	41.7	+15.85	December	0-4	0.0	-4.00

4-y-o+	W-R	Per cent	£1 Level Stake	Totals	W-R	Per cent	£1 Level Stake
January	2-4	50.0	-0.18	January	2-19	10.5	-15.18
February	2-4	50.0	+0.55	February	3-13	23.1	-6.72
March	0-7	0.0	-7.00	March	1-18	5.6	-15.00
April	1-6	16.7	+7.00	April	5-30	16.7	-1.95
May	1-6	16.7	+3.00	May	11-56	19.6	+12.35
June	2-7	28.6	-0.63	June	10-65	15.4	+71.28
July	0-6	0.0	-6.00	July	8-77	10.4	-49.26
August	2-10	20.0	+26.00	August	11-65	16.9	+6.43
September	0-6	0.0	-6.00	September	14-73	19.2	-10.13
October	0-4	0.0	-4.00	October	12-53	22.6	+18.25
November	0-4	0.0	-4.00	November	5-22	22.7	+3.63
December	0-1	0.0	-1.00	December	5-17	29.4	-5.00

DISTANCE

2-y-o	W-R	Per cent	£1 Level Stake	3-y-o	W-R	Per cent	£1 Level Stake
5f-6f	5-33	15.2	-19.06	5f-6f	10-44	22.7	+38.13
7f-8f	13-78	16.7	-21.75	7f-8f	19-127	15.0	-50.61
9f-13f	0-3	0.0	-3.00	9f-13f	29-153	19.0	+68.85
14f+	0-0	0.0	0.00	14f+	1-5	20.0	-1.75

4-y-o+	W-R	Per cent	£1 Level Stake	Totals	W-R	Per cent	£1 Level Stake
5f-6f	2-24	8.3	+6.00	5f-6f	17-101	16.8	+25.07
7f-8f	5-28	17.9	+7.80	7f-8f	37-233	15.9	-64.56
9f-13f	3-13	23.1	-6.05	9f-13f	32-169	18.9	+59.80
14f+	0-0	0.0	0.00	14f+	1-5	20.0	-1.75

TYPE OF RACE

Non-Handicaps	W-R	Per cent	£1 Level Stake	Handicaps	W-R	Per cent	£1 Level Stake
2-y-o	14-92	15.2	-46.81	2-y-o	4-22	18.2	+3.00
3-y-o	26-140	18.6	+42.78	3-y-o	33-189	17.5	+11.85
4-y-o+	3-26	11.5	+3.58	4-y-o+	7-39	17.9	+4.17

RACE CLASS

	W-R	Per cent	£1 Level Stake
Class 1	3-42	7.1	+6.00
Class 2	10-61	16.4	+31.00
Class 3	4-46	8.7	+32.75
Class 4	21-136	15.4	-42.72
Class 5	42-180	23.3	-3.79
Class 6	7-43	16.3	-4.67
Class 7	0-0	0.0	0.00

FIRST TIME OUT

	W-R	Per cent	£1 Level Stake
2-y-o	3-34	8.8	-21.40
3-y-o	9-67	13.4	-13.22
4-y-o+	4-15	26.7	+4.45
Totals	16-116	13.8	-30.17

JOCKEYS

	W-R	Per cent	£1 Level Stake
Josephine Gordon	24-142	16.9	+29.07
James Doyle	22-77	28.6	+21.13
Ben Curtis	12-32	37.5	+12.43
Jack Mitchell	8-38	21.1	+15.50
Jason Watson	5-20	25.0	+19.60
Nicola Currie	3-21	14.3	-7.42
Jim Crowley	2-8	25.0	-0.75
Louis Steward	2-27	7.4	+7.00
Stevie Donohoe	1-1	100.0	+2.50
Fran Berry	1-2	50.0	+1.75
Ray Dawson	1-2	50.0	+2.00
Georgia Cox	1-2	50.0	+3.50
Daniel Tudhope	1-3	33.3	+0.75
Luke Morris	1-6	16.7	+4.00
Danny Brock	1-6	16.7	-3.00
Silvestre De Sousa	1-7	14.3	+19.00
Pat Cosgrave	1-32	3.1	-26.50

COURSE RECORD

	Total W-R	Non-Hndcps 2-y-o	Non-Hndcps 3-y-o+	Hndcps 2-y-o	Hndcps 3-y-o+	Per cent	£1 Level Stake
Wolvhptn (A.W)	12-40	0-4	6-17	1-4	5-15	30.0	+5.96
Kempton (A.W)	10-55	5-13	0-15	1-5	4-22	18.2	-11.85
Chelmsford (A.W)	8-47	3-13	2-18	0-1	3-15	17.0	-14.15
Haydock	6-19	0-3	4-7	0-0	2-9	31.6	+78.60
Newcastle (A.W)	6-29	0-1	2-15	0-1	4-12	20.7	-0.50
Yarmouth	5-12	1-1	1-3	0-0	3-8	41.7	+23.19
Carlisle	4-6	0-1	3-4	0-0	1-1	66.7	+3.41
Doncaster	4-14	3-6	0-0	0-1	1-7	28.6	-3.63
Lingfield (A.W)	4-37	0-6	1-16	0-0	3-15	10.8	-15.00
Nottingham	3-11	1-3	0-4	0-0	2-4	27.3	+3.75
Newbury	3-25	1-10	1-5	0-0	1-10	12.0	+11.40
Southwell (A.W)	2-7	0-0	1-3	1-2	0-2	28.6	+7.50
Bath	2-8	0-0	0-3	0-0	2-5	25.0	+3.75
Ffos Las	2-9	0-2	1-1	0-0	1-6	22.2	-3.50
Ascot	2-16	0-0	0-6	0-0	2-10	12.5	-6.50
Windsor	2-18	0-1	2-6	0-2	0-9	11.1	-13.22
Hamilton	1-1	0-0	1-1	0-0	0-0	100.0	+0.44
Chepstow	1-2	0-0	1-1	0-0	0-1	50.0	+24.00
Catterick	1-3	0-0	0-0	0-0	1-3	33.3	+1.50
Ayr	1-4	0-0	1-1	0-0	0-3	25.0	-2.86
Beverley	1-4	0-1	1-2	0-0	0-1	25.0	-1.75
Lingfield	1-6	0-1	0-2	1-1	0-2	16.7	-2.25
Brighton	1-8	0-1	0-2	0-0	1-5	12.5	-5.00
Sandown	1-8	0-2	0-1	0-0	1-5	12.5	-4.75
Thirsk	1-9	0-1	1-4	0-0	0-4	11.1	-6.00
Goodwood	1-10	0-2	0-2	0-1	1-5	10.0	+11.00
York	1-13	0-3	0-4	0-1	1-5	7.7	+13.00
Newmarket	1-18	0-2	0-6	0-0	1-10	5.6	-9.00

WINNING HORSES

Horse	Races Run	1st	2nd	3rd	£
Almufti	4	1	0	1	5822

Arbalet (IRE)	5	1	1	1	4205
Artois	2	1	0	1	5822
Barend Boy	9	1	1	1	3752
Blonde Warrior (IRE)	5	2	2	0	8539
Breaking Records (IRE)	14	3	2	3	17596
Burford Brown	7	2	1	1	7245
Caliburn (IRE)	6	1	0	1	6469
Central City (IRE)*	7	1	1	0	3105
Collide	6	3	0	0	17683
Corrosive (USA)	8	3	1	1	26652
Debbonair (IRE)	4	1	0	0	3235
Deira Surprise	5	1	2	1	3752
Dragon Mountain	7	2	0	0	12938
Dukhan	7	1	1	2	12938
El Ghazwani (IRE)	6	1	0	0	5531
Employer (IRE)	7	1	0	2	3752
Encrypted	8	3	1	0	102640
Expensive Liaison (IRE)	3	1	0	0	4140
Exprompt (FR)	3	1	0	0	4852
Fajjaj (IRE)	5	1	1	1	4140
Fenjal (IRE)	6	1	1	0	3105
Formula One (IRE)	4	1	1	0	3817
Francis Xavier (IRE)*	1	1	0	0	5531
Ghayadh	6	2	1	1	8895
Gifted Master (IRE)	7	2	0	0	186750
Gododdin	8	3	0	1	9283
Heavenly Holly (IRE)	3	2	0	0	9186
Hostess	3	1	1	0	4787
Hot Team (IRE)	5	1	2	1	3752
Humbert (IRE)	9	3	3	0	35503
James Street (IRE)	5	3	1	0	12550
Labrega	4	1	1	0	4852
Leigh's Law (IRE)	5	1	0	1	5531
Mootasadir	5	3	0	0	18394
Morning Beauty	8	2	2	0	13456
Morning Skye (IRE)	12	3	2	2	12615
Mystic Meg	11	3	1	0	14102
Never Back Down (IRE)	5	2	0	0	51669
New Orleans (IRE)	13	1	3	1	3752
Ours Puissant (IRE)	3	1	1	0	5822
Pepper Street (IRE)*	6	1	0	1	3170
Power Of States (IRE)	1	1	0	0	4787
Power To Exceed (IRE)	5	1	3	0	4205
Rashdan (FR)	7	2	0	0	10092
Red October (IRE)	3	1	2	0	6728
Roystonia (IRE)	5	1	0	2	3752
Set Piece	1	1	0	0	3881
Silver Quartz*	6	2	0	1	22427
Stage Name	4	1	0	1	3752
Star Archer	6	2	0	1	15580
Sudona	5	1	0	0	3105
Summerseat Mist (IRE)	6	1	1	0	3105
Thunderbolt Rocks	4	1	0	0	5531
Unforgetable Filly	5	1	0	1	26654
Zofelle (IRE)	2	1	0	0	3752
Total winning prize-money					**£798681**
Favourites	**37-78**		**47.4%**		**9.22**

MARK PATTINSON

EPSOM, SURREY

	No. of Hrs	Races Run	1st	2nd	3rd	Unpl	Per cent	£1 Level Stake
2-y-o	*0*	*0*	*0*	*0*	*0*	*0*	*0.0*	*0.00*
3-y-o	*2*	*4*	*0*	*0*	*0*	*4*	*0.0*	*-4.00*
4-y-o+	*7*	*33*	*3*	*2*	*1*	*27*	*9.1*	*+8.00*
Totals	**9**	**37**	**3**	**2**	**1**	**31**	**8.1**	**+4.00**
2017	*7*	*31*	*3*	*1*	*2*	*25*	*9.7*	*-11.88*
2016	*1*	*1*	*0*	*1*	*0*	*0*	*0.0*	*-1.00*

JOCKEYS

	W-R	Per cent	£1 Level Stake
Mr Ross Birkett	1-1	100.0	+18.00
William Carson	1-2	50.0	+9.00
Paddy Bradley	1-10	10.0	+1.00

COURSE RECORD

	Total W-R	Non-Hndcps 2-y-o	Non-Hndcps 3-y-o+	Hndcps 2-y-o	Hndcps 3-y-o+	Per cent	£1 Level Stake
Bath	1-2	0-0	0-0	0-0	1-2	50.0	+9.00
Windsor	1-3	0-0	0-0	0-0	1-3	33.3	+16.00
Chelmsford (A.W)	1-4	0-0	0-0	0-0	1-4	25.0	+7.00

WINNING HORSES

Horse	Races Run	1st	2nd	3rd	£
Almanack	7	1	0	0	2911
*Our Oystercatcher	3	1	1	0	4464
*Tobacco Road (IRE)	5	1	0	0	2995
Total winning prize-money					**£10370**
Favourites	**0-2**		**0.0%**		**-2.00**

LYDIA PEARCE

NEWMARKET, SUFFOLK

	No. of Hrs	Races Run	1st	2nd	3rd	Unpl	Per cent	£1 Level Stake
2-y-o	*3*	*5*	*0*	*0*	*0*	*5*	*0.0*	*-5.00*
3-y-o	*0*	*0*	*0*	*0*	*0*	*0*	*0.0*	*0.00*
4-y-o+	*10*	*61*	*6*	*3*	*3*	*49*	*9.8*	*-17.00*
Totals	**13**	**66**	**6**	**3**	**3**	**54**	**9.1**	**-22.00**
2017	*13*	*68*	*4*	*3*	*4*	*57*	*5.9*	*+12.00*
2016	*16*	*59*	*5*	*3*	*2*	*49*	*8.5*	*-19.00*

JOCKEYS

	W-R	Per cent	£1 Level Stake
Jack Mitchell	3-23	13.0	+10.00
Gavin Ashton	1-2	50.0	+0.75
Darragh Keenan	1-8	12.5	-3.50
Joey Haynes	1-20	5.0	-16.25

COURSE RECORD

	Total W-R	Non-Hndcps 2-y-o	3-y-o+	Hndcps 2-y-o	3-y-o+	Per cent	£1 Level Stake
Yarmouth	5-22	0-0	0-1	0-0	5-21	22.7	+16.00
Leicester	1-4	0-0	0-0	0-0	1-4	25.0	+2.00

WINNING HORSES

Horse	Races Run	1st	2nd	3rd	£
Bartholomew J (IRE)	7	3	0	1	6857
Luna Magic	13	1	1	0	3752
Sexy Secret	10	2	1	1	6598
Total winning prize-money					**£17207**
Favourites	**1-2**		**50.0%**		**0.75**

OLLIE PEARS

NORTON, N YORKS

	No. of Hrs	Races Run	1st	2nd	3rd	Unpl	Per cent	£1 Level Stake
2-y-o	*12*	*52*	*2*	*3*	*7*	*40*	*3.8*	*-40.75*
3-y-o	*9*	*60*	*6*	*9*	*9*	*36*	*10.0*	*-13.13*
4-y-o+	*9*	*75*	*4*	*11*	*10*	*50*	*5.3*	*-41.50*
Totals	**30**	**187**	**12**	**23**	**26**	**126**	**6.4**	**-95.38**
2017	*30*	*162*	*16*	*9*	*22*	*115*	*9.9*	*-3.25*
2016	*24*	*131*	*7*	*13*	*15*	*96*	*5.3*	*-80.27*

BY MONTH

2-y-o	W-R	Per cent	£1 Level Stake	3-y-o	W-R	Per cent	£1 Level Stake
January	0-0	0.0	0.00	January	1-3	33.3	+0.75
February	0-0	0.0	0.00	February	0-1	0.0	-1.00
March	0-0	0.0	0.00	March	0-1	0.0	-1.00
April	0-2	0.0	-2.00	April	1-7	14.3	-1.00
May	0-7	0.0	-7.00	May	1-12	8.3	+5.00
June	0-6	0.0	-6.00	June	0-5	0.0	-5.00
July	1-6	16.7	-2.75	July	0-8	0.0	-8.00
August	0-6	0.0	-6.00	August	2-9	22.2	+0.13
September	0-10	0.0	-10.00	September	0-7	0.0	-7.00
October	1-9	11.1	-1.00	October	0-3	0.0	-3.00
November	0-4	0.0	-4.00	November	1-3	33.3	+8.00
December	0-2	0.0	-2.00	December	0-1	0.0	-1.00

4-y-o+	W-R	Per cent	£1 Level Stake	Totals	W-R	Per cent	£1 Level Stake
January	0-3	0.0	-3.00	January	1-6	16.7	-2.25
February	0-1	0.0	-1.00	February	0-2	0.0	-2.00
March	0-4	0.0	-4.00	March	0-5	0.0	-5.00
April	0-7	0.0	-7.00	April	1-16	6.3	-10.00
May	0-8	0.0	-8.00	May	1-27	3.7	-10.00
June	0-8	0.0	-8.00	June	0-19	0.0	-19.00
July	1-11	9.1	+4.00	July	2-25	8.0	-6.75
August	0-10	0.0	-10.00	August	2-25	8.0	-15.87
September	0-5	0.0	-5.00	September	0-22	0.0	-22.00
October	1-4	25.0	+3.50	October	2-16	12.5	-0.50
November	1-8	12.5	-0.50	November	2-15	13.3	+7.50
December	1-6	16.7	-2.50	December	1-9	11.1	-3.50

DISTANCE

2-y-o	W-R	Per cent	£1 Level Stake	3-y-o	W-R	Per cent	£1 Level Stake
5f-6f	0-26	0.0	-26.00	5f-6f	1-14	7.1	-10.25
7f-8f	2-26	7.7	-14.75	7f-8f	5-40	12.5	+3.13
9f-13f	0-0	0.0	0.00	9f-13f	0-6	0.0	-6.00
14f+	0-0	0.0	0.00	14f+	0-0	0.0	0.00

4-y-o+	W-R	Per cent	£1 Level Stake	Totals	W-R	Per cent	£1 Level Stake
5f-6f	2-29	6.9	-18.00	5f-6f	3-69	4.3	-54.25
7f-8f	1-24	4.2	-16.50	7f-8f	8-90	8.9	-28.12
9f-13f	1-20	5.0	-5.00	9f-13f	1-26	3.8	-11.00
14f+	0-2	0.0	-2.00	14f+	0-2	0.0	-2.00

TYPE OF RACE

Non-Handicaps	W-R	Per cent	£1 Level Stake	Handicaps	W-R	Per cent	£1 Level Stake
2-y-o	2-39	5.1	-27.75	2-y-o	0-13	0.0	-13.00
3-y-o	2-8	25.0	+6.75	3-y-o	4-52	7.7	-19.88
4-y-o+	0-3	0.0	-3.00	4-y-o+	4-72	5.6	-38.50

RACE CLASS

	W-R	Per cent	£1 Level Stake
Class 1	0-0	0.0	0.00
Class 2	0-0	0.0	0.00
Class 3	0-4	0.0	-4.00
Class 4	0-13	0.0	-13.00
Class 5	2-61	3.3	-46.25
Class 6	10-108	9.3	-31.13
Class 7	0-1	0.0	-1.00

FIRST TIME OUT

	W-R	Per cent	£1 Level Stake
2-y-o	0-12	0.0	-12.00
3-y-o	1-9	11.1	-5.25
4-y-o+	0-9	0.0	-9.00
Totals	1-30	3.3	-26.25

JOCKEYS

	W-R	Per cent	£1 Level Stake
Ben Robinson	5-25	20.0	+20.50
Shane Gray	2-31	6.5	-12.75
Andrew Mullen	2-78	2.6	-68.25
Silvestre De Sousa	1-1	100.0	+1.63
Joey Haynes	1-2	50.0	+6.00
Jamie Gormley	1-4	25.0	+3.50

COURSE RECORD

	Total W-R	Non-Hndcps 2-y-o	3-y-o+	Hndcps 2-y-o	3-y-o+	Per cent	£1 Level Stake
Newcastle (A.W)	4-31	0-4	1-1	0-8	3-18	12.9	-1.50
Wolvhptn (A.W)	2-18	1-2	0-3	0-1	1-12	11.1	-7.38
Southwell (A.W)	2-21	0-0	1-1	0-1	1-19	9.5	-11.25
Musselburgh	1-2	0-0	0-0	0-0	1-2	50.0	+4.50
Ripon	1-6	0-3	0-0	0-0	1-3	16.7	+9.00
Catterick	1-10	1-3	0-1	0-0	0-6	10.0	-6.75
Beverley	1-27	0-6	0-2	0-0	1-19	3.7	-10.00

WINNING HORSES

Horse	Races Run	1st	2nd	3rd	£

Horse	Races Run	1st	2nd	3rd	£
Amity Island	10	1	1	1	3105
Christmas Night	13	2	3	6	6210
Dandy Highwayman (IRE)	15	1	1	0	3105
Kroy	11	1	2	3	3105
Laydee Victoria (IRE)	7	1	0	0	3752
Mr C (IRE)	3	1	1	0	3105
Placebo Effect (IRE)	10	1	1	2	3752
Queen Of Scheme (IRE)	6	1	1	1	3105
Roaring Rory	6	1	1	1	3105
Smashing Lass (IRE)	10	1	1	3	3493
*Straight Ash (IRE)	6	1	1	0	3105
Total winning prize-money					**£38942**
Favourites	**1-6**		**16.7%**		**-3.38**

GEORGE PECKHAM

NEWMARKET, SUFFOLK

	No. of Hrs	Races Run	1st	2nd	3rd	Unpl	Per cent	£1 Level Stake
2-y-o	*10*	*25*	*3*	*3*	*2*	*17*	*12.0*	*-16.30*
3-y-o	*8*	*33*	*1*	*2*	*3*	*27*	*3.0*	*-28.00*
4-y-o+	*9*	*37*	*0*	*5*	*1*	*31*	*0.0*	*-37.00*
Totals	**27**	**95**	**4**	**10**	**6**	**75**	**4.2**	**-81.30**
2017	*25*	*91*	*7*	*1*	*5*	*78*	*7.7*	*-57.38*
2016	*13*	*46*	*7*	*4*	*5*	*30*	*15.2*	*+8.25*

JOCKEYS

	W-R	Per cent	£1 Level Stake
Luke Morris	2-14	14.3	-9.30
Jack Mitchell	1-3	33.3	+1.00
Daniel Muscutt	1-12	8.3	-7.00

COURSE RECORD

	Total W-R	Non-Hndcps 2-y-o	Non-Hndcps 3-y-o+	Hndcps 2-y-o	Hndcps 3-y-o+	Per cent	£1 Level Stake
Ascot	1-2	0-0	0-1	1-1	0-0	50.0	+0.20
Ripon	1-3	1-1	0-1	0-0	0-1	33.3	+1.00
Kempton (A.W)	1-13	0-3	0-2	0-0	1-8	7.7	-8.00
Chelmsford (A.W)	1-17	1-3	0-7	0-1	0-6	5.9	-14.50

WINNING HORSES

Horse	Races Run	1st	2nd	3rd	£
Red Island (IRE)	3	1	1	0	3429
Semoum (USA)	5	2	1	1	11644
Two Seas	6	1	0	1	3105
Total winning prize-money					**£18178**
Favourites	**2-6**		**33.3%**		**-1.30**

LINDA PERRATT

EAST KILBRIDE, S LANARKS

	No. of Hrs	Races Run	1st	2nd	3rd	Unpl	Per cent	£1 Level Stake
2-y-o	*4*	*17*	*2*	*0*	*2*	*13*	*11.8*	*+1.00*
3-y-o	*4*	*23*	*1*	*1*	*3*	*18*	*4.3*	*-16.50*
4-y-o+	*10*	*90*	*4*	*4*	*4*	*78*	*4.4*	*-58.50*
Totals	**18**	**130**	**7**	**5**	**9**	**109**	**5.4**	**-74.00**
2017	*13*	*126*	*8*	*7*	*14*	*97*	*6.3*	*-18.50*
2016	*19*	*156*	*5*	*4*	*9*	*138*	*3.2*	*-98.00*

JOCKEYS

	W-R	Per cent	£1 Level Stake
Ben Robinson	3-10	30.0	+16.50
Jamie Gormley	1-2	50.0	+1.50
P J McDonald	1-6	16.7	+5.00
Callum Rodriguez	1-11	9.1	-2.00
James Sullivan	1-15	6.7	-9.00

COURSE RECORD

	Total W-R	Non-Hndcps 2-y-o	Non-Hndcps 3-y-o+	Hndcps 2-y-o	Hndcps 3-y-o+	Per cent	£1 Level Stake
Musselburgh	4-25	0-1	0-1	1-4	3-19	16.0	+5.00
Ayr	2-54	0-2	0-2	0-2	2-48	3.7	-34.00
Newcastle (A.W)	1-21	0-0	0-2	1-3	0-16	4.8	-15.00

WINNING HORSES

Horse	Races Run	1st	2nd	3rd	£
Burmese Blazer (IRE)*	9	1	1	1	3105
Jordan Electrics	9	1	0	2	3105
Lucky Violet (IRE)	18	3	3	2	15526
*Popping Corks (IRE)	4	1	0	0	3105
Stardrifter	14	1	0	0	3493
Total winning prize-money					**£28334**
Favourites	**1-2**		**50.0%**		**1.50**

AMANDA PERRETT

PULBOROUGH, W SUSSEX

	No. of Hrs	Races Run	1st	2nd	3rd	Unpl	Per cent	£1 Level Stake
2-y-o	*13*	*39*	*4*	*3*	*5*	*27*	*10.3*	*-2.25*
3-y-o	*15*	*84*	*15*	*8*	*9*	*52*	*17.9*	*-11.38*
4-y-o+	*17*	*143*	*12*	*18*	*15*	*96*	*8.4*	*-56.95*
Totals	**45**	**266**	**31**	**29**	**29**	**175**	**11.7**	**-70.58**
2017	*53*	*244*	*16*	*28*	*28*	*171*	*6.6*	*-127.25*
2016	*52*	*250*	*30*	*32*	*26*	*162*	*12.0*	*-30.40*

BY MONTH

2-y-o	W-R	Per cent	£1 Level Stake	**3-y-o**	W-R	Per cent	£1 Level Stake
January	0-0	0.0	0.00	January	1-1	100.0	+2.75
February	0-0	0.0	0.00	February	1-2	50.0	+0.50
March	0-0	0.0	0.00	March	0-2	0.0	-2.00
April	0-0	0.0	0.00	April	0-5	0.0	-5.00
May	0-0	0.0	0.00	May	2-14	14.3	2.00
June	0-4	0.0	-4.00	June	1-11	9.1	-8.00
July	0-3	0.0	-3.00	July	0-11	0.0	-11.00
August	1-6	16.7	-3.63	August	6-12	50.0	+20.75
September	0-6	0.0	-6.00	September	2-11	18.2	-2.38

October	2-10	20.0	+22.00
November	1-8	12.5	-5.63
December	0-2	0.0	-2.00

October	2-12	16.7	-2.00
November	0-2	0.0	-2.00
December	0-1	0.0	-1.00

4-y-o+	W-R	Per cent	£1 Level Stake
January	0-6	0.0	-6.00
February	0-8	0.0	-8.00
March	0-2	0.0	-2.00
April	0-6	0.0	-6.00
May	3-23	13.0	+12.80
June	3-16	18.8	-2.75
July	0-22	0.0	-22.00
August	3-18	16.7	-1.00
September	1-24	4.2	-17.50
October	2-13	15.4	+0.50
November	0-3	0.0	-3.00
December	0-2	0.0	-2.00

Totals	W-R	Per cent	£1 Level Stake
January	1-7	14.3	-3.25
February	1-10	10.0	-7.50
March	0-4	0.0	-4.00
April	0-11	0.0	-11.00
May	5-37	13.5	+10.80
June	4-31	12.9	-14.75
July	0-36	0.0	-36.00
August	10-36	27.8	+16.12
September	3-41	7.3	-25.88
October	6-35	17.1	+20.50
November	1-13	7.7	-5.00
December	0-5	0.0	-3.00

DISTANCE

2-y-o	W-R	Per cent	£1 Level Stake
5f-6f	2-12	16.7	+1.38
7f-8f	1-25	4.0	-22.63
9f-13f	1-2	50.0	+19.00
14f+	0-0	0.0	0.00

3-y-o	W-R	Per cent	£1 Level Stake
5f-6f	3-12	25.0	-3.00
7f-8f	2-30	6.7	-22.00
9f-13f	8-39	20.5	+8.00
14f+	2-3	66.7	+5.63

4-y-o+	W-R	Per cent	£1 Level Stake
5f-6f	4-47	8.5	-27.25
7f-8f	5-48	10.4	-16.20
9f-13f	2-40	5.0	-26.50
14f+	1-8	12.5	+13.00

Totals	W-R	Per cent	£1 Level Stake
5f-6f	9-71	12.7	-28.87
7f-8f	8-103	7.8	-60.83
9f-13f	11-81	13.6	+0.50
14f+	3-11	27.3	+18.63

TYPE OF RACE

Non-Handicaps

	W-R	Per cent	£1 Level Stake
2-y-o	2-31	6.5	-7.63
3-y-o	3-34	8.8	-19.00
4-y-o+	2-8	25.0	-2.20

Handicaps

	W-R	Per cent	£1 Level Stake
2-y-o	2-8	25.0	+5.38
3-y-o	12-50	24.0	+7.63
4-y-o+	10-135	7.4	-54.75

RACE CLASS

	W-R	Per cent	£1 Level Stake
Class 1	1-4	25.0	0.00
Class 2	2-38	5.3	-14.50
Class 3	4-43	9.3	-17.00
Class 4	10-86	11.6	-25.63
Class 5	11-78	14.1	-7.75
Class 6	3-17	17.6	-4.70
Class 7	0-0	0.0	0.00

FIRST TIME OUT

	W-R	Per cent	£1 Level Stake
2-y-o	0-13	0.0	-13.00
3-y-o	3-15	20.0	+0.75
4-y-o+	1-17	5.9	+4.00
Totals	4-45	8.9	-8.25

JOCKEYS

	W-R	Per cent	£1 Level Stake
Jim Crowley	6-22	27.3	+1.93
Jason Watson	5-36	13.9	-10.63
Robert Havlin	4-29	13.8	+13.00
Joe Fanning	2-3	66.7	+5.63
Charles Bishop	2-7	28.6	+1.00
Kieran Shoemark	2-9	22.2	+25.00
Andrea Atzeni	2-13	15.4	-4.25
Joey Haynes	2-22	9.1	-15.75
Pat Dobbs	2-38	5.3	-26.00
Tom Eaves	1-1	100.0	+2.00
Frankie Dettori	1-1	100.0	+12.00
Richard Kingscote	1-4	25.0	+2.50
Martin Dwyer	1-16	6.3	-12.00

COURSE RECORD

	Total W-R	Non-Hndcps 2-y-o	Non-Hndcps 3-y-o+	Hndcps 2-y-o	Hndcps 3-y-o+	Per cent	£1 Level Stake
Kempton (A.W)	5-44	1-10	0-2	1-3	3-29	11.4	-14.50
Goodwood	4-27	0-2	1-4	0-0	3-21	14.8	+20.00
Lingfield (A.W)	4-33	0-4	1-7	0-0	3-22	12.1	-18.45
Epsom	3-5	0-0	0-0	0-0	3-5	60.0	+9.50
Brighton	3-10	0-0	0-0	1-1	2-9	30.0	+1.88
Windsor	3-26	0-0	2-5	0-0	1-21	11.5	-14.00
Salisbury	2-10	0-3	0-2	0-0	2-5	20.0	+0.25
Catterick	1-1	0-0	1-1	0-0	0-0	100.0	+2.00
Haydock	1-2	0-0	0-0	0-0	1-2	50.0	+4.00
Leicester	1-5	0-0	0-0	0-0	1-5	20.0	-1.50
Newmkt (Jly)	1-8	0-0	0-1	0-0	1-7	12.5	-5.25
Newmarket	1-9	0-2	0-3	0-0	1-4	11.1	+4.00
Chelmsford (A.W)	1-9	1-3	0-2	0-0	0-4	11.1	+12.00
Bath	1-11	0-0	0-3	0-1	1-7	9.1	-4.50

WINNING HORSES

Horse	Races Run	1st	2nd	3rd	£
Astromachia	7	2	1	1	11644
Count Otto (IRE)	14	3	2	2	28922
Dagian (IRE)*	5	1	2	0	3752
Desert Path	5	3	0	0	25036
Gather	2	1	0	0	5175
Inhale	2	1	0	1	3881
Lightening Dance	8	1	1	1	3817
Lightning Charlie	14	2	2	1	12000
Mr Bossy Boots (IRE)	7	1	1	1	3105
Open Wide (USA)	12	1	2	4	5757
Parnassian (IRE)	13	1	2	1	6469
Platitude	6	1	1	0	15753
Port Of Call	9	2	0	1	7763
Saluti (IRE)	9	2	0	0	7763
Sing A Rainbow (IRE)	6	1	0	0	3105
Spirit Ridge	4	2	1	0	10803
The Warrior (IRE)*	17	1	1	3	3752
Tinto	11	2	1	2	10221
Zhui Feng (IRE)	6	1	1	0	20983
Zuba	3	1	0	0	4787
Zzoro (IRE)	11	1	1	1	9338
Total winning prize-money					**£203826**
Favourites	**6-19**		**31.6%**		**-3.57**

PAT PHELAN

EPSOM, SURREY

	No. of Hrs	Races Run	1st	2nd	3rd	Unpl	Per cent	£1 Level Stake
2-y-o	*6*	*23*	*1*	*0*	*1*	*21*	*4.3*	*-16.00*
3-y-o	*7*	*31*	*3*	*2*	*2*	*24*	*9.7*	*+4.00*
4-y-o+	*10*	*61*	*8*	*7*	*6*	*40*	*13.1*	*-9.25*
Totals	**23**	**115**	**12**	**9**	**9**	**85**	**10.4**	**-21.25**
2017	*26*	*94*	*1*	*5*	*7*	*81*	*1.1*	*-86.00*
2016	*26*	*123*	*8*	*8*	*12*	*95*	*6.5*	*-68.75*

BY MONTH

2-y-o	W-R	Per cent	£1 Level Stake	3-y-o	W-R	Per cent	£1 Level Stake
January	0-0	0.0	0.00	January	0-4	0.0	-4.00
February	0-0	0.0	0.00	February	0-1	0.0	-1.00
March	0-0	0.0	0.00	March	0-3	0.0	-3.00
April	0-0	0.0	0.00	April	0-2	0.0	-2.00
May	0-0	0.0	0.00	May	0-5	0.0	-5.00
June	0-4	0.0	-4.00	June	0-2	0.0	-2.00
July	0-2	0.0	-2.00	July	0-2	0.0	-2.00
August	0-4	0.0	-4.00	August	0-1	0.0	-1.00
September	0-4	0.0	-4.00	September	1-2	50.0	+15.00
October	0-2	0.0	-2.00	October	0-3	0.0	-3.00
November	0-3	0.0	-3.00	November	2-3	66.7	+15.00
December	1-4	25.0	+3.00	December	0-3	0.0	-3.00

4-y-o+	W-R	Per cent	£1 Level Stake	Totals	W-R	Per cent	£1 Level Stake
January	2-5	40.0	+8.00	January	2-9	22.2	+4.00
February	2-4	50.0	+5.75	February	2-5	40.0	+4.75
March	0-3	0.0	-3.00	March	0-6	0.0	-6.00
April	2-8	25.0	+10.50	April	2-10	20.0	+8.50
May	1-8	12.5	-5.50	May	1-13	7.7	-10.50
June	0-6	0.0	-6.00	June	0-12	0.0	-12.00
July	0-4	0.0	-4.00	July	0-8	0.0	-8.00
August	0-8	0.0	-8.00	August	0-13	0.0	-13.00
September	0-3	0.0	-3.00	September	1-9	11.1	+8.00
October	0-4	0.0	-4.00	October	0-9	0.0	-9.00
November	1-3	33.3	+5.00	November	3-9	33.3	+20.00
December	0-5	0.0	-5.00	December	1-12	8.3	-8.00

DISTANCE

2-y-o	W-R	Per cent	£1 Level Stake	3-y-o	W-R	Per cent	£1 Level Stake
5f-6f	0-6	0.0	-6.00	5f-6f	0-10	0.0	-10.00
7f-8f	1-17	5.9	-10.00	7f-8f	0-8	0.0	-8.00
9f-13f	0-0	0.0	0.00	9f-13f	3-13	23.1	+22.00
14f+	0-0	0.0	0.00	14f+	0-0	0.0	0.00

4-y-o+	W-R	Per cent	£1 Level Stake	Totals	W-R	Per cent	£1 Level Stake
5f-6f	0-0	0.0	0.00	5f-6f	0-16	0.0	-16.00
7f-8f	3-13	23.1	+8.75	7f-8f	4-38	10.5	-9.25
9f-13f	5-42	11.9	-12.00	9f-13f	8-55	14.5	+10.00
14f+	0-6	0.0	-6.00	14f+	0-6	0.0	-6.00

TYPE OF RACE

Non-Handicaps	W-R	Per cent	£1 Level Stake	Handicaps	W-R	Per cent	£1 Level Stake
2-y-o	0-16	0.0	-16.00	2-y-o	1-7	14.3	0.00
3-y-o	0-7	0.0	-7.00	3-y-o	3-24	12.5	+11.00
4-y-o+	0-4	0.0	-4.00	4-y-o+	8-57	14.0	-5.25

RACE CLASS

	W-R	Per cent	£1 Level Stake
Class 1	0-0	0.0	0.00
Class 2	0-0	0.0	0.00
Class 3	0-0	0.0	0.00
Class 4	0-7	0.0	-7.00
Class 5	1-40	2.5	-27.00
Class 6	11-67	16.4	+13.75
Class 7	0-1	0.0	-1.00

FIRST TIME OUT

	W-R	Per cent	£1 Level Stake
2-y-o	0-6	0.0	-6.00
3-y-o	0-7	0.0	-7.00
4-y-o+	0-10	0.0	-10.00
Totals	0-23	0.0	-23.00

JOCKEYS

	W-R	Per cent	£1 Level Stake
Paddy Bradley	9-61	14.8	-4.25
Hector Crouch	1-1	100.0	+16.00
J F Egan	1-4	25.0	+3.00
Charlie Bennett	1-14	7.1	-1.00

COURSE RECORD

	Total W-R	Non-Hndcps 2-y-o	Non-Hndcps 3-y-o+	Hndcps 2-y-o	Hndcps 3-y-o+	Per cent	£1 Level Stake
Lingfield (A.W)	10-52	0-6	0-5	1-4	9-37	19.2	+24.25
Lingfield	1-7	0-1	0-0	0-0	1-6	14.3	-4.50
Kempton (A.W)	1-26	0-2	0-4	0-3	1-17	3.8	-11.00

WINNING HORSES

Horse	Races Run	1st	2nd	3rd	£
Hackbridge	9	3	0	0	9962
Hatsaway (IRE)	7	1	1	1	3105
Keep It Country Tv	9	1	0	1	3105
Pivotal Flame (IRE)	13	2	1	1	6210
Presence Process	12	3	1	2	9315
Settle Petal	14	2	3	2	6210
Total winning prize-money					**£37907**
Favourites	**4-10**		**40.0%**		**2.75**

RICHARD PHILLIPS

ADLESTROP, GLOUCS

	No. of Hrs	Races Run	1st	2nd	3rd	Unpl	Per cent	£1 Level Stake
2-y-o	*0*	*0*	*0*	*0*	*0*	*0*	*0.0*	*0.00*
3-y-o	*3*	*15*	*2*	*0*	*1*	*12*	*13.3*	*-1.00*
4-y-o+	*2*	*3*	*0*	*0*	*2*	*1*	*0.0*	*-3.00*
Totals	**5**	**18**	**2**	**0**	**3**	**13**	**11.1**	**-4.00**
2017	*4*	*14*	*0*	*0*	*2*	*12*	*0.0*	*-14.00*
2016	*6*	*27*	*1*	*1*	*4*	*21*	*3.7*	*-22.50*

JOCKEYS

	W-R	Per cent	£1 Level Stake
Joe Fanning	1-2	50.0	+7.00
Danny Brock	1-6	16.7	-1.00

COURSE RECORD

	Total W-R	Non-Hndcps 2-y-o	Non-Hndcps 3-y-o+	Hndcps 2-y-o	Hndcps 3-y-o+	Per cent	£1 Level Stake
Wolvhptn (A.W)	2-7	0-0	1-1	0-0	1-6	28.6	+7.00

WINNING HORSES

Horse	Races Run	1st	2nd	3rd	£
*Lady Of Authority	7	1	0	0	3105
Madame Ritz (IRE)	6	1	0	1	3752
Total winning prize-money					**£6857**
Favourites	**1-8**		**12.5%**		**-3.50**

TIM PINFIELD

UPPER LAMBOURN, BERKS

	No. of Hrs	Races Run	1st	2nd	3rd	Unpl	Per cent	£1 Level Stake
2-y-o	*1*	*2*	*0*	*0*	*0*	*2*	*0.0*	*-2.00*
3-y-o	*2*	*9*	*2*	*0*	*2*	*5*	*22.2*	*+5.00*
4-y-o+	*5*	*16*	*0*	*1*	*3*	*12*	*0.0*	*-16.00*
Totals	**8**	**27**	**2**	**1**	**5**	**19**	**7.4**	**-13.00**
2017	*2*	*7*	*0*	*0*	*0*	*7*	*0.0*	*-7.00*
2016	*0*							

JOCKEYS

	W-R	Per cent	£1 Level Stake
Martin Dwyer	2-11	18.2	+3.00

COURSE RECORD

	Total W-R	Non-Hndcps 2-y-o	Non-Hndcps 3-y-o+	Hndcps 2-y-o	Hndcps 3-y-o+	Per cent	£1 Level Stake
Newmarket	1-1	0-0	1-1	0-0	0-0	100.0	+5.00
Windsor	1-2	0-0	1-2	0-0	0-0	50.0	+6.00

WINNING HORSES

Horse	Races Run	1st	2nd	3rd	£
Sir Thomas Gresham (IRE)	3	2	0	1	12467
Total winning prize-money					**£12467**
Favourites	**0-0**		**0.0%**		**0.00**

DAVID PIPE

NICHOLASHAYNE, DEVON

	No. of Hrs	Races Run	1st	2nd	3rd	Unpl	Per cent	£1 Level Stake
2-y-o	*0*	*0*	*0*	*0*	*0*	*0*	*0.0*	*0.00*
3-y-o	*1*	*1*	*0*	*0*	*0*	*1*	*0.0*	*-1.00*
4-y-o+	*14*	*19*	*2*	*1*	*1*	*15*	*10.5*	*-7.00*
Totals	**15**	**20**	**2**	**1**	**1**	**16**	**10.0**	**-8.00**
2017	*10*	*18*	*0*	*1*	*0*	*17*	*0.0*	*-18.00*
2016	*12*	*16*	*3*	*0*	*1*	*12*	*18.8*	*-7.53*

JOCKEYS

	W-R	Per cent	£1 Level Stake
Miss Siobhan Doolan	1-1	100.0	+7.00
Finley Marsh	1-4	25.0	0.00

COURSE RECORD

	Total W-R	Non-Hndcps 2-y-o	Non-Hndcps 3-y-o+	Hndcps 2-y-o	Hndcps 3-y-o+	Per cent	£1 Level Stake
Newbury	1-2	0-0	0-0	0-0	1-2	50.0	+6.00
Ffos Las	1-2	0-0	0-0	0-0	1-2	50.0	+2.00

WINNING HORSES

Horse	Races Run	1st	2nd	3rd	£
Dell' Arca (IRE)	2	1	0	0	5865
*Jacbequick	2	1	1	0	3752
Total winning prize-money					**£9617**
Favourites	**12-32**		**37.5%**		**2.14**

JONATHAN PORTMAN

UPPER LAMBOURN, BERKS

	No. of Hrs	Races Run	1st	2nd	3rd	Unpl	Per cent	£1 Level Stake
2-y-o	*14*	*47*	*4*	*6*	*5*	*32*	*8.5*	*-25.88*
3-y-o	*25*	*150*	*21*	*18*	*13*	*97*	*14.0*	*+37.75*
4-y-o+	*10*	*46*	*8*	*5*	*8*	*25*	*17.4*	*+30.85*
Totals	**49**	**243**	**33**	**29**	**26**	**154**	**13.6**	**+42.72**
2017	*52*	*190*	*15*	*10*	*19*	*146*	*7.9*	*+59.69*
2016	*48*	*216*	*22*	*16*	*19*	*159*	*10.2*	*-48.51*

BY MONTH

2-y-o	W-R	Per cent	£1 Level Stake	3-y-o	W-R	Per cent	£1 Level Stake
January	0-0	0.0	0.00	January	0-8	0.0	-8.00
February	0-0	0.0	0.00	February	1-3	33.3	+6.00
March	0-0	0.0	0.00	March	1-6	16.7	+15.00
April	0-0	0.0	0.00	April	5-21	23.8	+58.00
May	0-1	0.0	-1.00	May	2-25	8.0	-15.75
June	0-2	0.0	-2.00	June	3-18	16.7	-3.25
July	0-6	0.0	-6.00	July	4-15	26.7	+4.55
August	1-6	16.7	-2.25	August	1-19	5.3	-16.80
September	2-14	14.3	+1.00	September	1-18	5.6	-7.00
October	1-12	8.3	-9.63	October	1-12	8.3	-4.00
November	0-2	0.0	-2.00	November	2-4	50.0	+10.00
December	0-4	0.0	-4.00	December	0-1	0.0	-1.00

4-y-o+	W-R	Per cent	£1 Level Stake	Totals	W-R	Per cent	£1 Level Stake
January	0-3	0.0	-3.00	January	0-11	0.0	-11.00
February	0-2	0.0	-2.00	February	1-5	20.0	+4.00
March	0-3	0.0	-3.00	March	1-9	11.1	+12.00
April	2-5	40.0	+7.00	April	7-26	26.9	+65.00

May	4-8	50.0	+48.85	May	6-34	17.6	+32.10
June	2-6	33.3	+2.00	June	5-26	19.2	-3.25
July	0-5	0.0	-5.00	July	4-26	15.4	-6.45
August	0-5	0.0	-5.00	August	2-30	6.7	-24.05
September	0-3	0.0	-3.00	September	3-35	8.6	-9.00
October	0-4	0.0	-4.00	October	2-28	7.1	-17.63
November	0-2	0.0	-2.00	November	2-8	25.0	+8.00
December	0-0	0.0	0.00	December	0-5	0.0	-1.00

DISTANCE

2-y-o	W-R	Per cent	£1 Level Stake	3-y-o	W-R	Per cent	£1 Level Stake
5f-6f	1-16	6.3	-7.00	5f-6f	7-25	28.0	+5.50
7f-8f	3-31	9.7	-18.88	7f-8f	11-59	18.6	+63.00
9f-13f	0-0	0.0	0.00	9f-13f	3-60	5.0	-24.75
14f+	0-0	0.0	0.00	14f+	0-6	0.0	-6.00
4-y-o+	W-R	Per cent	£1 Level Stake	**Totals**	W-R	Per cent	£1 Level Stake
5f-6f	0-1	0.0	-1.00	5f-6f	8-42	19.0	-2.50
7f-8f	0-4	0.0	-4.00	7f-8f	14-94	14.9	+40.12
9f-13f	4-29	13.8	-3.75	9f-13f	7-89	7.9	-28.50
14f+	4-12	33.3	+39.60	14f+	4-18	22.2	+33.60

TYPE OF RACE

Non-Handicaps	W-R	Per cent	£1 Level Stake	Handicaps	W-R	Per cent	£1 Level Stake
2-y-o	2-37	5.4	-25.63	2-y-o	2-10	20.0	-0.25
3-y-o	4-38	10.5	+3.10	3-y-o	17-112	15.2	+34.65
4-y-o+	0-2	0.0	-2.00	4-y-o+	8-44	18.2	+32.85

RACE CLASS

	W-R	Per cent	£1 Level Stake
Class 1	0-1	0.0	-1.00
Class 2	1-8	12.5	-2.00
Class 3	1-9	11.1	-5.00
Class 4	5-47	10.6	-20.50
Class 5	15-104	14.4	+36.60
Class 6	11-72	15.3	+36.63
Class 7	0-2	0.0	-2.00

FIRST TIME OUT

	W-R	Per cent	£1 Level Stake
2-y-o	0-14	0.0	-14.00
3-y-o	6-25	24.0	+63.00
4-y-o+	3-10	30.0	+12.00
Totals	9-49	18.4	+61.00

JOCKEYS

	W-R	Per cent	£1 Level Stake
Rob Hornby	23-151	15.2	+13.38
Richard Kingscote	7-23	30.4	+25.35
Luke Morris	1-5	20.0	+6.00
Mr James Harding	1-6	16.7	+35.00
Nicola Currie	1-9	11.1	+12.00

COURSE RECORD

	Total W-R	Non-Hndcps 2-y-o	Non-Hndcps 3-y-o+	Hndcps 2-y-o	Hndcps 3-y-o+	Per cent	£1 Level Stake
Lingfield	5-15	0-0	0-2	0-0	5-13	33.3	+3.60
Kempton (A.W)	5-40	2-10	1-5	0-3	2-22	12.5	+7.88
Wolvhptn (A.W)	4-19	0-2	0-5	0-0	4-12	21.1	+70.00
Lingfield (A.W)	4-19	0-2	2-12	0-1	2-4	21.1	+31.00
Newbury	3-16	0-5	0-2	1-1	2-8	18.8	-0.05
Windsor	3-28	0-3	1-5	0-0	2-20	10.7	-19.70
Chelmsford (A.W)	2-12	0-2	0-1	0-0	2-9	16.7	+4.50
Newmarket	1-2	0-0	0-0	1-1	0-1	50.0	+4.00
Yarmouth	1-4	0-0	0-0	0-0	1-4	25.0	-0.75
Ffos Las	1-4	0-0	0-0	0-0	1-4	25.0	+7.00
Leicester	1-7	0-1	0-1	0-0	1-5	14.3	-1.00
Goodwood	1-8	0-2	0-1	0-0	1-5	12.5	-4.00
Chepstow	1-9	0-1	0-1	0-0	1-7	11.1	-5.75
Brighton	1-11	0-1	0-0	0-0	1-10	9.1	-5.00

WINNING HORSES

Horse	Races Run	1st	2nd	3rd	£
Ashazuri	12	2	2	3	6857
Broad Appeal	7	1	1	1	3105
Choral Music*	8	4	1	0	13391
Even Keel (IRE)	8	2	4	1	16690
Folies Bergeres*	9	1	2	1	3235
Gainsay	10	3	1	1	9315
Golden Iris	11	2	4	1	10221
Goodnight Girl (IRE)	10	3	3	2	14814
Hewouldwouldnthe	4	1	0	1	3619
Homing Star	8	1	0	1	3170
Indiscretion (IRE)	5	1	2	0	3752
Invincibella	7	1	1	1	3881
Mancini	7	3	0	1	22532
Mandalayan (IRE)	7	1	0	3	3752
Orin Swift (IRE)	5	1	2	1	4787
Quick Breath	10	2	1	0	12097
Show Of Force*	10	1	1	0	3752
Toybox	5	1	1	0	3235
*Walk On Walter (IRE)	4	2	1	0	7504
Total winning prize-money					**£149709**
Favourites	**8-29**		**27.6%**		**-8.78**

BRENDAN POWELL

UPPER LAMBOURN, BERKS

	No. of Hrs	Races Run	1st	2nd	3rd	Unpl	Per cent	£1 Level Stake
2-y-o	*4*	*15*	*1*	*0*	*0*	*14*	*6.7*	*-9.00*
3-y-o	*5*	*33*	*3*	*1*	*8*	*21*	*9.1*	*-4.13*
4-y-o+	*11*	*54*	*7*	*5*	*3*	*39*	*13.0*	*+26.30*
Totals	**20**	**102**	**11**	**6**	**11**	**74**	**10.8**	**+13.17**
2017	*31*	*140*	*6*	*8*	*13*	*113*	*4.3*	*-64.75*
2016	*31*	*185*	*14*	*27*	*15*	*129*	*7.6*	*-53.88*

BY MONTH

2-y-o	W-R	Per cent	£1 Level Stake	3-y-o	W-R	Per cent	£1 Level Stake
January	0-0	0.0	0.00	January	0-2	0.0	-2.00
February	0-0	0.0	0.00	February	0-2	0.0	-2.00
March	0-0	0.0	0.00	March	0-0	0.0	0.00
April	0-0	0.0	0.00	April	0-3	0.0	-3.00
May	0-0	0.0	0.00	May	1-3	33.3	+14.00
June	0-1	0.0	-1.00	June	0-3	0.0	-3.00
July	0-4	0.0	-4.00	July	0-3	0.0	-3.00

	W-R	Per cent	£1 Level Stake
August	0-2	0.0	-2.00
September	0-0	0.0	0.00
October	0-4	0.0	-4.00
November	0-1	0.0	-1.00
December	1-3	33.3	+3.00

	W-R	Per cent	£1 Level Stake
August	0-3	0.0	-3.00
September	0-4	0.0	-4.00
October	0-4	0.0	-4.00
November	1-4	25.0	+5.00
December	1-2	50.0	+0.88

4-y-o+	W-R	Per cent	£1 Level Stake
January	1-4	25.0	+2.50
February	0-3	0.0	-3.00
March	1-8	12.5	-1.00
April	0-3	0.0	-3.00
May	0-3	0.0	-3.00
June	1-6	16.7	+11.00
July	0-4	0.0	-4.00
August	1-4	25.0	+13.00
September	0-6	0.0	-6.00
October	1-5	20.0	+8.00
November	2-5	40.0	+14.80
December	0-3	0.0	-3.00

Totals	W-R	Per cent	£1 Level Stake
January	1-6	16.7	+0.50
February	0-5	0.0	-5.00
March	1-8	12.5	-1.00
April	0-6	0.0	-6.00
May	1-6	16.7	+11.00
June	1-10	10.0	+7.00
July	0-11	0.0	-11.00
August	1-9	11.1	+8.00
September	0-10	0.0	-10.00
October	1-13	7.7	0.00
November	3-10	30.0	+19.80
December	2-8	25.0	-2.12

DISTANCE

2-y-o	W-R	Per cent	£1 Level Stake
5f-6f	0-2	0.0	-2.00
7f-8f	1-12	8.3	-6.00
9f-13f	0-1	0.0	-1.00
14f+	0-0	0.0	0.00

3-y-o	W-R	Per cent	£1 Level Stake
5f-6f	0-2	0.0	-2.00
7f-8f	0-16	0.0	-16.00
9f-13f	3-14	21.4	+14.88
14f+	0-1	0.0	-1.00

4-y-o+	W-R	Per cent	£1 Level Stake
5f-6f	0-2	0.0	-2.00
7f-8f	3-25	12.0	+1.30
9f-13f	4-26	15.4	+28.00
14f+	0-1	0.0	-1.00

Totals	W-R	Per cent	£1 Level Stake
5f-6f	0-6	0.0	-6.00
7f-8f	4-53	7.5	-20.70
9f-13f	7-41	17.1	+41.88
14f+	0-2	0.0	-2.00

TYPE OF RACE

Non-Handicaps

	W-R	Per cent	£1 Level Stake
2-y-o	0-9	0.0	-9.00
3-y-o	0-8	0.0	-8.00
4-y-o+	1-4	25.0	+13.00

Handicaps

	W-R	Per cent	£1 Level Stake
2-y-o	1-6	16.7	0.00
3-y-o	3-25	12.0	+3.88
4-y-o+	6-50	12.0	+13.30

RACE CLASS

	W-R	Per cent	£1 Level Stake
Class 1	1-2	50.0	+15.00
Class 2	0-2	0.0	-2.00
Class 3	1-4	25.0	+13.00
Class 4	0-10	0.0	-10.00
Class 5	0-26	0.0	-26.00
Class 6	9-58	15.5	+23.17
Class 7	0-0	0.0	0.00

FIRST TIME OUT

	W-R	Per cent	£1 Level Stake
2-y-o	0-4	0.0	-4.00
3-y-o	0-5	0.0	-5.00
4-y-o+	1-11	9.1	-4.50
Totals	1-20	5.0	-13.50

JOCKEYS

	W-R	Per cent	£1 Level Stake
Fergus Sweeney	3-7	42.9	+10.88
Martin Dwyer	2-26	7.7	-2.00
Martin Harley	1-1	100.0	+16.00
Cameron Noble	1-1	100.0	+5.50
Jack Mitchell	1-1	100.0	+12.00
Luke Morris	1-2	50.0	+15.00
Dougie Costello	1-2	50.0	+15.00
Cieren Fallon	1-3	33.3	-0.20

COURSE RECORD

	Total W-R	Non-Hndcps 2-y-o	Non-Hndcps 3-y-o+	Hndcps 2-y-o	Hndcps 3-y-o+	Per cent	£1 Level Stake
Lingfield (A.W)	4-17	0-1	0-2	1-1	3-13	23.5	+15.30
Kempton (A.W)	4-18	0-0	1-3	0-1	3-14	22.2	+17.88
Chelmsford (A.W)	2-13	0-0	0-0	0-1	2-12	15.4	+21.00
Wolvhptn (A.W)	1-9	0-1	0-1	0-1	1-6	11.1	+4.00

WINNING HORSES

Horse	Races Run	1st	2nd	3rd	£
Freedom And Wheat (IRE)	9	1	0	0	3105
Garth Rockett	11	2	2	1	6598
Kasperenko	4	2	0	0	50997
Mr Andros	13	1	2	0	3105
Udogo	9	2	0	1	6210
Zarrar (IRE)	13	3	0	3	9315
Total winning prize-money					**£79330**
Favourites	**2-6**		**33.3%**		**-0.33**

SIR MARK PRESCOTT BT

NEWMARKET, SUFFOLK

	No. of Hrs	Races Run	1st	2nd	3rd	Unpl	Per cent	£1 Level Stake
2-y-o	*29*	*105*	*9*	*6*	*6*	*84*	*8.6*	*-60.17*
3-y-o	*27*	*135*	*39*	*27*	*15*	*53*	*28.9*	*+49.70*
4-y-o+	*8*	*36*	*3*	*5*	*4*	*24*	*8.3*	*-26.25*
Totals	**64**	**276**	**51**	**38**	**25**	**161**	**18.5**	**-36.72**
2017	*60*	*282*	*48*	*32*	*37*	*163*	*17.0*	*-64.47*
2016	*61*	*278*	*55*	*45*	*23*	*155*	*19.8*	*-60.61*

BY MONTH

2-y-o	W-R	Per cent	£1 Level Stake
January	0-0	0.0	0.00
February	0-0	0.0	0.00
March	0-0	0.0	0.00
April	0-0	0.0	0.00
May	0-3	0.0	-3.00
June	1-10	10.0	-2.00
July	0-13	0.0	-13.00
August	1-10	10.0	-4.00
September	3-21	14.3	-7.75
October	3-37	8.1	-21.25
November	0-8	0.0	-8.00
December	1-3	33.3	-1.17

3-y-o	W-R	Per cent	£1 Level Stake
January	0-2	0.0	-2.00
February	0-1	0.0	-1.00
March	2-5	40.0	+3.67
April	0-1	0.0	-1.00
May	1-9	11.1	-1.00
June	6-19	31.6	-0.28
July	20-42	47.6	+46.69
August	2-22	9.1	-15.88
September	6-22	27.3	+3.00
October	1-9	11.1	+12.00
November	0-2	0.0	-2.00
December	1-1	100.0	+7.50

4-y-o+	W-R	Per cent	£1 Level Stake
January	1-6	16.7	-3.50
February	0-3	0.0	-3.00

Totals	W-R	Per cent	£1 Level Stake
January	1-8	12.5	-5.50
February	0-4	0.0	-4.00

	W-R	Per cent	£1 Level Stake		W-R	Per cent	£1 Level Stake
March	0-2	0.0	-2.00	March	2-7	28.6	+1.67
April	0-1	0.0	-1.00	April	0-2	0.0	-2.00
May	1-3	33.3	-0.25	May	2-15	13.3	-4.25
June	0-2	0.0	-2.00	June	7-31	22.6	-4.28
July	1-6	16.7	-1.50	July	21-61	34.4	+32.19
August	0-4	0.0	-4.00	August	3-36	8.3	-23.88
September	0-3	0.0	-3.00	September	9-46	19.6	-7.75
October	0-3	0.0	-3.00	October	4-49	8.2	-12.25
November	0-1	0.0	-1.00	November	0-11	0.0	-3.00
December	0-2	0.0	-2.00	December	2-6	33.3	+5.50

DISTANCE

2-y-o	W-R	Per cent	£1 Level Stake	3-y-o	W-R	Per cent	£1 Level Stake
5f-6f	3-32	9.4	-19.17	5f-6f	1-8	12.5	-6.27
7f-8f	4-70	5.7	-46.75	7f-8f	6-34	17.6	+32.17
9f-13f	2-3	66.7	+5.75	9f-13f	21-63	33.3	-8.08
14f+	0-0	0.0	0.00	14f+	11-30	36.7	+31.88

4-y-o+	W-R	Per cent	£1 Level Stake	Totals	W-R	Per cent	£1 Level Stake
5f-6f	0-0	0.0	0.00	5f-6f	4-40	10.0	-25.44
7f-8f	0-4	0.0	-4.00	7f-8f	10-108	9.3	-18.58
9f-13f	1-4	25.0	-1.25	9f-13f	24-70	34.3	-3.58
14f+	2-28	7.1	-21.00	14f+	13-58	22.4	+10.88

TYPE OF RACE

Non-Handicaps	W-R	Per cent	£1 Level Stake	Handicaps	W-R	Per cent	£1 Level Stake
2-y-o	6-88	6.8	-58.92	2-y-o	3-17	17.6	-1.25
3-y-o	1-23	4.3	+11.00	3-y-o	38-112	33.9	+38.70
4-y-o+	0-5	0.0	-5.00	4-y-o+	3-31	9.7	-21.25

RACE CLASS

	W-R	Per cent	£1 Level Stake
Class 1	0-8	0.0	-8.00
Class 2	1-9	11.1	-5.25
Class 3	0-4	0.0	-4.00
Class 4	16-75	21.3	+8.27
Class 5	18-129	14.0	-27.83
Class 6	16-51	31.4	+0.10
Class 7	0-0	0.0	0.00

FIRST TIME OUT

	W-R	Per cent	£1 Level Stake
2-y-o	1-29	3.4	-21.00
3-y-o	9-27	33.3	+48.10
4-y-o+	0-8	0.0	-8.00
Totals	10-64	15.6	+19.10

JOCKEYS

	W-R	Per cent	£1 Level Stake
Luke Morris	37-189	19.6	-39.40
Ryan Tate	11-65	16.9	+16.13
Gavin Ashton	2-6	33.3	+0.06
Adam Kirby	1-1	100.0	+1.50

COURSE RECORD

	Total W-R	Non-Hndcps 2-y-o	Non-Hndcps 3-y-o+	Hndcps 2-y-o	Hndcps 3-y-o+	Per cent	£1 Level Stake
Wolvhptn (A.W)	6-41	1-11	0-8	1-5	4-17	14.6	-8.33
Chelmsford (A.W)	6-42	1-16	1-5	2-4	2-17	14.3	+11.75
Bath	5-12	0-2	0-2	0-0	5-8	41.7	-3.76
Lingfield (A.W)	5-27	1-9	0-4	0-1	4-13	18.5	-7.83
Chepstow	4-7	0-2	0-0	0-0	4-5	57.1	+6.46
Newcastle (A.W)	4-22	0-7	0-0	0-0	4-15	18.2	+8.71
Brighton	3-6	1-1	0-0	0-0	2-5	50.0	+1.20
Yarmouth	3-7	0-1	0-0	0-0	3-6	42.9	+0.22
Lingfield	3-10	0-2	0-0	0-0	3-8	30.0	-5.08
Ffos Las	2-2	0-0	0-0	0-0	2-2	100.0	+4.13
Ayr	1-1	0-0	0-0	0-0	1-1	100.0	+0.73
Catterick	1-1	0-0	0-0	0-0	1-1	100.0	+2.50
Chester	1-1	0-0	0-0	0-0	1-1	100.0	+3.50
Musselburgh	1-1	0-0	0-0	0-0	1-1	100.0	+2.75
Hamilton	1-1	0-0	0-0	0-0	1-1	100.0	+9.00
Beverley	1-3	1-2	0-0	0-0	0-1	33.3	+0.25
Redcar	1-3	0-0	0-0	0-1	1-2	33.3	-0.90
Carlisle	1-5	1-4	0-0	0-0	0-1	20.0	+2.00
Doncaster	1-5	0-3	0-0	0-0	1-2	20.0	0.00
Salisbury	1-5	0-2	0-0	0-0	1-3	20.0	+10.00

WINNING HORSES

Horse	Races Run	1st	2nd	3rd	£
Albanita	3	1	0	0	7375
Alternate Route	2	1	0	0	4399
Altra Vita	9	6	0	1	26038
Anandita	7	1	1	2	3170
Bath And Tennis (IRE)	2	1	0	0	5531
Brassica (IRE)	2	1	0	0	5757
Buckman Tavern (FR)	3	1	0	0	6728
Calling The Wind (IRE)	9	2	2	1	9574
Done Deal (IRE)	4	1	0	0	4140
Dutch Monarch	8	1	2	1	3752
Elysees Palace	2	1	0	0	6081
Final Rock	6	3	3	0	9962
Grey Spirit (IRE)	3	2	1	0	6987
Harmonica	4	2	0	0	11533
Isle Of Avalon (IRE)	1	1	0	0	4787
Klass Action (IRE)	3	1	1	0	4787
Matchmaking (GER)	5	4	0	1	16140
Midnight Blue	4	3	1	0	9962
Miss Celestial (IRE)	4	2	0	1	8539
Piedita (IRE)	3	1	0	0	6081
Praeceps (IRE)*	10	3	1	2	12309
Rude Awakening	6	2	3	0	5531
Timoshenko	5	5	0	0	30962
Trouble And Strife (IRE)	10	3	5	1	14232
True North (IRE)	8	1	2	2	3493
Twister (IRE)	7	1	2	3	3752

Total winning prize-money **£231602**

Favourites **25-59** **42.4%** **-8.39**

RICHARD PRICE

ULLINGSWICK, H'FORDS

	No. of Hrs	Races Run	1st	2nd	3rd	Unpl	Per cent	£1 Level Stake
2-y-o	*1*	*6*	*0*	*0*	*0*	*6*	*0.0*	*-6.00*
3-y-o	*2*	*16*	*1*	*2*	*1*	*12*	*6.3*	*+5.00*
4-y-o+	*8*	*60*	*5*	*6*	*9*	*40*	*8.3*	*-35.25*

Totals	**11**	**82**	**6**	**8**	**10**	**58**	**7.3**	**-36.25**
2017	*13*	*92*	*10*	*8*	*15*	*58*	*10.9*	*-15.75*
2016	*10*	*60*	*3*	*4*	*9*	*43*	*5.0*	*-37.00*

JOCKEYS

	W-R	Per cent	£1 Level Stake
David Egan	1-1	100.0	+3.50
Dane O'Neill	1-1	100.0	+1.75
Ellie MacKenzie	1-3	33.3	0.00
Jonathan Fisher	1-9	11.1	+0.50
William Cox	1-10	10.0	+11.00
David Probert	1-13	7.7	-8.00

COURSE RECORD

	Total W-R	Non-Hndcps 2-y-o	Non-Hndcps 3-y-o+	Hndcps 2-y-o	Hndcps 3-y-o+	Per cent	£1 Level Stake
Lingfield	2-3	0-0	0-0	0-0	2-3	66.7	+4.25
Newbury	1-2	0-0	0-0	0-0	1-2	50.0	+7.50
Leicester	1-7	0-0	0-0	0-1	1-6	14.3	-4.00
Chepstow	1-13	0-1	0-0	0-0	1-12	7.7	-8.00
Wolvhptn (A.W)	1-25	0-2	0-2	0-1	1-20	4.0	-4.00

WINNING HORSES

Horse	Races Run	1st	2nd	3rd	£
Bellevarde (IRE)	13	2	3	3	7504
Champagne Bob	12	2	1	1	7121
Ocean Gale	6	1	0	2	3105
Our Man In Havana	14	1	2	1	3105
Total winning prize-money					**£20835**
Favourites	**2-4**		**50.0%**		**1.75**

MICK QUINN

NEWMARKET, SUFFOLK

	No. of Hrs	Races Run	1st	2nd	3rd	Unpl	Per cent	£1 Level Stake
2-y-o	*3*	*5*	*0*	*1*	*2*	*2*	*0.0*	*-5.00*
3-y-o	*4*	*42*	*5*	*4*	*8*	*25*	*11.9*	*-8.75*
4-y-o+	*4*	*45*	*4*	*5*	*4*	*32*	*8.9*	*-19.00*
Totals	**11**	**92**	**9**	**10**	**14**	**59**	**9.8**	**-32.75**
2017	*13*	*73*	*6*	*10*	*9*	*48*	*8.2*	*+19.00*
2016	*11*	*67*	*4*	*8*	*9*	*46*	*6.0*	*-44.92*

JOCKEYS

	W-R	Per cent	£1 Level Stake
Franny Norton	4-25	16.0	+6.00
Charles Bishop	2-6	33.3	+5.25
Pat Cosgrave	2-8	25.0	+6.00
Fran Berry	1-22	4.5	-19.00

COURSE RECORD

	Total W-R	Non-Hndcps 2-y-o	Non-Hndcps 3-y-o+	Hndcps 2-y-o	Hndcps 3-y-o+	Per cent	£1 Level Stake
Chelmsford (A.W)	2-13	0-0	0-2	0-0	2-11	15.4	+6.00
Yarmouth	2-20	0-2	0-0	0-0	2-18	10.0	-11.00
Ripon	1-1	0-0	0-0	0-0	1-1	100.0	+8.00
Brighton	1-3	0-0	0-0	0-0	1-3	33.3	0.00
Lingfield	1-4	0-0	0-0	0-0	1-4	25.0	+2.00
Southwell (A.W)	1-6	0-0	1-1	0-0	0-5	16.7	-3.75
Lingfield (A.W)	1-13	0-0	0-6	0-0	1-7	7.7	-2.00

WINNING HORSES

Horse	Races Run	1st	2nd	3rd	£
Colonel Frank	13	1	3	0	10082
Great Hall	12	1	1	2	15563
Princess Harley (IRE)	11	1	1	2	3752
Princess Keira (IRE)	10	1	2	3	3752
Tawaafoq	14	2	1	2	6857
*The Night King	14	3	1	2	11644
Total winning prize-money					**£51650**
Favourites	**3-4**		**75.0%**		**4.25**

JOHN QUINN

SETTRINGTON, N YORKS

	No. of Hrs	Races Run	1st	2nd	3rd	Unpl	Per cent	£1 Level Stake
2-y-o	*27*	*85*	*7*	*8*	*12*	*58*	*8.2*	*-4.42*
3-y-o	*20*	*121*	*13*	*12*	*17*	*79*	*10.7*	*-33.22*
4-y-o+	*29*	*188*	*25*	*18*	*22*	*123*	*13.3*	*+27.50*
Totals	**76**	**394**	**45**	**38**	**51**	**260**	**11.4**	**-10.14**
2017	*76*	*451*	*55*	*64*	*55*	*277*	*12.2*	*-52.30*
2016	*73*	*415*	*52*	*52*	*49*	*262*	*12.5*	*-127.41*

BY MONTH

2-y-o	W-R	Per cent	£1 Level Stake	3-y-o	W-R	Per cent	£1 Level Stake
January	0-0	0.0	0.00	January	0-2	0.0	-2.00
February	0-0	0.0	0.00	February	0-1	0.0	-1.00
March	0-1	0.0	-1.00	March	1-2	50.0	+7.00
April	1-2	50.0	+2.33	April	0-11	0.0	-11.00
May	2-5	40.0	+19.75	May	0-13	0.0	-13.00
June	1-5	20.0	+21.00	June	5-22	22.7	+10.41
July	1-6	16.7	+5.00	July	4-17	23.5	+1.38
August	0-13	0.0	-13.00	August	2-24	8.3	-11.00
September	1-22	4.5	-18.50	September	0-13	0.0	-13.00
October	1-22	4.5	-11.00	October	1-11	9.1	+4.00
November	0-8	0.0	-8.00	November	0-3	0.0	-3.00
December	0-1	0.0	-1.00	December	0-2	0.0	-2.00

4-y-o+	W-R	Per cent	£1 Level Stake	Totals	W-R	Per cent	£1 Level Stake
January	1-7	14.3	-3.00	January	1-9	11.1	-5.00
February	0-8	0.0	-8.00	February	0-9	0.0	-9.00
March	0-8	0.0	-8.00	March	1-11	9.1	-2.00
April	1-18	5.6	-3.00	April	2-31	6.5	-11.67
May	6-28	21.4	+46.25	May	8-46	17.4	+53.00
June	1-24	4.2	-15.00	June	7-51	13.7	+16.41
July	4-21	19.0	+9.50	July	9-44	20.5	+15.88
August	3-28	10.7	-3.00	August	5-65	7.7	-27.00
September	3-18	16.7	-3.75	September	4-53	7.5	-35.25
October	4-17	23.5	+12.00	October	6-50	12.0	+5.00

November	1-8	12.5	-2.50	November	1-19	5.3	-5.50
December	1-3	33.3	+6.00	December	1-6	16.7	+4.00

DISTANCE

2-y-o	W-R	Per cent	£1 Level Stake	3-y-o	W-R	Per cent	£1 Level Stake
5f-6f	5-52	9.6	+14.08	5f-6f	12-63	19.0	+18.28
7f-8f	2-32	6.3	-17.50	7f-8f	1-28	3.6	-21.50
9f-13f	0-1	0.0	-1.00	9f-13f	0-23	0.0	-23.00
14f+	0-0	0.0	0.00	14f+	0-7	0.0	-7.00

4-y-o+	W-R	Per cent	£1 Level Stake	Totals	W-R	Per cent	£1 Level Stake
5f-6f	10-73	13.7	+6.00	5f-6f	27-188	14.4	+38.36
7f-8f	8-52	15.4	+9.50	7f-8f	11-112	9.8	-29.50
9f-13f	3-43	7.0	-25.75	9f-13f	3-67	4.5	-49.75
14f+	4-20	20.0	+37.75	14f+	4-27	14.8	+30.75

TYPE OF RACE

Non-Handicaps	W-R	Per cent	£1 Level Stake	Handicaps	W-R	Per cent	£1 Level Stake
2-y-o	6-71	8.5	+6.08	2-y-o	1-14	7.1	-10.50
3-y-o	0-14	0.0	-14.00	3-y-o	13-107	12.1	-19.22
4-y-o+	1-13	7.7	-9.25	4-y-o+	24-175	13.7	+36.75

RACE CLASS

	W-R	Per cent	£1 Level Stake
Class 1	2-6	33.3	+41.00
Class 2	5-44	11.4	+12.00
Class 3	4-40	10.0	-14.00
Class 4	12-69	17.4	+36.03
Class 5	7-128	5.5	-70.92
Class 6	15-105	14.3	-11.25
Class 7	0-2	0.0	-2.00

FIRST TIME OUT

	W-R	Per cent	£1 Level Stake
2-y-o	0-27	0.0	-27.00
3-y-o	0-20	0.0	-20.00
4-y-o+	4-29	13.8	+22.50
Totals	4-76	5.3	-24.50

JOCKEYS

	W-R	Per cent	£1 Level Stake
Jason Hart	30-233	12.9	+19.49
Callum Rodriguez	2-6	33.3	+6.00
Jason Watson	2-10	20.0	-0.50
Adam McNamara	1-1	100.0	+4.50
Rossa Ryan	1-2	50.0	+11.00
David Egan	1-2	50.0	+13.00
Richard Kingscote	1-2	50.0	+1.25
Joe Fanning	1-3	33.3	+5.00
Cameron Noble	1-3	33.3	-0.13
Tony Hamilton	1-4	25.0	+2.50
Ben Robinson	1-5	20.0	+4.00
Oisin Murphy	1-6	16.7	+20.00
Silvestre De Sousa	1-7	14.3	-3.25
Kevin Stott	1-14	7.1	+3.00

COURSE RECORD

	Total W-R	Non-Hndcps 2-y-o	Non-Hndcps 3-y-o+	Hndcps 2-y-o	Hndcps 3-y-o+	Per cent	£1 Level Stake
Newcastle (A.W)	5-36	1-8	0-2	1-4	3-22	13.9	+2.00
Pontefract	4-14	1-5	0-0	0-0	3-9	28.6	+17.08
York	4-21	1-7	0-1	0-1	3-12	19.0	+36.50
Catterick	4-33	1-8	0-3	0-0	3-22	12.1	0.00
Ripon	3-15	0-2	0-0	0-1	3-12	20.0	+20.50
Musselburgh	3-19	0-1	0-0	0-2	3-16	15.8	-0.50
Windsor	2-4	0-1	0-0	0-0	2-3	50.0	+13.00
Newmkt (Jly)	2-5	0-0	0-0	0-0	2-5	40.0	+2.38
Haydock	2-12	0-2	0-1	0-0	2-9	16.7	+7.00
Chelmsford (A.W)	2-13	0-0	0-0	0-0	2-13	15.4	-4.75
Ayr	2-18	0-1	0-0	0-0	2-17	11.1	-3.75
Doncaster	2-25	0-1	0-4	0-0	2-20	8.0	+4.00
Bath	1-3	1-1	0-0	0-0	0-2	33.3	+0.75
Goodwood	1-3	0-0	0-0	0-0	1-3	33.3	+4.00
Lingfield (A.W)	1-4	0-0	0-0	0-0	1-4	25.0	+1.50
Ascot	1-7	1-1	0-1	0-0	0-5	14.3	+19.00
Epsom	1-7	0-1	0-1	0-0	1-5	14.3	-2.00
Chester	1-8	0-0	0-0	0-0	1-8	12.5	+5.00
Hamilton	1-11	0-2	0-0	0-0	1-9	9.1	-10.09
Wolvhptn (A.W)	1-21	0-0	0-5	0-1	1-15	4.8	-17.00
Redcar	1-24	0-11	1-3	0-1	0-9	4.2	-20.25
Thirsk	1-27	0-3	0-2	0-1	1-21	3.7	-20.50

WINNING HORSES

Horse	Races Run	1st	2nd	3rd	£
Acadian Angel (IRE)*	16	1	1	3	3493
Ascot Week (USA)	12	3	0	1	9704
Balance Of Power	4	1	1	1	7375
Big Storm Coming	7	2	1	0	13585
Bodacious Name (IRE)	6	2	1	1	7763
Breaking Free	3	1	0	0	3105
Captain Jameson (IRE)	10	1	1	1	9962
Carey Street (IRE)	3	1	0	0	3881
Chebsey Beau	5	1	1	2	4399
El Astronaute (IRE)	11	2	4	2	62250
Ghost	12	1	2	3	3105
Indian Pursuit (IRE)	16	3	0	1	10415
Look My Way	4	1	0	1	31125
Lord Riddiford (IRE)	8	3	0	1	37456
Master Of Irony (IRE)	2	1	0	0	5531
Military Madame (IRE)	6	1	1	1	3105
Mr Wagyu (IRE)	16	4	1	4	17337
My Ukulele (IRE)	10	1	2	2	3105
Naples Bay	9	2	2	2	6598
Reputation (IRE)	11	1	2	0	6301
Safe Voyage (IRE)	2	1	0	0	28013
Shaheen (IRE)	10	3	2	1	22016
Signora Cabello (IRE)	5	3	0	0	62381
Soie D'Leau	6	1	1	0	12938
Spirit Of Zebedee (IRE)	16	2	2	4	6598
The Cotswold Wasp	3	1	1	0	4787
Wotabreeze (IRE)	12	1	1	1	3752
Total winning prize-money					**£390080**
Favourites	**11-41**		**26.8%**		**-11.37**

DENIS QUINN

NEWMARKET, SUFFOLK

	No. of Hrs	Races Run	1st	2nd	3rd	Unpl	Per cent	£1 Level Stake
2-y-o	*5*	*19*	*1*	*2*	*1*	*15*	*5.3*	*+48.00*
3-y-o	*7*	*39*	*2*	*2*	*4*	*30*	*5.1*	*-31.50*
4-y-o+	*7*	*18*	*1*	*0*	*0*	*17*	*5.6*	*-9.00*
Totals	**19**	**76**	**4**	**4**	**5**	**62**	**5.3**	**+7.50**
2017	*20*	*74*	*5*	*3*	*10*	*56*	*6.8*	*-43.34*
2016	*17*	*89*	*6*	*9*	*2*	*72*	*6.7*	*-34.75*

JOCKEYS

	W-R	Per cent	£1 Level Stake
Adam Kirby	1-2	50.0	+3.00
Gina Mangan	1-4	25.0	+63.00
Harry Burns	1-4	25.0	+5.00
Luke Morris	1-13	7.7	-10.50

COURSE RECORD

	Total W-R	Non-Hndcps 2-y-o	Non-Hndcps 3-y-o+	Hndcps 2-y-o	Hndcps 3-y-o+	Per cent	£1 Level Stake
Wolvhptn (A.W)	2-7	1-2	0-1	0-1	1-3	28.6	+65.00
Kempton (A.W)	2-12	0-1	1-1	0-1	1-9	16.7	-0.50

WINNING HORSES

Horse	Races Run	1st	2nd	3rd	£
Arsenio Lupin	3	1	0	0	3752
Rockies Spirit	15	1	0	2	3752
Sir Hamilton (IRE)*	10	1	2	1	3881
The Galla Girl (IRE)	5	1	0	0	3105
Total winning prize-money					**£14490**
Favourites	**1-2**		**50.0%**		**0.50**

MARK RIMELL

LEAFIELD, OXON

	No. of Hrs	Races Run	1st	2nd	3rd	Unpl	Per cent	£1 Level Stake
2-y-o	*0*	*0*	*0*	*0*	*0*	*0*	*0.0*	*0.00*
3-y-o	*0*	*0*	*0*	*0*	*0*	*0*	*0.0*	*0.00*
4-y-o+	*2*	*14*	*2*	*1*	*1*	*10*	*14.3*	*-1.50*
Totals	**2**	**14**	**2**	**1**	**1**	**10**	**14.3**	**-1.50**
2017	*3*	*29*	*5*	*2*	*1*	*20*	*17.2*	*+44.75*
2016	*3*	*19*	*1*	*0*	*3*	*15*	*5.3*	*-10.00*

JOCKEYS

	W-R	Per cent	£1 Level Stake
Tom Marquand	1-4	25.0	+5.00
Rob Hornby	1-8	12.5	-4.50

COURSE RECORD

	Total W-R	Non-Hndcps 2-y-o	Non-Hndcps 3-y-o+	Hndcps 2-y-o	Hndcps 3-y-o+	Per cent	£1 Level Stake
Kempton (A.W)	2-11	0-0	0-0	0-0	2-11	18.2	+1.50

WINNING HORSES

Horse	Races Run	1st	2nd	3rd	£
Magic Mirror	11	2	1	1	7504
Total winning prize-money					**£7504**
Favourites	**1-2**		**50.0%**		**1.50**

BRIAN ROTHWELL

NORTON, N YORKS

	No. of Hrs	Races Run	1st	2nd	3rd	Unpl	Per cent	£1 Level Stake
2-y-o	*1*	*2*	*0*	*0*	*0*	*2*	*0.0*	*-2.00*
3-y-o	*0*	*0*	*0*	*0*	*0*	*0*	*0.0*	*0.00*
4-y-o+	*3*	*17*	*3*	*2*	*0*	*12*	*17.6*	*+23.00*
Totals	**4**	**19**	**3**	**2**	**0**	**14**	**15.8**	**+21.00**
2017	*7*	*30*	*0*	*1*	*2*	*27*	*0.0*	*-30.00*
2016	*10*	*38*	*0*	*3*	*2*	*33*	*0.0*	*-38.00*

JOCKEYS

	W-R	Per cent	£1 Level Stake
Connor Murtagh	2-5	40.0	+22.00
Cam Hardie	1-10	10.0	+3.00

COURSE RECORD

	Total W-R	Non-Hndcps 2-y-o	Non-Hndcps 3-y-o+	Hndcps 2-y-o	Hndcps 3-y-o+	Per cent	£1 Level Stake
Catterick	3-5	0-1	0-0	0-0	3-4	60.0	+35.00

WINNING HORSES

Horse	Races Run	1st	2nd	3rd	£
Rose Marmara	13	3	2	0	16949
Total winning prize-money					**£16949**
Favourites	**0-1**		**0.0%**		**-1.00**

MANDY ROWLAND

LOWER BLIDWORTH, NOTTS

	No. of Hrs	Races Run	1st	2nd	3rd	Unpl	Per cent	£1 Level Stake
2-y-o	*1*	*1*	*0*	*0*	*0*	*1*	*0.0*	*-1.00*
3-y-o	*0*	*0*	*0*	*0*	*0*	*0*	*0.0*	*0.00*
4-y-o+	*6*	*18*	*1*	*0*	*1*	*16*	*5.6*	*-5.00*
Totals	**7**	**19**	**1**	**0**	**1**	**17**	**5.3**	**-6.00**
2017	*8*	*36*	*0*	*0*	*1*	*35*	*0.0*	*-36.00*
2016	*9*	*33*	*3*	*1*	*0*	*29*	*9.1*	*+14.00*

JOCKEYS

	W-R	Per cent	£1 Level Stake
William Cox	1-6	16.7	+7.00

COURSE RECORD

	Total W-R	Non-Hndcps 2-y-o	Non-Hndcps 3-y-o+	Hndcps 2-y-o	Hndcps 3-y-o+	Per cent	£1 Level Stake
Southwell (A.W)	1-5	0-0	0-1	0-1	1-3	20.0	+8.00

WINNING HORSES

Horse	Races Run	1st	2nd	3rd	£
Jazz Legend (USA)	5	1	0	1	3105
Total winning prize-money					**£3105**
Favourites	**0-0**		**0.0%**		**0.00**

JOHN RYAN

NEWMARKET, SUFFOLK

	No. of Hrs	Races Run	1st	2nd	3rd	Unpl	Per cent	£1 Level Stake
2-y-o	*13*	*56*	*8*	*6*	*1*	*41*	*14.3*	*-8.25*
3-y-o	*12*	*95*	*8*	*4*	*7*	*76*	*8.4*	*-37.25*
4-y-o+	*11*	*86*	*12*	*5*	*8*	*61*	*14.0*	*+59.50*
Totals	**36**	**237**	**28**	**15**	**16**	**178**	**11.8**	**+14.00**
2017	*35*	*229*	*16*	*15*	*27*	*171*	*7.0*	*-102.70*
2016	*36*	*245*	*20*	*27*	*27*	*171*	*8.2*	*-97.80*

BY MONTH

2-y-o	W-R	Per cent	£1 Level Stake	3-y-o	W-R	Per cent	£1 Level Stake
January	0-0	0.0	0.00	January	0-0	0.0	0.00
February	0-0	0.0	0.00	February	0-0	0.0	0.00
March	0-0	0.0	0.00	March	0-1	0.0	-1.00
April	0-0	0.0	0.00	April	0-5	0.0	-5.00
May	0-2	0.0	-2.00	May	0-15	0.0	-15.00
June	0-4	0.0	-4.00	June	1-16	6.3	-8.50
July	0-6	0.0	-6.00	July	1-12	8.3	-4.50
August	0-12	0.0	-12.00	August	1-15	6.7	-8.00
September	1-10	10.0	-7.38	September	1-8	12.5	+5.00
October	2-10	20.0	+7.50	October	1-10	10.0	-0.50
November	4-8	50.0	+17.00	November	1-6	16.7	+0.50
December	1-4	25.0	-1.38	December	2-7	28.6	-0.25

4-y-o+	W-R	Per cent	£1 Level Stake	Totals	W-R	Per cent	£1 Level Stake
January	1-6	16.7	+3.00	January	1-6	16.7	+3.00
February	0-3	0.0	-3.00	February	0-3	0.0	-3.00
March	0-5	0.0	-5.00	March	0-6	0.0	-6.00
April	0-6	0.0	-6.00	April	0-11	0.0	-11.00
May	1-7	14.3	+44.00	May	1-24	4.2	+27.00
June	3-11	27.3	+8.50	June	4-31	12.9	-4.00
July	0-7	0.0	-7.00	July	1-25	4.0	-17.50
August	1-9	11.1	0.00	August	2-36	5.6	-20.00
September	2-11	18.2	+18.50	September	4-29	13.8	+16.12
October	1-12	8.3	-6.00	October	4-32	12.5	+1.00
November	1-4	25.0	+11.00	November	6-18	33.3	+11.50
December	2-5	40.0	+1.50	December	5-16	31.3	+1.25

DISTANCE

2-y-o	W-R	Per cent	£1 Level Stake	3-y-o	W-R	Per cent	£1 Level Stake
5f-6f	6-31	19.4	-2.75	5f-6f	2-27	7.4	-7.50
7f-8f	2-22	9.1	-2.50	7f-8f	0-22	0.0	-22.00
9f-13f	0-3	0.0	-3.00	9f-13f	4-41	9.8	-13.50
14f+	0-0	0.0	0.00	14f+	2-5	40.0	+5.75

4-y-o+	W-R	Per cent	£1 Level Stake	Totals	W-R	Per cent	£1 Level Stake
5f-6f	4-31	12.9	-6.00	5f-6f	12-89	13.5	-16.25
7f-8f	4-25	16.0	+27.00	7f-8f	6-69	8.7	+2.50
9f-13f	4-27	14.8	+41.50	9f-13f	8-71	11.3	+25.00
14f+	0-3	0.0	-3.00	14f+	2-8	25.0	+2.75

TYPE OF RACE

Non-Handicaps	W-R	Per cent	£1 Level Stake	Handicaps	W-R	Per cent	£1 Level Stake
2-y-o	2-37	5.4	-23.38	2-y-o	6-19	31.6	+15.13
3-y-o	0-16	0.0	-16.00	3-y-o	8-79	10.1	-21.25
4-y-o+	0-12	0.0	-12.00	4-y-o+	12-74	16.2	+71.50

RACE CLASS

	W-R	Per cent	£1 Level Stake
Class 1	0-7	0.0	-7.00
Class 2	3-24	12.5	+33.25
Class 3	5-23	21.7	+11.50
Class 4	5-41	12.2	-11.88
Class 5	6-71	8.5	-24.50
Class 6	8-70	11.4	+7.63
Class 7	1-1	100.0	+5.00

FIRST TIME OUT

	W-R	Per cent	£1 Level Stake
2-y-o	0-13	0.0	-13.00
3-y-o	0-12	0.0	-12.00
4-y-o+	0-11	0.0	-11.00
Totals	0-36	0.0	-36.00

JOCKEYS

	W-R	Per cent	£1 Level Stake
Darragh Keenan	4-32	12.5	-6.38
Adam Kirby	3-11	27.3	+2.00
Luke Morris	3-11	27.3	+9.00
Martin Harley	2-2	100.0	+4.75
Cieren Fallon	2-6	33.3	+35.00
Stevie Donohoe	2-9	22.2	+5.50
John Fahy	2-14	14.3	+0.50
Gerald Mosse	2-28	7.1	+32.00
Richard Kingscote	1-1	100.0	+6.50
Jason Watson	1-3	33.3	-0.38
Franny Norton	1-3	33.3	+0.50
Hayley Turner	1-4	25.0	+1.00
Paul Mulrennan	1-5	20.0	+4.00
Jack Osborn	1-11	9.1	-2.00
Brett Doyle	1-11	9.1	+2.00
Laura Pearson	1-11	9.1	-5.00

COURSE RECORD

	Total W-R	Non-Hndcps 2-y-o	Non-Hndcps 3-y-o+	Hndcps 2-y-o	Hndcps 3-y-o+	Per cent	£1 Level Stake
Wolvhptn (A.W)	5-27	0-2	0-5	1-2	4-18	18.5	+4.00
Chelmsford (A.W)	5-34	1-7	0-3	2-4	2-20	14.7	-3.75
Yarmouth	3-43	0-8	0-3	1-3	2-29	7.0	-24.00
Southwell (A.W)	2-3	0-0	0-0	1-1	1-2	66.7	+11.50
Catterick	2-4	0-0	0-1	0-0	2-3	50.0	+11.50
Lingfield	2-9	0-1	0-1	0-0	2-7	22.2	+5.50
Chester	1-1	0-0	0-0	0-0	1-1	100.0	+6.50
Leicester	1-2	0-0	0-0	0-0	1-2	50.0	+24.00
Brighton	1-8	1-1	0-0	0-2	0-5	12.5	-5.38
Doncaster	1-8	0-0	0-1	0-0	1-7	12.5	+7.00
Musselburgh	1-8	0-1	0-0	0-2	1-5	12.5	+1.00
Lingfield (A.W)	1-10	0-1	0-3	0-1	1-5	10.0	-6.50
Newmarket	1-16	0-4	0-4	0-0	1-8	6.3	+35.00
Kempton (A.W)	1-18	0-1	0-3	1-4	0-10	5.6	-15.38
Newmkt (Jly)	1-19	0-9	0-0	0-0	1-10	5.3	-10.00

WINNING HORSES

Horse	Races Run	1st	2nd	3rd	£
Aircraft Carrier (IRE)	4	2	0	0	37876
Battle Of Waterloo (IRE)	3	1	0	0	4787
Dark Side Jazz (IRE)	11	2	0	1	6857
Grey Britain	6	2	0	1	42953
Lady Freyja	9	3	1	2	21185
Max Liebermann (IRE)*	9	1	0	0	3752
Merhoob (IRE)	16	3	2	1	25036
Midnight Wilde	7	1	1	1	14940
Plucky Dip	15	2	0	1	5757
Queen Adelaide	12	1	1	2	3493
Red Armour	4	1	2	0	3105
Roland Rocks (IRE)	14	1	0	2	3105
Sandridge Lad (IRE)	11	2	3	0	8863
Shining Armor	8	4	1	0	18501
Spenny's Lass	14	1	2	0	3235
The Gay Cavalier	3	1	1	0	3105
Total winning prize-money					**£206550**
Favourites	**5-14**		**35.7%**		**-0.34**

KEVIN RYAN

HAMBLETON, N YORKS

	No. of Hrs	Races Run	1st	2nd	3rd	Unpl	Per cent	£1 Level Stake
2-y-o	*48*	*172*	*25*	*22*	*20*	*105*	*14.5*	*-29.26*
3-y-o	*43*	*205*	*31*	*30*	*29*	*115*	*15.1*	*-24.92*
4-y-o+	*35*	*243*	*20*	*29*	*30*	*163*	*8.2*	*-43.00*
Totals	**126**	**620**	**76**	**81**	**79**	**383**	**12.3**	**-97.18**
2017	*124*	*661*	*76*	*94*	*73*	*418*	*11.5*	*-216.46*
2016	*127*	*733*	*94*	*91*	*93*	*455*	*12.8*	*-102.24*

BY MONTH

2-y-o	W-R	Per cent	£1 Level Stake	3-y-o	W-R	Per cent	£1 Level Stake
January	0-0	0.0	0.00	January	2-6	33.3	+3.00
February	0-0	0.0	0.00	February	2-13	15.4	-7.50
March	0-0	0.0	0.00	March	3-13	23.1	-1.63
April	1-6	16.7	+7.00	April	8-33	24.2	+13.50
May	5-22	22.7	+0.13	May	4-27	14.8	-3.54
June	1-22	4.5	-19.80	June	1-27	3.7	-16.00
July	3-30	10.0	-22.58	July	2-21	9.5	-14.25
August	6-37	16.2	-11.25	August	3-21	14.3	-2.50
September	9-38	23.7	+34.25	September	2-24	8.3	-12.50
October	0-10	0.0	-10.00	October	2-8	25.0	+1.50
November	0-6	0.0	-6.00	November	1-9	11.1	+8.00
December	0-1	0.0	-1.00	December	1-3	33.3	+7.00

4-y-o+	W-R	Per cent	£1 Level Stake	Totals	W-R	Per cent	£1 Level Stake
January	1-13	7.7	-11.00	January	3-19	15.8	-8.00
February	3-16	18.8	+61.50	February	5-29	17.2	+54.00
March	4-19	21.1	+15.50	March	7-32	21.9	+13.87
April	2-21	9.5	-11.00	April	11-60	18.3	+9.50
May	2-29	6.9	-19.00	May	11-78	14.1	-22.41
June	1-27	3.7	-19.00	June	3-76	3.9	-54.80
July	0-30	0.0	-30.00	July	5-81	6.2	-66.83
August	1-27	3.7	-20.00	August	10-85	11.8	-33.75
September	1-26	3.8	-22.50	September	12-88	13.6	-0.75
October	2-17	11.8	+0.50	October	4-35	11.4	-8.00
November	3-14	21.4	+16.00	November	4-29	13.8	+24.00
December	0-4	0.0	-4.00	December	1-8	12.5	+3.00

DISTANCE

2-y-o	W-R	Per cent	£1 Level Stake	3-y-o	W-R	Per cent	£1 Level Stake
5f-6f	25-140	17.9	+2.74	5f-6f	11-72	15.3	-18.38
7f-8f	0-32	0.0	-32.00	7f-8f	18-98	18.4	+18.13
9f-13f	0-0	0.0	0.00	9f-13f	2-34	5.9	-23.67
14f+	0-0	0.0	0.00	14f+	0-1	0.0	-1.00

4-y-o+	W-R	Per cent	£1 Level Stake	Totals	W-R	Per cent	£1 Level Stake
5f-6f	5-100	5.0	-60.50	5f-6f	41-312	13.1	-76.14
7f-8f	9-69	13.0	+47.50	7f-8f	27-199	13.6	+33.63
9f-13f	6-73	8.2	-29.00	9f-13f	8-107	7.5	-52.67
14f+	0-1	0.0	-1.00	14f+	0-2	0.0	-2.00

TYPE OF RACE

Non-Handicaps	W-R	Per cent	£1 Level Stake	Handicaps	W-R	Per cent	£1 Level Stake
2-y-o	19-146	13.0	-35.26	2-y-o	6-26	23.1	+6.00
3-y-o	13-82	15.9	-13.92	3-y-o	18-123	14.6	-11.00
4-y-o+	6-23	26.1	+24.00	4-y-o+	14-220	6.4	-67.00

RACE CLASS / FIRST TIME OUT

RACE CLASS	W-R	Per cent	£1 Level Stake	FIRST TIME OUT	W-R	Per cent	£1 Level Stake
Class 1	4-32	12.5	+7.50	2-y-o	7-48	14.6	-11.00
Class 2	9-107	8.4	-24.13	3-y-o	6-43	14.0	-20.63

Class 3	11-55	20.0	+15.25	4-y-o+	4-35	11.4	-16.00
Class 4	14-135	10.4	-61.92				
Class 5	26-200	13.0	-83.88	Totals	17-126	13.5	-47.63
Class 6	12-91	13.2	+50.00				
Class 7	0-0	0.0	0.00				

JOCKEYS

	W-R	Per cent	£1 Level Stake
Kevin Stott	28-175	16.0	-35.75
Tom Eaves	13-155	8.4	-84.17
Shane Gray	12-92	13.0	-30.42
Andrew Mullen	4-32	12.5	+22.50
Nicola Currie	3-14	21.4	+4.50
Thomas Greatrex	2-7	28.6	+8.00
Miss Harriett Lees	2-12	16.7	+60.00
Josephine Gordon	2-13	15.4	+6.00
Jamie Spencer	2-16	12.5	+0.50
Cameron Noble	2-17	11.8	-10.00
Frankie Dettori	1-1	100.0	+5.00
Sebastian Woods	1-1	100.0	+16.00
Connor Murtagh	1-5	20.0	+3.00
Ben Robinson	1-6	16.7	-3.00
Daniel Tudhope	1-6	16.7	-4.33
Tom Queally	1-10	10.0	+3.00

COURSE RECORD

	Total W-R	Non-Hndcps 2-y-o	3-y-o+	Hndcps 2-y-o	3-y-o+	Per cent	£1 Level Stake
Wolvhptn (A.W)	9-44	0-7	1-7	0-2	8-28	20.5	+73.25
Hamilton	7-30	2-10	1-3	3-3	1-14	23.3	-0.63
Redcar	6-29	1-10	3-8	0-1	2-10	20.7	-0.63
Pontefract	5-19	1-4	1-3	0-1	3-11	26.3	+13.33
Beverley	5-36	3-16	1-4	0-0	1-16	13.9	-20.33
Musselburgh	4-16	1-5	1-1	0-1	2-9	25.0	+3.13
Southwell (A.W)	4-20	0-1	2-8	0-0	2-11	20.0	+16.50
Doncaster	4-28	1-6	1-4	0-2	2-16	14.3	+41.00
York	4-62	2-18	0-3	1-4	1-37	6.5	-36.75
Lingfield (A.W)	3-11	0-0	2-6	0-0	1-5	27.3	+9.00
Carlisle	3-24	2-7	0-1	1-1	0-15	12.5	-13.05
Haydock	3-30	1-10	0-5	0-2	2-13	10.0	-9.75
Thirsk	3-34	0-9	2-7	0-1	1-17	8.8	-22.25
Chester	2-11	1-1	0-3	1-1	0-6	18.2	+2.00
Newmarket	2-11	0-2	1-3	0-0	1-6	18.2	-1.00
Nottingham	2-17	1-2	0-4	0-0	1-11	11.8	-8.25
Chelmsford (A.W)	2-28	0-1	1-8	0-0	1-19	7.1	-20.50
Ayr	2-32	1-12	1-3	0-2	0-15	6.3	-17.75
Newcastle (A.W)	2-50	0-6	1-11	0-2	1-31	4.0	-42.50
Windsor	1-3	1-2	0-1	0-0	0-0	33.3	+10.00
Wetherby	1-4	0-0	0-1	0-0	1-3	25.0	+1.50
Leicester	1-5	1-1	0-1	0-0	0-3	20.0	-0.50
Kempton (A.W)	1-10	0-1	0-2	0-0	1-7	10.0	-7.00

WINNING HORSES

Horse	Races Run	1st	2nd	3rd	£
Al Khan (IRE)	9	2	0	2	6514
Aloysius Lilius (IRE)	8	1	2	0	3752
Armandihan (IRE)	11	1	3	0	8093
Ayutthaya (IRE)	6	1	2	0	4852
Bielsa (IRE)	1	1	0	0	4528
Brando	5	1	3	0	34026
Bungee Jump (IRE)*	8	3	2	1	6857
Celebrity Dancer (IRE)	5	2	0	1	9315
Commander Han (FR)	8	1	2	1	5434
Company Asset (IRE)	5	1	0	0	23680
Conga	1	1	0	0	4787
Dalawyna (FR)	6	1	2	1	4787
Dame Gladys	4	1	1	0	3881
East	1	1	0	0	5434
Elnadim Star (IRE)	4	2	1	1	36377
Emaraaty Ana	4	2	0	1	132385
Everything For You (IRE)	7	1	4	0	8715
Foxy Lady	10	1	0	4	3105
Glass Slippers	5	2	0	1	16590
Gold Stone	6	1	1	0	3752
Hello Youmzain (FR)	2	1	1	0	4205
How Bizarre	7	2	3	1	9704
Jungle Room (USA)	5	1	0	1	3752
Kings Full (IRE)	2	1	0	1	5175
Knighted (IRE)	8	4	0	0	27047
Laughton	12	1	2	1	3105
Lualiwa	10	1	1	1	12450
Magical Spirit (IRE)	3	1	0	1	4140
Major Jumbo	9	2	2	3	75188
Mont Kinabalu (IRE)	7	2	0	1	17174
Morning Wonder (IRE)	5	1	0	1	12938
Mount Tahan (IRE)	10	2	1	0	19218
Naadirr (IRE)	5	1	0	0	7763
Nearest Green	4	2	0	2	10194
New Show (IRE)*	2	1	0	0	4852
Princes Des Sables	8	4	3	1	33852
Queen Jo Jo	4	1	1	1	4140
Queen's Sargent (FR)	7	1	2	0	5175
Savalas (IRE)	8	3	1	1	33909
Savannah Moon (IRE)	9	1	1	0	4528
Scrutiny	16	2	1	4	6100
Secret Venture	3	1	0	1	5434
Tagur (IRE)	13	4	1	2	13010
The Great Heir (FR)	7	3	1	0	161707
Three Card Trick	5	1	2	0	9704
Triple Distilled	5	1	2	0	4205
Vj Day (USA)*	5	1	1	1	3752
Yousini	4	2	1	0	11903
Zarjaz (USA)	5	1	1	1	3752
Total winning prize-money					**£844940**
Favourites	**21-62**		**33.9%**		**-1.66**

MATTHEW SALAMAN

TONYREFAIL, RHONDDA CYNON TAFF

	No. of Hrs	Races Run	1st	2nd	3rd	Unpl	Per cent	£1 Level Stake
2-y-o	*0*	*0*	*0*	*0*	*0*	*0*	*0.0*	*0.00*
3-y-o	*0*	*0*	*0*	*0*	*0*	*0*	*0.0*	*0.00*

4-y-o+	*6*	*43*	*4*	*3*	*2*	*34*	*9.3*	*+37.00*
Totals	**6**	**43**	**4**	**3**	**2**	**34**	**9.3**	**+37.00**
2017	*10*	*46*	*3*	*1*	*2*	*40*	*6.5*	*-9.50*
2016	*9*	*32*	*1*	*0*	*1*	*30*	*3.1*	*-22.00*

JOCKEYS

	W-R	Per cent	£1 Level Stake
Franny Norton	2-8	25.0	+12.00
Tim Clark	1-2	50.0	+7.00
Mark Crehan	1-8	12.5	+43.00

COURSE RECORD

	Total W-R	Non Hndcps 2-y-o	Non Hndcps 3-y-o+	Hndcps 2-y-o	Hndcps 3-y-o+	Per cent	£1 Level Stake
Chelmsford (A.W)	1-3	0-0	0-0	0-0	1-3	33.3	+4.00
Bath	1-7	0-0	0-0	0-0	1-7	14.3	+2.00
Chepstow	1-7	0-0	0-0	0-0	1-7	14.3	+44.00
Lingfield (A.W)	1-9	0-0	0-0	0-0	1-9	11.1	+4.00

WINNING HORSES

Horse	Races Run	1st	2nd	3rd	£
Locommotion	14	1	2	1	3429
Major Assault	9	1	0	0	2264
Molly Jones	12	2	1	1	6210
Total winning prize-money					**£11903**
Favourites	**0-3**		**0.0%**		**-3.00**

JOSE SANTOS

UPPER LAMBOURN, BERKS

	No. of Hrs	Races Run	1st	2nd	3rd	Unpl	Per cent	£1 Level Stake
2-y-o	*1*	*2*	*0*	*0*	*0*	*2*	*0.0*	*-2.00*
3-y-o	*8*	*46*	*8*	*4*	*3*	*31*	*17.4*	*+3.50*
4-y-o+	*4*	*24*	*3*	*2*	*2*	*17*	*12.5*	*+1.50*
Totals	**13**	**72**	**11**	**6**	**5**	**50**	**15.3**	**+3.00**
2017	*14*	*45*	*5*	*3*	*5*	*32*	*11.1*	*-18.00*
2016	*12*	*55*	*6*	*6*	*2*	*41*	*10.9*	*+253.00*

BY MONTH

2-y-o	W-R	Per cent	£1 Level Stake	3-y-o	W-R	Per cent	£1 Level Stake
January	0-0	0.0	0.00	January	0-2	0.0	-2.00
February	0-0	0.0	0.00	February	0-1	0.0	-1.00
March	0-0	0.0	0.00	March	0-2	0.0	-2.00
April	0-0	0.0	0.00	April	0-4	0.0	-4.00
May	0-0	0.0	0.00	May	1-5	20.0	-1.00
June	0-0	0.0	0.00	June	0-2	0.0	-2.00
July	0-0	0.0	0.00	July	1-4	25.0	+1.50
August	0-0	0.0	0.00	August	0-5	0.0	-5.00
September	0-0	0.0	0.00	September	1-6	16.7	+1.00
October	0-0	0.0	0.00	October	1-8	12.5	-2.50
November	0-1	0.0	-1.00	November	2-4	50.0	+13.00
December	0-1	0.0	-1.00	December	2-3	66.7	+7.50

4-y-o+	W-R	Per cent	£1 Level Stake	Totals	W-R	Per cent	£1 Level Stake
January	0-0	0.0	0.00	January	0-2	0.0	-2.00
February	0-0	0.0	0.00	February	0-1	0.0	-1.00
March	0-3	0.0	-3.00	March	0-5	0.0	-5.00
April	1-4	25.0	+9.00	April	1-8	12.5	+5.00
May	1-5	20.0	0.00	May	2-10	20.0	-1.00
June	0-2	0.0	-2.00	June	0-4	0.0	-4.00
July	0-3	0.0	-3.00	July	1-7	14.3	-1.50
August	0-1	0.0	-1.00	August	0-6	0.0	-6.00
September	1-4	25.0	+3.50	September	2-10	20.0	+4.50
October	0-2	0.0	-2.00	October	1-10	10.0	-4.50
November	0-0	0.0	0.00	November	2-5	40.0	+13.00
December	0-0	0.0	0.00	December	2-4	50.0	+7.50

DISTANCE

2-y-o	W-R	Per cent	£1 Level Stake	3-y-o	W-R	Per cent	£1 Level Stake
5f-6f	0-0	0.0	0.00	5f-6f	2-12	16.7	+5.00
7f-8f	0-2	0.0	-2.00	7f-8f	6-30	20.0	+2.50
9f-13f	0-0	0.0	0.00	9f-13f	0-4	0.0	-4.00
14f+	0-0	0.0	0.00	14f+	0-0	0.0	0.00

4-y-o+	W-R	Per cent	£1 Level Stake	Totals	W-R	Per cent	£1 Level Stake
5f-6f	0-4	0.0	-4.00	5f-6f	2-16	12.5	+1.00
7f-8f	1-4	25.0	+9.00	7f-8f	7-36	19.4	+9.50
9f-13f	2-16	12.5	-3.50	9f-13f	2-20	10.0	-7.50
14f+	0-0	0.0	0.00	14f+	0-0	0.0	0.00

TYPE OF RACE

Non-Handicaps	W-R	Per cent	£1 Level Stake	Handicaps	W-R	Per cent	£1 Level Stake
2-y-o	0-2	0.0	-2.00	2-y-o	0-0	0.0	0.00
3-y-o	2-18	11.1	-2.50	3-y-o	6-28	21.4	+6.00
4-y-o+	0-3	0.0	-3.00	4-y-o+	3-21	14.3	+4.50

RACE CLASS

	W-R	Per cent	£1 Level Stake
Class 1	0-1	0.0	-1.00
Class 2	0-1	0.0	-1.00
Class 3	0-1	0.0	-1.00
Class 4	0-10	0.0	-10.00
Class 5	6-34	17.6	+12.50
Class 6	5-25	20.0	+3.50
Class 7	0-0	0.0	0.00

FIRST TIME OUT

	W-R	Per cent	£1 Level Stake
2-y-o	0-1	0.0	-1.00
3-y-o	1-8	12.5	-2.50
4-y-o+	0-4	0.0	-4.00
Totals	1-13	7.7	-7.50

JOCKEYS

	W-R	Per cent	£1 Level Stake
Raul Da Silva	10-48	20.8	+22.00
Richard Kingscote	1-1	100.0	+4.00

COURSE RECORD

	Total W-R	Non-Hndcps 2-y-o	Non-Hndcps 3-y-o+	Hndcps 2-y-o	Hndcps 3-y-o+	Per cent	£1 Level Stake
Wolvhptn (A.W)	3-11	0-0	0-1	0-0	3-10	27.3	+14.50

Leicester	2-5	0-0	1-4	0-0	1-1	40.0	+8.00
Chelmsford (A.W)	2-10	0-0	0-3	0-0	2-7	20.0	+1.00
Southwell (A.W)	1-4	0-1	0-2	0-0	1-1	25.0	-0.50
Bath	1-5	0-0	0-1	0-0	1-4	20.0	0.00
Lingfield (A.W)	1-7	0-0	0-1	0-0	1-6	14.3	0.00
Kempton (A.W)	1-12	0-1	1-5	0-0	0-6	8.3	-2.00

WINNING HORSES

Horse	Races Run	1st	2nd	3rd	£
*Caramuru (IRE)	10	1	1	0	3752
Formiga (IRE)	12	1	1	0	3429
Foxangel	6	1	0	1	3493
*Jabarout (USA)	6	3	0	1	9315
Lady Valdean	9	2	1	1	7892
Poeta Brasileiro (IRE)	4	2	0	1	7633
Precious Silk (IRE)	7	1	1	0	5434
Total winning prize-money					**£40948**
Favourites	**2-4**		**50.0%**		**3.50**

MALCOLM SAUNDERS

GREEN ORE, SOMERSET

	No. of Hrs	Races Run	1st	2nd	3rd	Unpl	Per cent	£1 Level Stake
2-y-o	*1*	*4*	*0*	*0*	*1*	*3*	*0.0*	*-4.00*
3-y-o	*0*	*0*	*0*	*0*	*0*	*0*	*0.0*	*0.00*
4-y-o+	*11*	*92*	*10*	*10*	*9*	*63*	*10.9*	*-25.25*
Totals	**12**	**96**	**10**	**10**	**10**	**66**	**10.4**	**-29.25**
2017	*19*	*124*	*19*	*11*	*18*	*76*	*15.3*	*-16.62*
2016	*16*	*112*	*20*	*19*	*12*	*61*	*17.9*	*+25.13*

BY MONTH

2-y-o	W-R	Per cent	£1 Level Stake	3-y-o	W-R	Per cent	£1 Level Stake
January	0-0	0.0	0.00	January	0-0	0.0	0.00
February	0-0	0.0	0.00	February	0-0	0.0	0.00
March	0-0	0.0	0.00	March	0-0	0.0	0.00
April	0-0	0.0	0.00	April	0-0	0.0	0.00
May	0-0	0.0	0.00	May	0-0	0.0	0.00
June	0-0	0.0	0.00	June	0-0	0.0	0.00
July	0-1	0.0	-1.00	July	0-0	0.0	0.00
August	0-2	0.0	-2.00	August	0-0	0.0	0.00
September	0-1	0.0	-1.00	September	0-0	0.0	0.00
October	0-0	0.0	0.00	October	0-0	0.0	0.00
November	0-0	0.0	0.00	November	0-0	0.0	0.00
December	0-0	0.0	0.00	December	0-0	0.0	0.00

4-y-o+	W-R	Per cent	£1 Level Stake	Totals	W-R	Per cent	£1 Level Stake
January	1-2	50.0	+6.00	January	1-2	50.0	+6.00
February	1-2	50.0	+3.50	February	1-2	50.0	+3.50
March	0-0	0.0	0.00	March	0-0	0.0	0.00
April	0-4	0.0	-4.00	April	0-4	0.0	4.00
May	3-15	20.0	+12.38	May	3-15	20.0	+12.38
June	0-14	0.0	-14.00	June	0-14	0.0	-14.00
July	2-11	18.2	-4.25	July	2-12	16.7	-5.25
August	2-19	10.5	-2.50	August	2-21	9.5	-4.50
September	0-10	0.0	-10.00	September	0-11	0.0	-11.00
October	0-8	0.0	-8.00	October	0-8	0.0	-8.00
November	1-6	16.7	-3.38	November	1-6	16.7	-3.38
December	0-1	0.0	-1.00	December	0-1	0.0	-1.00

DISTANCE

2-y-o	W-R	Per cent	£1 Level Stake	3-y-o	W-R	Per cent	£1 Level Stake
5f-6f	0-3	0.0	-3.00	5f-6f	0-0	0.0	0.00
7f-8f	0-1	0.0	-1.00	7f-8f	0-0	0.0	0.00
9f-13f	0-0	0.0	0.00	9f-13f	0-0	0.0	0.00
14f+	0-0	0.0	0.00	14f+	0-0	0.0	0.00

4-y-o+	W-R	Per cent	£1 Level Stake	Totals	W-R	Per cent	£1 Level Stake
5f-6f	8-64	12.5	-10.75	5f-6f	8-67	11.9	-13.75
7f-8f	0-22	0.0	-22.00	7f-8f	0-23	0.0	-23.00
9f-13f	2-6	33.3	+7.50	9f-13f	2-6	33.3	+7.50
14f+	0-0	0.0	0.00	14f+	0-0	0.0	0.00

TYPE OF RACE

Non-Handicaps	W-R	Per cent	£1 Level Stake	Handicaps	W-R	Per cent	£1 Level Stake
2-y-o	0-4	0.0	-4.00	2-y-o	0-0	0.0	0.00
3-y-o	0-0	0.0	0.00	3-y-o	0-0	0.0	0.00
4-y-o+	0-1	0.0	-1.00	4-y-o+	10-91	11.0	-24.25

RACE CLASS

	W-R	Per cent	£1 Level Stake
Class 1	0-0	0.0	0.00
Class 2	0-1	0.0	-1.00
Class 3	2-9	22.2	+4.50
Class 4	2-29	6.9	+3.00
Class 5	4-27	14.8	-12.88
Class 6	2-29	6.9	-21.88
Class 7	0-1	0.0	-1.00

FIRST TIME OUT

	W-R	Per cent	£1 Level Stake
2-y-o	0-1	0.0	-1.00
3-y-o	0-0	0.0	0.00
4-y-o+	3-11	27.3	+22.00
Totals	3-12	25.0	+21.00

JOCKEYS

	W-R	Per cent	£1 Level Stake
Franny Norton	2-6	33.3	+0.75
J F Egan	2-10	20.0	+15.00
Charlie Bennett	2-18	11.1	-9.88
Liam Keniry	2-19	10.5	-8.63
Georgia Cox	1-5	20.0	+0.50
Pat Cosgrave	1-5	20.0	+6.00

COURSE RECORD

	Total W-R	Non-Hndcps 2-y-o	Non-Hndcps 3-y-o+	Hndcps 2-y-o	Hndcps 3-y-o+	Per cent	£1 Level Stake
Bath	3-20	0-1	0-0	0-0	3-19	15.0	+7.75
Lingfield (A.W)	2-6	0-0	0-0	0-0	2-6	33.3	+7.50
Brighton	2-7	0-0	0-0	0-0	2-7	28.6	-0.63
Southwell (A.W)	1-2	0-0	0-0	0-0	1-2	50.0	+3.50
Kempton (A.W)	1-9	0-0	0-0	0-0	1-9	11.1	-6.38
Wolvhptn (A.W)	1-16	0-1	0-0	0-0	1-15	6.3	-5.00

WINNING HORSES

Horse	Races Run	1st	2nd	3rd	£
Amberine	9	1	0	2	3105
Easy Tiger	11	2	3	2	14492
Nutini (IRE)	11	2	2	0	6857
Secretfact	11	2	2	0	9283
Showmethewayavrilo	10	1	1	2	5434
Silverrica (IRE)	4	1	0	0	5531
Titus Secret	4	1	0	0	3752
Total winning prize-money					**£48454**
Favourites	**2-5**		**40.0%**		**-0.13**

DIANNE SAYER

HACKTHORPE, CUMBRIA

	No. of Hrs	Races Run	1st	2nd	3rd	Unpl	Per cent	£1 Level Stake
2-y-o	*0*	*0*	*0*	*0*	*0*	*0*	*0.0*	*0.00*
3-y-o	*0*	*0*	*0*	*0*	*0*	*0*	*0.0*	*0.00*
4-y-o+	*9*	*40*	*3*	*3*	*3*	*31*	*7.5*	*-22.00*
Totals	**9**	**40**	**3**	**3**	**3**	**31**	**7.5**	**-22.00**
2017	*12*	*39*	*2*	*3*	*6*	*28*	*5.1*	*-11.50*
2016	*15*	*39*	*3*	*5*	*4*	*27*	*7.7*	*-14.50*

JOCKEYS

	W-R	Per cent	£1 Level Stake
James Sullivan	2-8	25.0	+6.50
Graham Lee	1-5	20.0	-1.50

COURSE RECORD

	Total W-R	Non-Hndcps 2-y-o	Non-Hndcps 3-y-o+	Hndcps 2-y-o	Hndcps 3-y-o+	Per cent	£1 Level Stake
Ayr	3-10	0-0	0-0	0-0	3-10	30.0	+8.00

WINNING HORSES

Horse	Races Run	1st	2nd	3rd	£
Redarna	7	3	0	0	10156
Total winning prize-money					**£10156**
Favourites	**4-5**		**80.0%**		**7.88**

KATIE SCOTT

GALASHEILS, SCOTTISH BORDERS

	No. of Hrs	Races Run	1st	2nd	3rd	Unpl	Per cent	£1 Level Stake
2-y-o	*0*	*0*	*0*	*0*	*0*	*0*	*0.0*	*0.00*
3-y-o	*0*	*0*	*0*	*0*	*0*	*0*	*0.0*	*0.00*
4-y-o+	*1*	*15*	*2*	*4*	*1*	*8*	*13.3*	*-5.50*
Totals	**1**	**15**	**2**	**4**	**1**	**8**	**13.3**	**-5.50**
2017	*1*	*2*	*0*	*0*	*0*	*2*	*0.0*	*-2.00*
2016	*0*							

JOCKEYS

	W-R	Per cent	£1 Level Stake
Phil Dennis	2-4	50.0	+5.50

COURSE RECORD

	Total W-R	Non-Hndcps 2-y-o	Non-Hndcps 3-y-o+	Hndcps 2-y-o	Hndcps 3-y-o+	Per cent	£1 Level Stake
Catterick	1-1	0-0	0-0	0-0	1-1	100.0	+3.00
Hamilton	1-3	0-0	0-0	0-0	1-3	33.3	+2.50

WINNING HORSES

Horse	Races Run	1st	2nd	3rd	£
Rockley Point	15	2	4	1	6987
Total winning prize-money					**£6987**
Favourites	**1-1**		**100.0%**		**3.00**

JEREMY SCOTT

BROMPTON REGIS, SOMERSET

	No. of Hrs	Races Run	1st	2nd	3rd	Unpl	Per cent	£1 Level Stake
2-y-o	*0*	*0*	*0*	*0*	*0*	*0*	*0.0*	*0.00*
3-y-o	*1*	*2*	*0*	*0*	*0*	*2*	*0.0*	*-2.00*
4-y-o+	*1*	*6*	*2*	*0*	*1*	*3*	*33.3*	*+2.88*
Totals	**2**	**8**	**2**	**0**	**1**	**5**	**25.0**	**+0.88**
2017	*3*	*9*	*1*	*0*	*0*	*8*	*11.1*	*+8.00*
2016	*1*	*4*	*2*	*0*	*0*	*2*	*50.0*	*+4.50*

JOCKEYS

	W-R	Per cent	£1 Level Stake
Jason Watson	2-5	40.0	+3.88

COURSE RECORD

	Total W-R	Non-Hndcps 2-y-o	Non-Hndcps 3-y-o+	Hndcps 2-y-o	Hndcps 3-y-o+	Per cent	£1 Level Stake
Lingfield (A.W)	2-6	0-0	0-0	0-0	2-6	33.3	+2.88

WINNING HORSES

Horse	Races Run	1st	2nd	3rd	£
Miss Minuty	6	2	0	1	7504
Total winning prize-money					**£7504**
Favourites	**14-30**		**46.7%**		**11.60**

GEORGE SCOTT

NEWMARKET, SUFFOLK

	No. of Hrs	Races Run	1st	2nd	3rd	Unpl	Per cent	£1 Level Stake
2-y-o	*26*	*79*	*5*	*10*	*6*	*58*	*6.3*	*-57.39*
3-y-o	*20*	*81*	*11*	*6*	*6*	*58*	*13.6*	*-36.63*
4-y-o+	*8*	*33*	*3*	*4*	*4*	*22*	*9.1*	*-21.60*
Totals	**54**	**193**	**19**	**20**	**16**	**138**	**9.8**	**-115.62**

2017	*30*	*116*	*22*	*10*	*9*	*75*	*19.0*	*+9.97*
2016	*25*	*98*	*12*	*9*	*10*	*67*	*12.2*	*-11.38*

BY MONTH

2-y-o	W-R	Per cent	£1 Level Stake	3-y-o	W-R	Per cent	£1 Level Stake
January	0-0	0.0	0.00	January	0-3	0.0	-3.00
February	0-0	0.0	0.00	February	0-2	0.0	-2.00
March	0-0	0.0	0.00	March	0-6	0.0	-6.00
April	0-1	0.0	-1.00	April	1-10	10.0	-6.00
May	1-8	12.5	-5.75	May	1-19	5.3	-13.00
June	0-11	0.0	-11.00	June	1-14	7.1	-9.50
July	2-9	22.2	-5.64	July	5-9	55.6	+6.75
August	0-8	0.0	-8.00	August	2-6	33.3	+4.88
September	1-12	8.3	-5.00	September	1-5	20.0	-1.75
October	1-20	5.0	-11.00	October	0-4	0.0	-4.00
November	0-8	0.0	-8.00	November	0-3	0.0	-3.00
December	0-2	0.0	-2.00	December	0-0	0.0	0.00

4-y-o+	W-R	Per cent	£1 Level Stake	Totals	W-R	Per cent	£1 Level Stake
January	2-4	50.0	+1.40	January	2-7	28.6	-1.60
February	0-0	0.0	0.00	February	0-2	0.0	-2.00
March	0-4	0.0	-4.00	March	0-10	0.0	-10.00
April	0-5	0.0	-5.00	April	1-16	6.3	-12.00
May	1-5	20.0	+1.00	May	3-32	9.4	-17.75
June	0-3	0.0	-3.00	June	1-28	3.6	-23.50
July	0-1	0.0	-1.00	July	7-19	36.8	+0.11
August	0-2	0.0	-2.00	August	2-16	12.5	-5.12
September	0-6	0.0	-6.00	September	2-23	8.7	-12.75
October	0-2	0.0	-2.00	October	1-26	3.8	-17.00
November	0-0	0.0	0.00	November	0-11	0.0	-3.00
December	0-1	0.0	-1.00	December	0-3	0.0	-1.00

DISTANCE

2-y-o	W-R	Per cent	£1 Level Stake	3-y-o	W-R	Per cent	£1 Level Stake
5f-6f	5-53	9.4	-31.39	5f-6f	4-16	25.0	+1.75
7f-8f	0-26	0.0	-26.00	7f-8f	3-52	5.8	-38.25
9f-13f	0-0	0.0	0.00	9f-13f	4-13	30.8	-0.13
14f+	0-0	0.0	0.00	14f+	0-0	0.0	0.00

4-y-o+	W-R	Per cent	£1 Level Stake	Totals	W-R	Per cent	£1 Level Stake
5f-6f	2-13	15.4	-7.60	5f-6f	11-82	13.4	-37.24
7f-8f	1-13	7.7	-7.00	7f-8f	4-91	4.4	-71.25
9f-13f	0-7	0.0	-7.00	9f-13f	4-20	20.0	-7.13
14f+	0-0	0.0	0.00	14f+	0-0	0.0	0.00

TYPE OF RACE

Non-Handicaps	W-R	Per cent	£1 Level Stake	Handicaps	W-R	Per cent	£1 Level Stake
2-y-o	5-67	7.5	-45.39	2-y-o	0-12	0.0	-12.00
3-y-o	2-34	5.9	-26.75	3-y-o	9-47	19.1	-9.88
4-y-o+	0-6	0.0	-6.00	4-y-o+	3-27	11.1	-15.60

RACE CLASS

	W-R	Per cent	£1 Level Stake
Class 1	1-9	11.1	-5.00
Class 2	3-19	15.8	+2.00
Class 3	0-10	0.0	-10.00
Class 4	3-42	7.1	-29.00
Class 5	8-92	8.7	-65.49
Class 6	4-21	19.0	-8.13
Class 7	0-0	0.0	0.00

FIRST TIME OUT

	W-R	Per cent	£1 Level Stake
2-y-o	0-26	0.0	-26.00
3-y-o	1-20	5.0	-16.00
4-y-o+	1-8	12.5	-6.60
Totals	2-54	3.7	-48.60

JOCKEYS

	W-R	Per cent	£1 Level Stake
Silvestre De Sousa	5-31	16.1	-14.89
Jason Watson	3-8	37.5	+2.38
Joshua Bryan	2-2	100.0	+3.50
Fran Berry	2-14	14.3	-8.60
James Doyle	1-1	100.0	+7.00
Gabriele Malune	1-3	33.3	-0.25
Frankie Dettori	1-3	33.3	+1.00
Paul Hanagan	1-4	25.0	+3.00
Oisin Murphy	1-5	20.0	+4.00
Jessica Cooley	1-8	12.5	-4.75
Edward Greatrex	1-10	10.0	-4.00

COURSE RECORD

	Total W-R	Non-Hndcps 2-y-o	Non-Hndcps 3-y-o+	Hndcps 2-y-o	Hndcps 3-y-o+	Per cent	£1 Level Stake
Brighton	3-3	0-0	0-0	0-0	3-3	100.0	+6.38
Newcastle (A.W)	2-5	1-1	1-3	0-0	0-1	40.0	+7.25
Windsor	2-8	1-3	0-0	0-0	1-5	25.0	-2.00
Chester	1-1	0-0	0-0	0-0	1-1	100.0	+5.00
Lingfield	1-2	1-2	0-0	0-0	0-0	50.0	-0.64
Ffos Las	1-4	0-1	0-0	0-1	1-2	25.0	-2.50
Pontefract	1-5	1-3	0-1	0-0	0-1	20.0	+2.00
York	1-5	0-3	0-0	0-1	1-1	20.0	+1.00
Newmkt (Jly)	1-7	0-2	0-0	0-0	1-5	14.3	-3.25
Newbury	1-9	0-4	1-3	0-0	0-2	11.1	-5.00
Southwell (A.W)	1-9	0-0	0-3	0-1	1-5	11.1	-7.60
Nottingham	1-11	0-5	0-2	0-1	1-3	9.1	-6.50
Newmarket	1-12	1-4	0-4	0-0	0-4	8.3	-9.75
Yarmouth	1-13	0-7	0-2	0-1	1-3	7.7	-5.00
Chelmsford (A.W)	1-17	0-4	0-5	0-2	1-6	5.9	-13.00

WINNING HORSES

Horse	Races Run	1st	2nd	3rd	£
Advanced Virgo (IRE)	5	2	0	0	6275
Another Batt (IRE)	6	1	0	1	21165
Bella Ferrari	8	1	1	1	3752
Bright Saffron*	5	1	0	0	3105
Concierge (IRE)	8	3	1	1	23677
Crash Helmet	4	1	2	0	3752
Gilgamesh	9	1	1	0	15563
Jack The Truth (IRE)	11	2	2	2	9186
James Garfield (IRE)	5	1	0	0	34026
Olympic Odyssey*	5	1	1	0	3235

Reloaded (IRE)	3	1	0	1	5175
Starboy (IRE)	13	3	1	3	13973
Usain Boat (IRE)	6	1	3	0	5175
Total winning prize-money					**£148059**
Favourites	**10-25**		**40.0%**		**3.64**

MICHAEL SCUDAMORE

BROMSASH, H'FORDS

	No. of Hrs	Races Run	1st	2nd	3rd	Unpl	Per cent	£1 Level Stake
2-y-o	*0*	*0*	*0*	*0*	*0*	*0*	*0.0*	*0.00*
3-y-o	*1*	*1*	*0*	*0*	*0*	*1*	*0.0*	*-1.00*
4-y-o+	*7*	*28*	*2*	*0*	*2*	*24*	*7.1*	*+15.00*
Totals	**8**	**29**	**2**	**0**	**2**	**25**	**6.9**	**+14.00**
2017	*7*	*26*	*1*	*3*	*2*	*20*	*3.8*	*-23.38*
2016	*7*	*26*	*0*	*4*	*2*	*20*	*0.0*	*-26.00*

JOCKEYS

	W-R	Per cent	£1 Level Stake
Liam Keniry	2-10	20.0	+33.00

COURSE RECORD

	Total W-R	Non-Hndcps 2-y-o	Non-Hndcps 3-y-o+	Hndcps 2-y-o	Hndcps 3-y-o+	Per cent	£1 Level Stake
Newcastle (A.W)	1-2	0-0	0-1	0-0	1-1	50.0	+7.00
Kempton (A.W)	1-10	0-0	0-3	0-0	1-7	10.0	+24.00

WINNING HORSES

Horse	Races Run	1st	2nd	3rd	£
Lawmaking	6	2	0	0	12000
Total winning prize-money					**£12000**
Favourites	**2-15**		**13.3%**		**-11.17**

DEREK SHAW

SPROXTON, LEICS

	No. of Hrs	Races Run	1st	2nd	3rd	Unpl	Per cent	£1 Level Stake
2-y-o	*6*	*21*	*0*	*0*	*0*	*21*	*0.0*	*-21.00*
3-y-o	*11*	*59*	*3*	*3*	*8*	*45*	*5.1*	*-7.50*
4-y-o+	*23*	*152*	*19*	*8*	*12*	*113*	*12.5*	*-19.42*
Totals	**40**	**232**	**22**	**11**	**20**	**179**	**9.5**	**-47.92**
2017	*39*	*270*	*24*	*19*	*18*	*208*	*8.9*	*-12.71*
2016	*42*	*252*	*21*	*21*	*20*	*190*	*8.3*	*-26.67*

BY MONTH

2-y-o	W-R	Per cent	£1 Level Stake	3-y-o	W-R	Per cent	£1 Level Stake
January	0-0	0.0	0.00	January	0-11	0.0	-11.00
February	0-0	0.0	0.00	February	0-8	0.0	-8.00
March	0-0	0.0	0.00	March	1-6	16.7	+0.50
April	0-0	0.0	0.00	April	0-3	0.0	-3.00
May	0-2	0.0	-2.00	May	0-3	0.0	-3.00
June	0-4	0.0	-4.00	June	2-4	50.0	+41.00
July	0-2	0.0	-2.00	July	0-4	0.0	-4.00
August	0-6	0.0	-6.00	August	0-7	0.0	-7.00
September	0-0	0.0	0.00	September	0-2	0.0	-2.00
October	0-1	0.0	-1.00	October	0-1	0.0	-1.00
November	0-3	0.0	-3.00	November	0-6	0.0	-6.00
December	0-3	0.0	-3.00	December	0-4	0.0	-4.00

4-y-o+	W-R	Per cent	£1 Level Stake	Totals	W-R	Per cent	£1 Level Stake
January	5-21	23.8	-2.50	January	5-32	15.6	-13.50
February	3-14	21.4	+3.25	February	3-22	13.6	-4.75
March	5-27	18.5	+15.83	March	6-33	18.2	+16.33
April	2-18	11.1	-4.00	April	2-21	9.5	-7.00
May	0-7	0.0	-7.00	May	0-12	0.0	-12.00
June	1-8	12.5	-2.00	June	3-16	18.8	+35.00
July	0-9	0.0	-9.00	July	0-15	0.0	-15.00
August	1-12	8.3	+5.00	August	1-25	4.0	-8.00
September	0-12	0.0	-12.00	September	0-14	0.0	-14.00
October	2-8	25.0	+9.00	October	2-10	20.0	+7.00
November	0-6	0.0	-6.00	November	0-15	0.0	-12.00
December	0-10	0.0	-10.00	December	0-17	0.0	-14.00

DISTANCE

2-y-o	W-R	Per cent	£1 Level Stake	3-y-o	W-R	Per cent	£1 Level Stake
5f-6f	0-19	0.0	-19.00	5f-6f	2-43	4.7	+2.00
7f-8f	0-2	0.0	-2.00	7f-8f	1-11	9.1	-4.50
9f-13f	0-0	0.0	0.00	9f-13f	0-5	0.0	-5.00
14f+	0-0	0.0	0.00	14f+	0-0	0.0	0.00

4-y-o+	W-R	Per cent	£1 Level Stake	Totals	W-R	Per cent	£1 Level Stake
5f-6f	6-69	8.7	-21.00	5f-6f	8-131	6.1	-38.00
7f-8f	12-68	17.6	+7.58	7f-8f	13-81	16.0	+1.08
9f-13f	1-14	7.1	-5.00	9f-13f	1-19	5.3	-10.00
14f+	0-1	0.0	-1.00	14f+	0-1	0.0	-1.00

TYPE OF RACE

Non-Handicaps	W-R	Per cent	£1 Level Stake	Handicaps	W-R	Per cent	£1 Level Stake
2-y-o	0-13	0.0	-13.00	2-y-o	0-8	0.0	-8.00
3-y-o	0-13	0.0	-13.00	3-y-o	3-46	6.5	+5.50
4-y-o+	2-10	20.0	-6.50	4-y-o+	17-142	12.0	-12.92

RACE CLASS

	W-R	Per cent	£1 Level Stake
Class 1	0-0	0.0	0.00
Class 2	0-7	0.0	-7.00
Class 3	2-22	9.1	-0.67
Class 4	5-55	9.1	-14.50
Class 5	8-63	12.7	+20.75
Class 6	6-84	7.1	-49.50
Class 7	1-1	100.0	+3.00

FIRST TIME OUT

	W-R	Per cent	£1 Level Stake
2-y-o	0-6	0.0	-6.00
3-y-o	0-11	0.0	-11.00
4-y-o+	0-23	0.0	-23.00
Totals	0-40	0.0	-40.00

JOCKEYS

	W-R	Per cent	£1 Level Stake
Paddy Mathers	18-178	10.1	-20.92
Gary Mahon	1-2	50.0	+4.50
Tom Eaves	1-3	33.3	+10.00
Gabriele Malune	1-3	33.3	-1.50
Franny Norton	1-9	11.1	-3.00

COURSE RECORD

	Total W-R	Non-Hndcps 2-y-o	Non-Hndcps 3-y-o+	Hndcps 2-y-o	Hndcps 3-y-o+	Per cent	£1 Level Stake
Chelmsford (A.W)	8-55	0-3	1-5	0-2	7-45	14.5	-1.25
Southwell (A.W)	5-47	0-0	1-7	0-1	4-39	10.6	-23.17
Wolvhptn (A.W)	5-52	0-6	0-6	0-2	5-38	9.6	-4.50
Doncaster	1-9	0-0	0-1	0-0	1-8	11.1	-3.00
Leicester	1-10	0-2	0-0	0-0	1-8	10.0	+24.00
Kempton (A.W)	1-13	0-1	0-0	0-0	1-12	7.7	-7.00
Newcastle (A.W)	1-18	0-0	0-2	0-3	1-13	5.6	-5.00

WINNING HORSES

Horse	Races Run	1st	2nd	3rd	£
Bomad	10	2	0	1	7892
Captain Lars (SAF)*	3	1	1	0	3105
Dynamo Walt (IRE)	14	3	1	1	22900
Emigrated (IRE)	8	2	0	0	6210
Hammer Gun (USA)	15	2	1	2	12857
Loyalty	6	2	0	0	8086
Naralsaif (IRE)	11	3	0	0	10092
Political Slot	10	1	2	1	3105
Samphire Coast	13	3	1	2	14555
Top Boy	10	1	2	1	3752
Treaty Of Rome (USA)	5	1	0	1	4399
Welliesinthewater (IRE)	10	1	1	2	5531
Total winning prize-money					**£102484**
Favourites	**3-7**		**42.9%**		**-1.25**

LYNN SIDDALL

COLTON, N YORKS

	No. of Hrs	Races Run	1st	2nd	3rd	Unpl	Per cent	£1 Level Stake
2-y-o	*2*	*4*	*0*	*0*	*0*	*4*	*0.0*	*-4.00*
3-y-o	*1*	*11*	*0*	*0*	*0*	*11*	*0.0*	*-11.00*
4-y-o+	*7*	*42*	*3*	*2*	*6*	*31*	*7.1*	*-14.00*
Totals	**10**	**57**	**3**	**2**	**6**	**46**	**5.3**	**-29.00**
2017	*11*	*66*	*2*	*8*	*4*	*52*	*3.0*	*-50.50*
2016	*9*	*79*	*7*	*5*	*6*	*60*	*8.9*	*-6.50*

JOCKEYS

	W-R	Per cent	£1 Level Stake
Callum Rodriguez	1-6	16.7	+0.50
Jack Garritty	1-9	11.1	+8.00
Paddy Aspell	1-20	5.0	-15.50

COURSE RECORD

	Total W-R	Non-Hndcps 2-y-o	Non-Hndcps 3-y-o+	Hndcps 2-y-o	Hndcps 3-y-o+	Per cent	£1 Level Stake
Wolvhptn (A.W)	2-16	0-0	0-0	0-0	2-16	12.5	-5.00
Newcastle (A.W)	1-11	0-0	0-2	0-0	1-9	9.1	+6.00

WINNING HORSES

Horse	Races Run	1st	2nd	3rd	£
Astrophysics	11	1	1	1	3105
Servo (IRE)	5	2	0	1	6598
Total winning prize-money					**£9703**
Favourites	**0-1**		**0.0%**		**-1.00**

DAVID SIMCOCK

NEWMARKET, SUFFOLK

	No. of Hrs	Races Run	1st	2nd	3rd	Unpl	Per cent	£1 Level Stake
2-y-o	*28*	*58*	*7*	*5*	*4*	*42*	*12.1*	*-5.88*
3-y-o	*53*	*192*	*27*	*33*	*23*	*108*	*14.1*	*-70.35*
4-y-o+	*42*	*220*	*23*	*37*	*30*	*128*	*10.5*	*-74.27*
Totals	**123**	**470**	**57**	**75**	**57**	**278**	**12.1**	**-150.50**
2017	*129*	*515*	*64*	*63*	*82*	*306*	*12.4*	*-110.69*
2016	*114*	*457*	*85*	*61*	*76*	*234*	*18.6*	*-28.23*

BY MONTH

2-y-o	W-R	Per cent	£1 Level Stake	3-y-o	W-R	Per cent	£1 Level Stake
January	0-0	0.0	0.00	January	2-12	16.7	-6.59
February	0-0	0.0	0.00	February	2-14	14.3	-3.00
March	0-0	0.0	0.00	March	1-10	10.0	-8.80
April	0-0	0.0	0.00	April	0-6	0.0	-6.00
May	0-1	0.0	-1.00	May	3-26	11.5	-10.88
June	0-1	0.0	-1.00	June	4-36	11.1	-24.33
July	0-2	0.0	-2.00	July	6-25	24.0	+1.88
August	2-6	33.3	+7.75	August	6-26	23.1	-0.63
September	3-10	30.0	+23.50	September	1-17	5.9	-14.00
October	1-20	5.0	-18.39	October	1-9	11.1	0.00
November	1-15	6.7	-11.75	November	1-7	14.3	+6.00
December	0-3	0.0	-3.00	December	0-4	0.0	-4.00

4-y-o+	W-R	Per cent	£1 Level Stake	Totals	W-R	Per cent	£1 Level Stake
January	4-20	20.0	-5.42	January	6-32	18.8	-12.01
February	2-21	9.5	-16.67	February	4-35	11.4	-19.67
March	4-18	22.2	-2.01	March	5-28	17.9	-10.81
April	0-7	0.0	-7.00	April	0-13	0.0	-13.00
May	1-23	4.3	-17.50	May	4-50	8.0	-29.38
June	3-44	6.8	-7.80	June	7-81	8.6	-33.13
July	2-25	8.0	-8.00	July	8-52	15.4	-8.12
August	2-22	9.1	-5.50	August	10-54	18.5	+1.62
September	3-17	17.6	-3.88	September	7-44	15.9	+5.62
October	1-7	14.3	-1.50	October	3-36	8.3	-19.89
November	0-2	0.0	-2.00	November	2-24	8.3	+4.00
December	1-14	7.1	+3.00	December	1-21	4.8	-1.00

DISTANCE

2-y-o	W-R	Per cent	£1 Level Stake	3-y-o	W-R	Per cent	£1 Level Stake
5f-6f	1-6	16.7	-4.38	5f-6f	5-29	17.2	-15.30
7f-8f	5-48	10.4	-0.75	7f-8f	15-81	18.5	-12.22
9f-13f	1-4	25.0	-0.75	9f-13f	6-74	8.1	-39.83
14f+	0-0	0.0	0.00	14f+	1-8	12.5	-3.00

4-y-o+	W-R	Per cent	£1 Level Stake	Totals	W-R	Per cent	£1 Level Stake
5f-6f	2-23	8.7	-14.88	5f-6f	8-58	13.8	-34.56
7f-8f	9-87	10.3	-29.13	7f-8f	29-216	13.4	-42.10
9f-13f	12-87	13.8	-7.27	9f-13f	19-165	11.5	-47.85
14f+	0-23	0.0	-23.00	14f+	1-31	3.2	-26.00

TYPE OF RACE

Non-Handicaps	W-R	Per cent	£1 Level Stake	Handicaps	W-R	Per cent	£1 Level Stake
2-y-o	7-57	12.3	-4.88	2-y-o	0-1	0.0	-1.00
3-y-o	14-104	13.5	-39.72	3-y-o	13-88	14.8	-30.63
4-y-o+	8-68	11.8	-35.63	4-y-o+	15-152	9.9	-38.64

RACE CLASS

	W-R	Per cent	£1 Level Stake
Class 1	3-67	4.5	-45.00
Class 2	6-87	6.9	-13.00
Class 3	10-69	14.5	-11.05
Class 4	8-79	10.1	-40.13
Class 5	28-139	20.1	-18.57
Class 6	2-29	6.9	-22.76
Class 7	0-0	0.0	0.00

FIRST TIME OUT

	W-R	Per cent	£1 Level Stake
2-y-o	4-28	14.3	+15.75
3-y-o	4-53	7.5	-38.88
4-y-o+	3-42	7.1	-32.92
Totals	11-123	8.9	-56.05

JOCKEYS

	W-R	Per cent	£1 Level Stake
Jamie Spencer	20-120	16.7	-25.17
Oisin Murphy	9-52	17.3	-16.60
Andrea Atzeni	4-13	30.8	+24.75
Martin Harley	4-32	12.5	-11.80
Stevie Donohoe	4-57	7.0	-31.29
Paul Mulrennan	2-2	100.0	+4.17
Milly Naseb	2-10	20.0	+1.50
Poppy Bridgwater	1-1	100.0	+8.00
Joey Haynes	1-2	50.0	+11.00
Joe Fanning	1-2	50.0	+3.00
Ryan Moore	1-3	33.3	-1.71
Tom Eaves	1-4	25.0	-0.50
Pat Cosgrave	1-4	25.0	+13.00
Jim Crowley	1-6	16.7	+11.00
Tom Marquand	1-6	16.7	-2.75
Hayley Turner	1-6	16.7	-1.00
Sean Levey	1-9	11.1	-7.09
Harry Bentley	1-13	7.7	-6.50
Callum Shepherd	1-20	5.0	-14.50

COURSE RECORD

	Total W-R	Non-Hndcps 2-y-o	Non-Hndcps 3-y-o+	Hndcps 2-y-o	Hndcps 3-y-o+	Per cent	£1 Level Stake
Chelmsford (A.W)	16-82	2-7	4-21	0-0	10-54	19.5	-1.57
Yarmouth	5-28	1-6	0-1	0-1	4-20	17.9	-8.88
Wolvhptn (A.W)	5-36	0-6	3-16	0-0	2-14	13.9	-5.63
Newcastle (A.W)	5-36	1-3	3-13	0-0	1-20	13.9	-17.38
Windsor	4-12	0-0	2-6	0-0	2-6	33.3	+23.00
Doncaster	3-21	0-3	0-7	0-0	3-11	14.3	-10.63
Lingfield (A.W)	3-31	1-2	1-15	0-0	1-14	9.7	-14.09
Kempton (A.W)	3-42	0-7	0-12	0-0	3-23	7.1	-16.88
Southwell (A.W)	2-7	0-0	2-6	0-0	0-1	28.6	0.00
Lingfield	2-9	0-0	1-4	0-0	1-5	22.2	+5.00
Goodwood	2-28	0-2	2-14	0-0	0-12	7.1	-15.00
Beverley	1-2	0-0	1-1	0-0	0-1	50.0	-0.33
Pontefract	1-2	0-0	1-2	0-0	0-0	50.0	+0.88
Haydock	1-4	0-0	0-3	0-0	1-1	25.0	+0.50
Leicester	1-5	0-0	1-4	0-0	0-1	20.0	+0.50
Redcar	1-8	0-1	1-4	0-0	0-3	12.5	-2.50
York	1-12	1-2	0-6	0-0	0-4	8.3	-8.50
Newbury	1-15	1-2	0-8	0-0	0-5	6.7	+11.00

WINNING HORSES

Horse	Races Run	1st	2nd	3rd	£
Amandine	8	1	3	2	5175
Annecy	3	1	1	0	4140
Another Eclipse (IRE)	6	1	1	2	15563
Arod (IRE)	4	1	2	0	20983
Birch Grove (IRE)	2	1	0	0	3752
Calling Out (FR)	7	1	0	2	12938
Court Of Justice (FR)	3	1	0	0	4033
Courtside (FR)	7	1	1	1	4399
Desert Encounter (IRE)	6	1	1	2	20983
Dragon Mall (USA)*	5	1	1	1	4464
Encryption (IRE)	4	1	2	0	3881
Forward Thinker	4	2	1	0	8539
Furious	3	1	0	0	4787
Glory Awaits (IRE)	16	2	1	2	13456
Highland Sky (IRE)	7	1	0	2	3752
Intern (IRE)	3	1	0	0	4011
Late Change	7	3	1	1	13035
Lightning Spear	4	1	1	1	593392
Majeed	4	1	1	0	12938
Make Magic (IRE)	6	1	0	0	4787
Maverick Officer	7	2	1	1	21079
Maximinus Thrax (FR)	2	1	1	0	3752
Miss Latin (IRE)	5	1	1	1	6081
Mugatoo (IRE)	3	1	0	1	3752
New World Power (JPN)	1	1	0	0	3752
Nonios (IRE)	13	3	3	0	40496
Oasis Fantasy (IRE)	9	1	4	2	5531
Plentyinthetanksir	11	2	1	1	8927
Polybius	13	2	1	1	18675
Power And Peace (IRE)	2	1	1	0	3105
Raakib Alhawa (IRE)	2	1	0	0	9960
Red Bunting (IRE)	1	1	0	0	3881

Sarshampla (IRE)	5	1	1	1	4140
Silchester (USA)	3	1	2	0	3752
Singyoursong (IRE)	6	1	0	0	16173
Soul Silver (IRE)	7	1	1	1	12938
Spanish Mission (USA)	2	1	0	1	9704
Stone Of Destiny*	3	2	1	0	5531
Supernova	3	2	1	0	10706
Universal Order	2	1	1	0	3752
Veena (FR)	3	1	0	2	3752
Walk On Walter (IRE)*	6	2	2	0	8280
West Coast Flyer	6	1	0	0	9338
White Chocolate (IRE)	7	1	2	2	7561
Woven	2	1	0	0	9704
Total winning prize-money					**£993330**
Favourites	**20-53**		**37.7%**		**-6.42**

KENNETH SLACK

HILTON, CUMBRIA

	No. of Hrs	Races Run	1st	2nd	3rd	Unpl	Per cent	£1 Level Stake
2-y-o	*0*	*0*	*0*	*0*	*0*	*0*	*0.0*	*0.00*
3-y-o	*1*	*3*	*0*	*0*	*0*	*3*	*0.0*	*-3.00*
4-y-o+	*6*	*27*	*5*	*3*	*4*	*15*	*18.5*	*+10.16*
Totals	**7**	**30**	**5**	**3**	**4**	**18**	**16.7**	**+7.16**
2017	*8*	*27*	*4*	*4*	*5*	*14*	*14.8*	*-15.98*
2016	*12*	*27*	*5*	*0*	*3*	*19*	*18.5*	*+9.00*

JOCKEYS

	W-R	Per cent	£1 Level Stake
Paul Mulrennan	2-3	66.7	+21.75
Ross Turner	1-1	100.0	+3.50
Nathan Evans	1-2	50.0	+4.00
James Sullivan	1-7	14.3	-5.09

COURSE RECORD

	Total W-R	Non-Hndcps 2-y-o	Non-Hndcps 3-y-o+	Hndcps 2-y-o	Hndcps 3-y-o+	Per cent	£1 Level Stake
Catterick	3-9	0-0	0-0	0-0	3-9	33.3	+1.16
Southwell (A.W)	2-3	0-0	0-0	0-0	2-3	66.7	+24.00

WINNING HORSES

Horse	Races Run	1st	2nd	3rd	£
Calliope	9	1	1	4	3493
Italian Riviera	7	2	0	0	8927
Port Soif	4	2	0	0	6210
Total winning prize-money					**£18630**
Favourites	**4-10**		**40.0%**		**0.28**

PAM SLY

THORNEY, CAMBS

	No. of Hrs	Races Run	1st	2nd	3rd	Unpl	Per cent	£1 Level Stake
2-y-o	*4*	*18*	*3*	*3*	*1*	*11*	*16.7*	*+0.25*
3-y-o	*2*	*3*	*0*	*0*	*0*	*3*	*0.0*	*-3.00*
4-y-o+	*8*	*48*	*4*	*6*	*10*	*28*	*8.3*	*-31.20*
Totals	**14**	**69**	**7**	**9**	**11**	**42**	**10.1**	**-33.95**
2017	*13*	*74*	*9*	*12*	*11*	*42*	*12.2*	*-15.38*
2016	*11*	*53*	*5*	*6*	*6*	*36*	*9.4*	*+18.50*

JOCKEYS

	W-R	Per cent	£1 Level Stake
Rob Hornby	2-12	16.7	+2.50
Jamie Spencer	1-1	100.0	+0.80
Martin Harley	1-3	33.3	+0.25
William Cox	1-7	14.3	-1.00
Callum Shepherd	1-10	10.0	-4.50
John Fahy	1-21	4.8	-17.00

COURSE RECORD

	Total W-R	Non-Hndcps 2-y-o	Non-Hndcps 3-y-o+	Hndcps 2-y-o	Hndcps 3-y-o+	Per cent	£1 Level Stake
Wolvhptn (A.W)	2-10	0-2	0-1	0-0	2-7	20.0	-0.50
Leicester	2-10	1-3	0-1	1-1	0-5	20.0	+5.00
Ripon	1-1	0-0	0-0	0-0	1-1	100.0	+4.50
Doncaster	1-3	1-2	0-0	0-0	0-1	33.3	+0.25
Yarmouth	1-4	0-0	0-0	0-0	1-4	25.0	-2.20

WINNING HORSES

Horse	Races Run	1st	2nd	3rd	£
Dazzling Dan (IRE)	4	1	2	0	4663
Eskendash (USA)	4	1	0	1	5693
John Clare (IRE)	5	1	0	0	3752
Silkstone (IRE)	6	1	1	1	4528
Spinart	9	1	1	2	4787
Zafaranah (USA)	11	2	2	3	7504
Total winning prize-money					**£30927**
Favourites	**5-12**		**41.7%**		**4.75**

BRYAN SMART

HAMBLETON, N YORKS

	No. of Hrs	Races Run	1st	2nd	3rd	Unpl	Per cent	£1 Level Stake
2-y-o	*16*	*67*	*8*	*6*	*7*	*46*	*11.9*	*-6.63*
3-y-o	*17*	*75*	*4*	*6*	*5*	*60*	*5.3*	*-19.50*
4-y-o+	*19*	*114*	*12*	*13*	*17*	*72*	*10.5*	*-7.75*
Totals	**52**	**256**	**24**	**25**	**29**	**178**	**9.4**	**-33.88**
2017	*59*	*279*	*17*	*33*	*28*	*201*	*6.1*	*-122.55*
2016	*51*	*240*	*28*	*27*	*23*	*162*	*11.7*	*-16.57*

BY MONTH

2-y-o	W-R	Per cent	£1 Level Stake	**3-y-o**	W-R	Per cent	£1 Level Stake
January	0-0	0.0	0.00	January	0-4	0.0	-4.00
February	0-0	0.0	0.00	February	0-3	0.0	-3.00
March	0-0	0.0	0.00	March	0-0	0.0	0.00
April	1-2	50.0	+8.00	April	0-6	0.0	-6.00
May	0-5	0.0	-5.00	May	0-12	0.0	-12.00
June	1-9	11.1	-1.00	June	1-10	10.0	-5.00

July	2-10	20.0	-0.63	July	0-9	0.0	-9.00
August	3-14	21.4	+2.00	August	1-9	11.1	-5.50
September	1-12	8.3	+5.00	September	1-10	10.0	+16.00
October	0-13	0.0	-13.00	October	0-5	0.0	-5.00
November	0-2	0.0	-2.00	November	1-5	20.0	+16.00
December	0-0	0.0	0.00	December	0-2	0.0	-2.00

4-y-o+	W-R	Per cent	£1 Level Stake	Totals	W-R	Per cent	£1 Level Stake
January	1-4	25.0	+1.00	January	1-8	12.5	-3.00
February	0-3	0.0	-3.00	February	0-6	0.0	-6.00
March	0-4	0.0	-4.00	March	0-4	0.0	-4.00
April	1-8	12.5	-2.00	April	2-16	12.5	0.00
May	2-17	11.8	-6.50	May	2-34	5.9	-23.50
June	1-14	7.1	-7.00	June	3-33	9.1	-13.00
July	3-16	18.8	+1.75	July	5-35	14.3	-7.88
August	2-13	15.4	+34.50	August	6-36	16.7	+31.00
September	1-15	6.7	-9.50	September	3-37	8.1	+11.50
October	1-13	7.7	-6.00	October	1-31	3.2	-24.00
November	0-5	0.0	-5.00	November	1-12	8.3	+11.00
December	0-2	0.0	-2.00	December	0-4	0.0	-4.00

DISTANCE

2-y-o	W-R	Per cent	£1 Level Stake	3-y-o	W-R	Per cent	£1 Level Stake
5f-6f	5-52	9.6	-6.50	5f-6f	3-41	7.3	-11.50
7f-8f	3-14	21.4	+0.88	7f-8f	1-27	3.7	-1.00
9f-13f	0-1	0.0	-1.00	9f-13f	0-7	0.0	-7.00
14f+	0-0	0.0	0.00	14f+	0-0	0.0	0.00

4-y-o+	W-R	Per cent	£1 Level Stake	Totals	W-R	Per cent	£1 Level Stake
5f-6f	5-80	6.3	-15.25	5f-6f	13-173	7.5	-33.25
7f-8f	7-29	24.1	+12.50	7f-8f	11-70	15.7	+12.38
9f-13f	0-4	0.0	-4.00	9f-13f	0-12	0.0	-12.00
14f+	0-1	0.0	-1.00	14f+	0-1	0.0	-1.00

TYPE OF RACE

Non-Handicaps	W-R	Per cent	£1 Level Stake	Handicaps	W-R	Per cent	£1 Level Stake
2-y-o	8-51	15.7	+9.38	2-y-o	0-16	0.0	-16.00
3-y-o	1-15	6.7	-11.50	3-y-o	3-60	5.0	-8.00
4-y-o+	4-21	19.0	+33.75	4-y-o+	8-93	8.6	-41.50

RACE CLASS

	W-R	Per cent	£1 Level Stake
Class 1	1-14	7.1	+27.00
Class 2	2-15	13.3	-7.25
Class 3	1-25	4.0	-18.00
Class 4	6-46	13.0	+3.50
Class 5	9-86	10.5	-28.13
Class 6	5-68	7.4	-9.00
Class 7	0-2	0.0	-2.00

FIRST TIME OUT

	W-R	Per cent	£1 Level Stake
2-y-o	2-16	12.5	+2.00
3-y-o	0-17	0.0	-17.00
4-y-o+	3-19	15.8	+1.00
Totals	5-52	9.6	-14.00

JOCKEYS

	W-R	Per cent	£1 Level Stake
Graham Lee	18-160	11.3	-22.38
Harry Russell	5-51	9.8	+27.00
Tom Eaves	1-8	12.5	-1.50

COURSE RECORD

	Total W-R	Non-Hndcps 2-y-o	Non-Hndcps 3-y-o+	Hndcps 2-y-o	Hndcps 3-y-o+	Per cent	£1 Level Stake
Thirsk	4-20	2-4	1-3	0-0	1-13	20.0	-4.00
Beverley	3-25	1-9	0-3	0-0	2-13	12.0	-3.50
Redcar	3-27	2-7	0-3	0-0	1-17	11.1	-2.13
Newcastle (A.W)	3-39	1-7	1-4	0-3	1-25	7.7	+1.00
York	2-11	0-3	1-2	0-0	1-6	18.2	+37.00
Carlisle	2-13	1-6	0-1	0-2	1-4	15.4	+4.00
Musselburgh	2-13	0-2	0-2	0-3	2-6	15.4	+0.50
Haydock	2-13	1-2	1-4	0-2	0-5	15.4	-3.75
Kempton (A.W)	1-3	0-0	1-1	0-0	0-2	33.3	+2.00
Nottingham	1-4	0-1	0-0	0-1	1-2	25.0	+17.00
Ayr	1-6	0-0	0-2	0-0	1-4	16.7	0.00

WINNING HORSES

Horse	Races Run	1st	2nd	3rd	£
Aerosphere	2	1	0	0	4033
Alpha Delphini	5	1	3	1	198485
Antagonize	2	2	0	0	8668
Armageddon	4	1	0	2	6469
Fairy Falcon	3	1	0	1	4852
Fendale	9	1	1	2	15563
Helovaplan (IRE)	6	1	0	3	5693
Jeany (IRE)	2	1	0	0	4205
Legal Tender (IRE)	4	1	0	0	3493
Moojim (IRE)	8	1	2	2	6469
Mythmaker	10	2	2	1	29569
Northernpowerhouse	5	1	0	2	5822
Pepys	10	6	2	0	25466
She's Royal	6	1	0	0	3493
Stronsay (IRE)	8	1	2	0	3235
Wrenthorpe	7	2	1	1	10286
Total winning prize-money					**£335801**
Favourites	**5-16**		**31.3%**		**4.13**

R MIKE SMITH

GALSTON, E AYRSHIRE

	No. of Hrs	Races Run	1st	2nd	3rd	Unpl	Per cent	£1 Level Stake
2-y-o	*4*	*11*	*1*	*1*	*0*	*9*	*9.1*	*+6.00*
3-y-o	*1*	*11*	*3*	*1*	*0*	*7*	*27.3*	*+27.75*
4-y-o+	*15*	*90*	*8*	*13*	*6*	*63*	*8.9*	*+20.00*
Totals	**20**	**112**	**12**	**15**	**6**	**79**	**10.7**	**+53.75**
2017	*11*	*75*	*11*	*8*	*9*	*47*	*14.7*	*+5.75*
2016	*8*	*52*	*1*	*5*	*3*	*43*	*1.9*	*-43.50*

BY MONTH

2-y-o	W-R	Per cent	£1 Level Stake	3-y-o	W-R	Per cent	£1 Level Stake
January	0-0	0.0	0.00	January	0-0	0.0	0.00
February	0-0	0.0	0.00	February	0-0	0.0	0.00
March	0-0	0.0	0.00	March	0-0	0.0	0.00

	W-R	Per cent	£1 Level Stake
April	0-0	0.0	0.00
May	0-0	0.0	0.00
June	0-0	0.0	0.00
July	0-2	0.0	-2.00
August	0-1	0.0	-1.00
September	1-3	33.3	+14.00
October	0-2	0.0	-2.00
November	0-3	0.0	-3.00
December	0-0	0.0	0.00

	W-R	Per cent	£1 Level Stake
April	0-0	0.0	0.00
May	0-0	0.0	0.00
June	1-3	33.3	+26.00
July	2-2	100.0	+7.75
August	0-2	0.0	-2.00
September	0-3	0.0	-3.00
October	0-1	0.0	-1.00
November	0-0	0.0	0.00
December	0-0	0.0	0.00

4-y-o+	W-R	Per cent	£1 Level Stake
January	0-4	0.0	-4.00
February	1-3	33.3	+12.00
March	0-1	0.0	-1.00
April	0-1	0.0	-1.00
May	1-11	9.1	+40.00
June	2-18	11.1	+6.50
July	3-14	21.4	+2.00
August	1-13	7.7	-9.50
September	0-11	0.0	-11.00
October	0-11	0.0	-11.00
November	0-2	0.0	-2.00
December	0-1	0.0	-1.00

Totals	W-R	Per cent	£1 Level Stake
January	0-4	0.0	-4.00
February	1-3	33.3	+12.00
March	0-1	0.0	-1.00
April	0-1	0.0	-1.00
May	1-11	9.1	+40.00
June	3-21	14.3	+32.50
July	5-18	27.8	+7.75
August	1-16	6.3	-12.50
September	1-17	5.9	0.00
October	0-14	0.0	-14.00
November	0-5	0.0	-2.00
December	0-1	0.0	-1.00

DISTANCE

2-y-o	W-R	Per cent	£1 Level Stake
5f-6f	0-3	0.0	-3.00
7f-8f	1-8	12.5	+9.00
9f-13f	0-0	0.0	0.00
14f+	0-0	0.0	0.00

3-y-o	W-R	Per cent	£1 Level Stake
5f-6f	0-0	0.0	0.00
7f-8f	0-1	0.0	-1.00
9f-13f	3-10	30.0	+28.75
14f+	0-0	0.0	0.00

4-y-o+	W-R	Per cent	£1 Level Stake
5f-6f	0-0	0.0	0.00
7f-8f	0-32	0.0	-32.00
9f-13f	6-44	13.6	+30.00
14f+	2-14	14.3	+22.00

Totals	W-R	Per cent	£1 Level Stake
5f-6f	0-3	0.0	-3.00
7f-8f	1-41	2.4	-24.00
9f-13f	9-54	16.7	+58.75
14f+	2-14	14.3	+22.00

TYPE OF RACE

Non-Handicaps

	W-R	Per cent	£1 Level Stake
2-y-o	1-9	11.1	+8.00
3-y-o	1-4	25.0	+25.00
4-y-o+	0-3	0.0	-3.00

Handicaps

	W-R	Per cent	£1 Level Stake
2-y-o	0-2	0.0	-2.00
3-y-o	2-7	28.6	+2.75
4-y-o+	8-87	9.2	+23.00

RACE CLASS

	W-R	Per cent	£1 Level Stake
Class 1	0-1	0.0	-1.00
Class 2	0-3	0.0	-3.00
Class 3	0-5	0.0	-5.00
Class 4	3-28	10.7	-1.25
Class 5	6-45	13.3	+7.00
Class 6	3-30	10.0	+57.00
Class 7	0-0	0.0	0.00

FIRST TIME OUT

	W-R	Per cent	£1 Level Stake
2-y-o	1-4	25.0	+13.00
3-y-o	0-1	0.0	-1.00
4-y-o+	1-15	6.7	+6.00
Totals	2-20	10.0	+18.00

JOCKEYS

	W-R	Per cent	£1 Level Stake
Andrew Breslin	5-22	22.7	+48.50
Paddy Mathers	4-16	25.0	+39.75
James Sullivan	2-19	10.5	+17.00
Ben Curtis	1-1	100.0	+2.50

COURSE RECORD

	Total W-R	Non-Hndcps 2-y-o	Non-Hndcps 3-y-o+	Hndcps 2-y-o	Hndcps 3-y-o+	Per cent	£1 Level Stake
Ayr	7-52	0-5	1-4	0-0	6-43	13.5	+65.75
Haydock	1-2	0-0	0-0	0-0	1-2	50.0	+1.50
Thirsk	1-2	1-1	0-0	0-0	0-1	50.0	+15.00
Carlisle	1-4	0-0	0-0	0-0	1-4	25.0	-0.50
Newcastle (A.W)	1-11	0-0	0-0	0-0	1-11	9.1	+4.00
Hamilton	1-14	0-0	0-1	0-0	1-13	7.1	-5.00

WINNING HORSES

Horse	Races Run	1st	2nd	3rd	£
Akamanto (IRE)	9	3	3	1	13520
An Fear Ciuin (IRE)	4	1	0	0	4140
Archibelle	8	1	1	0	3493
*Five Amarones (IRE)	4	1	1	0	6301
*Four Kingdoms (IRE)	5	1	1	1	4140
Glasses Up (USA)	11	3	1	0	17596
Las Tunas (FR)	2	1	0	0	3493
*Pudding Chare (IRE)	9	1	0	0	3105
Total winning prize-money					**£55788**
Favourites	**3-12**		**25.0%**		**-1.50**

MARTIN SMITH

NEWMARKET, SUFFOLK

	No. of Hrs	Races Run	1st	2nd	3rd	Unpl	Per cent	£1 Level Stake
2-y-o	*2*	*2*	*0*	*0*	*0*	*2*	*0.0*	*-2.00*
3-y-o	*4*	*28*	*3*	*5*	*2*	*17*	*10.7*	*+5.50*
4-y-o+	*5*	*33*	*2*	*2*	*6*	*23*	*6.1*	*-18.00*
Totals	**11**	**63**	**5**	**7**	**8**	**42**	**7.9**	**-14.50**
2017	*20*	*70*	*3*	*4*	*6*	*57*	*4.3*	*-8.00*
2016	*20*	*82*	*7*	*8*	*8*	*59*	*8.5*	*+30.25*

JOCKEYS

	W-R	Per cent	£1 Level Stake
Paul Hanagan	1-1	100.0	+6.50
Silvestre De Sousa	1-1	100.0	+2.50
Josephine Gordon	1-2	50.0	+13.00
Tom Marquand	1-7	14.3	+0.50
Hector Crouch	1-8	12.5	+7.00

COURSE RECORD

	Total W-R	Non-Hndcps 2-y-o	Non-Hndcps 3-y-o+	Hndcps 2-y-o	Hndcps 3-y-o+	Per cent	£1 Level Stake
Haydock	1-1	0-0	0-0	0-0	1-1	100.0	+2.50
Nottingham	1-2	0-0	1-1	0-0	0-1	50.0	+5.50
Sandown	1-3	0-0	0-1	0-0	1-2	33.3	+12.00
Brighton	1-6	0-0	1-1	0-0	0-5	16.7	+9.00
Lingfield (A.W)	1-11	0-0	0-3	0-0	1-8	9.1	-3.50

WINNING HORSES

Horse	Races Run	1st	2nd	3rd	£
Arch My Boy	2	1	1	0	4140
In The Red (IRE)	15	1	1	2	3752
Roman River	4	1	1	0	7116
The Emperor Within (FR)	8	2	2	1	13090
Total winning prize-money					**£28098**
Favourites	**1-3**		**33.3%**		**0.50**

JOHN SPEARING

KINNERSLEY, WORCS

	No. of Hrs	Races Run	1st	2nd	3rd	Unpl	Per cent	£1 Level Stake
2-y-o	*0*	*0*	*0*	*0*	*0*	*0*	*0.0*	*0.00*
3-y-o	*0*	*0*	*0*	*0*	*0*	*0*	*0.0*	*0.00*
4-y-o+	*9*	*54*	*4*	*2*	*5*	*43*	*7.4*	*-11.75*
Totals	**9**	**54**	**4**	**2**	**5**	**43**	**7.4**	**-11.75**
2017	*10*	*83*	*9*	*13*	*7*	*54*	*10.8*	*-5.50*
2016	*13*	*76*	*6*	*3*	*2*	*65*	*7.9*	*-9.50*

JOCKEYS

	W-R	Per cent	£1 Level Stake
Franny Norton	1-1	100.0	+20.00
Jack Mitchell	1-2	50.0	+6.00
Robert Winston	1-4	25.0	+6.00
Jane Elliott	1-6	16.7	-2.75

COURSE RECORD

	Total W-R	Non-Hndcps 2-y-o	Non-Hndcps 3-y-o+	Hndcps 2-y-o	Hndcps 3-y-o+	Per cent	£1 Level Stake
Chepstow	1-3	0-0	0-0	0-0	1-3	33.3	+0.25
Nottingham	1-3	0-0	0-0	0-0	1-3	33.3	+18.00
Brighton	1-5	0-0	0-0	0-0	1-5	20.0	+3.00
Wolvhptn (A.W)	1-16	0-0	0-0	0-0	1-16	6.3	-6.00

WINNING HORSES

Horse	Races Run	1st	2nd	3rd	£
A Sure Welcome	11	1	2	1	3752
Captain Sedgwick (IRE)	8	1	0	1	3105
*Cool Strutter (IRE)	5	1	0	0	3105
Whitecrest	16	1	0	2	3235
Total winning prize-money					**£13197**
Favourites	**1-3**		**33.3%**		**0.25**

RICHARD SPENCER

NEWMARKET, SUFFOLK

	No. of Hrs	Races Run	1st	2nd	3rd	Unpl	Per cent	£1 Level Stake
2-y-o	*21*	*110*	*17*	*10*	*14*	*69*	*15.5*	*+24.50*
3-y-o	*11*	*46*	*2*	*2*	*2*	*40*	*4.3*	*-35.50*
4-y-o+	*12*	*80*	*13*	*13*	*11*	*43*	*16.3*	*-0.63*
Totals	**44**	**236**	**32**	**25**	**27**	**152**	**13.6**	**-11.63**
2017	*26*	*110*	*10*	*10*	*11*	*79*	*9.1*	*-16.22*
2016	*19*	*79*	*3*	*13*	*14*	*49*	*3.8*	*-68.25*

BY MONTH

2-y-o	W-R	Per cent	£1 Level Stake	**3-y-o**	W-R	Per cent	£1 Level Stake
January	0-0	0.0	0.00	January	0-2	0.0	-2.00
February	0-0	0.0	0.00	February	0-1	0.0	-1.00
March	0-0	0.0	0.00	March	1-3	33.3	+2.50
April	1-2	50.0	+6.00	April	0-5	0.0	-5.00
May	1-8	12.5	+3.00	May	0-9	0.0	-9.00
June	3-14	21.4	+8.50	June	0-3	0.0	-3.00
July	5-16	31.3	+14.50	July	0-2	0.0	-2.00
August	1-19	5.3	-13.00	August	0-1	0.0	-1.00
September	1-18	5.6	-11.00	September	0-3	0.0	-3.00
October	3-17	17.6	+28.50	October	0-6	0.0	-6.00
November	2-10	20.0	-6.00	November	1-7	14.3	-2.00
December	0-6	0.0	-6.00	December	0-4	0.0	-4.00

4-y-o+	W-R	Per cent	£1 Level Stake	**Totals**	W-R	Per cent	£1 Level Stake
January	1-3	33.3	+5.00	January	1-5	20.0	+3.00
February	0-1	0.0	-1.00	February	0-2	0.0	-2.00
March	0-2	0.0	-2.00	March	1-5	20.0	+0.50
April	0-10	0.0	-10.00	April	1-17	5.9	-9.00
May	0-12	0.0	-12.00	May	1-29	3.4	-18.00
June	2-10	20.0	0.00	June	5-27	18.5	+5.50
July	3-8	37.5	-0.83	July	8-26	30.8	+11.67
August	4-9	44.4	+15.20	August	5-29	17.2	+1.20
September	0-11	0.0	-11.00	September	1-32	3.1	-25.00
October	2-12	16.7	+13.00	October	5-35	14.3	+35.50
November	0-1	0.0	-1.00	November	3-18	16.7	-3.00
December	1-1	100.0	+4.00	December	1-11	9.1	0.00

DISTANCE

2-y-o	W-R	Per cent	£1 Level Stake	**3-y-o**	W-R	Per cent	£1 Level Stake
5f-6f	13-80	16.3	+30.00	5f-6f	1-14	7.1	9.00
7f-8f	4-30	13.3	-5.50	7f-8f	0-26	0.0	-26.00
9f-13f	0-0	0.0	0.00	9f-13f	1-6	16.7	-0.50
14f+	0-0	0.0	0.00	14f+	0-0	0.0	0.00

4-y-o+	W-R	Per cent	£1 Level Stake	**Totals**	W-R	Per cent	£1 Level Stake
5f-6f	4-24	16.7	+16.00	5f-6f	18-118	15.3	+37.00
7f-8f	6-35	17.1	-8.43	7f-8f	10-91	11.0	-39.93
9f-13f	1-13	7.7	-5.00	9f-13f	2-19	10.5	-5.50
14f+	2-8	25.0	-3.20	14f+	2-8	25.0	-3.20

TYPE OF RACE

Non-Handicaps

	W-R	Per cent	£1 Level Stake
2-y-o	14-78	17.9	+38.50
3-y-o	2-18	11.1	-7.50
4-y-o+	0-10	0.0	-10.00

Handicaps

	W-R	Per cent	£1 Level Stake
2-y-o	3-32	9.4	-14.00
3-y-o	0-28	0.0	-28.00
4-y-o+	13-70	18.6	+9.37

RACE CLASS

	W-R	Per cent	£1 Level Stake
Class 1	1-16	6.3	-10.00
Class 2	1-23	4.3	-16.00
Class 3	3-16	18.8	+19.00
Class 4	10-58	17.2	+21.00
Class 5	11-77	14.3	-15.50
Class 6	6-46	13.0	-10.13
Class 7	0-0	0.0	0.00

FIRST TIME OUT

	W-R	Per cent	£1 Level Stake
2-y-o	3-21	14.3	+25.00
3-y-o	0-11	0.0	-11.00
4-y-o+	1-12	8.3	-4.00
Totals	4-44	9.1	+10.00

JOCKEYS

	W-R	Per cent	£1 Level Stake
Tom Queally	12-101	11.9	-4.70
Daniel Muscutt	4-16	25.0	-1.63
Martin Dwyer	3-15	20.0	+30.00
Graham Lee	2-4	50.0	+6.50
Charles Bishop	2-5	40.0	+6.50
David Egan	1-1	100.0	+6.00
Luke Morris	1-1	100.0	+3.50
Oisin Murphy	1-1	100.0	+3.50
James Doyle	1-2	50.0	+0.50
Hollie Doyle	1-2	50.0	+3.50
Scott McCullagh	1-4	25.0	-1.80
Robert Winston	1-6	16.7	+2.00
Stevie Donohoe	1-13	7.7	-5.00
Rhiain Ingram	1-24	4.2	-19.50

COURSE RECORD

	Total W-R	Non-Hndcps 2-y-o	Non-Hndcps 3-y-o+	Hndcps 2-y-o	Hndcps 3-y-o+	Per cent	£1 Level Stake
Newcastle (A.W)	4-7	3-4	1-1	0-0	0-2	57.1	+4.50
Yarmouth	4-19	0-3	0-0	0-3	4-13	21.1	-6.93
Newbury	3-12	2-8	0-0	0-1	1-3	25.0	+46.00
Windsor	2-6	1-1	0-1	0-1	1-3	33.3	+6.50
Lingfield	2-7	0-1	0-1	0-0	2-5	28.6	+0.30
Southwell (A.W)	2-10	1-2	1-3	0-3	0-2	20.0	+3.00
Newmkt (Jly)	2-10	1-4	0-0	0-1	1-5	20.0	-1.00
Lingfield (A.W)	2-11	0-2	0-1	0-1	2-7	18.2	+2.00
Kempton (A.W)	2-24	1-5	0-6	1-8	0-5	8.3	-4.50
Chester	1-1	0-0	0-0	1-1	0-0	100.0	+3.50
Wetherby	1-1	1-1	0-0	0-0	0-0	100.0	+10.00
Ffos Las	1-1	0-0	0-0	0-0	1-1	100.0	+12.00
Thirsk	1-3	1-1	0-0	0-1	0-1	33.3	+6.00
Salisbury	1-4	1-2	0-2	0-0	0-0	25.0	+7.00
Brighton	1-5	0-1	0-0	0-0	1-4	20.0	-0.50
Goodwood	1-8	1-2	0-0	0-2	0-4	12.5	-2.00
Doncaster	1-21	0-10	0-1	1-3	0-7	4.8	-14.00
Chelmsford (A.W)	1-22	1-9	0-2	0-3	0-8	4.5	-19.50

WINNING HORSES

Horse	Races Run	1st	2nd	3rd	£
Alfie Solomons (IRE)	9	1	3	0	6728
Archie (IRE)	9	1	1	1	6728
Bernardo O'Reilly	8	3	1	1	22422
Bo Selecta (IRE)	3	1	0	0	3105
California Love	6	2	0	0	7633
Cococabala (IRE)	8	2	0	1	9639
Cookupastorm (IRE)	6	1	0	0	3752
*Fink Hill (USA)	6	1	0	0	3752
*Heather Lark (IRE)	4	1	1	0	3752
Its'afreebee (IRE)	10	2	4	0	7504
Keyser Soze (IRE)	7	1	1	2	7246
La Isla Bonita	14	3	1	1	9962
Louis Treize (IRE)	3	1	1	0	3752
No Diggity (IRE)*	8	1	0	0	3105
Rebel Surge (IRE)	11	1	2	2	6469
Revich (IRE)	8	1	1	2	6081
Rumble Inthejungle (IRE)	5	2	0	1	47643
Spencers Son (IRE)	3	1	0	1	3235
Stay Classy (IRE)	6	2	2	1	33142
Thistimenextyear	6	1	1	2	5531
Thrilla In Manila	1	1	0	0	4787
You Never Can Tell (IRE)	6	2	0	1	7633
Total winning prize-money					**£213601**
Favourites	**7-22**		**31.8%**		**-7.13**

HENRY SPILLER

NEWMARKET, SUFFOLK

	No. of Hrs	Races Run	1st	2nd	3rd	Unpl	Per cent	£1 Level Stake
2-y-o	*10*	*40*	*1*	*4*	*2*	*33*	*2.5*	*-23.00*
3-y-o	*12*	*57*	*3*	*1*	*7*	*46*	*5.3*	*-17.50*
4-y-o+	*16*	*81*	*10*	*3*	*7*	*61*	*12.3*	*+14.50*
Totals	**38**	**178**	**14**	**8**	**16**	**140**	**7.9**	**-26.00**
2017	*37*	*119*	*11*	*13*	*12*	*82*	*9.2*	*-35.20*
2016	*25*	*78*	*6*	*2*	*7*	*63*	*7.7*	*-2.00*

BY MONTH

2-y-o	W-R	Per cent	£1 Level Stake
January	0-0	0.0	0.00
February	0-0	0.0	0.00
March	0-0	0.0	0.00
April	1-1	100.0	+16.00
May	0-4	0.0	-4.00
June	0-5	0.0	-5.00
July	0-10	0.0	-10.00
August	0-7	0.0	-7.00
September	0-3	0.0	-3.00
October	0-5	0.0	-5.00
November	0-4	0.0	-4.00
December	0-1	0.0	-1.00

3-y-o	W-R	Per cent	£1 Level Stake
January	0-5	0.0	-5.00
February	1-1	100.0	+22.00
March	0-8	0.0	-8.00
April	0-6	0.0	-6.00
May	0-3	0.0	-3.00
June	0-7	0.0	-7.00
July	2-8	25.0	+8.50
August	0-6	0.0	-6.00
September	0-6	0.0	-6.00
October	0-2	0.0	-2.00
November	0-4	0.0	-4.00
December	0-1	0.0	-1.00

4-y-o+	W-R	Per cent	£1 Level Stake
January	3-7	42.9	+19.00
February	1-7	14.3	-3.50
March	1-3	33.3	+1.50
April	0-10	0.0	-10.00
May	0-4	0.0	-4.00
June	0-12	0.0	-12.00
July	2-11	18.2	+8.00
August	1-9	11.1	-4.50
September	0-7	0.0	-7.00
October	1-3	33.3	+6.00
November	1-5	20.0	+24.00
December	0-3	0.0	-3.00

Totals	W-R	Per cent	£1 Level Stake
January	3-12	25.0	+14.00
February	2-8	25.0	+18.50
March	1-11	9.1	-6.50
April	1-17	5.9	0.00
May	0-11	0.0	-11.00
June	0-24	0.0	-24.00
July	4-29	13.8	+6.50
August	1-22	4.5	-17.50
September	0-16	0.0	-16.00
October	1-10	10.0	-1.00
November	1-13	7.7	+20.00
December	0-5	0.0	-4.00

DISTANCE

2-y-o	W-R	Per cent	£1 Level Stake
5f-6f	1-26	3.8	-9.00
7f-8f	0-14	0.0	-14.00
9f-13f	0-0	0.0	0.00
14f+	0-0	0.0	0.00

3-y-o	W-R	Per cent	£1 Level Stake
5f-6f	2-19	10.5	+9.50
7f-8f	1-29	3.4	-18.00
9f-13f	0-9	0.0	-9.00
14f+	0-0	0.0	0.00

4-y-o+	W-R	Per cent	£1 Level Stake
5f-6f	5-36	13.9	-2.00
7f-8f	2-26	7.7	-6.00
9f-13f	3-15	20.0	+26.50
14f+	0-4	0.0	-4.00

Totals	W-R	Per cent	£1 Level Stake
5f-6f	8-81	9.9	-1.50
7f-8f	3-69	4.3	-38.00
9f-13f	3-24	12.5	+17.50
14f+	0-4	0.0	-4.00

TYPE OF RACE

Non-Handicaps	W-R	Per cent	£1 Level Stake
2-y-o	1-32	3.1	-15.00
3-y-o	1-22	4.5	+1.00
4-y-o+	1-4	25.0	+25.00

Handicaps	W-R	Per cent	£1 Level Stake
2-y-o	0-8	0.0	-8.00
3-y-o	2-35	5.7	-18.50
4-y-o+	9-77	11.7	-10.50

RACE CLASS

	W-R	Per cent	£1 Level Stake
Class 1	0-2	0.0	-2.00
Class 2	0-5	0.0	-5.00
Class 3	0-6	0.0	-6.00
Class 4	2-41	4.9	-27.50
Class 5	7-76	9.2	+33.00
Class 6	5-48	10.4	-18.50
Class 7	0-0	0.0	0.00

FIRST TIME OUT

	W-R	Per cent	£1 Level Stake
2-y-o	1-10	10.0	+7.00
3-y-o	0-12	0.0	-12.00
4-y-o+	2-16	12.5	+1.00
Totals	3-38	7.9	-4.00

JOCKEYS

	W-R	Per cent	£1 Level Stake
Liam Keniry	2-4	50.0	+8.50
Andrea Atzeni	2-5	40.0	+8.50
Adam Kirby	2-7	28.6	+1.50
David Probert	1-2	50.0	+3.50
Kevin Stott	1-3	33.3	+26.00
Martin Harley	1-5	20.0	+18.00
Marc Monaghan	1-6	16.7	+1.00
Cameron Noble	1-10	10.0	+1.00
Jimmy Quinn	1-11	9.1	+6.00
Ben Curtis	1-15	6.7	-3.00
Fran Berry	1-33	3.0	-20.00

COURSE RECORD

	Total W-R	Non-Hndcps 2-y-o	Non-Hndcps 3-y-o+	Hndcps 2-y-o	Hndcps 3-y-o+	Per cent	£1 Level Stake
Chelmsford (A.W)	4-34	0-11	0-5	0-3	4-15	11.8	-13.00
Wolvhptn (A.W)	3-19	1-4	0-5	0-0	2-10	15.8	+15.50
Yarmouth	2-18	0-2	0-1	0-1	2-14	11.1	-2.50
Lingfield (A.W)	2-21	0-0	1-7	0-0	1-14	9.5	+15.00
Newcastle (A.W)	1-12	0-2	1-1	0-1	0-8	8.3	+17.00
Newmkt (Jly)	1-14	0-4	0-0	0-0	1-10	7.1	-7.00
Kempton (A.W)	1-18	0-0	0-4	0-2	1-12	5.6	-9.00

WINNING HORSES

Horse	Races Run	1st	2nd	3rd	£
Arnoul Of Metz	8	1	0	0	3105
Captain Pugwash (IRE)*	5	2	0	1	11127
Daphinia	5	1	2	0	3752
Folie Douze	3	1	0	1	3752
Good Business (IRE)	10	3	0	1	9962
Herringswell (FR)	9	1	0	4	3105
*Kamra (USA)	5	2	1	1	10221
Kyoto Star (FR)	3	1	0	0	3752
Natalie Express (FR)	7	1	1	2	3752
Trulee Scrumptious	8	1	0	0	4528
Total winning prize-money					**£57056**
Favourites	**1-4**		**25.0%**		**0.50**

DANIEL STEELE

HENFIELD, W SUSSEX

	No. of Hrs	Races Run	1st	2nd	3rd	Unpl	Per cent	£1 Level Stake
2-y-o	*0*	*0*	*0*	*0*	*0*	*0*	*0.0*	*0.00*
3-y-o	*0*	*0*	*0*	*0*	*0*	*0*	*0.0*	*0.00*
4-y-o+	*13*	*37*	*2*	*1*	*2*	*32*	*5.4*	*-14.50*
Totals	**13**	**37**	**2**	**1**	**2**	**32**	**5.4**	**-14.50**
2017	*13*	*60*	*4*	*2*	*2*	*52*	*6.7*	*-33.00*
2016	*4*	*16*	*0*	*0*	*1*	*15*	*0.0*	*-16.00*

JOCKEYS

	W-R	Per cent	£1 Level Stake
Joshua Bryan	2-2	100.0	+20.50

COURSE RECORD

	Total W-R	Non-Hndcps 2-y-o	Non-Hndcps 3-y-o+	Hndcps 2-y-o	Hndcps 3-y-o+	Per cent	£1 Level Stake
Salisbury	1-1	0-0	0-0	0-0	1-1	100.0	+16.00
Goodwood	1-2	0-0	0-0	0-0	1-2	50.0	+3.50

WINNING HORSES

Horse	Races Run	1st	2nd	3rd	£
Chivers (IRE)*	4	2	0	0	8668

Total winning prize-money			**£8668**
Favourites	**1-1**	**100.0%**	**4.50**

ROBERT STEPHENS

PENHOW, NEWPORT

	No. of Hrs	Races Run	1st	2nd	3rd	Unpl	Per cent	£1 Level Stake
2-y-o	*0*	*0*	*0*	*0*	*0*	*0*	*0.0*	*0.00*
3-y-o	*1*	*2*	*0*	*0*	*1*	*1*	*0.0*	*-2.00*
4-y-o+	*18*	*68*	*3*	*9*	*10*	*46*	*4.4*	*-36.75*
Totals	**19**	**70**	**3**	**9**	**11**	**47**	**4.3**	**-38.75**
2017	*19*	*74*	*6*	*12*	*8*	*46*	*8.1*	*+13.50*
2016	*14*	*45*	*4*	*2*	*8*	*31*	*8.9*	*+1.38*

JOCKEYS

	W-R	Per cent	£1 Level Stake
Adam Kirby	2-8	25.0	-2.75
Liam Jones	1-7	14.3	+19.00

COURSE RECORD

	Total W-R	Non-Hndcps 2-y-o	Non-Hndcps 3-y-o+	Hndcps 2-y-o	Hndcps 3-y-o+	Per cent	£1 Level Stake
Chelmsford (A.W)	2-6	0-0	0-0	0-0	2-6	33.3	-0.75
Bath	1-3	0-0	0-0	0-0	1-3	33.3	+23.00

WINNING HORSES

Horse	Races Run	1st	2nd	3rd	£
Espresso Freddo (IRE)	12	1	1	2	4399
Noble Behest	1	1	0	0	0
Street Jester	6	1	0	1	3105
Total winning prize-money					**£7504**
Favourites	**2-5**		**40.0%**		**1.25**

WILLIAM STONE

WEST WICKHAM, CAMBS

	No. of Hrs	Races Run	1st	2nd	3rd	Unpl	Per cent	£1 Level Stake
2-y-o	*0*	*0*	*0*	*0*	*0*	*0*	*0.0*	*0.00*
3-y-o	*4*	*36*	*1*	*3*	*4*	*28*	*2.8*	*-31.00*
4-y-o+	*7*	*58*	*3*	*7*	*4*	*44*	*5.2*	*-30.00*
Totals	**11**	**94**	**4**	**10**	**8**	**72**	**4.3**	**-61.00**
2017	*10*	*88*	*11*	*12*	*5*	*60*	*12.5*	*-12.25*
2016	*9*	*72*	*4*	*9*	*7*	*52*	*5.6*	*-47.00*

JOCKEYS

	W-R	Per cent	£1 Level Stake
Hollie Doyle	4-47	8.5	-14.00

COURSE RECORD

	Total W-R	Non-Hndcps 2-y-o	Non-Hndcps 3-y-o+	Hndcps 2-y-o	Hndcps 3-y-o+	Per cent	£1 Level Stake
Wolvhptn (A.W)	1-8	0-0	1-2	0-0	0-6	12.5	-3.00
Brighton	1-12	0-0	0-0	0-0	1-12	8.3	-1.00
Lingfield (A.W)	1-15	0-0	0-0	0-0	1-15	6.7	-9.00
Chelmsford (A.W)	1-21	0-0	0-2	0-0	1-19	4.8	-10.00

WINNING HORSES

Horse	Races Run	1st	2nd	3rd	£
Hidden Stash	14	1	1	1	3105
Invisible Storm	11	1	1	1	3817
Tigerfish (IRE)	15	1	3	1	3105
Touch The Clouds	7	1	0	1	3429
Total winning prize-money					**£13456**
Favourites	**0-1**		**0.0%**		**-1.00**

WILF STOREY

MUGGLESWICK, CO DURHAM

	No. of Hrs	Races Run	1st	2nd	3rd	Unpl	Per cent	£1 Level Stake
2-y-o	*1*	*1*	*0*	*0*	*0*	*1*	*0.0*	*-1.00*
3-y-o	*1*	*2*	*0*	*0*	*0*	*2*	*0.0*	*-2.00*
4-y-o+	*8*	*63*	*2*	*5*	*6*	*50*	*3.2*	*-44.00*
Totals	**10**	**66**	**2**	**5**	**6**	**53**	**3.0**	**-47.00**
2017	*10*	*98*	*11*	*9*	*9*	*69*	*11.2*	*+17.25*
2016	*12*	*106*	*5*	*6*	*8*	*87*	*4.7*	*-26.00*

JOCKEYS

	W-R	Per cent	£1 Level Stake
Paula Muir	1-11	9.1	-3.00
Nathan Evans	1-24	4.2	-13.00

COURSE RECORD

	Total W-R	Non-Hndcps 2-y-o	Non-Hndcps 3-y-o+	Hndcps 2-y-o	Hndcps 3-y-o+	Per cent	£1 Level Stake
Musselburgh	1-5	0-0	0-0	0-0	1-5	20.0	+6.00
Newcastle (A.W)	1-25	0-1	0-3	0-0	1-21	4.0	-17.00

WINNING HORSES

Horse	Races Run	1st	2nd	3rd	£
Highway Robber	10	1	2	0	3105
Jan Smuts (IRE)	9	1	0	0	3493
Total winning prize-money					**£6598**
Favourites	**0-1**		**0.0%**		**-1.00**

SIR MICHAEL STOUTE

NEWMARKET, SUFFOLK

	No. of Hrs	Races Run	1st	2nd	3rd	Unpl	Per cent	£1 Level Stake
2-y-o	*42*	*88*	*13*	*13*	*10*	*52*	*14.8*	*-46.86*
3-y-o	*63*	*275*	*49*	*56*	*36*	*134*	*17.8*	*-68.76*
4-y-o+	*15*	*63*	*15*	*18*	*3*	*27*	*23.8*	*-19.66*
Totals	**120**	**426**	**77**	**87**	**49**	**213**	**18.1**	**-135.28**
2017	*135*	*438*	*82*	*68*	*47*	*241*	*18.7*	*-58.89*
2016	*140*	*505*	*111*	*93*	*66*	*234*	*22.0*	*-25.48*

BY MONTH

2-y-o	W-R	Per cent	£1 Level Stake
January	0-0	0.0	0.00
February	0-0	0.0	0.00
March	0-0	0.0	0.00
April	0-0	0.0	0.00
May	0-1	0.0	-1.00
June	0-5	0.0	-5.00
July	0-4	0.0	-4.00
August	3-15	20.0	-5.22
September	4-28	14.3	-13.65
October	4-22	18.2	-9.03
November	2-10	20.0	-5.90
December	0-3	0.0	-3.00

3-y-o	W-R	Per cent	£1 Level Stake
January	0-0	0.0	0.00
February	0-0	0.0	0.00
March	0-2	0.0	-2.00
April	3-22	13.6	+0.23
May	7-58	12.1	-35.22
June	10-45	22.2	+11.13
July	7-37	18.9	-14.17
August	11-49	22.4	-1.59
September	8-35	22.9	-12.63
October	3-23	13.0	-10.50
November	0-3	0.0	-3.00
December	0-1	0.0	-1.00

4-y-o+	W-R	Per cent	£1 Level Stake
January	0-0	0.0	0.00
February	0-2	0.0	-2.00
March	0-1	0.0	-1.00
April	1-7	14.3	-5.00
May	3-14	21.4	-8.93
June	4-11	36.4	+3.82
July	3-9	33.3	+1.50
August	2-9	22.2	-4.42
September	2-5	40.0	+1.38
October	0-5	0.0	-5.00
November	0-0	0.0	0.00
December	0-0	0.0	0.00

Totals	W-R	Per cent	£1 Level Stake
January	0-0	0.0	0.00
February	0-2	0.0	-2.00
March	0-3	0.0	-3.00
April	4-29	13.8	-4.77
May	10-73	13.7	-45.15
June	14-61	23.0	+9.95
July	10-50	20.0	-16.67
August	16-73	21.9	-11.23
September	14-68	20.6	-24.90
October	7-50	14.0	-24.53
November	2-13	15.4	-3.00
December	0-4	0.0	-1.00

DISTANCE

2-y-o	W-R	Per cent	£1 Level Stake
5f-6f	1-28	3.6	-25.25
7f-8f	12-60	20.0	-21.61
9f-13f	0-0	0.0	0.00
14f+	0-0	0.0	0.00

3-y-o	W-R	Per cent	£1 Level Stake
5f-6f	3-17	17.6	+4.50
7f-8f	23-117	19.7	-15.51
9f-13f	21-137	15.3	-61.00
14f+	2-4	50.0	+3.25

4-y-o+	W-R	Per cent	£1 Level Stake
5f-6f	0-6	0.0	-6.00
7f-8f	2-6	33.3	+0.38
9f-13f	13-46	28.3	-9.04
14f+	0-5	0.0	-5.00

Totals	W-R	Per cent	£1 Level Stake
5f-6f	4-51	7.8	-26.75
7f-8f	37-183	20.2	-36.74
9f-13f	34-183	18.6	-70.04
14f+	2-9	22.2	-1.75

TYPE OF RACE

Non-Handicaps

	W-R	Per cent	£1 Level Stake
2-y-o	13-83	15.7	-41.86
3-y-o	24-134	17.9	-25.64
4-y-o+	12-43	27.9	-10.03

Handicaps

	W-R	Per cent	£1 Level Stake
2-y-o	0-5	0.0	-5.00
3-y-o	25-141	17.7	-43.13
4-y-o+	3-20	15.0	-9.63

RACE CLASS

	W-R	Per cent	£1 Level Stake
Class 1	20-84	23.8	-7.70
Class 2	5-43	11.6	-24.25
Class 3	9-52	17.3	-25.01
Class 4	14-114	12.3	-43.21
Class 5	29-128	22.7	-30.11
Class 6	0-5	0.0	-5.00
Class 7	0-0	0.0	0.00

FIRST TIME OUT

	W-R	Per cent	£1 Level Stake
2-y-o	3-42	7.1	-29.63
3-y-o	10-63	15.9	-16.47
4-y-o+	3-15	20.0	-7.58
Totals	16-120	13.3	-53.68

JOCKEYS

	W-R	Per cent	£1 Level Stake
Ryan Moore	23-99	23.2	-28.63
Jim Crowley	9-41	22.0	-2.52
Pat Dobbs	7-40	17.5	-23.10
Richard Kingscote	6-28	21.4	-6.88
Daniel Tudhope	5-11	45.5	+2.51
James Doyle	4-10	40.0	+7.13
Kieran Shoemark	3-9	33.3	+7.50
David Probert	3-18	16.7	-6.75
William Buick	3-20	15.0	+0.25
Frankie Dettori	2-6	33.3	+7.00
Oisin Murphy	2-13	15.4	-5.17
Jimmy Quinn	2-17	11.8	-9.50
James McDonald	1-3	33.3	+6.00
Jamie Spencer	1-4	25.0	-1.63
Edward Greatrex	1-4	25.0	+4.00
Tristan Price	1-6	16.7	-3.00
Dane O'Neill	1-7	14.3	-1.50
Jason Watson	1-7	14.3	-4.25
Josephine Gordon	1-14	7.1	-12.27
Andrea Atzeni	1-18	5.6	-13.50

COURSE RECORD

	Total	Non-Hndcps		Hndcps		Per	£1 Level
	W-R	2-y-o	3-y-o+	2-y-o	3-y-o+	cent	Stake
Sandown	7-22	1-5	5-9	0-0	1-8	31.8	+8.23
Wolvhptn (A.W)	6-31	1-7	3-13	0-0	2-11	19.4	-6.25
Ascot	6-33	0-3	5-21	0-0	1-9	18.2	+4.82
Chelmsford (A.W)	6-33	2-6	0-10	0-0	4-17	18.2	-13.28
Doncaster	5-15	1-3	2-6	0-0	2-6	33.3	+1.60
Goodwood	5-21	0-1	5-12	0-1	0-7	23.8	-0.05
Kempton (A.W)	5-42	3-18	0-9	0-1	2-14	11.9	-21.00
Leicester	4-14	0-7	1-3	0-0	3-4	28.6	+3.50
Newmkt (Jly)	4-21	2-7	1-6	0-0	1-8	19.0	-6.75
Beverley	3-6	0-1	1-1	0-0	2-4	50.0	+2.35
Pontefract	3-9	0-1	2-4	0-0	1-4	33.3	-1.67
Newcastle (A.W)	3-10	1-1	2-4	0-0	0-5	30.0	-2.21
York	3-15	0-0	2-9	0-0	1-6	20.0	-8.67
Lingfield (A.W)	3-17	2-4	0-8	0-1	1-4	17.6	-5.25
Thirsk	2-2	0-0	2-2	0-0	0-0	100.0	+7.73
Haydock	2-8	0-0	0-4	0-0	2-4	25.0	-2.00
Nottingham	2-13	0-0	0-6	0-0	2-7	15.4	-6.38
Windsor	2-16	0-1	1-6	0-0	1-9	12.5	-7.25
Newbury	2-24	0-2	2-16	0-0	0-6	8.3	-20.69
Newmarket	2-29	0-7	1-15	0-1	1-6	6.9	-22.63
Salisbury	1-11	0-2	1-3	0-0	0-6	9.1	-9.20
Yarmouth	1-12	0-5	0-2	0-1	1-4	8.3	-8.25

WINNING HORSES

Horse	Races Run	1st	2nd	3rd	£
Accommodate (IRE)	3	1	0	0	6081
Adamant (GER)	3	1	1	0	16173
Allante (IRE)	6	1	1	1	5531
Almania (IRE)	2	1	0	0	4528
Baritone (IRE)	6	1	1	2	9338
Beachwalk	4	2	0	0	7504
Bedwyyah (IRE)	8	1	2	2	4852
Comrade In Arms (USA)	4	1	1	0	5531
Crystal Hope	5	1	0	1	6469
Crystal King	5	1	0	0	3752
Crystal Moonlight	5	2	1	1	19925
Crystal Ocean	6	3	3	0	224005
Desert Diamond	5	3	1	0	41811
Eqtidaar (IRE)	5	1	1	0	283550
Expert Eye	5	2	2	0	153117
Gabr	6	1	2	1	45368
Garden Oasis	3	1	1	0	4852
Georgian Manor (IRE)	6	2	1	1	11472
Gold At Midnight	3	1	0	1	5822
Hamlul (FR)	6	1	1	1	7719
Hareeq	4	1	1	1	5822
Homeopathic	7	1	1	1	9704
Karnavaal (IRE)	3	1	0	0	4787
Layaleena (IRE)	3	1	0	0	5175
Ledham (IRE)	5	2	2	1	13090
Loolwah (IRE)	1	1	0	0	3881
Lunar Corona	3	1	0	1	3752
Mekong	7	3	2	0	97903
Melting Dew	5	2	1	0	57001
Midi	4	2	0	0	7892
Mirage Dancer	6	2	3	0	85065
Mubakker (USA)	2	1	0	0	3752
Mustashry	4	3	1	0	140811
Phantasmic	5	1	2	1	5419
Poet's Word (IRE)	4	3	1	0	1173897
Procedure	12	2	5	1	10480
Qaroun	5	2	0	1	14513
Rapier (USA)	7	1	0	0	3752
Rawdaa	5	2	3	0	35006
Refrain (IRE)	7	1	2	1	3881
Regal Reality	4	1	0	2	56710
Romola	3	1	1	0	3752
Sangarius	3	2	0	0	22188
Sextant	3	1	2	0	9704
Sharp Practice	5	1	0	0	5531
Smart Call (SAF)	4	1	0	1	34026
Solid Stone (IRE)	3	1	1	0	4787
Sovereign Grant	3	1	0	1	3881
Sun Maiden	5	1	0	2	4787
Tahreek	6	2	0	0	9509
Veracious	4	1	0	2	39697
Vivionn	2	1	0	0	3752
Whitehall	8	1	1	3	3881
Zaaki	6	1	1	3	4852
Total winning prize-money					**£2760040**
Favourites	**44-115**		**38.3%**		**-5.90**

ALI STRONGE

EASTBURY, BERKS

	No. of Hrs	Races Run	1st	2nd	3rd	Unpl	Per cent	£1 Level Stake
2-y-o	*4*	*14*	*0*	*0*	*2*	*12*	*0.0*	*-14.00*
3-y-o	*6*	*37*	*2*	*5*	*1*	*28*	*5.4*	*-17.63*
4-y-o+	*14*	*68*	*5*	*6*	*10*	*47*	*7.4*	*-36.17*
Totals	**24**	**119**	**7**	**11**	**13**	**87**	**5.9**	**-67.80**
2017	*16*	*64*	*7*	*5*	*9*	*43*	*10.9*	*+23.50*
2016	*15*	*76*	*4*	*6*	*18*	*48*	*5.3*	*-25.38*

JOCKEYS

	W-R	Per cent	£1 Level Stake
Tom Marquand	2-38	5.3	-11.00
Harry Bentley	1-4	25.0	-1.63
Silvestre De Sousa	1-5	20.0	-0.67
Charles Bishop	1-6	16.7	+1.00
Thomas Greatrex	1-9	11.1	-5.50
Hollie Doyle	1-13	7.7	-6.00

COURSE RECORD

	Total W-R	Non-Hndcps 2-y-o	Non-Hndcps 3-y-o+	Hndcps 2-y-o	Hndcps 3-y-o+	Per cent	£1 Level Stake
Wolvhptn (A.W)	2-15	0-2	1-3	0-0	1-10	13.3	-1.50
Epsom	1-5	0-0	0-0	0-0	1-5	20.0	+2.00
Chepstow	1-6	0-0	0-1	0-0	1-5	16.7	-3.63
Brighton	1-8	0-3	0-0	0-0	1-5	12.5	-3.67
Newbury	1-8	0-3	0-0	0-0	1-5	12.5	+9.00
Lingfield (A.W)	1-13	0-0	0-2	0-0	1-11	7.7	-6.00

WINNING HORSES

Horse	Races Run	1st	2nd	3rd	£
Amanto (GER)	7	1	0	3	3235
He's Our Star (IRE)	9	2	1	0	7245
Let's Be Happy (IRE)*	7	2	1	0	6857
*Storm Melody	6	1	0	1	3105
*Zoffany Bay (IRE)	7	1	2	1	3105
Total winning prize-money					**£23547**
Favourites	**2-11**		**18.2%**		**-4.29**

SAEED BIN SUROOR

NEWMARKET, SUFFOLK

	No. of Hrs	Races Run	1st	2nd	3rd	Unpl	Per cent	£1 Level Stake
2-y-o	*40*	*100*	*19*	*17*	*17*	*47*	*19.0*	*-41.45*
3-y-o	*44*	*157*	*38*	*31*	*20*	*68*	*24.2*	*-36.26*
4-y-o+	*41*	*127*	*27*	*18*	*17*	*65*	*21.3*	*-16.49*
Totals	**125**	**384**	**84**	**66**	**54**	**180**	**21.9**	**-94.20**
2017	*94*	*280*	*65*	*51*	*36*	*128*	*23.2*	*-59.61*
2016	*123*	*319*	*68*	*62*	*33*	*156*	*21.3*	*-38.64*

BY MONTH

2-y-o	W-R	Per cent	£1 Level Stake
January	0-0	0.0	0.00
February	0-0	0.0	0.00
March	0-0	0.0	0.00
April	0-0	0.0	0.00
May	0-3	0.0	-3.00
June	2-6	33.3	-1.63
July	4-9	44.4	-0.47
August	1-8	12.5	-4.00
September	6-31	19.4	-2.90
October	4-25	16.0	-16.45
November	1-14	7.1	-11.75
December	1-4	25.0	-1.25

3-y-o	W-R	Per cent	£1 Level Stake
January	1-4	25.0	-1.13
February	1-1	100.0	+0.91
March	1-1	100.0	+0.67
April	0-11	0.0	-11.00
May	2-14	14.3	-3.50
June	8-35	22.9	-8.11
July	10-26	38.5	+7.20
August	7-20	35.0	+1.28
September	3-21	14.3	-11.00
October	3-19	15.8	-9.59
November	1-4	25.0	-2.09
December	1-1	100.0	+0.10

4-y-o+	W-R	Per cent	£1 Level Stake
January	1-2	50.0	+3.50
February	0-0	0.0	0.00
March	0-1	0.0	-1.00
April	5-9	55.6	+8.21
May	2-16	12.5	-12.59
June	1-24	4.2	-22.00
July	6-22	27.3	+1.23
August	2-22	9.1	-11.75
September	5-18	27.8	+4.13
October	2-10	20.0	+3.80
November	1-1	100.0	+1.63
December	2-2	100.0	+8.36

Totals	W-R	Per cent	£1 Level Stake
January	2-6	33.3	+2.37
February	1-1	100.0	+0.91
March	1-2	50.0	-0.33
April	5-20	25.0	-2.79
May	4-33	12.1	-19.09
June	11-65	16.9	-31.74
July	20-57	35.1	+7.96
August	10-50	20.0	-14.47
September	14-70	20.0	-9.77
October	9-54	16.7	-22.24
November	3-19	15.8	-0.46
December	4-7	57.1	+8.46

DISTANCE

2-y-o	W-R	Per cent	£1 Level Stake
5f-6f	6-31	19.4	-19.72
7f-8f	13-64	20.3	-16.73
9f-13f	0-5	0.0	-5.00
14f+	0-0	0.0	0.00

3-y-o	W-R	Per cent	£1 Level Stake
5f-6f	2-5	40.0	-1.53
7f-8f	18-62	29.0	-1.44
9f-13f	18-89	20.2	-32.28
14f+	0-1	0.0	-1.00

4-y-o+	W-R	Per cent	£1 Level Stake
5f-6f	1-10	10.0	-7.25
7f-8f	12-58	20.7	-7.35
9f-13f	13-52	25.0	-0.39
14f+	1-7	14.3	-1.50

Totals	W-R	Per cent	£1 Level Stake
5f-6f	9-46	19.6	-28.50
7f-8f	43-184	23.4	-25.52
9f-13f	31-146	21.2	-37.67
14f+	1-8	12.5	-2.50

TYPE OF RACE

Non-Handicaps	W-R	Per cent	£1 Level Stake
2-y-o	18-92	19.6	-36.07
3-y-o	26-94	27.7	-22.22
4-y-o+	7-38	18.4	-17.93

Handicaps	W-R	Per cent	£1 Level Stake
2-y-o	1-8	12.5	-5.38
3-y-o	12-63	19.0	-14.04
4-y-o+	20-89	22.5	+1.44

RACE CLASS

	W-R	Per cent	£1 Level Stake
Class 1	1-24	4.2	-17.00
Class 2	6-53	11.3	-24.88
Class 3	17-80	21.3	-14.01
Class 4	24-96	25.0	+2.67
Class 5	36-130	27.7	-39.97
Class 6	0-1	0.0	-1.00
Class 7	0-0	0.0	0.00

FIRST TIME OUT

	W-R	Per cent	£1 Level Stake
2-y-o	5-40	12.5	-17.88
3-y-o	10-44	22.7	-8.44
4-y-o+	8-41	19.5	-13.38
Totals	23-125	18.4	-39.70

JOCKEYS

	W-R	Per cent	£1 Level Stake
Oisin Murphy	14-53	26.4	-11.31
Jason Watson	12-35	34.3	+10.84
Hayley Turner	8-20	40.0	+12.88
Hector Crouch	8-32	25.0	+7.02
Pat Cosgrave	7-30	23.3	-13.65
Edward Greatrex	5-13	38.5	+2.33
William Cox	5-19	26.3	-7.92
Kevin Stott	5-21	23.8	-1.82
David Allan	3-6	50.0	+9.38
Jim Crowley	3-13	23.1	-4.18
David Egan	3-21	14.3	-10.50
Paul Hanagan	2-5	40.0	-0.40
Rossa Ryan	2-8	25.0	-3.63
George Wood	2-12	16.7	-4.75
Alistair Rawlinson	1-4	25.0	-2.47
Harry Bentley	1-6	16.7	-3.25
Gerald Mosse	1-7	14.3	-4.13
Marc Monaghan	1-9	11.1	-1.50
Graham Lee	1-10	10.0	-7.13

COURSE RECORD

	Total W-R	Non-Hndcps 2-y-o	Non-Hndcps 3-y-o+	Hndcps 2-y-o	Hndcps 3-y-o+	Per cent	£1 Level Stake
Wolvhptn (A.W)	11-32	4-11	2-9	0-0	5-12	34.4	+0.76
Chelmsford (A.W)	11-48	1-10	5-13	0-1	5-24	22.9	-13.27
Newmkt (July)	6-17	1-3	3-5	0-1	2-8	35.3	+4.07
Doncaster	6-18	2-5	3-7	0-1	1-5	33.3	+7.85
Lingfield (A.W)	6-19	2-6	2-7	0-1	2-5	31.6	-4.99
Kempton (A.W)	5-35	0-11	3-10	0-1	2-13	14.3	-13.21
Nottingham	4-6	1-1	2-4	0-0	1-1	66.7	+9.60
Leicester	4-12	1-4	3-5	0-0	0-3	33.3	-0.60
Salisbury	3-8	1-1	2-6	0-0	0-1	37.5	+5.03
Thirsk	3-8	0-0	2-5	0-0	1-3	37.5	+4.54
Beverley	2-3	0-0	1-1	0-0	1-2	66.7	+1.50
Epsom	2-4	1-1	0-1	0-0	1-2	50.0	+0.32
Catterick	2-5	0-0	1-2	1-2	0-1	40.0	-0.58
Brighton	2-8	1-3	1-2	0-0	0-3	25.0	-5.72
Ripon	2-8	0-0	1-3	0-0	1-5	25.0	+3.00
Sandown	2-9	0-2	0-2	0-0	2-5	22.2	+4.50
Newbury	2-12	0-2	0-3	0-1	2-6	16.7	+1.00
Windsor	2-12	1-2	0-5	0-0	1-5	16.7	-7.17
Southwell (A.W)	1-2	0-0	1-2	0-0	0-0	50.0	+0.38
Hamilton	1-3	0-0	1-1	0-0	0-2	33.3	-1.43
Ayr	1-5	0-0	0-1	0-0	1-4	20.0	-1.00
Redcar	1-8	1-3	0-1	0-0	0-4	12.5	-5.90
Yarmouth	1-10	1-3	0-4	0-0	0-3	10.0	-7.00
Haydock	1-12	0-2	0-3	0-0	1-7	8.3	-8.50
Ascot	1-14	0-3	0-7	0-0	1-4	7.1	-8.00
Newmarket	1-14	0-4	0-3	0-0	1-7	7.1	-10.25
Newcastle (A.W)	1-15	0-2	0-6	0-0	1-7	6.7	-12.13

WINNING HORSES

Horse	Races Run	1st	2nd	3rd	£
Alfurat River	4	1	1	1	6469
Arabian Coast (IRE)	2	1	0	0	5175
Asoof	8	3	0	2	28593
Beautiful Memory (IRE)	5	3	0	0	14102
Beauvais (IRE)	2	1	1	0	3881
Bedouin's Story	7	3	0	1	14717
Best Solution (IRE)	1	1	0	0	56710
Burj	7	2	0	1	7504
Cantiniere (USA)	3	2	1	0	7504
Commander Cole	6	1	0	0	12450
Dayking	3	1	1	0	5111
Desert Fire (IRE)	3	2	0	0	9574
Desert Frost (IRE)	8	1	3	2	9338
Diamond Oasis	2	1	0	0	3752
Dubai Beauty (IRE)	2	1	0	0	5175
Dubai Blue (USA)	2	1	0	0	4949
Dubai Horizon (IRE)	7	2	0	0	40505
Dubai Icon	2	1	0	0	3881
Dubai Legacy (USA)	3	2	0	0	9315
Dubai One (IRE)	4	1	0	1	7246
Estihdaaf (USA)	3	1	1	1	6469
Extra Mile	4	3	0	1	20561
Fitzsimmons (USA)	5	1	0	2	3752
Glassy Waters (USA)	3	2	0	0	13715
Global Hero	3	2	1	0	8863
Huge Future	3	1	1	1	14232
Jfoul (IRE)	6	2	0	0	12162
Laieth	2	1	1	0	3881
Leader's Legacy (USA)	4	1	0	1	7246
Madkhal (USA)	4	1	1	0	3752
Major Partnership (IRE)	5	3	1	1	17597
Midnight Meeting (IRE)	4	2	0	0	8668
Moqarrab (USA)	3	1	0	0	3752
Moving Forward (IRE)	6	1	0	3	3752
National Army	2	1	0	0	3752
Ocean Of Love	4	2	1	1	15591
Parting Clouds	6	1	1	1	5531
Perisher	6	1	0	1	4528
Piece Of History (IRE)	6	2	1	0	14814
Race Day (IRE)	5	1	0	0	9338
Racing Country (IRE)	2	2	0	0	13585
Recordman	6	1	1	3	8345
Right Direction (IRE)	6	2	2	1	13456
Royal Marine (IRE)	2	1	0	0	9704
Royal Meeting (IRE)	1	1	0	0	4787
Shoot For Gold	2	1	0	0	3752
Silent Attack	2	1	0	0	7246
Silver River	3	2	0	1	7763
Stealth Fighter (IRE)	3	1	1	0	5175
Swift Rose (IRE)	1	1	0	0	4787
Team Decision (IRE)	7	3	0	1	21024
Very Talented (IRE)	2	1	0	0	16173
Victory Wave (USA)	8	4	1	0	58489
Volcanic Sky	7	1	4	0	8345
Welsh Lord	3	1	2	0	8345
Total winning prize-money					**£628883**
Favourites	**49-119**		**41.2%**		**-18.15**

TOM TATE

TADCASTER, N YORKS

	No. of Hrs	Races Run	1st	2nd	3rd	Unpl	Per cent	£1 Level Stake
2-y-o	*2*	*4*	*0*	*0*	*0*	*4*	*0.0*	*-4.00*
3-y-o	*1*	*3*	*0*	*1*	*0*	*2*	*0.0*	*-3.00*
4-y-o+	*11*	*68*	*5*	*4*	*14*	*45*	*7.4*	*-3.00*
Totals	**14**	**75**	**5**	**5**	**14**	**51**	**6.7**	**-10.00**
2017	*13*	*83*	*14*	*12*	*7*	*50*	*16.9*	*+36.67*
2016	*10*	*51*	*3*	*1*	*8*	*38*	*5.9*	*-20.00*

JOCKEYS

	W-R	Per cent	£1 Level Stake
Andrew Mullen	2-23	8.7	-5.00
James Sullivan	2-25	8.0	-4.00
Mr Patrick Millman	1-1	100.0	+25.00

COURSE RECORD

	Total W-R	Non-Hndcps 2-y-o	Non-Hndcps 3-y-o+	Hndcps 2-y-o	Hndcps 3-y-o+	Per cent	£1 Level Stake
York	2-5	0-0	0-0	0-0	2-5	40.0	+16.00
Newmkt (Jly)	1-2	0-0	0-0	0-0	1-2	50.0	+9.00
Pontefract	1-5	0-0	0-0	0-0	1-5	20.0	+21.00
Newcastle (A.W)	1-14	0-0	0-0	0-0	1-14	7.1	-7.00

WINNING HORSES

Horse	Races Run	1st	2nd	3rd	£
Awake My Soul (IRE)	6	1	1	2	9704
Destroyer	10	1	0	2	6469
Equiano Springs	7	1	0	1	5531
First Dance (IRE)	9	1	0	2	3743
Waiting For Richie	1	1	0	0	12450
Total winning prize-money					**£37897**
Favourites	**0-3**		**0.0%**		**-3.00**

JAMES TATE

NEWMARKET, SUFFOLK

	No. of Hrs	Races Run	1st	2nd	3rd	Unpl	Per cent	£1 Level Stake
2-y-o	*36*	*114*	*23*	*13*	*15*	*63*	*20.2*	*-3.30*
3-y-o	*39*	*138*	*16*	*29*	*16*	*77*	*11.6*	*-57.62*
4-y-o+	*4*	*11*	*2*	*1*	*1*	*7*	*18.2*	*-2.92*
Totals	**79**	**263**	**41**	**43**	**32**	**147**	**15.6**	**-63.84**
2017	*54*	*241*	*34*	*39*	*36*	*132*	*14.1*	*-118.13*
2016	*77*	*302*	*54*	*39*	*51*	*157*	*17.9*	*-33.10*

BY MONTH

2-y-o	W-R	Per cent	£1 Level Stake
January	0-0	0.0	0.00
February	0-0	0.0	0.00
March	0-0	0.0	0.00
April	0-1	0.0	-1.00
May	1-6	16.7	-0.50
June	2-13	15.4	-7.88
July	2-15	13.3	-9.50
August	4-16	25.0	+5.25
September	6-19	31.6	+6.10
October	4-16	25.0	+4.75
November	1-12	8.3	-3.00
December	3-16	18.8	+2.48

3-y-o	W-R	Per cent	£1 Level Stake
January	0-6	0.0	-6.00
February	2-12	16.7	-3.00
March	2-12	16.7	+4.80
April	2-14	14.3	-3.50
May	3-11	27.3	-1.79
June	2-13	15.4	-2.00
July	1-17	5.9	-14.50
August	2-13	15.4	-4.00
September	1-19	5.3	-16.63
October	0-16	0.0	-16.00
November	0-2	0.0	2.00
December	1-3	33.3	+7.00

4-y-o+	W-R	Per cent	£1 Level Stake
January	1-1	100.0	+2.75
February	0-0	0.0	0.00
March	1-2	50.0	+2.33
April	0-2	0.0	-2.00
May	0-2	0.0	-2.00
June	0-0	0.0	0.00
July	0-1	0.0	-1.00
August	0-1	0.0	-1.00
September	0-1	0.0	-1.00
October	0-1	0.0	-1.00
November	0-0	0.0	0.00
December	0-0	0.0	0.00

Totals	W-R	Per cent	£1 Level Stake
January	1-7	14.3	-3.25
February	2-12	16.7	-3.00
March	3-14	21.4	+7.13
April	2-17	11.8	-6.50
May	4-19	21.1	-4.29
June	4-26	15.4	-9.88
July	3-33	9.1	-25.00
August	6-30	20.0	+0.25
September	7-39	17.9	-11.53
October	4-33	12.1	-12.25
November	1-14	7.1	-2.00
December	4-19	21.1	+7.00

DISTANCE

2-y-o	W-R	Per cent	£1 Level Stake
5f-6f	11-59	18.6	-7.88
7f-8f	11-54	20.4	+3.58
9f-13f	1-1	100.0	+1.00
14f+	0-0	0.0	0.00

3-y-o	W-R	Per cent	£1 Level Stake
5f-6f	5-36	13.9	-14.82
7f-8f	10-76	13.2	-22.29
9f-13f	1-25	4.0	-19.50
14f+	0-1	0.0	-1.00

4-y-o+	W-R	Per cent	£1 Level Stake
5f-6f	1-1	100.0	+3.33
7f-8f	0-7	0.0	-7.00
9f-13f	1-3	33.3	+0.75
14f+	0-0	0.0	0.00

Totals	W-R	Per cent	£1 Level Stake
5f-6f	17-96	17.7	-19.37
7f-8f	21-137	15.3	-25.71
9f-13f	3-29	10.3	-17.75
14f+	0-1	0.0	-1.00

TYPE OF RACE

Non-Handicaps	W-R	Per cent	£1 Level Stake
2-y-o	11-90	12.2	-23.25
3-y-o	9-66	13.6	-19.62
4-y-o+	1-4	25.0	+0.33

Handicaps	W-R	Per cent	£1 Level Stake
2-y-o	12-24	50.0	+19.95
3-y-o	7-72	9.7	-38.00
4-y-o+	1-7	14.3	-3.25

RACE CLASS

	W-R	Per cent	£1 Level Stake
Class 1	2-18	11.1	-9.63
Class 2	3-14	21.4	-0.17
Class 3	0-10	0.0	-10.00
Class 4	9-56	16.1	-12.38
Class 5	23-152	15.1	-31.64
Class 6	4-13	30.8	-0.02
Class 7	0-0	0.0	0.00

FIRST TIME OUT

	W-R	Per cent	£1 Level Stake
2-y-o	4-36	11.1	-1.50
3-y-o	5-39	12.8	-4.32
4-y-o+	2-4	50.0	+4.08
Totals	11-79	13.9	-1.74

JOCKEYS

	W-R	Per cent	£1 Level Stake
Luke Morris	7-68	10.3	-22.79
Oisin Murphy	5-18	27.8	-0.95
Jamie Spencer	4-14	28.6	+11.75
P J McDonald	4-15	26.7	+5.98
David Allan	4-32	12.5	-18.38
Ryan Moore	2-4	50.0	+3.00
Harry Bentley	2-5	40.0	+0.25
Adam Kirby	2-6	33.3	+1.75
Callum Shepherd	2-8	25.0	+5.00
Callum Rodriguez	1-1	100.0	+0.73
Franny Norton	1-2	50.0	+3.00
Tom Eaves	1-3	33.3	+0.25
Paul Mulrennan	1-3	33.3	+2.50
Fran Berry	1-4	25.0	+1.50
Robert Havlin	1-5	20.0	-2.63
Daniel Tudhope	1-5	20.0	-0.67
James Doyle	1-13	7.7	-7.00
Tom Marquand	1-15	6.7	-6.00

COURSE RECORD

	Total W-R	Non-Hndcps 2-y-o	Non-Hndcps 3-y-o+	Hndcps 2-y-o	Hndcps 3-y-o+	Per cent	£1 Level Stake
Wolvhptn (A.W)	9-41	2-16	0-8	3-3	4-14	22.0	-3.25
Kempton (A.W)	7-27	2-11	4-8	0-1	1-7	25.9	+18.38
Newcastle (A.W)	4-24	1-6	0-9	3-4	0-5	16.7	-13.80
Lingfield (A.W)	3-13	2-4	0-4	1-2	0-3	23.1	+7.75
Musselburgh	2-3	0-1	1-1	0-0	1-1	66.7	+6.33
Sandown	2-6	0-0	1-2	0-1	1-3	33.3	+5.50
Yarmouth	2-9	1-6	0-0	1-1	0-2	22.2	-0.88
Southwell (A.W)	2-10	0-1	2-6	0-0	0-3	20.0	+6.80
Chelmsford (A.W)	2-27	0-6	0-7	2-2	0-12	7.4	-18.75
Ripon	1-1	0-0	0-0	1-1	0-0	100.0	+2.25
Carlisle	1-2	0-0	0-0	0-0	1-2	50.0	+3.50
Ffos Las	1-2	0-0	0-0	1-1	0-1	50.0	+3.50
Beverley	1-4	1-3	0-1	0-0	0-0	25.0	-0.88
Catterick	1-5	1-2	0-2	0-1	0-0	20.0	+0.50
Thirsk	1-6	0-3	1-2	0-1	0-0	16.7	-4.17
Windsor	1-6	1-4	0-1	0-0	0-1	16.7	-2.00
Ascot	1-7	0-2	1-3	0-0	0-2	14.3	-4.63

WINNING HORSES

Horse	Races Run	1st	2nd	3rd	£
Across The Sea	7	1	1	0	4140
Astonished (IRE)	1	1	0	0	3881
Attainment	3	1	0	1	3752
Autumn Splendour (IRE)	7	2	1	1	10868
Battle Of Wills (IRE)	4	1	0	0	3752
Camelot Rakti (IRE)	6	1	1	0	3105

Fields Of Athenry (USA)	2	1	0	1	3752
Haddaf (IRE)	11	3	0	1	41999
Hard Taskmaster (IRE)	9	4	0	0	15008
Iconic Sunset	2	1	1	0	4075
Implicit (IRE)	10	3	4	1	14232
Influent (IRE)	1	1	0	0	5531
Intuitive (IRE)	2	1	0	0	3881
Invincible Army (IRE)	4	1	1	0	45368
Jumeirah Street (USA)	6	1	1	1	5175
Kings Highway (IRE)	3	1	1	0	3881
Kyllang Rock (IRE)	1	1	0	0	18675
Litigation	6	1	2	1	3752
Name The Wind	1	1	0	0	5822
New Graduate (IRE)	3	1	2	0	5175
Noble Lineage (IRE)	3	1	0	0	3752
Power Link (USA)	4	1	0	0	3752
Promote (IRE)	2	1	1	0	4787
Real Estate (IRE)*	8	1	2	0	3752
Royal Residence	7	1	3	0	6469
Sameem (IRE)	4	1	1	1	4140
Second Generation	6	2	0	0	15681
Top Rank (IRE)	1	1	0	0	4075
Tribal Warrior	6	3	0	1	14620
Ziarah (IRE)	4	1	2	0	5531
Total winning prize-money					**£272383**
Favourites	**15-43**		**34.9%**		**-4.04**

ROGER TEAL

GREAT SHEFFORD, BERKS

	No. of Hrs	Races Run	1st	2nd	3rd	Unpl	Per cent	£1 Level Stake
2-y-o	*5*	*17*	*2*	*2*	*2*	*11*	*11.8*	*0.00*
3-y-o	*6*	*28*	*2*	*4*	*0*	*22*	*7.1*	*-16.50*
4-y-o+	*13*	*80*	*6*	*6*	*5*	*63*	*7.5*	*+7.00*
Totals	**24**	**125**	**10**	**12**	**7**	**96**	**8.0**	**-9.50**
2017	*16*	*103*	*11*	*16*	*15*	*61*	*10.7*	*+12.00*
2016	*19*	*135*	*17*	*10*	*9*	*99*	*12.6*	*-10.50*

BY MONTH

2-y-o	W-R	Per cent	£1 Level Stake	3-y-o	W-R	Per cent	£1 Level Stake
January	0-0	0.0	0.00	January	0-0	0.0	0.00
February	0-0	0.0	0.00	February	0-0	0.0	0.00
March	0-0	0.0	0.00	March	0-0	0.0	0.00
April	0-0	0.0	0.00	April	0-2	0.0	-2.00
May	0-1	0.0	-1.00	May	0-5	0.0	-5.00
June	0-0	0.0	0.00	June	0-4	0.0	-4.00
July	0-1	0.0	-1.00	July	1-6	16.7	+0.50
August	0-2	0.0	-2.00	August	0-1	0.0	-1.00
September	0-3	0.0	-3.00	September	0-1	0.0	-1.00
October	0-3	0.0	-3.00	October	0-3	0.0	-3.00
November	2-6	33.3	+11.00	November	0-3	0.0	-3.00
December	0-1	0.0	-1.00	December	1-3	33.3	+2.00

4-y-o+	W-R	Per cent	£1 Level Stake	Totals	W-R	Per cent	£1 Level Stake
January	1-7	14.3	-0.50	January	1-7	14.3	-0.50
February	0-6	0.0	-6.00	February	0-6	0.0	-6.00
March	1-5	20.0	+46.00	March	1-5	20.0	+46.00
April	0-7	0.0	-7.00	April	0-9	0.0	-9.00
May	0-5	0.0	-5.00	May	0-11	0.0	-11.00
June	1-7	14.3	+2.00	June	1-11	9.1	-2.00
July	1-11	9.1	-5.50	July	2-18	11.1	-6.00
August	1-9	11.1	-4.00	August	1-12	8.3	-7.00
September	0-10	0.0	-10.00	September	0-14	0.0	-14.00
October	0-10	0.0	-10.00	October	0-16	0.0	-16.00
November	1-2	50.0	+8.00	November	3-11	27.3	+5.00
December	0-1	0.0	-1.00	December	1-5	20.0	+1.00

DISTANCE

2-y-o	W-R	Per cent	£1 Level Stake	3-y-o	W-R	Per cent	£1 Level Stake
5f-6f	0-11	0.0	-11.00	5f-6f	0-6	0.0	-6.00
7f-8f	1-2	50.0	+7.00	7f-8f	1-13	7.7	-6.50
9f-13f	1-4	25.0	+4.00	9f-13f	1-9	11.1	-4.00
14f+	0-0	0.0	0.00	14f+	0-0	0.0	0.00

4-y-o+	W-R	Per cent	£1 Level Stake	Totals	W-R	Per cent	£1 Level Stake
5f-6f	2-18	11.1	-7.50	5f-6f	2-35	5.7	-24.50
7f-8f	3-34	8.8	+36.00	7f-8f	5-49	10.2	+36.50
9f-13f	1-23	4.3	-16.50	9f-13f	3-36	8.3	-16.50
14f+	0-5	0.0	-5.00	14f+	0-5	0.0	-5.00

TYPE OF RACE

Non-Handicaps	W-R	Per cent	£1 Level Stake	Handicaps	W-R	Per cent	£1 Level Stake
2-y-o	0-10	0.0	-10.00	2-y-o	2-7	28.6	+10.00
3-y-o	0-10	0.0	-10.00	3-y-o	2-18	11.1	-6.50
4-y-o+	0-5	0.0	-5.00	4-y-o+	6-75	8.0	+12.00

RACE CLASS

	W-R	Per cent	£1 Level Stake
Class 1	0-3	0.0	-3.00
Class 2	1-3	33.3	+48.00
Class 3	0-3	0.0	-3.00
Class 4	0-21	0.0	-21.00
Class 5	4-54	7.4	-27.00
Class 6	5-38	13.2	-0.50
Class 7	0-3	0.0	-3.00

FIRST TIME OUT

	W-R	Per cent	£1 Level Stake
2-y-o	1-5	20.0	+3.00
3-y-o	0-6	0.0	-6.00
4-y-o+	1-13	7.7	-6.50
Totals	2-24	8.3	-9.50

JOCKEYS

	W-R	Per cent	£1 Level Stake
Robert Winston	3-14	21.4	+13.00
William Cox	2-10	20.0	+0.50
Oisin Murphy	1-3	33.3	+2.50
Daniel Muscutt	1-3	33.3	+3.50
Jack Mitchell	1-9	11.1	0.00
David Probert	1-13	7.7	+38.00
Rossa Ryan	1-16	6.3	-11.00

COURSE RECORD

	Total W-R	Non-Hndcps 2-y-o	3-y-o+	Hndcps 2-y-o	3-y-o+	Per cent	£1 Level Stake
Wolvhptn (A.W)	3-18	0-0	0-6	1-1	2-11	16.7	+6.50
Windsor	2-12	0-0	0-3	0-0	2-9	16.7	-0.50
Doncaster	1-4	0-1	0-0	0-0	1-3	25.0	+47.00
Salisbury	1-6	0-0	0-0	0-0	1-6	16.7	-0.50
Lingfield (A.W)	1-8	0-0	0-2	0-1	1-5	12.5	-3.00
Newbury	1-10	0-1	0-0	0-0	1-9	10.0	-1.00
Kempton (A.W)	1-13	0-1	0-1	1-2	0-9	7.7	-4.00

WINNING HORSES

Horse	Races Run	1st	2nd	3rd	£
Blistering Bob	8	1	0	0	3752
*Fitwood Star	1	1	0	0	3105
High Acclaim (USA)	8	1	0	0	28013
Jack Bear	7	1	0	1	3752
Langley Vale	9	1	0	0	3105
Look Surprised	9	2	1	3	7245
Lucky Louie	4	1	2	0	3752
Taurean Dancer (IRE)	9	1	2	0	3105
Whelans Way (IRE)	5	1	1	0	3235
Total winning prize-money					**£59064**
Favourites	**1-9**		**11.1%**		**-5.75**

HENRY TETT

LAMBOURN, BERKS

	No. of Hrs	Races Run	1st	2nd	3rd	Unpl	Per cent	£1 Level Stake
2-y-o	*1*	*2*	*0*	*0*	*0*	*2*	*0.0*	*-2.00*
3-y-o	*2*	*4*	*0*	*0*	*0*	*4*	*0.0*	*-4.00*
4-y-o+	*3*	*15*	*1*	*0*	*1*	*13*	*6.7*	*-4.00*
Totals	**6**	**21**	**1**	**0**	**1**	**19**	**4.8**	**-10.00**
2017	*7*	*38*	*3*	*4*	*3*	*28*	*7.9*	*+4.00*
2016	*7*	*20*	*0*	*0*	*0*	*20*	*0.0*	*-20.00*

JOCKEYS

	W-R	Per cent	£1 Level Stake
Mr Frederick Tett	1-4	25.0	+7.00

COURSE RECORD

	Total W-R	Non-Hndcps 2-y-o	3-y-o+	Hndcps 2-y-o	3-y-o+	Per cent	£1 Level Stake
Wolvhptn (A.W)	1-5	0-0	0-1	0-0	1-4	20.0	+6.00

WINNING HORSES

Horse	Races Run	1st	2nd	3rd	£
Mr Red Clubs (IRE)	8	1	0	0	3619
Total winning prize-money					**£3619**
Favourites	**0-0**		**0.0%**		**0.00**

DAVID THOMPSON

BOLAM, CO DURHAM

	No. of Hrs	Races Run	1st	2nd	3rd	Unpl	Per cent	£1 Level Stake
2-y-o	*0*	*0*	*0*	*0*	*0*	*0*	*0.0*	*0.00*
3-y-o	*3*	*17*	*0*	*0*	*0*	*17*	*0.0*	*-17.00*
4-y-o+	*12*	*95*	*6*	*12*	*12*	*65*	*6.3*	*-23.25*
Totals	**15**	**112**	**6**	**12**	**12**	**82**	**5.4**	**-40.25**
2017	*9*	*64*	*6*	*3*	*12*	*43*	*9.4*	*+5.83*
2016	*13*	*67*	*3*	*10*	*8*	*46*	*4.5*	*-30.00*

JOCKEYS

	W-R	Per cent	£1 Level Stake
Jamie Gormley	3-17	17.6	+14.25
Josephine Gordon	1-2	50.0	+4.50
Callum Rodriguez	1-8	12.5	-3.00
Andrew Mullen	1-14	7.1	+15.00

COURSE RECORD

	Total W-R	Non-Hndcps 2-y-o	3-y-o+	Hndcps 2-y-o	3-y-o+	Per cent	£1 Level Stake
Newcastle (A.W)	4-41	0-0	0-2	0-0	4-39	9.8	+14.75
Hamilton	1-13	0-0	0-0	0-0	1-13	7.7	-2.00
Redcar	1-15	0-0	0-5	0-0	1-10	6.7	-10.00

WINNING HORSES

Horse	Races Run	1st	2nd	3rd	£
Highwayman	17	2	2	1	6598
Lukoutoldmakezebak	12	2	0	3	6210
Someone Exciting	21	1	4	4	3493
Visitant	14	1	1	2	3493
Total winning prize-money					**£19794**
Favourites	**1-1**		**100.0%**		**2.25**

RONALD THOMPSON

STAINFORTH, S YORKS

	No. of Hrs	Races Run	1st	2nd	3rd	Unpl	Per cent	£1 Level Stake
2-y-o	*4*	*13*	*0*	*1*	*2*	*10*	*0.0*	*-13.00*
3-y-o	*4*	*32*	*0*	*5*	*7*	*20*	*0.0*	*-32.00*
4-y-o+	*4*	*31*	*4*	*2*	*1*	*24*	*12.9*	*-7.25*
Totals	**12**	**76**	**4**	**8**	**10**	**54**	**5.3**	**-52.25**
2017	*10*	*51*	*0*	*4*	*4*	*43*	*0.0*	*-51.00*
2016	*14*	*39*	*1*	*1*	*2*	*35*	*2.6*	*-28.00*

JOCKEYS

	W-R	Per cent	£1 Level Stake
Andrew Elliott	3-21	14.3	-1.25
Callum Rodriguez	1-1	100.0	+3.00

COURSE RECORD

	Total W-R	Non-Hndcps 2-y-o	3-y-o+	Hndcps 2-y-o	3-y-o+	Per cent	£1 Level Stake
Catterick	2-8	0-0	0-0	0-0	2-8	25.0	+1.75
Thirsk	1-2	0-0	0-0	0-0	1-2	50.0	+8.00
Southwell (A.W)	1-13	0-1	0-2	0-2	1-8	7.7	-9.00

WINNING HORSES

Horse	Races Run	1st	2nd	3rd	£
Mr Strutter (IRE)	19	4	2	1	13490
Total winning prize-money					**£13490**
Favourites	**1-4**		**25.0%**		**-0.25**

NIGEL TINKLER

LANGTON, N YORKS

	No. of Hrs	Races Run	1st	2nd	3rd	Unpl	Per cent	£1 Level Stake
2-y-o	*11*	*64*	*4*	*4*	*2*	*54*	*6.3*	*-18.63*
3-y-o	*14*	*84*	*19*	*7*	*9*	*49*	*22.6*	*+38.58*
4-y-o+	*17*	*166*	*14*	*20*	*11*	*121*	*8.4*	*-37.13*
Totals	**42**	**314**	**37**	**31**	**22**	**224**	**11.8**	**-17.18**
2017	*35*	*221*	*19*	*21*	*22*	*159*	*8.6*	*-114.42*
2016	*30*	*224*	*20*	*27*	*24*	*153*	*8.9*	*-32.00*

BY MONTH

2-y-o	W-R	Per cent	£1 Level Stake	3-y-o	W-R	Per cent	£1 Level Stake
January	0-0	0.0	0.00	January	0-3	0.0	-3.00
February	0-0	0.0	0.00	February	0-1	0.0	-1.00
March	0-0	0.0	0.00	March	0-1	0.0	-1.00
April	0-2	0.0	-2.00	April	2-8	25.0	+12.00
May	0-6	0.0	-6.00	May	4-17	23.5	+15.75
June	0-9	0.0	-9.00	June	4-17	23.5	+5.33
July	2-8	25.0	+17.50	July	4-12	33.3	+12.50
August	1-18	5.6	-1.00	August	5-14	35.7	+9.00
September	1-10	10.0	-7.13	September	0-6	0.0	-6.00
October	0-7	0.0	-7.00	October	0-5	0.0	-5.00
November	0-3	0.0	-3.00	November	0-0	0.0	0.00
December	0-1	0.0	-1.00	December	0-0	0.0	0.00

4-y-o+	W-R	Per cent	£1 Level Stake	Totals	W-R	Per cent	£1 Level Stake
January	0-1	0.0	-1.00	January	0-4	0.0	-4.00
February	1-4	25.0	-1.63	February	1-5	20.0	-2.63
March	1-9	11.1	-6.25	March	1-10	10.0	-7.25
April	1-7	14.3	+6.00	April	3-17	17.6	+16.00
May	1-23	4.3	-18.00	May	5-46	10.9	-8.25
June	5-29	17.2	+47.75	June	9-55	16.4	+44.08
July	0-20	0.0	-20.00	July	6-40	15.0	+10.00
August	4-27	14.8	-2.00	August	10-59	16.9	+6.00
September	0-20	0.0	-20.00	September	1-36	2.8	-33.13
October	1-17	5.9	-13.00	October	1-29	3.4	-25.00
November	0-4	0.0	-4.00	November	0-7	0.0	-4.00
December	0-5	0.0	-5.00	December	0-6	0.0	-5.00

DISTANCE

2-y-o	W-R	Per cent	£1 Level Stake	3-y-o	W-R	Per cent	£1 Level Stake
5f-6f	4-46	8.7	-0.63	5f-6f	13-46	28.3	+48.83
7f-8f	0-17	0.0	-17.00	7f-8f	4-26	15.4	-6.75
9f-13f	0-1	0.0	-1.00	9f-13f	2-11	18.2	-2.50
14f+	0-0	0.0	0.00	14f+	0-1	0.0	-1.00

4-y-o+	W-R	Per cent	£1 Level Stake	Totals	W-R	Per cent	£1 Level Stake
5f-6f	5-74	6.8	-44.50	5f-6f	22-166	13.3	+3.70
7f-8f	7-59	11.9	+24.88	7f-8f	11-102	10.8	+1.13
9f-13f	2-33	6.1	-17.50	9f-13f	4-45	8.9	-21.00
14f+	0-0	0.0	0.00	14f+	0-1	0.0	-1.00

TYPE OF RACE

Non-Handicaps	W-R	Per cent	£1 Level Stake	Handicaps	W-R	Per cent	£1 Level Stake
2-y-o	1-45	2.2	-24.00	2-y-o	3-19	15.8	+5.38
3-y-o	0-13	0.0	-13.00	3-y-o	19-71	26.8	+51.58
4-y-o+	0-5	0.0	-5.00	4-y-o+	14-161	8.7	-32.13

RACE CLASS

	W-R	Per cent	£1 Level Stake
Class 1	0-0	0.0	0.00
Class 2	2-18	11.1	+1.88
Class 3	4-43	9.3	-19.67
Class 4	10-59	16.9	+20.75
Class 5	10-93	10.8	-15.13
Class 6	11-99	11.1	-3.00
Class 7	0-2	0.0	-2.00

FIRST TIME OUT

	W-R	Per cent	£1 Level Stake
2-y-o	0-11	0.0	-11.00
3-y-o	2-14	14.3	+6.00
4-y-o+	1-17	5.9	-4.00
Totals	3-42	7.1	-9.00

JOCKEYS

	W-R	Per cent	£1 Level Stake
Lewis Edmunds	19-125	15.2	+30.96
Faye McManoman	6-82	7.3	-55.50
Andrew Mullen	4-11	36.4	+39.88
Silvestre De Sousa	3-12	25.0	+10.50
James Sullivan	1-1	100.0	+3.50
Theodore Ladd	1-2	50.0	+2.00
Robert Dodsworth	1-4	25.0	+1.50
Tom Eaves	1-13	7.7	+4.00
Rowan Scott	1-22	4.5	-12.00

COURSE RECORD

	Total W-R	Non-Hndcps 2-y-o	3-y-o+	Hndcps 2-y-o	3-y-o+	Per cent	£1 Level Stake
Beverley	5-31	1-11	0-0	0-1	4-19	16.1	+7.75
Ripon	4-18	0-6	0-0	0-0	4-12	22.2	+3.33
Newcastle (A.W)	4-43	0-2	0-5	0-3	4-33	9.3	-16.38
Carlisle	3-9	0-2	0-0	0-1	3-6	33.3	+8.50
Nottingham	3-14	0-0	0-0	0-2	3-12	21.4	+3.75
Thirsk	3-21	0-4	0-1	1-2	2-14	14.3	-8.00
Newmkt (Jly)	2-5	0-0	0-0	1-1	1-4	40.0	+22.00
Leicester	2-7	0-0	0-1	0-0	2-6	28.6	+20.00

Doncaster	2-25	0-3	0-2	0-0	2-20	8.0	0.00
Redcar	2-43	0-8	0-4	0-1	2-30	4.7	-37.00
Musselburgh	1-1	0-0	0-0	0-0	1-1	100.0	+1.50
Goodwood	1-1	0-0	0-0	1-1	0-0	100.0	+1.88
Wolvhptn (A.W)	1-3	0-0	0-0	0-0	1-3	33.3	+1.00
Catterick	1-4	0-1	0-0	0-1	1-2	25.0	+13.00
Chester	1-4	0-1	0-0	0-0	1-3	25.0	+0.50
Yarmouth	1-4	0-0	0-0	0-0	1-4	25.0	+1.00
Hamilton	1-11	0-0	0-0	0-1	1-10	9.1	+30.00

WINNING HORSES

Horse	Races Run	1st	2nd	3rd	£
Allux Boy (IRE)	13	1	2	1	3170
Archie Perkins (IRE)	8	2	3	0	6620
Athollblair Boy (IRE)	11	2	2	1	9283
Bashiba (IRE)	14	1	2	1	3781
Citron Major	12	3	0	3	9704
Cliff (IRE)	14	1	1	1	3398
Daffy Jane	11	3	2	2	11032
Dutch Coed	13	1	1	0	3493
Etienne Gerard	14	1	0	1	3105
Exclusive Waters (IRE)	13	1	1	2	3493
*Firmdecisions (IRE)	14	2	0	0	12032
Kaeso	9	2	2	2	13001
Kilbaha Lady (IRE)	12	1	1	1	3235
Princess Power (IRE)	9	4	1	0	54496
Rock On Bertie (IRE)*	7	1	0	0	3105
Roundhay Park	9	2	1	2	16324
Seen The Lyte (IRE)	12	4	0	1	21121
Sheepscar Lad (IRE)	10	1	2	0	5531
Whinmoor	9	4	1	0	19666
Total winning prize-money					**£205590**
Favourites	**15-32**		**46.9%**		**17.50**

MARTIN TODHUNTER

ORTON, CUMBRIA

	No. of Hrs	Races Run	1st	2nd	3rd	Unpl	Per cent	£1 Level Stake
2-y-o	*0*	*0*	*0*	*0*	*0*	*0*	*0.0*	*0.00*
3-y-o	*0*	*0*	*0*	*0*	*0*	*0*	*0.0*	*0.00*
4-y-o+	*2*	*13*	*2*	*1*	*1*	*9*	*15.4*	*+1.50*
Totals	**2**	**13**	**2**	**1**	**1**	**9**	**15.4**	**+1.50**
2017	*6*	*17*	*4*	*3*	*0*	*10*	*23.5*	*+0.83*
2016	*6*	*35*	*3*	*2*	*5*	*25*	*8.6*	*-19.00*

JOCKEYS

	W-R	Per cent	£1 Level Stake
Mr Simon Walker	1-1	100.0	+10.00
Callum Rodriguez	1-4	25.0	-0.50

COURSE RECORD

	Total W-R	Non-Hndcps 2-y-o	3-y-o+	Hndcps 2-y-o	3-y-o+	Per cent	£1 Level Stake
Catterick	1-3	0-0	0-0	0-0	1-3	33.3	+8.00
Ayr	1-4	0-0	0-0	0-0	1-4	25.0	-0.50

WINNING HORSES

Horse	Races Run	1st	2nd	3rd	£
Question Of Faith	10	2	1	1	11657
Total winning prize-money					**£11657**
Favourites	**2-6**		**33.3%**		**0.50**

MARK H TOMPKINS

NEWMARKET, SUFFOLK

	No. of Hrs	Races Run	1st	2nd	3rd	Unpl	Per cent	£1 Level Stake
2-y-o	*9*	*26*	*1*	*1*	*0*	*24*	*3.8*	*-9.00*
3-y-o	*14*	*62*	*6*	*2*	*3*	*51*	*9.7*	*+54.50*
4-y-o+	*8*	*31*	*1*	*1*	*3*	*26*	*3.2*	*-27.75*
Totals	**31**	**119**	**8**	**4**	**6**	**101**	**6.7**	**+17.75**
2017	*34*	*145*	*7*	*11*	*8*	*119*	*4.8*	*-112.24*
2016	*24*	*147*	*11*	*11*	*15*	*109*	*7.5*	*-92.21*

JOCKEYS

	W-R	Per cent	£1 Level Stake
Louis Steward	3-31	9.7	+27.00
Joey Haynes	2-29	6.9	-20.75
Theodore Ladd	1-3	33.3	+48.00
Paul Mulrennan	1-6	16.7	+0.50
Shane Kelly	1-11	9.1	+2.00

COURSE RECORD

	Total W-R	Non-Hndcps 2-y-o	3-y-o+	Hndcps 2-y-o	3-y-o+	Per cent	£1 Level Stake
Chelmsford (A.W)	3-36	0-8	0-3	0-0	3-25	8.3	+18.00
Newmarket	1-1	1-1	0-0	0-0	0-0	100.0	+16.00
Southwell (A.W)	1-5	0-0	0-2	0-0	1-3	20.0	+46.00
Newcastle (A.W)	1-6	0-0	1-2	0-1	0-3	16.7	+0.50
Wolvhptn (A.W)	1-10	0-0	0-2	0-0	1-8	10.0	-6.75
Lingfield (A.W)	1-21	0-1	0-5	0-1	1-14	4.8	-16.00

WINNING HORSES

Horse	Races Run	1st	2nd	3rd	£
Astrojewel	5	1	0	0	3105
Four Fifty Three	11	1	1	1	3493
Garrel Glen	2	1	0	0	3881
Indian Red	7	1	0	2	3105
Roof Garden	5	2	0	0	6987
Topapinion	1	1	0	0	3752
Velvet Vision	5	1	1	0	5175
Total winning prize-money					**£29498**
Favourites	**1-5**		**20.0%**		**-1.75**

MARCUS TREGONING

WHITSBURY, HANTS

	No. of Hrs	Races Run	1st	2nd	3rd	Unpl	Per cent	£1 Level Stake
2-y-o	*13*	*34*	*2*	*1*	*1*	*30*	*5.9*	*+6.00*
3-y-o	*15*	*71*	*12*	*7*	*6*	*46*	*16.9*	*-36.26*
4-y-o+	*13*	*68*	*4*	*6*	*9*	*49*	*5.9*	*-39.50*
Totals	**41**	**173**	**18**	**14**	**16**	**125**	**10.4**	**-69.76**
2017	*40*	*160*	*26*	*26*	*11*	*97*	*16.3*	*-35.19*
2016	*40*	*137*	*11*	*21*	*15*	*89*	*8.0*	*-70.63*

BY MONTH

2-y-o	W-R	Per cent	£1 Level Stake
January	0-0	0.0	0.00
February	0-0	0.0	0.00
March	0-0	0.0	0.00
April	0-0	0.0	0.00
May	0-0	0.0	0.00
June	0-0	0.0	0.00
July	0-0	0.0	0.00
August	0-4	0.0	-4.00
September	0-7	0.0	-7.00
October	2-11	18.2	+29.00
November	0-8	0.0	-8.00
December	0-4	0.0	-4.00

3-y-o	W-R	Per cent	£1 Level Stake
January	0-2	0.0	-2.00
February	0-1	0.0	-1.00
March	0-0	0.0	0.00
April	0-0	0.0	0.00
May	0-8	0.0	-8.00
June	3-8	37.5	+1.38
July	2-12	16.7	-6.00
August	2-10	20.0	-4.17
September	2-12	16.7	-8.09
October	2-7	28.6	0.00
November	1-8	12.5	-5.38
December	0-3	0.0	-3.00

4-y-o+	W-R	Per cent	£1 Level Stake
January	0-0	0.0	0.00
February	0-0	0.0	0.00
March	0-0	0.0	0.00
April	0-2	0.0	-2.00
May	1-9	11.1	-2.50
June	1-13	7.7	-9.50
July	0-8	0.0	-8.00
August	0-8	0.0	-8.00
September	1-11	9.1	-5.50
October	0-5	0.0	-5.00
November	1-7	14.3	+6.00
December	0-5	0.0	-5.00

Totals	W-R	Per cent	£1 Level Stake
January	0-2	0.0	-2.00
February	0-1	0.0	-1.00
March	0-0	0.0	0.00
April	0-2	0.0	-2.00
May	1-17	5.9	-10.50
June	4-21	19.0	-8.12
July	2-20	10.0	-14.00
August	2-22	9.1	-16.17
September	3-30	10.0	-20.59
October	4-23	17.4	+24.00
November	2-23	8.7	+0.62
December	0-12	0.0	-8.00

DISTANCE

2-y-o	W-R	Per cent	£1 Level Stake
5f-6f	1-8	12.5	-2.00
7f-8f	1-26	3.8	+8.00
9f-13f	0-0	0.0	0.00
14f+	0-0	0.0	0.00

3-y-o	W-R	Per cent	£1 Level Stake
5f-6f	1-9	11.1	-6.00
7f-8f	4-38	10.5	-28.29
9f-13f	7-22	31.8	+0.03
14f+	0-2	0.0	-2.00

4-y-o+	W-R	Per cent	£1 Level Stake
5f-6f	0-1	0.0	-1.00
7f-8f	3-27	11.1	-11.50
9f-13f	1-29	3.4	-16.00
14f+	0-11	0.0	-11.00

Totals	W-R	Per cent	£1 Level Stake
5f-6f	2-18	11.1	-9.00
7f-8f	8-91	8.8	-31.79
9f-13f	8-51	15.7	-15.97
14f+	0-13	0.0	-13.00

TYPE OF RACE

Non-Handicaps

	W-R	Per cent	£1 Level Stake
2-y-o	2-31	6.5	+9.00
3-y-o	5-27	18.5	-15.92
4-y-o+	0-5	0.0	-5.00

Handicaps

	W-R	Per cent	£1 Level Stake
2-y-o	0-3	0.0	-3.00
3-y-o	7-44	15.9	-20.34
4-y-o+	4-63	6.3	-34.50

RACE CLASS

	W-R	Per cent	£1 Level Stake
Class 1	1-3	33.3	+31.00
Class 2	2-22	9.1	-5.00
Class 3	2-15	13.3	-6.00
Class 4	3-38	7.9	-27.54
Class 5	5-69	7.2	-52.63
Class 6	5-26	19.2	-9.59
Class 7	0-0	0.0	0.00

FIRST TIME OUT

	W-R	Per cent	£1 Level Stake
2-y-o	0-13	0.0	-13.00
3-y-o	2-15	13.3	-10.00
4-y-o+	0-13	0.0	-13.00
Totals	2-41	4.9	-36.00

JOCKEYS

	W-R	Per cent	£1 Level Stake
Hayley Turner	9-72	12.5	-37.50
Jim Crowley	3-9	33.3	+3.83
Martin Dwyer	3-24	12.5	+25.38
Paul Hanagan	1-1	100.0	+1.38
Mr Ross Birkett	1-1	100.0	+1.63
Tyler Saunders	1-30	3.3	-28.47

COURSE RECORD

	Total W-R	Non-Hndcps 2-y-o	Non-Hndcps 3-y-o+	Hndcps 2-y-o	Hndcps 3-y-o+	Per cent	£1 Level Stake
Chelmsford (A.W)	3-12	0-1	2-3	0-0	1-8	25.0	-5.67
Ffos Las	2-6	0-0	0-1	0-0	2-5	33.3	+0.03
Salisbury	2-12	0-2	1-4	0-0	1-6	16.7	-5.00
Lingfield (A.W)	2-18	0-3	1-5	0-1	1-9	11.1	-11.63
Goodwood	2-23	0-4	0-6	0-0	2-13	8.7	-13.00
Kempton (A.W)	2-38	0-12	0-4	0-1	2-21	5.3	-31.38
Beverley	1-2	0-0	1-1	0-0	0-1	50.0	+0.38
Nottingham	1-2	1-2	0-0	0-0	0-0	50.0	+4.00
Newcastle (A.W)	1-2	0-0	0-0	0-0	1-2	50.0	+11.00
Leicester	1-3	0-0	0-0	0-0	1-3	33.3	+2.50
Newbury	1-6	1-4	0-0	0-0	0-2	16.7	+28.00

WINNING HORSES

Horse	Races Run	1st	2nd	3rd	£
Alrahaal (IRE)	4	1	0	0	4528
Barnay*	10	1	4	1	3105
Honourbound (IRE)	6	1	0	1	3170
Landue	10	5	1	1	20988
Margub	4	2	1	0	13779
Mohaather	3	2	1	0	26565
Mukalal	6	1	0	0	8086
Power Of Darkness	2	2	0	0	17237
Seafarer (IRE)	8	1	2	3	16173
Sir Titan	8	2	1	1	16179
Total winning prize-money					**£129810**
Favourites	**12-23**		**52.2%**		**12.24**

GRANT TUER

BIRKBY, N YORKS

	No. of Hrs	Races Run	1st	2nd	3rd	Unpl	Per cent	£1 Level Stake
2-y-o	*4*	*19*	*0*	*2*	*1*	*16*	*0.0*	*-19.00*
3-y-o	*4*	*17*	*4*	*3*	*1*	*9*	*23.5*	*+9.50*
4-y-o+	*7*	*49*	*4*	*5*	*4*	*36*	*8.2*	*+15.00*
Totals	**15**	**85**	**8**	**10**	**6**	**61**	**9.4**	**+5.50**
2017	*10*	*46*	*3*	*5*	*6*	*32*	*6.5*	*-20.50*
2016	*7*	*46*	*3*	*6*	*3*	*34*	*6.5*	*-5.00*

JOCKEYS

	W-R	Per cent	£1 Level Stake
Ben Curtis	2-4	50.0	+3.50
Phillip Makin	2-18	11.1	+6.00
Jack Mitchell	1-3	33.3	+1.00
Jack Garritty	1-4	25.0	+37.00
Connor Murtagh	1-7	14.3	0.00
Sam James	1-17	5.9	-10.00

COURSE RECORD

	Total W-R	Non-Hndcps 2-y-o	Non-Hndcps 3-y-o+	Hndcps 2-y-o	Hndcps 3-y-o+	Per cent	£1 Level Stake
Musselburgh	2-11	0-2	0-0	0-1	2-8	18.2	+13.00
Pontefract	1-4	0-1	0-1	0-0	1-2	25.0	-1.00
Wolvhptn (A.W)	1-5	0-0	0-0	0-0	1-5	20.0	-1.00
Ripon	1-5	0-2	0-1	0-0	1-2	20.0	-0.50
Carlisle	1-7	0-0	0-0	0-0	1-7	14.3	0.00
Thirsk	1-7	0-0	0-0	0-0	1-7	14.3	0.00
Newcastle (A.W)	1-14	0-0	0-2	0-5	1-7	7.1	+27.00

WINNING HORSES

Horse	Races Run	1st	2nd	3rd	£
Champarisi	7	1	0	1	3752
Etikaal	15	2	1	1	6987
Final Go	6	1	1	0	4205
Fyrecracker (IRE)	6	2	1	0	7569
Roundhead	2	2	0	0	7504
Total winning prize-money					**£30017**
Favourites	**2-5**		**40.0%**		**5.00**

JOSEPH TUITE

LAMBOURN, BERKS

	No. of Hrs	Races Run	1st	2nd	3rd	Unpl	Per cent	£1 Level Stake
2-y-o	*13*	*55*	*8*	*7*	*2*	*38*	*14.5*	*-1.79*
3-y-o	*13*	*64*	*8*	*11*	*4*	*41*	*12.5*	*-26.09*
4-y-o+	*17*	*132*	*14*	*7*	*22*	*89*	*10.6*	*-35.00*
Totals	**43**	**251**	**30**	**25**	**28**	**168**	**12.0**	**-62.88**
2017	*39*	*205*	*17*	*20*	*14*	*153*	*8.3*	*-84.50*
2016	*37*	*249*	*22*	*31*	*28*	*168*	*8.8*	*-111.51*

BY MONTH

2-y-o	W-R	Per cent	£1 Level Stake
January	0-0	0.0	0.00
February	0-0	0.0	0.00
March	0-0	0.0	0.00
April	0-2	0.0	-2.00
May	0-2	0.0	-2.00
June	0-7	0.0	-7.00
July	1-8	12.5	+13.00
August	2-14	14.3	-6.09
September	2-11	18.2	-4.50
October	3-9	33.3	+8.80
November	0-2	0.0	-2.00
December	0-0	0.0	0.00

3-y-o	W-R	Per cent	£1 Level Stake
January	2-5	40.0	+3.41
February	2-4	50.0	+1.63
March	0-3	0.0	-3.00
April	0-3	0.0	-3.00
May	0-12	0.0	-12.00
June	1-8	12.5	0.00
July	3-11	27.3	+4.88
August	0-7	0.0	-7.00
September	0-4	0.0	-4.00
October	0-3	0.0	-3.00
November	0-4	0.0	-4.00
December	0-0	0.0	0.00

4-y-o+	W-R	Per cent	£1 Level Stake
January	0-12	0.0	-12.00
February	0-6	0.0	-6.00
March	1-8	12.5	-4.75
April	1-14	7.1	-10.25
May	3-14	21.4	+5.00
June	1-9	11.1	0.00
July	2-8	25.0	+10.00
August	2-18	11.1	-5.00
September	2-10	20.0	+2.50
October	1-21	4.8	-8.00
November	1-7	14.3	-1.50
December	0-5	0.0	-5.00

Totals	W-R	Per cent	£1 Level Stake
January	2-17	11.8	-8.59
February	2-10	20.0	-4.37
March	1-11	9.1	-7.75
April	1-19	5.3	-15.25
May	3-28	10.7	-9.00
June	2-24	8.3	-7.00
July	6-27	22.2	+27.88
August	4-39	10.3	-18.09
September	4-25	16.0	-6.00
October	4-33	12.1	-2.20
November	1-13	7.7	-5.50
December	0-5	0.0	-5.00

DISTANCE

2-y-o	W-R	Per cent	£1 Level Stake
5f-6f	4-42	9.5	-1.25
7f-8f	4-12	33.3	+0.46
9f-13f	0-1	0.0	-1.00
14f+	0-0	0.0	0.00

3-y-o	W-R	Per cent	£1 Level Stake
5f-6f	3-39	7.7	-25.75
7f-8f	1-8	12.5	-1.50
9f-13f	4-15	26.7	+3.16
14f+	0-2	0.0	-2.00

4-y-o+	W-R	Per cent	£1 Level Stake
5f-6f	3-40	7.5	-27.50
7f-8f	4-36	11.1	-14.50
9f-13f	3-43	7.0	-15.50
14f+	4-13	30.8	+22.50

Totals	W-R	Per cent	£1 Level Stake
5f-6f	10-121	8.3	-54.50
7f-8f	9-56	16.1	-15.54
9f-13f	7-59	11.9	-13.34
14f+	4-15	26.7	+20.50

TYPE OF RACE

Non-Handicaps	W-R	Per cent	£1 Level Stake
2-y-o	3-34	8.8	-0.20
3-y-o	0-19	0.0	-19.00
4-y-o+	0-1	0.0	-1.00

Handicaps	W-R	Per cent	£1 Level Stake
2-y-o	5-21	23.8	-1.59
3-y-o	8-45	17.8	-7.09
4-y-o+	14-131	10.7	-34.00

RACE CLASS

	W-R	Per cent	£1 Level Stake
Class 1	0-1	0.0	-1.00
Class 2	0-18	0.0	-18.00

FIRST TIME OUT

	W-R	Per cent	£1 Level Stake
2-y-o	0-13	0.0	-13.00
3-y-o	1-13	7.7	-6.50

Class 3	3-24	12.5	+6.00
Class 4	5-34	14.7	+15.63
Class 5	7-90	7.8	-55.45
Class 6	15-84	17.9	-10.06
Class 7	0-0	0.0	0.00

4-y-o+	1-17	5.9	-13.75
Totals	2-43	4.7	-33.25

JOCKEYS

	W-R	Per cent	£1 Level Stake
Finley Marsh	6-22	27.3	+21.75
Nicola Currie	6-38	15.8	+9.38
Oisin Murphy	5-32	15.6	-13.32
Charles Bishop	4-20	20.0	-1.34
Liam Jones	1-1	100.0	+5.00
Oliver Stammers	1-1	100.0	+4.50
William Carver	1-2	50.0	+2.50
Andrea Atzeni	1-3	33.3	+10.00
Jack Mitchell	1-3	33.3	+0.75
Adam Kirby	1-4	25.0	-1.00
Franny Norton	1-4	25.0	+9.00
Fran Berry	1-9	11.1	0.00
Liam Keniry	1-12	8.3	-10.09

COURSE RECORD

	Total W-R	Non-Hndcps 2-y-o	Non-Hndcps 3-y-o+	Hndcps 2-y-o	Hndcps 3-y-o+	Per cent	£1 Level Stake
Chelmsford (A.W)	6-22	0-1	0-2	2-3	4-16	27.3	-0.93
Kempton (A.W)	5-42	0-4	0-2	0-3	5-33	11.9	-10.50
Bath	3-11	0-1	0-1	1-2	2-7	27.3	+0.50
Windsor	3-25	1-10	0-4	0-0	2-11	12.0	-12.57
Wolvhptn (A.W)	3-26	0-2	0-2	0-0	3-22	11.5	-8.38
Catterick	1-1	1-1	0-0	0-0	0-0	100.0	+10.00
Yarmouth	1-2	0-0	0-0	0-0	1-2	50.0	+1.75
Leicester	1-4	0-1	0-0	0-1	1-2	25.0	+7.00
Brighton	1-7	0-1	0-0	1-3	0-3	14.3	-4.25
Chester	1-7	0-1	0-0	0-0	1-6	14.3	+2.00
Nottingham	1-7	0-1	0-0	0-1	1-5	14.3	+6.00
Salisbury	1-7	0-2	0-1	0-0	1-4	14.3	-2.50
Ascot	1-8	0-0	0-0	0-0	1-8	12.5	+5.00
Newbury	1-11	1-2	0-0	0-0	0-9	9.1	+10.00
Lingfield (A.W)	1-27	0-0	0-4	1-2	0-21	3.7	-22.00

WINNING HORSES

Horse	Races Run	1st	2nd	3rd	£
All Back To Mine	10	1	2	0	3752
Angel Mead	2	1	0	0	6728
Avon Green	9	1	2	0	3105
Conkering Hero (IRE)	14	3	1	4	10350
Fast Dancer (IRE)	10	1	1	3	11828
Fortune And Glory (USA)	13	3	1	5	10997
Grecian Divine (IRE)	5	1	0	1	3429
Kimifive (IRE)	10	2	3	0	12712
Machine Learner	6	1	0	0	9704
Redgrave (IRE)	8	1	0	0	6469
Shabbah (IRE)	6	1	0	0	5822
Sophosc (IRE)	9	3	2	0	12032
Surrey Blaze (IRE)	10	5	0	1	7504
Surrey Thunder (FR)	2	1	0	1	3752
Sylvia's Mother	9	2	2	0	6987
Topology	10	1	2	4	3105
Who Told Jo Jo (IRE)	14	2	0	0	6210
Total winning prize-money					**£124486**
Favourites	**12-23**		**52.2%**		**7.87**

BILL TURNER

SIGWELLS, SOMERSET

	No. of Hrs	Races Run	1st	2nd	3rd	Unpl	Per cent	£1 Level Stake
2-y-o	*6*	*23*	*1*	*4*	*3*	*15*	*4.3*	*-18.50*
3-y-o	*5*	*27*	*3*	*3*	*3*	*18*	*11.1*	*-5.00*
4-y-o+	*4*	*27*	*1*	*1*	*3*	*22*	*3.7*	*-16.00*
Totals	**15**	**77**	**5**	**8**	**9**	**55**	**6.5**	**-39.50**
2017	*21*	*71*	*3*	*4*	*6*	*58*	*4.2*	*-41.25*
2016	*25*	*109*	*6*	*7*	*7*	*89*	*5.5*	*-35.13*

JOCKEYS

	W-R	Per cent	£1 Level Stake
Jason Watson	3-12	25.0	+12.00
Finley Marsh	2-13	15.4	+0.50

COURSE RECORD

	Total W-R	Non-Hndcps 2-y-o	Non-Hndcps 3-y-o+	Hndcps 2-y-o	Hndcps 3-y-o+	Per cent	£1 Level Stake
Brighton	2-15	0-1	0-1	0-0	2-13	13.3	+0.50
Kempton (A.W)	1-5	1-2	0-0	0-1	0-2	20.0	-0.50
Bath	1-9	0-2	0-1	0-0	1-6	11.1	0.00
Chepstow	1-9	0-3	0-1	0-0	1-5	11.1	-0.50

WINNING HORSES

Horse	Races Run	1st	2nd	3rd	£
Arthur's Spirit	8	1	1	0	3881
Bbob Alula	7	1	1	0	3105
*Born To Boogie	13	1	0	0	3105
Little Boy Blue	8	2	1	3	17790
Total winning prize-money					**£27881**
Favourites	**0-5**		**0.0%**		**-5.00**

KAREN TUTTY

OSMOTHERLEY, N YORKS

	No. of Hrs	Races Run	1st	2nd	3rd	Unpl	Per cent	£1 Level Stake
2-y-o	*0*	*0*	*0*	*0*	*0*	*0*	*0.0*	*0.00*
3-y-o	*2*	*19*	*2*	*1*	*2*	*14*	*10.5*	*-8.50*
4-y-o+	*14*	*125*	*12*	*4*	*11*	*98*	*9.6*	*+3.48*
Totals	**16**	**144**	**14**	**5**	**13**	**112**	**9.7**	**-5.02**
2017	*17*	*155*	*8*	*14*	*13*	*120*	*5.2*	*-86.29*
2016	*13*	*98*	*10*	*6*	*9*	*73*	*10.2*	*+24.00*

BY MONTH

2-y-o	W-R	Per cent	£1 Level Stake
January	0-0	0.0	0.00
February	0-0	0.0	0.00
March	0-0	0.0	0.00
April	0-0	0.0	0.00
May	0-0	0.0	0.00
June	0-0	0.0	0.00
July	0-0	0.0	0.00
August	0-0	0.0	0.00
September	0-0	0.0	0.00
October	0-0	0.0	0.00
November	0-0	0.0	0.00
December	0-0	0.0	0.00

3-y-o	W-R	Per cent	£1 Level Stake
January	0-2	0.0	-2.00
February	0-1	0.0	-1.00
March	0-1	0.0	-1.00
April	0-1	0.0	-1.00
May	0-1	0.0	-1.00
June	1-2	50.0	+3.50
July	1-2	50.0	+3.00
August	0-2	0.0	-2.00
September	0-2	0.0	-2.00
October	0-1	0.0	-1.00
November	0-3	0.0	-3.00
December	0-1	0.0	-1.00

4-y-o+	W-R	Per cent	£1 Level Stake
January	2-7	28.6	+7.73
February	0-4	0.0	-4.00
March	0-4	0.0	-4.00
April	0-8	0.0	-8.00
May	2-22	9.1	+8.00
June	2-15	13.3	+14.25
July	1-13	7.7	-6.50
August	2-16	12.5	+3.00
September	2-15	13.3	+5.00
October	0-7	0.0	-7.00
November	1-10	10.0	-1.00
December	0-4	0.0	-4.00

Totals	W-R	Per cent	£1 Level Stake
January	2-9	22.2	+5.73
February	0-5	0.0	-5.00
March	0-5	0.0	-5.00
April	0-9	0.0	-9.00
May	2-23	8.7	+7.00
June	3-17	17.6	+17.75
July	2-15	13.3	-3.50
August	2-18	11.1	+1.00
September	2-17	11.8	+3.00
October	0-8	0.0	-8.00
November	1-13	7.7	-4.00
December	0-5	0.0	-5.00

DISTANCE

2-y-o	W-R	Per cent	£1 Level Stake
5f-6f	0-0	0.0	0.00
7f-8f	0-0	0.0	0.00
9f-13f	0-0	0.0	0.00
14f+	0-0	0.0	0.00

3-y-o	W-R	Per cent	£1 Level Stake
5f-6f	0-11	0.0	-11.00
7f-8f	1-5	20.0	+0.50
9f-13f	1-3	33.3	+2.00
14f+	0-0	0.0	0.00

4-y-o+	W-R	Per cent	£1 Level Stake
5f-6f	7-68	10.3	+12.98
7f-8f	5-46	10.9	+1.50
9f-13f	0-10	0.0	-10.00
14f+	0-1	0.0	-1.00

Totals	W-R	Per cent	£1 Level Stake
5f-6f	7-79	8.9	+1.98
7f-8f	6-51	11.8	+2.00
9f-13f	1-13	7.7	-8.00
14f+	0-1	0.0	-1.00

TYPE OF RACE

Non-Handicaps

	W-R	Per cent	£1 Level Stake
2-y-o	0-0	0.0	0.00
3-y-o	1-1	100.0	+4.50
4-y-o+	0-3	0.0	-3.00

Handicaps

	W-R	Per cent	£1 Level Stake
2-y-o	0-0	0.0	0.00
3-y-o	1-18	5.6	-13.00
4-y-o+	12-122	9.8	+6.48

RACE CLASS

	W-R	Per cent	£1 Level Stake
Class 1	0-0	0.0	0.00
Class 2	0-0	0.0	0.00
Class 3	0-0	0.0	0.00
Class 4	0-12	0.0	-12.00
Class 5	5-46	10.9	-6.50
Class 6	8-84	9.5	+2.48
Class 7	1-2	50.0	+11.00

FIRST TIME OUT

	W-R	Per cent	£1 Level Stake
2-y-o	0-0	0.0	0.00
3-y-o	0-2	0.0	-2.00
4-y-o+	3-14	21.4	+13.73
Totals	3-16	18.8	+11.73

JOCKEYS

	W-R	Per cent	£1 Level Stake
Gemma Tutty	8-81	9.9	-26.02
Miss Amy Collier	2-9	22.2	+25.00
Tony Hamilton	1-1	100.0	+8.00
Connor Beasley	1-1	100.0	+16.00
Jessica Cooley	1-2	50.0	+11.00
Sam James	1-7	14.3	+4.00

COURSE RECORD

	Total W-R	Non-Hndcps 2-y-o	Non-Hndcps 3-y-o+	Hndcps 2-y-o	Hndcps 3-y-o+	Per cent	£1 Level Stake
Beverley	3-10	0-0	0-0	0-0	3-10	30.0	+14.50
Hamilton	2-10	0-0	0-0	0-0	2-10	20.0	+19.25
Newcastle (A.W)	2-24	0-0	0-0	0-0	2-24	8.3	+6.00
Chepstow	1-2	0-0	1-1	0-0	0-1	50.0	+3.50
Nottingham	1-5	0-0	0-0	0-0	1-5	20.0	+8.00
Chelmsford (A.W)	1-6	0-0	0-0	0-0	1-6	16.7	-4.27
Wolvhptn (A.W)	1-11	0-0	0-1	0-0	1-10	9.1	-2.00
Redcar	1-11	0-0	0-2	0-0	1-9	9.1	-3.00
Carlisle	1-12	0-0	0-0	0-0	1-12	8.3	-5.00
Thirsk	1-12	0-0	0-0	0-0	1-12	8.3	-1.00

WINNING HORSES

Horse	Races Run	1st	2nd	3rd	£
*Alfie's Angel (IRE)	12	1	0	2	3398
Dasheen	10	1	0	0	4033
Gaelic Wizard (IRE)	20	2	0	1	6862
Ideal Candy (IRE)	8	2	1	2	7138
Jorvik Prince	14	2	1	3	6534
Novabridge	13	2	0	1	5434
Thornaby Nash	12	3	0	1	12056
*Twin Appeal (IRE)	6	1	1	0	4033
Total winning prize-money					**£49488**
Favourites	**1-3**		**33.3%**		**-1.27**

NIGEL TWISTON-DAVIES

NAUNTON, GLOUCS

	No. of Hrs	Races Run	1st	2nd	3rd	Unpl	Per cent	£1 Level Stake
2-y-o	*0*	*0*	*0*	*0*	*0*	*0*	*0.0*	*0.00*
3-y-o	*0*	*0*	*0*	*0*	*0*	*0*	*0.0*	*0.00*
4-y-o+	*3*	*9*	*1*	*2*	*0*	*6*	*11.1*	*-3.50*
Totals	**3**	**9**	**1**	**2**	**0**	**6**	**11.1**	**-3.50**
2017	*7*	*24*	*1*	*2*	*2*	*19*	*4.2*	*-20.00*
2016	*6*	*20*	*2*	*4*	*2*	*12*	*10.0*	*+3.00*

JOCKEYS

	W-R	Per cent	£1 Level Stake
Kieran Shoemark	1-3	33.3	+2.50

COURSE RECORD

	Total W-R	Non-Hndcps 2-y-o	Non-Hndcps 3-y-o+	Hndcps 2-y-o	Hndcps 3-y-o+	Per cent	£1 Level Stake
Kempton (A.W)	1-4	0-0	0-0	0-0	1-4	25.0	+1.50

WINNING HORSES

Horse	Races Run	1st	2nd	3rd	£
Unblinking	4	1	2	0	3105
Total winning prize-money					**£3105**
Favourites	**26-71**		**36.6%**		**-3.92**

JAMES UNETT

WOLVERHAMPTON, WEST MIDLANDS

	No. of Hrs	Races Run	1st	2nd	3rd	Unpl	Per cent	£1 Level Stake
2-y-o	*1*	*1*	*0*	*0*	*0*	*1*	*0.0*	*-1.00*
3-y-o	*3*	*9*	*0*	*0*	*0*	*9*	*0.0*	*-9.00*
4-y-o+	*8*	*48*	*3*	*6*	*2*	*37*	*6.3*	*+2.75*
Totals	**12**	**58**	**3**	**6**	**2**	**47**	**5.2**	**-7.25**
2017	*11*	*57*	*2*	*6*	*4*	*45*	*3.5*	*-26.00*
2016	*16*	*85*	*4*	*6*	*5*	*69*	*4.7*	*-65.50*

JOCKEYS

	W-R	Per cent	£1 Level Stake
Liam Jones	2-6	33.3	+41.00
Hector Crouch	1-2	50.0	+1.75

COURSE RECORD

	Total W-R	Non-Hndcps 2-y-o	Non-Hndcps 3-y-o+	Hndcps 2-y-o	Hndcps 3-y-o+	Per cent	£1 Level Stake
Chester	1-1	0-0	0-0	0-0	1-1	100.0	+33.00
Newcastle (A.W)	1-2	0-0	0-0	0-0	1-2	50.0	+1.75
Wolvhptn (A.W)	1-32	0-1	0-4	0-0	1-27	3.1	-19.00

WINNING HORSES

Horse	Races Run	1st	2nd	3rd	£
Ebqaa (IRE)	5	1	0	0	6081
King Oswald (USA)	19	2	3	0	6210
Total winning prize-money					**£12291**
Favourites	**0-4**		**0.0%**		**-4.00**

MARK USHER

UPPER LAMBOURN, BERKS

	No. of Hrs	Races Run	1st	2nd	3rd	Unpl	Per cent	£1 Level Stake
2-y-o	*4*	*16*	*2*	*0*	*1*	*13*	*12.5*	*+14.00*
3-y-o	*10*	*76*	*3*	*6*	*10*	*57*	*3.9*	*-39.00*
4-y-o+	*16*	*159*	*13*	*20*	*20*	*105*	*8.2*	*-46.00*
Totals	**30**	**251**	**18**	**26**	**31**	**175**	**7.2**	**-71.00**
2017	*31*	*207*	*12*	*19*	*18*	*157*	*5.8*	*-104.92*
2016	*29*	*168*	*10*	*15*	*13*	*130*	*6.0*	*-79.00*

BY MONTH

2-y-o	W-R	Per cent	£1 Level Stake	3-y-o	W-R	Per cent	£1 Level Stake
January	0-0	0.0	0.00	January	0-1	0.0	-1.00
February	0-0	0.0	0.00	February	0-1	0.0	-1.00
March	0-0	0.0	0.00	March	0-3	0.0	-3.00
April	0-0	0.0	0.00	April	0-4	0.0	-4.00
May	0-0	0.0	0.00	May	0-11	0.0	-11.00
June	0-1	0.0	-1.00	June	0-7	0.0	-7.00
July	0-3	0.0	-3.00	July	1-9	11.1	+12.00
August	0-5	0.0	-5.00	August	1-11	9.1	-6.00
September	1-3	33.3	+12.00	September	0-10	0.0	-10.00
October	1-1	100.0	+14.00	October	0-8	0.0	-8.00
November	0-1	0.0	-1.00	November	1-8	12.5	+3.00
December	0-2	0.0	-2.00	December	0-3	0.0	-3.00

4-y-o+	W-R	Per cent	£1 Level Stake	Totals	W-R	Per cent	£1 Level Stake
January	1-19	5.3	-14.50	January	1-20	5.0	-15.50
February	1-16	6.3	-7.00	February	1-17	5.9	-8.00
March	2-17	11.8	-6.50	March	2-20	10.0	-9.50
April	3-11	27.3	+20.00	April	3-15	20.0	+16.00
May	2-17	11.8	+1.00	May	2-28	7.1	-10.00
June	0-5	0.0	-5.00	June	0-13	0.0	-13.00
July	1-17	5.9	-8.00	July	2-29	6.9	+1.00
August	2-22	9.1	0.00	August	3-38	7.9	-11.00
September	0-12	0.0	-12.00	September	1-25	4.0	-10.00
October	1-10	10.0	-1.00	October	2-19	10.5	+5.00
November	0-9	0.0	-9.00	November	1-18	5.6	-6.00
December	0-4	0.0	-4.00	December	0-9	0.0	-7.00

DISTANCE

2-y-o	W-R	Per cent	£1 Level Stake	3-y-o	W-R	Per cent	£1 Level Stake
5f-6f	0-4	0.0	-4.00	5f-6f	1-26	3.8	-5.00
7f-8f	2-12	16.7	+18.00	7f-8f	0-17	0.0	-17.00
9f-13f	0-0	0.0	0.00	9f-13f	2-30	6.7	-14.00
14f+	0-0	0.0	0.00	14f+	0-3	0.0	-3.00

4-y-o+	W-R	Per cent	£1 Level Stake	Totals	W-R	Per cent	£1 Level Stake
5f-6f	1-26	3.8	-11.00	5f-6f	2-56	3.6	-20.00
7f-8f	6-50	12.0	+4.50	7f-8f	8-79	10.1	+5.50
9f-13f	6-70	8.6	-26.50	9f-13f	8-100	8.0	-40.50
14f+	0-13	0.0	-13.00	14f+	0-16	0.0	-16.00

TYPE OF RACE

Non-Handicaps	W-R	Per cent	£1 Level Stake	Handicaps	W-R	Per cent	£1 Level Stake
2-y-o	0-11	0.0	-11.00	2-y-o	2-5	40.0	+25.00
3-y-o	0-15	0.0	-15.00	3-y-o	3-61	4.9	-24.00
4-y-o+	0-0	0.0	0.00	4-y-o+	13-159	8.2	-46.00

RACE CLASS

	W-R	Per cent	£1 Level Stake
Class 1	0-0	0.0	0.00
Class 2	0-0	0.0	0.00
Class 3	0-6	0.0	-6.00
Class 4	0-9	0.0	-9.00
Class 5	6-78	7.7	-28.00
Class 6	12-153	7.8	-23.00
Class 7	0-5	0.0	-5.00

FIRST TIME OUT

	W-R	Per cent	£1 Level Stake
2-y-o	0-4	0.0	-4.00
3-y-o	0-10	0.0	-10.00
4-y-o+	2-16	12.5	-6.00
Totals	2-30	6.7	-20.00

JOCKEYS

	W-R	Per cent	£1 Level Stake
Jason Watson	5-31	16.1	+9.00
Darragh Keenan	3-16	18.8	+29.00
Gary Mahon	2-6	33.3	+12.00
David Probert	2-10	20.0	+16.00
Jamie Spencer	1-1	100.0	+4.00
Toby Eley	1-2	50.0	+19.00
Silvestre De Sousa	1-3	33.3	0.00
Robert Havlin	1-5	20.0	+10.00
Nicola Currie	1-29	3.4	-24.50
Ryan Tate	1-36	2.8	-33.50

COURSE RECORD

	Total W-R	Non-Hndcps 2-y-o	Non-Hndcps 3-y-o+	Hndcps 2-y-o	Hndcps 3-y-o+	Per cent	£1 Level Stake
Chelmsford (A.W)	4-40	0-0	0-0	0-0	4-40	10.0	-14.50
Kempton (A.W)	4-48	0-1	0-3	2-4	2-40	8.3	-4.50
Wolvhptn (A.W)	2-42	0-3	0-2	0-0	2-37	4.8	-11.50
Newmkt (Jly)	1-1	0-0	0-0	0-0	1-1	100.0	+4.00
Yarmouth	1-4	0-0	0-0	0-0	1-4	25.0	-1.00
Salisbury	1-7	0-0	0-0	0-1	1-6	14.3	-1.50
Nottingham	1-8	0-0	0-1	0-0	1-7	12.5	+1.00
Leicester	1-10	0-0	0-0	0-0	1-10	10.0	+11.00
Newbury	1-14	0-2	0-4	0-0	1-8	7.1	-7.00
Windsor	1-14	0-1	0-1	0-0	1-12	7.1	+1.00
Lingfield (A.W)	1-20	0-0	0-1	0-0	1-19	5.0	-5.00

WINNING HORSES

Horse	Races Run	1st	2nd	3rd	£
Arlecchino's Leap	7	3	0	0	10933
Bayston Hill	13	2	1	1	7633
Bird For Life	14	1	4	3	3105
Born To Please	8	1	0	2	3493
Dreamboat Annie	14	1	2	2	3493
Marshall Aid (IRE)	9	1	4	0	3429
Mezmaar	7	1	1	1	3493
Mistry	12	1	0	0	3105
Misu Pete	17	2	2	4	6857
Padura Brave	7	2	0	1	6210
Point In Time (IRE)	8	2	0	2	8280
Shamonix (IRE)	12	1	1	0	3170
Total winning prize-money					**£63201**
Favourites	**3-15**		**20.0%**		**-6.50**

ROGER VARIAN

NEWMARKET, SUFFOLK

	No. of Hrs	Races Run	1st	2nd	3rd	Unpl	Per cent	£1 Level Stake
2-y-o	*66*	*161*	*30*	*21*	*26*	*84*	*18.6*	*-4.98*
3-y-o	*78*	*313*	*56*	*61*	*45*	*150*	*17.9*	*-45.29*
4-y-o+	*31*	*129*	*21*	*25*	*11*	*71*	*16.3*	*-60.18*
Totals	**175**	**603**	**107**	**107**	**82**	**305**	**17.7**	**-110.45**
2017	*162*	*558*	*109*	*113*	*91*	*244*	*19.5*	*-117.57*
2016	*167*	*554*	*97*	*72*	*65*	*317*	*17.5*	*-141.34*

BY MONTH

2-y-o	W-R	Per cent	£1 Level Stake
January	0-0	0.0	0.00
February	0-0	0.0	0.00
March	0-0	0.0	0.00
April	0-0	0.0	0.00
May	0-1	0.0	-1.00
June	1-7	14.3	-1.50
July	2-8	25.0	-3.42
August	2-18	11.1	-11.64
September	8-35	22.9	+10.94
October	9-43	20.9	+20.40
November	6-34	17.6	-10.34
December	2-15	13.3	-8.43

3-y-o	W-R	Per cent	£1 Level Stake
January	0-3	0.0	-3.00
February	0-1	0.0	-1.00
March	0-3	0.0	-3.00
April	2-49	4.1	-44.25
May	7-57	12.3	-4.38
June	11-50	22.0	+10.56
July	9-38	23.7	-5.87
August	8-36	22.2	-14.43
September	9-35	25.7	+9.07
October	5-28	17.9	-7.75
November	4-9	44.4	+18.25
December	1-4	25.0	+0.50

4-y-o+	W-R	Per cent	£1 Level Stake
January	0-2	0.0	-2.00
February	0-3	0.0	-3.00
March	1-5	20.0	-3.09
April	4-13	30.8	-0.50
May	8-26	30.8	+2.08
June	4-16	25.0	-8.17
July	0-15	0.0	-15.00
August	2-18	11.1	-12.00
September	1-18	5.6	-14.50
October	1-10	10.0	-1.00
November	0-3	0.0	-3.00
December	0-0	0.0	0.00

Totals	W-R	Per cent	£1 Level Stake
January	0-5	0.0	-5.00
February	0-4	0.0	-4.00
March	1-8	12.5	-6.09
April	6-62	9.7	-44.75
May	15-84	17.9	-3.30
June	16-73	21.9	+0.89
July	11-61	18.0	-24.29
August	12-72	16.7	-38.07
September	18-88	20.5	+5.51
October	15-81	18.5	+11.65
November	10-46	21.7	+15.25
December	3-19	15.8	+0.50

DISTANCE

2-y-o	W-R	Per cent	£1 Level Stake
5f-6f	8-36	22.2	-5.97
7f-8f	20-121	16.5	-2.51
9f-13f	2-4	50.0	+3.50
14f+	0-0	0.0	0.00

3-y-o	W-R	Per cent	£1 Level Stake
5f-6f	6-29	20.7	-8.69
7f-8f	32-179	17.9	-12.34
9f-13f	16-96	16.7	-23.01
14f+	2-9	22.2	-1.25

4-y-o+	W-R	Per cent	£1 Level Stake
5f-6f	0-29	0.0	-29.00
7f-8f	11-58	19.0	-12.84
9f-13f	9-40	22.5	-20.09
14f+	1-2	50.0	+1.75

Totals	W-R	Per cent	£1 Level Stake
5f-6f	14-94	14.9	-43.66
7f-8f	63-358	17.6	-27.69
9f-13f	27-140	19.3	-39.60
14f+	3-11	27.3	+0.50

TYPE OF RACE

Non-Handicaps	W-R	Per cent	£1 Level Stake	Handicaps	W-R	Per cent	£1 Level Stake
2-y-o	28-154	18.2	-6.98	2-y-o	2-7	28.6	+2.00
3-y-o	36-186	19.4	-1.12	3-y-o	20-127	15.7	-44.17
4-y-o+	8-35	22.9	-15.93	4-y-o+	13-94	13.8	-44.25

RACE CLASS

	W-R	Per cent	£1 Level Stake
Class 1	12-69	17.4	-4.93
Class 2	6-89	6.7	-64.25
Class 3	17-62	27.4	+24.83
Class 4	27-162	16.7	-26.33
Class 5	43-208	20.7	-32.31
Class 6	2-13	15.4	-7.47
Class 7	0-0	0.0	0.00

FIRST TIME OUT

	W-R	Per cent	£1 Level Stake
2-y-o	9-66	13.6	+11.50
3-y-o	7-78	9.0	-26.50
4-y-o+	12-31	38.7	+9.98
Totals	28-175	16.0	-5.02

JOCKEYS

	W-R	Per cent	£1 Level Stake
Andrea Atzeni	43-239	18.0	-78.81
David Egan	23-131	17.6	+15.48
Jack Mitchell	22-117	18.8	-10.69
Jim Crowley	8-32	25.0	-9.71
Dane O'Neill	2-15	13.3	-9.05
Tony Hamilton	1-1	100.0	+3.00
James Doyle	1-2	50.0	+7.00
William Buick	1-2	50.0	+11.00
Kieran Shoemark	1-2	50.0	+5.00
Luke Morris	1-3	33.3	-0.25
Daniel Tudhope	1-4	25.0	-0.25
Frankie Dettori	1-4	25.0	+1.50
Yuga Kawada	1-10	10.0	-8.17
Silvestre De Sousa	1-14	7.1	-9.50

COURSE RECORD

	Total W-R	Non-Hndcps 2-y-o	Non-Hndcps 3-y-o+	Hndcps 2-y-o	Hndcps 3-y-o+	Per cent	£1 Level Stake
Kempton (A.W)	14-55	7-27	3-11	0-0	4-17	25.5	-0.46
Doncaster	9-36	1-8	3-9	0-0	5-19	25.0	-9.84
Newmarket	9-52	3-13	4-21	0-1	2-17	17.3	+14.50
Newcastle (A.W)	8-31	1-13	5-10	0-0	2-8	25.8	-0.64
Wolvhptn (A.W)	7-49	1-13	4-23	1-3	1-10	14.3	+8.25
Lingfield (A.W)	6-27	1-6	3-16	0-0	2-5	22.2	+11.50
Nottingham	5-23	1-7	1-6	1-1	2-9	21.7	-6.09
Yarmouth	5-26	0-10	1-7	0-0	4-9	19.2	-4.00
Ascot	5-33	2-5	1-11	0-0	2-17	15.2	+4.91
Bath	4-8	0-0	3-4	0-0	1-4	50.0	+0.63
Newbury	4-25	2-9	2-12	0-0	0-4	16.0	+3.00
Redcar	3-7	1-1	2-5	0-0	0-1	42.9	+0.71
Goodwood	3-23	1-5	1-9	0-0	1-9	13.0	-9.75
Beverley	2-2	2-2	0-0	0-0	0-0	100.0	+3.58
Lingfield	2-4	0-0	2-3	0-0	0-1	50.0	+3.41
Epsom	2-7	0-1	0-1	0-0	2-5	28.6	-1.50
Hamilton	2-7	1-1	1-4	0-0	0-2	28.6	-4.06
Leicester	2-17	0-2	1-5	0-0	1-10	11.8	-9.42
Haydock	2-21	1-6	1-9	0-0	0-6	9.5	-13.93
Chelmsford (A.W)	2-29	1-6	1-14	0-0	0-9	6.9	-12.25
Wetherby	1-1	0-0	1-1	0-0	0-0	100.0	+0.67
Carlisle	1-2	0-0	1-2	0-0	0-0	50.0	-0.92
Chepstow	1-3	1-1	0-1	0-0	0-1	33.3	-0.25
Pontefract	1-5	0-1	1-2	0-0	0-2	20.0	-2.50
Ripon	1-6	0-0	0-2	0-0	1-4	16.7	-3.75
Thirsk	1-6	0-0	1-4	0-0	0-2	16.7	-2.00
Chester	1-9	0-0	0-3	0-0	1-6	11.1	-5.50
Windsor	1-10	0-0	1-7	0-0	0-3	10.0	-7.25
Salisbury	1-13	1-7	0-3	0-1	0-2	7.7	-8.00
Sandown	1-17	0-2	0-2	0-0	1-13	5.9	-14.25
Newmkt (Jly)	1-22	0-7	0-5	0-1	1-9	4.5	-18.25

WINNING HORSES

Horse	Races Run	1st	2nd	3rd	£
Ajman King (IRE)	2	2	0	0	68475
Angel's Glory	5	1	2	1	5175
Barsanti (IRE)	5	1	1	0	25520
Bayroot (IRE)	1	1	0	0	3881
Canvassed (IRE)	1	1	0	0	4787
Character Witness (IRE)	6	1	0	2	3752
Contrive (IRE)	12	4	2	0	27022
Daira Prince (IRE)	6	3	0	0	28257
Dashed	2	1	0	0	4528
Defoe (IRE)	2	2	0	0	93572
Dubawi Prince	3	1	0	0	6469
Elamirr (IRE)	3	1	0	0	3752
Elasia	6	3	1	0	44215
Emmaus (IRE)	4	1	1	0	34026
Epic Challenge	4	1	1	0	6469
Faadhel (GER)	7	2	1	2	12550
Flavius Titus	8	1	2	1	5531
Fujaira Prince (IRE)	2	2	0	0	8992
Game Player (IRE)	5	2	2	0	10221
Gilded Heaven	6	1	0	1	3105
Golden Slam	7	1	0	1	3752
Hermosita	3	1	0	1	4464
Howman (IRE)	5	2	0	1	9283
Ibraz	4	2	0	1	13841
Ideological (IRE)	4	2	1	1	7116
Imaginative (IRE)	5	1	1	1	3881
Impulsion (IRE)	5	1	0	1	4528
Inpromptu (IRE)	7	1	0	2	6469
Jamil (IRE)	4	1	1	0	5175
Jumira Prince (IRE)	4	1	2	0	5531
Kaanoon	6	3	1	0	14750
Khuzaam (USA)	2	1	1	0	3881
Lashabeeh (IRE)	5	1	2	0	5175
Lastochka	1	1	0	0	3881
Laugh A Minute	5	1	0	1	9338
Loveisili	7	1	2	2	4140
Mackaar (IRE)	2	1	0	0	4140
Manorah (IRE)	2	1	0	0	3881
Masaarr (USA)	5	1	0	2	7763

Mojika	6	1	3	0	3752
Mot Juste (USA)	4	2	0	0	38166
Mountain Angel (IRE)	6	1	2	2	6728
Mubhij (IRE)	3	1	1	0	4787
Mystic Flight (IRE)	5	2	1	1	13197
Nausha	1	1	0	0	5434
Nearooz	1	1	0	0	7763
Pilaster	5	3	0	1	192772
Prefontaine (IRE)	5	1	1	1	16173
Prince Eiji	2	1	0	1	7763
Qabala (USA)	1	1	0	0	6469
Qazyna (IRE)	4	1	0	2	6469
Queen Of Desire (IRE)	5	3	0	2	15202
Rasima	9	2	4	0	32300
Sam Gold (IRE)	4	1	0	1	5531
San Donato (IRE)	5	3	1	0	27363
Shabeeb (USA)	3	1	0	0	18675
Shagalla	4	1	0	0	3752
Sharja Bridge	5	1	1	0	155625
Sheikha Reika (FR)	4	2	1	0	34579
Spanish City	8	2	0	0	17466
Star Shield	3	1	0	1	4787
Surfman	2	1	0	1	3881
Tauteke	2	1	0	1	7763
The Chemist	7	1	2	1	3752
Three Comets (GER)	4	1	2	1	4140
Thriving	6	2	2	0	8539
Tomyris	4	1	0	0	34026
Turaya	1	1	0	0	9704
Turjomaan (USA)	2	2	0	0	11515
Watheeqa (USA)	4	1	1	0	3752
Wilbury Twist	6	1	1	2	3752
Willie John	1	1	0	0	3752
Yourtimeisnow	5	2	0	1	32451
Zabeel Prince (IRE)	3	1	1	0	20983
Zamandas (IRE)	6	2	0	0	8539
Total winning prize-money					**£1302678**
Favourites	**58-158**		**36.7%**		**-9.54**

ED VAUGHAN

NEWMARKET, SUFFOLK

	No. of Hrs	Races Run	1st	2nd	3rd	Unpl	Per cent	£1 Level Stake
2-y-o	*7*	*13*	*4*	*1*	*2*	*6*	*30.8*	*+8.00*
3-y-o	*18*	*65*	*7*	*5*	*4*	*49*	*10.8*	*-35.68*
4-y-o+	*3*	*18*	*0*	*2*	*3*	*13*	*0.0*	*-18.00*
Totals	**28**	**96**	**11**	**8**	**9**	**68**	**11.5**	**-45.68**
2017	*26*	*94*	*18*	*15*	*11*	*50*	*19.1*	*+44.39*
2016	*21*	*91*	*16*	*15*	*10*	*50*	*17.6*	*+16.20*

BY MONTH

2-y-o	W-R	Per cent	£1 Level Stake
January	0-0	0.0	0.00
February	0-0	0.0	0.00
March	0-0	0.0	0.00
April	0-0	0.0	0.00
May	0-0	0.0	0.00
June	0-1	0.0	-1.00
July	1-1	100.0	+2.25
August	0-1	0.0	-1.00
September	1-3	33.3	-0.25
October	0-3	0.0	-3.00
November	1-2	50.0	+9.00
December	1-2	50.0	+2.00

3-y-o	W-R	Per cent	£1 Level Stake
January	2-7	28.6	+6.00
February	1-5	20.0	-2.25
March	0-1	0.0	-1.00
April	1-10	10.0	-8.43
May	1-9	11.1	-3.00
June	1-9	11.1	-5.00
July	0-6	0.0	-6.00
August	1-6	16.7	-4.00
September	0-7	0.0	-7.00
October	0-4	0.0	-4.00
November	0-1	0.0	-1.00
December	0-0	0.0	0.00

4-y-o+	W-R	Per cent	£1 Level Stake
January	0-0	0.0	0.00
February	0-0	0.0	0.00
March	0-0	0.0	0.00
April	0-1	0.0	-1.00
May	0-3	0.0	-3.00
June	0-5	0.0	-5.00
July	0-1	0.0	-1.00
August	0-4	0.0	-4.00
September	0-3	0.0	-3.00
October	0-0	0.0	0.00
November	0-1	0.0	-1.00
December	0-0	0.0	0.00

Totals	W-R	Per cent	£1 Level Stake
January	2-7	28.6	+6.00
February	1-5	20.0	-2.25
March	0-1	0.0	-1.00
April	1-11	9.1	-9.43
May	1-12	8.3	-6.00
June	1-15	6.7	-11.00
July	1-8	12.5	-4.75
August	1-11	9.1	-9.00
September	1-13	7.7	-10.25
October	0-7	0.0	-7.00
November	1-4	25.0	-2.00
December	1-2	50.0	0.00

DISTANCE

2-y-o	W-R	Per cent	£1 Level Stake
5f-6f	1-3	33.3	-0.25
7f-8f	2-9	22.2	+5.25
9f-13f	1-1	100.0	+3.00
14f+	0-0	0.0	0.00

3-y-o	W-R	Per cent	£1 Level Stake
5f-6f	1-2	50.0	0.00
7f-8f	2-37	5.4	-29.43
9f-13f	4-26	15.4	-6.25
14f+	0-0	0.0	0.00

4-y-o+	W-R	Per cent	£1 Level Stake
5f-6f	0-6	0.0	-6.00
7f-8f	0-8	0.0	-8.00
9f-13f	0-3	0.0	-3.00
14f+	0-1	0.0	-1.00

Totals	W-R	Per cent	£1 Level Stake
5f-6f	2-11	18.2	-6.25
7f-8f	4-54	7.4	-32.18
9f-13f	5-30	16.7	-6.25
14f+	0-1	0.0	-1.00

TYPE OF RACE

Non-Handicaps	W-R	Per cent	£1 Level Stake
2-y-o	4-13	30.8	+8.00
3-y-o	5-27	18.5	-7.68
4-y-o+	0-0	0.0	0.00

Handicaps	W-R	Per cent	£1 Level Stake
2-y-o	0-0	0.0	0.00
3-y-o	2-38	5.3	-28.00
4-y-o+	0-18	0.0	-18.00

RACE CLASS

	W-R	Per cent	£1 Level Stake
Class 1	0-7	0.0	-7.00
Class 2	0-4	0.0	-4.00
Class 3	0-8	0.0	-8.00
Class 4	3-19	15.8	-9.00
Class 5	5-37	13.5	-7.68
Class 6	3-21	14.3	-10.00
Class 7	0-0	0.0	0.00

FIRST TIME OUT

	W-R	Per cent	£1 Level Stake
2-y-o	3-7	42.9	+10.75
3-y-o	2-18	11.1	-6.43
4-y-o+	0 3	0.0	-3.00
Totals	5-28	17.9	+1.32

JOCKEYS

	W-R	Per cent	£1 Level Stake
Stevie Donohoe	6-16	37.5	+16.32
P J McDonald	1-2	50.0	+4.00
Pat Cosgrave	1-4	25.0	-0.75
Oisin Murphy	1-4	25.0	-1.25
Jamie Spencer	1-5	20.0	-3.00
Jane Elliott	1-8	12.5	-4.00

COURSE RECORD

	Total	Non-Hndcps		Hndcps		Per	£1 Level
	W-R	2-y-o	3-y-o+	2-y-o	3-y-o+	cent	Stake
Yarmouth	4-9	1-2	1-3	0-0	2-4	44.4	+5.75
Wolvhptn (A.W)	3-8	1-1	2-3	0-0	0-4	37.5	+8.75
Lingfield (A.W)	1-5	0-0	1-3	0-0	0-2	20.0	-2.00
Newmkt (Jly)	1-8	1-1	0-2	0-0	0-5	12.5	-4.75
Kempton (A.W)	1-11	1-3	0-1	0-0	0-7	9.1	0.00
Chelmsford (A.W)	1-15	0-0	1-6	0-0	0-9	6.7	-13.43

WINNING HORSES

Horse	Races Run	1st	2nd	3rd	£
Ardiente	1	1	0	0	3881
Choco Box	4	1	1	0	3105
Dame Malliot	1	1	0	0	4787
Dancing Brave Bear (USA)	4	1	1	0	5175
Desert Wind (IRE)	6	3	1	0	10739
Dubai Dominion	4	1	1	2	5175
Magic J (USA)	1	1	0	0	6728
Peace Prevails*	6	1	1	1	3752
Rosedale Topping (IRE)	5	1	0	0	3105
Total winning prize-money					**£46447**
Favourites	**3-8**		**37.5%**		**-1.18**

LUCY WADHAM

NEWMARKET, SUFFOLK

	No. of Hrs	Races Run	1st	2nd	3rd	Unpl	Per cent	£1 Level Stake
2-y-o	*1*	*7*	*0*	*2*	*1*	*4*	*0.0*	*-7.00*
3-y-o	*4*	*22*	*4*	*4*	*4*	*10*	*18.2*	*-6.72*
4-y-o+	*2*	*11*	*1*	*3*	*0*	*7*	*9.1*	*-3.50*
Totals	**7**	**40**	**5**	**9**	**5**	**21**	**12.5**	**-17.22**
2017	*5*	*26*	*2*	*6*	*0*	*18*	*7.7*	*-16.00*
2016	*18*	*64*	*11*	*5*	*11*	*37*	*17.2*	*-17.69*

JOCKEYS

	W-R	Per cent	£1 Level Stake
Hayley Turner	2-6	33.3	+1.38
Jim Crowley	1-1	100.0	+5.00
David Probert	1-3	33.3	-1.09
Josephine Gordon	1-6	16.7	+1.50

COURSE RECORD

	Total	Non-Hndcps		Hndcps		Per	£1 Level
	W-R	2-y-o	3-y-o+	2-y-o	3-y-o+	cent	Stake
Southwell (A.W)	2-5	0-0	0-0	0-0	2-5	40.0	-0.22
Newbury	1-1	0-0	0-0	0-0	1-1	100.0	+3.50
Lingfield (A.W)	1-4	0-0	0-2	0-0	1-2	25.0	+2.00
Yarmouth	1-7	0-1	0-0	0-2	1-4	14.3	+0.50

WINNING HORSES

Horse	Races Run	1st	2nd	3rd	£
Anna Jammeela	10	2	1	1	6598
Dance To Paris	4	1	1	1	3752
Galmarley	7	1	2	1	25876
Potters Lady Jane	9	1	3	0	6243
Total winning prize-money					**£42469**
Favourites	**8-18**		**44.4%**		**3.94**

TRACY WAGGOTT

SPENNYMOOR, CO DURHAM

	No. of Hrs	Races Run	1st	2nd	3rd	Unpl	Per cent	£1 Level Stake
2-y-o	*2*	*7*	*0*	*1*	*2*	*4*	*0.0*	*-7.00*
3-y-o	*5*	*26*	*0*	*2*	*4*	*20*	*0.0*	*-26.00*
4-y-o+	*11*	*89*	*7*	*10*	*9*	*63*	*7.9*	*-48.25*
Totals	**18**	**122**	**7**	**13**	**15**	**87**	**5.7**	**-81.25**
2017	*17*	*140*	*11*	*18*	*17*	*94*	*7.9*	*-67.75*
2016	*21*	*142*	*7*	*6*	*14*	*115*	*4.9*	*-45.00*

JOCKEYS

	W-R	Per cent	£1 Level Stake
Barry McHugh	4-32	12.5	-3.00
Ben Curtis	2-16	12.5	-8.75
Royston Ffrench	1-6	16.7	-1.50

COURSE RECORD

	Total	Non-Hndcps		Hndcps		Per	£1 Level
	W-R	2-y-o	3-y-o+	2-y-o	3-y-o+	cent	Stake
Newcastle (A.W)	3-40	0-0	0-4	0-2	3-34	7.5	-28.25
Catterick	2-12	0-0	0-0	0-0	2-12	16.7	0.00
Pontefract	1-4	0-0	0-0	0-0	1-4	25.0	+5.00
Thirsk	1-15	0-0	0-3	0-0	1-12	6.7	-7.00

WINNING HORSES

Horse	Races Run	1st	2nd	3rd	£
Henley	8	2	0	1	13779
Rasolacad (IRE)	8	1	1	1	6728
Supreme Power (IRE)	14	2	3	1	6598
Windforpower (IRE)	20	2	2	1	6210
Total winning prize-money					**£33315**
Favourites	**2-8**		**25.0%**		**0.25**

MARK WALFORD

SHERRIFF HUTTON, N YORKS

	No. of Hrs	Races Run	1st	2nd	3rd	Unpl	Per cent	£1 Level Stake
2-y-o	*1*	*1*	*0*	*0*	*0*	*1*	*0.0*	*-1.00*
3-y-o	*4*	*18*	*3*	*1*	*1*	*13*	*16.7*	*+15.75*
4-y-o+	*12*	*75*	*11*	*4*	*16*	*44*	*14.7*	*+16.50*
Totals	**17**	**94**	**14**	**5**	**17**	**58**	**14.9**	**+31.25**
2017	*18*	*85*	*8*	*5*	*9*	*62*	*9.4*	*-44.38*
2016	*21*	*96*	*5*	*11*	*6*	*74*	*5.2*	*-34.50*

BY MONTH

2-y-o	W-R	Per cent	£1 Level Stake
January	0-0	0.0	0.00
February	0-0	0.0	0.00
March	0-0	0.0	0.00
April	0-0	0.0	0.00
May	0-0	0.0	0.00
June	0-0	0.0	0.00
July	0-1	0.0	-1.00
August	0-0	0.0	0.00
September	0-0	0.0	0.00
October	0-0	0.0	0.00
November	0-0	0.0	0.00
December	0-0	0.0	0.00

3-y-o	W-R	Per cent	£1 Level Stake
January	0-0	0.0	0.00
February	0-1	0.0	-1.00
March	0-2	0.0	-2.00
April	2-4	50.0	+25.75
May	1-3	33.3	+1.00
June	0-1	0.0	-1.00
July	0-2	0.0	-2.00
August	0-3	0.0	-3.00
September	0-1	0.0	-1.00
October	0-1	0.0	-1.00
November	0-0	0.0	0.00
December	0-0	0.0	0.00

4-y-o+	W-R	Per cent	£1 Level Stake
January	0-1	0.0	-1.00
February	0-1	0.0	-1.00
March	1-5	20.0	+2.00
April	0-8	0.0	-8.00
May	0-5	0.0	-5.00
June	3-12	25.0	+14.50
July	4-13	30.8	+19.00
August	1-9	11.1	-3.50
September	1-7	14.3	+6.00
October	1-7	14.3	+0.50
November	0-4	0.0	-4.00
December	0-3	0.0	-3.00

Totals	W-R	Per cent	£1 Level Stake
January	0-1	0.0	-1.00
February	0-2	0.0	-2.00
March	1-7	14.3	0.00
April	2-12	16.7	+17.75
May	1-8	12.5	-4.00
June	3-13	23.1	+13.50
July	4-16	25.0	+16.00
August	1-12	8.3	-6.50
September	1-8	12.5	+5.00
October	1-8	12.5	-0.50
November	0-4	0.0	-4.00
December	0-3	0.0	-3.00

DISTANCE

2-y-o	W-R	Per cent	£1 Level Stake
5f-6f	0-1	0.0	-1.00
7f-8f	0-0	0.0	0.00
9f-13f	0-0	0.0	0.00
14f+	0-0	0.0	0.00

3-y-o	W-R	Per cent	£1 Level Stake
5f-6f	3-14	21.4	+19.75
7f-8f	0-4	0.0	-4.00
9f-13f	0-0	0.0	0.00
14f+	0-0	0.0	0.00

4-y-o+	W-R	Per cent	£1 Level Stake
5f-6f	1-11	9.1	-3.50
7f-8f	3-24	12.5	+17.50
9f-13f	7-38	18.4	+4.50
14f+	0-2	0.0	-2.00

Totals	W-R	Per cent	£1 Level Stake
5f-6f	4-26	15.4	+15.25
7f-8f	3-28	10.7	+13.50
9f-13f	7-38	18.4	+4.50
14f+	0-2	0.0	-2.00

TYPE OF RACE

Non-Handicaps	W-R	Per cent	£1 Level Stake
2-y-o	0-1	0.0	-1.00
3-y-o	0-8	0.0	-8.00
4-y-o+	0-3	0.0	-3.00

Handicaps	W-R	Per cent	£1 Level Stake
2-y-o	0-0	0.0	0.00
3-y-o	3-10	30.0	+23.75
4-y-o+	11-72	15.3	+19.50

RACE CLASS

	W-R	Per cent	£1 Level Stake
Class 1	0-0	0.0	0.00
Class 2	0-0	0.0	0.00
Class 3	0-0	0.0	0.00
Class 4	3-14	21.4	+9.00
Class 5	7-38	18.4	+36.75
Class 6	4-42	9.5	-14.50
Class 7	0-0	0.0	0.00

FIRST TIME OUT

	W-R	Per cent	£1 Level Stake
2-y-o	0-1	0.0	-1.00
3-y-o	0-4	0.0	-4.00
4-y-o+	1-12	8.3	-5.00
Totals	1-17	5.9	-10.00

JOCKEYS

	W-R	Per cent	£1 Level Stake
Andrew Mullen	6-13	46.2	+34.50
Kevin Stott	1-1	100.0	+12.00
Martin Dwyer	1-1	100.0	+4.50
Ger O'Neill	1-2	50.0	+1.75
Tom Eaves	1-3	33.3	+2.00
Miss Emma Todd	1-3	33.3	+4.00
Josephine Gordon	1-3	33.3	+18.00
Luke Morris	1-4	25.0	+3.50
Jason Hart	1-27	3.7	-12.00

COURSE RECORD

	Total W-R	Non-Hndcps 2-y-o	Non-Hndcps 3-y-o+	Hndcps 2-y-o	Hndcps 3-y-o+	Per cent	£1 Level Stake
Beverley	4-12	0-0	0-1	0-0	4-11	33.3	+6.00
Chester	2-2	0-0	0-0	0-0	2-2	100.0	+15.50
Chepstow	1-1	0-0	0-0	0-0	1-1	100.0	+4.50
Ripon	1-2	0-0	0-0	0-0	1-2	50.0	+24.00
Ayr	1-3	0-0	0-0	0-0	1-3	33.3	+12.00
Newmkt (Jly)	1-4	0-0	0-0	0-0	1-4	25.0	+17.00
Doncaster	1-5	0-0	0-1	0-0	1-4	20.0	+2.00
Redcar	1-6	0-0	0-0	0-0	1-6	16.7	-2.00
Thirsk	1-9	0-0	0-2	0-0	1-7	11.1	-5.25
Wolvhptn (A.W)	1-13	0-1	0-4	0-0	1-8	7.7	-5.50

WINNING HORSES

Horse	Races Run	1st	2nd	3rd	£
Bit Of A Quirke	9	4	0	0	19142
Cape Hideaway	1	1	0	0	3619
Carlovian	18	2	1	5	6857
Cornborough	5	1	0	2	6728
Dream Free*	11	1	1	2	3105
Rickyroadboy	12	3	1	1	4464
Woody Bay	9	2	0	3	10059
Total winning prize-money					**£53974**
Favourites	**7-15**		**46.7%**		**7.40**

ED WALKER

UPPER LAMBOURN, BERKS

	No. of Hrs	Races Run	1st	2nd	3rd	Unpl	Per cent	£1 Level Stake
2-y-o	*33*	*105*	*14*	*9*	*12*	*70*	*13.3*	*-41.76*
3-y-o	*44*	*224*	*32*	*33*	*30*	*128*	*14.3*	*-62.08*
4-y-o+	*29*	*158*	*15*	*34*	*21*	*87*	*9.5*	*-75.90*
Totals	**106**	**487**	**61**	**76**	**63**	**285**	**12.5**	**-179.74**
2017	*89*	*387*	*54*	*53*	*56*	*224*	*14.0*	*-96.00*
2016	*63*	*267*	*27*	*31*	*33*	*175*	*10.1*	*-61.97*

BY MONTH

2-y-o	W-R	Per cent	£1 Level Stake	3-y-o	W-R	Per cent	£1 Level Stake
January	0-0	0.0	0.00	January	2-12	16.7	-7.58
February	0-0	0.0	0.00	February	1-6	16.7	-2.50
March	0-0	0.0	0.00	March	2-11	18.2	-3.13
April	0-2	0.0	-2.00	April	0-20	0.0	-20.00
May	1-7	14.3	-3.00	May	5-32	15.6	-14.50
June	1-6	16.7	+4.00	June	4-35	11.4	-11.75
July	1-9	11.1	-6.75	July	6-27	22.2	+0.38
August	2-13	15.4	-0.75	August	4-26	15.4	-9.50
September	5-23	21.7	-6.26	September	5-24	20.8	+6.00
October	3-24	12.5	-10.00	October	3-20	15.0	+11.50
November	1-17	5.9	-13.00	November	0-4	0.0	-4.00
December	0-4	0.0	-4.00	December	0-7	0.0	-7.00

4-y-o+	W-R	Per cent	£1 Level Stake	Totals	W-R	Per cent	£1 Level Stake
January	1-10	10.0	-5.50	January	3-22	13.6	-13.08
February	4-11	36.4	+7.25	February	5-17	29.4	+4.75
March	0-9	0.0	-9.00	March	2-20	10.0	-12.13
April	3-16	18.8	+2.10	April	3-38	7.9	-19.90
May	2-24	8.3	-16.75	May	8-63	12.7	-34.25
June	0-18	0.0	-18.00	June	5-59	8.5	-25.75
July	1-16	6.3	-13.00	July	8-52	15.4	-19.37
August	1-15	6.7	-3.00	August	7-54	13.0	-13.25
September	2-22	9.1	-10.50	September	12-69	17.4	-10.76
October	1-13	7.7	-5.50	October	7-57	12.3	-4.00
November	0-2	0.0	-2.00	November	1-23	4.3	-6.00
December	0-2	0.0	-2.00	December	0-13	0.0	-9.00

DISTANCE

2-y-o	W-R	Per cent	£1 Level Stake	3-y-o	W-R	Per cent	£1 Level Stake
5f-6f	8-53	15.1	-11.88	5f-6f	16-70	22.9	+7.17
7f-8f	6-51	11.8	-28.89	7f-8f	12-103	11.7	-49.75
9f-13f	0-1	0.0	-1.00	9f-13f	4-50	8.0	-18.50
14f+	0-0	0.0	0.00	14f+	0-1	0.0	-1.00

4-y-o+	W-R	Per cent	£1 Level Stake	Totals	W-R	Per cent	£1 Level Stake
5f-6f	2-27	7.4	-11.00	5f-6f	26-150	17.3	-15.71
7f-8f	2-43	4.7	-30.00	7f-8f	20-197	10.2	-108.64
9f-13f	9-75	12.0	-41.90	9f-13f	13-126	10.3	-61.40
14f+	2-13	15.4	+7.00	14f+	2-14	14.3	+6.00

TYPE OF RACE

Non-Handicaps	W-R	Per cent	£1 Level Stake	Handicaps	W-R	Per cent	£1 Level Stake
2-y-o	9-86	10.5	-42.13	2-y-o	5-19	26.3	+0.38
3-y-o	7-78	9.0	-41.08	3-y-o	25-146	17.1	-21.00
4-y-o+	1-18	5.6	-12.50	4-y-o+	14-140	10.0	-63.40

RACE CLASS

	W-R	Per cent	£1 Level Stake
Class 1	1-26	3.8	-16.00
Class 2	3-41	7.3	-21.00
Class 3	5-49	10.2	-25.63
Class 4	17-134	12.7	-50.16
Class 5	31-200	15.5	-51.71
Class 6	4-37	10.8	-15.25
Class 7	0-0	0.0	0.00

FIRST TIME OUT

	W-R	Per cent	£1 Level Stake
2-y-o	1-33	3.0	-29.00
3-y-o	3-44	6.8	-34.46
4-y-o+	5-29	17.2	-5.40
Totals	9-106	8.5	-68.86

JOCKEYS

	W-R	Per cent	£1 Level Stake
Liam Keniry	23-200	11.5	-73.75
Pat Cosgrave	8-66	12.1	-33.50
Luke Morris	6-29	20.7	-6.75
Gerald Mosse	6-58	10.3	-16.25
Richard Kingscote	4-22	18.2	+0.50
Jamie Spencer	4-23	17.4	+3.00
Andrea Atzeni	3-5	60.0	+4.21
Oisin Murphy	2-3	66.7	+10.00
Joe Fanning	1-1	100.0	+1.25
P J McDonald	1-1	100.0	+2.50
David Probert	1-2	50.0	+2.00
Oliver Stammers	1-4	25.0	-1.63
Adam McNamara	1-9	11.1	-7.33

COURSE RECORD

	Total W-R	Non-Hndcps 2-y-o	Non-Hndcps 3-y-o+	Hndcps 2-y-o	Hndcps 3-y-o+	Per cent	£1 Level Stake
Wolvhptn (A.W)	7-42	1-10	3-14	0-1	3-17	16.7	-19.48
Windsor	6-30	1-6	1-5	0-0	4-19	20.0	-6.13
Kempton (A.W)	6-54	1-5	0-10	0-3	5-36	11.1	-21.25
Haydock	5-25	1-2	0-5	0-0	4-18	20.0	-3.00
Lingfield (A.W)	5-41	0-7	1-7	0-0	4-27	12.2	-18.88
Ascot	4-21	0-2	0-3	0-0	4-16	19.0	+7.00
Ffos Las	3-9	1-1	0-2	1-2	1-4	33.3	+15.63
Newcastle (A.W)	3-14	0-2	1-6	1-3	1-3	21.4	+12.00
Yarmouth	3-14	0-2	0-0	1-3	2-9	21.4	+2.75
Newmarket	3-21	2-6	0-4	0-0	1-11	14.3	-5.00
Newbury	3-35	0-11	0-5	0-1	3-18	8.6	-22.13
Nottingham	2-14	0-4	0-2	0-1	2-7	14.3	-1.00
Salisbury	2-15	1-7	0-1	0-0	1-7	13.3	-6.88
Catterick	1-2	0-0	0-0	1-1	0-1	50.0	+0.25
Bath	1-4	0-0	0-1	1-1	0-2	25.0	0.00
Chester	1-6	0-0	1-1	0-0	0-5	16.7	-3.13
Brighton	1-7	0-3	1-1	0-0	0-3	14.3	-3.25
Leicester	1-8	0-1	0-2	0-0	1-5	12.5	-2.50

Newmkt (Jly)	1-11	1-4	0-0	0-0	0-7	9.1	-1.00
Sandown	1-18	0-1	0-3	0-0	1-14	5.6	-14.50
Goodwood	1-19	0-2	0-5	0-0	1-12	5.3	-15.25
Doncaster	1-20	0-4	0-4	0-0	1-12	5.0	-17.00

WINNING HORSES

Horse	Races Run	1st	2nd	3rd	£
Abel Tasman*	11	1	3	2	4852
Aeolus	7	1	0	1	16173
Agrotera (IRE)	5	2	1	0	59777
Akbar Shah (IRE)	7	1	3	0	6728
Arendelle	10	1	0	1	3752
Baba Ghanouj (IRE)	2	1	0	0	3752
Blackheath	8	2	2	1	7569
Burrumbeet (IRE)	4	1	1	0	3752
Cap Francais	3	2	1	0	11580
Caradoc (IRE)	2	1	1	0	5852
Catoca (USA)	7	1	2	1	3752
Dark Pearl (IRE)	6	1	1	1	6469
Desert Doctor (IRE)	11	3	1	1	16529
Fille De Reve	6	2	1	0	25791
Gallic	5	1	1	1	4787
Garbanzo (IRE)*	6	3	0	0	15978
Ginistrelli (IRE)	2	1	0	0	6469
Global Excel	6	1	1	2	4140
Glorious Army	7	1	3	0	3752
Glorious Charmer	8	2	0	2	7569
Glorious Lover (IRE)	3	1	1	1	3752
Hombre Casado (FR)	9	3	1	2	18750
Iconic Knight (IRE)	9	2	2	1	9283
Inlawed*	4	1	0	0	3105
Maygold	6	2	0	2	9057
Mountain Peak	8	3	1	1	18695
On The Stage	8	2	0	0	7633
Petruchio (IRE)	3	1	0	0	3752
Quality Seeker (USA)	7	1	0	2	5531
Reckless Wave (IRE)	8	1	1	0	4140
Royal Intervention (IRE)	3	1	2	0	17013
Sayem	7	1	1	1	6469
Simpson (IRE)	6	1	0	1	7246
Sky Eagle (IRE)	5	1	2	1	5757
Sky Marshal (IRE)	9	2	3	1	6210
Smiley Bagel (IRE)	9	2	2	1	6857
Soumei (IRE)	5	1	0	1	3752
Sunday Star	4	1	1	1	6469
Toshima (IRE)*	3	1	0	0	3752
Trevena	6	2	0	0	8539
Triggered (IRE)	6	2	0	1	10868
Total winning prize-money					**£385653**
Favourites	**21-69**		**30.4%**		**-3.49**

CHRIS WALL

NEWMARKET, SUFFOLK

	No. of Hrs	Races Run	1st	2nd	3rd	Unpl	Per cent	£1 Level Stake
2-y-o	*4*	*12*	*0*	*1*	*2*	*9*	*0.0*	*-12.00*
3-y-o	*11*	*55*	*6*	*8*	*3*	*38*	*10.9*	*-32.52*
4-y-o+	*16*	*89*	*11*	*7*	*4*	*67*	*12.4*	*+4.21*
Totals	**31**	**156**	**17**	**16**	**9**	**114**	**10.9**	**-40.31**
2017	*35*	*174*	*19*	*18*	*12*	*125*	*10.9*	*-67.95*
2016	*39*	*183*	*18*	*16*	*13*	*136*	*9.8*	*-76.61*

BY MONTH

2-y-o	W-R	Per cent	£1 Level Stake	**3-y-o**	W-R	Per cent	£1 Level Stake
January	0-0	0.0	0.00	January	0-0	0.0	0.00
February	0-0	0.0	0.00	February	0-0	0.0	0.00
March	0-0	0.0	0.00	March	0-0	0.0	0.00
April	0-0	0.0	0.00	April	0-2	0.0	-2.00
May	0-1	0.0	-1.00	May	0-4	0.0	-4.00
June	0-1	0.0	-1.00	June	0-8	0.0	-8.00
July	0-2	0.0	-2.00	July	1-6	16.7	-2.00
August	0-3	0.0	-3.00	August	2-14	14.3	-10.36
September	0-0	0.0	0.00	September	2-9	22.2	+4.00
October	0-2	0.0	-2.00	October	1-8	12.5	-6.17
November	0-3	0.0	-3.00	November	0-3	0.0	-3.00
December	0-0	0.0	0.00	December	0-1	0.0	-1.00

4-y-o+	W-R	Per cent	£1 Level Stake	**Totals**	W-R	Per cent	£1 Level Stake
January	0-0	0.0	0.00	January	0-0	0.0	0.00
February	0-0	0.0	0.00	February	0-0	0.0	0.00
March	0-0	0.0	0.00	March	0-0	0.0	0.00
April	0-6	0.0	-6.00	April	0-8	0.0	-8.00
May	4-14	28.6	+14.50	May	4-19	21.1	+9.50
June	4-14	28.6	+0.83	June	4-23	17.4	-8.17
July	0-14	0.0	-14.00	July	1-22	4.5	-18.00
August	1-14	7.1	-11.13	August	3-31	9.7	-24.49
September	0-12	0.0	-12.00	September	2-21	9.5	-8.00
October	1-10	10.0	+3.00	October	2-20	10.0	-5.17
November	1-4	25.0	+30.00	November	1-10	10.0	+27.00
December	0-1	0.0	-1.00	December	0-2	0.0	-2.00

DISTANCE

2-y-o	W-R	Per cent	£1 Level Stake	**3-y-o**	W-R	Per cent	£1 Level Stake
5f-6f	0-7	0.0	-7.00	5f-6f	0-6	0.0	-6.00
7f-8f	0-5	0.0	-5.00	7f-8f	1-11	9.1	-1.00
9f-13f	0-0	0.0	0.00	9f-13f	4-33	12.1	-22.36
14f+	0-0	0.0	0.00	14f+	1-5	20.0	-3.17

4-y-o+	W-R	Per cent	£1 Level Stake	**Totals**	W-R	Per cent	£1 Level Stake
5f-6f	5-36	13.9	+22.88	5f-6f	5-49	10.2	+9.88
7f-8f	5-35	14.3	-7.67	7f-8f	6-51	11.8	-13.67
9f-13f	1-18	5.6	-11.00	9f-13f	5-51	9.8	-33.36
14f+	0-0	0.0	0.00	14f+	1-5	20.0	-3.17

TYPE OF RACE

Non-Handicaps	W-R	Per cent	£1 Level Stake	Handicaps	W-R	Per cent	£1 Level Stake
2-y-o	0-10	0.0	-10.00	2-y-o	0-2	0.0	-2.00
3-y-o	0-13	0.0	-13.00	3-y-o	6-42	14.3	-19.52
4-y-o+	1-7	14.3	0.00	4-y-o+	10-82	12.2	+4.21

RACE CLASS

	W-R	Per cent	£1 Level Stake
Class 1	1-7	14.3	0.00
Class 2	1-11	9.1	+2.00
Class 3	2-10	20.0	-2.63
Class 4	2-40	5.0	-31.00
Class 5	6-49	12.2	+5.44
Class 6	5-39	12.8	-14.13
Class 7	0-0	0.0	0.00

FIRST TIME OUT

	W-R	Per cent	£1 Level Stake
2-y-o	0-4	0.0	-4.00
3-y-o	0-11	0.0	-11.00
4-y-o+	1-16	6.3	-8.00
Totals	1-31	3.2	-23.00

JOCKEYS

	W-R	Per cent	£1 Level Stake
Tom Queally	5-39	12.8	-9.00
James Doyle	3-5	60.0	+3.08
William Buick	3-6	50.0	+3.94
Gerald Mosse	2-15	13.3	-6.17
George Wood	2-52	3.8	-16.17
Richard Kingscote	1-1	100.0	+12.00
David Allan	1-3	33.3	+7.00

COURSE RECORD

	Total W-R	Non-Hndcps 2-y-o	Non-Hndcps 3-y-o+	Hndcps 2-y-o	Hndcps 3-y-o+	Per cent	£1 Level Stake
Yarmouth	5-29	0-1	0-1	0-0	5-27	17.2	-6.52
Doncaster	2-6	0-0	0-0	0-0	2-6	33.3	+13.00
Newmkt (Jly)	2-19	0-1	0-3	0-0	2-15	10.5	-12.13
Haydock	1-3	0-0	0-1	0-0	1-2	33.3	+1.00
Newcastle (A.W)	1-3	0-1	0-0	0-0	1-2	33.3	+7.00
Goodwood	1-4	0-0	1-2	0-0	0-2	25.0	+3.00
Newmarket	1-6	0-0	0-1	0-0	1-5	16.7	-1.50
Chelmsford (A.W)	1-6	0-0	0-0	0-0	1-6	16.7	-4.17
Wolvhptn (A.W)	1-8	0-0	0-3	0-0	1-5	12.5	+26.00
Windsor	1-14	0-1	0-2	0-0	1-11	7.1	-11.00
Kempton (A.W)	1-27	0-2	0-2	0-2	1-21	3.7	-24.00

WINNING HORSES

Horse	Races Run	1st	2nd	3rd	£
Black Lotus	6	2	2	1	8604
*Delilah Park	3	1	0	0	3752
First Sitting	5	1	0	0	28355
Hackney Road	5	2	1	0	12000
Ice Lord (IRE)	7	2	1	0	22154
Jumping Cats	8	1	1	1	3493
Marilyn	8	3	0	0	10739
Mountain Rescue (IRE)*	8	1	0	1	9704
Pentland Hills (IRE)	8	2	3	1	6857
Seyasah (IRE)	7	1	0	0	3752
*Summer Thunder (USA)	4	1	0	0	3105
Total winning prize-money					**£112515**
Favourites	**6-14**		**42.9%**		**-0.69**

CHARLIE WALLIS

ARDLEIGH, ESSEX

	No. of Hrs	Races Run	1st	2nd	3rd	Unpl	Per cent	£1 Level Stake
2-y-o	*2*	*3*	*0*	*0*	*0*	*3*	*0.0*	*-3.00*
3-y-o	*3*	*18*	*1*	*4*	*2*	*11*	*5.6*	*-10.00*
4-y-o+	*16*	*173*	*21*	*23*	*14*	*115*	*12.1*	*-34.21*
Totals	**21**	**194**	**22**	**27**	**16**	**129**	**11.3**	**-47.21**
2017	*19*	*134*	*9*	*6*	*11*	*108*	*6.7*	*-73.50*
2016	*16*	*108*	*9*	*11*	*10*	*78*	*8.3*	*-26.75*

BY MONTH

2-y-o	W-R	Per cent	£1 Level Stake	3-y-o	W-R	Per cent	£1 Level Stake
January	0-0	0.0	0.00	January	1-3	33.3	+5.00
February	0-0	0.0	0.00	February	0-2	0.0	-2.00
March	0-0	0.0	0.00	March	0-0	0.0	0.00
April	0-0	0.0	0.00	April	0-3	0.0	-3.00
May	0-0	0.0	0.00	May	0-0	0.0	0.00
June	0-0	0.0	0.00	June	0-0	0.0	0.00
July	0-0	0.0	0.00	July	0-2	0.0	-2.00
August	0-0	0.0	0.00	August	0-1	0.0	-1.00
September	0-0	0.0	0.00	September	0-3	0.0	-3.00
October	0-0	0.0	0.00	October	0-2	0.0	-2.00
November	0-0	0.0	0.00	November	0-1	0.0	-1.00
December	0-3	0.0	-3.00	December	0-1	0.0	-1.00

4-y-o+	W-R	Per cent	£1 Level Stake	Totals	W-R	Per cent	£1 Level Stake
January	1-15	6.7	-9.00	January	2-18	11.1	-4.00
February	3-15	20.0	+4.50	February	3-17	17.6	+2.50
March	2-18	11.1	-6.00	March	2-18	11.1	-6.00
April	5-17	29.4	+17.33	April	5-20	25.0	+14.33
May	1-16	6.3	-11.50	May	1-16	6.3	-11.50
June	1-18	5.6	-3.00	June	1-18	5.6	-3.00
July	1-11	9.1	-5.00	July	1-13	7.7	-7.00
August	0-11	0.0	-11.00	August	0-12	0.0	-12.00
September	3-9	33.3	+0.46	September	3-12	25.0	-2.54
October	0-11	0.0	-11.00	October	0-13	0.0	-13.00
November	1-12	8.3	-5.50	November	1-13	7.7	-6.50
December	3-20	15.0	+5.50	December	3-24	12.5	+4.50

DISTANCE

2-y-o	W-R	Per cent	£1 Level Stake	3-y-o	W-R	Per cent	£1 Level Stake
5f-6f	0-3	0.0	-3.00	5f-6f	1-8	12.5	0.00
7f-8f	0-0	0.0	0.00	7f-8f	0-1	0.0	-1.00
9f-13f	0-0	0.0	0.00	9f-13f	0-8	0.0	-8.00
14f+	0-0	0.0	0.00	14f+	0-1	0.0	-1.00

4-y-o+	W-R	Per cent	£1 Level Stake	Totals	W-R	Per cent	£1 Level Stake
5f-6f	18-126	14.3	-6.71	5f-6f	19-137	13.9	-9.71
7f-8f	2-36	5.6	-25.50	7f-8f	2-37	5.4	-26.50
9f-13f	1-11	9.1	-2.00	9f-13f	1-19	5.3	-10.00
14f+	0-0	0.0	0.00	14f+	0-1	0.0	-1.00

TYPE OF RACE

Non-Handicaps	W-R	Per cent	£1 Level Stake	Handicaps	W-R	Per cent	£1 Level Stake
2-y-o	0-1	0.0	-1.00	2-y-o	0-2	0.0	-2.00
3-y-o	0-2	0.0	-2.00	3-y-o	1-16	6.3	-8.00
4-y-o+	1-6	16.7	-1.50	4-y-o+	20-167	12.0	-32.71

RACE CLASS

	W-R	Per cent	£1 Level Stake
Class 1	0-0	0.0	0.00
Class 2	0-9	0.0	-9.00
Class 3	1-9	11.1	+4.00
Class 4	3-22	13.6	+5.50
Class 5	0-35	0.0	-35.00
Class 6	15-104	14.4	-19.21
Class 7	3-15	20.0	+6.50

FIRST TIME OUT

	W-R	Per cent	£1 Level Stake
2-y-o	0-2	0.0	-2.00
3-y-o	0-3	0.0	-3.00
4-y-o+	1-16	6.3	-7.00
Totals	1-21	4.8	-12.00

JOCKEYS

	W-R	Per cent	£1 Level Stake
William Carson	7-62	11.3	-17.17
Charles Bishop	6-16	37.5	+13.83
Hollie Doyle	2-10	20.0	+5.00
Jason Watson	2-12	16.7	-2.50
Adam Kirby	1-1	100.0	+8.00
Luke Morris	1-5	20.0	+3.00
David Egan	1-6	16.7	+7.00
Gabriele Malune	1-9	11.1	-6.38
Joshua Bryan	1-18	5.6	-3.00

COURSE RECORD

	Total W-R	Non-Hndcps 2-y-o	Non-Hndcps 3-y-o+	Hndcps 2-y-o	Hndcps 3-y-o+	Per cent	£1 Level Stake
Chelmsford (A.W)	9-64	0-0	0-0	0-0	9-64	14.1	-2.88
Southwell (A.W)	4-13	0-0	0-1	0-1	4-11	30.8	+10.83
Lingfield (A.W)	3-26	0-0	0-2	0-0	3-24	11.5	-6.50
Brighton	2-8	0-0	1-2	0-0	1-6	25.0	+2.50
Wolvhptn (A.W)	2-24	0-1	0-0	0-1	2-22	8.3	-14.17
Bath	1-2	0-0	0-0	0-0	1-2	50.0	+5.00
Chester	1-2	0-0	0-0	0-0	1-2	50.0	+13.00

WINNING HORSES

Horse	Races Run	1st	2nd	3rd	£
Billyoakes (IRE)	17	2	2	2	6534
Divine Call	13	2	0	1	6598
Fareeq	15	2	3	1	6210
George Dryden (IRE)	15	1	2	2	5531
*King Robert	1	1	0	0	6728
La Fortuna	23	8	1	1	24518
Sharp Operator	19	3	3	3	8798
Sir Hector (IRE)	8	1	3	1	3105
Zac Brown (IRE)	14	2	2	1	17402
Total winning prize-money					**£85424**
Favourites	**4-11**		**36.4%**		**1.96**

JASON WARD

MIDDLEHAM, N YORKS

	No. of Hrs	Races Run	1st	2nd	3rd	Unpl	Per cent	£1 Level Stake
2-y-o	*2*	*4*	*2*	*0*	*0*	*2*	*50.0*	*+12.50*
3-y-o	*2*	*18*	*3*	*1*	*2*	*12*	*16.7*	*+15.00*
4-y-o+	*8*	*44*	*5*	*4*	*5*	*30*	*11.4*	*-11.25*
Totals	**12**	**66**	**10**	**5**	**7**	**44**	**15.2**	**+16.25**
2017	*11*	*72*	*2*	*6*	*8*	*56*	*2.8*	*-58.00*
2016	*8*	*64*	*6*	*10*	*8*	*40*	*9.4*	*-22.75*

BY MONTH

2-y-o	W-R	Per cent	£1 Level Stake	3-y-o	W-R	Per cent	£1 Level Stake
January	0-0	0.0	0.00	January	0-1	0.0	-1.00
February	0-0	0.0	0.00	February	1-2	50.0	+8.00
March	0-0	0.0	0.00	March	0-0	0.0	0.00
April	0-0	0.0	0.00	April	1-1	100.0	+14.00
May	0-0	0.0	0.00	May	0-3	0.0	-3.00
June	0-1	0.0	-1.00	June	0-3	0.0	-3.00
July	2-2	100.0	+14.50	July	0-0	0.0	0.00
August	0-1	0.0	-1.00	August	1-1	100.0	+7.00
September	0-0	0.0	0.00	September	0-2	0.0	-2.00
October	0-0	0.0	0.00	October	0-2	0.0	-2.00
November	0-0	0.0	0.00	November	0-2	0.0	-2.00
December	0-0	0.0	0.00	December	0-1	0.0	-1.00

4-y-o+	W-R	Per cent	£1 Level Stake	Totals	W-R	Per cent	£1 Level Stake
January	0-6	0.0	-6.00	January	0-7	0.0	-7.00
February	0-0	0.0	0.00	February	1-2	50.0	+8.00
March	0-3	0.0	-3.00	March	0-3	0.0	-3.00
April	0-2	0.0	-2.00	April	1-3	33.3	+12.00
May	2-5	40.0	+11.00	May	2-8	25.0	+8.00
June	1-8	12.5	0.00	June	1-12	8.3	-4.00
July	0-6	0.0	-6.00	July	2-8	25.0	+8.50
August	1-5	20.0	-2.25	August	2-7	28.6	+3.75
September	1-5	20.0	+1.00	September	1-7	14.3	-1.00
October	0-3	0.0	-3.00	October	0-5	0.0	-5.00
November	0-1	0.0	-1.00	November	0-3	0.0	-3.00
December	0-0	0.0	0.00	December	0-1	0.0	-1.00

DISTANCE

2-y-o	W-R	Per cent	£1 Level Stake	3-y-o	W-R	Per cent	£1 Level Stake
5f-6f	0-1	0.0	-1.00	5f-6f	2-14	14.3	+4.00
7f-8f	2-3	66.7	+13.50	7f-8f	1-2	50.0	+13.00
9f-13f	0-0	0.0	0.00	9f-13f	0-2	0.0	-2.00
14f+	0-0	0.0	0.00	14f+	0-0	0.0	0.00

4-y-o+	W-R	Per cent	£1 Level Stake	Totals	W-R	Per cent	£1 Level Stake
5f-6f	0-9	0.0	-9.00	5f-6f	2-24	8.3	-6.00
7f-8f	3-20	15.0	+2.00	7f-8f	6-25	24.0	+28.50
9f-13f	2-15	13.3	-4.25	9f-13f	2-17	11.8	-6.25
14f+	0-0	0.0	0.00	14f+	0-0	0.0	0.00

TYPE OF RACE

Non-Handicaps	W-R	Per cent	£1 Level Stake	Handicaps	W-R	Per cent	£1 Level Stake
2-y-o	2-4	50.0	+12.50	2-y-o	0-0	0.0	0.00
3-y-o	2-8	25.0	+17.00	3-y-o	1-10	10.0	-2.00
4-y-o+	0-5	0.0	-5.00	4-y-o+	5-39	12.8	-6.25

RACE CLASS / FIRST TIME OUT

RACE CLASS	W-R	Per cent	£1 Level Stake	FIRST TIME OUT	W-R	Per cent	£1 Level Stake
Class 1	0-2	0.0	-2.00	2-y-o	0-2	0.0	-2.00
Class 2	0-10	0.0	-10.00	3-y-o	1-2	50.0	+13.00
Class 3	2-13	15.4	+2.00	4-y-o+	0-8	0.0	-8.00
Class 4	3-11	27.3	+6.25				
Class 5	5-25	20.0	+25.00	Totals	1-12	8.3	+3.00
Class 6	0-5	0.0	-5.00				
Class 7	0-0	0.0	0.00				

JOCKEYS

	W-R	Per cent	£1 Level Stake
Connor Murtagh	2-5	40.0	+11.50
Rachel Richardson	1-1	100.0	+9.00
Richard Kingscote	1-1	100.0	+1.75
Franny Norton	1-2	50.0	+4.00
Rossa Ryan	1-3	33.3	+4.00
Ben Curtis	1-4	25.0	+11.00
Harrison Shaw	1-4	25.0	+4.00
Luke Morris	1-5	20.0	+4.00
Andrew Breslin	1-7	14.3	+1.00

COURSE RECORD

	Total W-R	Non-Hndcps 2-y-o	Non-Hndcps 3-y-o+	Hndcps 2-y-o	Hndcps 3-y-o+	Per cent	£1 Level Stake
Haydock	3-6	0-0	0-0	0-0	3-6	50.0	+10.75
Beverley	2-3	0-0	1-1	0-0	1-2	66.7	+20.00
Newmarket	1-1	0-0	0-0	0-0	1-1	100.0	+8.00
Ayr	1-2	1-1	0-0	0-0	0-1	50.0	+4.50
Hamilton	1-3	0-0	0-1	0-0	1-2	33.3	+4.00
Musselburgh	1-4	1-1	0-2	0-0	0-1	25.0	+6.00
Newcastle (A.W)	1-6	0-0	1-2	0-0	0-4	16.7	+4.00

WINNING HORSES

Horse	Races Run	1st	2nd	3rd	£
King's Pavilion (IRE)	11	1	1	2	9338
Maifalki (FR)	7	3	2	1	18456
Meerpat	15	2	1	2	9315
Roll On Rory*	8	1	0	0	9704
*Shakour (IRE)	3	1	0	0	4140
Wee Jim (IRE)	3	2	0	0	8539

Total winning prize-money			**£59492**
Favourites	**1-3**	**33.3%**	**-0.25**

FRED WATSON

SEDGEFIELD, CO DURHAM

	No. of Hrs	Races Run	1st	2nd	3rd	Unpl	Per cent	£1 Level Stake
2-y-o	*0*	*0*	*0*	*0*	*0*	*0*	*0.0*	*0.00*
3-y-o	*1*	*1*	*0*	*0*	*0*	*1*	*0.0*	*-1.00*
4-y-o+	*6*	*26*	*1*	*3*	*2*	*20*	*3.8*	*-17.50*
Totals	**7**	**27**	**1**	**3**	**2**	**21**	**3.7**	**-18.50**
2017	*7*	*24*	*1*	*2*	*2*	*19*	*4.2*	*-13.00*
2016	*7*	*28*	*1*	*0*	*2*	*25*	*3.6*	*-23.50*

JOCKEYS

	W-R	Per cent	£1 Level Stake
Andrew Mullen	1-4	25.0	+4.50

COURSE RECORD

	Total W-R	Non-Hndcps 2-y-o	Non-Hndcps 3-y-o+	Hndcps 2-y-o	Hndcps 3-y-o+	Per cent	£1 Level Stake
Newcastle (A.W)	1-12	0-0	0-3	0-0	1-9	8.3	-3.50

WINNING HORSES

Horse	Races Run	1st	2nd	3rd	£
Joyful Star	5	1	1	1	3105

Total winning prize-money			**£3105**
Favourites	**0-0**	**0.0%**	**0.00**

ARCHIE WATSON

UPPER LAMBOURN, W BERKS

	No. of Hrs	Races Run	1st	2nd	3rd	Unpl	Per cent	£1 Level Stake
2-y-o	*58*	*227*	*54*	*46*	*30*	*96*	*23.8*	*-20.44*
3-y-o	*37*	*150*	*25*	*22*	*14*	*89*	*16.7*	*-22.69*
4-y-o+	*22*	*151*	*26*	*20*	*23*	*82*	*17.2*	*-30.04*
Totals	**117**	**528**	**105**	**88**	**67**	**267**	**19.9**	**-73.17**
2017	*48*	*275*	*56*	*31*	*39*	*148*	*20.4*	*-2.17*
2016	*7*	*29*	*4*	*5*	*6*	*14*	*13.8*	*-6.00*

BY MONTH

2-y-o	W-R	Per cent	£1 Level Stake	3-y-o	W-R	Per cent	£1 Level Stake
January	0-0	0.0	0.00	January	2-6	33.3	+17.00
February	0-0	0.0	0.00	February	3-9	33.3	+0.35
March	0-1	0.0	-1.00	March	4-15	26.7	+0.85
April	0-7	0.0	-7.00	April	3-19	15.8	-12.71
May	3-15	20.0	-4.90	May	1-16	6.3	-12.50
June	8-22	36.4	+25.28	June	0-11	0.0	-11.00
July	10-25	40.0	+3.38	July	4-15	26.7	-1.43
August	15-46	32.6	+1.72	August	0-14	0.0	-14.00
September	11-39	28.2	-1.54	September	1-15	6.7	0.00
October	3-37	8.1	-15.50	October	3-9	33.3	+8.00

	W-R	Per cent	£1 Level Stake
November	3-20	15.0	-9.38
December	1-15	6.7	-11.50

	W-R	Per cent	£1 Level Stake
November	1-9	11.1	-5.25
December	3-12	25.0	+8.00

4-y-o+	W-R	Per cent	£1 Level Stake
January	6-19	31.6	+17.13
February	4-20	20.0	-5.53
March	6-24	25.0	+5.13
April	0-8	0.0	-8.00
May	3-18	16.7	-5.84
June	1-14	7.1	-10.50
July	1-13	7.7	-10.50
August	0-5	0.0	-5.00
September	3-6	50.0	+2.58
October	0-5	0.0	-5.00
November	1-9	11.1	-2.00
December	1-10	10.0	-2.50

Totals	W-R	Per cent	£1 Level Stake
January	8-25	32.0	+34.13
February	7-29	24.1	-5.18
March	10-40	25.0	+4.98
April	3-34	8.8	-27.71
May	7-49	14.3	-23.24
June	9-47	19.1	+3.78
July	15-53	28.3	-8.55
August	15-65	23.1	-17.28
September	15-60	25.0	+1.04
October	6-51	11.8	-12.50
November	5-38	13.2	-7.25
December	5-37	13.5	+5.50

DISTANCE

2-y-o	W-R	Per cent	£1 Level Stake
5f-6f	39-128	30.5	+18.04
7f-8f	15-93	16.1	-32.48
9f-13f	0-6	0.0	-6.00
14f+	0-0	0.0	0.00

3-y-o	W-R	Per cent	£1 Level Stake
5f-6f	8-40	20.0	+0.35
7f-8f	10-52	19.2	-15.54
9f-13f	7-46	15.2	+4.50
14f+	0-12	0.0	-12.00

4-y-o+	W-R	Per cent	£1 Level Stake
5f-6f	16-52	30.8	-2.54
7f-8f	3-34	8.8	-3.00
9f-13f	7-58	12.1	-17.50
14f+	0-7	0.0	-7.00

Totals	W-R	Per cent	£1 Level Stake
5f-6f	63-220	28.6	+15.85
7f-8f	28-179	15.6	-51.02
9f-13f	14-110	12.7	-19.00
14f+	0-19	0.0	-19.00

TYPE OF RACE

Non-Handicaps

	W-R	Per cent	£1 Level Stake
2-y-o	40-180	22.2	-31.33
3-y-o	11-57	19.3	-12.32
4-y-o+	8-29	27.6	-1.21

Handicaps

	W-R	Per cent	£1 Level Stake
2-y-o	14-47	29.8	+10.89
3-y-o	14-93	15.1	-10.38
4-y-o+	18-122	14.8	-28.83

RACE CLASS

	W-R	Per cent	£1 Level Stake
Class 1	3-41	7.3	-14.50
Class 2	7-42	16.7	-4.65
Class 3	2-32	6.3	-12.38
Class 4	20-109	18.3	-44.69
Class 5	51-233	21.9	-23.97
Class 6	22-71	31.0	+28.01
Class 7	0-0	0.0	0.00

FIRST TIME OUT

	W-R	Per cent	£1 Level Stake
2-y-o	11-58	19.0	-7.25
3-y-o	9-37	24.3	+25.85
4-y-o+	4-22	18.2	+7.00
Totals	24-117	20.5	+25.60

JOCKEYS

	W-R	Per cent	£1 Level Stake
Edward Greatrex	33-197	16.8	-47.35
Hollie Doyle	22-95	23.2	-9.07
Oisin Murphy	19-78	24.4	-11.55
Daniel Tudhope	9-32	28.1	+10.43
Thomas Greatrex	4-13	30.8	+9.75
Luke Morris	4-30	13.3	-0.38
Pierre-Louis Jamin	4-32	12.5	-9.25
Mr Simon Walker	3-8	37.5	+1.13
Ben Curtis	2-5	40.0	+1.41
Andrew Mullen	2-14	14.3	-0.63
James Doyle	1-1	100.0	+2.00
David Probert	1-2	50.0	-0.67
Rob Hornby	1-5	20.0	-3.00

COURSE RECORD

	Total W-R	Non-Hndcps 2-y-o	Non-Hndcps 3-y-o+	Hndcps 2-y-o	Hndcps 3-y-o+	Per cent	£1 Level Stake
Lingfield (A.W)	22-74	4-11	7-21	1-5	10-37	29.7	+33.10
Wolvhptn (A.W)	15-62	4-17	2-8	3-8	6-29	24.2	-4.33
Kempton (A.W)	11-60	2-20	3-10	2-9	4-21	18.3	-5.13
Chelmsford (A.W)	8-62	3-21	0-4	0-4	5-33	12.9	-16.50
Catterick	4-10	3-5	0-0	0-0	1-5	40.0	-0.12
Lingfield	3-13	1-4	2-6	0-0	0-3	23.1	-4.63
Musselburgh	2-2	1-1	0-0	0-0	1-1	100.0	+10.11
Thirsk	2-3	1-2	0-0	1-1	0-0	66.7	+4.40
Hamilton	2-6	1-1	1-1	0-1	0-3	33.3	-3.10
Sandown	2-6	1-1	0-0	0-0	1-5	33.3	+7.00
Chepstow	2-7	1-3	0-1	0-0	1-3	28.6	-1.75
Redcar	2-7	2-5	0-0	0-0	0-2	28.6	-2.00
Ffos Las	2-7	0-1	0-0	1-2	1-4	28.6	+1.20
Bath	2-8	2-3	0-0	0-1	0-4	25.0	-3.00
Beverley	2-8	1-5	0-0	1-1	0-2	25.0	-1.38
Yarmouth	2-8	1-4	0-1	1-1	0-2	25.0	-0.50
Brighton	2-9	2-4	0-1	0-0	0-4	22.2	-0.50
Salisbury	2-9	2-5	0-0	0-0	0-4	22.2	-3.75
Haydock	2-10	1-2	0-1	1-2	0-5	20.0	-1.97
Leicester	2-10	0-4	1-2	1-2	0-2	20.0	-1.50
Nottingham	2-10	1-6	0-0	0-0	1-4	20.0	+2.50
Southwell (A.W)	2-25	0-1	1-10	1-2	0-12	8.0	-17.43
Wetherby	1-2	1-1	0-0	0-0	0-1	50.0	+2.50
Carlisle	1-5	1-3	0-0	0-1	0-1	20.0	+0.50
Doncaster	1-7	1-3	0-0	0-2	0-2	14.3	-2.00
Ripon	1-7	0-2	1-1	0-0	0-4	14.3	-4.63
Windsor	1-7	1-4	0-3	0-0	0-0	14.3	-5.33
Chester	1-8	0-2	0-2	1-3	0-1	12.5	-5.80
Goodwood	1-10	0-6	0-2	0-0	1-2	10.0	-6.75
Newbury	1-10	1-6	0-1	0-0	0-3	10.0	-1.50
Ascot	1-12	1-7	0-1	0-0	0-4	8.3	+1.00
Newcastle (A.W)	1-21	0-6	1-6	0-0	0-9	4.8	-18.90

WINNING HORSES

Horse	Races Run	1st	2nd	3rd	£
Anycity (IRE)*	3	1	2	0	5434
Attain	19	4	7	3	14897
Barys	5	1	0	2	3752
*Beleaguerment (IRE)	2	1	0	0	3881
Black Sails*	5	1	2	0	3105
Brandon Castle*	4	1	0	0	62250
Bungle Inthebistro	1	1	0	0	3752
*Capla Gilda	6	4	0	1	14426
*Captain Lars (SAF)	29	10	4	5	44733
Casima	7	2	0	1	6857
Chevallier	13	2	1	3	19074

Concello (IRE)	6	3	1	1	14361
Corinthia Knight (IRE)	8	4	1	0	140215
Daddys Poppit (USA)	2	1	0	0	3493
De Medici (IRE)	7	2	1	2	10221
Federal Law (CAN)	4	1	2	0	5111
Felix The Poet	4	2	0	0	4787
Fognini (IRE)	7	3	3	1	14361
Full Suit*	10	1	2	2	3105
Gallovie	4	1	1	1	3752
Ghost Serge (IRE)*	5	1	0	0	4140
Gold Arrow	4	2	1	0	8539
*Gratified (IRE)	3	1	1	0	3105
Grenadier	3	1	0	1	3752
Herecomesthesun (IRE)	4	1	0	1	3881
Isaan Queen (IRE)	7	2	3	0	8415
Isstoora (IRE)	8	1	1	0	3881
It's All A Joke (IRE)	6	2	2	0	9186
It's Not Unusual	9	2	2	0	6598
Izvestia (IRE)	4	2	0	2	12097
Julius Limbani (IRE)	2	1	0	0	4528
Karijini (GER)	4	2	1	0	6469
Kheros	2	1	0	1	3235
Luchador	5	2	0	1	11256
Mango Tango (FR)	2	1	0	0	11972
*Mankind (FR)	6	1	0	0	3493
Mercer's Troop (IRE)*	6	1	0	1	3881
Meringue (IRE)	4	2	1	0	6987
Nate The Great	6	2	1	2	8992
*Poetic Imagination	4	1	1	2	5531
*Proceed (IRE)	1	1	0	0	3105
Pulsating (IRE)*	12	3	3	3	9962
Quiet Endeavour (IRE)	8	4	0	0	19925
Quiet Waters (IRE)	4	2	0	0	7633
Rockin Roy (IRE)	9	4	2	1	13158
*Sary Arqa	1	1	0	0	3752
Showout	4	2	1	0	9186
Shumookhi (IRE)	6	2	2	0	19248
So Brave	5	2	0	1	7504
Soldier's Call	5	3	1	1	97205
Summer Blossom (IRE)	10	1	3	4	4140
Times Past (IRE)	6	1	3	1	3752
Warmhearted (IRE)	9	1	2	1	4140
We Are The World	9	1	2	0	3752
Yabass (IRE)	6	1	2	0	3881
Zenovia (IRE)	2	1	0	0	2995
Total winning prize-money					**£724843**
Favourites	**43-124**		**34.7%**		**-28.19**

SHARON WATT

BROMPTON-ON-SWALE, N YORKS

	No. of Hrs	Races Run	1st	2nd	3rd	Unpl	Per cent	£1 Level Stake
2-y-o	*0*	*0*	*0*	*0*	*0*	*0*	*0.0*	*0.00*
3-y-o	*1*	*5*	*0*	*0*	*0*	*5*	*0.0*	*-5.00*
4-y-o+	*3*	*16*	*1*	*3*	*0*	*12*	*6.3*	*-11.00*
Totals	**4**	**21**	**1**	**3**	**0**	**17**	**4.8**	**-16.00**
2017	*5*	*28*	*4*	*1*	*1*	*22*	*14.3*	*+17.41*
2016	*4*	*24*	*0*	*1*	*1*	*22*	*0.0*	*-24.00*

JOCKEYS

	W-R	Per cent	£1 Level Stake
Phil Dennis	1-9	11.1	-4.00

COURSE RECORD

	Total W-R	Non-Hndcps 2-y-o	3-y-o+	Hndcps 2-y-o	3-y-o+	Per cent	£1 Level Stake
Wolvhptn (A.W)	1-4	0-0	0-0	0-0	1-4	25.0	+1.00

WINNING HORSES

Horse	Races Run	1st	2nd	3rd	£
Champagne Rules	10	1	3	0	3493
Total winning prize-money					**£3493**
Favourites	**0-0**		**0.0%**		**0.00**

ADAM WEST

EPSOM, SURREY

	No. of Hrs	Races Run	1st	2nd	3rd	Unpl	Per cent	£1 Level Stake
2-y-o	*12*	*51*	*0*	*2*	*3*	*46*	*0.0*	*-51.00*
3-y-o	*12*	*82*	*7*	*6*	*7*	*62*	*8.5*	*+11.75*
4-y-o+	*4*	*13*	*0*	*2*	*0*	*11*	*0.0*	*-13.00*
Totals	**28**	**146**	**7**	**10**	**10**	**119**	**4.8**	**-52.25**
2017	*16*	*64*	*5*	*2*	*9*	*48*	*7.8*	*+11.25*
2016	*10*	*29*	*1*	*0*	*2*	*26*	*3.4*	*+38.00*

JOCKEYS

	W-R	Per cent	£1 Level Stake
Toby Eley	3-16	18.8	+35.00
Paddy Mathers	1-10	10.0	+5.00
Charlie Bennett	1-11	9.1	+6.00
John Fahy	1-20	5.0	-17.25
Nicky Mackay	1-20	5.0	-12.00

COURSE RECORD

	Total W-R	Non-Hndcps 2-y-o	3-y-o+	Hndcps 2-y-o	3-y-o+	Per cent	£1 Level Stake
Wolvhptn (A.W)	2-13	0-2	0-0	0-2	2-9	15.4	+6.00
Pontefract	1-1	0-0	0-0	0-0	1-1	100.0	+1.75
Sandown	1-5	0-2	0-0	0-1	1-2	20.0	+21.00
Lingfield	1-6	0-0	0-1	0-1	1-4	16.7	+2.00
Windsor	1-10	0-3	0-0	0-0	1-7	10.0	+11.00
Chelmsford (A.W)	1-18	0-3	0-0	0-3	1-12	5.6	-1.00

WINNING HORSES

Horse	Races Run	1st	2nd	3rd	£
Bambino Lola	4	1	0	1	12450
Couldn't Could She	14	1	1	1	3752
Peggie Sue	10	3	1	1	11385
*Rainbow Jazz (IRE)	14	2	3	1	6598
Total winning prize-money					**£34185**
Favourites	**1-2**		**50.0%**		**0.75**

SIMON WEST

MIDDLEHAM MOOR, N YORKS

	No. of Hrs	Races Run	1st	2nd	3rd	Unpl	Per cent	£1 Level Stake
2-y-o	*0*	*0*	*0*	*0*	*0*	*0*	*0.0*	*0.00*
3-y-o	*0*	*0*	*0*	*0*	*0*	*0*	*0.0*	*0.00*
4-y-o+	*5*	*32*	*1*	*2*	*2*	*27*	*3.1*	*-6.00*
Totals	**5**	**32**	**1**	**2**	**2**	**27**	**3.1**	**-6.00**
2017	*10*	*44*	*0*	*3*	*5*	*36*	*0.0*	*-44.00*
2016	*11*	*87*	*1*	*7*	*8*	*71*	*1.1*	*-70.00*

JOCKEYS

	W-R	Per cent	£1 Level Stake
Andrew Elliott	1-5	20.0	+21.00

COURSE RECORD

	Total W-R	Non-Hndcps 2-y-o	Non-Hndcps 3-y-o+	Hndcps 2-y-o	Hndcps 3-y-o+	Per cent	£1 Level Stake
Carlisle	1-3	0-0	0-0	0-0	1-3	33.3	+23.00

WINNING HORSES

Horse	Races Run	1st	2nd	3rd	£
Amood (IRE)	14	1	1	1	7439
Total winning prize-money					**£7439**
Favourites	**0-0**		**0.0%**		**0.00**

SHEENA WEST

FALMER, E SUSSEX

	No. of Hrs	Races Run	1st	2nd	3rd	Unpl	Per cent	£1 Level Stake
2-y-o	*0*	*0*	*0*	*0*	*0*	*0*	*0.0*	*0.00*
3-y-o	*2*	*6*	*0*	*0*	*0*	*6*	*0.0*	*-6.00*
4-y-o+	*5*	*8*	*1*	*2*	*1*	*4*	*12.5*	*-5.00*
Totals	**7**	**14**	**1**	**2**	**1**	**10**	**7.1**	**-11.00**
2017	*3*	*13*	*0*	*1*	*0*	*12*	*0.0*	*-13.00*
2016	*6*	*8*	*0*	*0*	*1*	*7*	*0.0*	*-8.00*

JOCKEYS

	W-R	Per cent	£1 Level Stake
Silvestre De Sousa	1-1	100.0	+2.00

COURSE RECORD

	Total W-R	Non-Hndcps 2-y-o	Non-Hndcps 3-y-o+	Hndcps 2-y-o	Hndcps 3-y-o+	Per cent	£1 Level Stake
Nottingham	1-1	0-0	0-0	0-0	1-1	100.0	+2.00

WINNING HORSES

Horse	Races Run	1st	2nd	3rd	£
*Lyrica's Lion (IRE)	3	1	1	1	15563
Total winning prize-money					**£15563**
Favourites	**1-2**		**50.0%**		**1.00**

JOHN WEYMES

MIDDLEHAM MOOR, N YORKS

	No. of Hrs	Races Run	1st	2nd	3rd	Unpl	Per cent	£1 Level Stake
2-y-o	*2*	*3*	*0*	*0*	*0*	*3*	*0.0*	*-3.00*
3-y-o	*2*	*5*	*0*	*1*	*0*	*4*	*0.0*	*-5.00*
4-y-o+	*4*	*32*	*2*	*0*	*7*	*22*	*6.3*	*-10.00*
Totals	**8**	**40**	**2**	**1**	**7**	**29**	**5.0**	**-18.00**
2017	*15*	*63*	*3*	*5*	*3*	*52*	*4.8*	*-33.75*
2016	*5*	*28*	*1*	*1*	*6*	*20*	*3.6*	*-18.00*

JOCKEYS

	W-R	Per cent	£1 Level Stake
Phil Dennis	2-31	6.5	-9.00

COURSE RECORD

	Total W-R	Non-Hndcps 2-y-o	Non-Hndcps 3-y-o+	Hndcps 2-y-o	Hndcps 3-y-o+	Per cent	£1 Level Stake
Southwell (A.W)	2-13	0-0	0-1	0-0	2-12	15.4	+9.00

WINNING HORSES

Horse	Races Run	1st	2nd	3rd	£
Deben	15	1	0	5	3105
Dream Ally (IRE)	10	1	0	1	3105
Total winning prize-money					**£6210**
Favourites	**0-0**		**0.0%**		**0.00**

DONALD WHILLANS

HAWICK, BORDERS

	No. of Hrs	Races Run	1st	2nd	3rd	Unpl	Per cent	£1 Level Stake
2-y-o	*1*	*1*	*0*	*0*	*0*	*1*	*0.0*	*-1.00*
3-y-o	*0*	*0*	*0*	*0*	*0*	*0*	*0.0*	*0.00*
4-y-o+	*2*	*8*	*2*	*1*	*0*	*5*	*25.0*	*+5.00*
Totals	**3**	**9**	**2**	**1**	**0**	**6**	**22.2**	**+4.00**
2017	*2*	*13*	*0*	*2*	*3*	*8*	*0.0*	*-13.00*
2016	*1*	*2*	*0*	*0*	*0*	*2*	*0.0*	*-2.00*

JOCKEYS

	W-R	Per cent	£1 Level Stake
Rachel Richardson	2-2	100.0	+11.00

COURSE RECORD

	Total W-R	Non-Hndcps 2-y-o	Non-Hndcps 3-y-o+	Hndcps 2-y-o	Hndcps 3-y-o+	Per cent	£1 Level Stake
Musselburgh	1-1	0-0	0-0	0-0	1-1	100.0	+8.00
Ayr	1-2	0-0	0-1	0-0	1-1	50.0	+2.00

WINNING HORSES

Horse	Races Run	1st	2nd	3rd	£
Wor Lass	3	2	1	0	9445
Total winning prize-money					**£9445**
Favourites	**2-5**		**40.0%**		**0.25**

ALISTAIR WHILLANS

NEWMILL-ON-SLITRIG, BORDERS

	No. of Hrs	Races Run	1st	2nd	3rd	Unpl	Per cent	£1 Level Stake
2-y-o	*2*	*4*	*0*	*0*	*0*	*4*	*0.0*	*-4.00*
3-y-o	*4*	*15*	*0*	*0*	*1*	*14*	*0.0*	*-15.00*
4-y-o+	*16*	*132*	*8*	*13*	*12*	*99*	*6.1*	*-47.50*
Totals	**22**	**151**	**8**	**13**	**13**	**117**	**5.3**	**-66.50**
2017	*18*	*147*	*8*	*11*	*20*	*108*	*5.4*	*-95.15*
2016	*18*	*143*	*17*	*21*	*16*	*89*	*11.9*	*-6.25*

JOCKEYS

	W-R	Per cent	£1 Level Stake
Paul Hanagan	2-6	33.3	+3.00
P J McDonald	2-8	25.0	+10.50
Connor Murtagh	2-8	25.0	+34.00
Hayley Turner	1-2	50.0	+3.00
Graham Lee	1-8	12.5	+2.00

COURSE RECORD

	Total W-R	Non-Hndcps 2-y-o	Non-Hndcps 3-y-o+	Hndcps 2-y-o	Hndcps 3-y-o+	Per cent	£1 Level Stake
Newcastle (A.W)	4-56	0-2	0-7	0-1	4-46	7.1	-7.50
Chelmsford (A.W)	1-1	0-0	0-0	0-0	1-1	100.0	+12.00
Haydock	1-4	0-0	0-1	0-0	1-3	25.0	+4.00
Ayr	1-8	0-0	0-1	0-0	1-7	12.5	+2.00
Carlisle	1-9	0-0	0-0	0-0	1-9	11.1	-4.00

WINNING HORSES

Horse	Races Run	1st	2nd	3rd	£
Alexandrakollontai (IRE)	14	2	1	1	8604
Full Intention*	9	1	2	0	5434
Gun Case	16	1	2	2	3493
Henpecked	4	2	1	1	10063
Royal Shaheen (FR)	13	2	1	1	14814
Total winning prize-money					**£42408**
Favourites	**2-5**		**40.0%**		**-0.13**

RICHARD WHITAKER

SCARCROFT, W YORKS

	No. of Hrs	Races Run	1st	2nd	3rd	Unpl	Per cent	£1 Level Stake
2-y-o	*1*	*7*	*0*	*1*	*1*	*5*	*0.0*	*-7.00*
3-y-o	*3*	*17*	*0*	*0*	*1*	*16*	*0.0*	*-17.00*
4-y-o+	*8*	*65*	*6*	*3*	*4*	*52*	*9.2*	*-15.75*
Totals	**12**	**89**	**6**	**4**	**6**	**73**	**6.7**	**-39.75**
2017	*17*	*95*	*11*	*11*	*9*	*64*	*11.6*	*-28.54*
2016	*26*	*158*	*13*	*9*	*16*	*120*	*8.2*	*-26.50*

JOCKEYS

	W-R	Per cent	£1 Level Stake
Lewis Edmunds	2-17	11.8	-8.50
Phil Dennis	2-29	6.9	-12.25
Ben Curtis	1-1	100.0	+14.00
Rob J Fitzpatrick	1-1	100.0	+8.00

COURSE RECORD

	Total W-R	Non-Hndcps 2-y-o	Non-Hndcps 3-y-o+	Hndcps 2-y-o	Hndcps 3-y-o+	Per cent	£1 Level Stake
Pontefract	3-16	0-0	0-0	0-0	3-16	18.8	+0.25
Newcastle (A.W)	2-13	0-0	0-0	0-0	2-13	15.4	+15.00
Nottingham	1-2	0-0	0-0	0-1	1-1	50.0	+3.00

WINNING HORSES

Horse	Races Run	1st	2nd	3rd	£
Penny Pot Lane	12	1	0	1	5822
Round The Island	16	3	0	3	12291
Silk Mill Blue	12	2	1	0	5757
Total winning prize-money					**£23870**
Favourites	**1-4**		**25.0%**		**-0.50**

MICHAEL WIGHAM

NEWMARKET, SUFFOLK

	No. of Hrs	Races Run	1st	2nd	3rd	Unpl	Per cent	£1 Level Stake
2-y-o	*6*	*30*	*2*	*2*	*1*	*25*	*6.7*	*0.00*
3-y-o	*1*	*4*	*0*	*0*	*0*	*4*	*0.0*	*-4.00*
4-y-o+	*15*	*119*	*13*	*17*	*10*	*78*	*10.9*	*-42.15*
Totals	**22**	**153**	**15**	**19**	**11**	**107**	**9.8**	**-46.15**
2017	*16*	*86*	*14*	*10*	*5*	*57*	*16.3*	*-1.63*
2016	*20*	*87*	*10*	*11*	*8*	*58*	*11.5*	*-38.09*

BY MONTH

2-y-o	W-R	Per cent	£1 Level Stake	**3-y-o**	W-R	Per cent	£1 Level Stake
January	0-0	0.0	0.00	January	0-0	0.0	0.00
February	0-0	0.0	0.00	February	0-0	0.0	0.00
March	0-0	0.0	0.00	March	0-0	0.0	0.00
April	0-0	0.0	0.00	April	0-0	0.0	0.00
May	0-2	0.0	-2.00	May	0-0	0.0	0.00
June	0-0	0.0	0.00	June	0-0	0.0	0.00
July	0-3	0.0	-3.00	July	0-0	0.0	0.00
August	0-6	0.0	-6.00	August	0-0	0.0	0.00
September	1-6	16.7	+20.00	September	0-2	0.0	-2.00
October	0-5	0.0	-5.00	October	0-2	0.0	-2.00
November	0-3	0.0	-3.00	November	0-0	0.0	0.00
December	1-5	20.0	-1.00	December	0-0	0.0	0.00

4-y-o+	W-R	Per cent	£1 Level Stake	**Totals**	W-R	Per cent	£1 Level Stake
January	0-7	0.0	-7.00	January	0-7	0.0	-7.00
February	0-8	0.0	-8.00	February	0-8	0.0	-8.00
March	0-10	0.0	10.00	March	0-10	0.0	10.00
April	0-5	0.0	-5.00	April	0-5	0.0	-5.00
May	0-7	0.0	-7.00	May	0-9	0.0	-9.00
June	1-12	8.3	-9.90	June	1-12	8.3	-9.90
July	3-15	20.0	-1.50	July	3-18	16.7	-4.50

	W-R	Per cent	£1 Level Stake		W-R	Per cent	£1 Level Stake
August	3-17	17.6	+5.25	August	3-23	13.0	-0.75
September	1-11	9.1	-6.50	September	2-19	10.5	+11.50
October	2-7	28.6	+1.50	October	2-14	14.3	-5.50
November	1-9	11.1	-5.00	November	1-12	8.3	-5.00
December	2-11	18.2	+11.00	December	3-16	18.8	+11.00

DISTANCE

2-y-o	W-R	Per cent	£1 Level Stake	3-y-o	W-R	Per cent	£1 Level Stake
5f-6f	1-14	7.1	+12.00	5f-6f	0-4	0.0	-4.00
7f-8f	1-16	6.3	-12.00	7f-8f	0-0	0.0	0.00
9f-13f	0-0	0.0	0.00	9f-13f	0-0	0.0	0.00
14f+	0-0	0.0	0.00	14f+	0-0	0.0	0.00

4-y-o+	W-R	Per cent	£1 Level Stake	Totals	W-R	Per cent	£1 Level Stake
5f-6f	11-67	16.4	-10.40	5f-6f	12-85	14.1	-2.40
7f-8f	2-47	4.3	-26.75	7f-8f	3-63	4.8	-38.75
9f-13f	0-4	0.0	-4.00	9f-13f	0-4	0.0	-4.00
14f+	0-1	0.0	-1.00	14f+	0-1	0.0	-1.00

TYPE OF RACE

Non-Handicaps	W-R	Per cent	£1 Level Stake	Handicaps	W-R	Per cent	£1 Level Stake
2-y-o	2-21	9.5	+9.00	2-y-o	0-9	0.0	-9.00
3-y-o	0-0	0.0	0.00	3-y-o	0-4	0.0	-4.00
4-y-o+	0-7	0.0	-7.00	4-y-o+	13-112	11.6	-35.15

RACE CLASS

	W-R	Per cent	£1 Level Stake
Class 1	0-0	0.0	0.00
Class 2	3-22	13.6	+7.00
Class 3	1-17	5.9	-12.50
Class 4	1-24	4.2	-12.00
Class 5	5-45	11.1	-6.15
Class 6	5-44	11.4	-21.50
Class 7	0-1	0.0	-1.00

FIRST TIME OUT

	W-R	Per cent	£1 Level Stake
2-y-o	0-6	0.0	-6.00
3-y-o	0-1	0.0	-1.00
4-y-o+	0-15	0.0	-15.00
Totals	0-22	0.0	-22.00

JOCKEYS

	W-R	Per cent	£1 Level Stake
Franny Norton	4-46	8.7	-17.75
Joe Fanning	2-4	50.0	+27.00
Josephine Gordon	2-11	18.2	+8.00
J F Egan	2-14	14.3	-4.50
James Doyle	1-1	100.0	+3.50
David Egan	1-3	33.3	+0.50
P J McDonald	1-3	33.3	+0.50
Silvestre De Sousa	1-4	25.0	-1.90
David Probert	1-8	12.5	-2.50

COURSE RECORD

	Total W-R	Non-Hndcps 2-y-o	Non-Hndcps 3-y-o+	Hndcps 2-y-o	Hndcps 3-y-o+	Per cent	£1 Level Stake
Newcastle (A.W)	3-15	0-0	0-2	0-0	3-13	20.0	+10.50
Newmkt (Jly)	2-4	0-0	0-0	0-0	2-4	50.0	+10.10
Yarmouth	2-7	0-2	0-0	0-0	2-5	28.6	+1.00
Chelmsford (A.W)	2-26	0-1	0-0	0-1	2-24	7.7	-14.50
Wolvhptn (A.W)	2-27	1-4	0-2	0-1	1-20	7.4	-17.50
Pontefract	1-1	1-1	0-0	0-0	0-0	100.0	+25.00
Doncaster	1-3	0-0	0-0	0-0	1-3	33.3	+0.25
Kempton (A.W)	1-12	0-2	0-0	0-3	1-7	8.3	-8.00
Lingfield (A.W)	1-16	0-2	0-2	0-1	1-11	6.3	-11.00

WINNING HORSES

Horse	Races Run	1st	2nd	3rd	£
*Anycity (IRE)	2	1	0	0	3752
Charleston Belle	7	1	0	0	3105
Clear Water (IRE)	6	1	1	1	6469
Deeds Not Words (IRE)	24	4	0	1	12420
Flying Foxy	9	1	1	2	4528
Glenamoy Lad	3	1	0	0	18675
Nick Vedder	13	2	6	1	7504
Red Saree (IRE)	4	1	0	0	4528
Sanaadh	2	1	0	0	15753
Verne Castle	12	2	1	1	32992
Total winning prize-money					**£109726**
Favourites	**4-15**		**26.7%**		**-0.65**

IAN WILLIAMS

PORTWAY, WORCS

	No. of Hrs	Races Run	1st	2nd	3rd	Unpl	Per cent	£1 Level Stake
2-y-o	*1*	*3*	*0*	*0*	*0*	*3*	*0.0*	*-3.00*
3-y-o	*28*	*132*	*22*	*18*	*13*	*79*	*16.7*	*-7.09*
4-y-o+	*54*	*314*	*44*	*31*	*38*	*200*	*14.0*	*-56.07*
Totals	**83**	**449**	**66**	**49**	**51**	**282**	**14.7**	**-66.16**
2017	*69*	*388*	*51*	*46*	*38*	*252*	*13.1*	*-61.57*
2016	*56*	*251*	*38*	*23*	*28*	*162*	*15.1*	*-31.62*

BY MONTH

2-y-o	W-R	Per cent	£1 Level Stake	3-y-o	W-R	Per cent	£1 Level Stake
January	0-0	0.0	0.00	January	0-5	0.0	-5.00
February	0-0	0.0	0.00	February	0-3	0.0	-3.00
March	0-0	0.0	0.00	March	0-4	0.0	-4.00
April	0-0	0.0	0.00	April	0-3	0.0	-3.00
May	0-0	0.0	0.00	May	3-14	21.4	+18.00
June	0-0	0.0	0.00	June	1-16	6.3	-13.63
July	0-0	0.0	0.00	July	3-13	23.1	-1.63
August	0-0	0.0	0.00	August	6-27	22.2	-1.75
September	0-2	0.0	-2.00	September	6-19	31.6	+6.91
October	0-1	0.0	-1.00	October	1-10	10.0	+7.00
November	0-0	0.0	0.00	November	1-6	16.7	+2.00
December	0-0	0.0	0.00	December	1-12	8.3	-9.00

4-y-o+	W-R	Per cent	£1 Level Stake	Totals	W-R	Per cent	£1 Level Stake
January	1-9	11.1	0.00	January	1-14	7.1	-5.00
February	3-22	13.6	-12.57	February	3-25	12.0	-15.57
March	1-7	14.3	-1.50	March	1-11	9.1	-5.50
April	3-15	20.0	+2.00	April	3-18	16.7	-1.00

May	3-35	8.6	-15.00	May	6-49	12.2	+3.00
June	6-35	17.1	-10.25	June	7-51	13.7	-23.88
July	4-25	16.0	-5.00	July	7-38	18.4	-6.63
August	3-46	6.5	-15.00	August	9-73	12.3	-16.75
September	9-39	23.1	+17.00	September	15-60	25.0	+21.91
October	9-39	23.1	+10.75	October	10-50	20.0	+16.75
November	0-22	0.0	-22.00	November	1-28	3.6	-20.00
December	2-20	10.0	-4.50	December	3-32	9.4	-13.50

DISTANCE

2-y-o	W-R	Per cent	£1 Level Stake	3-y-o	W-R	Per cent	£1 Level Stake
5f-6f	0-0	0.0	0.00	5f-6f	0-9	0.0	-9.00
7f-8f	0-3	0.0	-3.00	7f-8f	3-46	6.5	-12.50
9f-13f	0-0	0.0	0.00	9f-13f	18-74	24.3	+15.03
14f+	0-0	0.0	0.00	14f+	1-3	33.3	-0.63

4-y-o+	W-R	Per cent	£1 Level Stake	Totals	W-R	Per cent	£1 Level Stake
5f-6f	6-32	18.8	+4.00	5f-6f	6-41	14.6	-5.00
7f-8f	8-69	11.6	-14.17	7f-8f	11-118	9.3	-29.67
9f-13f	16-140	11.4	-66.40	9f-13f	34-214	15.9	-51.37
14f+	14-73	19.2	+20.50	14f+	15-76	19.7	+19.87

TYPE OF RACE

Non-Handicaps	W-R	Per cent	£1 Level Stake	Handicaps	W-R	Per cent	£1 Level Stake
2-y-o	0-3	0.0	-3.00	2-y-o	0-0	0.0	0.00
3-y-o	4-21	19.0	+2.88	3-y-o	18-111	16.2	-9.97
4-y-o+	1-15	6.7	-8.50	4-y-o+	43-299	14.4	-47.57

RACE CLASS

	W-R	Per cent	£1 Level Stake
Class 1	1-9	11.1	-2.50
Class 2	12-114	10.5	-47.00
Class 3	6-55	10.9	-19.25
Class 4	13-91	14.3	-21.88
Class 5	23-99	23.2	+60.08
Class 6	11-75	14.7	-29.62
Class 7	0-6	0.0	-6.00

FIRST TIME OUT

	W-R	Per cent	£1 Level Stake
2-y-o	0-1	0.0	-1.00
3-y-o	2-28	7.1	-11.50
4-y-o+	5-54	9.3	-21.00
Totals	7-83	8.4	-33.50

JOCKEYS

	W-R	Per cent	£1 Level Stake
Fran Berry	7-32	21.9	+18.50
Kieran O'Neill	6-25	24.0	-2.25
Jim Crowley	6-33	18.2	-3.88
P J McDonald	5-18	27.8	+20.75
Richard Kingscote	4-25	16.0	-5.03
Stevie Donohoe	4-31	12.9	+2.50
Ryan Moore	3-9	33.3	+3.38
James Doyle	3-18	16.7	-7.25
Paddy Mathers	3-22	13.6	+5.75
Dr Misha Voikhansky	2-4	50.0	+4.50
Martin Dwyer	2-5	40.0	+6.00
Andrea Atzeni	2-6	33.3	+14.00
William Buick	2-10	20.0	-1.00
Ben Curtis	2-11	18.2	+2.50
David Egan	2-14	14.3	-7.63
Ted Durcan	1-1	100.0	+10.00
Liam Keniry	1-1	100.0	+0.91
Nick Scholfield	1-1	100.0	+2.50
Callum Rodriguez	1-1	100.0	+5.00
Miss Brodie Hampson	1-1	100.0	+2.75
Pat Cosgrave	1-3	33.3	+1.50
Phillip Makin	1-3	33.3	+1.00
Paul Hanagan	1-4	25.0	+0.50
Mr Charlie Todd	1-5	20.0	+2.00
Jamie Spencer	1-6	16.7	-4.17
Gabriele Malune	1-7	14.3	+2.00
Silvestre De Sousa	1-7	14.3	-0.50
Adam Kirby	1-8	12.5	-2.50

COURSE RECORD

	Total W-R	Non-Hndcps 2-y-o	Non-Hndcps 3-y-o+	Hndcps 2-y-o	Hndcps 3-y-o+	Per cent	£1 Level Stake
Nottingham	7-20	0-1	1-3	0-0	6-16	35.0	+16.88
Chelmsford (A.W)	7-27	0-0	0-0	0-0	7-27	25.9	+6.24
Doncaster	6-21	0-0	2-3	0-0	4-18	28.6	+11.13
Chester	5-26	0-2	0-2	0-0	5-22	19.2	-1.25
Newmkt (Jly)	4-21	0-0	0-0	0-0	4-21	19.0	+3.00
Wolvhptn (A.W)	4-57	0-0	0-6	0-0	4-51	7.0	-32.15
Haydock	3-13	0-0	0-1	0-0	3-12	23.1	+0.38
Newmarket	3-21	0-0	0-0	0-0	3-21	14.3	+9.00
Goodwood	3-22	0-0	0-2	0-0	3-20	13.6	-13.50
Lingfield (A.W)	3-26	0-0	0-2	0-0	3-24	11.5	+1.50
Ayr	2-4	0-0	0-0	0-0	2-4	50.0	+12.00
Salisbury	2-6	0-0	1-1	0-0	1-5	33.3	+1.75
Bath	2-7	0-0	0-1	0-0	2-6	28.6	-1.00
Leicester	2-12	0-0	0-1	0-0	2-11	16.7	-3.50
Kempton (A.W)	2-28	0-0	0-3	0-0	2-25	7.1	-14.63
Carlisle	1-2	0-0	0-0	0-0	1-2	50.0	+4.00
Catterick	1-3	0-0	0-0	0-0	1-3	33.3	-0.50
Pontefract	1-3	0-0	0-1	0-0	1-2	33.3	+14.00
Lingfield	1-5	0-0	0-0	0-0	1-5	20.0	+0.50
Redcar	1-5	0-0	0-0	0-0	1-5	20.0	+10.00
Beverley	1-9	0-0	0-1	0-0	1-8	11.1	-5.25
Windsor	1-10	0-0	0-2	0-0	1-8	10.0	-4.50
Epsom	1-11	0-0	0-0	0-0	1-11	9.1	-4.50
Newbury	1-13	0-0	0-2	0-0	1-11	7.7	-9.25
Sandown	1-14	0-0	1-2	0-0	0-12	7.1	-7.50
Ascot	1-18	0-0	0-0	0-0	1-18	5.6	-14.00

WINNING HORSES

Horse	Races Run	1st	2nd	3rd	£
Aces (IRE)	6	2	0	0	47298
Artic Nel	8	1	0	0	3235
Bamako Du Chatelet (FR)	14	2	0	2	6857
*Bezos (IRE)	6	1	1	1	3881
Born To Spend (IRE)	4	1	0	0	3120
Boy In The Bar	14	1	1	2	25876
Byron Flyer	9	3	1	2	37990
*Central City (IRE)	4	1	0	1	6728
Darksideoftarnside (IRE)	6	1	0	0	11644
Dr Doro (IRE)	5	3	0	1	3752
Faithful Mount	8	1	0	2	6081

Gala Celebration (IRE)	6	1	3	1	5434
Gossip Column (IRE)	8	4	1	0	30469
Jack Regan	10	3	2	1	20917
Jam Session (IRE)	4	2	0	0	17725
Jumping Around (IRE)	2	1	1	0	3493
Kreb's Cycle (IRE)	8	1	1	2	5531
Lucky's Dream	7	2	1	0	6987
Magic Circle (IRE)	2	2	0	0	132082
Matewan (IRE)	4	2	1	1	12943
Miss Mumtaz (IRE)	9	1	3	1	4205
Misty Birnam (SAF)	12	1	0	2	4787
Monjeni	6	1	0	1	5531
My Fantasea (IRE)	12	3	3	1	10609
Oi The Clubb Oi'S	4	1	0	1	3881
Paddy A (IRE)	15	3	4	4	14749
Paddy The Chef (IRE)	9	1	0	2	3881
Pretty Jewel	9	4	0	2	26083
Pure Shores	9	2	1	1	8345
Reshoun (FR)	7	1	0	1	38814
Restorer	9	2	1	0	33767
Saunter (FR)	4	1	0	0	16173
Shuhood (IRE)	10	2	1	3	13294
Speedo Boy (FR)	6	1	0	1	18675
Stars Over The Sea (USA)	5	1	2	0	31125
Swordbill	10	3	2	0	12032
Turanga Leela	9	2	0	0	7504
War Brigade (FR)	3	1	0	1	3619
Total winning prize-money					**£649117**
Favourites	**36-102**		**35.3%**		**-0.17**

OLLY WILLIAMS

MARKET RASEN, LINCS

	No. of Hrs	Races Run	1st	2nd	3rd	Unpl	Per cent	£1 Level Stake
2-y-o	*1*	*8*	*0*	*0*	*2*	*6*	*0.0*	*-8.00*
3-y-o	*3*	*23*	*0*	*4*	*3*	*16*	*0.0*	*-23.00*
4-y-o+	*6*	*39*	*1*	*4*	*1*	*33*	*2.6*	*-22.00*
Totals	**10**	**70**	**1**	**8**	**6**	**55**	**1.4**	**-53.00**
2017	*8*	*38*	*2*	*4*	*4*	*28*	*5.3*	*-26.50*
2016	*4*	*25*	*4*	*2*	*1*	*18*	*16.0*	*+19.00*

JOCKEYS

	W-R	Per cent	£1 Level Stake
Paddy Vaughan	1-14	7.1	+3.00

COURSE RECORD

	Total W-R	Non-Hndcps 2-y-o	Non-Hndcps 3-y-o+	Hndcps 2-y-o	Hndcps 3-y-o+	Per cent	£1 Level Stake
Southwell (A.W)	1-24	0-0	0-1	0-0	1-23	4.2	-7.00

WINNING HORSES

Horse	Races Run	1st	2nd	3rd	£
*Essential	10	1	1	0	3105
Total winning prize-money					**£3105**
Favourites	**0-4**		**0.0%**		**-4.00**

NOEL WILLIAMS

BLEWBURY, OXON

	No. of Hrs	Races Run	1st	2nd	3rd	Unpl	Per cent	£1 Level Stake
2-y-o	*1*	*1*	*0*	*0*	*0*	*1*	*0.0*	*-1.00*
3-y-o	*2*	*6*	*1*	*1*	*3*	*1*	*16.7*	*0.00*
4-y-o+	*2*	*7*	*0*	*0*	*1*	*6*	*0.0*	*-7.00*
Totals	**5**	**14**	**1**	**1**	**4**	**8**	**7.1**	**-8.00**
2017	*4*	*15*	*2*	*0*	*0*	*13*	*13.3*	*+5.50*
2016	*1*	*3*	*0*	*0*	*0*	*3*	*0.0*	*-3.00*

JOCKEYS

	W-R	Per cent	£1 Level Stake
Rob Hornby	1-2	50.0	+4.00

COURSE RECORD

	Total W-R	Non-Hndcps 2-y-o	Non-Hndcps 3-y-o+	Hndcps 2-y-o	Hndcps 3-y-o+	Per cent	£1 Level Stake
Windsor	1-1	0-0	0-0	0-0	1-1	100.0	+5.00

WINNING HORSES

Horse	Races Run	1st	2nd	3rd	£
Percy Prosecco	5	1	1	2	3105
Total winning prize-money					**£3105**
Favourites	**3-10**		**30.0%**		**1.13**

STUART WILLIAMS

NEWMARKET, SUFFOLK

	No. of Hrs	Races Run	1st	2nd	3rd	Unpl	Per cent	£1 Level Stake
2-y-o	*15*	*62*	*7*	*7*	*7*	*41*	*11.3*	*-19.45*
3-y-o	*19*	*115*	*16*	*14*	*14*	*71*	*13.9*	*-37.49*
4-y-o+	*30*	*248*	*35*	*37*	*32*	*142*	*14.1*	*-23.32*
Totals	**64**	**425**	**58**	**58**	**53**	**254**	**13.6**	**-80.26**
2017	*61*	*344*	*32*	*37*	*38*	*234*	*9.3*	*-143.69*
2016	*63*	*369*	*51*	*31*	*38*	*248*	*13.8*	*-50.01*

BY MONTH

2-y-o	W-R	Per cent	£1 Level Stake	**3-y-o**	W-R	Per cent	£1 Level Stake
January	0-0	0.0	0.00	January	2-11	18.2	-7.20
February	0-0	0.0	0.00	February	0-7	0.0	-7.00
March	0-0	0.0	0.00	March	0-6	0.0	-6.00
April	0-0	0.0	0.00	April	0-6	0.0	-6.00
May	0-2	0.0	-2.00	May	2-10	20.0	-2.00
June	2-6	33.3	+11.00	June	3-16	18.8	-1.17
July	2-7	28.6	-2.45	July	1-15	6.7	-9.50
August	1-11	9.1	+1.00	August	2-16	12.5	-8.50
September	0-12	0.0	-12.00	September	3-11	27.3	+13.50
October	2-13	15.4	-4.00	October	2-10	20.0	-3.63
November	0-8	0.0	-8.00	November	1-5	20.0	+2.00
December	0-3	0.0	-3.00	December	0-2	0.0	-2.00

4-y-o+	W-R	Per cent	£1 Level Stake
January	3-34	8.8	-14.25
February	4-20	20.0	-2.63
March	4-20	20.0	-2.17
April	2-15	13.3	+6.50
May	1-23	4.3	-16.50
June	1-23	4.3	-18.00
July	4-20	20.0	+7.75
August	4-23	17.4	+12.75
September	2-26	7.7	-13.50
October	4-15	26.7	+3.22
November	3-16	18.8	+12.00
December	3-13	23.1	+1.50

Totals	W-R	Per cent	£1 Level Stake
January	5-45	11.1	-21.45
February	4-27	14.8	-9.63
March	4-26	15.4	-8.17
April	2-21	9.5	+0.50
May	3-35	8.6	-20.50
June	6-45	13.3	-8.17
July	7-42	16.7	-4.20
August	7-50	14.0	+5.25
September	5-49	10.2	-12.00
October	8-38	21.1	-4.41
November	4-29	13.8	+14.00
December	3-18	16.7	-0.50

DISTANCE

2-y-o	W-R	Per cent	£1 Level Stake
5f-6f	7-43	16.3	-0.45
7f-8f	0-18	0.0	-18.00
9f-13f	0-1	0.0	-1.00
14f+	0-0	0.0	0.00

3-y-o	W-R	Per cent	£1 Level Stake
5f-6f	10-56	17.9	-8.83
7f-8f	2-34	5.9	-18.00
9f-13f	4-25	16.0	-10.67
14f+	0-0	0.0	0.00

4-y-o+	W-R	Per cent	£1 Level Stake
5f-6f	13-102	12.7	-24.03
7f-8f	16-101	15.8	+12.88
9f-13f	6-45	13.3	-12.17
14f+	0-0	0.0	0.00

Totals	W-R	Per cent	£1 Level Stake
5f-6f	30-201	14.9	-33.31
7f-8f	18-153	11.8	-23.12
9f-13f	10-71	14.1	-23.84
14f+	0-0	0.0	0.00

TYPE OF RACE

Non-Handicaps	W-R	Per cent	£1 Level Stake
2-y-o	4-45	8.9	-22.20
3-y-o	3-23	13.0	-3.00
4-y-o+	0-13	0.0	-13.00

Handicaps	W-R	Per cent	£1 Level Stake
2-y-o	3-17	17.6	+2.75
3-y-o	13-92	14.1	-34.49
4-y-o+	35-235	14.9	-10.32

RACE CLASS

	W-R	Per cent	£1 Level Stake
Class 1	0-10	0.0	-10.00
Class 2	10-92	10.9	-14.00
Class 3	4-55	7.3	-30.00
Class 4	14-103	13.6	-15.25
Class 5	21-103	20.4	+15.48
Class 6	8-60	13.3	-28.49
Class 7	1-2	50.0	+2.00

FIRST TIME OUT

	W-R	Per cent	£1 Level Stake
2-y-o	1-15	6.7	-2.00
3-y-o	2-19	10.5	-8.20
4-y-o+	1-30	3.3	-26.75
Totals	4-64	6.3	-36.95

JOCKEYS

	W-R	Per cent	£1 Level Stake
Oisin Murphy	8-32	25.0	+19.88
Sean Levey	6-31	19.4	+14.75
P J McDonald	6-33	18.2	-2.95
Silvestre De Sousa	5-17	29.4	+14.00
Daniel Muscutt	5-27	18.5	-0.13
Richard Kingscote	4-25	16.0	+1.00
Martin Dwyer	3-12	25.0	-3.20
Harry Bentley	3-28	10.7	-8.92
Fran Berry	3-38	7.9	-14.00
Jamie Spencer	2-4	50.0	+4.75
Cameron Noble	2-4	50.0	+0.73
Rossa Ryan	2-8	25.0	-1.00
Milly Naseb	2-42	4.8	-31.00
Hayley Turner	1-1	100.0	+3.50
Miss Serena Brotherton	1-1	100.0	+3.33
William Carver	1-2	50.0	+19.00
Stevie Donohoe	1-3	33.3	+1.00
Joe Fanning	1-5	20.0	-3.00
Edward Greatrex	1-11	9.1	0.00
Aaron Jones	1-19	5.3	-16.00

COURSE RECORD

	Total W-R	Non-Hndcps 2-y-o	Non-Hndcps 3-y-o+	Hndcps 2-y-o	Hndcps 3-y-o+	Per cent	£1 Level Stake
Chelmsford (A.W)	10-71	0-4	0-4	0-7	10-56	14.1	-18.25
Yarmouth	9-40	0-4	2-2	0-1	7-33	22.5	+11.25
Wolvhptn (A.W)	7-33	0-1	0-2	0-0	7-30	21.2	-0.52
Kempton (A.W)	5-40	0-2	0-9	1-3	4-26	12.5	-12.00
Newcastle (A.W)	3-18	0-0	1-3	0-1	2-14	16.7	-7.20
Windsor	3-18	1-7	0-1	0-0	2-10	16.7	+5.83
Bath	2-2	0-0	0-0	0-0	2-2	100.0	+5.50
Lingfield	2-6	1-1	0-1	0-0	1-4	33.3	+1.00
Brighton	2-10	1-2	0-0	0-0	1-8	20.0	+0.50
Goodwood	2-12	0-1	0-1	1-1	1-9	16.7	+4.50
Ascot	2-13	0-0	0-0	0-0	2-13	15.4	+2.50
Epsom	2-14	0-1	0-0	0-0	2-13	14.3	+6.00
Lingfield (A.W)	2-29	0-0	0-6	0-0	2-23	6.9	-16.17
Newmkt (Jly)	2-31	0-5	0-4	0-0	2-22	6.5	-6.25
Chepstow	1-1	1-1	0-0	0-0	0-0	100.0	+0.80
Haydock	1-1	0-0	0-0	0-0	1-1	100.0	+5.50
Nottingham	1-9	0-6	0-0	1-1	0-2	11.1	-6.25
Sandown	1-18	0-1	0-0	0-0	1-17	5.6	-13.00
Newmarket	1-26	0-5	0-0	0-1	1-20	3.8	-11.00

WINNING HORSES

Horse	Races Run	1st	2nd	3rd	£
Able Jack	6	3	0	0	20927
Alaadel	6	1	0	1	15753
Allegiant (USA)	4	1	0	0	5434
Bajan Gold (IRE)	6	2	1	1	7504
Breathtaking Look	3	2	0	0	7504
Broughton Excels	4	1	1	0	2588
Compas Scoobie	21	2	2	5	10544
Daschas	10	3	2	1	21962
Derek Duval (USA)	13	3	3	1	13973
Don Armado (IRE)	8	2	1	1	19634
Examiner (IRE)	6	1	0	0	16173
Excellent George	11	3	1	2	13779
Glenn Coco	10	1	2	1	5434
Hanakotoba (USA)	6	1	0	0	3105
Hart Stopper	8	2	1	1	38814
Human Nature (IRE)	14	1	3	1	5531
Jan's Joy	11	1	0	0	3105
*Juanito Chico (IRE)	6	1	0	0	6469
Lalania	8	1	0	3	3752

Lethal Angel	12	1	3	1	3493
Lunar Deity	12	1	3	3	3105
Maratha (IRE)	11	1	3	1	5531
Marronnier (IRE)	3	1	0	1	3752
My Boy Sepoy	8	2	1	0	6857
Oakley Mimosa	9	1	1	1	3493
Pactolus (IRE)	17	3	5	2	36656
Pinnata (IRE)	6	2	1	1	16065
Relevant (IRE)	4	1	0	0	2995
Restless Rose	6	1	1	2	3752
Shamshon (IRE)	20	2	4	2	10221
Stellar Surprise	5	1	0	1	16808
Street Parade	5	2	1	0	7504
Swift Approval (IRE)	20	1	4	3	11972
Via Serendipity	8	2	1	2	53256
Watchmyeverymove (IRE)	6	1	2	1	3752
Wiff Waff	15	3	4	2	10609
Total winning prize-money					**£421806**
Favourites	**19-62**		**30.6%**		**-3.26**

LISA WILLIAMSON

RIDLEY WOOD, WREXHAM

	No. of Hrs	Races Run	1st	2nd	3rd	Unpl	Per cent	£1 Level Stake
2-y-o	*3*	*8*	*0*	*0*	*0*	*8*	*0.0*	*-8.00*
3-y-o	*5*	*34*	*2*	*3*	*3*	*26*	*5.9*	*-12.00*
4-y-o+	*18*	*166*	*4*	*11*	*14*	*137*	*2.4*	*-93.00*
Totals	**26**	**208**	**6**	**14**	**17**	**171**	**2.9**	**-113.00**
2017	*28*	*169*	*8*	*7*	*11*	*142*	*4.7*	*-58.50*
2016	*22*	*151*	*5*	*9*	*12*	*125*	*3.3*	*-92.00*

JOCKEYS

	W-R	Per cent	£1 Level Stake
Gabriele Malune	2-31	6.5	+15.00
Callum Shepherd	1-3	33.3	+18.00
Raul Da Silva	1-10	10.0	-4.00
Kevin Lundie	1-34	2.9	-19.00
Elisha Whittington	1-34	2.9	-27.00

COURSE RECORD

	Total W-R	Non-Hndcps 2-y-o	Non-Hndcps 3-y-o+	Hndcps 2-y-o	Hndcps 3-y-o+	Per cent	£1 Level Stake
Chelmsford (A.W)	3-37	0-0	0-1	0-0	3-36	8.1	-5.00
Wolvhptn (A.W)	2-72	0-4	0-5	0-0	2-63	2.8	-16.00
Ffos Las	1-6	0-0	0-0	0-0	1-6	16.7	+1.00

WINNING HORSES

Horse	Races Run	1st	2nd	3rd	£
Blue Rocks	5	1	0	0	3817
Brandy Station (IRE)	14	2	1	1	6275
Mighty Zip (USA)	16	1	1	1	3493
Red Stripes (USA)	28	1	6	5	4399
*Sayesse	5	1	0	0	5434
Total winning prize-money					**£23418**
Favourites	**0-6**		**0.0%**		**-6.00**

NOEL WILSON

MARWOOD, CO DURHAM

	No. of Hrs	Races Run	1st	2nd	3rd	Unpl	Per cent	£1 Level Stake
2-y-o	*2*	*11*	*0*	*0*	*1*	*10*	*0.0*	*-11.00*
3-y-o	*7*	*26*	*0*	*0*	*0*	*26*	*0.0*	*-26.00*
4-y-o+	*13*	*80*	*10*	*5*	*6*	*59*	*12.5*	*-8.92*
Totals	**22**	**117**	**10**	**5**	**7**	**95**	**8.5**	**-45.92**
2017	*21*	*130*	*15*	*10*	*11*	*94*	*11.5*	*+126.85*
2016	*18*	*102*	*3*	*3*	*11*	*84*	*2.9*	*-76.00*

BY MONTH

2-y-o	W-R	Per cent	£1 Level Stake	3-y-o	W-R	Per cent	£1 Level Stake
January	0-0	0.0	0.00	January	0-0	0.0	0.00
February	0-0	0.0	0.00	February	0-0	0.0	0.00
March	0-0	0.0	0.00	March	0-0	0.0	0.00
April	0-0	0.0	0.00	April	0-0	0.0	0.00
May	0-0	0.0	0.00	May	0-2	0.0	-2.00
June	0-0	0.0	0.00	June	0-3	0.0	-3.00
July	0-2	0.0	-2.00	July	0-3	0.0	-3.00
August	0-4	0.0	-4.00	August	0-6	0.0	-6.00
September	0-3	0.0	-3.00	September	0-3	0.0	-3.00
October	0-2	0.0	-2.00	October	0-3	0.0	-3.00
November	0-0	0.0	0.00	November	0-5	0.0	-5.00
December	0-0	0.0	0.00	December	0-1	0.0	-1.00

4-y-o+	W-R	Per cent	£1 Level Stake	Totals	W-R	Per cent	£1 Level Stake
January	0-1	0.0	-1.00	January	0-1	0.0	-1.00
February	1-1	100.0	+6.00	February	1-1	100.0	+6.00
March	0-1	0.0	-1.00	March	0-1	0.0	-1.00
April	0-6	0.0	-6.00	April	0-6	0.0	-6.00
May	0-12	0.0	-12.00	May	0-14	0.0	-14.00
June	1-7	14.3	-2.00	June	1-10	10.0	-5.00
July	1-15	6.7	0.00	July	1-20	5.0	-5.00
August	3-17	17.6	+10.50	August	3-27	11.1	+0.50
September	2-10	20.0	-1.25	September	2-16	12.5	-7.25
October	1-6	16.7	-2.50	October	1-11	9.1	-7.50
November	1-3	33.3	+1.33	November	1-8	12.5	-3.67
December	0-1	0.0	-1.00	December	0-2	0.0	-2.00

DISTANCE

2-y-o	W-R	Per cent	£1 Level Stake	3-y-o	W-R	Per cent	£1 Level Stake
5f-6f	0-11	0.0	-11.00	5f-6f	0-16	0.0	-16.00
7f-8f	0-0	0.0	0.00	7f-8f	0-9	0.0	-9.00
9f-13f	0-0	0.0	0.00	9f-13f	0-1	0.0	-1.00
14f+	0-0	0.0	0.00	14f+	0-0	0.0	0.00

4-y-o+	W-R	Per cent	£1 Level Stake	Totals	W-R	Per cent	£1 Level Stake
5f-6f	8-58	13.8	+1.75	5f-6f	8-85	9.4	-25.25
7f-8f	1-10	10.0	-5.67	7f-8f	1-19	5.3	-14.67
9f-13f	1-12	8.3	-5.00	9f-13f	1-13	7.7	-6.00
14f+	0-0	0.0	0.00	14f+	0-0	0.0	0.00

TYPE OF RACE

Non-Handicaps

	W-R	Per cent	£1 Level Stake
2-y-o	0-7	0.0	-7.00
3-y-o	0-9	0.0	-9.00
4-y-o+	0-3	0.0	-3.00

Handicaps

	W-R	Per cent	£1 Level Stake
2-y-o	0-4	0.0	-4.00
3-y-o	0-17	0.0	-17.00
4-y-o+	10-77	13.0	-5.92

RACE CLASS

	W-R	Per cent	£1 Level Stake
Class 1	0-1	0.0	-1.00
Class 2	0-0	0.0	0.00
Class 3	0-2	0.0	-2.00
Class 4	1-14	7.1	-8.00
Class 5	2-30	6.7	-21.50
Class 6	7-69	10.1	-12.42
Class 7	0-1	0.0	-1.00

FIRST TIME OUT

	W-R	Per cent	£1 Level Stake
2-y-o	0-2	0.0	-2.00
3-y-o	0-7	0.0	-7.00
4-y-o+	1-13	7.7	-6.00
Totals	1-22	4.5	-15.00

JOCKEYS

	W-R	Per cent	£1 Level Stake
Phil Dennis	5-48	10.4	-12.75
David Nolan	1-1	100.0	+3.33
Jamie Gormley	1-1	100.0	+6.00
Miss Becky Smith	1-1	100.0	+2.50
Jack Garritty	1-4	25.0	+2.00
Connor Beasley	1-22	4.5	-7.00

COURSE RECORD

	Total W-R	Non-Hndcps 2-y-o	Non-Hndcps 3-y-o+	Hndcps 2-y-o	Hndcps 3-y-o+	Per cent	£1 Level Stake
Musselburgh	4-24	0-0	0-0	0-2	4-22	16.7	+1.25
Wolvhptn (A.W)	1-3	0-0	0-0	0-0	1-3	33.3	+1.33
Newcastle (A.W)	1-9	0-0	0-2	0-0	1-7	11.1	-2.00
Hamilton	1-10	0-1	0-0	0-0	1-9	10.0	+5.00
Ripon	1-10	0-1	0-2	0-0	1-7	10.0	-5.00
Ayr	1-12	0-0	0-1	0-0	1-11	8.3	-6.00
Catterick	1-13	0-0	0-1	0-1	1-11	7.7	-4.50

WINNING HORSES

Horse	Races Run	1st	2nd	3rd	£
Ghostly Arc (IRE)	6	1	0	1	3493
Kinloch Pride	12	1	1	2	3493
Longroom	9	2	0	0	11127
Majdool (IRE)	7	1	0	1	3105
Our Place In Loule	9	3	1	1	9704
Pavers Pride	11	2	3	1	6724
Total winning prize-money					**£37646**
Favourites	**2-6**		**33.3%**		**0.25**

ADRIAN WINTLE

WESTBURY-ON-SEVERN, GLOUCS

	No. of Hrs	Races Run	1st	2nd	3rd	Unpl	Per cent	£1 Level Stake
2-y-o	*0*	*0*	*0*	*0*	*0*	*0*	*0.0*	*0.00*
3-y-o	*1*	*2*	*0*	*0*	*0*	*2*	*0.0*	*-2.00*
4-y-o+	*9*	*51*	*5*	*3*	*2*	*41*	*9.8*	*-7.00*
Totals	**10**	**53**	**5**	**3**	**2**	**43**	**9.4**	**-9.00**
2017	*12*	*50*	*3*	*4*	*6*	*37*	*6.0*	*-28.50*
2016	*4*	*7*	*2*	*0*	*0*	*5*	*28.6*	*+11.00*

JOCKEYS

	W-R	Per cent	£1 Level Stake
Hollie Doyle	3-19	15.8	+15.50
Rhiain Ingram	1-2	50.0	+3.50
Jane Elliott	1-3	33.3	+1.00

COURSE RECORD

	Total W-R	Non-Hndcps 2-y-o	Non-Hndcps 3-y-o+	Hndcps 2-y-o	Hndcps 3-y-o+	Per cent	£1 Level Stake
Chepstow	2-5	0-0	0-0	0-0	2-5	40.0	+4.50
Lingfield	1-3	0-0	0-0	0-0	1-3	33.3	+6.00
Lingfield (A.W)	1-5	0-0	0-0	0-0	1-5	20.0	+16.00
Wolvhptn (A.W)	1-13	0-0	0-0	0-0	1-13	7.7	-8.50

WINNING HORSES

Horse	Races Run	1st	2nd	3rd	£
Gold Hunter (IRE)	7	1	1	1	6553
Kenstone (FR)	7	1	1	0	5531
Rock'n Gold	9	1	0	0	3105
Three C's (IRE)	12	2	1	0	6210
Total winning prize-money					**£21399**
Favourites	**1-5**		**20.0%**		**0.00**

STEVE WOODMAN

EAST LAVANT, W SUSSEX

	No. of Hrs	Races Run	1st	2nd	3rd	Unpl	Per cent	£1 Level Stake
2-y-o	*0*	*0*	*0*	*0*	*0*	*0*	*0.0*	*0.00*
3-y-o	*1*	*8*	*0*	*0*	*0*	*8*	*0.0*	*-8.00*
4-y-o+	*1*	*15*	*2*	*2*	*0*	*11*	*13.3*	*+7.00*
Totals	**2**	**23**	**2**	**2**	**0**	**19**	**8.7**	**-1.00**
2017	*3*	*21*	*0*	*1*	*0*	*20*	*0.0*	*-21.00*
2016	*3*	*27*	*4*	*3*	*4*	*16*	*14.8*	*+27.50*

JOCKEYS

	W-R	Per cent	£1 Level Stake
Jack Mitchell	1-2	50.0	+9.00
Nicola Currie	1-3	33.3	+8.00

COURSE RECORD

	Total W-R	Non-Hndcps 2-y-o	Non-Hndcps 3-y-o+	Hndcps 2-y-o	Hndcps 3-y-o+	Per cent	£1 Level Stake
Kempton (A.W)	1-3	0-0	0-1	0-0	1-2	33.3	+8.00
Brighton	1-9	0-0	0-1	0-0	1-8	11.1	+2.00

WINNING HORSES

Horse	Races Run	1st	2nd	3rd	£
Solveig's Song	15	2	2	0	6210
Total winning prize-money					**£6210**
Favourites	**0-0**		**0.0%**		**0.00**

LEADING FLAT TRAINERS AT ASCOT (SINCE 2014)

	Total W-R	2yo Stks	3yo Stks	Other Stks	2yo H'caps	3yo H'caps	Other H'caps	App'ce	Amateurs	Per cent	£1 Level stake
John Gosden	44-259	6-27	10-66	18-91	0-0	5-33	5-42	0-0	0-0	17.0	-14.97
A P O'Brien	29-206	7-35	10-66	10-85	0-0	1-15	1-5	0-0	0-0	14.1	-22.70
Richard Hannon	27-350	17-114	1-38	4-51	0-6	4-71	1-64	0-3	0-3	7.7	-171.70
William Haggas	24-188	3-31	1-25	7-45	1-1	7-37	5-48	0-1	0-0	12.8	-45.94
Sir Michael Stoute	22-157	2-9	4-30	10-58	0-0	3-33	3-27	0-0	0-0	14.0	-3.93
Charlie Appleby	22-162	8-31	5-27	2-24	0-1	3-35	4-44	0-0	0-0	13.6	-21.85
Mark Johnston	22-251	7-61	2-26	2-9	2-5	4-77	5-71	0-2	0-0	8.8	-88.38
Roger Varian	17-134	4-21	2-19	2-33	0-0	3-18	5-42	1-1	0-0	12.7	-25.27
Saeed bin Suroor	14-106	3-16	1-18	4-29	0-0	3-14	3-29	0-0	0-0	13.2	-24.79
Clive Cox	13-129	6-33	0-9	2-22	0-1	2-24	3-40	0-0	0-0	10.1	-33.92
Andrew Balding	13-176	0-16	0-12	3-44	0-0	4-39	5-60	1-5	0-0	7.4	-86.00
Jamie Osborne	12-52	0-12	0-0	1-1	0-0	2-5	6-30	1-1	2-3	23.1	**66.25**
Roger Charlton	12-67	2-9	1-3	3-22	0-0	2-11	4-21	0-1	0-0	17.9	-9.00
Marco Botti	10-75	2-9	0-8	8-27	0-0	0-15	0-16	0-0	0-0	13.3	-17.50
Michael Bell	9-74	3-18	1-7	1-9	1-3	1-18	0-15	2-3	0-1	12.2	**15.33**
Richard Fahey	9-182	0-29	1-9	3-30	0-0	1-22	4-88	0-1	0-3	4.9	-48.40
Robert Cowell	8-74	1-7	0-1	1-13	0-0	0-1	6-52	0-0	0-0	10.8	**9.00**
Wesley A Ward	8-41	5-29	0-4	2-5	0-0	1-1	0-2	0-0	0-0	19.5	**22.50**
James Fanshawe	7-61	0-1	0-0	4-34	0-0	1-5	2-20	0-1	0-0	11.5	-17.50
David Simcock	7-97	0-7	2-7	3-37	0-0	0-9	2-37	0-0	0-0	7.2	-22.67
Hugo Palmer	7-66	3-9	2-16	0-10	0-1	1-15	1-14	0-1	0-0	10.6	-33.63
Ralph Beckett	7-89	0-18	1-13	3-26	0-1	0-9	3-22	0-0	0-0	7.9	-46.25
David Elsworth	6-63	0-11	0-6	2-16	0-0	0-3	4-26	0-1	0-0	9.5	-1.00
Ed Walker	6-45	0-5	0-4	1-7	0-0	1-10	4-17	0-2	0-0	13.3	-6.00
Luca Cumani	6-55	0-1	0-4	3-15	0-0	0-9	3-25	0-1	0-0	10.9	-26.63
David O'Meara	6-154	0-9	0-2	1-30	0-0	1-7	4-105	0-0	0-1	3.9	-38.50
Marcus Tregoning	5-36	0-4	0-0	1-4	0-0	2-10	2-15	0-3	0-0	13.9	**11.25**
Patrick Chamings	5-20	0-0	0-0	0-3	0-0	0-0	4-15	1-2	0-0	25.0	**12.88**
Ed Dunlop	5-57	1-8	0-5	1-13	0-0	2-12	1-18	0-1	0-0	8.8	-11.25
Dean Ivory	5-52	0-2	0-2	1-16	0-0	1-5	3-27	0-0	0-0	9.6	-17.50

LEADING FLAT TRAINERS AT AYR (SINCE 2014)

	Total W-R	2yo Stks	3yo Stks	Other Stks	2yo H'caps	3yo H'caps	Other H'caps	App'ce	Amateurs	Per cent	£1 Level stake
Keith Dalgleish	59-498	13-67	0-0	7-61	1-25	4-19	33-301	1-22	0-3	11.8	-11.23
Jim Goldie	58-640	0-12	0-1	6-65	0-1	2-8	49-516	0-25	1-12	9.1	-126.55
Michael Dods	34-278	9-43	0-0	3-32	0-8	2-13	18-171	2-7	0-4	12.2	-0.87
David O'Meara	34-212	0-17	0-0	8-31	0-4	0-5	26-153	0-1	0-1	16.0	-25.89
Richard Fahey	34-382	6-61	0-1	2-47	3-31	1-17	20-215	2-9	0-1	8.9	-151.50
K R Burke	26-128	9-31	0-0	6-23	1-7	3-10	6-55	1-1	0-1	20.3	-5.65
Ruth Carr	24-184	0-0	0-0	1-12	0-0	0-1	21-165	0-4	2-2	13.0	-4.55
Linda Perratt	23-348	0-10	1-1	2-30	0-3	0-5	18-277	2-17	0-5	6.6	-111.25
Iain Jardine	21-187	0-16	0-0	0-20	1-4	0-3	15-126	4-11	1-7	11.2	-43.25
R Mike Smith	19-157	0-5	0-0	3-18	0-0	1-1	12-118	2-12	1-3	12.1	**54.50**
Adrian Paul Keatley	16-78	0-3	0-0	1-10	0-0	1-1	12-57	2-6	0-1	20.5	**29.37**
Mark Johnston	16-147	7-45	0-1	3-18	1-14	0-5	4-58	0-5	1-1	10.9	-86.76
John Quinn	14-101	3-17	0-0	2-7	0-5	0-3	8-64	1-5	0-0	13.9	**1.87**
Brian Ellison	13-83	0-3	0-0	0-5	1-5	0-5	10-61	1-3	1-1	15.7	-4.88
Tim Easterby	12-142	0-7	0-1	3-13	0-10	1-9	7-95	1-1	0-6	8.5	-35.09
Kevin Ryan	12-162	6-45	0-0	2-19	2-8	0-5	2-80	0-4	0-1	7.4	-77.95
Lucy Normile	10-82	1-4	0-0	2-8	0-0	0-0	7-63	0-5	0-2	12.2	**53.62**
Shaun Harris	9-53	0-1	0-0	0-2	0-1	1-2	7-37	1-7	0-3	17.0	**19.50**
Marjorie Fife	9-50	0-1	0-0	0-1	0-1	0-0	7-42	0-1	2-4	10.0	**27.00**
Dianne Sayer	8-43	0-1	0-0	0-3	0-0	0-1	8-34	0-1	0-3	18.6	**29.50**
Richard Guest	7-74	0-5	0-0	1-4	0-2	0-4	6-55	0-2	0-2	9.5	**4.50**
Jedd O'Keeffe	7-33	2-5	0-0	0-1	0-2	0-0	5-23	0-0	0-2	21.2	**5.50**
Roger Fell	5-34	0-1	0-0	1-2	0-2	0-0	4-27	0-2	0-0	14.7	-7.38
John James Feane	7-21	0-1	0-0	1-2	0-0	1-1	3-15	2-2	0-0	33.3	**7.13**
Alistair Whillans	7-117	0-1	0-0	0-12	0-0	0-1	7-95	0-7	0-1	6.0	-52.25
Declan Carroll	6-31	0-2	0-0	0-0	1-1	1-1	4-23	0-4	0-0	19.4	**16.25**
Paul Midgley	6-45	0-1	0-0	0-5	0-2	0-0	6-36	0-0	0-1	13.3	-16.63
Rebecca Bastiman	6-82	0-0	0-0	0-6	0-0	0-0	4-69	2-7	0-0	7.3	-23.25
Gordon Elliott	5-15	0-2	0-0	0-0	0-0	0-0	4-12	0-0	1-1	33.3	**2.17**
David Barron	5-69	1-3	0-0	1-6	0-2	1-3	2-51	0-3	0-1	7.2	-40.00

LEADING FLAT TRAINERS AT BATH (SINCE 2014)

	Total W-R	2yo Stks	3yo Stks	Other Stks	2yo H'caps	3yo H'caps	Other H'caps	App'ce	Amateurs	Per cent	£1 Level stake
Malcolm Saunders	31-150	0-5	1-1	1-7	0-2	3-13	22-109	4-13	0-0	20.7	**21.91**
Richard Hannon	28-171	12-63	3-8	2-17	3-18	6-41	2-22	0-2	0-0	16.4	-49.19
Mick Channon	27-157	6-36	1-4	2-14	2-7	10-44	5-47	1-5	0-0	17.2	-18.30
Clive Cox	22-114	6-20	0-6	3-20	1-4	8-25	3-37	1-2	0-0	19.3	-24.58
Charles Hills	21-89	5-21	3-6	3-21	0-4	2-13	7-23	1-1	0-0	23.6	**15.41**
Mark Johnston	19-82	5-19	0-3	3-9	1-3	8-30	2-18	0-0	0-0	23.2	-10.96
Rod Millman	18-104	2-12	1-3	0-4	0-4	3-25	12-54	0-2	0-0	17.3	**54.88**
Roger Charlton	17-52	4-8	1-3	4-8	0-1	3-15	5-16	0-1	0-0	32.7	**18.44**
Tony Carroll	17-144	0-5	0-2	1-9	0-2	1-13	12-102	3-11	0-0	11.8	-13.42
Ronald Harris	17-178	2-27	0-3	2-8	1-2	3-24	9-104	0-10	0-0	9.6	-42.75
Brian Meehan	16-57	5-21	1-1	2-6	0-2	4-16	4-11	0-0	0-0	28.1	**64.48**
Sir Mark Prescott Bt	16-44	0-3	1-1	0-2	0-1	7-20	8-17	0-0	0-0	36.4	-8.98
Andrew Balding	15-92	2-12	0-1	3-15	0-1	2-24	8-39	0-0	0-0	16.3	-5.34
Marcus Tregoning	12-43	1-4	2-2	2-4	0-0	2-14	5-18	0-1	0-0	27.9	**4.46**
David Evans	12-138	3-33	0-3	0-8	2-14	2-23	5-55	0-2	0-0	8.7	-54.10
Tony Newcombe	10-67	0-0	0-1	0-3	0-0	0-3	10-54	0-6	0-0	14.9	**3.25**
Ed de Giles	10-57	0-1	1-1	0-2	0-0	0-2	9-49	0-2	0-0	17.5	**31.63**
Roger Varian	9-27	1-4	0-0	4-9	1-2	0-4	3-8	0-0	0-0	33.3	-3.41
John Flint	8-61	0-1	0-0	0-3	0-0	0-1	7-54	1-2	0-0	13.1	**5.83**
Sylvester Kirk	8-71	4-8	0-9	1-7	0-1	2-22	1-24	0-0	0-0	11.3	**17.63**
Jo Hughes	8-85	2-28	1-6	3-11	0-7	1-14	1-18	0-1	0-0	9.4	-11.38
George Baker	8-58	3-9	0-3	0-5	1-1	0-10	4-29	0-1	0-0	13.8	-13.38
Ron Hodges	7-57	0-1	0-0	0-4	0-0	0-3	7-47	0-2	0-0	12.3	**13.50**
Hugo Palmer	7-16	2-3	0-0	1-5	0-1	2-3	2-4	0-0	0-0	43.8	**30.80**
Brendan Powell	7-45	0-3	2-3	0-5	0-2	0-7	5-24	0-1	0-0	15.6	**32.50**
Robert Cowell	7-43	0-7	0-1	2-11	0-1	4-10	1-12	0-1	0-0	16.3	-11.32
William Haggas	7-32	3-7	0-0	2-10	0-0	1-10	1-5	0-0	0-0	21.9	-14.73
Amanda Perrett	7-48	0-1	0-1	0-7	0-2	1-12	6-24	0-1	0-0	14.6	-19.63
Jonathan Geake	6-26	0-0	0-0	1-2	0-0	0-1	5-23	0-0	0-0	23.1	**11.50**
J S Moore	6-67	1-21	0-1	0-2	0-12	2-15	3-16	0-0	0-0	9.0	**13.00**

LEADING FLAT TRAINERS AT BEVERLEY (SINCE 2014)

	Total W-R	2yo Stks	3yo Stks	Other Stks	2yo H'caps	3yo H'caps	Other H'caps	App'ce	Amateurs	Per cent	£1 Level stake
Richard Fahey	54-366	21-130	3-12	4-43	2-13	15-60	9-98	0-6	0-4	14.8	-123.42
Mark Johnston	50-273	17-79	1-16	4-19	2-7	11-73	14-77	1-2	0-0	18.3	-50.14
David O'Meara	40-262	2-48	1-14	6-32	0-2	4-30	26-131	1-4	0-1	15.3	-8.67
Tim Easterby	37-342	6-94	1-12	3-20	0-10	7-75	20-117	0-6	0-8	10.8	-128.08
Kevin Ryan	20-178	9-63	1-7	3-17	0-1	3-39	4-50	0-1	0-0	11.2	-8.67
Brian Ellison	17-148	8-41	3-14	2-13	1-3	2-18	1-52	0-6	0-1	11.5	-35.06
Michael Dods	15-77	10-28	0-2	0-5	0-3	1-12	3-24	1-3	0-0	19.5	**3.25**
Richard Guest	15-79	2-9	0-1	1-4	0-0	2-8	8-46	1-3	1-8	19.0	**40.75**
Ollie Pears	15-138	1-32	2-11	2-13	0-0	2-20	6-53	1-7	1-2	10.9	**43.25**
Les Eyre	15-113	1-10	0-3	1-8	0-2	1-13	12-71	0-4	0-2	13.3	-10.95
Bryan Smart	14-102	5-44	0-5	4-21	0-2	0-10	4-17	1-3	0-0	13.7	-5.50
Paul Midgley	12-113	1-21	0-1	3-31	0-0	0-4	7-52	1-2	0-2	10.6	-33.00
Karen Tutty	11-75	0-1	0-1	3-16	0-0	0-3	7-45	0-3	1-6	14.7	**26.25**
David Loughnane	11-42	0-4	0-3	3-7	0-0	2-6	5-21	1-1	0-0	26.2	**76.75**
Michael Easterby	11-167	1-32	0-3	0-15	0-1	1-22	7-82	0-7	2-5	6.6	-17.25
Ann Duffield	11-123	4-63	1-3	0-6	1-3	0-11	5-35	0-2	0-0	8.9	-68.88
William Haggas	10-29	3-8	3-5	3-10	0-0	1-6	0-0	0-0	0-0	34.5	**1.04**
Declan Carroll	10-93	0-17	0-2	1-9	0-0	0-3	8-56	1-6	0-0	10.8	-24.38
John Quinn	10-100	3-33	1-2	1-13	1-2	3-22	1-23	0-3	0-2	10.0	-44.65
Nigel Tinkler	10-145	4-54	0-4	0-17	0-3	3-15	2-41	1-8	0-3	6.9	-68.75
Tony Coyle	9-108	4-28	1-7	0-10	0-0	0-15	4-44	0-3	0-1	8.3	**2.70**
David C Griffiths	9-50	0-2	0-1	2-6	0-0	0-5	6-34	1-1	0-1	18.0	**6.50**
Michael Bell	8-34	1-5	1-5	2-3	0-1	3-12	1-6	0-2	0-0	23.5	-2.25
Roger Varian	8-22	6-9	1-5	1-5	0-0	0-1	0-2	0-0	0-0	36.4	**8.56**
Mark Walford	7-31	0-0	0-0	1-4	0-0	0-5	6-20	0-2	0-0	22.6	**6.75**
Lawrence Mullaney	7-60	0-6	0-1	1-9	0-1	1-6	4-32	1-3	0-2	11.7	**11.87**
David Nicholls	7-45	1-2	0-0	3-10	0-0	0-1	3-31	0-1	0-0	15.6	**22.00**
K R Burke	7-42	2-25	2-4	0-1	0-1	2-6	1-5	0-0	0-0	16.7	-0.50
Julie Camacho	7-42	0-4	0-1	3-10	0-0	0-3	4-24	0-0	0-0	16.7	-7.76
Keith Dalgleish	7-50	1-10	0-2	0-6	0-2	4-13	2-15	0-2	0-0	14.0	-15.25

LEADING FLAT TRAINERS AT BRIGHTON (SINCE 2014)

	Total W-R	2yo Stks	3yo Stks	Other Stks	2yo H'caps	3yo H'caps	Other H'caps	App'ce	Amateurs	Per cent	£1 Level stake
Richard Hannon	38-153	19-58	0-4	4-16	2-13	6-29	7-30	0-3	0-0	24.8	**33.99**
Tony Carroll	36-208	0-4	0-0	5-33	0-1	1-8	27-152	2-7	1-3	17.3	**3.88**
Gary Moore	34-209	5-18	1-4	2-27	0-4	1-15	24-128	1-7	0-6	16.3	**21.10**
John Gallagher	21-103	0-8	0-2	6-18	1-3	2-4	11-65	1-3	0-0	20.4	**57.26**
John Bridger	21-151	0-4	0-0	8-31	0-1	0-5	11-100	2-9	0-1	13.9	-6.55
Richard Hughes	20-78	4-15	1-1	3-6	0-3	4-11	8-39	0-3	0-0	25.6	**10.57**
Mick Channon	20-147	4-35	1-2	2-17	3-10	2-24	7-55	1-4	0-0	13.6	**11.45**
Eve Johnson Houghton	18-86	1-16	0-1	2-12	0-3	3-10	11-42	1-2	0-0	20.9	-6.96
Mark Johnston	16-92	4-32	1-2	2-11	1-4	2-18	6-25	0-0	0-0	17.4	-24.53
Philip Hide	15-80	1-4	0-1	2-10	0-0	3-8	7-53	2-3	0-1	18.8	-8.82
Sylvester Kirk	14-86	5-17	0-0	1-15	0-2	3-23	4-25	1-4	0-0	16.3	**11.83**
George Baker	14-94	1-7	1-2	2-9	1-2	2-16	6-51	0-4	1-3	14.9	**55.50**
Andrew Balding	12-66	2-11	0-3	1-6	0-2	2-10	5-30	0-0	0-0	20.0	-2.99
Luca Cumani	11-28	3-11	0-0	3-4	0-0	1-3	4-10	0-0	0-0	39.3	**3.86**
Paul Cole	11-42	4-10	0-2	0-3	0-0	1-4	6-22	0-1	0-0	26.2	**14.60**
John Berry	11-34	0-0	0-0	0-5	0-0	0-0	9-24	0-3	2-2	32.4	**38.20**
Clive Cox	10-29	3-5	1-1	0-1	0-1	2-8	4-13	0-0	0-0	34.5	**13.50**
Stuart Williams	10-69	1-5	1-1	0-7	0-0	0-14	8-41	0-1	0-0	14.5	-38.07
Ronald Harris	9-67	0-7	0-0	3-8	0-0	0-4	6-48	0-0	0-0	13.4	**15.00**
William Muir	9-50	1-3	0-1	1-4	0-0	3-15	4-27	0-0	0-0	18.0	-3.54
Malcolm Saunders	8-38	0-1	0-0	0-1	0-0	1-6	7-29	0-1	0-0	21.1	**7.38**
Jim Boyle	8-70	0-5	0-0	0-10	0-0	2-8	6-42	0-4	0-1	11.4	**18.50**
Amanda Perrett	8-51	0-4	0-3	0-5	1-2	3-11	4-26	0-0	0-0	15.7	-5.00
John Spearing	8-65	0-3	0-0	1-8	0-0	0-3	7-48	0-3	0-0	12.3	-13.25
Michael Attwater	8-84	0-3	1-3	2-10	0-0	1-6	4-57	0-5	0-0	9.5	-35.38
Dean Ivory	7-50	0-5	0-0	3-8	1-3	0-4	3-30	0-0	0-0	14.0	**18.75**
Laura Mongan	7-53	0-0	0-2	1-8	0-0	0-4	4-35	2-4	0-0	13.2	-4.17
Sir Mark Prescott Bt	7-35	2-8	1-1	1-6	0-1	2-8	1-10	0-0	0-1	20.0	-7.76
Chris Dwyer	6-24	0-2	0-0	2-5	0-0	0-3	4-14	0-0	0-0	25.0	**0.13**
Rae Guest	6-24	1-4	0-0	0-1	0-0	1-7	4-12	0-0	0-0	25.0	**1.75**

LEADING FLAT TRAINERS AT CARLISLE (SINCE 2014)

	Total W-R	2yo Stks	3yo Stks	Other Stks	2yo H'caps	3yo H'caps	Other H'caps	App'ce	Amateurs	Per cent	£1 Level stake
Keith Dalgleish	34-261	2-37	1-5	0-19	1-10	5-44	25-141	0-4	0-1	13.0	-55.84
Richard Fahey	31-260	8-86	1-6	4-23	4-17	7-38	7-86	0-3	0-1	11.9	-91.81
K R Burke	24-108	15-43	0-0	1-8	1-10	4-16	3-28	0-3	0-0	22.2	**47.95**
Mark Johnston	24-144	5-40	0-2	4-20	2-6	6-23	7-52	0-1	0-0	16.7	-32.68
Tim Easterby	24-234	3-49	0-2	1-21	0-18	5-35	15-103	0-3	0-3	10.3	-67.03
Kevin Ryan	16-105	7-37	0-2	0-3	1-3	1-21	7-36	0-2	0-1	15.2	-25.95
Michael Dods	15-129	6-37	0-0	0-8	2-6	2-25	5-49	0-2	0-2	11.6	-47.63
Ann Duffield	10-74	5-29	0-2	0-4	1-5	0-13	3-20	1-1	0-0	13.5	-3.02
Brian Ellison	10-74	1-14	0-0	0-9	0-2	0-4	9-44	0-0	0-1	13.5	-23.81
Alan Swinbank	9-60	0-5	0-0	1-11	0-0	0-5	8-38	0-0	0-1	15.0	**15.75**
David Barron	8-41	2-7	1-1	1-6	0-3	1-6	3-18	0-0	0-0	19.5	**19.27**
Bryan Smart	8-67	4-31	0-1	1-5	0-4	2-9	1-15	0-2	0-0	11.9	-1.50
Karen Tutty	8-57	0-2	0-1	3-9	0-0	0-0	5-43	0-2	0-0	14.0	-4.00
Roger Fell	7-41	0-1	0-0	0-0	0-1	1-7	6-32	0-0	0-0	17.1	-0.00
William Haggas	7-21	1-2	0-3	1-6	0-0	4-9	1-1	0-0	0-0	33.3	**2.58**
Nigel Tinkler	7-36	0-6	0-0	1-3	1-2	4-7	0-12	0-4	1-2	19.4	**20.00**
David Nicholls	7-20	0-0	0-0	3-6	0-0	0-0	3-13	1-1	0-0	35.0	**28.50**
Iain Jardine	7-71	0-7	0-1	1-11	0-2	2-12	4-34	0-2	0-2	9.9	-30.50
Sir Mark Prescott Bt	6-22	1-6	0-1	2-4	0-0	1-6	2-5	0-0	0-0	27.0	**1.44**
Paul Midgley	6-32	0-2	0-0	0-1	0-1	1-5	3-20	2-2	0-1	18.8	**6.62**
Ruth Carr	6-70	0-1	0-0	1-9	0-0	0-3	5-53	0-2	0-2	8.6	-33.50
David O'Meara	6-84	0-8	0-1	2-9	1-4	1-19	1-40	1-3	0-0	7.1	-42.17
John Davies	5-22	0-1	0-0	2-7	0-0	0-1	3-13	0-0	0-0	22.7	**4.00**
Tony Coyle	5-29	0-3	0-0	0-2	0-2	2-4	3-17	0-0	0-1	17.2	**24.25**
Hugo Palmer	5-11	0-3	0-1	4-5	0-0	0-0	1-2	0-0	0-0	45.5	-0.06
Sir Michael Stoute	5-9	1-1	0-0	4-6	0-0	0-1	0-1	0-0	0-0	55.6	-0.30
Mick Channon	5-25	0-5	1-2	1-3	1-4	1-4	1-7	0-0	0-0	20.0	-5.00
Jedd O'Keeffe	5-39	1-12	0-0	0-1	0-2	3-5	1-19	0-0	0-0	12.8	-20.50
John Quinn	5-51	0-16	0-1	1-3	0-5	2-8	2-18	0-0	0-0	9.8	-21.75
Michael Easterby	5-92	0-5	0-2	0-14	0-1	2-9	2-56	0-2	1-3	5.4	-54.25

LEADING FLAT TRAINERS AT CATTERICK (SINCE 2014)

	Total W-R	2yo Stks	3yo Stks	Other Stks	2yo H'caps	3yo H'caps	Other H'caps	App'ce	Amateurs	Per cent	£1 Level stake
Richard Fahey	42-223	12-59	1-6	5-26	8-31	2-20	14-79	0-2	0-0	18.8	-12.58
John Quinn	29-168	4-36	0-1	6-21	3-10	2-18	13-74	1-3	0-5	17.3	**10.71**
Mark Johnston	27-152	11-41	1-2	2-11	4-30	3-27	6-40	0-0	0-1	17.8	-39.76
Tim Easterby	24-230	1-25	0-2	2-23	2-24	6-36	12-111	0-3	1-6	10.4	-59.65
David O'Meara	23-193	7-33	0-2	2-22	0-6	4-21	10-106	0-0	0-3	11.9	-79.95
Ruth Carr	20-158	1-3	1-2	2-18	0-1	0-7	14-117	2-6	0-4	12.7	-40.00
Keith Dalgleish	18-101	5-28	0-2	2-8	0-7	3-15	8-39	0-1	0-1	17.8	**34.83**
Brian Ellison	16-102	2-10	1-2	2-18	1-5	4-11	6-51	0-2	0-3	15.7	-0.60
Michael Bell	14-32	1-5	0-1	3-4	1-3	4-8	4-10	0-0	1-1	43.8	**27.69**
Michael Easterby	14-145	0-19	0-1	1-21	0-3	5-14	5-76	2-5	1-6	9.7	-49.38
Scott Dixon	13-125	1-7	0-0	1-7	0-3	1-4	8-93	0-8	2-3	10.4	-12.09
Michael Appleby	12-104	1-7	0-0	3-19	1-3	2-11	5-58	0-3	0-3	11.5	-13.80
Kevin Ryan	12-91	1-16	0-2	3-13	2-8	1-21	4-29	1-2	0-0	13.2	-18.87
Ann Duffield	12-118	2-30	0-2	4-19	1-15	2-10	3-36	0-3	0-3	10.2	-36.92
David Nicholls	11-81	1-2	0-0	5-14	0-1	1-3	3-57	1-4	0-0	13.6	**5.00**
K R Burke	10-67	4-20	0-0	3-12	0-6	0-12	3-17	0-0	0-0	14.9	**4.39**
Declan Carroll	9-66	1-5	0-1	1-7	0-2	1-9	6-39	0-3	0-0	13.6	**51.75**
Marjorie Fife	9-89	0-1	0-2	2-11	0-1	0-3	7-66	0-3	0-2	10.1	-29.25
Paul Midgley	8-76	1-17	1-2	1-12	0-2	1-9	3-30	0-0	1-4	10.5	-20.50
Eric Alston	7-29	0-2	0-0	0-4	0-0	2-6	4-14	1-1	0-2	24.1	**20.25**
David Barron	7-55	4-12	0-0	1-7	0-1	0-4	2-27	0-4	0-0	12.7	-8.02
Alan Swinbank	7-52	0-1	0-0	0-9	0-0	2-6	5-35	0-0	0-1	13.5	-16.80
Kenneth Slack	6-20	0-0	0-0	1-2	0-0	0-0	4-13	1-3	0-2	30.0	**0.51**
Martin Todhunter	6-31	0-0	0-0	0-4	0-0	0-0	6-23	0-3	0-1	19.4	**7.60**
James Bethell	6-33	0-4	0-1	0-4	0-2	1-2	5-20	0-0	0-0	18.2	**8.88**
Noel Wilson	6-52	0-3	0-0	1-6	0-2	0-5	3-32	1-2	1-2	11.5	**16.00**
David Loughnane	6-30	0-2	0-1	1-2	1-2	1-2	3-21	0-0	0-0	20.0	**18.88**
Sir Mark Prescott Bt	6-20	1-2	0-0	0-1	1-4	0-2	4-10	0-0	0-1	30.0	-0.17
Iain Jardine	6-45	1-6	0-0	2-8	0-0	1-2	1-26	0-1	1-2	13.3	-1.75
William Haggas	6-12	4-8	0-0	2-2	0-0	0-1	0-1	0-0	0-0	50.0	-2.14

LEADING FLAT TRAINERS AT CHELMSFORD (SINCE 2014)

	Total W-R	2yo Stks	3yo Stks	Other Stks	2yo H'caps	3yo H'caps	Other H'caps	App'ce	Amateurs	Per cent	£1 Level stake
Mark Johnston	59-370	18-88	5-25	13-58	6-33	5-43	12-119	0-4	0-0	15.9	-80.39
David Simcock	45-221	6-25	3-10	7-67	0-0	5-11	20-101	4-7	0-0	20.4	**20.59**
Saeed bin Suroor	43-142	10-30	3-7	15-49	0-3	2-8	13-44	0-1	0-0	30.3	-12.99
Stuart Williams	41-268	3-14	0-2	4-35	2-13	0-11	32-184	0-9	0-0	15.3	-0.13
William Haggas	41-162	9-38	3-7	16-58	2-9	2-15	9-34	0-1	0-0	25.3	-12.07
John Gosden	40-174	9-53	4-14	18-65	0-7	1-13	8-21	0-1	0-0	23.0	-41.42
Marco Botti	39-278	12-71	5-17	7-73	1-11	4-28	10-77	0-1	0-0	14.0	-4.86
Michael Appleby	39-398	0-13	2-6	2-66	0-7	2-15	28-275	4-13	1-3	9.8	-154.88
Derek Shaw	36-279	0-15	0-2	7-39	1-13	1-7	26-196	1-7	0-0	12.9	-3.71
Chris Dwyer	33-205	1-16	0-3	6-29	2-9	4-12	20-133	0-1	0-2	16.1	**20.03**
Jamie Osborne	33-238	2-36	2-5	6-40	4-30	3-16	16-109	0-2	0-0	13.9	-4.98
Richard Hannon	31-274	10-77	3-21	4-40	5-48	3-24	4-58	2-6	0-0	11.3	-103.99
Dean Ivory	29-207	0-12	1-3	6-41	0-11	1-11	20-121	1-8	0-0	14.0	-40.83
Sir Michael Stoute	27-127	5-31	1-10	6-36	0-2	4-17	11-31	0-0	0-0	21.3	-9.15
Sir Mark Prescott Bt	27-155	4-49	0-4	5-26	4-11	5-20	8-43	1-2	0-0	17.4	-17.74
Charlie Appleby	25-100	7-28	1-7	8-19	1-10	5-18	3-18	0-0	0-0	25.0	-31.52
Andrew Balding	25-172	0-17	1-10	13-56	0-4	4-17	7-65	0-3	0-0	14.5	-75.20
Hugo Palmer	24-124	9-36	1-7	6-38	0-8	3-10	4-24	1-1	0-0	19.4	-3.70
Phil McEntee	22-326	0-11	0-7	2-54	1-12	0-6	19-218	0-16	0-2	6.7	-105.88
Richard Hughes	21-105	5-24	2-5	6-23	4-17	2-9	1-23	1-4	0-0	20.0	-18.11
Ian Williams	20-89	0-1	3-3	3-11	0-0	1-3	12-67	1-3	0-1	22.5	-0.54
Michael Easterby	20-100	0-1	0-0	3-13	0-8	1-6	14-66	1-4	1-2	20.0	-9.53
Simon Crisford	19-99	4-32	1-5	7-28	0-5	2-7	5-22	0-0	0-0	19.2	-2.11
John Best	18-108	0-8	1-4	1-11	1-6	2-5	13-74	0-0	0-0	16.7	**46.63**
Hughie Morrison	18-87	2-14	0-2	1-14	1-3	2-8	12-43	0-3	0-0	20.7	-7.61
Roger Varian	18-115	2-18	1-6	9-45	1-4	2-10	3-32	0-0	0-0	15.7	-33.73
Charlie Wallis	17-140	0-7	0-1	1-19	0-2	0-2	16-107	0-2	0-0	12.1	-20.38
Ed Dunlop	17-153	1-29	1-8	2-36	1-14	3-16	9-48	0-2	0-0	11.1	-65.59
Gary Moore	16-108	0-6	1-1	1-22	0-9	2-8	12-59	0-2	0-1	14.8	-21.64
Mark H Tompkins	16-145	0-24	3-9	3-30	1-4	1-17	7-58	1-3	0-0	11.0	-35.58

LEADING FLAT TRAINERS AT CHEPSTOW (SINCE 2014)

	Total W-R	2yo Stks	3yo Stks	Other Stks	2yo H'caps	3yo H'caps	Other H'caps	App'ce	Amateurs	Per cent	£1 Level stake
David Evans	26-217	4-54	1-7	4-23	3-14	0-19	13-97	1-3	0-0	12.0	-7.95
Richard Hannon	26-149	13-48	1-8	4-20	3-10	1-23	4-38	0-2	0-0	17.4	-46.71
Andrew Balding	21-109	3-16	2-11	1-24	0-1	4-18	10-35	1-4	0-0	19.3	-9.09
Ralph Beckett	18-60	2-16	1-2	5-19	0-0	2-7	8-16	0-0	0-0	30.0	-7.08
John O'Shea	17-130	0-0	0-0	4-27	0-0	0-1	13-95	0-7	0-0	13.1	**1.33**
Eve Johnson Houghton	17-64	5-15	1-6	1-11	0-4	1-7	9-21	0-0	0-0	26.6	**24.68**
Ed de Giles	17-62	0-4	0-2	3-15	0-0	2-3	12-38	0-0	0-0	27.4	**57.25**
Ronald Harris	14-167	1-26	0-5	2-25	0-6	1-16	10-88	0-1	0-0	8.4	-36.90
Bernard Llewellyn	13-110	0-0	0-0	3-22	0-0	0-0	7-73	3-12	0-3	11.8	**6.66**
Clive Cox	12-54	4-13	1-3	1-14	0-1	1-5	5-18	0-0	0-0	22.2	**2.90**
Mick Channon	12-91	1-23	0-5	4-15	1-7	3-13	3-25	0-1	0-2	13.2	-5.34
Richard Price	12-83	0-1	0-1	3-20	0-1	0-2	9-54	0-4	0-0	14.5	-24.18
William Haggas	11-30	1-8	1-1	6-11	0-1	1-3	2-5	0-0	0-0	37.0	**4.64**
John Flint	11-66	0-0	0-2	2-10	0-0	1-5	8-49	0-0	0-0	16.7	**6.00**
Tony Carroll	9-101	1-2	0-2	0-21	0-2	0-5	7-67	1-2	0-0	8.9	-25.50
Charles Hills	8-46	4-15	0-1	3-12	0-3	0-5	1-9	0-1	0-0	17.4	**2.25**
Richard Hughes	8-47	3-12	1-5	1-4	0-5	0-1	2-19	1-1	0-0	17.0	-7.20
Patrick Chamings	7-33	0-0	1-2	1-9	0-0	0-4	5-18	0-0	0-0	21.2	**4.87**
Ed Dunlop	7-27	0-2	1-2	1-5	0-2	2-5	3-11	0-0	0-0	25.9	**9.38**
Grace Harris	7-69	0-1	0-1	0-8	0-0	0-3	7-52	0-4	0-0	10.1	**56.50**
David Simcock	7-31	3-8	0-1	2-9	0-0	0-3	2-10	0-0	0-0	22.6	-5.69
Malcolm Saunders	7-91	0-10	0-1	2-19	0-3	1-4	4-53	0-1	0-0	7.7	-42.50
Paul Henderson	6-12	0-0	0-0	2-3	0-0	1-1	3-8	0-0	0-0	50.0	**15.29**
Paul Cole	6-25	1-4	0-2	1-3	0-2	2-3	2-10	0-1	0-0	24.0	**38.25**
Hughie Morrison	6-30	0-1	1-1	0-5	2-3	1-7	2-11	0-2	0-0	20.0	-6.96
George Baker	6-49	0-4	1-3	1-8	0-1	0-3	3-28	1-2	0-0	12.2	-7.38
Sir Mark Prescott Bt	6-32	0-13	0-0	0-1	0-0	3-5	3-12	0-1	0-0	18.8	-14.16
Rod Millman	6-61	0-10	0-2	1-9	1-4	0-9	4-26	0-1	0-0	9.8	-27.67
Neil Mulholland	5-24	0-0	0-0	1-5	0-1	0-3	4-15	0-0	0-0	20.8	**10.25**
Michael Mullineaux	5-49	0-0	0-1	3-8	0-0	0-4	0-33	1-1	1-2	10.2	**31.00**

LEADING FLAT TRAINERS AT CHESTER (SINCE 2014)

	Total W-R	2yo Stks	3yo Stks	Other Stks	2yo H'caps	3yo H'caps	Other H'caps	App'ce	Amateurs	Per cent	£1 Level stake
Richard Fahey	64-517	12-62	0-5	8-42	2-31	9-68	27-281	4-23	2-5	12.4	-93.86
Andrew Balding	44-183	5-20	1-18	10-37	2-7	9-36	9-51	8-12	0-2	24.0	**73.27**
Mark Johnston	41-263	12-54	0-9	3-20	3-21	11-67	11-79	1-12	0-1	15.6	-63.06
Tom Dascombe	38-299	14-90	3-15	5-24	5-26	3-39	7-87	1-14	0-4	12.7	-112.60
Tim Easterby	18-130	2-12	0-1	0-10	0-3	3-15	13-83	0-5	0-1	13.8	-3.75
Kevin Ryan	15-77	5-12	0-0	3-10	2-3	3-16	2-32	0-4	0-0	19.5	**8.91**
Richard Hannon	15-94	9-31	1-8	1-14	2-12	1-16	1-9	0-4	0-0	16.0	-15.85
A P O'Brien	12-34	0-0	10-28	2-5	0-0	0-1	0-0	0-0	0-0	35.3	-1.33
William Haggas	12-40	3-3	2-7	2-7	1-3	3-10	1-7	0-3	0-0	30.0	-3.78
Brian Ellison	10-71	0-4	1-2	0-12	0-1	1-8	6-36	1-4	1-4	14.1	-3.50
Sir Michael Stoute	10-47	1-3	1-8	6-14	0-0	1-12	1-10	0-0	0-0	21.3	-19.04
Roger Varian	8-44	1-4	1-5	2-15	0-0	3-10	1-10	0-0	0-0	18.2	-6.79
Ian Williams	8-73	0-4	0-1	1-8	1-1	1-10	5-44	0-4	0-1	11.0	-32.75
John Gosden	7-31	0-1	4-13	3-11	0-0	0-5	0-1	0-0	0-0	22.6	-6.54
John Quinn	6-60	0-7	0-0	0-3	1-4	0-8	5-31	0-7	0-0	10.0	-11.00
Ralph Beckett	6-48	0-1	0-4	2-12	1-1	3-17	0-12	0-1	0-0	12.5	-23.13
Eric Alston	6-70	0-10	0-2	0-4	0-0	1-6	5-46	0-2	0-0	8.6	-27.50
Bernard Llewellyn	5-38	0-0	0-1	0-3	0-0	0-3	4-28	0-2	1-1	13.2	**21.38**
Michael Appleby	5-43	0-3	0-1	0-4	0-2	0-4	5-26	0-1	0-2	11.6	**25.50**
Charlie Appleby	5-25	0-2	0-4	2-8	1-2	1-4	1-5	0-0	0-0	20.0	-3.93
Ruth Carr	5-46	0-0	0-0	0-2	0-0	0-1	5-41	0-0	0-2	10.9	-7.50
David Barron	5-47	0-0	0-0	1-4	0-0	0-6	4-36	0-1	0-0	10.6	-18.00
Charles Hills	5-60	1-7	1-17	0-9	0-4	1-15	2-8	0-0	0-0	8.3	-40.63
David Evans	5-125	1-41	0-1	0-5	0-12	1-20	3-39	0-2	0-5	4.0	-67.50
Ed Dunlop	4-23	0-1	0-2	0-5	0-0	2-4	2-10	0-1	0-0	17.4	**1.75**
Alan King	4-22	0-2	0-0	0-2	0-0	1-4	3-14	0-0	0-0	18.2	**10.33**
James Fanshawe	4-8	0-0	0-0	1-2	0-0	0-1	3-5	0-0	0-0	50.0	**11.63**
Iain Jardine	4-27	0-0	0-0	0-1	0-1	2-4	2-18	0-2	0-1	14.8	-2.17
Saeed bin Suroor	4-20	0-3	0-3	2-6	0-0	1-2	1-6	0-0	0-0	20.0	-2.33
Michael Easterby	4-31	0-1	0-0	0-2	1-2	0-5	2-17	0-1	1-3	12.9	-4.25

LEADING FLAT TRAINERS AT DONCASTER (SINCE 2014)

	Total W-R	2yo Stks	3yo Stks	Other Stks	2yo H'caps	3yo H'caps	Other H'caps	App'ce	Amateurs	Per cent	£1 Level stake
Richard Fahey	44-462	10-101	4-20	2-57	2-25	4-66	17-157	5-29	0-7	9.5	-84.75
Richard Hannon	39-309	13-129	1-18	7-51	4-25	6-48	7-36	1-1	0-1	12.6	-27.52
Roger Varian	38-156	4-32	6-13	16-50	0-2	4-27	8-32	0-0	0-0	24.4	**29.11**
John Gosden	28-160	8-43	3-27	9-50	2-3	3-18	3-18	0-1	0-0	17.5	-56.00
Sir Michael Stoute	26-77	4-19	3-9	10-26	0-0	4-10	5-13	0-0	0-0	33.8	**49.81**
Luca Cumani	25-89	2-11	4-11	6-21	0-1	5-11	7-31	1-3	0-0	28.1	**43.51**
Mark Johnston	25-176	11-66	1-15	0-11	3-14	5-26	5-40	0-3	0-1	14.2	-36.36
Charlie Appleby	23-115	7-43	3-10	3-17	2-5	4-20	4-20	0-0	0-0	20.0	-9.18
David O'Meara	23-261	4-15	2-11	2-44	0-0	1-19	9-150	3-15	2-7	8.8	-95.60
Saeed bin Suroor	21-68	4-14	3-5	6-22	1-3	3-9	4-14	0-1	0-0	30.9	**7.48**
William Haggas	21-112	10-28	1-10	6-36	0-4	1-14	3-19	0-1	0-0	18.8	-27.42
David Simcock	20-96	2-16	1-6	4-28	0-2	2-12	10-29	1-3	0-0	20.8	**19.20**
James Fanshawe	15-95	1-5	1-10	7-39	0-0	1-5	4-35	1-1	0-0	15.8	-2.44
Andrew Balding	14-91	3-17	2-9	4-28	2-3	1-9	2-22	0-2	0-1	15.4	**21.88**
K R Burke	14-144	8-32	1-15	1-22	0-7	1-17	2-36	1-13	0-2	9.7	-7.87
Charles Hills	14-142	4-46	1-15	5-35	0-2	2-14	2-30	0-0	0-0	9.9	-15.91
Ralph Beckett	14-105	4-25	3-12	3-21	0-6	1-16	3-22	0-2	0-1	13.3	-32.87
Ian Williams	13-70	0-5	0-2	2-9	0-1	1-6	7-37	1-8	2-2	18.6	-3.46
Hugo Palmer	12-64	5-21	0-0	4-18	0-4	1-8	2-12	0-1	0-0	18.8	-8.13
Michael Easterby	12-129	0-10	1-9	2-15	0-2	0-2	6-65	1-18	2-8	9.3	-15.13
Michael Appleby	12-137	0-9	0-2	1-27	0-2	1-8	7-75	3-13	0-1	8.8	-17.25
Kevin Ryan	12-167	1-46	0-5	1-21	1-5	3-23	6-59	0-7	0-1	7.2	-37.00
Marco Botti	11-114	5-33	2-8	2-21	0-1	1-23	1-26	0-1	0-1	9.6	-37.18
David Barron	10-112	0-6	0-5	0-12	0-0	0-7	9-75	1-7	0-0	8.9	-10.25
John Quinn	10-95	0-12	0-1	0-12	1-4	3-11	5-43	0-7	1-5	10.5	-17.50
Jeremy Noseda	9-39	2-9	1-7	4-11	0-0	1-5	1-7	0-0	0-0	23.1	-7.90
Jedd O'Keeffe	9-63	0-5	0-4	1-6	0-2	4-12	4-29	0-4	0-1	14.3	-12.50
Mick Channon	9-88	3-24	0-6	1-12	1-6	2-10	2-27	0-2	0-1	10.2	-23.22
Tim Easterby	9-249	0-41	0-12	2-33	2-13	3-21	1-109	1-8	0-12	3.6	-155.50

LEADING FLAT TRAINERS AT EPSOM (SINCE 2014)

	Total W-R	2yo Stks	3yo Stks	Other Stks	2yo H'caps	3yo H'caps	Other H'caps	App'ce	Amateurs	Per cent	£1 Level stake
Mark Johnston	22-138	10-28	1-11	2-10	1-3	3-23	5-59	0-3	0-1	15.9	-28.84
Mick Channon	15-65	2-16	0-3	2-8	0-4	5-14	4-14	2-4	0-2	23.1	**26.04**
John Gosden	14-50	1-6	8-27	4-10	0-0	0-5	1-2	0-0	0-0	28.0	-2.53
Andrew Balding	13-105	3-12	0-8	2-13	0-2	1-18	6-50	1-1	0-1	12.4	-0.30
Richard Hannon	13-91	7-27	0-5	2-12	1-8	0-17	3-22	0-0	0-0	14.3	-30.93
Richard Fahey	12-113	1-11	0-3	1-7	1-9	1-16	7-64	0-2	1-1	10.6	-24.88
Roger Varian	10-37	0-4	2-5	1-9	0-0	1-9	6-9	0-1	0-0	27.0	**8.38**
George Baker	10-46	2-4	0-1	4-10	0-0	0-4	4-22	0-3	0-2	21.7	**40.50**
Eve Johnson Houghton	9-41	0-4	0-0	1-4	0-1	2-8	5-23	1-1	0-0	22.0	**9.48**
Ralph Beckett	9-52	1-5	0-8	2-12	0-0	1-7	5-20	0-0	0-0	17.3	-9.44
Hughie Morrison	7-28	2-3	0-2	1-3	1-1	0-4	3-13	0-2	0-0	25.0	**22.00**
Saeed bin Suroor	7-29	3-6	0-8	1-5	0-2	1-2	2-6	0-0	0-0	24.1	-7.50
Jim Boyle	7-64	0-8	0-1	0-8	0-2	0-7	6-31	1-7	0-0	10.9	-16.00
Stuart Williams	6-51	0-2	0-0	0-2	0-0	0-6	5-39	1-2	0-0	11.8	**2.00**
Sylvester Kirk	6-46	0-4	0-1	0-2	1-4	3-13	1-18	1-3	0-1	13.0	**7.25**
A P O'Brien	6-49	0-0	5-43	1-6	0-0	0-0	0-0	0-0	0-0	12.2	**58.53**
David O'Meara	6-47	0-0	1-2	0-9	0-0	0-1	5-35	0-0	0-0	12.8	-9.90
Pat Phelan	6-52	0-8	0-0	0-2	0-1	0-5	5-29	1-7	0-0	11.5	-10.38
John Quinn	5-26	0-2	0-0	0-3	0-1	1-4	3-14	0-0	1-2	19.2	**17.75**
Charlie Appleby	5-33	2-7	1-11	1-6	0-3	0-3	1-3	0-0	0-0	15.2	-1.78
Charles Hills	5-42	1-9	0-2	0-3	0-0	0-10	4-18	0-0	0-0	11.9	-20.15
Gary Moore	5-74	0-8	0-0	0-8	0-0	1-7	2-41	2-6	0-4	6.8	-25.90
John Gallagher	4-20	0-1	0-0	0-1	0-0	0-0	4-18	0-0	0-0	20.0	**5.50**
Tony Carroll	4-31	0-0	0-0	0-5	0-1	0-1	4-22	0-0	0-2	12.9	**7.50**
Brian Meehan	4-29	3-14	1-2	0-2	0-1	0-3	0-7	0-0	0-0	13.8	**8.50**
William Knight	4-24	0-2	0-0	2-4	1-2	0-7	1-9	0-0	0-0	16.7	**9.50**
Paul Cole	4-14	1-3	0-0	1-2	0-1	0-2	2-6	0-0	0-0	28.6	**11.00**
Amanda Perrett	4-23	0-1	0-0	0-0	0-0	2-3	2-17	0-2	0-0	17.4	**12.50**
Peter Hedger	4-8	0-0	0-0	0-1	0-0	0-0	3-4	0-1	1-2	50.0	**19.75**
John Bridger	4-42	0-3	0-0	0-2	0-1	0-1	4-31	0-4	0-0	9.5	-18.50

LEADING FLAT TRAINERS AT FFOS LAS (SINCE 2014)

	Total W-R	2yo Stks	3yo Stks	Other Stks	2yo H'caps	3yo H'caps	Other H'caps	App'ce	Amateurs	Per cent	£1 Level stake
David Evans	19-150	6-30	0-0	2-10	2-20	0-11	9-78	0-1	0-0	12.7	**35.24**
Andrew Balding	16-62	3-12	0-0	5-12	0-3	1-6	7-29	0-0	0-0	25.8	**42.53**
Rod Millman	10-54	1-14	0-0	1-8	1-7	1-5	6-20	0-0	0-0	18.5	-10.00
William Muir	9-44	3-12	0-1	1-5	2-5	2-5	1-16	0-0	0-0	20.5	**13.75**
Richard Hannon	8-46	6-22	0-0	0-5	0-11	1-4	1-4	0-0	0-0	17.4	-12.50
Roger Charlton	7-27	4-7	0-0	1-6	0-1	1-2	1-11	0-0	0-0	25.9	**29.48**
Hughie Morrison	5-25	0-3	0-1	2-6	0-2	1-1	2-12	0-0	0-0	20.0	-0.00
William Knight	5-20	1-3	0-0	0-1	0-1	0-2	4-13	0-0	0-0	25.0	**1.50**
Richard Hughes	5-27	1-5	0-0	2-5	0-6	0-2	2-9	0-0	0-0	18.5	**8.17**
Charles Hills	5-26	3-8	0-0	2-7	0-4	0-0	0-7	0-0	0-0	19.2	**10.16**
Tony Carroll	5-35	0-1	0-0	1-9	0-2	0-1	4-22	0-0	0-0	14.3	-2.00
Sir Mark Prescott Bt	4-10	0-2	0-0	0-0	2-2	0-0	2-6	0-0	0-0	40.0	**1.48**
Ed Walker	4-21	[illegible]	0-0	0-0	[illegible]	0-0	[illegible]	0-0	0-0	19.0	**7.03**
Peter Makin	4-9	0-0	0-0	0-0	0-0	0-0	4-9	0-0	0-0	44.4	**12.17**
Stuart Kittow	4-22	0-0	0-0	2-6	0-1	0-3	2-12	0-0	0-0	18.2	-5.10
Ralph Beckett	4-31	2-8	0-0	2-5	0-4	0-2	0-12	0-0	0-0	12.9	-16.34
Bernard Llewellyn	3-33	0-0	0-0	0-6	0-0	0-0	3-25	0-2	0-0	9.1	-0.00
Archie Watson	3-11	0-2	0-0	1-3	1-2	0-1	1-3	0-0	0-0	27.3	**0.45**
Jamie Osborne	3-15	0-0	0-0	0-5	0-3	1-2	2-5	0-0	0-0	20.0	**0.75**
Brian Meehan	3-15	1-5	0-0	1-4	0-3	0-0	1-3	0-0	0-0	20.0	**1.00**
Luca Cumani	3-5	1-1	0-0	0-1	1-1	0-0	1-2	0-0	0-0	60.0	**12.75**
William Haggas	3-7	0-0	0-0	1-3	1-1	0-0	1-3	0-0	0-0	42.9	-0.93
John O'Shea	3-19	0-0	0-0	0-6	0-0	0-0	3-13	0-0	0-0	15.8	-1.00
Hugo Palmer	3-10	0-2	0-0	2-3	0-0	0-0	1-5	0-0	0-0	30.0	-2.83
Roger Varian	3-9	1-2	0-0	0-1	0-0	0-0	2-6	0-0	0-0	33.3	-2.95
David Simcock	3-20	0-3	0-0	2-6	0-0	0-1	1-10	0-0	0-0	15.0	-7.38
Richard Price	3-24	0-2	0-0	0-2	0-0	0-4	3-16	0-0	0-0	12.5	-9.25
Ronald Harris	3-36	0-4	0-1	0-3	1-5	0-3	2-20	0-0	0-0	8.3	-10.50
Ed de Giles	3-25	0-3	1-1	0-8	0-0	0-1	1-11	1-1	0-0	12.0	-12.80
Mick Channon	3-41	0-7	0-1	0-3	1-8	2-6	0-16	0-0	0-0	7.3	-25.25

LEADING FLAT TRAINERS AT GOODWOOD (SINCE 2014)

	Total W-R	2yo Stks	3yo Stks	Other Stks	2yo H'caps	3yo H'caps	Other H'caps	App'ce	Amateurs	Per cent	£1 Level stake
Mark Johnston	48-309	13-66	1-15	4-27	3-31	12-83	13-76	2-10	0-1	15.5	**68.83**
Richard Hannon	44-409	19-136	5-22	4-57	4-40	7-84	3-55	2-15	0-0	10.8	-138.61
Mick Channon	27-216	12-57	2-16	1-37	3-18	2-29	6-55	1-4	0-0	12.5	-11.54
Sir Michael Stoute	24-120	2-7	7-20	9-41	0-1	4-31	2-20	0-0	0-0	20.0	-30.89
William Haggas	22-112	2-12	6-13	5-30	0-8	5-25	4-21	0-3	0-0	19.6	-16.35
John Gosden	22-111	5-20	2-25	11-45	0-0	1-10	3-11	0-0	0-0	19.8	-26.18
Charlie Appleby	21-106	8-30	2-13	5-22	2-4	2-18	2-19	0-0	0-0	19.8	-4.10
Andrew Balding	19-169	2-29	4-14	5-33	0-11	3-24	4-49	1-8	0-1	11.2	-55.01
David Simcock	17-124	1-8	1-11	9-49	0-1	3-18	3-34	0-3	0-0	13.7	**17.49**
Gary Moore	14-110	2-18	1-6	1-12	0-3	6-14	4-51	0-2	0-4	12.7	**106.21**
Clive Cox	13-104	3-25	0-1	2-19	0-4	2-24	4-28	2-3	0-0	12.5	-16.45
Amanda Perrett	13-179	0-14	2-16	3-33	0-0	5-32	3-73	0-10	0-1	7.3	-67.75
Charles Hills	13-128	4-42	0-8	6-27	1-8	1-16	1-25	0-2	0-0	10.2	-70.04
Henry Candy	12-66	1-11	2-7	1-10	1-1	2-8	4-24	1-5	0-0	18.2	-1.58
Roger Varian	12-84	4-16	0-10	6-28	0-0	0-5	2-25	0-0	0-0	14.3	-29.13
Ian Williams	11-57	0-0	0-0	1-12	0-0	0-3	8-38	0-0	2-4	19.3	**50.15**
Ralph Beckett	11-88	3-18	0-10	3-29	0-2	2-12	3-16	0-0	0-1	12.5	-2.62
Roger Charlton	10-67	0-3	3-6	4-23	0-1	2-16	1-17	0-1	0-0	14.9	**3.00**
Marcus Tregoning	10-88	1-24	1-5	2-11	0-3	4-15	2-26	0-3	0-1	11.4	**1.00**
Hughie Morrison	10-94	0-18	1-10	2-14	0-2	2-12	4-32	1-4	0-2	10.6	-8.50
A P O'Brien	8-39	4-9	1-5	3-24	0-0	0-0	0-1	0-0	0-0	20.5	-20.95
Sylvester Kirk	8-69	0-22	1-4	0-3	1-3	2-15	1-13	1-4	2-5	11.6	-31.13
Richard Fahey	8-155	1-16	0-2	0-20	2-15	2-22	3-76	0-4	0-0	5.2	-85.00
George Baker	7-92	1-14	0-1	0-6	0-2	0-4	6-56	0-7	0-2	7.6	**68.00**
Ed Dunlop	7-61	0-7	0-8	2-15	1-4	1-9	3-16	0-2	0-0	11.5	-4.75
Saeed bin Suroor	7-67	4-16	0-6	2-20	0-1	0-8	1-16	0-0	0-0	10.4	-38.70
William Knight	7-99	1-9	0-4	1-17	0-1	1-16	4-43	0-6	0-3	7.1	-40.79
Jonathan Portman	6-54	1-11	0-6	0-8	0-1	0-8	3-13	1-4	1-3	11.1	**4.00**
Paul Cole	6-59	2-17	0-6	0-9	1-1	0-5	3-19	0-1	0-1	10.2	-18.50
John Bridger	6-69	0-6	0-4	1-3	0-0	0-9	4-27	1-15	0-5	8.7	-18.75

LEADING FLAT TRAINERS AT HAMILTON (SINCE 2014)

	Total W-R	2yo Stks	3yo Stks	Other Stks	2yo H'caps	3yo H'caps	Other H'caps	App'ce	Amateurs	Per cent	£1 Level stake
Keith Dalgleish	61-482	9-75	2-7	8-55	1-13	6-35	32-279	3-14	0-4	12.7	-87.39
Mark Johnston	41-217	18-58	0-9	3-30	1-10	2-17	17-90	0-3	0-0	18.9	-41.43
Richard Fahey	37-282	8-64	0-4	5-47	1-25	6-23	16-113	1-4	0-2	13.1	-81.88
Kevin Ryan	33-154	5-35	1-3	8-27	7-11	2-15	10-62	0-0	0-1	21.4	**15.72**
David O'Meara	28-143	1-13	2-6	10-31	0-3	2-10	12-77	1-3	0-0	19.6	-29.29
Tim Easterby	20-102	3-7	0-1	2-12	1-3	2-14	11-57	0-3	1-5	19.6	**40.65**
John Patrick Shanahan	20-104	0-5	0-3	6-25	0-0	0-8	13-61	0-1	1-1	19.2	-1.23
Jim Goldie	20-197	0-2	0-0	3-33	0-2	1-6	15-138	1-11	0-5	10.2	-29.35
Iain Jardine	19-154	3-16	0-0	0-19	0-2	0-9	15-96	1-8	0-4	12.3	**30.55**
Michael Dods	14-75	3-8	1-2	1-8	0-4	1-12	8-37	0-2	0-2	18.7	-11.17
Paul Midgley	10-75	0-2	0-1	3-17	0-0	0-2	7-49	0-1	0-3	13.3	-18.50
Alan Swinbank	10-72	0-0	0-2	2-17	0-0	1-4	7-47	0-1	0-1	13.9	-32.58
K R Burke	10-95	4-27	0-2	1-16	1-5	0-15	4-27	0-2	0-1	10.5	-50.99
Alistair Whillans	10-115	0-2	0-0	3-21	0-0	0-1	5-83	1-6	1-2	8.7	-52.75
Ruth Carr	9-96	0-1	0-0	0-2	0-1	0-4	8-81	0-1	1-6	9.4	**18.50**
Kristin Stubbs	9-41	1-1	0-2	0-0	0-2	0-0	8-33	0-0	0-3	22.0	**22.50**
Alan Berry	9-106	0-3	0-1	0-20	0-0	0-8	9-63	0-5	0-6	8.5	**36.00**
David Brown	9-40	1-9	1-1	0-2	2-2	1-4	4-22	0-0	0-0	22.5	-0.96
Rebecca Bastiman	9-57	0-0	0-0	1-5	0-0	1-3	6-45	1-3	0-1	15.8	-3.63
Ann Duffield	9-86	1-23	0-0	0-8	1-7	3-13	3-34	1-1	0-0	10.5	-40.45
Ben Haslam	8-44	0-5	0-1	1-4	0-1	0-3	5-25	1-2	1-3	18.2	**0.97**
Marjorie Fife	8-69	0-1	0-0	1-8	0-1	1-2	6-49	0-5	0-3	11.6	-2.17
Linda Perratt	8-233	0-7	0-1	1-33	0-2	0-5	7-168	0-11	0-6	3.4	-133.00
Michael Easterby	7-31	0-0	1-1	0-1	0-1	0-3	4-20	1-2	1-3	22.6	**2.41**
Bryan Smart	7-83	2-17	0-2	1-16	1-6	0-9	3-33	0-0	0-0	8.4	**28.87**
Jedd O'Keeffe	7-37	1-7	0-0	2-5	0-0	0-3	3-21	1-1	0-0	18.9	-3.51
Patrick Holmes	7-72	0-1	0-1	2-9	0-0	0-3	4-46	1-10	0-2	9.7	-4.00
Eric Alston	7-70	0-2	0-1	2-15	0-0	0-4	5-47	0-1	0-0	10.0	-7.00
Michael Appleby	6-27	0-1	1-1	1-3	0-0	0-1	3-17	0-3	1-1	22.2	**21.99**
David Barron	6-50	0-5	0-4	4-12	0-0	0-2	2-26	0-0	0-1	12.0	-13.40

LEADING FLAT TRAINERS AT HAYDOCK (SINCE 2014)

	Total W-R	2yo Stks	3yo Stks	Other Stks	2yo H'caps	3yo H'caps	Other H'caps	App'ce	Amateurs	Per cent	£1 Level stake
Tom Dascombe	64-364	17-107	1-12	5-33	4-22	14-67	23-121	0-2	0-0	17.6	**224.92**
Mark Johnston	39-248	14-78	0-7	1-16	1-6	12-70	11-70	0-1	0-0	15.7	-10.80
William Haggas	35-122	6-22	4-12	8-39	0-3	10-29	7-17	0-0	0-0	28.7	**3.70**
Richard Fahey	35-374	10-78	1-5	4-30	1-23	10-73	8-163	1-2	0-0	9.4	-157.90
John Gosden	30-100	13-32	1-4	10-37	0-1	2-13	4-13	0-0	0-0	30.0	**46.60**
David O'Meara	29-248	0-4	0-3	6-51	0-3	3-25	19-157	1-5	0-0	11.7	**15.46**
Richard Hannon	24-220	6-77	0-6	6-36	3-13	6-53	3-34	0-1	0-0	10.9	-66.06
K R Burke	22-204	5-62	1-10	4-19	0-7	5-43	7-60	0-3	0-0	10.8	-37.42
Tim Easterby	20-222	3-32	0-3	1-15	1-12	2-30	11-125	2-4	0-1	9.0	-28.00
Hugo Palmer	18-59	7-14	3-7	3-12	0-2	2-14	3-10	0-0	0-0	30.5	**81.19**
Roger Varian	17-110	3-26	1-8	9-39	0-1	0-20	4-15	0-1	0-0	15.5	-42.69
Kevin Ryan	16-159	5-47	0-2	1-23	2-10	4-32	4-44	0-1	0-0	10.1	-53.00
Andrew Balding	15-101	4-11	0-4	4-24	0-1	2-27	5-30	0-4	0-0	14.9	-29.85
Clive Cox	13-60	5-16	1-3	3-13	0-4	3-12	1-12	0-0	0-0	21.7	**21.07**
Charles Hills	13-94	0-19	1-7	5-21	3-5	1-17	3-24	0-1	0-0	13.8	-7.01
Charlie Appleby	13-81	4-34	1-2	6-19	0-0	2-19	0-7	0-0	0-0	16.0	-47.17
Sir Michael Stoute	12-57	1-6	1-2	2-22	0-0	6-12	2-15	0-0	0-0	21.1	-2.62
Michael Bell	12-61	2-15	0-0	1-5	0-2	7-24	1-13	1-2	0-0	19.7	-10.22
Michael Dods	12-79	1-3	1-2	1-7	0-3	1-22	7-41	1-1	0-0	15.2	-11.24
Brian Ellison	10-66	0-3	0-1	1-8	0-1	3-11	5-39	1-3	0-0	15.2	**24.25**
Ed Walker	10-67	2-10	0-3	0-10	0-1	2-23	6-19	0-1	0-0	14.9	-23.90
Iain Jardine	9-39	0-1	0-0	0-1	0-1	1-3	7-29	1-3	0-1	23.1	**33.50**
Mick Channon	9-92	2-18	0-3	2-14	2-11	2-23	1-23	0-0	0-0	9.8	-17.13
Brian Meehan	8-65	3-19	0-4	2-7	0-5	2-15	1-15	0-0	0-0	12.3	-11.30
Ian Williams	7-58	0-5	0-0	1-6	0-0	1-9	5-36	0-1	0-1	12.1	-19.12
Luca Cumani	7-56	0-5	0-3	4-22	0-0	2-11	1-15	0-0	0-0	12.5	-37.88
Roger Fell	6-35	0-1	0-1	0-2	0-0	0-4	4-24	2-3	0-0	17.1	-2.50
Paul Midgley	6-51	0-0	0-0	1-9	1-2	0-6	3-33	1-1	0-0	11.8	-4.50
David Barron	6-69	0-1	0-1	1-9	0-2	3-14	2-41	0-1	0-0	8.7	-12.00
Ismail Mohammed	6-34	0-9	0-1	0-4	0-1	2-8	4-11	0-0	0-0	17.6	-14.63

LEADING FLAT TRAINERS AT KEMPTON - All-Weather (SINCE 2014)

	Total W-R	2yo Stks	3yo Stks	Other Stks	2yo H'caps	3yo H'caps	Other H'caps	App'ce	Amateurs	Per cent	£1 Level stake
John Gosden	77-310	28-139	7-21	29-89	3-16	5-20	5-24	0-1	0-0	24.8	**12.18**
Richard Hannon	75-656	25-215	5-33	14-86	10-99	6-95	13-123	2-5	0-0	11.4	-197.53
Charlie Appleby	66-221	33-107	2-10	8-39	6-18	8-18	9-29	0-0	0-0	29.9	-2.53
James Fanshawe	59-326	6-42	2-10	14-83	1-6	10-38	26-142	0-5	0-0	18.1	-50.30
Ralph Beckett	49-305	23-114	1-10	7-52	1-17	8-46	9-66	0-0	0-0	16.1	**18.45**
Roger Varian	46-226	18-93	1-4	14-52	2-8	2-19	9-49	0-1	0-0	20.4	-28.46
Andrew Balding	45-364	7-66	4-20	10-86	0-8	12-47	11-127	1-10	0-0	12.4	-97.90
Saeed bin Suroor	42-181	10-66	2-5	13-39	2-4	2-11	13-55	0-1	0-0	23.2	-24.41
Tony Carroll	40-509	0-17	1-1	4-67	0-9	0-23	32-355	3-37	0-0	7.9	-230.26
Jeremy Noseda	36-128	12-34	3-8	9-28	0-3	2-9	10-45	0-1	0-0	28.1	**3.15**
Clive Cox	36-245	5-62	1-5	7-40	3-12	6-31	14-95	0-0	0-0	14.7	**16.05**
William Haggas	35-181	9-56	3-13	7-38	3-15	7-26	6-32	0-1	0-0	19.3	-41.30
Roger Charlton	34-228	11-74	1-7	6-40	0-12	4-31	11-61	1-3	0-0	14.9	-19.16
Marco Botti	34-357	6-103	2-12	7-71	5-18	3-62	11-87	0-4	0-0	9.5	-139.65
Hugo Palmer	33-185	14-74	0-7	3-32	1-11	2-13	13-45	0-3	0-0	17.8	**3.93**
Gary Moore	33-327	1-24	0-3	7-45	2-9	1-34	21-202	1-10	0-0	10.1	-92.58
Mark Johnston	33-281	10-72	0-10	7-41	4-30	6-41	5-78	0-6	1-3	11.7	-131.22
Sir Michael Stoute	31-203	16-95	2-11	6-44	0-2	3-18	4-33	0-0	0-0	15.3	-80.19
David Simcock	30-230	8-54	0-8	5-57	2-2	1-26	13-75	1-8	0-0	13.0	-10.93
William Knight	30-237	1-19	0-2	4-33	0-3	4-28	20-147	1-5	0-0	12.7	-25.42
Dean Ivory	28-311	1-29	0-7	6-56	0-2	1-20	19-192	1-5	0-0	9.0	-25.87
Charles Hills	28-216	6-57	1-5	9-51	2-24	5-26	5-51	0-2	0-0	13.0	-36.95
Ed Walker	28-205	6-51	0-10	4-31	3-13	2-25	13-74	0-1	0-0	13.7	-51.92
Amanda Perrett	28-238	7-49	0-6	5-35	3-9	2-25	11-111	0-1	0-2	11.8	-54.80
Stuart Williams	25-182	0-15	0-2	2-25	2-8	3-22	17-106	1-4	0-0	13.7	-8.90
David Elsworth	25-156	6-47	0-5	4-27	1-14	1-13	12-49	1-1	0-0	16.0	-9.63
Richard Hughes	25-203	3-47	0-0	3-25	6-30	2-20	8-72	3-8	0-1	12.3	-26.38
Jamie Osborne	25-239	3-52	0-5	5-28	2-24	7-41	8-85	0-3	0-1	10.5	-66.81
Simon Dow	23-211	1-25	1-4	1-21	3-11	3-23	14-124	0-3	0-0	10.9	-42.77
James Tate	22-119	9-53	0-1	9-25	0-7	4-17	0-16	0-0	0-0	18.5	**26.47**

LEADING FLAT TRAINERS AT LEICESTER (SINCE 2014)

	Total W-R	2yo Stks	3yo Stks	Other Stks	2yo H'caps	3yo H'caps	Other H'caps	App'ce	Amateurs	Per cent	£1 Level stake
Richard Fahey	32-172	8-45	3-6	2-16	5-22	5-29	9-52	0-1	0-1	18.6	**8.80**
Richard Hannon	31-212	16-78	5-20	2-21	4-28	1-37	2-26	1-2	0-0	14.6	-49.35
Mark Johnston	29-143	7-44	1-4	3-8	3-17	4-25	11-44	0-1	0-0	20.3	-14.62
Charles Hills	20-87	8-31	1-5	4-12	0-8	5-16	2-14	0-1	0-0	23.0	**21.61**
Mick Channon	20-95	7-29	2-8	4-9	2-12	4-20	1-15	0-1	0-1	21.1	**28.17**
Sir Michael Stoute	19-82	3-33	4-9	3-18	0-1	1-7	8-14	0-0	0-0	23.2	-16.82
Roger Varian	15-85	2-25	2-10	6-16	0-1	3-19	2-14	0-0	0-0	17.6	-23.58
David Evans	13-140	2-35	1-15	3-20	2-20	2-15	3-29	0-3	0-3	9.3	-31.00
Saeed bin Suroor	12-43	4-12	2-8	5-7	0-1	1-6	0-9	0-0	0-0	27.9	**0.47**
David O'Meara	12-84	0-3	1-5	1-7	0-5	1-13	8-49	1-2	0-0	14.3	-33.70
Hughie Morrison	11-55	0-9	0-2	3-10	0-1	4-7	4-25	0-0	0-1	20.0	**21.13**
John Gosden	10-65	5-25	1-14	3-13	0-0	0-9	1-4	0-0	0-0	15.4	-24.39
Ralph Beckett	9-59	5-19	1-6	2-5	0-2	1-14	0-13	0-0	0-0	15.3	-7.34
Michael Bell	9-67	1-17	0-4	0-3	2-7	2-18	4-16	0-1	0-1	13.4	-12.43
Henry Candy	9-63	1-10	2-2	0-7	0-1	1-15	5-27	0-1	0-0	14.3	-20.58
Clive Cox	9-92	3-31	0-6	0-6	0-5	4-23	2-21	0-0	0-0	9.8	-40.77
Michael Appleby	9-134	0-16	0-4	2-21	1-5	2-10	3-64	1-9	0-5	6.7	-62.25
George Baker	8-50	0-7	2-8	1-8	1-3	1-3	3-17	0-2	0-2	16.0	**2.75**
Charlie Appleby	8-44	5-22	1-5	1-4	0-4	1-7	0-2	0-0	0-0	18.2	-21.38
Andrew Balding	8-73	0-9	1-7	0-12	0-0	5-20	2-23	0-2	0-0	11.0	-32.63
William Haggas	8-66	3-25	2-6	1-13	0-4	2-11	0-7	0-0	0-0	12.1	-41.02
David Barron	7-31	1-1	1-2	2-5	0-2	2-8	1-13	0-0	0-0	22.6	**4.10**
Jamie Osborne	7-25	2-10	1-1	3-6	0-3	1-2	0-3	0-0	0-0	28.0	**16.50**
Rae Guest	7-34	2-7	0-8	1-3	0-0	1-5	3-10	0-1	0-0	20.6	**36.75**
Roger Charlton	7-33	1-7	0-3	1-6	0-0	1-9	4-8	0-0	0-0	21.2	-2.49
Hugo Palmer	7-32	3-8	0-3	2-6	0-3	1-7	1-5	0-0	0-0	21.9	-9.34
Tom Dascombe	7-66	2-29	1-6	2-9	0-7	1-7	1-8	0-0	0-0	10.6	-14.90
Luca Cumani	7-45	3-11	0-4	0-4	0-0	0-9	4-17	0-0	0-0	15.6	-18.63
Nigel Tinkler	6-35	0-3	1-7	0-3	0-3	2-7	3-7	0-4	0-1	17.1	**16.00**
Mike Murphy	6-32	0-2	0-2	0-2	0-1	0-3	4-19	1-2	1-1	18.8	**20.50**

LEADING FLAT TRAINERS AT LINGFIELD - Turf (SINCE 2014)

	Total W-R	2yo Stks	3yo Stks	Other Stks	2yo H'caps	3yo H'caps	Other H'caps	App'ce	Amateurs	Per cent	£1 Level stake
Richard Hannon	25-148	8-48	3-11	4-26	2-9	1-20	7-34	0-0	0-0	16.9	-12.51
William Haggas	24-53	9-18	4-7	7-20	2-2	1-3	1-3	0-0	0-0	45.3	**40.96**
John Bridger	16-119	1-12	0-2	0-12	2-5	1-6	9-74	3-5	0-3	13.4	**40.13**
Andrew Balding	14-57	1-8	1-8	4-14	0-1	2-6	6-20	0-0	0-0	24.6	**1.00**
Jim Boyle	14-58	2-11	0-0	0-4	0-0	3-12	9-28	0-3	0-0	24.1	**49.50**
Roger Varian	11-46	1-11	2-4	5-16	1-1	1-4	1-10	0-0	0-0	23.9	-9.21
Gary Moore	11-86	1-9	0-3	0-14	0-0	2-6	7-51	0-2	1-1	12.8	-18.25
David Evans	10-71	3-16	0-1	2-9	3-15	1-5	1-22	0-2	0-1	14.1	**1.77**
Mick Channon	10-103	5-28	0-5	1-16	1-7	0-15	3-30	0-1	0-1	9.7	-38.05
Patrick Chamings	9-32	1-4	0-0	4-10	0-0	1-1	3-17	0-0	0-0	28.1	**36.33**
Jonathan Portman	8-43	2-9	0-4	0-3	0-0	1-10	5-17	0-0	0-0	18.6	**16.85**
Richard Hughes	8-52	2-14	0-2	1-7	1-1	0-5	2-19	1-3	1-1	15.4	-16.26
Charlie Appleby	7-30	4-17	1-5	1-4	0-1	0-0	1-3	0-0	0-0	23.3	**1.26**
Henry Candy	7-28	2-11	0-1	0-6	0-0	3-3	2-7	0-0	0-0	25.0	**14.74**
John Ryan	7-41	1-10	0-4	1-6	0-0	2-8	3-12	0-1	0-0	17.1	**20.00**
Ed Vaughan	7-31	0-4	0-0	1-6	0-0	1-6	5-14	0-1	0-0	22.6	-3.18
Ed Dunlop	7-45	1-13	1-6	1-4	1-2	1-11	2-9	0-0	0-0	15.6	-7.25
David Simcock	7-40	3-9	1-3	1-10	0-1	1-4	1-13	0-0	0-0	17.5	-8.12
Sir Mark Prescott Bt	7-27	0-8	0-0	2-3	0-1	0-6	5-8	0-1	0-0	25.9	-10.29
John Best	7-54	0-10	1-1	0-8	1-3	1-8	4-24	0-0	0-0	13.0	-13.52
Jamie Osborne	7-41	3-15	0-2	0-7	0-4	1-4	3-9	0-0	0-0	17.1	-14.79
Chris Wall	6-18	1-3	0-0	1-3	0-0	1-2	3-10	0-0	0-0	33.3	**6.50**
Roger Charlton	6-24	2-6	0-1	3-6	0-3	1-4	0-4	0-0	0-0	25.0	-7.07
John Spearing	6-29	0-3	0-0	0-3	0-1	1-3	5-19	0-0	0-0	20.7	**8.00**
Hugo Palmer	6-20	3-7	0-3	1-5	2-2	0-1	0-2	0-0	0-0	30.0	**8.32**
Luca Cumani	6-19	0-0	1-4	5-11	0-0	0-1	0-3	0-0	0-0	31.6	**11.25**
Saeed bin Suroor	6-27	2-7	1-6	3-11	0-0	0-0	0-3	0-0	0-0	22.2	-5.60
Brian Meehan	6-30	2-9	0-4	1-8	0-2	2-3	1-4	0-0	0-0	20.0	-8.35
J R Jenkins	6-51	0-0	0-1	1-10	0-0	1-2	4-34	0-2	0-2	11.8	-10.50

LEADING FLAT TRAINERS AT LINGFIELD - All Weather (SINCE 2014)

	Total W-R	2yo Stks	3yo Stks	Other Stks	2yo H'caps	3yo H'caps	Other H'caps	App'ce	Amateurs	Per cent	£1 Level stake
Richard Hannon	73-412	19-83	14-63	11-60	7-40	10-72	11-86	1-8	0-0	17.7	**2.98**
Mark Johnston	63-352	7-39	11-65	6-55	3-10	18-74	17-100	1-8	0-1	17.9	-41.24
Charlie Appleby	52-164	6-27	12-35	15-47	2-7	6-14	11-31	0-3	0-0	31.7	**6.83**
John Gosden	49-242	11-67	12-54	15-78	0-4	6-24	5-15	0-0	0-0	20.2	-58.55
Andrew Balding	45-283	2-22	10-39	9-86	1-3	4-22	18-99	1-10	0-2	15.9	-63.48
William Haggas	42-153	10-42	8-28	14-46	1-5	4-18	5-13	0-1	0-0	27.5	**0.69**
David Evans	42-366	5-29	7-38	3-62	2-18	8-56	16-145	0-11	1-7	11.5	-153.09
Ralph Beckett	40-173	3-27	10-46	7-40	5-8	4-20	11-32	0-0	0-0	23.1	-4.28
Simon Dow	36-280	3-16	1-13	5-51	1-9	5-17	20-168	1-5	0-1	12.9	**0.77**
David Simcock	33-199	2-10	12-42	7-54	0-1	1-18	11-64	0-9	0-1	16.6	-3.47
Gary Moore	33-316	0-13	0-14	9-73	0-4	3-17	21-174	0-9	0-12	10.4	-114.56
Tony Carroll	32-273	2-4	1-3	9-68	0-1	1-12	17-162	2-19	0-4	11.7	-81.91
Saeed bin Suroor	31-99	10-30	2-5	9-33	3-4	2-8	5-19	0-0	0-0	31.3	**6.32**
Sir Mark Prescott Bt	30-147	3-32	0-8	3-27	0-2	9-30	14-43	1-5	0-0	20.4	-8.40
Jamie Osborne	30-272	3-35	4-42	11-61	1-12	4-43	7-74	0-5	0-0	11.0	-69.99
Archie Watson	29-116	6-16	3-8	5-25	1-8	1-3	10-49	0-4	3-3	25.0	**30.86**
Amanda Perrett	28-169	0-11	2-11	10-41	0-2	6-22	10-80	0-2	0-0	16.6	-9.85
Stuart Williams	28-205	2-6	3-11	7-52	0-5	1-26	14-97	0-7	1-1	13.7	-13.57
Lee Carter	28-361	0-4	1-15	12-76	0-0	0-15	14-226	1-21	0-4	7.8	-152.88
Marco Botti	27-200	5-23	3-22	8-60	0-5	3-30	8-59	0-1	0-0	13.5	-38.08
Richard Fahey	27-230	2-15	4-16	5-48	1-11	3-21	10-108	2-9	0-2	11.7	-46.90
Tom Dascombe	26-138	1-15	3-11	7-45	1-9	2-13	10-43	2-2	0-0	18.8	-26.92
Roger Varian	25-121	4-19	4-21	7-43	0-0	3-10	7-28	0-0	0-0	20.7	**0.56**
Michael Attwater	25-375	1-19	0-15	5-50	0-5	2-26	15-232	1-26	1-2	6.7	-97.25
Roger Charlton	24-102	2-15	4-15	8-27	1-5	3-17	5-22	1-1	0-0	23.5	**11.42**
Dean Ivory	24-192	0-13	1-13	4-37	0-3	4-19	15-100	0-7	0-0	12.5	-24.00
James Tate	22-110	4-20	2-13	8-36	1-5	2-18	5-18	0-0	0-0	20.0	-11.56
David Elsworth	21-116	1-9	6-31	7-33	1-5	3-8	2-27	1-3	0-0	18.1	-19.07
James Fanshawe	21-110	0-11	1-7	10-39	2-5	2-14	6-34	0-0	0-0	19.1	-25.13
Ed Walker	21-151	1-32	2-17	3-26	1-6	3-25	11-44	0-1	0-0	13.9	-26.96

LEADING FLAT TRAINERS AT MUSSELBURGH (SINCE 2014)

	Total W-R	2yo Stks	3yo Stks	Other Stks	2yo H'caps	3yo H'caps	Other H'caps	App'ce	Amateurs	Per cent	£1 Level stake
Keith Dalgleish	51-415	11-59	0-2	6-36	6-28	5-61	22-219	1-3	0-7	12.3	-91.69
Mark Johnston	50-249	17-66	0-0	3-15	0-11	11-64	19-93	0-0	0-0	20.1	-5.34
Richard Fahey	45-242	13-50	0-1	6-27	3-17	8-51	15-95	0-1	0-0	18.6	**59.32**
Jim Goldie	29-324	0-2	0-0	3-39	0-4	0-12	26-244	0-10	0-13	9.0	-72.09
Kevin Ryan	22-105	6-26	0-0	2-13	1-4	3-19	8-41	1-1	1-1	21.0	**22.63**
David O'Meara	20-146	3-21	0-0	4-17	2-13	2-23	9-69	0-2	0-1	13.7	-53.16
Tim Easterby	18-155	3-12	0-0	0-19	1-14	5-25	8-78	0-1	1-6	11.6	-36.55
Iain Jardine	17-167	1-15	0-1	0-13	0-3	1-17	11-106	2-5	2-7	10.2	-81.98
Linda Perratt	15-226	0-3	0-0	1-23	1-5	1-13	11-158	1-14	0-10	6.6	-43.50
Rebecca Bastiman	14-83	0-2	0-0	0-9	0-0	0-5	14-63	0-3	0-1	16.9	**4.25**
John Quinn	14-81	4-17	0-0	2-4	0-6	2-17	6-35	0-0	0-2	17.3	-7.47
Michael Easterby	13-72	0-1	0-0	1-7	1-5	0-8	8-44	0-2	3-5	18.1	**11.75**
Ruth Carr	12-106	0-0	0-0	1-9	0-0	1-[illegible]	10-91	0-0	0-1	11.0	-10.00
Paul Midgley	11-89	1-3	0-0	4-21	0-7	1-5	5-46	0-3	0-4	12.4	**6.40**
Richard Guest	11-62	0-5	0-0	2-8	1-7	2-6	5-34	1-1	0-1	17.7	**28.63**
Noel Wilson	11-74	0-7	0-0	1-3	0-2	0-10	6-44	3-7	1-1	14.9	-0.90
Bryan Smart	11-81	2-19	0-0	3-14	1-9	1-6	4-31	0-2	0-0	13.6	-1.55
Brian Ellison	10-83	1-11	0-0	0-11	0-3	0-10	9-47	0-0	0-1	12.0	-16.42
Alistair Whillans	10-107	0-3	0-0	0-12	0-0	1-1	8-83	0-2	1-6	9.3	-48.30
William Haggas	9-27	3-4	0-0	1-6	0-0	3-12	2-5	0-0	0-0	33.3	**12.92**
Michael Appleby	8-28	0-1	0-0	2-8	0-0	0-1	5-15	0-2	1-1	28.6	**30.82**
K R Burke	8-47	2-11	0-0	1-5	1-7	2-14	2-10	0-0	0-0	17.0	-7.75
Alan Swinbank	8-51	0-1	0-0	1-4	0-0	1-9	3-30	0-0	3-7	15.7	-9.13
Michael Dods	8-54	1-8	0-0	1-3	3-10	1-11	2-21	0-1	0-0	14.8	-19.50
Garry Moss	6-17	0-0	0-0	0-1	0-0	1-3	5-13	0-0	0-0	35.3	**3.38**
Tracy Waggott	6-42	0-0	0-0	1-4	0-1	1-5	4-29	0-3	0-0	14.3	-17.50
Robert Cowell	5-14	1-2	0-0	2-7	1-1	0-0	1-4	0-0	0-0	35.7	**2.82**
David Brown	5-28	1-8	0-0	0-3	0-3	1-5	3-9	0-0	0-0	17.9	**5.00**
Ollie Pears	5-25	1-2	0-0	0-0	1-3	1-4	1-12	1-3	0-1	20.0	**6.50**
R Mike Smith	5-38	0-1	0-0	1-5	0-0	0-4	3-25	1-1	0-2	13.2	**8.00**

LEADING FLAT TRAINERS AT NEWBURY (SINCE 2014)

	Total W-R	2yo Stks	3yo Stks	Other Stks	2yo H'caps	3yo H'caps	Other H'caps	App'ce	Amateurs	Per cent	£1 Level stake
Richard Hannon	57-532	25-261	6-61	5-48	6-30	10-67	2-57	2-6	1-2	10.7	-145.85
John Gosden	47-198	17-60	18-71	5-36	0-2	3-18	4-11	0-0	0-0	23.7	**20.85**
William Haggas	38-181	9-68	7-32	5-25	2-4	4-21	10-29	0-1	1-1	21.0	-1.67
Charles Hills	18-199	8-90	2-33	3-24	2-5	0-12	3-33	0-2	0-0	9.0	-44.12
Brian Meehan	17-187	6-97	3-28	2-15	1-6	1-12	4-28	0-0	0-1	9.1	**11.37**
Ralph Beckett	17-139	6-49	3-31	3-16	0-2	2-15	2-24	0-0	1-2	12.2	-28.21
Sir Michael Stoute	17-123	5-26	4-30	5-28	0-1	3-19	0-19	0-0	0-0	13.8	-47.22
Andrew Balding	16-173	4-55	4-32	1-24	0-1	3-25	4-30	0-2	0-4	9.2	-19.83
Roger Charlton	15-120	4-42	3-35	0-15	0-0	5-12	3-16	0-0	0-0	12.5	-11.30
Luca Cumani	14-62	0-3	3-17	5-16	0-0	3-9	3-16	0-1	0-0	22.6	**17.50**
Charlie Appleby	14-67	3-18	3-6	6-21	1-1	0-11	1-10	0-0	0-0	20.9	-13.76
Roger Varian	14-111	5-36	3-36	5-18	0-1	1-9	0-11	0-0	0-0	12.6	-30.75
Mark Johnston	13-91	6-31	1-5	2-8	0-6	1-14	3-27	0-0	0-0	14.3	-7.53
Eve Johnson Houghton	11-99	2-34	0-8	1-10	0-2	3-14	4-27	1-3	0-1	11.1	**12.87**
Hughie Morrison	11-137	3-40	0-22	1-12	0-2	2-13	4-40	1-7	0-1	8.0	-66.50
David Simcock	10-70	2-15	0-9	6-28	0-0	0-3	2-15	0-0	0-0	14.3	**1.00**
Ed Walker	10-78	3-22	0-14	0-5	0-1	3-12	1-20	3-4	0-0	12.8	**3.62**
Richard Fahey	10-88	6-42	0-8	2-13	0-0	0-6	2-18	0-0	0-1	11.4	**15.13**
Hugo Palmer	9-74	4-26	2-7	0-20	0-0	0-6	3-15	0-0	0-0	12.2	**0.00**
Jonathan Portman	9-89	4-33	0-8	0-0	1-2	1-11	2-18	0-9	1-8	10.1	-9.05
Saeed bin Suroor	9-55	0-10	2-8	3-14	0-1	1-8	3-14	0-0	0-0	16.4	-13.59
Henry Candy	8-66	4-23	0-9	1-7	0-0	0-7	3-20	0-0	0-0	12.1	-4.38
Mick Channon	8-182	2-74	2-35	2-14	2-11	0-18	0-26	0-4	0-0	4.4	-96.25
Sylvester Kirk	7-112	4-40	0-6	0-6	0-5	0-12	2-34	1-8	0-1	6.3	**2.87**
David Evans	7-99	1-45	0-3	0-4	0-9	1-13	4-17	0-4	1-4	7.1	-19.50
Tom Dascombe	6-43	3-16	0-1	0-4	0-4	0-5	3-12	0-0	0-1	14.0	**5.25**
Paul Cole	6-63	2-28	3-14	0-1	0-1	0-5	1-14	0-0	0-0	9.5	-10.50
Alan King	6-64	0-12	0-4	0-5	0-0	1-12	3-25	1-4	1-2	9.4	-39.72
Denis Coakley	5-27	1-3	0-1	0-1	0-0	0-4	4-17	0-1	0-0	18.5	**12.50**
Rod Millman	5-68	0-13	1-10	0-3	1-3	2-8	0-24	0-1	1-6	7.4	**69.50**

LEADING FLAT TRAINERS AT NEWCASTLE - All Weather (SINCE 2016)

	Total W-R	2yo Stks	3yo Stks	Other Stks	2yo H'caps	3yo H'caps	Other H'caps	App'ce	Amateurs	Per cent	£1 Level stake
Richard Fahey	44-379	4-74	1-15	5-37	9-47	6-32	18-166	1-8	0-0	11.6	-56.88
Jim Goldie	29-243	0-0	0-2	1-24	1-4	2-7	24-192	1-14	0-0	11.9	**21.33**
John Gosden	28-77	12-28	6-15	4-20	2-2	3-4	1-8	0-0	0-0	36.4	-2.51
Michael Easterby	25-186	1-23	0-1	2-20	4-9	0-9	16-116	2-8	0-0	13.4	**78.09**
Mark Johnston	25-235	7-54	2-17	1-31	3-46	2-18	9-65	1-3	0-1	10.6	-77.51
David O'Meara	21-253	1-19	2-5	3-55	2-14	1-8	12-144	0-8	0-0	8.3	-78.41
Hugo Palmer	20-85	8-23	1-9	7-18	0-7	1-2	3-26	0-0	0-0	23.5	-0.47
Brian Ellison	20-239	1-23	0-7	2-39	0-7	0-12	17-143	0-8	0-0	8.4	-39.59
Kevin Ryan	20-178	3-21	3-16	0-15	2-16	3-22	9-81	0-7	0-0	11.2	-40.19
Richard Guest	20-172	0-11	0-1	3-14	0-4	1-5	14-121	2-16	0-0	11.6	-42.80
William Haggas	19-50	4-13	3-7	4-12	2-5	1-5	5-8	0-0	0-0	38.0	**8.24**
Michael Dods	19-161	4-32	2-11	4-18	1-8	3-12	5-73	0-7	0-0	11.8	-25.49
K R Burke	18-177	5-43	3-16	3-27	2-19	3-16	1-50	1-6	0-0	10.2	**27.70**
Roger Varian	18-83	3-29	1-6	9-20	0-1	0-2	5-25	0-0	0-0	21.7	-23.50
David Simcock	18-103	6-20	3-16	5-22	1-2	1-6	2-35	0-2	0-0	17.5	-26.88
James Bethell	17-115	1-17	0-4	2-15	0-3	1-5	13-71	0-0	0-0	14.8	**26.75**
Keith Dalgleish	17-247	3-31	1-12	0-24	1-16	1-15	10-139	1-10	0-0	6.9	-112.08
Ruth Carr	16-148	0-0	0-0	3-15	0-0	1-7	11-120	1-6	0-0	10.8	**20.33**
Sir Mark Prescott Bt	16-64	0-14	0-1	0-5	2-3	5-12	9-28	0-1	0-0	25.0	**25.40**
Iain Jardine	16-208	0-8	0-3	3-24	0-7	0-5	10-141	3-18	0-2	7.7	-46.25
David Barron	14-152	0-7	2-12	4-22	2-8	1-19	4-78	1-6	0-0	9.2	-71.91
Ben Haslam	12-108	0-18	0-4	1-14	2-14	2-16	7-37	0-5	0-0	11.1	**29.25**
Julie Camacho	12-103	1-7	1-2	2-12	0-2	0-9	6-61	2-10	0-0	11.7	-9.25
Alistair Whillans	12-136	1-9	0-1	1-18	0-2	0-1	10-96	0-8	0-1	8.8	-14.40
John Quinn	12-151	2-24	0-5	1-17	1-19	0-16	6-62	2-7	0-1	7.9	-68.47
James Fanshawe	11-53	0-7	0-1	6-24	0-0	0-1	5-20	0-0	0-0	20.8	-9.43
Saeed bin Suroor	11-49	3-12	0-2	2-12	1-3	0-2	5-18	0-0	0-0	22.4	-13.50
James Tate	11-55	2-11	1-6	0-11	3-6	2-5	3-16	0-0	0-0	20.0	-19.92
Karen McLintock	11-99	0-4	0-1	0-14	0-4	1-5	9-67	1-4	0-0	11.1	-23.00
Roger Fell	11-181	0-12	0-0	3-21	0-11	4-13	4-113	0-11	0-0	6.1	-85.38

LEADING FLAT TRAINERS AT NEWMARKET - JULY COURSE (SINCE 2014)

	Total W-R	2yo Stks	3yo Stks	Other Stks	2yo H'caps	3yo H'caps	Other H'caps	App'ce	Amateurs	Per cent	£1 Level stake
Richard Hannon	55-408	25-177	3-23	2-26	9-38	8-85	8-59	0-0	0-0	13.5	-68.39
Mark Johnston	46-228	9-51	2-6	2-12	5-22	10-59	18-78	0-0	0-0	20.2	**13.60**
Charlie Appleby	43-211	25-101	3-20	4-28	2-8	2-24	7-30	0-0	0-0	20.4	-33.73
John Gosden	38-220	11-79	4-38	8-44	1-2	7-38	7-19	0-0	0-0	17.3	-7.61
Saeed bin Suroor	24-105	6-30	3-11	5-22	0-1	3-10	7-31	0-0	0-0	22.9	**4.12**
William Haggas	23-145	4-30	3-16	6-34	0-7	5-34	5-24	0-0	0-0	15.9	-40.60
Richard Fahey	20-161	2-24	0-6	1-18	3-20	5-39	9-54	0-0	0-0	12.4	**11.50**
Charles Hills	19-159	5-51	1-7	1-21	1-2	6-34	5-44	0-0	0-0	11.9	-48.05
Ralph Beckett	17-97	2-27	1-10	1-14	1-6	4-14	8-26	0-0	0-0	17.5	-8.38
Sir Michael Stoute	17-137	5-46	1-8	5-33	0-2	2-34	4-14	0-0	0-0	12.4	-77.45
Andrew Balding	14-104	3-27	1-5	1-17	0-0	8-22	1-33	0-0	0-0	13.5	-1.90
Chris Wall	12-70	0-8	0-1	1-13	0-0	1-4	10-44	0-0	0-0	17.1	**2.62**
Marco Botti	12-84	3-28	2-5	0-14	2-3	1-15	4-19	0-0	0-0	14.3	**13.54**
Michael Bell	12-122	3-41	0-4	2-11	0-9	4-29	3-28	0-0	0-0	9.8	-25.50
Jeremy Noseda	10-49	4-16	1-4	0-9	0-0	4-9	1-11	0-0	0-0	20.4	-11.72
Luca Cumani	10-85	0-22	0-5	4-22	0-1	2-13	4-22	0-0	0-0	11.8	-46.60
Ed Dunlop	10-102	7-49	0-5	0-9	0-5	1-7	2-27	0-0	0-0	9.8	-48.55
James Fanshawe	9-63	0-6	2-6	2-15	0-0	2-10	3-26	0-0	0-0	14.3	-0.00
A P O'Brien	9-37	4-16	2-6	3-15	0-0	0-0	0-0	0-0	0-0	24.3	**1.28**
Mick Channon	9-93	3-25	0-2	2-8	1-12	2-23	1-23	0-0	0-0	9.7	-12.67
Brian Meehan	9-71	1-26	2-6	2-8	0-7	3-17	1-7	0-0	0-0	12.7	-27.75
David Elsworth	9-98	4-34	1-4	1-15	0-3	0-11	3-31	0-0	0-0	9.2	-50.34
David Simcock	9-94	0-12	0-8	3-25	0-1	1-10	5-37	0-1	0-0	9.6	-55.90
Roger Varian	9-100	1-27	0-6	3-21	0-2	2-19	3-25	0-0	0-0	9.0	-57.34
Hugo Palmer	9-95	1-35	0-5	3-13	1-4	2-16	2-22	0-0	0-0	9.5	-61.79
Ed Walker	8-57	3-18	0-3	0-4	0-1	3-11	2-19	0-1	0-0	14.0	-3.67
Henry Candy	8-51	0-7	0-0	4-16	0-0	4-18	0-10	0-0	0-0	15.7	-9.50
Stuart Williams	8-122	0-17	0-5	1-10	0-0	1-13	6-76	0-1	0-0	6.6	-23.50
Kevin Ryan	7-59	2-8	0-4	0-8	0-4	3-23	2-12	0-0	0-0	11.9	**19.50**
Ian Williams	7-41	0-0	0-0	0-3	0-0	1-9	6-29	0-0	0-0	17.1	-0.20

LEADING FLAT TRAINERS AT NEWMARKET - ROWLEY MILE (SINCE 2014)

	Total W-R	2yo Stks	3yo Stks	Other Stks	2yo H'caps	3yo H'caps	Other H'caps	App'ce	Amateurs	Per cent	£1 Level stake
John Gosden	63-326	23-109	21-106	13-55	0-8	3-14	3-34	0-0	0-0	19.3	-1.70
Charlie Appleby	52-207	14-74	13-46	7-26	2-6	9-28	7-27	0-0	0-0	25.1	**50.92**
Richard Hannon	39-350	11-123	16-74	3-34	2-30	5-47	2-41	0-1	0-0	11.1	**39.38**
A P O'Brien	31-142	19-79	6-39	5-21	0-0	1-2	0-1	0-0	0-0	21.8	**23.63**
Saeed bin Suroor	27-146	10-41	8-37	1-23	1-3	2-19	4-22	1-1	0-0	18.5	**1.61**
Mark Johnston	27-250	12-84	4-32	2-16	3-19	0-40	6-57	0-2	0-0	10.8	-46.75
Roger Varian	22-201	8-61	5-49	3-36	0-2	2-14	4-39	0-0	0-0	10.9	-41.50
William Haggas	20-196	4-77	3-33	6-43	1-6	2-16	4-20	0-1	0-0	10.2	-37.80
Sir Michael Stoute	19-171	3-47	5-39	7-39	0-4	2-19	2-23	0-0	0-0	11.1	-61.38
Ralph Beckett	15-119	4-32	1-16	2-28	1-7	3-16	4-19	0-1	0-0	12.6	-19.22
Andrew Balding	14-157	3-43	2-19	4-27	0-5	0-14	5-48	0-1	0-0	8.9	-50.03
Richard Fahey	14-187	3-38	1-11	1-19	0-14	2-34	7-71	0-0	0-0	7.5	-75.95
Mick Channon	13-100	2-33	3-16	3-17	0-8	1-10	4-10	0-0	0-0	13.0	-5.88
Charles Hills	13-167	4-62	2-40	3-19	0-5	2-14	2-26	0-1	0-0	7.8	-96.43
Martyn Meade	11-47	5-16	1-8	1-9	1-4	2-4	1-6	0-0	0-0	23.4	**147.50**
Hugo Palmer	11-116	5-47	2-21	1-16	1-4	1-17	1-11	0-0	0-0	9.5	-34.93
Henry Candy	9-55	2-15	0-7	4-14	0-1	1-4	2-14	0-0	0-0	16.4	-5.90
Hughie Morrison	8-54	0-7	1-3	4-15	0-2	0-2	3-24	0-1	0-0	14.8	-5.88
Kevin Ryan	8-57	0-11	0-5	4-13	0-3	1-6	3-19	0-0	0-0	14.0	-7.75
Roger Charlton	8-58	3-13	0-6	2-12	0-3	0-11	3-13	0-0	0-0	13.8	-15.09
Luca Cumani	8-114	6-33	1-24	1-18	0-4	0-9	0-25	0-1	0-0	7.0	-71.76
K R Burke	7-65	3-23	0-8	1-8	1-3	0-8	2-15	0-0	0-0	10.8	-8.42
Ed Walker	6-63	2-15	1-7	1-15	1-4	0-8	1-13	0-0	0-1	9.5	-21.63
Stuart Williams	6-102	0-27	0-3	0-10	0-3	2-6	3-52	1-1	0-0	5.9	-29.67
A Fabre	5-19	1-4	1-4	3-11	0-0	0-0	0-0	0-0	0-0	26.3	**2.82**
Amanda Perrett	5-34	1-7	0-6	1-5	0-0	0-2	3-14	0-0	0-0	14.7	**6.00**
Owen Burrows	5-36	1-11	2-11	0-4	0-0	1-4	1-6	0-0	0-0	13.9	**12.00**
Ian Williams	5-42	0-0	0-1	0-6	0-0	2-6	3-29	0-0	0-0	11.9	-2.17
Michael Appleby	5-58	0-4	0-1	0-5	0-2	1-3	4-43	0-0	0-0	8.6	-16.75
Clive Cox	5-66	2-20	0-4	1-10	1-7	1-9	0-16	0-0	0-0	7.6	-27.00

LEADING FLAT TRAINERS AT NOTTINGHAM (SINCE 2014)

	Total W-R	2yo Stks	3yo Stks	Other Stks	2yo H'caps	3yo H'caps	Other H'caps	App'ce	Amateurs	Per cent	£1 Level stake
Michael Appleby	38-261	1-17	1-10	5-33	0-6	7-38	19-136	2-16	3-5	14.6	**13.19**
Richard Fahey	38-221	12-55	2-19	2-17	2-23	8-43	12-59	0-1	0-4	17.2	**37.00**
Richard Hannon	26-177	8-61	3-26	3-12	4-24	3-24	5-29	0-1	0-0	14.7	-39.67
John Gosden	22-130	7-46	8-38	3-19	2-5	2-11	0-11	0-0	0-0	16.9	-15.68
Mick Channon	19-136	7-35	3-14	3-7	2-13	1-30	1-28	0-5	2-4	14.0	**47.40**
Clive Cox	19-99	3-20	2-13	3-13	1-8	4-23	6-22	0-0	0-0	19.2	-2.55
Roger Varian	19-108	3-37	2-22	2-12	1-3	3-10	8-24	0-0	0-0	17.6	-27.12
Mark Johnston	19-143	7-47	1-12	0-12	5-23	4-21	2-26	0-1	0-1	13.3	-61.35
Sir Michael Stoute	17-87	2-15	5-31	3-14	0-2	6-16	1-9	0-0	0-0	19.5	-0.54
K R Burke	16-98	4-17	1-17	1-8	1-5	2-25	6-22	1-1	0-3	16.3	**22.75**
William Haggas	15-75	4-27	4-19	4-16	0-2	2-4	1-6	0-0	0-1	20.0	-7.85
Hughie Morrison	13-68	1-15	2-6	0-5	0-0	4-11	6-31	0-0	0-0	19.1	**21.50**
Ralph Beckett	13-82	3-25	3-9	3-10	0-7	2-13	2-17	0-0	0-1	15.9	-6.81
Ian Williams	12-66	0-3	1-3	0-8	0-2	2-10	8-36	0-1	1-3	18.2	**2.13**
James Fanshawe	12-83	1-18	2-21	2-16	0-0	1-3	5-24	1-1	0-0	14.5	-7.87
Robert Cowell	11-86	2-19	0-0	3-19	0-2	1-6	5-40	0-0	0-0	12.8	-0.00
Saeed bin Suroor	11-35	6-14	3-8	1-10	0-2	0-0	1-1	0-0	0-0	31.4	**4.50**
Andrew Balding	11-58	4-21	0-6	3-9	0-2	0-4	2-12	0-2	2-2	19.0	**8.43**
Michael Easterby	10-68	0-2	0-1	0-3	0-1	3-14	4-36	3-9	0-2	14.7	**0.75**
Scott Dixon	10-79	1-5	0-2	1-5	0-1	1-13	7-47	0-6	0-0	12.7	**25.70**
Richard Guest	10-101	0-10	0-0	2-11	0-0	1-7	6-52	1-11	0-10	9.9	-15.50
Declan Carroll	9-63	1-8	1-2	2-8	0-2	0-6	4-29	1-7	0-1	14.3	**74.54**
Charlie Appleby	9-50	6-20	1-10	2-10	0-2	0-5	0-3	0-0	0-0	18.0	-8.00
Simon Crisford	8-37	5-13	0-10	0-3	1-2	0-3	2-6	0-0	0-0	21.6	**5.96**
William Muir	8-48	2-9	0-4	0-3	0-0	3-8	3-24	0-0	0-0	16.7	**6.53**
Eric Alston	8-38	0-0	0-0	2-5	0-0	1-2	5-30	0-1	0-0	21.1	**26.50**
Kevin Ryan	8-74	2-17	1-5	1-12	1-4	2-21	1-13	0-1	0-1	10.8	-33.63
Ed de Giles	7-46	0-5	0-3	1-3	0-1	1-6	5-24	0-3	0-1	15.2	**36.00**
David Elsworth	7-35	1-5	4-9	0-1	0-4	1-7	1-9	0-0	0-0	20.0	**62.38**
David Evans	7-77	1-14	0-4	0-6	3-11	1-18	1-19	1-2	0-3	9.1	-2.00

LEADING FLAT TRAINERS AT PONTEFRACT (SINCE 2014)

	Total W-R	2yo Stks	3yo Stks	Other Stks	2yo H'caps	3yo H'caps	Other H'caps	App'ce	Amateurs	Per cent	£1 Level stake
Richard Fahey	55-314	17-79	2-9	6-36	5-21	11-41	14-121	0-7	0-0	17.5	**42.37**
Mark Johnston	34-197	13-52	4-14	7-31	1-12	3-28	6-54	0-5	0-1	17.3	-71.06
Tim Easterby	25-197	2-37	2-6	3-21	0-10	3-32	15-86	0-4	0-1	12.7	-28.67
David O'Meara	18-163	0-14	1-5	7-34	0-2	2-14	8-90	0-4	0-0	11.0	-53.50
Kevin Ryan	15-109	5-29	1-6	0-14	0-2	4-22	5-36	0-0	0-0	13.8	**8.71**
Micky Hammond	15-154	1-11	0-0	3-28	0-1	2-8	8-96	1-8	0-2	9.7	-41.75
Sir Michael Stoute	13-56	0-5	2-11	6-19	0-2	0-2	4-16	1-1	0-0	23.2	-17.06
Michael Appleby	13-105	0-8	0-0	3-28	1-4	0-3	6-54	3-7	0-1	12.4	-33.84
Richard Whitaker	12-60	2-6	0-2	0-6	0-0	0-1	8-42	2-3	0-0	20.0	**13.08**
Mick Channon	12-58	2-12	0-3	2-14	3-8	1-7	4-13	0-1	0-0	20.7	**41.50**
Charlie Appleby	11-32	4-9	0-1	2-9	0-3	3-4	2-6	0-0	0-0	34.4	-0.44
Michael Easterby	11-100	0-8	0-1	1-15	0-3	1-5	6-61	3-7	0-0	11.0	-29.92
Michael Dods	11-125	1-16	0-2	2-17	0-3	1-15	7-68	0-2	0-2	8.8	-60.34
John Quinn	10-81	1-21	2-5	0-11	1-4	2-14	4-24	0-2	0-0	12.3	**0.21**
Ralph Beckett	10-21	3-3	1-2	2-5	1-4	1-1	2-6	0-0	0-0	47.6	**16.82**
David Barron	10-53	2-7	2-2	1-4	0-0	1-7	4-33	0-0	0-0	18.9	**17.75**
Les Eyre	9-71	0-5	0-2	2-6	0-2	0-7	7-48	0-1	0-0	12.7	-4.00
Saeed bin Suroor	8-32	1-6	1-5	5-13	0-0	0-3	1-5	0-0	0-0	25.0	-5.92
William Haggas	8-44	1-12	2-6	4-14	1-4	0-6	0-2	0-0	0-0	18.2	-10.14
Paul Midgley	8-107	0-9	0-3	0-10	0-0	0-6	8-77	0-2	0-0	7.5	-22.50
Ruth Carr	8-89	0-0	0-0	1-10	0-0	0-5	6-70	1-4	0-0	9.0	-23.25
K R Burke	8-83	5-19	0-5	1-11	0-6	0-16	2-24	0-2	0-0	9.6	-47.41
Luca Cumani	7-20	0-0	1-2	3-6	0-1	0-0	2-9	1-2	0-0	35.0	**3.04**
James Given	7-38	0-4	0-4	2-6	0-0	0-3	4-20	1-1	0-0	18.4	**22.75**
Richard Guest	6-56	1-9	0-0	1-9	0-2	1-5	3-25	0-6	0-0	10.7	**10.63**
Alan Swinbank	6-42	0-1	0-1	2-8	0-0	0-4	4-27	0-1	0-0	14.3	-11.92
Declan Carroll	5-48	1-8	0-0	1-6	0-1	0-2	2-30	1-1	0-0	10.4	**13.83**
Karen McLintock	5-20	0-1	0-0	0-4	1-1	1-2	3-12	0-0	0-0	25.0	**50.00**
Jedd O'Keeffe	5-46	0-5	0-2	0-5	0-2	2-13	3-18	0-1	0-0	10.9	-8.75
Tom Dascombe	5-54	3-18	0-5	1-8	0-3	1-4	0-16	0-0	0-0	9.3	-19.50

LEADING FLAT TRAINERS AT REDCAR (SINCE 2014)

	Total W-R	2yo Stks	3yo Stks	Other Stks	2yo H'caps	3yo H'caps	Other H'caps	App'ce	Amateurs	Per cent	£1 Level stake
Richard Fahey	51-322	23-134	0-9	16-58	0-16	2-33	10-63	0-4	0-5	15.8	-9.87
David O'Meara	38-251	7-41	0-12	7-62	0-7	7-27	16-96	0-3	1-3	15.1	-19.61
Tim Easterby	33-432	0-95	3-18	6-69	2-30	4-63	17-147	1-5	0-5	7.6	-165.44
Michael Dods	25-211	7-62	2-10	5-38	1-12	3-23	7-60	0-3	0-3	11.8	-18.09
Kevin Ryan	23-161	8-56	0-5	7-31	1-7	5-18	2-40	0-2	0-2	14.3	-54.16
Mark Johnston	20-126	5-38	0-4	3-20	0-7	1-15	11-40	0-1	0-1	15.9	-12.50
David Barron	15-102	3-19	1-3	4-25	0-3	2-12	5-38	0-0	0-2	14.7	**48.63**
William Haggas	14-35	5-14	0-1	5-10	0-3	4-5	0-2	0-0	0-0	40.0	**5.54**
Michael Easterby	14-149	1-35	0-3	3-31	0-2	3-16	5-53	0-6	2-3	9.4	-52.13
Ruth Carr	14-170	0-3	0-2	5-43	0-0	1-14	6-96	0-6	2-6	8.2	-74.50
Keith Dalgleish	11-99	5-31	1-5	1-14	0-6	2-22	2-21	0-0	0-0	11.1	-0.25
Declan Carroll	10-82	1-13	0-1	2-19	3-6	1-10	3-30	0-1	0-2	12.2	**3.25**
Nigel Tinkler	10-141	1-31	0-4	1-17	0-7	7-29	1-47	0-4	0-2	7.1	-37.67
John Quinn	10-118	2-49	0-5	7-21	0-7	0-13	1-20	0-2	0-1	8.5	-81.23
Paul Midgley	9-91	1-15	1-5	1-13	0-2	0-13	5-42	0-0	1-1	9.9	-28.83
Ed Walker	8-32	2-7	0-1	3-6	3-6	0-4	0-8	0-0	0-0	25.0	**15.20**
Richard Hannon	8-27	3-13	1-1	3-10	0-1	1-2	0-0	0-0	0-0	29.6	**34.58**
Iain Jardine	8-68	0-13	0-1	1-13	0-6	0-7	6-24	1-3	0-1	11.8	-17.72
Bryan Smart	8-126	6-48	1-7	0-21	0-3	0-18	1-27	0-1	0-1	6.3	-87.15
Brian Ellison	8-128	0-13	0-2	6-40	0-4	0-19	1-44	1-3	0-3	6.3	-96.05
Geoffrey Harker	7-61	0-1	0-1	2-23	0-0	0-0	5-35	0-0	0-1	11.5	**10.00**
Scott Dixon	7-48	0-4	0-1	1-8	0-3	3-11	3-19	0-1	0-1	14.6	**57.16**
Charlie Appleby	7-23	4-12	1-1	2-7	0-0	0-3	0-0	0-0	0-0	30.4	-4.94
Tom Dascombe	7-43	3-18	0-2	0-6	0-3	3-7	1-7	0-0	0-0	16.3	-9.21
Jim Goldie	7-82	0-2	0-1	3-24	0-1	0-5	3-40	0-6	1-3	8.5	-22.00
Tracy Waggott	7-137	0-5	0-4	3-58	0-1	0-8	4-58	0-1	0-2	5.1	-46.00
Alan Swinbank	6-59	0-4	0-4	3-23	0-0	1-7	2-20	0-0	0-1	10.2	**0.25**
Keith Reveley	6-51	0-9	0-0	2-16	0-0	0-7	2-16	1-2	1-1	11.8	**16.25**
Garry Moss	6-26	0-3	1-1	2-8	1-2	1-3	1-9	0-0	0-0	23.1	**38.00**
Roger Fell	6-42	0-5	0-2	2-8	0-0	1-4	2-22	1-1	0-0	14.3	-12.50

LEADING FLAT TRAINERS AT RIPON (SINCE 2014)

	Total W-R	2yo Stks	3yo Stks	Other Stks	2yo H'caps	3yo H'caps	Other H'caps	App'ce	Amateurs	Per cent	£1 Level stake
David O'Meara	46-291	6-31	2-15	4-28	0-5	7-40	25-166	2-6	0-0	15.8	**4.21**
Tim Easterby	44-419	7-99	2-22	3-26	1-10	10-70	19-184	1-7	1-1	10.5	-94.13
Richard Fahey	43-339	12-98	1-14	4-18	2-11	13-60	10-131	1-7	0-0	12.7	-96.83
Mark Johnston	33-211	11-51	1-11	2-20	2-8	8-47	8-71	1-1	0-2	15.6	**0.86**
William Haggas	22-49	3-12	6-7	9-14	0-1	3-12	1-2	0-1	0-0	44.9	**11.19**
Ruth Carr	12-111	0-1	0-1	1-4	0-0	0-9	11-86	0-8	0-2	10.8	**40.75**
Richard Whitaker	11-77	1-9	0-3	2-11	0-0	2-11	6-39	0-4	0-0	14.3	**27.25**
David Barron	11-114	3-17	0-6	1-10	0-0	1-17	5-61	1-3	0-0	9.6	-40.40
Tom Dascombe	10-59	4-28	1-6	0-1	1-4	0-5	4-13	0-1	0-1	16.9	**7.29**
John Quinn	10-73	3-22	0-2	2-3	0-3	1-14	4-26	0-3	0-0	13.7	**7.60**
Roger Varian	10-41	1-6	3-8	1-6	0-1	2-8	3-12	0-0	0-0	24.4	-13.27
Paul Midgley	10-88	1-13	0-0	0-2	1-2	1-11	7-50	0-9	0-1	11.4	-13.63
Ann Duffield	10-83	7-29	0-1	0-0	1-2	1-12	1-17	0-7	0-0	12.0	-15.21
K R Burke	9-90	5-33	0-7	0-7	0-3	1-15	3-24	0-1	0-0	10.0	**93.13**
Micky Hammond	9-109	0-6	0-5	1-12	0-1	0-15	8-65	0-4	0-1	8.3	-2.50
Nigel Tinkler	9-68	1-23	0-3	1-4	0-3	5-14	1-13	1-7	0-1	13.2	-10.67
Mick Channon	9-53	6-18	0-0	0-7	1-4	1-6	1-15	0-3	0-0	17.0	-21.88
Kevin Ryan	9-125	1-25	1-13	0-6	0-5	2-26	5-49	0-1	0-0	7.2	-62.00
Keith Dalgleish	8-75	0-21	0-1	4-10	0-4	1-10	3-29	0-0	0-0	10.7	-27.13
Bryan Smart	7-55	1-10	2-7	0-0	0-1	0-10	4-25	0-2	0-0	12.7	**15.00**
James Given	7-42	1-11	0-1	0-4	0-0	0-6	6-18	0-2	0-0	16.7	-7.12
Michael Dods	7-74	2-17	1-3	0-5	0-4	3-16	1-27	0-2	0-0	9.5	-28.09
James Tate	6-14	1-6	1-2	0-0	1-1	1-1	2-4	0-0	0-0	42.9	-0.33
Les Eyre	6-27	0-0	0-0	0-3	0-0	1-5	5-18	0-1	0-0	22.2	**0.21**
Saeed bin Suroor	6-24	1-3	1-1	2-8	1-1	0-4	1-7	0-0	0-0	25.0	**2.92**
Richard Hannon	6-24	1-7	1-1	1-2	1-1	1-7	1-6	0-0	0-0	25.0	-3.06
Jedd O'Keeffe	6-38	2-13	0-3	0-2	0-0	1-6	3-14	0-0	0-0	15.8	-4.43
Roger Fell	6-60	0-1	0-2	1-4	0-0	3-12	1-35	1-5	0-1	10.0	-14.75
Brian Ellison	6-55	0-9	1-5	2-4	0-0	1-6	2-28	0-3	0-0	10.9	-22.63
Michael Easterby	6-101	0-17	0-7	1-6	0-1	1-11	3-54	1-4	0-1	5.9	-70.67

LEADING FLAT TRAINERS AT SALISBURY (SINCE 2014)

	Total W-R	2yo Stks	3yo Stks	Other Stks	2yo H'caps	3yo H'caps	Other H'caps	App'ce	Amateurs	Per cent	£1 Level stake
Richard Hannon	58-409	35-172	2-18	11-70	1-32	3-55	5-51	1-11	0-0	14.2	-56.22
Andrew Balding	30-172	10-50	2-13	6-35	0-3	6-27	6-32	0-12	0-0	17.4	-15.47
Ralph Beckett	25-152	8-54	1-6	4-32	0-4	6-21	6-32	0-3	0-0	16.4	-19.97
Clive Cox	17-116	5-35	1-6	4-23	2-6	1-16	4-26	0-4	0-0	14.7	-35.90
Rod Millman	16-153	5-45	0-7	1-13	3-9	2-20	2-45	2-11	1-3	10.5	-40.58
Mick Channon	14-158	2-52	3-12	1-25	1-8	3-27	4-28	0-6	0-0	8.9	-55.07
John Gosden	13-44	2-9	2-7	9-23	0-0	0-4	0-1	0-0	0-0	29.5	**37.69**
Charles Hills	13-92	0-32	1-7	7-25	0-4	2-13	3-10	0-1	0-0	14.1	-10.40
Roger Charlton	13-74	3-23	2-6	3-20	0-2	3-12	2-9	0-2	0-0	17.6	-26.97
Roger Varian	12-65	3-17	1-6	4-25	0-1	2-6	2-9	0-1	0-0	18.5	**2.06**
William Haggas	11-43	2-13	1-7	6-14	0-3	2-3	0-3	0-0	0-0	25.6	-6.07
Henry Candy	11-92	3-26	1-6	3-33	0-0	0-7	3-16	1-4	0-0	12.0	-22.15
Sir Michael Stoute	11-79	1-19	1-11	5-23	0-1	3-16	1-9	0-0	0-0	13.9	-30.19
David Evans	10-117	4-48	2-10	0-4	2-9	1-17	1-22	0-7	0-0	8.5	-8.34
Amanda Perrett	10-69	0-13	0-1	2-11	0-0	1-11	7-32	0-1	0-0	14.5	-13.42
Eve Johnson Houghton	10-87	4-34	0-4	2-8	0-4	3-10	1-22	0-5	0-0	11.5	-21.78
Joseph Tuite	9-50	1-15	0-1	0-4	0-0	2-7	1-14	5-8	0-1	18.0	-0.67
Hughie Morrison	8-56	0-18	0-2	3-10	0-0	1-7	4-14	0-5	0-0	14.3	**7.75**
Ian Williams	8-29	0-5	1-1	0-0	0-1	1-2	5-17	1-2	0-1	27.6	**9.00**
Harry Dunlop	8-77	3-33	0-2	0-6	0-3	1-8	4-21	0-4	0-0	10.4	-8.17
Ed Walker	8-56	1-21	0-1	2-12	0-1	2-4	3-16	0-1	0-0	14.3	-11.26
Sylvester Kirk	8-92	4-29	0-4	1-11	0-8	2-19	0-12	1-9	0-0	8.7	-36.40
Saeed bin Suroor	7-29	3-6	0-3	3-13	0-0	0-1	1-6	0-0	0-0	24.1	**1.47**
David Elsworth	7-40	0-4	0-1	2-13	1-1	0-2	3-18	1-1	0-0	17.5	-7.50
Mark Johnston	7-35	4-14	0-1	2-6	1-5	0-4	0-5	0-0	0-0	20.0	**7.60**
Luca Cumani	7-39	0-4	1-6	1-15	0-0	1-5	4-9	0-0	0-0	17.9	-10.63
Marcus Tregoning	7-49	3-15	0-2	1-11	0-1	1-7	2-13	0-0	0-0	14.3	-12.50
Richard Hughes	6-58	1-18	0-2	1-6	0-3	1-8	3-17	0-4	0-0	10.3	-22.59
Malcolm Saunders	5-54	0-9	0-0	0-5	0-0	1-3	4-32	0-5	0-0	9.3	**3.50**
Stuart Kittow	5-45	1-10	0-0	0-10	0-0	1-4	3-20	0-1	0-0	11.1	**4.00**

LEADING FLAT TRAINERS AT SANDOWN (SINCE 2014)

	Total W-R	2yo Stks	3yo Stks	Other Stks	2yo H'caps	3yo H'caps	Other H'caps	App'ce	Amateurs	Per cent	£1 Level stake
Richard Hannon	41-298	20-109	3-21	3-27	1-10	7-75	6-53	1-3	0-0	13.8	-23.88
John Gosden	34-154	11-40	7-32	7-31	0-0	8-42	1-9	0-0	0-0	22.1	-7.41
Sir Michael Stoute	33-130	3-22	6-18	8-22	0-0	10-44	6-24	0-0	0-0	25.4	**16.43**
Clive Cox	20-109	4-22	2-10	2-9	1-3	5-36	6-29	0-0	0-0	18.3	**22.71**
William Haggas	17-69	5-14	1-7	3-11	0-1	5-23	3-13	0-0	0-0	24.6	**7.00**
Roger Varian	16-79	1-15	2-14	1-11	0-0	7-17	5-22	0-0	0-0	20.3	-18.63
Andrew Balding	16-162	3-40	2-12	3-24	0-1	0-45	6-36	1-1	1-3	9.9	-29.48
Charlie Appleby	13-75	7-26	0-7	1-13	0-2	4-23	1-4	0-0	0-0	17.3	-15.27
Mark Johnston	13-115	8-34	0-5	1-9	0-4	2-28	2-35	0-0	0-0	11.3	-61.54
Roger Charlton	12-66	2-14	0-2	2-14	0-1	6-20	2-15	0-0	0-0	18.2	-21.28
Saeed bin Suroor	9-39	0-8	0-4	3-8	0-0	2-10	4-9	0-0	0-0	23.1	**0.08**
Mick Channon	9-79	2-21	0-8	0-7	1-7	2-24	4-9	0-3	0-0	11.4	**6.55**
Ralph Beckett	9-84	1-19	3-8	0-15	0-0	2-22	3-19	0-1	0-0	10.7	-30.55
K R Burke	8-55	2-12	0-2	0-2	0-1	3-20	3-15	0-2	0-1	14.5	**12.00**
William Muir	8-44	0-5	0-3	0-6	0-0	3-15	5-15	0-0	0-0	18.2	**16.75**
Henry Candy	8-61	2-9	1-7	0-7	0-1	1-14	4-21	0-2	0-0	13.1	-10.38
Eve Johnson Houghton	8-74	1-9	1-3	1-6	0-0	3-24	2-30	0-2	0-0	10.8	-10.50
Hughie Morrison	8-45	0-3	0-3	3-14	0-0	3-12	1-11	0-0	1-2	17.8	-16.65
Charles Hills	8-75	2-17	2-14	1-8	1-4	1-18	1-14	0-0	0-0	10.7	-20.00
Brian Meehan	8-72	2-21	0-4	1-9	0-3	3-15	2-17	0-3	0-0	11.1	-25.27
Michael Bell	7-41	1-6	0-3	2-5	0-1	1-10	3-14	0-1	0-1	17.1	-18.04
David Elsworth	6-34	0-3	1-4	0-5	0-0	3-8	2-14	0-0	0-0	17.6	**1.00**
Simon Crisford	5-26	2-6	0-2	0-2	0-0	2-9	1-7	0-0	0-0	19.2	-2.25
Ed Walker	5-42	1-5	0-4	0-3	0-1	1-8	3-21	0-0	0-0	11.9	**1.25**
Jamie Osborne	5-25	1-4	0-0	0-2	1-2	0-5	3-12	0-0	0-0	20.0	**1.25**
Sir Mark Prescott Bt	5-18	0-1	0-0	1-5	1-1	1-8	1-2	0-0	1-1	27.8	**8.23**
David Menuisier	5-20	0-4	0-2	0-1	0-0	1-4	4-9	0-0	0-0	25.0	**23.10**
Ed Dunlop	5-50	2-17	0-6	0-5	0-0	0-7	3-15	0-0	0-0	10.0	-22.00
Hugo Palmer	5-43	3-16	0-5	0-4	0-1	0-11	2-6	0-0	0-0	11.6	-26.25
Rod Millman	5-54	0-6	1-4	0-3	0-2	2-15	1-19	0-1	1-4	9.3	-32.63

LEADING FLAT TRAINERS AT SOUTHWELL - All Weather (SINCE 2014)

	Total W-R	2yo Stks	3yo Stks	Other Stks	2yo H'caps	3yo H'caps	Other H'caps	App'ce	Amateurs	Per cent	£1 Level stake
Michael Appleby	117-753	0-18	2-10	23-144	4-21	6-35	79-501	2-19	1-5	15.5	-189.88
Scott Dixon	53-568	1-24	1-9	16-131	1-19	5-26	28-345	1-13	0-1	9.3	-8.10
Derek Shaw	35-261	0-2	0-2	5-52	0-3	2-33	24-159	4-10	0-0	13.4	**33.88**
Richard Fahey	35-198	7-22	1-6	9-32	2-21	3-24	11-83	1-8	1-2	17.7	-32.98
K R Burke	32-144	2-9	4-9	12-43	2-14	4-23	8-40	0-3	0-3	22.2	**132.67**
David Evans	31-219	1-13	2-13	4-31	2-16	8-42	12-90	2-11	0-3	14.2	**10.05**
Andrew Balding	28-100	2-6	0-3	12-36	0-1	6-15	7-36	1-2	0-1	28.0	-1.46
Roy Bowring	25-181	0-2	0-1	8-38	0-0	1-11	16-125	0-4	0-0	13.8	-17.60
Keith Dalgleish	24-162	1-10	2-6	1-18	0-5	7-26	12-90	0-5	1-2	14.8	-9.08
Mark Johnston	24-134	2-18	0-3	6-22	1-5	4-25	10-57	1-4	0-0	17.9	-24.54
David Barron	22-101	3-6	0-4	8-27	0-2	2-10	9-51	0-1	0-0	21.8	-0.44
Conor Dore	22-157	1-1	1-2	5-30	1-4	0-4	12-108	2-8	0-0	14.0	-2.39
Declan Carroll	20-103	0-0	0-0	2-9	0-0	1-3	17-86	0-4	0-1	19.4	**20.87**
J R Jenkins	19-221	0-1	0-3	9-87	0-1	0-12	10-109	0-4	0-4	8.6	-13.90
Brian Ellison	19-137	3-10	1-5	6-34	0-4	2-10	5-60	1-7	1-7	13.9	-42.03
John Balding	18-158	0-1	0-0	1-35	0-0	0-4	17-117	0-1	0-0	11.4	-30.25
James Given	17-135	1-11	0-3	7-37	1-6	2-16	6-58	0-3	0-1	12.6	**23.46**
David O'Meara	17-131	0-5	2-5	7-40	0-5	0-8	8-67	0-1	0-0	13.0	-34.17
Julia Feilden	16-115	0-0	0-1	2-16	1-3	3-11	8-68	0-7	2-9	13.9	**13.20**
Gay Kelleway	16-92	2-5	2-6	6-18	0-1	0-8	5-50	1-3	0-1	17.4	**38.29**
Alan Swinbank	15-103	0-0	0-1	4-26	0-0	0-1	9-68	0-4	2-3	14.6	-26.30
David Brown	14-65	0-7	0-1	3-11	2-5	7-19	1-20	1-2	0-0	21.5	-8.07
Hughie Morrison	14-72	1-9	1-2	2-14	0-2	0-5	10-36	0-2	0-2	19.4	-12.28
John Butler	14-88	0-0	1-1	7-19	0-2	0-4	6-58	0-4	0-0	15.9	-19.66
David C Griffiths	14-136	0-4	1-2	1-24	0-3	2-12	9-89	1-2	0-0	10.3	-52.75
Ivan Furtado	13-91	0-0	0-1	1-18	0-0	1-4	10-63	0-3	1-2	14.3	**4.00**
Roger Fell	13-66	0-1	0-0	3-8	1-2	0-0	9-45	0-1	0-0	10.7	[illegible]
Marjorie Fife	12-86	0-0	0-0	3-12	0-0	0-1	8-69	1-3	0-1	14.0	**18.38**
Alan McCabe	12-59	0-5	1-1	1-14	1-2	3-9	6-28	0-0	0-0	20.3	**22.15**
Chris Dwyer	12-75	0-2	0-0	2-24	0-2	1-3	8-40	1-2	0-2	16.0	-12.52

LEADING FLAT TRAINERS AT THIRSK (SINCE 2014)

	Total W-R	2yo Stks	3yo Stks	Other Stks	2yo H'caps	3yo H'caps	Other H'caps	App'ce	Amateurs	Per cent	£1 Level stake
Richard Fahey	49-301	13-94	5-17	15-39	1-18	7-40	8-88	0-3	0-2	16.3	**9.20**
David O'Meara	32-241	7-31	4-17	6-49	1-4	1-20	13-118	0-2	0-0	13.3	-27.83
Tim Easterby	29-370	5-95	2-33	4-52	1-15	3-37	11-133	3-4	0-1	7.8	-95.88
Michael Dods	26-233	3-45	2-20	3-25	2-9	4-34	12-97	0-2	0-1	11.2	-42.37
Kevin Ryan	23-202	5-48	5-16	3-30	3-7	3-32	4-69	0-0	0-0	11.4	-51.70
Keith Dalgleish	15-66	5-18	1-7	0-11	1-4	2-5	6-21	0-0	0-0	22.7	**47.94**
Paul Midgley	14-100	0-12	0-3	2-16	0-1	2-8	9-58	0-1	1-1	14.0	**9.25**
Ruth Carr	14-202	0-3	1-11	4-42	0-0	0-16	8-126	1-2	0-2	6.9	-68.30
Brian Ellison	12-109	0-16	0-9	3-29	1-4	1-7	6-40	1-4	0-0	11.0	**1.88**
Bryan Smart	11-72	3-11	0-6	4-14	1-6	1-12	2-23	0-0	0-0	15.3	**14.38**
Michael Appleby	11-67	1-4	0-3	2-16	0-0	4-10	3-33	1-1	0-0	16.4	**105.25**
Michael Easterby	11-150	0-28	0-11	1-21	0-4	2-18	8-67	0-1	0-0	7.3	-69.25
William Haggas	10-41	4-14	1-4	4-14	0-1	1-4	0-2	0-2	0-0	24.4	-16.63
John Quinn	10-103	3-23	1-7	3-16	0-7	1-12	2-37	0-1	0-0	9.7	-35.55
Declan Carroll	9-92	4-7	0-6	1-19	0-1	1-9	3-49	0-1	0-0	9.8	**13.75**
Alan Swinbank	8-57	0-2	1-5	1-21	0-0	0-3	6-26	0-0	0-0	14.0	**7.62**
Sir Michael Stoute	8-17	0-1	1-1	6-8	1-1	0-3	0-2	0-1	0-0	47.1	**9.07**
Richard Guest	8-74	1-14	2-5	1-12	0-0	2-11	2-29	0-2	0-1	10.8	-4.27
Scott Dixon	7-63	0-4	0-2	3-19	0-0	1-4	3-33	0-1	0-0	11.1	**1.25**
Saeed bin Suroor	7-19	1-3	2-2	4-10	0-0	0-1	0-3	0-0	0-0	36.8	**1.53**
Hugo Palmer	7-30	2-10	2-6	0-4	0-0	2-2	1-7	0-1	0-0	23.3	-6.87
Mick Channon	7-42	4-16	0-2	2-7	0-4	0-6	1-5	0-2	0-0	16.7	-7.55
Ralph Beckett	6-14	3-5	1-2	2-5	0-0	0-2	0-0	0-0	0-0	42.9	**5.34**
James Tate	6-23	1-9	0-2	3-6	0-0	1-3	1-3	0-0	0-0	26.1	**6.71**
David Evans	6-16	4-8	0-3	0-1	1-1	0-1	1-2	0-0	0-0	37.5	**38.97**
Charlie Appleby	6-21	2-7	1-2	2-9	0-0	0-1	1-2	0-0	0-0	28.6	-0.02
Tom Dascombe	6-38	1-7	1-2	2-11	0-1	1-3	1-14	0-0	0-0	15.8	-19.38
Nigel Tinkler	6-94	0-24	2-11	2-18	1-5	1-8	0-24	0-3	0-1	6.4	-57.00
Mark Johnston	6-85	3-24	0-3	0-11	1-12	0-11	1-22	1-2	0-0	7.1	-61.35
David Barron	6-124	1-19	0-8	2-28	1-3	0-8	2-57	0-1	0-0	4.8	-85.62

LEADING FLAT TRAINERS AT WETHERBY (SINCE 2015)

	Total W-R	2yo Stks	3yo Stks	Other Stks	2yo H'caps	3yo H'caps	Other H'caps	App'ce	Amateurs	Per cent	£1 Level stake
Richard Fahey	6-29	2-8	1-1	0-3	0-0	2-9	1-8	0-0	0-0	20.7	**16.25**
Tim Easterby	5-34	0-5	2-4	0-1	0-0	1-13	1-9	1-2	0-0	14.7	**9.80**
David O'Meara	5-28	0-3	1-2	0-1	0-0	1-6	3-16	0-0	0-0	17.9	**45.75**
John Gosden	3-4	0-0	0-0	3-4	0-0	0-0	0-0	0-0	0-0	75.0	**8.00**
Mark Johnston	3-15	1-5	1-2	0-0	0-0	1-6	0-2	0-0	0-0	20.0	**10.10**
Declan Carroll	3-11	0-0	0-0	1-3	0-0	0-1	1-6	1-1	0-0	27.3	**11.00**
Kevin Ryan	3-19	1-2	0-1	1-6	0-0	1-5	0-5	0-0	0-0	15.8	**24.50**
Ruth Carr	3-22	0-0	0-1	1-1	0-0	0-1	2-18	0-1	0-0	13.6	-3.00
William Haggas	2-8	0-0	0-1	1-4	0-0	0-1	1-2	0-0	0-0	25.0	**0.67**
Jedd O'Keeffe	2-9	0-0	1-1	1-2	0-0	0-1	0-5	0-0	0-0	22.2	**1.00**
John Davies	2-10	0-0	0-0	0-1	0-0	0-2	2-7	0-0	0-0	20.0	**1.50**
Tony Coyle	2-10	0-1	0-2	0-2	0-0	0-0	2-4	0-1	0-0	20.0	**3.50**
Roger Charlton	2-2	0-0	0-0	0-0	0-0	1-1	1-1	0-0	0-0	100.0	**5.38**
Antony Brittain	2-10	0-0	0-0	0-1	0-0	0-1	2-7	0-1	0-0	20.0	**5.50**
Eric Alston	2-7	0-0	0-0	0-0	0-0	0-0	2-6	0-1	0-0	28.6	**16.00**
George Margarson	2-4	1-1	0-1	0-0	0-0	1-2	0-0	0-0	0-0	50.0	**17.00**
David Brown	2-2	0-0	0-0	0-0	0-0	2-2	0-0	0-0	0-0	100.0	**26.00**
Tina Jackson	2-4	0-0	0-0	0-0	0-0	0-0	2-4	0-0	0-0	50.0	**28.00**
David Loughnane	2-5	0-0	0-0	0-1	0-0	0-1	2-3	0-0	0-0	40.0	**41.00**
Michael Dods	2-18	0-2	0-0	0-3	0-0	1-3	1-9	0-1	0-0	11.1	-1.00
Roger Fell	2-16	0-1	0-0	0-1	0-0	0-3	2-11	0-0	0-0	12.5	-5.00
Ed Dunlop	1-3	0-1	0-0	1-2	0-0	0-0	0-0	0-0	0-0	33.3	**0.25**
Archie Watson	1-4	1-2	0-0	0-1	0-0	0-1	0-0	0-0	0-0	25.0	**0.50**
Geoffrey Harker	1-8	0-0	0-0	0-2	0-0	0-0	1-5	0-1	0-0	12.5	**1.00**
Lawrence Mullaney	1-8	0-0	0-0	0-0	0-0	0-1	0-5	1-2	0-0	12.5	**1.00**
Ron Barr	1-4	0-0	0-0	0-0	0-0	0-1	1-2	0-1	0-0	25.0	**1.50**
Wilf Storey	1-4	0-0	0-0	0-1	0-0	0-0	0-2	1-1	0-0	25.0	**1.50**
Luca Cumani	1-2	0-0	0-0	1-2	0-0	0-0	0-0	0-0	0-0	50.0	**1.50**
Tom Dascombe	1-7	1-2	0-1	0-1	0-0	0-2	0-1	0-0	0-0	14.3	**2.00**
Dianne Sayer	1-7	0-1	0-0	0-2	0-0	0-0	1-4	0-0	0-0	14.3	**2.00**

LEADING FLAT TRAINERS AT WINDSOR (SINCE 2014)

	Total W-R	2yo Stks	3yo Stks	Other Stks	2yo H'caps	3yo H'caps	Other H'caps	App'ce	Amateurs	Per cent	£1 Level stake
Richard Hannon	63-409	33-155	2-27	5-62	4-24	10-62	9-76	0-3	0-0	15.4	-104.80
Clive Cox	40-187	12-39	1-9	10-39	0-3	7-33	10-64	0-0	0-0	21.4	**26.48**
Roger Varian	31-100	1-12	5-13	11-34	0-1	5-14	9-26	0-0	0-0	31.0	**25.18**
Ralph Beckett	26-128	5-28	3-15	5-27	0-3	7-23	6-29	0-2	0-1	20.3	-9.53
David Evans	24-241	13-86	0-11	2-24	0-14	1-23	5-70	2-6	1-7	10.0	-106.08
Henry Candy	22-122	4-21	3-12	7-40	1-2	1-9	5-34	1-4	0-0	18.0	**7.75**
Ed Walker	22-103	3-27	0-5	3-16	1-3	0-15	15-37	0-0	0-0	21.4	-7.75
Andrew Balding	21-150	7-25	3-12	7-45	1-3	0-20	3-43	0-2	0-0	14.0	-55.11
Charles Hills	20-146	6-52	0-13	4-22	0-4	3-18	7-36	0-1	0-0	13.7	-5.75
Roger Charlton	20-103	2-26	1-7	7-35	0-0	2-13	7-21	1-1	0-0	19.4	-8.82
John Gosden	19-81	3-9	2-12	9-35	1-2	2-13	2-10	0-0	0-0	23.5	-28.21
William Haggas	17-70	4-24	2-6	6-19	0-2	2-6	3-13	0-0	0-0	24.3	-24.84
Saeed bin Suroor	16-48	3-9	1-1	5-19	1-1	1-3	5-15	0-0	0-0	33.3	**0.92**
John Bridger	16-156	1-16	0-10	4-33	1-1	0-6	9-78	0-5	1-7	10.3	-42.50
Mick Channon	15-162	3-48	2-9	3-23	0-8	2-39	4-29	0-4	1-2	9.3	-55.12
Eve Johnson Houghton	14-114	3-28	1-4	1-15	0-2	0-17	9-45	0-3	0-0	12.3	**0.71**
Jamie Osborne	14-75	2-33	2-5	5-13	0-4	2-4	2-14	1-2	0-0	18.7	**41.85**
Gary Moore	13-128	0-16	0-5	5-31	1-2	1-12	5-54	0-1	1-7	10.2	-3.54
Mark Johnston	13-67	7-15	0-3	0-6	1-8	1-14	4-20	0-1	0-0	19.4	-15.62
Rod Millman	13-122	1-27	0-3	2-17	1-4	5-18	4-44	0-5	0-4	10.7	-45.75
Dean Ivory	12-129	2-25	2-5	2-31	0-0	0-3	6-58	0-7	0-0	9.3	-42.75
K R Burke	11-44	1-12	1-1	1-2	0-2	5-12	3-14	0-1	0-0	25.0	**8.67**
Richard Hughes	11-100	1-32	0-2	2-16	0-3	1-8	6-36	0-2	1-1	11.0	-27.23
David Simcock	10-62	0-10	0-4	4-17	0-0	0-5	6-26	0-0	0-0	16.1	-2.52
Luca Cumani	10-46	1-4	0-5	7-22	0-0	0-2	2-13	0-0	0-0	21.7	-6.69
Michael Bell	10-63	2-18	0-6	3-12	1-4	2-9	2-13	0-0	0-1	15.9	-15.67
Jeremy Noseda	10-70	3-16	0-6	3-21	0-0	0-7	4-20	0-0	0-0	14.3	-22.97
Sir Michael Stoute	10-86	1-7	1-11	4-39	0-1	1-12	3-16	0-0	0-0	11.6	-53.38
Charlie Appleby	9-48	1-8	1-3	3-19	0-1	3-11	1-6	0-0	0-0	18.8	-15.57
Marco Botti	9-67	1-12	1-7	2-20	1-1	3-11	1-16	0-0	0-0	13.4	-16.35

LEADING FLAT TRAINERS AT WOLVERHAMPTON - All Weather (SINCE 2014)

	Total W-R	2yo Stks	3yo Stks	Other Stks	2yo H'caps	3yo H'caps	Other H'caps	App'ce	Amateurs	Per cent	£1 Level stake
Mark Johnston	80-491	12-93	7-42	7-65	4-37	20-84	29-161	1-8	0-1	16.3	-115.78
Richard Fahey	74-598	13-128	3-18	13-93	1-53	6-60	36-228	2-15	0-3	12.4	-82.62
David Evans	72-706	7-93	5-36	17-95	5-54	10-101	24-294	3-23	1-10	10.2	-238.72
Michael Appleby	70-603	0-7	0-11	9-112	1-11	3-29	53-395	3-31	1-7	11.6	-145.54
Tom Dascombe	60-433	12-106	4-16	15-82	2-27	3-35	23-158	1-4	0-5	13.9	**33.02**
John Gosden	60-187	25-75	5-20	23-50	4-11	3-16	0-15	0-0	0-0	32.1	-2.73
Daniel Mark Loughnane	59-669	0-41	2-28	12-133	0-11	1-42	39-374	5-38	0-2	8.8	-200.40
Charlie Appleby	57-173	11-52	4-11	15-42	4-11	5-18	17-37	1-2	0-0	32.9	-24.13
Tony Carroll	55-528	1-14	2-6	13-106	0-7	6-27	31-333	2-29	0-6	10.4	-123.73
Jamie Osborne	52-363	11-68	2-27	15-75	5-33	6-57	13-99	0-3	0-1	14.3	-112.68
Marco Botti	50-318	12-81	4-26	16-80	3-16	7-42	8-70	0-3	0-0	15.7	-47.88
Richard Hannon	46-277	16-92	9-29	9-38	5-41	1-32	5-40	1-3	0-2	16.6	-53.38
David O'Meara	46-451	1-38	3-10	9-84	1-19	4-39	24-245	4-16	0-0	10.2	-139.78
Saeed bin Suroor	45-128	12-38	1-3	13-38	3-5	2-5	14-38	0-1	0-0	35.2	**4.92**
James Tate	43-245	5-47	6-21	10-59	4-17	5-45	12-53	1-3	0-0	17.6	-43.67
William Haggas	38-133	15-40	4-11	13-45	0-7	2-12	4-18	0-0	0-0	28.6	-15.96
David Simcock	37-238	1-29	5-25	12-77	1-2	0-11	18-92	0-2	0-0	15.5	-47.70
Roger Varian	36-167	3-39	2-16	17-59	3-8	4-14	6-27	1-4	0-0	21.6	**23.49**
Ian Williams	35-290	1-7	0-3	9-40	0-4	2-18	20-200	2-14	1-4	12.1	-31.23
Sir Mark Prescott Bt	34-204	4-62	1-15	8-39	0-14	7-25	12-46	1-2	1-1	16.7	-22.71
Kevin Ryan	32-208	1-28	1-12	9-42	0-13	8-32	12-76	0-3	1-2	15.4	**34.33**
Ralph Beckett	29-131	7-35	3-8	7-28	2-7	4-17	6-35	0-1	0-0	22.1	**15.04**
Stuart Williams	28-155	0-5	0-4	3-22	1-4	3-24	19-91	2-5	0-0	18.1	-35.79
Michael Easterby	28-226	0-13	0-6	2-26	0-7	4-23	18-135	0-8	4-8	12.4	-51.39
Hugo Palmer	27-98	6-18	0-7	11-37	3-11	3-10	4-15	0-0	0-0	27.6	**19.29**
Keith Dalgleish	27-262	1-20	2-10	6-40	0-11	2-20	15-153	0-6	1-2	10.3	-123.82
K R Burke	26-194	7-42	0-17	7-28	1-16	3-32	8-55	0-4	0-0	13.4	-1.34
Sylvester Kirk	26-229	3-37	2-15	3-22	2-19	5-31	8-92	3-11	0-2	11.4	-49.29
Charles Hills	25-155	8-38	1-14	3-40	2-10	3-14	8-37	0-1	0-1	16.1	-21.44
Ed Walker	25-130	2-26	4-8	7-28	2-4	2-15	7-46	1-3	0-0	19.2	-27.11

LEADING FLAT TRAINERS AT YARMOUTH (SINCE 2014)

	Total W-R	2yo Stks	3yo Stks	Other Stks	2yo H'caps	3yo H'caps	Other H'caps	App'ce	Amateurs	Per cent	£1 Level stake
William Haggas	33-131	12-53	3-12	5-18	1-5	6-23	6-20	0-0	0-0	25.2	-3.43
David Simcock	26-100	4-16	2-7	5-16	1-2	3-9	11-48	0-2	0-0	26.0	**52.38**
Roger Varian	24-98	8-33	1-5	4-17	0-2	4-12	7-29	0-0	0-0	24.5	**0.73**
John Gosden	23-73	9-35	4-8	4-11	1-2	1-8	4-9	0-0	0-0	31.5	**21.69**
Stuart Williams	18-99	0-10	1-3	4-13	0-2	5-17	7-50	1-4	0-0	18.2	-0.38
Chris Wall	18-93	1-11	0-1	6-16	0-0	4-12	7-53	0-0	0-0	19.4	-19.83
Chris Dwyer	17-108	2-15	1-3	3-16	1-3	1-3	8-66	1-2	0-0	15.7	**29.13**
Michael Bell	16-98	5-35	0-9	1-6	0-3	3-17	7-28	0-0	0-0	16.3	**1.91**
Mark Johnston	15-75	4-13	0-4	1-7	2-8	3-16	5-27	0-0	0-0	20.0	**59.22**
Sir Michael Stoute	13-66	3-28	0-1	2-7	1-3	1-11	6-16	0-0	0-0	19.7	-22.50
Luca Cumani	12-63	3-19	0-4	3-13	0-1	1-9	5-17	0-0	0-0	19.0	**19.32**
James Tate	12-68	4-19	0-4	2-6	1-3	0-6	5-30	0-0	0-0	17.6	-21.10
Michael Appleby	12-114	0-5	0-1	2-21	0-2	1-7	7-74	2-4	0-0	10.5	-32.42
John Ryan	12-118	1-23	0-10	1-18	1-4	0-13	9-49	0-1	0-0	10.2	-37.45
Hugo Palmer	11-49	4-15	2-5	1-8	0-3	1-5	3-13	0-0	0-0	22.4	**14.19**
Lydia Pearce	10-74	0-2	0-1	2-11	0-0	1-8	7-50	0-2	0-0	13.5	**13.00**
George Margarson	10-95	0-17	0-6	1-15	0-2	4-14	5-39	0-2	0-0	10.5	**22.75**
Philip McBride	10-50	1-12	0-3	2-8	0-5	3-9	4-13	0-0	0-0	20.0	**68.13**
Gay Kelleway	10-79	1-11	1-5	2-15	0-2	1-11	4-33	1-2	0-0	12.7	-1.01
Marco Botti	10-78	2-25	2-6	1-10	0-3	2-17	3-17	0-0	0-0	12.8	-17.24
K R Burke	9-50	4-9	0-5	0-5	0-5	2-8	3-15	0-3	0-0	18.0	**22.80**
Mick Quinn	9-71	0-7	0-4	1-8	0-1	0-8	8-43	0-0	0-0	12.7	-13.70
Sir Mark Prescott Bt	9-45	0-16	0-0	0-2	0-0	1-6	8-21	0-0	0-0	20.0	-21.56
Phil McEntee	9-88	0-3	1-3	0-19	0-0	1-5	6-52	1-6	0-0	10.2	-21.63
Julia Feilden	9-136	0-8	0-9	1-19	0-2	1-17	7-75	0-6	0-0	6.6	-83.50
James Fanshawe	8-60	1-4	0-1	2-17	0-1	1-6	4-31	0-0	0-0	13.3	**1.25**
Anthony Carson	8-44	1-6	1-3	1-10	0-0	1-1	4-24	0-0	0-0	18.2	**15.88**
Charlie Fellowes	8-33	0-6	1-3	0-3	0-1	1-3	6-17	0-0	0-0	24.2	**16.75**
Ed Vaughan	7-28	2-5	0-4	2-7	0-0	1-5	2-6	0-1	0-0	25.0	**0.13**
Rae Guest	7-46	0-7	0-2	2-11	0-0	1-11	4-14	0-1	0-0	15.2	-15.00

LEADING FLAT TRAINERS AT YORK (SINCE 2014)

	Total W-R	2yo Stks	3yo Stks	Other Stks	2yo H'caps	3yo H'caps	Other H'caps	App'ce	Amateurs	Per cent	£1 Level stake
Richard Fahey	44-646	13-165	1-29	4-61	5-45	3-64	17-245	1-26	0-11	6.8	-191.50
William Haggas	34-187	11-39	2-12	7-42	1-10	2-23	10-51	1-10	0-0	18.2	**3.54**
David O'Meara	31-423	0-21	1-11	7-64	0-8	3-20	19-271	1-25	0-3	7.3	-134.75
Mark Johnston	27-265	13-74	2-11	0-23	2-34	5-45	4-72	1-4	0-2	10.2	-17.64
Tim Easterby	26-360	4-55	1-11	2-39	0-10	1-29	12-190	4-20	2-6	7.2	-86.50
Kevin Ryan	25-284	11-85	2-16	2-32	3-20	2-25	4-91	1-14	0-1	8.8	-93.16
Sir Michael Stoute	21-104	2-4	2-13	11-46	0-0	1-13	5-28	0-0	0-0	20.2	**1.15**
John Gosden	21-86	0-6	8-20	9-42	0-0	2-11	2-7	0-0	0-0	24.4	-0.34
Charlie Appleby	15-73	5-11	1-9	3-23	1-4	3-8	2-17	0-1	0-0	20.5	**1.30**
Michael Dods	13-99	0-3	2-3	5-19	0-5	0-11	4-52	1-5	1-1	13.1	**3.66**
Richard Hannon	12-145	7-60	2-12	0-21	1-16	0-25	2-10	0-0	0-1	8.3	-38.13
John Quinn	11-114	4-24	0-1	0-8	2-12	0-9	4-51	0-6	1-3	9.6	**9.08**
Andrew Balding	11-108	1-20	0-4	4-25	0-1	1-18	5-39	0-1	0-0	10.2	**15.00**
Ralph Beckett	11-81	2-9	0-8	3-20	0-4	1-9	5-29	0-0	0-2	13.6	**16.08**
Saeed bin Suroor	10-79	2-13	1-5	3-17	0-0	0-2	4-41	0-1	0-0	12.7	-18.84
Brian Ellison	10-153	0-18	0-2	2-22	0-3	0-5	6-79	1-12	1-12	6.5	-25.25
Roger Varian	10-90	1-11	1-11	2-21	0-2	1-7	5-35	0-3	0-0	11.1	-45.65
Charles Hills	9-89	3-23	0-8	1-25	0-5	0-3	5-24	0-1	0-0	10.1	-7.50
Michael Easterby	9-203	1-34	0-6	1-19	0-2	1-4	5-118	1-15	0-5	4.4	-104.50
Tom Dascombe	8-60	2-18	2-2	0-7	3-8	0-5	1-19	0-0	0-1	13.3	-4.30
K R Burke	8-98	3-40	0-5	0-9	2-6	0-12	2-21	1-4	0-1	8.2	-36.00
David Simcock	7-71	1-4	1-7	3-24	0-0	0-5	1-30	1-1	0-0	9.9	**36.50**
Hugo Palmer	6-66	1-21	2-10	1-11	0-3	1-6	1-15	0-0	0-0	9.1	**8.00**
Luca Cumani	6-52	2-3	1-4	1-19	0-0	1-7	0-16	1-3	0-0	11.5	-0.50
Michael Appleby	6-83	0-4	0-1	2-13	0-0	0-6	3-52	1-7	0-0	7.2	-29.25
David Barron	6-100	2-12	0-2	0-13	0-2	0-11	2-49	2-11	0-0	6.0	-33.00
David C Griffiths	5-32	0-3	0-0	3-12	1-2	0-1	1-12	0-2	0-0	15.6	**15.00**
Sir Mark Prescott Bt	5-15	1-1	0-0	3-7	0-0	0-0	0-6	1-1	0-0	33.3	**23.25**
Bryan Smart	5-50	0-9	0-3	3-9	0-2	1-3	1-23	0-1	0-0	10.0	**24.50**
Clive Cox	5-33	1-6	2-6	1-10	0-1	1-3	0-6	0-1	0-0	15.2	**26.19**

LEADING TRAINERS BY MONTH 2014-2018

JANUARY

	Total W-R	2-y-o	3-y-o	4-y-o+	Per cent	£ Level Stake
Michael Appleby	51-372	0-0	3-30	48-342	13.7	-114.39
Charlie Appleby	47-159	0-0	13-41	34-118	29.6	**14.80**
David Simcock	43-187	0-0	15-47	28-140	23.0	**39.84**
David Evans	36-320	0-0	15-113	21-207	11.3	-107.64
Mark Johnston	35-170	0-0	18-82	17-88	20.6	-42.20
Saeed bin Suroor	34-145	0-0	7-18	27-127	23.4	**5.41**
Stuart Williams	31-160	0-0	7-34	24-126	19.4	-15.84
Richard Fahey	29-258	0-0	8-65	21-193	11.2	-76.70
Tony Carroll	28-282	0-0	3-12	25-270	9.9	-62.43
Jamie Osborne	27-204	0-0	10-76	17-128	13.2	-67.91
John Gosden	24-92	0-0	14-48	10-44	26.1	-17.07
Ian Williams	20-108	0-0	0-9	20-99	18.5	**17.11**
Kevin Ryan	20-107	0-0	5-34	15-73	18.7	-17.88
Daniel Mark Loughnane	20-161	0-0	0-24	20-137	12.4	-55.21
Marco Botti	19-126	0-0	6-38	13-88	15.1	**7.85**
Andrew Balding	19-130	0-0	5-26	14-104	14.6	-53.61
Keith Dalgleish	18-110	0-0	5-19	13-91	16.4	**14.26**
Derek Shaw	18-159	0-0	3-33	15-126	11.3	-28.42
Phil McEntee	18-115	0-0	0-8	18-107	15.7	-28.88
Sir Mark Prescott Bt	16-57	0-0	5-18	11-39	28.1	**10.95**
K R Burke	16-124	0-0	6-46	10-78	12.9	**94.11**
Richard Hannon	16-127	0-0	10-67	6-60	12.6	-24.56
Michael Easterby	15-87	0-0	3-10	12-77	17.2	-7.62
Scott Dixon	15-156	0-0	0-19	15-137	9.6	-13.18
Gary Moore	15-109	0-0	0-16	15-93	13.8	-25.77
William Haggas	14-60	0-0	8-35	6-25	23.3	-15.66
J R Jenkins	14-137	0-0	1-4	13-133	10.2	-34.25
Dean Ivory	13-119	0-0	2-18	11-101	10.9	-52.38
Michael Bell	12-54	0-0	8-26	4-28	22.2	-3.63
Tom Dascombe	12-75	0-0	3-15	9-60	16.0	-5.93
Ed Walker	12-64	0-0	3-19	9-45	18.8	-6.33
John Butler	12-72	0-0	1-6	11-66	16.7	-12.64
James Tate	12-67	0-0	7-40	5-27	17.9	-19.49
Simon Dow	12-86	0-0	5-23	7-63	14.0	-26.84
David Barron	12-91	0-0	3-19	9-72	13.2	-38.78
David O'Meara	12-131	0-0	0-6	12-125	9.2	-65.15
Conor Dore	11-100	0-0	0-3	11-97	11.0	**0.25**
Neil Mulholland	11-61	0-0	1-3	10-58	18.0	**3.85**
Archie Watson	11-37	0-0	2-7	9-30	29.7	**38.63**
Robert Cowell	11-72	0-0	4-16	7-56	15.3	-2.80
Chris Dwyer	11-67	0-0	3-11	8-56	16.4	-27.97
Richard Guest	10-72	0-0	1-11	9-61	13.9	**1.20**
Ivan Furtado	10-53	0-0	3-9	7-44	18.9	**11.38**
Shaun Harris	10-90	0-0	0-2	10-88	11.1	-31.07
James Given	10-97	0-0	2-30	8-67	10.3	-40.51
Gay Kelleway	9-107	0-0	3-20	6-87	8.4	-36.58
Simon Crisford	8-39	0-0	4-16	4-23	20.5	**9.41**
Anthony Carson	8-33	0-0	1-6	7-27	24.2	**19.08**
Brian Ellison	8-59	0-0	2-9	6-50	13.6	**45.00**
William Knight	8-38	0-0	0-5	8-33	21.1	-5.86
Richard Hughes	8-47	0-0	2-12	6-35	17.0	-13.60
Iain Jardine	8-63	0-0	0-2	8-61	12.7	-15.22

FEBRUARY

	Total W-R	2-y-o	3-y-o	4-y-o+	Per cent	£ Level Stake
Michael Appleby	40-276	0-0	2-16	38-260	14.5	-53.30
David Evans	36-256	0-0	17-89	19-167	14.1	**5.06**
Saeed bin Suroor	36-141	0-0	10-27	26-114	25.5	**21.24**
Tony Carroll	35-291	0-0	2-16	33-275	12.0	-65.10
Charlie Appleby	33-171	0-0	10-48	23-123	19.3	-55.97
Richard Fahey	30-190	0-0	5-55	25-135	15.8	-20.26
Mark Johnston	30-178	0-0	12-76	18-102	16.9	-36.49
David Simcock	26-172	0-0	5-39	21-133	15.1	-58.97
Andrew Balding	22-120	0-0	10-28	12-92	18.3	-21.29
Stuart Williams	20-128	0-0	3-22	17-106	15.6	-16.66
Daniel Mark Loughnane	19-132	0-0	0-10	19-122	14.4	**29.58**
Jamie Osborne	19-141	0-0	9-65	10-76	13.5	-14.75
Ian Williams	18-113	0-0	0-4	18-109	15.9	-20.47
Marco Botti	18-125	0-0	6-32	12-93	14.4	-34.94
Gary Moore	17-96	0-0	2-9	15-87	17.7	**3.57**
Ed Walker	16-44	0-0	5-16	11-28	36.4	**21.42**
James Tate	15-69	0-0	5-26	10-43	21.7	-20.31
Ralph Beckett	14-51	0-0	6-19	8-32	27.5	**2.24**
Kevin Ryan	14-98	0-0	4-29	10-69	14.3	**51.00**
John Best	14-73	0-0	1-12	13-61	19.2	-11.10
Keith Dalgleish	14-90	0-0	6-20	8-70	15.6	-33.84
Roger Varian	13-37	0-0	5-11	8-26	35.1	**4.04**
David Barron	13-81	0-0	4-20	9-61	16.0	-10.01
John Gosden	13-60	0-0	5-28	8-32	21.7	-11.13
Tom Dascombe	12-63	0-0	1-7	11-56	19.0	-11.60
Dean Ivory	12-103	0-0	3-17	9-86	11.7	-29.37
K R Burke	11-81	0-0	1-25	10-56	13.6	**5.25**
Alan Bailey	11-62	0-0	3-10	8-52	17.7	**36.75**
Chris Dwyer	11-72	0-0	4-14	7-58	15.3	**65.88**
Simon Dow	11-74	0-0	3-8	8-66	14.9	-20.50
Richard Hannon	11-86	0-0	6-36	5-50	12.8	-34.68
Michael Easterby	10-59	0-0	2-6	8-53	16.9	**1.58**
Michael Attwater	10-108	0-0	0-10	10-98	9.3	**11.05**
Jeremy Noseda	10-28	0-0	3-6	7-22	35.7	-3.07
Neil Mulholland	10-51	0-0	0-3	10-48	19.6	-13.35
Lee Carter	10-88	0-0	0-6	10-82	11.4	-18.63
Derek Shaw	10-127	0-0	1-29	9-98	7.9	-69.13
Conor Dore	9-76	0-0	1-3	8-73	11.8	**0.37**
Mick Channon	9-76	0-0	3-27	6-49	11.8	**0.67**
Julia Feilden	9-66	0-0	3-15	6-51	13.6	**14.45**
Ronald Harris	9-90	0-0	4-14	5-76	10.0	-5.50
Archie Watson	9-42	0-0	4-6	5-36	21.4	-9.43
Clive Cox	8-37	0-0	1-7	7-30	21.6	**3.75**
Joseph Tuite	8-52	0-0	4-17	4-35	15.4	**4.12**
Charles Hills	8-56	0-0	4-22	4-34	14.3	**6.16**
Mark H Tompkins	8-46	0-0	1-14	7-32	17.4	**9.95**
Gay Kelleway	8-88	0-0	3-34	5-54	9.1	-4.05
Robert Cowell	8-53	0-0	3-14	5-39	15.1	-10.42
John Butler	8-80	0-0	3-11	5-69	10.0	-39.65
Charlie Fellowes	7-26	0-0	2-6	5-20	26.9	**9.75**
Pat Phelan	7-39	0-0	2-9	5-30	17.9	**16.00**
Sir Mark Prescott Bt	7-29	0-0	2-6	5-23	24.1	-3.78

MARCH

	Total W-R	2-y-o	3-y-o	4-y-o+	Per cent	£ Level Stake
Mark Johnston	67-288	6-9	27-115	34-164	23.3	-24.95
Michael Appleby	50-305	0-0	3-17	47-288	16.4	-2.26
Charlie Appleby	40-132	0-0	15-46	25-86	30.3	-4.80
Richard Fahey	34-234	0-4	8-63	26-167	14.5	-14.78
Andrew Balding	33-137	0-0	12-33	21-104	24.1	-36.05
Richard Hannon	26-124	1-4	9-50	16-70	21.0	**14.05**
Saeed bin Suroor	21-100	0-0	3-16	18-84	21.0	**31.42**
Tony Carroll	20-215	0-0	3-19	17-196	9.3	-116.13
Derek Shaw	18-144	0-1	2-18	16-125	12.5	**84.41**
David Barron	18-97	0-0	5-22	13-75	18.6	-12.62
Stuart Williams	18-120	0-0	0-18	18-102	15.0	-40.38
Kevin Ryan	18-122	0-1	7-36	11-85	14.8	-42.90
David Simcock	18-158	0-0	2-28	16-130	11.4	-78.03
William Haggas	17-43	0-0	5-14	12-29	39.5	**9.99**
Daniel Mark Loughnane	16-113	0-0	1-12	15-101	14.2	-11.04
Ian Williams	15-86	0-0	1-9	14-77	17.4	**18.47**
James Given	15-76	0-3	3-28	12-45	19.7	**41.49**
Phil McEntee	15-119	0-1	1-8	14-110	12.6	**71.25**
James Tate	15-69	0-0	4-31	11-38	21.7	-13.77
Ed Dunlop	15-73	0-0	6-18	9-55	20.5	-23.92
John Gosden	15-76	0-0	5-30	10-46	19.7	-29.74
Marco Botti	15-120	0-0	7-40	8-80	12.5	-44.29
Ralph Beckett	14-51	0-0	7-26	7-25	27.5	**8.88**
Conor Dore	14-74	0-0	0-2	14-72	18.9	**10.87**
John Butler	14-78	0-0	0-4	14-74	17.9	-6.83
K R Burke	14-111	0-2	8-40	6-69	12.6	-18.65
Scott Dixon	14-141	1-4	4-17	9-120	9.9	-19.17
Tom Dascombe	14-84	0-4	2-17	12-63	16.7	-21.54
David Evans	14-233	0-18	4-75	10-140	6.0	-122.67
J R Jenkins	13-113	0-0	0-4	13-109	11.5	**12.50**
Archie Watson	13-57	0-1	5-16	8-40	22.8	-3.27
Mick Channon	13-85	2-3	3-30	8-52	15.3	-26.04
Roger Varian	12-43	0-0	2-10	10-33	27.9	-0.49
Ruth Carr	12-122	0-0	1-7	11-115	9.8	-9.67
David O'Meara	12-131	1-3	4-25	7-103	9.2	-56.02
Michael Attwater	11-90	0-0	2-11	9-79	12.2	**8.11**
Alan Bailey	11-70	0-1	0-9	11-60	15.7	**17.75**
Jeremy Noseda	11-33	0-0	4-9	7-24	33.3	-5.52
Robert Cowell	11-54	0-1	6-16	5-37	20.4	-11.31
Dean Ivory	11-91	0-1	0-13	11-77	12.1	-20.88
Jamie Osborne	11-120	0-0	3-46	8-74	9.2	-72.65
David Brown	10-51	0-0	6-32	4-19	19.6	-14.32
Brian Ellison	10-89	0-1	1-10	9-78	11.2	-23.25
Chris Dwyer	10-91	0-2	4-17	6-72	11.0	-38.38
Charles Hills	9-57	0-1	6-26	3-30	15.8	**2.98**
William Knight	9-47	0-0	1-1	8-46	19.1	**17.71**
Neil Mulholland	9-42	0-0	0-0	9-42	21.4	**19.10**
Michael Easterby	9-89	0-2	0-9	9-78	10.1	-57.88
Alan Swinbank	8-40	0-0	0-2	8-38	20.0	**6.75**
Michael Bell	8-49	0-0	4-18	4-31	16.3	**6.79**
Richard Guest	8-93	0-1	1-6	7-86	8.6	-5.00
Richard Hughes	8-65	0-1	1-14	7-50	12.3	-12.02

APRIL

	Total W-R	2-y-o	3-y-o	4-y-o+	Per cent	£ Level Stake
Richard Fahey	102-601	21-80	35-201	46-320	17.0	**22.37**
John Gosden	98-319	1-1	69-229	28-89	30.7	**79.72**
Richard Hannon	83-532	16-69	39-309	28-154	15.6	-16.96
Mark Johnston	63-510	11-75	27-235	25-200	12.4	-200.99
Charlie Appleby	49-175	3-10	31-115	15-50	28.0	**20.37**
David O'Meara	48-338	2-14	7-72	39-252	14.2	-14.32
Roger Varian	43-237	0-3	18-128	25-106	18.1	-89.19
Kevin Ryan	39-320	3-28	14-110	22-182	12.2	-84.77
William Haggas	38-143	1-5	22-95	15-43	26.6	-13.29
Sir Michael Stoute	38-224	0-0	19-132	19-92	17.0	-72.10
Saeed bin Suroor	37-131	1-2	18-72	18-57	28.2	**5.71**
Ralph Beckett	37-195	1-13	22-113	14-69	19.0	**41.55**
Mick Channon	36-280	7-47	16-138	13-95	12.9	-40.90
Andrew Balding	36-270	0-0	16-126	20-144	13.3	-87.66
Michael Easterby	34-244	0-7	6-41	28-196	13.9	**23.11**
Michael Appleby	33-275	0-6	6-41	27-228	12.0	-103.04
K R Burke	32-262	2-26	6-104	24-132	12.2	**21.13**
Tom Dascombe	31-233	7-68	6-76	18-89	13.3	-2.57
David Evans	29-288	13-85	6-83	10-120	10.1	-53.40
Marco Botti	27-206	0-3	9-113	18-90	13.1	-33.15
Ruth Carr	27-263	0-2	2-18	25-243	10.3	-40.25
Michael Dods	26-184	2-14	8-55	16-115	14.1	**20.84**
Charles Hills	26-242	1-15	14-142	11-85	10.7	-73.59
Keith Dalgleish	25-206	3-21	6-51	16-134	12.1	**17.44**
Clive Cox	25-131	4-7	9-69	12-55	19.1	**34.36**
John Quinn	24-141	1-13	9-45	14-83	17.0	**23.49**
Hugo Palmer	24-118	4-18	10-61	10-39	20.3	**26.88**
Tony Carroll	23-180	0-0	1-17	22-163	12.8	-38.14
Roger Charlton	22-100	0-0	9-55	13-45	22.0	**26.12**
Tim Easterby	20-345	3-33	4-104	13-208	5.8	-133.17
Brian Ellison	19-233	2-14	6-48	11-171	8.2	-101.69
Chris Dwyer	18-102	0-5	4-21	14-76	17.6	-11.60
Rod Millman	17-135	4-22	8-49	5-64	12.6	**101.63**
Ed Dunlop	17-179	0-4	8-104	9-71	9.5	-98.69
David Barron	16-161	3-13	1-36	12-112	9.9	-87.90
Richard Guest	15-136	1-5	2-22	12-109	11.0	-18.40
Eve Johnson Houghton	15-130	0-7	5-63	10-60	11.5	-25.55
Michael Bell	15-139	0-5	8-78	7-56	10.8	-35.94
James Tate	15-104	1-15	11-56	3-33	14.4	-44.12
David Brown	14-85	3-17	5-39	6-29	16.5	**12.69**
Eric Alston	14-83	0-1	1-9	13-73	16.9	**35.00**
Gary Moore	14-106	1-1	1-11	12-94	13.2	-23.63
J R Jenkins	14-119	0-0	1-8	13-111	11.8	-25.15
Alan Swinbank	14-116	0-0	1-15	13-101	12.1	-31.17
Brian Meehan	13-86	1-9	5-43	7-34	15.1	**84.73**
William Knight	13-119	0-0	2-46	11-73	10.9	-62.56
Ed de Giles	12-61	0-0	3-17	9-44	19.7	**40.55**
William Muir	12-85	0-3	6-39	6-43	14.1	-21.88
Robert Cowell	12-104	1-7	2-20	9-77	11.5	-34.05
Daniel Mark Loughnane	12-118	0-1	1-19	11-98	10.2	-60.75
Philip Kirby	11-97	0-3	2-15	9-79	11.3	**1.00**
Paul Cole	11-94	2-8	5-40	4-46	11.7	-35.13

MAY

	Total W-R	2-y-o	3-y-o	4-y-o+	Per cent	£ Level Stake
Richard Hannon	155-925	57-233	63-460	35-232	16.8	**43.45**
Mark Johnston	133-852	45-199	53-359	35-294	15.6	-109.57
Richard Fahey	131-1032	37-224	32-312	62-496	12.7	-238.19
John Gosden	86-433	4-30	42-254	40-149	19.9	-67.02
William Haggas	77-340	9-39	37-161	31-140	22.6	-16.99
David O'Meara	76-636	6-41	16-118	54-477	11.9	-83.72
Sir Michael Stoute	72-342	0-7	35-181	37-154	21.1	-9.45
Roger Varian	63-367	5-31	20-156	38-180	17.2	-74.44
Charlie Appleby	62-284	16-60	25-138	21-86	21.8	-14.51
Ralph Beckett	57-307	9-35	23-138	25-134	18.6	-18.34
Tim Easterby	57-598	3-96	20-173	34-329	9.5	-168.35
Andrew Balding	49-462	2-28	19-183	28-251	10.6	-177.93
Charles Hills	45-363	13-79	12-153	20-131	12.4	-99.08
Mick Channon	45-475	21-120	12-186	12-169	9.5	-169.75
Clive Cox	44-275	9-49	20-115	15-111	16.0	-26.50
Kevin Ryan	43-435	14-93	14-126	15-216	9.9	-193.57
Keith Dalgleish	42-365	3-43	8-69	31-253	11.5	-93.82
Tom Dascombe	41-324	8-82	20-117	13-125	12.7	-24.58
Michael Appleby	40-374	1-16	7-55	32-303	10.7	-94.80
Saeed bin Suroor	38-195	7-18	11-86	20-91	19.5	-8.28
Robert Cowell	37-207	3-23	10-35	24-149	17.9	-4.64
Hughie Morrison	36-207	0-5	16-81	20-121	17.4	**36.56**
K R Burke	35-326	11-66	9-135	15-125	10.7	-136.45
David Evans	34-364	5-111	10-94	19-159	9.3	-74.14
Brian Ellison	31-318	3-36	8-65	20-217	9.7	-88.34
Ruth Carr	31-334	0-5	0-23	31-306	9.3	-100.43
David Barron	30-240	5-15	8-62	17-163	12.5	**10.75**
David Simcock	30-264	0-3	7-82	23-179	11.4	-29.78
Michael Bell	27-220	8-42	13-110	6-68	12.3	-29.82
Ed Dunlop	27-241	4-26	12-109	11-106	11.2	-93.52
Jim Goldie	26-272	0-4	1-14	25-254	9.6	-8.50
Hugo Palmer	26-191	3-33	12-90	11-68	13.6	-26.39
Ian Williams	24-166	0-2	3-29	21-135	14.5	**4.16**
Richard Guest	24-177	1-12	6-28	17-137	13.6	**35.50**
John Quinn	24-212	6-36	3-59	15-117	11.3	-27.64
Roger Charlton	24-183	1-6	13-92	10-85	13.1	-52.13
Michael Easterby	24-276	0-26	2-45	22-205	8.7	-89.37
Michael Dods	24-243	7-29	7-69	10-145	9.9	-97.51
Alan Swinbank	23-143	0-3	2-25	21-115	16.1	-2.51
Paul Midgley	22-223	1-23	4-30	17-170	9.9	-43.31
Eve Johnson Houghton	21-204	4-34	7-76	10-94	10.3	-42.87
Scott Dixon	20-160	2-16	3-33	15-111	12.5	**82.50**
David Elsworth	19-108	4-11	8-38	7-59	17.6	**39.21**
Paul Cole	19-136	4-21	11-54	4-61	14.0	-0.27
Marco Botti	19-266	1-20	5-108	13-138	7.1	-129.47
James Tate	18-132	3-35	7-55	8-42	13.6	-14.70
Ed Walker	18-176	1-11	4-69	13-96	10.2	-108.80
Gary Moore	17-164	2-10	3-25	12-129	10.4	-5.09
Alan King	17-108	0-1	7-37	10-70	15.7	-20.98
Brian Meehan	17-195	4-51	7-79	6-65	8.7	-34.75
Sir Mark Prescott Bt	16-82	0-9	6-36	10-37	19.5	-14.46
George Baker	16-158	0-20	2-41	14-97	10.1	-62.28

JUNE

	Total W-R	2-y-o	3-y-o	4-y-o+	Per cent	£ Level Stake
Mark Johnston	184-1033	86-313	43-343	55-377	17.8	-143.31
Richard Fahey	152-1128	36-291	38-278	78-559	13.5	-91.74
Richard Hannon	132-986	68-376	38-360	26-250	13.4	-275.57
William Haggas	86-404	17-70	31-167	38-167	21.3	-94.41
David O'Meara	83-705	8-66	12-120	63-519	11.8	-105.78
Roger Varian	78-404	10-49	25-154	43-201	19.3	-69.07
Tim Easterby	76-643	8-129	19-143	49-371	11.8	-48.58
John Gosden	74-417	10-57	32-212	32-148	17.7	-87.44
Andrew Balding	70-465	3-49	31-177	36-239	15.1	-71.70
Sir Michael Stoute	69-316	4-22	30-157	35-137	21.8	**9.05**
Ralph Beckett	55-306	9-44	15-119	31-143	18.0	-28.27
Charlie Appleby	53-318	18-93	14-105	21-120	16.7	-32.79
David Simcock	53-302	5-25	15-71	33-206	17.5	[illegible]
Mick Channon	51-481	16-135	14-151	21-195	10.6	-139.51
Keith Dalgleish	48-493	10-81	9-76	29-336	9.7	-193.32
Roger Charlton	45-191	4-20	20-82	21-89	23.6	-10.68
Ruth Carr	44-331	0-5	1-19	43-307	13.3	**30.58**
K R Burke	44-350	15-84	15-129	14-137	12.6	-67.04
Tom Dascombe	44-329	13-120	10-87	21-122	13.4	-137.25
Brian Ellison	43-376	6-56	6-57	31-263	11.4	-50.00
Charles Hills	43-361	6-93	15-126	22-142	11.9	-53.37
Saeed bin Suroor	38-231	6-25	13-77	19-129	16.5	-109.67
Jim Goldie	37-291	0-2	3-11	34-278	12.7	**25.06**
Michael Dods	37-278	6-58	14-71	17-149	13.3	-57.59
James Fanshawe	35-184	0-5	9-49	26-130	19.0	**37.22**
Michael Appleby	35-325	1-16	7-48	27-261	10.8	-73.56
Clive Cox	35-299	6-63	17-129	12-107	11.7	-76.38
Michael Easterby	33-317	1-38	8-55	24-224	10.4	-107.48
Hugo Palmer	31-191	12-51	9-71	10-69	16.2	**47.13**
Luca Cumani	30-178	0-6	7-66	23-106	16.9	-63.67
Tony Carroll	28-289	0-15	2-34	26-240	9.7	-84.89
David Evans	28-387	7-135	5-83	16-169	7.2	-195.60
Eve Johnson Houghton	27-216	7-55	7-67	13-94	12.5	**10.89**
Paul Midgley	27-216	2-23	1-14	24-179	12.5	-3.76
Ed Walker	27-203	2-26	9-74	16-103	13.3	-36.06
James Tate	27-176	10-57	8-52	9-67	15.3	-58.26
Richard Hughes	26-154	6-43	7-43	13-68	16.9	-29.09
Robert Cowell	26-215	2-32	6-37	18-146	12.1	-35.33
Hughie Morrison	26-206	1-15	11-65	14-126	12.6	-39.46
Ian Williams	26-205	0-6	2-33	24-166	12.7	-66.38
Henry Candy	25-171	5-21	11-59	9-91	14.6	**15.80**
Chris Wall	25-131	1-7	4-29	20-95	19.1	**49.56**
Dean Ivory	24-166	5-28	1-30	18-108	14.5	**144.38**
John Quinn	24-251	8-56	5-62	11-133	9.6	-46.94
Sir Mark Prescott Bt	24-157	5-39	12-65	7-53	15.3	-52.14
Marco Botti	24-231	6-47	12-88	6-96	10.4	-71.85
Rod Millman	23-160	5-31	8-50	10-79	14.4	-3.82
Sylvester Kirk	23-212	6-53	6-76	11-83	10.8	-22.64
Kevin Ryan	23-343	9-80	7-103	7-160	6.7	-138.67
Iain Jardine	21-192	2-25	1-26	18-141	10.9	**31.62**
George Baker	21-196	3-37	3-35	15-124	10.7	-15.07
Jamie Osborne	21-183	7-56	5-44	9-83	11.5	-36.92

JULY

	Total W-R	2-y-o	3-y-o	4-y-o+	Per cent	£ Level Stake
Mark Johnston	208-1071	82-355	41-220	85-496	19.4	**59.50**
Richard Hannon	152-1064	86-530	24-207	42-327	14.3	-172.87
Richard Fahey	126-1199	44-418	25-180	57-601	10.5	-350.77
William Haggas	117-440	28-98	31-127	58-215	26.6	**19.02**
David O'Meara	87-687	11-82	10-88	66-517	12.7	-186.28
Tim Easterby	81-686	8-148	22-144	51-394	11.8	-46.59
Andrew Balding	77-462	19-91	21-129	37-242	16.7	**29.68**
Roger Varian	77-330	11-59	21-75	45-196	23.3	-35.43
John Gosden	72-350	17-84	15-106	40-160	20.6	-77.45
Charlie Appleby	71-326	31-122	13-66	27-138	21.8	-26.19
Keith Dalgleish	70-481	13-92	11-48	46-341	14.6	-120.21
Kevin Ryan	66-522	32-171	14-111	20-240	12.6	-38.39
Saeed bin Suroor	62-278	11-58	11-44	40-176	22.3	-39.68
Sir Michael Stoute	61-309	2-42	18-93	41-174	19.7	-54.30
Charles Hills	56-438	15-144	9-75	32-219	12.8	-148.00
Michael Bell	52-245	12-68	11-84	29-93	21.2	**49.69**
Ralph Beckett	52-322	7-79	9-61	36-182	16.1	-83.37
K R Burke	51-354	23-142	8-74	20-138	14.4	-10.50
Sir Mark Prescott Bt	49-218	2-45	14-59	33-114	22.5	-1.16
Clive Cox	48-275	14-76	12-74	22-125	17.5	-34.09
Mick Channon	48-465	16-166	14-100	18-199	10.3	-110.82
Hugo Palmer	47-249	22-82	4-49	21-118	18.9	-21.63
Michael Dods	46-333	8-80	4-63	34-190	13.8	-54.40
Tom Dascombe	43-367	22-161	7-52	14-154	11.7	-69.19
David Evans	42-406	21-158	0-46	21-202	10.3	-84.71
Roger Charlton	41-189	4-33	9-51	28-105	21.7	-26.53
Ruth Carr	39-350	1-1	2-26	36-323	11.1	-71.85
Brian Ellison	39-326	2-46	2-30	35-250	12.0	-82.97
Luca Cumani	36-187	0-21	9-40	27-126	19.3	-40.22
John Quinn	36-283	10-84	7-52	19-147	12.7	-48.96
Hughie Morrison	35-213	0-13	3-46	32-154	16.4	**8.62**
Brian Meehan	33-225	17-107	8-49	8-69	14.7	-65.63
Michael Appleby	31-295	2-20	3-37	26-238	10.5	**4.78**
Jim Goldie	31-367	0-3	0-9	31-355	8.4	-87.37
Michael Easterby	30-301	0-49	5-33	25-219	10.0	-99.47
Eve Johnson Houghton	29-227	4-68	7-53	18-106	12.8	-61.95
Iain Jardine	28-205	3-23	2-14	23-168	13.7	-16.20
James Tate	28-159	13-64	1-23	14-72	17.6	-44.27
Sylvester Kirk	27-214	6-61	10-56	11-97	12.6	-43.51
Paul Midgley	27-250	0-29	1-22	26-199	10.8	-72.63
David Simcock	27-271	0-25	9-53	18-193	10.0	-88.53
Marco Botti	26-206	7-57	4-43	15-106	12.6	-36.29
Ed Walker	25-199	1-43	1-31	23-125	12.6	-90.22
Marcus Tregoning	23-124	3-20	5-38	15-66	18.5	-16.90
Bryan Smart	23-182	8-60	4-29	11-93	12.6	-50.63
Stuart Williams	23-196	2-22	3-39	18-135	11.7	-53.78
Archie Watson	22-88	13-44	2-7	7-37	25.0	-5.72
Rod Millman	22-170	3-39	4-28	15-103	12.9	-22.75
David Barron	22-198	4-42	6-32	12-124	11.1	-65.96
James Fanshawe	22-171	0-13	5-26	17-132	12.9	-74.61
Ed Dunlop	22-243	8-69	3-46	11-128	9.1	-126.68
Simon Crisford	21-119	8-44	3-20	10-55	17.6	-33.57

AUGUST

	Total W-R	2-y-o	3-y-o	4-y-o+	Per cent	£ Level Stake
Richard Hannon	158-1079	106-591	13-154	39-334	14.6	-274.71
Richard Fahey	152-1182	65-457	21-150	66-575	12.9	-207.32
Mark Johnston	127-922	62-352	12-160	53-410	13.8	-284.52
William Haggas	96-434	26-136	28-105	42-193	22.1	-28.79
David O'Meara	93-697	12-94	15-92	66-511	13.3	-186.71
Sir Michael Stoute	82-397	18-99	13-73	51-225	20.7	-100.79
John Gosden	80-304	19-92	13-58	48-154	26.3	**58.84**
Andrew Balding	77-477	24-125	18-80	35-272	16.1	**2.48**
Kevin Ryan	71-511	27-192	14-100	30-219	13.9	-55.73
Tim Easterby	71-724	14-198	13-121	44-405	9.8	-219.90
Charlie Appleby	68-326	40-154	15-68	13-104	20.9	-67.75
Mick Channon	67-504	24-212	14-103	29-189	13.3	-43.79
Charles Hills	62-413	25-170	9-49	28-194	15.0	-70.01
K R Burke	58-364	31-172	8-51	19-141	15.9	**52.29**
Keith Dalgleish	55-433	14-117	6-53	35-263	12.7	-29.38
Michael Dods	53-385	23-115	6-52	24-218	13.8	-95.14
David Simcock	52-309	12-56	3-39	37-214	16.8	-10.43
Sir Mark Prescott Bt	49-211	11-62	10-35	28-114	23.2	-32.61
Ralph Beckett	48-310	11-100	5-50	32-160	15.5	-47.34
Roger Varian	47-321	7-71	3-41	37-209	14.6	-121.04
Michael Bell	45-279	19-91	13-74	13-114	16.1	-104.49
Saeed bin Suroor	44-213	11-54	3-16	30-143	20.7	-53.26
Luca Cumani	43-203	8-39	10-44	25-120	21.2	-28.16
John Quinn	41-288	12-94	7-43	22-151	14.2	-24.82
Tom Dascombe	39-333	23-172	4-39	12-122	11.7	**20.36**
Eve Johnson Houghton	39-256	9-71	8-50	22-135	15.2	**21.34**
Hugo Palmer	38-227	14-88	3-23	21-116	16.7	-14.81
Michael Appleby	38-318	1-24	7-37	30-257	11.9	-25.38
Henry Candy	37-181	7-42	5-25	25-114	20.4	**34.33**
David Evans	36-396	17-154	1-36	18-206	9.1	-117.07
Hughie Morrison	35-233	6-39	3-45	26-149	15.0	-30.14
Clive Cox	35-301	11-101	6-48	18-152	11.6	-112.36
Sylvester Kirk	34-225	13-78	7-57	14-90	15.1	**12.71**
Brian Ellison	34-302	2-59	5-28	27-215	11.3	-89.54
Tony Carroll	33-295	3-25	3-15	27-255	11.2	-20.63
Marco Botti	32-234	14-88	3-35	15-111	13.7	**14.88**
Gary Moore	32-231	4-39	7-30	21-162	13.9	**51.93**
Ruth Carr	32-341	1-3	1-27	30-311	9.4	-67.40
Paul Midgley	31-224	2-29	2-21	27-174	13.8	**11.23**
Chris Wall	31-157	0-14	12-37	19-106	19.7	-19.88
James Tate	30-173	13-78	4-11	13-84	17.3	-11.83
Iain Jardine	30-201	2-22	3-23	25-156	14.9	-22.45
William Muir	28-200	8-53	5-40	15-107	14.0	-24.50
Nigel Tinkler	27-209	5-64	10-39	12-106	12.9	**13.25**
James Fanshawe	27-188	1-18	6-26	20-144	14.4	-42.92
David Barron	27-246	4-45	7-36	16-165	11.0	-54.33
Ed Dunlop	27-237	9-86	6-34	12-117	11.4	-84.65
Roger Charlton	27-200	8-56	4-41	15-103	13.5	-114.74
Archie Watson	26-103	20-57	1-11	5-35	25.2	**19.20**
Brian Meehan	26-190	9-97	7-27	10-66	13.7	-28.66
Simon Crisford	25-121	10-52	3-14	12-55	20.7	**56.37**
George Baker	25-161	4-32	1-14	20-115	15.5	**100.46**

SEPTEMBER

	Total W-R	2-y-o	3-y-o	4-y-o+	Per cent	£ Level Stake
Richard Fahey	109-1105	48-453	13-65	48-587	9.9	-251.84
Mark Johnston	106-821	54-386	12-83	40-352	12.9	-270.33
William Haggas	105-466	41-203	15-69	49-194	22.5	**0.51**
Richard Hannon	96-932	65-591	3-71	28-270	10.3	-360.09
John Gosden	93-380	47-173	6-36	40-171	24.5	**39.48**
Saeed bin Suroor	79-291	26-100	4-17	49-174	27.1	**14.05**
Roger Varian	74-385	28-152	9-33	37-200	19.2	-5.27
Andrew Balding	74-464	17-146	11-72	46-246	15.9	-103.73
Charlie Appleby	71-325	50-198	7-33	14-94	21.8	-98.13
Sir Michael Stoute	64-370	25-158	8-52	31-160	17.3	-94.08
Kevin Ryan	61-438	29-189	5-37	27-212	13.9	-29.12
David O'Meara	61-609	7-90	4-33	50-486	10.0	-157.54
Mick Channon	55-441	26-218	7-53	22-170	12.5	-69.98
Clive Cox	52-290	24-106	7-34	21-150	17.9	**107.69**
Hugo Palmer	52-277	23-136	9-18	20-123	18.8	-32.39
Sir Mark Prescott Bt	51-251	12-107	6-30	33-114	20.3	-31.09
Tim Easterby	50-645	9-203	8-40	33-402	7.8	-230.40
Ralph Beckett	49-317	26-151	6-26	17-140	15.5	**20.86**
K R Burke	44-393	23-196	0-30	21-167	11.2	-95.50
Keith Dalgleish	44-406	11-112	5-37	28-257	10.8	-110.28
Charles Hills	42-405	20-193	2-27	20-185	10.4	-175.80
David Simcock	41-259	10-75	4-25	27-159	15.8	-47.84
Roger Charlton	37-211	14-72	4-35	19-104	17.5	**31.85**
James Fanshawe	37-219	4-31	5-21	28-167	16.9	-18.99
Luca Cumani	35-197	11-56	4-19	20-122	17.8	-8.16
Tom Dascombe	34-332	19-177	1-13	14-142	10.2	**10.85**
Hughie Morrison	33-252	6-56	4-30	23-166	13.1	-52.98
Ian Williams	32-172	1-14	6-23	25-135	18.6	**12.32**
Michael Dods	32-298	8-93	4-29	20-176	10.7	-59.45
Ed Walker	31-230	14-97	0-19	17-114	13.5	-42.83
Simon Crisford	27-132	15-76	3-10	9-46	20.5	**14.75**
Tony Carroll	27-249	0-24	1-9	26-216	10.8	-55.59
David Evans	27-298	14-138	3-27	10-133	9.1	-81.40
Michael Appleby	27-276	1-38	1-16	25-222	9.8	-89.08
Henry Candy	26-198	9-62	3-28	14-108	13.1	-34.20
George Baker	25-171	2-38	0-11	23-122	14.6	-13.79
Brian Ellison	25-253	5-50	1-12	19-191	9.9	-26.22
Jamie Osborne	24-182	6-70	0-14	18-98	13.2	-29.38
Sylvester Kirk	24-208	9-74	4-41	11-93	11.5	-41.13
John Quinn	24-258	9-104	0-13	15-141	9.3	-113.44
Gary Moore	23-176	1-38	2-23	20-115	13.1	**5.25**
Archie Watson	23-106	13-55	2-8	8-43	21.7	-2.75
Ed Dunlop	23-273	9-119	3-19	11-135	8.4	-91.88
Marco Botti	22-216	14-98	1-28	7-90	10.2	-83.71
David Elsworth	20-120	7-42	1-11	12-67	16.7	**13.08**
Robert Cowell	20-164	7-48	1-6	12-110	12.2	-14.57
Iain Jardine	19-185	1-22	3-17	15-146	10.3	-17.67
Paul Midgley	19-209	2-23	0-5	17-181	9.1	-35.50
Eve Johnson Houghton	19-218	3-81	5-33	11-104	8.7	-55.52
Jim Goldie	19-256	0-7	0-8	19-241	7.4	-77.80
William Knight	18-139	4-27	1-13	13-99	12.9	-2.88
David Barron	18-195	5-32	1-11	12-152	9.2	-8.07

OCTOBER

	Total W-R	2-y-o	3-y-o	4-y-o+	Per cent	£ Level Stake
Richard Fahey	95-868	49-342	7-50	39-476	10.9	-213.22
John Gosden	89-462	53-258	4-33	32-171	19.3	-74.55
Richard Hannon	76-758	50-507	5-27	21-224	10.0	-221.44
Saeed bin Suroor	72-295	38-133	3-19	31-143	24.4	-13.46
William Haggas	65-409	36-223	4-30	25-156	15.9	-96.23
Mark Johnston	64-669	29-365	3-53	32-251	9.6	-118.91
Roger Varian	53-367	26-193	4-23	23-151	14.4	-34.14
Charlie Appleby	51-236	27-143	5-13	19-80	21.6	**11.77**
Charles Hills	47-343	21-176	1-16	25-151	13.7	**15.09**
Ralph Beckett	47-300	27-143	5-23	15-134	15.7	-57.90
David O'Meara	45-509	3-69	5-22	37-418	8.8	-152.72
Sir Michael Stoute	41-269	28-144	1-12	12-113	15.2	-57.43
Andrew Balding	40-369	16-138	2-30	22-201	10.8	**35.81**
Mick Channon	39-367	21-194	3-26	15-147	10.6	-7.70
Hugo Palmer	39-244	24-135	2-15	13-94	16.0	-28.37
Keith Dalgleish	34-330	15-110	2-11	17-209	10.3	-1.00
Ed Walker	33-215	18-92	2-13	13-110	15.3	**19.09**
Roger Charlton	33-209	14-93	2-15	17-101	15.8	-21.76
K R Burke	33-303	16-143	3-33	14-127	10.9	-43.13
Michael Appleby	33-361	5-55	3-12	25-294	9.1	-43.62
Marco Botti	33-256	16-135	4-16	13-105	12.9	-63.16
Hughie Morrison	31-263	7-80	3-28	21-155	11.8	-53.72
Tim Easterby	31-445	7-127	0-19	24-299	7.0	-200.25
Luca Cumani	30-174	10-70	2-16	18-88	17.2	**8.82**
Tom Dascombe	30-240	20-131	0-15	10-94	12.5	-24.48
James Fanshawe	30-184	7-40	5-13	18-131	16.3	-25.45
Kevin Ryan	29-299	12-114	2-19	15-166	9.7	-88.40
Sir Mark Prescott Bt	27-244	7-131	1-8	19-105	11.1	-87.55
Ian Williams	26-177	0-17	1-10	25-150	14.7	-9.40
Clive Cox	24-251	11-111	1-15	12-125	9.6	-93.11
David Simcock	23-227	10-102	3-14	10-111	10.1	-65.47
Jamie Osborne	22-136	8-64	1-3	13-69	16.2	**9.75**
Simon Crisford	22-96	10-51	1-3	11-42	22.9	**10.68**
William Muir	22-158	8-61	1-12	13-85	13.9	**71.83**
David Evans	22-291	8-123	0-14	14-154	7.6	-108.52
Gary Moore	21-197	6-49	0-6	15-142	10.7	**10.19**
Michael Easterby	20-264	5-54	0-5	15-205	7.6	-4.87
James Tate	20-146	9-69	0-5	11-72	13.7	-9.87
Henry Candy	20-145	5-44	0-5	15-96	13.8	-10.32
John Quinn	20-200	7-91	1-9	12-100	10.0	-33.60
Harry Dunlop	18-136	8-66	1-7	9-63	13.2	**26.84**
Paul Cole	18-149	7-66	2-11	9-72	12.1	-32.87
Richard Guest	18-206	1-40	0-5	17-161	8.7	-43.50
Michael Bell	18-197	7-101	1-26	10-70	9.1	-109.79
Michael Dods	17-221	7-67	1-6	9-148	7.7	-84.25
Eve Johnson Houghton	16-158	6-53	1-14	9-91	10.1	-17.38
Richard Hughes	16-130	7-67	0-4	9-59	12.3	-43.72
Tony Carroll	16-249	0-25	1-11	15-213	6.4	-122.13
Stuart Williams	15-150	4-49	0-8	11-93	10.0	-55.41
Marcus Tregoning	14-115	2-32	4-18	8-65	12.2	**2.05**
Charlie Fellowes	14-100	3-41	0-4	11-55	14.0	-37.58
Robert Cowell	14-187	4-60	0-2	10-125	7.5	-70.24

NOVEMBER

	Total W-R	2-y-o	3-y-o	4-y-o+	Per cent	£ Level Stake
John Gosden	57-274	43-196	1-9	13-69	20.8	-27.48
Charlie Appleby	40-119	22-71	2-3	16-45	33.6	**29.57**
Richard Fahey	38-369	16-147	1-8	21-214	10.3	-95.26
William Haggas	36-153	23-92	0-4	13-57	23.5	-31.23
Saeed bin Suroor	33-132	19-71	1-1	13-60	25.0	-20.95
Ralph Beckett	31-157	16-90	3-7	12-60	19.7	**43.63**
Roger Varian	29-155	13-96	1-4	15-55	18.7	-0.18
Jamie Osborne	28-178	15-97	2-3	11-78	15.7	**14.94**
David O'Meara	28-268	3-45	0-0	25-223	10.4	-68.30
Michael Appleby	28-309	2-41	0-3	26-265	9.1	-113.75
Richard Hannon	27-240	19-163	0-7	8-70	11.3	-54.34
Mark Johnston	26-249	16-158	1-5	9-86	10.4	-101.85
Andrew Balding	24-182	8-72	0-6	16-104	13.2	-43.61
David Evans	23-198	8-78	0-3	15-117	11.6	-69.25
Marco Botti	19-169	11-78	2-6	6-85	11.2	-41.55
Roger Charlton	18-97	7-63	0-2	11-32	18.6	**16.31**
Clive Cox	18-107	11-58	2-7	5-42	16.8	-6.63
Dean Ivory	18-126	1-21	0-2	17-103	14.3	-10.13
Hugo Palmer	18-94	5-49	0-3	13-42	19.1	-19.10
Stuart Williams	17-105	2-27	2-3	13-75	16.2	**15.35**
Richard Guest	17-124	0-24	1-2	16-98	13.7	-31.55
Richard Hughes	16-103	7-50	1-1	8-52	15.5	-9.60
Paul Cole	14-75	8-44	1-1	5-30	18.7	**25.65**
K R Burke	14-147	5-54	0-8	9-85	9.5	**42.19**
David Simcock	14-99	8-50	0-2	6-47	14.1	-3.09
Keith Dalgleish	14-155	3-41	0-3	11-111	9.0	-34.63
James Fanshawe	14-99	1-33	1-5	12-61	14.1	-38.33
Simon Crisford	13-68	6-38	0-1	7-29	19.1	-8.20
Michael Easterby	13-125	1-26	0-3	12-96	10.4	-17.50
Tony Carroll	13-155	0-12	1-3	12-140	8.4	-46.00
Kevin Ryan	11-103	1-30	1-3	9-70	10.7	-14.05
Sylvester Kirk	12-118	4-48	1-7	7-63	10.2	**28.25**
William Muir	11-59	4-22	0-2	7-35	18.6	**1.65**
Tom Dascombe	11-77	2-27	0-0	9-50	14.3	-18.93
Sir Mark Prescott Bt	11-95	5-53	0-4	6-38	11.6	-23.70
Ed Walker	11-107	7-70	1-2	3-35	10.3	-28.90
John Ryan	10-81	5-18	0-5	5-58	12.3	**32.50**
Brendan Powell	10-59	1-5	1-2	8-52	16.9	**88.55**
Jim Goldie	10-79	1-2	0-1	9-76	12.7	-0.62
Rae Guest	10-61	2-20	0-3	8-38	16.4	-7.00
Luca Cumani	10-67	3-31	0-3	7-33	14.9	-16.40
Jeremy Noseda	9-34	2-19	1-3	6-12	26.5	**0.02**
Michael Bell	9-80	6-49	0-4	3-27	11.3	**44.85**
James Tate	9-65	6-48	0-0	3-17	13.8	-1.17
Sir Michael Stoute	9-73	6-51	0-2	3-20	12.3	-19.17
David Elsworth	8-53	1-21	0-0	7-32	15.1	**4.75**
Roger Fell	8-78	1-12	1-2	6-64	10.3	**6.13**
Declan Carroll	8-59	2-9	0-1	6-49	13.6	**13.37**
Archie Watson	8-74	2-33	0-1	6-40	10.8	-40.38
Tim Easterby	8-112	4-34	0-1	4-77	7.1	-43.92
Hughie Morrison	8-117	1-57	0-3	7-57	6.8	-64.00
Scott Dixon	8-146	0-27	0-1	8-118	5.5	-76.05

DECEMBER

	Total W-R	2-y-o	3-y-o	4-y-o+	Per cent	£ Level Stake
John Gosden	38-142	31-118	0-1	7-23	26.8	-22.80
Michael Appleby	37-343	3-29	1-13	33-301	10.8	-130.19
David Evans	27-222	8-84	3-6	16-132	12.2	-51.17
Charlie Appleby	26-88	10-48	0-0	16-40	29.5	**4.01**
Richard Fahey	24-244	6-92	0-6	18-146	9.8	-11.00
Richard Hannon	24-191	20-130	0-5	4-56	12.6	-43.48
David O'Meara	22-188	0-34	0-4	22-150	11.7	-21.40
Jamie Osborne	22-172	10-77	0-6	12-89	12.8	-27.23
David Simcock	20-93	9-25	0-0	11-68	21.5	**70.89**
Simon Dow	20-94	5-20	0-4	15-70	21.3	**89.87**
Stuart Williams	18-117	2-19	0-1	16-97	15.4	-10.50
William Haggas	17-68	11-44	0-3	6-21	25.0	**4.94**
Saeed bin Suroor	17-47	8-28	0-0	9-19	36.2	**8.26**
Tony Carroll	17-182	0-11	0-3	17-168	9.3	-37.31
Scott Dixon	16-177	2-30	1-4	13-143	9.0	**60.88**
Andrew Balding	16-111	1-35	1-4	14-72	14.4	-49.33
Archie Watson	15-78	3-23	2-4	10-51	19.2	**5.72**
Mark Johnston	15-126	8-67	1-5	6-54	11.9	-38.68
Marco Botti	15-135	6-64	0-0	9-71	11.1	-75.09
Richard Hughes	14-75	6-32	0-2	8-41	18.7	-14.54
Ian Williams	14-114	0-12	3-7	11-95	12.3	-16.86
Gay Kelleway	13-98	4-18	0-4	9-76	13.3	-14.67
Dean Ivory	13-120	2-12	1-4	10-104	10.8	-27.50
Milton Bradley	12-70	0-3	0-0	12-67	17.1	**15.60**
Roger Varian	12-64	6-36	0-3	6-25	18.8	-25.42
Ralph Beckett	12-76	10-55	0-1	2-20	15.8	-31.03
J R Jenkins	11-105	1-7	0-1	10-97	10.5	**50.80**
Michael Easterby	11-87	2-18	0-2	9-67	12.6	-6.60
Derek Shaw	11-115	1-16	0-0	10-99	9.6	-30.50
Gary Moore	11-107	0-17	2-4	9-86	10.3	-50.00
Keith Dalgleish	10-78	2-10	0-0	8-68	12.8	**16.75**
James Tate	10-65	7-47	0-0	3-18	15.4	-18.48
Clive Cox	10-76	3-39	0-2	7-35	13.2	-19.75
Julia Feilden	9-70	1-6	0-6	8-58	12.9	**2.50**
Tom Dascombe	9-66	1-14	1-3	7-49	13.6	**3.57**
Ivan Furtado	9-70	3-12	0-2	6-56	12.9	-7.37
K R Burke	9-84	4-35	1-4	4-45	10.7	-30.11
Kevin Ryan	8-56	1-17	0-1	7-38	14.3	**8.33**
Neil Mulholland	8-36	0-5	0-2	8-29	22.2	**43.25**
Daniel Mark Loughnane	8-132	0-20	1-9	7-103	6.1	-7.00
Hugo Palmer	8-46	6-31	0-0	2-15	17.4	-9.78
Michael Bell	8-49	2-24	1-1	5-24	16.3	-23.95
George Margarson	7-41	1-5	0-0	6-36	17.1	**3.25**
Charlie Fellowes	7-37	2-13	0-1	5-23	18.9	**6.23**
Hughie Morrison	7-61	4-37	1-5	2-19	11.5	**7.50**
David Elsworth	7-32	3-19	0-0	4-13	21.9	**14.35**
Alan King	7-28	0-2	0-1	7-25	25.0	**20.25**
Sir Mark Prescott Bt	7-48	2-22	0-3	5-23	14.6	-4.00
Amanda Perrett	7-43	4-15	1-4	2-24	16.3	-8.93
John Butler	7-66	1-13	0-1	6-52	10.6	-11.50
Iain Jardine	7-54	0-5	1-4	6-45	13.0	-12.27
Ed Walker	7-68	2-37	0-1	5-30	10.3	-12.63

Season Statistics Trainers - GB Flat 2018 (Jan 1-Dec 31)

NAME	WINS-RUNS	%	2ND	3RD	4TH	WIN PRIZE	TOTAL PRIZE	£1 STAKE
J Gosden	177-705	25%	131	91	69	£6,628,123	£8,511,288	-58.66
A P O'Brien	24-229	10%	20	37	24	£3,534,704	£6,276,315	-107.66
Sir Michael Stoute	77-426	18%	87	49	52	£2,760,039	£4,569,453	-135.28
M Johnston	226-1440	16%	194	203	200	£2,357,974	£4,329,621	-339.17
C Appleby	88-313	28%	55	40	32	£2,821,438	£3,735,625	-17.32
R Fahey	190-1599	12%	200	191	184	£2,067,729	£3,377,935	-249.92
R Hannon	172-1401	12%	191	161	151	£1,859,206	£3,183,585	-345.26
W Haggas	145-657	22%	105	79	83	£2,151,803	£3,060,943	-109.22
A Balding	123-772	16%	104	107	94	£1,418,462	£2,600,151	-59.03
R Varian	107-603	18%	108	83	77	£1,302,677	£2,041,332	-110.45
D O'Meara	113-1074	11%	151	110	126	£741,205	£1,912,467	-298.78
D Simcock	57-470	12%	75	58	61	£998,503	£1,690,564	-150.51
K A Ryan	76-620	12%	82	79	65	£848,043	£1,627,892	-97.18
T Easterby	118-1085	11%	127	112	99	£944,581	£1,525,376	-174.87
R Beckett	88-522	17%	89	62	54	£881,765	£1,310,293	-78.51
C Hills	62-541	11%	59	59	69	£737,104	£1,281,828	-72.59
H Palmer	87-508	17%	61	55	64	£802,559	£1,165,920	+18.57
K Burke	70-634	11%	89	81	64	£600,753	£1,141,681	-65.80
Clive Cox	68-486	14%	71	45	52	£637,906	£1,126,565	-82.15
A Watson	105-528	20%	88	67	50	£734,873	£1,108,646	-73.48
D Elsworth	28-161	17%	23	14	15	£712,957	£1,077,780	+0.25
M Channon	92-679	14%	69	102	82	£622,534	£1,058,276	-117.15
S Crisford	70-337	21%	69	47	39	£542,653	£1,023,318	-30.11
T Dascombe	77-494	16%	66	66	61	£633,829	£1,019,457	+132.24
I Williams	66-449	15%	50	51	45	£655,714	£1,006,764	-66.16
S bin Suroor	84-384	22%	66	54	42	£628,883	£944,596	-94.19
M Appleby	94-790	12%	99	97	80	£562,270	£933,447	-158.51
Eve Johnson Houghton	37-373	10%	43	49	31	£633,427	£852,282	-152.91
K Dalgleish	73-735	10%	70	93	90	£491,399	£849,118	-96.59
M Dods	52-445	12%	52	52	43	£436,866	£827,250	-65.64
E Walker	61-487	13%	77	63	64	£385,653	£820,242	-179.74
J Fanshawe	38-308	12%	55	43	43	£491,359	£808,722	-108.03
W Mullins	6-30	20%	4	1	2	£525,902	£803,564	+3.75
S C Williams	58-424	14%	59	54	46	£427,564	£727,042	-79.26
R Charlton	48-307	16%	29	36	28	£444,679	£716,839	-76.54
J Goldie	42-399	11%	44	44	39	£442,604	£694,034	+18.83
H Morrison	44-394	11%	41	46	51	£384,292	£688,838	-112.48
Michael Bell	56-379	15%	44	51	42	£402,362	£679,332	-75.64
R G Fell	56-473	12%	48	45	47	£468,722	£667,835	-34.57
M Botti	34-373	9%	53	44	68	£402,730	£657,841	-111.90
Mrs J Harrington	3-16	19%	2	1	0	£452,971	£620,670	-7.56
J J Quinn	45-394	11%	38	51	31	£429,170	£617,839	-10.09
R Hughes	62-456	14%	69	71	53	£326,552	£589,633	-135.02
P Midgley	39-408	10%	36	47	45	£346,938	£589,362	-97.03
D Ivory	39-359	11%	37	36	29	£382,474	£567,535	-54.28

Course Records

ASCOT

Distance	Time	Age	Weight	Going	Horse	Date
5f	58.80	2	9-1	Good To Firm	No Nay Never	Jun 20 2013
5f	57.44	6	9-1	Good To Firm	Miss Andretti	Jun 19 2007
6f	1m 12.39	2	9-1	Good To Firm	Rajasinghe	Jun 20 2017
6f	1m 11.05	3	9-1	Good To Firm	Blue Point	May 3 2017
7f	1m 26.55	2	9-0	Good To Firm	Malabar	Jly 25 2014
7f	1m 24.28	4	8-11	Good To Firm	Galician	Jly 27 2013
7f 213y	1m 39.55	2	8-12	Good	Joshua Tree	Sep 26 2009
7f 213y	1m 35.89	3	9-0	Good To Firm	Alpha Centauri	Jun 22 2018
1m	1m 36.60	4	9-0	Good To Firm	Ribchester	Jun 20 2017
1m 1f 212y	2m 1.90	5	8-11	Good To Firm	The Fugue	Jun 18 2014
1m 3f 211y	2m 24.60	4	9-7	Good To Firm	Novellist	Jly 27 2013
1m 7f 209y	3m 24.12	4	8-12	Good To Firm	Mizzou	Apr 29 2015
2m 3f 210y	4m 16.92	6	9-2	Good To Firm	Rite of Passage	Jun 17 2010
2m 5f 143y	4m 45.24	9	9-2	Good To Firm	Pallasator	Jun 23 2018

AYR

Distance	Time	Age	Weight	Going	Horse	Date
5f	56.98	2	8-11	Good	Boogie Street	Sep 18 2003
5f	55.68	3	8-11	Good To Firm	Look Busy	Jun 21 2008
6f	1m 9.73	2	7-10	Firm	Sir Bert	Sep 17 1969
6f	1m 8.37	5	8-6	Good To Firm	Maison Dieu	Jun 21 2008
7f 50y	1m 28.99	2	9-0	Good	Tafaahum	Sep 19 2003
7f 50y	1m 26.43	4	9-4	Good To Firm	Hajjam	May 22 2018
1m	1m 39.18	2	9-7	Good	Moonlightnavigator	Sep 18 2014
1m	1m 36.00	4	7-13	Firm	Sufi I	Sep 16 1959
1m 1f 20y	1m 50.30	4	9-3	Good	Retirement	Sep 19 2003
1m 2f	2m 4.02	4	9-9	Good To Firm	Endless Hall	Jly 17 2000
1m 5f 26y	2m 45.81	4	9-7	Good To Firm	Eden's Close	Sep 18 1993
1m 7f	3m 13.16	3	9-4	Good	Romany Rye	Sep 19 1991
2m 1f 105y	3m 45.20	4	6-13	Firm	Curry	Sep 16 1955

BATH

Distance	Time	Age	Weight	Going	Horse	Date
5f 10y	59.50	2	9-2	Firm	Amour Propre	Jly 24 2008
5f 10y	58.75	3	8-12	Firm	Enticing	May 1 2007
5f 160y	1m 8.70	2	8-12	Firm	Qalahari	Jly 24 2008
5f 160y	1m 8.10	6	9-0	Firm	Madraco	May 22 1989
1m 5y	1m 39.51	2	9-2	Firm	Natural Charm	Sep 14 2014
1m 5y	1m 37.20	5	8-12	Good To Firm	Adobe	Jun 17 2000
1m 5y	1m 37.20	3	8-7	Firm	Alasha	Aug 18 2002
1m 2f 37y	2m 5.80	3	9-0	Good To Firm	Connoisseur Bay	May 29 1998
1m 3f 137y	2m 25.74	3	9-0	Hard	Top The Charts	Sep 8 2005
1m 5f 11y	2m 47.20	4	10-0	Firm	Flown	Aug 13 1991
2m 1f 24y	3m 43.41	6	7-9	Firm	Yaheska	Jun 14 2003

BEVERLEY

Distance	Time	Age	Weight	Going	Horse	Date
5f	1m 0.89	2	8-12	Good To Firm	Langavat	Jun 8 2013
5f	59.77	5	9-3	Good To Firm	Judicial	Jun 20 2017
7f 96y	1m 31.10	2	9-7	Good To Firm	Champagne Prince	Aug 10 1995
7f 96y	1m 31.10	2	9-0	Firm	Majal	Jly 30 1991
7f 96y	1m 29.50	3	7-8	Firm	Who's Tef	Jly 30 1991
1m 100y	1m 43.30	2	9-0	Firm	Arden	Sep 24 1986
1m 100y	1m 42.20	3	8-4	Firm	Legal Case	Jun 14 1989
1m 1f 207y	2m 1.00	3	9-7	Good To Firm	Eastern Aria	Aug 29 2009
1m 4f 23y	2m 33.35	5	9-2	Good To Firm	Two Jabs	Apr 23 2015
2m 32y	3m 28.62	4	9-11	Good To Firm	Corpus Chorister	Jly 18 2017

BRIGHTON

Distance	Time	Age	Weight	Going	Horse	Date
5f 60y	1m 0.10	2	9-0	Firm	Bid for Blue	May 6 1993
5f 60y	59.30	3	8-9	Firm	Play Hever Golf	May 26 1993
5f 215y	1m 8.10	2	8-9	Firm	Song Mist	Jly 16 1996
5f 215y	1m 7.30	5	9-1	Good To Firm	Blundell Lane	May 4 2000
5f 215y	1m 7.30	3	8-9	Firm	Third Party	Jun 3 1997
6f 210y	1m 19.90	2	8-11	Hard	Rain Burst	Sep 15 1988
6f 210y	1m 19.40	4	9-3	Good To Firm	Sawaki	Sep 3 1991
7f 211y	1m 32.80	2	9-7	Firm	Asian Pete	Oct 3 1989
7f 211y	1m 30.50	5	8-11	Firm	Mystic Ridge	May 27 1999
1m 1f 207y	2m 4.70	2	9-0	Good To Soft	Esteemed Master	Nov 2 2001
1m 1f 207y	1m 57.20	3	9-0	Firm	Get The Message	Apr 30 1984
1m 3f 198y	2m 25.80	4	8-2	Firm	New Zealand	Jly 4 1985

CARLISLE

Distance	Time	Age	Weight	Going	Horse	Date
5f	1m 0.10	2	8-5	Firm	La Tortuga	Aug 2 1999
5f	58.80	3	9-8	Good To Firm	Esatto	Aug 21 2002
5f 193y	1m 12.30	2	9-2	Good To Firm	Burrishoole Abbey	Jun 22 2016
5f 193y	1m 10.83	4	9-0	Good To Firm	Bo McGinty	Sep 11 2005
6f 195y	1m 24.30	3	8-9	Good To Firm	Marjurita	Aug 21 2002
7f 173y	1m 35.84	5	8-12	Good To Firm	Waarif	Jun 27 2018
1m 1f	1m 53.84	3	9-0	Firm	Little Jimbob	Jun 14 2004
1m 3f 39y	2m 20.46	5	10-0	Good To Firm	Aasheq	Jun 27 2018
1m 6f 32y	3m 2.20	6	8-10	Firm	Explosive Speed	May 26 1994
2m 1f 47y	3m 46.20	3	7-10	Good To Firm	Warring Kingdom	Aug 25 1999

CATTERICK

Distance	Time	Age	Weight	Going	Horse	Date
5f	57.60	2	9-0	Firm	H Harrison	Oct 8 2002
5f	57.10	4	8-7	Firm	Kabcast	Jly 6 1989
5f 212y	1m 11.40	2	9-4	Firm	Captain Nick	Jly 11 1978
5f 212y	1m 9.86	9	8-13	Good To Firm	Sharp Hat	May 30 2003
7f 6y	1m 24.10	2	8-11	Firm	Linda's Fantasy	Sep 18 1982
7f 6y	1m 22.56	6	8-7	Firm	Differential	May 31 2003
1m 4f 13y	2m 30.50	3	8-8	Good To Firm	Rahaf	May 30 2003
1m 5f 192y	2m 54.80	3	8-5	Firm	Geryon	May 31 1984
1m 7f 189y	3m 20.80	4	7-11	Firm	Bean Boy I	Jly 8 1982

CHELMSFORD (A.W)

Distance	Time	Age	Weight	Going	Horse	Date
5f	58.52	2	9-6	Standard	Prince Of Rome	Sep 20 2018
5f	57.30	7	8-13	Standard	Brother Tiger	Feb 7 2016
6f	1m 11.19	2	8-13	Standard	Florencio	Oct 15 2015
6f	1m 10.00	4	9-2	Standard	Raucous	Apr 27 2017
7f	1m 22.59	7	8-0	Standard	Boy In The Bar	Sep 22 2018
1m	1m 37.15	2	9-3	Standard	Dragon Mall	Sep 26 2015
1m	1m 35.46	4	9-7	Standard	Mindurownbusiness	Nov 23 2015
1m 2f	2m 2.33	8	9-7	Standard	Bancnuanaheireann	Nov 5 2015
1m 5f 66y	2m 47.00	4	8-7	Standard	Coorg	Jan 6 2016
1m 6f	2m 55.65	4	10-0	Standard	Castle Combe	Sep 3 2015
2m	3m 22.37	5	9-3	Standard	Notarised	Mar 3 2016

CHEPSTOW

Distance	Time	Age	Weight	Going	Horse	Date
5f 16y	57.60	2	8-11	Firm	Micro Love	Jly 8 1986
5f 16y	56.80	3	8-4	Firm	Torbay Express	Sep 15 1979
6f 16y	1m 8.50	2	9-2	Firm	Ninjago	Jly 27 2012
6f 16y	1m 8.10	3	9-7	Firm	America Calling	Sep 18 2001
7f 16y	1m 20.80	2	9-0	Good To Firm	Royal Amaretto	Sep 12 1996
7f 16y	1m 19.30	3	9-0	Firm	Taranaki	Sep 18 2001
1m 14y	1m 33.10	2	8-11	Good To Firm	Ski Academy	Aug 28 1995
1m 14y	1m 31.60	3	8-13	Firm	Stoli	Sep 18 2001
1m 2f 36y	2m 4.10	3	8-5	Good To Firm	Ela Athena	Jly 23 1999
1m 2f 36y	2m 4.10	5	8-9	Hard	Leonidas	Jly 5 1983
1m 2f 36y	2m 4.10	5	7-8	Good To Firm	It's Varadan	Sep 9 1989
1m 4f 23y	2m 31.00	5	8-11	Hard	The Friend	Aug 29 1983
1m 4f 23y	2m 31.00	3	8-9	Good To Firm	Spritsail	Jly 13 1989
2m 49y	3m 27.70	4	9-0	Good To Firm	Wizzard Artist	Jly 1 1989
2m 2f	3m 56.40	5	8-7	Good To Firm	Laffah	Jly 8 2000

CHESTER

Distance	Time	Age	Weight	Going	Horse	Date
5f 15y	59.94	2	9-2	Good To Firm	Leiba Leiba	Jun 26 2010
5f 15y	58.88	3	8-7	Good To Firm	Peterkin	Jly 11 2014
5f 110y	1m 6.39	2	8-7	Good To Soft	Kinematic	Sep 27 2014
5f 110y	1m 4.54	5	8-5	Good	Bossipop	Sep 1 2018
6f 17y	1m 10.54	2	8-12	Good	Glass Slippers	Sep 1 2018
6f 17y	1m 12.02	5	9-5	Good To Firm	Deauville Prince	Jun 13 2015
7f 1y	1m 25.29	2	9-0	Good To Firm	Due Respect	Sep 25 2002
7f 1y	1m 23.75	5	8-13	Good To Firm	Three Graces	Jly 9 2005
7f 127y	1m 32.29	2	9-0	Good To Firm	Big Bad Bob	Sep 25 2002
7f 127y	1m 30.62	5	9-10	Good	Oh This Is Us	Sep 1 2018
1m 2f 70y	2m 7.15	3	8-8	Good To Firm	Stotsfold	Sep 23 2006
1m 3f 75y	2m 22.17	3	8-12	Good To Firm	Perfect Truth	May 6 2009
1m 4f 63y	2m 33.70	3	8-10	Good To Firm	Fight Your Corner	May 7 2002
1m 5f 84y	2m 45.43	5	8-11	Firm	Rakaposhi King	May 7 1987
1m 7f 196y	3m 20.33	4	9-0	Good To Firm	Grand Fromage	Jly 13 2002
2m 2f 140y	3m 58.89	7	9-2	Good To Firm	Greenwich Meantime	May 9 2007

DONCASTER

Distance	Time	Age	Weight	Going	Horse	Date
5f 3y	58.04	2	9-1	Good	Gutaifan	Sep 11 2015
5f 3y	57.31	7	9-10	Good	Tabaret	Aug 14 2010
5f 143y	1m 5.38	4	9-7	Good	Muthmir	Sep 13 2014
6f 2y	1m 10.33	2	9-4	Good To Firm	Comedy	Jun 29 2018
6f 2y	1m 9.56	3	8-10	Good To Firm	Proclaim	May 30 2009
6f 111y	1m 17.19	2	8-9	Good	Mr Lupton	Sep 10 2015
7f 6y	1m 22.78	2	9-5	Good	Basateen	Jly 24 2014
7f 6y	1m 21.81	6	8-7	Good To Firm	Signor Peltro	May 30 2009
7f 213y	1m 38.37	2	8-6	Good To Soft	Antoniola	Oct 23 2009
7f 213y	1m 34.46	4	8-12	Good To Firm	Staying On	Apr 18 2009
1m	1m 36.72	2	8-12	Good	Dance Of Fire	Sep 13 2014
1m	1m 34.95	6	8-9	Firm	Quick Wit	Jly 18 2013
1m 2f 43y	2m 4.81	4	8-13	Good To Firm	Red Gala	Sep 12 2007
1m 3f 197y	2m 27.48	3	8-4	Good To Firm	Swift Alhaarth	Sep 10 2011
1m 6f 115y	3m 0.44	3	9-0	Good To Firm	Masked Marvel	Sep 10 2011
2m 109y	3m 34.52	7	9-0	Good To Firm	Inchnadamph	Nov 10 2007
2m 1f 197y	3m 48.41	4	9-4	Good To Firm	Septimus	Sep 14 2007

EPSOM

Distance	Time	Age	Weight	Going	Horse	Date
5f	55.02	2	8-9	Good To Firm	Prince Aslia	Jun 9 1995
5f	53.60	4	9-5	Firm	Indigenous	Jun 2 1960
6f 3y	1m 7.85	2	8-11	Good To Firm	Showbrook	Jun 5 1991
6f 3y	1m 7.21	5	9-13	Good To Firm	Mac Gille Eoin	Jly 2 2009
7f 3y	1m 21.30	2	8-9	Good To Firm	Red Peony	Jly 29 2004
7f 3y	1m 20.15	4	8-7	Firm	Capistrano I	Jun 7 1972
1m 113y	1m 42.80	2	8-5	Good To Firm	Nightstalker	Aug 30 1988
1m 113y	1m 40.75	3	8-6	Good To Firm	Sylva Honda	Jun 5 1991
1m 2f 17y	2m 3.50	5	7-11	Firm	Crossbow I	Jun 7 1967
1m 4f 6y	2m 31.33	3	9-0	Good To Firm	Workforce	Jun 5 2010

FFOS LAS

Distance	Time	Age	Weight	Going	Horse	Date
5f	57.06	2	9-3	Good To Firm	Mr Majeika	May 5 2011
5f	56.35	5	8-8	Good	Haajes	Sep 12 2009
6f	1m 9.00	2	9-5	Good To Firm	Wonder Of Qatar	Sep 14 2014
6f	1m 7.80	8	8-4	Good To Firm	The Jailer	May 5 2011
1m	1m 39.36	2	9-2	Good To Firm	Hala Hala	Sep 2 2013
1m	1m 37.12	5	9-0	Good To Firm	Zebrano	May 5 2011
1m 2f	2m 4.85	8	8-12	Good To Firm	Pelham Crescent	May 5 2011
1m 3f 209y	2m 31.58	4	8-9	Good To Firm	Men Don't Cry	Jly 23 2013
1m 6f	2m 58.61	4	9-7	Good To Firm	Lady Eclair	Jly 12 2010
2m	3m 25.42	4	9-3	Good To Firm	Long John Silver	Jly 24 2018

GOODWOOD

Distance	Time	Age	Weight	Going	Horse	Date
5f	57.14	2	9-1	Good	Yalta	Jly 27 2016
5f	56.01	5	9-0	Good To Firm	Rudi's Pet	Jly 27 1999
6f	1m 9.81	2	8-11	Good To Firm	Bachir	Jly 28 1999
6f	1m 9.10	6	9-0	Good To Firm	Tamagin	Sep 12 2009
7f	1m 24.99	2	8-11	Good To Firm	Ekraar	Jly 29 1999
7f	1m 23.88	3	8-7	Firm	Brief Glimpse	Jly 25 1995
1m	1m 37.21	2	9-0	Good	Caldra	Sep 9 2006
1m	1m 35.61	4	8-9	Good To Firm	Spectait	Aug 4 2006
1m 1f 11y	1m 56.27	2	9-3	Good To Firm	Dordogne	Sep 22 2010
1m 1f 11y	1m 52.81	3	9-6	Good	Vena	Jly 27 1995
1m 1f 197y	2m 2.81	3	9-3	Good To Firm	Road To Love	Aug 3 2006
1m 3f 44y	2m 22.77	3	9-3	Good	Khalidi	May 26 2017
1m 3f 218y	2m 31.39	3	9-1	Good To Firm	Cross Counter	Aug 4 2018
1m 6f	2m 57.61	4	9-6	Good To Firm	Meeznah	Jly 28 2011
2m	3m 21.55	5	9-10	Good To Firm	Yeats	Aug 3 2006

HAMILTON

Distance	Time	Age	Weight	Going	Horse	Date
5f 7y	57.95	2	8-8	Good To Firm	Rose Blossom	May 29 2009
5f 7y	57.95	2	8-8	Good To Firm	Rose Blossom	May 29 2009
6f 6y	1m 10.00	2	8-12	Good To Firm	Break The Code	Aug 24 1999
6f 6y	1m 9.03	6	9-5	Good To Firm	George Bowen	Jly 20 2018
1m 68y	1m 45.46	2	9-5	Good To Firm	Laafiraaq	Sep 20 2015
1m 68y	1m 42.70	6	7-7	Firm	Cranley	Sep 25 1972
1m 1f 35y	1m 53.60	5	9-6	Good To Firm	Regent's Secret	Aug 10 2005
1m 3f 15y	2m 18.66	3	9-3	Good To Firm	Postponed	Jly 18 2014
1m 4f 15y	2m 30.52	5	9-10	Good To Firm	Record Breaker	Jun 10 2009
1m 5f 16y	2m 45.10	6	9-6	Firm	Mentalasanythin	Jun 14 1995

HAYDOCK

Distance	Time	Age	Weight	Going	Horse	Date
5f	58.51	2	9-1	Good	Four Dragons	Oct 14 2016
5f	58.56	2	8-2	Good To Firm	Barracuda Boy	Aug 11 2012
5f	56.39	5	9-4	Firm	Bated Breath	May 26 2012
5f	57.38	7	9-12	Good To Firm	Foxy Forever	Jly 21 2017
6f	1m 10.98	4	9-9	Good To Firm	Wolfhound	Sep 4 1993
6f	1m 10.58	2	9-2	Good To Firm	Prestbury Park	Jly 21 2017
6f	1m 8.56	3	9-0	Firm	Harry Angel	May 27 2017
6f	1m 9.40	7	9-3	Good To Firm	Markab	Sep 4 2010
6f 212y	1m 27.29	2	9-2	Good To Firm	Drogon	Jly 5 2018
6f 212y	1m 27.29	2	9-2	Good To Firm	Nayef Road	Aug 10 2018
6f 212y	1m 25.28	3	9-8	Good To Firm	Mystic Flight	Jun 7 2018
7f 37y	1m 27.57	2	9-2	Good To Firm	Contrast	Aug 5 2016
7f 37y	1m 25.50	3	8-11	Good	Forge	Sep 1 2016
7f 212y	1m 37.80	3	9-4	Good To Firm	Sidewinder	May 26 2017
1m 37y	1m 38.50	4	8-11	Good To Firm	Express Himself	Jun 10 2015
1m 2f 42y	2m 7.25	3	8-9	Good To Firm	Laraaib	May 26 2017
1m 2f 100y	2m 7.53		-		Teodoro	Aug 6 2016
1m 3f 140y	2m 27.01	3	9-7	Good To Firm	Quantatmental	Jun 7 2018
1m 3f 175y	2m 25.53	4	8-12	Good To Firm	Number Theory	May 24 2012
1m 6f	2m 55.20	5	9-9	Good To Firm	Huff And Puff	Sep 7 2012
2m 45y	3m 26.98	5	8-13	Good To Firm	De Rigueur	Jun 8 2013

KEMPTON (A.W)

Distance	Time	Age	Weight	Going	Horse	Date
5f	58.96	2	8-6	Standard	Glamorous Spirit	Nov 28 2008
5f	58.07	5	8-12	Standard	A Momentofmadness	Apr 7 2018
6f	1m 11.02	2	9-1	Standard To Slow	Invincible Army	Sep 9 2017
6f	1m 9.79	4	8-11	Standard	Trinityelitedotcom	Mar 29 2014
7f	1m 23.79	2	8-0	Standard	Elsaakb	Nov 8 2017
7f	1m 23.10	6	9-9	Standard	Sirius Prospect	Nov 20 2014
1m	1m 37.26	2	9-0	Standard	Cecchini	Nov 8 2017
1m	1m 35.73	3	8-9	Standard	Western Aristocrat	Sep 15 2011
1m 1f 219y	2m 2.93	3	8-11	Standard To Slow	Ply	Sep 25 2017
1m 2f 219y	2m 16.09	4	8-7	Standard	Salutation	Mar 29 2014
1m 3f 219y	2m 28.99	6	9-3	Standard	Spring Of Fame	Nov 7 2012
1m 7f 218y	3m 21.50	4	8-12	Standard	Colour Vision	May 2 2012

LEICESTER

Distance	Time	Age	Weight	Going	Horse	Date
1m 53y	1m 44.05	2	8-11	Good To Firm	Congressional	Sep 6 2005
1m 53y	1m 41.89	5	9-7	Good To Firm	Vainglory	Jun 18 2009
1m 1f 216y	2m 5.30	2	9-1	Good To Firm	Windsor Castle	Oct 14 1996
1m 1f 216y	2m 2.40	4	9-6	Good To Firm	Lady Angharad	Jun 18 2000
1m 1f 216y	2m 2.40	3	8-11	Firm	Effigy I	Nov 4 1985
1m 3f 179y	2m 27.10	5	8-12	Good To Firm	Murghem	Jun 18 2000

LINGFIELD

Distance	Time	Age	Weight	Going	Horse	Date
4f 217y	56.76	2	9-2	Good	Glory Fighter	May 11 2018
4f 217y	56.09	3	9-4	Good To Firm	Whitecrest	Sep 16 2011
6f	1m 8.36	2	8-12	Good To Firm	Folly Bridge	Sep 8 2009
6f	1m 8.13	6	9-8	Firm	Clear Praise	Aug 10 2013
7f	1m 20.55	2	8-11	Good To Firm	Hiking	Aug 17 2013
7f	1m 20.05	3	8-5	Good To Firm	Perfect Tribute	May 7 2011
7f 135y	1m 29.32	2	9-3	Good To Firm	Dundonnell	Aug 4 2012
7f 135y	1m 26.73	3	8-6	Good To Firm	Hiaam	Jly 11 1987
1m 1f	1m 52.40	4	9-2	Good To Firm	Quandary	Jly 15 1995
1m 2f	2m 4.61	3	9-3	Firm	Usran	Jly 15 1989
1m 3f 133y	2m 23.95	3	8-5	Firm	Night-Shirt	Jly 14 1990
1m 6f	2m 59.10	5	9-5	Firm	Ibn Bey	Jly 1 1989
2m 68y	3m 23.71	3	9-5	Good To Firm	Lauries Crusador	Aug 13 1988

LINGFIELD (A.W)

Distance	Time	Age	Weight	Going	Horse	Date
5f 6y	58.11	2	9-5	Standard	Ivors Rebel	Sep 23 2014
5f 6y	56.67	5	8-12	Standard	Ladies Are Forever	Mar 16 2013
6f 1y	1m 9.76	2	9-4	Standard	Red Impression	Nov 24 2018
6f 1y	1m 8.75	7	9-2	Standard	Tarooq	Dec 18 2013
7f 1y	1m 22.67	2	9-3	Standard	Complicit	Nov 23 2013
7f 1y	1m 21.92	5	9-6	Standard	Grey Mirage	Feb 22 2014
1m 1y	1m 35.84	2	9-5	Standard	Brave Hero	Nov 25 2015
1m 1y	1m 33.90	6	9-5	Standard	Lucky Team	Mar 30 2018
1m 2f	2m 0.99	4	9-0	Standard	Farraaj	Mar 16 2013
1m 4f	2m 26.99	6	9-11	Standard	Flinzulu	Jan 01 2017
1m 5f	2m 39.70	3	8-10	Standard	Hidden Gold	Oct 30 2014
1m 7f 169y	3m 15.18	4	9-1	Standard	Winning Story	Apr 14 2017

MUSSELBURGH

Distance	Time	Age	Weight	Going	Horse	Date
5f 1y	57.66	2	9-2	Good To Firm	It Dont Come Easy	Jun 3 2017
5f 1y	56.77	9	9-10	Good To Firm	Caspian Prince	Jun 9 2018
7f 33y	1m 27.46	2	8-8	Good	Durham Reflection	Sep 14 2009
7f 33y	1m 25.00	9	8-8	Good To Firm	Kalk Bay	Jun 4 2016
1m 2y	1m 40.34	2	8-12	Good To Firm	Succession	Sep 26 2004
1m 2y	1m 36.83	3	9-5	Good To Firm	Ginger Jack	Jly 13 2010
1m 208y	1m 50.42	8	8-11	Good To Firm	Dhaular Dhar	Sep 3 2010
1m 4f 104y	2m 36.80	3	8-3	Good To Firm	Harris Tweed	Jun 5 2010
1m 5f	2m 46.41	3	9-5	Good To Firm	Alcaeus	Sep 29 2013
1m 5f 216y	2m 57.98	7	8-5	Good To Firm	Jonny Delta	Apr 18 2014
1m 7f 217y	3m 25.62	4	8-3	Good To Firm	Aldreth	Jun 13 2015

NEWBURY

Distance	Time	Age	Weight	Going	Horse	Date
5f 34y	59.19	2	8-6	Good To Firm	Superstar Leo	Jly 22 2000
5f 34y	58.44	5	9-1	Good To Firm	Robot Boy	Apr 17 2015
6f 110y	1m 18.06	2	9-5	Good To Firm	Twin Sails	Jun 11 2015
7f	1m 23.04	2	8-11	Good To Firm	Haafhd	Aug 15 2003
7f	1m 20.80	3	9-0	Good To Firm	Muhaarar	Apr 18 2015
1m	1m 37.50	2	9-1	Good To Firm	Winged Cupid	Sep 16 2005
1m	1m 33.59	6	9-0	Firm	Rakti	May 14 2005
1m 1f	1m 40.05	3	8-0	Good To Firm	Holtye	May 21 1995
1m 2f	2m 1.29	3	8-7	Good To Firm	Wall Street II	Jly 20 1996
1m 3f 5y	2m 16.54	3	8-9	Good To Firm	Grandera	Sep 22 2001
1m 4f 5y	2m 28.26	4	9-7	Good To Firm	Azamour	Jly 23 2005
1m 5f 61y	2m 44.90	5	10-0	Good To Firm	Mystic Hill	Jly 20 1996
2m	3m 25.42	8	9-12	Good To Firm	Moonlight Quest	Jly 19 1996

NEWCASTLE (A.W)

Distance	Time	Age	Weight	Going	Horse	Date
5f	57.78	3	8-9	Standard	Astraea	Dec 15 2018
6f	1m 9.86	3	9-2	Standard	Unabated	Mar 22 2017
7f 14y	1m 24.48	4	9-7	Standard	Alice Thornton	Oct 14 2016
1m 5y	1m 36.28	5	9-10	Standard	Auspicion	Sep 12 2017
1m 2f 42y	2m 4.88	3	8-6	Standard	Palisade	Oct 16 2016
1m 4f 98y	2m 36.76	3	8-7	Standard	Ajman Prince	Oct 14 2016
2m 56y	3m 29.87	4	9-8	Standard	Dannyday	Jun 25 2016

NEWMARKET

Distance	Time	Age	Weight	Going	Horse	Date
5f	58.69	2	8-12	Good To Firm	Mrs Danvers	Oct 7 2016
5f	56.81	6	9-2	Good To Firm	Lochsong	Apr 30 1994
6f	1m 9.56	2	8-12	Good To Firm	Bushranger	Oct 3 2008
6f	1m 10.19	5	9-6	Good To Firm	Brando	Apr 20 2017
6f	1m 9.55	3	9-1	Good To Firm	Captain Colby	May 16 2015
7f	1m 22.37	2	9-1	Good	U S Navy Flag	Oct 14 2017
7f	1m 21.98	3	9-0	Good To Firm	Tupi	May 16 2015
1m	1m 35.67	2	8-12	Good	Steeler	Sep 29 2012
1m	1m 34.07	4	9-0	Good To Firm	Eagle Mountain	Oct 3 2008
1m 1f	1m 47.26	5	8-12	Good To Firm	Manduro	Apr 19 2007
1m 2f	2m 2.76	2	9-2	Good	Kew Gardens	Oct 14 2017
1m 2f	2m 0.13	3	8-12	Good	New Approach	Oct 18 2008
1m 4f	2m 29.13	3	9-0	Good	First Nation	Oct 13 2017
1m 4f	2m 26.07	3	8-9	Good To Firm	Mohedian Lady	Sep 22 2011
1m 6f	2m 51.59	3	8-7	Good	Art Eyes	Sep 29 2005
2m	3m 18.64	5	9-6	Good To Firm	Times Up	Sep 22 2011
2m 2f	3m 45.59	4	8-8	Good	Withhold	Oct 14 2017
2m 2f	3m 47.50	3	7-12	Hard	Whiteway	Oct 15 1947

NEWMARKET (JULY)

Distance	Time	Age	Weight	Going	Horse	Date
5f	58.52	2	8-10	Good	Seductress	Jly 10 1990
5f	56.09	6	9-11	Good	Borderlescott	Aug 22 2008
5f	57.91	3	9-3	Good To Firm	Embour	Jun 23 2018
6f	1m 10.35	2	8-11	Good	Elnawin	Aug 22 2008
6f	1m 10.34	2	9-0	Good To Firm	Clemmie	Jly 14 2017
6f	1m 9.68	4	9-1	Good To Firm	Gifted Master	Aug 26 2017
6f	1m 9.11	4	9-5	Good To Firm	Lethal Force	Jly 13 2013
7f	1m 23.33	2	9-1	Good To Firm	Birchwood	Jly 11 2015
7f	1m 22.59	3	9-7	Firm	Ho Leng	Jly 9 1998
1m	1m 37.47	2	8-13	Good	Whippers Love	Aug 28 2009
1m	1m 34.42	3	8-12	Good To Firm	Alice Springs	Jly 8 2016
1m	1m 36.01	3	8-12	Good To Firm	Roly Poly	Jly 14 2017
1m 2f	2m 2.21	7	8-10	Good	Kapstadt	Jun 16 2017
1m 2f	2m 0.91	3	9-5	Good To Firm	Maputo	Jly 11 2013
1m 4f	2m 25.11	3	8-11	Good	Lush Lashes	Aug 22 2008
1m 4f	2m 30.01	4	9-8	Good To Firm	Reverend Jacobs	Aug 3 2018
1m 5f	2m 40.75	5	9-10	Good	Wadi Al Hattawi	Aug 29 2015
1m 5f	2m 44.06	4	9-12	Good To Firm	Pumblechook	Jun 24 2017
1m 6f	2m 53.98	4	8-11	Good	Jaameh	Jun 10 2017

NOTTINGHAM

Distance	Time	Age	Weight	Going	Horse	Date
5f 8y	59.05	2	9-0	Good To Firm	Main Desire	May 2 2017
5f 8y	57.90	2	8-9	Firm	Hoh Magic	May 13 1994
5f 8y	57.40	3	9-6	Good To Firm	Carlton Frankie	May 2 2017
5f 8y	57.58	5	7-11	Good To Firm	Penny Dreadful	Jun 19 2017
6f 18y	1m 11.40	2	8-11	Firm	Jameelapi	Aug 8 1983
6f 18y	1m 10.00	4	9-2	Firm	Ajanac	Aug 8 1988
1m 72y	1m 45.14	2	9-6	Good	Rashford's Double	Nov 2 2016
1m 72y	1m 43.22	4	9-7	Good To Firm	Reaver	Apr 22 2017
1m 75y	1m 44.75	2	9-0	Good	Vivid Diamond	Oct 3 2018
1m 75y	1m 42.02	3	9-0	Good To Firm	Ganayem	May 11 2018
1m 2f 50y	2m 7.13	5	9-8	Good To Firm	Vasily	Jly 19 2013
1m 2f 52y	2m 16.66	2	9-3	Soft	Lethal Glaze	Oct 1 2008
1m 2f 52y	2m 9.40	3	9-5	Good	Centurius	Apr 20 2013
1m 6f	2m 57.80	3	8-10	Firm	Buster Jo	Oct 1 1985
2m	3m 25.25	3	9-5	Good	Bulwark	Sep 27 2005

PONTEFRACT

Distance	Time	Age	Weight	Going	Horse	Date
5f 3y	1m 1.10	2	9-0	Firm	Golden Bounty	Sep 20 2001
5f 3y	1m 0.49	5	9-5	Good To Firm	Judicial	Apr 24 2017
6f	1m 14.00	2	9-3	Firm	Fawzi	Sep 6 1983
6f	1m 12.60	3	7-13	Firm	Merry One	Aug 29 1970
1m 6y	1m 42.80	2	9-13	Firm	Star Spray	Sep 6 1983
1m 6y	1m 42.80	2	9-0	Firm	Alasil	Sep 26 2002
1m 6y	1m 40.60	4	9-10	Good To Firm	Island Light	Apr 13 2002
1m 2f 5y	2m 10.10	2	9-0	Firm	Shanty Star	Oct 7 2002
1m 2f 5y	2m 8.20	4	7-8	Hard	Happy Hector	Jly 9 1979
1m 2f 5y	2m 8.20	3	7-13	Hard	Tom Noddy	Aug 21 1972
1m 4f 5y	2m 33.72	3	8-7	Firm	Ajaan	Aug 8 2007
2m 1f 27y	3m 40.67	4	8-7	Good To Firm	Paradise Flight	Jun 6 2005
2m 2f 2y	3m 51.10	3	8-8	Good To Firm	Kudz	Sep 9 1986
2m 5f 139y	4m 47.80	4	8-4	Firm	Physical	May 14 1984

REDCAR

Distance	Time	Age	Weight	Going	Horse	Date
5f	56.88	2	9-7	Good To Soft	Wolfofwallstreet	Oct 27 2014
5f	56.01	10	9-3	Firm	Henry Hall	Sep 20 2006
5f 217y	1m 8.84	2	8-3	Good To Firm	Obe Gold	Oct 2 2004
5f 217y	1m 8.60	3	9-2	Good To Firm	Sizzling Saga	Jun 21 1991
7f	1m 21.28	2	9-3	Firm	Karoo Blue	Sep 20 2006
7f	1m 21.00	3	9-1	Firm	Empty Quarter	Oct 3 1995
7f 219y	1m 34.37	2	9-0	Firm	Mastership	Sep 20 2006
7f 219y	1m 32.42	4	10-0	Firm	Nanton	Sep 20 2006
1m 1f	1m 52.44	2	9-0	Firm	Spear	Sep 13 2004
1m 1f	1m 48.50	5	8-12	Firm	Mellottie	Jly 25 1990
1m 2f 1y	2m 10.10	2	8-11	Good	Adding	Nov 10 1989
1m 2f 1y	2m 1.40	5	9-2	Firm	Eradicate	May 28 1990
1m 5f 218y	2m 59.54	6	8-5	Good To Firm	Leodis	Jun 23 2018
1m 7f 217y	3m 24.90	3	9-3	Good To Firm	Subsonic	Oct 8 1991

RIPON

Distance	Time	Age	Weight	Going	Horse	Date
5f	57.80	2	8-8	Firm	Super Rocky	Aug 5 1991
5f	57.28	5	8-12	Good	Desert Ace	Sep 24 2016
6f	1m 10.40	2	9-2	Good	Cumbrian Venture	Aug 17 2002
6f	1m 9.09	5	8-13	Good To Firm	Sandra's Secret	May 20 2018
1m	1m 38.77	2	9-4	Good	Greed Is Good	Sep 28 2013
1m	1m 36.62	4	8-11	Good To Firm	Granston	Aug 29 2005
1m 1f	1m 49.97	6	9-3	Good To Firm	Ginger Jack	Jun 20 2013
1m 1f 170y	1m 59.12	5	8-9	Good To Firm	Wahoo Sam	Aug 30 2005
1m 4f 10y	2m 31.40	4	8-8	Good To Firm	Dandino	Apr 16 2011
2m	3m 27.07	5	9-12	Good To Firm	Greenwich Meantime	Aug 30 2005

SALISBURY

Distance	Time	Age	Weight	Going	Horse	Date
5f	59.30	2	9-0	Good To Firm	Ajigolo	May 12 2005
5f	59.18	7	8-10	Good To Firm	Edged Out	Jun 18 2017
6f	1m 12.10	2	8-0	Good To Firm	Parisian Lady	Jun 10 1997
6f	1m 11.09	3	9-0	Firm	L'Ami Louis	May 1 2011
6f 213y	1m 25.97	2	9-0	Firm	More Royal	Jun 29 1995
6f 213y	1m 24.91	3	9-4	Firm	Chilworth Lad	May 1 2011
1m	1m 40.48	2	8-13	Firm	Choir Master	Sep 17 2002
1m	1m 38.29	3	8-7	Good To Firm	Layman	Aug 11 2005
1m 1f 198y	2m 4.00	4	9-2	Good To Firm	Chain Of Daisies	Aug 10 2016
1m 4f 5y	2m 31.69	3	9-5	Good To Firm	Arrive	Jun 27 2001
1m 6f 44y	3m 0.48	7	9-2	Good To Firm	Highland Castle	May 23 2015

SANDOWN

Distance	Time	Age	Weight	Going	Horse	Date
5f 10y	59.48	2	9-3	Firm	Times Time	Jly 22 1982
5f 10y	58.57	3	8-12	Good To Firm	Battaash	Jly 8 2017
7f	1m 26.56	2	9-0	Good To Firm	Raven's Pass	Sep 1 2007
7f	1m 26.36	3	9-0	Firm	Mawsuff	Jun 14 1986
1m	1m 39.21	4	8-12	Good To Firm	El Hayem	Jly 8 2017
1m 14y	1m 41.14	2	8-11	Good To Firm	Reference Point	Sep 23 1986
1m 14y	1m 38.87	7	9-10	Good To Firm	Prince Of Johanne	Jly 6 2013
1m 1f	1m 54.63	2	8-8	Good To Firm	French Pretender	Sep 20 1988
1m 1f	1m 52.40	7	9-3	Good To Firm	Bourgainville	Aug 11 2005
1m 1f 209y	2m 2.14	4	8-11	Good	Kalaglow	May 31 1982
1m 6f	3m 3.19	3	9-2	Good To Firm	Dominating	Jun 16 2017
1m 6f	2m 56.90	4	8-7	Good To Firm	Lady Rosanna	Jly 19 1989
2m 50y	3m 29.38	6	9-0	Good To Firm	Caucus	Jly 6 2013

SOUTHWELL (A.W)

Distance	Time	Age	Weight	Going	Horse	Date
4f 214y	57.71	2	8-4	Standard	Scale Force	Dec 29 2018
4f 214y	56.80	5	9-7	Standard	Ghostwing	Jan 3 2012
6f 16y	1m 14.00	2	8-5	Standard	Panalo	Nov 8 1989
6f 16y	1m 13.50	4	10-0	Standard	Saladan Knight	Dec 30 1989
7f 14y	1m 26.82	2	8-12	Standard	Winged Icarus	Aug 28 2012
7f 14y	1m 26.38	4	8-6	Standard	Moon River	Mar 30 2016
1m 13y	1m 38.00	2	8-10	Standard	Andrew's First	Dec 30 1989
1m 13y	1m 38.00	2	8-9	Standard	Alpha Rascal	Nov 13 1990
1m 13y	1m 37.25	3	8-6	Standard	Valira	Nov 3 1990
1m 3f 23y	2m 21.50	4	9-7	Standard	Tempering	Dec 5 1990
1m 4f 14y	2m 33.90	4	9-12	Standard	Fast Chick	Nov 8 1989
1m 6f 21y	3m 1.60	3	7-8	Standard	Erevnon	Dec 29 1990
2m 102y	3m 37.60	9	8-12	Standard	Old Hubert	Dec 5 1990

THIRSK

Distance	Time	Age	Weight	Going	Horse	Date
5f	57.20	2	9-7	Good To Firm	Proud Boast	Aug 5 2000
5f	56.92	5	9-6	Firm	Charlie Parkes	Apr 11 2003
6f	1m 9.20	2	9-6	Good To Firm	Westcourt Magic	Aug 25 1995
6f	1m 8.80	6	9-4	Firm	Johayro	Jly 23 1999
7f	1m 23.70	2	8-9	Firm	Courting	Jly 23 1999
7f	1m 22.80	4	8-5	Firm	Silver Haze I	May 21 1988
7f 218y	1m 37.97	2	9-0	Firm	Sunday Symphony	Sep 4 2004
7f 218y	1m 34.80	4	8-13	Firm	Yearsley I	May 5 1990
1m 4f 8y	2m 29.90	5	9-12	Firm	Gallery God	Jun 4 2001
2m 13y	3m 22.30	3	9-0	Firm	Tomaschek	Jly 17 1981

WETHERBY

Distance	Time	Age	Weight	Going	Horse	Date
5f 110y	1m 4.25	3	9-1	Good To Firm	Dapper Man	Jun 19 2017
7f	1m 24.72	4	9-2	Good	Slemy	Jly 21 2015
1m	1m 38.79	4	9-4	Good To Firm	Thomas Cranmer	Jun 6 2018
1m 2f	2m 5.13	5	9-5	Good	First Sargeant	Jly 21 2015
1m 6f	3m 0.41	3	9-7	Good To Firm	Davy's Dilemma	Jun 19 2017

WINDSOR

Distance	Time	Age	Weight	Going	Horse	Date
5f 21y	58.69	2	9-0	Good To Firm	Charles The Great	May 23 2011
5f 21y	58.08	5	8-13	Good To Firm	Taurus Twins	Apr 4 2011
6f 12y	1m 10.50	2	9-5	Good To Firm	Cubism I	Aug 17 1998
6f 12y	1m 9.58	7	9-0	Good To Firm	Tropics	Jun 1 2015
1m 31y	1m 41.73	2	9-5	Good To Firm	Salouen	Aug 7 2016
1m 31y	1m 39.81	5	9-7	Good	French Navy	Jun 29 2013
1m 1f 194y	2m 1.62	6	9-1	Good	Al Kazeem	Aug 23 2014
1m 3f 99y	2m 21.50	3	9-2	Firm	Double Florin	May 19 1980

WOLVERHAMPTON (A.W)

Distance	Time	Age	Weight	Going	Horse	Date
5f 21y	59.75	2	9-6	Standard	Quatrieme Ami	Nov 13 2015
5f 21y	59.39	5	9-8	Standard	Boom The Groom	Feb 22 2016
6f 20y	1m 12.16	2	9-2	Standard	Mubakker	Nov 1 2018
6f 20y	1m 11.44	5	9-6	Standard	Kachy	Dec 26 2018
7f 36y	1m 27.45	2	8-13	Standard	Fox Power	Sep 26 2018
7f 36y	1m 25.35	4	9-3	Standard	Mister Universe	Mar 12 2016
1m 142y	1m 47.38	2	9-5	Standard	Jack Hobbs	Dec 27 2014
1m 142y	1m 45.43	4	9-4	Standard	Keystroke	Nov 26 2016
1m 1f 104y	1m 56.64	8	8-13	Standard	Perfect Cracker	Mar 19 2016
1m 4f 51y	2m 33.92	3	8-13	Standard	Natural Scenery	Oct 21 2016
1m 5f 194y	2m 58.68	3	9-2	Standard	Instrumentalist	Oct 9 2012
1m 5f 194y	2m 57.55	6	9-7	Standard	Entihaa	Dec 6 2014
2m 120y	3m 31.92	7	9-3	Standard	Watersmeet	Jan 15 2018

YARMOUTH

Distance	Time	Age	Weight	Going	Horse	Date
5f 42y	1m 0.37	2	8-11	Good To Firm	Pink Iceburg	Jly 11 2018
5f 42y	59.74	3	8-11	Good To Firm	Haveoneyerself	Jun 29 2018
6f 3y	1m 10.40	2	9-0	Firm	Lanchester	Sep 15 1988
6f 3y	1m 9.14	3	9-0	Good To Firm	Cartographer	May 24 2017
7f 3y	1m 22.20	2	9-0	Good To Firm	Warrshan	Sep 14 1988
7f 3y	1m 22.12	4	9-4	Good To Firm	Glenbuck	Apr 26 2007
1m 3y	1m 36.30	2	8-2	Firm	Out Run	Sep 15 1988
1m 3y	1m 33.49	7	9-0	Firm	Bint Dandy	May 16 2018
1m 1f 21y	1m 52.00	3	9-5	Good To Firm	Touch Gold	Jly 5 2012
1m 2f 23y	2m 2.83	3	8-8	Firm	Reunite	Jly 18 2006
1m 3f 104y	2m 23.10	3	8-9	Firm	Rahil I	Jly 1 1993
1m 6f 17y	2m 57.80	3	8-2	Good To Firm	Barakat	Jly 24 1990

YORK

Distance	Time	Age	Weight	Going	Horse	Date
5f	57.11	2	9-0	Good	Big Time Baby	Aug 20 2016
5f	56.16	3	9-3	Good To Firm	Dayjur	Aug 23 1990
5f 89y	1m 3.20	2	9-3	Good To Firm	The Art Of Racing	Sep 9 2012
5f 89y	1m 1.72	4	9-7	Good To Firm	Bogart	Aug 21 2013
6f	1m 8.90	2	9-0	Good	Tiggy Wiggy	Aug 21 2014
6f	1m 8.23	3	8-11	Good To Firm	Mince	Sep 9 2012
7f	1m 22.32	2	9-1	Good To Firm	Dutch Connection	Aug 20 2014
7f	1m 21.83	4	9-8	Good To Firm	Dimension	Jly 28 2012
7f 192y	1m 36.92	2	9-5	Good	Awesometank	Oct 14 2017
7f 192y	1m 35.10	4	8-12	Good	Home Cummins	Jly 9 2016
1m 177y	1m 46.76	5	9-8	Good To Firm	Echo Of Light	Sep 5 2007
1m 2f 56y	2m 5.29	3	8-11	Good To Firm	Sea The Stars	Aug 18 2009
1m 3f 188y	2m 26.28	6	8-9	Firm	Bandari	Jun 18 2005
1m 5f 188y	2m 53.48	5	9-9	Good To Firm	Muntahaa	Aug 25 2018
2m 56y	3m 28.97	5	9-5	Good To Firm	Gabrial's King	Jly 12 2014

Notes

Notes

Notes

Notes

Notes

FIFTY SHADES OF HAY
THE EXTRAORDINARY WORLD OF RACEHORSE NAMES
David Ashforth
£12.99

01933 304858